GERMANY

2020

CONTENTS

Welcome to Rick Steves' Europe

Travel is intensified living—maximum thrills per minute and one of the last great sources of legal adventure. Travel is freedom. It's recess, and we need it.

I discovered a passion for European travel as a teen and have been sharing it ever since—through my tours, public television and radio shows, and travel guidebooks. Over the years, I've taught thousands of travelers how to best enjoy Europe's blockbuster sights—and experience "Back Door" discoveries that most tourists miss.

This book offers a balanced mix of Germany's cities and villages. I've also included a taste of neighboring Austria, with side-trips into Tirol and Salzburg. It's selective: Rather than covering dozens of castles along the Rhine, I focus on the best: Rheinfels and Marksburg. And it's in-depth: My self-guided museum tours and city walks give insight into Germany's vibrant history and today's living, breathing culture.

I advocate traveling simply and smartly. Take advantage of my money- and time-saving tips on sight-seeing, transportation, and more. Try local, characteristic alternatives to expensive hotels and restaurants. In many ways, spending more money only builds a thicker wall between you and what you traveled so far to see.

We visit Germany to experience it—to become temporary locals. Thoughtful travel engages us with the world, as we learn to appreciate other cultures and new ways to measure quality of life.

Judging by the positive feedback I receive from readers, this book will help you enjoy a fun, affordable, and rewarding vacation—whether it's your first trip or your tenth.

Gute Reise! Happy travels!

Rick Steves

GERMANY

Germany is blessed with some of Europe's most high-powered sights. It has spectacular scenery—the jagged Alps, flower-filled meadows, rolling hills of forests and farms, and rivers such as the raging Rhine and moseying Mosel. And it has hundreds of castles, some ruined and mysterious; others stout, crenellated, and imposing; and still others right out of a Disney fairy tale.

And of course there are the cultural clichés, kept alive more by tradition-loving Germans than by tourist demand. The country is dotted with idyllic half-timbered villages where you can enjoy strudel at the bakery or sip a stein of beer while men in lederhosen play oompah music. Peruse a wonderland of chocolates and stock up on cuckoo clocks.

These traditions stand at sharp contrast with the "real" Germany of today. The muscleman of Europe, Germany is the European Union's most populous country and has the biggest economy. This land that's roughly the size of Montana creates a gross domestic product that's one-fifth the size of the United States'. Germany has risen from the ashes of World War II to become the world's fourth-largest industrial power. At the forefront of human progress, Germany is a world of high-tech transportation, gleaming cities, social efficiency, and world-class museums celebrating many of history's greatest cultural achievements.

German inventions range from Gutenberg's printing press to Zeppelin's zeppelins to Röntgen's X-rays to Daim-

Medieval Nürnberg hosted Holy Roman Emperors and Adolf Hitler, while Martin Luther shook up the Church and reshaped Christianity.

ler's and Benz's cars to Geiger's counter. Musically, Germany dominated the scene for more than two centuries—Bach, Beethoven, Brahms, Handel, Pachelbel, and Wagner. Germans have a reputation as profound analytical thinkers, sprouting philosophers such as Kant, Hegel, Nietzsche, Marx, and Engels.

Germany's roots run deep; the southern half was ruled by ancient Rome. After Rome fell, German lands fragmented into hundreds of small feudal kingdoms, each with its own coinage, king, and castle—many of which still dot the countryside today. These lands became an important European hub for trade and transportation.

It was from Germany that a humble monk named Martin Luther rocked Europe with religious reform. Germany became a Europe-wide battleground for Protestants and Catholics in a series of religious wars.

Traditionally—and in some ways even today—German culture divides at a sort of north-south Mason-Dixon Line. Northern Germany was barbarian, is predominantly Protestant, and tackles life aggressively, while southern Germany was Roman, is largely Catholic, and enjoys a more relaxed tempo.

As a nation, Germany is less than 150 years old ("born" in 1871). Though quite young compared with most of its European neighbors, it quickly became a cultural powerhouse. Its

Beer Halls and Beer Gardens

For traditional Bavarian fun, nothing beats an old-fashioned beer hall (*Brauhaus*) or beer garden (*Biergarten*). Though the best are in Munich, you'll find them all over Germany —with rivers of beer, cheap food, noisy fun, and oompah music.

Beer is truly a drink of the people. Beer hall meals are inexpensive, and surly beer maids pull mustard packets from their cleavage. Unlike with wine, spending more money on beer doesn't get you a better drink. The big question among connoisseurs is, "Which brew today?"

Beer gardens go back to the days when monks brewed and sold beer. They stored their beer in cellars under courtyards kept cool by the shade of bushy chestnut trees. Eventually, tables were set up, and these convivial eateries evolved. The tradition (complete with chestnut trees) survives, and any real beer garden will keep a few tables (those without tablecloths) available for customers who buy only beer and bring their own food.

Huge liter beers (called *eine Mass* in German, or "*eine* pitcher" in English) cost about €8. (Men's rooms come with vomitoriums.) If you order a half-liter (*eine Halbe*), the barmaid is likely to say, "Why don't you go home and come back when you are thirsty?" You can order your beer *Helles* (light in color but not "lite" in calories), *Dunkles* (dark), or ask for a *Weissbier* or *Weizen* ("white" or wheat-based beer cloudy and sweet) or a *Radler* (half lemon soda, half beer).

Most beer gardens have a deposit (*Pfand*) system for their big ▶▶▶

Oompah music, hearty sausages, and fresh beer are the perfect ingredients for beer hall fun.

▶▶▶ glass steins: You pay €1 extra, and when you're finished, you can take the mug and your deposit token *(Pfandmarke)* to the return man *(Pfandrückgabe)* for your refund, or leave it on the table and lose your money. If you buy a bottled beer, pour it into the glass before you check out; otherwise you'll pay two deposits (one for the glass, the other for the bottle).

Many beer halls have a cafeteria system. The food is usually *Selbst-bedienung*—self-service. If two prices are listed, *Selbstbedieung* is for self-service *(Bitte bedienen Sie sich selbst* means "please serve yourself"), while *Bedienung* is for table service.

At a large *Biergarten,* assemble your dream feast by visiting various counters, marked by type of food *(Bier* or *Bierschänke* for beer, *Bratwürste* for sausages, *Brotzeiten* for lighter fare served cold, and so on). After the meal, reclaim your deposit and bus your dirty dishes *(Geschirr)*—look for *Geschirrrückgabe* or *Geschirrabgabe* signs.

You'll notice many tables marked *Stammtisch* (reserved for regulars and small groups). Beer halls have a long tradition of being launch pads for grassroots action. In the days before radio and television, aspiring leaders connected with the public here.

A beer hall is a classic *gemütliche* scene. *Gemütlich* is a word for Bavaria's special coziness and the knack of savoring the moment. Experience it by spending time in a frothy beer hall, clinking mugs with new friends, immersed in a boisterous and belching Bavarian atmosphere. ■

Buy a big beer, skip the Stammtisch *section (for regular customers only), and settle into Germany's inviting beer gardens.*

prosperity ended in the humiliating defeat of World War I, followed by Hitler's cruel rule and Germany's near destruction in World War II.

Many visitors can't help but associate Germany with its dark Nazi past. While a small neo-Nazi skinhead element still survives in the back alleys of German culture, for the most part the nation is surprisingly progressive. A genuine sense of responsibility for World War II and the Holocaust pervades much of German society. If you visit a concentration camp memorial, you'll likely see several field-trip groups of German teens visiting there to learn the lessons of their country's past.

At war's end, Germany was divided East-West between the victorious Allies, and the Cold War set in (1945-1990). More than 25 years after reunification, despite billions of dollars of economic aid, the East lags behind the West, with a lower income and a higher unemployment rate.

The historic divisions in Germany, between the north/south and the east/west, are growing less pronounced as Germany becomes a more mobile society. Germans love to travel, throughout their own country and beyond. They're cosmopolitan and outward-looking. Two-thirds speak at least one other language (mostly English). Watch out—they may know American politics and history better than you do.

Germany was a founding member of the European Union and continues to lead the way in creating a healthy Europe for the future—with peace, unity, tolerance (e.g.,

Ponder Berlin's memorials to politicians who opposed Hitler (left) and to Sinti and Roma victims (right).

The many faces of modern Germany

legalized gay marriage), and human rights as its central motivations. It has taken a tough stance on bailing out EU nations that haven't shown fiscal responsibility, but it remains a generous country—it's one of the world's biggest foreign-aid donors.

Looking ahead, Germany is faced with a number of challenges—none bigger than immigration. Today, more than 11 million immigrants live within its borders—more than any country except the US and Russia. Nearly 3 million are Turkish; many were *Gastarbeiter* (guest workers) invited by Germany to help boost its labor force. In 2015 alone, Germany welcomed more than a million refugees, mostly from Syria and Iraq. Many newcomers are Muslims—not always the easiest fit within a traditionally Christian nation.

Today, three decades after the end of the Cold War, Germany is reunited, with Berlin as its capital. *Deutschland* is energetic, efficient, and organized. It's a nation of cutting-edge industry, medieval castles, speedy autobahns, old-time beer halls, soaring skyscrapers, and the best wurst. This young country with a long past continues to make history.

Germany's Top Destinations

Herzlich Willkommen! There's so much to see in Germany and so little time. This overview breaks the country's top destinations into must-see sights (to help first-time travelers plan their trip) and worth-it sights (for those with extra time or special interests). I've also suggested a minimum number of days to allow per destination.

PLACES COVERED
IN THIS BOOK
▲▲▲ Must See
▲▲ Try Hard to See
▲ Worthwhile

DENMARK

SWEDEN

North Sea

Baltic Sea

HAMBURG

NETH.

POLAND

BERLIN

LUTHERLAND

LEIPZIG

COLOGNE

DRESDEN

RHINE VALLEY

MOSEL VALLEY

FRANKFURT

CZECH REPUBLIC

TRIER

WÜRZBURG

LUX.

ROTHENBURG & THE ROMANTIC ROAD

NÜRNBERG

FRANCE

BADEN-BADEN & THE BLACK FOREST

MUNICH

SALZBURG

BAVARIAN ALPS

BELGIUM

100 Kilometers

100 Miles

AUSTRIA

SWITZ.

MUST-SEE DESTINATIONS

These four destinations give you an excellent and diverse sampler of Germany (and dip into nearby Austria).

▲▲▲Munich (allow 2 days)

The thriving city has a glorious main square and a traffic-free center, with a fun open-air market/beer garden, the Viktualienmarkt. Well-stocked with sights, Munich serves up Baroque palaces, stately churches, and excellent museums on art, science, and history. This in-love-with-life city enjoys its lush parks (such as the vast English Garden) and rowdy beer halls (rowdier at Oktoberfest). Sights near Munich include a beer-loving monastery, more palaces, and most important, the sobering concentration camp memorial at Dachau. With limited time, the Bavarian Alps region and Salzburg can be done as day trips (though each merit a longer stay).

▲▲▲Bavarian Alps (2 days)

This Alps-straddling region, with Germany on one side and Austria on the other, boasts the fairy-tale castles of "Mad" King Ludwig II: Neuschwanstein, Hohenschwangau, and Linderhof. Choose among inviting home bases: handy Füssen (with a nearby spa), the Austrian retreat of Reutte (with a ruined castle of its own), and adorable Oberammergau (known for wood-carving and its Passion Play). For alpine fun, try hikes, luge rides, and a lift to the top of the towering Zugspitze, Germany's highest point.

▲▲▲Salzburg (1-2 days)

Just south of the German border, the Austrian city of Salzburg is a musical mecca for fans of Mozart and *The Sound of Music,* offering S.O.M. tours and concerts in Baroque

Marvel at Munich's Residenz, ride a luge in Bavaria, make friends at Ehrenberg (Austria), and enjoy snowy Neuschwanstein Castle.

churches, along with riverside promenades, grand gardens, and beer gardens. The picturesque old town—with winding lanes, shops, and Mozart's birthplace—is surrounded by hills laced with trails and topped by a sky-high fortress. Near Salzburg is Berchtesgaden (in Germany) with serene alpine scenery and Hitler's mountain-top retreat.

▲▲▲Berlin (2-3 days)

Germany's vibrant, sprawling capital features world-class art and history museums, the Brandenburg Gate, trendy nightlife, leafy boulevards, striking modern architecture, and remnants of the Berlin Wall, which once divided the city and country. Thought-provoking memorials and museums throughout the city commemorate the many victims of World War II. Near Berlin are Potsdam's palaces and the former Sachsenhausen concentration camp.

Stroll Salzburg's elegant streets, explore Berlin's courtyards, and pay homage to its symbol of reunification—the Brandenburg Gate.

WORTH-IT DESTINATIONS

You can weave any of these destinations—rated ▲ or ▲▲—into your itinerary. It's easy to add some destinations based on convenience (if you're heading from Frankfurt to Munich, Rothenburg is on the way), though some farther-flung places (like Hamburg) can merit the journey, depending on your time and interests. Germany's excellent train system brings everything within reach; most destinations in this book are within a two- to four-hour ride from Frankfurt's airport, a popular arrival point with its own train station.

▲Baden-Baden and the Black Forest (1-2 days)
Baden-Baden is a tourist-friendly resort, offering two kinds of bath experiences (sedate and lively), a riverside stroll, and a grand casino in a small-town package. With a second day, delve into Black Forest sights: the university town of Freiburg, the cozy village of Staufen, and forested hills rife with hikes, folk museums, cute hamlets, and cuckoo clocks.

▲▲Rothenburg and the Romantic Road (1-2 days)
Rothenburg is a well-preserved medieval town full of half-timbered buildings, small museums, fun tours, and cobbled lanes surrounded by walkable medieval walls. With extra time, explore the Romantic Road's scenic route through the lovely countryside and time-passed towns of Dinkelsbühl and Nördlingen.

▲Würzburg (half-day to 1 day)
This university town is home to the impressive, fun-to-tour Residenz palace (with manicured gardens and a dazzling Rococo chapel), a hilltop fortress, atmospheric wine bars, and a bridge that's perfect for strolling at sunset.

Germany has storybook villages like Bacharach, medieval festivals in Rothenburg, fine wood carving—a Germany specialty—in Nürnberg, and skyscrapers in Frankfurt.

▲Frankfurt (half-day to 1 day)

The country's bustling banking center, with a skyscraping skyline, gives you a good look at modern Germany. Rebuilt after World War II, Frankfurt has a charming old town (Römerberg), riverside parks, and a string of museums across the river. It's also a major transportation hub, with an international airport and major train stations.

▲▲Rhine Valley (1-2 days)

Steeped in legend, the mighty Rhine River is lined with storybook villages capped by imposing castles. Good home bases are cute Bacharach and St. Goar (with the best castle, Rheinfels). A thoroughfare since ancient times, the Rhine Valley is easy to explore by boat, car, bike, and train.

▲▲Mosel Valley (1 day)

This sleepy meandering river, near the Rhine Valley, harbors wine-loving cobbled towns, such as handy Cochem and tiny, quaint Beilstein. Nestled within a forest is my favorite European castle, Burg Eltz, which feels lived in, because it is. Farther west is Trier, easy to add for Mosel fans.

▲Trier (half-day to 1 day)

On the banks of the Mosel, Germany's oldest city has a fun market square, a huge cathedral, a fine archaeological museum, and massive Roman monuments such as the Porta Nigra gate and the basilica.

▲Cologne (half-day to 1 day)

Busy Cologne, on the Rhine River, has a spectacular Gothic cathedral looming over its train station, making it a rewarding, quick stop that's especially convenient for train travelers. The city's engaging museums—from Roman-Germanic to art (old masters and modern art) to chocolate—may entice visitors to stay longer.

▲▲Nürnberg (1-2 days)

This city has an engaging old town (rebuilt after World War II), a famous Christmas market, a variety of great museums, and haunting reminders of its Nazi past (the Nazi Documentation Center and Rally Grounds).

▲Lutherland (1-2 days)

Martin Luther made an impact on each of these places: the charming university town of Erfurt, where he spent his youth; Wartburg Castle, where he hid out from the pope's goons; and Wittenberg (with the most Luther sights), where he taught, preached, and revolutionized Christianity.

▲Leipzig (half-day to 1 day)

This rejuvenated city, which was once the derelict "second city" of East Germany, has wonderful Bach and Cold War museums. The city is architecturally drab, but has a classic café scene and the trendy Karli restaurant-and-nightlife zone.

▲▲Dresden (1-2 days)

The art-filled city, midway between Nürnberg and Berlin, offers exquisite museums (with the Green Vault's Saxon treasures), Baroque palaces, a pleasant riverside promenade, and the landmark Frauenkirche church, symbolizing Dresden's rebirth after the notorious WWII firebombing.

▲Hamburg (half-day to 1 day)

The big port city is awash with history and museums—from emigration to World War II to the Beatles. Its harbor tour is fun, its harbor boardwalk is inviting, its architecture is avant-garde (Elbphilharmonie Concert Hall), and its nightlife is Las Vegas-style. Hamburg makes an easy stop between Germany and Denmark.

Pause for a coffee break in Dresden's museum complex, and relax on a harbor tour in Hamburg.

Planning Your Trip

To plan your trip, you'll need to design your itinerary—choosing where and when to go, how you'll travel, and how many days to spend at each destination. For my best advice on sightseeing, accommodations, restaurants, and transportation, see the Practicalities chapter.

DESIGNING AN ITINERARY

As you read this book and learn your options...

Choose your top destinations.

My recommended itinerary (on the next page) gives you an idea of how much you can reasonably see in 21 days, but you can adapt it to fit your own interests and time frame.

My itinerary is heavy on half-timbered towns. But if a little cuteness goes a long way for you, spend less time in smaller towns and more time in the bigger cities, which offer more sights and nightlife.

If you love to go a wandering, you could easily spend a week in the Bavarian Alps area, touring castles, hiking, luge-riding, and spa-soaking. The region is easier by car, but doable without.

If rivers lined with castles, vineyards, and charming villages appeal to you, the Rhine and Mosel would fill a good week, including a day trip to Cologne for its stunning cathedral.

For beer hall fun, raise your glass in Munich. Wine connoisseurs enjoy Würzburg, the Rhine, and Mosel. For spa relaxation, Baden-Baden is your best bet.

Germany's Best Three-Week Trip by Car and Train

Day	Plan	Sleep in
1	Fly into Frankfurt, pick up car, drive to Rhine Valley	Bacharach
2	Rhine Valley	Bacharach
3	To Burg Eltz and Mosel, then drive to Baden-Baden	Baden-Baden
4	Relax and soak in Baden-Baden	Baden-Baden
5	Explore the Black Forest	Freiburg or Staufen
6	To the Bavarian Alps	Füssen or Reutte
7	Neuschwanstein, other castles, Bavaria, Tirol	Füssen or Reutte
8	More Bavaria/Tirol, then drive to Salzburg	Salzburg
9	Salzburg	Salzburg
10	To Munich	Munich
11	Munich	Munich
12	To Dachau, then follow Romantic Road to Rothenburg	Rothenburg
13	Rothenburg	Rothenburg
14	Rothenburg (or Würzburg), drive to Nürnberg, drop off car	Nürnberg
15	Nürnberg	Nürnberg
16	Train to Dresden	Dresden
17	Dresden	Dresden
18	Train to Berlin	Berlin
19	Berlin	Berlin
20	Berlin	Berlin
21	Fly home	

With Less Time: Go directly from Baden-Baden to Füssen/Reutte instead of overnighting in Freiburg/Staufen. Skip your choice of Salzburg, Nürnberg, Dresden, or Berlin.

   With More Time: You could stay a day in Frankfurt (upon arrival), add another day for the Rhine to day-trip to Cologne from

Historians can study their particular passion on site: ancient Roman monuments (Trier), medieval towns and castles (Rothenburg, Rhine), Reformation (Lutherland), World War II sights (Berlin, Nürnberg, Munich), and much more.

Salzburg strikes a chord for classical-music lovers, offering concerts nearly nightly. Art lovers are drawn to Munich, Berlin, and Dresden for their outstanding museums. Photographers want to go everywhere.

Bacharach, or add a stay in the quieter Mosel Valley. The Martin Luther towns (Erfurt and Wittenberg) and Leipzig fit well as mid-point stops if you're connecting Frankfurt or Nürnberg with Berlin or Dresden. Berlin merits several days more. Hamburg isn't on the way to anything in Germany, but it's a worthwhile detour to see a thriving, historic German port city.

By Train Only: Skip the southern Black Forest and take the train from Baden-Baden to Füssen, then Salzburg, then Munich. Take the train or bus to Rothenburg; from there, Nürnberg and Dresden are on the way to Berlin.

Decide when to go.

Peak season (roughly May-Sept) offers the best weather, long days (light until after 21:00), and the busiest schedule of tourist fun. Late spring and fall generally have decent weather and lighter crowds. Winter can be cold and dreary, but Germany's famous Christmas markets brighten main squares from late November until Christmas. For weather specifics, see the climate chart in the appendix.

Statues in Leipzig poke fun at communism, while people sip wine at sunset in Würzburg.

Connect the dots.

Link your destinations into a logical route. Determine which cities you'll fly into and out of. Begin your search for transatlantic flights at Kayak.com.

Decide if you'll travel by car or public transportation, or a combination of both. A car is useless in big cities (park it), but it's helpful for exploring countryside regions, where bus and train connections are relatively infrequent and time-consuming.

Trains in Germany are either fast and pricey (book ahead for discounts, or use a rail pass), or slow and cheap (even cheaper with one of several day passes). Long-distance buses are inexpensive, though it's wise to book several days in advance.

For the best of both worlds, use trains to connect major cities, and rent a car strategically to explore the countryside, such as the Bavarian Alps region, which has many scattered sights. Other candidates are the sleepy Mosel Valley, quaint Black Forest, and Romantic Road towns and sights (but if just Rothenburg's your aim, it's easily reached by train).

To determine approximate transportation times between your destinations, study the driving chart (see the Practicalities chapter) or train schedules (www.bahn.com). Compare the cost of any long train ride in Europe with a short budget flight; check Skyscanner.com for intra-European flights.

Trip Costs Per Person

Run a reality check on your dream trip. You'll have major transportation costs in addition to daily expenses.

Flight: A round-trip flight from the US to Frankfurt costs about $1,000-2,000, depending on where you fly from and when.

Public Transportation: For a three-week trip, allow $400 for second-class trains and buses ($500 for first-class trains). A rail pass is generally a good value because it covers the pricey, fast trains. In some cases, a short flight can be cheaper than taking the train.

Car Rental: Allow roughly $250 per week, not including tolls, gas, parking, and insurance. If you need the car for three weeks or more, leasing can be cheaper.

AVERAGE DAILY EXPENSES PER PERSON

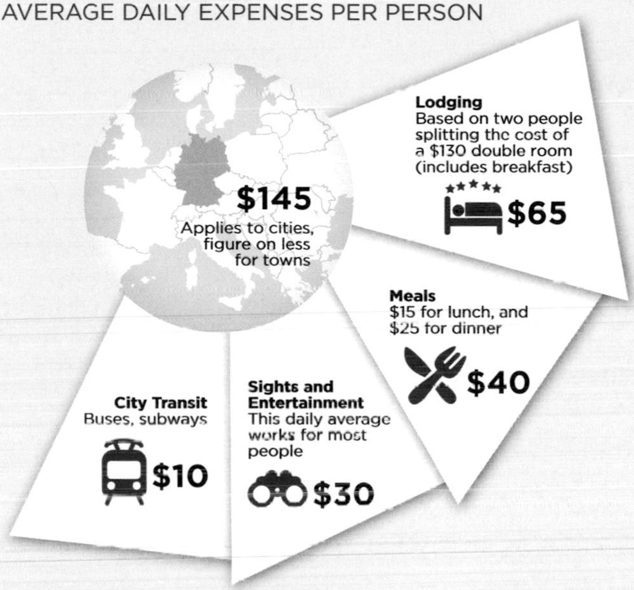

$145
Applies to cities, figure on less for towns

Lodging
Based on two people splitting the cost of a $130 double room (includes breakfast)
★★★★★ **$65**

Meals
$15 for lunch, and $25 for dinner
$40

City Transit
Buses, subways
$10

Sights and Entertainment
This daily average works for most people
$30

Budget Tips

You can cut my suggested average daily expenses by taking advantage of the deals you'll find throughout Germany and mentioned in this book.

City transit passes (for multiple rides or all-day usage) decrease your cost per ride.

If using trains, opt for the cheaper slow trains, and use day passes for further savings (most cost-effective for groups of 2-5).

Avid sightseers buy combo-tickets or passes that cover multiple museums. If a town doesn't offer deals, visit only the sights you most want ▶▶▶

▶▶▶ to see, and seek out free sights and experiences (people-watching counts).

Some businesses—especially hotels and walking-tour companies—offer discounts to my readers (look for the RS% symbol in the listings in this book).

Book your rooms directly with the hotel. Some hotels offer a discount if you pay in cash and/or stay three or more nights (check online or ask). Rooms cost less outside of peak season (May-Sept). And even seniors can sleep cheap in hostels (some have double rooms) for about $30 per person. Or check Airbnb-type sites for deals.

It's easy to eat cheap in Germany. Restaurants offer among the most reasonable prices in Europe. You can get tasty, inexpensive meals at bakeries (many sell sandwiches), department-store cafeterias, and fast-food stands. Cultivate the art of picnicking in atmospheric settings.

When you splurge, choose an experience you'll always remember, such as a concert, spa, or alpine lift. Minimize souvenir shopping; focus instead on collecting wonderful memories. ◼▮

Write out a day-by-day itinerary.

Figure out how many destinations you can comfortably fit in your time frame. Don't overdo it—few travelers wish they'd hurried more. Allow enough days per stop (see estimates in "Germany's Top Destinations," earlier). Minimize one-night stands. It can be worth taking a late-afternoon drive or train ride to settle into a town for two consecutive nights—and gain a full day for sightseeing. Include sufficient time for transportation; whether you travel by train or car, it'll take you a half-day to get between most destinations.

Staying in a home base (such as Munich) and making day trips can be more time-efficient than changing locations and hotels.

Take sight closures into account. Avoid visiting a town on the one day a week its must-see sights are closed. Check if any holidays or festivals fall during your trip—these attract crowds and can close sights (for the latest, visit Germany's tourist website, www.germany.travel).

Give yourself some slack. Every trip, and every traveler, needs downtime for doing laundry, picnic shopping, people-watching, and so on. Pace yourself. Assume you will return.

BEFORE YOU GO

You'll have a smoother trip if you tackle a few things ahead of time. For more info on these topics, see the Practicalities chapter (and www.ricksteves.com, which has helpful travel tips and talks).

Make sure your travel documents are valid. If your passport is due to expire within six months of your ticketed date of return, you need to renew it. Allow up to six weeks to renew or get a passport (www.travel.state.gov). Beginning in 2021, you will also need to register with the European Travel Information and Authorization System (ETIAS). A useful private website with more details is www.schengenvisainfo.com/etias.

Arrange your transportation. Book your international flights. Figure out your transportation options: It's worth thinking about buying train tickets online in advance, getting a rail pass, renting a car, or booking cheap European flights. (You can wing it once you're there, but it may cost more.)

Book rooms well in advance, especially if your trip falls during peak season or any major holidays or festivals.

Make reservations or buy tickets ahead for major sights. Reserve ahead for Neuschwanstein Castle. For a Munich BMW factory tour, sign up at least two months in advance. To visit the Reichstag dome in Berlin, reserve a free entry slot online a week or two in advance. To see Dresden's Historic Green Vault, book your tickets online well in advance, or play it loose and line up early for same-day tickets.

Tickets for the music-packed Salzburg Festival (mid-July through August) go fast; buy tickets far in advance (on sale in January).

Consider travel insurance. Compare the cost of the insurance to the cost of your potential loss. Check whether your existing insurance (health, homeowners, or renters) covers you and your possessions overseas.

Call your bank. Alert your bank that you'll be using your debit and credit cards in Europe. Ask about transaction fees, and get the PIN number for your credit card. You don't need to bring euros for your trip; you'll withdraw euros from cash machines in Europe.

Use your smartphone smartly. Sign up for an international service plan to reduce your costs, or rely on Wi-Fi in Europe instead. Download any apps you'll want on the road, such as maps, translation, transit schedules, and Rick Steves Audio Europe (see sidebar).

Rip up this book! Turn chapters into mini guidebooks: Break the book's spine and use a utility knife to slice apart chapters, keeping gummy edges intact. Reinforce the chapter spines with clear wide tape; use a heavy-duty stapler; or make or buy a cheap cover (see Travel Store at www.ricksteves.com), swapping out chapters as you travel.

Pack light. You'll walk with your luggage more than you think. Bring a single carry-on bag and a daypack. Use the packing checklist in the appendix as a guide.

Travel Smart

If you have a positive attitude, equip yourself with good information (this book), and expect to travel smart, you will.

Read—and reread this book. To have an "A" trip, be an "A" student. Note opening hours of sights, closed days, crowd-beating tips, and whether reservations are required or advisable. Check the latest at www.ricksteves.com/update.

Be your own tour guide. As you travel, get up-to-date info on sights, reserve tickets and tours, reconfirm hotels and travel arrangements, and check transit connections. Visit local tourist information offices (TIs). Upon arrival in a new town, lay the groundwork for a smooth departure; confirm the train, bus, or road you'll take when you leave.

Outsmart thieves. Pickpockets abound in crowded places where tourists congregate. Treat commotions as smoke-screens for theft. Keep your cash, credit cards, and passport secure in a money belt tucked under your clothes; carry only a day's spending money in your front pocket. Don't set valuable items down on counters or café tabletops, where they can be quickly stolen or easily forgotten.

Minimize potential loss. Keep expensive gear to a minimum. Bring photocopies or take photos of important documents (passport and cards) to aid in replacement if they're lost or stolen. Back up photos and files frequently.

Guard your time and energy. Taking a taxi can be a good value if it saves you a long wait for a cheap bus or an exhausting walk across town. To avoid long lines, follow my crowd-beating tips, such as making advance reservations, or sightseeing early or late.

Be flexible. Even if you have a well-planned itinerary, expect changes, closures, sore feet, bad weather, and so on. Your Plan B could turn out to be even better.

Attempt the language. Most Germans—especially in the tourist trade and in cities—speak English, but if you learn some German, even just a few phrases, you'll get more smiles and make more friends. Practice the survival phrases near the end of this book, and even better, bring a phrase book.

Connect with the culture. Interacting with locals carbonates your experience. Enjoy the friendliness of the German people. Ask questions; most locals are happy to point you in their idea of the right direction. Set up your own quest for the best beer-and-bratwurst, castle, or cathedral. When an opportunity pops up, make it a habit to say "yes."

Germany...here you come!

MUNICH

München

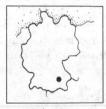

Munich ("München" in German), often called Germany's most livable city, is also one of its most historic, artistic, and entertaining. While another nickname is "Germany's biggest village," it's big and growing, with a population of 1.5 million. Until 1871, it was the capital of an independent Bavaria. Its royal palaces, jewels, and grand boulevards remind visitors that Munich has long been a political and cultural powerhouse. Meanwhile, the concentration camp in nearby Dachau reminds us that eight decades ago, Munich provided a springboard for Nazism.

Orient yourself in Munich's old center, with its colorful pedestrian zones. Immerse yourself in the city's art and history—crown jewels, Baroque theater, Wittelsbach palaces, great paintings, and beautiful parks. Spend your Munich evenings in a frothy beer hall or outdoor *Biergarten*, prying big pretzels from buxom, no-nonsense beer maids amidst an oompah, bunny-hopping, and belching Bavarian atmosphere.

PLANNING YOUR TIME

Munich is worth two days, including a half-day side-trip to Dachau (about an hour from Munich by public transportation). If all you have is one day, follow my "Munich City Walk" (visiting museums along the way), tour one of the royal palaces (the Residenz or Nymphenburg), and drink in the beer-hall culture for your evening's entertainment. With a second day, choose from the following: Tour the Dachau Concentration Camp Memorial, rent a bike to enjoy the English Garden, or—if you're into art—tour your choice of the city's many fine art museums (especially the Alte Pinakothek). With numerous worthwhile sights and activities, the city could easily fill three days. And many visitors spend an entire day side-tripping south to "Mad" King Ludwig's Castles (covered in the Bavarian Alps chapter). Salzburg, Austria (about 2 hours one-way by direct train) is also within day-trip distance.

Orientation to Munich

The tourist's Munich is circled by a ring road (site of the old town wall) marked by four old gates: Karlstor (near the main train station—the Hauptbahnhof), Sendlinger Tor, Isartor (near the river), and Odeonsplatz (no surviving gate, near the palace). Marienplatz marks the city's center. A great pedestrian-only zone (Kaufinger-strasse and Neuhauser Strasse) cuts this circle in half, running neatly from the Karlstor and the train station through Marienplatz to the Isartor. Orient yourself along this east-west axis. Most of the sights and hotels I recommend are within a 20-minute walk of Marienplatz and each other.

Despite its large population, Munich feels small. Its elegance stems from its determination to be pedestrian- and bike-friendly and because by law no building in the town center can be taller than the church spires.

TOURIST INFORMATION

Munich's helpful city-run TI (www.muenchen.de) is on the main square, **Marienplatz**, below the glockenspiel (Mon-Sat 9:30-19:30, Sun 10:00-18:00, sometimes closed Sun off-season, tel. 089/2339-6500--answered Mon-Fri 9:00-17:00). Munich's other TI, previously located outside the main train station, is closed during the Hauptbahnhof's extensive renovation project.

At the TI, buy the inexpensive city map (which is better than the free map in your hotel lobby—especially for public transit), and confirm your sightseeing plans. Pick up the *Discovering Munich* brochure, which describes transportation options, and the free, twice-monthly magazine *In München*, which lists movies and entertainment (in German, organized by date). If you're interested in tours offered by Gray Line or Munich Walk, don't buy your ticket at the TI; instead, purchase discounted tickets at EurAide (see next).

EurAide Train Assistance and Tour Discounts: At counter #1 in the train station's main *Reisezentrum* (travel center, opposite track 21), the hardworking, eager-to-help EurAide desk is a godsend for Eurailers and budget travelers. Alan Wissenberg and his staff answer train-travel and day-trip questions in English. Paid by the German rail company to help you design your train travels, EurAide makes reservations and sells tickets and sleepers for the train at the same price you'd pay at the other counters (May-Oct

Mon-Fri 8:30-20:00, Sat until 14:00, closed Sun; Nov-April Mon-Fri 10:00-19:00—except Jan-Feb 8:00-13:00, Sat 10:00-12:00, closed Sun). EurAide also sells an inexpensive city map and offers a free newsletter, *The Inside Track*, packed with regional train travel information (also see www.euraide.com). A line can form at this popular service; do your homework and have a list of questions ready.

EurAide sells cash-only tickets at a discount for travelers with this book for Munich Walk city walking tours and Gray Line city bus tours, as well as for Gray Line tours to Neuschwanstein and Linderhof castles (all described later, under "Tours in Munich").

ARRIVAL IN MUNICH

By Train: A complete renovation of Munich's main train station—München Hauptbahnhof, a sight in itself—is in progress as the city

builds a new €3.9 billion S-Bahn tunnel (see the architect's futuristic renderings in front of track 17). The locations of some services mentioned here will likely change as construction progresses.

The Hauptbahnhof is a hive of activity, with a vast **shopping mall** stretching for blocks underground (open daily). Clean, high-tech, pay **WCs** and **showers** are downstairs near tracks 11 and 26. Check out the bright and modern **food court** or the Dean & David kiosk opposite track 14. For sandwiches and prepared meals to bring on board, I shop at **Yorma's** (four branches: by track 26, by track 32, at street level, and in Bahnhofplatz, the underground passageway).

You'll find **lockers** opposite track 26 and near track 17. **Press P & B Books** (across from track 23) sells English-language books, newspapers, and magazines. **Radius Tours** (at track 32) rents bikes and organizes tours (see listings later under "Getting Around Munich" and "Tours in Munich").

Up the escalators opposite track 22 are **car-rental agencies,** a quiet, nonsmoking **waiting room** *(Warteraum)* that's open to anybody, and the **DB Lounge** (limited to those with a first-class ticket issued by the Deutsche Bahn).

Subway lines, trams, and buses connect the station to the rest of the city (though many of my recommended hotels are within walking distance of the station). If you get lost in the underground maze of subway corridors while you're trying to get to the train station, follow the signs for *DB* (Deutsche Bahn) to surface success-

MUNICH

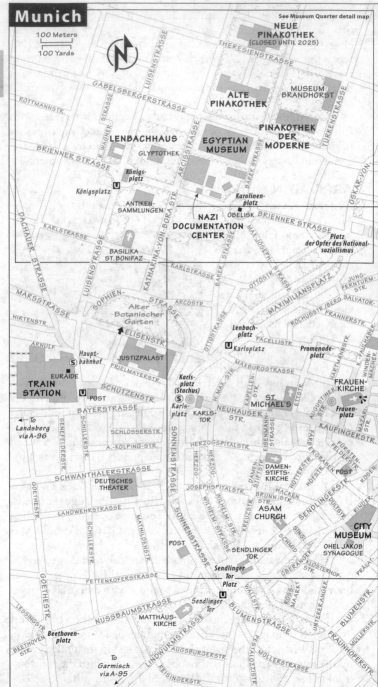

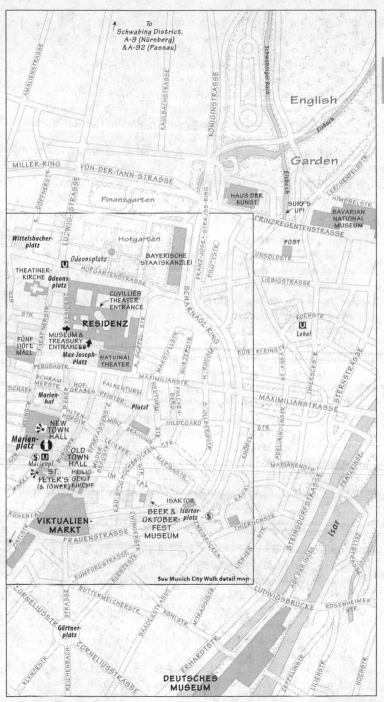

To
Schwabing District,
A-9 (Nürnberg)
& A-92 (Passau)

English

Garden

Schwabinger Bach

AMALIENSTRASSE

KAULBACHSTRASSE

KÖNIGINSTRASSE

Eisbach

LERCHENFELDSTR.

MILLER-RING

VON-DER-TANN-STRASSE

K. DÖPFNER STR.

LUDWIG-STRASSE

Finanzgarten

HAUS DER
KUNST

SURF'S
UP!

Eisbach

HIMBSELSTR.

BAVARIAN
NATIONAL
MUSEUM

PRINZREGENTENSTRASSE

POST

UNSÖLDSTR.

LIEBIGSTRASSE

Wittelsbacher-
platz

Hofgarten

THEATINER-
KIRCHE

STR.

Odeonsplatz

Odeons-
platz

HOFGARTENSTRASSE

BAYERISCHE
STAATSKANZLEI

FRANZ-JOSEF-STRAUSS-RING

PILOTYSTR.

KOCHSTR.

Lehel

LEAT HERSTR.

RESIDENZ STR.

CUVILLIÉS
THEATER
ENTRANCE

RESIDENZ

SCHARNAGL-RING

FÜNF
HÖFE
MALL

MUSEUM &
TREASURY
ENTRANCES

Max-Joseph-
platz

NATIONAL
THEATER

A. GABEL STR.

MARSTALLSTR.

WURZERSTR.

H. SACHS STR.

DÜR. EIFENSTR.

ST. ANNA

THIERSCH STR.

STERNSTRASSE

SCHRAM-
MERSTR.

SCHÄFF.

HOF-
GRABEN

DIENER

FALKENTURM

MAXIMILIANSTR.

FALCKE-
BERG

HILDEGARD

R. STRAUSS STR.

STR.

MARIENSTR.

MAXIMILIANSTRASSE

STR.

ADELGUND STR.

MARIANNEN STR.

PRATERINSEL

Marien-
hof

PFISTER

Platzl

WEINSTR.

ALTEN-
HOFSTR.

BURGSTR.

NEW TOWN
HALL

LEDERER STR.

BRÄUHAUS

Marien-
platz

OLD
TOWN
HALL

Marienpl.

ST.
PETER'S
(& TOWER)

GEIST.
KIRCHE

HEILIG-

IM
TAL

RAD. STEIG

HOCHBRÜCKEN

KNÖBEL

KANAL

STEINSDORFSTRASSE

Isar

ZEILE STR.

ROSENTA

VIKTUALIEN-
MARKT

ISARTOR

BEER &
OKTOBER-
FEST
MUSEUM

Isartor-
platz

WEINBRÜCKEN

THIERSCH STR.

AUF DER INSEL

ZELLSTR.

RABL STR.

FRAUENSTRASSE

ZWINGERSTR.

KLENZESTR.

KUMFÖRDSTRASSE

BUTTERMEICHERSTR.

BAADERSTR.

KOHLSTR.

MORASSISTR.

LUDWIGSBRÜCKE

ROSENHEIMER
STR.

See Munich City Walk detail map

CORNELIUSSTR.

STRASSE

Gärtner-
platz

CORNELIUSSTRASSE

REICHENBACH STR.

KLENZE STR.

ERHARDTSTR.

DEUTSCHES
MUSEUM

ZEPPELIN STR.

LILIENSTR.

HOCHSTR.

fully. Watch out for the hallways with blue ticket-stamping machines in the middle—these lead to the subway, where you could be fined if you don't have a validated ticket.

The Lufthansa **airport bus** leaves from the north side of the train station (exit by track 26).

By Bus: Munich's central bus station (ZOB) is by the Hackerbrücke S-Bahn station (from the train station, it's a short walk or one hop on the S-Bahn; www.muenchen-zob.de). The Romantic Road bus leaves from here, as do many buses to Eastern Europe and the Balkans. Upstairs you'll find ticket offices, eateries, shops, and waiting areas.

By Plane: For airport information, see "Munich Connections" near the end of this chapter.

HELPFUL HINTS

Museum Tips: Museums closed on Monday include the Alte Pinakothek, Egyptian Museum, Nazi Documentation Center, and the BMW Museum. The art museums are generally open late one night a week.

Half-Price Tickets: Your ticket to the Jewish History Museum, Munich City Museum, Nazi Documentation Center, Lenbachhaus, or Villa Stuck gets you half-price admission to any of the others up to two days later (e.g., show your €5 Nazi Documentation Center ticket to get €5 off your €10 Lenbachhaus ticket).

Palace Sightseeing Passes: The Bavarian Palace Department offers a 14-day ticket (the *Mehrtagesticket*) that covers admission to Munich's Residenz and Nymphenburg Palace complexes, as well as other castles and palaces in Bavaria (for details, see page 141; purchase at participating sights, www.schloesser. bayern.de). For avid castle-goers planning to visit castles beyond Munich, this can be a good deal.

Festivals: It's hard to visit Munich without running into at least one festival. For a complete list, see the TI website (www. muenchen.de), download the handy brochure *einfach erleben*, or ask at the TI.

Oktoberfest lasts around two weeks (Sept 19-Oct 4 in 2020; Sept 18-Oct 3 in 2021), usually ending on the first Sunday in October (www.oktoberfest.de). The same fairgrounds also host a **Spring Festival** (*Frühlingsfest,* two weeks in late April-early May, www.fruehlingsfest-muenchen.de). **Tollwood,** an artsy, multicultural event, happens twice a year—in summer (late June-July) and winter (alternative Christmas market, late Nov-Dec, www.tollwood.de).

Concerts: The München Ticket office sells concert and event tickets in the New Town Hall (Mon-Fri 10:00-19:00, Sat until

14:00, closed Sun, Dienerstrasse 20, next to Ratskeller restaurant, tel. 089/5481-8181, www.muenchenticket.de).

Wi-Fi: The city offers free Wi-Fi at many spots around town, including Marienplatz, Karlsplatz (known locally as Stachus), and the train station (connect to M-WLAN network, then click to accept terms).

WCs: Munich had outdoor urinals until the 1972 Olympics and then decided to beautify the city by doing away with them. What about the people's needs? By law, any place serving beer must admit the public (whether or not they're customers) to use the WCs.

Laundry: A 10-minute walk from the train station, **Waschcenter** is convenient (self-service daily 7:00-23:00; drop-off Mon-Fri 7:00-19:00, Sat 9:00-16:00; English instructions; Paul-Heyse-Strasse 21, near intersection with Landwehrstrasse—see the "Munich Hotels" map, later; U-Bahn: Theresienwiese, mobile 0171-734-2094).

Bikes and Pedestrians: Signs painted on the sidewalk or blue-and-white street signs show designated lanes for pedestrians and cyclists. The strip of pathway closest to the street is usually reserved for bikes. Pedestrians wandering into the bike path may hear the cheery ding-ding of a cyclist's bell just before being knocked unconscious.

Taxi: Call 089/21610 for a taxi.

Private Driver: Reliable **Johann Fayoumi** speaks English (€70/hour, mobile 0174-183-8473, www.firstclasslimousines.de, johannfayoumi@gmail.com).

Car Rental: Several car-rental agencies are located upstairs at the train station, opposite track 21 (open daily, hours vary).

Great Views in the Town Center: Downtown Munich's best city viewpoints are from the towers of St. Peter's Church (stairs only) and New Town Hall (elevator, fast and easy). The Frauenkirche towers usually make this list, but are closed for renovation.

What's with Monaco? People walking around with guidebooks to Monaco aren't lost. "Monaco di Baviera" is *Italiano* for "Munich."

GETTING AROUND MUNICH

Much of Munich is walkable. But given that the city is laced by many trams, buses, and subways, it's worth learning the system and considering getting a day pass. Public transit also makes it easy to access sights outside the historic core, such as Dachau or Nymphenburg Palace (see the "Munich Transportation" map). Taxis are honest and professional, but expensive (about €12 between the Hauptbahnhof and Marienplatz) and generally unnecessary.

By Public Transit

Munich's transit system uses the same ticket for its subway/trains, buses, and trams. There are two types of trains: The U-Bahn—like a subway, making lots of short hops around town—is run by the local transit authority (Munich Transit Corporation, MVG); the S-Bahn, a light rail that goes faster and stops only at major stations, is operated by German Railways (Deutsche Bahn, DB).

Transit lines are numbered (for example, S-3 or U-5). U-Bahn lines mainly run north-south, while S-Bahn lines are generally east-west. There are four concentric zones—Zone 1 (inner zone where you'll spend most of your time), Zone 2 (Dachau), Zone 3, and Zone 4 (airport).

Information: Pick up a transit map at the TI or station, use the journey planner at www.mvv-muenchen.de, or download the MVV app. You can also head straight to an **MVG customer service center** where real people are waiting to help (underground at the train station, Mon-Fri 8:00-20:00, Sat 9:00-16:00, Sun 9:00-20:00; and at Marienplatz, same hours except closed Sun; kiosks outside open long hours daily; tel. 0800-344-226-600, www.mvg.de).

Ticket Options

Transit tickets are sold at booths in the subway and at any ticket machine that has an MVG (blue machines) or DB (red machines) logo. Though operated by different companies, the machines work much the same way (and accept coins, bills, and credit cards).

A one-zone **regular ticket** *(Einzelfahrkarte)* costs €2.90 and is good for three hours in one direction, including changes and stops. For short rides (four stops max, only two of which can be on the subway lines), buy the €1.50 **short-stretch ticket** *(Kurzstrecke)*, good for one ride. The €6.70 **all-day pass** *(Single-Tageskarte)* for Zone 1 is a great deal for a single traveler. If you're going to Dachau, buy the *XXL* version of the *Single-Tageskarte*, which also includes Zone 2 (€8.90); the **airport-city day ticket** *(Flughafen)* covers all four zones and gets you to the airport and other out-of-the-way destinations (€11.60/single ride; €13/all-day pass).

All-day small-group passes *(Partner-Tageskarte)* are an even better deal—they cover all public transportation for up to five adults (or up to two adults and six kids). A *Partner-Tageskarte* for Zone 1 costs €12.80. The *XXL* version, which includes Dachau, costs €16.10; and the **airport-city day ticket** *(Flughafen)* costs €24.30

and includes all four zones. These partner tickets—while seemingly impossibly cheap—are for real. Read it again and do the arithmetic. Even two people traveling together save money, and for groups, it's a real steal. The only catch is that you've got to stay together.

For longer stays, consider a **three-day ticket** (€16.80/person, €29.60/partner ticket for the gang, Zone 1 only, does not include Dachau).

The **City Tour Card,** which covers public transportation and adds stingy discounts on a few sights and tours, costs a little more than a transit pass (Zone 1 single traveler-€12.90/1 day, €24.90/3 days; Zone 1 partner ticket-€19.90/1 day, €39.90/3 days; www.citytourcard-muenchen.com). The partner tickets are the best value—four adults can save money with just one visit to Nymphenburg Palace on public transit. For single travelers, the card usually isn't worth it. Students, seniors, and readers of this book qualify for many of the same discounts without buying this card.

Using the System

To find the right platform, look for the name of the last station in the direction *(Richtung)* you want to travel. For example, *Richtung: Marienplatz* means that that particular subway, bus, or tram is traveling in the direction of Marienplatz. Know where you're going relative to Marienplatz, the Hauptbahnhof, and Ostbahnhof, as these are often referred to as end points.

You must stamp tickets with the date and time prior to using them (for an all-day or multiday pass, stamp it only the first time you use it; some tickets bought at a machine come prestamped—check to be sure). For the subway, punch your ticket in the blue machine *before* going down to the platform. For buses and trams, stamp your ticket once on board. Plainclothes ticket checkers enforce this honor system, rewarding freeloaders—even jet-lagged travelers—with stiff €60 fines.

Useful Transit Lines

Several subway lines, trams, and buses are especially convenient for tourists (be aware that ongoing construction work might impact the use of some lines). All the main S-Bahn lines (S-1 through S-8) run east-west along the main tourist axis between the Hauptbahnhof, Marienplatz, and the Ostbahnhof. For travel within the city center, just find the platform for lines S-1 through S-8. One track *(Gleis)* will be headed east to the Ostbahnhof, the other west to the Hauptbahnhof. Hop on any train going your direction.

The U-3 goes to Olympic Park and the BMW sights, and the S-2 goes to Dachau. Bus #100 is useful for getting to the English Garden (from the train station) and to the Museum Quarter (from Odeonsplatz). Tram #17 goes to Nymphenburg Palace (from the

MUNICH

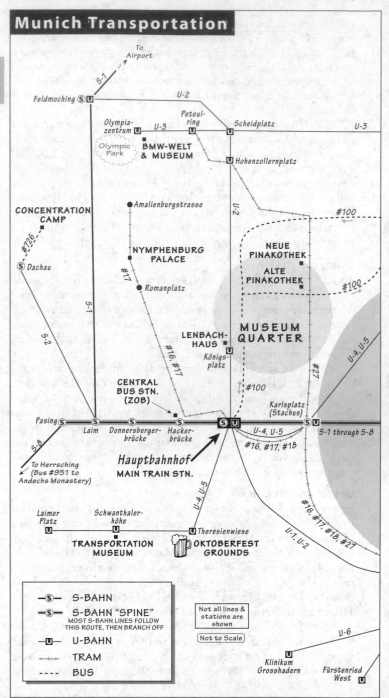

Munich Transportation

To Airport

S-1

Feldmoching Ⓢ Ⓤ   U-2

Olympia-   Peteul-
zentrum Ⓤ U-3   ring   Scheidplatz   U-3

Olympic   ■ BMW-WELT   Ⓤ Hohenzollernplatz
Park   & MUSEUM

CONCENTRATION   ● Amalienburgstrasse
CAMP   NEUE   #100
                                        PINAKOTHEK
#726   NYMPHENBURG   ALTE
Ⓢ Dachau   PALACE   PINAKOTHEK   #100

S-1   #17   ● Romanplatz
S-2   M U S E U M

          LENBACH-   Q U A R T E R   U-4, U-5
          HAUS
          #16 #17   Königs-
          platz   Ⓤ   #27
                                        #100

          CENTRAL   #100
          BUS STN.
          (ZOB)   Karlsplatz
Pasing Ⓢ   Ⓢ   Ⓢ   Ⓢ   (Stachus)
          Laim Donnersberger- Hacker- Ⓢ Ⓤ   Ⓢ Ⓤ   S-1 through S-8
          brücke   brücke   U-4, U-5
S-8   #16, #17, #18

To Herrsching   *Hauptbahnhof*
(Bus #951 to   MAIN TRAIN STN.
Andechs Monastery)

                    U-4, U-5   #16, #17, #18, #27

Laimer   Schwanthaler-
Platz   höhe
Ⓤ   Ⓤ   Ⓤ Theresienwiese
                              U-1, U-2
TRANSPORTATION   🍺 OKTOBERFEST
MUSEUM   GROUNDS

—Ⓢ— S-BAHN

—Ⓢ— S-BAHN "SPINE"   Not all lines &
      MOST S-BAHN LINES FOLLOW   stations are
      THIS ROUTE, THEN BRANCH OFF   shown

—Ⓤ— U-BAHN   Not to Scale   U-6

++++ TRAM   Ⓤ   Ⓤ
                    Klinikum   Fürstenried
---- BUS   Grosshadern   West

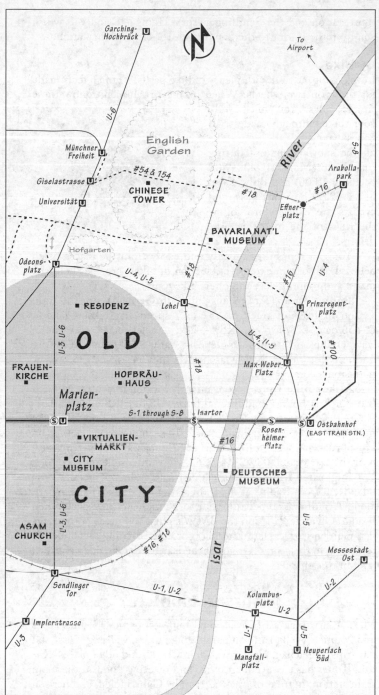

MUNICH

train station and the Sendlinger Tor). Trams #16 and #18 whisk you from the Isartor to the Sendlinger Tor or the train station.

By Bike

Level, compact, and with plenty of bike paths, Munich feels made for those on two wheels. When biking in Munich, follow these simple rules: You must walk your bike through pedestrian zones; you can take your bike on the subway, but not during rush hour (Mon-Fri 6:00-9:00 & 16:00-18:00) and only if you buy a €2.60 bike day pass; and cyclists are expected to follow the rules of the road, just like drivers.

You can **rent bikes** quickly and easily from the places listed below. Each has an extensive selection of bikes; provides helmets, maps, and route advice; and offers bike tours.

Radius Tours (*Rad* means "bike" in German) is in the train station in front of track 32 (3- to 7-speed city bikes-€4/hour, €14.50/day, €28/2 days, RS%—ask, fancier bikes cost more, leave credit-card number as deposit, daily 8:30-19:00, May-Aug until 20:00, closed Nov-March, tel. 089/543-487-7730, www.radiustours.com).

Mike's Bike Tours is conveniently located in central Munich (€10 for first hour, €2/additional hour, €18/day, RS%—ask; daily 10:00-19:30, shorter hours Oct-mid-April, closed mid-Nov-Feb; most of the year at Bräuhausstrasse 10—enter around corner on Hochbrückenstrasse; off-season at Thomas-Wimmer-Ring 16, near the Isartor; tel. 089/2314-0263, www.mikesbiketours.com).

Suggested Ride: For a great city ride, consider this day on a bike: Rent from Radius at the train station, and take the bike path along Arnulfstrasse, pedaling out to Nymphenburg Palace. Then head to Olympic Park and the BMW sights, and finish at the English Garden (for the late-afternoon or early-evening scene) before returning to the center. Or go for the Isar River bike ride described later in this chapter.

Tours in Munich

Munich's two largest conventional tour companies, Radius Tours and Munich Walk, run comparable bike tours, walking tours, and day trips to Dachau, Neuschwanstein Castle, and other places. **Radius Tours** has a convenient office and meeting point in the main train station, in front of track 32 (run by Gaby Holder and her son

Daniel, tel. 089/543-487-7740, www.radiustours.com). **Munich Walk,** run by Ralph Lünstroth, uses Marienplatz as its meeting point (tel. 089/2423-1767, www.munichwalktours.de).

There's also **Gray Line,** which runs sightseeing buses around town and for day trips (tel. 089/5490-7560, www.stadtrundfahrten-muenchen.de). You can buy discounted cash-only tickets for Gray Line and Munich Walk tours at the train station EurAide office.

"Free" Tours: Marienplatz is chaotic with "free" tour guides jockeying to gather their groups. You'll encounter brochures advertising these "free" walking and biking tours. The tours aren't really free—tips are expected, and the guides actually have to pay the company for each person who takes the tour—so unless you tip more than they owe the company, they don't make a penny. The tours tend to be light on history, and the guides work hard to promote their company's other tours (which are not free).

TOURS WITHIN MUNICH

🎧 To sightsee on your own, download my free **Munich City Walk audio tour** (see sidebar on page 26 for details).

Walking Tours

These companies all offer RS% discounts to my readers. Just show your book and ask at the time of booking (online reservations not required).

Munich Walk offers two daytime tours: a daily city walk (€14, year-round at 10:45, May-Oct also daily at 14:45, 2 hours) and "Third Reich in Munich" (€16, daily year-round at 10:15, 2.5 hours, extended €25 six-hour version Mon and Sat only). Their "Beer and Brewery" tour is more mature than your typical hard-partying pub crawl. You visit Paulaner, Munich's oldest brewery, to learn, eat, and drink in the city that made beer famous. The price includes two beers in the brewery; afterward, the tour ends at the Hofbräuhaus (€30, May-mid-Sept Mon, Wed, and Fri-Sat at 18:15, less frequent and at 17:30 off-season, 3.5 hours). All Munich Walk tours depart from in front of the TI on Marienplatz.

Radius Tours runs two city walking tours with reliably good guides: a daily city tour (€15, at 10:15, 2.5 hours) and "Birthplace of the Third Reich" (€17.50, April-mid-Oct daily at 15:00, off-season daily at 11:30; 2.5 hours). They also offer an educational "Bavarian Beer and Food" tour (€36; April-mid-Oct Mon-Sat 18:00, off-season Tue, Thu, and Sat at 18:00; 3.5 hours; no tours during Oktoberfest except their Oktoberfest tour—reserve well in advance, www.radiustours.com). All tours depart from the Radius office in front of track 32 at the train station. Reserve a day ahead in summer (if booking online, use the "student rate"); otherwise just show up.

MUNICH

Munich at a Glance

In the Center

▲▲**Marienplatz** Munich's main square, at the heart of a lively pedestrian zone, watched over by New Town Hall (and its glockenspiel show). **Hours:** Glockenspiel jousts daily at 11:00 and 12:00, plus 17:00 March-Oct; New Town Hall tower elevator runs daily 10:00-19:00; Oct-April Mon-Fri 10:00-17:00, closed Sat-Sun. See page 46.

▲▲**Viktualienmarkt** Munich's "small-town" open-air market, perfect for a quick snack or meal. **Hours:** Market closed Sun; beer garden open daily 10:00-22:00 (weather permitting). See page 52.

▲▲**Hofbräuhaus** World-famous beer hall, worth a visit even if you're not chugging. **Hours:** Daily 9:00-23:30. See page 62.

▲▲**The Residenz** Elegant family palace of the Wittelsbachs, awash in Bavarian opulence. Complex includes the Residenz Museum (lavish apartments), Residenz Treasury (Wittelsbach family crowns and royal knickknacks), and the impressive, heavily restored Cuvilliés Theater. **Hours:** Museum and treasury—daily 9:00-18:00, mid-Oct-mid-March 10:00-17:00; theater—generally Mon-Sat 14:00-18:00, Sun from 9:00, longer hours Aug-mid-Sept. See page 69.

▲▲**Alte Pinakothek** Bavaria's best painting gallery, with a wonderful collection of European masters from the 14th through the 19th century. **Hours:** Wed-Sun 10:00-18:00, Tue until 20:00, closed Mon. See page 81.

▲▲**Egyptian Museum** Easy-to-enjoy collection of ancient Egyptian treasures. **Hours:** Wed-Sun 10:00-18:00, Tue until 20:00, closed Mon. See page 87.

▲▲**Lenbachhaus** Three stages of German art: 19th-century, Blue Rider, and post-WWI—most important for its Blue Rider collection. **Hours:** Wed-Sun 10:00-18:00, Tue until 20:00, closed Mon. See page 87.

▲▲**Nazi Documentation Center** Thoughtful look at Munich's role in the rise of Nazism. **Hours:** Tue-Sun 10:00-19:00, closed Mon. See page 89.

▲**Munich City Museum** The city's history in five floors. **Hours:** Tue-Sun 10:00-18:00, closed Mon. See page 79.

▲**Asam Church** Private church of the Asam brothers, dripping with Baroque. **Hours:** Sat-Thu 9:00-18:00, Fri from 13:00. See page 55.

▲**Pinakothek der Moderne** Munich's modern art museum with works by Picasso, Dalí, Miró, Magritte, and Ernst. **Hours:** Tue-Sun 10:00-18:00, Thu until 20:00, closed Mon. See page 86.

▲**English Garden** The largest city park on the Continent, packed with locals, tourists, surfers, and nude sunbathers. (On a bike, I'd rate this ▲▲.) See page 91.

▲**Deutsches Museum** Germany's version of our Smithsonian Institution, with 10 miles of science and technology exhibits at its main branch. **Hours:** Daily 9:00-17:00. See page 93.

Outside the City Center

▲▲▲**Dachau Concentration Camp Memorial** Notorious Nazi camp on the outskirts of Munich, now a powerful museum and memorial. **Hours:** Daily 9:00-17:00. See page 129.

▲▲**Nymphenburg Palace** The Wittelsbachs' impressive summer palace, featuring a hunting lodge, coach museum, fine royal porcelain collection, and vast park. **Hours:** Park—daily 6:00-dusk; palace buildings—daily April-mid-Oct 9:00-18:00, mid-Oct-March 10:00-16:00. See page 98.

▲**BMW-Welt and Museum** The carmaker's futuristic museum and floating-cloud showroom, highlighting BMW past, present, and future in unforgettable architecture. **Hours:** BMW-Welt showroom exhibits—daily 9:00-18:00; museum—Tue-Sun 10:00-18:00, closed Mon. See page 105.

▲**Museum of Transportation** Deutsches Museum's cross-town annex devoted to travel. **Hours:** Daily 9:00-17:00. See page 95.

▲**Schleissheim Palace** Another Wittelsbach palace, highlighted by Baroque architecture, a fine garden, and fewer tourists than the other palaces. **Hours:** Tue-Sun 9:00-18:00, Oct-March 10:00-16:00, closed Mon year-round. See page 97.

▲**Andechs Monastery** Baroque church, hearty food, and Bavaria's best brew, in the nearby countryside. **Hours:** Beer garden daily 10:00-20:00, church open until 18:00. See page 136.

The **Size Matters Beer Tour,** run by Kenyan-German-American Tim and his associate John, stops at the Augustiner Biergarten, Löwenbräu, and Park Café. Depart from Euro Youth Hotel, near the train station, at Senefelderstrasse 5 (€16, daily at 18:45, less frequent in winter, www.sizemattersbeertour.de).

Local Guides

A guide can be a great value—especially if you assemble a small group. Six people splitting the cost can make the luxury of a private guide affordable. I've had great days with two good guides: **Georg Reichlmayr,** who has helped me generously with this chapter (€200/3 hours, tel. 08131/86800, mobile 0170-341-6384, program explained on his website, www.muenchen-stadtfuehrung.de, info@muenchen-stadtfuehrung.de), and **Birgit Stempfle** (€180/3 hours, mobile 0171-718-1465, www.sightseeing-munich.de, info@sightseeing-munich.de).

Bike Tours

Munich lends itself to bike touring. The following outfits fit the bill and offer similar RS% discounts to my readers. You don't need to reserve ahead—just show up—but do confirm times. Prices include bike rental (you'll pick up your bike after meeting your guide).

Munich Walk offers 3.5-hour bike tours around Munich (€25, daily 10:45, no tours Nov-March, depart from Marienplatz TI, www.munichwalktours.de).

Radius Tours has similar 3-hour bike tours (€29.50, April-mid-Oct daily at 10:00, no tours off-season, www.radiustours.com). Tours leave from the Radius office at track 32 in the train station.

Mike's Bike Tours packs four hours of "edutainment" on wheels into their "Classic" bike tour (€29, reservations recommended, 1-hour break in Chinese Tower beer garden, daily at 11:30, mid-April-Sept also at 16:00, more tour options in summer, meet under tower of Old Town Hall at east end of Marienplatz—near toy museum at Marienplatz 15, tel. 089/2554-3987, www.mikesbiketours.com).

Hop-On, Hop-Off Bus Tour

Gray Line Tours has hop-on, hop-off bus tours that leave from in front of the Karstadt department store at Bahnhofplatz, directly across from the train station. Choose from a basic, one-hour "Express Circle" that heads past the Pinakotheks, Marienplatz, and Karlsplatz; or the more extensive "Grand Circle" that lasts 2.5 hours and also includes Nymphenburg Palace and BMW-Welt/Museum (both tours depart 3/hour, 9:40-18:00). If you plan on visiting Nymphenburg and the BMW center, this is a very efficient way to see both—just plan your visits to these sights around the tour schedule (bus generally leaves from Nymphenburg at :30 past the hour, and from BMW at :45 past). The tour itself is also worthwhile: Sitting upstairs on the topless double-decker bus, you'll see

lots of things missed by the typical visitor wandering around the center. It complements the information in this book, though the live narration (in German and English) is delivered as stiffly as a recording. Just show up and pay the driver (€17 Express tour—valid 24 hours, €22/€27 Grand tour—valid 24/48 hours, daily in season, tel. 089/5490-7560, www.stadtrundfahrten-muenchen.de). You'll get a small discount by buying your ticket in advance on their website or at EurAide (cash only).

DAY TRIPS BEYOND MUNICH

While you can do many day trips from Munich on your own by train (see "Day Trips from Munich," at the end of this chapter), going as part of an organized group can be convenient. Many of the companies offering tours in Munich also have options for getting to **Dachau,** Neuschwanstein, Nürnberg, Salzburg, and other destinations.

An organized bus tour can be especially convenient for getting to **Neuschwanstein.** Though they're a little more expensive, I prefer the guided private bus tours (as opposed to the escorted tours by public transportation)—you're guaranteed a seat (public transport to Neuschwanstein is routinely standing-room only in summer), and you get to see more. All these tours can sell out, especially in summer, so it's wise to buy your ticket in advance. **Gray Line Tours** offers rushed all-day bus tours of Neuschwanstein that also include Ludwig's Linderhof Castle and 30 minutes in Oberammergau (€54, does not include castle admissions, RS% if you buy your ticket at EurAide and pay cash, daily at 8:30, meets across from main train station in front of Karstadt department store, www.stadtrundfahrten-muenchen.de). **Munich Walk** advertises a similar tour—they're simply selling tickets for this Gray Line trip. A luxury version from Gray Line offers a smaller group and more amenities (€139, includes castle admission, daily Jan-Oct at 8:30, www.sightseeing-munich.com).

Bus Bavaria (run by Mike's Bike Tours) offers a private bus tour for the able-bodied with a focus on the outdoors—a bike ride, hike, and short swim near Neuschwanstein are included (€59, RS%—ask, does not include castle admission or lunch; Tue, Thu,

Sat, and Sun mid-May–mid-Aug; otherwise Mon, Wed, Fri, Sat; meet at 8:30 at Mike's Bike Tours office near Hofbräuhaus, Bräuhausstrasse 10—enter around corner on Hochbrückenstrasse, tel. 089/2554-3987, mobile 0172-852-0660, www.mikesbiketours. com).

Radius Tours runs all-day tours to Neuschwanstein using public transportation. Your guide will escort you onto the train to Füssen and then the bus from there to the castle, and help you into the castle for the standard tour that's included with any admission ticket (€49, €42 with rail pass, RS%—use "student rate" when you book online, does not include castle admission; daily April–Dec at 9:30, also May–mid-Oct and Dec at 10:30; Jan–March tours run Mon, Wed, and Fri–Sun at 9:30; smart to reserve ahead online, departs from the Radius office near track 32 in the train station, www.radiustours.com). The 10:30 tour is the same as the 9:30 but comes with less-crowded trains.

Munich City Walk

Munich is big and modern, with a million and a half citizens, but, with its pedestrian-friendly historic core, it feels a lot like an easygoing Bavarian town. On this self-guided walk, rated ▲▲▲, we'll start in the central square, see its famous glockenspiel, stroll through a thriving open-air market, and visit historic churches with lavish Baroque decor. We'll sample edibles at a venerable gourmet deli and take a spin through the world's most famous beer hall. Allow two to three hours for this walk through a thousand years of Munich's history. Allow extra time if you want to take a break from the walk to tour the museums—details on visiting the sights are given later, under "Sights in Munich."

🎧 Download my free Munich City Walk audio tour, and use the "Munich City Walk" map to help find your way.

• *Begin your walk at the heart of the old city, with a stroll through...*

❶ Marienplatz

Riding the escalator out of the subway into sunlit Marienplatz (mah-REE-en-platz, "Mary's Square," rated ▲▲) gives you a fine first look at the glory of Munich: great buildings, outdoor cafés, and people bustling and lingering like the birds and breeze with which they share this square.

The square is both old and new: For a thousand years, it's been the center of Munich. It was the town's marketplace and public forum, standing at a crossroads along the Salt Road, which ran between Salzburg and Augsburg.

Lining one entire side of the square is the impressive facade of the **New Town Hall** (Neues Rathaus), with its soaring 280-foot spire. The structure looks medieval, but it was actually built in the late 1800s (1867-1908). The style is "Neo"-Gothic—pointed arches over the doorways and a roofline bristling with prickly spires. The 40 statues look like medieval saints, but they're from around 1900, depicting more recent Bavarian kings and nobles. This medieval-looking style was all the rage in the 19th century as Germans were rediscovering their historical roots and uniting as a modern nation.

The New Town Hall is famous for its **glockenspiel.** A carillon in the tower chimes a tune while colorful figurines come out on the balcony to spin and dance. It happens daily at 11:00 and 12:00 all year (also at 17:00 March-Oct) and lasts about 10 minutes. The *Spiel* of the glocken-spiel tells the story of a noble wedding that took place on the market square in 1568. You see the wedding procession and the friendly joust of knights on horseback. The duke and his bride watch the action as the groom's Bavarian family (in Bavarian white and blue) joyfully jousts with the bride's French family (in red and white). Below, the barrelmakers—famous for being the

first to dance in the streets after a deadly plague lifted—do their popular jig. Finally, the solitary cock crows.

At the very top of the New Town Hall is a statue of a child with outstretched arms, dressed in monk's garb and holding a book in its left hand. This is the **Münchner Kindl,** the symbol of Munich. The town got its name from the people who first settled here: the monks *(Mönchen).* You'll spot this mini monk all over town, on everything from the city's coat of arms to souvenir shot glasses to ad campaigns (often holding not a book, but maybe a beer or a smartphone). The city symbol was originally depicted as a grown man, wearing a gold-lined black cloak and red shoes. By the 19th century, artists were representing him as a young boy, then a gender-neutral child, and, more recently, a young girl.

These days, a teenage girl dressed as the *Kindl* kicks off the annual Oktoberfest by leading the opening parade on horseback, and then serves as the mascot throughout the festivities.

New Town Hall Tower Views: Enter the New Town Hall and take an elevator to the fourth floor (where you purchase your ticket), then ride another elevator to the top of the New Town Hall

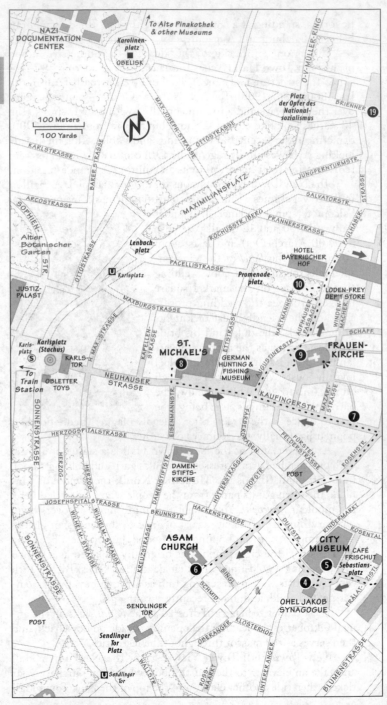

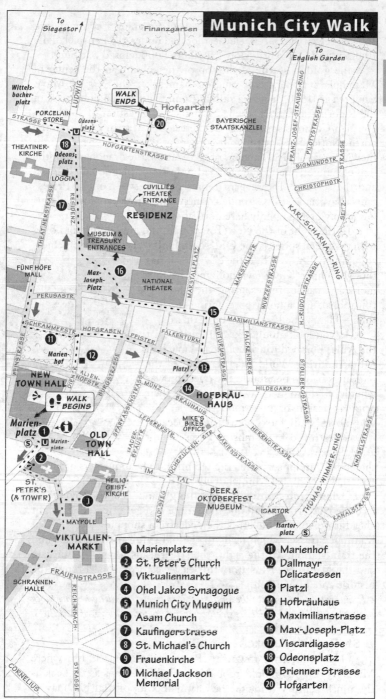

Munich City Walk

MUNICH

1. Marienplatz
2. St. Peter's Church
3. Viktualienmarkt
4. Ohel Jakob Synagogue
5. Munich City Museum
6. Asam Church
7. Kaufingerstrasse
8. St. Michael's Church
9. Frauenkirche
10. Michael Jackson Memorial
11. Marienhof
12. Dallmayr Delicatessen
13. Platzl
14. Hofbräuhaus
15. Maximilianstrasse
16. Max-Joseph-Platz
17. Viscardigasse
18. Odeonsplatz
19. Brienner Strasse
20. Hofgarten

tower—where, from a small perch, you can enjoy a commanding 360-degree city view (€3, elevator located under glockenspiel; daily 10:00-19:00; Oct-April Mon-Fri 10:00-17:00, closed Sat-Sun).

The **golden statue** at the top of the column in the center of Marienplatz honors the square's namesake, the Virgin Mary. Sculpted in 1590, it was a rallying point in the religious wars of the Reformation. Back then, Munich was a bastion of southern-German Catholicism against the heresies of Martin Luther to the north. Notice how, at the four corners of the statue, cherubs fight the four great biblical enemies of civilization: the dragon of war, the lion of hunger, the rooster-headed monster of plague and disease, and the serpent. The serpent represents heresy—namely, Protestants. Bavaria is still Catholic country, and Protestants weren't allowed to worship openly here until about 1800.

To the right of the New Town Hall, the gray pointy building with the green spires is the **Old Town Hall** (Altes Rathaus). On its

adjoining bell tower, find the city seal. It has the Münchner Kindl (symbolizing the first monks), a castle (representing the first fortifications), and a lion (representing the first ruler—Henry the Lion, who built them).

As you look around, keep in mind that the Allies bombed Marienplatz and much of Munich during World War II. Most of the buildings had to be rebuilt; the question was whether to do so in a way that matched their original design or in a modern style. The Old Town Hall looks newer now because it was destroyed by bombs and was rebuilt after the war. The New Town Hall survived the bombs, and it served as the US military headquarters after the Americans occupied Munich in 1945.

Orientation Spin: Back on the ground, before moving on, face the New Town Hall one more time and get oriented. Straight ahead is north. To the left is the pedestrian shopping street called Kaufingerstrasse, which leads to the old gate called Karlstor and the train station. To the right, the street leads to the Isartor gate and the Deutsches Museum. This east-west axis cuts through the historic core of Munich.

• *Turn around and notice the small street to the left leading a short block to St. Peter's Church, with its steeple poking up above a row of buildings.*

❷ St. Peter's Church

The oldest church in town, St. Peter's stands on the hill where Munich's original monks probably settled—perhaps as far back as the ninth century (though the city marks its official birthday as

1158). Today's church (from 1368) replaced the original monastery church.

St. Peter's ("Old Peter" to locals) is part of the soul of the city. There's even a popular song about it that goes, "Munich is not Munich without St. Peter's."

Cost and Hours: Church-free, tower climb-€3, Mon-Fri 9:00-18:30, Sat-Sun from 10:00.

Visiting the Church: On the outside of the church, notice the 16th- and 17th-century tombstones plastered onto the wall. Origi-

nally, people were buried in the holy ground around the church. But in the Napoleonic age, the cemeteries were dug up and relocated outside the city walls for hygienic and space reasons. They kept a few tombstones here as a reminder.

Step inside. (If there's a Mass in progress, visitors are welcome, but stay in the back. If there's no Mass, feel free to explore.) Typical of so many Bavarian churches, it's whitewashed and light-filled, with highlights in pastel pinks and blues framed by gold curli-cues. The ceiling painting opens up to the heavens, where Peter is crucified upside down.

Photos (on a pillar near the entrance) show how St. Peter's was badly damaged in World War II—the roof caved in, and the tower was demolished during an air raid. But the beloved church was rebuilt and restored, thanks to donations—half from the Augustiner brewery, the rest from private donors. (The accuracy of the restoration was possible thanks to Nazi catalog photos—see "The History of Munich" sidebar later in this chapter.) For decades after World War II, the bells played a popular tune that stopped just before the last note, reminding locals that the church still needed money to rebuild.

Explore further. The nave is lined with bronze statues of the apostles, and the altar shows a statue of St. Peter being adored by four Church fathers. The finely crafted, gray iron fences that line the nave were donated after World War II by the local blacksmiths of the national railway. The precious and fragile sandstone Gothic chapel altar (to the left of the main altar) survived the war only because it was buried in sandbags.

Find the second chapel from the back on the left side. Now there's something you don't see every day: a skeleton in a box. As the red Latin inscription says, this is St. Munditia. In the fourth century, she was beheaded by the Romans for her Christian faith.

Munich has more relics of saints than any city outside Rome. That's because it was the Pope's Catholic bastion against the rising tide of Protestantism in northern Europe during the Reformation. In 1675, St. Munditia's remains were given to Munich by the Pope as thanks for the city's devoted service. It was also a vivid reminder to the faithful that those who die for the cause of the Roman Church go directly to heaven without waiting for Judgment Day.

• *Leave St. Peter's out the door opposite the one you entered. Then, head to the right to the tower entrance. It's a long climb to the top of the **tower** (306 steps, no elevator)—much of it with two-way traffic on a one-lane staircase—but the view is dynamite. Try to be two flights from the top when the bells ring at the top of the hour. Then, when your friends back home ask you about your trip, you'll say, "What?" After your tower climb, head downhill to join the busy commotion of the...*

❸ Viktualienmarkt

The market (rated ▲▲, closed Sun) is a lively world of produce stands and budget eateries. Browse your way through the stalls and pavilions, as you make your way to the market's main landmark, the blue-and-white striped may-pole. Early in the morning, you can still feel small-town Munich here. Remember, Munich has been a market town since its ear-liest days as a stop on the salt-trade crossroads. By the 1400s, the market bustled, most likely beneath a traditional maypole, just like you see today.

Besides salt, Munich gained a reputation for beer. By the 15th century, more than 30 breweries pumped out the golden liquid, brewed by monks, who were licensed to sell it. They stored their beer in cellars under courtyards kept cool by the shade of bushy chestnut trees—a tradition Munich's breweries still stick to.

The market's centerpiece seems to be its **beer garden** (daily 10:00-22:00, weather permitting). Its picnic tables are filled with hungry and thirsty locals, all in the shade of the traditional chest-nut trees.

As this beer garden is city-owned and needs to be equitable, the beverage selection rotates week to week to feature beer from six leading brewers. Step up to the beer kiosk where you'll see a sign explaining which beer is on tap.

Shoppers often pause here for a late-morning snack of *Weiss-wurst*—white sausage—served with mustard, a pretzel, and a beer. Here, you can order just a half-liter—unlike some other beer gardens that only sell by the full liter. This is handy for shoppers who want just a quick sip. As is the tradition at all the city's beer gardens, some tables—those without tablecloths—are set aside for patrons who bring their own food; they're welcome here as long as they buy a drink. The Viktualienmarkt is ideal for a light meal (see "Eating in Munich," later in this chapter).

Now make your way to the towering **maypole.** Throughout Bavaria, colorfully ornamented maypoles decorate town squares. Many are painted, like this one, in Bavaria's colors, white and blue. The decorations are festively replaced every year on the first of May. Traditionally, rival communities try to steal each other's maypole. Locals guard their new pole day and night as May Day approaches. Stolen poles are ransomed only with lots of beer for the clever thieves.

As was standard in any village, the decorations that line each side of the pole explain which merchants are doing business in the market. Munich's maypole gives prominence (on the bottom level) to a horse-drawn wagon bringing in beer barrels. And you can't have a kegger without coopers—find the merry barrelmakers, the four cute guys dancing. Today, traditional barrel making is enjoying a comeback as top breweries like to have real wooden kegs.

The bottom of the pole celebrates the world's oldest food law. The German Beer Purity Law *(Reinheitsgebot)* of 1487 actually originated here in Munich, was later adopted in Bavaria, and eventually spread throughout the rest of Germany. It stipulated that beer could consist only of three ingredients: barley, hops, and water, with no additives. (Later they realized that a fourth ingredient, yeast, is always present in fermentation.) Why was beer so treasured? Back in the Middle Ages, it was considered liquid food.

From the maypole, take in the bustling scene around you. The market was modernized in the 1800s as the city grew. Old buildings were torn down, replaced with stalls and modern market halls. Now, in the 21st century, it's a wonder such a traditional place survives—especially because it sits on the most expensive real estate in town. But locals love their market, so the city protects these old-time shops, charging them only a small percentage of their gross income, enabling them to carry on. The city also bans most fast-food chains. This keeps the market classy and authentic. Münchners consider the produce here to be top quality, if on the expensive side.

• *At the far end of the Viktualienmarkt, across the street and to the right of Der Pschorr, spot* **Café Frischhut** *with its colorful old-time sign hanging out front (at Prälat-Zistl-Strasse 8). This is Munich's favorite place to stop for a fresh* Schmalznudel—*pop in to pick up one of these traditional fried-dough treats (best enjoyed warm with a sprinkling of sugar).*

Continue straight to a modern glass-and-iron building, the

Schrannenhalle. This 1800s grain exchange has been renovated into a high-end paradise for foodies, especially those seeking Italian edibles. Stroll through Eataly, past enticing bottles of olive oil and delectable pasta. Pause to watch bakers tending to the day's bread, and make your way to the far end, where wine connoisseurs could detour downstairs for a vast wine collection (and a good WC).

*When you're ready to move on, exit the Schrannenhalle midway down on the right-hand side. You'll spill out into **Sebastiansplatz**, a small square lined with healthy eateries. Continue through Sebastians-platz and veer left, where you'll see a cube-shaped building, the...*

❹ Ohel Jakob Synagogue

This modern synagogue anchors a revitalized Jewish quarter. In the 1930s, about 10,000 Jews lived in Munich, and the main syna-gogue stood near here. Then, in 1938, Hitler demanded that the synagogue be torn down. By the end of World War II, Munich's Jewish community was gone. But thanks to Germany's accep-tance of religious refugees from former Soviet states, the Jewish population has now reached its prewar size. The new synagogue was built in 2006. There's also a kindergarten and day school, play-ground, fine kosher restaurant (at #18), and bookstore. Notice the low-key but efficient security.

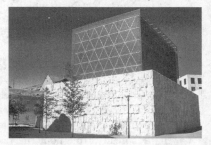

While the synagogue is shut tight to nonworshippers, its ar-chitecture is striking from the outside. Lower stones of travertine evoke the Wailing Wall in Jerusalem, while an upper section rep-resents the tent that held important religious wares during the 40 years of wandering through the desert. The synagogue's door fea-tures the first 10 letters of the Hebrew alphabet, symbolizing the Ten Commandments.

The cube-shaped **Jewish History Museum** (behind the cube-shaped synagogue) is stark, windowless, and as inviting as a bomb shelter. While the museum's small permanent collection is disap-pointing, good temporary exhibits might justify the entry fee (€6; ticket gets you half-price admission to Munich City Museum, Nazi Documentation Center, Lenbachhaus, or Villa Stuck—or use any of those tickets to get half-price admission here; Tue-Sun 10:00-18:00, closed Mon, St.-Jakobs-Platz 16, tel. 089/2339-6096, www.juedisches-museum-muenchen.de).

• Facing the synagogue, on the same square, is the...

MUNICH

❺ Munich City Museum (Münchner Stadtmuseum)

The highs and lows of Munich's history are covered in this surprisingly honest municipal museum (rated ▲). It covers the cultural upheavals of the early 1900s, Munich's role as the birthplace of the Nazis, and the city's renaissance during Germany's postwar "economic miracle." There's scant information posted in English, but an included audioguide can fill in the gaps.

• *You can stop and tour the museum now (see listing on page 79). Otherwise, continue through the synagogue's square, past the fountain, across the street, and one block farther to the pedestrianized Sendlinger Strasse. Take a left and walk 100 yards until you see a fancy facade on your right (at #32), which marks the...*

❻ Asam Church (Asamkirche)

This tiny church (rated ▲) is a slice of heaven on earth—a gooey, drippy Baroque-concentrate masterpiece by Bavaria's top two Rococonuts—the Asam brothers. Just 30 feet wide, it was built in 1740 to fit within this row of homes. Originally, it was a private chapel where these two brother-architects could show off their work (on their own land, next to their home and business headquarters—to the left), but it's now a public place of worship.

Cost and Hours: Free, Sat-Thu 9:00-18:00, Fri from 13:00, tel. 089/2368-7989. The church is small, so visitors are asked not to enter during Mass.

Visiting the Church: This place of worship served as a promotional brochure to woo clients, and is packed with every architectural trick in the books. Imagine approaching the church not as a worshipper, but as a shopper representing your church's building committee. First stand outside: Hmmm, the look of those foundation stones really packs a punch. And the legs hanging over the portico...nice effect. Those starbursts on the door would be a hit back home, too.

Then step inside: I'll take a set of those over-the-top golden capitals, please. We'd also like to order the gilded garlands draping the church in jubilation, and the twin cupids capping the confessional. And how about some fancy stucco work, too? (Molded-and-painted plaster was clearly an Asam brothers specialty.) Check out the illusion of a dome painted on the flat ceiling—that'll save us lots of money. The yellow glass above the altar has the effect of the thin-sliced alabaster at St. Peter's in Rome, but it's within our bud-

The History of Munich

Born from Salt and Beer (1100-1500): Munich began in the 12th century, when Henry the Lion (Heinrich der Löwe) established a lucrative salt trade near a monastery of "monks"—München. After Henry's death, an ambitious merchant family, the Wittelsbachs, took over. By the 1400s, Munich's maypole-studded market bustled with trade in salt and beer, the twin-domed Frauenkirche drew pilgrims, and the Wittelsbachs made their home in the Residenz. When the various regions of Bavaria united in 1506, Munich (pop. 14,000) was the natural capital.

Religious Wars, Plagues, Decline (1500-1800): While Martin Luther and the Protestant Reformation raged in northern Ger-
many, Munich became the
ultra-Catholic heart of the
Counter-Reformation, decorated in the ornate Baroque
and Rococo style of its Italian
Catholic allies. The religious
wars and periodic plagues left
the city weakened. Now the
Wittelsbachs took their cultural cues from more-powerful

France (Nymphenburg Palace is a miniature Versailles), England (the English Garden), and Italy (the Pitti Palace-inspired Residenz). While the rest of Europe modernized, Munich remained behind the times.

The Golden Age of Kings (1806-1886): When Napoleon invaded, the Wittelsbach dukes surrendered hospitably, and were prompt-ly rewarded with an even grander title: King of Bavaria. Munich boomed. **Maximilian I** (r. 1806-1825), a.k.a. Max Joseph, rebuilt in Neoclassical style—grand columned buildings connected by broad boulevards. **Ludwig I** (r. 1825-1848) turned Munich into a modern railroad hub, budding industrial city, and fitting capital (pop. 90,000). But the skirt-chasing Ludwig was brought down in a sex scandal with the notorious Irish dancer Lola Montez. His son **Maximilian II** (r. 1848-1864) continued Ludwig's moderniza-tion program, while studiously avoiding dancers. In 1864, 18-year-

get! And, tapping the "marble" pilasters to determine that they are just painted fakes, we decide to take that, too. Crammed between two buildings, light inside this narrow church is limited, so there's a big, clear window in the back for maximum illumination—we'll order one to cut back on our electricity bill.

Visiting the Asam Church, you can see why the Asam broth-ers were so prolific and successful. (You'll find black-and-white portraits of the two Asams in oval frames flanking the altar.) On the way out, say goodbye to the gilded grim reaper in the narthex old **Ludwig II** (r. 1864-1886) became king. Ludwig didn't much like Munich, preferring to build castles in the Bavarian countryside. (For more on Ludwig, see the Bavarian Alps chapter.)

End of the Wittelsbachs (1886-1918): When Bavaria became part of the newly united Germany, Berlin overtook Munich as Germany's power center. Turn-of-the-century Munich was culturally rich, giving birth to the abstract art of the Blue Rider group. But World War I devastated Munich. After the war, mobs of poor, hungry, disillusioned, and angry Münchners roamed the streets. In 1918, they drove the last Bavarian king out, ending 700 years of Wittelsbach rule.

Nazis, World War II, and Munich Bombed (1918-1945): In the power vacuum, a fringe group emerged—the Nazi party, headed by charismatic war veteran Adolf Hitler. Hitler rallied the Nazis in a Munich beer hall, leading a failed coup d'état known as the Beer Hall Putsch (1923). When the Nazis eventually took power in Berlin, they remembered their roots, dubbing Munich "Capital of the Movement." In World War II, nearly half the city was leveled by Allied air raids. The once-grand city lay in waste.

Munich Rebuilds (1945-Present): After the war, with generous American aid, Münchners rebuilt. Nazi authorities had taken care during the early war years to create a photographic archive of historic sights, which now came in handy. The city faced a choice—rebuild in the old style or go with modern skyscrapers. Munich chose to preserve the low-rise, medieval feel, but with a modern infrastructure. For the 1972 Olympic Games, they built a futuristic stadium, a sleek new subway system, and one of Europe's first pedestrian-only zones—Kaufingerstrasse. In 1990, when Germany reunited, Berlin once again became the country's focal point, relegating Munich to the role of sleepy Second City.

These days, Munich seems to be comfortable just being itself rather than trying to keep up with Berlin. Though rich and modern—home to BMW and Siemens, and a producer of software, books, movies, and the latest fashions—it remains safe, clean, and cultured. It's a university town, built on a human scale, and close to the beauties of nature.

(left side as you're leaving) as he cuts the thread of life—reminding all who visit of our mortality...and, by the way, that shrouds have no pockets.

• *Leaving the church, look to your right, noticing the Sendlinger Tor at the end of the street—part of the fortified town wall that circled Munich in the 14th century. Then turn left and walk straight up Sendlinger Strasse. Walk toward the Münchner Kindl, still capping the spire of the New Town Hall in the distance, and then up (pedestrian-only) Rosenstrasse, until you hit Marienplatz and the big, busy...*

❼ Kaufingerstrasse

This car-free street leads you through a great shopping district, past cheap department stores, carnivals of street entertainers, and good old-fashioned slicers and dicers. As far back as the 12th century, this was the town's main commercial street. Traders from Salzburg and Augsburg would enter the town through the fortified Karlstor. This street led past the Augustiner beer hall (opposite St. Michael's Church to this day), right to the main square and cathedral.

Up until the 1970s, the street was jammed with car traffic. Then, for the 1972 Olympics, it was turned into one of Europe's first pedestrian zones. At first, shopkeepers were afraid that would ruin business. Now it's Munich's living room. Nearly 9,000 shoppers pass through it each hour. Merchants nearby are begging for their streets to become traffic-free, too. Imagine this street in Hometown, USA.

The 1972 Olympics transformed this part of Munich—the whole area around Marienplatz was pedestrianized and the transit system expanded. Since then, Munich has become one of the globe's greenest cities. Skyscrapers have been banished to the suburbs, and the nearby Frauenkirche is still the tallest building in the center.

• *Stroll a few blocks away from Marienplatz toward the Karlstor, until you arrive at the imposing church on the right.*

❽ St. Michael's Church (Michaelskirche)

This is one of the first great Renaissance buildings north of the Alps. The ornate facade, with its sloped roofline, was inspired by the Gesù Church in Rome—home of the Jesuit order. Jesuits saw themselves as the intellectual defenders of Catholicism. St. Michael's was built in the late 1500s—at the height of the Protestant Reformation—to serve as the northern outpost of the Jesuits. Appropriately, the facade features a statue of Michael fighting a Protestant demon.

Cost and Hours: Church-free, generally daily 8:00-19:00, until later on Sun and summer evenings; crypt-€2, Mon-Fri 9:30-16:30, Sat until 14:30, closed Sun; frequent concerts—check schedule posted outside; tel. 089/231-7060.

Visiting the Church: Inside, admire the ornate Baroque interior, topped with a barrel vault, the largest of its day. Stroll up the nave to the ornate pulpit, where Jesuit priests would hammer away at Reformation heresy. The church's acoustics are spectacular, and the choir—famous in Munich—sounds heavenly singing from the organ loft high in the rear.

The crypt (*Fürstengruft*, down the stairs to the right by the altar) contains 40 stark, somewhat forlorn tombs of Bavaria's ruling family, the Wittelsbachs.

The most ornate tomb (center of back wall, facing altar) holds the illustrious Ludwig II, known for his fairy-tale castle at Neuschwanstein. Ludwig didn't care much for Munich. He escaped to the Bavarian countryside where he spent his days building castles, listening to music, and dreaming about knights of old. His excesses earned him the nickname "Mad" King Ludwig. But of all the Wittelsbachs, it's his tomb that's decorated with flowers—placed here by romantics still mad about their "mad" king.

Also on the back wall is the tomb of Wilhelm V (right), who built this church, and Maximilian I (left), who saved Munich from Swedish invaders during the Thirty Years' War.

Finally (center of right wall as you enter) there's Otto, who went insane and was deposed in 1916, virtually bringing the Wittelsbachs' seven-century reign to an end.

• *Our next stop, the Frauenkirche, is a few hundred yards away. Backtrack a couple of blocks up Kaufingerstrasse to the wild boar statue, which marks the German Hunting and Fishing Museum. This place has outdoorsy regalia, kid-friendly exhibits, and the infamous Wolpertinger—a German "jackalope" created by very creative local taxidermists. At the boar statue, turn left on Augustinerstrasse, which leads to Munich's towering, twin-domed cathedral.*

❾ Frauenkirche

These twin onion domes are the symbol of the city. They're unusual in that most Gothic churches have either pointed steeples or square towers. Some say Crusaders, inspired by the Dome of the Rock in Jerusalem, brought home the idea. Or it may be that, due to money problems, the towers weren't completed until Renaissance times, when domes were popular. Whatever the reason, the

Frauenkirche's domes may be the inspiration for the characteristic domed church spires that mark villages all over Bavaria.

Cost and Hours: Free, generally open daily 7:00-20:30, tel. 089/290-0820.

Restorations: The church towers are under restoration and may not be open for climbing during your visit.

Visiting the Church: The church was built in just 22 years, from 1466 to 1488. Note that it's made of brick, not quarried stone—easy to make locally, and cheaper and faster to build with than stone. Construction was partly funded with the sale of indulgences (which let sinners bypass purgatory on the way to heaven). It's dedicated to the Virgin—Our Lady *(Frau)*—and has been the city's cathedral since 1821.

Step inside, and remember that much of this church was destroyed during World War II. The towers survived, and the rest was rebuilt essentially from scratch.

Near the entrance is a big, black, ornate, tomb-like monument honoring Ludwig IV the Bavarian (1282-1347), who was elected Holy Roman Emperor—a big deal. The Frauenkirche was built a century later with the express purpose of honoring his memory. His monument was originally situated in front at the high altar, right near Christ. Those Wittelsbachs—always trying to be associated with God. This alliance was instilled in people through the prayers they were forced to recite: "Virgin Mary, mother of our duke, please protect us."

Nearby, a relief (over the back pew on the left) honors one of Munich's more recent citizens. Joseph Ratzinger was born in Bavaria in 1927, became archbishop of the Frauenkirche (1977-1982), then moved to the Vatican where he later served as Pope Benedict XVI (2005-2013).

Now walk slowly up the main aisle, enjoying stained glass right and left. This glass is obviously modern, having replaced the original glass that was shattered in World War II. Ahead is the high altar, under a huge hanging crucifix. Find the throne—the ceremonial seat of the local bishop. From here, look up to the tops of the columns, and notice the tiny painted portraits. They're the craftsmen from five centuries ago who helped build the church.

Now walk behind the altar to the apse, where the three tall windows still have their original 15th-century glass. To survive the bombs of 1944, each pane was lovingly removed and stored safely away.

• *Our next stop is on Promenadeplatz, just 400 yards north of here. Facing the altar, take the left side exit and walk straight 50 yards until you see a door marking a tiny but well-signed passageway (on the left) called the Aufhauser Passage. Follow it through a modern building, where you'll emerge at a little park called* **Promenadeplatz.** *Detour a few steps left into the park, where you'll find a colorful modern memorial. (If the Aufhauser Passage is closed, use the "Munich City Walk" map to circle around the block to the next stop.)*

❿ Michael Jackson Memorial

When Michael Jackson was in town, he'd stay at the Hotel Bayer-

ischer Hof, like many VIPs. Fans would gather in the park waiting for him to appear at his window. He'd sometimes oblige (but his infamous baby-dangling incident happened in Berlin, not here). When Jackson died in 2009, devotees created this memorial by taking over a statue of Renaissance composer Orlando di Lasso. They still visit daily, leave a memento, and keep it tidy.

• *Now exit the park at the end with the giant silver statue and turn left down Kardinal-Faulhaber-Strasse, lined with former 18th-century mansions that have since become offices and bank buildings. At #11, turn right and enter a modern shopping mall called the Fünf Höfe Passage. The place takes your basic shopping mall and gives it more class. It's divided into five connecting courtyards (the "fünf Höfe"), spruced up with bubbling fountains, exotic plants, and a hanging garden.*

Emerging on a busy pedestrian street, turn right, and head down the street (noticing the Münchner Kindl again high above), to a big green square: Marienhof, with the most aristocratic grocery store in all of Germany.

⓫ Marienhof

This square, tucked behind the New Town Hall, was left as a green island after the 1945 bombings. For now, the square's all dug up while Munich builds an additional subway tunnel here. With virtually the entire underground system converging on nearby Marienplatz, this new tunnel will provide a huge relief to the city's congested subterranean infrastructure.

• *On the far side of Marienhof, the stately yellow building is...*

⓬ Dallmayr Delicatessen

When the king called out for dinner, he called Alois Dallmayr. This place became famous for its exotic and luxurious food items: tropical fruits, seafood, chocolates, fine wines, and coffee (there are meat and cheese counters, too). As you enter, read the black plaque with the royal seal by the door: *Königlich Bayerischer Hof-Lieferant* ("Deliverer for the King of Bavaria and his Court"). Catering to royal and aristocratic tastes (and budgets) since 1700, it's still the choice of Munich's old rich. Today, it's most famous for its sweets, chocolates, and coffee—dispensed from fine hand-painted Nymphenburg porcelain jugs (Mon-Sat 9:30-19:00, closed Sun; Dienerstrasse 13, www.dallmayr.com). Imagine picking up a royal picnic to munch in the grassy park out front.

• *Leaving Dallmayr, turn right and then right again to continue along Hofgraben. Walk straight three blocks, gently downhill, to Platzl— "small square." (If you get turned around, just ask any local to point you toward the Hofbräuhaus.)*

⓭ Platzl

As you stand here—admiring classic facades in the heart of medieval Munich—recall that everything around you was flattened in World War II. Here on Platzl, reconstruction happened in stages: From 1945 to 1950, they removed 12 million tons of bricks and replaced roofs to make buildings weather-tight. From 1950 to 1972, they redid the exteriors. From 1972 to 2000, they refurbished the interiors. Today, the rebuilt Platzl sports new—but old-looking—facades.

Officials estimate that hundreds of unexploded bombs still lie buried under Munich. As recently as 2012, a 550-pound bomb was found in Schwabing, a neighborhood just north of the old city center. They had to evacuate the neighborhood and detonate the bomb, which created a huge fireball—a stark reminder of Munich's scary past.

Today's Platzl hosts a lively mix of places to eat and drink—chains like Starbucks and Hard Rock Café alongside local spots like Schuhbecks Eissalon, a favorite for ice cream (Pfisterstrasse 11).

• *At the bottom of the square (#9), you can experience the venerable...*

⓮ Hofbräuhaus

The world's most famous beer hall (rated ▲▲) is a trip. Whether or not you slide your lederhosen on its polished benches, it's a great experience just to walk through the place in all its rowdy glory (with its own gift shop).

Cost and Hours: Free to enter, daily 9:00-23:30, live oompah music at lunch and dinner; a 5-minute walk northeast of Marienplatz at Platzl 9, tel. 089/2901-36100, www.hofbraeuhaus.de. For details on eating here, see the "Beer Halls, Beer Gardens, and Bavarian Food" section, later.

Visiting the Hofbräuhaus: Before going in, check out the huge arches at the entrance and the crown logo. The original brewery was built here in 1589. As the crown suggests, it was the Wittelsbachs' personal brewery, to make the "court brew" *(Hof Brau)*. In 1880, the brewery moved out, and this 5,000-seat food-and-beer palace was built in its place. After being bombed in World War II, the Hofbräuhaus was one of the first places to be rebuilt (German priorities).

Now, take a deep breath and go on in. Dive headlong into the sudsy Hofbräu mosh pit. Don't be shy. Everyone's drunk anyway. The atmosphere is thick with the sounds of oompah music, played here every night of the year.

You'll see locals stuffed into lederhosen and dirndls, giant gingerbread cookies that sport romantic messages, and kiosks selling postcards of the German (and apparently beer-drinking) ex-pope. Notice the quirky 1950s-style painted ceiling, with Bavarian colors, grapes, chestnuts, and fun "eat, drink, and be merry" themes. You'll see signs on some tables reading *Stammtisch*, meaning they're reserved for regulars, and their racks of old beer steins made of pottery and pewter. Beer halls like the Hofbräuhaus sell beer only by the liter mug, called a *Mass* (mahs). You can get it light *(helles)* or dark *(dunkles)*. A slogan on the ceiling above the band reads, *Durst ist schlimmer als Heimweh*—"Thirst is worse than homesickness."

You can explore upstairs, too. Next to the entrance, a grand staircase leads up to the big folk-show hall on the top floor. There, at the far end of the hall, is a balcony with a humble little (free) Hofbräuhaus museum.

• *Leaving the Hofbräuhaus, turn right and walk two blocks, then turn left when you reach the street called...*

⓮ Maximilianstrasse

This broad east-west boulevard, lined with grand buildings and exclusive shops, introduces us to Munich's golden age of the 1800s. In that period, Bavaria was ruled by three important kings: Max Joseph, Ludwig I, and Ludwig II. They transformed Munich from a cluster of medieval lanes to a modern city of spacious squares, Neoclassical monuments, and wide boulevards. At the east end of this boulevard is the palatial home of the Bavarian parliament.

The street was purposely designed for people and for shopping, not military parades. And to this day, Maximilianstrasse is busy with shoppers browsing Munich's most exclusive shops. Many are wealthy visitors from the Middle East, places like Dubai and the United Arab Emirates. These families often come here for medical treatment. And they make a vacation out of it, bringing the whole family and often even their own car and driver. The shopping is great, there's no stress (like they might feel in a more frenetic city, like London), security is excellent, the weather is cool, and they're

Oktoberfest

The 1810 marriage reception of King Ludwig I was such a success that It turned into an annual bash. These days, the Oktoberfest lasts just over two weeks, starting on a Saturday in September and usually ending on the first Sunday in October (www.oktoberfest.de).

Oktoberfest is held at the Theresienwiese fairground south of the main train station, in a meadow known as the "Wies'n" (VEE-zen). Huge tents are set up that together can seat nearly 120,000 beer drinkers. The festivities kick off with an opening parade of about 9,500 participants. Then, for the next two weeks, it's a frenzy of drinking, dancing, music, and food. There's a huge Ferris wheel, and the triple-loop roller coaster must be the wildest on earth (best before the beer-drinking). Total strangers stroll arm-in-arm down rows of picnic tables amid a carnival of beer, pretzels, and wurst, drawing visitors from all over the globe. A million gallons of beer later, they roast the last ox.

If you'll be here during the festivities, it's best to reserve a room early, but if you arrive in the morning (except Fri or Sat) and haven't called ahead, the TI may be able to help. During the fair, the city functions even better than normal, but is admittedly more expensive and crowded. It's a good time to sightsee, even if beer-

free of the societal constraints that keep them on the straight and narrow back home. Germans just politely provide the services, happy to make back some of the money that pours eastward every time they pull up to a gas station.

• *Maximilianstrasse leads to a big square—Max-Joseph-Platz.*

⑯ Max-Joseph-Platz

The square is fronted by two big buildings: the National Theater (with its columns) and the Residenz (with its intimidating stone facade).

The **Residenz,** the former "residence" of the royal Wittelsbach family, started as a crude castle (c. 1385). Over the centuries, it evolved into one of Europe's most opulent palaces. The facade takes its cue from Pitti Palace in Florence. Today, you can visit the Residenz for its lavish Rococo interior, its crown jewels, and exquisite Cuvilliés Theater (all described under "Sights in Munich," later in this chapter).

The square's centerpiece is a grand statue of **Maximilian I—**

hall rowdiness isn't your cup of tea.

Even though the beer tents are enormous, they're often full, especially on weekends—if possible, avoid going on a Friday or Saturday night. If you find yourself inside a tent with nowhere to sit, be bold—find an underused table and ask some potential new friends to scoot (or at least keep your elbows sharp). For some cultural background with your Wies'n visit, consider hiring a local guide or going with a group (Radius Tours, for example, offers a €140 tour that includes two beers, half a chicken, and guaranteed seating, Sun-Fri at 10:00, none on Sat, reserve ahead, www.radiustours.com; Size Matters Beer Tour runs options for €129-209 that include breakfast, lunch, four beers, and reserved seating, www.sizemattersbeertour.de).

If you're not visiting while the party's on, don't worry: You can still dance to oompah bands, munch huge pretzels, and show off your stein-hoisting skills any time of year at Munich's classic beer halls, including the venerable Hofbräuhaus. See the "Beer Halls, Beer Gardens, and Bavarian Food" section, later, for descriptions of my favorites.

In the city center, the humble **Beer and Oktoberfest Museum** (Bier- und Oktoberfestmuseum) offers a low-tech and underwhelming take on beer history. Exhibits and artifacts outline the centuries-old quest for the perfect beer (apparently achieved in Munich) and the origins of the city's Oktoberfest celebration (€4, Tue-Sat 13:00-18:00, closed Sun-Mon, between the Isartor and Viktualienmarkt at Sterneckerstrasse 2, tel. 089/2423-1607, www.bier-und-oktoberfestmuseum.de).

a.k.a. Max Joseph. In 1806, Max was the city's duke, serving in

the long tradition of his Wittelsbach family...until Napoleon invaded and deposed the duke. But then Napoleon—eager to marry into the aristocracy—agreed to reinstate Max, with one condition: that his daughter marry Napoleon's stepson. Max Joseph agreed, and was quickly crowned not duke but king of Bavaria.

Max Joseph and his heirs ruled as constitutional monarchs. Now a king, Max Joseph was popular; he emancipated Protestants and Jews, revamped the Viktualienmarkt, and graced Munich with grand buildings like the **National Theater.** This Neoclassical building, opened in 1818, celebrated Bavaria's strong culture, deep roots, and legitimacy as a nation; four of Richard Wagner's operas were first performed here. It's now where the Bavarian State Opera and the Bavarian State Orchestra perform. (The Roman numerals MCMLXIII in the frieze mark the year the theater reopened after WWII bombing restoration—1963.)

• *Leave Max-Joseph-Platz opposite where you entered, walking alongside the Residenz on Residenzstrasse for about 100 yards to the next grand square. But before you get to Odeonsplatz, pause at the first corner on the left and look down Viscardigasse at the gold-cobbled swoosh in the pavement.*

⑰ Viscardigasse

The cobbles in Viscardigasse recall one of Munich's most dramatic moments: It was 1923, and Munich was in chaos. World War I had left Germany in shambles. Angry mobs roamed the streets. Out of the fury rose a new and frightening movement—Adolf Hitler and the Nazi Party. On November 8, Hitler launched a coup, later known as the Beer Hall Putsch, to try to topple the German government. It started with a fiery speech by Hitler in a beer hall a few blocks from here (the beer hall no longer exists). The next day, Hitler and his mob of Nazis marched up Residenzstrasse. A block ahead, where Residenzstrasse spills into Odeonsplatz, stood a hundred government police. Shots were fired. Hitler was injured, and 16 Nazis were killed, along with four policemen. The coup was put down, and Hitler was sent to a prison outside Munich. During his nine months there, he wrote down his twisted ideas in his book *Mein Kampf.*

Ten years later, when Hitler finally came to power, he made a memorial at Odeonsplatz to honor the "first martyrs of the Third Reich." Germans were required to raise their arms in a *Sieg Heil* salute as they entered the square. The only way to avoid the indignity of saluting Nazism was to turn left down Viscardigasse instead. That stream of shiny cobbles marks the detour taken by those brave dissenters.

• *But now that Hitler's odious memorial is long gone, you can continue to...*

⑱ Odeonsplatz

This square links Munich's illustrious past with the Munich of today. It was laid out by the Wittelsbach kings in the 1800s. They incorporated the much older (yellow) church that was already on the square, the Theatinerkirche. This church contains about half of the Wittelsbach tombs. The church's twin towers and 230-foot-high dome are classic Italian Baroque, reflecting Munich's strong Catholic bent in the 1600s.

Overlooking the square from the south is an arcaded loggia filled with statues. In the 1800s the Wittelsbachs commissioned this Hall of Heroes to honor Bavarian generals. It was modeled after the famous Renaissance loggia in Florence. Odeonsplatz was part of the Wittelsbachs' grand vision of modern urban planning, designed to connect the historic core with the expanding metropolis.

At the far end of the square, several wide boulevards lead away from here. Look west (left) down ❶ **Brienner Strasse** (watch out for bikes). In the distance, and just out of sight, a black obelisk commemorates the 30,000 Bavarians who marched with Napoleon to Moscow and never returned. Beyond the obelisk is the grand Königsplatz, or "King's Square," with its Neoclassical buildings. Back in the 1930s, Königsplatz was the center of the Nazi party. Remember, Munich was the cradle of Nazism. (For more on the Nazi sights in Königsplatz, see page 89). Today, the Nazi shadow has largely lifted from that square (only two buildings from that era remain) and Königsplatz is home to Munich's cluster of great art museums. A few miles beyond Königsplatz is the Wittelsbachs' impressive summer home, Nymphenburg Palace.

Now turn your attention 90 degrees to the right. The boulevard heading north from Odeonsplatz is **Ludwigstrasse.** It stretches a full mile, flanked by an impressive line of uniform 60-foot-tall buildings in the Neo-Gothic style. In the far distance is the city's Triumphal Arch, the Siegestor, capped with a figure of Bavaria, a goddess riding a lion-drawn chariot. She's looking out, away from the city, to welcome home returning soldiers. The street is named for the great Wittelsbach builder-king Ludwig I, the grandfather of "Mad" King Ludwig. It was Ludwig I who truly made Munich into a grand capital. ("I won't rest," he famously swore, "until Munich looks like Athens.") The street that bears his name, Ludwigstrasse, was used for big parades and processions, as it leads to that Roman style arch.

Beyond the arch—and beyond what you can see—lie the suburbs of modern Munich, including the city's modern skyscrapers, Olympic Park, and the famous BMW headquarters.

As you enjoy the busy scene on Odeonsplatz, let's bring Munich's 850-year history up to the present. Munich today, with a population of 1.5 million, is Germany's third-largest city, after Berlin and Hamburg. It's the capital of the independent-minded German state of Bavaria, and proudly waves two flags: the white-and-blue diamonds of Bavaria and the black-and-gold of the city of Munich. Munich is home to more banks and financial firms than any German city besides Frankfurt. It's a center for book publishing and hosts two TV networks. Information technology is big, as well—it's home to electronics giant Siemens and the German branch of Microsoft. And, of course, Munich is home to makers of some of the world's finest cars—BMW (for "Bayerische Motoren Werke"—Bavarian Motor Works). Yes, Munich is a major metropolis, but you'd hardly know it by walking through its pleasant streets and parks.

• *We'll finish our walk in the pleasant Hofgarten. Its formal gate is to your right as you're facing up Ludwigstrasse. Step through the gate and enter the...*

⑳ Hofgarten

The elegant "garden of the royal court" is a delight. Built by the Wittelsbachs as their own private backyard to the Residenz palace, it's now open to everyone.

Just inside the gate is an arcade decorated with murals commissioned by Ludwig I in the early 1800s. While faded, they still tell the glorious story of Bavaria from 1155 until 1688. The garden's 400-year-old centerpiece is a Renaissance-style temple with great acoustics. (There's often a musician performing here for tips.) It's decorated with the same shell decor as was popular inside the Residenz.

• *With this city walk completed, you've seen the essential Munich. From here, a path leads to the government offices of Bavaria (Bayerischen Staatskanzlei), housed in an impressive Neoclassical building flanked by modern glass halls. Look for the war memorial in front, which honors the "fallen heroes" of World War I, but only the "fallen" of World War II. To reach the English Garden, angle downhill to the northeast, walk under a bridge, and then make your way to the main street—Von-der-Tann Strasse—that runs just north of the Hofgarten. Along the way, you pass the stern Haus der Kunst (a rare fascist building surviving in Munich) and a happy place where locals surf in the river—the gateway into Munich's sprawling English Garden, described later.*

From the Hofgarten you're within easy reach of Munich's top sights. You could make the quick walk back to tour the museum and treasury at the Residenz; or descend into the U-Bahn from the Odeonsplatz stop for points elsewhere (the BMW Museum/Olympic Park is just a few stops away on this line). If you're ready to eat, you have several choices. Café Luitpold (best for coffee and cake) and the elegant Spatenhaus are nearby (see "Eating in Munich," later).

Sights in Munich

CITY CENTER

The other top sights in the city center are covered earlier, on my self-guided walk.

▲▲The Residenz

For 500 years, this was the palatial "residence" and seat of power of the ruling Wittelsbach family. It began (1385) as a crude castle with a moat around it. The main building was built from 1550 to 1650, and decorated in Rococo style during the 18th century. The final touch (under Ludwig I) was the grand south facade modeled after Florence's Pitti Palace. In March 1944, Al-  lied air raids left the Residenz in shambles, so much of what we see today—like much of historic Munich—is a reconstruction.

The vast Residenz complex is divided into three sections: The **Residenz Museum** is a long hike through 90 lavishly decorated rooms. The **Residenz Treasury** shows off the Wittelsbach crown jewels. The **Cuvilliés Theater** is an ornate Rococo opera house. While each has its own admission, I'd just get the combo-ticket and see them all.

If you're unsure about which of Munich's top two palaces to visit, the Residenz is more central and has the best interior, while Nymphenburg (described on page 98) has the finest garden, grounds, and outdoor views.

Planning Your Time: Start your visit with the Residenz Treasury—small, manageable, and dazzling. Then hike through the sprawling palace called the Residenz Museum. The Cuvilliés Theater is a quick dollop of architectural whipped cream at the end. If you run out of time or energy, you can reenter with the same ticket on another day to visit anything you missed. The entrances on Max-Joseph-Platz and Residenzstrasse both lead to the ticket office, gift shop, and start of the treasury and Residenz Museum tours.

Cost and Hours: Residenz Museum-€7, Residenz Treasury-€7 (both include essential audioguides), Cuvilliés Theater-€3.50; €11 combo-ticket covers museum and treasury; €13 version covers all three; treasury and museum open daily 9:00-18:00, mid-Oct-mid-March 10:00-17:00; theater generally open Mon-Sat 14:00-18:00, Sun from 9:00, longer hours Aug-mid-Sept; last entry one hour be-

MUNICH

fore closing for all three sights, mandatory bag check, tel. 089/290-671, www.residenz-muenchen.de.

Residenz Treasury (Schatzkammer)

The treasury shows off a thousand years of Wittelsbach crowns and knickknacks. You'll see the regalia used in Bavaria's coronation ceremonies, the revered sacred objects that gave the Wittelsbachs divine legitimacy, and miscellaneous wonders that dazzled their European relatives. It's the best treasury in Bavaria, with fine 13th- and 14th-century crowns and delicately carved ivory and glass. Pick up the audioguide, slow down, and narrow your focus to fully appreciate the tiniest details (punch in the number for whichever treasures catch your eye for the audio commentary). Here are the highlights.

Visiting the Treasury: In **Room 1,** the oldest jewels are 200 years older than Munich itself. Treasures of particular interest line the left wall. The gem-studded Crown of Kunigunde is associated with the saintly Bavarian queen, who was crowned Holy Roman Empress in 1014 by the pope in St. Peter's Basilica in Rome. The pearl-studded prayer book of Charles the Bald (Charlemagne's grandson) allowed the book's owner to claim royal roots dating all the way back to that first Holy Roman Emperor crowned in 800. The spiky Crown of an English Queen (a.k.a. the Palatine Crown, c. 1370) is actually England's oldest crown, brought to Munich by an English princess who married a Wittelsbach duke. In the last case, the angel and gilt-embellished Crown of Henry II (c. 1270-1280) dates from Munich's roots, when the town was emerging as a regional capital.

Along the right side of the room are religious objects such as reliquaries and portable altars. The tiny mobile altar allowed a Carolingian king (from Charlemagne's family of kings) to pack light in 890—and still have a little Mass while on the road. Many of the precious and very old objects in this room came from various prince-bishops' collections when they were secularized (and their realms came under Bavarian rule in the Napoleonic era, c. 1800).

Room 3: Study the reliquary with St. George killing the dragon—sparkling with more than 2,000 precious stones. Get up close (it's OK to walk around the rope posts)...you can almost hear the dragon hissing. A gold-armored St. George, seated atop a ruby-studded ivory horse, tramples an emerald-green dragon. The golden box below contained the supposed relics of St. George, who was the patron saint of the Wittelsbachs.

If you could lift the minuscule visor, you'd see that the carved ivory face of St. George is actually the Wittelsbach Duke Wilhelm V—the great champion of the Catholic Counter-Reformation—slaying the dragon of Protestantism.

Room 4: The incredibly realistic carved ivory crucifixes from 1630 were done by local artist Georg Petel, who was inspired by his friend Peter Paul Rubens' painting (now in the Alte Pinakothek). Look at the flesh of Jesus' wrist pulling around the nails. In the center of the room is the intricate portable altarpiece (1573-74) of Duke Albrecht V, the Wittelsbach ruler who (as we'll see in the Residenz Museum) made a big mark on the Residenz.

Room 5: The freestanding glass case (#245) holds the impressive royal regalia of the 19th-century Wittelsbach kings—the crown, scepter, orb, and sword that were given to the king during the coronation ceremony. (The smaller pearl crown was for the queen.) They date from the early 1800s when Bavaria had been conquered by Napoleon. The Wittelsbachs struck a

deal that allowed them to stay in power, under the elevated title of "king" (not just "duke" or "prince-elector" or "prince-archbishop"). These objects were made in France by the same craftsmen who created Napoleon's crown. For the next century-plus, Wittelsbach kings (including Ludwig II) received these tokens of power. However, during the coronation ceremony, the crown you see was not actually placed on the king's head. It was brought in on a cushion (as it's displayed) and laid at the new monarch's feet.

Rooms 6-10: The rest of the treasury has objects that are more beautiful than historic. Admire the dinnerware made of rock crystal (Room 6), stone (Room 7), and gold and enamel (Room 8). Room 9 has a silver-gilt-and-marble replica of Trajan's Column. Finally, explore the "Exotica" of Room 10, including an ancient green Olmec figure encased in a Baroque niche and a Chinese rhino-horn bowl with a teeny-tiny Neptune inside.

• From the micro-detail of the treasury, it's time to visit the expansive Residenz Museum. Stop by the audioguide desk to have your wand reprogrammed for the museum, cross the hall, and enter the...

Residenz Museum (Residenzmuseum)

Though called a "museum," what's really on display here are the 90 rooms of the Residenz itself: the palace's spectacular banquet and reception halls, and the Wittelsbachs' lavish private apartments.

The rooms are decorated with period (but generally not original) furniture: chandeliers, canopied beds, Louis XIV-style chairs, old clocks, tapestries, and dinnerware of porcelain and silver. It's the best place to glimpse the opulent lifestyle of Bavaria's late, great royal family.

(Whatever happened to the Wittelsbachs, the longest continuously ruling family in European history? They're still around, but they're no longer royalty, so most of them have real jobs now—you may well have just passed one on the street.)

⊖ Self-Guided Tour: The place is big. Follow the museum's prescribed route (often a one-way route employing red arrows), using this section to hit the highlights and supplementing it with the audioguide. Grab a free museum floor plan as you enter to help locate specific room numbers mentioned here. Be flexible. The route can vary because rooms are occasionally closed off. Despite that, you should see most of the rooms I've described in approximately this order.

• *One of the first "rooms" you encounter (it's actually part of an outdoor courtyard) is the...*

❶ Shell Grotto (Room 6): This artificial grotto is made of volcanic tuff and covered completely in Bavarian freshwater shells.

In its day, it was an exercise in man controlling nature—a celebration of the Renaissance humanism that flourished in the 1550s. Mercury—the pre-Christian god of trade and business—oversees the action. Check out the statue in the courtyard—in the Wittelsbachs' heyday, red wine would have flowed from the mermaid's breasts and dripped from Medusa's severed head.

The grotto courtyard is just one of 10 such courtyards in the complex. Like the rest of the palace, this courtyard and its grotto were destroyed by Allied bombs. After World War II, Germans had no money to contribute to the reconstruction—but they could gather shells. All the shells you see here were donated by small-town Bavarians, as the grotto was rebuilt using Nazi photos as a guide (see "The History of Munich" sidebar, earlier in this chapter).

• *Before moving on, note the door marked* OO, *leading to handy WCs. Now continue into the next room, the...*

❷ Antiquarium (Room 7): This long, low, arched hall stretches 220 feet end to end. It's the oldest room in the Residenz, built around 1550. The room was, and still is, a festival banquet hall. The ruler presided from the raised dais at the near end (warmed by the

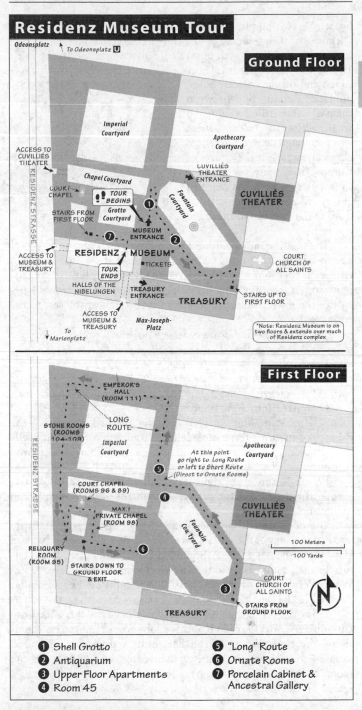

Residenz Museum Tour

MUNICH

Odeonsplatz — To Odeonsplatz Ⓤ

Ground Floor

Imperial Courtyard

Apothecary Courtyard

ACCESS TO CUVILLIÉS THEATER

RESIDENZ STRASSE

CUVILLIÉS THEATER ENTRANCE

Chapel Courtyard

COURT CHAPEL

TOUR BEGINS

Fountain Courtyard

CUVILLIÉS THEATER

STAIRS FROM FIRST FLOOR

Grotto Courtyard

⑦

① MUSEUM ENTRANCE

②

ACCESS TO MUSEUM & TREASURY

RESIDENZ MUSEUM*

TOUR ENDS

TICKETS

COURT CHURCH OF ALL SAINTS

HALLS OF THE NIBELUNGEN

TREASURY ENTRANCE

TREASURY

STAIRS UP TO FIRST FLOOR

ACCESS TO MUSEUM & TREASURY

Max-Joseph-Platz

*Note: Residenz Museum is on two floors & extends over much of Residenz complex

To Marienplatz

First Floor

EMPEROR'S HALL (ROOM 111)*

LONG ROUTE

STONE ROOMS (ROOMS 104-109)

Imperial Courtyard

Apothecary Courtyard

At this point go right to Long Route or left to Short Route (Direct to Ornate Rooms)

RESIDENZ STRASSE

⑤

COURT CHAPEL (ROOMS 96 & 89)

④

MAX I PRIVATE CHAPEL (ROOM 98)

Fountain Courtyard

CUVILLIÉS THEATER

RELIQUARY ROOM (ROOM 95)

⑥

100 Meters

100 Yards

STAIRS DOWN TO GROUND FLOOR & EXIT

COURT CHURCH OF ALL SAINTS

Ⓝ

TREASURY

③

STAIRS FROM GROUND FLOOR

① Shell Grotto
② Antiquarium
③ Upper Floor Apartments
④ Room 45
⑤ "Long" Route
⑥ Ornate Rooms
⑦ Porcelain Cabinet & Ancestral Gallery

fireplace). Two hundred dignitaries can dine here, surrounded by allegories of the goodness of just rule on the ceiling.

The hall is lined with busts of Roman emperors. In the mid-16th century, Europe's royal families (such as the Wittelsbachs) col-

lected and displayed such busts, implying a connection between themselves and the enlightened ancient Roman rulers. There was such huge demand for these classical statues in the courts of Europe that many of the "ancient busts" were fakes cranked out by crooked Romans. Still, a third of the statuary you see here is original.

The small paintings around the room (which survived WWII bombs because they were painted in arches) show 120 Bavarian villages as they looked in 1550. Even today, when a Bavarian historian wants a record of how his village once looked, he comes here. Notice the town of Dachau in 1550 (in the archway closest to the entrance door).

• *Keep following the red arrows through a few more rooms, then up a stairway to the upper floor. Pause in the Black Hall (Room 13) to admire the head-spinning trompe l'oeil ceiling, which makes the nearly flat roof appear to be a much grander arched vault. From here, the prescribed route winds through a number of rooms surrounding a large courtyard.*

❸ **Upper Floor Apartments** (Rooms 14-45): In this series of rooms (after some fine porcelain) we get the first glimpse of the Residenz Museum's forte: chandeliered rooms decorated with ceiling paintings, stucco work, tapestries, parquet floors, and period furniture.

Rooms to the left of the Black Hall are the **Electoral Apartments** (Rooms 22-31), the private apartments of the monarch and his consort.

The door from the Black Hall that's opposite the staircase leads to the long **All Saints' Corridor** (Room 32), where you can glance into the adjoining All Saints' Chapel. This early-19th-century chapel, commissioned by Ludwig I, was severely damaged in World War II, didn't reopen until 2003, and now hosts popular concerts in the evening.

From the All Saints' Corridor you can reach the **Charlotte Chambers/Court Garden Rooms,** a long row of impressive rooms across the courtyard from the Electoral Apartments, first used to house visiting rulers. Some of them later served as the private rooms of Princess Charlotte, Max Joseph's daughter.

• *Your visit eventually reaches a hallway—* ❹ *Room 45—where you*

MUNICH

have a choice: To the left is the "short" route that heads directly to the stunning Ornate Rooms (described later). But we'll take the "long" route to the right (starting in Room 47) that adds a dozen-plus rooms to your visit.

❺ **The "Long" Route:** Walk through the lavish rooms that border the courtyard. The large **Emperor's Hall** (Room 111) was once the most important room for grand festivities; the **Stone Rooms** (104-109) are so-called for their colorful marble—both real and fake. Then come several small rooms, where the centerpiece painting on the ceiling is just blank black, as no copy of the original survived World War II. These rooms were built specifically to house the Holy Roman Emperor and his wife during their visits to Munich.

The **Reliquary Room** (Room 95) harbors a collection of gruesome Christian relics (bones, skulls, and even several mummified hands) in ornate golden cases. The case in the middle supposedly contains skeletons of three babies from the Massacre of the Innocents in Bethlehem (where Herod, in an attempt to murder Baby Jesus, ordered all boys of a certain age killed).

• *A few more steps brings you to the balcony of the...*

Court Chapel (Rooms 96/89): Dedicated to Mary, this late-Renaissance/early-Baroque gem was the site of "Mad" King Lud-

wig's funeral after his mysterious murder—or suicide—in 1886. (He's buried in St. Michael's Church, described in my "Munich City Walk," earlier.) Though Ludwig II was not popular in political circles, he was beloved by his people, and his funeral drew huge crowds. About 75 years earlier, in 1810, his grandfather and namesake (Ludwig I) was married here. After the wedding ceremony, carriages rolled his guests to a rollicking reception, which turned out to be such a hit that it became an annual tradition—Oktoberfest.

Ahead is the **Private Chapel of Maximilian I** (Room 98). Duke Maximilian I, the dominant Bavarian figure in the Thirty Years' War, built one of the most precious rooms in the palace. The miniature pipe organ (from about 1600) still works. The room is sumptuous, from the gold leaf ceiling and the fine altar with silver reliefs to the miniature dome and the walls made of *scagliola*—fake marble—a special mix of stucco, applied and polished. Designers liked it because it was less expensive than real marble and the color could be controlled. Note the post-Renaissance perspective tricks decorating the walls; they were popular in the 17th century.

• *Whichever route you take—long or short—you'll eventually reach a set of rooms known as the...*

❻ Ornate Rooms (Rooms 55-62): As the name implies, these are some of the richest rooms in the palace. The Wittelsbachs were always trying to keep up with the Habsburgs, and this long string of ceremonial rooms—used for official business—was designed to impress. The decor and furniture are Rococo—over-the-top Baroque. The family art collection, now in the Alte Pinakothek, once decorated these walls.

The rooms were designed in the 1730s by François de Cuvilliés. The Belgian-born Cuvilliés first attracted notice as the clever court dwarf for the Bavarian ruler. He was sent to Paris to study art and returned to become the court architect. Besides the Residenz, he went on to also design the Cuvilliés Theater and Amalienburg at Nymphenburg Palace. Cuvilliés' style, featuring incredibly intricate stucco tracery twisted into unusual shapes, defined Bavarian Rococo. The stucco work frames paintings and mirrors. His assistant in the stucco department was Johann Baptist Zimmermann, who also did the Wieskirche (in southern Bavaria, near Füssen). As you glide through this section of the palace, be sure to appreciate the gilded stucco ceilings above you.

The **Green Gallery** (Room 58)—named for its green silk damask wallpaper—was the ballroom. Imagine the parties they had here—aristocrats in powdered wigs, a string quartet playing Baroque tunes, a card game going on, while everyone admired the paintings on the walls or themselves reflected in the mirrors.

The **State Bedroom** (Room 60), though furnished with a canopy bed, wasn't an actual bedroom—it was just for show. Rulers invited their subjects to come at morning and evening to stand at the railing and watch their boss ceremonially rise from his slumber to symbolically start and end the working day.

Perhaps the most ornate of these Ornate Rooms is the **Cabinet of Mirrors** (Room 61) and the adjoining **Cabinet of Miniatures** (Room 62) from 1740. In the Cabinet of Mirrors, notice the fun visual effects of the mirrors around you—the corner mirrors make things go on forever. Then peek inside the coral red room and imagine visiting the duke and having him take you here to ogle miniature copies of the most famous paintings of the day, composed with one-haired brushes.

• *After exploring the Ornate Rooms (and the many other elaborate rooms here on the upper floor), find the staircase (past Room 69) that heads back downstairs. On the ground floor, you emerge in the long Ancestral Gallery (Room 4). Before walking down it, detour to the right, into Room 5.*

❼ **Porcelain Cabinet** (Room 5) and **Ancestral Gallery** (Room 4): In the 18th century, the royal family bolstered their status with an in-house porcelain works: Nymphenburg porcelain. See how the mirrors enhance the porcelain vases, creating the effect of infinite pedestals. If this inspires you to acquire some pieces of your own, head to the Nymphenburg Porcelain Store at Odeonsplatz (listed under "Shopping in Munich," later).

The Ancestral Gallery (Room 4) was built in the 1740s to display portraits of the Wittelsbachs. All official guests had to

pass through here to meet the duke (and his 100 Wittelsbach relatives). The room's symbolism reinforced the Wittelsbachs' claims to being as powerful as the Habsburgs of Vienna. Standing here, you're essentially surrounded by a scrapbook covering centuries of royal family history.

Midway down the hall, find the family tree labeled (in Latin) "genealogy of an imperial family." The tree is shown being planted by Hercules, to boost their royal street cred. Opposite the tree are two notable portraits: Charlemagne, the first Holy Roman Emperor, and to his right, Louis IV (wearing the same crown), the first Wittelsbach H.R.E., crowned in 1328. For the next 500 years, this lineage was used to substantiate the family's claim to power as they competed with the Habsburgs. (After failing to sort out their differences through strategic weddings, the two families eventually went to war.)

Allied bombs took their toll on this hall. The central ceiling painting has been restored, but since there were no photos documenting the other two ceiling paintings, those spots remain empty. Looking carefully at the walls, you can see how each painting was hastily cut out of its frame. That's because—though most of Munich's museums were closed during World War II—the Residenz remained open to instill confidence in local people. It wasn't until 1944, when bombs were imminent, that the last-minute order was given to hide the paintings away.

Also on the ground floor are the **Halls of the Nibelungen** (*Nibelungensäle*, Rooms 74-79), featuring mythological scenes that were the basis of Wagner's *Der Ring des Nibelungen.*

• *Your Residenz Museum tour is over. The doorway at the end of the hall leads back to the museum entrance.*

If you're visiting the Cuvilliés Theater, exit the museum and return to Residenzstrasse. Enter the Chapel Courtyard by passing between the green lions standing guard. Walk to the far end of the lane until you reach a fountain. Just above a doorway to the left you'll see a nondescript sign that says Cuvilliés Theater.

Cuvilliés Theater

In 1751, this was Germany's ultimate Rococo theater. Mozart conducted here several times. Designed by the same brilliant architect who did the Amalienburg (see page 104), this theater is dazzling enough to send you back to the days of divine monarchs.

Your visit consists of just one small-but-plush theater hall. It's an intimate, horseshoe-shaped performance venue, seating fewer than 400. The four tiers of box seats were for the four classes of society: city burghers on bottom, royalty next up (in the most elaborate seats), and lesser courtiers in the two highest tiers. The ruler occupied the large Royal Box directly opposite the stage (i.e., over the entrance doorway). "Mad" King Ludwig II occasionally bought out the entire theater to watch performances here by himself.

François Cuvilliés' interior is exquisite. Red, white, and gold hues dominate. Most of the decoration is painted wood, even parts that look like marble. Even the proscenium above the stage—seemingly draped with a red-velvet "curtain"—is actually made of carved wood. Also above the stage is an elaborate Wittelsbach coat of arms. The balconies seem to be supported by statues of the four seasons and are adorned with gold garlands. Cuvilliés achieved the Rococo ideal of giving theater-goers a multimedia experience—uniting the beauty of his creation with the beautiful performance on stage. It's still a working theater.

WWII bombs completely obliterated the old Cuvilliés Theater, which originally stood at a different location a short distance from here. Fortunately, much of the carved wooden interior had been removed from the walls and stored away for safekeeping. After the war, this entirely new building was built near the ruins of the old theater and paneled with the original decor. It's so heavily restored, you can almost smell the paint.

▲Munich City Museum (Münchner Stadtmuseum)

The museum's permanent exhibit on Munich's history (called "Typically Munich!") is interesting, but it's an exhaustive and con-

fusing maze, and there's no posted English information. Use the following mini tour for an overview, then supplement it with the audioguide and English booklet.

Cost and Hours: €4, includes good audioguide, €7 includes temporary exhibits; ticket gets you half-price admission to Jewish History Museum, Nazi Documentation Center, Lenbachhaus, or Villa Stuck—or use any of those tickets to get half-price admission here; Tue-Sun 10:00-18:00, closed Mon; no crowds, pick up English handout, St.-Jakobs-Platz 1, tel. 089/2332-2370, www. muenchner-stadtmuseum.de. The humorous Servus Heimat souvenir shop in the courtyard is worth a stop.

Eating: The museum's recommended Stadt Café is handy for a light meal.

Visiting the Museum: Start in the ticketing hall with the wooden model showing Munich today. Find the Frauenkirche, Isar River, New Town Hall, Residenz...and no skyscrapers. The city looks remarkably similar in scale to the model (in the next room) from 1570.

Ground Floor (Medieval): An imposing gray statue of Henry the Lion introduces us to the city's 12th-century founder. The eight statues of Morris dancers (1480) became a symbol of the vibrant market town (and the tradition continued with the New Town Hall glockenspiel's dancing coopers). On the rest of the ground floor, paintings, swords, and cherubs clad in armor (these are the original statues that stood under the Virgin Mary's column on Marienplatz) capture more medieval ambience.

First Floor (1800s): The "New Munich" was created when the city was expanded beyond the old medieval walls (see the illuminated view of the city from 1761 in the "Canaletto-Blick" opposite the top of the stairs). The city was prosperous, as evidenced by the furniture and paintings on display. In the center of the room, find big paintings ("Effigies") of the century's magnificent kings—Maximilian I, Maximilian II, and Ludwig I (as well as Lola Montez, Ludwig I's most famous mistress).

Second Floor (Munich 1900): As Munich approached its 700th birthday, it was becoming aware of itself as a major capital. The Münchner Kindl logo was born. It was a city of artists

(Wagner operas, Lenbach portraits, Von Stuck soirées), *Jugendstil* furniture, beer, and a cosmopolitan outlook (see the "Kaiser Panorama," the big barrel-shaped 3-D peep show of Indian/Asian peoples). But after the destruction of World War I, Munich became a hotbed of discontent. The "revue" room shows the city's clash of ideas: communists, capitalists, Nazis, and the anarchic theater of comedian Karl Valentin and early works by playwright Bertolt Brecht. A nearby display gives some background on Munich's role as the birthplace of Nazism (much more thoroughly covered in the museum's National Socialism wing).

Third Floor (Puppetry and Fairground Art): Consider a trip to the third floor to see the puppetry exhibit (though not part of the "Typically Munich!" exhibit, it's worthwhile and included with your ticket). The collection of objects from the 19th century onward highlights Germany's long tradition of puppetry. You'll see everything from rod-and-shadow puppets to glove puppets to marionnettes—along with the reconstructed Munich workshop of puppet maker Walter Oberholzer and traveling marionette theaters from southern Germany. Fair and Oktoberfest items such as carousel animals may attract children, but beware that horror-house displays may scare the daylights out of them (and you).

Video Finish: End your visit back on the first floor with a kaleidoscope of video images capturing the contemporary Munich scene—rock music, World Cup triumphs, beer gardens, and other things that are..."typically Munich."

National Socialism Wing: Your permanent-exhibit ticket includes this small but worthwhile exhibit (located in a separate building across the courtyard) of photos and uniforms that takes you chronologically through the Nazi years, focused on Munich: the post-WWI struggles, Hitler's 1923 Beer Hall Putsch, his writing of *Mein Kampf*, the mass rallies in Königsplatz and Odeonsplatz, establishment of the Dachau concentration camp, the destruction rained on Munich in World War II, and postwar reconstruction.

MUNICH'S MUSEUM QUARTER (KUNSTAREAL)

This quarter, northwest of the city center, has an impressive cluster of fine museums displaying art spanning from 3000 BC right up to the present (Egyptian Museum, Glyptothek, Alte Pinakothek, Lenbachhaus, Moderne Pinakothek, and the Museum Brandhorst). Most people don't come to Munich for the art, but this group makes a case for the city's world-class status. The Alte Pinakothek is the best of the bunch, but modern art is also surprisingly well represented. Consider spending an afternoon here (and maybe an evening; most of these museums are open late one night of the week). Café Ella, in the Lenbachhaus, is a good option for

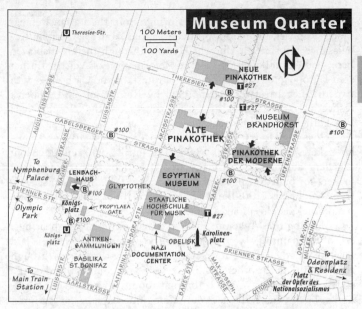

lunch or dinner (closed Mon). Also in this area is the excellent Nazi Documentation Center.

Getting There: The Glyptothek and Lenbachhaus are right by the Königsplatz stop on the U-2 subway line. The three Pinakothek museums, the Egyptian Museum, and the Brandhorst are a few blocks to the northeast. Handy tram #27 whisks you right to the Pinakothek stop from Karlsplatz (between the train station and Marienplatz). You can also take bus #100 from the train station, or walk 10 minutes from the Theresienstrasse or Königsplatz stops on the U-2 line.

Tickets: A €12 pass covers the Pinakotheks, plus the Brandhorst and Schack Collection (more 19th-century German Romanticism) on a single day. A €29 combo-ticket covers five visits to any of those museums (no time restriction, sharable with travel companions). On Sundays, these museums let you in for just a token €1, but charge €4.50 for the useful audioguides (normally included).

▲▲Alte Pinakothek

The Alte Pinakothek ("Old Art Gallery") shows off a world-class collection of European masterpieces from the 14th to 19th century, starring the two tumultuous centuries (1450-1650) when Europe went

from medieval to modern. See paintings from the Italian Renaissance (Raphael, Leonardo, Botticelli, Titian) and the German Renaissance it inspired (Albrecht Dürer). Through the art displayed here, you can follow along as the Reformation of Martin Luther split Europe into two subcultures—Protestant and Catholic—with two distinct art styles (exemplified by Rembrandt and Rubens, respectively). You may also see paintings from the (closed) Neue Pinakothek across the street.

Cost and Hours: €7, €1 on Sun, covered by day pass and combo-ticket; Wed-Sun 10:00-18:00, Tue until 20:00, closed Mon; excellent audioguide is usually free (€4.50 on Sun), mandatory lockers for big bags, pleasant Café Klenze; U-2: Theresienstrasse, tram #27, or bus #100; Barer Strasse 27, tel. 089/2380-5216, www.pinakothek.de/alte-pinakothek.

Visiting the Museum: Pick up a map and get your bearings. All of the paintings we'll see are on the upper floor, which is laid out like a barbell. Start at one fat end and work your way through the "handle" to the other end. From the ticket counter, head up the stairway to the left to reach the first rooms. I've listed the highlights, but as you walk, let your audioguide explain any painting that catches your interest.

German Renaissance (Room II): Albrecht Altdorfer's *The Battle of Issus (Schlacht bei Issus)* shows a world at war. Masses of soldiers are swept along in the currents and tides of a battle completely beyond their control, their confused motion reflected in the swirling sky. We see the battle from a great height, giving us a godlike perspective. Though the painting depicts Alexander the Great's history-changing victory over the Persians (find the Persian king Darius turning and fleeing), it could as easily have been Germany in the 1520s. Christians were fighting Muslims, peasants battled masters, and Catholics and Protestants were squaring off for a century of conflict. The armies melt into a huge landscape, leaving the impression that the battle goes on forever.

Albrecht Dürer's larger-than-life *Four Apostles (Johannes und Petrus* and *Paulus und Marcus)* are saints of a radical new religion: Martin Luther's Protestantism. Just as Luther challenged Church authority, Dürer—a friend of

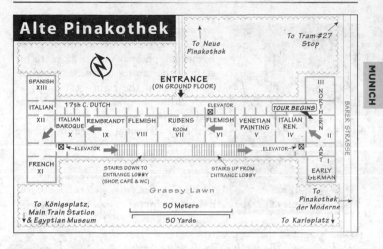

Alte Pinakothek

To Neue Pinakothek

To Tram #27 Stop

ENTRANCE (ON GROUND FLOOR)

SPANISH XIII

ITALIAN — 17th C. DUTCH

ELEVATOR

TOUR BEGINS

III N O R T H E R N

XII

ITALIAN BAROQUE X

REMBRANDT IX

FLEMISH VIII

RUBENS ROOM VII

FLEMISH VI

VENETIAN PAINTING V

ITALIAN REN. IV

II

ELEVATOR

ELEVATOR

A R T I

FRENCH XI

STAIRS DOWN TO ENTRANCE LOBBY (SHOP, CAFÉ & WC)

STAIRS UP FROM ENTRANCE LOBBY

EARLY GERMAN

Grassy Lawn

To Pinakothek der Moderne

To Königsplatz, Main Train Station & Egyptian Museum

50 Meters

50 Yards

To Karlsplatz

BARER STRASSE

MUNICH

Luther's—strips these saints of any rich clothes, halos, or trappings of power and gives them down-to-earth human features: receding hairlines, wrinkles, and suspicious eyes. The inscription warns German rulers to follow the Bible rather than Catholic Church leaders. The figure of Mark—a Bible in one hand and a sword in the other—is a fitting symbol of the dangerous times.

Dürer's *Self-Portrait in Fur Coat (Selbstbildnis im Pelzrock)* looks like Jesus Christ but is actually 28-year-old Dürer himself (per his inscription: "XXVIII"), gaz-

ing out, with his right hand solemnly giving a blessing. This is the ultimate image of humanism: the artist as an instrument of God's continued creation. Get close and enjoy the intricately braided hair, the skin texture, and the fur collar. To the left of the head is Dürer's famous monogram—"A.D." in the form of a pyramid.

Italian Renaissance (Room IV): With the Italian Renaissance—the "rebirth" of interest in the art and learning of ancient Greece and Rome—artists captured the realism, three-dimensionality, and symmetry found in classical statues. Twenty-one-year-old Leonardo da Vinci's *Virgin and Child (Maria mit dem Kinde)* need no halos—they radiate purity. Mary is a solid pyramid of maternal love, flanked by Renaissance-arch windows that look out on the hazy distance. Baby Jesus reaches out to play innocently with a carnation, the blood-colored symbol of his eventual death.

Raphael's *Holy Family at the Canigiani House (Die hl. Familie*

aus dem Hause Canigiani) takes Leonardo's pyramid form and runs with it. Father Joseph forms the peak, with his staff as the strong central axis. Mary and Jesus (on the right) form a pyramid-within-the-pyramid, as do Elizabeth and baby John the Baptist on the left. They all exchange meaningful eye contact, safe within the bounds of the stable family structure.

In Botticelli's *Lamentation over Christ (Die Beweinung Christi)*, the Renaissance "pyramid" implodes, as the weight of the dead Christ drags everyone down, and the tomb grins darkly behind them.

Venetian Painting (Room V): In Titian's *Christ Crowned with Thorns (Die Dornenkrönung)*, a powerfully built Christ sits silently enduring torture by prison guards. The painting is by Venice's greatest Renaissance painter, but there's no symmetry, no pyramid form, and the brushwork is intentionally messy and Impressionistic. By the way, this is the first painting we've seen done on canvas rather than wood, as artists experimented with vegetable oil-based paints.

Rubens and Baroque (Room VII): Europe's religious wars split the Continent in two—Protestants in the northern countries, Catholics in the south. (Germany itself was divided, with Bavaria remaining Catholic.) The Baroque style, popular in Catholic countries, featured large canvases, bright colors, lots of flesh, rippling motion, wild emotions, grand themes... and pudgy winged babies, the sure sign of Baroque. This room holds several canvases by the great Flemish painter Peter Paul Rubens.

In Rubens' 300-square-foot *Great Last Judgment (Das Grosse Jüngste Gericht)*, Christ raises the righteous up to heaven (left side) and damns the sinners to hell (on the right). This swirling cycle of

MUNICH

nudes was considered risqué and kept under wraps by the very monks who'd commissioned it.

Rubens and Isabella Brant in the Honeysuckle Bower shows the artist with his first wife, both of them the very picture of health, wealth, and success. They lean together unconsciously, as people in love will do, with their hands clasped in mutual affection. When his first wife died, 53-year-old Rubens found a replacement—16-year-old Hélène Fourment, shown in an adjacent painting (just to the left) in her wedding dress. You may recognize Hélène's face in other Rubens paintings.

The Rape of the Daughters of Leucippus (Der Raub der Töchter des Leukippos) has many of Rubens' most typical elements—fleshy, emotional, rippling motion; bright colors; and a classical subject. The legendary twins Castor and Pollux crash a wedding and steal the brides as their own. The chaos of flailing limbs and rearing horses is all held together in a subtle X-shaped composition. Like the weaving counterpoint in a Baroque fugue, Rubens balances opposites.

Notice that Rubens' canvases were—to a great extent—cranked out by his students and assistants from small "cartoons" the master himself made (displayed in the side room).

Rembrandt and Dutch (Room IX): From Holland, Rembrandt van Rijn's *Six Paintings from the Life of Christ* are a down-to-earth look at supernatural events. *The Holy Family (Die Heilige Familie)* is set in a carpenter's workshop (with tools on the wall). The canvases are dark brown, lit by strong light. The *Holy Family*'s light source is the Baby Jesus himself—literally the "light of the world." In the *Raising of the Cross (Kreuzaufrichtung)*, a man dressed in blue is looking on—a self-portrait of Rembrandt.

In the *Deposition (Kreuzabnahme)*, the light bounces off Christ's pale body onto his mother Mary, who has fainted in the shadows, showing how his death also hurts her. The drama is underplayed, with subdued emotions.

▲Neue Pinakothek

The Alte Pinakothek's younger sister is an easy-to-like collection located just across the street, showing paintings from 1800 to 1920. The museum's highlights are its world-class Impressionist paintings and one of Van Gogh's *Sunflowers*, but it is closed for renovations through 2025. During construction, highlights from the collection will be displayed at the Alte Pinakothek and at the Schack Collection (Prinzregentenstrasse 9, near the Bavarian National Museum).

Cost and Hours: When open, likely €7, €1 on Sun, covered by day pass and combo-ticket; Thu-Mon 10:00-18:00, Wed until 20:00, closed Tue; well-done audioguide is usually free (€4.50 on Sun), classy **$$ Café Hunsinger** in basement spills into park; U-2: Theresienstrasse, tram #27, or bus #100; Barer Strasse 29 but enter on Theresienstrasse, tel. 089/2380-5195, www.pinakothek.de/neue-pinakothek.

▲Pinakothek der Moderne

This museum picks up where the other two Pinakotheks leave off, covering the 20th and 21st centuries. Most of the building houses temporary exhibits and constantly rotating collections, but there are two (fairly) permanent exhibits, with excellent English descriptions throughout. The striking, white, high-ceilinged building is itself worth a look—it's free to step into the atrium.

Cost and Hours: €10, €1 on Sun, covered by day pass and combo-ticket; Tue-Sun 10:00-18:00, Thu until 20:00, closed Mon; audioguide is usually free (€4.50 on Sun), mandatory bag check for big bags; café in atrium with outdoor patio; U-2: Theresienstrasse, tram #27, or bus #100; Barer Strasse 40, tel. 089/2380-5360, www.pinakothek.de/pinakothek-der-moderne.

Visiting the Museum: The manageably sized Classical Modernism wing, upstairs near the entrance, covers many of the stars of modern art—Picasso, Dalí, Miró, and so on. The museum's strength is the German contribution. The Expressionists rendered reality in deep colors and bold black outlines. Munich's Blue Rider Group (Kandinsky, Klee, Marc) took it to the next level by abandoning reality altogether and expressing themselves with only color and line. One or two rooms display "degenerate art"—paintings confiscated by the Nazis and eventually rescued by an art lover. Max Beckmann (whose work is usually in Room 11) witnessed the rise of Nazism—and was branded a degenerate—and his symbol-laced works chronicle the cynicism of the time.

The design wing, in the basement, is worth a quick look. From chairs to bikes to blenders to cars and computers, these are every-day objects that work efficiently but also have a sleek artistic flair.

▲▲Egyptian Museum (Staatliches Museum Ägyptischer Kunst)

To enjoy this museum, you don't need a strong interest in ancient Egypt (but you may have one by the time you leave). This modern space was custom-made to evoke the feeling of being deep in an ancient tomb, from the wide, easy-to-miss staircase outside that descends to the narrow entry, to the twisty interior rooms that grow narrower and more catacomb-like as you progress. The art here  is beautifully lit, explained well in English, and accompanied by touch-screen terminals that give the curious more background. The museum's clever design creates a low-stress visit (just follow the one-way route marked by brass arrows in the floor), and makes up for the fact that the collection lacks a rock-star showpiece (such as Nefertiti, who still holds her head high in Berlin's Neues Museum).

Cost and Hours: €7, €1 on Sun, Wed-Sun 10:00-18:00, Tue until 20:00, closed Mon, audioguide is usually free (€1 on Sun); U-2 or U-8 to Königsplatz, tram #27 to Karolinenplatz, or bus #100 to Pinakothek stop; 10-minute walk from main train station, Gabelsbergerstrasse 35, tel. 089/2892-7630, www.smaek.de.

▲▲Lenbachhaus

Locals like to say, "Berlin had generals, Munich had artists." And that was particularly true in the decades before World War I. Little ol' Munich blew the art world's mind when a bunch of art-school cronies got fed up with being told how and what to paint, and together as the revolutionary "Blue Rider" *(Blaue Reiter)* group galloped toward a brand-new horizon—abstract art. In the Lenbachhaus' series of pleasant galleries you can witness the birth of Modernist nonrepresentational art, with paintings by Kandinsky, Klee, and Marc, then stroll the rest of the building's offerings (including the apartments of painter Franz von Lenbach, whose original villa and studio are now largely enclosed by the modern museum building).

Cost and Hours: €10, includes well-done audioguide; ticket gets you half-price admission to Jewish History Museum, Nazi Documentation Center, Munich City Museum, or Villa Stuck (or use any of those tickets to get half-price admission here); Wed-Sun 10:00-18:00, Tue until 20:00, closed Mon; Luisenstrasse 33, tel. 089/2333-2000, www.lenbachhaus.de.

Cuisine Art: The museum has a good, upscale Italian restaurant, **Café Ella,** that's open much later than the museum (Tue-Sat 9:00-24:00, Sun until 21:00, closed Mon, tel. 089/7008-8177).

Visiting the Museum: The collection includes three distinct sections: 19th century (conservative, colorful, optimistic); Blue Rider (emotional, inspired, modern); and Post-1945 (abstract). The Blue Rider revolution begins on the second floor, with seemingly innocuous paintings of the cute Bavarian town of Murnau. It was here in 1908 that two Munich couples—Wassily Kandinsky, Alexej Jawlensky, and their artist girlfriends—came for vacation. The four painted together—it's hard to tell their work apart—employing intense colors, thick paint, and bold black outlines. Over the next few years (c. 1911-1914), they'd gather together into a group of Munich-based artists calling themselves the Blue Rider, which included Paul Klee and Franz Marc. They were all devoted to expressing the spiritual truths they felt within by using intense colors and geometric shapes.

The Blue Rider School was blown apart by World War I: The artists who survived the Great War went on to pioneer abstract art. Over time, they paid less attention to re-creating the physical world realistically on canvas and more attention to the colors and lines alone. Kandinsky's "Improvisations"—like a jazz musician improvising a new pattern of notes from a set scale— eventually became the art world's first purely abstract canvases. Soon Kandinsky was teaching at the famous Bauhaus school in Weimar, and his style spread everywhere. Jawlensky and Klee also went  on to develop a simpler and more abstract style. This is the art that infuriated Hitler, art that he termed "degenerate."

One floor down, in the "Art After 1945" section, you'll see big, empty canvases by the Abstract Expressionists who—like Kandinsky and his Blue Rider contemporaries—tried to "express" deep truths through "abstract" color and line alone. You'll see other recent pieces, most of them provocative.

This floor also has a section devoted to several oddball installations by Joseph Beuys. (Is that art, or did the janitor just leave a

MUNICH

broom here?) The far wing's stash of 19th-century paintings (on both floors) provides a nice contrast to all the abstract stuff.

Finally, across the entry hall from the ticket desk and up one floor, enter the luxe villa of Franz von Lenbach, who made a successful living here executing portraits of 19th-century notables. His paintings fill the walls of ornate rooms accentuated by fine 15th- to 19th-century furnishings.

More Art Museums
The museum quarter has several more highly regarded museums, but for the typical tourist on a quick visit they probably don't merit a stop.

The **Museum Brandhorst** (closed Mon) covers the end of the 20th century and the beginning of the 21st, with a particular emphasis on Andy Warhol and Cy Twombly. Its collection is contained in a striking building with thousands of colored cylinders lining the outside. The **Glyptothek,** an impressive collection of Greek and Roman sculpture started by Ludwig I, is closed for a years-long renovation.

▲▲Nazi Documentation Center
(NS-Dokumentationszentrum München)
This center—housed in a stark, light-filled, cube-shaped building—documents the rise and fall of Nazism with a focus on Munich's role and the reasons behind it, as this city, like the rest of Germany, is determined to learn from its 20th-century nightmare. While there are no actual artifacts here, the learning experience is moving and a worthwhile companion to visiting the Dachau Concentration Camp Memorial.

Cost and Hours: €5 includes well-done and techic audio guide; ticket gets you half-price admission to Jewish History Museum, Munich City Museum, Villa Stuck, or Lenbachhaus—or use any of those tickets to get half-price admission here; Tue-Sun 10:00-19:00, closed Mon, U-2: Königsplatz, Brienner Strasse 34, tel. 089/2336-7001, www.ns-dokuzentrum-muenchen.de.

Background: Munich was the birthplace of the National Socialist German Workers' Party (NSDAP—or Nazi Party), and even after the Nazis took power and moved to Berlin, it remained the official Nazi Party headquarters. It was in Munich that Hitler and other disillusioned World War I veterans gathered to lick their wounds. The Nazi Party was founded here in 1919, and this is where Hitler staged his attempted coup (the Beer Hall Putsch).

He was imprisoned in nearby Landsberg where he wrote his *Mein Kampf* manifesto.

As soon as the Nazis took power (in 1933), they opened their first concentration camp, outside Munich in Dachau. Munich was the site of the infamous failed peace pact, the Munich Agreement of 1938, where Britain's prime minister tried to avoid war by appeasing Hitler. Once in power, Hitler officially proclaimed Munich "Capital of the Movement."

Königsplatz was ground zero for Nazi activities. (Remember that Hitler fancied himself an artist, and with its world-class museums, art academies, and artists' villas, this square was at the heart of the German art world—thus making it a perfect stage for Hitler's ego; the monumental Neoclassical buildings that surround the square were also right up his alley.) Mass rallies were held on Königsplatz, where they burned forbidden books. Some 68 buildings in the neighborhood housed dozens of Nazi departments and 6,000 employees. While WWII bombs left much of the city in rubble, the Nazi-built structures were so strong that, ironically, they were among the rare buildings in the center still standing in 1945. Most of the Nazi-built architecture is gone now, but at Arcisstrasse 12, once the Führerbau ("Führer building," now used as a music academy), you can still see the window of Hitler's personal office above the entrance porch. The official Nazi Party headquarters (called the Brown House) was next door, along Brienner Strasse. That structure was destroyed in the war and has now been replaced by this brand-new building.

Visiting the Museum: The museum is arranged chronologically and begins on the top floor. (Take the elevator to avoid confusion.) The top floor covers the end of World War I and the beginning of Hitler's movement in Munich (1918-1933). It includes gripping biographies of the early opponents of the Nazi Party.

The third floor (covering 1933-1939) documents the establishment of the racially pure *Volksgemeinschaft* ("people's community") and the effect of Nazi domination on everyday life, including a timeline that illustrates the restrictions and ordinances that worsened Jewish isolation. Look out onto Königsplatz and envision Hitler's rise to power, which started right here. The second floor (1939-1945) covers the horrors of war, the Holocaust, and the "denazification" period after the end of Nazi rule. Find the video showing Munich in ruins immediately following the war and compare the footage to what you see today.

The first floor (after 1945) examines the faith people put in the Nazi regime and the difficulty in coming to terms with the past. The Learning Center, in the basement, encourages reflection, with a collection of books banned during Nazi rule and research stations where you can delve into topics of interest.

NEAR THE RIVER
▲English Garden (Englischer Garten)

Munich's "Central Park," the largest urban park on the Continent, was laid out in 1789 by an American. More than 100,000 locals

commune with nature here on sunny summer days (including lots of students from the nearby university). The park stretches three miles from the center, past the university and the trendy Schwabing quarter. For the best quick visit, take bus #100 or tram #18 to the Nationalmuseum/Haus der Kunst stop. Under the bridge, you'll see surfers. (The surf's always up here—even through the night; surfers bring their own lights.) Follow the path, to the right of the surfing spot, downstream until you reach the big lawn. The Chinese Tower beer garden (described in the "Beer Halls, Beer Gardens, and Bavarian Food" section, later) is just beyond the tree-covered hill to the right. Follow the oompah music and walk to the hilltop temple, with a postcard view of the city on your way. Afterward, instead of retracing your steps, you can walk (or take bus #54 a couple of stops) to the Giselastrasse U-Bahn station and return to town on the U-3 or U-6.

A rewarding respite from the city, the park is especially fun and worth ▲▲—on a bike under the summer sun and on warm evenings (unfortunately, there are no bike-rental agencies in or near the park; to rent some wheels, see page 40). Caution: While local law requires sun worshippers to wear clothes on the tram, the park is sprinkled with buck-naked sunbathers—quite a shock to prudish Americans (they're the ones riding their bikes into the river and trees).

Haus der Kunst

Built by Hitler as a temple of Nazi art, this bold and fascist building—a rare surviving example of a purpose-built Nazi structure—is now an impressive shell for various temporary art exhibits. Ironically, the art now displayed in Hitler's "house of art" is the kind that annoyed the Führer most—modern. Its cellar, which served

Green Munich

Although the capital of a very conservative part of Germany, Munich has long been a liberal stronghold. For nearly two decades, the city council has been controlled by a Social Democrat/Green Party coalition. The city policies are pedestrian-friendly—you'll find much of the town center closed to normal traffic, with plenty of bike lanes and green spaces. As you talk softly and hear birds rather than motors, it's easy to forget you're in the center of a big city. On summer Mondays, the peace and quiet make way for "blade Monday"—when streets in the center are closed to cars and as many as 30,000 inline skaters swarm around town in a giant rolling party.

as a nightclub for GIs in 1945, is now the extremely exclusive P-1 nightclub.

Cost and Hours: €14, daily 10:00-20:00, Thu until 22:00, exhibits usually well-explained in English, at south end of English Garden, tram #18 or bus #100 from station to Nationalmuseum/Haus der Kunst, Prinzregentenstrasse 1, tel. 089/2112-7113, www.hausderkunst.de.

Cuisine Art: The Goldene Bar, where a 1930s atmosphere survives (on the back side of the building, overlooking the English Garden), is one of Germany's most interesting cafés (café open daily 10:00-20:00; bar open Mon-Sat until late, closed Sun).

Nearby: Just beyond the Haus der Kunst, where Prinzregentenstrasse crosses the Eisbach canal, you can get another view of surfers in the rapids created as the small river tumbles underground.

Bavarian National Museum (Bayerisches Nationalmuseum)

This tired but interesting collection features Tilman Riemenschneider wood carvings, manger scenes, traditional living rooms, and old Bavarian houses. For those with a keen interest in Baroque and Rococo art, it's worth the trip.

Cost and Hours: €7, €1 on Sun; Tue-Sun 10:00-17:00, Thu until 20:00, closed Mon; tram #18 or bus #100 from station to Nationalmuseum/Haus der Kunst, Prinzregentenstrasse 3, tel. 089/211-2401, www.bayerisches-nationalmuseum.de.

Villa Stuck

Franz von Stuck, Munich's top Art Nouveau artist and fin-de-siècle tastemaker, designed this mansion for himself, then lived and worked (and partied) here from 1898 until his death in 1928. Within Munich's cutting-edge art scene, you were nobody until you were invited to an evening here. The rooms' original dark-wood/gold-leaf decor dazzle Jugendstil fans; upstairs in Von Stuck's former studio is his "Sin Altar" with a version of his most famous (and perhaps most erotically charged) painting, *The Sin (Die Sünde)*.

Cost and Hours: €9; ticket gets you half-price admission to Jewish History Museum, Munich City Museum, Nazi Documentation Center, or Lenbachhaus—or use any of those tickets to get half-price admission here; Tue-Sun 11:00-18:00, closed Mon; U-4: Prinzregentenplatz or tram #17 or bus #100 to Friedensengel/Villa Stuck, just a short ride across the river from the north end of the city center, Prinzregentenstrasse 60, tel. 089/455-5510, www.villastuck.de.

▲Deutsches Museum (Main Branch)

Germany's answer to our Smithsonian Institution, the Deutsches Museum traces the evolution of science and technology. The main branch is centrally located. The two other branches—the Museum of Transportation and the Flight Museum—are situated outside the city center, but are worth the effort for enthusiasts (both described later). You can pay separately for each museum, or buy a combo-ticket that covers all three.

Here at the main branch, enjoy wandering through rooms of historic airplanes, spaceships, mining, the harnessing of wind and water power, hydraulics, musical instruments, printing, chemistry, computers, astronomy, and nanotechnology...it's the Louvre of technical know-how. The museum feels a bit dated, and not all the displays have English descriptions—but major renovations are underway to get this museum up to speed. About a third of the collection will likely be closed during your visit, but even those on roller skates will still need to be selective. Use my mini tour to get oriented, then study the floor plan and choose which sections interest you. The museum is designed to be hands-on; if you see a button, push it.

Cost and Hours: €12, €19 combo-ticket with other Deutsches Museum branches, €25 family ticket, €3 extra for planetarium show, daily 9.00-17:00, no guided tours in English but English map available, several small cafés in the museum, tel. 089/217-9333, www.deutsches-museum.de.

Getting There: Take tram #17 to the Deutsches Museum stop. Alternatively, take the S-Bahn or tram #18 to Isartor, then walk 300 yards over the river and turn right, following the signs (if you can find them). The entrance is near the far end of the building along the riverside. See the "Munich" map near the start of this chapter.

Visiting the Museum: After buying your ticket at the kiosk outside, head inside and stop by the information desk to ask about the day's schedule of demonstrations (for example, electric power or glass-blowing). Pick up an essential floor plan (you'll get lost without it) and then walk toward the vast high-ceilinged room dominated by a tall-masted ship.

Ground Floor: Get oriented and locate the handy elevator behind you—it's one of the few elevators in this labyrinthine building that goes to all six floors. Use the diagram (outlining the exhibits on each floor) near the elevators to make a plan. Now, let's explore.

The exhibit on **marine navigation** is anchored by the 60-foot sailing ship *Maria*. Take the staircase down, where you can look inside her cut-away hull and imagine life below decks. Before heading back upstairs, find the bisected U1 submarine (on the wall farthest from the entrance)—the first German *U-Boot* (undersea boat), dating from 1906.

Now make your way to several technology exhibits—DNA and nanotechnology (downstairs). Children will enjoy the "Kinderreich" (past the cloakroom to the left as you enter) and the exciting twice-daily high-voltage demonstrations (ground floor) showing the noisy creation of a five-foot bolt of lightning.

First Floor: The **historic aviation** collection occupies the center of the first floor. You'll see early attempts at flight—gliders, hot-air balloons, and a model of the airship pioneered by Germany's Count Zeppelin. The highlight is a Wright Brothers double-decker airplane from 1909—six years after their famous first flight, when they began to manufacture multiple copies of their prototype. By World War I, airplanes were becoming a formidable force. The Fokker tri-plane was made famous by Germany's war ace the Red Baron (Manfred von Richthofen).

Second Floor: Gathered together near the main elevator, you'll find a replica of prehistoric **cave paintings** and daily **glass-blowing** demonstrations. Don't miss the flight simulator—a training device that is almost identical to flying a real airplane.

Third Floor: The third floor traces the history of **measurement,** including time (from a 16th-century sundial and an 18th-century clock to a scary Black Forest wall clock complete with grim reaper), weights, and geodesy (surveying and mapping). In the **computer** section, you go from the ancient abacus to a 1956 Univac computer—as big as a room, with a million components, costing a million dollars, and with less computing power than your smartphone.

Floors 4-6: The focus here is on **astronomy.** A light-show exhibit traces the evolution of the universe. The **planetarium** lecture is in German, but might be worthwhile if you love the stars. Finally, you emerge on the museum rooftop—the **"sundial garden"**—with great views. On a clear day, you can see the Alps.

SIGHTS OUTSIDE THE CITY CENTER

The following sights are 30 minutes or less from the city center. A little farther out are several excellent day-trip options, including the Dachau Concentration Camp Memorial (about an hour away by public transportation) and Andechs Monastery. King Ludwig's castles of Bavaria, Nürnberg, Salzburg, and Berchtesgaden also make good day trips.

Deutsches Museum Branches
▲Museum of Transportation (Verkehrszentrum)

While it veers a little toward the wonky, this fun museum has enough to interest the casual visitor—and it's heaven for any driving enthusiast. You'll see all aspects of transport, from old big-wheeled bikes to Benz's first car (a three-wheeler from the 1880s) to sleek ICE super-trains (serious train buffs going to Nürnberg will be more excited by the German Railway Museum there). The museum asks what our lives would be like without transportation, and the exhibits show how modes of transportation developed from Neolithic "bone" skates (predecessors to today's in-line skates) to 19th-century Lapland skis, to today's snowboards and

fast cars. This annex of the Deutsches Museum is housed in three giant hangar-like exhibition halls near the Oktoberfest grounds, a.k.a. Theresienwiese.

Cost and Hours: €7, €19 combo-ticket with other Deutsches Museum branches, €15 family ticket; daily 9:00-17:00, Am Bavariapark 5—but if arriving by GPS try Theresienhöhe 14a, tel. 089/500-806-123, www.deutsches-museum.de.

Getting There: Take the U-4 or U-5 to Schwanthalerhöhe and follow signs for *Deutsches Museum* from the platform. The museum is just a few steps from the station exit.

Visiting the Museum: True to the Deutsches Museum's interactive spirit, the Museum of Transportation is engaging and well-explained in English.

Hall I focuses on urban transport, with special attention to Munich. Climb into the original 1927 prototype of a Berliner S-Bahn car, marvel at a cross-section of the intricate and multilayered subway system, learn about the history of the bicycle, and admire the vintage cars—including a deluxe 1930s Mercedes-Benz 370—arrayed into mock traffic jams. Twice a day (10:30 and 15:00) they fire up an S-Bahn simulator and let visitors pretend to drive the train.

Hall II gives you a look at the development of long-distance overland travel. The focus here is on trains and bus travel. Don't miss the Maffei S3/6, a.k.a. "The Pride of Bavaria" (in its heyday the fastest steam engine, at nearly 80 miles per hour); climb aboard the clever old postal train car (complete with a mail slot on the side); and check out the 1950s panorama bus that shuttled eager tourists to fashionable destinations such as Italy. If your timing is right (or you see a tour in progress), be sure to take a ride in the old carriage. The metal track simulates what it would have felt like to travel in the 18th century over different terrain (grass and cobblestones—pretty uncomfortable).

Hall III is all about fun: motorcycles, bicycles, skis, and race cars. Famous prewar models include the Mercedes-Benz SS and the Auto Union Type C "Grand Prix" race car. Other tiny racers—which resemble metal pickles to the uninitiated—include the 1950s Mercedes-Benz 300 SLR and the famous Messerschmitt 200. You'll also find early-18th-century bicycles based on Leonardo da Vinci's drawings. Before the invention of the pedal crank, bikes were just silly-looking scooters for adults.

Flight Museum (Flugwerft Schleissheim)

Fans of all things winged will enjoy the Deutsches Museum's Flight Museum, with more than 50 planes, helicopters, gliders, and an original Europa rocket housed in a historical aerodrome on a former military airfield. Expect to find a few extras here while the main Deutsches Museum is under renovation, particularly aircraft designed after World War I. Inside the museum, try a helicopter simulator (for an extra charge, usually available on weekends) and watch antique planes being restored in the glass-walled workshop. The museum is well conceived and has some English explanations, but probably only those interested in the history of flight will find the trek to this out-of-the-way museum worthwhile.

Cost and Hours: €7, €19 combo-ticket with other Deutsches Museum branches, €15 family ticket, daily 9:00-17:00, tiny café, tel. 089/3157-1410, www.deutsches-museum.de.

Getting There: It's easiest by car, or you can ride the S-1 about 20 minutes from Marienplatz (direction: Freising Flughafen) and get off at Oberschleissheim (trip covered by Munich XXL day pass). Walk over the bridge, following *Museen* signs, for 15 minutes until the street turns into Effnerstrasse.

MUNICH

Greater Munich

2 Kilometers
2 Miles

To Airport & Nürnberg
A-92

FLIGHT MUSEUM & SCHLEISSHEIM PALACE

To Airport & Nürnberg
99

To Dachau
99

BMW-WELT & MUSEUM

FRANKFURTER-RING

A-9

DACHAUER STRASSE

To Rothenburg & Romantic Road
A-8

VERDISTR.

WINTRICH RING

TOWER

Olympic Park

PETUEL-RING

LEOPOLDSTR.

UNGERERSTR.

99

NYMPHENBURG PALACE & GARDENS

304

ARNULF STR.

MAIN TRAIN STATION

SIEGESTOR

CHINESE TOWER BEER GARDEN

English Garden

See detail maps

LANDSBERGERSTR.

OLD CITY

PRINZREGENTENSTR.

VILLA STUCK

A-94

To Landsberg & Füssen (via Romantic Road)

MUSEUM OF TRANSPORTATION

LINDWURM STR.

DEUTSCHES MUSEUM

ROSENHEIMER

OSTBAHNHOF

OKTOBERFEST SITE (THERESIENWIESE)

BÖSCH.

Isar River

CHIEMGAUSTR.

A-96 To Landsberg, Füssen (via Romantic Road) & Lindau

A-95 To Andechs Monastery & Garmisch

A-8

A-995

99 To Salzburg

Nearby: Consider a visit to opulent Schleissheim Palace (described next), a two-minute walk from the Flight Museum.

▲Schleissheim Palace

Tucked just outside central Munich, Schleissheim Palace is a hidden gem of High Baroque architecture and Wittelsbach wealth. As a way of wielding his political power, Max Emanuel commissioned French and Italian artists to create a mini Versailles (the New Palace) to house his impressive art collection and show off his beautifully manicured Baroque garden. Porcelain collectors shouldn't miss the Meissen porcelain exhibit in the Lustheim Palace at the far end of the gardens—about a 30-minute walk. Rarely visited, this expansive palace is worth a stop, especially for those with a car.

Cost and Hours: New Palace-€4.50, gardens-free, €8 combo-ticket covers New Palace, Old Palace (skippable), and porcelain collection; Tue-Sun 9:00-18:00, Oct-March 10:00-16:00, closed

MUNICH

Mon year-round; nice beer garden, tel. 089/315-8720, www.schloesser-schleissheim.de.

Getting There: Schleissheim Palace is a two-minute walk from the Flight Museum (see previous listing).

▲▲Nymphenburg Palace Complex

For 200 years, this oasis of palaces and gardens was the Wittelsbach rulers' summer vacation home, a getaway from the sniping politics of court life in the city. Their kids could play, picnic, ride horses, and frolic in the ponds and gardens, while the adults played cards, listened to music, and sipped coffee on the veranda. It was at Nymphenburg that a seven-year-old Mozart gave a widely heralded concert, that 60-year-old Ludwig I courted the femme fatale Lola Montez, and that "Mad" King Ludwig II (Ludwig I's grandson) was born and baptized.

Today, Nymphenburg Palace and the surrounding one-square-mile park are a great place for a royal stroll or discreet picnic. Indoors, you can tour the Bavarian royal family's summer quarters and visit the Royal Stables Museum (carriages, sleighs, and porcelain). If you have time, check out playful extras such as a hunting lodge (Amalienburg), bathhouse (Badenburg), pagoda (Pagodenburg), and fake ruins (Magdalenenklause). The complex also houses a humble natural history museum and Baroque chapel. Allow at least three hours (including travel time) to see the palace complex at a leisurely pace.

Cost and Hours: Palace-€6; combo-ticket-€11.50 (€8.50 off-season) covers the palace, Royal Stables Museum, and outlying sights. All of these sights are open daily April-mid-Oct 9:00-18:00, mid-Oct-March 10:00-16:00—except for Amalienburg and the other small palaces in the park, which are closed in winter; park open daily 6:00-dusk and free to enter; audioguide-€3.50, mandatory bag check for big bags, tel. 089/179-080, www.schloss-nymphenburg.de.

Getting There: The palace is three miles northwest of central Munich. Take tram #17 (direction: Amalienburgstrasse) from the train station or Karlsplatz. In 15 minutes you reach the Schloss Nymphenburg stop. From the bridge by the tram stop, you'll see the palace—a 10-minute walk away. The palace is a pleasant 30-minute bike ride from the main train station (either follow Arnulfstrasse all the way to Nymphenburg, or turn up Landshuter Allee—at Donersburgerbrücke—then follow Nymphenburger Strasse until you hit the canal that stretches to the palace). Be aware that biking in the palace grounds is not permitted.

Eating: A **$$** café serves lunch and snacks in a winter garden or on a nice terrace, a five-minute walk behind and to the right

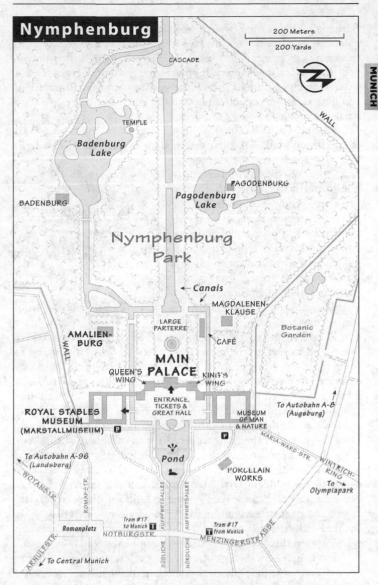

of the palace (open year-round). More eating options are near the tram stop.

Nymphenburg Palace

In 1662, after 10 years of trying, the Bavarian ruler Ferdinand Maria and his wife, Henriette Adelaide of Savoy, finally had a son, Max Emanuel. In gratitude for a male heir, Ferdinand gave this land to his Italian wife, who proceeded to build an Italian-style

MUNICH

Baroque palace as their summer residence. Their son expanded the palace to its current size. (Today's Wittelsbachs, who still refer to themselves as "princes" or "dukes," live in one wing of the palace.)

The palace interior, while interesting, is much less extensive than Munich's Residenz. The place is stingy on free information; you'll need the serviceable audioguide if you'd like more info than what I've provided below.

⮕ **Self-Guided Tour:** Your visit starts in the **Great Hall** (a.k.a. **Stone Hall**). As the central room of the palace, this light and airy space was the dining hall, site of big Wittelsbach family festivals. One of the grandest and best-preserved Rococo rooms in Bavaria (from about 1760), it sports elaborate stucco work and a ceiling fresco by Johann Baptist Zimmermann (of Wieskirche fame). Imagine the feasts and celebrations held in this room; you can practically hear the musicians playing from the balcony.

Zimmermann's fresco opens a sunroof to the heavens, where Greek gods cavort. In the sunny center, Apollo drives his chariot to bring the dawn, while bearded Zeus (astride an eagle) and peacock-carrying Juno look on. The rainbow symbolizes the peace brought by the enlightened Wittelsbachs. Around the borders of the painting, notice the fun optical illusions: For example, a painted dog holds a stucco bird in its mouth. The painting's natural setting and *joie de vivre* reflect the pastoral pleasures enjoyed here at the Wittelsbachs' summer home. Find the woman with the crescent moon above her head: That's Princess-Electress Maria Amelia, depicted as the Greek goddess Diana (you can visit the hunting lodge her husband, Prince-Elector Karl Albrecht, built for her nearby). And at one end of the fresco (away from the windows) lounges a lovely maiden with flowers in her hair: It's Flora, the eponymous nymph who inspired this "nymph's castle"—Nymphenburg.

From here, two wings stretch to the left and right. They're mirror images of one another: antechamber, audience chamber, bedchamber, and private living quarters. Guests would arrive here in the Great Hall for an awe-inspiring first impression, then make their way through a series of (also-impressive) waiting rooms for their date with the Wittelsbach nobility.

• *The tour continues to the left (as you look out the big windows).*

North Wing (Rooms 2-9): Breeze quickly through this less interesting wing, filled with tapestries and Wittelsbach portraits (including curly-haired Max Emanuel, who built this wing). Pause in the long corridor **(the North Gallery)** lined with paintings of various Wittelsbach palaces. The names of each are labeled on gilded plaques above the paintings. The ones of Nymphenburg show the place around 1720, back when there was nothing but countryside between it and downtown (and gondolas plied the canals). Imagine the logistics when the royal family—with their entourage of 200—decided to move out to the summer palace. Find the painting of Fürstenried Palace (in another Munich suburb), and look for the twin onion domes of the Frauenkirche in the distance.

Take a short detour into the **North Apartment Antechamber** (Room 3), where audiences would patiently wait to meet with the Bavarian ruler. Notice the portraits of his children that adorn the wall and the exquisite black marble table, inlaid with expensive gemstones, given to Max Emanuel's oldest son (Prince-Elector Karl Albrecht, later Holy Roman Emperor Charles VII, seated in the center portrait) upon a visit to the Medicis in Florence. Next, the former bedroom houses the **Little Gallery of Beauties,** with portraits of ladies at the French court and mistresses of the Sun King, commissioned by Max Emanuel while he was exiled in France.

• *Return to the Great Hall and enter the other wing.*

South Wing (Rooms 10-20): Pass through the gold-and-white Room 10 and turn right into the red-walled **South Apartment Antechamber.** The room calls up the exuberant time of Nymphenburg's founding couple, Ferdinand and Henriette. A portrait on the wall shows them posing together in their rich courtly dress. The large painting on the left depicts the family in a Greek myth: Henriette (as the moon goddess) leads her youngest son Joseph Clemens by the hand, while her first son Max Emanuel (as Hercules) receives the gift of a sword. On the right side of the room, Ferdinand is represented as Endymion, a mortal loved by the moon goddess. The ceiling painting (of the earth goddess Cybele) also dates from the time of Nymphenburg's first family.

After admiring the Queen's Bedroom and Chinese lacquer cabinet, head back down the long hall to **King Ludwig I's Gallery of Beauties.** The room is decorated top to bottom with portraits of 36 beautiful women (all of them painted by Joseph Stieler between 1826 and 1850). Ludwig I was a consummate girl-watcher.

Ludwig prided himself on his ability to appreciate beauty regardless of social rank. He enjoyed picking out the prettiest women from the general public and, with one of the most effective pickup lines of all time, inviting them to the palace for a portrait. Who could refuse? The portraits were on public display in the Residenz, and catapulted their subjects to stardom. The women range from commoners to princesses, but notice that they share one physical trait—Ludwig obviously preferred brunettes. The portraits are done in the modest and slightly sentimental Biedermeier style popular in central Europe, as opposed to the more flamboyant Romanticism (so beloved of Ludwig's "mad" grandson) also thriving at that time.

Most of these portraits have rich stories behind them (each of the following is at eye level): With the door you entered as your "6 o'clock," work your way counterclockwise, starting from "7 o'clock." There you'll find Helene Sedlmayr, a humble cobbler's daughter who caught Ludwig's eye; she poses in a blue-and-gray dress way beyond her budget. Though poor, she was considered Munich's comeliest Fräulein, and she eventually married the king's valet and had 10 children. Back near the door is Lady Jane Ellenborough—an elegant English baroness who went through four marriages and numerous affairs, including one with Ludwig (and, much later, with his son Otto, after Otto had become king of Greece). She was fluent in nine languages, including Arabic, after marrying a Syrian sheik 20 years her junior.

Continuing to your left near another door is Lola Montez, the king's most notorious mistress, who led him to his downfall. The portrait shows her the year she met Ludwig (she was 29, he was 60), wearing the black-lace mantilla and red flowers of a Spanish dancer. This Irish beauty (born Maria Gilbert) lived in India for a time, became Franz Liszt's lover in Paris, and eventually made her way to Munich. Ludwig was so bedazzled that he gave her a title—Countess of Landsfeld—along with a hefty annual income. Near Lola, the woman half-cloaked in a red-and-ermine robe is Princess Marie of Prussia—Ludwig's daughter-in-law—who once lived in the last rooms we'll visit. (And where in the Gallery of Beauties is the portrait of Ludwig's wife, Queen Therese? She's not here...you'll have to duck into the elegant, green Queen's Study to see her portrait.)

Pass through the blue Audience Room (with elaborate curtain rods and mahogany furniture in the French-inspired Empire style) and into the (other) **Queen's Bedroom.** The room has much the same furniture it had on August 25, 1845, when Princess Marie gave birth to the future King Ludwig II. Little Ludwig (see his bust, next to brother Otto's) was greatly inspired by Nymphenburg—riding horses in summer, taking sleigh rides in winter, reading poetry at Amalienburg. The love of nature and solitude he absorbed at Nymphenburg eventually led Ludwig to abandon Munich for his castles in the remote Bavarian countryside. By the way, note the mirror in this bedroom. Royal births were carefully witnessed, and the mirror allowed for a better view. While Ludwig's birth was well-documented, his death was shrouded in mystery (see page 165).

Palace Grounds

The wooded grounds extend far back beyond the formal gardens and are popular with joggers and walkers. Find a bench for a low-profile picnic. The park is laced with canals and small lakes, where court guests once rode on Venetian-style gondolas.

Royal Stables Museum (Marstallmuseum)

These former stables (to the left of the main palace as you approach the complex) are full of gilded coaches that will make you think of Cinderella's journey to the king's ball. Upstairs, a porcelain exhibit shows off some of the famous Nymphenburg finery. If you don't want to visit the main palace, you can buy a €4.50 ticket just for this museum (no audioguide available).

Visiting the Museum: Wandering through the collection, you can trace the evolution of 300 years of coaches—getting lighter and with better suspension as they were harnessed to faster horses. In the big entrance hall is a golden carriage drawn by eight fake white horses. In 1742, it carried Karl Albrecht Wittelsbach to Frankfurt to be crowned Holy Roman Emperor. As emperor, he got eight horses—kings got only six. The event is depicted in a frieze on the museum wall; Karl's carriage is #159.

Other objects bear witness to the good times of the relaxed Nymphenburg lifestyle and are a window into the pomp and circumstance surrounding the royals.

Just around the corner, on the right, is a painting of "Mad" King Ludwig on his sleigh at night. Next up are some over-the-top objects—sleighs, golden carriages, and (in the glass cases) harnesses—owned by Ludwig II. In his later years, Ludwig was a Howard Hughes-type recluse who stayed away from the public eye and only went out at night. (At his nearby Linderhof Palace, he actually had a hydraulic-powered dining table that would rise from the kitchen below, completely set for the meal—so he wouldn't be seen by his servants.) Ludwig's over-the-top coaches were Baroque. But this was 1870. The coaches, like the king, were in the wrong century.

Notice the photos (c. 1865, in the glass case) of Ludwig and the Romantic composer Richard Wagner. Ludwig cried on the day Wagner was married.

Backtrack to the entrance, then pass the courtyard into another hall, this one filled with more practical coaches for everyday use. At the end of the hall, Ludwig II's favorite horse, "Cosa-Rara," is stuffed and mounted.

Head upstairs to a collection of **Nymphenburg porcelain.** You'll see plates and cups painted in various styles, from ancient Greek to Old Masters, Romantic, and Art Nouveau. Historically, royal families such as the Wittelsbachs liked to have their own porcelain factories to make fit-for-a-king plates, vases, and so on. The Nymphenburg Palace porcelain works is still in operation (not open to the public—but the factory store on Odeonsplatz is happy to see you—see "Shopping in Munich," later). Find the large room with copies of 17th-century Old Masters' paintings from the Wittelsbach art collection (now at the Alte Pinakothek). Ludwig I had these paintings copied onto porcelain for safekeeping into the distant future. Take a close look—they're exquisite.

Amalienburg

Three hundred yards from Nymphenburg Palace, hiding in the park (head into the sculpted garden and veer to the left, following signs), you'll find a fine little Rococo hunting lodge, which takes just a few minutes to tour. In 1734, Prince-Elector Karl Albrecht had it built for his wife, Maria Amalia. Amalienburg was designed by François de Cuvilliés (of Residenz fame) and decorated by Johann Baptist Zimmermann. It's the most  worthwhile of the four small "extra" palaces buried in the park that are included on the combo-ticket. The others are the Pagodenburg, a Chinese-inspired pavilion; Badenburg, an opulent bathing house and banquet hall; and the Magdalenenklause, a mini palace that looks like a ruin from the outside but has an elaborate altar and woody apartments inside.

Visiting Amalienburg: As you approach, circle around and notice the facade. Above the pink-and-white grand entryway, Diana, goddess of the chase, is surrounded by themes of the hunt and flanked by busts of satyrs. The queen would shoot from the perch atop the roof. Behind a wall in the garden, dogs would scare nonflying pheasants. When they jumped up in the air above the wall, the sporting queen—as if shooting skeet—would pick the birds off.

Tourists now enter this tiny getaway through the back door. Doghouses under gun cupboards fill the first room. In the fine yellow-and-silver bedroom, the bed is flanked by portraits of Karl

Albrecht and Maria Amalia—decked out in hunting attire. She liked her dogs. The door under her portrait leads to stairs to the rooftop pheasant-shooting perch. The relief on the door's lower panel shows Vulcan forging arrows for amorous cupids.

The mini Hall of Mirrors is a blue-and-silver commotion of Rococo nymphs designed by Cuvilliés. In the next room, paintings depict court festivities, formal hunting parties, and no-contest kills (where the animal is put at an impossible disadvantage—like shooting fish in a barrel). Finally, the sparse kitchen is decorated with Chinese-style drawings on Dutch tile.

Other Sights Outside the Center
▲BMW-Welt and Museum

At the headquarters of BMW ("beh-em-VEH" to Germans), Beamer dreamers can visit two space-age buildings to learn more about this brand's storied heritage (worth ▲▲ to enthusiasts). The renowned *Autos* and *Motorräder* are beautifully displayed (perhaps even fetishized by car enthusiasts). This vast complex—built on the site of Munich's first airstrip and home to the BMW factory since 1920—has four components: the headquarters (in the building nicknamed "the Four Cylinders"—not open to the public), the factory (tourable with advance reservations), the showroom (called BMW-Welt—"BMW World"), and the BMW Museum. Everything comes with fine English translations.

Cost and Hours: Museum-€10, €3 discount with Olympic Park ticket; Tue-Sun 10:00-18:00, closed Mon; BMW-Welt showroom-free, building open daily until 24:00, exhibits staffed 9:00-18:00; tel. 089/125-016-001, www.bmw-welt.com.

Tours: English tours are offered of both the museum (€13, 1 hour, call or email ahead for times) and BMW-Welt (€7.50, discount with Olympic Park ticket; 1 hour, Mon-Wed and Sat at 15:30). Factory tours must be booked at least two months in advance (€9, 2.5 hours, Mon-Fri only, ages 6 and up, reservations tel. 089/125-016-001, infowelt@bmw-welt.com).

Getting There: From the city center, ride the U-3 to Olympia-Zentrum. Follow *Ausgang* signs to BMW-Welt/BMW Museum. Leaving the station, climb the stairs and get oriented: Ahead is the BMW-Welt (showroom) entry, the massive multicornered building across the street is the BMW factory, the quadruple "piston" towers are for the corporate offices, and the BMW Museum is marked by the gray "soup bowl." Across the highway bridge (beyond the southeast corner of BMW-Welt) is the Olympic Park and stadium. To reach the BMW Museum, head down Lerchenauer Strasse, staying parallel to the factory on your left, and cross at the stoplight just before the bridge.

Visiting BMW: The futuristic, bowl-shaped **museum** encloses

a world of floating walkways linking exhibits highlighting BMW motorcycle and car design and technology through the years. The museum traces the Bavarian Motor Works' history since 1917, when the company began making airplane engines. Motorcycles came next, followed by the first BMW sedan in 1929. You'll see how design was celebrated here from the start. Exhibits showcase motorsports, roadsters, and luxury cars. Stand on an *E* for English to hear the chief designer talk about his favorite cars in the "treasury." And the 1956 BMW 507 is enough to rev almost anyone's engine.

When you finish your visit at the museum, cross over the swoopy bridge to enter **BMW-Welt** on the first floor. The building itself—a cloud-shaped, glass-and-steel architectural masterpiece—is reason enough to visit. It's free and filled with exhibits designed to enthuse car lovers so they'll find a way to afford a Beamer. While the adjacent museum reviews the BMW past, BMW-Welt shows you the present (including new electric models) and gives you a breathtaking look at the future. With interactive stations, high-powered videos, an inviting cafeteria, and lots of horsepower, this is where customers come to pick up their new Beamers (stand on the sky bridge viewpoint to watch in envy), and where hopeful customers-to-be come to nurture their automotive dreams.

Olympic Park (Olympiapark München) and TV Tower (Olympiaturm)

After the construction of Munich's Allianz Arena for the 2006 World Cup, the city's great 1972 Olympic stadium and sports complex were left in the past, and have melded into the neighborhood as simply a huge park and swimming pool. You can get a good look at the center's striking "cobweb" style of architecture while enjoying the park's picnic potential. In addition, there are plenty of activities at the park, including a TV tower (Olympiaturm), minigolf, paddleboats, and an excellent swimming pool, the Olympia-Schwimmhalle.

The TV tower has commanding views from 620 feet. Walk completely around, enjoying the vista, with sights identified on the windows. You can see the Alps on a good day. The strange little rock-and-roll museum (with Freddie Mercury's black leather pants) is a bonus for some. Two floors higher is the open rooftop. And downstairs is the revolving Restaurant 181 (named for its altitude—see "Eating in Munich," later).

Cost and Hours: Tower-€7, €6 with BMW Museum ticket; daily 9:00-24:00, tel. 089/3067-2750, www.olympiapark.de; pool-€4.80, daily 7:00-23:00, tel. 089/2361-5050, www.swm.de.

Getting There: The U-3 runs from Marienplatz directly to the Olympia-Zentrum stop. Emerging from the station, you'll face the BMW-Welt (described earlier). Turn right and follow the path closest to BMW-Welt to a bridge over the highway and into Olympic Park. From this bridge, from left to right, you can see the ice rink and sports center, the Olympiaturm TV tower, the swimming facility, the Olympiahalle arena and concert venue, and Olympic Stadium. In the distance, the grassy hill (likely with people on top enjoying the view) was made from the rubble of WWII bomb damage.

▲Isar River Bike Ride

Munich's river, lined by a gorgeous park, leads bikers into the pristine countryside in just a few minutes. From downtown (easy access from the English Garden or Deutsches Museum), follow the riverside bike path south (upstream) along the east (left) bank. You can't get lost. Just stay on the lovely bike path. It crosses the river after a while, passing tempting little beer gardens and lots of Bavarians having their brand of fun—including gangs enjoying Munich's famous river-party rafts. Go as far as you like, then retrace your route to get home. The closest bike rental is Mike's Bike Tours (see "Getting Around Munich" near the beginning of this chapter).

Shopping in Munich

While the whole city is great for shopping, the most glamorous area is around Marienplatz. It's fun to window shop, even if you have no plans to buy. Here are a few stores and streets to consider.

Bavarian Souvenirs

Servus Heimat's amusing shops are a good source of unusual gifts that remind Bavarians of their childhood. Ask for the inside scoop behind T-shirt logos, books, and quirky kitchen utensils (City Museum store, tucked between the Munich City Museum and the Stadt Café: daily 10:00-18:00, St.-Jakobs-Platz 1, tel. 089/2370-2380; also stores at Im Tal 20—between Marienplatz and the Isartor—and at Brunnstrasse 3—near Asam Church, Mon-Sat 10:00-19:00, closed Sun; www.servusheimat.com).

Books

The **Hugendubel bookstore** on Karlsplatz has some English offerings (Mon-Sat 10:00-20:00, closed Sun, Karlsplatz 12, tel. 089/3075-7575, www.hugendubel.de).

Dirndls and Lederhosen

For fine-quality (and very expensive) traditional clothing (*Trachten* in German), head to **Loden-Frey Verkaufshaus.** The third floor of this fine department store is dedicated to classic Bavarian wear for men and women (Mon-Sat 10:00-20:00, closed Sun, a block west of Marienplatz at Maffeistrasse 7, tel. 089/210-390, www. loden-frey.com). For less expensive (but still good quality) gear, visit **Angermaier Trachten,** near the Viktualienmarkt (Mon-Fri 10:00-19:00, Sat until 18:00, closed Sun; Rosental 10, tel. 089/2300-0199, www.trachten-angermaier.de).

Toys

Obletter, right on Karlsplatz, has a good selection of wooden toys in its underground level and a fun section full of puppets (Mon-Sat 9:30-20:00, closed Sun, Karlsplatz 11, tel. 089/5508-9510).

Porcelain

For contemporary and classic dinnerware and figurines, find the **Nymphenburg Porcelain Store** on Odeonsplatz (Mon-Sat 10:00-18:00, closed Sun, Odeonsplatz 1, tel. 089/282-428, www. nymphenburg.com).

Window Shopping and Malls

Shoppers will want to stroll from Marienplatz down the pedestrianized Weinstrasse (to the left as you face the New Town Hall). Look for **Fünf Höfe** on your left, a delightful indoor/outdoor mall filled with Germany's top shops (Mon-Fri 10:00-19:00, Sat until 18:00, closed Sun). Named for its five courtyards, this is where tradition meets modern. Note how its Swiss architects play with light and color. Even if you're not a shopper, wander through the **Kunsthalle** to appreciate the architecture, the elegant window displays, and the sight of Bavarians living very well.

Built by Maximilian II in the 1850s, the nearby **Maximilianstrasse** was designed for shoppers. Today it's home to Munich's most exclusive shops.

Department Stores

Ludwig Beck, an upscale department store at Marienplatz, has been a local institution since 1861. With six floors of expensive designer clothing (plus some music, stationery, and cosmetics), this is the place to go for a €200 pair of jeans. Beck has long been to fabrics what Dallmayr is to fine food—too expensive a place to buy, but fun to browse (Mon-Sat 10:00-20:00, closed Sun). For more reasonable prices near Marienplatz, try **C&A** (considered cheap yet respected; sells only clothing) and **Galeria Kaufhof** (midrange; sells everything), or the more upmarket **Karstadt** near the train station.

Lowbrow Tips

For that beer stein you promised to take home to your uncle, try the shops on the pedestrian zone by St. Michael's Church and the gift shops that surround the Hofbräuhaus. If you're looking for a used cell phone or exotic groceries, the area south of the train station fits the bill.

Nightlife in Munich

Here are a few nightlife alternatives to the beer-and-oompah scene.

Music and Dance

Ballet and opera fans can check the schedule at the **Bayerisch Staatsoper,** centrally located next door to the Residenz. These shows are popular, so book at least two months ahead—seats range from reasonable to very pricey (Max-Joseph-Platz 2, tel. 089/2185-1920, www.bayerische.staatsoper.de). The **Hotel Bayerischerhof**'s nightclub has live music—major jazz acts plus pop/soul/disco—in a posh, dress-up, expensive setting (Promenadeplatz 2, tel. 089/212-0994, www.bayerischerhof.de). **Café am Beethovenplatz** is another option for live classical, jazz, and swing music (see listing later, under "Eating in Munich"). For familiar Broadway-style musicals (usually in German), try the **Deutsches Theatre,** conveniently located near my train-station hotels (Schwanthalerstrasse 13, tel. 089/5523-4444, www.deutsches-theater.de).

Pubs

A good, untouristed area known for its nightlife—both gay and straight—is **Gärtnerplatz,** a 30-minute walk due south of Marienplatz (bus #52 from Marienplatz, or U-1 or U-2 to Fraunhoferstrasse).

Jodlerwirt ("Yodeling Innkeeper") is a smart-alecky pub with a small menu and a big attitude. The ambience is as Bavarian as you'll find—even if it's just you and the accordionist, it's fun. Lots of belly laughs...and completely incomprehensible to the average tourist (Mon-Sat 17:00-late, accordion act from 20:00, closed Sun, near the Old Town Hall, just off Marienplatz, at Tal 1, tel. 089/221-249, www.jodlerwirt.com, Paola speaks English). For some travelers, this quirky place is just plain awkward. For others, it's a trip highlight.

Sleeping in Munich

Unless you hit Munich during a fair, convention, or big holiday, you can sleep reasonably here. Student hotels around the station house anyone who's young at heart for as low as €25, and it's possible to find a fine double with breakfast in a good basic hotel for €100. I've listed accommodations in two main neighborhoods: within a few blocks of the central train station (Hauptbahnhof), and in the old center, between Marienplatz and Sendlinger Tor. Many of these places have complicated, slippery pricing schemes. During major conventions and events, prices increase from 20 percent to as much as 300 percent (worst at Oktoberfest; reserve well in advance). Sunday is very slow and usually comes with a huge discount if you ask.

NEAR THE TRAIN STATION

Good-value hotels cluster in the multicultural area immediately south of the station. To some this is a colorful neighborhood, for others it feels seedy after dark, but it's sketchy only for those in search of trouble. Still, hotels in the old center (listed later) might feel more comfortable to some.

$$$$ Hotel Deutsches Theater, filled with brass and marble, has 27 well-worn, three-star rooms. The back rooms face the courtyard of a neighboring theater—when there's a show, there can be some noise (breakfast extra, elevator, Landwehrstrasse 18, tel. 089/545-8525, www.hoteldeutschestheater.de, info@hoteldeutschestheater.de).

$$$$ Hotel Uhland is a stately mansion that rents 29 rooms with modern bathrooms in a safe-feeling, genteel residential neighborhood a slightly longer walk from the station than other places listed here (toward the Theresienwiese Oktoberfest grounds). It's been in the Hauzenberger and Reim families for 60 years (family rooms, some waterbeds, limited parking, Uhlandstrasse 1, tel. 089/543-350, www.hotel-uhland.de, info@hotel-uhland.de). From the station, take bus #58 (direction: Silberhornstrasse) to Georg-Hirth-Platz, or walk 15 minutes: Out the station's south exit, cross Bayerstrasse, take Paul-Heyse-Strasse three blocks to Georg-Hirth-Platz, then take a soft right on Uhlandstrasse.

$$$$ Hotel Schiller5 is convenient to the train station, and its dark wood elegance makes the splurge feel worthwhile. The hotel is divided in half: The "Old Style" section is somewhat contemporary but the "Modern" section is more polished. Most of their 62 rooms come with a kitchenette (family rooms, air-con, pay parking, includes minibar and lounge drinks, Schillerstrasse 5, tel. 089/515-040, www.schiller5.com, info@schiller5.com).

$$$ Hotel Monaco is a delightful and welcoming little hideaway, tucked inside three floors of a giant, nondescript building two blocks from the station. Emerging from the elevator, you're warmly welcomed by Christine and her staff into a flowery, cherub-filled oasis. It's homey, with 22 clean rooms and lots of feminine touches (breakfast extra, cash preferred, cheaper rooms with shared bath, family rooms, pay parking nearby, Schillerstrasse 9, entrance on Adolf-Kolping-Strasse, reception on fifth floor, tel. 089/545-9940, www.hotel-monaco.de, info@hotel-monaco.de).

$$$ **Marc München**—polished, modern, and with 80 rooms—is a good option if you need a little more luxury than the other listings here and are willing to pay the price. It's just a half-block from the station, and has four-star comforts like a refined lobby and classy breakfast spread (RS%, air-con, pay parking, Senefelderstrasse 12, tel. 089/559-820, www.hotel-marc.de, info@hotel-marc.de).

$$ **Hotel Belle Blue,** three blocks from the station, has 30 brightly colored rooms and air-conditioning. Run by Irmgard, this hotel has been in the family for 90 years and offers a good value. The breakfast is tops, and several stylish apartments with kitchenettes are perfect for families (elevator, pay parking, Schillerstrasse 21, tel. 089/550-6260, www.hotel-belleblue.de, info@hotel-belleblue.com).

$$ **Hotel Europäischer Hof,** across the street from the station, is a huge, impersonal hotel with 150 decent rooms. During cool weather, when you can keep the windows shut, the street-facing rooms are an acceptable option. The quieter, courtyard-facing rooms are more expensive and a lesser value (RS%, includes breakfast when you book directly, cheaper rooms with shared bath, elevator, pay parking, Bayerstrasse 31, tel. 089/551-510, www.heh.de, info@heh.de).

$$ **Hotel Royal** is one of the best values in the neighborhood (if you can ignore the strip joints flanking the entry). While a bit institutional, it's plenty comfortable and clean. Most importantly, it's energetically run by Pasha and Christiane. Each of its 40 rooms is sharp and bright (RS%, family rooms, comfort rooms on the quiet side cost extra—worth it in summer when you'll want the window open, elevator, Schillerstrasse 11a, tel. 089/5998-8160, www.hotel-royal.de, info@hotel-royal.de).

$$ **Hotel Cocoon Hauptbahnhof** is part of a trendy chain but it's a good value. This location has a rustic countryside/alpine theme. Ride the elevator like a personal gondola up to one of their 103 rooms (breakfast extra, air-con, bike rental, pay parking, Mittererstrasse 9, tel. 089/5999-3905, www.hotel-cocoon.de, info@hotel-cocoon.de).

$$ **Hotel St. Paul** is a clean, simple, no-nonsense 40-room place to rest your head and comes with a cheery courtyard and the charming sound of bells from the nearby church. Rooms at the

MUNICH

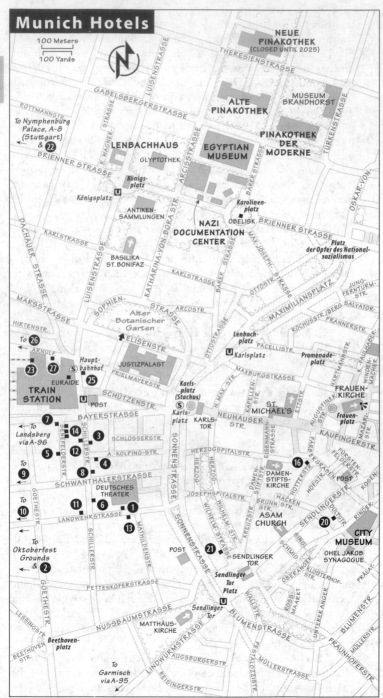

Munich Hotels

100 Meters
100 Yards

NEUE PINAKOTHEK
(CLOSED UNTIL 2025)

THERESIENSTRASSE

ALTE PINAKOTHEK

MUSEUM BRANDHORST

PINAKOTHEK DER MODERNE

GABELSBERGERSTRASSE

LUISENSTRASSE

TÜRKENSTRASSE

ROTTMANNSTR.

To Nymphenburg Palace, A-8 (Stuttgart) & 22

LENBACHHAUS

GLYPTOTHEK

EGYPTIAN MUSEUM

OSKAR-VON-

BRIENNER STRASSE

Königsplatz

Königsplatz

ANTIKEN-SAMMLUNGEN

ARCISSTRASSE

KATHARINA-VON-BORA-STR.

NAZI DOCUMENTATION CENTER

Karolinen-platz

OBELISK

BRIENNER STRASSE

Platz der Opfer des National-sozialismus

KARLSTRASSE

BASILIKA ST. BONIFAZ

BAYER-STRASSE

MAX-JOSEPH-STRASSE

OTTOSTR./STRASSE

MAXIMILIANSPLATZ

JUNG-FERNTURM-STR.

DACHAUER STRASSE

LUISENSTRASSE

KARLSTRASSE

MARSSTRASSE

SOPHIEN-STRASSE

ARCOSTR.

KOCHSTR./BERG SALVATOR-

PRANNERSTR.

JUNG-

HIRTENSTR.

Alter Botanischer Garten

ELISENSTR.

Lenbach-platz

PACELLISTR.

Promenade-platz

To 26

ARNULF

Haupt-bahnhof

JUSTIZPALAST

U Karlsplatz

KARTMANNSTR.

K. FAULHABER-

23 27

EURAIDE

S

PRIELMAYERSTR.

Karls-platz (Stachus)

MAXBURGSTRASSE

KAPELLEN STR.

WINDEN-MACHER-

FRAUEN-KIRCHE

TRAIN STATION

25

U POST

SCHÜTZENSTR.

Karls-platz

KARLSTOR

H. MAX.STR.

NEUHAUSER-STR.

ST. MICHAEL'S

AUGUSTINER-STR.

Frauen-platz

7

BAYERSTRASSE

SCHLOSSERSTR.

HERZOGSPITALSTR.

EISENMANN-STRASSE

BAYER

ETTSTR.

KAUFINGERSTR.

To Landsberg via A-96

14

3

SCHILLERSTR.

SENDEFELDERSTR.

A. KOLPING-STR.

HERZOG-

DAMEN-STIFTS-

HOFSTR.

FÜRSTEN-FELDER-

ROSEN-

5

12

4

16

POST

8

SCHWANTHALERSTRASSE

JOSEPHSPITALSTR.

DAMEN-STIFTS-KIRCHE

HACKEN-

SENDLINGER-STR.

CITY MUSEUM

To 9

DEUTSCHES THEATER

BRUNN-STR.

ASAM CHURCH

SINGL.

20

11

6

1

KREUZSTR.

WILHELM-STR.

OHEL JAKOB SYNAGOGUE

To 10

LANDWEHRSTRASSE

13

SCHILLERSTR.

MATHILDENSTR.

SONNENSTRASSE

SCHMID-

OBERANGER-

KLOSTERHOF-STR.

ROSS-MARKT

To Oktoberfest Grounds & 2

POST

21

SENDLINGER TOR

WALLSTR.

UNTERERANGER

PRALAT-STR.

PETTENKOFERSTRASSE

Sendlinger Tor Platz

BLUMENSTRASSE

BLUMENSTR.

MÜLLERSTR.

LESSINGSTR.

GOETHESTR.

NUSSBAUMSTRASSE

U Sendlinger Tor

FRAUNHOFERSTR.

Beethoven-platz

BEETHOVEN-STR.

MATTHÄUS-KIRCHE

LINDWURMSTRASSE

AUGSBURGERSTR.

MÜLLERSTRASSE

PESTALOZZISTR.

To Garmisch via A-95

REISINGERSTR.

MUNICH

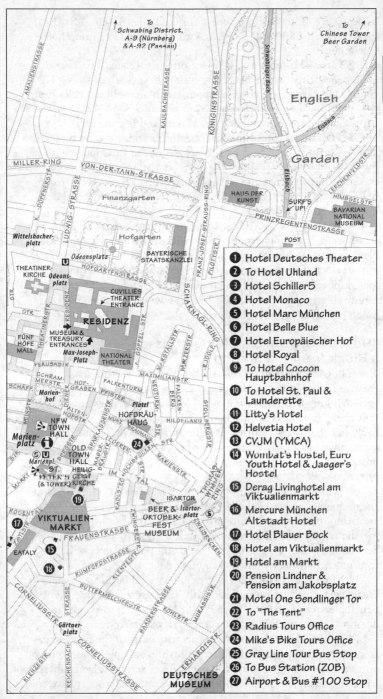

To Schwabing District, A-9 (Nürnberg) & A-92 (Passau)

To Chinese Tower Beer Garden

English

Garden

MILLER-RING

VON-DER-TANN-STRASSE

Finanzgarten

HAUS DER KUNST

SURF'S UP!

PRINZREGENTENSTRASSE

BAVARIAN NATIONAL MUSEUM

POST

Wittelsbacher-platz

Hofgarten

THEATINER-KIRCHE

Odeonsplatz

BAYERISCHE STAATSKANZLEI

HOFGARTENSTRASSE

CUVILLIES THEATER ENTRANCE

RESIDENZ

FÜNF HÖFE MALL

MUSEUM & TREASURY ENTRANCES

Max-Joseph-Platz

NATIONAL THEATER

Marienhof

HOF-GRABEN

FALKENTURM

Platzl

HOFBRÄU-HAUS

NEW TOWN HALL

Marien-platz

OLD TOWN HALL

ST. PETER'S (& TOWER)

HEILIG-GEIST-KIRCHE

ISARTOR

Isartor-platz

BEER & OKTOBER-FEST MUSEUM

VIKTUALIEN-MARKT

FRAUENSTRASSE

EATALY

DEUTSCHES MUSEUM

Gärtner-platz

CORNELIUSSTRASSE

❶	Hotel Deutsches Theater
❷	To Hotel Uhland
❸	Hotel Schiller5
❹	Hotel Monaco
❺	Hotel Marc München
❻	Hotel Belle Blue
❼	Hotel Europäischer Hof
❽	Hotel Royal
❾	To Hotel Cocoon Hauptbahnhof
❿	To Hotel St. Paul & Launderette
⓫	Litty's Hotel
⓬	Helvetia Hotel
⓭	CVJM (YMCA)
⓮	Wombat's Hostel, Euro Youth Hotel & Jaeger's Hostel
⓯	Derag Livinghotel am Viktualienmarkt
⓰	Mercure München Altstadt Hotel
⓱	Hotel Blauer Bock
⓲	Hotel am Viktualienmarkt
⓳	Hotel am Markt
⓴	Pension Lindner & Pension am Jakobsplatz
㉑	Motel One Sendlinger Tor
㉒	To "The Tent"
㉓	Radius Tours Office
㉔	Mike's Bike Tours Office
㉕	Gray Line Tour Bus Stop
㉖	To Bus Station (ZOB)
㉗	Airport & Bus #100 Stop

back do not have elevator access (limited free parking, St. Paul Strasse 7, tel. 089/5440-7800, www.hotel-stpaul.de, info@hotel-stpaul.de).

$ Litty's Hotel is a basic place offering 42 small rooms with little personality. Some first-floor rooms have a street-facing balcony (breakfast extra, cheaper rooms with shared bath, elevator, pay parking, Landwehrstrasse 32c, tel. 089/5434-4211, www.littyshotel.de, info@littyshotel.de, Verena and Bernd Litty).

$ Helvetia Hotel unapologetically provides rooms that are modern (except for dated bathrooms)—they're functional with a Swiss sensibility. Ask about the pop art throughout the hotel—the artist has a connection to the owners (breakfast extra, air-con, Schillerstrasse 6, tel. 089/590-6850, www.helvetia-hotel.com, info@helvetia-hotel.com).

¢ The CVJM (YMCA), open to all ages, rents 87 beds in clean, slick, and simple rooms, each with its own bathroom. Doubles are head-to-head; triples are like doubles with a bunk over one of the beds (family rooms available, reserve at least 6 months ahead for Oktoberfest weekdays, a year ahead for Oktoberfest weekends; Landwehrstrasse 13, tel. 089/552-1410, www.cvjm-muenchen.org/hotel, hotel@cvjm-muenchen.org).

"Hostel Row" on Senefelderstrasse, a Block from the Station

The following hostels are casual and well-run, with friendly and creative management, and all cater expertly to the needs of young beer-drinking backpackers enjoying Munich on a shoestring. With 900 cheap dorm beds, this is a spirited street. Each place has a lively bar that rages until the wee hours. All have 24-hour receptions, none has a kitchen, but each offers a reasonably priced buffet breakfast. Sleep cheap in big dorms, or spend a little more for a private room.

¢ Wombat's Hostel, perhaps the most hip and colorful, rents cheap doubles and dorm beds, plus some private rooms. The dorms are fresh, modern, and contain bathrooms. The bright rooms facing the winter garden have huge windows (family room available, Senefelderstrasse 1, tel. 089/5998-9180, www.wombats-hostels.com/munich, office@wombats-munich.de).

¢ Euro Youth Hotel fills a rare pre-WWII building (includes breakfast for private rooms, bar with live music and game nights, Senefelderstrasse 5, tel. 089/5990-8811, www.euro-youth-hotel.de, info@euro-youth-hotel.de, run by Alfio and Andy).

¢ Jaeger's Hostel rounds out this trio, with all the fun and efficiency you'd hope for in a hostel—plus the only air-conditioning on the street. Popular with the backpacker set and also business travelers, this is the quietest hostel of the group. All rooms have en suite bathrooms, and the classy bar is a congenial gathering place (family rooms available, Senefelderstrasse 3, tel. 089/555-281, www.jaegershostel.de, office@jaegershostel.de).

IN THE OLD CENTER

A few good deals remain in the area south of Marienplatz, going toward the Sendlinger Tor. This neighborhood feels more genteel than the streets around the train station, and is convenient for sightseeing.

$$$$ Derag Livinghotel am Viktualienmarkt rents 83 rooms in two connected buildings. One building is elegant and tech-savvy, with great views of the Viktualienmarkt. The other has stylish rooms with kitchenettes but no views, and is geared toward longer-stay business guests, although short-term visitors are welcomed. Both buildings share the same homey breakfast room (breakfast extra, complimentary minibar, air-con, elevator, laundry facilities, pay parking, entrance facing the market on Frauenstrasse 4, tel. 089/885-6560, www.deraghotels.de, res.vik@derag.de).

$$$$ Mercure München Altstadt Hotel is reliable, with all the modern comforts in its 80 pricey business-class rooms, and is well-located on a boring, quiet street very close to the Marienplatz action. It's a chain, and a bit bland, but has fine service (family rooms, air-con, laundry service, a block south of the pedestrian zone at Hotterstrasse 4, tel. 089/232-590, www.mercure-muenchen-altstadt.de, h3709@accor.com).

$$$ Hotel Blauer Bock, formerly a dormitory for Benedictine monks, has been on the same corner near the Munich City Museum since 1841. Its 69 contemporary Bavarian rooms are classy, the breakfast is top-notch, and the location is great, with some views of the nearby Viktualienmarkt (family rooms, elevator, guest iPads at front desk, pay parking, Sebastiansplatz 9, tel. 089/231-780, www.hotelblauerbock.de, info@hotelblauerbock.de).

$$$ Hotel am Viktualienmarkt rents 26 rooms on a small side street a couple of blocks from the Viktualienmarkt. Everything is small but well-designed—including the elevator and three good-value, tiny single rooms (family rooms, apartment, Utzschneider-strasse 14, tel. 089/231-1090, www.hotel-am-viktualienmarkt.de, reservierung@hotel-am-viktualienmarkt.de).

$$ Hotel am Markt, right next to the Viktualienmarkt, has old-feeling hallways and 32 simple rooms with lots of wainscoting. Light sleepers might need earplugs—the neighboring church's bells ring hourly (save money by skipping expensive breakfast, elevator, Heiliggeiststrasse 6, tel. 089/225-014, www.hotel-am-markt.eu, service@hotel-am-markt.eu).

$$ Pension Lindner is clean and quiet, with nine pleasant, pastel-bouquet rooms off a bare stairway. Frau Marion Sinzinger offers a warm welcome and good buffet breakfasts (cheaper rooms with shared bath, tiny elevator, Dultstrasse 1, tel. 089/263-413, www.pension-lindner.com, info@pension-lindner.com).

$$ Pension am Jakobsplatz, downstairs from Pension Lindner and well-run by Christoph, makes you feel like you're visiting friends. It's a good value with an ideal location, cheap prices, and plenty of good local recommendations. It has four basic but pleasant rooms—two have full private facilities, and the others have a sink and shower but share a toilet (Dultstrasse 1, tel. 089/2323-1556, mobile 0173-973-4598, www.pension-jakobsplatz.de, info@pension-jakobsplatz.de).

$$ Motel One Sendlinger Tor, around the corner from the Sendlinger Tor tram and U-Bahn stop, is a huge, posh-feeling, 241-room, inexpensive chain hotel with rushed-but-pleasant staff in a fine location. The stylish, modern rooms are fairly tight and lack some basic amenities (phones, minibars), but otherwise are a good value—and tend to sell out a few weeks in advance. Street-side rooms on upper floors have great views for a little extra—I'd request one of these. When booking on their website, make sure to choose the Sendlinger Tor location—they have several other hotels in Munich (breakfast extra, air-con, guest iPad at front desk, pay parking, Herzog-Wilhelm-Strasse 28, tel. 089/5177-7250, www.motel-one.com, muenchen-sendlingertor@motel-one.com).

AWAY FROM THE CENTER

¢ The Tent—a venerable Munich institution officially known as the International Youth Camp Kapuzinerhölzl—offers 400 spots in three huge circus tents near Nymphen-burg Palace. It never fills up, though you are encouraged to reserve online. Choose a mattress on a wooden floor or a bunk bed, or pitch your own tent. Blankets, hot showers, lockers (bring or buy a lock), and a kitchen are all included; breakfast is extra. A fun but noisy experience (a cross between a slumber party and Woodstock), it feels wholesome, but I wouldn't bring kids. It's really for young adults, with a cool table-tennis-and-Frisbee atmosphere throughout the day, nightly campfires, and no curfew, though silence is requested after 1:00 (open early June–early 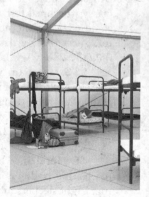 Oct only, prices a little higher during Oktoberfest, cash only, bikes-€9/day, catch tram #17 from train station for 18 minutes to Botanischer Garten, direction: Amalienburgstrasse, then go right down Franz-Schrank-Strasse—it's behind the trees at the end of the street, tel. 089/141-4300, www.the-tent.com, cu@the-tent.com).

MORE HOTELS IN MUNICH

If my listings above are full, consider these.

Within walking distance of the Viktualienmarkt, artsy **$$$$ Hotel Olympic** has 37 fresh, relaxing rooms (Hans-Sachs-Strasse 4, tel. 089/231-890, www.hotel-olympic.de); **$$$$ Hotel Admiral** is classy yet homey (Kohlstrasse 9, tel. 089/216-350, www.hotel-admiral.de); and **$$$$ Hotel Isartor** has 68 comfortable but plain rooms (Baaderstrasse 2, tel. 089/216-3340, www.hotel-isartor.de).

Near Sendlinger Tor, alpine-bright and sunny **$$$$ Hotel Müller Munich** offers 44 cozy rooms (Fliegenstrasse 4, tel. 089/232-3860, www.carahotels.dc), while **$$$ Carathotel München City** is a glossy slumber-mill popular with groups. Its streetside rooms have rare air-conditioning, and its 48 apartments have kitchenettes (Lindwurmstrasse 13, tel. 089/230-380, www.carahotels.de).

An easy tram or U-Bahn ride from Marienplatz, **$$$$ Hotel Europa** has four-star American-style comfort and amenities in an impersonal, blocky structure (Dachauerstrasse 115, U-1 to Stiglmaicrplatz or U-2 to Theresienstrasse, tel. 089/542-420, www.hotel-europa.de).

Eating in Munich

Munich's cuisine is traditionally seasoned with beer. In beer halls, beer gardens, or at the Viktualienmarkt, try the most typical meal in town: *Weisswurst* (white-colored veal sausage—peel off the skin before eating, often available only until noon) with *susser Senf* (sweet mustard), a salty *Brezel* (pretzel), and *Weissbier* ("white" wheat beer). Another traditional favorite is *Obatzter,* a mix of soft cheeses, butter, paprika, and often garlic or onions that's spread on bread. *Brotzeit,* literally "bread time," gets you a wooden platter of cold cuts, cheese, and pickles and is a good option for a light dinner. Also look for these Munich specialties: *Fleischpfanzerl,* a.k.a. *Fleischklösse* or *Frikadellen* (meatballs); *Hendl* or *Brathähnchen* (roasted chicken); *Radi* (radish that's thinly spiral-cut and salted); *Schweinrollbraten* (pork belly); *Schweinshax'n,* or just *Hax'n* (pork knuckle); spareribs; and *Steckerlfisch* (a whole fish—usually mackerel—herbed and

grilled on a stick). Many restaurants claim to have the best Bavarian classics (schnitzel and pork knuckle)—find your own favorite. (For more on food in Germany, see the Practicalities chapter.)

I'm here for the beer-hall and beer-garden fun (my first several listings). But when the *Wurst und Kraut* get to be too much for you, Munich has plenty of good alternatives; I've listed my favorites later in this section.

Bavarian restaurants are smoke-free. The only ashtrays you'll see throughout Bavaria are outside.

BEER HALLS, BEER GARDENS, AND BAVARIAN FOOD

Nothing beats the Hofbräuhaus (the only beer hall in town where you'll find oompah music) for those in search of the boisterous, clichéd image of the beer hall. Locals prefer the innumerable beer gardens. On a warm day, when you're looking for the authentic outdoor beer-garden experience, your best options are the Augustiner (near the train station), the small beer garden at the Viktualienmarkt (near Marienplatz), or the sea of tables in the English Garden. Eating outside is made more pleasant by the *Föhn* (warm winds that come over the Alps from Italy), which gives this part of Germany 30 more days of sunshine than the North—and sometimes even an Italian ambience. (Many natives attribute the city's huge increase in outdoor dining to global warming.)

For tips on eating in beer halls and beer gardens, see the sidebar in this book's introductory chapter.

Near Marienplatz

$$ The **Hofbräuhaus** (HOAF-broy-howz) is the world's most famous beer hall. While it's grotesquely touristy and filled with sloppy backpackers and tour groups, it's still a lot of fun—a Munich must. Even if you don't eat here, check it out to see hundreds of tourists drinking beer in a German beer hall...across from a Hard Rock Café. Germans go for the entertainment—to sing "Country Roads," see how Texas girls party, and watch tourists try to chug beer.

You can drop by anytime for a large or light meal (my favorite: €9 for *Vier Stück gebratene Schweinswürstl auf Sauerkraut*—four small pork sausages with sauerkraut), or just for a drink. Even though visitors outnumber locals, the food here is decent. Except for *Weissbier*, the Hofbräuhaus sells beer only by the *Mass* (one-liter mug) after 18:00—and they claim to sell 10,000 of these liters every day. Choose from four zones: the rowdy main hall on the ground floor, a quieter courtyard under the stars, a dainty restaurant with mellow music (zither, oboe, harp) where the locals gather on the first floor up, or the giant festival hall (*Festsaal*, sometimes reserved for events) under a big barrel vault on the top floor.

The Hofbräuhaus main hall/restaurant offers regular live oompah music. This music-every-night atmosphere is irresistible, and the fat, shiny-leather bands get even church mice to stand up and conduct three-quarter time with breadsticks. The festival hall, notorious as the place where Hitler gave his first public speech in 1920, today is a vacuous venue where tour groups come for a nightly folk show. While kitschy, it's a fun and tasty way to enjoy traditional live folk music and dance (main hall/restaurant—daily 9:00-23:30, music during lunch and dinner only—daily 12:00-16:00 & 18:00-23:30; festival hall—nightly 19:00-22:00, free show with food or drink, same prices as the ground-floor beer hall, reservations generally unnecessary; 5-minute walk from Marienplatz at Platzl 9, tel. 089/2901-36100). For more on this Munich institution, see my "Munich City Walk," earlier in this chapter.

$$$ Haxnbauer, stark and old-school, is a hit with German tourists for one reason: the best pork knuckle in town (half *Schweinshaxe*—€19, slightly less if you just get some slices). You'll pay a little extra, but it's clearly the place for what looks like a pork knee—notice the rotisserie window luring customers inside (daily 11:00-24:00, two blocks from Hofbräuhaus at Sparkassenstrasse 6, tel. 089/216-6540).

$$ Andechser am Dom sits at the rear of the twin-domed Frauenkirche on a breezy square. Charming Sepp runs this local favorite, serving Andechs beer brewed by monks and great food to appreciative regulars. Some customers are more famous than others—how many do you recognize from the photos blanketing the walls? Münchners favor the dark beer (ask for *dunkles*), but I love the light *(helles)*. The *Gourmetteller* is a great sampler of their specialties, but you can't go wrong with *Rostbratwurst* with kraut (daily 10:00-24:00, Frauenplatz 7, reserve during peak times, tel. 089/2429-2920, www.andechser-am-dom.de).

$$ Nürnberger Bratwurst Glöckl am Dom, around the corner from Andechser am Dom, is popular with tourists and offers a more traditional, fiercely Bavarian evening. Dine outside under the trees or in the dark, medieval, cozy interior. Enjoy the tasty little *Nürnberger* sausages with kraut and their popular shredded pancake for dessert (daily 10:00-24:00, Frauenplatz 9, tel. 089/291-9450).

$$$ Altes Hackerhaus is popular with locals and tourists for its traditional *Bayerisch* (Bavarian) fare served with a slightly fancier feel in one of the oldest buildings in town. It offers a small courtyard and a fun forest of characteristic nooks festooned with a veritable museum of family pictures and nostalgic treasures. Naturally, Hacker-Pschorr beer is popular, especially the *Weisse* ("small

MUNICH

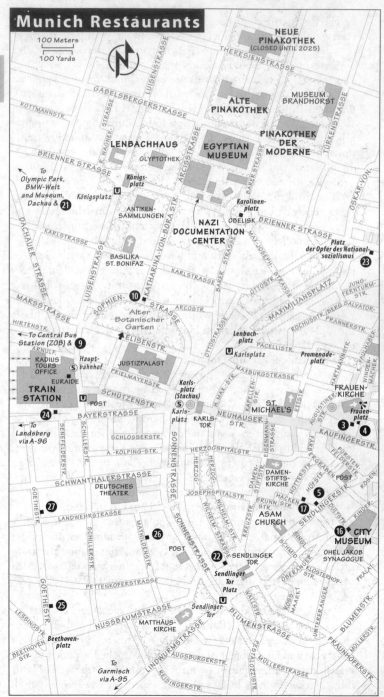

Munich Restaurants

100 Meters
100 Yards

NEUE PINAKOTHEK (CLOSED UNTIL 2025)

THERESIENSTRASSE

ALTE PINAKOTHEK

MUSEUM BRANDHORST

PINAKOTHEK DER MODERNE

LENBACHHAUS

GLYPTOTHEK

EGYPTIAN MUSEUM

GABELSBERGERSTRASSE

KOTTMANNSTR.

BRIENNER STRASSE

To Olympic Park, BMW-Welt and Museum, Dachau & **21**

Königsplatz

ANTIKEN-SAMMLUNGEN

Königsplatz

NAZI DOCUMENTATION CENTER

Karolinen-platz

OBELISK

BRIENNER STRASSE

Platz der Opfer des National-sozialismus **23**

KARLSTRASSE

BASILIKA ST. BONIFAZ

KARLSTRASSE

KARLSTRASSE

SOPHIEN-STRASSE

10

Alter Botanischer Garten

MARSSTRASSE

HIRTENSTR.

To Central Bus Station (ZOB) & **9**

ELISENSTR.

Haupt-bahnhof

JUSTIZPALAST

PRIELMAYERSTR.

Lenbach-platz

Karlsplatz

Promenade-platz

RADIUS TOURS OFFICE

EURAIDE

TRAIN STATION

POST

24

SCHÜTZENSTR.

BAYERSTRASSE

To Landsberg via A-96

SCHILLERSTR.

SCHLOSSERSTR.

A.-KOLPING-STR.

Karls-platz (Stachus)

Karlsplatz

KARLS-TOR

KARLSTR.

NEUHAUSER-STR.

ST. MICHAEL'S

FRAUEN-KIRCHE

Frauen-platz

3

4

KAUFINGERSTR.

FÜRSTEN-FELDERST.

SCHWANTHALERSTRASSE

DEUTSCHES THEATER

LANDWEHRSTRASSE

27

HERZOGSPITALSTR.

JOSEPHSPITALSTR.

DAMEN-STIFTS-KIRCHE

HACKEN-STR.

5

17

ASAM CHURCH

SENDLINGERSTR.

16 CITY MUSEUM

OHEL JAKOB SYNAGOGUE

POST

26

SONNENSTRASSE

POST

22

SENDLINGER TOR

Sendlinger Tor Platz

Sendlinger Tor

PETTENKOFERSTRASSE

25

NUSSBAUMSTRASSE

MATTHÄUS-KIRCHE

BLUMENSTRASSE

Beethoven-platz

LINDWURMSTRASSE

AUGSBURGERSTR.

To Garmisch via A-95

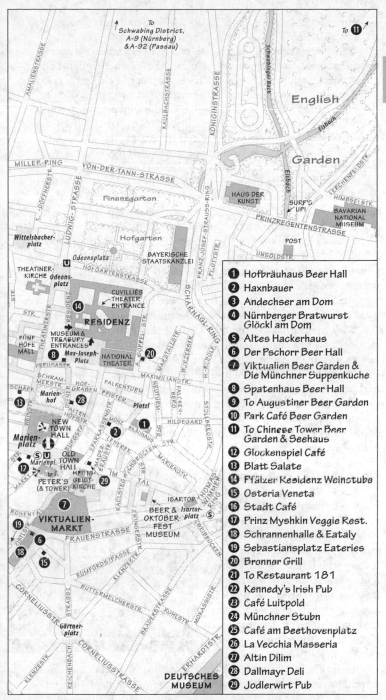

1. Hofbräuhaus Beer Hall
2. Haxnbauer
3. Andechser am Dom
4. Nürnberger Bratwurst Glöckl am Dom
5. Altes Hackerhaus
6. Der Pschorr Beer Hall
7. Viktualien Beer Garden & Die Münchner Suppenkuche
8. Spatenhaus Beer Hall
9. To Augustiner Beer Garden
10. Park Café Beer Garden
11. To Chinese Tower Beer Garden & Seehaus
12. Glockenspiel Café
13. Blatt Salate
14. Pfälzer Residenz Weinstube
15. Osteria Veneta
16. Stadt Café
17. Prinz Myshkin Veggie Rest.
18. Schrannenhalle & Eataly
19. Sebastiansplatz Eateries
20. Bronner Grill
21. To Restaurant 181
22. Kennedy's Irish Pub
23. Café Luitpold
24. Münchner Stubn
25. Café am Beethovenplatz
26. La Vecchia Masseria
27. Altin Dilim
28. Dallmayr Deli
29. Jodlerwirt Pub

appetite" menu available, daily 10:30-24:00, Sendlinger Strasse 14, tel. 089/260-5026).

$$$ Der Pschorr, an upscale beer hall occupying a former slaughterhouse, has a terrace overlooking the Viktualienmarkt and serves what many consider Munich's finest beer in chilled glasses. With organic "slow food" including vegan and vegetarian options, this place mixes modern concepts—no candles, industrial-strength conviviality—with traditional, quality, classic dishes. They tap classic wooden kegs every few minutes with gusto. The sound of the hammer tapping wooden kegs lets patrons know their beer is good and fresh (seasonal specials, daily 10:00-24:00, Viktualienmarkt 15, at end of Schrannenhalle, tel. 089/442-383-940).

$ Viktualien Beer Garden, at the center of the Viktualienmarkt, taps you into about the best budget eating in town. It's just steps from Marienplatz (daily 10:00-22:00 in good weather). There's table service wherever you see a tablecloth; to picnic, choose a table without one—but you must buy a drink from the counter. Countless stalls surround the beer garden and sell wurst, sandwiches, produce, and so on. This B.Y.O.F. tradition recalls a time when monastery beer gardens served beer but not food. This is a good spot to grab a typical Munich *Weisswurst*—and some beer.

$$$ Spatenhaus is the opera-goers' classy beer hall, serving elegant food in a rustic, traditional setting since 1896—maybe it's not even right to call it a "beer hall." You can also eat outside, on the square facing the opera and palace. It's pricey, but you won't find better-quality Bavarian cuisine. The upstairs restaurant serves international cuisine to locals in a more formal dining room—reservations recommended (daily 9:30-23:00, on Max-Joseph-Platz opposite opera, Residenzstrasse 12, tel. 089/290-7060, www.spatenhaus.de).

Near the Train Station

$$ Augustiner Beer Garden is a sprawling haven for local beer lovers. A true under-the-leaves beer garden packed with Münchners, this is a delight. In fact, most Münchners consider Augustiner the best beer garden in town—which may be why it has 6,000 seats. There's no music, it's away from the tourist hordes, and it serves up great beer, good traditional food, huge portions, reasonable prices, and perfect conviviality. The outdoor self-service (at the opposite end from the entrance) is best on a nice summer evening, and it's easy to make new friends at the communal picnic tables. Parents with kids can sit at tables adjoining a sizable playground. There's also indoor and outdoor seating at a more expensive **$$$** restaurant with table service by the entrance (daily 11:30-24:00, Arnulfstrasse 52, 3 looooong blocks from station going away from the center—or take tram #16/#17 one stop to Hopfenstrasse, taxis always waiting at the gate, tel. 089/594-393).

$$ Park Café Beer Garden is a nice hideaway in good weather, tucked inside the Alter Botanischer Garden, just north of the train station. Order Bavarian food from self-service counters (don't forget to reclaim your deposit at the counter for your plate and mug). The indoor **$$$** restaurant is a modern and cozy pricier option, and often features DJs or live music in the late evening (daily 11:00-24:00, beer garden open until 19:00 in nice weather, Sophienstrasse 7, tel. 089/5161-7980).

In the English Garden

$$ The Chinese Tower beer garden *(Chinesischer Turm Biergarten)*, deep in the English Garden, is famed for outdoor ambience and a cheap meal; it's a great place for a balmy, relaxed evening. You're welcome to B.Y.O. food and grab a table, or buy from the cafeteria-style food stalls with clear English descriptions. Don't bother to phone ahead—they have 6,000 seats. This is a fine opportunity to try a *Steckerlfisch*, sold at a separate kiosk. Take your blue token and your beer mug around back to redeem your refund (daily, long hours in good weather, usually live music, playground, tel. 089/383-8730; take tram #18 from main train station or Sendlinger Tor to Tivolistrasse, or U-3 or U-6 to Giselastrasse and then bus #54 or #154 two stops).

$$$$ Seehaus, deeper into the English Garden (and worth the effort to find), is a 10-minute walk past the Chinese Tower or a fun pedicab ride. It's famous among Münchners for its idyllic lakeside setting and excellent Mediterranean and traditional Bavarian cooking (seafood emphasized), served in two separate restaurants. It's dressy and a bit snobbish, and understandably filled with locals who fit the same description. Choose from classy indoor or lakeside seating (daily 10:00-24:00; take U-3 or U-6 to Münchner Freiheit and walk 10 minutes, or get off at Dietlindenstrasse and then take bus #144 one stop to Osterwaldstrasse; Kleinhesslohe 3, tel. 089/381-6130).

$$ Seehaus Beer Garden, adjacent to the fancy Seehaus restaurant, offers the same waterfront atmosphere in a less expensive, more casual setting. There's all the normal wurst, kraut, pretzels, and fine beer at typical prices (daily 11:00-22:00 in good weather).

BEYOND BEER HALLS

Man does not live by beer alone. Well, maybe some do. But for the rest of us, I recommend the following alternatives to the beer-and-wurst circuit.

On and near Marienplatz

$$$ **Glockenspiel Café** is good for a coffee or a meal with a bird's-eye view down on the Marienplatz action—I'd come for the view more than the Italian food. Locals like the open terrace without a view (drinks and meals served anytime). Regardless of the weather, I grab a seat overlooking Marienplatz—but after 18:00, you must order dinner for view seating (Mon-Sat 9:00-24:00, Sun 10:00-19:00, ride elevator from Rosenstrasse entrance, opposite glockenspiel at Marienplatz 28, tel. 089/264-256).

$$ **Blatt Salate** is a self-serve salad bar on a side street between the Frauenkirche and the New Town Hall; it's a great little hideaway for a healthy, quick lunch—a yummy salad with fresh bread and a drink (vegetarian and meat salads and soups, Mon-Sat 11:00-19:00, closed Sun, Schäfflerstrasse 7, tel. 089/2102-0281).

$$ **Pfälzer Residenz Weinstube,** a very traditional German dining hall actually in the Residenz complex, is dedicated to food and wine from the Rhineland (Palatine)—which, while not part of Bavaria, was ruled by the Wittelsbach family. Serving lots of small wine-friendly dishes and a big variety of German wines by the tiny glass, it's ideal for wine lovers needing a break from beer (daily 10:30-24:00, Residenzstrasse 1, tel. 089/225-628).

Around the Viktualienmarkt

$$$ **Osteria Veneta,** hidden on a quiet street just behind the Viktualienmarkt, provides a nice escape from the traditional Bavarian beer hall. It's perfect for a leisurely meal, with indoor and outdoor seating; a chalkboard lists daily specials (Mon-Sat 18:00-24:00, closed Sun, Utzschneiderstrasse 4, tel. 089/2602-2093).

$ **Die Münchner Suppenküche** ("Munich Soup Kitchen"), a soup tent at the Viktualienmarkt, is a fine place for a small, cozy sit-down lunch at picnic tables under a closed-in awning. The red sign lists the soups of the day—I go for the goulash or the Bavarian potato soup (Mon-Sat 10:00-18:00, closed Sun, near corner of Reichenbachstrasse and Frauenstrasse, tel. 089/260-9599).

$$ **Stadt Café** is a lively café serving a selection of sandwiches, with a nice wine list and cakes. This informal, no-frills restaurant draws newspaper readers, stroller moms, and locals meeting

for a drink after work. Dine in the quiet cobbled courtyard, inside, or outside facing the new synagogue (open daily 10:00-24:00, in same building as Munich City Museum, St.-Jakobs-Platz 1, tel. 089/266-949).

$$$ Prinz Myshkin Vegetarian Restaurant is an upscale vegetarian eatery in the old center—a rare find in this wurst-loving part of the world. The decor is trendy, the arched ceilings are cool but provide poor acoustics, and the outside seating is on a quiet street. Don't miss the enticing appetizer selection on display as you enter (they do a fine €14 mixed-appetizer plate). They also have vegetarian sushi, pastas, Indian dishes, and their own baker, so they're proud of their sweets (lunch specials, seasonal menu, daily 11:00-late, Hackenstrasse 2, tel. 089/265-596).

$$ Eataly at Schrannenhalle, the former grain exchange just off Viktualienmarkt, is a sparkling, pricey food court full of Italian taste treats. It's a foodie's paradise with a variety of restaurants serving pizza, pasta, and main courses with Italian gusto and fresh ingredients. You can sit at your choice of bars to watch the cooking, and get pizza by the slice to go. While overpriced, it's a festival of Italian food fun with great seating inside the old market hall and outside overlooking the square (café open Mon-Sat 8:00-20:00, Sun 10:00-19:00; restaurants open Mon-Sat 11:30-22:30, Sun until 21:30, Viktualienmarkt 15, tel. 089/248-817-711).

Eateries on Sebastiansplatz: Looking for a no-schnitzel-or-dumplings alternative? Sebastiansplatz is a long, pedestrianized square across from Eataly, between the Viktualienmarkt and the synagogue, lined with **$$** bistros handy for a healthy and quick lunch. Options range from French to Italian to Asian to salads. You can eat out on the busy cobbled square or inside—just survey the scene and choose.

Other Memorable Options

$$$ Brenner Grill is just right for an upscale yet fun break from heavy Bavarian fare. It's in a big, modern, high-energy place with hundreds of local diners and almost no tourists. Diners enjoy steak, fish, international dishes, and a popular pasta bar under a forest of modern pillars adjacent to two big open grills, or outside behind the National Theater. Save room for what's in the dessert case (long hours daily, Maximilianstrasse 15, tel. 089/452-2880).

$$$$ Restaurant 181, the fine revolving restaurant atop the TV tower in Olympic Park (named for its height in meters above the ground), is where locals go for anniversaries and birthdays. Dinner is formal and pricey (seatings at 18:00 with €54 three-course menu and at 20:30 with a €74 four-course menu); lunch is more casual (à la carte, 12:00-14:30). The offerings are international and diners ride the lift free (daily from 11:00, reserve for dinner, tel. 089/350-948-181, www.drehrestaurant.de).

$$ Kennedy's Irish Pub, at Sendlinger Tor, is a hit with millennials for quality hamburgers, ribs, sandwiches, and nightly music from 22:00 (karaoke Mon and Wed, live band Tue and Thu-Fri). The basement interior has a family-friendly pub feel, and outside tables are under trees and a medieval gate (long hours daily, Sendlinger Torplatz 11, tel. 089/5998-8460).

$$ Café Luitpold is where Munich's high society comes to sip its coffee and nibble on exquisite cakes. The café is proudly home to the original *Luitpoldtorte* (sponge cake with layers of marzipan and buttercream, covered in dark chocolate). Some say this is Munich's answer to Vienna's Sacher torte—though I prefer their strawberry-cream cake (Tue-Sat 8:00-23:00, Sun-Mon 9:00-19:00, Brienner Strasse 11, tel. 089/242-8750).

Near the Train Station

$$$ Münchner Stubn, just across the street from the train station, is a rare traditional German find in a neighborhood full of ethnic eateries. The air-conditioned bright modern interior with folkloric touches is worth a few extra euros. It's a nice escape while waiting for a train. They offer traditional dishes with a modern twist as well as reasonably priced lunch specials (daily 10:00-24:00, Bayerstrasse 35, tel. 089/551-113-330).

$$$ Café am Beethovenplatz feels like an old Vienna café with its inviting, woody interior and charming garden. While just a 10-minute walk from the station, it's in a leafy and quiet residential neighborhood. They serve a mix of Italian, Bavarian, and vegetarian fare, offer cheap lunch specials and homemade cakes, and have live music almost nightly (from 20:00, classical Mon and Tue, jazz or swing otherwise). Popular with university students, it feels both trendy and classy (daily 9:00-24:00, at Mariandl Hotel, Goethestrasse 51, tel. 089/552-9100).

$$$ La Vecchia Masseria, between Sendlinger Tor and the train station hotels, serves Italian food in a cozy Tuscan farmhouse-style interior, or outside in a beautiful flowery courtyard. Pasta, pizzas, and seasonal, more expensive main courses are served by bustling waiters who likely speak more Italian than German. Can't decide which pasta to get? Ask for a *bis,* half-portions of two pastas (daily 11:30-23:30, garden dining until 21:30, reservations smart, Mathildenstrasse 3, tel. 089/550-9090, www.lavecchiamasseria. de).

$$ Altin Dilim, a cafeteria-style Turkish restaurant, is a standout among the many hole-in-the-wall Middle Eastern places in the ethnic area near the station. It feels like a trip to Istanbul—complete with a large selection, a handy pictorial menu that helps you order, and interesting decor. Pay at the counter (cheap *döner kebabs,* daily 6.00-24:00, Goethestrasse 17, tel. 089/9734-0869).

PICNICS

For a truly elegant picnic (costing as much as a restaurant meal), **Dallmayr** is the place to shop. The crown in their emblem reflects that even the royal family assembled its picnics at this historic delicatessen. Pretend you're a Bavarian aristocrat—King Ludwig himself, even—and put together a royal spread to munch in the nearby Hofgarten. Or visit the classy but pricey café that serves light meals on the first floor (Mon-Sat 9:30-19:00, closed Sun, behind New Town Hall, Dienerstrasse 14, tel. 089/213-5110). For more about this famous spot, see page 61.

A **Budget Picnic:** To save money, browse at Dallmayr but buy at a **supermarket** (generally open Mon-Sat until 20:00, closed Sun). The ones that hide in the basements of department stores are on the upscale side: **Galeria Kaufhof** stores at Marienplatz and Karlsplatz, or the even more upmarket **Karstadt** across from the train station. Cheaper grocery stores include the **REWE** in the basement at Fünf Höfe (entrance is in Viscardihof), **Lidl** at Schwanthalerstrasse 31 (near the train-station hotels), or **Yorma's** (several branches at the train station).

Munich Connections

Munich is a super transportation hub (one reason it was the target of so many WWII bombs), with easy train and bus connections to most Bavarian destinations, as well as international trains.

BY TRAIN

For quick help at the main train station, stop by the service counter in front of track 18. For better English and more patience, drop by the EurAide desk in the *Reisezentrum* (see page 30). Train info: www.bahn.com.

From Munich to: **Füssen** (hourly, 2 hours, half with easy transfer in Buchloe; for a Neuschwanstein Castle day trip, leave as early as possible), **Reutte,** Austria (hourly, about 3 hours, half with transfer), **Oberammergau** (nearly hourly, 2 hours, transfer in Murnau), **Salzburg,** Austria (2/hour, 1.5 hours on fast train), **Berchtesgaden** (hourly, 2.5 hours, transfer in Freilassing), **Nürnberg** (2/hour, 1 hour on fast train), **Cologne** (2/hour, 4.5 hours, some with transfer), **Würzburg** (1-2/hour, 2 hours), **Rothenburg** (hourly, 3.5 hours, 2-3 transfers), **Frankfurt** (hourly, 3.5 hours), **Frankfurt Airport** (hourly, 3.5 hours), **Leipzig** (8/day direct, 3 hours; more with transfer in Nürnberg, Erfurt, or Halle/Saale), **Erfurt** (hourly, 2.5 hours), **Dresden** (every 2 hours, 5 hours, transfer in

Leipzig), **Hamburg** (hourly direct, 6.5 hours), **Berlin** (hourly, 4-5 hours), **Vienna** (direct trains every 2 hours, 4 hours; more with transfer in Salzburg; 1 night train with early arrival), **Venice** (6/day, 7.5 hours with transfer in Verona or Villach; 1 direct daytime, 6.5 hours; 1 direct night train, 9 hours), **Paris** (1/day direct, 6/day with transfer at Stuttgart or Mannheim, all 6 hours, reservation required in France), **Prague** (7/day direct, 6 hours; or 5 hours by bus—see below), **Zürich** (3/day direct, 4.5 hours, more by direct bus). To use a rail pass for any train to Italy, your pass must include all countries on the train route (i.e., Austria or Switzerland), or you'll have to buy the segment that's not included; EuroCity trains to Italy via Innsbruck also require pass holders to make a reservation (not indicated in online schedules, and not required if you're buying a point-to-point ticket instead of using a pass).

BY BUS

Munich's Central Bus Station (ZOB) is by the Hackerbrücke S-Bahn station (one S-Bahn stop or a short walk from the main train station; www.muenchen-zob.de). Those traveling beyond Germany on a tight budget should consider the Deutsche Bahn buses, which leave from the Central Bus Station for Prague, Milan, Zürich, Split, and Zagreb.

Romantic Road Bus: The Romantic Road bus (April-Oct only; run by EurAide) connects Munich's main train station north to Rothenburg, Würzburg, Frankfurt, and other destinations en route. This slower but more scenic alternative to the train provides a glimpse of towns such as Nördlingen and Dinkelsbühl. For more information, see page 400.

BY PLANE

Munich Airport (Flughafen München) is 17 miles northeast of town (airport code: MUC, tel. 089/97500, www.munich-airport.de). It has two large terminals linked by shuttle buses: Older Terminal 1 serves Air France, Air Europa, American, British Airways, Delta, EasyJet, and others. Lufthansa, United, Germanwings, and minor airlines use Terminal 2.

The Munich Airport Center (MAC) is a public space that connects the two terminals with plenty of shops, a supermarket, ATMs, and an S-Bahn station. (It even hosts a Christmas market, with 50 market stalls and an ice-skating rink, in November and December.)

Both terminals have ATMs and plenty of eateries in the gate areas. Terminal 1 has a lost-and-found office, and Terminal 2 and the MAC each have a pharmacy.

Getting Between the Airport and Downtown

Munich's airport is an easy 40-minute ride on the S-1 or S-8 **subway** (both run every 20 minutes, from 4:00 to after midnight) between the airport and Marienplatz and the train station. The S-8 is a bit quicker and easier; the S-1 line has two branches and some trains split—if you ride the S-1 to the airport, be certain your train is going to the *Flughafen* (airport). A single **airport ticket** costs €11.20, but the all-day pass (€12.80) is worth getting if you'll be making even one more public transport trip that day. Groups of two or more should buy the €23.90 all-day partner ticket *(Partner-Tageskarte)*, which covers up to five adults for the day (see "Getting Around Munich," earlier in this chapter, for details on tickets and passes). The trip is also free with a validated and dated rail pass.

Another alternative is the **Lufthansa airport bus,** which links the airport with the main train station (€10.50, €17 round-trip, 4/hour, 45 minutes, buses depart airport 6:30-22:30, depart train station 5:15-20:00, buy tickets on bus; from inside the station, exit near track 26 and look for yellow *Airport Bus* signs; www.airportbus-muenchen.de). If you're traveling alone, going round-trip, and not using other public transport the same day, the bus saves a few euros. Avoid taking a **taxi** from the airport—it's a long, expensive drive (roughly €65). Take public transit to the city and then switch to a taxi if needed.

Day Trips from Munich

The Dachau Concentration Camp Memorial and Andechs Monastery are at opposite ends of the day-trip spectrum. Dachau, less than an hour by public transportation, makes for a serious, thought-provoking visit while Andechs, doable by public transportation but easier by car, serves up some of my favorite beer in Germany in a serene rural setting. Other day-trip possibilities —including the King's Castles, Nürnberg, Salzburg, and Berchtesgaden—are summarized at the end of this section.

▲▲▲DACHAU CONCENTRATION CAMP MEMORIAL (GEDENKSTÄTTE DACHAU)

Dachau was the first Nazi concentration camp (1933). Today, it's an easily accessible camp for travelers and an effective voice from our recent but grisly past, pleading, "Never again." A visit to Dachau is a powerful and valuable experience and, when approached thoughtfully, well worth the trouble. Many visitors come away from here with more respect for history and the dangers of mixing fear, the promise of jobs, blind patriotism, and an evil government. You'll likely see lots of students here, as all Bavarian schoolchildren are required to visit a concentration camp. It's interesting to think that little more than a couple of generations ago, people greeted each other with a robust *"Sieg Heil!"* Today, almost no Germans know the lyrics of their national anthem, and German flags are a rarity outside of major soccer matches.

Cost and Hours: Free, daily 9:00-17:00. Some areas of the camp may begin to close before 17:00—plan your visit to wrap up by 16:40 to allow time to walk back to the entrance. The museum discourages parents from bringing children under age 14.

Planning Your Time: Allow yourself about five hours—giving you at least two and a half hours at the camp, plus round-trip travel from central Munich. With limited time you could do the whole trip in as little as three and a half hours by concentrating on the museum and skipping the powerful-but-long walk to the memorials and crematorium.

Getting There on Your Own: The camp is a 45-minute trip from downtown Munich. Take the S-2 (direction: Petershausen) from any of the central S-Bahn stops in Munich to Dachau (3/hour, 20-minute trip from Hauptbahnhof). Then, at Dachau station, go down the stairs and follow the crowds out to the bus platforms; find the one marked *KZ-Gedenkstätte-Concentration Camp Memorial Sight.* Here, catch bus #726 and ride it seven minutes to the KZ-Gedenkstätte stop (3/hour). Before you leave this bus stop, be sure to note the return times back to the station.

The Munich XXL day pass covers the entire trip, both ways (€8.90/person, €16.10/partner ticket for up to 5 adults). If you've already invested in a three-day Munich transport pass (which covers only the inner zone), you can save a couple of euros by buying and stamping single tickets (€2.90/person each way) to cover the Dachau part of the trip.

Drivers follow Dachauer Strasse from downtown Munich to Dachau-Ost, then follow *KZ-Gedenkstätte* signs.

Getting There by Guided Tour: The camp is easy to see on your own. But if you'd prefer a guided visit, Radius and Munich Walk tours are a great value, considering how good and passionate their guides are—and that you're paying less than €20 for the guiding, once you factor in transportation costs. Allow roughly five hours total. Both companies charge about the same price. It's smart to reserve the day before, especially for the morning tours. Choose between **Radius** (€28, RS%—select "student rate" when

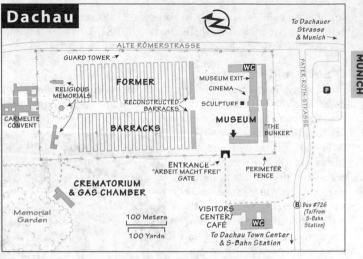

MUNICH

booking online; tours run daily year round at 9:15, also at 12:15 April-mid-Oct and at 10:15 June-July, tel. 089/543-487-7740, www.radiustours.com) and **Munich Walk** (€25, daily year-round at 10:15, also at 13:15 April-Oct, tel. 089/2423-1767, www. munichwalktours.de).

The Town: The town of Dachau—quiet, tree-lined, and residential—is more pleasant than its unfortunate association with the camp on its outskirts, and it tries hard to encourage you to visit its old town and castle (www.dachau.de). With 40,000 residents and quick access to downtown Munich, Dachau is now a high-priced and in-demand place to live.

Visitors Center: Coming from the bus stop or parking lot, you'll first see the visitors center, outside the camp wall. It lacks exhibits, but does have a small cafeteria (sandwiches and pasta dishes), a bookstore with English-language books on Holocaust themes, and a WC (more WCs inside the camp). At the information desk, pick up the English pamphlet, rent an audioguide, or sign up for a tour. Also consider buying the excellent 200-page book with a CD (€18) that contains the same text and images that you'll be seeing in the museum.

Tours: The €4 **audioguide** covers the grounds and museum; its basic itinerary includes 1.5 hours of information (cash only, leave ID). It gives you a few extras (mainly short reminiscences by several camp survivors and members of the Allied forces who liberated the camp), but isn't essential, since the camp is fully labeled in English (rental desk closes at 17:00 sharp). Two different **guided walks** in English are offered, starting from the visitors center (€3, daily at 11:00 and 13:00, 2.5 hours; limited to 30 people, so show up early—especially in summer, 11:00 walk fills up first; call or visit website to confirm times, tel. 08131/669-970, www. kz-gedenkstaette-dachau.de).

◔ Self-Guided Tour

From the visitors center, you approach the main compound. You enter, like the inmates did, through the infamous **iron gate** that held the taunting slogan *Arbeit macht frei* ("Work makes you free").

The original sign was stolen in 2014 and replaced with a replica. Inside are the four key experiences: the museum, the bunker behind the museum, the restored barracks, and a pensive walk across the huge but now-empty camp to the memorials and crematorium at the far end.

Enter the museum, housed in a former camp maintenance building. Just inside is a small bookshop that funds a nonprofit organization (founded by former prisoners) that researches and preserves the camp's history. Immediately to the right of the door you entered, check show times for the museum's powerful 22-minute documentary film (described later). The museum is organized chronologically, everything is thoughtfully described in English, and touch-screens let you watch early newsreels.

The Camp Is Founded (Rooms 1-2)

On January 30, 1933, Adolf Hitler took power. Two months later, Dachau opened. It was a "concentration" camp, to gather together and isolate enemies of the state

so they could not infect the rest of society. The camp was built well outside Dachau's residential zone, surrounded by a mile-wide restricted area.

A map of the Nazi camp system shows that Dachau was just one of many such camps. Some were concentration camps (marked with a square, like Dachau). Others (marked with a triangle with a V) were extermination camps—Auschwitz, Sobibor—built with the express purpose of executing people on a mass scale. Nearby, photos and posters chronicle the rise of Hitler in the 1920s: the resentment bred by Germany's defeat in World War I, the weak Weimar Republic, Hitler's solution to Germany's problems (blame the Jews), his failed Beer Hall Putsch, his participation in mainstream politics. No sooner did he take power than he suspended democracy and began squelching all opposition.

Life at the Camp (Rooms 3-7)

In 1933, the first prisoners passed through the *Arbeit macht frei* gates. They were classified and labeled with a badge (see the chart in Room 4) according to their "crime" against the state. Besides political activists (communists and leftist intellectuals), prisoners included homosexuals, Jehovah's Witnesses, Roma and Sinti (Gypsies), so-called career criminals, "asocials," and Germans who had tried to flee the country. A special badge—the yellow Star of David—was reserved for a group the Nazis particularly loathed: Jews.

The camp was run by the SS, the organization (headed by mastermind Heinrich Himmler) charged with Germany's internal security. Dachau was a training center for future camp managers. Rudolf Höss, who worked at Dachau from 1934 to 1938, went on to become the first commandant of Auschwitz.

Life at Dachau was horrific. It was a work camp, where inmates were expected to pay for their "crimes" with slave labor. And it was clear that work camps were also death camps: Prisoners sent there were sentenced to "extermination through works." The camp was strictly regimented: a wake-up call at 4:00, an 11-hour workday, roll call at 5:15 and 19:00, lights out at 21:00. The work was hard, whether quarrying or hauling loads or constructing the very buildings you see today. The rations were meager. Rule-breakers were punished severely—all manner of torture took place here. The most common punishment was being forced to stand at attention until you collapsed.

On September 1, 1939, Germany invaded Poland, World War II began, and Dachau's role changed.

Cinema

The 22-minute film is a sobering, graphic, and sometimes grisly account of the rise of Hitler and the atrocities of the camp. Since the 1969 film doesn't reflect current research, an update is in the works (usually shown in English at 10:00, 11:30, 12:30, 14:00, and 15:00; not recommended for children under 14).

The War Years (Rooms 8-15)

Once the war began, conditions at Dachau deteriorated. The original camp had been designed to hold just under 3,000 inmates. In 1937 and 1938, the camp was expanded and the building that now houses the museum was built, as well as barracks intended to hold 6,000 prisoners. With the war, the prisoner population swelled, and the Nazis found other purposes for the camp. It was less a concentration camp for German dissidents and more a dumping ground for foreigners, POWs, and even 2,000 Catholic priests. From Dachau, Jewish prisoners were sent east to the gas chambers. Inmates were used as slave labor for the German war machine—many were shipped to nearby camps to make armaments. Prisoners were used as human guinea pigs for war-related medical experiments of human tolerance for air pressure, hypothermia, and biological agents like malaria; the photos of these victims may be the most painful to view.

As the Allies closed in on both fronts, Dachau was bursting with more than 30,000 prisoners jammed into its 34 barracks. In the winter of 1944-1945, disease broke out (including typhus and dysentery), and food ran short. Deaths in the camp increased dramatically—from 403 (October 1944) to nearly 3,991 (February 1945). With coal for the crematorium running low, those who died were buried in mass graves outside the camp site. The Allies arrived on April 29. After 12 years of existence, Dachau was finally liberated, but more than 1,000 prisoners were so weak or sick that they died soon after.

Postscript

All told, about 40,000 people died at Dachau between 1933 and 1945. (By comparison, more than a million were killed at Auschwitz in Poland.) But Dachau remains notorious because it was the Nazis' first camp. Oddly, Dachau actually housed people longer *after* the war than during the war. First, it housed Nazi officials arrested by the Allies, as they awaited trial at Nürnberg for war crimes. From 1948 to 1964, the camp became cheap housing for ethnic Germans expelled from Eastern Europe, complete with a cinema, shops, and so on. The last of the barracks was torn down in 1964, and the museum opened the following year.

• *Consider using the WC before leaving the museum building (there aren't any bathrooms elsewhere within the camp walls). Find the side door, at the end of the exhibition, which leads out to the long, low bunker behind the museum building.*

Bunker

This was a cellblock for prominent "special prisoners," such as failed Hitler assassins, German religious leaders, and politicians who challenged Nazism. Most of the 136 cells are empty, but exhibits in a few of them (near the entrance) profile the inmates and the SS guards who worked at Dachau, and allow you to listen to some inmates' testimonies. Cell #2 was the interrogation room. Cell #9 was a "standing

cell"—inmates were tortured here by being forced to stay on their feet for days at a time.

• *Exit the bunker, and walk around past the* Arbeit macht frei *gate to the big square between the museum and the reconstructed barracks, which was used for roll call. In front of the museum, notice the powerful memorial to the victims created in 1968 by Nandor Glid, a Jewish Holocaust survivor and artist, which includes humanity's vow: Never Again. Cross the square to the farther of the two reconstructed...*

Barracks

Take a quick look inside to get an idea of what sleeping and living conditions were like in the camp. There were 34 barracks, each

measuring about 10 yards by 100 yards. When the camp was at its fullest, there was only about one square yard of living space per inmate.

• *Now walk between the two reconstructed barracks and down the tree-lined path past the foundations of the other barracks. At the end of the camp, in space that once housed the camp vegetable garden, rabbit farm, and brothel, there are now three places of meditation and worship (Jewish to your right, Catholic straight ahead, and Protestant to your left). Beyond them, just outside the camp, is a Carmelite convent. Turn left toward the corner of the camp and find the small bridge leading to the...*

Camp Crematorium

A memorial garden surrounds the two camp crematorium buildings, which were used to burn the bodies of prisoners who had died

or been killed. The newer, larger concrete crematorium was built to replace the smaller wooden one. One of its rooms is a **gas chamber,** which worked on the same principles as the much larger one at Auschwitz, and was originally disguised as a shower

room (the fittings are gone now). It was never put to use at Dachau for mass murder, but survivors have testified that small groups were killed in it "experimentally." In the garden near the buildings is a Russian Orthodox shrine.

• *Our tour is over. To return to Munich by public transit, retrace your steps to the bus stop, where bus #726 takes you back to the Dachau train station. Then catch the S-2 to downtown Munich (direction: Erding or Markt Schwaben). The ride back to Munich gives you ample time to process all you've seen and experienced on your visit.*

▲ANDECHS MONASTERY

This monastery crouches quietly with a big smile between two lakes just south of Munich. For a fine Baroque church in a rural Bavarian setting at a monastery that serves hearty cafeteria-quality food—and perhaps the best beer in Germany—consider a short side-trip here. The cafeteria terrace offers first-class views and second-class prices. Don't miss the stroll up to the church, where you can sit peacefully and ponder the striking contrasts a trip through Germany offers.

Cost and Hours: Free, beer garden open daily 10:00-20:00, church open until 18:00, tel. 08152/376-261, www.andechs.de.

Getting There: Reaching Andechs from Munich without a car is doable with a little planning. Bus #951 stops at the monastery on its run between Herrsching (at the end of the S-8 subway line) and Starnberg Nord (on the S-6 line). Bus #958 runs to Andechs from Tutzing (also on the S-6 line). Check the schedules at www. bahn.com or www.mvv-muenchen.de to find a convenient connection (use Kloster Andechs as your destination; trip takes 1-1.5 hours, buy Munich airport-city day ticket for €13 or pay €24.20 for the partner pass good for up to 5 people). You can also take the S-8 train to Herrsching, then hike, bike, or catch a taxi for the three miles to the monastery.

MORE DAY TRIPS FROM MUNICH

Below I've listed other fine day-trip options from Munich. If traveling by train, consider buying the **Regional Day Ticket for Bavaria,** also known as a Bayern-Ticket, which covers up to five people from Munich to anywhere in Bavaria (plus Salzburg) and back for a very low price (€25 for the first person plus €6 for each additional person, €2 more if bought at counter instead of machine—but worth the extra cost if you need help, not valid before 9:00 Mon-Fri, valid only on slower "regional" trains—most of them labeled on schedules as either "RB," "RE," or "IRE," also valid on city transport). The ticket is sold at train stations and at EurAide (for details on purchasing tickets, see the "Transportation" section of the Practicalities chapter).

"Mad" King Ludwig's Castles: The spectacular castles of Neuschwanstein and Linderhof each make a great day trip (it's possible to do both in a day, but exhausting). Your easiest option is to take a tour (reserve at least a day ahead, as tours sell out in summer; see "Tours in Munich" near the beginning of this chapter). Without a tour, only Neuschwanstein is easy (2 hours by train to

Füssen, then 10-minute bus ride to the castle). Or spend the night in Füssen. For all the details, see the next chapter.

Nürnberg: A handy but expensive ICE express train zips you to Nürnberg in about an hour (departures several times an hour), making this very historic city a viable day trip from Munich. Cheaper RE trains, covered by the Regional Day Ticket, take a little longer. It's also accessible via a Radius Tours all-day excursion (www.radiustours.com). For details, see the Nürnberg chapter.

Salzburg: This Austrian city is an easy day trip and offers some exciting sightseeing (fast train from Munich gets you there in around 1.5 hours; also reachable via Radius Tours package). For details, see the Salzburg chapter.

Berchtesgaden: This resort, near Hitler's Eagle's Nest getaway, is easier as a side-trip from Salzburg (just 15 miles from there). For details, see the Salzburg chapter

BAVARIAN ALPS

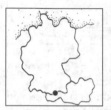

In this picturesque corner of the Alps, you'll find a timeless land of fairy-tale castles, painted buildings shared by cows and farmers, and locals who still dress in dirndls and lederhosen and yodel when they're happy.

This area (2 hours south of Munich) straddles the border between Bavaria (part of Germany) and Tirol (part of Austria). On the German side, you can tour "Mad" King Ludwig II's ornate Neuschwanstein Castle, Europe's most spectacular. Stop by the Wieskirche, a lavishly decorated Baroque church, and browse through Oberammergau, Germany's woodcarving capital and home

of the famous Passion Play (next performed in 2020). A smaller yet still-impressive Ludwig castle (Linderhof), an important monastery (Ettal), and the highest point in Germany (Zugspitze) round out southern Bavaria's top attractions.

Just over the border in Austria, you can explore the ruined Ehrenberg Castle and scream down a mountain at one of the area's many luge runs. In this chapter, I'll first cover the German side (with the most sights), then the Austrian side around Reutte.

CHOOSING A HOME BASE

My hotel recommendations in this chapter cluster in three areas: Füssen and Oberammergau (in Germany), and Reutte (in Austria). When selecting a home base, consider these factors:

Füssen offers the easiest access to the region's biggest attraction—the "King's Castles" (Neuschwanstein and Hohenschwangau)—and is the handiest base for train travelers. The town itself is a mix of real-world and cutesy-cobbled, and has some of the glitziest hotels in the area (as well as more affordable options).

Oberammergau is the best-known, most touristy, and cutest town of the bunch. World-famous for its once-per-decade Passion Play, it's much sleepier the other nine years. It's a long bus ride or a 45-minute drive from Oberammergau to the King's Castles. Three lesser yet worthwhile sights are close by: Ettal Monastery, Linderhof Castle, and the German lift to the Zugspitze.

Reutte is the least appealing town and is less practical for train travelers, but the villages around it are home to some of the region's coziest, most pleasant rural accommodations—making it a particularly good option for drivers. Reutte butts up against the ruined Ehrenberg Castle. The King's Castles, Linderhof, and the Austrian approach to the Zugspitze are all within a 30-minute drive.

For specifics on public transit logistics from each town, see "By Public Transportation," later.

PLANNING YOUR TIME AND GETTING AROUND THE BAVARIAN ALPS

While Germans and Austrians vacation here for a week at a time, the typical speedy American traveler will find two days' worth of sightseeing. The basic visit ranges anywhere from a long day trip from Munich to a three-night, two-day stay. If the weather's good, be sure to ride a lift to an alpine peak.

By Car

This region is best by car, and all the sights are within an easy 60-mile loop from Füssen or Reutte. Even if you're doing the rest of your trip by train, consider renting a car for your time here (for local rental offices, see page 148). Here's a good plan for a one-day circular drive from **Reutte** (from **Füssen,** you can start about 30 minutes later):

7:30	Depart hotel (breakfast at hotel)
8:00	Arrive at the King's Castles to pick up tickets for the two castles (Neuschwanstein and Hohenschwangau)
9:30	Tour Hohenschwangau
11:30	Tour Neuschwanstein
13:30	Drive to Oberammergau (with a 15-minute stop at the Wieskirche), and spend an hour there browsing the carving shops and grabbing a quick lunch
15:30	Drive to Ettal Monastery for a half-hour stop
16:30	Tour Linderhof Castle
18:30	Drive along the scenic Plansee lake

BAVARIAN ALPS

19:30   Back at hotel
20:00   Dinner

Off-season (mid-Oct-March), start your day an hour later, since Neuschwanstein and Hohenschwangau tours don't depart until 10:00; and skip Linderhof, which closes at 16:30.

The next morning, you could stroll through Reutte, hike to the Ehrenberg ruins and the pedestrian bridge, and ride a mountain luge on your way to your next destination.

If you're based in **Oberammergau** instead, get an early start and hit Neuschwanstein and Hohenschwangau first. If the weather's good, hike to the top of Ehrenberg Castle (in Reutte). Drive along the Plan-see and tour Linderhof and Ettal Monastery on your way back home.

By Public Transportation

Where you stay determines which sights you can see most easily. Train travelers use **Füssen** as a base and bus or bike the three miles to the King's Castles and the Tegelberg luge or cable car. Staying in **Oberammergau** gives you easy access to Linderhof and Ettal Monastery, and you can day-trip to the top of the Zugspitze via Garmisch. **Reutte** is the least convenient base if you're carless, but travelers staying there can easily bike or hike to the Ehrenberg ruins and can reach Neuschwanstein by bus (via Füssen) or bike (1.5 hours); if you stay at the recommended Gutshof zum Schluxen hotel (between Reutte and Füssen, in Pinswang, Austria) it's an easy 1.5-hour hike through the woods to Neuschwanstein—a fun opportunity to cross the border on foot.

Visiting sights farther from your home base by local bus re-quires planning. The Deutsche Bahn (German Railway) website (www.bahn.com) and DB Navigator app are helpful tools when planning your journey, on both sides of the border. (Schedules are also available in German at www.rvo-bus.de.) Those staying in **Füssen** can day-trip by bus to Reutte and the Ehrenberg ruins (but you'll have to taxi back to the train station to catch the bus back to Füssen), to the Wieskirche, or, with some planning, to Oberam-mergau. From **Oberammergau,** you can reach Neuschwanstein and Füssen by bus if you plan ahead. From **Reutte,** you can take the train to Ehrwald to reach the Zugspitze from the Austrian side, but side trips to Oberammergau and Linderhof are impractical.

Staying overnight in this region is rewarding, but travelers in a hurry can see the highlights as a **day trip from Munich.** If you can postpone leaving Munich until after 9:00 on a weekday morning, the **Regional Day Ticket for Bavaria** is a great deal for getting to Füssen or Oberammergau: It covers buses and slower regional trains throughout Bavaria (plus Salzburg) for up to five people at a very low price (€25/day for the first person plus €6 for each ad-ditional person; see "More Day Trips from Munich" at the end of the Munich chapter). If you're interested only in Ludwig's castles, consider an all-day organized bus tour from Munich to the Bavarian biggies (see page 45).

By Bike

This is great biking country. Some hotels loan bikes to guests, and shops in Reutte and Füssen rent bikes for €10-15 per day. The ride from Füssen or Reutte to Neuschwanstein and the Tegelberg luge (1.5 hours) is a breeze. Simply joyriding in the meadows that stretch out from Neuschwanstein is unforgettable. For a bit more adventure, consider a ride around the Forggensee (about 3 hours; see "Activities near Füssen," later) or the Hopfensee (1-2 hours). The Füssen TI has a map with a multitude of biking tours.

By Tour

Without a car, **House LA's** full-day tour of Neuschwanstein, Hohenschwangau, Linderhof, and Oberammergau from Füssen can be a time-efficient option (€90/person—price includes Neuschwanstein and Linderhof admission but not Hohenschwangau, mobile 0170-624-8610, www.fussen-info.com). They also offer private, half-day, and bike tours; book at least two days in advance; tours depart from House LA at 9:00—see listing in "Sleeping in Füssen," later.

HELPFUL HINTS

Sightseeing Pass: The Bavarian Palace Department offers a **14-day ticket** (the *Mehrtagesticket*) that covers admission to Neuschwanstein (but not Hohenschwangau) and Linderhof; the Residenz, Nymphenburg Palace, and Amalienburg Palace in Munich; the Imperial Palace in Nürnberg; the Residenz and Marienberg Fortress in Würzburg; and many other castles and palaces not mentioned in this book. If you're planning to visit at least three of these sights within a two-week period, the pass will likely pay for itself (one person-€26, family/partner version for up to two adults plus children-€48, sold online and at all covered castles, www.schloesser.bayern.de). Don't confuse this with the pointless combination ticket for Ludwig II's castles, which costs €26 but only covers three castles—Neuschwanstein, Linderhof, and Herrencheimsee (farther east and not described in this book).

Visiting Churches: To immerse yourself in traditional southern German culture, consider attending a church service. Road signs for *Heilige Messe* (holy Mass) often indicate the day and time for Mass; otherwise look for a schedule posted at the church. Services are usually on Saturday *(Sa.)* evening or Sunday *(So.)* morning.

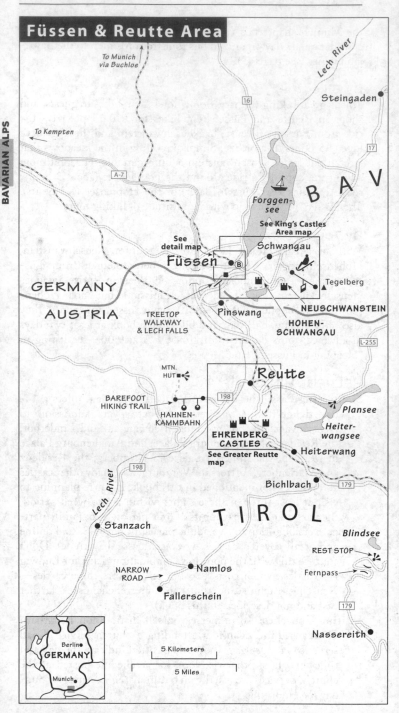

Füssen & Reutte Area

BAVARIAN ALPS

To Munich
via Buchloe

Lech River

Steingaden

To Kempten

16

17

A-7

Forggen-
see

BAV

See King's Castles
Area map

See
detail map

Füssen   B

Schwangau

GERMANY

AUSTRIA

Pinswang

Tegelberg

NEUSCHWANSTEIN

TREETOP
WALKWAY
& LECH FALLS

HOHEN-
SCHWANGAU

L-255

MTN.
HUT

Reutte

198

Plansee

BAREFOOT
HIKING TRAIL

HAHNEN-
KAMMBAHN

EHRENBERG
CASTLES
See Greater Reutte
map

Heiter-
wangsee

Heiterwang

Lech River

198

Bichlbach

179

TIROL

Stanzach

Blindsee

REST STOP

NARROW
ROAD

Namlos

Fernpass

Fallerschein

179

Nassereith

Berlin

GERMANY

Munich

5 Kilometers

5 Miles

BAVARIAN ALPS

Romantic Road to Landsberg & Rothenburg

To Munich

17

2059

ECHELSBACHER BRIDGE (GORGE)

Staffel-see

Murnau

23

B

WIES-KIRCHE

Saulgrub

Ammer

A R I A

N

To Munich

A-95

Unterammergau

STECKEN-BERG

See detail map

Oberammergau

LINDERHOF

Kofel ▲

2060

MONASTERY

Ettal

Oberau

TUNNEL

Garmisch-Partenkirchen

187

SKI JUMP

To Mittenwald &Innsbruck

Eibsee

COG TRAIN

Partnach Gorge

187

Lermoos

Zugspitze 9718'

GERMANY

Ehrwald

AUSTRIA

TUNNEL

Biberwier

Luge

Telfs

179

A-12

To Zürich

Stams

To Innsbruck

Füssen, Germany

Dramatically situated under a renovated castle on the lively Lech River, Füssen (FEW-sehn) has been a strategic stop since ancient times. Its main street was once part of the Via Claudia Augusta, the Roman road across the Alps. Going north, early travelers could follow the Lech River downstream to the Danube and then cross over to the Main and Rhine valleys—a route now known to modern travelers as the "Romantic Road." Today, while Füssen is overrun by tourists in the summer, few venture to the back streets...which is where you'll find the real charm. Apart from my self-guided walk and the Füssen Heritage Museum, there's little to do here—but it's a fine base for visiting the King's Castles and other surrounding attractions.

Orientation to Füssen

Füssen's roughly circular old town huddles around its castle and monastery, along the Lech River. The train station, TI, and many shops are at the north end of town, and my recommended hotels and eateries are within easy walking distance. Roads spin off in all directions (to Neuschwanstein, to Austria, and to numerous lakes). Halfway between Füssen and the German border (as you drive, or a nice woodsy walk from town) is Lech Falls, a thunderous waterfall (with a handy WC).

TOURIST INFORMATION

The TI is in the center of town (July-mid-Sept Mon-Fri 9:00-18:00, Sat 9:30-13:30, Sun until 12:30; off-season Mon-Fri 9:00-17:00, Sat 9:30-13:30, closed Sun; 3 blocks from station at Kaiser-Maximilian-Platz 1, tel. 08362/93850, www.fuessen.de).

Bavarian Craftsmanship

The scenes you'll see painted on the sides of houses in Bavaria
are called *Lüftlmalerei*. The
term came from the name of
the house ("Zum Lüftl") owned
by a man from Oberammergau
who pioneered the practice in
the 18th century. As the paintings became popular during
the Counter-Reformation Baroque age, themes tended to
involve Christian symbols,
saints, and stories (such as
scenes from the life of Jesus),
to reinforce the Catholic Church's authority in the region.
Some scenes also depicted an important historical event that
took place in that house or town.

Especially in the northern part of this region (for example,
in Rothenburg), you'll see *Fachwerkhäuser*—half-timbered
houses. A timber frame outlines the wall, which was traditionally filled in with a
mixture of wicker and
clay. These are most
often found inside
fortified cities that
were once strong and
semi-independent
(such as Rothenberg,
Nürnberg, and Din-
kelsbühl). Farther
south, you'll see stur-
dy, white-walled ma-
sonry houses with woodwork on the upper stories and an
overhanging roof. The interiors of many Bavarian homes and
hotels have elaborate wooden paneling and furniture, often
beautifully carved or made from special sweet-smelling wood.

ARRIVAL IN FÜSSEN

By Train: The train station is three blocks from the center of town
and the TI. Buses to Neuschwanstein, Reutte, and elsewhere leave
from a parking lot next to the station.

By Car: Füssen is known for its traffic jams, and you can't
drive into the old town. The most convenient lots (follow signs) are
the underground P-5 (near the TI, €13/day) and the aboveground
P-3 (off Kemptener Strasse, €12/day).

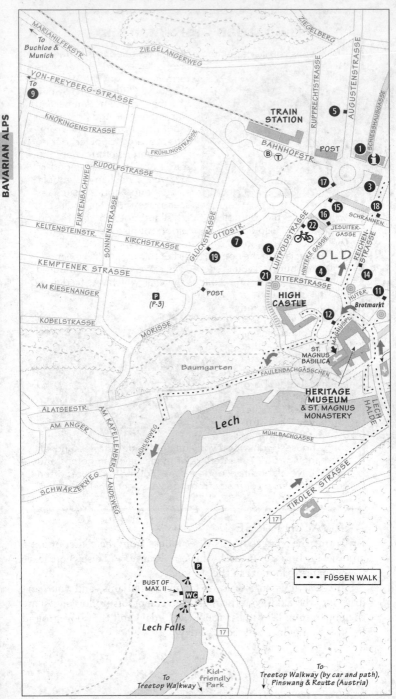

BAVARIAN ALPS

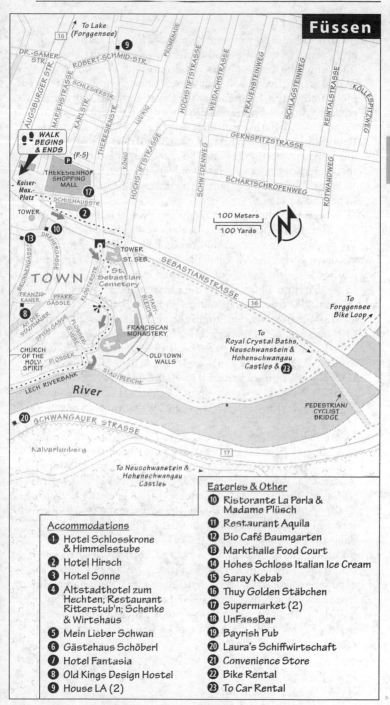

BAVARIAN ALPS

Füssen

To Lake (Forggensee)

16

9

DR.-SAMER-STR.

ROBERT-SCHMID-STR.

PROMENADE

AUGSBURGER STR.

MARIENSTRASSE

SCHLESIERSTR.

KARLSTR.

THERESIENSTR.

HOCHSTIFTSTRASSE

WEIDACHSTRASSE

FRAUENSTEINWEG

SCHLAGSTEINWEG

REINTALSTRASSE

KÖLLESPITZWEG

KÖNIG LUDWIG

GERNSPITZSTRASSE

WALK BEGINS & ENDS (P-5)

P

THERESIENHOF SHOPPING MALL

17

Kaiser-Max.-Platz

SCHULHAUSSTR.

2

TOWER

DREHERGASSE

10

13

SCHW.-DENWEG

HOCHSTIFTSTRASSE

SCHARTSCHROFENWEG

ROTWANDWEG

TOWER ST. SEB.

SEBASTIANSTRASSE

16

100 Meters

100 Yards

N

T O W N

BRUNNENGASSE

St. Sebastian Cemetery

STADTBLEICHE

FRANZIS-KANER

PFARR-GASSLE

KLOSTERSTR.

FLOSSER GASSE

To Forggensee Bike Loop

AN DER STADTMAUER

SPITAL GASSE

FRANCISCAN MONASTERY

To Royal Crystal Baths, Neuschwanstein & Hohenschwangau Castles &

23

CHURCH OF THE HOLY SPIRIT

FLOSSER

OLD TOWN WALLS

STADTBLEICHE

LECH RIVERBANK

River

PEDESTRIAN/CYCLIST BRIDGE

20

SCHWANGAUER STRASSE

Kalvarienberg

17

To Neuschwanstein & Hohenschwangau Castles

Accommodations

1 Hotel Schlosskrone & Himmelsstube

2 Hotel Hirsch

3 Hotel Sonne

4 Altstadthotel zum Hechten; Restaurant Ritterstub'n; Schenke & Wirtshaus

5 Mein Lieber Schwan

6 Gästehaus Schöberl

7 Hotel Fantasia

8 Old Kings Design Hostel

9 House LA (2)

Eateries & Other

10 Ristorante La Perla & Madame Plüsch

11 Restaurant Aquila

12 Bio Café Baumgarten

13 Markthalle Food Court

14 Hohes Schloss Italian Ice Cream

15 Saray Kebab

16 Thuy Golden Stäbchen

17 Supermarket (2)

18 UnFassBar

19 Bayrish Pub

20 Laura's Schiffwirtschaft

21 Convenience Store

22 Bike Rental

23 To Car Rental

BAVARIAN ALPS

HELPFUL HINTS

Hotel Card: Be sure to ask your hotel for a **Füssen Card,** which gives you free use of public transit in the immediate region (including the bus to Neuschwanstein and Wieskirche), as well as €1-2 discounts at many attractions: Neuschwanstein, Hohenschwangau, Museum of the Bavarian Kings, Forggensee boat trip, Füssen Heritage Museum, Tegelberg cable car, Royal Crystal Baths, and Hahnenkammbahn cable car near Reutte. Some accommodations won't tell you about the card unless you request it. You may be asked for a €3-5 deposit; be sure to return the card before you leave town. After the hotel activates the card, it can take an hour or two before it works at sights and on buses.

Wi-Fi: Füssen Card holders can access free Wi-Fi hotspots at the TI, Markthalle, and other places in town; look for orange Wi-Fi signs and enter the number on your card to log on.

Convenience Store: For a catchall convenience and drugstore, **Müller** is on the west side of the old town (Mon-Fri 8:30-19:00, Sat until 18:00, closed Sun, Kemptener Strasse 1).

Bike Rental: Ski Sport Luggi outfits sightseers with good bikes and tips on two-wheeled fun in the area (prices per 24 hours: €10-city bike, €15-mountain bike, €25-electric bike; Mon-Fri 9:00-12:00 & 14:00-18:00, Sat until 13:00, Sun until 12:00 or by reservation; shorter hours off-season, call ahead to reserve, ID required, Luitpoldstrasse 11, tel. 08362/505-9155, mobile 0151-2700-0930, www.ski-sport-luggi.de). For a strenuous but enjoyable 20-mile loop trip, see "Activities near Füssen," later.

Taxi: Call 08362/6222 for taxi service to Neuschwanstein Castle (€11), Tegelberg cable car (€14), and other places.

Car Rental: Hertz Rental Car is an easy taxi ride from the center. Andreas speaks English well and Valbona does her best with help from the Google Translate app (Mon-Fri 8:00-12:00 & 14:00-18:00, Sat 8:00-12:00, Sun and holidays by appointment, Füssener Strasse 112, tel. 08362/986-580, www.hertz.de).

Local Guide: Silvia Skelac, an American born to German parents, moved to Europe two decades ago. She is available as a guide—for private tours, hard-to-reach sights, mountain hikes, and alpine herb walks—and as a ski instructor (€80/half-day, €160/full day, up to 4 people, includes transportation in Silvia's SUV, Austrian mobile 0664-978-7488, info@crossroads-services.com).

Füssen Walk

For most, Füssen is just a home base for visiting Ludwig's famous castles. But the town has a rich history and hides some evocative corners, as you'll see when you follow this self-guided orientation walk. This 45-minute stroll is designed to get you out of the cutesy old cobbled core where most tourists spend their time. Throughout the town, "City Tour" information plaques explain points of interest in English (in more detail than I've provided).

• *Begin at the square in front of the TI, three blocks from the train station.*

Kaiser-Maximilian-Platz: The entertaining "Seven Stones" fountain on this square, by sculptor Christian Tobin, was built in 1995 to celebrate Füssen's 700th birthday. The stones symbolize community, groups of people gathering, conviviality...each is different, with "heads" nodding and talking. It's granite on granite. The moving heads are not connected and nod only with waterpower. It's frozen in winter but is a popular and splashy play zone for kids on hot summer days.

• *Walk along the pedestrian street toward the glass building. To your right, you'll soon see...*

Hotel Hirsch and Medieval Towers: Recent renovations have restored some of the original Art Nouveau flavor to Hotel Hirsch, which opened in 1904. In those days, aristocratic tourists came here to appreciate the castles and natural wonders of the Alps. Across the busy street stands one of two surviving towers from Füssen's medieval town wall (c. 1502), and next to it is a passageway into the old town.

• *Walk along the busy street and cross at the second light to another tower. Head to the information plaque and archway where a small street called Klosterstrasse emerges through a surviving piece of the old town wall. Step through the smaller pedestrian archway, walk along Klosterstrasse for a few yards, and turn left through the gate into the...*

Historic Cemetery of St. Sebastian (Alter Friedhof): This peaceful oasis of Füssen history, established in the 16th century, fills a corner between the town wall and the Franciscan monastery.

It's technically full, and only members of great and venerable Füssen families (who already own plots here) can join those who are buried (free, daily 8:00-19:00, off-season until 17:00).

Immediately inside the gate and on the right is the tomb of Domenico Quaglio, who, in 1835, painted the Romantic scenes decorating the walls of Hohenschwangau Castle. Across the cemetery, on the old city wall (beyond the church), is the World War I memorial, listing all the names of men from this small town killed in that devastating conflict (along with each one's rank and place of death). A bit to the right, also along the old wall, is a statue of the hand of God holding a fetus—a place to remember babies who died before being born. And in the corner, farther to the right, is a gated area with the simple wooden crosses of Franciscans who lived just over the wall in the monastery. Strolling the rest of the grounds, note the fine tomb art from many ages collected here, and the loving care this community gives its cemetery.

• *Exit on the far side, just past the dead Franciscans. Turn left just outside the gate and walk toward the picket fence across the street.*

Town View from Franciscan Monastery (Franziskanerkloster): Enjoy a fine view over the medieval town with an alpine backdrop. In the distance, you'll see the dome and clock tower of the Church of St. Magnus and the aptly named High Castle (the former summer residence of the Bishops of Augsburg), where this walk ends. The tall, skinny smokestack (c. 1886) is a reminder that when Ludwig built Neuschwanstein the textile industry (linen and flax) was very big here. Retrace your steps and follow the wall of the Franciscan Monastery, which still has big responsibilities but only a handful of monks in residence.

• *Go around the corner and down the stairway. At the bottom, turn left through the medieval "Bleachers' Gate" (marked 5½, under the mural of St. George slaying the dragon) to the...*

Lech Riverbank: This low end of town, the flood zone, was the home of those whose work depended on the river—bleachers, rafters, and fishermen. In its heyday, the Lech River was an expressway to Augsburg (about 70 miles to the north). Around the year 1500, the rafters established the first professional guild in Füssen. Cargo from Italy passed here en route to big German cities farther north. Rafters would assemble rafts and pile them high with wine, olive oil, and other goods—or with people needing a lift. If the water was high, they could float all the way to Augsburg in as little as one day. There they'd disassemble their raft and sell off the lumber along with the goods they'd carried, then make their way home to raft again. Today you'll see no modern-day rafters here, as there's a hydroelectric plant just downstream.

• *Walk upstream a bit, appreciating the river's milky color (from mountain rocks, pulverized to a sediment over the long journey from the Alps), and turn right to head inland immediately after crossing under the bridge.*

Church of the Holy Spirit, Bread Market, and Lutemakers: Climbing uphill, you pass the colorful Church of the Holy Spirit

(Heilig-Geist-Spitalkirche) on the right. As this was the church of the rafters, their patron, St. Christopher (with the Baby Jesus on his shoulder), is prominent on the facade. Today it's the church of Füssen's old folks' home (it's adjacent—notice the easy-access skyway). Step inside to take in the details packed into this tiny space, from the carved sides of the pews to the trompe l'oeil dome ceiling. Notice also the painting of a raft disaster on the Lech River—once a common fate of those in the dangerous rafting trade.

Farther up the hill on the right is Bread Market Square (Brotmarkt), with a fountain honoring a famous 16th-century lutemaking family, the Tieffenbruckers. In its day, Füssen (surrounded by forests) was a huge center of violin- and lutemaking, with about 200 workshops. Today only three survive.

• *Backtrack and go through the archway into the courtyard of the former...*

St. Magnus Monastery (Kloster St. Mang): From 1717 until secularization in 1802, this Benedictine monastery was the power center of town. Today the courtyard is popular for concerts, and the building houses the City Hall and the Füssen Heritage Museum.

Füssen Heritage Museum: This is Füssen's one must-see sight, spanning a thousand years of the town's history, with industrial artifacts, medieval cloisters, and Baroque halls (€6, €7 combo-ticket includes High Castle painting gallery and tower; Tue-Sun 11:00-17:00, closed Mon; shorter hours and closed Mon-Thu Nov-March; tel. 08362/903-146, www.museum.fuessen.de).

Pick up the loaner English translations and follow the signs to the St. Anna Chapel, with its famous *Dance of Death.* This was painted shortly after a plague devastated the community in 1590. It shows 20 social classes, each dancing with the Grim Reaper—starting with the pope and the emperor. The words above say, essentially, "You can say yes or you can say no, but you must ultimately

BAVARIAN ALPS

dance with death." Leaving the chapel, you walk over the metal lid of the crypt. Upstairs, exhibits illustrate Füssen's important trades: ropemaking, rafting, and violin- and lutemaking (with a complete workshop)—but the building itself outshines these creaky displays. Among the exquisitely decorated Baroque rooms are an ornate imperial ballroom and a two-tiered oval library displaying cupid statues and frescoes dating from 1719, with an opening to the refectory below.

• *Leaving the courtyard, hook left around the old monastery and go slightly uphill to the square tower. This marks...*

St. Magnus Basilica (Basilika St. Mang): St. Mang (or Magnus) is Füssen's favorite saint. In the eighth century, he worked miracles all over the area with his holy rod. For centuries, pilgrims came to this medieval basilica from far and wide to enjoy art depicting the great works of St. Magnus. Then, in the 18th century, the basilica got a Baroque facelift. Above the altar dangles a glass cross containing the saint's relics (including that holy stick). At the rear of the church is a chapel bright with primary colors that honors a much more modern saint—Franz Seelos (1819-1867), the local boy who went to America (Pittsburgh and New Orleans) and lived such a righteous life that in 2000 he was beatified by Pope John Paul II.

• *From the church, find the grassy knolls and the trail ahead of you, and walk uphill toward the castle entrance.*

High Castle (Hohes Schloss): This castle, long the summer residence of the Bishop of Augsburg, houses a painting gallery (the upper floor is labeled in English) and a tower with a view over the town and lake (€6, €7 combo-ticket includes Füssen Heritage Museum, same hours as museum). The courtyard (with handy WCs under the sundial, just before the tower climb) is worth even a few minutes to admire the striking perspective tricks painted onto its flat walls.

• *Exit the castle wall, and follow the call of the Lech River through the ivy-covered archway to the right. It's a 15-minute walk from here to the falls.*

Baumgarten and Lech Falls: As you explore the castle garden, notice the impressive walls that kept the High Castle safe from pesky invaders. Wander toward the Lech River and follow the signs (away from town and into a quaint neighborhood) that point you toward Lech Falls—it's just beyond the tall, skinny smokestack you saw earlier.

Cross the bridge to enjoy a bit of impressive natural beauty tucked away just outside town. Some say that the name "Füssen" is derived from the Latin word for gorge. Royals and tourists alike have enjoyed this gorge for centuries. Imagine "Mad" King Ludwig coming here with his family to enjoy a special tea arranged on top of the gorge. High above looms a bust of his father (Maximilian II); down below, the interesting rock formations bulge and twist above the roaring water.

• *The Treetop Walkway (described later) is just a 10-minute walk ahead on Tiroler Strasse. Otherwise, from here you can walk downhill to return to town, enjoying a backside view of St. Magnus Monastery where it borders the Lech River. Take a left at the bridge and head back uphill to find the city's main drag (once the Roman Via Claudia and now Reichenstrasse), which leads from a grand statue of St. Magnus past lots of shops, cafés, and strolling people to Kaiser-Maximilian-Platz and the TI...where you began.*

Activities near Füssen

The following sights lie within a few miles of Füssen. All can be reached by car, bike, or foot. See the "King's Castles Area" map, later in this chapter, for locations.

▲Royal Crystal Baths (Königliche Kristall-Therme)

This pool/sauna complex just outside Füssen is the perfect way to relax on a rainy day or to cool off on a hot one. The main part of the complex (downstairs), called the *Therme*, contains two heated indoor pools and a café; outside you'll find a shallow kiddie pool, a lap pool, a heated *Kristallbad* with massage jets and a whirlpool, and a salty mineral bath. The extensive saunas upstairs are well worth the few extra euros, if you're OK with nudity. (Swimsuits are required in the downstairs pools but *verboten* in the upstairs saunas.) Pool and sauna rules are posted in German, but don't worry—just follow the locals' lead.

To enter the baths, first choose the length of your visit and your focus (big outdoor pool only, all ground-floor pools but not the saunas, or the whole enchilada—a flier explains all the prices in English). You'll get a wristband and a credit card-sized ticket with a bar code. Insert that ticket into the entry gate, note your entry time, and keep your ticket—you'll need it to get out. Enter through the changing stalls—where you'll change into your bathing suit (use the clever lever at knee level to lock the door). Then choose a storage locker (€1 coin deposit). When it's time to leave, reinsert your ticket in the gate—if you've gone over the time limit, feed extra euros into the machine.

Cost and Hours: Baths only-€14.50/2 hours, €19/4 hours,

€24/all day; saunas-about €6 extra, towel rental-€3, bathrobe rental -€5, bathing suits sold but not rented; daily 9:00-22:00, Fri-Sat until 23:00; nude swimming everywhere Tue and Fri after 19:00; tel. 08362/819-630, www.kristalltherme-schwangau.de.

Getting There: From Füssen, drive, take the bus (#73 or #78, ask driver for best stop), bike, or walk (30 minutes) across the river, turn left toward Schwangau, and then, about a mile later, turn left at signs for *Kristall-Therme*. It's at Am Ehberg 16. If biking from Füssen, it's easy to see the castle, enjoy the spa, and then roll back into town (about an hour of pedaling altogether).

Bike or Boat Around the Forggensee

On a beautiful day, nothing beats a **bike ride** around the bright-turquoise Forggensee, a nearby lake. This 20-mile loop is exclusively on bike paths (give it a half-day; it's tight to squeeze it into the afternoon after a morning of castle visits, but possible with an early start). Locals swear that going clockwise is less work, but either way has a couple of strenuous uphill parts (total elevation gain of about 600 feet). Still, the amazing views of the surrounding Alps will distract you from your churning legs—so this is still a great way to spend the afternoon. Rent a bike (ideally a 21-speed), pack a picnic lunch, and figure about a three-hour round-trip. From Füssen, follow *Festspielhaus* signs; once you reach the theater, follow *Forggensee Rundweg* signs.

You can also take a **boat ride** on the Forggensee, leaving either from the Füssen "harbor" *(Bootshafen)* or the theater *(Festspielhaus),* a 20- to 30-minute walk north of town (€9/50-minute cruise, 5/day; €13/2-hour cruise, 3/day; runs daily June-mid-Oct, no boats off-season, tel. 08362/921-363, www.stadt-fuessen.de). Unless it's very crowded in the summer, you can bring your bike onto the boat and get off across the lake—shortening the total loop.

Treetop Walkway (Baumkronenweg Ziegelwies)

This elevated wooden "treetop path" lets you stroll for a third of a mile, high in the trees on a graceful yet sturdy suspension-bridge-like structure 60 feet in the air.
The walkway crosses the Austria-Germany border and offers views of the surrounding mountains and the "wild" alpine Lech River, which can be a smooth glacier-blue mirror one day and a muddy torrent the next. Located east of Füssen, just past Lech Falls on the road to Reutte, the  walkway can be accessed at either end. The Austrian end (closer to Reutte) has a large parking lot and a tiny ticket booth. At the

German end (closer to Füssen) there is a nature center and café, and parking is scarce. Stairs (kids can take the slide) lead down to a riverside trail that loops about a mile through a kid-friendly park, with a log raft to cross a little creek, a wonky little bridge, and a sandy stream great for wading. Those with more energy to burn can try the slightly longer mountain loop, accessed by a tunnel under the road.

Cost and Hours: €5, free for kids 15 and under, daily 10:00-17:00, April and Nov until 16:00, closed Dec-March and in bad weather, Tiroler Strasse 10, tel. 08362/938-7550, www. baumkronenweg.eu.

Sleeping in Füssen

Convenient Füssen is just three miles from Ludwig's castles and offers a cobbled, riverside retreat. My recommended accommodations are within a few handy blocks of the train station and the town center. Parking is easy, and some hotels also have their own lot or garage. Many hotels give a 5-10 percent discount for two-night stays—always ask—and prices drop by 10-20 percent off-season. Competition is fierce, so shop around. Remember to ask your hotelier for a Füssen Card (see page 148).

BIG, FANCY HOTELS IN THE CENTER OF TOWN

$$$ Hotel Schlosskrone is formal, with 62 rooms in two wings and all the amenities you need to pamper yourself after a long castle visit. It also runs two restaurants and a fine pastry shop (some rooms with balconies, family rooms, air-con, elevator, free sauna and fitness center, spa, playroom, pay parking, Prinzregentenplatz 2, tel. 08362/930-180, www.schlosskrone.de, rezeption@schlosskrone. de, Norbert Schöll and family).

$$$ Hotel Hirsch is a well-maintained, family-run, 71-room, old-style hotel that takes pride in tradition. Most of their standard rooms are cozy with modern bathrooms, and their rooms with historical and landscape themes are a fun splurge (family rooms, elevator, nice rooftop terrace, free parking, Kaiser-Maximilian-Platz 7, tel. 08362/93980, www.hotelfuessen.de, info@hotelhirsch.de, sibling owners Harold and Eva).

$$$ Hotel Sonne takes pride in its decorating (some would say overdecorating). From eclectic to classic, its 50 rooms are a convenient home base for a night or two (some rooms with balconies, family rooms, air-con in some rooms, elevator, free laundry machine, free sauna and fitness center, pay parking, kitty-corner from TI at Prinzregentenplatz 1, on GPS you may need to enter Reichenstrasse 37, tel. 08362/9080, www.hotel-sonne.de, info@ hotel-sonne.de).

SMALLER, MIDPRICED HOTELS AND PENSIONS

$$ Altstadthotel zum Hechten offers 35 rooms (some with balconies) in a friendly, family-run hotel with bright, comfortable rooms and a borderline-kitschy breakfast room. It's a good value, with a few fun extras including a travel-resource/game room, borrowable hiking gear, and a recommended restaurant (two buildings, family rooms, elevator, pay parking, situated right under Füssen Castle in the old-town pedestrian zone at Ritterstrasse 6, on GPS you may need to enter Hinteregasse 2, tel. 08362/91600, www.hotel-hechten.com, info@hotel-hechten.com, Pfeiffer and Tramp families).

$$ Mein Lieber Schwan, a block from the train station, is run by Herr Bletschacher, a hometown boy who's proud of his accommodations' personality and charm. He offers four superbly outfitted apartments, each with a double bed, sofa bed, kitchen, and antique furnishings (cash or PayPal only, no breakfast, free parking, laundry facilities, garden, Augustenstrasse 3, tel. 08362/509-980, www.meinlieberschwan.de, fewo@meinlieberschwan.de). Herr Bletschacher also has two slightly larger apartments at Klosterstrasse 10.

$ Gästehaus Schöberl, run by Pia and her husband Georg (who co-manages Altstadthotel zum Hechten), makes you feel like you're staying with friends. Its six bright and spacious rooms are a great value and set on a quiet street just off the main drag. One room is in the owners' house, and the rest are in the building next door (cash only, family room, free parking, closed in Nov, Luitpoldstrasse 14—check-in at #16 around back, tel. 08362/922-411, www.schoeberl-fuessen.de, info@schoeberl-fuessen.de).

$ Hotel Fantasia, the little sister of Hotel Sonne, has 16 trendy rooms adorned with violet paint and lots of pictures of King Ludwig that might make the nuns who once lived here blush. The price is right, but the reception is often unmanned (breakfast extra, family rooms, pay parking, peaceful garden, trampoline, Ottostrasse 1, tel. 08362/9080, www.hotel-fantasia.de, info@hotel-fantasia.de).

BUDGET BEDS

¢ Old Kings Design Hostel shoehorns two dorm rooms and three private doubles into an old townhouse that doesn't resemble a typical hostel. While the quarters are tight (all rooms share bathrooms), the central location, creative decor, and reasonable prices are enticing (bike rental, reception open daily 7:00-11:00 & 16:00-21:00, buried deep in the pedestrian zone at Franziskanergasse 2, tel. 08362/883-4090, www.oldkingshostel.com, info@oldkingshostel.com).

¢ House LA, run by energetic mason Lahdo Algül and hardworking Aga, has two branches. The backpacker house has 11 basic, clean dorm rooms at rock-bottom prices about a 10-minute walk from the station (private room available, free parking, Wachsbleiche 2). A second building has five family apartments with kitchen and bath (RS%, breakfast extra, free parking, 6-minute walk back along tracks from station to von Freybergstrasse 26; contact info for both: tel. 08362/607-366, mobile 0170-624-8610, www.housela.de, info@housela.de). Both locations rent bikes and have laundry facilities.

Eating in Füssen

$$ Restaurant Ritterstub'n offers delicious, reasonably priced German grub plus salads, veggie plates, and a fun kids' menu. They have three eating zones: modern decor in front, traditional Bavarian in back, and a courtyard. Ask about their €19 three-course fixed-price dinners. Their single-trip salad buffet is a great value—pile it high, as you're charged by the plate size. Demure Gabi serves while her husband Claus cooks (cheap lunch specials, Tue-Sun 11:30-14:00 & 17:30-21:30, closed Mon, Ritterstrasse 4, tel. 08362/7759).

$$ Schenke & Wirtshaus (inside the recommended Altstadthotel zum Hechten) dishes up hearty, traditional Bavarian dishes from goulash to pork knuckle in a classic interior. Their specialty is pike *(Hecht)* pulled from the Lech River, served with a tasty fresh-herb sauce (daily 11:00-21:00, Ritterstrasse 6, tel. 08362/91600).

$$$ Ristorante La Perla is an Italian restaurant run with pride by Michael and his family. Sit either in the classic rosy interior, at streetside tables on a quiet Old Town lane, or in the hidden courtyard out back (cheaper pizzas and pastas, daily 11:00-22:00, Nov-Jan closed 14:30-17:30 and all day Mon, Drehergasse 44, tel. 08362/7155).

$$$ The **Himmelsstube** is the restaurant inside Hotel Schlosskrone, right on Füssen's main traffic circle. It offers a weekday lunch buffet and live Bavarian zither music most Fridays and Saturdays during dinner. Choose between a traditional dining room and a pastel winter garden (daily 11:30-14:30 & 18:00-22:00, Prinzregentenplatz 2, tel. 08362/930-180, www.schlosskrone.de).

$$ Restaurant Aquila serves modern German and Italian-influenced dishes and serious salads in a simple indoor setting, but I prefer the outdoor tables on delightful Brotmarkt square (Wed-Mon 11:30-21:00, closed Tue, reservations smart, Brotmarkt 9, tel. 08362/6253, www.aquila-fuessen.de).

$$$ Madame Plüsch, old-school and elegant, serves tasty Bavarian dishes (fish, pork, beef, and veggie options), prepared and seasoned with care. Dine in a cozy interior or at tables on the square (Thu-Mon 11:30-15:00 & 17:00-23:00, Wed 17:00-23:00, closed

Tue, reservations recommended, Drehergasse 48, tel. 08362/938-0949, www.madame-pluesch.de).

$ Bio Café Baumgarten is a tiny healthy oasis near the St. Magnus Basilica tower, with tables inside and out on the square. Its organic fare includes breakfast, smoothies, salads, and sweet and savory crêpes, plus homemade cakes (daily 9:00-18:00, Magnusplatz 6, tel. 08362/989-9750).

Food Court: The fun **$ Markthalle** offers a wide selection of reasonably priced, wurst-free food. Located in a former warehouse from 1483, it's now home to a fishmonger, deli counters, a fruit stand, a bakery, and a wine bar. Buy your food from one of the vendors, park yourself at any one of the tables, then look up and admire the Renaissance ceiling (Mon-Fri 8:00-18:30, Sat until 15:00, closed Sun, corner of Schrannengasse and Brunnengasse).

Brewpub near the Castles: If you have a car, consider heading to **Schloss Brauhaus,** in the village of Schwangau, for local brew and an unbeatable view (described on page 173).

Gelato: Hohes Schloss Italian Ice Cream is a popular *gelateria* on the main drag with a huge menu of decadent sundaes and an inviting people-watching perch (Reichenstrasse 14).

Cheap Eats: $ Saray Kebab is the town's favorite Middle Eastern takeaway joint (Mon-Sat 11:00-23:00, closed Sun, Luitpoldstrasse 1, tel. 08362/2847). **$ Thuy Golden Stäbchen** serves a mix of Vietnamese, Chinese, and Thai food on a deserted back street with outdoor tables and a castle view (Tue-Sun 10:00-22:00, closed Mon, Hinteregasse 29, tel. 08362/939-7714).

Picnic Supplies: Bakeries and butcher shops *(Metzger)* abound and frequently have ready-made sandwiches. For groceries, try the discount **Netto** supermarket, at the roundabout across from Hotel Schlosskrone, or the midrange **REWE** in the Theresienhof shopping complex (both supermarkets open Mon-Sat 7:00-20:00, closed Sun).

Nightlife: At the **UnFassBar,** on Füssen's main drag, locals crowd at streetside tables or inside the cozy interior for drinks and small bites (Wed-Sat 10:00-22:00, closed Sun-Tue, Reichenstrasse 32, tel. 08362/929-6688). **Bayrish Pub** is popular for soccer viewing, live music, and conviviality (Tue-Fri 17:30-late, Sat from 14:30, closed Sun-Mon, Ottostrasse 7, tel. 08362/930-7444). **Laura's Schiffwirtschaft,** just across the river, attracts a younger crowd with live music, a foosball table, and basic bar food. The early-evening river views are exceptional (Wed-Sat 17:00-24:00, closed Sun-Tue, tel. 08362/924-3370).

Füssen Connections

BY BUS AND TRAIN

Bus schedules from Füssen can be very confusing. The website www.bahn.com is good for figuring out your options for a particular day and route. The DB Navigator app is also useful for planning your journey.

From Füssen to: **Neuschwanstein** (bus #73 or #78, departs from train station, most continue to Tegelberg cable car station after castles, at least hourly, 10 minutes, €2.30 one way, buses #9606 and #9651 also make the trip); **Wieskirche** (bus #73, #9606, or #9651; 2-6 buses/day, 45-60 minutes); **Oberammergau** (bus #9606, 1-3/day, 1.5 hours, bus sometimes starts as #73 and changes number to #9606 en route—confirm with driver that bus is bound for Oberammergau); **Reutte** (bus #74 in Germany, changes number to #4258 in Austria, Mon-Fri 7/day, Sat-Sun 6/day, last bus 19:00, 30-50 minutes, €4.50 one-way); **Zugspitze** (possible as day trip via bus #74 to Reutte, then train to Ehrwald for Austrian ascent or Garmisch, allow up to 3.5 hours total to reach the top); **Munich** (hourly trains, 2 hours, half with easy transfer in Buchloe); **Innsbruck** (fastest via bus #4258/#74 to Reutte, then train from Reutte to Innsbruck via Garmisch, every 2 hours, 2.5 hours; otherwise via Munich); **Salzburg** (roughly hourly, 4 hours on fast trains, 5 hours on slow trains—included with Regional Day Ticket for Bavaria, transfer in Munich and sometimes in Kaufbeuren or Buchloe); **Rothenburg ob der Tauber** (hourly trains, 5-6 hours, look for connections with only 3 transfers—often in Augsburg, Treuchtlingen, and Steinach); **Frankfurt** (hourly trains, 5-6 hours, 1-2 changes). Train info: www.bahn.com.

The Best of the Bavarian Alps

Within a short drive of Füssen and Reutte, you'll find some of the most enjoyable—and most tourist filled—sights in Germany. The otherworldly "King's Castles" of Neuschwanstein and Hohenschwangau capture romantics' imaginations, the ornately decorated Wieskirche puts the faithful in a heavenly mood, and the little town of Oberammergau overwhelms visitors with cuteness. Yet another impressive castle (Linderhof), another fancy church (Ettal), and a sky-high viewpoint (the Zugspitze) round out this region's top attractions.

The King's Castles: Neuschwanstein and Hohenschwangau

The most popular tourist destinations in southern Bavaria are the two "King's Castles" (Königsschlösser) near Füssen. The older Hohenschwangau, King Ludwig's boyhood home, is less famous but more historic. The more dramatic Neuschwanstein, which inspired Walt Disney, is the one everyone visits. I recommend visiting both and hiking above Neuschwanstein to Mary's Bridge. Reservations are a magic wand that smooth out your visit. With fairy-tale turrets built by a fairy-tale king in a fairy-tale alpine setting, these castles are understandably a huge hit.

GETTING THERE

If arriving by **car,** note that road signs in the region refer to the sight as *Königsschlösser.* There's plenty of parking (all lots-€6). The first lots require more walking. The most convenient lot, by the lake (#4, *Parkplatz am Alpsee*), is up the small road past the souvenir shops and ticket center.

From **Füssen,** those without cars can catch **bus** #73 or #78 (at least hourly, generally departs Füssen's train station at :05 past the hour, extra buses often run when crowded, €2.30 each way, 10 minutes; a few departures of #9606 and #9651 also make this trip). A Regional Day Ticket for Bavaria (see "Planning Your Time and Getting Around the Bavarian Alps," earlier) or the Füssen Card available from your hotel (see page 148) let you ride for free. You can also take a **taxi** (€11 one-way), ride a rental **bike** (3 level miles), or—if you're in a pinch—**walk** (less than an hour). The bus drops you at the tourist office (note return times so you aren't stuck waiting); it's a one-minute walk from there to the ticket office. When returning, note that buses #73 and #78 pointing left (with your back to the TI) are headed to Füssen, while the same numbers pointing right are going elsewhere.

From **Reutte,** take the bus to the Füssen train station (#4258, number changes to #74 in Germany, Mon-Fri 8/day, Sat-Sun 6/day). Once in Füssen, hop on bus #73 or #78 to the castles (see earlier).

ORIENTATION TO THE KING'S CASTLES

Cost: Timed-entry tickets for Neuschwanstein and Hohenschwangau cost €13 apiece. A "Königsticket" combo-ticket for both castles costs €25—the Bavarian Palace Department's 14-day ticket may be a better deal if you're only touring Neuschwanstein but seeing other Bavarian sights (see "Helpful Hints" at the beginning of this chapter). A "Schwanenticket," which also covers the Museum of the Bavarian Kings—described later—costs €31.50. Children under age 18 (accompanied by an adult) get in free.

Hours and Entry Times: The ticket center, located at street level between the two castles, is open daily (7:30-17:00, mid Oct-March 8:30-15:00). The first castle tour of the day departs at 9:00 (10:00 in off-season); the last tour departs at 17:00 (15:30 in off-season).

Tickets, whether reserved in advance or bought on the spot, come with admission times. If you miss your appointed tour time, you can't get in. To tour both castles, you must do Hohenschwangau first (logical, since this gives a better introduction to King Ludwig's short life). You'll get two entry times: Hohenschwangau and then, two hours later, Neuschwanstein. If you're planning to hike up to Mary's Bridge prior to your Neuschwanstein tour, allow plenty of time: There's often a line to get onto the bridge for that famous view.

Information: Tel. 08362/930-830, www.hohenschwangau.de.

King's Castles Area

Forggensee

BOAT RENTAL

To Munich via Kaufbeuren

AUGSBURGER STRASSE

RUPPRECHT-STRASSE

THERESIENSTRASSE

SCHELLEWEG

FRAUENBERGSTR.

Füssen

VON-FREYBERG-STR.

To Car Rental

TRAIN STATION

(P-5)

SHOPPING MALL

Horn

#73 & 78

KEMPTENER STR.

SEBASTIANSTR.

HERITAGE MUSEUM

HIGH CASTLE

(P-3)

FRANCISCAN MONASTERY

FORGGENWEG

AM LECHRAIN

ST. MAGNUS MONASTERY

ALATSEESTR.

TIROLER STR.

SCHWANGAUER STR.

17

Lech Falls

KID-FRIENDLY PARK

NATURE CENTER

Lech River

TREETOP WALKWAY

Schwansee

17

To Reutte

AUSTRIA

GERMANY

To Pinswang

Horse Carriage Stops

Alpsee

Eateries & Other
- ❸ Schloss Brauhaus
- ❹ Sauerwein Alois Café-Konditorei-Bäckerei
- ❺ Supermarket

Accommodations
- ❶ Alpenhotel Allgäu
- ❷ Beim "Landhannes"

400 Meters

400 Yards

Reservations: It's just plain smart to reserve ahead, particularly for holidays and weekends during peak season (June-Oct—especially July-Aug) when slots can book up several days in advance. Reservations cost €2.50 per person per castle and must be made online at least two days in advance (no later than 15:00 local time, www.hohenschwangau.de). With enough notice, a few hotels can book tickets for you. You must pick up reserved tickets an hour before your appointed entry time, as it takes a while to get up to the castles. Show up late and they may have given your slot to someone else (but will likely help you book a new reservation). If you know a few hours in

advance that you're running late and can call the office (tel. 08362/930-830), they'll likely rebook you.

If you're staying in Reutte and depending on buses for transportation, make your reservation for midday (noon or later) to give yourself ample time to arrive at Neuschwanstein.

Note that you need a reservation even with the Bavarian Palace Department's 14-day ticket (covers Neuschwanstein only, described earlier). Reserve online; your credit card will be charged only for the booking fee.

Without a Reservation: A percentage of castle tickets are set aside for in-person purchase, so if reservations for your day of choice are sold out online, you can still get a ticket if you arrive early. Because day-trippers from Munich tend to take the morning train—with a bus connection arriving at the castles by about 11:15—if you need to buy a ticket on the spot, arrive by 11:00 to beat the crowd. During August, the busiest month, tickets for English tours can run out by around noon.

Arrival: Make the **ticket center** your first stop. If you have a reservation, stand in the short line for picking up tickets. If you don't have a reservation...welcome to the very long line. Arrive by 7:30 in summer, and you'll likely be touring around 9:00.

Tips for Munich Day-Trippers: Rather than buy point-to-point train tickets, it's a no-brainer to buy the Regional Day Ticket for Bavaria (described under "Planning Your Time and Getting Around the Bavarian Alps," earlier); not only is it cheaper, but it also covers the bus between Füssen and the castles (the only catch is that on weekdays, the pass isn't valid before 9:00). Take a train that departs for Füssen at least four hours before your reserved castle entry time. (It's a 2-hour train ride, followed by a 30-minute bus trip to the castle ticket office—and you must be there to pick up your tickets an hour before your tour.) Trains from Munich leave hourly at :51 past the hour. So, if you take the 9:51 train, you can make a 14:00 castle tour. If you reserve a castle tour for 11:00, you'll need to pack breakfast and take the 6:53 train (confirm train times in advance).

Getting Up to the Castles: From the ticket booth, Hohenschwangau is an easy 10-minute **walk** up the paved path past the bus parking (for a quicker ascent zigzag up to the big yellow castle using the ramp/stairs behind Hotel Müller). Neuschwanstein is a moderately steep, 30-minute hike in the other direction (also well signed—the most direct and least steep approach begins near the Schlossbräustüberl restaurant).

To minimize hiking to Neuschwanstein, you can take a shuttle bus or a horse-drawn carriage. Neither option gets you to the castle doorstep. The **shuttle bus** departs about every 20 minutes from the parking lot just below Hohenschwangau and drops you off near Mary's Bridge (Marienbrücke), leaving you a steep, 10-minute downhill walk to the castle—so be sure to see the view from Mary's Bridge *before* hiking down (€2.50 uphill, €1.50 downhill, €3 round-trip). **Horse-drawn carriages,** which leave from in front of Hotel Müller, are slower than walking and stop below Neuschwanstein, leaving you a five-minute uphill hike (€6 up, €3 down). Carriages also run to Hohenschwangau (€4.50 up, €2 down).

Be warned that both buses and carriages can have long lines at peak times—especially if it's raining. You might wait up to 45 minutes, making it slower than walking. If you're

"Mad" King Ludwig (1845-1886)

A tragic figure, Ludwig II (a.k.a. "Mad" King Ludwig) ruled Bavaria for 22 years until his death in 1886 at the age of 40. Bavaria was weak. Politically, Ludwig's reality was to "rule" as either a pawn of Prussia or a pawn of Austria. Rather than deal with politics in Bavaria's capital, Munich, Ludwig frittered away most of his time at his family's hunting palace, Hohenschwangau. He spent much of his adult life constructing his fanciful Neuschwanstein Castle—like a kid builds a tree house—on a neighboring hill upon the scant ruins of a medieval castle. Here and in his other projects (such as Linderhof Castle and the never-built Falkenstein Castle), even as he strove to evoke medieval grandeur, he embraced the state-of-the-art technology of the Industrial Age in which he lived. Neuschwanstein had electricity, running water, and a telephone (but no Wi-Fi).

Ludwig was a true romantic living in a Romantic age. His best friends were artists, poets, and composers such as Richard Wagner. His palaces are wallpapered with misty medieval themes—especially those from Wagnerian operas.

Although Ludwig spent 17 years building Neuschwanstein, he lived in it only 172 days. Soon after he moved in (and before his vision for the castle was completed), Ludwig was declared mentally unfit to rule Bavaria and taken away. Two days after this eviction, Ludwig was found dead in a lake. To this day, people debate whether the king was murdered or committed suicide.

cutting it close to your appointed time, you may need to hoof it. Note that buses don't run in snowy or icy conditions, which can happen even in spring.

With time, here's the most economical and least strenuous plan: Ride the bus to Mary's Bridge for the view, hike down to Neuschwanstein, and then catch the horse carriage from below the castle down to the parking lot (round-trip cost: €5.50). If you're on a tight schedule, consider taking the bus back down, as carriages can be unpredictable.

Entry Procedure: At each castle, tourists jumble in the courtyard, waiting for their ticket number to light up on the board. When it does, power through the mob and go to the turnstile. Warning: You must use your ticket while your number is still on the board. If you space out, you'll miss your entry window.

Renovations: Neuschwanstein is undergoing restoration work, so you may encounter scaffolding, and some furnishings may have protective coverings when you visit (photos in rooms show the space without the coverings).

Services: A TI (run by helpful Thomas), bus stop, ATM, pay WC, lockers, and post machine cluster around the main intersection a couple hundred yards before you get to the ticket office (TI open daily April-Oct 10:00-17:30, Nov-March Sat-Sun until 16:00, closed Mon-Fri, tel. 08362/81980, www.schwangau. de). While the tiny bathrooms inside the castles themselves are free, you'll pay to use the WCs elsewhere.

Wi-Fi: You can get an hour of free Wi-Fi at the TI and other hotspots near the castles. Look for signs with the orange logo.

Best Views: In the morning, the light comes in just above the mountains—making your initial view of Neuschwanstein hazy and disappointing (though views from the ticket center up to Hohenschwangau are nice). Later in the day, the sun drops down into the pasture, lighting up Neuschwanstein magnificently. Regardless of time of day, the best accessible Neuschwanstein view is from Mary's Bridge (or, for the bold, from the little bluff just above it)—a 10-minute hike from the castle. (Many of the postcards and posters you'll see are based on photos taken high in the hills, best left to avid hikers.)

Eating at the Castles: I prefer to bring a packed lunch. The park by the Alpsee (the nearby lake) is ideal for a picnic, although you're not allowed to sit on the grass—only on the benches (or eat out on the lake in one of the old-fashioned rowboats—see "After Your Castle Visit," next). The restaurants in the "village" at the foot of Europe's Disney castle are mediocre and overpriced, serving endless droves of hungry, shop-happy tourists. You can find decent German fare at the snack stand across from the TI or next to Hotel Alpenstuben (between the TI and ticket center). Up near Neuschwanstein itself (near the horse carriage drop-off) is a cluster of overpriced eateries, and inside the castle is a café with remarkable views, solid sustenance, and unremarkable coffee.

If you have a car or a bike, see "Eating Near the King's Castles," later, for better options.

After Your Castle Visit: If you follow my advice, you could be done with your castle tours in the early afternoon. With a car, you could try to squeeze in a nearby sight (such as Linderhof Castle, Ehrenberg Castle ruins, Highline 179 suspension footbridge, or Wieskirche). To stick closer by, here are some ideas: The hike from Neuschwanstein up to **Mary's Bridge** is easy and rewarding; the hike back down to the valley through the **Pöllat Gorge** is also highly recommended (may be closed). When the sun is shining, rent a **pedal boat** or **rowboat** for a scenic float around the **Alpsee,** the lake below Hohenschwangau. With a **bike,** you could pedal through the mostly flat countryside that spreads out in front of Neuschwanstein (perhaps partway around the Forggensee). And nearby—an easy drive or bus ride away—the Tegelberg area has both a high-mountain **cable car** and a fun **luge** ride. All of these options are described later. Yet another option is to walk all the way around the Alpsee (about 1.5 hours, clockwise is less strenuous, some steps). And for some relaxation, the **Royal Crystal Baths** in the town of Schwangau are ideal (described earlier).

SIGHTS AT THE KING'S CASTLES

The two castles complement each other perfectly. But if you have to choose one, Neuschwanstein's wow factor—inside and out—is undeniable.

▲▲▲Hohenschwangau Castle

Standing quietly below Neuschwanstein, the big, yellow Hohenschwangau Castle is where Ludwig spent his summers as a young boy. Originally built in the 12th century, it was ruined by Napoleon. Ludwig's father, King Maximilian II, rebuilt it in 1830. Hohenschwangau (hoh-en-SHVAHN-gow, loosely translated as "High Swanland") was used by the royal family as a summer hunting lodge until 1912. The Wittelsbach family (which ruled Bavaria for nearly seven centuries) still owns the place (and lived in the annex—today's shop—until the 1970s).

The interior decor (mostly Neo-Gothic, like the castle itself) is harmonious, cohesive, and original—all done in 1835, with paintings inspired by Romantic themes. As you tour the castle, imagine how the paintings must have inspired young Ludwig. For 17 years, he lived here at his dad's place and followed the construction of his dream castle across the way—you'll see the telescope still set up and directed at Neuschwanstein.

The excellent 30-minute tour gives a better glimpse of Ludwig's life than the more visited and famous Neuschwanstein Castle tour. Tours here are smaller (35 people rather than 60) and more relaxed. You'll explore rooms on two floors—the queen's rooms, and then, upstairs, the king's. (Conveniently, their bedrooms were connected by a secret passage.) You'll see photos and busts of Ludwig and his little brother, Otto; some Turkish-style flourishes (to please the king, who had been impressed after a visit to the Orient); countless swans—try to find them (honoring the Knights of Schwangau, whose legacy the Wittelsbachs inherited); over-the-top gifts the Wittelsbachs received from their adoring subjects; and paintings of VIGs (very important Germans, including Martin Luther—who may or may not have visited here—and an infant Charlemagne).

One of the most impressive rooms is the Banquet Hall (also known as the Hall of Heroes); one vivid wall mural depicts a savage, yet bloodless, fifth-century barbarian battle. Just as the castle itself had running water and electricity despite its historic appearance (both were installed in the 1900s under King Luitpold, Ludwig's uncle), its Romantic decor presents a sanitized version of the medieval past, glossing over inconvenient details. You'll also see Ludwig's bedroom, which he inherited from his father. He kept most of the decor (including the nude nymphs frolicking over his bed) but painted the ceiling black and installed transparent stars that could be lit from the floor above to create the illusion of a night sky.

After the tour is over, wind through the castle gardens and imagine Ludwig frolicking here with his sights set on the hill far in the distance.

▲▲▲Neuschwanstein Castle

Imagine "Mad" King Ludwig as a boy, climbing the hills above his dad's castle, Hohenschwangau, dreaming up the ultimate fairy-tale castle. Inheriting the throne at the young age of 18, he had the power to make his dream concrete and stucco. Neuschwanstein (noy-SH-VAHN-shtine, roughly "New Swanstone") was designed first by a theater-set designer...then by an architect. While it was built upon the ruins of an old

castle and looks medieval, Neuschwanstein is modern iron-and-brick construction with a sandstone veneer—only about as old as the Eiffel Tower. It feels like something you'd see at a home show for 19th-century royalty. Built from 1869 to 1886, it's the epitome of the Romanticism popular in 19th-century Europe. Construction stopped with Ludwig's death (only a third of the interior was finished), and within six weeks, tourists were paying to go through it.

During World War II, the castle took on a sinister role. The

Nazis used Neuschwanstein as one of their primary secret store-houses for stolen art. After the war, Allied authorities spent a year sorting through and redistributing the art, which filled 49 rail cars from this one location alone. It was the only time the unfinished rooms were put to use.

Today, guides herd groups of 60 through the castle, giving an interesting—yet often unenthusiastic and rushed—30-minute tour. (While you're waiting for your tour time to pop up on the board, climb the stairs to the upper courtyard to see more of the exterior, which isn't covered on your tour.) Once inside, you'll go up and down more than 300 steps (keep an eye out for a spiral stair case column that becomes a palm tree), visiting 15 lavish rooms with their original furnishings and fanciful wall paintings—mostly based on Wagnerian opera themes. While renovations are under way, furnishings may be covered up, but the opulence of the building itself delivers plenty of drama.

Ludwig's extravagant throne room, modeled in a Neo-Byzantine style to emphasize his royal status, celebrates six valiant Christian kings (whose mantle Ludwig clearly believed he had donned) under a huge gilded-bronze, crown-like chandelier. The exquisite two-million-stone mosaic floor is a visual encyclopedia of animals and plants. While you're standing on a replica, original segments ring the perimeter. The most memorable stop may be the king's gilded-lily bedroom, with his elaborately carved canopy bed (with a forest of Gothic church spires on top), washstand (filled with water piped in from the Alps), and personal chapel. After passing through Ludwig's living room and a faux grotto, you'll climb to the fourth floor for the grand finale: the Singers' Hall, an ornately decorated space filled with murals depicting the story of Parzival, the legendary medieval knight with whom Ludwig identified.

After the tour, weave through the crowded gift shop and past the WCs and café to see the 13-minute video (runs continuously, English subtitles). This uses historical drawings and modern digital modeling to tell the story of how the castle was built, and illustrates all the unfinished parts of Ludwig's vision (more prickly towers, a central chapel, a fancy view terrace, an ornate bathhouse, and more). Finally, you'll see a digital model of Falkenstein—a whimsical, over-the-top, never-built castle that makes Neuschwanstein look stubby. Falkenstein occupied Ludwig's fantasies the year he died.

Then head downstairs to the kitchen (state-of-the-art for this high-tech king in its day), where you'll see a room lined with fascinating drawings of the castle plans (described in English), as well as a large castle model.

SIGHTS NEAR THE CASTLES

The first three listings are right at the castles, while the cable car and luge are a few miles away.

▲▲Mary's Bridge (Marienbrücke)

Before or after the Neuschwanstein tour, climb up to Mary's Bridge (named for Ludwig's mom) to marvel at Ludwig's castle, just as Ludwig did. Jockey with a United Nations of tourists for the best angle—there's usually a line just to get onto the structure. This bridge was quite an engineering accomplishment 100 years ago. (Access to the bridge is closed in bad winter weather, but many travelers walk around the barriers to get there—at their own risk, of course.)

For an even more glorious castle view, the frisky can hike even higher: After crossing the bridge, you'll see very rough, steep, unofficial trails crisscrossing the hillside on your left. If you're willing to ignore the *Lebensgefahr* (risk of death) signs, you can scamper up to the bluff just over the bridge.

The trail connecting Neuschwanstein to Mary's Bridge is also scenic, with views back on Neuschwanstein's facade in one direction, and classic views of Hohenschwangau—perched on its little hill between lakes, with cut-glass peaks on the horizon—in the other.

▲Pöllat Gorge (Pöllatschlucht)

If it's open, the river gorge that slices into the rock just behind Neuschwanstein's lofty perch is a more interesting and scenic—and less crowded—alternative to shuffling back down the main road. While it takes an extra 15 minutes or so, it's well worth it. You'll find the trailhead just above the Neuschwanstein exit, on the path toward Mary's Bridge (look for *Pöllatschlucht* signs; trail closed in winter and sometimes impassable due to rockslides).

You'll begin by walking down a steep, well-maintained set of concrete stairs, with Germany's finest castle looming through the trees. Then you'll pop out along the river, passing a little beach (with neatly stacked stones) offering a view up at the grand waterfall that gushes beneath Mary's Bridge. From here, follow the river as it goes over several smaller waterfalls—and stroll for a while along steel walkways and railings that make this slippery area safer. After passing an old wooden channel used to harness the power of all that water, you'll hit level ground; turn left and walk through a pleasantly untouristy residential settlement back toward the TI.

Museum of the Bavarian Kings
(Museum der Bayerischen Könige)

About a five-minute walk from the castles' ticket center, in a former grand hotel on the shore of the Alpsee, this modern, well-presented exhibit documents the history of the Wittelsbachs, Bavaria's former royal family. On display are plenty of family portraits and busts, as well as treasures including Ludwig II's outlandish royal robe and elaborately decorated fairy-tale sword, and the impressive dining set given as a golden-anniversary present to his cousin Ludwig III and his wife, the last reigning Wittelsbachs. After losing the throne, the family spoke out against the Nazis, and some were sent to concentration camps as a result. A free audioguide lends some context to the family's history, albeit in more detail than you'll probably want. The museum is worthwhile only if you're captivated by this clan and have time to kill. (But trying to squeeze it between your two castle visits is rushing it —especially if you like to linger.)

Cost and Hours: €11, includes audioguide and map; combo-ticket with Hohenschwangau or Neuschwanstein-€22, with both castles-€31.50; daily 9:00-19:00, Oct-March 10:00-18:00; no reservations required, mandatory lockers, Alpseestrasse 27, tel. 08362/887-250, www.hohenschwangau.de.

▲Tegelberg Cable Car (Tegelbergbahn)

Just north of Neuschwanstein is a fun play zone around the mighty Tegelberg cable car, a scenic ride to the mountain's 5,500-foot summit. At the top on a clear day, you get great views of the Alps and Bavaria and the vicarious thrill of watching hang gliders and paragliders leap into airborne ecstasy. Weather permitting, scores of adventurous Germans line up and leap from the

launch ramp at the top of the lift. With someone leaving every two or three minutes, it's great for spectators. Thrill seekers with exceptional social skills may talk themselves into a tandem ride with a paraglider. From the top of Tegelberg, it's a steep and demanding 2.5-hour hike down to Ludwig's castle. (Avoid the treacherous trail directly below the cable car.) Around the cable car's valley station, you'll find a playground, a cheery eatery, the stubby remains of an ancient Roman villa, and a summer luge ride (described next).

Cost and Hours: €20.60 round-trip, €13.30 one-way; first ascent daily at 9:00; last descent April-Oct at 17:00, mid-Dec-March at 16:00, closed Nov-mid-Dec; 4/hour, 5-minute ride to the top, in bad weather call first to confirm, tel. 08362/98360, www.tegelbergbahn.de.

Getting There: From the castles, most #73 and #78 buses from Füssen continue to the Tegelbergbahn valley station (5-minute ride). It's a 30-minute walk or 10-minute bike ride from the castles.

▲Tegelberg Luge

Next to the cable car's valley station is a summer luge course *(Sommerrodelbahn)*. A summer luge is like a bobsled on wheels (for more details, see "Luge Lesson" on page 204). This course's stainless steel track is heated, so it's often dry and open even when drizzly weather shuts down the concrete luges. A funky cable system pulls riders (in their sleds) to the top without a ski lift. It's not as long, fast, or scenic as Austria's Biberwier luge (described on page 203), but it's handy, harder to get hurt on, and half the price.

Cost and Hours: €3.90/ride, shareable 6-ride card-€16.30; hours typically April-Sept daily 10:00-17:00 depending on weather; call first to confirm, waits can be long in good weather, no children under age 3, ages 3-8 may ride with an adult, tel. 08362/98360, www.tegelbergbahn.de.

SLEEPING NEAR THE KING'S CASTLES

Though best for drivers, both of these places are a quick taxi ride from the Füssen train station and also close to bus stops. In return for paying the Schwangau hotel tax, you get a card with the same benefits as the Füssen Card (see page 148).

$$ Alpenhotel Allgäu is a small, family-run hotel with 18 decent rooms in a bucolic setting perched just below Ludwig's dream castle. It's a 15-minute walk from the castle ticket office and a nice place to frolic when the crowds depart (most rooms with balconies or porches—some with castle views; family rooms, elevator, free parking, just before tennis courts at Schwangauer Strasse 37 in the town of Schwangau—don't let your GPS take you to Schwangauer Strasse 37 in Füssen, tel. 08362/81152, www.alpenhotel-allgaeu.de, info@alpenhotel-allgaeu.de, Frau Reiss).

$ Beim "Landhannes," a 200-year-old working organic dairy farm run by Conny Schön, is a great value for drivers and a unique experience for all. They rent three creaky but sunny rooms and five apartments with kitchenettes, and keep flowers on the balconies, big bells and antlers in the halls, and cows in the yard (cash only, free parking, nearby bike rental, in the village of Horn on the Füssen side of Schwangau—see the "King's Castles Area" map, 100 yards in front of Hotel Kleiner König down a tiny lane through the meadow, Am Lechrain 22, tel. 08362/8349, www.landhannes.de, info@landhannes.de).

EATING NEAR THE KING'S CASTLES

For quick, functional eateries in the immediate castle area, see "Orientation to the King's Castles," earlier.

If you have a car and want to eat at a good-value, nontouristy place with stunning castle views, consider **$$ Schloss Brauhaus,** a sprawling microbrewery restaurant in the village of Schwangau, about 1.5 miles from the castles. They brew five types of beer (dark, light, wheat, and two seasonal brews) and serve classic German fare with limited but hearty vegetarian options. Choose between the woody-industrial interior—with big copper vats and a miniature bowling alley (€8/hour)—and the outdoor *Biergarten,* with minigolf (€5.50, €3/child) and views of Neuschwanstein (food served Mon-Thu 14:00-21:00, Fri-Sun from 11:00; beer served until 23:00; Gipsmühlweg 5 in Schwangau—coming from Füssen, watch for signs on the main street, Füssener Strasse, see the "King's Castles Area" map; tel. 08362/926-4680, www.schlossbrauhaus. de).

Also in Schwangau, try **Sauerwein Alois Café-Konditorei-Bäckerei** for huge, fresh, and cheap sandwiches. They also have tempting pastries (Mon-Fri 6:00-18:00, Sat until 17:00, Sun 13:00-18:00 but no sandwiches, Füssener Strasse 15, tel. 08362/8220). Farther down the road is a **REWE** supermarket, handy for picnic items, hearty sandwiches, hot deli foods, and build-your-own salads (daily 7:00-20:00, König-Ludwig Strasse 2, tel. 08362/98270).

Wieskirche

Germany's greatest Rococo-style church, this "Church in the Meadow"—worth ▲▲—looks as brilliant now as the day it floated down from heaven. Overripe with decoration but bright and bursting with beauty, this church is a divine droplet,

a curly curlicue, the final flowering of the Baroque movement.

GETTING THERE

By **car,** the Wieskirche is a 30-minute drive north of Neuschwanstein or Füssen. Head north, turn right at Steingaden, and follow the brown signs to pay parking. With careful attention to schedules, you can day-trip here from Füssen by **bus** (#73, #9606, or #9651; 2-6/day, 45-60 minutes), but it's a long round-trip for a church that most see in 10-15 minutes.

ORIENTATION TO WIESKIRCHE

Cost and Hours: Donation requested, daily 8:00-20:00, Nov-March until 17:00. The interior is closed to sightseers during services: Sun 8:00-13:00; Tue, Wed, and Sat 10:00-12:00; and Fri 17:00-20:00.

Information: Tel. 08862/932-930, www.wieskirche.de.

Tours: Free tours in English are possible, but must be arranged at least one week in advance by telephone or by fax (fax tel. 08862/932-9310).

Services: Trinket shops, snack stands (one sells freshly made doughnuts—look for *Wieskücherl* sign), and a WC clog the parking area in front of the church; take a commune-with-nature-and-smell-the-farm detour back through the meadow to the parking lot.

VISITING THE CHURCH

This pilgrimage church is built around the much venerated statue of a scourged (or whipped) Christ, which supposedly wept in 1738. The carving—too graphic to be accepted by that generation's Church—was the focus of worship in a peasant's barn. Miraculously, it shed tears—empathizing with all those who suffer. Pilgrims came from all around. A tiny and humble chapel was built to house the statue in 1739. (You can see it where the lane to the church leaves the parking lot.) Bigger and bigger crowds came. Two of Bavaria's top Rococo architects, the Zimmermann brothers (Johann Baptist and Dominikus), were commissioned to build the Wieskirche that stands here today.

Follow the theological sweep from the altar to the ceiling: Jesus whipped, chained, and then killed (notice the pelican above the altar—recalling a pre-Christian story of a bird that opened its

breast to feed its young with its own blood); the painting of Baby Jesus posed as if on the cross; the golden sacrificial lamb; and finally, high on the ceiling, the resurrected Christ before the Last Judgment. This is the most positive depiction of the Last Judgment around. Jesus, rather than sitting on the throne to judge, rides high on a rainbow—a symbol of forgiveness—giving any sinner the feeling that there is still time to repent, with plenty of mercy on hand. In the back, above the pipe organ, notice the closed door to paradise, and at the opposite end (above the main altar), the empty throne—waiting for Judgment Day.

Above the doors flanking the altar are murky glass cases with

18th-century handkerchiefs. People wept, came here, were healed, and no longer needed their hankies. Walk through either of these doors and up an aisle flanking the high altar to see votives—requests and thanks to God (for happy, healthy babies, and healing for sick loved ones). Notice how the kneelers are positioned so that worshippers can meditate on scenes of biblical miracles painted high on the ceiling and visible through the ornate scalloped frames. A priest here once told me that faith, architecture, light, and music all combine to create the harmony of the Wieskirche.

Two paintings flank the door at the rear of the church. The one on the right shows the ceremonial parade in 1749 when the white clad monks of Steingaden carried the carved statue of Christ from the tiny church to its new big one. The second painting (on the left), from 1757, is a votive from one of the Zimmermann brothers, the artists and architects who built this church. He is giving thanks for the successful construction of the new church.

If you can't visit the Wieskirche, visit one of the other churches that came out of the same heavenly spray can: Oberammergau's church, Munich's Asamkirche, Würzburg's Hofkirche Chapel (at the Residenz), the splendid Ettal Monastery (near Oberammergau), and, on a lesser scale, Füssen's basilica.

ROUTE TIPS FOR DRIVERS

Driving from Wieskirche to Oberammergau: Cross the **Echelsbacher Bridge,** which arches 230 feet over the Pöllat Gorge. Thoughtful drivers let their passengers walk across to enjoy the views, then meet them at the other side. Notice the painting of the traditional village woodcarver (who used to walk from town to town with his art on his back) on the first big house on the Oberammergau side. It holds the Almdorf Ammertal shop, with a huge selection of overpriced carvings and commission-hungry tour guides.

Oberammergau

The Shirley Temple of Bavarian villages, and exploited to the hilt by the tourist trade, Oberammergau wears too much makeup. During its famous Passion Play (every 10 years, next in 2020), the crush is unbearable—and the prices at the hotels and restaurants can be as well. The village has about 1,200 beds for the 5,000 playgoers coming daily. But the rest of the

time, Oberammergau—while hardly "undiscovered"—is a pleasant, and at times even sleepy, Bavarian village.

If you're passing through, Oberammergau is a ▲ sight—worth a wander among the half-timbered, frescoed *Lüftlmalerei* houses (see sidebar on page 145). It's also a relatively convenient home base for visiting Linderhof Castle, Ettal Monastery, and the Zugspitze (via Garmisch). A smaller (and less conveniently located) alternative to Füssen and Reutte, it's worth considering for drivers who want to linger in the area. A day trip to Neuschwanstein from Oberammergau is manageable if you have a car, but train travelers do better to stay in Füssen.

GETTING TO OBERAMMERGAU

Trains run from Munich to Oberammergau (nearly hourly, 2 hours, change in Murnau). From Füssen, you can take the **bus** (#9606, 1-3/day, 1.5 hours, bus may start as #73 and change to #9606 en route—confirm with driver that bus is going to Oberammergau). **Drivers** can get here from Reutte in less than 30 minutes via the pretty Plansee lake, or from Munich in about an hour.

Orientation to Oberammergau

This village of about 5,000 feels even smaller, thanks to its remote location. The downtown core, huddled around the onion-domed church, is compact and invites strolling; all of my recommended sights, hotels, and restaurants are within about a 10-minute walk of each other. While the town's name sounds like a mouthful, it's based on the name of the local river (the Ammer) and means, roughly, "Upper Ammerland."

Tourist Information: The helpful, well-organized TI provides English information on area hikes and will store your bags for free during opening hours (Mon-Fri 9:00-18:00, Sat-Sun until 13:00; closed Sun mid-Sept-mid-June, also closed Sat Nov-Dec; Eugen-Papst-Strasse 9A, tel. 08822/922-740, www.oberammergau.de).

Arrival in Oberammergau: The town's train station is a short walk from the center: Turn left, cross the bridge, and you're already downtown.

If you're **driving,** you'll find that there are two exits from the main road into Oberammergau—at the north and south ends. Either way, make your way to the free lot between the TI and the river. While there's ample street parking in town, most is time limited and/or requires payment—be sure to read signs carefully. Hotels and sights are well signed in the town.

Helpful Hints: Travelers staying in the Oberammergau area are entitled to a Gäste-Karte—be sure to ask your hotel for one. The TI has a sheet explaining the card's benefits, such as free travel

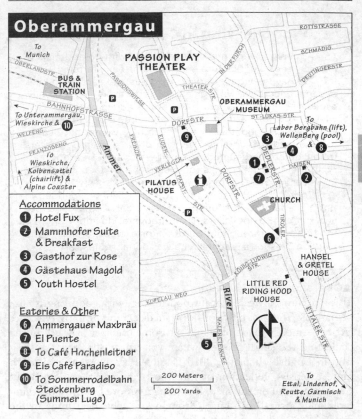

Oberammergau

To Munich

PASSION PLAY THEATER

BUS & TRAIN STATION

BAHNHOFSTRASSE

To Unterammergau, Wieskirche & 🔟

WELFENG.

FRANZOSENG.

To Wieskirche, Kolbensattel (chairlift) & Alpine Coaster

ROTTSTRASSE

SCHMÄDIG

DEUTINGERSTR.

OBERLANDSTR.

PASSIONSWIESE

THEATER STR.

IN DER FURCH

OBERAMMERGAU MUSEUM

DORFSTR.

ST.-LUKAS-STR.

To Laber Bergbahn (lift), WellenBerg (pool) & 🔟

EUGEN-PAPST-STR.

FEIERAG.

VERLEGER

DEDLERSTR.

DAISEN.

DORFSTR.

TIROLER STR.

CHURCH

PILATUS HOUSE

KÖNIG-LUDWIG-STR.

HANSEL & GRETEL HOUSE

KOPELAU WEG

LITTLE RED RIDING HOOD HOUSE

River

MAISENTENWEG

ETTALER STR.

Ammer

Accommodations
1. Hotel Fux
2. Mammhofer Suite & Breakfast
3. Gasthof zur Rose
4. Gästehaus Magold
5. Youth Hostel

Eateries & Other
6. Ammergauer Maxbräu
7. El Puente
8. To Café Hochenleitner
9. Eis Café Paradiso
10. To Sommerrodelbahn Steckenberg (Summer Luge)

200 Meters
200 Yards

To Ettal, Linderhof, Reutte, Garmisch & Munich

on mountain lifts and local buses (including Garmisch, Linderhof, Füssen, and Ettal Monastery) and free admission to the Oberammergau Museum, Passion Play Theater, and WellenBerg swimming pool.

Sights in Oberammergau

▲Local Arts and Crafts

The town's best sight is its woodcarving shops *(Holzschnitzerei)*. Browse through these small art galleries filled with very expensive whittled works. The beautifully frescoed **Pilatus House** at Ludwig-Thoma-Strasse 10 has an open workshop where you can watch woodcarvers and painters at work on summer afternoons (free, late May–mid-Oct Tue-Sun 13:00-17:00, closed Mon and off-season, open weekends in Dec, tel. 08822/949-511). Upstairs in the Pilatus House is a small exhibit of "reverse glass" paintings *(verre églomisé)* that's worth a quick glance.

Woodcarving in Oberammergau

The Ammergau region is relatively poor, with no appreciable industry and no agriculture, save for some dairy farming. What they *do* have is wood. Carving religious and secular themes became a lucrative way for the locals to make some money, especially when confined to the house during the long, cold winter. And with a major pilgrimage site—Ettal Monastery—just down the road, there was a built-in consumer base eager to buy hand-carved crucifixes and other souvenirs. Carvers from Oberammergau peddled their wares across Europe, carrying them on their backs (on distinctive wooden backpack-racks called *Kraxe*) as far away as Rome.

Today, the Oberammergau Carving School (founded in 1887) is a famous institution that takes only 20 students per year out of 450 applicants. Their graduates do important restoration work throughout Europe. For example, much of the work on Dresden's Frauenkirche was done by these artists.

▲Oberammergau Museum

This museum showcases local woodcarving, with good English explanations. The ground floor has a small exhibit of nativity scenes (*Krippe*—mostly made of wood, but some of paper or wax). In the back, find the small theater, where you can watch an interesting film in English about the 2010 Passion Play. Upstairs is a much more extensive collection of the wood carvings that helped put Oberammergau on the map, including a room of old woodcarving tools, plus a small exhibit on Roman archaeological finds in the region. Your ticket also lets you into the lobby of the Passion Play Theater, described next.

Cost and Hours: €3.50; €6 combo-ticket includes museum and theater lobby; Easter-Oct and Dec-mid-Jan Tue-Sun 10:00-17:00, closed Mon and off-season; Dorfstrasse 8, tel. 08822/94136, www.oberammergaumuseum.de.

Passion Play Theater (Festspielhaus)

Back in 1633, in the midst of the bloody Thirty Years' War and with horrifying plagues devastating entire cities, the people of Oberammergau promised God that if they were spared from extinction, they'd "perform a play depicting the suffering, death, and resurrection of our Lord Jesus Christ" every decade thereafter. The town survived, and as it heads into its 42nd decade, the people of Oberammergau are still making good on the deal. For 100 days every 10 years, about half of the town's population (a cast of 2,000) are involved in the production of this extravagant five-hour Passion Play—telling the story of Jesus' entry into Jerusalem, the Crucifixion, and the Resurrection.

If you're not visiting during the Passion Play performances, you'll have to settle for reading the book, seeing Nicodemus tool around town in his VW, or taking a quick look at the theater, a block from the center of town.

Visiting the Theater: The theater lobby hosts a modest exhibit on the history of the performances. A long wall of photographs of past performers shows the many generations of Oberammergauers who have participated in this tradition. Climb the stairs and peek into the theater itself, which has an unusual indoor/outdoor design and a real-life alpine backdrop.

To learn more, take a 45-minute guided tour of the theater, organized by the museum (€3.50, €6 combo-ticket with Oberammergau Museum, €8 with guided tour; tours run Easter-Oct only, Tue-Sun at 11:00 in English, additional tour times in German; theater open same hours as museum, tel. 08822/94136, www.oberammergaumuseum.de).

Oberammergau Church

The town church is typical Bavarian Baroque but a poor cousin of the one at Wieskirche not too far from here. Being in a woodcarving center, it's only logical that all the statues are made of wood and then stuccoed and gilded to look like marble or gold. Saints Peter and Paul flank the altar, where the central painting can be raised to reveal a small stage decorated to celebrate special times during the church calendar. In the central dome, a touching painting shows Peter and Paul bidding each other farewell (with the city of Rome as a backdrop) on the day of their execution—the same day, in the year AD 67. On the left, Peter is crucified upside-down. On the right, Paul is beheaded with a sword. On your way out look for the wooden cross once used in the Passion Play (open daily 8:00-19:30).

Wander through the lovingly maintained **graveyard,** noticing the wide variety in headstones. A towering stone WWI memorial at the gate has an imposing look and sternly worded celebrations of the "heroes" of that war. But around the other side, below it on the outer fence, find the newer glass panel that modifies the sentiment: "We honor and remember the victims of the violence that our land gave the world."

Lüftlmalerei Painted Houses

Wealthy merchants, farmers, and artisans had their houses painted using a special fresco technique called *Lüftlmalerei* that still sets Oberammergau apart today (see sidebar). The motifs are mostly biblical scenes and famous fairy-tale characters. While you'll see plenty of these houses, locals recommend the "Little Red Riding Hood" and "Hansel and Gretel" houses on Ettaler Strasse, the

Passion Play 2020

Anticipation is high for the once-a-decade experience encompassing spirituality and entertainment: Oberammergau's Passion Play. Its 2020 run is from May 16 through October 4. Tickets are so in demand that bookings went on sale more than two years before its opening day.

Throughout the run, the tiny village expects some 450,000 visitors—about half from outside Germany. Performances are five hours long and take place five days a week. The play begins in the afternoon, pauses for a three-hour dinner break, and lets out late in the evening (mid-May-mid-Aug 14:30-22:30, from mid-Aug 13:30-21:30). While this experience is a big investment in money, time, and energy, those who've seen it say it's unforgettably moving and well worth it.

Tickets are easiest to obtain in a one- or two-night package deal that includes hotel, ticket, dinner, shuttle, and a book (€324-1,000+, tel. 08822/949-8857, www.passionsspiele-oberammergau.de). Travelers will most likely have difficulty booking hotel rooms on their own during the Passion Play performance dates (though apartment rentals or pensions are still sometimes possible).

main drag into town (see "Oberammergau" map). If you want to see more, ask the TI for a map.

NEAR OBERAMMERGAU

These attractions are a long walk from town but easy to reach by car or bike.

Mountain Lifts, Luges, and More

Laber Bergbahn, a gondola that lifts you up to fine views, is at the east end of town. For an easy hike take the lift up and walk down in about 2.5 hours (www.laber-bergbahn.de).

Kolbensattel, across town to the west, is a family-friendly park with a chairlift, a mountain playground, a high-ropes course, and a speedy 1.5-mile-long **Alpine Coaster** (similar to a luge, closed off-season; €7.50 each for chairlift or coaster, €11.50 coaster combo-ticket with lift, €26 combo-ticket for coaster, ropes course, and lift, daily April-Nov 10:00-17:00 in good weather, tel. 08822/4760, www.kolbensattel.de). From the top, you can hike along the ridge to a series of mountain huts: In about 1.5 hours, you'll reach Pürschling; two hours later is Brunnenkopf (from which you could hike down to Linderhof Castle). Get tips and maps from the TI before doing these hikes.

WellenBerg Swimming Pool
Near the Laber Bergbahn lift and a 25-minute walk from town is this sprawling complex of indoor and outdoor pools and saunas (€8/3 hours, €12/day, €4.50 extra for sauna, daily 10:00-21:00, Himmelreich 52, tel. 08822/92360, www.wellenberg-oberammergau.de).

Sommerrodelbahn Steckenberg
The next town over, Unterammergau, hosts a stainless steel summer luge track that's faster than the Tegelberg luge but not nearly as wicked as the one in Biberwier. This one has double seats (allowing a parent to accompany kids) and two sticks—one for each hand; be careful of your elbows. Unlike other luges, children under age three are allowed, and you only pay one fare when a parent and child ride together.

Cost and Hours: €3.50/ride, €15/6 rides; May-late Oct Mon-Fri 13:00-17:00, Sat-Sun 10:00-18:00, closed off-season and when wet; Liftweg 1 in Unterammergau, clearly marked and easy 2.5-mile bike ride to Unterammergau along Bahnhofstrasse/Rottenbucherstrasse, take the first left when entering Unterammergau, tel. 08822/4027, www.steckenberg.de.

Sleeping in Oberammergau

Accommodations in Oberammergau tend to be affordable (compared to Füssen or Reutte) and friendly. All offer free parking. I've ranked these based on summer prices (generally May-Oct).

$$ Hotel Fux—quiet, romantic, and well run—rents 10 large rooms and six apartments decorated in the Bavarian *Landhaus* style (free sauna, indoor playground, Mannagasse 2a, tel. 08822/93093, www.hotel-in-oberammergau.de, info@firmafux.de).

$$ Mammhofer Suite & Breakfast, run by friendly Josef, offers nine contemporary-Bavarian rooms (mostly suites and most with views) in a quiet, residential neighborhood just across the street from the town center (Daisenbergerstrasse 10, tel. 08822/923-753, www.mammhofer.com, stay@mammhofer.com).

$ Gasthof zur Rose is big and centrally located, with 19 mostly small but comfortable rooms run by the friendly Frank family. At the reception desk, look at the several decades' worth of photos showing the family performing in the Passion Play (family rooms, Dedlerstrasse 9, tel. 08822/4706, www.rose-oberammergau.de, info@rose-oberammergau.de).

$ Gästehaus Magold, homey and family-friendly, has three bright and spacious rooms and two apartments—twice as nice as the cheap hotel rooms in town, and for much less (cash only, immediately behind Gasthof zur Rose at Kleppergasse 1, tel. 08822/4340, www.gaestehaus-magold.de, info@gaestehaus-magold.de, hard-working Christine).

¢ **Oberammergau Youth Hostel,** on the river, is just a short walk from the center (family rooms, reception open 8:00-10:00 & 17:00-19:00, closed mid-Nov-Dec, Malensteinweg 10, tel. 08822/4114, www.oberammergau.jugendherberge.de, oberammergau@jugendherberge.de).

Eating in Oberammergau

$$$ Ammergauer Maxbräu, in the Hotel Maximilian on the edge of downtown, serves high-quality, thoughtfully presented Bavarian fare with a modern, international twist. The rustic-yet-mod interior—with big copper vats where they brew their own beer—is cozy on a rainy day. And in nice weather, locals fill the beer garden out front (daily 11:00-22:00, right behind the church, Ettaler Strasse 5, tel. 08822/948-740, www.maximilian-oberammergau.de).

$$ Gasthof zur Rose, a couple of blocks off the main drag, serves reasonably priced Bavarian food in its dining room and at a few outdoor tables (Tue-Sun 11:30-14:00 & 17:30-21:00, closed Mon, Dedlerstrasse 9, tel. 08822/4706, www.rose-oberammergau. de).

$$ El Puente may vex Mexican-food purists, but it's the most hopping place in town, with margaritas and cocktails attracting young locals and tourists alike. Come not for the burritos and enchiladas but for the bustling energy (pricier steaks, Mon-Sat 18:00-23:30, closed Sun, Daisenbergerstrasse 3, tel. 08822/945-777).

$ Café Hochenleitner, just a few minutes from the center, is quiet with nice outdoor seating and run by a family whose young son is winning awards for his creative confections (Tue-Sun 12:00-18:00, closed Mon, Faistenmantlgasse 7, tel. 08822/1312).

Dessert: Eis Café Paradiso serves up good gelato along the main street. In nice weather, Germans sunbathe with their big €5 sundaes on the generous patio out front (daily 9:00-23:00 in summer, Dorfstrasse 4, tel. 08822/6279).

Oberammergau Connections

From Oberammergau to: Linderhof Castle (bus #9622, 5-6/day Mon-Fri, 4/day Sat-Sun, 30 minutes; many of these also stop at **Ettal Monastery**), **Hohenschwangau** (for Neuschwanstein) and **Füssen** (bus #9606, 3-4/day, 1.5 hours, some transfer or change number to #73 at Echelsbacher Brücke), **Garmisch** (bus #9606, nearly hourly, better frequency in morning, 40 minutes; possible by train with transfer in Murnau, 1.5 hours; from Garmisch, you can ascend the **Zugspitze**), **Munich** (nearly hourly trains, 2 hours, change in Murnau). Train info: www.bahn.com.

Linderhof Castle

This homiest of "Mad" King Ludwig's castles is a small, comfortably ex-quisite mini Versailles—good enough for a minor god, and worth ▲▲. Set in the woods 15 minutes from Oberammergau and surrounded by fountains and sculpted, Italian-style gardens, it's the only palace I've toured that actually had me feeling envious.

BAVARIAN ALPS

GETTING THERE

Without a car, getting to (and back from) Linderhof is a royal headache, unless you're staying in Oberammergau. Buses from Oberammergau take 30 minutes (#9622, 5-6/day Mon-Fri, 4/day Sat-Sun). If you're driving, pay to park near the ticket office. If driving from Reutte, take the scenic Plansee route.

ORIENTATION TO LINDERHOF CASTLE

Cost: €8.50, €7.50 in winter

Hours: Daily April-mid-Oct 9:00-18:00, mid-Oct-March 10:00-16:30. Outlying buildings are closed mid-Oct-mid-April.

Information: Tel. 08822/92030, www.linderhof.de.

Crowd-Beating Tips: July and August crowds can mean an hour's wait between when you buy your ticket and when you start your tour. It's most crowded in the late morning. During this period, you're wise to arrive after 15:00. Any other time of year, your wait to tour the palace should be brief. If you do wind up with time to kill, consider it a blessing—the gardens are fun to explore, and some of the smaller buildings can be seen quickly while you're waiting for your appointment.

Sightseeing Tips and Procedure: The complex sits isolated in nat-ural splendor. Plan for lots of walking and a two-hour stop to fully enjoy this royal park. Bring rain gear in iffy weather. Your ticket comes with an entry time to tour the palace, which is a 10-minute walk from the ticket office. At the palace entrance, wait in line at the turnstile listed on your ticket (A through D) to take the required 30-minute English tour. Afterward, ex-plore the rest of the park (grotto closed through 2021) and the other royal buildings dotting the king's playground if you like. You can eat lunch at a **$$** café across from the ticket office.

Renovations: Expect cranes and construction equipment on the grounds while the grotto behind the palace undergoes restoration.

VISITING THE CASTLE

The main attraction here is the **palace** itself. While Neuschwanstein is Neo-Gothic—romanticizing the medieval glory days of Bavaria —Linderhof is Baroque and Rococo, the frilly, overly ornamented styles more associated with Louis XIV, the "Sun King" of France. And, while Neuschwanstein is full of swans, here you'll see fleur-de-lis (the symbol of French royalty) and multiple portraits of Louis XIV, Louis XV, Madame Pompadour, and other pre-Revolutionary French elites. Though they lived a century apart, Ludwig and Louis were spiritual contemporaries: Both clung to the notion of absolute monarchy, despite the realities of the changing world around them. Capping the palace roofline is one of Ludwig's favorite symbols:

Atlas, with the weight of the world literally on his shoulders. Oh, those poor, overburdened, misunderstood absolute monarchs!

Ludwig was king for 22 of his 40 years. He lived much of his last eight years here—the only one of his castles that was finished in his lifetime. Frustrated by the limits of being a "constitutional monarch," he retreated to Linderhof, inhabiting a private fantasy world where extravagant castles glorified his otherwise weakened kingship. You'll notice that the castle is small—designed for a single occupant. Ludwig, who never married or had children, lived here as a royal hermit.

The castle tour includes 10 rooms on the upper floor. (The downstairs, where the servants lived and worked, now houses the gift shop.) You'll see room after room exquisitely carved with Rococo curlicues, wrapped in gold leaf. Up above, the ceiling paintings have 3-D legs sticking out of the frame. Clearly inspired by Versailles, Linderhof even has its own (much smaller) hall of mirrors—decorated with over a hundred Nymphenburg porcelain vases and a priceless ivory chandelier. The bedroom features an oversized crystal chandelier, delicate Meissen porcelain flowers framing the mirrors, and a literally king-size bed—a two-story canopy affair draped in blue velvet. Perhaps the most poignant sight, a sad commentary on Ludwig's tragically solitary lifestyle, is his dinner table—preset with dishes and food—which could rise from the kitchen below into his dining room so he could eat alone. (Examine the incredibly delicate flowers in the Meissen porcelain centerpiece.)

The palace is flanked on both sides with grand, terraced **fountains** (peopled by gleaming golden gods) that erupt at the top and bottom of each hour. If you're waiting for your palace tour to begin, hike up to the top of the terrace for a fine view.

Ludwig's **grotto,** behind the palace, is currently undergoing restoration work. Inspired by Wagner's *Tannhäuser* opera, this artificial cave (300 feet long and 70 feet tall) is actually a performance space. Its rocky walls are made of cement poured over an iron frame. (While Ludwig exalted the distant past, he took full advantage of then-cutting-edge technology to bring his

fantasies to life.) The grotto provided a private theater for the reclusive king to enjoy his beloved Wagnerian operas—he was usually the sole member of the audience. The grotto features a waterfall, fake stalactites, and a swan boat floating on an artificial lake (which could be heated for swimming). Brick ovens hidden in the walls could be used to heat the huge space. The first electricity in Bavaria was generated here, to change the colors of the stage lights and to power Ludwig's fountain and wave machine.

Other Sights at Linderhof: Several other smaller buildings are scattered around the grounds; look for posted maps and directional signs to track them down. Most interesting are the **Moroccan House** and **Moorish Kiosk.** With over-the-top decor seemingly designed by a sultan's decorator on acid, these allowed Ludwig to "travel" to exotic lands without leaving the comfort of Bavaria. (The Moorish Kiosk is more interesting; look for its gilded dome in the woods beyond the grotto.) At the far edge of the property is **Hunding's Hut,** inspired by Wagner's *The Valkyrie*—a rustic-cottage stage-set with a fake ash tree inside it. And closer to the entrance—along the path between the ticket booth and the palace—is the **King's Cottage,** used for special exhibitions (often with an extra charge).

Ettal Monastery

In 1328, the Holy Roman Emperor was returning from Rome with what was considered a miraculous statue of Mary and Jesus. He was in political and financial trouble, so to please God, he founded a monastery with this statue as its centerpiece. The monastery, located here because it was suitably off the beaten path, became important as a place of pilgrimage, and today Ettal is on one of the most traveled tourist routes in Bavaria. Stopping here (free

and easy for drivers) offers a convenient peek at a splendid Baroque church, worth ▲. Restaurants across the road serve lunch.

GETTING THERE

Ettal Monastery dominates the village of Ettal—you can't miss it. Ettal is a few minutes' **drive** (or a delightful **bike** ride) from Oberammergau. Just park (€1/4 hours in larger lots; free in small, crowded lot near the *Klosterladen*, alongside the building) and wander in. Some Oberammergau-to-Linderhof **buses** stop here (see "Oberammergau Connections," earlier).

ORIENTATION TO ETTAL MONASTERY

Cost and Hours: The church is free and open daily 8:00-19:45 in summer, until 18:00 off-season. It's best not to visit during Mass (usually Sun at 9:30 and 11:00). If you're moved to make a donation, you can drop a coin in one of the old-fashioned collection boxes.

Information: Tel. 08822/740, www.kloster-ettal.de.

VISITING THE MONASTERY

As you enter the more than 1,000-square-foot **courtyard**, imagine the 14th-century Benedictine abbey, an independent religious community. It produced everything it needed right here. In the late Middle Ages, abbeys like this had jurisdiction over the legal system, administration, and taxation of their district. Since then, the monastery has had its ups and downs. Secularized during the French Revolution and Napoleonic age, the

20 + C + M + B + 20

All over Germany (and much of Catholic Europe), you'll likely see written on doorways a mysterious message: "20 + C + M + B + 20." This is marked in chalk on Epiphany (Jan 6), the Christian holiday celebrating the arrival of the Magi to adore the newborn Baby Jesus. In addition to being the initials of the three wise men (Caspar, Melchior, and Balthazar), the letters also stand for the Latin phrase *Christus mansionem benedicat*—"May Christ bless the house." The numbers represent the year (20+20), and the little crosses remind all who enter that the house has been blessed in this year. Epiphany is a bigger deal in Catholic Europe than in the US. The holiday includes gift-giving, feasting, and caroling door to door—often collecting for a charity organization. Those who donate get their doors chalked up in thanks, and these marks are left on the door through the year.

Benedictines' property was confiscated by the state and sold. Religious life returned a century later. Today the abbey survives, with 50 or 60 monks. It remains a self-contained community, with living quarters for the monks, workshops, and guests' quarters. Along with their religious responsibilities, the brothers make their famous liqueur, brew beer, run a hotel, and educate 380 students in their private high school. The monks' wares are for sale at two shops (look for the *Klosterladen* by the courtyard or the *Kloster-Markt* across the street).

After entering the outer door, notice the **tympanum** over the inner door dating from 1350. It shows the founding couple, Emperor Louis the Bavarian and his wife Margaret, directing our attention to the crucified Lord and inviting us to enter the church contemplatively.

Stepping inside, the light draws our eyes to the **dome** (it's a double-shell design, 230 feet high) rather than to the high altar. Illusions—with the dome opening right to the sky—merge heaven and earth. The dome fresco shows hundreds of Benedictines worshipping the Holy Trinity...the glory of the Benedictine Order. This is classic "south-German Baroque."

Statues of the **saints** on the altars are either engaged in a holy conversation with each other or singing the praises of God. Gilded curlicues seem to create constant movement, with cherubs adding to the energy. Side altars and confessionals seem to grow out of the architectural structure; its decorations and furnishings become part of an organic whole. Imagine how 18th-century farmers and woodcutters, who never traveled, would step in here on Sunday and be inspired to praise their God.

The origin of the monastery is shown over the **choir arch** directly above the altar: An angel wearing the robe of a Benedictine monk presents the emperor with a marble Madonna and commissions him to found this monastery. (In reality, the statue was made in Pisa, circa 1300, and given to the emperor in Italy.)

Dwarfed by all the magnificence and framed by a monumental tabernacle is that tiny, most precious statue of the abbey—the miraculous **statue of Mary and the Baby Jesus.**

Nearby: The fragrant **demonstration dairy** *(Schaukäserei)* about a five-minute walk behind the monastery is worth a quick look. The farmhouse displays all the steps in the production line, starting with the cows themselves (next to the house), to the factory staff hard at work, and through to the end products, which you can sample in the shop (try the beer cheese). Better yet, enjoy a snack on the deck while listening to the sweet music/incessant clanging of cowbells (free; daily 10:00-17:00, off-season closed Mon; best cheese-making action 10:00-11:00; Mandlweg 1, tel. 08822/923-926, www.schaukaeserei-ettal.de). To walk there from the monastery's exit, take a left and go through the passageway; take another left when you get to the road, then yet another left at the first street (you'll see it up the road, directly behind the abbey).

Zugspitze

The tallest point in Germany, worth ▲▲ in clear weather, is also a border crossing. Lifts from both Austria and Germany meet at the 9,700-foot summit of the Zugspitze (TSOOG-shpit-seh). You can straddle the border between two great nations while enjoying an incredible view. Restaurants, shops,  and telescopes await you at the summit.

SUMMITING THE ZUGSPITZE

German Approach: There are several ways to ascend from this side, but they all cost the same (€58 round-trip, less in winter, tel. 08821/7970, www.zugspitze.de).

If relying on public transit, first head to Garmisch (for details on getting there from Füssen, see "Füssen Connections," earlier; from Oberammergau, see "Oberammergau Connections," earlier). From there, ride a train to Eibsee (30 minutes, hourly departures daily 8:15-14:15), at which point you have a choice. You can walk across the parking lot and zip up to the top in a cable car (10 minutes, daily 8:30-16:45, departs at least every 30 minutes; in busy times departs every 10 minutes, but since each car fits only 35—which the electronic board suspensefully counts down as each passenger goes through the turnstile—you may have to wait to board). Or you can transfer to a cogwheel train (45 minutes to the top, departs hourly—coordinated with Garmisch train; once up top, transfer from the train to a short cable car for the quick, 3-minute ascent to the summit).

Drivers can go straight to Eibsee (about 10 minutes beyond Garmisch—head through town following signs for *Fernpass/ Reutte*, and watch for the Zugspitze turnoff on the left); once there, you have the same cable car vs. cog railway choice described above. (Even though they're not taking the train from Garmisch, drivers pay the same—€58 round-trip, plus another €4 for parking.)

You can choose how you want to go up and down at the spur of the moment: both ways by cable car, both by cog train, or mix and match. Although the train ride takes longer, many travelers enjoy the more involved cog railway experience—at least one way. The disadvantage of the train is that more than half of the trip is through dark tunnels deep in the mountains; aside from a few fleeting glimpses of the Eibsee sparkling below, it's not very scenic.

Arriving at the top, you'll want to head up to the third floor (elevators recommended, given the high altitude)—follow signs for *Gipfel* (summit).

To get back down to Eibsee, keep in mind that the last cable car departs the summit at 16:45, and the last cogwheel train at 16:30. On busy days, you may have to reserve a return time once you reach the top—if it's crowded, look for signs and prebook your return to avoid getting stuck up top longer than you want. In general, allow plenty of time for afternoon descents: If bad weather hits in the late afternoon, cable cars can be delayed at the summit, causing tourists to miss their train connection from Eibsee back to Garmisch.

Hikers can enjoy the easy six-mile walk around the lovely Eibsee (start 5 minutes downhill from cable car station).

Austrian Approach: The Tiroler Zugspitzbahn ascent is less crowded and cheaper than the Bavarian one. Make your way to the village of Ehrwald (drivers follow signs for *Tiroler Zugspitzbahn;* free parking). Departing from above Ehrwald, a lift zips you to the top in 10 minutes (€46.50 round-trip, departures in each direction at :00, :20, and :40 past the hour, daily 8:40-16:40 except

closed during bad weather May-
June and Oct-Nov, last ascent at
16:00, Austrian tel. 05673/2309,
www.zugspitze.at). While those
without a car will find the German ascent from Garmisch easier, the Austrian ascent is also
doable. It's a 30-minute train
trip from Reutte to Ehrwald
(train runs every 2 hours); then

either hop the bus from the Ehrwald train station to the lift (departures nearly hourly), or pay about €10 for the five-minute taxi ride
from the train station.

VISITING THE SUMMIT

Whether you've ascended from the Austrian or German side,
you're high enough now to enjoy a little tour of the summit. The
two terraces—Bavarian and Tirolean—are connected by a narrow
walkway, which was the border station before Germany and Austria opened their borders. The Austrian (Tirolean) side was higher
until the Germans blew its top off in World War II to make a flak
tower, so let's start there.

Tirolean Terrace: Before you stretches the Zugspitzplatt
glacier. Is it melting? A reflector once stood here to slow it from
shrinking during summer months. Many ski lifts fan out here, as
if reaching for a ridge that defines the border between Germany
and Austria. The circular metal building is the top of the cog railway line that the Germans cut through the mountains in 1931.
Just above that, find a small square building—the *Hochzeitskapelle*
(wedding chapel) consecrated in 1981 by Cardinal Joseph Ratzinger (a.k.a. the retired Pope Benedict XVI).

Both Germany and Austria use this rocky pinnacle for communication purposes. The square box on the Tirolean Terrace provides the Innsbruck airport with air traffic control, and a tower
nearby is for the German *Katastrophenfunk* (civil defense network).

This highest point in Germany (there are many higher points
in Austria) was first climbed in 1820. The Austrians built a cable
car that nearly reached the summit in 1926. (You can see it just over
the ridge on the Austrian side—look for the ghostly, abandoned
concrete station.) In 1964, the final leg, a new lift, was built connecting that 1926 station to the actual summit, where you stand
now. Before then, people needed to hike the last 650 feet to the top.
Today's lift carries half a million people up to the Zugspitze every
year. The Austrian station, which is much nicer than the German
station, has a fine little museum—free with Austrian ticket, €4 if
you came up from Germany—that shows three interesting vid-

eos (6-minute 3-D mountain show, 30-minute making-of-the-lift documentary, and 45-minute look at the nature, sport, and culture of the region).

Looking up the valley from the Tirolean Terrace, you can see the towns of Ehrwald and Lermoos in the distance, and the valley that leads to Reutte. Looking farther clockwise, you'll see the Eibsee below. Hell's Valley, stretching to the right of the Eibsee, seems to merit its name.

Bavarian Terrace: The narrow passage connecting the two terraces used to be a big deal—you'd show your passport here at the little blue house and shift from Austrian schillings to German marks. Notice the regional pride here: no German or Austrian national banners, but regional ones instead—*Freistaat Bayern* (Bavaria) and *Land Tirol*.

The German side features a golden cross marking the summit...the highest point in Germany. A priest and his friends hauled it up in 1851. The historic original was shot up by American soldiers using it for target practice in the late 1940s, so what you see today is a modern replacement. In the summer, it's easy to "summit" the Zugspitze, as there are steps and handholds all the way to the top. Or you can just stay behind and feed the birds. The yellow-beaked ravens get chummy with those who share a little pretzel or bread. Below the terrace, notice the restaurant that claims—irrefutably—to be the "highest *Biergarten* in Deutschland."

The oldest building up here is the first mountaineers' hut, built in 1897 and entwined with mighty cables that cinch it down. In 1985, observers clocked 200-mph winds up here—those cables were necessary. Step inside the restaurant to enjoy museum-like photos and paintings on the wall (including a look at the team who hiked up with the golden cross in 1851).

Near the waiting area for the cable cars and cogwheel train is a little museum (in German only) that's worth a look if you have some time to kill before heading back down. If you're going down on the German side, remember you must choose between the cable car (look for the *Eibsee* signs) or cog railway (look for *Talfahrt/Descent*, with a picture of a train; you'll board a smaller cable car for the quick trip to the train station).

Reutte, Austria

Reutte (ROY-teh, with a guttural *r*), a relaxed Austrian town of 6,000, is a 20-minute drive across the border from Füssen. While overlooked by the international tourist crowd, it's popular with Germans and Austrians for its climate. Doctors recommend its "grade 1" air.

Although its setting—surrounded by alpine peaks—is striking, the town itself is pretty unexceptional. But that's the point. I enjoy Reutte for the opportunity it offers to simply be in a real community. As an example of how the town is committed to its character, real estate can be sold only to those using it as a primary residence. (Many formerly vibrant alpine towns made a pile of money but lost their sense of community by becoming resorts. They allowed wealthy foreigners—who just drop in for a week or two a year—to buy up all the land, and are now shuttered up and dead most of the time.)

Reutte has one claim to fame among Americans: As Nazi Germany was falling in 1945, Hitler's top rocket scientist, Werner von Braun, joined the Americans (rather than the Russians) in Reutte. You could say that the American space program began here.

Reutte isn't featured in any other American guidebook. Its charms are subtle. It was never rich or important. Its castle is ruined, its buildings have painted-on "carvings," its churches are full, its men yodel for each other on birthdays, and its energy is spent soaking its Austrian and German guests in *Gemütlichkeit* (cozy conviviality). Most guests stay for a week, so the town's attractions are more time-consuming than thrilling.

Some travelers tell me this town is over-Reutte-d. Füssen's tidy pedestrian core and glitzy hotels make it an easier home base. But in my view, Reutte's two big trump cards are its fine countryside accommodations (the farther from the town center, the more rustic, authentic, and relaxing) and its proximity to one of my favorite ruined castles, Ehrenberg. Since you need a car to take best advantage of these pluses (as well as to reach the King's Castles quickly), Reutte is a good place for drivers to spend the night.

Orientation to Reutte

Reutte feels spread out, because it's really a web of several villages that fill a basin hemmed in by mountains and cut through by the Lech River. Drivers find its tangle of crisscrossing roads bewildering at first; know where you're going and follow signs to stay on track (see the "Greater Reutte" map).

Reutte proper, near the train station, has a one-street downtown where you'll find the TI, museum, and a couple of hotels and eateries. The area's real charm lies in the abutting hamlets, and that's where my favorite hotels and restaurants are located: **Breitenwang,** flowing directly from Reutte to the east, marked by its pointy steeple; **Ehenbichl,** a farming village cuddled up against the mountains to the south; **Höfen,** squeezed between an airstrip and a cable car station, just across the river from Ehenbichl; and remote **Pinswang,** stranded in a forgotten valley halfway to Germany, just over the mountain from Neuschwanstein. Watching over it all to the south are the **Ehrenberg Castle** ruins—viewable from just about everywhere and evocatively floodlit at night—two miles out of town on the main Innsbruck road.

TOURIST INFORMATION

Reutte's TI is a block from the train station (Mon-Fri 8:00-18:00, Sat 9:00-12:30 & 13:00-18:00, off-season Mon-Fri 8:00-17:00, Sat 10:00-14:00, closed Sun year-round, Untermarkt 34, tel. 05672/62336, www.reutte.com). Go over your sightseeing plans, ask about a Tirolean folk evening performance (summer only), and pick up city and biking/hiking maps, bus schedules, the *Griiss Enk* twice-yearly events schedule (in German and English), a free town info booklet (with a good self-guided walk), and a brochure explaining the Aktiv-Card (available at hotels; described later, under "Helpful Hints").

ARRIVAL IN REUTTE

By Car: From the expressway, always take the south *(Süd)* exit into town (even if you pass the *Nord* exit first). For parking in town, blue lines denote pay-and-display spots. There are a few spaces just outside the TI that are free for up to 30 minutes—handy for stopping by with a few questions en route to your out-of-town hotel. For longer stays, there's a free lot (P-1) just past the train station on Mühler Strasse (about a 10-minute walk from the town center and TI).

While Austria requires a **toll sticker** *(Vignette)* for driving on its expressways (€9/10 days, buy at the border, gas stations, car-rental agencies, or *Tabak* shops), those just dipping into Tirol from Bavaria don't need one—even on the expressway-like bypass around Reutte.

By Train or Bus: When traveling by train make sure to get off at Reutte Bahnhof, not Reutte Schulzentrum. From the tidy little train/bus station (no baggage storage, usually unstaffed), exit straight ahead and walk three minutes straight up Bahnhofstrasse. After the park on your left, you'll see the TI.

HELPFUL HINTS

Welcome to Austria: Remember, Reutte is in Austria. If calling from a German phone number to an Austrian one, dial 00-43 and then the number (omitting the initial zero). To call from an Austrian phone to a German one, dial 00-49 and then the number (again, omitting the initial zero; see page 996 for dialing instructions).

Hotel Card: Guests staying in the Reutte area (and, therefore, paying the local hotel tax) are entitled to an **Aktiv-Card**—be sure to ask your hotel for one. The TI has a brochure explaining the card's benefits, including free travel on some local buses, low-cost taxi service on most routes in high season, free admission to the recommended museum below Ehrenberg Castle, 50 percent off the Alpentherme bath complex, plus free days and discounts on many outdoor activities.

Laundry: There's no launderette, but a couple of recommended hotels let nonguests use their laundry services: **Hotel Maximilian** (wash, dry, and fold) and **Alpenhotel Ernberg** (self-service).

Bike Rental: Try **Sport 2000 Paulweber** (city bike-€20/day, mountain bike-€25/day, electric bike-€30-35/day, Mon-Fri 8:30-12:00 & 14:00-18:00, Sat 8:30-12:00, closed Sun, Allgäuer Strasse 15, tel. 05672/62232), or check at the Hotel Maximilian.

Taxi: Inexpensive taxi service is available to hotel guests with an Aktiv-Card (described earlier). Those without a card can call **Reutte Taxi** (tel. 0699-1050-4949).

Sights in and near Reutte

▲▲EHRENBERG CASTLE ENSEMBLE

If Neuschwanstein was the medieval castle dream, Ehrenberg *(Festungsensemble Ehrenberg)* is the medieval castle reality. Once the largest fortification in Tirol, its brooding ruins lie about two miles outside Reutte. What's here is actually an "ensemble" of four castles, built to defend against the Bavarians and to bottle up the strategic Via Claudia trade route, which cut through the Alps as it connected Italy and Germany. Half-forgotten and overgrown only a decade ago, they've been transformed into a fine attraction with hiking paths, a museum, guesthouse, and a recent addition: a 1,200-foot pedestrian suspension bridge. The European Union helped fund the project because it promotes the heritage of a multinational region—Tirol—rather than a country.

In Roman times, the Via Claudia—the road below Ehrenberg—was the main route between northern Italy (Verona) and southern Germany (Augsburg), and was broad enough for wheeled traffic. Historians estimate that in medieval times, about 10,000 tons of precious salt passed through this valley each year, so it's no wonder the locals built this complex of fortresses and castles to control traffic and levy tolls on all who passed.

Ehrnberger Clause. *Schloß Ehrnberg*

The complex has four parts: the old toll buildings on the valley floor, where you park (the Klause); the oldest castle, on the hilltop directly above (Ehrenberg); a mightier castle on a higher peak of the same hill (Schlosskopf); and a smaller fortification across the valley (Fort Claudia). All four were once a single complex connected by walls. Signs posted throughout the site help orient visitors and explain some background on the region's history, geology, flora, and fauna, and colorful, fun boards relate local folktales.

Cost and Hours: The castle ruins themselves are free and always open, but the museum and suspension bridge charge admission (for details, see individual listings).

Information and Services: A helpful information desk has maps of trails leading up to the castle. Take advantage of the WC stop before you begin your ascent.

Getting There: The castles are on the road to Lermoos and Innsbruck, just five minutes by **car** from Reutte (parking-€4/day). It's a pleasant but steep 30-minute **walk** or a short **bike** ride from town; bikers can use the *Radwanderweg* along the Lech River (the TI has a good map).

Local **bus** #4250 runs sporadically from Reutte's main train station to Ehrenberg (5-8/day Mon-Sat, 1-3/day Sun, 10 minutes, €2.90; see www.vvt.at for schedules—the stop name is "Ehrenberger Klause"). However, no buses run directly *back* to Reutte from the castle. If you aren't driving, a taxi is your only option here (see "Helpful Hints," earlier).

BAVARIAN ALPS

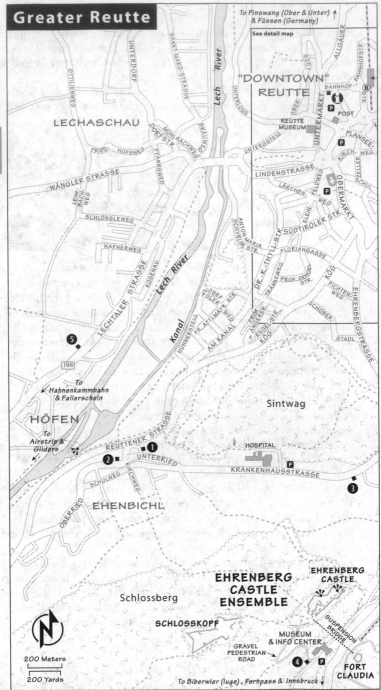

Greater Reutte

To Pinswang (Ober & Unter)
& Füssen (Germany)

See detail map

"DOWNTOWN" REUTTE

BAHNHOF

B

REUTTE MUSEUM

POST

PLANSEE

LINDENSTRASSE

LECHASCHAU

OBERMARKT

SÜDTIROLER STR.

FLORIANGASSE

Sintwag

HOSPITAL

KRANKENHAUSSTRASSE

To Hahnenkammbahn
& Fallerschein

HÖFEN

Airstrip &
Gliders

REUTTENER STRASSE

UNTERRIED

EHENBICHL

EHRENBERG
CASTLE
ENSEMBLE

EHRENBERG
CASTLE

Schlossberg

SCHLOSSKOPF

SUSPENSION
BRIDGE

MUSEUM
& INFO CENTER

GRAVEL
PEDESTRIAN
ROAD

FORT
CLAUDIA

N

200 Meters
200 Yards

To Biberwier (luge), Fernpass & Innsbruck

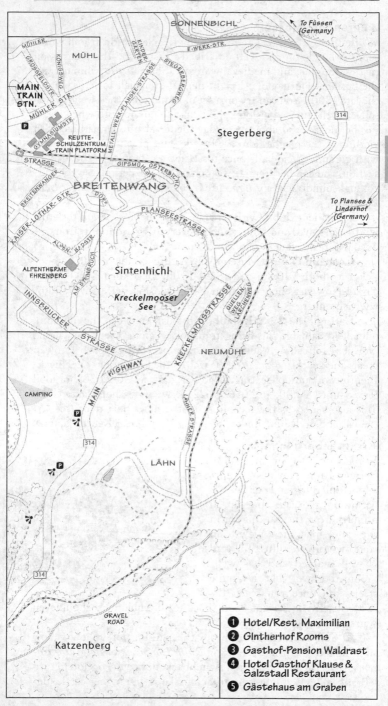

BAVARIAN ALPS

To Füssen (Germany)

SONNENBICHL

E-WERK-STR.

MÜLLER

MÜHL

KÖNIGSWEG

GROSSFELDSTR.

KINDER GARTEN

MÜHLER STR.

STEGERBERGWEG

MAIN TRAIN STN.

GYMNASIUMSTR.

METALL-WERK-PLANSEE-STRASSE

Stegerberg

314

REUTTE-SCHULZENTRUM TRAIN PLATFORM

STRASSE

GIPSMÜHLER

OSTERBICHL

BREITENWANGER STR.

BREITENWANG

DORF

PLANSEESTRASSE

To Plansee & Linderhof (Germany)

KAISER-LOTHAR-STR.

ALPEN-BLDSTR.

AM STEINBRUCH

ALPENTHERME EHRENBERG

Sintenhichl

Kreckelmooser See

KRECKELMOOSSTRASSE

QUELLEN WEG

KIRCHENWEG

INNSBRUCKER STRASSE

NEUMÜHL

MAIN HIGHWAY

CAMPING

LÄHNER STRASSE

314

LÄHN

314

GRAVEL ROAD

Katzenberg

1 Hotel/Rest. Maximilian

2 Glntherhof Rooms

3 Gasthof-Pension Waldrast

4 Hotel Gasthof Klause & Salzstadl Restaurant

5 Gästehaus am Graben

▲Ehrenberg Museum

While there are no real artifacts here, the clever, kid-friendly museum is hands-on and well described in English. The focus is on castles, knights, and medieval warcraft. Some of the exhibits trace the fictional journey of a knight named Heinrich to Jerusalem in the late 1300s. You can try on a set of armor (and then weigh yourself), see the limited vision knights had to put up with when wearing helmets, learn about everyday medieval life, empathize with victims of the plague, join a Crusade, and pretend to play soccer with gigantic stone balls once tossed by a catapult. In the armory section, you can heft replica weapons from the period. Several videos and soundtracks spring to life if you press a button (select *E* for English).

A smaller exhibit (with separate entry fee) focuses on the still-wild Lech River and how it affects everything around it, from industry (rafting trade) to flora and fauna.

Cost and Hours: Museum-€8, nature exhibit-€5.50, combo-ticket for both-€10.80, daily 9:00-17:00, Dec-April 10:00-16:00, closed Nov, last entry one hour before closing, tel. 05672/62007, www.ehrenberg.at.

Eating: The **$$ Salzstadl** ("salt barn"), next to the museum, once held valuable salt being transported along the Via Claudia. Now it's a refreshingly authentic restaurant serving typical Tirolean meals and snacks *(Brotzeiten)*, as well as the local brew—Lechweg-Bier (lots of outdoor seating, salad bar; daily 11:30-22:30, hot food served until 20:00; tel. 05672/62213, www.gasthof-klause.com). This also serves as the reception for the hotel next door (see "At the Ehrenberg Ruins" under "Sleeping in and near Reutte," later).

▲▲Ehrenberg Ruins

Ehrenberg, a romantic 13th-century ruin, provides a super opportunity to let your imagination off its leash. Hike up 30 minutes from the parking lot in the valley for a great view from your own private ruins. The trail is well marked and has well-groomed gravel, but it's quite steep, and once you reach the  castle itself, you'll want good shoes to scramble over the uneven stairs. The castle is always open.

❷ **Self-Guided Tour:** From the parking lot, follow yellow signs up into the woods, tracking *Ruine Ehrenberg* or *Bergruine Ehrenberg*. At the top of the first switchback, notice the option to turn left and hike 45 minutes up to Schlosskopf, the higher castle (described next; this is an easier ascent than the very steep route you can take from closer to Ehrenberg). But we'll head right and continue up the path through the lower entrance bastion of Ehrenberg.

Emerging from the woods, you'll pop out at a saddle between two steep hills. As you face Reutte, the hill on the left is Schlosskopf (notice the steeper ascent here to reach the top), and to the right is Ehrenberg. Ehrenberg is the older of the two, built around 1290. Thirteenth-century castles were designed to stand boastfully tall. Later, with the advent of gunpowder, castles dug in. (Notice the 18th-century ramparts around the castle.)

Now continue twisting up the path to Ehrenberg Castle. As you approach its outer gate, look for the small **door** to the left. It's the night entrance (tight and awkward, and therefore safer against a surprise attack). But we'll head through the **main gate**—actually, two of them. Castles were designed with layered defenses—outer bastion down below, outer gate here, inner gate deeper within—which allowed step-by-step retreat, giving defenders time to regroup and fight back against invading forces.

After you pass through the outer gate, but before climbing to the top of the castle, follow the path around to the right to a big, grassy courtyard with commanding views and a fat, restored **turret**. This stored gunpowder and held a big cannon that enjoyed a clear view of the valley below. In medieval times, all the trees approaching the castle were cleared to keep an unobstructed view.

Look out over the valley. The pointy spire marks the village of **Breitenwang,** which was the site of a Roman camp in AD 46. In 1489, after a bridge was built across the Lech River at Reutte (marked by the onion-domed church with the yellow tower), Reutte was made a market town and eclipsed Breitenwang in importance. Any gliders circling? They launch from just over the river in Höfen.

For centuries, this castle was the seat of government—ruling an area called the "judgment of Ehrenberg" (roughly the same as today's "district of Reutte"). When the emperor came by, he stayed here. In 1604, the ruler moved downtown into more comfortable quarters, and the castle was no longer a palace.

Now climb to the top of Ehrenberg Castle. Take the high ground. There was no water supply here—just kegs of wine, beer, and a cistern to collect rain. Up at the top, appreciate how strategic this lofty position is—with commanding views over Reutte and its broad valley, as well as the narrow side-valley where the pedestrian bridge looms over the highway down below. But also notice that you're sandwiched between two higher hilltops: Schlosskopf in one direction and Falkenberg (across the narrow valley) in the other. In the days before gunpowder, those higher positions offered no real threat. But in the age of cannonballs, Ehrenberg was suddenly very vulnerable...and very obsolete.

Still, Ehrenberg repelled 16,000 Swedish soldiers in the defense of Catholicism in 1632. But once Schlosskopf was fortified a few decades later, Ehrenberg's days were numbered, and its end was not glorious. In the 1780s, a local businessman bought the castle in order to sell off its parts. Later, in the late 19th century, when vagabonds moved in, the roof was removed to make squatting miserable. With the roof gone, deterioration quickened, leaving only this evocative shell and a whiff of history.

Scramble around the ruined walls a bit—nocking imaginary arrows—and head back down through the main gate, returning to the valley the way you came. If you have more energy and castle curiosity, you could try conquering the next castle over: Schlosskopf.

▲Schlosskopf

When Bavarian troops captured Ehrenberg in 1703, the Tiroleans climbed up to the bluff above it to rain cannonballs down on their former fortress. In 1740, a mighty new castle—designed to defend against modern artillery—was built on this sky-high strategic location: Schlosskopf ("Castle Head"). But it too fell into ruin, and by the end of the 20th century, the castle was completely overgrown with trees—you literally couldn't see it from Reutte. But today the trees have been shaved away, and the castle has been excavated. In 2008, the Castle Ensemble project, led by local architect Armin Walch, opened the site with English descriptions and view platforms. One spot gives spectacular views of the strategic valley. The other looks down on the older Ehrenberg Castle ruins, illustrating the strategic problems presented with the advent of the cannon.

Getting There: There are two routes to Schlosskopf, both steep and time-consuming. The steeper of the two (about 30 minutes straight up) starts at the little saddle of land between the two castles (described earlier). The second, which curls around the back of the hill, is less steep but takes longer (45-60 minutes); this one begins from partway down the gravel switchbacks between Ehrenberg and the valley floor—just watch for *Schlosskopf* signs.

Highline 179 Suspension Footbridge

At more than 1,200 feet long, this suspended pedestrian bridge hangs more than 300 feet above the valley floor, connecting Ehrenberg with the previously difficult-to-reach Fort Claudia across the valley. It was the vision of architect and local trailblazer Armin Walch, who helped restore the Ehrenberg ruins and wanted to do something to draw attention to the region. Designed by Swiss engineers and paid for by private investors, the bridge was erected in just six months. With your ticket, the turnstile lets you in, then you walk to the far side where you're welcome to leave the bridge and enjoy the viewpoint. With the same ticket, you can walk back across the bridge to your starting point.

I'm not much into adventure sports, but for me, this wobbly ramble is a thrill. If you look down, directly beneath you is the Via Claudia, which in Roman times was the main route between Italy and Germany. Now this bridge is at the foot of all these great castles, allowing travelers a fun way to reach them—if you like a little adventure.

Cost and Hours: €8 round-trip, better to purchase ticket at the complex's information desk (at parking lot level, credit cards accepted) in case the cash-only machines at the top aren't working, children's tickets available only at information desk; daily 8:00-22:00, open rain or shine unless too windy, tel. 05672/62007, www.highline179.com.

IN REUTTE TOWN

Reutte Museum (Museum Grünes Haus)

Reutte's cute city museum offers a quick look at the local folk culture and the story of the castles. There are exhibits on Ehrenberg and the Via Claudia, local painters, and more—ask to borrow the English translations.

Cost and Hours: €3; Tue-Sat 13:00-17:00, closed Sun-Mon; shorter hours and closed Sun-Tue off-season; closed Easter-end of April and Nov-early Dec; in the green building with trompe l'oeil columns and window trim at Untermarkt 25, around corner from Hotel Goldener Hirsch, tel. 05672/72304, www.museum-reutte.at.

▲▲Tirolean Folk Evening

Ask the TI or your hotel if there's a Tirolean folk evening scheduled. During the summer (July-Sept), nearby towns (such as Höfen on Tue) occasionally put on an evening of yodeling, slap dancing, and Tirolean frolic. These are generally free and worth the short drive. Off-season, you'll have to do your own yodeling. Free open-air concerts *(Platzkonzerte)* are held in Reutte and the surrounding communities in the summer. For listings of these and other local events, pick up a copy of the *Griass Enk* entertainment listings at the TI.

Alpentherme Ehrenberg

This extensive swimming pool and sauna complex, a 15-minute walk from downtown Reutte, is a tempting retreat. The Badewelt section features two indoor pools and a big outdoor saltwater pool, and two indoor waterslides. The all-nude Saunaparadies section (no kids under age 16) consists of three indoor saunas, three freestanding outdoor saunas, and a big outdoor swimming pool. You'll be given a wristband that lets you access your locker and buy snacks on credit without needing a key or cash. Those staying in the Reutte area get a 50 percent discount with an Aktiv-Card (see "Helpful Hints," earlier); it's a nice way to relax after hiking around castles all day.

Cost and Hours: Pools only-€10.50/2 hours, €12.50/4 hours, €14.50/day; sauna and pools-€21/3 hours, €27/day; towel rental-€3, robe rental-€5, swimsuits sold but not rented; daily 10:00-21:00, sauna until 22:00, closes for one week every May; Thermenstrasse 10, tel. 05672/72222, www.alpentherme-ehrenberg.at.

ACROSS THE RIVER, IN HÖFEN

Just over the Lech River are two very different ways to reach high-altitude views. To get here from Reutte, head up Lindenstrasse (where the cobbled Obermarkt ends), cross the bridge, and turn left down Lechtaler Strasse; as you enter the village of Höfen, you'll see the cable car to your right and the airstrip to your left.

▲Scenic Flights

For a major thrill on a sunny day, drop by the tiny airport in Höfen, where small single-prop planes and gliders take passengers on scenic flights (April-Oct). Al-though I've listed contact infor-mation below, your best bet is to show up at the airstrip on a good-weather afternoon and ask around. Prop planes can buzz the Zugspitze and Ludwig's castles and give you a bird's-eye peek at the Ehrenberg ruins (tel. 05672/632-0729 or mobile  0664-221-2233, www.flugsportverein-reutte.at). The prop planes and gliders are based out of two different restaurants that face the airstrip. From the main road, watch for the big building marked *Flugplatz* down below.

Hahnenkammbahn

This mountain lift swoops you in small, enclosed cars high above the tree line to an attractive panoramic restaurant and starting point for several hikes. In the alpine flower park, special paths lead you past countless varieties of local flora. Unique to this lift is a barefoot hiking trail *(Barfusswanderweg)*, designed to be walked without shoes—no joke.

Cost and Hours: €13.50 one-way, €19 round-trip, runs June-Oct daily 9:00-16:30, also in good weather late May and early Nov, flowers best in late July, base station across the river in Höfen, tel. 05672/62420, www.reuttener-seilbahnen.at.

NEAR REUTTE
Sights Along the Lech River
The Lech River begins high in the Alps and meanders 75 miles (including right past Reutte) on its way to the Lechfall, where it becomes navigable, near Füssen. This stretch of the Lech River Valley (Lechtal) has been developed as a popular hiking trail, called the **Lechweg,** divided into 15 stages *(Strecken);* part of the area has also been designated as a nature park. A variety of glossy brochures—mostly in German and available at local TIs and hotels—explain the importance of the Lech to local culture and outline some enticing hikes.

Within the pristine Tiroler Lech Nature Park, a little outside Reutte, is an impressive wooden **lookout tower** from which you can observe the vibrant bird life in the wetlands along the Lech River (110 species of birds nest here). Look for *Vogelerlebnispfad* signs as you're driving through the village of Pflach (on the road between Reutte and Füssen; www.naturpark-tiroler-lech.at).

▲▲Biberwier Luge Course
Near Lermoos, on the road between Reutte and Innsbruck, you'll find the Biberwier *Sommerrodelbahn.* At 4,250 feet, it's the longest summer luge in Tirol. The drawbacks are its brief season, short hours, and a proclivity for shutting down sporadically—even at the slightest bit of rain. This is clearly the most exciting (and dangerous) of the region's luge rides. Keep your knees and elbows in tight, keep both hands on the stick, and watch your speed on corners. Every day some hotshot leaves a big chunk of skin on the course—a painful souvenir that lasts a very long time.

If you don't have a car, this is not worth the trouble; consider the luge near Neuschwanstein instead (see "Tegelberg Luge" on page 172). The ugly cube-shaped building marring the countryside near the luge course is a hotel for outdoor adventure enthusiasts. You can ride your mountain bike right into your room, or skip the elevator by using its indoor climbing wall.

Cost and Hours: €7.80/ride, cheaper with multiride tickets; daily mid-May-early Oct 8:30-17:00, stays open later July-Aug, closed off-season; tel. 05673/2323, www.bergbahnen-langes.at.

Getting There: It's 20 minutes from Reutte on the main road toward Innsbruck; Biberwier is the first exit after a long tunnel.

Luge Lesson

Taking a wild ride on a summer luge (pronounced "loozh") is a quintessential alpine experience. In German, it's called a *Sommerrodelbahn* ("summer toboggan run"). To try one of Europe's great accessible thrills, take the lift up to the top of a mountain, grab a wheeled sled-like go-cart, and scream back down the mountainside on a banked course. Then take the lift back up and start all over again.

Luge courses are highly weather dependent and can close at the slightest hint of rain. If the weather's questionable, call ahead to confirm that your preferred luge is open. Stainless steel courses are more likely than concrete ones to stay open in drizzly weather.

Operating the sled is simple: Push the stick forward to go faster, pull back to apply brakes. Even a novice can go very, very fast. Most are cautious on their first run, speed demons on their second... and bruised and bloody on their third. A woman once showed me her travel journal illustrated with her husband's dried five-inch-long luge scab. He had disobeyed the only essential rule of luging: Keep both hands on your stick. To avoid a bumper-to-bumper traffic jam, let the person in front of you get as far ahead as possible before you start. You'll emerge from the course with a windblown hairdo and a smile-creased face.

Key Luge Terms

Lenkstange	lever
drücken / schneller fahren	push / go faster
ziehen / bremsen	pull / brake
Schürfwunde	scrape
Schorf	scab

▲Fallerschein

Easy for drivers and a special treat for those who may have been Kit Carson in a previous life, this extremely remote log cabin village, south of Reutte, is a 4,000-foot-high flower-speckled world of serene slopes and cowbells. Thunderstorms roll down the valley like it's God's bowling alley, but the pint-size church on the high ground, blissfully simple in a land of Baroque, seems to promise that this huddle of houses will survive, and the river and breeze will just keep flowing. The couples sitting on benches are mostly Austrian vacationers who've rented cabins here. Some of them, appreciating the remoteness of Fallerschein, are having affairs.

Getting There: From Reutte, it's a 45-minute drive. Take road 198 to Stanzach (passing Weissenbach am Lech, then Forchach), then turn left toward Namlos. Follow the L-21 Berwang road for about five miles to a parking lot. From there, it's a two-mile walk down a drivable but technically closed one-lane road. Those driving in do so at their own risk.

Sleeping in Fallerschein: ¢ Michl's Fallerscheiner Stube is a family-friendly mountain-hut restaurant with a low-ceilinged attic space that has basic dorm beds for up to 17 sleepy hikers. The accommodations aren't fancy, but if you're looking for remote, this is it (May-Oct only, wildlife viewing deck, reservations best made by phone, mobile 0676-727-9681, www.alpe-fallerschein.com, michael@alpe-fallerschein.com, Knitel family).

Sleeping in and near Reutte

While it's not impossible by public transport, staying here makes most sense for those with a car. Reutte is popular with Austrians and Germans, who visit year after year for one- or two-week vacations. Prices stay fairly even throughout the year. Remember to ask for the Aktiv-Card (see page 194). My recommendations all have free parking and a great breakfast.

Most of my listings are in the "villages" around Reutte (such as Breitenwang, Ehenbichl, and Höfen), which basically feel like the suburbs. For even more options, ask the Reutte TI for their list of private homes that rent out rooms. These average about €30 per person per night in a room with breakfast and facilities down the hall.

Remember, to call Reutte from a German phone, dial 00-43 and then the number (minus the initial zero).

IN CENTRAL REUTTE

$ Hotel "Das Beck" offers 16 simple, sunny rooms (most with balconies) filling a modern building in the heart of town close to the train station. This is the most practical option for those coming by train or bus. It's a great value, and guests are personally taken care of by Hans, Inge, Tamara, and Manuela. Their small café offers tasty snacks and specializes in Austrian and Mediterranean wines. Expect good conversation, overseen by Hans (family rooms, Untermarkt 11, tel 05672/62522, www.hotel-das-beck.at, info@hotel-das-beck.at).

IN BREITENWANG

Now basically a part of Reutte, the older and quieter village of Breitenwang has good *Zimmer* and a fine bakery. It's a 20-minute walk from the Reutte train station: From the post office, follow

Planseestrasse past the onion-dome church to the pointy straight-dome church near the two hotels. The Hosp family—as well as some others renting private rooms—have places along Kaiser-Lothar-Strasse, the first right past this church. Reutte's Alpentherme indoor pool complex, 50 percent off with your Aktiv-Card, is just around the block.

If staying in Breitenwang and traveling by train, take advantage of the tiny Reutte-Schulzentrum station, just a five-minute walk from these listings. All trains on the Garmisch-Reutte line stop here, but only on demand—which means you have to let the conductor know in advance where you want to get off. To board at Reutte-Schulzentrum, stand on the platform and flag the train down; you'll be able to buy a ticket from the conductor with no penalty.

$$ Alpenhotel Ernberg's 26 comfortable rooms, with wooden accents and colorful terraces, are run with great care by friendly and hardworking Hermann, who combines alpine elegance with modern touches. Nestle in for some serious coziness among the carved-wood eating nooks, tiled stoves, and family-friendly backyard (RS%, family rooms, self-service laundry, popular restaurant, bar, Planseestrasse 50, tel. 05672/71912, www.ernberg.at, info@ernberg.at).

$$ Moserhof Hotel has 40 traditional rooms with alpine accents and balconies plus an elegant dining room and sitting areas throughout (elevator, restaurant, sauna and whirlpool, Planseestrasse 44, tel. 05672/62020, www.hotel-moserhof.at, info@hotel-moserhof.at, Hosp family).

IN EHENBICHL, NEAR THE EHRENBERG RUINS

These listings are a bit farther from central Reutte, a couple of miles upriver in the village of Ehenbichl. From central Reutte, go south on Obermarkt and turn right on Kög, which becomes Reuttener Strasse, following signs to *Ehenbichl*. These places are inconvenient by public transit (you'll need to brave infrequent local buses; see www.vvt.at for schedules). For taxi service, ask your hotelier. For locations, see the "Greater Reutte" map, earlier.

$$ Hotel Maximilian offers 32 rooms and a fine restaurant (evenings only, closed Wed). Friendly Gabi, Monika, and the rest of the Koch family proudly leave no detail unattended and keep guests entertained with table tennis, a pool table, play areas for children (indoors and out), a piano, and a sauna (family rooms, some view rooms, elevator, laundry service, hotel closed late Oct-mid-Dec, Reuttener Strasse 1 in Ehenbichl—don't let your GPS take you to Reuttener Strasse in Pflach, tel. 05672/62585, www.maxihotel.com, info@hotelmaximilian.at). They rent cars to guests

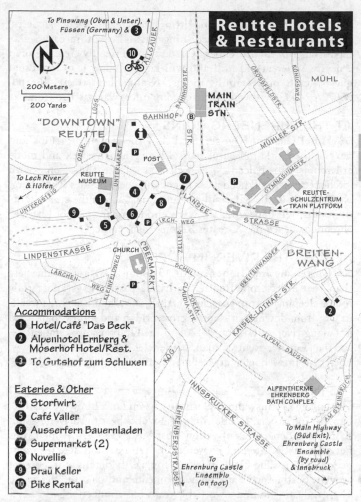

BAVARIAN ALPS

Reutte Hotels & Restaurants

To Pinswang (Ober & Unter),
Füssen (Germany) & ❸

200 Meters
200 Yards

"DOWNTOWN" REUTTE

MAIN TRAIN STN.

BAHNHOF-

MÜHL

KÖNIGSWEG

GROSSFELDSTR.

MÜHLER STR.

GYMNASIUMSTR.

REUTTE-SCHULZENTRUM TRAIN PLATFORM

POST

REUTTE MUSEUM

PLANSEE-STRASSE

To Lech River & Höfen

UNTERGSSIEG

LINDENSTRASSE

LÄRCHEN-WEG

KLEINFELDWEG

CHURCH

KIRCH-WEG

ZEITLER

SCHUL

PORTA

CLAUDIA-STR.

BREITENWANGER

BREITEN-WANG

KAISER-LOTHAR-STR.

ALPEN-DADSTR.

ÜBERMARKT

INNSBRUCKER STRASSE

EHRENBERGSTRASSE

KOG

AM STEINBRUCH

ALPENTHERME EHRENBERG BATH COMPLEX

To Main Highway (Süd Exit), Ehrenberg Castle Ensemble (by road) & Innsbruck

To Ehrenburg Castle Ensemble (on foot)

Accommodations
❶ Hotel/Café "Das Beck"
❷ Alpenhotel Ernberg & Moserhof Hotel/Rest.
❸ To Gutshof zum Schluxen

Eateries & Other
❹ Storfwirt
❺ Café Valier
❻ Ausserfern Bauernladen
❼ Supermarket (2)
❽ Novellis
❾ Bräu Keller
❿ Bike Rental

only (€0.72/km, automatic transmission) and bikes to anyone (guests-€5/half-day, €8/day; nonguests-€6/half-day, €12/day).

$ Gintherhof is a working dairy farm that provides its guests with fresh milk, butter, and homemade jam. Kind, hardworking Annelies Paulweber offers a warm welcome, geranium-covered balconies, four cozy rooms, and one apartment (with kitchenette), all complete with free hiking gear and a Madonna in every corner (cash only, Unterried 7, just up the road behind Hotel Maximilian, tel. 05672/67697, www.gintherhof.com, info@gintherhof.com).

$ Gasthof-Pension Waldrast is run by the Huter family and their dog, Picasso. Built in 1928, the place feels hauntingly quiet and has no restaurant, but it's inexpensive and offers 10 pleasant, spacious rooms with generous sitting areas, castle-view balconies, and traditional Austrian furnishings. It's also within easy walking distance of the Ehrenberg Castle ruins. Friendly Gerd restored a nearly 500-year-old mill and will happily show it to interested guests (cash only, family rooms, Krankenhausstrasse 16, tel. 05672/62443, www.waldrasttirol.com, info@waldrasttirol.com).

AT THE EHRENBERG RUINS

$$ Hotel Gasthof Klause, just below the Ehrenberg ruins and next to the castle museum, rents 12 surprisingly sleek and modern rooms with balconies, as well as 15 apartments (some with kitchenettes). You'll need a car to get anywhere besides Ehrenberg. Reception is in the Salzstadl restaurant just across the street (family rooms, tel. 05672/62213, www.ehrenberg.at, gasthof-klause@ ehrenberg.at, see the "Greater Reutte" map, earlier).

ACROSS THE RIVER, IN HÖFEN

$$ Gästehaus am Graben, with 13 rooms, is a good value less than two miles from Reutte, with fine castle views and family rooms sleeping four to six (closed April, Nov, and last three weeks in Jan; from downtown Reutte, cross bridge and follow main road left along river, or take bus #4268 to the Graben stop; Graben 1— see the "Greater Reutte" map, earlier, tel. 05672/626-440, www. hoefen.at, info@hoefen.at, Reyman family).

IN PINSWANG

The village of Pinswang is closer to Füssen (and Ludwig's castles), but still in Austria. While this hotel works best for drivers, about half of the departures of yellow post bus #4258/#74, which runs between the Reutte and Füssen train stations, stop here (3-4/day, get off at Pinswang Gemeindeamt stop, verify details with hotel or at www.postbus.at, or use www.bahn.com and plug in "Pinswang Gemeindeamt" to find a workable train-bus connection).

$$ Gutshof zum Schluxen gets the "Remote Old Hotel in an Idyllic Setting" award. This family-friendly farm, with 24 rooms and a playground, offers rustic elegance and lots of wooden accents. Its picturesque meadow setting will turn you into a dandelion-picker, and its proximity to Neuschwanstein will turn you into a hiker—the castle is about an hour's walk away (family room, some rooms with balconies, laundry service, free loaner bikes for Rick Steves readers, restaurant closed Mon-Tue, between Reutte and Füssen in village of Pinswang, tel. 05677/53217, www.schluxen.at, info@schluxen.at, Mathias).

To reach Neuschwanstein from this hotel by foot or bike, follow the dirt road up the hill behind the hotel. When the road forks at the top of the hill, go right (downhill), cross the Austria-Germany border (marked by a sign and deserted hut), and follow the narrow, paved path to the castles. It's a 1- to 1.5-hour hike or a great circular bike trip (allow 30 minutes; cyclists can return to Schluxen from the castles on a different 30-minute bike route via Füssen).

Eating in Reutte

The nicer restaurants in Reutte are all in hotels. **$$$ Alpenhotel Ernberg,** the **$$$ Moserhof Hotel,** and **$$$ Hotel Maximilian** (evenings only) all have fine restaurants. On weekdays, Alpenhotel Ernberg serves good three-course lunches for €11.

$ Storfwirt is ideal for a quick and cheap weekday lunch. This rustic cafeteria in downtown Reutte serves some 300 happy eaters every day (salad bar, daily soup-and-main-course specials, always something for vegetarians). Their adjacent **deli** is a great place to shop for a Tirolean picnic; choose from the local meats, cheeses, and prepared salads in the glass case, pick up a schnitzel with potato salad, or ask them to make you a sandwich to order. You can take your food away or eat at informal tables (Storfwirt and deli both open Mon-Fri 11:00-14:00, closed Sat-Sun; next door to the big Müller pharmacy at Schrettergasse 15, tel. 05672/62640, www. storfwirt.at, helpful manager Rainer).

$ Café Valier, perfect for coffee and cake, is a local mainstay that has been run by the same family for five generations (Mon-Sat 7:00-18:00, closed Sun, Untermarkt 5, tel. 05672/62462).

Picnic Supplies: Along Mühler Strasse, near the intersection with Untermarkt, is the **Ausserfern Bauernladen** (farmer's shop), where local farmers sell their own products. You can buy picnic fixings (cheeses, spreads, and yummy *Heuwürstchen* sausages cooked in hay), or ask them to make you a rustic sandwich to eat at one of the tables (Wed-Fri 9:00-18:00, Sat until 12:00, closed Sun-Tue, Obermarkt 3, mobile 0676-575-4588). **Eurospar** has groceries and a handy deli section with salads, sandwiches, and hot meals (Mon-Fri 7:15-19:30, Sat until 18:00, Sun until 11:00; Mühler Strasse 20). **Billa** supermarket also has picnic supplies (across from TI at Untermarkt 33, Mon-Fri 7:15-19:30, Sat until 18:00, closed Sun).

Nightlife: $ Novellis is the most happening joint in town, with live music on Fridays and Saturdays. Its salads, burgers, and wraps offer a nice escape from typical Bavarian food (Mon-Fri 9:00-24:00, Sat from 10:00, closed Sun; Mühler Strasse 12, tel. 05672/64612). **Bräu Keller,** behind Hotel "Das Beck," offers a classier lounge with a nice drink menu and small bites (Thu-Sat 17:00-24:00, closed Sun-Wed, Untermarkt 7a). A strip of bars, dance clubs, and Italian restaurants lines Lindenstrasse.

Reutte Connections

BY PUBLIC TRANSPORTATION

From Reutte by Train to: Ehrwald (at base of Zugspitze lift, every 2 hours, 30 minutes), **Garmisch** (same train, every 2 hours, 1 hour), **Innsbruck** (every 2 hours, 2.5 hours, transfer in Garmisch), **Munich** (hourly, about 3 hours, some with 1 transfer), **Salzburg** (every 2 hours, 5 hours, transfer in Garmisch and Munich). Austrian train info: Tel. 051-717 (to get an operator, dial 2, then 2), www.oebb.at; German train info: www.bahn.com.

By Bus to: Füssen (#4258—but known as #74 in Germany, 6-7/day, last bus at 18:05, 30-50 minutes, €4.50 one-way, buses depart from train station, pay driver).

ROUTE TIPS FOR DRIVERS

From downtown Reutte, *Fernpass* signs lead you out to the main Innsbruck road, which is also the best way to reach the Ehrenberg ruins. To reach the Ehrenberg Castle ruins, the Biberwier luge, the Zugspitze (either the Austrian ascent at Ehrwald or the German ascent at Garmisch), or Innsbruck, turn right for the on-ramp (marked *Fernpass* and *Innsbruck*) to highway 179. But if you're headed for Germany via the scenic Plansee, Linderhof Castle, Ettal Monastery, or Oberammergau, continue straight (bypassing the highway on-ramp).

SALZBURG

Salzburg • Berchtesgaden

Salzburg, just over the Austrian border, makes a fun day trip from Munich (1.5 hours by direct train). Thanks to its charmingly preserved Old Town, splendid gardens, Baroque churches, and one of Europe's largest intact medieval fortresses, Salzburg feels made for tourism. As a musical mecca, the city puts on a huge annual festival, as well as constant concerts. Salzburgers are forever smiling to the tunes of Mozart and *The Sound of Music*. It's a city with class. Vagabonds visiting here wish they had nicer clothes.

In the mountains just outside Salzburg is Berchtesgaden, a German alpine town that was once a favorite of Adolf Hitler but today thrills a better class of nature lover.

PLANNING YOUR TIME

While Salzburg doesn't have blockbuster museums, the town itself is a Baroque showpiece of cobbled streets and elegant buildings —a touristy stroller's delight. If you're a fan of the movie, allow half a day for the *Sound of Music* tour, which kills a nest of sightseeing birds with one ticket (city overview, *S.O.M.* sights, and a fine drive by the lakes).

You'd probably enjoy at least two nights in Salzburg—one to swill beer in an atmospheric local garden and another to attend a concert in a Baroque hall or chapel. Seriously consider one of Salzburg's many evening musical events, even if you're not normally a music lover (some are free).

When the weather's good, take advantage of the city's proximity to alpine splendor. Bike down the river or hike across the Mönchsberg, Salzburg's mini mountain. Or consider visiting scenic Berchtesgaden, just 15 miles away, in Germany (also the site of Hitler's Eagle's Nest; see the end of this chapter).

A day trip from Salzburg to Hallstatt (the small-town highlight of the Salzkammergut Lake District) is doable by car (1.5 hours each way) but makes for a very long day by public transit (five hours round-trip). An overnight in Hallstatt is better (or take a bus tour; see page 224).

Salzburg, Austria

Today, eight million tourists crawl Salzburg's cobbles each year. That's a lot of Mozart balls—and all that popularity has led to a glut of businesses hoping to catch the tourist dollar. Still, Salzburg is both a must and a joy.

Even without Mozart and the Von Trapps, Salzburg is steeped in history. In about AD 700, Bavaria gave Salzburg to Bishop Rupert in return for his promise to Christianize the area. For centuries, Salzburg remained an independent city-state, ruled by prince-archbishops—a cross between a king and a pope, but less powerful than either one. Salzburg's mighty fortress—looming protectively over the city—helped deter invaders.

At its peak, Salzburg controlled an area about half the size of today's Austria. Its power was funded by salt—the "white gold" of the day. It's said one barrel of salt was worth the cost of one house.

Salzburgers enjoy throwing around the names of their obscure prince-archbishops (who built various fanciful palaces and elegant squares), but only one is worth remembering: Wolf Dietrich von Raitenau (1559-1617). It was his vision of making Salzburg a mini Rome north of the Alps that gave the city an Italian flair and created much of what tourists enjoy today.

Napoleon finally put an end to Salzburg's independence in 1803 (they handed him the keys to the fortress without putting up a fight). Then, after the fall of Napoleon, Salzburg became part of Austria and was ruled by Vienna.

Thanks in part to its formidable fortress, Salzburg managed to avoid the ravages of war for 1,200 years...until World War II. Allied bombing destroyed much of the city (especially around the train station), but the historic Old Town survived.

Music lovers adore Salzburg, where you can shell out for classy performances...or are just as likely to hear musicians practicing through an open window. The city also has a beautiful setting, wrapped in alpine wonder; a stout castle with great panoramas over cut-glass peaks; a tidy—almost sterile—Old Town of interlocking squares and Baroque domes, giving it a nearly Italian feel; some engaging museums; and, overall, the most accessible taste of Austria you'll find anywhere.

Orientation to Salzburg

Salzburg, a city of 150,000 (Austria's fourth largest), is divided into old and new. The Old Town (Altstadt), between the Salzach River and Salzburg's Mönchsberg mountain, holds nearly all the charm and most of the tourists. The New Town (Neustadt), across the river, has the train station, a few sights and museums, and some good accommodations.

TOURIST INFORMATION

Salzburg has two helpful TIs (main tel. 0662/889-870, www. salzburg.info): at the **train station** (9:00-18:00, until 19:00 in summer; tel. 0662/8898-7340) and on **Mozartplatz** in the old center (daily 9:00-18:00, July-Aug often until 19:00, closed Sun in winter; tel. 0662/8898-7330).

At any TI, you can pick up a free city-center map (or purchase a map with broader coverage if biking out of town), the free bus map *(Liniennetz)*, and an events guide. Inside the Mozartplatz TI is the privately run Salzburg Ticket Service counter, where you can book concert tickets.

Salzburg Card: TIs sell the Salzburg Card, which covers all public transportation (including the Mönchsberg elevator and funicular to the fortress) and admission to all the city sights (including Hellbrunn Palace and a river cruise). The card can be a convenience and a money saver if you'll be seeing lots of sights (€29/24 hours, €38/18 hours, €44/72 hours, cheaper off-season, half-price for kids ages 6-15, www.salzburg.info). As Salzburg's major sights are pricey, busy sightseers can save plenty. Do the math on the places you want to see to evaluate whether the card makes financial sense.

ARRIVAL IN SALZBURG
By Train

The Salzburg station has tourist information, luggage lockers, a pay WC (by platform 5), and a handy Spar supermarket. Ticket counters and ticket machines for both the Austrian and German railways are off the main hall. To find the TI, follow the green-

and-white information signs (the blue-and-white ones lead to a railway "InfoPoint"). Next to the train station is Forum 1, a sizable shopping mall.

Getting downtown from the station is a snap. Simply step outside, find bus **platform C** (labeled *Zentrum-Altstadt*), and buy a ticket from the machine (€2 *Stundenkarte*). Buses #1, #3, #5, and #6 all do the same route into the city center before diverging. Bus #25 (from **platform B**) follows the same path to the center and continues to Hellbrunn Palace. For most sights and Old Town hotels, get off just after the bridge (either Rathaus or Hanuschplatz, depending on the bus). For my recommended New Town hotels, get off at Makartplatz, just before the bridge.

A **taxi** from the station to most hotels is about €8.

To **walk** downtown (15 minutes), turn left as you leave the station, and walk straight down Rainerstrasse, which leads under the tracks past Mirabellplatz, turning into Dreifaltigkeitsgasse. From here, you can turn left onto Linzer Gasse for many of my recommended New Town hotels, or cross the river to the Old Town. For a slightly longer but more dramatic approach, leave the station the same way but follow the tracks to the river, turn left, and walk the riverside path toward the hilltop fortress.

By Car

Mozart never drove in Salzburg's Old Town, and neither should you. Carefully heed the *rising bollards* signs at the entrance to pedestrian zones—they mean business. (The hydraulic bollards are designed to essentially destroy the car of anyone who tries to sneak through behind a car with permission.)

The best place to park is the **park-and-ride** lot at the Alpensiedlung bus stop, near the Salzburg Süd autobahn exit. Coming on A-8 from Munich, cross the border into Austria (for tips on driving from Germany to Salzburg, see "Route Tips for Drivers" on page 281). Take A-10 toward Hallein, and then take the next exit (Salzburg Süd) in the direction of Anif. Stay on the Alpenstrasse (road 150) for about 2.5 miles, following *P+R* signs, to arrive at the park-and-ride (€5/24 hours). From the parking lot, catch bus #3 or #8 into town (for ticket info, see "Getting Around Salzburg," later). Alternatively, groups of up to five people can buy a combo-ticket from the parking lot attendant, which includes the 24-hour parking fee and a 24-hour transit pass for the whole group (€14, group must stay together).

If you don't want to park-and-ride, head to the easiest, cheapest, most central parking lot: the 1,500-car Altstadtgarage, in the tunnel under the Mönchsberg (€18/day, note your slot number and which of the twin lots you're in). Your hotel may provide discounted parking passes. If staying in Salzburg's New Town, the Mirabell-Congress garage makes more sense (see page 265 for directions).

By Plane

Salzburg's airport sits just behind its Mönchsberg mountain (code: SZG, tel. 0662/85800, www.salzburg-airport.com). A taxi into town runs about €15. To take a bus, cross the parking lot to the row of bus stops: Bus #10 goes to the Old Town (20 minutes); bus #2 goes to the train station, then terminates at Mirabellplatz (near several of my New Town accommodations; about 30 minutes). For either bus, buy a €2 *Stundenkarte* ticket at the machine, or pay the driver €2.60 (each bus runs every 10 minutes, less frequent on Sun).

HELPFUL HINTS

Welcome to Austria: If calling from a German phone to an Austrian one, dial 00-43 and then the number (omitting the initial zero). To call from an Austrian phone to a German one, dial 00-49 and then the number (again omitting the initial zero; see page 996 for dialing instructions). **Drivers** should note that Austria requires a toll sticker *(Vignette)* for using its expressways; for details, see "Route Tips for Drivers" on page 281.

Recommendations Skewed by Kickbacks: Salzburg is addicted to the tourist dollar, and it can never get enough. Virtually all hotels are on the take when it comes to concert and tour recommendations, so take any entertainment advice with a grain of salt. If you book a concert through your hotel, you'll probably lose any discounts I've negotiated for my readers who book directly.

Festivals: The Salzburg Festival runs each year from mid-July to the end of August (for more details on this and other big annual musical events, see page 264). In mid-September, the St. Rupert's Fair (Ruperti Kirtag), celebrating Salzburg's favorite saint, fills the sky with fireworks and Salzburg's Old Town with music and food stands (www.rupertikirtag.at). And from mid-November throughout Advent, Salzburg boasts a handful of Christmas markets—the biggest sprawling across Domplatz and Residenzplatz (www.christkindlmarkt.co.at), with smaller ones up at the fortress (mostly just Fri-Sun), on Mirabellplatz (daily), and elsewhere around town (www. weihnachtsmarkt-salzburg.at).

SALZBURG

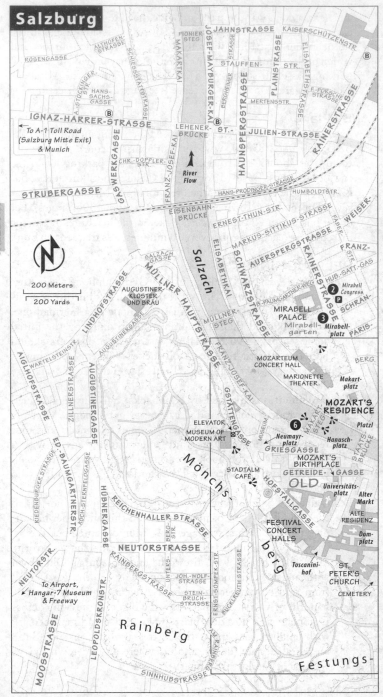

SALZBURG

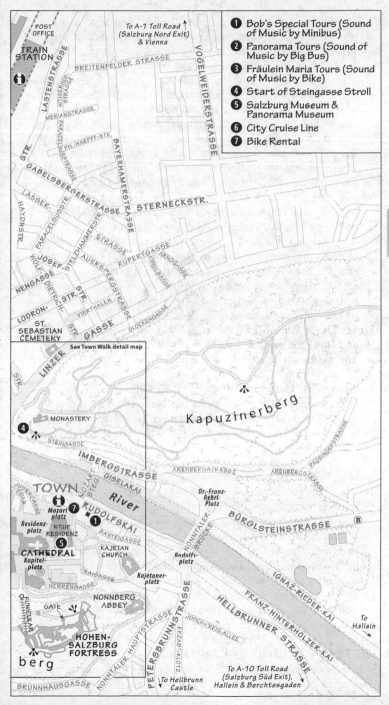

1. Bob's Special Tours (Sound of Music by Minibus)
2. Panorama Tours (Sound of Music by Big Bus)
3. Fräulein Maria Tours (Sound of Music by Bike)
4. Start of Steingasse Stroll
5. Salzburg Museum & Panorama Museum
6. City Cruise Line
7. Bike Rental

Wi-Fi: The city has free hotspots at Mirabell Gardens, Mozart-platz, and Kapitelplatz (choose *Salzburg surft!* and click *Agree*).

Laundry: A handy launderette with a few self-serve machines is at Paris-Lodron-Strasse 16, at the corner of Wolf-Dietrich-Strasse, near my recommended Linzer Gasse hotels—take bus #2, #4, or #21 to the Wolf-Dietrich-Strasse stop (self-service or same-day full-service, Mon-Fri 7:30-18:00, Sat 8:00-12:00, closed Sun, tel. 0662/876-381). If they're closed, head for **Green and Clean,** three stops from the train station on the #1 or #2 bus; board from platform D at station, get off at the Gaswerkgasse stop (daily 6:00-22:00, Ignaz-Harrer-Strasse 32, tel. 0800-102-559). See the map on page 268 for locations.

Cinema: An art-house movie theater, **Das Kino** plays films in their original language (a block off the river and Linzer Gasse on Steingasse, tel. 0662/873-100, www.daskino.at).

Smoking Policies: Unlike Germany, which can implement sweeping reforms overnight, conservative Austria has been slow to embrace the smoke-free movement. Big restaurants must offer smoke-free zones (and smoking zones, if they choose). Smaller places choose to be either smoking or nonsmoking, indicated by red or green stickers on the door.

Market Days: Pop-up farmers markets are a fun local tradition and ideal for picking up picnic supplies or artisan trinkets. The **Grünmarkt** at Universitätsplatz in the Old Town runs Monday-Friday (7:00-19:00) and expands onto Wiener-Philharmoniker Gasse on Saturday (7:00-13:00). Around the Andräkirche and Mirabellplatz in the New Town on Thursday (5:00-13:00) is the huge **Schrannenmarkt,** Salzburg's longest running market, dating from 1906. The **Salzach Galerien**, with arts-and-crafts booths and food, stretches along the south side of the river between Makartsteg and Müllnersteg bridges on most summer weekends (10:00-20:00).

Morning Joggers: Salzburg is a great place for jogging. Within minutes you can be huffing and puffing "The hills are alive..." in green meadows outside of town. The obvious best bets in town are through the Mirabell Gardens along its riverbank pedestrian lanes.

Public Swimming Pool: The **Freibad Leopoldskron** complex, a few miles out of town and across the lake from Leopoldskron Palace (of *Sound of Music* fame), is a first-class place for a swim while surrounded by nature (and it's on the hop-on, hop-off bus route because of the palace's connection to the movie).

GETTING AROUND SALZBURG

By Bus: Most Salzburg sights I list are within the *Kernzone* (core zone) of the city's extensive bus system. I've listed prices for buying tickets from the driver; you'll pay less if you buy them ahead at a *Tabak/Trafik* shop or streetside ticket machine (these are scarce in town, but look around tram stops at major hubs—such as the main train station). Note that "09/17" tickets and one-week *Wochenkarte* passes are sold only at ticket machines or *Tabak/Trafik* shops. These are your options:

- Basic single-ride ticket *(Einzelfahrt):* €2.60 (at a machine, select *Stundenkarte*)
- Ticket for 1-2 stops in a single direction *(Kurzstrecke):* €1.30
- "09/17" ticket (valid Mon-Sat 9:00-17:00, not valid Sun or holidays: €1.50)
- 24-hour ticket *(24-Stundenkarte):* €5.70
- One-week pass *(Wochenkarte,* valid 7 calendar days: €15.50— usually pays for itself if you're staying at least four days) Remember to validate your ticket by inserting it in the machine on board.

Get oriented using the free bus map *(Liniennetz),* available at the TI. Many lines converge at Hanuschplatz, on the Old Town side of the river, between the Makartsteg and Staatsbrücke bridges. To get from the Old Town to the train station, catch bus #1 from the inland side of Hanuschplatz. From the other side of the river, find the Makartplatz/Theatergasse stop and catch bus #1, #3, #5, or #6. Busy stops like Hanuschplatz and Mirabellplatz have several bus shelters; look for your bus number.

For more information, visit www.svv-info.at, call 0662/632-900 (answered 24/7), or visit the O pbus transit info office downstairs from bus platform C in front of the train station (Mon-Fri 6:00-18:00, Sat 7:00-15:00, closed Sun).

By Bike: Salzburg is great fun for cyclists. **A'Velo Radladen** rents bikes in the Old Town, just outside the TI on Mozartplatz (€12/4 hours, €18/24 hours, more for electric or mountain bikes, RS%—10 percent off with this book; daily 9:30-18:00, possibly later in summer, shorter hours off-season and in bad weather; passport number for security deposit, mobile 0676-435 5950, run by George). Some of my recommended hotels and pensions also rent or loan bikes to guests.

By Funicular and Elevator: The Old Town is connected to the top of the Mönchsberg mountain (and great views) via funicular and elevator. The funicular *(Festungsbahn)* whisks you up into the imposing Hohensalzburg Fortress (included in castle admission, goes every few minutes). The elevator (Mönchsberg Aufzug) on the west side of the Old Town lifts you to the recommended Stadtalm Café, the Museum of Modern Art and its chic café, wooded paths, and more great views (for details on both options, see page 245).

By Buggy: The horse buggies *(Fiaker)* that congregate at

Residenzplatz charge €48 for a 25-minute trot around the Old Town (www.fiaker-salzburg.at).

Tours in Salzburg

IN SALZBURG

Walking Tours

Any day of the week, you can take a one-hour, informative guided walk of the Old Town without a reservation—just show up at the TI on Mozartplatz at the tour time and pay the guide (€10, daily at 12:15 and 14:00, tel. 0662/8898-7330).

To save money (and probably learn more), use this chapter's self-guided walk or ∩ download my free Salzburg Town Walk audio tour (see page 26).

Local Guides

Salzburg has many good guides. Two I have worked with and enjoyed are **Sabine Rath** (€160/2 hours, €225/4 hours, €335/8 hours, mobile 0664-201-6492, www.tourguide-salzburg.com, info@tourguide-salzburg.com) and **Anna Stellnberger** (€150/2 hours, €220/4 hours, €320/8 hours, mobile 0664-787-5177, anna. stellnberger@aon.at). Salzburg has many other guides (for a list, see www.salzburgguides.at).

Boat Tours

City Cruise Line (a.k.a. Stadt Schiff-Fahrt) runs a basic 40-minute round-trip river cruise with recorded commentary (€15, 9/day July-Aug, 6-8/day May-June and Sept, 3-4/day April and Oct, no boats Nov-March). For a longer cruise, ride to Hellbrunn (€18, €30 includes palace admission and a ride back to the Old Town on a double-decker bus—a good value; daily April-Oct at 14:00, 40 minutes one-way). Boats leave from the Old Town side of the river just downstream of the Makartsteg bridge (tel. 0662/825-858, www.salzburghighlights.at). While views can be cramped, passengers are treated to a cute finale just before docking, when the captain twirls a fun "waltz."

Hop-On, Hop-Off Bus

While most of Salzburg's top sights are concentrated in its walkable Old Town, several are scattered around the city—making a hop-on, hop-off bus tour practical here. I'd skip the sky (blue) line, which mostly hits walkable sights, and opt for the yellow line, which stretches into the outskirts (Hellbrunn Palace and several *Sound of Music* sights). Both have simple and sleepy recorded commentary (one line: €19/1 day, €23/2 days; both lines: €24/1 day, €28/2 days, RS%—10% off with this book; includes all-day transit pass for city buses, both routes run 2/hour, buy tickets and start tour at Mirabellplatz 2, tel. 0662/881-616, www.salzburg-sightseeingtours.at). To see the countryside, consider their green line, which makes a 2.5-hour loop into the Salzkammergut Lake District (€29/all day, runs 7/day).

Segway Tours

This can be an efficient, fun way to cover a lot of ground. Choose a 1.5-hour version that combines a city tour with a trip up the Mönchsberg mountain (€49), or the two-hour version that also heads into the nearby countryside (€65). Reserve ahead (3/day, daily June-Aug; Wed-Sun March-May and Sept-Oct; no tours Nov-Feb; office near recommended New Town hotels at Wolf-Dietrich-Strasse 3, tel. 0676/674-4425, www.segway-salzburg.at).

▲▲*The Sound of Music* Tours

Salzburg is the joyful setting of *The Sound of Music*. The Broadway musical and 1965 movie tell the story of a stern captain who hires a governess for his unruly children and ends up marrying her. Though the movie took plenty of Hollywood liberties (see *"The Sound of Music:* Fact and Fiction" sidebar), it's based on the actual Von Trapp family from Austria. They really did come from Salzburg. Maria really was a governess who became the captain's wife. They did sing in the Festival Hall, they did escape from the Nazis, and they ended up after the war in Vermont, where Maria passed away in 1987. The movie screens nightly at the recommended International Youth Hostel (nonguests welcome; details on page 267).

Salzburg has a number of *Sound of Music* sights—mostly locations where the movie was shot, but also some places associated with the real Von Trapps:

- Mirabell Gardens, with its arbor and Pegasus statue, where the kids sing "Do-Re-Mi."
- Festival Hall, where the real-life Von Trapps performed, and where (in the movie) they sing "Edelweiss" after nervously waiting in the Toscaninihof courtyard.
- St. Peter's Cemetery, the inspiration for the scene where the family hides from Nazi guards (it was actually filmed on a Hollywood set).
- Nonnberg Abbey, where the nuns sing "How Do You Solve a Problem like Maria?"
- Leopoldskron Palace, which serves as the Von Trapps' idyllic lakeside home in the movie (though it wasn't their actual home).
- Summer Riding School's iconic arcaded stage, the setting for the Von Trapp family's final public performance in the movie.
- Hellbrunn Palace gardens, now home to the famous gazebo where Liesl, the Von Trapp's oldest daughter, sings the words, "I am sixteen going on seventeen."

SALZBURG

The Sound of Music: Fact and Fiction

Rather than visit the real-life sights from the life of Maria von Trapp and family, most tourists want to see the places where Hollywood chose to film this fanciful story. Local guides are happy not to burst any *S.O.M.* pilgrim's bubble, but keep these points in mind:

"Edelweiss": The song is not a cherished Austrian folk tune or national anthem. Like all the "Austrian" music in *S.O.M.*, it was composed for Broadway by Rodgers and Hammerstein. It was the last composition that the famed team wrote together, as Hammerstein died in 1960.

Religious Calling: *S.O.M.* implies that Maria was devoutly religious throughout her life, but Maria's foster parents raised her as a socialist and atheist. Maria discovered her religious calling while studying to be a teacher. After completing school, she entered the convent as a novitiate.

Job Description: Maria's position was not as governess to all the children, but specifically as governess and teacher for the Captain's second-oldest daughter, also called Maria, who was bedridden with rheumatic fever.

Whistling: The Captain didn't run a tight domestic ship—but he did use a whistle to call his children—each kid was trained to respond to a certain pitch.

Name Changes: Though the Von Trapp family did have seven children, the show changed all their names and even their genders. As an adult, Rupert, the eldest child, responded to the often-asked question, "Which one are you?" with "I'm Liesl!" Maria and the Captain later had three more children together.

Escape: The family didn't escape by hiking to Switzerland (which

There are many more sights—the horse pond, the wedding church in Mondsee, the fountain in Residenzplatz. Since they're scattered throughout greater Salzburg, taking a tour is the best way to see them efficiently.

I took a *S.O.M.* tour skeptically (as part of my research)—and enjoyed it. The bus tour version includes a quick general city tour, hits the *S.O.M.* spots, and shows you a lovely stretch of the Salzkammergut Lake District. Warning: Many think rolling through the Austrian countryside with 30 Americans singing "Doe, a deer..." is pretty schmaltzy. Locals don't understand all the com-is a five-hour drive away). Rather, they pretended to go on one of their frequent mountain hikes. With only the possessions in their backpacks, they "hiked" all the way to the station at the edge of their estate and took a train to Italy. The movie scene showing them climbing into Switzerland was filmed near Berchtesgaden, Germany...home to Hitler's Eagle's Nest, and certainly not a smart place to flee to.

Family Home: The actual Von Trapp house exists...but it's not the one in the film. The mansion in the movie is actually two different buildings—one used for the front, the other for the back. The interiors were filmed on Hollywood sets. And the much-vaunted "Sixteen Going on Seventeen" gazebo you'll see at Hellbrunn Palace was built just for the movie, then moved twice to reach its current location.

Set Shots: For the film, Boris Levin designed a reproduction of the Nonnberg Abbey courtyard so faithful to the original (down to its cobblestones and stained-glass windows) that many still believe the cloister scenes were really shot at the abbey. And no matter what you hear in Salzburg, the graveyard scene (in which the Von Trapps hide from the Nazis) was also filmed on the Fox lot.

Swindled!: In 1956, a German film producer offered Maria $9,000 cash for the rights to her book. Because it was more money than the family had seen in all their years of singing, she accepted the deal. The agent claimed that German law forbids film companies from paying royalties to foreigners (Maria had by then become a US citizen). She agreed to the contract and unknowingly signed away all film rights to her story. Later, she discovered the agent had swindled the family—no such law existed.

Restitution: Rodgers, Hammerstein, and other producers gave the Von Trapps a percentage of the royalties, even though they weren't required to—but it was a fraction of what they otherwise would have earned. But Maria wasn't bitter. She said, "The great good the film and the play are doing to individual lives is far beyond money."

motion (many have never seen the movie). Guides are professional, but can be (understandably) jaded.

Taking a Tour: Two companies do *S.O.M.* tours by bus (Bob's and Panorama), while a third company does a bike version. It's best to reserve ahead. Note: Your hotel will be eager to call to reserve for you—to get their commission—but you won't get the discount I've negotiated.

By Minibus: Most of **Bob's Special Tours** use an eight-seat minibus (and occasionally a 16-seat bus) and therefore promote a more laid-back camaraderie with your fellow *S.O.M.* pilgrims, and waste less time loading and unloading. Online bookings close three days prior to the tour date—after that, email, call, or stop by the office to reserve (€55 for adults; RS%—student price with this book if you pay cash and book directly, €50 for kids 7-21 and students with ID, €45 for kids 6 and under—includes required car seat but must reserve in advance; daily at 9:00 and 14:00 year-round, tours leave from Bob's office along the river just east of Mozartplatz at Rudolfskai 38, tel. 0662/849-511, www.bobstours.com, office@bobstours.com). Nearly all of Bob's tours stop for a fun luge ride in Fuschl am See when the weather is dry (mountain bobsled-€5 extra, generally April-Oct, confirm beforehand).

By Big Bus: Panorama Tours uses larger buses that depart from their smart kiosk at Mirabellplatz daily at 9:15 and 14:00 year-round (€45, RS%—€5 discount for *S.O.M.* tours if you pay in cash and book by phone or in person, book by calling 0662/874-029 or 0662/883-2110, www.panoramatours.com). While they lack the personal touch of Bob's, Panorama's big buses have a higher vantage point, and the guides have a more polished (some might say *too* polished) spiel.

By Bike: Fräulein Maria's Bicycle Tour offers some exercise—and much better access to the in-town sights, which are skipped or viewed from afar on the bus tours. Meet your guide (more likely a *herr* than a *fräulein*) at the Mirabell Gardens (at Mirabellplatz 4, 50 yards to the left of palace entry). The main attractions of the eight-mile pedal include the Mirabell Gardens, the horse pond, St. Peter's Cemetery, Nonnberg Abbey, Leopoldskron Palace, and, of course, the gazebo. The tour is very family-friendly, and there'll be lots of stops for goofy photo ops (€35 includes bike, €20 for kids 13-18, €15 for kids under 13, RS%—€2 discount with this book; daily April-Oct at 9:30, June-Aug also at 16:30, allow 3.5 hours, reservations required, mobile 0650-342-6297, www.mariasbicycletours.com).

BEYOND SALZBURG

Both Bob's and Panorama Tours offer day trips from Salzburg (such as Berchtesgaden/Eagle's Nest, salt mines, Hallstatt, and Salzkammergut lakes and mountains). One efficient tour worth considering is Bob's full-day *Sound of Music*/Hallstatt Tour, which first covers everything in the standard four-hour *S.O.M.* tour, then continues for a four-hour look at the scenic, lake-speckled Salzkammergut, with free time to explore charming Hallstatt (€110, RS%—student price with this book if you pay cash and book directly; doesn't include entrance fees to optional Hallstatt activities such as boat ride; departs daily at 9:00; Rudolfskai 38, tel. 0662/849-511, www.bobstours.com, office@bobstours.com).

Salzburg at a Glance

▲▲▲**Salzburg Town Walk** Old Town's best sights in handy orientation walk. See page 226.

▲▲**Salzburg Cathedral** Glorious, harmonious Baroque main church of Salzburg. **Hours:** Mon-Sat 8:00-19:00, Sun from 13:00; March-April, Oct, and Dec until 18:00; Jan-Feb and Nov until 17:00. See page 230.

▲▲**Getreidegasse** Picturesque old shopping lane with characteristic wrought-iron signs. See page 237.

▲▲**Hohensalzburg Fortress** Imposing mountaintop castle, with small museums, commanding views, and concerts most evenings. **Hours:** Museums open daily May-Sept 9:00-19:00, Oct-April 9:30-17:00. See page 245.

▲▲**Salzburg Museum** Best place for city history. **Hours:** Tue-Sun 9:00-17:00, closed Mon. See page 240.

▲▲*The Sound of Music* **Tours** Bus or bike through *S.O.M.* sights of Salzburg and surrounding countryside. See page 221.

▲▲**Mozart's Birthplace** House where Mozart was born in 1756, featuring his instruments and other exhibits. **Hours:** Daily July-Aug 8:30-19:00, Sept-June 9:00-17:30. See page 242.

▲▲**Hellbrunn Palace** Lavish palace on the outskirts of town featuring gardens with trick fountains. **Hours:** Daily 9:00-17:30, July-Aug until 21:00, April and Oct until 16:30, closed Nov-March. See page 258.

▲**DomQuartier Museums** Prince-Archbishop Wolf Dietrich's Residenz palace, cathedral viewpoint, and religious art. **Hours:** Wed-Mon 10:00-17:00, Wed until 20:00 in July-Aug, closed Tue except in July-Aug. See page 239.

▲**Panorama Museum** Vivid peek at a panorama painting of the city in 1829. **Hours:** Daily 9:00-17:00. See page 241.

▲**Mozart's Residence** Restored house where the composer lived. **Hours:** Daily July-Aug 8:30-19:00, Sept-June 9:00-17:30. See page 254.

▲**Mönchsberg Walk** "The hills are alive" stroll right in downtown Salzburg. See page 252.

▲**Mirabell Gardens and Palace** Beautiful palace grounds and concert venue with fine views and *Sound of Music* memories. **Hours:** Gardens—open till dusk; palace—daily 8:00-18:00; summer concerts in the park on Sun and Wed. See page 253.

▲**Steingasse** Historic cobbled lane with trendy pubs in a tourist-free part of old Salzburg. See page 255.

Salzburg Town Walk

I've linked the best sights in the Old Town into this handy self-guided orientation walk (rated ▲▲▲). Allow about 1.5 hours.

🎧 Download my free Salzburg Town Walk audio tour.

• *Begin at the Mozartsteg, the wrought-iron, Art Nouveau pedestrian bridge over the Salzach River.*

❶ Mozartsteg

Get your bearings: The milky-green Salzach River thunders under your feet. On the north bank is the New Town. The south side is the Old Town, dominated by a castle on a hill.

Take in the charming, well-preserved, historic core of Salzburg's Old Town. The skyline bristles with Baroque steeples and green, copper domes. Salzburg has 38 Catholic churches, plus two Protestant churches and a synagogue. The biggest green dome is the cathedral, which we'll visit shortly. Overlooking it all is the castle called the Hohensalzburg Fortress. Far to the right of the fortress, find the Museum of Modern Art—a blocky modern building atop the hill. The castle-like structure behind it is a water reservoir.

The Salzach is called "salt river" not because it's salty, but because of the precious cargo it once carried. The salt mines of Hallein are just 12 miles upstream. For 2,000 years, barges carried salt from here to the wider world—to the Danube, the Black Sea, and on to the Mediterranean. As barges passed through, they had to pay a toll on their salt. The city was made great from the trading of salt *(Salz)* defended by a castle *(Burg)*—"Salz-burg."

The embankments and roads were built when the river was regulated in the 1850s. Before that, the Salzach was much wider and slower moving. Houses opposite the Old Town fronted the river with docks and "garages" for boats.

Looking upstream, notice the peak with the TV tower. This stands atop the 4,220-foot-high Gaisberg hill. The summit is a favorite destination for local nature lovers and strong bikers.

• *Now let's plunge into Salzburg's Old Town. From the bridge, walk one block toward the hill-capping castle into the Old Town. Leaving the bridge, notice Michaelstor—the remains of the 17th-century town wall (with gun holes). It was built in 1620 when Salzburg cleverly barricaded itself with a wall and neutrality to avoid the tumult of the Thirty Years' War (Catholics vs. Protestants, 1618-1648). Pass the traffic barriers (that keep this quiet town free of too much traffic) and turn right into a big square, called...*

❷ Mozartplatz

All the tourists around you probably wouldn't be here if not for the man honored by this statue—Wolfgang Amadeus Mozart. The great composer spent most of his first 25 years (1756-1781) in Salzburg. He was born just a few blocks from here. He and his father both served Salzburg's rulers before Wolfgang went on to seek his fortune in Vienna. The statue (considered a poor likeness)

was erected in 1842, just after the 50th anniversary of Mozart's death. The music festival of that year planted the seed for what would become the now world-renowned Salzburg Festival.

Mozart stands atop the spot where the first Salzburgers settled. Two thousand years ago, the Romans had a salt-trading town here called Juvavum. In the year 800, Salzburg—by then Christian and home to an important abbey—joined Charlemagne's Holy Roman Empire as an independent city. The Church of St. Michael (whose yellow tower overlooks the square) dates from that time. It's Salzburg's oldest, if not biggest, church.

• *Before moving on, note the TI (which also sells concert tickets). The entrance to the Salzburg Museum is across the square (described on page 240). Now walk toward the cathedral and into the big square with the huge fountain.*

❸ Residenzplatz

As Salzburg's governing center, this square has long been ringed with important buildings. The cathedral borders the south side.

The Residenz—the former palace of Salzburg's rulers—is to the right (as you face the cathedral). To the left is the New Residenz, with its bell tower.

In the 1600s, this square got a makeover in the then-fashionable Italian Baroque style. The rebuilding started under energetic Prince Archbishop Wolf Dietrich, who ruled from 1587 to 1612. Dietrich had been raised in Rome. He counted the Medicis as his cousins, and had grandiose Italian ambitions for Salzburg. Fortunately for him, the existing cathedral conveniently burned down in 1598. Dietrich set about rebuilding it as part of his grand vision to make Salzburg the "Rome of the North."

The fountain is as Italian as can be, an over-the-top version of Bernini's famous Triton Fountain in Rome. It shows Triton on top

SALZBURG

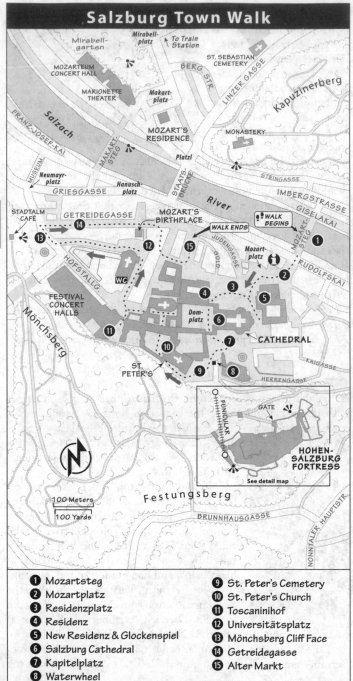

Salzburg Town Walk

- ❶ Mozartsteg
- ❷ Mozartplatz
- ❸ Residenzplatz
- ❹ Residenz
- ❺ New Residenz & Glockenspiel
- ❻ Salzburg Cathedral
- ❼ Kapitelplatz
- ❽ Waterwheel
- ❾ St. Peter's Cemetery
- ❿ St. Peter's Church
- ⓫ Toscaninihof
- ⓬ Universitätsplatz
- ⓭ Mönchsberg Cliff Face
- ⓮ Getreidegasse
- ⓯ Alter Markt

blowing his conch-shell horn. The water cascades down the basins and sprays playfully in the wind.

Notice that Salzburg's buildings are made from three distinctly different types of stone. Most common is the chunky gray conglomerate (like the cathedral's side walls) quarried from the nearby cliffs. There's also white marble (like the cathedral's towers and windows) and red marble (best seen in monuments inside buildings), both from the Alps near Berchtesgaden.

• *Turn your attention to the building on the right, the...*

❹ Residenz

This was the palace of Salzburg's powerful ruler, the prince-archbishop—that is, a ruler with both the political powers of a prince and the religious authority of an archbishop. The ornate Baroque entrance attests to the connections these rulers had with Rome. You can step inside the Residenz courtyard to get a glimpse of the impressive digs (to see the fancy interior with state rooms and an impressive collection of paintings, you must buy a DomQuartier ticket—see page 239).

Notice that the Residenz has a white-stone structure (called the Cathedral Terrace) connecting it with the cathedral. This skyway gave the prince-archbishops an easy commute to church and a chance to worship while avoiding the public.

• *At the opposite end of Residenzplatz from the Residenz is the...*

❺ New (Neue) Residenz

In the days of the prince-archbishops, this building hosted parties in its lavish rooms. These days, the New Residenz houses both the

Salzburg Museum (entrance on Mozartplatz) and the Panorama Museum (entrance between the New Residenz and the cathedral; for details on both museums, see "Sights in Salzburg," later). It's also home to the Heimatwerk, a fine shop showing off local handicrafts like dirndls and locally made jelly.

The New Residenz bell tower has a famous **glockenspiel**. This 17th-century carillon has 35 bells (cast in Antwerp) and chimes daily at 7:00, 11:00, and 18:00. It also plays little tunes appropriate to the season. The mechanism is a big barrel with adjustable tabs that turns like a giant music box, pulling the right bells in the right rhythm. (Twice-weekly tours let you get up close to watch the glockenspiel action: €4, April-Oct Thu at 17:30 and Fri at 10:30, no tours Nov-March, buy ticket and meet for tour at Panorama Muse-

SALZBURG

um, no reservations needed—but get tickets at least a few minutes ahead as it often sells out in nice weather, ask for English handout.)

Notice the tower's ornamental top: an upside-down heart in flames surrounds the solar system, representing how God loves all of creation.

Residenzplatz sets the tone for the whole town. From here, a series of interconnecting squares—like you'll see nowhere else—make a grand procession through the Old Town. Everywhere you go, you'll see similar Italian architecture. As you walk from square to square, notice how easily you slip from noisy and commercial to peaceful and reflective.

But it wasn't always so charming and peaceful. On Residenz-platz in 1938, a huge crowd—responding to the promise of jobs and the scapegoating of immigrants and minorities—welcomed Hitler's Nazi takeover and celebrated the Anschluss (the "unification" of Germany and Austria).

• *Exit the square by walking under the prince–archbishop's skyway. You'll step into Domplatz (Cathedral Square). A good place to view the cathedral facade is from the far end of the square.*

❻ Salzburg Cathedral (Salzburger Dom)

Salzburg's cathedral (rated ▲▲) was one of the first Italian Ba-roque buildings north of the Alps. The dome stands 230 feet high, and two domed towers flank the very Italian-esque entrance.

The church was consecrated in 1628. Experts differ on what motivated the build-ers. As it dates from the years of Catholic-Protestant warfare, it may have been meant to emphasize Salzburg's commitment to the Roman Catholic cause. Or it may have repre-sented a peaceful alternative to the religious strife. Regardless, Salzburg's archbishop was the top papal official north of the Alps, and the city was the pope's northern outpost. With its rich salt production, Salzburg had enough money to stay out of the conflict and earn the nickname "The Fortified Island of Peace."

The cathedral was the center of power for the prince-archbishop in his religious role, and the government buildings surrounding it served his needs as a secular prince. But for now, it's time to visit the cathedral.

Cost and Hours: Free, donation requested, Mon-Sat 8:00-19:00, Sun from 13:00; March-April, Oct, and Dec until 18:00; Jan-Feb and Nov until 17:00; www.salzburger-dom.at. If the Je-dermann theater production is under way (July and Aug), you'll find a 1,500-seat temporary theater filling the cathedral square. (And you may need to enter the cathedral through the back door.)

Visiting the Cathedral: As you approach the church, pause at the **iron gates.** The dates on the doors are milestones in the church's history. In the year 774, the first church, built in Romanesque style, was consecrated by St. Virgil (see his statue on the left), an Irish monk who became Salzburg's bishop. It was destroyed by fire in 1167, rebuilt, and then burned again in 1598. It was replaced in 1628 by the one you see today. The year 1959 marks the completion of repairs after a WWII bomb severely damaged the dome.

Because it was built in just 14 years (from 1614 to 1628), the church boasts an unusually harmonious Baroque architecture. And

it's big—330 feet long, 230 feet tall—built with sturdy pillars and broad arches. When Pope John Paul II visited in 1998, some 5,000 people packed the place.

Inside, notice how you're drawn toward the light—closer to God. Imagine being part of a sacred procession, passing from the relatively dim entrance to the bright altar with its painting of Christ's resurrection, bathed in light from the dome overhead. The church never had stained glass, just clear windows to let light power the message.

Under the soaring dome, look up and admire the exceptional stucco work, by an artist from Milan. It's molded into elaborate garlands, angels, and picture frames, some of it brightly painted. You're surrounded by the tombs (and portraits) of 10 archbishops.

You're also surrounded by four organs. (Actually, five. Don't forget the biggest organ, over the entrance.) Mozart served as organist here for two years, and he composed several Masses still played today. Salzburg's prince-archbishops were great patrons of music, with a personal orchestra that played religious music in the cathedral and dinner music in the Residenz. The tradition of music continues today. Sunday Mass here can be a musical spectacle—all five organs playing, balconies filled with singers and musicians, creating glorious surround-sound. Think of the altar in Baroque terms, as the center of a stage, with sunrays serving as spotlights in this dramatic and sacred theater.

Directly under the dome, Roman-numeral plaques commemorate the visits here by Pope John Paul II in 1988 and 1998 (notice the extra X).

At the collection box by the back pew, black-and-white photos show the bomb damage of October 16, 1944, which left a gaping hole where the dome once was. In the first chapel on the left is a dark bronze baptismal font. It dates from 1320—a rare survivor from the medieval cathedral. The lions upon which it sits are older yet, from the 12th century...back when this part of Europe didn't really know what lions looked like. In 1756, little Wolfgang Amadeus Mozart was baptized here. For the next 25 years, this would be his home church. Amadeus, by the way, means "beloved by God."

Other Cathedral Sights: The **crypt,** with more tombs and a prayer chapel, is underwhelming (downstairs from the left transept, free). To learn more about the church, you can visit the **Cathedral Museum** as part of the DomQuartier Museums tour (see page 239). In summer, the **Cathedral Excavations Museum** (Domgrabungsmuseum, outside the church on Residenzplatz and down the stairs) shows off the church's medieval foundations and a few Roman mosaics—worthwhile only for Roman-iacs (€3, daily 9:00-17:00, closed Sept-June, www.salzburgmuseum.at).

• *As you leave the cathedral, check out the concert and Mass schedules posted near the entrance. Exiting the cathedral, turn left, heading in the direction of the distant fortress on the hill. You'll soon reach a spacious square with a golden orb.*

❼ Kapitelplatz

The playful modern sculpture in the square shows a man atop a golden orb. Every year, a foundation commissions a different artist to create a new work of public art somewhere in the city; this one's from 2007. Kapitelplatz is a pleasant square—notice the giant chessboard that often draws a crowd.

Follow the orb-man's gaze up the hill to **Hohensalzburg Fortress.** (I think he's trying to decide whether to shell out for the funicular or save money by hiking up.) Construction of the fortress began in 1077. Over the centuries, the small castle grew into a mighty, whitewashed fortress—so impressive that no army even tried attacking for over 800 years. These days, you can tour the castle grounds, visit some interior rooms and museums, and enjoy incredible views. You can walk up (Festungsgasse leads up from Kapitelplatz—follow the lane straight up from the golden ball) or, for a few euros more, take the funicular (for details, see page 245). While the castle's earliest funicular dates back to the 1500s, when animals pulled cargo up its tracks, today's funicular is electric, from 1910.

Now walk across the square to the pond surrounded by a balustrade and adorned with a Trevi-fountain-like **statue of Neptune**. It looks fancy, but the pond was built as a horse bath, the 18th-century equivalent of a car wash. Notice the gold lettering above Neptune. It reads, "Leopold the Prince Built Me." But the artist added a clever twist. The inscription uses the letters "LLDVI," and so on. Those are also Roman numerals—add 'em up: L is 50, D is 500, and so on. It all adds up to 1732—the year the pond was built.

This square hosts many free events and concerts (including videos of great Salzburg Festival performances on a jumbo screen).
• *With your back to the cathedral, leave the square, exiting through the gate in the far-right corner.*

❽ Waterwheel (Wasserrad)

The waterwheel is part of a clever, still-functioning canal system built in the 12th century to bring water to Salzburg from the foothills of the Alps, 10 miles away. When the stream reached Salzburg, it was divided into five smaller canals for the citizens' use. The rushing water was harnessed to waterwheels, which powered factories. There were more than 100 watermill-powered firms as late as the 19th century. Residents also used the water to fight fires and, once a week, to flush the streets clean. Hygienic Salzburg never suffered from a plague...it's probably the only major town in Austria with no plague monument. For more on the canal system, you might want to visit the nearby Alm River Canal exhibit (which you enter after exiting the funicular on the way down; see page 251).

This particular waterwheel (actually, it's a modern replacement) once ground grain into flour to make bread for the monks of St. Peter's Abbey. Nowadays, you can pop into the adjacent **bakery**—fragrant and traditional—and buy a fresh-baked roll for about a euro (closed Wed and Sun).
• *You've entered the borders of the former St. Peter's Abbey, a monastic complex of churches, courtyards, businesses (like the bakery), and a cemetery. Find the Katakomben sign and step through the wrought-iron gates into...*

❾ St. Peter's Cemetery (Petersfriedhof)

This collection of lovingly tended graves abuts the sheer rock face of the Mönchsberg (free, silence requested, daily 6:30-20:00, Oct-March until 18:00, www.stift-stpeter.at). Walk in about 50 yards past a well to a junction of lanes in the middle of the cemetery. (Stop at the round stone ball on the right—perfect for stretching that stiff back.) You're surrounded by three churches, each founded in the early Middle Ages atop a pagan Celtic holy site. The biggest church, St. Peter's, sticks its big Romanesque apse into the cemetery. Notice the fancy tombstones lining the church's wall.

The graves surrounding you are tended by descendants of the deceased. In Austria (and many other European countries), gravesites are rented, not owned. Rent bills are sent out every 10 years. If no one cares enough to make the payment, your tombstone is removed. Note the well you passed, used to fill the watering cans for the family members who keep these flowery graves so pretty.

The cemetery plays a role in *The Sound of Music.* The Captain and his large family were well known in Salzburg for their musical talents. But when Nazi Germany annexed Austria in 1938, the Von Trapps decided to flee so that the father would not be pressed into service again. In the movie, they hid here as they made their daring escape. The scene was actually filmed on a Hollywood set inspired by St. Peter's Cemetery.

Look up the cliff, which has a few buildings attached—called (not quite accurately) "catacombs." Legendary medieval hermit-monks are said to have lived in the hillside here. For a small fee, you can enter the *Katakomben* and climb lots of steps to see a few old caves, a chapel, and some fine city views (entrance at the base of the cliff, under the arcade—look for #LIV over the arch; €2, visit takes 10 minutes; daily 10:00-12:30 & 13:00-18:00, Oct-April until 17:00).

Explore the arcade at the base of the cliff with its various burial chapels. Alcove #XXI has the tomb of the cathedral architect Santino Solari—forever facing his creation. At the catacombs entry (#LIV) are two interesting tombs marked by plaques on the floor. "Marianne" is Mozart's sister, nicknamed "Nannerl." As children, Mozart and his sister performed together on grand tours of Europe's palaces. Michael Haydn was the brother of Joseph Haydn. He succeeded Mozart as church cathedral organist.

• *Exit the cemetery through the green door at the opposite end. Just outside, you enter a large courtyard anchored by...*

⑩ St. Peter's Church (Stiftskirche St. Peter)

You're standing at the birthplace of Christianity in Salzburg. St. Peter's Abbey—the monastery that surrounds this courtyard—was founded in 696, barely two centuries after the fall of Rome. The recommended Stiftskeller St. Peter restaurant in the courtyard (known these days for its Mozart Dinner Concert) brags that

Charlemagne ate here in the year 803, making it (perhaps) the oldest restaurant in Europe. St. Peter's Church dates from 1147.

Cost and Hours: Free, daily 8:00-21:00, Nov-March until 19:00, www.stift-stpeter.at.

Visiting the Church: Enter the church, pausing in the atrium to admire the Romanesque **tympanum** (from 1250) over the inner doorway. Jesus sits on a rainbow, flanked by Peter and Paul. Beneath them is a stylized Tree of Life, and overhead, a Latin inscription reading, "I am the door to life, and only through me can you find eternal life."

Enter the **nave**. The once purely Romanesque interior (you may find a few surviving bits of faded 13th-century frescoes) now lies hidden under a sugary Rococo finish. It's Salzburg's only Rococo interior—all whitewashed, with highlights of pastel green, gold, and red. If it feels Bavarian, it's because it was done by Bavarian artists. The ceiling paintings feature St. Peter receiving the keys from Christ (center painting), walking on water, and joining the angels in heaven.

The monastery was founded by **St. Rupert** (c. 650-718). Find his statue at the main altar—he's the second gold statue from the left. Rupert arrived as a Christian missionary in what was then a largely pagan land. He preached the gospel, reopened the Roman salt mines, and established the city. It was he who named it "Salzburg."

Rupert's tomb is midway up the right aisle. It's adorned with a painting of him praying for his city. Beneath him is a depiction of Salzburg circa 1750 (when this was painted): one bridge, salt ships sailing the river, and angels hoisting barrels of salt to heaven.

• *Exit the courtyard at the opposite side from where you entered, through the arch under the blue-and-yellow sundial. The passageway takes you past dorms still used for student monks. At the T-intersection (where you bump into the Franciscan Church), turn right for a quick detour to appreciate another view of Domplatz.*

You're just in time for "the coronation of the Virgin Mary." The Baroque style was all about putting on a show, which is wonderfully illustrated by the **statue of Mary** (1771) that welcomes visitors in this square. As you approach her from the center of this lane, walking between the little brass rails in the cobblestones, keep an eye on the golden crown above and far behind Mary on the cathedral's facade. Just as you get to the middle arch, watch as she's crowned Queen of Heaven by the two angels on the church facade. Bravo!

Notice one more time the very Italian look of the cathedral facade: the false-front roofline; the windows flanked by classical half-columns and topped with heavy pediments; and the Baroque balustrade, decorated with garlands and masks, and studded with statues.

• *Do a U-turn and head back down Franziskanergasse. Pass beneath the archway painted with a modern Lamentation scene (1926) to enter a square called Max-Reinhardt-Platz. Pause here to admire the line of impressive Salzburg Festival concert halls ahead of you. Then turn left, through a square archway, into a small square called...*

⓫ Toscaninihof

In this small courtyard, you get a peek at the back end of the large Festival Hall complex (on your right). The Festival Hall has three theaters and seats 5,000 people (see photo on the wall). It's very busy during the Salzburg Music Festival each summer. The festival was started in the austere 1920s, after World War I, and Salzburg couldn't afford a new concert hall, so they remodeled what were once the prince-archbishop's stables and riding school.

The tunnel you see to the left leads to the actual concert hall. It's generally closed, but you might be able to look through nearby doorways and see carpenters building stage sets or hear performers practicing for an upcoming show.

The Von Trapp family performed in the Festival Hall. In the movie, this backstage courtyard is where Captain von Trapp nervously waited before walking onstage to sing "Edelweiss." Then the family slipped away to begin their escape from the Nazis.

The Toscaninihof also has the entrance to the city's huge, 1,500-space, inside-the-mountain parking lot. It originated in 1944 as the Mönchsberg air raid shelter—an underground system that offered 18,000 locals refuge from WWII bombs. The stone stairway in the courtyard leads a few flights up to a panoramic view.

• *Return to Max-Reinhardt-Platz. Continue straight along the right side of the big church, passing popular sausage stands and a public WC, then enter...*

⓬ Universitätsplatz

This square, home to the huge Baroque Kollegienkirche (University Church), also hosts Salzburg's liveliest open-air produce market (and a lot of touristy food stands). It generally runs mornings, Monday through Saturday. It's at its best early Saturday morning, when the farmers are in town. The fancy yellow facade overlooking the square marks the back end of Mozart's Birthplace, which we'll see shortly.

Find the fountain—it's about 50 yards past the church, on the right. As with public marketplaces elsewhere, it's for washing fruit and vegetables. This fountain—though modern in design—is still part of a medieval-era water system. The water plummets down a hole and on to the river. The sundial over the water hole shows both the time and the date.

• *Continue toward the end of the long, tapering square. Along the way, you'll pass several nicely arcaded medieval passageways (on the right), which lead to Salzburg's old main street, Getreidegasse. (Try weaving back and forth through some.) When you reach the traffic-control bollards, you're looking at the...*

⓭ Mönchsberg Cliff Face

Rising some 1,700 feet above you is the Mönchsberg, Salzburg's mountain. Today you see the remains of an aborted attempt in the 1600s to cut through the Mönchsberg. It proved too big a job, and when new tunneling technology arrived, that project was abandoned. The stones cut did serve as a quarry for the city's 17th-century growth spurt—the bulk of the cathedral, for example, is built of this economical and local conglomerate stone.

Early one morning in 1669, a huge landslide killed more than 200 townspeople who lived close to where the elevator is now (to the right). Since then, the cliffs have been carefully checked each spring and fall. Even today, you might see crews on the cliff, monitoring its stability.

Walk to the base of the cliff, where you'll see what was the giant horse trough for the prince-archbishops' stables. Paintings show the various breeds and temperaments of horses in the stable. Like Vienna, Salzburg had a passion for the equestrian arts.

• *Walk a block (past the toy museum —Spielzeug Museum—on your left) toward the river. (The elevator up the Mönchsberg is just ahead.) Opposite the church, turn right onto the long pedestrian street called...*

⓮ Getreidegasse

Old Salzburg's colorful main drag, Getreidegasse (rated ▲▲) has been a center of trade since Roman times. Check out all the old

wrought-iron signs that advertise what's sold inside. This was the Salzburg of prosperous medieval burghers (businessmen). These days it bustles with the tourist trade. Dating mainly from the 15th century, the buildings are tall and narrow because this was prime real estate, and there was nowhere to build but up. Space was always tight, as the town was squeezed between the river and the mountain, and lots of land was set aside for the church. The architecture still looks much as it did in Mozart's day—though many of the buildings themselves are now inhabited by chain outlets.

Enjoy the traditional signs, and try to guess what they sold. There are signs advertising spirits, a book maker, and a horn indicating a place for the postal coach. A brewery has a star for the name of the beer, "Sternbräu." There's a window maker, a key maker, a pastry shop, a tailor, a pretzel maker, a pharmacy, a hat maker, and...ye olde hamburger shoppe, McDonald's.

On the right at #39, **Sporer** pours homemade spirits (about €4/shot, Mon-Fri 9:30-19:00, Sat 8:30-17:00, closed Sun). This has been a family-run show for a century—fun-loving, proud, and English-speaking. *Nuss* is nut, *Marille* is apricot (typical of Austria), the *Kletzen* cocktail is like a super-thick Baileys with pear, and *Edle Brande* is the stronger schnapps. The many homemade firewaters are in jugs at the end of the bar.

After noticing building #39's old doorbells—one per floor—continue down Getreidegasse. On the left at #40, **Eisgrotte** serves good ice cream. Across from Eisgrotte, a tunnel leads to the recommended **Balkan Grill** (sign reads *Bosna Grill*), the local choice for the very best wurst in town. Down the tunnel at #28 (a blacksmith shop since the 1400s), Herr Wieber, an ironworker and locksmith, welcomes the curious. Next door, McDonald's is required to keep its arches Baroque and low-key.

At Getreidegasse #9, the knot of excited tourists marks the home of Salzburg's most famous resident. Mozart was born here in 1756. It was here that he composed most of his boy-genius works. Inside you see paintings of his family, letters, personal items (a lock of his hair, a clavichord he may have played), all trying to bring life to the Mozart story (see the description on page 242).

• *A bit farther along, at Getreidegasse #3, turn right, into the passageway. You'll walk under a whale bone (likely symbolizing the wares of an exotic import shop) and reach the Old World time-capsule café called* **Schatz Konditorei** *(worth a stop for coffee and pastry). At Schatz Konditorei, turn left through the tunnel-like passage. When you reach Sigmund-Haffner-Gasse, glance to the left (for a nice view of the city hall tower), then turn right. Walk along Sigmund-Haffner-Gasse and take your first left to reach a square called...*

⑮ Alter Markt

This is Salzburg's old marketplace. Here you'll find a sausage stand and the venerable and recommended Café Tomaselli.

• *Our walk is over. If you're up for more sightseeing, most everything's a short walk from here. The Old Town has several museums, or you can head up to the Hohensalzburg Fortress. To visit sights across the river in the New Town, cross the pedestrian bridge nearby.*

Sights in Salzburg

IN THE OLD TOWN
▲DomQuartier Museums

The interconnected museums of the DomQuartier, ringing the Domplatz, focus on religious art and the history of Salzburg's prince-archbishops. Your DomQuartier ticket admits you to a circular, indoor route through the Residenz (the ornate former palace), the cathedral (which you view from the organ loft), and a couple of adjoining buildings. For me, the highlight isn't the apartments or paintings, but the chance to walk across the gallery to the organ loft and peer into the cavernous cathedral (not permitted during Sun morning Mass, so plan accordingly).

Cost and Hours: €12, includes good audioguide, Wed-Mon 10:00-17:00, Wed until 20:00 July-Aug, closed Tue except July-Aug, last entry one hour before closing, Residenzplatz 1, tel. 0662/8042-2109, www.domquartier.at.

Visiting the DomQuartier Museums: If you enter at the Residenz (you can also enter at the cathedral), signs will guide you along the following circuit:

Once Salzburg's center of power, the **Residenz State Rooms** were the home of the prince-archbishop. Walking through these 15 chandeliered, stuccoed, tapestried, and frescoed "stately rooms" (*Prunkräume*), you'll see elements of Renaissance, Baroque, and Classicist styles—200 years of let-them eat-cake splendor.

The painting collection, one floor up in the **Residenz Gallery,** is strongest in Baroque paintings—not surprising in this bastion of Catholicism. The collection is always changing, but look for these highlights: Rubens' *Allegory on Charles V* shows the pope's great champion with a sword in one hand and a scepter in the other. Rembrandt's teeny-tiny *Old Woman Praying* glows, despite her wrinkled face and broken teeth (the model was probably his mother). Other highlights include Federico Barocci's intense *Self-Portrait*, Bernardo Strozzi's *Sleeping Child*, and Boucher's rosy-cheeked *Dreaming Shepherdess*. Austria is represented by F. G. Waldmüller's cheery, sun-drenched *Children at the Window*, Salzburg's own Hans Makart's honest portrait of his first wife Amalie, and lots of Romantic alpine landscapes.

In good weather, you can cross over to the cathedral the same way the prince-archbishops did—walking across their marble skyway (the **Panorama Terrace**), high above the unwashed masses. (If it's raining, you'll be sent one floor down to the indoor walkway.)

Though you don't actually tour the cathedral interior, you do glance down on the nave from high above. On this level, you can visit two small museums: the **Nordoratorium** (North Oratory) and the **Cathedral Museum,** with rich religious objects from the cathedral's long history.

Then you'll head downstairs to the **Cabinet of Curiosities** and follow the Long Gallery to the **Museum of St. Peter's Abbey**—introducing you to work and life at the abbey (which claims to be the oldest monastery north of the Alps).

▲▲Salzburg Museum

This is your best look at Salzburg's history. As the building was once the prince-archbishop's New Residence, many exhibits are in the lavish rooms where Salzburg's rulers entertained.

Cost and Hours: €9, €10 combo-ticket with Panorama Museum, includes heavy-but-handy high-tech audio/videoguide (ID required), Tue-Sun 9:00-17:00, closed Mon, café, on Residenzplatz, tel. 0662/620-8080, www.salzburgmuseum.at.

Visiting the Museum: The first floor and the *Kunsthalle* in the basement house temporary exhibits. But the centerpiece of the museum is the permanent **Salzburg Myth** exhibit on the second floor. You'll learn how the town's physical beauty—nestled among the Alps, near a river—attracted 19th-century Romantics who made it one of Europe's first tourist destinations, an "Alpine Arcadia." Visitors are challenged to consider how people then—as today—filtered out certain harsh realities (like poor living conditions) in favor of romanticized images of the places they visited.

Room 2.01 displays lots of gauzy landscapes of Salzburg from this era (and earlier), all remarkably recognizable. The side room holds musical instruments and plentiful audio samples, and explains how the arrival of the music festival in the 1920s spurred Salzburg's status still more, drawing high-class visitors from across the globe. The exhibit includes strings, woodwinds, and keyboards dating back as far as the 1600s. Highlights include the enormous bassoon-like *Grossbass Pommer,* the single-stringed *tromba marina* (nicknamed "the nun's violin," its buzz resembles a trumpet), and the tiny *pochette* (pocket-sized violin).

After that prelude, several rooms address the notion of tourism in the context of city development, and the conflict of modernization versus conservation. The exhibit then focuses mostly on the glory days of the prince-archbishops (1500-1800), with displays housed in impressive ceremonial rooms. Portraits of the prince-archbishops (in Room 2.07) show them to be cultured men, with sensitive eyes and soft hands, and carrying books. But they were also powerful secular rulers of an independent state that extended far beyond today's Salzburg (see the map in Room 2.08).

Room 2.09 displays Daniel Miller's paintings of the city as seen from Kapuzinerberg and from Mönchsberg. Even though both paintings are from 1635, almost everything in them is still identifiable.

The heart of the exhibit is Room 2.11, the big, colorful hall where the Salzburg Diet (the legislature) met. The elaborate painted relief ceiling depicts heroic Romans who sacrificed for their country. Spend some time here with the grab-bag of interesting displays, including old guns, rock crystals, and coins. A portrait shows the prince-archbishop who sums up Salzburg's golden age—Wolf Dietrich von Raitenau (1559-1617). Here he is at age 28, having just assumed power. Educated, well-traveled, a military strategist, and fluent in several languages, Wolf Dietrich epitomized the kind of Renaissance man who could lead both church and state. He largely created the city we see today—the rebuilt cathedral, Residenz, Residenzplatz, and Mirabell Palace—done in the Italian Baroque style. Interactive screens describe the strict ordinances issued by this notable archbishop, including the Mandate of Religion (1588), which ordered all non-Catholics to leave the city. Today, about 95 percent of Salzburg is (nominally) Catholic, and there's only one Lutheran church.

Nearby exhibits flesh out Wolf Dietrich the man and his associates. Room 2.13 holds a portrait of the Italian architect Vincenzo Scamozzi, who contributed to the city's Baroque appearance during Wolf Dietrich's tenure. You'll also see a portrait of Salome Alt, Wolf Dietrich's mistress, a merchant's daughter which whom he shared 15 children and a retreat outside the city walls (which was later rebuilt as Mirabell Palace). This liaison prevented Wolf Dietrich's promotion to cardinal, but the couple's love never faltered. After Raitenau's death, Alt dressed as a widow for the rest of her life.

In Room 2.12, find the oldest known painted view of Salzburg (1599), and try to spot the burnt ruins of the second Romanesque church, now the site of Salzburg Cathedral.

▲Panorama Museum

Located in the New Residence, the Panorama Museum displays a wrap-around painting of the city, giving a 360-degree look at Salzburg in the year 1829.

Cost and Hours: €4 includes Panorama and temporary exhibits, €10 combo-ticket with Salzburg Museum, daily 9:00-17:00, Residenzplatz 9, tel. 0662/620-808-730, www.salzburgmuseum.at.

Visiting the Museum: From the Salzburg Museum entryway, find the underground "Panorama Passage" that leads to this unique exhibit. The passage itself is lined with archaeological finds (Roman and early medieval), helping set the stage for the Salzburg you're about to see.

In the early 19th century, before the advent of photography, 360-degree panorama paintings of great cities or events were popular. When this one was created, the 1815 Treaty of Vienna had just divvied up post-Napoleonic Europe, and Salzburg had become part of the Habsburg realm. This photo-realistic painting served as a town portrait done at the emperor's request.

Painted by Johann Michael Sattler, the view shows the city as seen from the top of its castle. It took Sattler four years to complete (1825-29), after which the painting spent 10 years touring the great cities of Europe, showing off Salzburg's breathtaking setting. Donated to the city by Sattler's son in 1870, it was displayed at Mirabell Palace until 1937 and then stored in Salzburg fortress. Today, the exquisitely restored painting, hung in a circular room, offers a fascinating look at the city as it was in the early 19th century. The river was slower and had beaches, but the Old Town looks essentially as it does today.

▲▲Mozart's Birthplace (Geburtshaus)

In 1747, Leopold Mozart—a musician in the prince-archbishop's band—moved into this small rental unit with his new bride. Soon

they had a baby girl (Nannerl), and in 1756, a little boy was born—Wolfgang Amadeus Mozart. It was here that Mozart learned to play piano and violin, and composed his first boy-genius works. Even after the family gained fame, touring Europe's palaces and becoming the toast of Salzburg, they continued living in this rather cramped apartment.

Today this is the most popular Mozart sight in town—for fans, it's almost a pilgrimage. Shuffling through with the crowds, you'll peruse three floors of rooms displaying paintings, letters, personal items, and lots of context, all bringing life to the Mozart story.

Cost and Hours: €11, €18 combo-ticket with Mozart's Residence, daily 9:00-17:30, July-Aug 8:30-19:00, Getreidegasse 9, tel. 0662/844-313, www.mozarteum.at. Avoid shoulder-to-shoulder crowds by visiting right when it opens or late in the day.

Visiting Mozart's Birthplace: You'll begin on the top floor

Mozart's Salzburg

Salzburg was Mozart's home for the first 25 years of his brief, 35-year life. He was born on Getreidegasse and baptized in the cathedral. He played his first big concert, at age six, at the Residenz. He was the organist for the cathedral, conducted the prince-archbishop's orchestra, and dined at (what's now called) Café Tomaselli. It was from Salzburg that he gained Europe-wide fame, touring the continent with his talented performing family. At age 17, Mozart and his family moved into lavish digs at (today's) Mozart's Residence.

As his fame and ambitions grew, Mozart eventually left Salzburg to pursue his dreams in Vienna. His departure from Salzburg's royal court in 1/81 is the stuff of legend. Mozart, full of himself, announced that he was quitting. The prince-archbishop essentially said, "You can't quit; you're fired!" and as Mozart walked out, he was literally kicked in the ass.

Mozart Sights in Salzburg: Both Mozart sights in Salzburg—the Birthplace and the Residence—are expensive and equally good. If I had to choose, I'd go with the Birthplace as the best overall introduction (though it's more crowded), and consider the Residence extra credit. If you're truly interested in Mozart and his times, buy the combo-ticket and see both.

in the actual apartment—five small rooms, including the kitchen and the bedroom where Mozart was born. The rooms are bare of any furnishings. Instead, you see Mozart's "square piano," detailed biographies and portraits of the famous family, and some memorabilia: Mozart's childhood viola, some (possible) locks of his hair, buttons from his jacket, and a letter to his wife, whom he calls his "little rascal, pussy-pussy." Snippets of correspondence between Mozart's family members (beneath the portraits) are filled with warmth and humor, revealing their individual personalities.

The museum portion begins with an exhibition on Mozart's life after he left Salzburg for Vienna: He jams with Haydn and wows the Viennese with electrifying concerts and new compositions. Despite his fame, Mozart fell on hard times, and died young and in debt. But, as the museum shows, his legacy lived on. Using computers, you can hear his music while following along on his handwritten scores.

Downstairs, the Mozart und Oper room examines the operas he wrote (*Don Giovanni*, *The Magic Flute*, *The Marriage of Figaro*), with stage sets and video clips. The prize piece is an old clavichord on which Mozart supposedly composed his final work—the *Requiem*, which was played for his own funeral. (A predecessor of the more complicated piano, the clavichord's keys hit the strings with a simple teeter-totter motion that allows you to play very softly—ideal for composers living in tight apartment quarters.)

The lower-floor Wunderkind Mozart exhibit takes you on the road with the child prodigy, and gives a slice-of-life portrait of what it was like to live and travel in the 1700s (Mozart spent a third of his life journeying throughout Europe—during a time when it took 29 hours to travel just from Salzburg to Munich). The restful, oval-shaped listening room allows you to take a break from the crowds and be immersed in beautiful music and perfect acoustics.

Summer Riding School (Felsenreitschule)

Built into the mountainside, the Summer Riding School was established in 1683 by Prince-Archbishop Johann Ernst von Thun adjacent to his massive stables, now the next-door Large Festival Hall (Grosses Festspielhaus). The complex took on many uses before Austrian-American theater director Max Reinhardt took on the venue for the Salzburg Festival in 1926. While fans will recognize its iconic arcaded stage as the setting for the Von Trapp family's final public performance in *The Sound of Music*, it's worthwhile to take a guided tour of this venue to understand its architecture, artwork, and theatrical and technical feats.

Cost and Hours: Visit possible only with guided tour, €7, tours run daily at 14:00, mid-July-Aug also at 9:30 & 15:30, closed during performances or rehearsals, buy ticket at least 15 minutes in advance, departs from Salzburger Festspiele Shop (Hofstallgasse 1, www.salzburgerfestspiele.at, info@salzburgfestival.at).

Sound of Music World

This exhibition works hard to tell the story of the real Von Trapp family. The pricey "museum" has a few artifacts, an interview video with one of the Von Trapp children, and some fun photos taken of the film cast in Salzburg during filming here. The exhibit is best left to diehards, but the gift shop is fun for all.

Cost and Hours: Museum-€8, store-free to enter; daily 10:00-18:00, Getreidegasse 47—across from funicular, tel. 0662/630-860, www.soundofmusicworld.com.

ATOP THE CLIFFS ABOVE THE OLD TOWN

Atop the Mönchsberg, the mini mountain that rises behind the Old Town, is a tangle of paved walking paths with great views, a couple of cafés (one cheap, one expensive, both with million-dollar views), a modern art museum, a neighborhood of very fancy homes, and one major sight: Hohensalzburg Fortress (perched on the Festungsberg, the Mönchsberg's southern arm).

Getting There: There are three ways to get up to the cliffs: climb, take an elevator, or ride the funicular.

The **climb** up or down is steep but quick and saves a few euros. Paths or stairs lead up from the Augustiner Bräustübl beer hall/garden, Toscaninihof (near the Salzburg Festival concert halls), and Festungsgasse (at the base of the fortress).

The Mönchsberg **elevator** *(Aufzug)* starts where Gstättengasse and Griesgasse meet, on the west side of the Old Town—look for the Museum of Modern Art entry (€2.30 one-way, €3.60 round-trip—can descend via funicular at Hohensalzburg Fortress, normally Tue-Sun 8:00-23:00, Mon until 19:00).

The **funicular** starts from Festungsgasse (just off Kapitelplatz, by the cathedral) and comes up inside the fortress complex. It's pricey—€6.50 to go up or €8 round-trip—but you can purchase a fortress ticket that includes the funicular.

If you plan to do it all, the fortress, modern art museum, and both the elevator and funicular are covered by the Salzburg Card (see under "Tourist Information," earlier). I'd do it in this order: Take the funicular to the fortress in the morning (to potentially avoid the worst crowds), take the Mönchsberg Walk over to the museum, and then take the elevator down to the Old Town. Cheapskates can see the Museum of Modern Art first, use that ticket to cover elevator and funicular rides, and then buy the "by foot" ticket to enter the fortress.

Cafés: The elevator deposits you right at the recommended Mönchsberg 32, a chic café/bar/restaurant adjacent to the modern art museum and a fine place for a drink or splurge meal. From there, it's a five-minute walk to the rustic, recommended Stadtalm Café, with wooden picnic tables and a one-with-nature allure.

▲▲Hohensalzburg Fortress (Festung)

Construction of Hohensalzburg Fortress was begun about 1077 by Archbishop Gebhard of Salzburg as a show of the Catholic Church's power (see sidebar on page 247). Built on a rock (called Festungsberg) 400 feet above the Salzach River, the fortress was never really used. That was the idea. It was a good investment—so foreboding, nobody attacked the town for over 800 years. The city was never taken by force, but when Napoleon stopped by, Salzburg wisely surrendered. After a stint as a military barracks, the fortress was opened to the public in the 1860s by Habsburg Emperor Franz Josef. Today, it remains one of Europe's mightiest castles, dominating Salzburg's skyline and offering impressive views in both directions, cafés, and a handful of mediocre museums. It's a pleasant place to grab an ice-cream cone and wander the whitewashed maze of buildings while soaking up some medieval ambience.

Cost: Don't get bogged down in the many ticket variations; the basic choices are whether to walk or ride the funicular up, and whether you want to add on the finest rooms. Most visitors avoid the short but steep walk by opting for the one-minute trip on the funicular *(Festungsbahn)*.

The **"basic" ticket** (€12.90 by funicular, €10 by foot) covers most castle sights: a brief audioguide tour of a small historical exhibit and a tower-top view (signed as *A*); a variety of museums, including the modern Fortress Museum and the military-oriented Rainer Regiment museums (B); and the Marionette Exhibit.

The **"all-inclusive" ticket** (€16.30 by funicular—cheaper online and before 10:00, €12.40 by foot) covers everything in the "basic" ticket plus a brief visit to the well-presented Regency Rooms (signed as *C*). Even with a "basic" ticket, you can pay €3.50 at the door to enter the Regency Rooms (worth seeing but skippable if your time is short).

Hours: The museums are open daily 9:00-19:00, Oct-April 9:30-17:00.

Information: Tel. 0662/8424-3011, www.salzburg-burgen.at.

Avoiding Crowds: Avoid waits for the funicular ascent with the Salzburg Card (which lets you skip to the head of the line) or by walking up. In summer, there can be long waits to start the audioguide tour (only 60 people are admitted at a time). To avoid ticket-line queues, buy your ticket online before you visit. To avoid crowds in general, visit early in the morning or late in the day.

Concerts: The fortress serves as a venue for evening concerts (the Festungskonzerte), which are held in the old banquet rooms on the upper floor of the palace museum. Concerts take place 300 nights a year and are a good way to see the fortress without crowds. For concert details, see page 262.

Eating: The **$$ cafés** to either side of the upper funicular station are a great place to linger while taking in the jaw-

Popes vs. Emperors

Salzburg was on the frontline of a medieval power struggle  between the Roman Catholic Church and the Holy Roman Emperors. The town's mighty Hohensalzburg Fortress—a symbol of the Church's determination to assert its power here—was built around 1077, just as the conflict was heating up.

The argument was a classic tug-of-war between papal and imperial power. The prize: the right to appoint (or "invest") church officials. Such appointments traditionally came from the Church, but in the early Middle Ages, rulers began picking bishops and abbots themselves (which Rome more or less rubber-stamped). These appointed bishops and abbots were then under considerable obligation to support their king, both spiritually and materially.

For a while, Rome put up with this turned-around system, but things came to a head under Pope Gregory VII. To remind the uppity kings of their place below God and pope, he prohibited investiture by secular ("lay") rulers in 1074. But Holy Roman Emperor Henry IV bucked the system, continuing to appoint his own church leaders and boldly renouncing Gregory VII as pope. In retaliation, Gregory excommunicated both Henry and the bishops he'd appointed.

Salzburg's Archbishop Gebhard took the pope's side against Henry. As a visible sign of ecclesiastical strength, he started construction of the massive Hohensalzburg Fortress. Henry hit back by expelling Gebhard from Salzburg in 1085. Undeterred, Gebhard spent a decade in exile mustering support for the pope and raising forces against Henry.

Gebhard eventually returned to Salzburg and resumed his position as archbishop. But the investiture back-and-forth continued until 1122, when the next pope and emperor finally reached a power-sharing accord.

dropping view (daily 11:30-22:00, food served until about 20:30, closed Jan-Feb).

❷ **Self-Guided Tour:** The fortress is an eight-acre complex of some 50 buildings, with multiple courtyards and multiple rings of protective walls.

• *At the top of the funicular, turn right, head to the panoramic terrace, and bask in the* **view** *toward the Alps. Continue up through the fortress gates— two defensive rings for double protection. Emerging into the light, go left (uphill) to find the entrance to the...*

Audioguide Tour (A): The audioguide leads you through a

SALZBURG

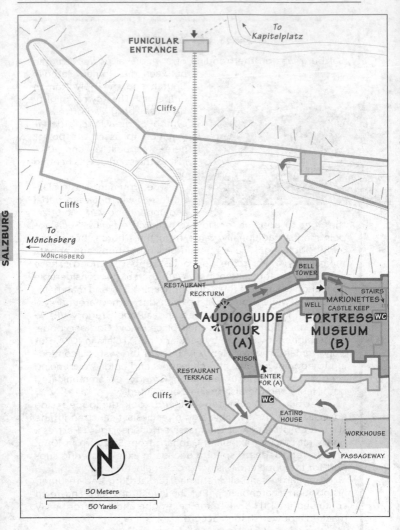

To Kapitelplatz

FUNICULAR ENTRANCE

Cliffs

Cliffs

To Mönchsberg

MÖNCHSBERG

RESTAURANT

RECKTURM

BELL TOWER

WELL

STAIRS

MARIONETTES

CASTLE KEEP

AUDIOGUIDE TOUR (A)

FORTRESS MUSEUM (B)

WC

PRISON

RESTAURANT TERRACE

Cliffs

ENTER FOR (A)

WC

EATING HOUSE

WORKHOUSE

PASSAGEWAY

N

50 Meters

50 Yards

few (mostly bare) rooms. The **Stable Block** highlights 17 prince-archbishops and displays models showing the fortress' growth, starting in 1460. The last model (1810) shows it at its peak. The fortress was never taken by force, but it did make a negotiated surrender with Napoleon, and never saw action again.

The tour then takes you to the base of the **prison tower,** with a room dedicated to the art of "enhanced interrogation" (to use American military jargon)—filled with tools of that gruesome trade. One of the most esteemed prisoners held here was Prince-Archbishop Wolf Dietrich, who lost favor with the pope, was captured by a Bavarian duke, and spent his last seven years

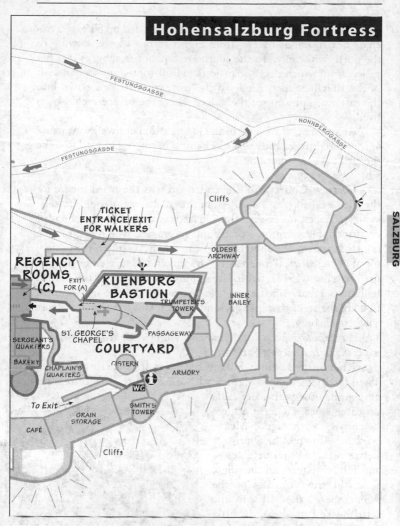

Hohensalzburg Fortress

FESTUNGSGASSE

NONNBERGGASSE

FESTUNGSGASSE

Cliffs

TICKET
ENTRANCE/EXIT
FOR WALKERS

OLDEST
ARCHWAY

**REGENCY
ROOMS
(C)** EXIT
FOR (A)

**KUENBURG
BASTION**

TRUMPETER'S
TOWER

INNER
BAILEY

ST. GEORGE'S
CHAPEL

PASSAGEWAY

SERGEANT'S
QUARTERS

COURTYARD

BAKERY

CHAPLAIN'S
QUARTERS

CISTERN

ARMORY

WC

To Exit →

GRAIN
STORAGE

SMITH'S
TOWER

CAFÉ

Cliffs

in Hohensalzburg. It's a complicated story—basically, the pope counted on Salzburg to hold the line against the Protestants for several generations following the Reformation. Wolf Dietrich was a good Catholic, as were most Salzburgers. But the town's important businessmen and the region's salt miners were Protestant, and for Salzburg's financial good, Wolf Dietrich dealt with them in a tolerant and pragmatic way. Eventually the pope—who allowed zero tolerance for Protestants in those heady Counter-Reformation days—had Wolf Dietrich locked up and replaced.

Next, climb a spiral staircase to the top of one of the castle's towers, the **Reckturm.** Jockey your way to the railing at the upper platform and survey the scene. (If it's too crowded up here, you can enjoy nearly-as-good views from bigger terraces lower down.) To the north is the city. To the south are Salzburg's suburbs in a flat valley, from which rises the majestic 6,000-foot Untersberg massif of the Berchtesgaden Alps. To the east, you can look down into the castle complex to see the palace where the prince-archbishops lived.

As you exit, at the end of the long battlement walkway, pause at the **"Salzburger Bull"**—a mechanical barrel organ used to wake the citizens every morning.

• *Exit the tour into the...*

Fortress Courtyard: The courtyard was the main square for the medieval fortress's 1,000-some residents, who could be self-sufficient when necessary. The square was ringed by the shops of craftsmen, blacksmiths, bakers, and so on. The well dipped into a rain-fed cistern. The church is dedicated to St. George, the protector of horses (logical for an army church) and decorated by fine red marble reliefs (1512). Behind the church is the top of the old lift (still in use) that helped supply the fortress. Under the archway next to it are the steps that lead back into the city, or to the paths across the Mönchsberg.

• *Just downhill from the chapel, find an opening in the wall that leads to a balcony with a view of Salzburg.*

Kuenburg Bastion: Survey Salzburg from here and think about fortifying an important city by using nature. The fortress sits atop a ridgeline with sheer cliffs on three sides, giving it a huge defensive advantage. Meanwhile, the town of Salzburg sits between the natural defenses of the Salzach River and the ridge. (The ridgeline consists of the Mönchsberg, the cliffs to the left, and Festungsberg, the little mountain you're on.) The fortress itself has three concentric rings of defense: the original keep in the center (where the museums we're about to visit are located), the vast whitewashed walls (near you), and still more beefed-up fortifications (on the hillside below you, added against an expected Ottoman invasion). With all these defenses, the city only required a few more touches: The New Town across the river needed a bit of a wall arcing from the river to its hill. Back then, only one bridge crossed the Salzach into town, and it had a fortified gate. Cradled amid the security of its defenses—both natural and man-made—independent Salzburg thrived for nearly a thousand years.

• *Back in the main courtyard, with the chapel on your right, head uphill*

through the stone gate and go straight ahead up the stairs. At the very top of the long staircase is the entrance to the...

Fortress Museum (Festungsmuseum, B): The first part of this extensive museum covers the history of the fortress, including a great town model and smaller models illustrating how the castle was constructed, and military artifacts. Follow the one-way route, exploring the exhibits on this floor, then head one floor up.

• *At this level, you have the chance to enter the Regency Rooms.*

Regency Rooms (C): These recently restored rooms are the most beautiful in the palace, with richly painted and gilded woodwork. You'll begin by viewing a fun seven-minute video presentation/puppet show setting the historical context for when the prince-archbishop built these rooms around the year 1500—the High Middle Ages. Then you'll see the Golden Hall, where evening concerts are held, and the Royal Apartment, consisting of two rooms—one with a colorfully painted tile stove in the corner, and the other featuring a toilet with a several-hundred-foot drop.

• *You'll loop right back to where you started. From here, you can proceed into...*

More Museums: The rest of this floor belongs to the **Rainer Regiments Museum,** dedicated to the Salzburg soldiers who fought mountain-to-mountain on the Italian front during World War I. Heading downstairs, you'll find the second part of the **Fortress Museum,** with a 16th-century kitchen, torture devices (including a chastity belt), a creatively displayed collection of pikes and swords, carved-wood furniture, and a fine collection of everyday decorative arts (dishes).

• *Exiting the museums and gift shop, turn left up the passage, head back down the long staircase, then hook a U-turn at the bottom to find the...*

Marionette Exhibit: Marionette shows are a Salzburg tradition (think of the "Lonely Goatherd" scene in *The Sound of Music*). Two fun rooms show off various puppets and scenery backdrops. Videos show glimpses of the Marionette Theater performances of Mozart classics (see page 263).

• *Our tour is over. To **walk**—either down to Salzburg or across the Mönchsberg (see "Mönchsberg Walk," later)—you can take any trail downhill. Eventually you'll pass through the ticket checkpoint and come to a T-intersection. Head right (downhill) to return to the Old Town (following Altstadt signs); or turn left (uphill), and go under the funicular tracks to make your way across Mönchsberg (following Museum der Moderne signs).*

*To reach the **funicular,** backtrack to the station between the two cafés. At the bottom of the lift, spend a minute or two at the fine little **Alm River Canal Exhibit,** which focuses on how the river powered the city before steam took over.*

SALZBURG

▲Mönchsberg Walk

The paved, wooded walking path along the narrow ridgeline between the Mönchsberg elevator and the fortress is less than a mile long and makes for a great quiet and shady, 30-minute hike. There's some up and down, but the total elevation gain is about equal in either direction.

Frequent signposts direct you between all the key points, so it's hard to get lost. (*Festung Hohensalzburg* and *Museum der Moderne Salzburg* refer to the fortress and elevator ends of the mountain, respectively; the spots where you can go down the stairs into town are signed *Altstadt*.) Along the way, you'll see stunning views of Salzburg, rustic homes, a few unique little castle-like homes to ogle, a modern art museum (and occasional modern art sculptures in yards), a couple places to eat or enjoy a scenic drink, the sheer cliff face with its layers of sediment, and parts of the medieval wall. You can also pause to read information plaques about Salzburg's first settlers and the quarrying of the cliffs. At one point, the route forks to either a paved road or a footpath. Either works, as they converge later on.

The recommended Augustiner Bräustübl beer hall/garden is 10 minutes downhill past the Museum of Modern Art (follow signs for *Mülln;* see description on page 277).

Museum of Modern Art (Museum der Moderne Salzburg)

This stark concrete-and-glass exhibition space features artworks from the 19th and 20th centuries to the present day, with a particular emphasis on photography and graphic arts. It's located right at the top of the Mönchsberg elevator. Next to the museum is the "Sky Space," a cylindrical stone tower intended to let you contemplate the sky.

Cost and Hours: €13.30, includes round-trip elevator between Old Town and Mönchsberg—descent via funicular allowed, Tue-Sun 10:00-18:00, Wed until 20:00, closed Mon except during festival, tel. 0662/842-220-351, www.museumdermoderne.at.

IN THE NEW TOWN, NORTH OF THE RIVER

The following sights are across the river from the Old Town. I've connected them with walking instructions (to trace the route, see map on page 274).

• *Begin at the Makartsteg pedestrian bridge, where you can enjoy the...*

Salzach River View

Scan the cityscape and notice all the churches. Salzburg has 40 of them, justifying its nickname as the "Rome of the North." The grand buildings just across the bridge (with their elegant promenades and cafés) were built on reclaimed land in the late 19th century. Find the five streams gushing into the river. These date from the 13th

century, when the river was split into five canals running through the town to power its mills. Facing upstream, the Hotel Stein (just left of next bridge) has a popular roof-terrace restaurant (see "Seven Senses Rooftop Terrace," later). Also upstream on the left, between here and the next bridge, is the recommended Café Bazar (a fine place for a drink with a view). Downstream, high overhead on the left, atop the Mönchsberg, notice the Museum of Modern Art (with a view restaurant) and a faux castle (actually a water reservoir). The Romanesque bell tower with the green copper dome in the distance is the Augustine church, site of the best beer hall in town (the recommended Augustiner Bräustübl).

• *Cross the bridge, walk two blocks inland, and take a left past the heroic statues into...*

▲Mirabell Gardens and Palace (Mirabellgarten und Schloss)

These bubbly gardens, laid out in 1730 for the prince-archbishop, have been open to the public since 1850 (thanks to Emperor Franz Josef, who was rattled by the popular revolutions of 1848). The gardens are free and open until dusk. The palace is open daily 8:00-18:00 and during concerts. The statues and the arbor (far left) were featured in *The Sound of Music*.

Walk through the gardens toward the palace and find the statue of the horse (on the river side of the palace). Look back, enjoy the garden/cathedral/castle view, and imagine how the prince-archbishop must have reveled in a vista that reminded him of all his secular and religious power.

The rearing **Pegasus statue** is the site of a famous *Sound of Music* scene where the kids all danced before lining up on the stairs with Maria (30 yards farther along). The steps lead to a small mound in the park (made of rubble from a former theater). Notice that Pegasus is missing what locals call "his best part." (They claim it made the prince feel less impressive, so he had it removed.)

Nearest the horse, stairs lead between two lions to a pair of tough gnomes welcoming you to Salzburg's **Dwarf Park.** Cross the elevated walk (noticing the city's fortified walls) to meet whimsical marble statues modeled after a dozen dwarfs who served in the court of the prince-archbishop in the 17th century.

There's plenty of **music** here, both in the park and in the palace. A brass band plays free park concerts (May-Aug Sun at 10:30 and Wed at 20:30). To properly enjoy the lavish Mirabell Palace—once the prince-archbishop's summer palace and now the seat of the mayor—get a ticket to a Schlosskonzerte (my favorite venue for a classical concert—see page 262).

• *Backtrack out of the park the way you came in, into the park-like square called Makartplatz (with the big-domed church at the top of the square). Across the square—opposite the big and bright Hotel Bristol—you'll find...*

▲Mozart's Residence (Wohnhaus)

In the fall of 1773, when Wolfgang was 17—and his family was flush with money from years of touring—the Mozarts moved here from their cramped apartment on Getreidegasse. Aimed toward the Mozart connoisseur, the exhibits feature original Mozart family instruments, a good introductory video, and includes an informative audioguide. The building itself, bombed in World War II, is a reconstruction.

MOZART'S WOHNHAUS
Salzburg 1760-1780

Cost and Hours: €11, €18 combo-ticket with Mozart's Birthplace, daily July-Aug 8:30-19:00, Sept-June 9:00-17:30, Makartplatz 8, tel. 0662/8742-2740, www.mozarteum.at.

Visiting Mozart's Residence: The exhibit—seven rooms on one floor—starts in the main hall, which was used by the Mozarts to entertain Salzburg's high society. Consider spending time with the good introductory video in this room. Here, you can see Mozart's pianoforte from 1782, as well as his violin. The family portrait on the wall (from around 1780) shows Mozart with his sister Nannerl at the piano, their father on violin, and their mother—who'd died two years earlier in Paris. You'll also see three circular targets high on the wall, and—in the glass case nearby—the air rifle that Mozart and his family used to shoot at them.

Room 2 trumpets the successes the Mozart family enjoyed while living here: portraits of Salzburg bigwigs they hung out with, letters from Mozart bragging about his musical successes, and the publication of Leopold's treatise on playing violin.

Room 3 is dedicated to father Leopold—*Kapellmeister* of the prince—a member of the archbishop's orchestra, musician, and composer in his own right. Was Leopold a loving nurturer of young Wolfgang or an exploiting Svengali?

Room 4 stars "Nannerl" (Maria Anna), Mozart's sister, who was five years older. Though both were child prodigies, playing four-hand showpieces for Europe's crowned heads, Nannerl went on to lead a stable life as a wife and mother.

Room 5 boasts letters and music books from the nearby Mozarteum library. Rooms 6 describes the "cult of Mozart" and the use of his image in advertising, and Room 7 displays many portraits of Mozart (some authentic, some not), all a testament to his long legacy. By the time Mozart was 25, he'd grown tired of his father, this house, and Salzburg, and he went on to Vienna—to more triumphs, but ultimately, a sad end. You'll also learn about his son, Franz Xaver, and about Mozarteum—the organization dedicated to the "advancement of music" in Salzburg.

Nearby: Tucked inside the shop (near the WCs) is the free Mozart Sound and Film Collection, an archive of audio recordings, historic concerts on video, documentaries, and even the film *Amadeus*. Music aficionados and those with at least 30 minutes to spare will find this intriguing (Mon-Tue and Fri 9:00-13:00, Wed-Thu 13:00-17:00, closed Sat-Sun).

• *Leaving the museum, hook left around the corner and walk a few short blocks back to the main bridge (Staatsbrücke), where you'll find the Platzl, a square once used as a hay market. Pause to enjoy the kid-pleasing little fountain. Look up handsome Linzer Gasse, with its attractive small shops (we'll go there later). Just past the fountain (with your back to the river), Steingasse leads darkly to the right.*

▲Steingasse Stroll

Heading up dim, narrow Steingasse, you get a rare glimpse of medieval Salzburg. It's not the Church's Salzburg of grand squares and Baroque facades, but the people's Salzburg, of cramped quarters and humble cobbled lanes. Inviting cocktail bars along here come alive at night (see "Steingasse Pub Crawl" on page 280).

Stop at #9 (which sticks out into the lane) and look across the river into the Old Town; the city's original bridge once connected Salzburg's two halves right here. According to town lore, this building is where Joseph Mohr, who wrote the words to "Silent Night," was born—poor and illegitimate—in 1792. The popular Christmas carol was composed and first sung just outside Salzburg, in the village of Oberndorf, in 1818. Stairs lead from near here up to a 17th-century Capuchin monastery.

On the next corner, the wall is gouged out. This scar was left even after the building was restored, to serve as a reminder of the American GI who tried to get a tank down this road during a visit to the town brothel—two blocks farther up Steingasse. Within steps of here is the art cinema (showing movies in their original language, schedule in window) and three recommended bars (described on page 280).

Go deeper. At #19 (on the left), find the carvings on the old door. Some say these are notices from beggars to the begging community (more numerous after post-Reformation religious wars, which forced many people out of their homes and towns)—a kind of "hobo code" indicating whether the residents would give or not. Trace the wires of the old-fashioned doorbells to the highest floors.

Farther on, you step through the old fortified gate (at #20) and find a commanding Salzburg view across the river. Under the fortress and to the left, notice the red dome marking Nonnberg Abbey, with the oldest nunnery in the German-speaking world (established in 712). The real Maria, who inspired *The Sound of Music*, taught in this nunnery's school. In 1927, she and Captain von Trapp were married in the abbey's church. He was 47. She was 22.

From here, look back above the arch you just passed through, and up at part of the town's medieval fortification. The coat of arms on the arch is of the prince-archbishop who paid Bavaria a huge ransom to stay out of the Thirty Years' War (smart move). He then built this fortification (in 1634) in anticipation of rampaging armies from both sides.

Today, this street is for making love, not war. The Maison de Plaisir (a few doors down on the right, at #24) has for centuries been a Salzburg brothel. But the climax of this walk is more touristic.

• *For a grand view, head back to the Platzl and the bridge, enter the Hotel Stein (left corner, overlooking the river), and ride the elevator to the...*

Seven Senses Rooftop Terrace

This **$$$** restaurant-terrace offers one of the best views in town. Hidden from the tourist crush, it's a trendy, professional, local scene. You can discreetly peek at the view, enjoy a drink or meal, or come back later to gaze into the eyes of your travel partner as you sip a nightcap (reservations smart for outdoor seating, indoor dining also offered, food served daily until 22:00, tel. 0662/877-277, www.7-senses.at).

• *Back at the Platzl and the bridge, you can head straight up...*

Linzer Gasse

The old road leading out of Salzburg toward Linz (and, beyond that, Vienna) is refreshingly traffic-free after 11:00. It's lined with good hotels, shops, and eateries, and is a delight to stroll. It feels almost like an unglitzy Getreidegasse. Just above Steingasse, at #14, is the gateway leading up to Kapuzinerberg (described later).

• *Higher up on Linzer Gasse you'll reach the...*

▲St. Sebastian Cemetery

This wonderfully evocative cemetery dates from around 1600, when, after picking up modern ideas while studying in Rome, Prince-Archbishop Wolf Dietrich emptied the cathedral square of its tombs and estab-

lished this more modern (and Italian-feeling) place of burial. When he had it moved, people didn't like it. To help popularize it, he had his own mausoleum built as its centerpiece.

Cost and Hours: Free, daily 9:00-18:00, Nov-March until 16:00,

entry at Linzer Gasse 43 in summer; in winter go through the arch at #37 and around the building to the doorway under the blue seal.

Visiting the Cemetery: Wander through this quiet oasis. While regular citizens are buried in the middle, the arcade is lined with the fine tombs of fine families. Stroll the entire square, enjoying the art of the dead. Mozart is buried in Vienna, his mom's in Paris, and his sister is in Salzburg's Old Town (St. Peter's)—but Wolfgang's wife Constanze ("Constantia") and his father, Leopold, are buried here (from the black iron gate entrance on Linzer Gasse, walk 19 paces and look left). Continue straight past the Mozart tomb to the circular building that is Wolf Dietrich's mausoleum (English description at door).

• *If you're ready for a bite, the cemetery is within a few steps of several good eateries (see page 278). For a grand finale to your New Town explorations, head back down Linzer Gasse to #14 and the trailhead up to...*

Kapuzinerberg City View

Kapuzinerberg, a small park-like mountain, rises from the river opposite Salzburg's castle. From Linzer Gasse 14, a lane and steps lead past 12 Stations of the Cross to a Capuchin monastery (the mountain's namesake) and a commanding city viewpoint. Once an alp used for grazing animals by the town's farmers, today Kapuzinerberg is a peaceful escape with trails and a beer garden at its far end (at the little Franziskischlössl castle). To get to the scenic viewpoint over the river and across from the castle, follow the shorter loop, circling right (find the viewpoint on the left, just before the trail descends to Steingasse and the river).

NEAR SALZBURG

The following sights and activities take you just outside Salzburg for easy side-trips.

▲▲Hellbrunn Palace and Gardens

In about 1610, Prince-Archbishop Markus Sittikus decided he needed a lavish palace with a vast and ornate garden purely for pleasure (I imagine after meditating on stewardship and Christ-like values). He built this summer palace and hunting lodge, and just loved inviting his VIP guests from throughout Europe to have some fun with his trick fountains. Today, Hellbrunn is a popular side-trip.

While the formal garden may be one of the oldest in Europe (with a gazebo made famous by *The Sound of Music*), it's nothing special. The real draws here are those amazing fountains and the surprisingly engaging exhibits inside the palace. Perhaps most of all, Hellbrunn provides an ideal excuse to get out of the city.

Cost and Hours: €12.50 ticket includes fountain tour and palace audioguide, daily 9:00-17:30, July-Aug until 21:00—but tours after 18:00 don't include the palace interior, April and Oct until 16:30, these are last-tour times, closed Nov-March, tel. 0662/820-3720, www.hellbrunn.at.

Getting There: Hellbrunn is nearly four miles south of Salzburg. Take **bus** #25 from the train station or the Rathaus stop by the Staatsbrücke bridge, and get off at the Schloss Hellbrunn stop (2-3/hour, 20 minutes). Or, in good weather, the trip out to Hellbrunn is a delightful 30-minute **bike** excursion (see "Riverside or Meadow Bike Ride," later, and ask for a map when you rent your bike).

Visiting the Palace: Upon arrival, buy your **fountain tour** ticket and get a tour time (generally on the half-hour—if there's a wait until your fountain tour starts, you can see the palace first). The 40-minute English/German tours take you laughing and scrambling through a series of amazing 17th-century garden settings with lots of splashy fun and a guide who seems almost sadistic in the joy he has in soaking his group. (Hint: When you see a wet place, cover your camera.) You'll see ponds, grottoes, canals, fountains, and lots of little mechanical figures—all of them (quite remarkably) powered by 17th-century hydraulic engineering.

After the fountain tour you're free to wander the delightful

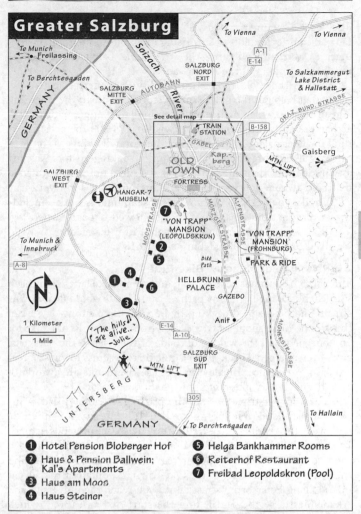

Greater Salzburg

To Vienna
To Vienna
To Munich • Freilassing
Salzach River
SALZBURG NORD EXIT
To Berchtesgaden
AUTOBAHN
A-1
E-14
SALZBURG MITTE EXIT
To Salzkammergut Lake District & Hallstatt
GRAZ. BUND. STRASSE
See detail map
TRAIN STATION
B-158
GABEL
Gaisberg
SALZBURG WEST EXIT
OLD TOWN
Kap.-berg
MTN. LIFT
HANGAR-7 MUSEUM
FORTRESS
MOOSSTRASSE
To Munich & Innsbruck
A-8
❼
❷
"VON TRAPP" MANSION (LEOPOLDSKRON)
MORZGER STRASSE
ALPENSTRASSE
"VON TRAPP" MANSION (FROHNBURG)
❺
Bike Path
PARK & RIDE
❶ ❹
HELLBRUNN PALACE
❻
❸
GAZEBO
N
AIGNERSTRASSE
1 Kilometer
"The hills are alive.." ~Julie
Anif •
1 Mile
E-14
A-10
SALZBURG SUD EXIT
MTN. LIFT
305
UNTERSBERG
To Hallein
GERMANY
To Berchtesgaden

❶ Hotel Pension Bloberger Hof
❷ Haus & Pension Ballwein; Kai's Apartments
❸ Haus am Moos
❹ Haus Steiner
❺ Helga Bankhammer Rooms
❻ Reiterhof Restaurant
❼ Freibad Leopoldskron (Pool)

garden and see the **gazebo** made famous by the song "Sixteen Going on Seventeen" from *The Sound of Music* (from the palace, head up the long, yellow-walled gravel road, then look right for *Sound-of-Music Pavilion* signs).

The **palace** was built in a style inspired by the Venetian architect Palladio, who was particularly popular around 1600, and it quickly became a cultural destination (enjoy the sounds of shrieking, fountain-taunted tourists below). This was the era when the aristocratic ritual was to go hunting in the morning (hence the wildlife-themed decor) and enjoy an opera in the evening. The first opera north of the Alps, imported from Italy, was performed here.

The decor is Mannerist (between Renaissance and Baroque), with faux antiquities and lots of surprising moments—intentional irregularities were in vogue after the strict logic, balance, and Greek-inspired symmetry of the Renaissance.

Today, those old rooms are filled with modern, creative exhibits that help put the palace into historical context: the emerging Age of Reason, when man was determined to conquer nature (such as harnessing hydropower to soak visiting VIPs). The eclectic exhibit includes palace models and architectural drawings, a statue of Sittikus at age three (when the dream of soaking visitors was just a twinkle in his demented little eye), a stuffed unicorn, a frescoed ballroom (where you can sit on a giant turntable for a very lazy tour), and a good exhibit on how all those fountains work—including an original pipe made out of a hollowed-out larchwood log. You'll also see a wrap-around animated film reenacting the wild Carnival celebrations of Salzburg circa 1618.

▲▲Riverside or Meadow Bike Ride

The Salzach River has smooth, flat, and scenic bike lanes along each side (thanks to medieval tow paths—cargo boats would float downstream and be dragged back up by horses). On a sunny day, I can think of no more shout-worthy escape from the city. Rent a bike for an hour, pedal all the way up one side of the river to the outskirts, cross over, and pedal back. Even a quickie ride across town is a great Salzburg experience. In the evening, the riverbanks are a world of floodlit spires. For bike-rental information, see page 219.

For a longer trip, consider the pristine, meadow-filled farm-country path along Hellbrunner Allee. It's an easy four-mile ride with a worthy destination—Hellbrunn Palace (see previous listing): From the middle of town, head along the river on Rudolfskai, with the river on your left and the fortress on your right. After passing the last bridge at the edge of the Old Town (Nonntaler Brücke), cut inland along Petersbrunnstrasse until you reach the university and Akademiestrasse. Beyond it find the start of Freisaalweg, which becomes the delightful Hellbrunner Allee bike path...which leads directly to the palace (paralleling Morzgerstrasse; see map on previous page). To make the trip a loop, you can come back along the river: Head out on Fürstenweg (past the *S.O.M.* gazebo), and follow it—carefully crossing highway 150—until you hit the river just south of the Hellbrunner Bridge. From here, you can turn left and follow the riverside path three miles back into town.

For a nine-mile ride, continue from Hellbrunn on to Hallein (where you can tour a salt mine—see next listing). If heading to Hallein directly from Salzburg, head out from the north bank of the river—the New Town side—which is more scenic.

▲Hallein Salt Mine (Salzwelten)

Of the many different salt-mine excursions from Salzburg, this one (in Bad Dürrnberg, just below the town of Hallein, 12 miles from Salzburg) is a good choice. Wearing white overalls and sliding down sleek wooden chutes, you'll cross underground from Austria into Germany while learning about the old-time salt-mining process. The tour entails lots of time on your feet as you walk from cavern to cavern, learning the history of the mine by watching a series of video skits with an actor channeling Prince-Archbishop Wolf Dietrich. The visit also includes a "Celtic Village" open-air museum.

Cost and Hours: €21, allow 2 hours for the visit, daily 9:00-17:00, Nov-mid-March 10:00-15:00, these are last-tour times, closed Jan, English-speaking guides—but let your linguistic needs be known loud and clear, tel. 06132/200-8511, www.salzwelten.at.

Getting There: Ride the train to Hallein (3/hour, about 20 minutes), where you can catch Postbus #41 to the salt mines in Bad Dürrnberg (runs hourly, 10 minutes). To save a few euros, buy the "ÖBB Plus" ticket, which includes the round-trip bus ride from the Hallein station and admission to the salt mine (€23.90).

Hangar-7

This hangar at the Salzburg airport (across the runways from the terminal) houses the car and aircraft collection of Dietrich Mateschitz, the flamboyant founder of the Red Bull energy-drink empire. Under the hangar's modern steel-and-glass dome are 20 or so glittering planes, helicopters, and racecars, plus three eateries designed to brandish the Red Bull "culture." For gearheads, this rates ▲▲▲; for anyone else, it's a worthwhile curiosity if you have a little extra time on your way into or out of town. Mateschitz (now in his 70s) remains Salzburg's big personality: He has a mansion at the edge of town, sponsors the local "Red Bull" soccer and hockey teams, owns several chic Salzburg eateries and cocktail bars, and employs thousands of mostly good-looking Salzburgers. He seems much like the energy drink that made him

rich and powerful—a high-energy, anything's-possible cultural Terminator.

Cost and Hours: Free, daily 9:00-22:00, bus #10 from Hanuschplatz to the Pressezentrum/Kuglhof stop—don't get off at the airport terminal, Wilhelm-Spazier-Strasse 7a, tel. 0662/2197, www.hangar-7.com.

Eating: Two floors up, the **$$$ Mayday Bar** has light meals and an experimental menu; in good weather, they close the bar and open an outdoor grill restaurant with similar prices. On the first floor, you'll probably want to skip the **$$$$ Ikarus Restaurant** (with a €180 fixed-price meal). By the entrance is the **$$ Carpe Diem** café.

Music in Salzburg

Music lovers come to Salzburg in late July and August for the Salzburg Festival, but there are also smaller, less expensive festivals at other times. And all year long, you can enjoy pleasant, if touristy, concerts held in historic venues around town—or a musical Mass on Sunday morning. Pick up the events calendar brochure at the TI (free, bimonthly) or check www.salzburg.info (under "Events," click on "Classical Music"). I've never planned in advance, and I've enjoyed great concerts with every visit.

DAILY MUSICAL EVENTS

The following concerts are mostly geared to tourists and can have a crank-'em-out feel, but they still provide good value, especially outside festival times. Or consider Salzburg's much-loved marionette theater, with nearly daily performances.

Concerts at Hohensalzburg Fortress (Festungskonzerte)

Nearly nightly concerts—Mozart's greatest hits for beginners—are held in the "prince's chamber" of the fortress atop the hill, featuring small chamber groups (assigned seat in first six rows-€44, open seating farther back-€36, funicular ride included if you come within an hour of the concert; at 20:00 or 20:30; doors open 30 minutes early, can combine with three-course dinner beforehand, reserve at tel. 0662/825-858 or via www.salzburghighlights.at, pick up tickets at the door). The medieval-feeling chamber has windows overlooking the city, and the concert gives you a chance to enjoy the grand city view and a stroll through the castle courtyard. Purists may object to hearing Baroque music in an incongruously Gothic space.

Concerts at the Mirabell Palace (Schlosskonzerte)

The nearly nightly chamber music concerts at the Mirabell Palace are performed in the lavishly Baroque Marble Hall. They come with more sophisticated programs and better musicians than the

fortress concerts...and Baroque music flying around a Baroque hall
is a happy bird in the right cage (assigned seat in first five rows-€38,
open seating farther back-€32; RS%—10 percent discount, use
code "RICK10"; usually at 20:00 but check flier for times, doors
open one hour ahead, tel. 0662/828-695, www.salzburg-palace-
concerts.com).

Mozart Dinner Concert

The elegant Stiftskeller St. Peter restaurant (see page 276) offers a
traditional candlelit meal with Mozart's greatest hits performed by
a string quintet and singers in historic costumes gavotting among
the tables. In this elegant Baroque setting, tourists clap between
movements and get three courses of food (from Mozart-era recipes)
mixed with three 20-minute courses of crowd-pleasing music—
structured much as such evenings were in Baroque-era times (€63,
RS%—use code "RICK9" to receive €9 discount, music starts
nightly, fewer nights in Feb, at 19:30, arrive 30 minutes before
that, dress is "smart casual," to reserve email office@skg.co.at or
call 0662/828-695, www.mozart-dinner-concert-salzburg.com).

Residenzkonzerte

On most afternoons, you can catch a 45-minute concert of 16th-
century music ("from Baroque through Mozart") played on Renaissance instruments at the Residenz (€22, discount with Salzburg
Card or DomQuartier ticket, daily at 15:00 for harpsichord and
17:00 for harpsichord and violin, tickets available 30 minutes before performance, mobile 0664-423-5645, www.agenturorpheus.
at).

Marionette Theater

Spellbinding marionettes star in these operas performed to recorded
music. A troupe of 10 puppeteers—actors themselves—brings to
life the artfully created puppets at the end of their five-foot strings.
The 180 performances a year alternate between *The Sound of Music*
and various German-language operas (with handy superscripts in
English). While the 300-plus-seat venue is forgettable, the art of
the marionettes enchants adults and children alike. For a sneak
preview, check out the videos on their website.

Cost and Hours: €20-37, kids-€15, June-Aug and Oct nearly
nightly at 19:30 plus matinees on some days, fewer shows off-season, near Mozart's Residence at Schwarzstrasse 24, tel. 0662/872-
406, www.marionetten.at.

WEEKLY MUSICAL EVENTS
Mozart Piano Sonatas (Klaviersonaten)

These short (45-minute) and fairly inexpensive weekend concerts in
St. Peter's Abbey are ideal for families (€22, €11 for kids, €55 for a

family of four, almost every Fri and Sat at 19:00 year-round, in the abbey's Romanesque Hall—a.k.a. Romanischer Saal, enter from inner courtyard 20 yards left of St. Peter's Church, mobile 0664-423-5645, www.agenturorpheus.at).

Free Brass Band Concerts
Traditional brass bands play in the Mirabell Gardens on Sundays and Wednesdays (May-Aug Sun at 10:30 and Wed at 20:30, may be canceled in bad weather).

Music at Sunday Mass
Each Sunday morning, three great churches offer a Mass, generally with glorious music. The **Salzburg Cathedral** is likely your best bet for fine music to worship by. The 10:00 service generally features a Mass written by a well-known composer performed by choir, organist, or other musicians. The worship service is often followed at 11:30 by a free organ concert (music program at www.kirchen.net/dommusik). Nearby (just outside Domplatz, with the pointy green spire), the **Franciscan Church** is the locals' choice and is enthusiastic about its musical Masses (at 9:00, www.franziskanerkirche-salzburg.at—click on "Programm"). **St. Peter's Church** sometimes has music (often at 10:15, www.stift-stpeter.at—click on "Kirchenmusik," then "Jahresprogramm").

ANNUAL MUSIC FESTIVALS
Salzburg Festival (Salzburger Festspiele)
Each summer, from mid-July to the end of August, Salzburg hosts its famous Salzburg Festival, founded in 1920 to employ Vienna's musicians in the summer. This fun and festive time is crowded—as many as 200,000 tickets are sold to festival events annually—but there are usually plenty of beds (except for a few August weekends). Events are pricey (€50-430) and take place primarily in three big halls: the Opera and Orchestra venues in the Festival House, and the Landestheater, where German-language plays are performed. The schedule is announced in November, tickets go on sale in January, and most seats are sold out by March. But many "go to the Salzburg Festival" by seeing smaller, nonfestival events that occur during the same weeks. For these unofficial events, same-day tickets are normally available—ask at the TI for details. For specifics on the festival schedule and tickets, visit www.salzburgfestival.at.

Music lovers in town during the festival who don't have tickets (or money) can still enjoy **Festival Nights,** a free series of videos of previous years' festival performances, projected on a big screen on Kapitelplatz (behind the cathedral). It's a fun scene, with plenty of folding chairs and a food circus of temporary eateries. For info and schedules, go to www.salzburg.info and search for "Festival Nights."

Other Annual Musical Festivals

The Salzburg Festival stages a week of Baroque concerts over the **Whitsunday** holiday weekend in early June (a school holiday in Austria and Bavaria). Offerings and prices are similar to those in July and August (www.salzburgerfestspiele.at/whitsun).

Mozart Week (Mozartwoche) is a high-quality, more affordable option held each year in late January. Run by the Mozarteum Foundation, it features up to three daily performances of works by both the great composer and his contemporaries (www.mozarteum.at; click on "Mozart Week" for details). Then comes the **Easter Music Festival** (Osterfestspiele), with reasonably priced concerts and operas (www.osterfestspiele-salzburg.at). The series of concerts and plays held during late October's **Culture Days** (Kulturtage) are also designed to give locals a chance to take in some high culture at a low price. And in late October, **Jazz & the City** offers free concerts scattered throughout dozens of venues in the city (www.salzburgjazz.com).

Sleeping in Salzburg

Peak season is May through October, with rates rising significantly during the summer music festival, during the four Advent weeks leading up to Christmas (when street markets are at full blast), and around Easter. Many of my Salzburg listings will let you skip breakfast to save about €10 per person—if you don't need a big breakfast, ask about this option. Remember, to call an Austrian number from a German one, dial 00-43 and then the number (minus the initial zero).

IN THE NEW TOWN, NORTH OF THE RIVER
Near Linzer Gasse

These listings cluster around Linzer Gasse, a lively pedestrian shopping street a 15-minute walk or quick bus ride from the train station (for directions, see "Arrival in Salzburg") and a 10-minute walk to the Old Town. If you're coming from the Old Town, cross the main bridge (Staatsbrücke), and Linzer Gasse is straight ahead. If driving, exit the highway at Salzburg-Nord, follow Vogelweiderstrasse straight to its end, and turn right. Parking is easy at the nearby Mirabell-Congress garage (€18/day, your hotel may be able to get you a €1-2 discount, Mirabellplatz).

$$$$ Altstadthotel Wolf-Dietrich, around the corner from Linzer Gasse on pedestrian-only Wolf-Dietrich-Strasse, has 40 well-located, tastefully plush rooms (10 overlook St. Sebastian Cemetery; some are in an annex across the street). Prices include a huge breakfast spread (RS%, family rooms, nonsmoking, elevator, annex rooms have air-con, pool with loaner swimsuits, sauna,

Wolf-Dietrich-Strasse 7, tel. 0662/871-275, www.salzburg-hotel. at, office@wolf-dietrich.at).

$$ Cityhotel Trumer Stube, well-located three blocks from the river just off Linzer Gasse, is a cozy, well-run, welcoming home base with 20 comfortable and attractive rooms (family rooms, in-room smartphones for free calls and navigation during your stay, nonsmoking, elevator, look for the flower boxes at Bergstrasse 6, tel. 0662/874-776, www.trumer-stube.at, info@trumer-stube.at, Vivienne).

$$ Gästehaus im Priesterseminar Salzburg occupies part of the Salzburg Seminary, where two floors have been turned into a comfortable, superbly located hotel with 60 high-ceilinged rooms. Each room has a Bible and a cross (and no TV), but guests are not required to be in a contemplative frame of mind. There's also a little guests' chapel, which looks down into the big church where Mozart used to play the organ. This is a rare place that doesn't charge extra during the Salzburg Festival—but for those dates you have to book by phone or email (family rooms, bike rental, elevator, communal kitchen, laundry facilities, reception closes at 20:00—arrange ahead if arriving later; Dreifaltigkeitsgasse 14, tel. 0662/8774-9510, www.gaestehaus-priesterseminar-salzburg.at, gaestehaus@priesterseminar.kirchen.net).

$$ Hotel Krone 1512, about five blocks from the river, offers 23 decent, simply furnished rooms in a building that dates to medieval times. Back-facing rooms are quieter than the streetside ones (earplugs smart as nearby church bells ring from 7:00-22:00). Cheapskates can save by requesting the nearly windowless "student" double. Stay awhile in their pleasant cliffside garden (RS%, email reservation for discount, higher discounts if paying cash, family rooms, elevator, Linzer Gasse 48, tel. 0662/872-300, www. krone1512.at, hotel@krone1512.at, run by Ukrainian-Austrian-Canadian Niko).

$$ Hotel Schwarzes Rössl is a university dorm that becomes a student-run hotel for the months of July, August, and September. The location couldn't be handier, and its 56 rooms, while a bit spartan, are comfortable (family rooms, cheaper rooms with shared bath, no breakfast, just off Linzer Gasse at Priesterhausgasse 6, July-Sept tel. 0662/874-426, otherwise tel. 1401-7655, www. academiahotels.at, salzburg@academiahotels.at).

$ Institute St. Sebastian is in a somewhat sterile but clean historic building next to St. Sebastian Cemetery. From October through June, it houses students but also rents 60 beds for travelers. From July through September, the students are gone, and they rent all 118 beds (including 20 twin rooms) to travelers. The building has spacious public areas, a roof garden, a piano, and some of the best rooms and dorm beds in town for the money. The immaculate doubles come with modern baths and head-to-toe twin beds (family rooms, cheaper rooms with shared bath, nonsmoking, elevator, self-service laundry, pay parking—request when you reserve; reception closes at 18:00; Linzer Gasse 41—enter through arch at #37, tel. 0662/871-386, www.st-sebastian-salzburg.at, office@st-sebastian-salzburg.at). Students like the ¢ dorms.

On Rupertgasse

These two well-run hotels are about five blocks farther from the river on Rupertgasse—a breeze for drivers, but with more street noise than the places on Linzer Gasse. They're good values if you don't mind being a 15- to 20-minute walk or quick bus ride from the Old Town or paying extra for breakfast. From the station, take bus #2 to the Bayerhammerstrasse stop; from Hanuschplatz, take #4 to Grillparzerstrasse.

$$ Hotel Jedermann is tastefully quirky and stylishly minimalist, with an artsy painted-concrete ambience (look for the owner's street-art mural), a backyard garden, and 30 rooms (family rooms, nonsmoking, elevator, pay parking, Rupertgasse 25, tel. 0662/873-2410, www.hotel-jedermann.com, office@hotel-jedermann.com, Herr und Frau Gmachl).

$$ Bergland Hotel is charming, classy, and a great value, renting 18 comfortable rooms with an oddly stylish leather-wicker-beach theme (breakfast extra, elevator, free parking if you book direct, Rupertgasse 15, tel. 0662/872-318, www.berglandhotel.at, office@berglandhotel.at, Kuhn family).

Near the Train Station

$ Motel One Salzburg-Mirabell is an inexpensive chain hotel right along the river. Its 119 cookie-cutter rooms are small, but the staff is helpful, the decor is fun, and the lounge is inviting. It's six blocks (or a two-stop bus ride) from the train station, and a 15-minute riverside walk or short bus ride from the Old Town (breakfast extra, elevator, pay parking, Elisabethkai 58, bus #1 or #2 from platform D at station to St.-Julien-Strasse—use underpass to cross road safely, tel. 0662/885-200, www.motel-one.com, salzburg-mirabell@motel-one.com).

¢ International Youth Hostel, a.k.a. the "Yo Ho," is a youthful, easygoing backpacker haven with cheap meals, lockers, a lively bar, and showings of *The Sound of Music* every evening at 20:00 (nonguests are welcome) with a pre-show happy hour at the bar. They welcome guests of any age—if you don't mind the noisy atmosphere (private rooms available, family rooms, breakfast extra, no curfew, laundry facilities, 6 blocks from station toward Linzer Gasse and 6 blocks from river at Paracelsusstrasse 9, tel. 0662/879-649, www.yoho.at, yoho@yoho.at).

SALZBURG

SALZBURG

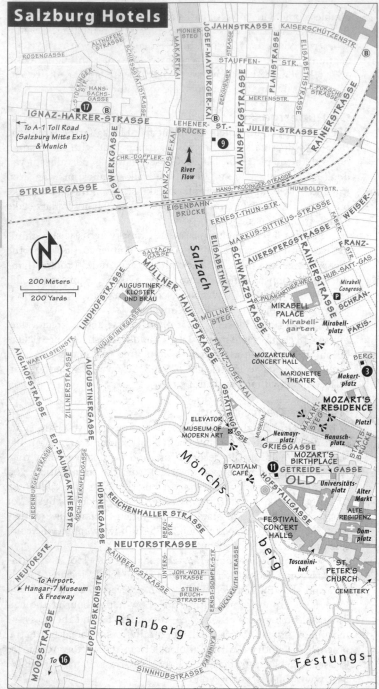

Salzburg Hotels

ROSENGASSE

ALTHOFEN-STRASSE

SCHIESSSTATTSTRASSE

STOCKINGER GASSE

HANS-SACHS-GASSE

17 B

IGNAZ-HARRER-STRASSE

← To A-1 Toll Road
(Salzburg Mitte Exit)
& Munich

GASWERKGASSE

CHR.-DOPPLER-STR.

STRUBERGASSE

JAHNSTRASSE

KAISERSCHÜTZENSTR.

PIONIER STEG

MAKARTKAI

JOSEF-MAYBURGER-KAI

STAUFFEN-

STR.

BERGHEIMER STRASSE

PLAINSTRASSE

ELISABETHSTRASSE

F.-PORSCHE STRASSE

B

HAUNSPERGSTRASSE

MERTENSSTR.

RAINERSTRASSE

LEHENER-BRÜCKE

B ST.-

JULIEN-STRASSE

9

FRANZ-JOSEF-KAI

↑
River
Flow

Salzach

EISENBAHN-BRÜCKE

HANS-PRODINGER-STRASSE

HUMBOLDTSTR.

ERNEST-THUN-STR.

ELISABETHKAI

MARKUS-SITTIKUS-STRASSE

AUERSPERGSTRASSE

RAINERSTRASSE

FABER-STR.

WEISER

FRANZ-STR.-GAS.

HUB.-SATT-GAS.

N

200 Meters

200 Yards

SALZACH GASSE

MÜLLNER HAUPTSTRASSE

LINDHOFSTRASSE

AUGUSTINER-KLOSTER
UND BRÄU

AUGUSTINERGASSE

MÜLLNER-STEG

FRANZ-JOSEF-KAI

B.-PAUMGARTNER-WEG

MIRABELL
PALACE

Mirabell-garten

Mirabell Congress

P

SCHRAN-

PARIS-

Mirabell-platz

BERG-

AIGLHOFSTRASSE

WARTELSTEINSTR.

ZILLNERSTRASSE

AUGUSTINERGASSE

MOZARTEUM
CONCERT HALL

MARIONETTE
THEATER

Makart-platz

3

ED.-BAUMGARTNERSTR.

RIEDENBURGER STRASSE

KOCH-STERNFELDGASSE

HÜBNERGASSE

Mönchs-

ELEVATOR
MUSEUM OF
MODERN ART

GSTÄTTENGASSE

MUSEUM

MOZART'S
RESIDENCE

MAKART STEG

Platzl

Neumayr-platz

Hanusch-platz

STAATS-BRÜCKE

GRIESGASSE

MOZART'S
BIRTHPLACE

STADTALM
CAFÉ

11

GETREIDE- GASSE

OLD

Universitäts-platz

Alter
Markt

REICHENHALLER STRASSE

NEUTORSTRASSE

RAINBERGSTRASSE

UNTERSBERG STR.

JOH.-WOLF-STRASSE

STEIN-BRUCH-STRASSE

ERNST-SOMPEK-STR.

BÜRGLSTEIN STRASSE

berg

HOFSTALLGASSE

FESTIVAL
CONCERT
HALLS

ALTE
RESIDENZ

Dom-platz

Toscanini-hof

ST.
PETER'S
CHURCH

CEMETERY

NEUTORSTR.

To Airport,
↙Hangar-7 Museum
& Freeway

LEOPOLDSKRONSTR.

MOOSSTRASSE

To 16
↓

AM RAINBERG

SINNHUBSTRASSE

Rainberg

Festungs-

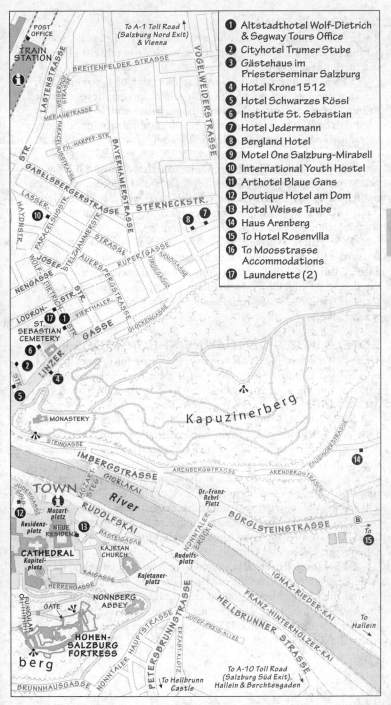

SALZBURG

1. Altstadthotel Wolf-Dietrich & Segway Tours Office
2. Cityhotel Trumer Stube
3. Gästehaus im Priesterseminar Salzburg
4. Hotel Krone 1512
5. Hotel Schwarzes Rössl
6. Institute St. Sebastian
7. Hotel Jedermann
8. Bergland Hotel
9. Motel One Salzburg-Mirabell
10. International Youth Hostel
11. Arthotel Blaue Gans
12. Boutique Hotel am Dom
13. Hotel Weisse Taube
14. Haus Arenberg
15. To Hotel Rosenvilla
16. To Moosstrasse Accommodations
17. Launderette (2)

IN THE OLD TOWN

These pricier hotels are nicely located in the heart of the Old Town. Although cars are restricted in this area, your hotel will give you instructions for driving in to unload and for parking.

$$$$ Arthotel Blaue Gans, at the start of Getreidegasse, comes with class and polish. Its 35 spacious and bright rooms mix minimalist modernity with old beams and bare wood. While pricey, it's worth considering if you can score a deal (family rooms, air-con, elevator, Getreidegasse 41, tel. 0662/842-491, www.blauegans.at, office@blauegans.at).

$$$ Boutique Hotel am Dom, on the narrow Goldgasse pedestrian street, offers 15 chic, upscale, boldly decorated (read: borderline gaudy) rooms, some with original wood-beam ceilings (family rooms, air-con, elevator, Goldgasse 17, tel. 0662/842-765, www.hotelamdom.at, office@hotelamdom.at).

$$$ Hotel Weisse Taube has 31 rooms—some straight-forward and comfortable, some modern and chic—all in a quiet, 14th-century building with a cozy breakfast room. It's well located about a block off Mozartplatz (RS%, family rooms, elevator, tel. 0662/842-404, Kaigasse 9, www.weissetaube.at, hotel@weissetaube.at).

HOTELS IN RESIDENTIAL NEIGHBORHOODS

These two modern hotels are worth considering for drivers in need of no-stress comfort. They come with a bit more space and free parking, but are a longish walk or bus ride to the Old Town. Get detailed driving instructions from your hosts.

$$$ Haus Arenberg rents 13 big, breezy rooms—most with generous balconies—in a modern, ranch-style mansion with a quiet garden. Though in a tony neighborhood with Porsches lining the narrow hillside lanes, it's relaxed and unpretentious. Figure a 15-minute downhill walk to the center of town (along atmospheric Steingasse) and 20 minutes back up, or take bus #6, #7, or #10 to the Volksgarten stop and hike five minutes uphill (family room, no elevator, library, electric bike rental, Blumensteinstrasse 8, tel. 0662/640-097, www.arenberg-salzburg.at, info@arenberg-salzburg.at, Leobacher family).

$$$ Hotel Rosenvilla, simpler and farther out than Haus Arenberg, offers 15 colorful rooms surrounded by a leafy garden, around the corner from a stop for the bus into town (family room, no elevator, Höfelgasse 4—take bus #7 from Hanuschplatz to the Finanzamt stop, tel. 0662/621-765, www.rosenvilla.com, hotel@rosenvilla.com, Stefanie).

PENSIONS ON MOOSSTRASSE

Tucked behind Salzburg's mountain, Moosstrasse was laid out a century ago through reclaimed marsh-land that was meant for farms, some of which are still there. But now the street is also lined with great-value pensions that offer a roomy, comfortable alternative to pricey in-town hotels. Each one comes with free parking, farm-fresh scents, mountains in the distance, and a good breakfast (extra charge at Haus Steiner). With easy and frequent buses zipping into town in 15 minutes, the seemingly remote location shouldn't keep you away. Some places charge about 10 percent extra for one-night stays. For locations, see the map on page 259.

Handy **bus** #21 connects Moosstrasse to the center frequently (Mon-Fri 4/hour until 19:00, Sat 4/hour until 17:00, evenings and Sun 2/hour, last bus leaves downtown around 23:00). To get to these pensions from the train station, take any bus heading toward the center to Makartplatz, where you'll change to #21. If you're coming from the Old Town, catch bus #21 from Hanuschplatz, just downstream of the Staatsbrücke bridge, by the Fisch Krieg Restaurant. When traveling to your pension, the bus stops only when requested—so press the button as soon as you hear your stop announced.

If you're **driving** from the center, go through the tunnel, continue straight on Neutorstrasse, and take the fourth left onto Moosstrasse. From the autobahn, exit at *Süd* and head in the direction of *Grödig*.

$$ Hotel Pension Bloberger Hof, the most hotelesque of these options, is comfortable and friendly, with a peaceful location and 20 farmer-plush, good-value rooms—including some bigger and pricier rooms (RS%, some rooms with balcony, family rooms, family apartment with kitchen, dinner for guests available Mon-Sat 18:00-21:00, nonsmoking, elevator, free loaner bikes, free airport pickup if staying 3 nights, Hammerauer Strasse 4, bus stop: Hammerauer Strasse then head left, tel. 0662/830-227, www.blobergerhof.at, office@blobergerhof.at, Inge and daughter Sylvia).

$ Haus Ballwein offers 11 cozy, charming, and fresh rooms in a delightful, family-friendly farmhouse. Some rooms have balconies with intoxicating views (family rooms, 2-bedroom apartment for up to 5 people, cash only, farm-fresh breakfasts amid hanging teapot collection, nonsmoking, 2 free loaner bikes, Moosstrasse

69a, bus stop: Gsengerweg then cross street, tel. 0662/824-029, www.haus-ballwein.at, haus.ballwein@gmx.net, Frau Ballwein).

The 11 rooms at **$$ Pension Ballwein,** across the yard—run by Frau Ballwein's son and his wife—are more polished and modern, and cost more. But the place is also fresh and roomy, and each room has a balcony (family rooms, nonsmoking, elevator, free loaner bikes, mobile 0664-222-5396, www.pension-ballwein.at, pension-ballwein@a1.net, Simon and Daniela).

Frau Ballwein's daughter has four modern and slick apartments—called **$ Kal's Apartments**—just a few doors up the street (no breakfast, Moosstrasse 63b, mobile 0650-552-1116, www.kalssalzburg.at, office@kalssalzburg.at, Brigitte).

$ Haus am Moos has nine older rooms—with less rustic wood and more classy antiques—in a relaxed country atmosphere. It comes with a garden, swimming pool, breakfast buffet with mountain views, and a tiny private chapel (family rooms, nonsmoking, Moosstrasse 186a, bus stop: Lehrbauhof then head right, tel. 0662/824-921, www.ammoos.at, ammoos186a@yahoo.de, Strasser family).

$ Haus Steiner's six rooms—some with great views—are straightforward and quiet, with older modern furnishings; there's a minimum two-night stay (breakfast extra, family rooms, nonsmoking, Moosstrasse 156c, bus stop: Hammerauer Strasse then head right, tel. 0662/830-031, www.haussteiner.com, info@haussteiner.com, Rosemarie Steiner).

$ Helga Bankhammer rents four inexpensive, nondescript rooms in a farmhouse, with a real dairy farm out back (cheaper rooms with shared bath, nonsmoking, pay laundry, Moosstrasse 77, bus stop: Marienbad then cross street and turn right, tel. 0662/830-067, www.haus-bankhammer.at, bankhammer@aon.at).

Eating on Moosstrasse: $$ Reiterhof, by the Hammerauer Strasse bus stop, is a popular restaurant near these listings. They have a cozy, woody dining room that looks down into a horse-training area (Wed-Sat dinner only, Sun lunch and dinner, closed Mon-Tue, Moosstrasse 151, tel. 0662/8250).

Eating in Salzburg

Many of the restaurants and cafés listed below are open longer hours and extra days during the Salzburg Festival. On the flip side, when business is slow, eateries may close early—no matter what hours they post.

On menus, look for a local dessert specialty called *Salzburger Nockerl*. This soufflé is made to resemble mountain peaks—including a snowy dusting of powdered sugar on top. Sometimes served with raspberry sauce, this rich dessert is designed to share.

IN THE OLD TOWN
Restaurants in the Center

$$ Gasthaus zum Wilder Mann is a good bet in bad weather for traditional dishes. For a quick lunch, get the *Bauernschmaus*, a mountain of dumplings, kraut, and peasant's meats. Notice the century-old flood photos on the wall. While they have a few outdoor tables, the atmosphere is all indoors, and the menu is more geared to cold weather (kitchen open Mon-Sat 11:00-21:00, closed Sun, 2 minutes from Mozart's Birthplace, Getreidegasse 20 or Griesgasse 17, tel. 0662/841-787, www.wildermann.co.at; Robert, Kurt, and Reinhold).

$$ St. Paul Stubm Beer Garden is tucked away under the fortress with a decidedly untouristy atmosphere. The food is better than at beer halls, and a young, bohemian-chic clientele fills its two troll-like rooms and its idyllic tree-shaded garden. *Kasnock'n* is a tasty dish of *Spätzle* with cheese served in an iron pan—hearty enough for two. Reservations are smart (Mon-Sat 17:00-22:00, open later for drinks only, closed Sun, Herrengasse 16, tel. 0662/843-220, www.paul-stube.at, Bernard).

$$ Zirkelwirt serves Austrian standards (schnitzel, goulash, *Spätzle* with kraut) and big salads in an updated *Gasthaus* dining room and exotic plant-screened terrace. Just a block off Mozartplatz, it's a world away from the tourism of the Old Town (daily 11:30-22:00, Pfeifergasse 14, tel. 0662/842-796).

$$ Café Tomaselli (with its Kiosk annex and terrace seating diagonally across the way) has long been Salzburg's top place for lingering and people-watching. Tomaselli serves light meals and lots of drinks, keeps long hours, and has fine seating on the square, a view terrace upstairs, and indoor tables. Despite its fancy wood paneling, 19th-century portraits, and chandeliers, it's surprisingly low-key (Mon-Sat 7:00-19:00, Sun from 8:00, Aug until 21:00, Alter Markt 9, tel. 0662/844-488).

$ Wokman, fragrant with fresh cilantro, is where the Nguyen family dishes up Vietnamese noodle soups and other Asian standards in a six-table restaurant a long block from the cathedral (eat

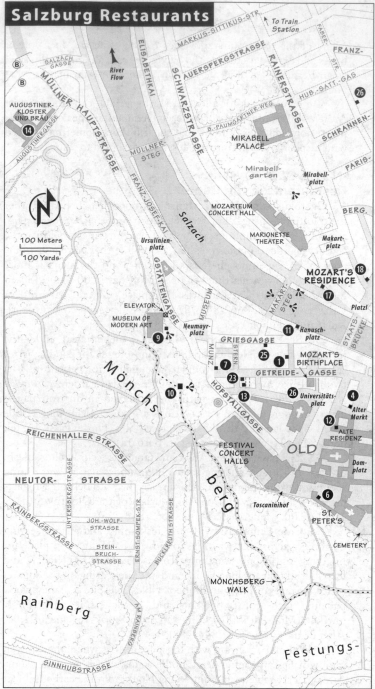

Salzburg Restaurants

SALZBURG

To Train Station

B

B

SALZACH GASSE

MÜLLNER HAUPTSTRASSE

AUGUSTINER-KLOSTER UND BRÄU

14

AUGUSTINERGASSE

MÜLLNER STEG

River Flow

ELISABETHKAI

FRANZ-JOSEF-KAI

Salzach

MARKUS-SITTIKUS-STR.

AUERSPERGSTRASSE

SCHWARZSTRASSE

B.-PAUMGARTNER-WEG

MIRABELL PALACE

Mirabell-garten

RAINERSTRASSE

FABER-STR.

HUB.-SATT.-GAS.

26

SCHRANNEN-

PARIS-

Mirabell-platz

BERG.

MOZARTEUM CONCERT HALL

MARIONETTE THEATER

Makart-platz

N

100 Meters
100 Yards

Ursulinen-platz

GSTÄTTENGASSE

ELEVATOR

MUSEUM OF MODERN ART

9

Mönchs-

MUSEUM

Neumayr-platz

MAKART-STEG

MOZART'S RESIDENCE

18

17

Platzl

STAATS-BRÜCKE

11

Hanusch-platz

berg

REICHENHALLER STRASSE

10

MÜNZ.

GRIESGASSE

STERN.

7

25

23

HOFSTALLGASSE

13

1

MOZART'S BIRTHPLACE

GETREIDE-GASSE

26

Universitäts-platz

12

4

Alter Markt

ALTE RESIDENZ

Dom-platz

NEUTOR-STRASSE

RAINBERGSTRASSE

UNTERSBERGSTRASSE

JOH.-WOLF-STRASSE

STEIN-BRUCH-STRASSE

ERNST-SOMPEK-STR.

BÜRGLREUTH STRASSE

AM RAINBERG

Rainberg

SINNHUBSTRASSE

FESTIVAL CONCERT HALLS

Toscaninihof

OLD

6

ST. PETER'S

CEMETERY

MÖNCHSBERG WALK

Festungs-

SALZBURG

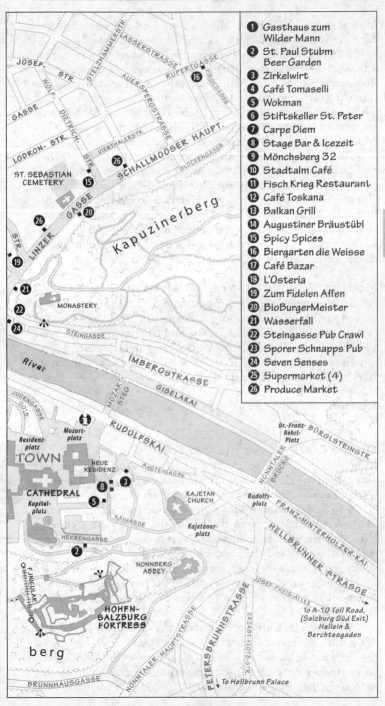

1. Gasthaus zum Wilder Mann
2. St. Paul Stubm Beer Garden
3. Zirkelwirt
4. Café Tomaselli
5. Wokman
6. Stiftskeller St. Peter
7. Carpe Diem
8. Stage Bar & Icezeit
9. Mönchsberg 32
10. Stadtalm Café
11. Fisch Krieg Restaurant
12. Café Toskana
13. Balkan Grill
14. Augustiner Bräustübl
15. Spicy Spices
16. Biergarten die Weisse
17. Café Bazar
18. L'Osteria
19. Zum Fidelen Affen
20. BioBurgerMeister
21. Wasserfall
22. Steingasse Pub Crawl
23. Sporer Schnapps Pub
24. Seven Senses
25. Supermarket (4)
26. Produce Market

in or take out, daily 11:30-21:00, closed Sun and weekday afternoons in winter, Kapitelgasse 11, mobile 0660-257-5588).

$$$$ Stiftskeller St. Peter has been in business for more than 1,000 years—it was mentioned in the biography of Charlemagne. These days it's classy and high-end touristy, serving uninspired traditional Austrian cuisine with indoor/outdoor seating (daily 11:30-22:00 or later, next to St. Peter's Church at foot of Mönchsberg, tel. 0662/841-268, www.stpeter.at). They host the recommended Mozart Dinner Concert described on page 263.

$$$$ Carpe Diem is a project by Red Bull tycoon Dietrich Mateschitz. Salzburg's beautiful people, fueled by Red Bull, present themselves here in the chic ground-floor **café** and trendy "lifestyle bar," which serves quality cocktails and fine finger food in cones (daily 8:30-23:00). Upstairs is an expensive **restaurant** boasting a Michelin star (Mon-Sat 12:00-14:00 & 18:30-22:00, closed Sun; Getreidegasse 50, tel. 0662/848-800, www.carpediemfinestfingerfood.com).

Modern, Eclectic Cuisine in Kaiviertel

An oasis of contemporary, international restaurants and shops is tucked just behind the Salzburg Museum in the Kaiviertel quarter (around the intersection of Kaigasse and Chiemseegasse). Among the offerings are Polish, Irish, Vietnamese, and Mexican cuisine, as well as organic coffee. For cocktails, pizza, and snacks try **Stage Bar,** which hosts live music nightly (Tue-Sat 19:00-late, closed Sun-Mon, Chiemseegasse 2, mobile 0650-453-0547). Popular **Icezeit** serves ice cream in exotic flavors and has vegan options (Chiemseegasse 1).

On the Cliffs Above the Old Town

Riding the Mönchsberg elevator from the west end of the Old Town up to the clifftop deposits you near two very different eateries, but each has commanding city views.

$$$$ Mönchsberg 32 is a sleek, modern café/bar/restaurant overlooking Salzburg from the top of the Mönchsberg elevator. Even if you're not hiking anywhere, this makes for a great place to enjoy a €5 coffee and the view. Or settle in for a pricey but high-quality meal (weekday lunch specials, Tue-Sun 9:00-24:00, closed Mon, popular breakfasts served until 12:00, buy a one-way elevator ticket—they give customers a free pass to descend, tel. 0662/841-000, www.m32.at).

$$ Stadtalm Café sits high above the Old Town on the edge of the cliff, with good traditional food and great views. Nearby are the remnants of the old city wall. If hiking across the Mönchsberg, make this a stop (cliff-side garden seating or cozy-mountain-hut indoor seating, generally Mon-Sat 11:30-23:00 or later, Sun until

18:00; closes earlier off-season, 5 minutes from top of Mönchsberg elevator, also reachable by stairs from Toscaninihof, Mönchsberg 19C, tel. 0662/841-729, Peter).

Eating Cheaply in the Old Town

$ Fisch Krieg Restaurant, on the river where the fishermen used to sell their catch, is a great value, serving fast, fresh, and inexpensive fish. Get your fishwich to go, or order from the affordable eat-in menu to enjoy the casual dining room—where trees grow through the ceiling—and the great riverside seating (Mon-Fri 8:30-18:30, Sat until 13:00, closed Sun, Hanuschplatz 4, tel. 0662/843-732).

$ Café Toskana is the university lunch canteen, very basic but fast and cheap—with drab indoor seating and a great courtyard for good weather. Choose between two daily soup and main course specials (vegetarian options available, open Mon-Fri but also Sat in summer, closed Sun, generally 8:30-17:00, hot meals served 11:30-13:30 only, behind the Residenz, in the courtyard opposite Sigmund-Haffner-Gasse 16, tel. 0662/8044-6909).

$ Sausage stands *(Würstelstände)* serve the town's favorite "fast food." The best stands (like those on Universitätsplatz) use the same boiling water all day, which gives the weenies more flavor. For a list of helpful terms, see page 987. **$ Balkan Grill,** run by chatty Frau Ebner, has been a Salzburg institution since 1950, selling just one type of spicy sausage—*Bosna*—with your choice of toppings (choose one of the numbered options; takeout only, steady and sturdy local crowd, Mon-Sat 11:00-19:00, Sun 14:00-19:00, hours vary with demand, Jan-Feb closed Sun, hiding down the tunnel at Getreidegasse 33 across from Eisgrotte).

Picnics: Picnickers will appreciate the well-stocked **Billa supermarket** at Griesgasse 19a, across from the Hanuschplatz bus stop (Mon-Fri 7:40-20:00, Sat until 18:00, Sun 11:00-15:00).

AWAY FROM THE CENTER

$$ Augustiner Bräustübl, a huge 1,000-seat beer garden within a monk-run brewery in the Kloster Mülln, is rustic and raw. When it's cool outside, enjoy a historic indoor setting in any of several beer-sloshed and smoke-stained halls (one of which is still for smokers). On busy nights, it's like a Munich beer hall with no music but the volume turned up. On balmy evenings, it's like a Renoir painting outdoors under chestnut trees—but with beer breath and cigarette smoke. Local students mix with tourists eating hearty slabs of grilled meat with their fingers, while children frolic on the playground kegs. For your beer: Pick up a half-liter or full-liter mug, pay the lady (*Schank* means self-serve price, *Bedienung* is the price with waiter service), wash your mug, give Mr. Keg your receipt and empty mug, and you will be made happy. Waiters only bring beer; for food, go up the stairs, grab a tray, and assemble your meal from the deli counters (or, as long as you buy a drink, you can bring in a picnic—many do). Classic pretzels from the bakery and spiraled, salty radishes make great beer even better. Locals

agree that the hot food here is not as good as the beer. Stick with the freshly cooked meat dishes: I made the mistake of choosing schnitzel, which was reheated in the microwave. For dessert—after a visit to the strudel kiosk—enjoy the incomparable floodlit view of old Salzburg from the nearby Müllnersteg pedestrian bridge and a riverside stroll home (daily 15:00-23:00, Augustinergasse 4, tel. 0662/431-246).

Getting There: It's about a 15-minute walk along the river (with the river on your right) from the Old Town side of the Staatsbrücke bridge. After passing the Müllnersteg pedestrian bridge, just after Café am Kai, follow the stairs up to a busy street, and cross it. From here, either continue up more stairs into the trees and around the small church (for a scenic approach to the monastery), or stick to the sidewalk as it curves around to Augustinergasse. Either way, your goal is the huge yellow building. Don't be fooled by second-rate gardens serving the same beer nearby. You can also take a bus from Hanuschplatz (#4, #7, #21, #24, #27, or #28) two stops to the Landeskrankenhaus stop, right in front of the beer garden. Or you can walk down from Mönchsberg (follow signs for *Mülln;* see "Mönchsberg Walk" on page 252).

NORTH OF THE RIVER
Restaurants near Linzer Gasse Hotels

$$ Spicy Spices is a trippy vegetarian-Indian restaurant where Suresh Syal (a.k.a. "Mr. Spicy") serves tasty curry and rice, samosas, organic salads, soups, and fresh juices. It's a *namaste* kind of place where everything's organic, and most items are vegan (Mon-Fri 11:00-21:00, Sat 11:30-21:00, closed Sun, Wolf-Dietrich-Strasse 1, tel. 0662/870-712).

$$ Biergarten die Weisse, close to the hotels on Rupertgasse and away from the tourists, is a longtime hit with the natives. If a beer hall can be happening, this one—modern yet with antlers—is it. Their famously good beer is made right there; favorites include fizzy wheat beer (Die Weisse Original) as well as seasonal beers (ask what's on offer). Enjoy the beer with their good, cheap, traditional food in the great garden setting or in the wide variety of indoor rooms—sports bar, young and noisy, or older and more elegant (Mon-Sat 10:00-24:00, closed Sun, Rupertgasse 10, bus #2 to Bayerhamerstrasse or #4 to Grillparzerstrasse, tel. 0662/872-246).

$$ Café Bazar overlooks the river between the Mirabell Gardens and the Staatsbrücke bridge. Its interior is as close as you'll get to a Vienna coffee house in Salzburg. While service is hit-or-miss, their outdoor terrace is a venerable spot for a classy drink with an Old Town and castle view (Mon-Sat 7:30-19:30, Sun 9:00-18:00, July-Aug daily until 23:00 or later, Schwarzstrasse 3, tel. 0662/874-278).

$$ L'Osteria, a local standby for Italian, has a fun energy, a youthful interior, and plenty of outside tables. It's a hit with locals for its pizza and weekly specials, and is one of the livelier hangouts for after-hours drinks when most of the town is closed (daily 11:00-24:00, Dreifaltigkeitsgasse 10, tel. 0662/8706-5810).

$$ Zum Fidelen Affen ("The Funky Monkey") is a reliable neighborhood eatery serving mostly traditional Austrian dishes and a few international items (pastas, big salads). The wood interior is cozy, but the big draw is the outdoor seating, which sprawls through an inviting people zone (Mon-Sat 17:00-24:00, closed Sun, Priesterhausgasse 8, tel. 0662/877-361).

$ BioBurgerMeister is a hip, crowded, order-at-the-counter place specializing in tasty American-style burgers and fries (including veggie and vegan burgers). The indoor seating is cramped—barely more than stools—but the outdoor tables on the street are pleasant (daily 11:00-22:00, across from the big church at Linzer Gasse 54, tel. 0662/265-101).

$$$$ Wasserfall is a splurge right on Linzer Gasse, serving a mostly Italian menu of pastas, meat, and fish. The sophisticated, dressy interior has an actual waterfall trickling underfoot. This is also where Salzburgers come to celebrate special occasions (Tue-Sat 17:30-24:00, closed Sun-Mon and July-mid-Aug, reservations smart, Linzer Gasse 10, tel. 0662/873-331, www.restaurant wasserfall.at).

Groceries: The **Spar supermarket** has multiple locations around the New Town (Mon-Sat generally 7:30-18:00, closed Sun). The bustling morning **Grünmarkt produce market** (closed Sun) on Universitätsplatz, behind Mozart's Birthplace, is fun but expensive.

Steingasse Pub Crawl

For a fun post-concert activity, drop in on a couple of atmospheric bars at the Linzer Gasse end of Steingasse (described on page 255). These dark bars, filled with well-dressed Salzburgers lazily smoking cigarettes and talking philosophy as laid-back tunes play, are all within about 100 yards of each other (all open until the wee hours). Most don't serve food, but **$ Reyna,** a convenient four-table pizzeria and *döner kebab* shop (at #3), stays open late.

Pepe Cocktail Bar, with Mexican decor and Latin music, serves cocktails and nachos (Wed-Sat 19:00 until late, closed Sun-Tue, live DJs on Sat, Steingasse 3, tel. 0662/873-662).

Saiten Sprung wins the "Best Atmosphere" award. The door is kept closed to keep out the crude and rowdy. Just ring the bell and enter its hellish interior—lots of stone and red decor, with mountains of melted wax beneath age-old candlesticks and an ambience of classic '70s and '80s music. Stelios, who speaks English with Greek charm, serves cocktails and fine wine, though no food (Tue-Sat 21:00-late, closed Sun-Mon except in Dec, Steingasse 11, tel. 0662/881-377).

Fridrich, two doors down, is an intimate little place under an 11th-century vault, with lots of mirrors and a silver ceiling fan. Bernd Fridrich is famous for his martinis and passionate about Austrian wines, and has a tattered collection of vinyl that keeps the 1970s alive. Their Yolanda cocktail (grapefruit and vodka) is a favorite. He and his partner Ferdinand serve little dishes designed to complement the focus on socializing and drinking, though their €16 "little bit of everything dish" can be a meal for two (Thu-Tue from 18:00, closed Wed except during festivals and Dec, Steingasse 15, tel. 0662/876-218).

Salzburg Connections

BY TRAIN

By train, Salzburg is the first stop over the German-Austrian border. This means that if Salzburg is your only stop in Austria, and you're using a rail pass that covers Germany (including the Regional Day Ticket for Bavaria) but not Austria, you don't have to pay extra or add Austria to your pass to get here. Deutsche Bahn (German Railway) ticket machines at the Salzburg train station make it easy to buy tickets to German destinations. Austrian train info: Tel. 051-717 (to get an operator, dial 2, then 2), from German phone call 00-43-51-717, www.oebb.at.

From Salzburg by Train to: Füssen (roughly hourly, 4 hours on fast trains, 5 hours on slow trains—included with Regional Day Ticket for Bavaria, change in Munich and sometimes in Kaufbeuren or Buchloe), **Reutte** (roughly hourly, 5 hours, change in Augsburg and Kempten, or in Munich and Garmisch), **Nürnberg** (hourly with change in Munich, 3 hours), **Hallstatt** (every 30-90 minutes, 50 minutes to Attnang-Puchheim, short wait, then 1.5 hours to Hallstatt; also works well by bus—see later), **Innsbruck** (hourly, 2 hours), **Vienna** (3/hour, 3 hours), **Melk** (almost hourly, 2.5 hours, transfer in Amstetten), **Munich** (2/hour, 1.5 hours on fast trains, 2 hours on slower trains—included with Regional Day Ticket for Bavaria), **Frankfurt** (4/day direct, 6 hours), **Ljubljana** (3/day, 4.5 hours, some with change in Villach), **Prague** (3/day, 5.5 hours with change in Linz; 7 hours with change in Landshut or Vienna), **Venice** (5/day, 7 hours, change in Innsbruck or Villach, short night train option). German train info: www.bahn.com.

BY BUS

To reach **Berchtesgaden,** bus #840 is easier than the train (for details see next page).

The bus trip to **Hallstatt** via Bad Ischl is cheaper, more scenic (with views of the Wolfgangsee), and only slightly slower than the train via Attnang-Puchheim—but the bus trip isn't covered by rail passes (bus #150 to Bad Ischl—Mon-Fri nearly hourly, fewer on Sat-Sun, 1.5 hours, leaves from platform F outside Salzburg train station, also stops at Mirabellplatz and Hofwirt, tel. 0810-222-333, www.postbus.at; at Bad Ischl station, change to the train—20-minute ride to Hallstatt, then ride the boat across the lake—or continue by bus #542/543 to the Lahn section of Hallstatt with a change in Gosaumühle).

ROUTE TIPS FOR DRIVERS

To drive on expressways in Austria, you need a **toll sticker** called a *Vignette* (€9/10 days, buy at the border, gas stations, car-rental agencies, or *Tabak* shops). You can skip the sticker if you stay off toll roads.

From Germany to Salzburg: To avoid the A-1 toll road between the German border and Salzburg, you can exit the A-8 autobahn at Bad Reichenall while you're still in Germany, take B-20, and then B-21, which becomes B-1 as it crosses the border (this adds about 10 minutes to the drive).

From Salzburg to Innsbruck: To leave town driving west, go through the Mönchsberg tunnel and follow blue *A-1* signs for Munich. It's 1.5 hours from Salzburg to Innsbruck.

From Salzburg to Hallstatt: To avoid tolls, stick to the most direct route (B-158 via St. Gilgen). If you're in a hurry, get on the Munich-Vienna autobahn (follow blue *A-1* signs, toll sticker required), head for Vienna, exit at Thalgau (#274), and follow signs to Hof, Fuschl, and St. Gilgen. The Salzburg-Hallstatt road passes two luge rides and the towns of St. Gilgen (pleasant but touristy) and Bad Ischl (the center of the Salzkammergut, with a spa, a Habsburg summer palace, and a good TI, www.badischl.at).

Berchtesgaden

This alpine ski region, in a finger of German territory that pokes south into Austria, is famous for its fjord-like lake and its moun-taintop Nazi retreat. Long be-fore its association with Hitler, Berchtesgaden (BERKH-tehs-gah-dehn) was one of the classic Romantic corners of Germany. In fact, Hitler's propagandists capitalized on the Führer's love of this region to establish the notion that the native Austrian was "truly" German at heart.

Today, the Berchtesgaden area still exerts a powerful pull on visitors. World War II buffs come here to see a top-notch documentation center, the remains of the Nazis' elaborate last-ditch bunkers, and Hitler's mountain retreat. For nature lovers, the pristine alpine setting is perfect for cruising up the romantic Königssee to get in touch with the soul of Bavarian Romanticism—or for a hike along a secluded gorge to a high waterfall. And if you have yet to do a salt-mine tour in Austria, Berchtesgaden has a good one.

Remote little Berchtesgaden can be inundated with Germans during peak season, when you may find yourself in a traffic jam of tourists. Plan your time carefully to avoid getting stuck in lines and crowds (more tips later).

GETTING THERE

From Salzburg: Berchtesgaden is 15 miles from Salzburg, and easily connected by bus #840 (runs about hourly Mon-Fri from 8:15, 6-8/day Sat-Sun from 9:15, usually at :15 past each hour, 50 minutes, buy tickets from driver, *Tageskarte* day pass covers your round trip plus local buses in Berchtesgaden—except special bus #849 up to the Eagle's Nest; check schedules at www.svv-info.at). While bus #840 originates in front of Salzburg's main train station, for many travelers it's easiest to catch it at Mirabellplatz (near many recommended New Town hotels) or in Salzburg's Old Town (on Rudolfskai, near Mozartplatz). The last bus #840 back to Salzburg from Berchtesgaden departs at 18:15 (on weekends, this bus requires an easy change at the border; the 17:15 departure is direct).

In a pinch, you can also take the train between Salzburg and

Berchtesgaden (via Freilassing)—but it takes twice as long and isn't as scenic.

From Munich: It's easiest to take the train (hourly, 2.5-3 hours, change in Freilassing).

PLANNING YOUR TIME

Berchtesgaden's sights are excellent, but especially packed during the busy summer months of June through September (sunny weekends attract huge crowds).

If your priority is the Nazi sites, plan your day around David and Christine Harper's half-day tour (see "Tours in Berchtesgaden," later). For a leisurely pace, take the bus at 10:15 or 11:15, poke around a bit, and meet the tour at the TI at 13:15. The tour ends in time for the last bus back at 18:15.

To squeeze in more sights, leave Salzburg on the 8:15 bus (Mon-Fri) and head directly for the salt mines, Königssee (boat trip), or the Almbach Gorge (hiking; closed in winter); as long as you're at any of these sights by 9:00 or 9:30, you should avoid the worst of the crowds and still make it to the 13:15 Nazi sites tour in time. (This is trickier on weekends, when the first bus is at 9:15—expect a longer wait at sights.) Bus #840 stops at both the salt mines and the gorge on the way into town; to reach Königssee, you'll have to change buses at the Berchtesgaden station. (Doing more than one of these in addition to the tour is not realistic unless you have a car.)

Note that the Eagle's Nest is open mid-May to mid-October (confirm at www.kehlsteinhaus.de). Even if it's closed, it's still worthwhile to tour the excellent documentation center and visit the area's other sights.

Orientation to Berchtesgaden

Most of the area's major sights are just outside the small town of Berchtesgaden (pop. 7,500). The hub of activity is the train station and bus terminal, which face a huge roundabout that spans the confluence of two rivers; the TI and parking lots are across the roundabout from the station. From here, buses fan out to the various outlying sights: To the north (along the road to Salzburg) are  the salt mine and the Almbach Gorge; in the foothills to the east is Obersalzberg, with the documentation center and the remains of some Hitler-era bunkers; high on the adjacent mountaintop to the east (called Kehlstein in German) is the Eagle's Nest; and to the south is the long, skinny Königssee, which cuts deep into alpine peaks. The old center of Berchtesgaden, bypassed by most tourists, is up the hill behind the station (use the underground passage below the train tracks and cross the parking lot to reach a footpath to the old center).

Remember, you're in Germany. To call a Berchtesgaden phone number from an Austrian phone, dial 00-49 and then the number (dropping the initial zero).

ARRIVAL IN BERCHTESGADEN

By Bus: Berchtesgaden's central bus terminal (ZOB) is just in front of the train station, which is where you'll find baggage lockers (along the train platform), free WCs (near the Burger King), a few basic eateries, and history (specifically, its vintage 1937 Nazi architecture and the murals in the main hall). The oversized station was built to accommodate (and intimidate) the hordes of Hitler fans who flocked here in hopes of seeing the Führer. The building next to the station, just beyond the round tower, was Hitler's own V.I.P. reception area.

By Car: Drivers follow signs for *P-Zentrum-i*, which lead you to the main roundabout at the station. You can park free for 30 minutes in front of the TI (marked with a red *i*). For a longer stay, use the lot across the street (free, 2-hour limit but rarely enforced) or the pay Salinenplatz lot by the train station. All the outlying sights have their own parking.

TOURIST INFORMATION

The TI is across the roundabout from the train station, in the yellow building with green shutters (daily 9:00-18:00; shorter hours and closed Sun Nov-April; German tel. 08652/656-6070, www.berchtesgaden.com). You may want to pick up the local-bus schedule *(Fahrplan)*.

GETTING AROUND BERCHTESGADEN

All buses (except #849) leave from the train station, run about hourly, and are covered by the *Tageskarte* from Salzburg. Check timetables at www.rvo-bus.de, or call German tel. 08652/94480.

Bus **#840** connects Berchtesgaden to Salzburg, also stopping at the salt mine (Salzbergwerk stop, 7 minutes from Berchtesgaden) and the Almbach Gorge (Kugelmühle stop, 12 minutes)—allowing you to hop off at either sight on your way into or out of town. For more on this bus, see "Getting There," earlier.

Buses **#837** and **#848** also go to the salt mine.

SALZBURG

Bus **#838** goes to the Obersalzberg Documentation Center and Bunker (Obersalzberg stop, 12 minutes).

Bus **#841** goes to the Königssee (Königssee stop, 9 minutes).

Bus **#849** is the only way to reach the Eagle's Nest, connecting from the Obersalzberg Documentation Center (for details, see the "Eagle's Nest" listing, later).

In a pinch, **taxis** are standing by at the train station (figure €8 to the salt mine, €12 to the Königssee, or €14 to Obersalzberg).

Tours in Berchtesgaden

Eagle's Nest Historical Tours

Since 1990, David and Christine Harper—who rightly consider this visit more an educational opportunity than simple sightseeing—have organized thoughtful tours of the Hitler-related sites near Berchtesgaden. Their bus tours, usually led by native English speakers, depart from the TI. Tours start by driving through the remains of the Nazis' Obersalzberg complex, then visit the bunkers underneath the documentation center, and end with a guided visit to the Eagle's Nest (€55/person, RS%—€3 discount with this book, includes admissions, daily at 13:15 mid-May-late Oct, 4 hours, 30 people maximum, reservations strongly recommended, private tours available, German tel. 08652/64971, www.eagles-nest-tours.com). Near the beginning or end of the season, tours are canceled if it's snowing at the Eagle's Nest.

David and Christine also do half-day private tours, which are more flexible and tailored to your interests (€250 for up to 4 people, €300 for up to 8 people); they also do great *Sound of Music* tours to Salzburg that begin in Berchtesgaden.

Bus Tours from Salzburg

While Salzburg-based tour companies (including Bob's Special Tours, www.bobstours.com, and Panorama tours, www.panoramatours.com) offer half- and full-day tours to Berchtesgaden, I don't recommend them except as a last resort. They take you to (but not into) the sights described here—meaning that you pay the tour price for the same transport that you can buy yourself for about €10 from Salzburg. Even on the full-day tours, you cannot see both the Eagle's Nest and the Obersalzberg Documentation Center—you must choose one. Instead, take David and Christine Harper's tour, or visit the documentation center and Eagle's Nest on your own by bus.

Sights near Berchtesgaden

NAZI SITES

Early in his career as a wannabe tyrant, Adolf Hitler had a radical friend who liked to vacation in Berchtesgaden, and through him Hitler came to know and love this dramatic corner of Bavaria. Berchtesgaden's part-Bavarian, part-Austrian character held a special appeal to the Austrian-German Hitler. In the 1920s, just out of prison, he checked into an alpine hotel in Obersalzberg, three miles uphill from Berchtesgaden, to finish work on his memoir and Nazi primer,  *Mein Kampf.* Because it was here that he claimed to be inspired and laid out his vision, some call Obersalzberg the "cradle of the Third Reich."

In the 1930s, after becoming the German Chancellor, Hitler

chose Obersalzberg as the place to build his mountain retreat, a supersized alpine farmhouse called the Berghof—the Nazis' answer to Camp David. His handlers crafted Hitler's image here—surrounded by nature, gently receiving alpine flowers from adoring little children, lounging around with farmers in lederhosen...no modern arms industry, no big-time industrialists, no ugly extermination camps. In reality, Obersalzberg was home to much more than Hitler's alpine chalet. It was a huge compound of 80 buildings—fenced off from the public after 1936, and connected by extensive bunkers—where the major decisions leading up to World War II were hatched. Hitler himself spent about a third of his time at the Berghof, hosted world leaders in the compound, and later had it prepared for his last stand.

Some mistakenly call the entire area "Hitler's Eagle's Nest." That name actually belongs only to the Kehlsteinhaus, a small mountaintop chalet on a 6,000-foot peak that juts up two miles south of Obersalzberg. (A visiting diplomat humorously dubbed it the "Eagle's Nest," and the name stuck.) In April 1945, Britain's Royal Air Force bombed the Obersalzberg compound nearly flat, but missed the difficult-to-target Eagle's Nest entirely. Before the Allies turned the site over to the German government in 1952, they blew up most of what had survived the bombing, wanting to leave nothing to attract future neo-Nazi pilgrims. The most extensive surviving remains are of the Nazis' bunker system, intended as a last resort for the regime as the Allies closed in. In the 1990s, a museum—the Obersalzberg Documentation Center—was built on top of one of the bunkers.

▲▲▲Obersalzberg Documentation Center and Bunker

With a fine museum and the chance to walk through a network of bunkers (all that survives from Hitler's original Berghof complex), this site provides an informative and sobering look at Nazi history.

Cost and Hours: €3 covers both museum and bunker; daily 9:00-17:00; Nov-March Tue-Sun 10:00-15:00, closed Mon; bunker may close temporarily for construction; last entry one hour before closing, allow 1.5 hours for visit, essential €2 audioguide, German tel. 08652/947-960, www.obersalzberg.de.

Getting There: Hop on bus #838 from Berchtesgaden's train station (Obersalzberg stop, then a 5-minute walk). Drivers follow signs for Obersalzberg and Kehlstein, then park for free at the documentation center (lot P1 is near the Eagle's Nest bus stop, while P2 is closer to the museum and bunker).

Visiting the Museum and Bunker: From the parking lot or bus stop, walk down past the big restaurant to reach the entrance.

The small but well-presented **museum** has few actual artifacts but does a fine job of explaining the history of the site, and offers a concise and powerful overview of Nazi history. If you're visiting other documentation centers on your trip (in Nürnberg or Berlin, for example), this is a rerun. If not, it's well worth your time. There's very little English, so rent the audioguide and follow the one-way route.

First head upstairs, with exhibits about this notorious site, including the propagandists based here who cultivated a gauzy cult of personality around their mountain-loving Führer. (A subtitled 28-minute film gives eyewitness accounts of the Berghof during Hitler's heyday.) Head back down to the main floor for a look at the Nazi state and their crimes: profiles of 15 key players, from Himmler to Goebbels to Göring; the *Volksgemeinschaft* propaganda that convinced everyday Germans of their ethnic purity; and methods of terror, from the SS to concentration camps. A children's book is filled with anti-Semitic stereotypes, and a map of the concentration camp network illustrates how all roads led to Auschwitz.

Head downstairs. On your way to the bunkers, you'll pass a series of exhibits on World War II, demonstrating how this place was Hitler's "second center of power" after Berlin.

Finally, you enter the vast and complex **Platterhof bunker system.** Construction began in 1943, after the Battle of Stalingrad ended the Nazi aura of invincibility. This is a professionally engineered underground town, which held meeting rooms, offices, archives for the government, and lavish living quarters for Hitler—all connected by four miles of tunnels cut through solid rock by slave labor. You can't visit all of it, and what you can see was stripped and looted bare after the war. (Look for graffiti from French soldiers, Italian forced laborers, and American GIs.) But enough is left that you can wander among the concrete and marvel at megalomania gone mad.

▲▲▲Eagle's Nest (Kehlsteinhaus)

In 1939, the Kehlsteinhaus chalet was given to the Führer for his 50th birthday. While a fortune was spent building this perch and the road up to it, Hitler, who was afraid of heights, visited only 14 times. Hitler's mistress, Eva Braun, though, liked to hike up to the Eagle's Nest to sunbathe.

Today, the chalet that Hitler ignored is basically a three-room, reasonably priced restaurant with a scenic terrace, 100 yards below the summit of a mountain. You could say it's like any alpine hiking hut, just more massively built. On a nice day, the views are magnificent (but it's often fogged in). Bring a jacket, and go early or late in the day to avoid crowds in summer.

From the upper bus stop, a finely crafted tunnel leads to the original polished-brass elevator, which takes you the last 400 feet up to the Eagle's Nest. Wander into the fancy back dining room (the best preserved from Hitler's time), where you can see the once-sleek marble fireplace chipped up by souvenir-seeking troops in 1945.

Cost and Hours: Free, generally open mid-May–late Oct, snowfall sometimes forces a later opening or earlier closing—dates listed at www.kehlsteinhaus.de.

Getting There: The only way to reach the Eagle's Nest—even if you have your own car—is by specially equipped bus #849, which leaves from the documentation center and climbs steeply up the one-way, private road—Germany's highest (every 25 minutes, 15-minute ride, €16.60 round-trip, *Tageskarte* day passes not valid, look for *Kehlstein Busahfahrt* signs, buy ticket from bus depot window, last bus up 16:00, last bus down 16:50, free parking at documentation center).

OTHER SIGHTS NEAR BERCHTESGADEN
▲Salt Mines (Salzbergwerk Berchtesgaden)
At the Berchtesgaden salt mines, you put on traditional miners' outfits, get on funny little trains, and zip deep into the mountain. On the 1.5-hour tour (which includes time to get into and back out of your miner's gear), you'll cruise subterranean lakes; slide speedily down two long, slick, wooden banisters; and learn how locals mined salt so long ago. Tours are in German, but English speakers get audioguides.

Cost and Hours: €17—book online to see available tour times and avoid waiting in line, daily 9:00-17:00, Nov-April 11:00-15:00—these are last-entry times, German tel. 08652/600-20, www.salzbergwerk.de.

Getting There: Reach the mines from Berchtesgaden with a 20-minute walk along the river or a quick bus ride (#837, #840, or #848—see "Getting around Berchtesgaden," earlier). If you have extra time, you can take the interesting 35-minute walking route from the station to the mines through Berchtesgaden's Old Town. Drivers look for the *Salzbergwerk* and *P* signs at the northern edge of town (on the Salzburg road). Park in the pay lot, then walk five

SALZBURG

minutes to the mine (follow signs through the pedestrian under-pass and over the river).

▲Königssee

Three miles south of Berchtesgaden, the idyllic Königssee stretches like a fjord through pristine mountain scenery to the dramatically

situated Church of St. Bartholomä and beyond. This is a stunner on a nice day (less so when it's socked in). If you plan to sail the Königssee, allow at least two hours round-trip to St. Bartholomä and three hours round-trip to Salet.

Getting There: Bus #841 goes from the Berchtesgaden train station to Königssee. Walkers can take the scenically woodsy, reasonably flat 1.5-hour walk (well-signed). From the pay parking lot and bus stop (with WCs, ATMs, and a TI), a brick path leads five minutes downhill to the lakeshore

through a thicket of souvenir stores selling marmot-fat ointment, quartz chunks, carved birdhouses, lederhosen, dirndls, and "super-pretzels."

Boat Trips: The big draw at Königssee is the scenic boat trips. Most visitors simply go as far as St. Bartholomä, poke around the

church there, eat some smoked fish, then take the boat back (35 minutes each way, €15 round-trip). You can stay on the boat 15 minutes longer to Salet, which is less crowded and offers a fine 15-minute hike to the smaller lake called Obersee (€18.50 round-trip). Boats, going at a sedate Bavarian speed, are filled

with Germans chuckling at the captain's commentary. For the best view, sit on the right going out, and on the left heading back. At a rock cliff midway through the journey, your captain stops, and the first mate pulls out a trumpet to demonstrate the fine echo. Boats leave with demand; you'll get a departure time when you buy your ticket (generally 2-4/hour, first boat around 8:30, last boat back between 18:00 and 19:00 depending on season—ask at ticket desk, runs late April-mid-Oct, no boats off-season, German tel. 08652/96360, www.seenschifffahrt.de). Boats fill up in nice weather (especially in July-Aug between 10:00 and 11:00). Later in the day, return boats (especially from St. Bartholomä) can be packed; if you're rushing to get back to town, keep an eye on queues for the return boats.

St. Bartholomä: The remote, red-onion-domed Church of St. Bartholomä sits on a little peninsula (once also the home of a monastery, then a hunting lodge of the Bavarian royal family). It's surrounded by a fine beer garden, rustic fishermen's pub, and inviting lakeside trails. The family next to St. Bartholomä's lives in the middle of this national park and has a license to fish— so very fresh, caught-and-smoked-today trout is the lunchtime favorite. (Look for the *Fischerei,* where you can get a filet on a baguette to go.) For a heartier meal, there's also an outpost of the Hofbräuhaus. Just up from the boat-dock area is a cluster of houses with a national park center (small German-only exhibit). Here you can get advice for hikes, which are well-signposted. The Eiskapelle "glacier" is about 1.25 hours one-way; for an easier hike, go only partway, to the river called Eisgraben. Or follow the easy 30-minute *St. Bartholomä-Rundweg* loop along the lakeshore.

Almbach Gorge (Almbachklamm)

This short, popular hike is a good option for nature lovers who come to see Berchtesgaden's Nazi sites, then want to fill up the rest of the day hiking along a stream-filled gorge. Though not a world-class attraction, it is an enjoyable way to spend two or three hours. Most visitors do it as roughly a four-mile round-trip, though you can go farther if you wish.

Getting There: Take bus #840 to the Kugelmühle stop (12 minutes toward Salzburg from Berchtesgaden) and check the next bus times—two hours between buses is enough for a quick visit, three hours for a leisurely one. Walk five minutes along Kugelmühlweg (following the *Almbachklamm* signs) to the trailhead. Drivers simply turn off the Salzburg road at *Almbachklamm* signs and turn left along Kugelmühlweg to reach the free parking lot.

Visiting the Gorge: First you'll see the **$$ Gasthaus zur Kugelmühle,** which serves meals and drinks in a pleasant setting (cash only, daily 11:30-19:30, German tel. 08650/461, www.gasthaus-kugelmuehle.de). In front of the restaurant is an old wooden apparatus for shaping marble blocks into round toy spheres (hence the name—*Kugel* means ball, *Mühle* means mill).

Just beyond is a gate where you pay €3 to enter the gorge; pick up a map and get hiking advice here (daily May-Oct 8:00-18:00; gorge closed in winter). A rushing stream cascades through the gorge, which the trail crosses and recrosses on numbered steel bridges. The trail is well maintained and exciting, and accessible to anyone who is reasonably fit, sure-footed, and wearing sturdy shoes. It's not recommended for young children because the path has some steep, unguarded drop-offs. Expect some narrow and slippery parts. The high Sulzer waterfall by bridge #19 is a traditional turnaround point. The walk there and back can be done in two hours at a good clip, but allowing three hours makes for a more pleasant visit. To gain some altitude, on the way back, at bridge #17, hike up to the Mesnerwirt Chapel.

BADEN-BADEN & THE BLACK FOREST

*Baden-Baden • Freiburg • Staufen •
Best of the Black Forest*

Locals and out-of-towners alike go cuckoo for this most romantic of German regions—famous for its mineral spas, clean air, hiking trails, cheery villages...and cuckoo clocks. The Black Forest ("Schwarzwald" in German) is a range of hills stretching along the French border 100 miles from Switzerland north to Karlsruhe (the highest peak is the 4,900-foot Feldberg). Ancient Romans found the thick forest here inaccessible and mysterious, so they called it "black."

Until the last century, the Schwarzwald was cut off from the German mainstream. The poor farmland drove medieval locals to become foresters, glassblowers, and clockmakers. Today, the Black Forest is where Germans come to recuperate from their hectic workaday lives, as well as from medical ailments—often compliments of Germany's generous public health system. Key words you'll see everywhere are *Bad* (or *Baden*), meaning "bath"; and *Kur,* loosely, "cure." Either term is synonymous with "spa" and directs you to a place to relax, soak, and recover. The region is also known for its favorite dessert, *Schwarzwälder Kirschtorte*—Black Forest cake, a mouthwatering concoction with alternating layers of schnapps-soaked chocolate cake, cherries, and whipped cream.

Germans use the term "Schwarzwald" to refer to the entire southwestern corner of Germany (forested or not). The region's two major (and very different) towns are Baden-Baden in the north and Freiburg in the south. Neither feels particularly woodsy—instead, their proximity to France lends both cities a sunny elegance. Baden-Baden is Germany's grandest 19th-century spa resort—old, elegant, and sedate. Stroll through its stylish streets and casino, then soak in its famous baths. Youthful and lively Freiburg is the

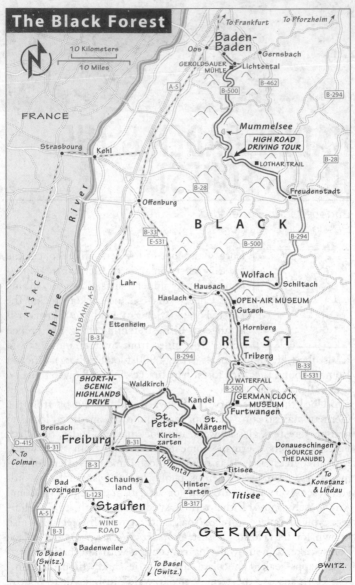

The Black Forest

10 Kilometers

10 Miles

To Frankfurt

To Pforzheim

Baden-Baden

Oos

Gernsbach

GEROLDSAUER MÜHLE

Lichtental

B-462

A-5

B-500

B-294

FRANCE

Mummelsee

HIGH ROAD DRIVING TOUR

Strasbourg

Kehl

LOTHAR TRAIL

B-28

Offenburg

B-28

Freudenstadt

B L A C K

B-33

E-531

B-500

B-294

Lahr

Hausach

Wolfach

Schiltach

Haslach

OPEN-AIR MUSEUM

Ettenheim

Gutach

Hornberg

B-3

F O R E S T

B-294

Triberg

B-33

E-531

WATERFALL

B-500

GERMAN CLOCK MUSEUM

SHORT-N-SCENIC HIGHLANDS DRIVE

Waldkirch

Kandel

Furtwangen

Breisach

St. Peter

St. Märgen

Freiburg

B-31

Kirchzarten

D-415

B-31

B-3

Höllental

Donaueschingen (SOURCE OF THE DANUBE)

To Colmar

Titisee

To Konstanz & Lindau

Bad Krozingen

Schauinsland

Hinterzarten

Titisee

L-123

A-5

Staufen

B-317

B-3

WINE ROAD

G E R M A N Y

To Basel (Switz.)

Badenweiler

To Basel (Switz.)

SWITZ.

Black Forest's de facto capital and main university town. For a small-town experience, hang your hat in cozy Staufen.

Back up in the hills, a pair of worthwhile museums show off two different sides of the local culture—the Vogtsbauernhof Black Forest Open-Air Museum near Gutach, and the German Clock Museum in Furtwangen. You'll also find plenty of opportunity for lazy drives and hikes. The area's two biggest tourist traps are the tiny Titisee (a lake not quite as big as its parking lot—skip it) and Triberg, a small town bisected by a waterfall and filled with cuckoo-clock shops.

PLANNING YOUR TIME

By **train,** Freiburg and Baden-Baden are easy. Exploring the more rural delights of the region by public transit is tougher, but not impossible. Baden-Baden has enough sightseeing to merit two nights and a day. Tour Freiburg for at least an afternoon, and consider sleeping in overlooked Staufen.

With more time and a **car,** do the whole thing: two nights and a relaxing day in Baden-Baden, a busy day doing the small-town forest medley south (with stops at the Vogtsbauernhof Black Forest Open-Air Museum and Furtwangen's German Clock Museum), and a quick visit to Freiburg (sleeping either there or in Staufen).

Baden-Baden

Of all the high-class resort towns I've seen, Baden-Baden is the easiest to enjoy in jeans with a picnic. The town makes a great first—or last—stop in Germany (an easy 1.5 hours from Frankfurt's airport by train).

Baden-Baden was the playground of Europe's high-rolling elite around 150 years ago. Royalty and aristocracy came from all corners of the continent to take the *Kur*—a soak in the curative mineral waters—and enjoy the world's top casino. Wrought-iron balconies on handsome 19th-century apartment buildings give Baden-Baden an elegant, almost Parisian feel. The town acquired its hyphenated double name—short for "Baden in Baden" (that is, Baden in the state of Baden, like New York, New York)—in 1931, to distinguish it from other places named Baden (German for "baths").

With its appealing combination of Edenism and hedonism, the town remains popular today. How popular? It's known among hoteliers as unique: In your typical convention town hoteliers expect that 85 percent of their guests will need single rooms and 15 percent will need doubles; here they flip-flop those figures, as spouses insist on coming to conventions held in Baden-Baden.

The town has also become popular among Russia's elite, and direct flights from Moscow land at Baden-Baden's airport. Many of the town's top hotels—and increasingly, cafés and other smaller businesses—are now Russian-owned. Around town, expect to see Russian on multilingual signs...and Russian-style customer service behind counters.

Along with conventioneers and rich Russians, a middle-class crowd of European tourists in search of a slower pulse—including Germans enjoying the fruits of their health-care system—flock to this lush resort town.

Orientation to Baden-Baden

Baden-Baden, with 55,000 residents, is made for strolling...with a poodle. Feel yourself relax and settle in to the slow pace. Except for the train station and a few accommodations, everything that matters is clustered within a 10-minute walk between the baths and the casino.

Although you'll barely notice if you just stick around the center, Baden-Baden is actually a long, skinny town, strung over several miles along the narrow valley of the Oosbach River (conveniently accessed by bus #201—see "Getting Around Baden-Baden," later). The train station is at the lower (northern) end of the valley, in a suburb called Baden-Oos, three miles from downtown; the Lichtentaler Abbey marks the upper end of the valley. The casino and town center are about halfway between, at the point where a small side valley joins the Oosbach Valley. The church, castle, baths, and oldest sections of town are a few blocks uphill on the north slope of this side valley.

TOURIST INFORMATION

Baden-Baden's TI is in the **Kurhaus** (daily 10:00-18:00, free WC, tel. 07221/275-200, www.baden-baden.de). Pick up their free monthly events program, *Baden-Baden Aktuell* (German only) and a map. Hikers like the TI's *Panoramaweg* map (German only). (Unfortunately, Baden-Baden is one of the worst towns for English translations. Throughout town, non-German-speaking tourists are generally left in the dark.) If you're driving into the countryside, consider buying the *Outline Map*, which helps you get your bearings for the region, and the Black Forest guidebook.

A ticket agency for theater, opera, orchestra, and musicals is at Bäderstrasse 2 (Tue-Sat 10:00-18:00, Sun 14:00-17:00, closed Mon, tel. 07221/932-700, www.tickets-baden-baden.de).

Another TI is at the **B-500 autobahn exit** (Mon-Sat 9:00-18:00, closed Sun, Schwarzwaldstrasse 52).

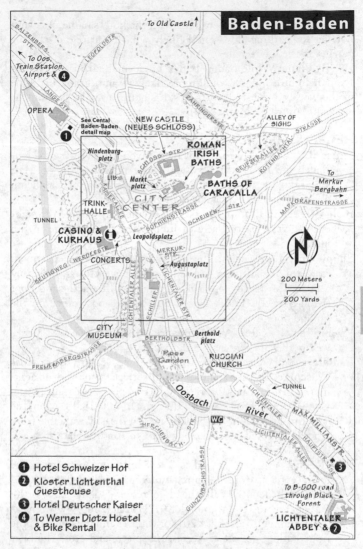

Baden-Baden

To Old Castle ↑

BALZENBERG-STR.
LEOPOLDSTR.
To Oos,
Train Station,
Airport & **4**
LANGE STR.
ZÄHRINGERSTR.
OPERA
1
See Cental
Baden-Baden
detail map
NEW CASTLE
(NEUES SCHLOSS)
ALLEY OF
SIGHS
SEUFZERALLEE
ROTENBACHTAL STRASSE
Hindenburg-
platz
SCHLOSS-STR.
ROMAN-
IRISH
BATHS
To
Merkur
Bergbahn
LIB.
Markt
platz
BATHS OF
CARACALLA
MARGRÄFENSTRASSE
TRINK-
HALLE
KAISER ALLEE
CITY
CENTER
SOPHIENSTRASSE
SCHEIBEN-
STR.
TUNNEL
CASINO &
KURHAUS
Leopoldsplatz
MERKUR-
STR.
BEUTIGWEG
WERDERSTR.
CONCERTS
Augustaplatz
LICHTENTALER ALLEE
SCHILLER
LICHTENTALER STR.
200 Meters
200 Yards
CITY
MUSEUM
BERTHOLDSTR.
Berthold
platz
FREMERSBERGSTRASSE
Rose
Garden
RUSSIAN
CHURCH
TUNNEL
Oosbach
LICHTENTALER STR.
MAXIMILLIANSTR.
River
HERCHENBACH-STR.
WC
LICHTENTALER ALLEE
HAUPTSTR.
GÜNZERBACHSTRASSE
3

1 Hotel Schweizer Hof
2 Kloster Lichtenthal
Guesthouse
3 Hotel Deutscher Kaiser
4 To Werner Dietz Hostel
& Bike Rental

To B-500 road
through Black
Forest

LICHTENTALER
ABBEY & **2**

ARRIVAL IN BADEN-BADEN

By Train: The train station has lockers (platform 1) and a handy *Reisezentrum* that sells tickets (long hours daily). To get from there to downtown in 15 minutes, catch frequent bus #201 (see "Getting Around Baden-Baden," later). A taxi to the center costs about €20.

By Car: Because most traffic goes underneath Baden-Baden (through long tunnels), finding your way to your hotel can be counterintuitive. Most hotels I recommend are in the town center; to reach them, first follow the blue *Therme* signs to the baths neighborhood, then look for green signs with the hotel's name. Ask your hotelier for parking tips (you'll likely wind up at one of the big garages in the town center).

By Plane: While Baden-Baden has a small airport (served by Ryanair from London), you'll more likely fly into Frankfurt. One of the world's busiest airports, it's 1.5 hours away by car (on the autobahn) or train (hourly, €50).

HELPFUL HINTS

Horse Races: Book well in advance if you'll be visiting Baden-Baden during its three annual horse races (usually in May, Aug, and Oct; races are held in nearby town of Iffezheim, check dates at www.baden-racing.com).

Baden-Baden in Bloom: Gardening events draw people throughout the year, particularly in June when the roses are in full bloom.

Shopping and Groceries: The big **Wagener Galerie** department store at Lange Strasse 44 has just about everything, including a huge *über*-trendy supermarket and a café on the top floor (Mon-Sat 9:00-19:00, closed Sun) and a post office on the ground floor.

Wi-Fi: The city's free Wi-Fi network "BADEN-WLAN" works well in the city center.

Laundry: A dry-cleaning shop in the town center, **Klara Ross Wäscherei** also does laundry (full service, same-day or next-morning turnaround). Friendly Klara speaks Russian, but no English (Mon-Sat 8:00-12:00, also 14:00-18:00 Mon-Tue and Thu-Fri, closed Sun; Eichstrasse 14, easily walkable from city center hotels—or take bus #201 to Augustaplatz stop, tel. 07221/22676).

Bike Rental: You can rent bikes a few bus stops away from the town center at **Rent-A-Sportsman** (€10-15/day, show ID and leave cash deposit, call ahead to reserve, daily 8:30-21:00; Eisenbahnstrasse 1a, mobile 0172/721-4280, www.rent-a-sportsman.de). Take bus #201 (or walk 15 minutes) toward the train station, get off at Verfassungsplatz, and cross the busy street; the rental office is behind the Olive restaurant. Active Klaus-Peter also offers lessons in the sport of Nordic walking.

Train Info: The **Derpart** travel agency, between Leopoldsplatz and the casino, posts a train schedule outside. They charge €7 to sell you a ticket—pricey, but it saves you a trip to the station (Mon-Fri 9:00-18:00, Sat 10:00-14:00, closed Sun, Sophienstrasse 1B, tel. 07221/21050).

GETTING AROUND BADEN-BADEN

Within town, only one bus really matters: **Bus #201** runs straight through Baden-Baden, connecting the train station in Oos, the town center (Leopoldsplatz), and Lichtentaler Abbey at the southeast end of town (every 10 minutes or so; €2.50/person single ticket, Citysolo day pass for 1 adult-€6.40, Cityplus day pass for up to 5 adults-€10.60; bus info at www.kvv.de). Buy tickets (valid for 1.5 hours in one direction) from the driver or machines, then validate them in the machine on board. With convenient bus #201, drivers staying at my recommended places outside the center don't need to mess with downtown parking.

Bus #208 can serve as a fun sightseeing bus, though it only runs five times a day and not at all on Sunday. Hop on at Augustaplatz or Leopoldsplatz and enjoy the full, hour-long, figure-eight trip looping through the countryside around town. **Buses #204** and **#205** end at the Merkur funicular (about 2/hour).

City-Bahn Baden-Baden is a putt-putt tourist train that chugs from the casino to the base of the Merkur funicular and back, with a stop near the Baths of Caracalla (€7, recorded English narration, hourly, departs the Kurhaus at about :40, 45 minutes).

Baden-Baden Walk

This self-guided walk starts at the casino, loops through the Old Town to both of the famous baths, and ends back at the river, where you can stroll up to the abbey. In other words, it covers everything. Consider interrupting this route with a visit to the casino and actually taking the waters at your choice of baths.

• *Start on the steps of the...*

Casino

The impressive building called the Kurhaus is wrapped around a grand casino. Designed to resemble Versailles, it still looks like it did when it was built in the 1850s. You can tour it in the morning, and gamble away the afternoon and evening.

To get a visual overview of the town from the casino, stand between the second and third big white columns of the entrance portico and survey the surroundings from left to right: Find the ruined castle near the top of the hill, then the rock-climbing cliffs, the new castle (top of town) next to the copper-topped brick spire of the Catholic church (the famous baths are just behind that), the Merkur peak (marked by a modern observatory tower, 2,000 feet above sea level, easy to reach by bus and then funicular), and the bandstand in the Kurhaus garden. The Baden-Baden orchestra plays free concerts here (most Sundays, March-Oct except in Aug, usually at 16:00).

While you're here, consider popping inside for a tour (in the morning), or to gamble or watch the action in the afternoon or evening—if you're properly dressed (described later, under "Sights in Baden-Baden"). Or, visit the TI.

• *Leaving the casino, walk about 100 yards to the left, past the five 19th-century gas lampposts (still lit by hand each night) to the...*

Trinkhalle

Beyond the trees is the old Trinkhalle—with a long entrance hall decorated with nymphs and romantic legends. This grand corridor

was designed for 19th-century needs: drinking the spa water while promenading out of the sun and rain. It's now home to a recommended café, In der Trinkhalle. Wander around its fancy portico, studying the romantic circa-1850 paintings that spa-goers a century ago could easily relate to. For a sample of the warm spring water, go inside and look for the tap at the central column.

Despite the label, a sip of this water is indeed safe (but quite hot, about 110 degrees)—even supposedly curative. (EU laws require these *Kein Trinkwasser* warnings on any water that isn't safe to drink day in and day out, and this water's high mineral concentration makes it unwise to drink much more than a cup or two at a time.)

From the Trinkhalle, walk down the steps and tip your hat to Kaiser Wilhelm. Locals like this Prussian king because in 1848 he used military force to silence revolutionaries demanding liberal reforms, ensuring that Germany's elites could continue to enjoy this fine town undisturbed. Look up at the charming spa-promotion provided by the relief in the pediment of the Trinkhalle: People come to the goddess of the spa sick and tired. They leave young, beautiful, ready to dance, and suddenly quite fertile. Spa is an acronym for the Latin "Sanus per Aquam," which means "health through water."

• *Cross the mighty Oos River.*

Centuries ago, this stream flowed outside the town walls,

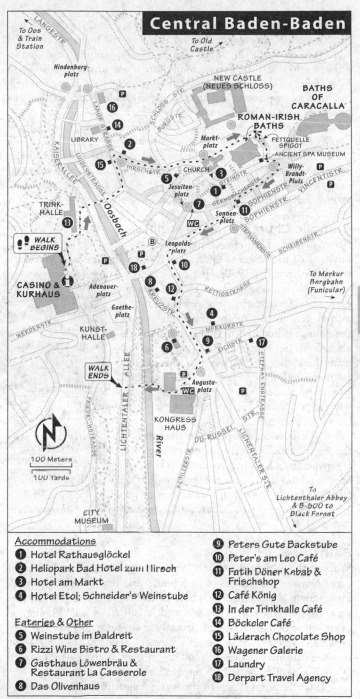

Central Baden-Baden

To Oos & Train Station

LANGESTR.

Hindenburg-platz

To Old Castle

NEW CASTLE (NEUES SCHLOSS)

BATHS OF CARACALLA

ROMAN-IRISH BATHS

SCHLOSS STR.

BURGSTR.

LIBRARY

LANGE STRASSE

Markt-platz

FETTQUELLE SPIGOT

ANCIENT SPA MUSEUM

KAISERALLEE

LUISENSTRASSE

Oosbach

HIRSCHSTR.

CHURCH

Jesuiten-platz

STEINSTR.

GERNSBACHERSTR.

SOPHIENSTR.

SOPHIENSTR.

Willy-Brandt-Platz

VINCENTISTR.

TRINK-HALLE

Sonnen-platz

STEPHANIENSTR.

SCHEIBENSTR.

WALK BEGINS

Leopolds-platz

CASINO & KURHAUS

Adenauer-platz

Goethe-platz

KUNST-HALLE

WALK ENDS

LICHTENTALER ALLEE

FRIEDRICHSTRASSE

WERDERSTR.

KREUZSTR.

RETTIGSTRASSE

MERKURSTR.

EICHSTR.

To Merkur Bergbahn (Funicular)

Augusta-platz

STEPHANIENSTRASSE

LICHTENTALER STR.

KONGRESS HAUS

River

SCHILLERSTR.

DU-RUSSEL

CITY MUSEUM

100 Meters

100 Yards

N

To Lichtenthaler Abbey & B-500 to Black Forest

Accommodations

❶ Hotel Rathausglöckel
❷ Heliopark Bad Hotel zum Hirsch
❸ Hotel am Markt
❹ Hotel Etol; Schneider's Weinstube

Eateries & Other

❺ Weinstube im Baldreit
❻ Rizzi Wine Bistro & Restaurant
❼ Gasthaus Löwenbräu & Restaurant La Casserole
❽ Das Olivenhaus

❾ Peters Gute Backstube
❿ Peter's am Leo Café
⓫ Fatih Döner Kebab & Frischshop
⓬ Café König
⓭ In der Trinkhalle Café
⓮ Böckeler Café
⓯ Läderach Chocolate Shop
⓰ Wagener Galerie
⓱ Laundry
⓲ Derpart Travel Agency

which would have been ahead of you at this point. As the city had little strategic importance and no reason to be fortified, its walls were torn down in the 1830s. Baden-Baden was not damaged in either world war. (The French made sure it was unscathed in World War II—they knew they'd be setting up occupation here, and why not have a nice place to call headquarters?) Baden-Baden's seen as a fine place to relax by whomever may be its ruler.

• *Walk one block inland, then go left on the pedestrian Lange Strasse past fine shops. Three feet below you is the ancient Roman road. And a block in front of you on the left is the Läderach shop—air-conditioned and fragrant with a tempting array of fine Swiss chocolate. At the Hotel zum Hirsch (look for the* Hirsch, *or deer), take a hard right, and climb up Hirschstrasse until you hit a big church.*

Catholic Church and Marktplatz

Baden-Baden's Catholic church looks over the marketplace that has marked the center of town since Roman times. Inside you'll see windows from the 1950s. The fine crucifix, carved out of a single stone in the 15th century, stood in a nearby cemetery until it was moved here in the 1960s. The front part of the church is lined with tombs and memorials to local big shots (counts and margraves) from the 16th to the 18th century. The fanciest memorial, filling most of the right wall, is Baroque and honors a local military figure who helped defend Europe against the Turks in the 17th century.

Back outside, you can see the edge of the "new castle" towering above the square. It's owned by a Kuwaiti woman who hopes to open a fabulous five-star hotel at a cost of €500 million (if she can clear the hurdles that come with renovating a historic building).

• *Now we'll explore the area around Baden-Baden's namesake and claim to fame.*

Baths Area

Walk to the back of the church, under a modern art installation (of jugs on stilts—reminders of the Roman spa that once stood here). Head down the cobbled lane behind the Roman-Irish Bath complex. Because the soil is spa-warmed, a garden of lush Mediterranean vegetation stretches left from here up towards the castle (an area nicknamed "Florentine Hill"). At the end (top of stairs), enjoy the **viewpoint;** Baden-Baden's high-rent district—nicknamed "Paradise"—climbs the hills opposite.

Take the steps down to the water spigot that taps the underground spring called the **Fettquelle** ("rich water source"). It's 105 degrees—as hot as a spa open to the public can legally be. Until recently, this was a practical source of hot water for Baden-Baden residents. Older locals remember being sent here to fetch hot water for their father's shave.

Walk to the sensuous (if armless) statue 50 yards ahead. To your left (her right, but it's missing) is the modern Baths of Caracalla. To your right (her left, still missing) is the venerable and more traditional Roman-Irish Bath (both described later).

• *Return halfway to the Fettquelle spigot and take the stairs down into the parking level (signposted* Römische Badruinen*) into the small tunnel to find the...*

Ancient Spa Museum

This ancient bath, now in ruins, was built for Roman soldiers. It's just one room—most of which you can see through the big windows—and worth the entry fee only if you want to use the included audioguide to learn its story, including how it was engineered (€2.50, open only two hours a day—11:00-12:00 & 15:00-16:00, closed in winter). As it was only for soldiers, this spa is just a simple terra-cotta structure with hollow walls and elevated floors to let the heat circulate.

• *Walking past the museum, you hit daylight, jog left, hook right around an outdoor café, then head down the pedestrian shopping lane called...*

Gernsbacher Strasse

Walking down Gernsbacher Strasse, consider the 2,000-year heritage of guests who have been housed, fed, and watered here at the spa. Fyodor Dostoyevsky, Mark Twain, Johannes Brahms, and Russian princes all called this neighborhood home in its 19th-century heyday. Germany's oldest tennis and golf clubs were created here (for the English community) in the 19th century.

In the late 20th century, Germany's healthcare system was very, very good for Baden-Baden. The government provided lavishly for spa treatment for its tired citizens. Times have changed, and now doctors must make the case to insurance companies that their patients are more than tired...they must actually be sick to have their visit subsidized by taxpayers. And the insurance company then dictates where they'll go. The government will still pay for up to two weeks of recreation at a spa like this, but patients must go to the spa that's recommended and sleep in its clinic. If they sleep in a hotel, the jig is up—and they lose their government funding (that's austerity, German style).

• *After two blocks, you hit Sonnenplatz. Hang a left, then a right, and continue down...*

Sophienstrasse

This street enjoys the reliable shade of a long row of tall chestnut trees. In the 1870s, when it was lined exclusively by hotels, this was the town's aristocratic promenade. Back then there were 15,000 bedrooms for rent in Baden-Baden (triple what the city has today).

• *After a short block you'll see a fine little heron fountain. Turn right there, down Rittergasse, to the recommended ivy-and-flower-bedecked Löwenbräu beer garden (a festival of Bavarian clichés even though we're not in Bavaria). Head left, past the lederhosen and dirndls, and peek back right up some stairs to the stern stone statue of Otto von Bismarck. Nicknamed the "Iron Chancellor," he spearheaded German unification under Prussia in 1871 (and gave Germany its national healthcare system shortly after unification). Directly ahead is Leopoldsplatz, Baden-Baden's main square.*

Leopoldsplatz

Until 1985, this square was a busy traffic hub, with 30,000 cars muscling through it each day. Now a 1.5-mile-long tunnel takes the east-west traffic under the city, and the peace and quiet you'd expect in a spa town has returned. Actually, Baden-Baden had to get rid of the noise and pollution caused by the traffic in order to maintain its top rating as a spa resort—lose that, and Baden-Baden would lose half its business. The main city bus stop is just off the square, on Luisenstrasse.

• *From Leopoldsplatz, head left on Lichtentaler Strasse. You'll pass jewelry stores, plenty of high-end shops, and the venerable and recommended Café König (on the right). Head for the big fountain in the distance, which marks Augustaplatz (public WC nearby). At the fountain, go right, through the park, and over the petite bridge, where you'll come to a sweet riverside path called Lichtentaler Allee (described under "Sights in Baden-Baden," next).*

    From here the casino is ahead and to your right. A stroll to the left—down Lichtentaler Allee—takes you to the rose garden, City Museum (an elegant old mansion with a humble but well-displayed collection of artifacts and etchings showing the history of the spa town), and out to Lichtentaler Abbey.

Sights in Baden-Baden

THE BATHS

Baden-Baden's top sights—two much-loved but very different baths—stand side by side in a park at the top of the Old Town. The Roman-Irish Bath is traditional, stately, indoors, contemplative, and extremely relaxing...just you, the past, and your body. The perky, fun, and modern Baths of Caracalla are less expensive, both indoor and outdoor, and more social. Some hotels sell discounted tickets (10-15 percent off) to one or both of the baths—ask.

At either bath, you'll get an electronic wristband, which you'll need when you're ready to leave. If you overstay your allotted time, you pay extra. You can relax while your valuables are stowed in very secure lockers. The baths share the huge underground Bäder-Garage (reduced price for bathers if you validate your parking ticket before leaving either bath, entrance on Rotenbachtalstrasse).

▲▲▲Roman-Irish Bath (Friedrichsbad)

The highlight of most visits to Baden-Baden is a sober 17-step ritual called the Roman-Irish Bath. This bathhouse pampered the

rich and famous in its elegant surroundings when it opened in 1877. Today, this steamy world of marble, brass columns, tropical tiles, herons, lily pads, and graceful nudity welcomes gawky tourists as well as locals.

Cost and Hours: €25/3 hours, €12 more gets you a soap-and-brush massage, another €12 for final crème massage; daily 9:00-22:00, last entry 2 hours before closing; no kids under age 14, Römerplatz 1, tel. 07221/275-920, www.friedrichsbad.eu. It's possible to speed through the bath in an hour, but the whole idea is to...slow down.

Dress Code: Everyone in these baths is always nude (even prudish American tourists). On Mondays, Thursdays, and Saturdays, men and women use separate and nearly identical facilities—but the sexes can mingle briefly in the pool under the grand dome in the center of the complex (yes, everyone's nude there, too). Shy bathers should avoid Tuesdays, Wednesdays, Fridays, Sundays, and holidays, when all the rooms are mixed—including the steam and massage rooms. If you're concerned, you needn't be; there's no ogling going on. It's a classy and respectful ritual, and a shame to miss just because you're intimidated by nudity.

Procedure: You'll pay, get a wristband, and activate it as you enter. Choose a locker (where you'll find your bed-sheet-like towel), and change in a changing cabin. Lock your locker by pressing on the button with your wristband. Remember your locker number; for security, it's not indicated on your wristband. Inside the baths, the complex routine is written (in English) on the walls with recommended times—simply follow the room numbers from 1 to 17. Instructions are repeated everywhere. And English-speaking attendants are there when necessary. For the first couple of stops only, you use plastic slippers and a towel for hygienic reasons and because the slats are too hot to sit on directly.

You'll start by taking a shower. Grab a towel and put on plastic slippers before hitting the warm-air bath for 15 minutes and the hot-air bath for five. Shower again. If you paid extra, take the rough and slippery soap-brush massage—which may finish with a good Teutonic spank for the gents and a gentler tap-tap for the ladies. Play Gumby in the shower; lounge under sunbeams in one of several thermal steam baths; and glide like a swan under a divine dome in the mixed-gender royal pool. Don't skip the invigorating cold plunge, but do go in all at once—the relaxation you'll experience after emerging is worth it. Dry off with warmed towels. If you prepaid for the eight-minute crème massage, now's the time. Then you'll be wrapped like a baby to lie on a bed for 30 minutes, thinking prenatal thoughts, in the mellow, yellow silent room. At the end, there's a reading room with refreshing drinks, chaise lounges, and magazines. You don't appreciate how clean you are after this experience until you put your dirty socks back on. Ewwww (bring a clean pair).

All you need is money. Hair dryers are available, and clocks are prominently displayed throughout. If you wear glasses, consider leaving them in your locker (it's more relaxing without them). Otherwise, you'll find trays throughout for you to park your specs.

Afterward, before going downstairs, sip just a little of the terrible but "magic" hot water *(Thermalwasser)* from the elegant fountain (locals ignore the "no drinking water" sign), and stroll down the broad royal stairway, feeling, as they say, five years younger—or at least, after all that sweating, a pound or two lighter.

▲▲Baths of Caracalla (Caracalla Therme)

For a more modern experience, spend a few hours at the Baths of Caracalla, a huge palace of water, steam, and relaxed people. More like a mini water park, and with bathers clothed, this is a fun and accessible experience, and is recommended for those who'd prefer less nudity (sauna-goers upstairs, however, are nude).

Cost and Hours: €15/1.5 hours, €16/2 hours, €19/3 hours, €23 buys the whole day, a few euros more for the sauna, multiple-visit tickets available and can be split among your group, discounts with hotel guest card *(Kurkarte);* massages and other spa treatments available; daily 8:00-22:00, last entry 1.5 hours before closing, no kids under age 7, kids 7-14 must be with parents (it's not really a splashing and sliding kind of pool); tel. 07221/275-940, www.caracalla.de.

Procedure: At this bath, you need to bring a towel (or rent one for €6) and a swimsuit (shorts are OK for men, no swimsuit rental available but you can buy one in the shop).

Find a locker, change clothes, strap the band around your wrist, and go play. Your wristband gets you into another poolside locker if you want to lock up your glasses. You won't need your wallet inside, but if you get something to eat or drink, you'll pay on exit (it's recorded on your wristband). Bring your towel to the pool. The baths are an indoor/outdoor wonderland of steamy pools, waterfalls, neck showers, hot tubs, hot springs, cold pools, lounge chairs, saunas, a wellness lounge/massage area, a cafeteria, and a bar. After taking a few laps around the fake river, you can join some kinky Germans for water spankings. Then join the gang in the central cauldron. The steamy "inhalation" room seems like purgatory's waiting room, with a misty minimum of visibility, filled with strange, silently aging bodies.

Nudity is limited to the sauna zone upstairs. The grand spiral staircase leads to a naked world of saunas, tanning lights, cold plunges, and sunbathing outside on lounge chairs. At the top of the stairs everyone stows their suit in a cubbyhole and wanders around with their towel (some are modest and wrapped; others just run around buck naked). There are three eucalyptus-scented saunas of varying temperatures (80, 90, and 95 degrees) and two saunas in outdoor log cabins (with mesmerizing robotic steam-makers). Follow the instructions on the wall. Towels are required, not for modesty but to separate your body from the wood benches. The highlight is the arctic bucket in the shower room. Pull the chain. Rarely will you ever feel so good.

MORE SIGHTS IN BADEN-BADEN
▲▲Casino and Kurhaus
Baden-Baden's grand casino occupies a classy building called the Kurhaus. It still looks like it did in the 1850s when it was built. Inspired by the Palace of Versailles, it's filled with rooms honoring French royalty who never actually set foot in the place. But many other French people did. Gambling was illegal in 19th-century

France...just over the border. The casino is state-owned, and the revenue it generates (about $25 million a year) funds all sorts of social services and city projects. The staff of 180 is paid mostly by tips from happy gamblers.

You can visit the casino on a guided tour in the mornings, when it's closed to gamblers, but it is most interesting to see in action. (While gambling starts at 14:00, there's a much better scene and energy later in the evening.) You can gamble if you want, but a third of the visitors come only to people-watch under the chandeliers. The scene is more subdued than at an American casino; anyone showing emotion is more likely a tourist than a se-

rious gambler. Lean against a gilded statue and listen to the graceful reshuffling of personal fortunes. Do some imaginary gambling or buy a few chips at the window near the entrance (an ATM is downstairs). The Russian novelist Fyodor Dostoyevsky came here, lost his fortune in these very rooms, and wrote a book about it: *The Gambler.*

The casino has a pricey restaurant (with a lovely garden), and the Equipage cocktail bar has live music and hanky-panky most nights (from 21:00 until late, closed Mon).

Cost and Hours: €5 entry, free with voucher from guided tour (described below), €2 minimum bet; open daily 14:00 until very late, livelier after dinner and liveliest after 22:00; no athletic shoes, no sandals or short sleeves for men, coat and collared shirt required for men and ties are encouraged—coat can be rented for €8, collared shirt can be purchased for €18, nice jeans OK; passport required—driver's license isn't enough, under 21 not admitted, no photos, pick up game rules as you enter; tel. 07221/30240, www.casino-baden-baden.de.

Lower rollers and budget travelers can try their luck downstairs at the casino's slot machines (called *Automatenspiel*), or give video poker or video roulette a go (€1 entry or included in €5 casino admission, opens at 12:00—otherwise same hours and age restrictions, passport still required, but no dress code).

Tours: The casino gives 40-minute German tours every morning (€7, €1 discount with hotel guest card—*Kurkarte;* April-Oct at 9:30, 10:15, 11:00, and 11:45; Nov-March at 10:00, 10:45, and 11:30; grab the succinct yellow English information sheet, some guides might add short English summaries if asked; tel. 07221/30240). Even peasants wearing T-shirts, shorts, and sandals, with cameras and kids in tow, are welcome on tours. After the guided visit, tour-takers (21 and up) receive a voucher for free entry during regular gambling hours.

▲▲Strolling Lichtentaler Allee

Imagine yourself dressed as a 19th-century aristocrat as you promenade down elegant Lichtentaler Allee, a pleasant, picnic-perfect 1.5-mile-long lane. Stroll through a park along the babbling brick-lined Oosbach River, past old mansions and under hardy oaks and exotic trees (street-lit all night), with people on horseback and horse-drawn carriages parading by. The lane is nicknamed "The Green Mile" for the huge variety of trees planted here back in the 19th century, when nature was all the rage (and appreciating it was part of the ritual of the *Kur*). It's also called "The Culture Mile" for the many museums that line it. The most interesting is the **City Museum** (€5, includes an "A" for effort audioguide, Tue-Sun 11:00-18:00, closed Mon).

By the tennis courts (gear rentable), cross the footbridge into the free Art Nouveau **Rose Garden** (Gönneranlage, hundreds of labeled kinds of roses bloom May-June, great tables and benches). Next to the courts is a popular Italian restaurant (Rosso Bianco). The promenade leads all the way to Lichtentaler Abbey (described next).

You can either walk round-trip, or walk one way and take city bus #201 back (runs every 10 minutes along the main street, parallel to the promenade, on the other side of the river). Many bridges cross the river, making it easy to shortcut to the bus anytime. Biking is another option (see "Helpful Hints," earlier), but you'll have to stay on the road in the bike lane, since the footpath is only for pedestrians.

Lichtentaler Abbey

An active Cistercian convent founded in 1245, Lichtentaler Abbey welcomes the public into its tranquil, gated world. And since 1245, here in what they call "a school for the service of the Lord," the Cistercians have embraced the teaching of St. Benedict: to live with moderation, show compassion for all, be unselfish, and follow the Golden Rule. The abbey has survived nearly eight centuries of threats, including the dissolutions of the abbeys in Napoleonic times and the destruction of both world wars. When you walk through its gate into the courtyard, ringed by trees and so peaceful, you sense that the place is blessed.

You can visit its 13th-century chapel, check out the shop (with herbs, liquors, etc.), and have lunch or a drink at Café Lumen (heavenly homemade cakes, Tue-Sun 11:00-18:00, closed Mon). They host sometimes-free concerts on Sundays in summer at 15:00. They also run the delightful Kloster Lichtenthal Guesthouse (see "Sleeping in Baden-Baden," later).

BADEN-BADEN & THE BLACK FOREST

Cost and Hours: Free, gate closes at 20:00, Hauptstrasse 40, tel. 07221/504-910, www.abtei-lichtenthal.de.

Russian Baden-Baden

The town's Russian link dates back to 1793, when the future Czar Alexander I took Louise, Princess of Baden, as his wife. Later, many Russians, including Dostoyevsky and Tolstoy, flocked here after gambling was banned in their motherland. Some lost their fortunes, borrowed a pistol, and did themselves in on the "Alley of Sighs" (Seufzerallee, near the Caracalla baths).

The **Russian Orthodox church** is just south of the town center—step in (€1 donation requested, daily 10:00-17:00 or according to whim, services Sat evening and Sun morning, Lichtentaler Strasse 76, near rose garden across river from Lichtentaler Allee, or take bus #201 to Bertholdplatz stop). Why no pews? In Orthodox churches the congregation stands throughout the service—sometimes for hours.

While the church dates from about 1900, the Russian community has been invigorated in recent years. In the 1990s, Russians of German ethnic origin were allowed to emigrate to Germany, and many settled in Baden-Baden. More recently, ultra-wealthy Russians seeking safe property investments have poured their rubles into Baden-Baden, and a new wave of Russian visitors and business owners have come in their wake.

▲Funicular to the Summit of Merkur

This delightful trip to a hilltop overlooking Baden-Baden is easy, quick, and a good reason to explore beyond the main drag. Catch bus #204 or #205 from the city center (departing 2/hour from Leopoldsplatz, on Sophienstrasse in front of Volksbank) and ride 11 minutes through the ritzy "Paradise" neighborhood to the end of the line at the base of the Merkur Bergbahn. Take the ear-popping funicular to the 2,000-foot summit.

At the top, you can enjoy a meal or drink (restaurant open until 18:00 or later) or explore some hiking trails. And, if the weather's good (with winds from the south or west), you can watch the paragliders leap into ecstasy. Take the funicular back down, or risk getting lost and walk down the lane to the base of the funicular (2.5 miles, signposted *Merkurbahn Talstation*). From the bottom of the funicular, buses depart back to Baden-Baden twice hourly.

Cost and Hours: €2 each way, departs frequently, daily 10:00-22:00, ticket office closes at 18:00, tickets also available at machines at both departure points, restaurant tel. 07221/31640.

Mini Black Forest Walks

Baden-Baden is at the northern end of the Black Forest. If you're not going south, but want a taste of Germany's favorite woods, consider one of several hikes from town. The TI has details and can suggest routes. If you're serious about hiking, invest in the TI's good (but German-only) *Panoramaweg* map, which outlines a 25-mile trail leading all the way around Baden-Baden's perimeter and nearby Geroldsau Valley (it's easy to do just part of the trail, since you're never far from the town center or a bus stop).

Sleeping in Baden-Baden

While Baden-Baden has some grand hotels, my recommended places are mostly small, family-run, and more budget-friendly (though all accommodations are pricey in this posh town). Hotel am Markt is a particularly great value and worth reserving in advance. Note that most hotels here don't have 24-hour reception desks; most close for the night at 21:00 or earlier, though they can wait up for you if they know you're arriving later. Call ahead with your specific arrival details if you'll be coming after 17:00.

While weekends and summer are generally more expensive, demand—and prices—change from day to day based on conventions, theater performances, and other events.

All hotels and pensions are required to charge an additional €3.80 per person, per night "spa tax." This comes with a "guest card" *(Kurkarte),* offering small discounts on tourist admissions around town (including the casino and the Caracalla Spa). If you're coming into town by car or foot, look for helpful green signs that direct you to each hotel by name.

IN THE CENTER, NEAR THE BATHS

These well-located options stick you right in the heart of Baden-Baden, in a pleasant, stepped pedestrian zone a short saunter from the baths. For locations, see the "Central Baden-Baden" map, earlier.

$$$ Hotel Rathausglöckel is a 16th-century guesthouse that has undergone a tasteful 21st-century renovation. Zoia, Sebastian, and Jasmine make this classic little place one of the town's most inviting hotels. Steep stairs lead to 15 antique-furnished rooms (plus a few grand suites) and an inviting rooftop deck (RS%, family rooms, no elevator, church bells every 15 minutes 8:15-22:00, pay parking, Steinstrasse 7, tel. 07221/90610, www.rathausgloeckel.de, info@rathausgloeckel.de).

$$$ Heliopark Bad Hotel zum Hirsch—hardly a "bad hotel"—is an "antique-boutique" resort hotel. Its 71 rooms, many of them quite spacious, come with stylish furniture (some traditional, some modern) and all the fixin's. It's wonderfully located in the middle of the pedestrian zone, an easy walk from the baths (ex-

cellent breakfast, elevator, Hirschstrasse 1, tel. 07221/9390, www.
heliopark-hirsch.de, info@heliopark-hirsch.de).

$$ Hotel am Markt is Baden-Baden's best little hotel. Family-run since 1951, this 21-room place offers all the modern comforts a commoner could want in a peaceful, central, nearly traffic-free location, two cobbled blocks from the baths. The church bells ring every 15 minutes from 8:15 until 22:00. Otherwise, quiet rules. The ambience makes it a joy to have breakfast or just kill time on the small terrace (elevator, pay parking; Marktplatz 18, tel. 07221/27040, www.hotel-am-markt-baden.de, info@hotel-am-markt-baden.de; run by sisters Frau Jung and Frau Bogner-Schindler, and daughters Lisa and Laura).

IN THE MODERN TOWN

$$ Hotel Etol is in the quiet courtyard of a renovated industrial complex, which celebrates its history as a tile and bathtub factory from around the year 1900. You'll climb the stairs to reach any of the 18 rooms, each named for a town in the Black Forest. Natural light, tasteful design, friendly staff, and a central location make this a winning choice (RS%, family rooms, pay laundry, pay parking; Merkurstrasse 7, 2-minute walk from Augustaplatz stop of bus #201—for location, see the "Central Baden-Baden" map, earlier; tel. 07221/973-470, www.hotel-etol.de, info@hotel-etol.de).

$$ Hotel Schweizer Hof's 39 rooms mix classic style and modern comfort. It's about a seven-minute walk north of the pedestrian district, on a little square next to the opera house (elevator, pay parking, nearby six-room apartment available; Lange Strasse 73—for location see the "Baden-Baden" map, earlier; bus #201 stop: Festspielhaus/Alter Bahnhof—then walk 50 yards past the opera house, drivers follow *Festspielhaus/Casino* signs, tel. 07221/30460, www.schweizerhof.de, mail@schweizerhof.de).

OUTSIDE THE CENTER

The following listings are a few stops from the center on bus #201. For locations, see the "Baden-Baden" map, earlier.

$ Kloster Lichtenthal Guesthouse lets you be a part of the peaceful cloistered world of a working Cistercian abbey. Its 45 rooms are monastic chic with meditative simplicity under historic beams, and your money supports the work of the sisters here. Their rooms with only a sink (modern bathrooms down the hall) cost about a third less than the en suite rooms. There is no TV and no Wi-Fi. When the abbey gate closes at 20:00, you feel quite special (reception open Mon-Fri 8:00-17:00, Sat-Sun until 15:00, free parking, Hauptstrasse 40, tel. 07221/504-9119, www.abtei-lichtenthal.de, gaestehaus@abtei-lichtenthal.de).

$ Hotel Deutscher Kaiser, a good choice for those looking to spend less, is a traditional guesthouse with 14 spacious and modern rooms, run by Frau Peter. Don't confuse this with the independent "Hotel Deutscher Kaiser" near Augustaplatz, which has different owners and offers much less value. The one you want is just before the Eckerlestrasse bus stop—in a peaceful neighborhood just a two-minute walk from the abbey, and steps away from Lichtentaler Allee park (bus #201, 6/hour, 10 minutes from center, 20 minutes from train station) or a 25-minute stroll from the city center (free and easy public parking nearby, Hauptstrasse 35, tel. 07221/72152, www.hoteldk.de, info@hoteldk.de). Drivers: Get directions in advance.

¢ **Werner Dietz Hostel,** between the station and the center, is big, modern, and has the cheapest beds in town (private rooms available, 23:30 curfew, outdoor swimming pool next door, Hardbergstrasse 34, tel. 07221/52223, www.jugendherberge-baden-baden.de, info@jugendherberge-baden-baden.de). To reach the hostel from the train station or downtown, take bus #201 to Grosse Dollenstrasse (also announced as *Jugendherberge*); it's a steep, well-marked 10-minute climb from there. Drivers: Call the hostel for directions.

Eating in Baden-Baden

DINING WITH ELEGANCE AND ATMOSPHERE

$$$ Weinstube im Baldreit, with both a cozy cellar and a leafy back courtyard, is ideal on a hot evening. Dining here, I feel like a pampered salamander in a Monet terrarium. While her French husband Philippe cooks near-gourmet regional dishes, Nicole is happy to translate the daily specials chalked in German on the board. Reservations are smart (Tue-Sat 17:00-22:00, closed Sun-Mon; from Lange Strasse 10, walk up the higgledy-piggledy street called Küferstrasse, follow *Weinstube* signs, Küferstrasse 3, tel. 07221/23136).

$$$$ Schneider's Weinstube, in a convivial space just outside the main tourist zone, is not nearly as atmospheric as Weinstube im Baldreit and has no outdoor seating option. But Herr *und* Frau Schneider serve what many locals consider the town's best cuisine and offer a fine selection of wines. Reservations are smart. While game and meat are the specialty, there is always a good vegetarian dish (Mon-Sat 17:00-22:00, closed Sun, Merkurstrasse 3, tel. 07221/976-6929, www.schneiders-weinstube.de).

$$$$ Rizzi Wine Bistro & Restaurant is the stylish choice for VIPs, offering formal service, good Mediterranean cuisine, and just a dash of pretense. It's chic and designed so you feel like you're eating in a park. Reserve in advance (daily 12:00-23:00, in the park at Augustaplatz 1, tel. 07221/25838, www.rizzi-baden-baden.de).

BAVARIAN AND FRENCH ON JESUITENPLATZ

$$ Gasthaus Löwenbräu, a sloppy, Bavarian-style *Biergarten,* slings good beer and basic schnitzel fare under a vine-covered trellis. This place is so very Bavarian they serve lederhosen wedgies in season (daily 10:00-23:00, Gernsbacher Strasse 9, tel. 07221/22311).

$$ Restaurant La Casserole, with a delightful interior and good seating on the peaceful square, is ideal if you feel like an Alsatian-style pizza. *Flammkuchen* comes with all the topping options popular at any pizza place and makes a nice budget meal (Mon-Sat dinner from 17:00, also Thu-Sat lunch 11:30-15:00, closed Sun, Gernsbacher Strasse 18, tel. 07221/22221).

QUICK AND SIMPLE MEALS IN THE CENTER

$$ Das Olivenhaus, a delightful little haven tucked sweetly into a modern gallery, serves creative plates mixing German and French influence in a quiet space designed to make you feel at home (Tue-Sat 11:30-16:00, closed Sun-Mon, Kreuzstrasse 3 in Kreuzpassage, tel. 07221/271-810, Olivia Pallas).

$ Peters Gute Backstube is a fast, healthy salad-and-sandwich place with nice seating inside and outside facing Augustaplatz (Mon-Sat 6:00-19:00, Sun 8:00-18:00, Lichtentalestrasse 17).

$ Peter's am Leo Café is a self-service joint offering big breakfasts, sandwiches, salads, pastries, and a few outdoor tables with views over Baden-Baden's central square (Mon-Sat 6:30-19:00, Sun from 8:00, on Leopoldsplatz at Sophienstrasse 10, tel. 07221/392817).

$ Fatih Döner Kebab and Frischshop is a basic falafel joint with a few stools and an attached deli serving fresh produce and picnic goodies (Mon-Fri 7:00-19:00 or later, Sat until 17:00, closed Sun, Sonnenplatz 1).

PRIME PEOPLE-WATCHING CAFÉS

Baden-Baden's many cafés are variations on a genteel theme. They serve chocolates, coffee, cakes (including the famous *Schwarzwälder Kirschtorte*—Black Forest cake), and light meals. Figure around €5-6 to savor a slice of cake and cup of coffee, or €8 or so for light food (such as sandwiches and salads). Most cafés close for dinner. I like the following three:

$ Café König is *the* place to bring your poodle and spend too much for an elegant cup of coffee and a slice of Black Forest cake.

Grab a seat and then go to the counter to choose your cake (daily 9:30-18:30, fine shady patio, between Leopoldsplatz and Augustaplatz at Lichtentaler Strasse 12, tel. 07221/23573). This little slice of Vienna also serves light meals.

$ In der Trinkhalle, a café that shares the handsome Trinkhalle building with the TI, has comfy leather sofas, international newspapers and magazines, a casino-view terrace, and a club-like ambience on Friday and Saturday nights (daily 10:00-18:00, Kaiserallee 3, tel. 07221/302905).

$ Böckeler Café, a good but less fancy option, has an extensive dessert counter, a modern interior, and outdoor tables along a lively pedestrian street (Mon-Fri 8:30-18:30, Sat-Sun until 18:00, Lange Strasse 40, tel. 07221/949594).

Nightlife in Baden-Baden

You can dress to the nines (the eights are fine, too) and head to the casino, where most of the action takes place at night (see "More Sights in Baden-Baden," earlier). If you'd rather keep it casual, several other places in town stay open late. For a hint of swank and lots of riverside ambience, the recommended **Rizzi Wine Bistro & Restaurant** serves food until 23:00 and drinks until even later. For a Bavarian Oktoberfest kind of atmosphere, the recommended **Gasthaus Löwenbräu** on the Jesuitenplatz is lively until late, with beer guzzlers young and old. See details on both earlier, under "Eating in Baden-Baden."

Baden-Baden Connections

From Baden-Baden by Train to: Freiburg (direct fast trains every hour or so, 45 minutes; cheaper regional trains take 1.5 hours with change in Offenburg), **Triberg** (hourly, 1.5 hours), **Munich** (hourly, 4 hours, change in Mannheim or Karlsruhe), **Frankfurt** (hourly, 2 hours, direct or with a change in Karlsruhe), **Frankfurt Airport** (roughly hourly, 1.5 hours, mostly with a change), **Bacharach** (hourly, 3 hours, 1-3 changes), **Strasbourg,** France (every 1-2 hours, usually 1.5 hours with a change in Appenweier), **Bern** or **Zürich,** Switzerland (every 1-2 hours, 3 hours, change in Basel). Train info: www.bahn.com.

Freiburg

Freiburg (FRY-boorg) is the capital of the Schwarzwald. This "sunniest town in Germany," with 30,000 students, is a lively and youthful complement to more sedate Baden-Baden. While its old center was almost entirely rebuilt after a November 1944 bombing (and feels that way), this university town is a hive of small shops, cozy cafés, and people living well. Less touristy than Baden-Baden, mostly traffic-free, and generously served by sleek and silent trams, it exudes an "I could live here" appeal. Freiburg's striking red-sandstone cathedral and its leading Augustiner Museum are world-class. And with

lush forested hills reaching above its venerable town gates, it's a handy springboard for Black Forest adventures.

Orientation to Freiburg

With about 230,000 people, Freiburg is a happening midsize city. Most points of interest to visitors are concentrated in the compact Old Town (Altstadt), bounded to the west by the train station and to the east by Freiburg's mountain, Schlossberg, and circled by a ring road. You can walk from one end of this zone to the other in about 20 minutes. The town's centerpiece, always in view, is the spiny spire of its cathedral. A center of higher education for centuries, its image is a town of highly educated, politically correct people with a smart opinion about everything.

TOURIST INFORMATION

Freiburg's helpful TI, on Rathausplatz, is a good info source for the entire Black Forest region (Mon-Fri 8:00-20:00, Sat 9:30-17:00, Sun 10:30-15:30; Oct-May Mon-Fri until 18:00, Sat until 14:30, Sun 10:00-12:00; tel. 0761/388-1880, www.freiburg.de).

ARRIVAL IN FREIBURG

By Train: The bustling train station has lockers (near track 1), a pay WC (downstairs), and a useful *Reisezentrum* that dispenses rail info and sells tickets (long hours daily). The bus station is next door (under the bridge; follow signs for "*ZOB*"—the German initials for central bus station). To get to the city center, you can take a taxi (€10), tram, or walk. To access **trams,** take the escalators up to the bridge above the tracks. Cross to the other side and take tram #1, #3, or #5 to get downtown. Get off at the second stop, Bertoldsbrunnen.

To reach the city center by **foot** (about 15 minutes), walk straight through the train station, cross the busy street, and continue ahead up the tree-lined Eisenbahnstrasse (passing the post office). Within three blocks, you'll cross the ring road, then continue straight (on the pedestrian-only Rathausgasse) to Rathausplatz, with the TI and where my self-guided walk begins. Most of my recommended hotels are within a 10-minute walk of here.

By Plane: EuroAirport Basel-Mulhouse-Freiburg is connected to cities across Europe by both major carriers and discount airlines (www.euroairport.com). FlixBus serves downtown Freiburg (€20, hourly, 1 hour, handy app, www.flixbus.com).

HELPFUL HINTS

Sightseeing Pass: The €7 entry to the Augustiner Museum (or the "city pass" ticket, sold at any other museum) includes all the city museums.

Farmers Market: A wonderful market surrounds the cathedral each morning (except Sunday), with the most action on Wednesday and Saturday.

Festivals: Freiburg's favorite block party, **Oberlindenhock,** takes place the last weekend of June on Oberlinden and Herrenstrasse near the Swabian Gate (Schwabentor), featuring street food, beer, wine, live music, and conviviality (www.oberlindenhock.de). The town's low-key **Weinfest** goes on for six evenings in early July, when Münsterplatz fills up with happy Freiburgers enjoying local wines and live music (www.freiburger-weinfest.de). Later in July comes the **Schlossbergfest,** with live music up on the town mountain (www.schlossbergfest-freiburg.de). And December sees one of Germany's better **Christmas markets** (on Rathausplatz, www.weihnachtsmarkt.freiburg.de).

Laundry: A self-service laundrette, **Waschsalon SB,** is at Adelhauser Strasse 24 (Mon-Fri 8:00-20:00, Sat 7:00-17:00, closed Sun, in passageway behind hair salon at corner with Marienstrasse, tel. 0761/35656).

Bike Rental/Tours: Freiburg Bikes, across the tracks from the train station, rents bikes and has free route maps (€10/4 hours, €15/24 hours, show ID, €50 cash deposit; June-Sept Mon-Sat 9:30-19:00, Sun 10:00-18:00, usually closed around lunchtime; Oct-May Mon-Sat generally 10:00-17:00, closed Sun; from station, cross tram bridge over train tracks, walk away from center to round building on left and go downstairs, look for *Radstation* and *Fahrradverleih* signs; Wentzingerstrasse 15, tel. 0176/5432-9898, www.freiburgbikes.de).

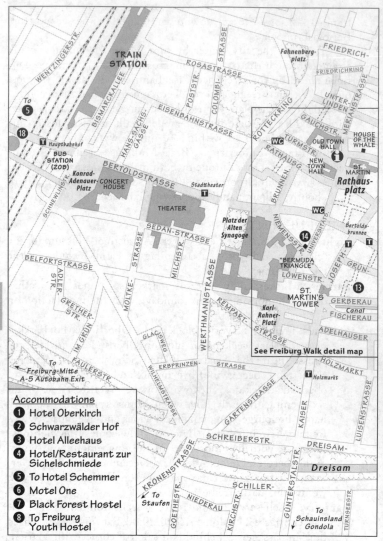

BADEN-BADEN & THE BLACK FOREST

Accommodations
1. Hotel Oberkirch
2. Schwarzwälder Hof
3. Hotel Alleehaus
4. Hotel/Restaurant zur Sichelschmiede
5. To Hotel Schemmer
6. Motel One
7. Black Forest Hostel
8. To Freiburg Youth Hostel

Local Guides: Iris Bürklin leads good tours around Freiburg (€100/2 hours, mobile 0162/595-6876, www.iris-freiburg.de, contact@iris-freiburg.de).

GETTING AROUND FREIBURG AND SURROUNDINGS

The city center (which includes most of my recommended hotels) is completely walkable. Trams are useful to reach outlying sights, such as the Schauinsland lift (€2.30/ride, €6.20/24-hour pass, €12.40/24-hour pass for 2-5 people, buy tickets from machine at

Freiburg

Karlsplatz

Münsterplatz

CATHEDRAL

HIST. MERCH. HOUSE

CITY HISTORY MUSEUM

AUGUSTINER MUSEUM

Augustiner-platz

SWABIAN GATE

ELEVATOR

FOOTBRIDGE

Canal

Schlossberg

LOOKOUT TOWER

Kanonen-platz

PLATEAU   BASTION

200 Meters

200 Yards

Eateries & Other

9 Wolfshöhle
10 Hausbrauerei Feierling
11 Restaurant Skajo
12 Manna Die Spezerei
13 Markthalle & Edo's Hummus Küche
14 UC/Uni-Café
15 Greiffenegg Schlössle & Biergarten Kastaniengarten
16 Karstadt Dep't Store (REWE Grocery)
17 Alte Wache Wine Bar
18 Bike Rental
19 Launderette

BADEN-BADEN & THE BLACK FOREST

train station or inside cars). For local transport info in English, see www.vag-freiburg.de.

To visit **Staufen, St. Peter,** or **St. Märgen** by regional train and bus, you'll need a two-zone ticket (€4 each way) or a 24-hour regional pass (€12.40 for 1 adult, €24.80 for 2-5 adults, sold at ticket machines and TI). If you're staying in one of those towns (but not Freiburg), your hotel tax includes a KONUS card, giving you free access to all public transit in the region (see "Sleeping in Staufen," later).

Freiburg Walk

This self-guided orientation walk, starting at Rathausplatz (and the TI), leads you through the top sights in the old center of Freiburg in about an hour.

• *Begin on the square in front of the Town Hall buildings.*

❶ Rathausplatz

The relaxing square with the fountain used to be an enclosed courtyard—the cloister of the neighboring Franciscan Church of St. Martin. The gothic arcade (on the far side) is part of a still-active monastery. Today, the square's fronted by twin city administration buildings (both with big clocks): the red Old Town Hall (on the right, with the TI inside) and the two-tone New Town Hall (on the left). The double eagle adorning the Old Town Hall recalls four centuries of Habsburg rule (until Napoleon in 1806).

Embedded in the cobbles in front of both of the Town Hall buildings are mosaic coats of arms representing each of Freiburg's

sister cities. Many of them—including Padua (Italy), Madison (Wisconsin), and Isfahan (Iran) are university towns, like Freiburg. The New Town Hall was originally the headquarters of Freiburg's first university. The town has been a university center since the mid-15th century, and the prestigious university is still the town's biggest employer.

The statue in the square honors Berthold the Black, a medieval monk credited (wrongly) with inventing gunpowder. Look into his face and then, speaking of explosives, think of the medieval city of Freiburg—almost entirely destroyed in the last months of World War II. Nearly all of what surrounds you (and that you'll see on this walk) has been rebuilt since.

Now, listen to the silence. No traffic. You can even hear the trickle of the little stream in the pavement.

• *Curl around the far side of St. Martin's Church and head up Franziskanerstrasse. As you walk, notice the small canal lining the street. Such canals are called...*

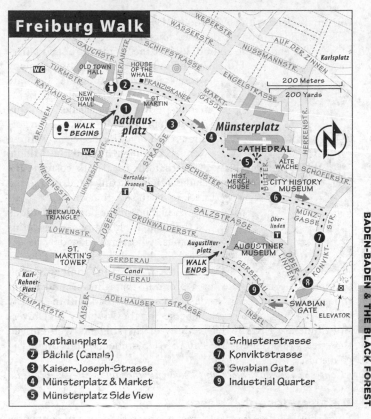

Freiburg Walk

1 Rathausplatz
2 Bächle (Canals)
3 Kaiser-Joseph-Strasse
4 Münsterplatz & Market
5 Münsterplatz Side View
6 Schusterstrasse
7 Konviktstrasse
8 Swabian Gate
9 Industrial Quarter

② Bächle

These "stream-lets," as their name translates, have been running down nearly every Freiburg street since the 13th century. Origi-

nally they were designed to keep fires from spreading (they could be quickly dammed to flood the street). And they did the job—Freiburg had no major fires after it introduced its *Bächle*.

The canals also provided a constantly replenishing source of water for people and cattle. These days, Freiburg's trademark canals are just fun: A sunny day turns any kid-at-heart into a puddle-jumper. Toddlers like to sail little boats and splash in the water to cool off when it's hot. Freiburg still employs two *Bächleputzer* to scrub the canals clean with steel brooms. Local lore promises that if you fall into a *Bächle*, you are destined to marry a Freiburger.

At the end of the church, look at the facade of the red building on the left, the **House of the Whale,** featuring one of many

whimsical little statues that decorate Freiburg. Look closely at the right-hand gargoyle on the facade. The veiny growth hanging from her neck is a goiter (a result of iodine deficiency). These were so common here in the Middle Ages that the local folk costume includes a tightly fitting band around the neck to disguise a goiter.

A plaque on the building reminds us that Dutch philosopher Desiderius Erasmus, who traveled widely to expand his knowledge and worldview, once lived here. The humanist and scholar is the namesake for a program that allows hundreds of thousands of European students to study abroad within the EU (European Region Action Scheme for the Mobility of University Students, ERASMUS). Many of the students who enliven the streets of Freiburg are ERASMUS students from other EU countries.

• *Continue ahead one block, until you reach the wide cross-street called...*

❸ Kaiser-Joseph-Strasse

Since the Middle Ages, this street has been the center of commerce in Freiburg, and is now lined with its biggest department stores and malls.

Look before crossing the street: Virtually silent trams glide along here constantly. Laced with tram and bus lines, Freiburg is proud of its reputation as a "green" city where most trips are made by public transit, bike, or on foot. The city is home to a large solar-panel factory, and it started the annual Intersolar trade fair.

Looking down the street to the right, you can see one of the two surviving towers of Freiburg's former town wall, **St. Martin's Tower** (or as some call it, the McDonald's Tower). If you were to head in that direction, then turn right just before you reached the tower, you'd wind up in the colorful student quarter called the "Bermuda Triangle." The tower is dedicated to the beloved saint who is celebrated with children's parades all over Germany every November 11. (For a commanding terrace view, ride the elevator from here to the rooftop Skajo Restaurant.)

• Jog a half-block to the right, then left, and continue straight to the towering church spire at...

❹ Münsterplatz and Market

The square surrounding the cathedral hosts a bustling outdoor produce and crafts market six mornings a week (Mon-Fri 7:30-13:30, Sat until 14:00, biggest Wed and Sat, no market on Sun). On the north side of the cathedral (to the left) vendors sell local produce; in front of the cathedral's door, flowers and herbs; and to the south (right), imported goods (Alsatian, Italian, crafts). Around the left side, you'll also find stands selling Freiburg's distinctive type of bratwurst—long, red, and skinny, called a *lange Rote*. If you order one, they'll ask you *"Mit oder ohne?"*—"with or without" onions.

Carved into the church's stones is evidence that the town market goes way back. On the giant buttress to the left of the

cathedral's main door look for the **engravings** with different years (e.g., ADMCCLXX—that's AD 1270) next to oval and circular shapes. These were the officially decreed sizes for a loaf of bread; customers could bring their purchases here to be sure they weren't being cheated. Deceitful merchants faced immediate punishment. Notice that the size of the standard loaf shrunk between 1270 and 1317...medieval inflation.

In the alcove in front of the cathedral entrance are more official measures. For example, to the left, you'll see the standard measures for a basket (the circle plus the line), an "elbow" (the line), and a barrel (the square with a diagonal line). On the right are measures dictating standard sizes for home-construction supplies (bricks, roof tiles, floor tiles, and beams). Nearby, the inscription boasts that since the 16th century, Freiburg has enjoyed the right to hold a large-scale market twice a year (a rare privilege in the Holy Roman Empire).

• Now's a good time to visit the cathedral if it's open (described later,

under "Sights in Freiburg"). When you're done, exit the cathedral out the side door (around the right side of the building) to continue this walk.

❺ Münsterplatz, Side View

For many, the most memorable part of the cathedral is its **gargoyles.** Find the "mooning" gargoyle (facing the entrance, walk around the right side—or if leaving the church from the side exit, walk to your right—and count from the corner to the fourth buttress)...and wait for rain.

Do an about-face and salute the Habsburgs, who are represented by the statues and the coat of arms on the **Historical Merchant House** (Historisches Kaufhaus, from 1532). This was the trading and customs center in the 16th century.

To the left as you face the Merchant House is the gray building that houses the **City History Museum** (described later, under "Sights in Freiburg"). Then, farther to the left, just next to the church, is the **Alte Wache.** A former police station, this was recently turned into a wine bar and is a fine place to sample local wines, either indoors or on the square (self-service, an *"achtel"* is an eighth of a liter). Most of the wine made here uses grape varieties from Burgundy. This corner of Germany enjoys some of the country's balmiest weather, thanks to the so-called "Burgundy Gate"— a gap between the Vosges and Jura mountains, which channels in warm Mediterranean air from the south of France.

• *Leave Münsterplatz via Buttergasse, the narrow lane between the City History Museum and the Merchant House. On the way, notice two Stolpersteine in the pavement. Then turn left and head up...*

❻ Schusterstrasse

This pleasant street is typical of old Freiburg, lined with a *Bächle,* with historic labels on many of the houses, and mosaic seals (made of rounded Rhine River stones) in front of most doors. For example, the building at #35 (on the left) is labeled *Haus zur kleinen Meise* (House of the Little Bird), with a knife mosaic out front. While the house labels date from the Middle Ages, the mosaics are typically more modern, paid for by today's merchants to match the purpose of the building. This one is a knife shop. The mosaics are portable, so if the vendor moves shop, he can just lift his up and take it with him.

• *Cross Herrenstrasse and continue up the narrow lane called Münzgasse. Turn right onto...*

❼ Konviktstrasse

Named not for a convict but for a convent, this is another typical Freiburg
street. Not long ago a seedy zone with
prostitutes, today it's known for its
high rents. Chain stores and chain restaurants are forbidden along this sto
rybook lane, and in the springtime it
is draped with fragrant purple wisteria.
Walk slowly to take it all in.

• Konviktstrasse brings you to a major
street right in front of the...

❽ Swabian Gate (Schwabentor)

This second of Freiburg's surviving gates is named for the Swabi-
ans, the historical rivals of the Freiburgers (the gate leads to where
you'd head to meet them).

The painting on the arch features a dandy salt merchant with a
wagonload of salt kegs—a reminder that salt mining was big in the

Black Forest back in the 13th century. You're
standing on Salzstrasse ("salt street"), and
just inside this gate were Freiburg's original
pubs and hotels (like Hotel Bären, with the
golden bear).

Just below the big painting, at the apex
of the arch, look for the little figure pulling
a thorn out of his foot. This is the last thing
Freiburgers would see before leaving town,
to remind them to stay on the right path and
avoid the "thorns" of sinful living.

• Freiburg's little mountain, Schlossberg, is nearby. It's best at sunset, but if you want to head up
now, simply climb the stairs at the Schwabentor,
use the pedestrian overpass to cross the busy road,
and take the free elevator on up (see page 330).

Or, for some back-street experiences, stick with me for a few more
minutes. Cross the busy Oberlinden, passing the Schwabentor, and then
make a hard right onto the downhill road, toward a canal.

❾ Freiburg's Canalside Industrial Quarter

While Freiburg turns its back on its river, water from that river is
channeled throughout the town. Walking downhill to reach the
canal, you can see how the street level of town was actually raised to
create a steeper incline to power the Bächle system of tiny streams
that trickle throughout the town. A delightful district of shops
and cafés today, this used to be Freiburg's industrial quarter—the

smelly tanners' and millers' quarter, with waterwheels powering everything.

Follow the canal for a while and soon you'll reach two recommended eateries: On the left is the picturesque Hotel/Restaurant Sichelschmiede; a few more steps up (also on the left—beware of the crocodile) is the modern Hausbrauerei Feierling microbrewery. Its inviting beer garden is across the street in the shade of chestnut trees, near a playground handy for parents needing a place to park their kids when it's beer o'clock. Just beyond that is Augustiner-platz, a popular hangout for students.

• *Your town walk is finished and you have options: Overlooking Augustinerplatz is Freiburg's leading museum, the Augustiner Museum. Continuing along the little street called Grünwälderstrasse (directly across from the Augustiner Museum entrance) brings you to a thriving neighborhood of cafés and eateries (including the wonderful Markthalle food circus, described later, under "Eating in Freiburg"). Or maybe it's time for that beer.*

Sights in Freiburg

▲▲Cathedral (Münster)

The lacy spire rocketing up from Freiburg's skyline marks its impressive main church. While Germany may have bigger and better cathedrals, Freiburg's is well worth a visit.

Cost and Hours: Cathedral interior-free, usually Mon-Sat 10:00-17:00, Sun 13:00-19:00; choir—€2, includes helpful English pamphlet, open most days 10:00-11:30 & 12:30-16:00; tower—€4, Tue-Sat 10:00-16:00, Sun 13:00-16:00, closed Mon. Enter from outside church on right and pay at top.

Tours: For €5, you can take a one-hour guided tour in English (daily at 14:00).

Organ Concerts: The powerful cathedral pipe organ gets lots of use. There are free concerts on Saturdays (at 11:30). And on Tuesday evenings at 20:15, guest organists from around the world perform (€9, www.freiburgermuenster.info).

❸ **Self-Guided Tour:** Begin out front. The scaffolding is an almost permanent feature as the cathedral walls are made from a soft local sandstone that's easy to work—but also extremely fragile. Decorations made from this distinctive pink stone need to be replaced every 30 to 60 years, so keeping the church from falling apart is a never-ending task. Elderly locals who've lived here their entire lives report having never seen the church without at least some scaffolding.

The frilly **tower** *(Münsterturm)* is as tall as the church is long (127 yards)...but not worth the 329-step ascent. Up in the tower are 16 different bells, each one with a different name and purpose. Traditionally, Catholics could not eat meat on Fridays, so instead they'd eat *Spätzle* (German egg noodles)—giving the oldest bell, rung just before lunchtime on Fridays, its nickname: the "*Spätzle* Bell."

Before going inside, enjoy the ornately decorated **entryway.** The 418 colorfully painted statues (protected with netting from destructive pigeons) ooze with medieval church symbolism. Each has an identifying symbol. As you look back out to the square, the first figure on the left is St. Catherine, holding a "breaking wheel." This kind of wheel was a torture device used during the Middle Ages; a victim's limbs were stretched along a cart wheel and crushed (after this saint was sentenced to be executed with one, it also became known as a "Catherine Wheel").

Two particularly memorable characters have become mascots of Freiburg. In the tympanum (over the door), find Jesus on the cross. Just below him and a bit to the right is the "Praying Devil." This potbellied devil greedily rubs his hands together as he watches the Archangel Michael weigh the goodness of a person's soul (while two other devils try to fix the results). Then, along the left wall, notice the strange little character under the third statue from the right (with the realistic green robe)—playing his nose like a trumpet.

Now go **inside.** Head right and look along the back of the side wall, where you'll find a photo of Freiburg after it was devastated by WWII bombs. The city made it through most of the war virtually unscathed—until November 27, 1944, when, in just 20 minutes, about 80 percent of Freiburg's buildings were destroyed by an Allied bombing run. The cathedral was one of the few structures that survived. Some credit divine intervention, while others claim the bombers intentionally avoided it; either way, the steeple's latticework top and underground lead anchors probably saved it, since shockwaves from explosions all around it would have leveled a solid, less-supported tower.

Ringing the nave are the church's original **stained-glass windows** from the 13th and 14th centuries, which were hidden away and protected during World War II. Each one is marked with the seal of a local merchant who sponsored it (go on a scavenger hunt to find the pretzel, from the baker; the barrel, from the cooper; the scissors, from the tailor; and the hammer, tongs, and snake—representing fire—from the blacksmith).

Looking around, you might notice that the cathedral's architecture doesn't entirely conform to the pointed-arch Gothic style. That's because most of what we see today was built on the site of an earlier church. After its thriving market and Black Forest silver mine made Freiburg rich, work began on a new church in about 1200, and most of the structure was finished relatively quickly (it has the only Gothic steeple in Germany that was actually completed during Gothic times, in 1330). For a time it was the tallest spire in Europe.

Many churches from this era have 12 **pillars** lining the nave, each one with the statue of an apostle. But after the primary construction on this cathedral was finished, a large choir was added beyond the altar, so two more pillars were needed—bringing the total to 14. The new pillars were granted to Paul and Jesus himself. Look at the statues on the two pillars flanking the altar: On the right is Jesus, and on the left is Thomas—pointing two fingers because of his insistence on touching Jesus before he'd believe in the Resurrection. Thomas' privileged position in this church is based on the philosophy that nonbelievers should be closest to Christ.

At the front of the nave, over the choir, hangs a 12th-century silver triumphal crucifix. The finest chapels with exquisite paintings, carvings, and glass are in the choir (well worth the small fee that supports the ongoing renovation work; follow their English flier).

When you're finished, head outside using the side door (right transept). You'll emerge on Münsterplatz near the tower entrance. Take a moment to get a sense of the statuary high up in the exterior niches. While these are mostly replicas, you can admire the original stone prophets nearby in the Augustiner Museum.

▲▲Augustiner Museum

Freiburg's top museum (refreshingly air-conditioned) does a great job of displaying local fine art and medieval artifacts in inventive ways around the reconstructed shell of an Augustinian church.

Cost and Hours: €7, includes entry to the City History Museum, Tue-Sun 10:00-17:00, closed Mon, enter on Augustinerplatz, tel. 0761/201-2531, www.freiburg.de/museen.

Visiting the Museum: Start by taking the elevator up to the top floor, then work your way down. The top floors show off beautiful, regional 19th-century paintings, unique eye-level view of some gargoyles, and a peek-a-boo view of a Baroque pipe organ. The second and first floors have 16th- through 19th-century stained glass and religious artwork. The ground floor offers close-up looks at some of the cathedral's original 13th-century medieval statuary. Imagine the 10 gigantic prophet statues that once adorned the cathedral (with proportions elongated so they'd appear normal from far below) slowly floating down from the sky to where they stand now—which is indeed how they got in here: lowered by crane through the open ceiling, the only way they'd fit.

Also on the ground floor, be sure to look for original work by Lucas Cranach the Elder, as well as a feisty *Cupid with the Flaming Arrow* (Hans Baldung Grien, c. 1530), a 14th-century painted-wood *Christ on a Donkey* (Christus auf Palmesel), and *The Fall of Man*, an exquisite, early-16th-century boxwood sculpture by an artist known mysteriously as Master H. L.

City History Museum

Telling the story of Freiburg (in German only), this museum is worthwhile if only to see the two town models in the cellar and the cathedral model upstairs. Downstairs, one model shows medieval Freiburg circa 1590, with the city wall and all five city gates intact. Notice the little wall around the cathedral (today's Münsterplatz). This was the town cemetery, and the little house huddled next to the grand church was the charnel house, where exhumed bones were stored. The other model, from the early 1700s, shows how the French King Louis XIV turned the whole city into one gigantic fortress—and built out from the medieval hilltop castle to create what became one of Europe's largest fortifications at the time (see next listing). Upstairs you'll find other exhibits and artifacts documenting town history, with limited English descriptions. Linger at the wooden model of the cathedral mid-construction and the delightful miniatures depicting daily medieval life on the Münsterplatz.

Cost and Hours: €3, covered by Augustiner Museum ticket, Tue-Sun 10:00–17:00, closed Mon, Münsterplatz 30, tel. 0761/201-2515.

Schlossberg (Castle Hill)

Schlossberg towers over the east end of Freiburg's Old Town. A monstrous 18th-century fort once stood here on "Castle Hill," built by the French to control the citizens of Freiburg during a period of French occupation. The giant fortress garrisoned as many as 150,000 soldiers at once. (The

long-running debate about where the border between France and Germany should be was only put to rest after World War II.) The French destroyed the fortress when they retreated, leaving behind only a few stony walls. Today Schlossberg is Freiburg's playground, popular for its views over the city. A modern lookout tower (100 feet high) stands where the French Fort d'Aigle (Eagle Fort) once stood.

To get to the top of Schlossberg, you can hike or take a free elevator. From the Schwabentor, the half-timbered tower at the east end of the Old Town, look for the pedestrian walkway over the busy ring road. Once across, if you want to walk, bear left and hike up the steep switchbacks for 10 minutes. Or, to take the elevator *(Aufzug)*, continue straight through the cave-like tunnel to access it.

For even better views, keep hiking to higher perches. About a seven-minute hike above the restaurant is a broad, flat plateau with benches overlooking the town's rooftops. From there, you can hike about five more minutes up to a stubby stone bastion. Don't bother with the 20-minute trek up to the modern lookout tower; it's closed.

Eating: For a cheap meal atop Castle Hill, consider the self-service open-air **$ Biergarten Kastaniengarten** (open in good weather only, April-Oct daily 12:00-22:00). There's also the more expensive **$$$$ Greiffenegg Schlössle Restaurant.**

Schauinsland

Freiburg's own mountain, little more than an oversized hill, is nine miles southeast of the center. The viewpoint at its 4,000-foot summit offers the handiest panorama view of the Schwarzwald for those without wheels. The gondola system that takes you up—one of Germany's oldest—was designed for Freiburgers relying on public transportation. At the top, you'll find a view restaurant, pleasant circular walks, and the Schniederlihof, a 1592 farmhouse museum. A tower on a nearby peak offers an even more commanding Black Forest view.

Cost and Hours: €12.50 round-trip for gondola, €25.50 family ticket includes 2 adults and up to 4 kids, daily 9:00-18:00, Oct-June until 17:00; catch tram #2—direction: Günterstal—from town center until the final stop, then take bus #21 to the Talstation stop; city center to gondola takes 25 minutes, gondola ride lasts 20 minutes; tel. 0761/451-1777, www.schauinslandbahn.de.

Hikes

If you want to hike, consider the St. Peter-St. Märgen trail described under "Black Forest Highlands" on page 350, which is cheaper and quicker to reach from Freiburg than the Schauinsland.

Sleeping in Freiburg

For sleeping in this region, choose between quieter and less-expensive little Staufen (see "Sleeping in Staufen," later), or livelier and easier-for-non-drivers Freiburg. This area tends to get pretty hot for a few days every summer, and like most non-chain hotels in Germany, my listings lack air conditioning (though most offer fans on request). If you have a car, hotels can usually get €12/day deals in city parking garages that otherwise charge twice that. The busiest months with the highest rates are May, June, September, and October. Most hotels don't have 24-hour reception desks. If you'll be arriving after 20:00, call ahead.

$$$ Hotel Oberkirch is pricey but ideally situated. Nine of its 26 rooms sit right on the main square (facing the cathedral and above a restaurant—earplugs included); the rest (and reception) are in a nearby building on Schusterstrasse. While some rooms feel a bit dated, all are clean and comfortable (family rooms, reception at Schusterstrasse 11, main-square rooms at Münsterplatz 22, tel. 0761/202-6868, www.hotel-oberkirch.de, info@hotel-oberkirch.de, friendly Dina).

$$ Schwarzwälder Hof, just a block behind the cathedral, has 25 bright, modern rooms over a reasonably priced restaurant, and 15 more around the corner on pedestrian, wisteria-covered Konviktstrasse. Guests get a free regional transport card (see "Sleeping in Staufen," later), making their prices a particularly good deal (Herrenstrasse 43, from station take tram #1 in direction: Littenweiler three stops to Oberlinden, tel. 0761/38030, www.shof.de, info@schwarzwaelder-hof.com, Engler family).

$$ Hotel Alleehaus lies in a big, creaky-floored house that retains a bit of its 19th-century elegance. Its 21 rooms (some in an annex) are nothing fancy and somewhat overpriced, but they're comfortable and spacious. While close to the action, it's on a quiet, leafy street a short walk south of the Old Town, and is warmly run by Sabine and her team (family rooms, pay parking, Marienstrasse 7, tel. 0761/387-600, www.hotel-alleehaus.de, wohlfuehlen@hotel-alleehaus.de). From the station, take tram #3 or #5 three stops to Holzmarkt.

$ Hotel zur Sichelschmiede rents five small, comfy rooms with attractive, traditional decor. To reach them, you'll climb a dark-wood staircase above a recommended restaurant in the cutest part of town, overlooking a canal (family room, Insel 1, tel. 0761/35037, www.sichelschmiede.de, info@sichelschmiede.de, Gerdi Stark and family).

$ Hotel Schemmer, though literally on the wrong side of the tracks, is close to public transport and a workable option if you're on a tight budget. It has 16 basic but more-than-adequate rooms on five floors (no elevator). Rooms with a private bath, which face the back, are quieter than shared-bath rooms, which front a busy street (family rooms, cheaper rooms with shared bath; Eschholzstrasse 63; take tram #1, #3, or #5 one stop to Eschholzstrasse—or on foot just follow the tracks 10 minutes from the station to the tram stop, then turn left on Eschholzstrasse, and walk a block and a half; tel. 0761/207-490, www.hotel-schemmer.de, kontakt@hotel-schemmer.de).

$$ Motel One is a stylish, simple, and economic hotel chain with a motto that nails what they offer: great design for little money. The Freiburg Motel One is in a modern building a short walk from both the train station and the Old Town (Friedrichring 1, tel. 0761/1206-9900, www.motel-one.com, freiburg@motel-one.com).

HOSTELS

¢ Black Forest Hostel has the cheapest beds in Freiburg. Run by friendly Tania and Cori, with a young, bohemian attitude, it's bare-bones simple (private rooms available, cash only, no curfew, no Wi-Fi, free parking nearby, Kartäuser Strasse 33—look for anchor sign and go down driveway; 20-minute walk from station or take tram #1—direction: Littenweiler—to Oberlinden stop, then walk 7 more minutes; tel. 0761/881-7870, www.blackforest-hostel.de, backpacker@blackforest-hostel.de). If full, try the much larger, more distant **¢ Freiburg Youth Hostel** at Kartäuser Strasse 151 (tel. 0761/67656, www.jugendherberge-freiburg.de, info@jugendherberge-freiburg.de).

Eating in Freiburg

As a university town, Freiburg is heavy on inexpensive eateries serving traditional German cuisine. Many of Freiburg's best choices are conveniently concentrated within a block or two of Augustinerplatz, along Grünwälderstrasse, and just beyond the cathedral on Konviktstrasse. (See the "Freiburg" map, earlier, for locations.)

$$$$ Wolfshöhle makes "casual fine dining" an art form. While owner/chef Sascha Weiss has earned a Michelin star here, there's no pretense—just a focus on great modern cuisine with a sleek, stylish ambience. If you'd like to trust the chef, his "surprise menu" is a popular option (always two serious vegetarian dishes, plan on €60 for dinner, €30 for lunch, closed Sun-Mon, reservations smart, Konviktstrasse 8, tel. 0761/30303, www.wolfshoehle-freiburg.de).

$$ Hausbrauerei Feierling is a rollicking microbrewery that also serves good meals. The cozy upstairs seating looks down over the big copper vats. Order the local brew—*Inselhopf*. On pleasant summer evenings, their **$** beer garden across the street offers cool, leafy shade and a bustling atmosphere. While a cheap, cold-cuts-oriented menu is offered at both places, hot meals are served only inside (daily 11:00-24:00, food until 22:00, indoor section closed on warm, sunny summer afternoons, Gerberau 46, tel. 0761/243-480).

$$ Sichelschmiede is a good option rain or shine. Its timbered alcoves and cluttered interior give it a cozy living-room feel, and its creekside seating is nice when it's hot. Come here for easygoing seasonal regional cuisine, good value, and a family-friendly ambience (daily 12:00-22:00, Insel 1, tel. 0761/35037; also rents rooms—see "Sleeping in Freiburg").

$$$ Restaurant Skajo is a trendy rooftop place popular with locals for contemporary European dishes, cocktails, and a fine city view. The service, food, and view are worth the splurge (Mon-Sat 11:00-22:00, Sun 13:00-21:00, fifth floor of building at Kaiser-Joseph-Strasse 192, tel. 0761/2025-1240).

$$ Manna Die Spezerei, a modern self-serve place with fine seating inside and out, overlooks the Augustinerplatz scene. It's popular for its gourmet sandwiches made to order, soup, and fancy juices. Portions are small and it's not cheap, but you'll get healthy, top-notch food (daily 8:30-21:00, Nov-April until 19:00. Salzstrasse 28, tel. 0761/290-9664).

$ Markthalle is a wonderful food court where you can pick up fresh produce and choose cuisines from around the world—German, French, Swiss, Italian, Indian, Brazilian, Chinese, Middle Eastern, and more. Sa Su Bar is good for soups and hearty salads (eat at shared tables, Mon-Thu 11:00-20:00, Fri-Sat until 24:00, closed Sun, live music or DJ on weekends after 20:00 —no cover, Grünwälderstrasse 4).

$ Edo's Hummus Küche, a modern place serving Middle Eastern dishes, is understandably popular with students (Mon-Thu 11:30-21:00, Fri-Sat until 22:00, closed Sun; in Dietler Passage—from Markthalle exit behind the sushi bar, tel. 0761/5195-8605).

Supermarket: Pick up picnic supplies at **REWE** (Mon-Sat 9:30-20:00, closed Sun, in basement of Karstadt department store on Kaiser-Joseph-Strasse, near the cathedral). Their rooftop cafeteria offers a fine budget buffet at lunch.

IN THE "BERMUDA TRIANGLE" NEIGHBORHOOD

Night owls flock around St. Martin's Tower (Martinstor), in the area affectionately called Freiburg's "Bermuda Triangle." Take the street to your right just before going through the gate, and get sucked into the party in this zone rife with students.

$ UC/Uni-Café, which spills onto the square in good weather, is the place to join the cerebral grad-student crowd for cheap, all-day breakfast options, crêpes, salads, and light meals, including €5 *Flammkuchen*—German-style flatbread. Or just hang out with the cocktail of the week (daily 8:00-23:00, Niemensstrasse 7, at Universitätsstrasse, tel. 0761/383-355).

Freiburg Connections

The full name of the town—and the station—is Freiburg im Breisgau, often abbreviated as "Freiburg (Brsg)" on schedules.

By Train to: Staufen (hourly until about 24:00, 30 minutes, most require transfer at Bad Krozingen), **Baden-Baden** (direct fast trains hourly, 45 minutes; cheaper regional trains take 1.5 hours with change in Offenburg), **Munich** (hourly, 4.5 hours, most with 1 change), **Interlaken**, Switzerland (hourly, 3 hours), **Colmar,** France (hourly, 1.5 hours; train to Breisach, then bus); **Basel,** Switzerland (about 3/hour, 40 minutes; 1 hour on cheaper regional train), **Bern,** Switzerland (about 2/hour, 2 hours, some transfer in Basel), **Frankfurt** (hourly, 2 hours, most direct), **Frankfurt Airport** (hourly, 2 hours, most with 1 change). Train info: www.bahn.com.

Staufen

Hemmed in by vineyards and watched over by the ruins of a protective castle, Staufen (SHTOW-fehn) is small and peaceful. Staufen's quiet pedestrian zone of colorful old buildings and reasonably priced hotels makes it a delightful home base for your exploration of the southern trunk of the Black Forest. You can also make Staufen a half-day outing from Freiburg.

Orientation to Staufen

Staufen (pop. 8,000) is simple. The main square is an easy 10-minute walk from the train station, and everything I list is along the way (or just off it). Though Staufen feels small, its high school, courthouse, and shopping district serve all the villages in the Münstertal valley.

Tourist Information: Staufen's helpful TI is on the main square in the Rathaus (Mon-Fri 9:00-12:30 & 14:00-17:30, Sat 10:00-12:00, closed Sun, shorter hours Nov-March; tel. 07636/70740, www.muenstertal-staufen.de). The City Museum is upstairs (free, same hours as TI).

Arrival in Staufen: The **train station** is often unstaffed and has no lockers. To get to town, exit the station with your back to the pond and angle right up Bahnhofstrasse. Turn right onto Hauptstrasse, which leads through the town center to the Rathaus and TI.

If you're arriving by **car,** be sure you're going to Staufen im Breisgau, and follow signs for *Stadtmitte* to find the town center. If your hotel is in the pedestrian zone, it's OK to drive there to park. If you're day-tripping, you'll find a handy parking lot right at the entrance to the center (and at the start of my self-guided walk).

Helpful Hints: Market days are Wednesday and Saturday on the main square (8:00-13:00). **Local guide** Marianne Pfadt enjoys taking visitors on a casual but insightful tour around her hometown's back streets (€50/1.5-hour walk, tel. 07633/982-529, siegfried.pfadt@t-online.de).

Staufen Walk

Staufen is an enjoyable town to explore—it feels real and is welcoming to visitors without being a tourist trap. This self-guided stroll begins at the start of the

cobbled pedestrian zone, near the parking lot; if you're coming from the train station, this is the first part of the old center you'll reach.

• *Begin on the square with the big tree, fountain, and giant wine press.*

"Wine Fountain"

Don't get too excited about this spot's nickname; unfortunately there's no magical spring spouting free wine here. The big old oak wine press adjacent is a reminder that wine has indeed flowed from this spot for years—produced from the vineyards just uphill from here. The winery facing the square, Weingut Peter Landmann, has long housed the local vintners' shared bottling cooperative (now run by a privately owned winery).

Wine (along with taxes levied on silver, which was mined deeper in the Black Forest) once brought Staufen wealth...and it still helps out.

At the benches between the fountain and the gigantic wine press, look for the photo of a red-sandstone courthouse that once stood here. That building, like much of Staufen, was devastated by an Allied bombing late in World War II (February 8, 1945)—you'll see other photos of the damage around town.

• Now walk up Staufen's main street called...

Hauptstrasse

Like its big sister Freiburg, Staufen has little canals called *Bächle* running along its main street. While back in the 12th century this was state-of-the-art city planning for hygiene and fire protection, today these little canals are simply part of the atmosphere. The charm of this colorful town center is governed by strict building codes: Only certain colors can be used, and the shutters are uniform. But locals grumble that sometimes the rules go too far. Notice the rain gutters that empty out onto the cobbles. These used to run underground, but were relocated to be more authentically historic—and now the streets turn into an ice rink when it freezes.

Notice the painting at the **Gasthaus Die Krone** (#30). It recalls an event in 1848 when the owner of the inn (and his sad wife)—supporters of democracy—stood up to government troops who put down a revolution. The adjacent fountain is dedicated to Mary as the town was thankful to have survived a plague.

Just before you reach the main square, on the left (at #47), look for the red **Gasthaus zum Löwen.** In the early 16th century, a popular and successful doctor/scientist/fortune-teller/alchemist named Johann Georg Faust was brought to Staufen to find a way to literally create gold for the town. He lived and worked in this house, experimenting with chemical processes until an accidental explosion killed him around the year 1540. The townspeople assumed that the devil must have had a hand in his death, and legends began to swirl. Over time, these stories grabbed the attention of various writers, including Goethe (the "German Shakespeare"). In Goethe's seminal work *Faust,* the title character sells his soul to a demon in exchange for unlimited earthly powers. (You might see a costumed demon leading tours through the streets of Staufen.) The building is now run as a guesthouse—you can sleep in Faust's actual room.

Across the street, at #56 (marked *Stubenhaus Stadtmuseum*), duck into one of Staufen's oldest **courtyards,** where historically the townsfolk gathered for social and cultural events. Concerts are still held here (and the public toilets are always open).

• *Continue out to Staufen's main square.*

Marktplatz (Market Square)

Looking around the square, notice the intentionally clever design: The four converging streets are offset, making the square feel es-

pecially cozy (and stopping the cold winter wind from howling through the town).

The soldier atop the **fountain** holds the shield of Staufen, with its symbol: three golden goblets on a red field. The medieval word *Stuff* meant "goblet"; Staufen was named for its castle hill, which resembles an upside-down goblet.

This has long been the town's marketplace (busy markets these days on Saturday and Wednesday mornings). The Kornhaus (or grain house) is where farmers would bring their taxes—a tithe, or tenth of their produce. Dominating the square is the **Town Hall** (Rathaus). The left part (Gothic) is older than the right part (Renaissance). The coats of arms represent the various powers that have controlled Staufen over the centuries. The golden seashell at the top on the right indicates that this was a stop along the Camino de Santiago, the medieval pilgrimage route that leads all the way to the northwest corner of Spain. And the iron neck collar was the pillory—for public shaming of anyone so deserving. Inside the Town Hall are the TI and a very humble town **museum** (Stadtmuseum, upstairs, a few town artifacts, not a word of English, free).

Look for **cracks** in the Town Hall's walls. In 2007, Staufen proudly embarked on an innovative plan to drill 460 feet down

and tap into a geothermal power source. For a few weeks, things worked great. Then cracks like these began to show on buildings around town. Catastrophically, the drills had pierced a layer of anhydrite and broken into an underground reservoir. From its contact with water, the anhydrite became gypsum and expanded, which caused parts of the town to sink and rise by up to four inches a year. The entire town's underground infrastructure needed to be dug up and replaced. Now hundreds of buildings are suddenly structurally

unsound. Insurance companies and the government are at an impasse regarding who should pay, so no one can sell anything. It's a terrible mess. For a better look at the damage, walk into the Town Hall and check out the old spiral staircase leading to the City Museum in the back.

• *Before moving on, put your back to the Town Hall and look out toward the busy street in the distance. The yellow building on the right with the big* CAFE *sign is Café Decker, a good place for cakes and chocolates. A five-minute walk beyond that is Staufen's fascinating little cemetery (explained later).*

Now, to see a side of Staufen most visitors miss, walk through...

Staufen's Back Streets *(Hinterstädtle)*

Leave Marktplatz on the little lane (called Freihofgasse) between the Kornhaus and the Volksbank. Stick with this lane as it curls around to the left, passing a butcher shop on the right (with fine Schwarzwälder—Black Forest—ham in gift packs). The street leads through a residential neighborhood. Then continue moseying straight along Spitalstrasse, the oldest quarter of town. Until the 1980s, this was a poor neighborhood. But now

it's become gentrified. As you stroll, listen to the constant sound of running water from little fountains. Look for the former town wall (on the right). Where the street does a little jog and hits a bigger road, the big building on the left was a hospice *(Spital),* which wealthy townspeople financed to house people who were ill and too poor to care for themselves. After renovation it will continue to be a home for the elderly and needy.

Turn left and head for the church. This area has some fun boutique shops: Around the right side of the church is a local **coffee roaster** (Alexandra's Coffee & More Kaffeerösterei), good for a delightful break.

Facing the church, look left, and notice the big doorway at #9, marked *Jägergasse.* Go into the passage and continue. Peek into the classic old winery at #10. Meiergasse leads to the left and back to the cobbled pedestrian zone.

• *If you still have time and energy, consider poking around Staufen's evocative cemetery, just across the river, or hiking up to its hilltop castle (both described next).*

To reach the cemetery, leave Market Square toward Café Decker. Cross the bridge and head to the right along the river until you reach the small footbridge on your right. Then turn left down Wettelbrunner Strasse, where the onion-domed chapel marks Staufen's cemetery.

Sights in Staufen

Cemetery (Friedhof)

In this atmospherically shady, even comforting cemetery, ornate headstones stand among flowering shrubs and a number of old trees—some of which grow right up from the graves. As in much of Europe, plots in this cemetery are not purchased, only leased. Notice that some headstones have several added-on plaques identifying the remains of many generations of ten-ants. Locals lovingly tend to the graves, tidying the ivy and planting flowers.

Nearby: On your way back to Market Square, you'll see Staufen's **pottery museum,** in the building labeled Keramik-Museum.

For another detour, go down the street on the right side of the Hotel Kreuz-Post, where you'll find the Schladerer **distillery** and its outlet shop—look for the *Verkauf* sign.

Castle

Staufen's own little vineyard-covered mountain is topped by the remains of a castle (once the residence of the Lords of Staufen) that was destroyed by Swedish troops in 1632. The most direct route to visit these ruins is to charge right on up, but you can also take one of the less-steep roundabout trails.

Sleeping in Staufen

Your hotel will add a local tax of €1.50 per person per night, which provides you with a KONUS card *(KONUS Gästekarte).* This covers all transit for the entire Black Forest region, including unlimited use of buses, regional trains, and local transit (such as buses or trams in Freiburg or Baden-Baden), but doesn't cover express ICE or IC trains. All the following listings have free parking.

$$$ Hotel-Gasthof Kreuz-Post, in the pedestrian zone just off Marktplatz, is the town splurge. It rents 12 bright, tidy rooms over a well-regarded but pricey restaurant (some rooms have elevator access, Hauptstrasse 65, tel. 07633/95320, www.kreuz-post-staufen.de, info@kreuz-post-staufen.de).

$$ Gasthaus Krone, the town's top value, sits in the middle of Staufen's main pedestrian drag like it owns it. Charming, friendly, and with nine comfortable rooms, it's a winner. Try here first (some rooms with balconies, Hauptstrasse 30, tel. 07633/5840, www.die-krone-staufen.de, info@die-krone.de, Lahn family).

$$ Gasthaus zum Hirschen, also family-run and with a storybook location on the main pedestrian street, has 15 rooms, a roof deck, and a traditional restaurant on the ground floor (family rooms, most rooms with balconies, elevator, Hauptstrasse 19, tel. 07633/5297, www.hirschen-staufen.de, hotel@hirschen-staufen.de, Dieter and Isabelle).

$ Gästehaus Kaltenbach is a great deal in a rural-feeling location. It's a 10-minute, uphill walk from the station or town center; they'll pick you up if you arrive by train with luggage. English teacher Gabriele Kaltenbach and her policeman-turned-farmer husband Günter rent six rooms in a huge farmhouse with horses out back. They have maps of local hiking trails (laundry facilities, yard with swing set; Bötzenstrasse 37, tel. 07633/95310, www.gaestehaus-kaltenbach.de, info@gaestehaus-kaltenbach.de). From the station, walk toward town and after a block look for the Bacchus statue at the corner of Bahnhofstrasse and Hauptstrasse. Head up Sixtgasse behind the statue, then turn left at the T-intersection onto Bötzenstrasse.

Eating in Staufen

Many of the hotels listed earlier also have their own good restaurants. For fine dining, head for **$$$$ Gasthaus Krone,** which proudly uses regional products (closed Sat, Hauptstrasse 30, tel. 07633/5840). For a midrange option, try **$$$ Gasthaus zum Löwen** (tables on main square next to Town Hall, or in comfy interior, daily, Rathausgasse 8, tel. 07633/908-9390). Across the square, the informal **$$ Kornhaus** is a less-expensive, family-friendly option (seasonal menu, daily, Hauptstrasse 57, tel. 07633/5401).

Dessert: Every sweet-tooth in Staufen adores **Café Decker** for its 50 types of chocolates (€7/100 grams) and long display case showing off a wide array of cakes. The dining room is genteel, and the rooftop terrace has nice views (full breakfasts, light lunch specials, and good sandwiches to go; Mon-Sat 6:30-18:00, closed Sun; Hauptstrasse 70, tel. 07633/5316).

Staufen Connections

Staufen is on a tiny branch line (called the Münstertalbahn) that connects to the main line at Bad Krozingen. Keep in mind that the Staufen train station is rarely staffed (but ticket machines are on hand and schedules are posted).

From Staufen by Train to: Freiburg (hourly until late, 30 minutes, a few direct, most require transfer in Bad Krozingen; covered by a single €4 two-zone local transport ticket, available from ticket machines, covered by KONUS Card).

The Black Forest

Baden-Baden, Freiburg, and Staufen are appealing towns and fine places to stay overnight. But the charms of the Black Forest are rural and best experienced by delving into the countryside of this land of cuckoo clocks and healthy hikes. You can enjoy picturesque driving tours, a hike between charming small towns, and some fun museums and scenic nature spots. Fair warning: The Black Forest is what I'd call "gently scenic." Do it before you delve into the bigger, better Alps in Switzerland or Bavaria; otherwise, you might be underwhelmed.

PLANNING YOUR TIME

On Your Own: Consider the Black Forest in three zones from Baden-Baden in the north to Freiburg/Staufen in the south: 1) The Black Forest High Road, a scenic drive through 30 miles of pine forests (an easy side-trip from Baden-Baden); 2) The sights in the middle, such as an open-air folk museum and a clock museum; and 3) The gentle southern area known as Black Forest Highlands, full of idyllic towns and easy hikes (most easily explored from

Freiburg). Drivers have their choice of any of these options, while those using public transportation can day-trip from Freiburg to the small town of St. Märgen and then walk (2 hours) to St. Peter. Everything that can be done from Freiburg can also be done from Staufen (add another 30 minutes or so each way).

With a Driver/Guide: Freiburg-based Simone Brixel offers hiking and sightseeing tours of the Black Forest in her comfortable car or minibus. She enjoys tailoring a trip to your interests (€500/6-hour guided tour for up to 4, €280/4 hours, transport-only tours with custom itinerary available for up to 7; tel. 0761/5147-0551, www.the-black-forest.com, simone@the-black-forest.com).

Black Forest High Road Drive

The Black Forest was named by the Romans for its mysterious impermeability. And it wasn't until the 20th century that the High Road (Schwarzwaldhochstrasse) was built along a ridge through the densest stretch of this fabled pine forest. This road takes you 30 miles (about one hour) on route B-500. Once on the High Road, there's no way to get lost—just follow signs for *Freudenstadt* if heading south (or *Baden-Baden* if heading north).

Here are the highlights if driving south out of Baden-Baden:

Geroldsauer Mühle: A bit more than a half-mile out of Baden-Baden is Geroldsauer Mühle, the palatial wooden market hall that stands as if welcoming you to the Black Forest. Its prize-winning building is filled with local produce, a bakery, and enticing shops, including the Mühlenmarkt, a festival of Black Forest produce (Tue-Sun 8:30-19:00, closed Mon).

Top of the High Road: You'll share the road with bikers, motorbikers, joy-riders, and Germans enjoying their hot cars. While this forest was just a black hole for the ancient Romans, in the 17th century the trees of this region were a much-needed resource for Amsterdam. Much of the Black Forest was deforested, made into huge log rafts, and floated down the Rhine to Amsterdam, where they were disassembled and used to build mighty ships and provide foundations for that city. (They say if you turned Amsterdam over, you'd find the Black Forest.)

B-500 was built in the 1930s; and many of the **grand hotels** you'll pass were also built during the Third Reich. Today, clinics buried deep in the forest here provide places for German celebrities with various struggles to convalesce. Along with lots of *Kliniks,* you'll pass trailheads with parking lots and (in August) locals picking blueberries.

This northern stretch of the forest, nicknamed **"the Jungle,"** is a high ridge with small views. Occasionally you'll hit an opening on the east with views stretching across Alsace all the way to the Vosges Mountains. (Alsace, a region of France bounded by the Rhine River and the Vosges Mountains, has long been disputed: Germans have always thought the mountains are the rightful border and the French think the river is. Accordingly, Alsace changed hands several times over the centuries.)

Mummelsee: This tiny mountain lake at about 3,300 feet altitude is a classic German nature stop. It's fun to park and check out the Mummelsee scene: a lakeside restaurant, an easy stroll around the lake, and lots of souvenirs and walking sticks for sale. This area was made a national park in 2014, and a big park center nearby is under construction (to open in 2020).

Lothar Trail (Black Forest National Park): In 1999, Hurricane Lothar blew down about 50,000 acres of the Black Forest. Germany decided to give visitors a front seat to the slow-motion spectacle of nature healing itself; they built Lothar Path (Lotharpfad), a family-friendly, half-mile-long boardwalk through the changing forest. It's a delightful 20-minute circular walk (free, easy parking).

Three miles farther south, B-500 meets B-28. Your Black Forest High Road drive is done. From here you can return to Baden-Baden, or continue on to one or more of the sights described next.

Black Forest Sights in the Center

Between the High Road in the north and the Highlands in the south is a middle zone with the main sightseeing stops of the Black Forest. Towns and various attractions are well-signposted and distances are short. Wolfach is the nicest town of the region (no actual sights, but well worth an hour's wander). The Black Forest Open-Air Museum is by far the most important stop in the area (with traditional life and amazing old farm buildings on display in a sprawling park). Triberg is a touristy town with a famous waterfall and a smaller folk museum. And the clock museum in Furtwangen is exciting for people who get excited about old clocks.

▲Wolfach

The main Black Forest road takes you right through this delightful town nestled in the forest on the Kinzig River. It's an old logging town—essentially one main street lined with fountains, fine facades, and inviting shops and cafés. The TI has a town walk brochure.

The Town Hall, rebuilt after a 19th-century fire, has a facade worth studying. Things are livelier on market days (Sat and Wed), but otherwise the town generally feels like it's on Valium. At its south end is a castle with a chapel (note its 14th-century pietà) and a museum that explores the history of log rafting—a big part of this town's economy in centuries past.

Sleeping in Wolfach: If you're tempted to spend the night, two good hotels are on the main street—**$ Hotel Krone** (25 rooms, breakfast extra, Hauptstrasse 33, tel. 07834/83780, www.krone-wolfach.de) and **$$ Gasthaus Hecht** (17 rooms, Hauptstrasse 51, tel. 07834/83510, http://hecht-wolfach.de).

▲▲▲Black Forest Open-Air Museum (Schwarzwälder Freilichtmuseum Vogtsbauernhof)

This museum offers the best look at this region's traditional folk architecture. Built around one grand old farmhouse, the museum is a collection of several old farm buildings, some of which house exhibits on the local dress and lifestyles. While English information is sparse, the place gives you a good sense of traditional rural life in the Black Forest.

Cost and Hours: €10, April-Oct daily 9:00-18:00, Aug until 19:00, last entry one hour before closing, closed Nov-March, English audioguide-€4, along B-33/E-531 between the towns of Gutach and Hausach, tel. 07831/93560, www.vogtsbauernhof.de.

Demonstrations: In July and August the park is busy with costumed docents and live presentations; look for a schedule when you buy your ticket or on the TV monitor in the entryway. One-hour English tours are offered daily for free in July and August (at 13:00). Off-season, the museum can be pretty sleepy.

Visiting the Museum: From the parking lot, it's a five-minute walk past eateries and under the railroad tracks to the ticket windows and main building. Pick up the map of the complex. The various buildings are identified out front (find English on the spinning language board), but the explanations inside are in German only.

Hippenseppenhof, the building directly across from the entry, dates from 1599. The oldest home in the park, it's a Catholic house with all the clichés on display. This is the closest thing to a museum in this park, where you'll see costumes, logging exhibits, clock-making, and more. The huge attic is like a barn on top of a house, with its own back-door access. The museum is named for the **Vogtsbauern-hof,** the district governor's farm—the biggest building and the prize of the museum. It's the only original structure on the premises, around which the rest of the complex grew as other buildings were

relocated here from around the region. Built in 1612 and occupied until 1965, this giant farmhouse has distinctive Black Forest features that you'll also see on a smaller scale in the surrounding buildings. The characteristic "semi-hipped" roof is wider than the frame of the house, which creates ample dry storage space under the eaves as well as shelter during storms.

The house is built into the side of a hill, allowing easy ramp access to any of its levels—including the vast "attic." From here, hay would be unloaded into the middle level, and then could easily be dropped down to where the livestock lived below.

Farmers and their animals lived under one roof. Explore the people's quarters. The kitchen occupied the center of the building, where its stove radiated heat to the other living areas. Notice the lack of a chimney and the blackened walls in the kitchen. The stove was open to the roof to allow smoke to flow through the house, dry out the air (which was otherwise made uncomfortably humid by the animals), and seep out through the thatch. The two-story kitchen allowed farmers to smoke meat above while they cooked meals below. The soot also helped to coat and preserve the wood frame. Windows were a sure sign of wealth and status.

Surrounding the main building are several smaller ones to explore. The **farm mill** is popular during its live grain-grinding demonstrations, when water power sets the giant gears in motion. The **day laborer's cottage,** which once housed a family with 14 kids, shows life in the early 20th century, when farm families had both electricity and outhouses. The **bakery and distillery** has a communal oven where families from the community baked their bread all at once. The **saw mill,** which runs sporadically, saws planks of wood from huge trunks. One house is dedicated to children's activities and another to cooking demonstrations.

Eating: The shops and restaurants scattered between the parking lot and museum entrance, while touristy, are a fair source for local specialties. At the outdoor stands you can try *Frikadelle* (a spiced pork-and-beef patty) or *Schupfnudeln* (potato-based noodles, fried up with sauerkraut). Don't be shy to try a little of everything; the friendly ladies ladling the portions will fill up your plate with whatever you point to for a reasonable price. Indulge in a creamy slice of *Schwarzwälder Kirschtorte.*

Nearby: Just a few minutes down the road toward Triberg is the **Sommerrodelbahn Gutach** luge course (daily March-Oct 10:00-18:00, tel. 07831/965580, www.sommerrodelbahn-gutach.de).

Triberg

Deep in the Black Forest along B-500, Triberg is a midsize town that exploits its cuckoo-clock heritage to the hilt. Despite the kitsch, it's a pleasant place to stretch your legs under giant cuckoo-clock facades. Triberg's two main attractions—the Black Forest Museum and Triberg Waterfall—are near each other. The **TI** is located in the Black Forest Museum (daily 9:00-17:00, closed off-season weekends, tel. 07722/866490, www.triberg.de).

▲Black Forest Museum (Schwarzwaldmuseum)

Not to be confused with the Black Forest Open-Air Museum described earlier, this collection gives a fine look at the regional culture. As you explore its three floors, you'll find insightful exhibits on various facets of Black Forest heritage, with a special emphasis on engineering (clockmaking, railways, mineral mining, locally built SABA radios) and crafts (woodcarving, glassmaking). The only English you'll encounter are the "do not touch" signs.

The main hall contains dozens of dolls wearing traditional dress from the region, including the distinctive maidens' hats, piled with gigantic cranberries (married women's hats have black puffballs). Player pianos, barrel organs, orchestrions ("orchestras-in-a-box"), and other music-making machines—which were built here alongside cuckoo clocks—were extremely popular in the days before recorded music. You'll also see a replica of a farmer's traditional quarters, a winter sports exhibit, and creepy masks used to celebrate the Germanic Mardi Gras, called "Fasnacht."

Cost and Hours: €6; daily 10:00-18:00, Nov-Easter Tue-Sun until 17:00 and closed Mon; Wallfahrtstrasse 4, tel. 07722/4434, www.schwarzwaldmuseum.de.

Triberg Waterfall (Triberger Wasserfall)

Triberg's other claim to fame is Germany's highest waterfall, where the Gutach River tumbles 500 feet in several bounces. Although paying €5 to see a waterfall feels like a rip-off, this one really is impressive—especially if you have time to walk through its steep, misty gorge. You'll hike five minutes to the falls and 20 minutes to the top of the falls. For added entertainment, buy a bag of peanuts to feed the squirrels (or yourself). The gorge has three entrances at different altitudes along the twisty main road toward Furtwangen, each open daily. The main—and lowest—entrance *(Haupt-eingang),* in the town center across from the Black Forest Museum, is most convenient.

▲German Clock Museum
(Deutsches Uhrenmuseum)

The only reason to stop in Furtwangen is to see the interesting German Clock Museum. More than a chorus of cuckoo clocks, this modern museum is practically evangelical in tracing the development of clocks from the Dark Ages to the Space Age. With the help of a staffer turning things on, this exhibit brings the history of timekeeping to fascinating life. (Consider a few demonstrations included in your ticket and ask for some action.)

Cost and Hours: €6, daily 9:00-18:00, Nov-March 10:00-17:00, Robert-Gerwig-Platz 1, tel. 07723/920-2800, www.deutsches-uhrenmuseum.de.

Getting There: It's hiding out in the town center of Furtwangen; as you approach the town, closely track the low-profile signs to *Deutsches Uhrenmuseum* or simply *Uhrenmuseum*.

Visiting the Museum: Borrow the English descriptions as you enter. The collection is displayed chronologically, starting on the first floor, then follow the *Rundgang* (tour) signs.

Floor 1: Starting with Stonehenge (which is thought to be a celestial calendar) and early sundials, the exhibit takes in the full breadth of timepiece history. In the display case of celestial clocks, find the highly detailed **astronomical-geographical clock** from 1787, which used just 24 gears to tell not only the time, but also the position of the stars in the night sky, which saint's day it was, and the phase of the moon.

Black Forest clockmakers achieved a breakthrough when they simplified the timekeeping mechanism so that it could be built almost entirely of wood, allowing clocks to be sold at a lower price (and leading to a worldwide boom in clock sales). You can watch **Black Forest clocks** evolve from rough-hewn wood to delicately painted white lacquer faces. Locals also figured out how to make musical clocks with wooden flutes and bellows.

The vast collection of **cuckoo clocks** (*Kuckucksuhren* in German) traces the evolution of the Black Forest's most iconic product. The cuckoo clock as we know it was created for a contest in 1850 by Friedrich Eisenlohr, a railway architect who modeled his *Bahnhäusleuhr* clock after a railroad house. While the clocks strike us as quaint and kitschy now, Eisenlohr's idea of shaping a clock like a little house was revolutionary at the time. Cuckoo clocks became very popular—especially among tourists during the late-19th-century heyday of the romantic Grand Tour era—and were eventually copied by clockmakers in Switzerland. (If you even hint that cuckoo clocks are Swiss, proud Black Forest natives will quickly set you straight.)

On the way downstairs, ogle the gigantic **"Astronomical World Clock."** The smaller dials show different time zones—a

The Black Forest Clockmaker Diaspora

Black Forest clockmakers specialized in affordable, everyday timepieces. Because they could be pro-duced and sold cheaply, Black Forest clocks became popular around the world. Between 1800 and 1850 alone, 15 million Black Forest clocks were sold worldwide. This demand—combined with a need for steady employment among a growing pop-ulation—persuaded many Black Forest na-tives to leave home and sell clocks in for-eign lands.

From the 1770s through the early 1900s, roving Black Forest clockmakers (called *Uhrenhändler*) traveled far and wide. They'd load their wares onto a wood-frame rucksack and cry, *Ins Uhrenland!*—"To clock country!"...that is, wherever peo-ple were buying clocks. Once they found a good market abroad, they'd settle in, set up shop, and create a lucrative little business. Many clockmakers were away from home for months, or even years—and quite a few married into their adopted local communities. (Emigrants from this part of Germany likely started out as clock-sellers.)

Most of these *Uhrenhändler* sold simple "shield clocks" (*Schilduhr*), with a face that hid the mechanical workings. The face of the clock could be painted to match the local tastes of the buyer. But no matter how far from home the clockmak-ers wandered, and no matter how different the clocks looked, they were still Black Forest at heart.

new concept in the slow-travel era when this was created. When the clock springs into action, Jesus blesses the 12 apostles as they shuffle past. (Ask the front desk to turn it on for you.) Next, head downstairs to...

Floor -1: Now in the 20th century, the exhibit shows off pocket watches with precious details. Wristwatches became popular first among women, who didn't have pockets, but were later adopted by men in World War I for easy access while using a rifle. But even as tech-nology advanced, Black Forest clockmakers still specialized in straightforward, affordable, everyday timepieces. Quartz technol-ogy allowed for far greater accuracy at a much lower price, which effectively crippled the cuckoo clock industry. Furtwangen no longer makes clocks, but it's still a respected industrial town.

Ponder this: If Germany is known for its engineering prowess, you can thank clocks. As technology evolved, German knowhow came to be applied to more and more complicated machines. And so, in a way, precision BMWs are the direct descendant of the rough wooden cuckoo clocks that have been made in the Black Forest for centuries.

Floor -2: The bottom level brings the story up to the modern day, from punch-clocks to atomic clocks. One fascinating exhibit explains how increasingly faster transportation in the late 19th century made it necessary to standardize time across locales. Along with the advent of trains, the innovation of the telegraph sealed it: The world's clocks needed to be in sync. Only in the 1870s did scientists begin to pursue standardization, leading in 1884 to the creation of the prime meridian (to use as a starting point for calculating world time zones). Germany adopted a standardized time zone in 1893.

The grand finale is an upbeat combo of mechanical musical instruments, from player pianos to giant wind-up carnival organs. To hear some of the thunderous music, ask at the desk. Hearing the amazing variety of sounds, it's fun to imagine how the simple "cuck-oo" of a clock with a little wooden bird evolved into a self-playing musical band in a box.

Black Forest Highlands

The "Black Forest" conjures up images of a dark, thick forest. But the southern end of the region—called the Black Forest Highlands—is more gentle, with onion-domed churches, idyllic lakes, and hikes through peaceful meadows. This is the kind of country you'd expect a doctor to send you to when you need some tranquility. In this region (most easily accessible from Freiburg), you'll find both the biggest tourist trap (Titisee) and my favorite commune-with-nature walk (from St. Märgen to St. Peter).

Joy riding through the area, you'll pass fields of corn (mostly for biofuel and pigs rather than people), lots of trucks (mostly from Eastern Europe, which are taking the small roads to avoid autobahn tolls), and lots of Swiss vacationers. Locals are down on the Swiss for crossing the border in droves to flaunt their relative wealth. For the Swiss, Germany is a bargain basement. To many locals, the Swiss are just driving up real estate prices while acting like big shots.

The Black Forest Highlands is a land of classic rural beauty, where huge traditional farms house the family downstairs and the animals upstairs. With solar panels on ancient roofs and little chapels out back, they are a delightful mix of modern and traditional. Most of these farms make ends meet by renting rooms *(Ferienwohnungen)*.

▲St. Märgen to St. Peter Hike

This five-mile, two-hour hike offers a delightful path through the bucolic Black Forest countryside, punctuated by scenic picnic benches for a memorable lunch. Connecting the charming towns of St. Märgen and St. Peter, this fresh-air walk is the quintessential Black Forest experience.

Planning Your Time: If you have a **car,** you can drive to St. Peter, park there, catch the bus to St. Märgen (1-2/hour, 10 minutes), then hike back to your car. Without a car, the hike is accessible by **public transportation** from Freiburg. Before you start, buy two €4 two-zone local transport tickets or a 24-hour regional pass (€11 for 1 adult, €22 for 2-5 adults, available from ticket machines). From Freiburg, ride the train to Kirchzarten (2/hour, 45 minutes), then catch bus #7216 to St. Märgen (1-2/hour, 35 minutes). Once you've walked to St. Peter, dip into the abbey church, then catch the bus back to Kirchzarten (2-3/hour, 25 minutes) and the train back to Freiburg. Confirm transit times at www.bahn.com or at the Freiburg train station.

St. Märgen: This sleepy town (pop. 1,900) is dominated by its Augustinian abbey (not really open to the public). St. Märgen is cute, but offers little reason to stop (other than to pick up a picnic for your hike). The bus drops you in the village center, near the Town Hall (Rathaus), abbey, supermarket, and bakery. The St. Märgen TI, in the back of the Rathaus, offers advice and maps for the hike to St. Peter (open Mon-Fri mornings only, tel. 07652/1206-8390, www.hochschwarzwald.de).

The Hike: The first 40 minutes of this hike are gently uphill (a 500-foot gain)—from the St. Märgen bus stop, follow the signposts marked *St. Peter (Höhenweg, 8km)* through the village. At Hotel Hirsch, make a left turn up a small paved road that leads directly to a tiny paved farm service road. Take a quick 100-yard detour right to see the mill *(Rankmuhle),* then at the first fork head left. Be careful to follow signs to St. Peter Höhenweg, not St. Peter. Eventually you'll reach a small chapel, the **Kapfenkapelle.**

The trail is level for the next half-hour, with views down into the valley. At a clearing in the woods, you'll find the **Vogesenkapelle,** built in 1938 by a local man who had fought during World War I in France's

BADEN-BADEN & THE BLACK FOREST

Vosges mountains. On a clear winter evening at sunset in the Vosges, the man was able to see all the way to the Black Forest—and could even make out his own farm. He vowed to build a chapel near his home if the Black Forest was spared the horrors of the war. And he did.

From the Vogesenkapelle, the path leads down about 45 minutes through farms into **St. Peter,** depositing you just below the abbey at the St. Peter bus stop.

St. Peter: This inviting town (pop. 2,500) is one of those healthy, go-take-a-walk-in-the-clean-air places that doctors actually prescribe for people from all over Germany. The well-organized little **TI,** under the archway across from the Benedictine abbey, has details on the region and walks (closed midday and Sat-Sun, Klosterhof 11, tel. 07652/1206-8370). To find a public WC and reasonably priced eating options, go through the archway to the square.

The town of St. Peter is dominated by its giant, namesake **Bene-dictine abbey.** Step into the courtyard *(Klosterhof)* and imagine a

monastery founded within these walls 700 years ago (then secularized under Napoleon in 1806). The red sandstone church dominates. Its Baroque interior, finished in 1727, is a dazzling white. While you'll see bigger and better in Bavaria, this is the best abbey in the Black Forest (free and open daily, enter at Geistliches Zentrum next door to church, tel. 07660/91010).

Returning to Freiburg: Just below St. Peter's abbey is the town bus stop, called Zähringer Eck, where you can catch bus #7216 back to Kirchzarten; from there, catch the train to Freiburg.

Short-and-Scenic Black Forest Highlands Drive

This pleasant loop starts in Freiburg and takes you through the most representative chunk of the area, including the towns of St. Märgen and St. Peter. This basically passes through much the same scenery as the hike described above, but by car.

Freiburg-St. Märgen-St. Peter Loop: Leave Freiburg on Schwarzwaldstrasse (signs to *Donaueschingen*), which becomes scenic road B-31 up the dark **Höllental** ("Hell's Valley"). Here the cliffs on either side begin to close in.

As you enter the narrowest part of the valley, watch for the *Hirschensprung* sign (where you can pull off). On the top of the cliff on the right, spot the bronze statue of a deer *(Hirsch)* preparing to leap *(sprung)* over the chasm to escape a hunter, a feat memorialized in a local legend.

After the moody, narrow stretch of the valley, you'll hit a straightaway, and then the road begins a series of switchbacks up and out of the canyon. En route, you're sure to see signs for overrated, overcrowded Titisee.

Titisee, a famous lake with a giggle-inducing name, is improbably popular among Germans. This town of 2,000 is built for tourism. One glance and you'll be wondering why they even bothered to develop this dull spot into a tourist attraction—and yet it's a huge hit. Don't let morbid curiosity take you to Titisee...or you'll squander valuable Black Forest time.

Instead, at Hinterzarten (just before Titisee), turn onto B-500 toward Furtwangen and St. Märgen. Soon you'll come to a fork in the road, where you can choose between heading straight to Furtwangen (and its **German Clock Museum**) or turning off for **St. Märgen,** then **St. Peter** (both described earlier; St. Peter is better if you have to choose).

From St. Peter, continue about 15 minutes through idyllic Black Forest scenery to the pass over **Mount Kandel** (head for Glottertal; just outside St. Peter, turn right at Elmehof to follow brown signs to *Kandel*). At the summit is the Berghotel Kandel, with parking and fine views on either side of the ridge. A short hike takes you to the 4,000-foot peak (Kandelgipfel), where on a nice day you can watch paragliders psych themselves up and take off.

On the other side of the pass, the road winds steeply down through a dense forest to Waldkirch, where a fast road takes you down to the Freiburg Nord autobahn (A-5) entrance. From here you can return south to Freiburg or drive north to Baden-Baden.

ROTHENBURG & THE ROMANTIC ROAD

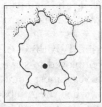

The Romantic Road takes you through Bavaria's medieval heartland, a route strewn with picturesque villages, farmhouses, onion-domed churches, Baroque palaces, and walled cities. The route, which runs from Würzburg to Füssen, is the most scenic way to connect Frankfurt with Munich. No trains run along the full length of the Romantic Road, but Rothenburg (ROH-tehn-burg), the most interesting town along the way, is easy to reach by rail. Drivers can either zero in on Rothenburg or take some extra time to meander from town to town on the way. For nondrivers, a tour bus travels the Romantic Road once daily in each direction.

Countless travelers have searched for the elusive "untouristy Rothenburg." There are many contenders (such as Michelstadt, Miltenberg, Bamberg, Bad Windsheim, and Dinkelsbühl), but none holds a candle to the king of medieval German cuteness. Even with crowds, overpriced souvenirs, Japanese-speaking night watchmen, and, yes, even *Schneeballen*, Rothenburg is best. Save time and mileage and be satisfied with the winner.

Rothenburg ob der Tauber

In the Middle Ages, when Berlin and Munich were just wide spots on the road, Rothenburg ob der Tauber was a "free imperial city" beholden only to the Holy Roman Emperor. During Rothenburg's heyday, from 1150 to 1400, it was a strategic stop on the trade routes between northern and southern Europe. Because of its privileged position, along with the abundant resources of its surrounding countryside (textile-producing sheep and fertile farmlands), Rothenburg thrived. With a whopping population of 6,000, it was one of Germany's largest towns. But as with many of Europe's best time-warp towns, Rothenburg's fortunes tumbled suddenly. (In this case, it was an occupation/ransacking during the Thirty Years' War, and a plague that followed soon after, that did the town in.) With no money to fix up its antiquated, severely leaning buildings, the town was left to languish in this state. Today, it's the country's best-preserved medieval walled town, enjoying tremendous tourist popularity without losing its charm.

Rothenburg's great trade these days is tourism: Two-thirds of the 2,500 people who live within its walls are employed to serve you. While roughly 2 million people visit each year, most come only on day trips. Rothenburg is yours after dark, when the groups vacate and the town's floodlit cobbles wring some romance out of any travel partner.

Too often, Rothenburg brings out the shopper in visitors before they've had a chance to see the historic town. True, this is a fine place to do your German shopping. But appreciate Rothenburg's great history and sights, too.

Germany has several towns named Rothenburg, so make sure you're going to Rothenburg ob der Tauber (not "ob der" any other river); people really do sometimes drive or ride the train to nondescript Rothenburgs by accident.

PLANNING YOUR TIME

Rothenburg in one day is easy. If time is short, you can make just a two- to three-hour midday stop in Rothenburg, but the town is really best appreciated after the day-trippers have gone home. Ideally, spend at least one night in Rothenburg (hotels are cheap and good).

With two nights and a full day, you'll be able to see more than the essentials and actually relax a little. I'd suggest starting your day with my self-guided town walk, including a visit to St. Jakob's Church (for the carved altarpiece) and the Rothenburg Museum (historic artifacts). Then spend the afternoon visiting the Medieval Crime and Punishment Museum and taking my "Schmiedgasse-Spitalgasse Shopping Stroll," followed by a walk on the wall (from Spitaltor to Klingentor). Cap your day with the entertaining Night Watchman's Tour (at 20:00). Locals love *"Die blaue Stunde"* (the blue hour)—the time just before dark when city lamps and the sky hold hands. Be sure to be out enjoying the magic of the city at this time.

For nature lovers, there are plenty of relaxing walks and bike rides in the forested environs around the town.

Rothenburg is very busy through the summer and in the Christmas Market month of December. Spring and fall are a joy, but it's pretty bleak in November and from January through March—when most locals are hibernating or on vacation. Legally, shops are only allowed to remain open 40 Sundays a year; this means that many close on Sundays during the slow off-season months.

Orientation to Rothenburg

To orient yourself in Rothenburg, think of the town map as a human head. Its nose—the castle garden—sticks out to the left, and the skinny lower part forms a neck, with the youth hostel and a recommended hotel being the Adam's apple. The town is a delight on foot. No sights or hotels are more than a 15-minute walk from the train station or each other.

Most of the buildings you'll see were in place by 1400. The city was born around its long-gone castle fortress—built in 1142, destroyed in 1356—which was located where the castle garden is now. You can see the shadow of the first town wall, which defines the oldest part of Rothenburg, in its contemporary street plan. Two gates from this wall still survive: the Markus Tower and the White Tower. The richest and biggest houses were in this central part. The commoners built higgledy-piggledy (read: picturesque) houses farther from the center but still inside the present walls.

Although Rothenburg is technically in Bavaria, the region around the town is called—and strongly identifies itself as—"Franken," one of Germany's many medieval dukedoms ("Franconia" in English).

ROTHENBURG & THE ROMANTIC ROAD

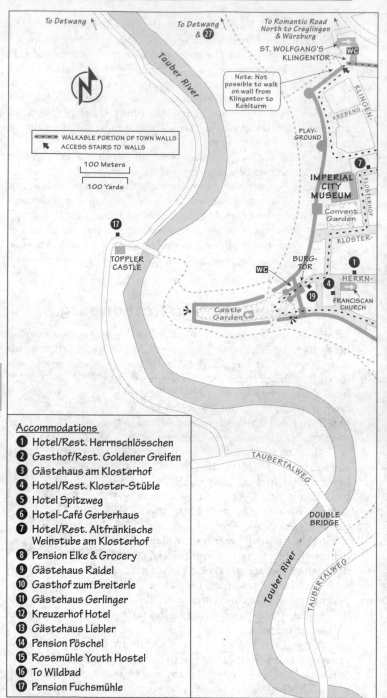

To Detwang

To Detwang & 27

To Romantic Road North to Creglingen & Würzburg

ST. WOLFGANG'S KLINGENTOR

WC

Tauber River

KLINGEN-

KREBENG-

Note: Not possible to walk on wall from Klingentor to Kohlturm

PLAY-GROUND

N

WALKABLE PORTION OF TOWN WALLS
ACCESS STAIRS TO WALLS

100 Meters
100 Yards

7

IMPERIAL CITY MUSEUM

KLOSTERHOF

Convent Garden

17

TOPPLER CASTLE

KLOSTER-

BURG-TOR

WC

1

HERRN-

4

19

FRANCISCAN CHURCH

Castle Garden

TAUBERTALWEG

DOUBLE BRIDGE

Tauber River

TAUBERTALWEG

Accommodations

1. Hotel/Rest. Herrnschlösschen
2. Gasthof/Rest. Goldener Greifen
3. Gästehaus am Klosterhof
4. Hotel/Rest. Kloster-Stüble
5. Hotel Spitzweg
6. Hotel-Café Gerberhaus
7. Hotel/Rest. Altfränkische Weinstube am Klosterhof
8. Pension Elke & Grocery
9. Gästehaus Raidel
10. Gasthof zum Breiterle
11. Gästehaus Gerlinger
12. Kreuzerhof Hotel
13. Gästehaus Liebler
14. Pension Pöschel
15. Rossmühle Youth Hostel
16. To Wildbad
17. Pension Fuchsmühle

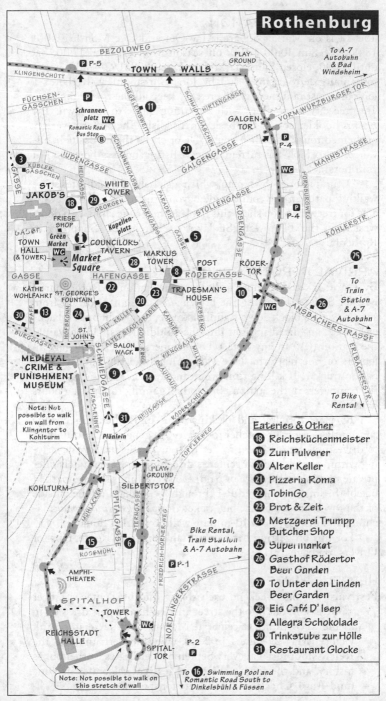

Rothenburg

BEZOLDWEG

P-5

TOWN WALLS

PLAY GROUND

KLINGENSCHÜTT

To A-7 Autobahn & Bad Windsheim

FÜCHSEN-GÄSSCHEN

SCHEGELEINSWEIHER

SCHMID-HIRTENGASSE

VORM WÜRZBURGER TOR

11

GALGEN-TOR

MANNSTRASSE

Schrannenplatz WC
Romantic Road Bus Stop B

JUDENGASSE

HEIGASSE

SCHRANNENGASSE

GALGENGASSE

21

P-4

WC

3

KÜBLER-GASSCHEN

GASSE

WHITE TOWER

GEORGEN.

PFARRGASSE

PARADEIS

GASSE

STOLLENGASSE

ROSENGASSE

P-4

KÖHLERSTR.

ST. JAKOB'S

18

29

FRIESE SHOP

Kapellen-platz

5

25

TOWN HALL (& TOWER)

Green Market WC

Market Square

COUNCILORS TAVERN

MARKUS TOWER

POST

RÖDER-TOR-

28

8

RÖDERGASSE

To Train Station & A-7 Autobahn

GASSE

KÄTHE WOHLFAHRT

HAFENGASSE

TRADESMAN'S HOUSE

10

26

30

13

ST. GEORGE'S FOUNTAIN

22

2

24

20

23

ALT. STAD GRABEN

ERBSENG.

WC

ANSBACHERSTRASSE

ERLBACHERSTR.

PFAFF.

HOFBRONN.

ALTER KELLER

GOLD RING

RAINEN-G.

MILLER

ST. JOHN'S

BURGGASSE

SCHMIEDGASSE

SALON WACK.

BRAUHAUS.

WENGGASSE

To Bike Rental

MEDIEVAL CRIME & PUNISHMENT MUSEUM

9

14

12

HIRSCHENWEG

NEUGASSE

RÖDERSCHÜTT

Note: Not possible to walk on wall from Klingentor to Kohlturm

31

Plönlein

TOPFERWEG

KOHLTURM

PLAY GROUND

SIEBERTSTOR

SPITALGASSE

STERNGASSE

FRIEDRICH-HÖRNER-WEG

KOHLTURM

MÜHLACKER

To Bike Rental, Train Station & A-7 Autobahn

15

ROSSMÜHL.

6

P-1

AMPHI-THEATER

SPITALHOF

TOWER

NOEDLINGERSTRASSE

REICHSSTADT HALLE

WC

SPITAL-TOR

P-2

Note: Not possible to walk on this stretch of wall

To **16**, Swimming Pool and Romantic Road South to Dinkelsbühl & Füssen

Eateries & Other

- **18** Reichsküchenmeister
- **19** Zum Pulverer
- **20** Alter Keller
- **21** Pizzeria Roma
- **22** TobinGo
- **23** Brot & Zeit
- **24** Metzgerei Trumpp Butcher Shop
- **25** Supermarket
- **26** Gasthof Rödertor Beer Garden
- **27** To Unter den Linden Beer Garden
- **28** Eis Café D' Isep
- **29** Allegra Schokolade
- **30** Trinkstube zur Hölle
- **31** Restaurant Glocke

TOURIST INFORMATION

The TI is on Market Square (May-Oct and Dec Mon-Fri 9:00-18:00, Sat-Sun 10:00-17:00; off-season Mon-Fri until 17:00, Sat until 13:00, closed Sun; Marktplatz 2, tel. 09861/404-800, www.rothenburg.de/tourismus, run by Jörg Christöphler). If there's a long line, just raid the rack where they keep all the free pamphlets. The free city map comes with a walking guide to the town. The *Events* booklet covers the basics in English. They offer a variety of themed tours; ask when you arrive or check their website in advance. Also look for current concert-listing posters here (and at your hotel).

A fun pictorial town map, which also helpfully indicates some walking paths in the countryside beyond the town walls, is available for free when you show this book at the Friese shop, two doors west from the TI (toward St. Jakob's Church; see "Shopping in Rothenburg," later).

ARRIVAL IN ROTHENBURG

By Train: It's a 10-minute walk from the station to Rothenburg's Market Square (following the brown *Altstadt* signs, exit left from station, walk a block down Bahnhofstrasse, turn right on Ansbacher Strasse, and head straight into the Middle Ages). Taxis wait at the station (€10 to any hotel). Day-trippers can leave luggage in lockers on the platform. Free WCs are behind the Speedy snack bar on track 1. If killing time, you can pay to get online on one of the computers in the station's Spielothek gaming room (long hours daily).

By Car: Driving and parking rules in Rothenburg change constantly—ask your hotelier for advice. In general, you're allowed to drive into the old town to get to your hotel. Otherwise, driving within the old walled center is discouraged. Some hotels offer private parking (either free or paid). To keep things simple, park in one of the lots—numbered P-1 through P-5—that line the outside of the town walls (€5/day, buy ticket from *Parkscheinautomat* machines and display, 5- to 10-minute walk to Market Square).

For tips on getting here from Frankfurt, see "Route Tips for Drivers" on page 391.

HELPFUL HINTS

Festivals: For one weekend each spring (during Pentecost), beer gardens spill out into the street and Rothenburgers dress up in medieval costumes to celebrate Mayor Nusch's **Meistertrunk** victory (May 29-June 1 in 2020, www.meistertrunk.de). The **Reichsstadt festival** every September celebrates Rothenburg's history, and the town's **Weindorf festival** celebrates its wine (mid-Aug). Check the TI website for specifics.

Christmas Market: Rothenburg is dead for much of the winter except in December (its busiest month), when the entire town cranks up the medieval cuteness with concerts and costumes, shops with schnapps, stalls filling squares, hot spiced wine, giddy nutcrackers, and mobs of ear-muffed Germans. Christmas markets are big all over Germany, and Rothenburg's is considered one of the best. The market takes place each year during Advent. Try to avoid Saturdays and Sundays, when big-city day-trippers really clog the grog.

Wi-Fi: Free Wi-Fi (Network: rothenburg.freifunk.net) is available at varying strengths around town. As it requires no password, it's not a secure signal—use it to look up info (train schedules, museum hours) but not to check email or make purchases.

Mailing Your Goodies Home: You can get handy yellow €2.50 boxes at the old town **post office** (Mon-Fri 9:00-13:00 & 14:00-17:30 except closed Wed afternoon, Sat 9:00-12:00, closed Sun, inside photo shop at Rödergasse 11). The main post office is in the shopping center across from the train station.

Bike Rental: A ride through the nearby countryside is enjoyable on nice days (follow route described on page 381). **Rad & Tat** rents bikes for €14 for a 24-hour day (otherwise €10/6 hours, electric bike-€28/day; Mon-Fri 9:00-18:00, Sat until 13:00, closed Sun; Bensenstrasse 17, tel. 09861/87984, www.mietraeder.de). To reach it, leave the old town toward the train station, take a right on Erlbacher Strasse, cross the tracks, and look across the street from the Lidl supermarket.

Taxi: For a taxi, call 09861/2000 or 09861/7227.

Haircuts: At **Salon Wack** (pronounced "vahk," not "whack"), Horst and his team speak English and welcome both men and women (Tue-Fri 8:00-12:00 & 13:30-18:00, Sat 8:30-14:00, closed Sun-Mon; off Wenggasse at Goldene Ringgasse 8, tel. 09861/7834).

Swimming: Rothenburg has a fine swimming complex, with a heated outdoor pool *(Freibad)* from mid-May to mid-Sept (when the weather's good), and an indoor pool and sauna the rest of the year. It's about a 15-minute walk south of Spitaltor along the main road toward Dinkelsbuhl (€3.50, kids-€2; outdoor pool daily 9:00-20:00; indoor pool Tue-Thu 9:00-21:00, Fri-Sun until 18:00, Mon 14:00-21:00; Nördlinger Strasse 20, tel. 09861/4565).

Tours in Rothenburg

▲▲Night Watchman's Tour

This tour is flat-out the most entertaining hour of medieval wonder anywhere in Germany and the best evening activity in town. The Night Watchman (a.k.a. Hans-Georg Baumgartner) jokes like a medieval John Cleese as he lights his lamp and takes tourists on his rounds, telling slice-of-gritty-life tales of medieval Rothenburg (€8, teens-€4, free for kids 12 and under, mid-March-Dec nightly at 20:00, in English, meet at Market Square, www.

nightwatchman.de). What's almost as entertaining as the tour is watching the parade of tourists following this pied piper through town each night.

▲Old Town Historic Walk

The TI offers engaging 1.5-hour guided walking tours in English (€8, Easter-Oct and Dec daily at 14:00, departs from Market Square). Just show up and pay the guide directly—there's always room. Take this tour for the serious side of Rothenburg's history, and to make sense of the town's architecture; you won't get as much of that on the fun—and completely different—Night Watchman's Tour. Taking both tours is a smart way to round out your overall Rothenburg experience.

Local Guides

A local historian can really bring the ramparts alive. Reserve a guide by emailing the TI (info@rothenburg.de; more info at www.tourismus.rothenburg.de—look under "Guided Tours"; €90/1.5 hours, €110/2 hours). I've had good experiences with **Martin Kamphans** (mobile 1577-0220-513, www.stadtfuehrungen-rothenburg.de, kamphans@posteo.de) and **Daniel Weber** (to get rates listed above ask for Rick Steves discount, mobile 0795-8311, www.toot-tours.com, mail@toot-tours.com).

Town Wall Walk

It's free to walk along Rothenburg's town wall, and 20 info plaques provide good English descriptions. (Ask at the TI for a pamphlet with narrated walk.) For details, see "Walk the Wall" on page 378.

Walks in Rothenburg

My self-guided circular "Rothenburg Town Walk" weaves the town's top sights together, takes about an hour without stops, and starts and ends on Market Square. (Note that this is roughly the same route followed by city guides on their daily Old Town Historic Walk, described earlier.) It flows into my "Schmiedgasse-Spitalgasse Shopping Stroll," which traces a straight shot from Market Square to Spitaltor, passing traditional shops and eateries on the way. Both walks are shown on the "Walks in Rothenburg" map.

🎧 Download my free Rothenburg Town Walk audio tour.

ROTHENBURG TOWN WALK

This loop walk, worth ▲▲▲, links Market Square to St. Jakob's Church, the Rothenburg Museum, the castle garden, and Herrngasse.

• *Start the walk on Market Square.*

Market Square Spin-Tour

Stand in front of the fountain at the bottom of Market Square (watch for occasional cars) and spin 360 degrees clockwise, starting with the Town Hall tower. Now do it again, this time more slowly to take in some details:

Town Hall and Tower: Rothenburg's tallest spire is the Town Hall tower (Rathausturm). At 200 feet, it stands atop the old Town Hall, a white, Gothic, 13th-century building. Notice the tourists enjoying the best view in town from the black top of the tower (see "Sights in Rothenburg" for details on climbing the tower). After a fire in 1501 burned down part of the original building, a new Town Hall was built alongside what survived of the old one (fronting the square). This half of the rebuilt complex is in the Renaissance style from 1570. The double eagles you see decorating many buildings here are a repeated reminder that this was a "free imperial city" belonging directly to the (Habsburg) Holy Roman Emperor, a designation that came with benefits.

Meistertrunk Show: At the top of Market Square stands the proud Councilors' Tavern (clock tower from 1466). In its day, the city council—the rich guys who ran the town government—drank here. Today, it's the **TI** and the focus of most tourists' attention when the little doors on either side of the clock flip open and the wooden figures (from 1910) do their thing. Be on Market Square at the top of any hour (between 10:00 and 22:00) for the ritual gath-

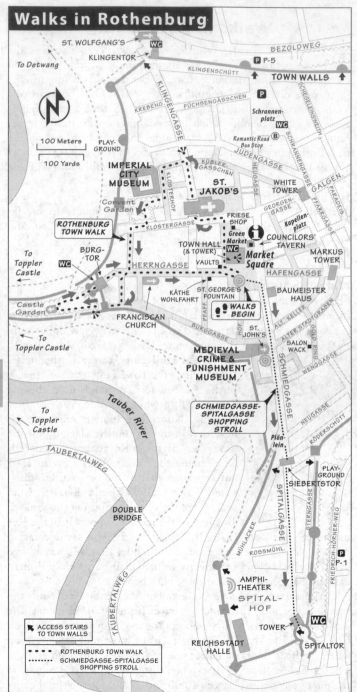

Walks in Rothenburg

ROTHENBURG & THE ROMANTIC ROAD

ST. WOLFGANG'S
WC
KLINGENTOR

BEZOLDWEG

To Detwang

KLINGENSCHÜTT
P P-5
TOWN WALLS

KREBENGASSE
FÜCHSENGÄSSCHEN
P
SCHRANNENGASSE

KLINGENGASSE
Schrannen-platz
WC

PLAYGROUND
Romantic Road
Bus Stop
B

100 Meters
100 Yards

IMPERIAL CITY MUSEUM

KÜBLER-GÄSSCHEN
HEUGASSE
JUDENGASSE

KLOSTERHOF
ST. JAKOB'S
WHITE TOWER
GALGEN
PARADEIS
PFARRG.

Convent Garden
GEORGEN-GASSE
Kapellenplatz

ROTHENBURG TOWN WALK

KLOSTERGASSE
FRIESE SHOP
Green Market
COUNCILORS' TAVERN

BURGTOR
TOWN HALL (& TOWER)
WC
Market Square
MARKUS TOWER

WC
HERRNGASSE
VAULTS
HAFENGASSE

To Toppler Castle

KÄTHE WOHLFAHRT
ST. GEORGE'S FOUNTAIN
BAUMEISTER HAUS

Castle Garden
PFAFF
WALKS BEGIN
ALT. KELLER
ALTER STADTGRABEN
SALON WACK

FRANCISCAN CHURCH
BURGGASSE
HOF
ST. JOHN'S
WENGGASSE

To Toppler Castle
MEDIEVAL CRIME & PUNISHMENT MUSEUM
SCHMIEDGASSE
NEUGASSE
RÖDERSCHÜTT

Tauber River
SCHMIEDGASSE-SPITALGASSE SHOPPING STROLL
Plönlein

To Toppler Castle
PLAYGROUND
SIEBERTSTOR

TAUBERTALWEG
SPITALGASSE
STERNGASSE
FRIEDRICH-HÖRNER-WEG
P P-1

DOUBLE BRIDGE
MÜHLACKER
ROSSMÜHL.

AMPHI-THEATER
SPITAL-HOF

TAUBERTALWEG
TOWER
WC

REICHSSTADT HALLE
SPITALTOR

ACCESS STAIRS TO TOWN WALLS
• • • • ROTHENBURG TOWN WALK
. . . . . SCHMIEDGASSE-SPITALGASSE SHOPPING STROLL

ering of the tourists to see the less-than-breathtaking reenactment of the Meistertrunk ("Master Draught") story:

In 1631, in the middle of the Thirty Years' War, the Catholic army took this Protestant town and was about to do its rape, pillage, and plunder thing. As was the etiquette, the mayor had to give the conquering general a welcoming drink. The general enjoyed a huge tankard of local wine. Feeling really good, he told the mayor, "Hey, if you can drink this entire three-liter tankard of wine in one gulp, I'll spare your town." The mayor amazed everyone by drinking the entire thing, and Rothenburg was saved. (While this is a nice story, it was dreamed up in the late 1800s for a theatrical play designed—effectively—to promote a romantic image of the town. In actuality, if Rothenburg was spared, it had likely bribed its way out of the jam.) The city was occupied and ransacked several times in the Thirty Years' War, and it never recovered—which is why it's such a well-preserved time capsule today.

For the best show, don't watch the clock; watch the open-mouthed tourists gasp as the old windows flip open. At the late shows, the square flickers with camera flashes.

Bottom of Market Square: As this was the most prestigious address in town, it's ringed by big homes with big carriage gates. One of the finest is just downhill from the bottom end of the square—the **Baumeister** ("master builder") **Haus,** where the man who designed and built the Town Hall lived. It features a famous Renaissance facade with statues of the seven virtues and the seven vices. The statues are copies; the originals are in the Rothenburg Museum (described later on this walk). While "Gluttony" is easy to find, see if you can figure out what his companions represent.

Behind you, take in the big 17th-century **St. George's fountain.** Its long metal gutters could slide to deposit the water into villagers' buckets. It's part of Rothenburg's ingenious water system: Built on a rock, the town had one real source above, which was plumbed to serve a series of fountains; water flowed from high to low through Rothenburg. Its many fountains had practical

functions beyond providing drinking water—some were stocked with fish on market days and during times of siege, and their water was useful for fighting fire. Because of its plentiful water supply—and its policy of requiring relatively wide lanes as fire breaks—the town never burned entirely, as so many neighboring villages did.

Two fine half-timbered buildings behind the fountain show

ROTHENBURG & THE ROMANTIC ROAD

the old-time lofts with warehouse doors and pulleys on top for hoisting. All over town, lofts like these were filled with grain. A year's supply was required by the city so it could survive any siege. The building behind the fountain is an art gallery showing off work by members of the local artists' association. To the right is Marien Apotheke, an old-time pharmacy mixing old and new in typical Rothenburg style.

The broad street running under the Town Hall tower is **Herrngasse.** The town originated with its castle fortress (built in 1142 but now long gone; a lovely garden now fills that space). Herrngasse connected the castle to Market Square. The last leg of this circular walking tour will take you from the castle garden up Herrngasse and back here.

For now, walk a few steps down Herrngasse and stop by the arch under the Town Hall tower (between the new and old town halls). On the wall to the left of the gate are the town's measuring rods—a reminder that medieval Germany was made of 300 independent little countries, many with their own weights and measures. Merchants and shoppers knew that these were the local standards: the rod (4.3 yards), the *Schuh* ("shoe," roughly a foot), and the *Ell* (from elbow to fingertip—four inches longer than mine... climb up and try it). The protruding cornerstone you're standing on is one of many all over town—intended to protect buildings from careening horse carts. In German, going recklessly fast is called "scratching the cornerstone."

• *Careen around that stone and under the arch to find the...*

▲Historical Town Hall Vaults (Historiengewölbe)

The vaults house an eclectic and grade-schoolish little museum that gives a waxy but interesting look at Rothenburg during the Catholics-vs.-Protestants Thirty Years' War. Popping in here can help prep your imagination to filter out the tourists and picture ye olde Rothenburg along the rest of this walk. With helpful English descriptions, it offers a look at "the fateful year 1631," a replica of the mythical Meistertrunk tankard, an alchemist's workshop, and a dungeon—used as a bomb shelter during World War II—complete with three dank cells and some torture lore.

Cost and Hours: €3.50, daily 9:30-17:30, shorter hours Nov-April, closed Jan, weekends only Feb, tel. 09861/86751, www.meistertrunk.de.

• *Leaving the museum, turn left (past a venerable and much-sketched-and-photographed door) and find a posted copy of a centuries-old map showing the territory of Rothenburg.*

Map of Rothenburg City Territory

In 1537 Rothenburg actually ruled a little country—one of about

300 petty dukedoms like this that made up what is today's Germany. The territory spanned a 12-by-12-mile area (about 400 square kilometers), encompassing 180 villages—a good example of the fragmentation of feudal Germany. While not to scale (Rothenburg is actually less than a mile wide), the map is fun to study. In the 1380s, Mayor Toppler purchased much of this territory. In 1562 the city sold off some of its land to neighboring dukes, which gave it the money for all the fine Renaissance buildings that embellish the town to this day.

• *Continue through the courtyard and into a square called...*

Green Market (Grüner Markt)

Once a produce market, this parking lot fills with Christmas stands during December. Notice the clay-tile roofs. These "beaver tail" tiles became standard after thatched roofs were outlawed to prevent fires. Today, all the town's roofs are made of these. The little fences stop heaps of snow from falling off the roof and onto people below. A free public WC is on your left, and the recommended Friese gift shop (see listing under "Shopping in Rothenburg," later) is on your right.

• *Continue straight ahead to St. Jakob's Church. Study the exterior first, then pay to go inside.*

▲▲St. Jakob's Church (St. Jakobskirche)

Rothenburg's main church is home to Tilman Riemenschneider's breathtaking, wood-carved *Altar of the Holy Blood*.

Cost and Hours: €2.50, daily April-Oct 9:00-17:00, Dec 10:00-16:45, off-season 10:00-12:00 & 14:00-16:00, on Sun wait to enter until services end at 10:45.

Tours and Information: A free, helpful English info sheet is available. Concerts and a tour schedule are posted near the door. Guided tours in English run on Sat at 15:30 (April-Oct) for no extra charge. Or get the worthwhile audioguide (€2, 45 minutes) to tailor your education with dual commentary—historical and theological—for a handful of important stops in the church.

Visiting the Church: Start by viewing the exterior. Next, enter the church, where you'll see the main nave first, then climb above the pipe organ (in the back) to finish with the famous carved altar.

Exterior: Outside the church, under the little roof at the base of the tower, you'll see 14th-century statues (mostly original) showing Jesus praying at Gethsemane, a common feature of Gothic churches. The sculptor is anonymous—in the Gothic age (pre-Albrecht Dürer), artists were just nameless craftspeople working only for the glory of God. Five yards to the left (on the wall), notice the nub of a sandstone statue—a rare original, looking pretty bad after 500 years of weather and, more recently, pollution. Most original statues are now in the city museum. The better-preserved statues you see on the church are copies. Also outside the church is a bronze model of the city. Look closely to appreciate the detail, including descriptions in braille.

Before entering, notice how the church was extended to the west and actually built over the street. The newer chapel was built to accommodate pilgrims and to contain the sumptuous Riemenschneider carved altarpiece.

If it's your wedding day, take the first entrance—marked by a very fertile Eve and, around the corner, Adam showing off an impressive six-pack. Otherwise, head toward the church's second (downhill) door. Before going inside, notice the modern statue at the base of the stairs. This is **St. James** (a.k.a. Sankt Jakob in German, Santiago in Spanish, and Saint-Jacques in French). You can tell this important saint by his big, floppy hat, his walking stick, the gourd on his hip (used by pilgrims to carry water), and—most importantly—the scallop shell in his hand. St. James' remains are entombed in the grand cathedral of Santiago de Compostela, in the northwestern corner of Spain. The medieval pilgrimage route called the Camino de Santiago passed through here on its way to that distant corner of Europe. Pilgrims would wear the scallop shell as a symbol of their destination (where that type of marine life was abundant). To this day, the word for "scallop" in many languages carries the name of this saint: *Jakobsmuschel* in German, *coquille Saint-Jacques* in French, and so on.

Inside the Church: Built in the 14th century, this church has been Lutheran since 1544. The interior was "purified" by Romantics in the 19th century—cleaned of everything Baroque or not original and refitted in the Neo-Gothic style. (For example, the baptismal font—in the middle of the choir—and the pulpit above the second pew *look* Gothic but are actually Neo-Gothic.) The stained-glass windows behind the altar, which are most colorful in the morning light, are originals from the 1330s. Admiring this church, consider what it says about the priorities of a town of just a few thousand people, who decided to use their collective wealth to build such a place. The size of a church is a good indication of the town's wealth when it was built. Medallions and portraits of Rothenburg's leading families and church leaders line the walls above the choir in the front of the church.

The **main altar,** from 1466, is by Friedrich Herlin. Below Christ are statues of six saints—including St. James (a.k.a. Jakob), with the telltale shell on his floppy hat. Study the painted panels—ever see Peter with spectacles (below the carved saints)? Go around the back of the altarpiece to look at the doors. In the upper left, you'll see a painting of Rothenburg's Market Square in the 15th century, looking much like it does today, with the exception of the full-Gothic Town Hall (as it was before the big fire of 1501). Notice Christ's face on the white "veil of Veronica" (center of back side, bottom edge). It follows you as you walk from side to side—this must have given the faithful the religious heebie-jeebies four centuries ago.

The **Tabernacle of the Holy Eucharist** (just left of the main altar—on your right as you walk back around) is a century older. It stored the wine and bread used for Holy Communion. Before the Reformation this was a Roman Catholic church, which meant that the bread and wine were considered to be the actual body and blood of Jesus (and therefore needed a worthy repository). Notice the unusual Trinity: The Father and Son are bridged by a dove, which represents the Holy Spirit. Stepping back, you can see that Jesus is standing on a skull—clearly "overcoming death."

Now, as pilgrims did centuries ago, climb the stairs at the back of the church that lead up behind the pipe organ to a loft-like chapel. Here you'll find the artistic highlight of Rothenburg and perhaps the most wonderful wood carving in all of Germany: the glorious 500-year-old, 35-foot-high *Altar of the Holy Blood*. Tilman Riemenschneider, the Michelangelo of German woodcarvers, carved this from 1499 to 1504 (at the same time Michelangelo was working on his own masterpieces). The altarpiece was designed to hold a rock-crystal capsule—set in the cross you see high above—that contains a precious scrap of tablecloth stained in the shape of a cross by a drop of communion wine considered to be the actual blood of Christ.

The altar is a realistic commotion, showing that Riemenschneider—a High Gothic artist—was ahead of his time. Below, in the scene of the Last Supper, Jesus gives Judas a piece of bread, marking him as the traitor, while John lays his head on Christ's lap. Judas, with his big bag of cash, could be removed from the scene (illustrated by photos on the wall nearby), as was the tradition for the four days leading up to Easter.

Everything is portrayed exactly as described in the Bible. In the relief panel on the left, Jesus enters the walled city of Jerusalem.

Notice the exacting attention to detail—down to the nails on the horseshoe. In the relief panel on the right, Jesus prays in the Garden of Gethsemane.

Before continuing on, take a moment to simply linger over the lovingly executed details: the curly locks of the apostles' hair and beards, and the folds of their garments; the delicate vines intertwining above their heads; Jesus' expression, at once tender and accusing.

• *After leaving the church, walk around the corner to the right and under the chapel (built over the road). Go two blocks down Klingengasse and stop at the corner of the street called Klosterhof. Looking farther ahead of you down Klingengasse, you see the...*

Klingentor

This cliff tower was Rothenburg's water reservoir. From 1595 until 1910, a 900-liter (240-gallon) copper tank high in the tower provided clean spring water—pumped up by river power—to the privileged. To the right of the Klingentor is a good stretch of wall rampart to walk. To the left, the wall is low and simple, lacking a rampart because it guards only a cliff.

Now find the shell decorating a building on the street corner next to you. That's once again the symbol of St. James, indicating that this building is associated with the church.

• *Turn left down Klosterhof, passing the shell and, on your right, the colorful, recommended Altfränkische Weinstube am Klosterhof pub. As you approach the next stop, notice the lazy Susan embedded in the wall (to the right of the museum door), which allowed cloistered nuns to give food to the poor without being seen.*

▲▲Rothenburg Museum

You'll get a vivid and artifact-filled sweep through Rothenburg's history at this excellent museum, housed in a former Dominican convent. The highlight for many is the painted glass mug said to have prompted the myth of the Meistertrunk.

Cost and Hours: €6; daily 9:30-17:30, Nov-Dec 13:00-16:00, closed Jan-March; English info sheet at entrance, Klosterhof 5, tel. 09861/939-043, www.rothenburgmuseum.de.

Visiting the Museum: As you follow the *Rundgang/Tour* signs to the left, watch for the following highlights:

Immediately inside the entry, a glass case shows off the 1616 Prince Elector's colorful glass tankard (which inspired the famous legend of the Meistertrunk, created in 1881 to drive tourism) and a set of golden Rothenburg coins. Down the hall, find a modern city model and trace the city's growth, its walls expanding like rings on a big tree. Before going upstairs, you'll see medieval and Renaissance sculptures, including original sandstone statues from St. Jakob's Church and original statues that once decorated the Baumeister Haus near Market Square. Upstairs in the nuns' dormitory are craftsmen's signs that once hung outside shops (see if you can guess the craft before reading the museum's label), ornate locks, tools for various professions, and a valuable collection of armor and weapons. You'll then go through two levels of rooms showcasing old furniture, housewares, and the Baroque statues that decorated the organ loft in St. Jakob's Church from 1669 until the 19th century, when they were cleared out to achieve "Gothic purity." Take time to enjoy the several rooms and shop fronts outfitted as they would have been centuries ago.

The painting gallery is lined with Romantic paintings of Rothenburg, which served as the first tourist promotion and give visitors today a chance to envision the city as it appeared in centuries past. Look for the large, gloomy work by Englishman Arthur Wasse (labeled *"Es spukt"*)—does that door look familiar?

Back downstairs near where you entered, circle left around the cloister to see a 14th-century convent kitchen *(Klosterküche)* with a working model of a lazy Susan (the kind that nuns would have used to share food with the poor outside the convent—go ahead, give it a swing) and a massive chimney (step inside and look up). Continue around to an exhibit of Jewish culture in Rothenburg through the ages *(Judaika)*, then see the grand finale (in the *Konventsaal*), the *Rothenburger Passion*. This 12-panel series of paintings showing scenes leading up to Christ's Crucifixion—originally intended for the town's Franciscan church (which we'll pass later)—dates from 1492.

• *Leaving the museum, go around to the right and into the Convent Garden (when locked at night, continue straight to the T-intersection and turn right).*

Convent Garden

This spot is a peaceful place to work on your tan...or mix a poisoned potion. Monks and nuns—who were responsible for concocting herbal cures in the olden days, finding disinfectants, and coming up with ways to disguise the taste of rotten food—often tended herb gardens. Smell (but don't pick) the *Pfefferminze* (peppermint), *Heidewacholder* (juniper/gin), *Rosmarin* (rosemary), *Lavandel* (lavender), and the tallest plant, *Hopfen* (hops...monks were the great medieval brewers). Don't smell the plants that are poisonous (potency indicated by the number of crosses, like stars indicating spiciness on a Thai food menu). Appreciate the setting, taking in the fine architecture and expansive garden—all within the city walls, where land was at such a premium. It's a reminder of the power of the pre-Reformation Church.

• *Exit opposite from where you entered, angling left through the nuns' garden, leaving via an arch along the far wall. Then turn right and go downhill to the...*

Town Wall

This part of the wall takes advantage of the natural fortification provided by the cliff (view through bars, look to far right) and is therefore much shorter than the ramparts.

• *Angle left along the wall. Cross the big street (Herrngasse, with the Burgtor tower on your right—which we'll enter from outside soon) and continue downhill on Burggasse until you hit another section of the town wall. Turn right, go through a small tower gate, and park yourself at the town's finest viewpoint.*

Castle Garden Viewpoint

From here enjoy a fine view of fortified Rothenburg. You're looking at the Spitaltor end of town (with the most interesting gate and the former hospital). After

this walk, you can continue with my "Schmiedgasse-Spitalgasse Shopping Stroll," which leads from Market Square down to this end of town, known as Plönlein, and then enter the city walls and walk the ramparts 180 degrees to the Klingentor tower (which we saw earlier on our walk, in the distance just after St. Jakob's Church). The droopy-eyed building at the far end of town (today's youth hostel) was the horse mill—which provided grinding power when the water mill in the valley below was not working (during drought or siege). Stretching below you is the fine park-like land around the Tauber River, nicknamed the "Tauber Riviera."

• *Now explore deeper into the park.*

Castle Garden (Burggarten) and the Burgtor Gate

The park before you was a castle fortress until it was destroyed in the 14th century. The chapel (50 yards straight into the park, on the left) is the only surviving bit of the original castle. In front of the chapel is a memorial to local Jews killed in a 1298 slaughter. A few steps beyond that is a flowery trellis that provides a fine picnic spot. If you walk all the way out to the garden's far end, you'll find another great viewpoint (well past the tourists, and considered by local teenagers the best place to make out).

When you're ready to leave the park, approach the Burgtor, the ornate fortified gate flanked by twin stubby towers, and imagine being locked out in the year 1400. (There's a WC on the left.) The tall tower behind the gate was accessed by a wooden drawbridge—see the chain slits above the inner gate, and between them the "pitch" mask with holes designed to allow defenders to pour boiling Nutella on attackers. High above is the town coat of arms: a red *(roten)* castle *(Burg)*.

As you go through the gate, study the big wooden door with the tiny "eye of the needle" door cut into it. If you were trying to enter town after curfew, you could have bribed the guard to let you through this door, which was small enough to keep out any fully armed attackers. Note also the square hole on the right and imagine the massive timber that once barricaded the gate.

• *Now climb up the big street, Herrngasse, as you return to your starting point.*

Herrngasse

Many towns have a Herrngasse, where the richest patricians and merchants (the *Herren*) lived. Predictably, it's your best chance to see the town's finest old mansions. Strolling back to Market Square, you'll pass, on the right, the **Franciscan Church** (from 1285—the oldest in town). Across the street, the mint-green house at #18 is the biggest patrician house on this main drag. The front door was big enough to allow a carriage to drive through it; a human-sized door cut into it was used by those on foot. The family, which has lived here for three centuries, has disconnected the four tempting old-time doorbells. The gift shop at #11 (Hornburghaus, on the right) offers a chance to poke into one of these big landowners' homes and appreciate their structure: living quarters in front above carriage-sized doors, courtyard out back functioning as a garage, stables, warehouse, servants' quarters, and a private well.

Farther up, also on the right, is Hotel Eisenhut, Rothenburg's fanciest hotel and worth a peek inside. Finally, passing the Käthe Wohlfahrt Christmas headquarters/shop (described under "Shopping in Rothenburg," later), you'll be back at Market Square, where you started this walk.

• *From here, you can continue walking by following my "Schmiedgasse-Spitalgasse Shopping Stroll," next. This stroll ends at the city gate called Spitaltor, a good access point for a walk on the town walls.*

▲▲SCHMIEDGASSE-SPITALGASSE SHOPPING STROLL

After doing the basic town walk and visiting the town's three essential interior sights (Rothenburg Museum, Medieval Crime and Punishment Museum, and St. Jakob's Church), your next priority might be Rothenburg's shops and its town wall. I'd propose this fun walk, which goes from Market Square in a straight line south (past the best selection of characteristic family-run shops) to the city's most impressive fortification (Spitaltor).

Standing on Market Square, with your back to the TI, you'll see a street sloping downward toward the south end of town. That's where you're headed. This street changes names as you walk, from **Obere Schmiedgasse** (upper blacksmith street) to **Spitalgasse** (hospital street), and runs directly to the **Spitaltor** tower and gate. From Spitaltor you can access the town wall and walk the ramparts 180 degrees around the city to the Klingentor tower.

As you stroll down this delightful lane, feel welcome to pop in and explore any shop along this cultural and historical scavenger hunt. I've provided the street number and "left" or "right" to indicate the side of the street (see the "Walks in Rothenburg" map, earlier).

Market Square to Burggasse

The facade of the fine Renaissance **Baumeister Haus** at #3 (left) celebrates a secular (rather than religious) morality, with statues representing the seven virtues and the seven vices. Which ones do you recognize?

At #5 (left), **Gasthof Goldener Greifen** was once the home of the illustrious Mayor Toppler (d. 1408). By the looks of its door (right of the main entrance), the mayor must have had an impressive wine cellar. Note the fine hanging sign (much nicer than "hanging out your shingle") of a gilded griffin. Business signs in a mostly illiterate medieval world needed to be easy for all to read. The entire street is ornamented with fun signs like this one. Nearby, a pretzel marks the bakery, and the crossed swords advertise the weapon-maker.

Shops on both sides of the street at #7 display examples of *Schneeballen* gone wild. These "snowballs," once a humble way to bake extra flour into a simple treat, are now iced and dolled up a million ways—none of which would be recognizable to the kids who originally enjoyed them. Long ago locals used a fork to pierce the middle, but today's tourists eat them like an apple. Watch them crumble.

Waffenkammer, at #9 (left), is "the weapons chamber," where Johannes Wittmann works hard to make a wonderland in which young-at-heart tourists can shop for (and try out) medieval weapons, armor, and clothing. Fun photo ops abound, especially downstairs—where you can try on a set of chain mail and pose with a knight in shining armor (ask about Rick Steves discount).

At #18 (right), **Metzgerei Trumpp,** a top-end butcher, is a carnivores' heaven. Check out the endless wurst offerings in the window—a reminder that in the unrefrigerated Middle Ages meat needed to be smoked or salted. Locals who love bacon opt for fat slices of pork with crackling skins.

Burggasse to Plönlein

At the next corner, with **Burggasse,** find the Catholic St. John's Church. The Medieval Crime and Punishment Museum (just down the lane to the right) marks the site of Rothenburg's first town wall. Below the church (on the right) is an old fountain. Behind and below that find a cute little dog park complete with a doggie WC.

The **Jutta Korn** shop, on the right at #4, showcases the work of a local artisan who designs her own jewelry. She's been a jewelry master here for more than 30 years. At #6 (right), **Leyk** sells "light-houses" made in town, many modeled after local buildings. The **Kleiderey,** an offbeat clothing store at #7 (left), is run by Tina, the Night Watchman's wife. The clothing is inspired by their southeast Asian travels.

At #13 (left), look opposite to find a narrow lane **(Ander Eich)** that leads to a little viewpoint in the town wall. Overlooking the "Tauber Riviera," it's a popular romantic perch in the evening.

The **Sumiko Ishii** souvenir shop, on the corner on the left, is a reminder that tourism from Asia is big business, and German shops are learning to cater to that crowd.

Continuing along, at #17 (left), the **Lebe Gesund Vegetarian** shop is all about healthy living. This charming little place (run by tasty-sample-dealing Universalist Christians who like to think of Jesus as a vegan) seems designed to offer forgiveness to those who loved the butcher's shop but are ready to repent.

On the right at #18, the **Da Vinci Lounge** café is decorated as if out of *Clockwork Orange*. Its modern interior is a stark contrast to this medieval city.

The **Käthe Wohlfahrt** shop at #19 (left) is one of the six Wohlfahrt stores around town, all owned by a local family and selling German clichés with gusto. Also on the left, at #21, the **An Ra** shop is where Annett Perner designs and sells her flowery clothes. You can pop in to see the actual work in the back. (There's more of An Ra across the street at #26.) Annett was behind a recent initiative, called "Handmade in Rothenburg," that formed a coalition between 10 local business owners who make everything from chocolate to jewelry to ceramics. They meet once a week to support each other and collaborate on ideas to strengthen the community, an example of the special bond of Rothenburg's town members.

At this point, stop and take a moment to notice the "vernacular architecture" (developed to meet local needs), with the cute gables and higgledy-piggledy rooflines, tiny doors closing narrow slits between homes, and the fountain that's hooked into pipes plumbed in the 1590s. In the Middle Ages, nothing was standard. Everything was built to order.

At #29 (left), **Glocke Weinladen am Plönlein** is an inviting shop of wine glasses and related accessories. The **Gasthof Glocke**, next door, with its wine-barrel-sized cellar door just waiting for some action, is a respected restaurant and home to the town's last vintner—a wonderful place to try local wines, as they serve a flight of five tiny glasses (several different flights: half-dry, dry, red, and sweet dessert wines) for those ready to appreciate this production.

Plönlein to Spitalhof

The corner immediately to your right is dubbed **Plönlein** and is famously picturesque. Plönlein is named for the carpenter's plumb line—a string that dangles exactly straight down when anchored by a plumb (a lead weight; the Latin word for lead is *plumbum*). The line helps carpenters build things straight, but of course, here, nothing is made "to plumb." If this scene brings you back to your childhood, that's because Rothenburg was  the inspiration for the village in the 1940 Disney animated film *Pinocchio*.

Walk a few more yards and look far up the lane **(Neugasse)** to the left. You'll see some cute pastel buildings with uniform windows and rooflines—clues that the buildings were rebuilt after WWII bombings hit that part of town. Straight ahead, the **Siebertstor Tower** marks the next layer of expansion to the town wall. Continue through the tower. The former tannery is now a pub featuring **Landwehr Bräu,** the local brew.

Farther along, at #14 (right), **Antiq & Trödel,** which smells like an antique shop should, is fun to browse through.

Still farther down, on the left at #25, **Hotel-Café Gerberhaus** is a fine stop for a coffee and cake, with a delicate dining room and a peaceful courtyard hiding out back under the town wall.

Spitalhof and Spitaltor

From here, the town runs out of energy and the remaining stretch is a bit glum. This is Spitalhof—the former Hospital Quarter—with some nice architecture and the town's retirement home. Stick with me and continue a few blocks to Spitaltor, the gate with the tall tower marking the end of town (and a good place to begin a ramparts ramble, if you're up for it).

In any walled city, the gate—made of wood—was the weak point. A bastion is an architectural shield, built beyond the wall proper to protect its wooden doors from cannon fire. Spitaltor is a double bastion, built around 1600 with the advent of stronger artillery. Walk through the gate (taking note of the stairs to the right—that's where you could begin your wall walk). Notice how the entry is curved. Any cannon that got past the first door and tried to blow the second door down would be vulnerable to cannon fire from the ramparts and arrows from the slits above.

Outside the fortified gate is the ditch that kept artillery at a distance (most medieval moats were dry like this one; water and alligators were mostly added by Hollywood). Standing outside the wall, ponder this sight as if approaching the city 400 years ago. The wealth of a city was shown by its walls and towers. (Stone was costly—in fact, the German saying for "filthy rich" is "stone rich.")

Circle around to the right. Look up at the formidable tower. The guardhouse atop it, one of several in the wall, was manned 24/7. Above the entry gate, notice the emblem: Angels bless the double eagle of the Holy Roman Emperor, which blesses the town (symbolized by the two red towers).

Cross the wooden bridge ahead and take a right. Past the first arch, you can access the cannon gallery upstairs in the double bastion—with stone ramps rather than stairs so that horse-drawn caissons bearing ammunition could make deliveries easily (free, always open, worth exploring but very dark). To the right of the second arch are the stairs that lead to the ramparts (from where you can start your ramparts walk around the east side of town; see "Walk the Wall" on page 378). Or you can hike back up the street you just walked down to return to the town center.

Sights in Rothenburg

ON AND NEAR MARKET SQUARE

▲Town Hall Tower

From Market Square you can see tourists on the crow's nest capping the Town Hall's tower. For a commanding view from the town's tallest perch, climb the steps of the tower. It's a rigorous but interesting 214-step climb that gets narrow and steep near the top—watch your head. Be here during the first or last hour of the day to avoid day-tripping crowds.

Cost and Hours: €2.50, pay at top, daily in season 9:30-12:30 & 13:00-17:00, enter from the grand steps overlooking Market Square.

▲▲Medieval Crime and Punishment Museum (Mittelalterliches Kriminalmuseum)

Specializing in everything connected to medieval criminal justice, this exhibit (well described in English) is a cut above all the tacky

and popular torture museums around Europe. Nearly everything on display here is an actual medieval artifact. In addition to ogling spiked chairs, thumbscrews, and shame masks, you'll learn about medieval police and criminal law. The museum is more eclectic than its name and includes exhibits on general history, superstition, biblical art, and so on.

A special exhibit, **Rothenburg as Landscape Garden**, features works by British painters circa 1900 that celebrate the town's artistic setting. In the same building as the museum's café, you can explore two floors of original artifacts and multimedia displays on the history and lore of witchcraft, sorcery, and medieval and early Renaissance Christianity.

Cost and Hours: €7, includes art exhibit; daily 10:00-18:00, Nov-March 13:00-16:00; last entry 45 minutes before closing, fun cards and posters, Burggasse 3-5, tel. 09861/5359, www.kriminalmuseum.eu.

Visiting the Museum: It's a one-way route. Just follow the yellow arrows and you'll see it all. Keep an eye out for several well-done interactive media stations that provide extra background on the museum's highlights.

From the entrance, head downstairs to the **cellar** to see some enhanced-interrogation devices. Torture was common in the Middle Ages—not to punish, but to extract a confession (medieval "justice" required a confession). Just the sight of these tools was often enough to make an innocent man confess. You'll see the rack, "stretching ladder," thumb screws, spiked leg screws, and other items that would make Dick Cheney proud. Medieval torturers also employed a waterboarding-like technique—but here, the special ingredient was holy water.

Upstairs, on the **first and second floors,** the walls are lined with various legal documents of the age, while the dusty glass cases show off law-enforcement tools—many of them quite creative. Shame was a big tool back then. The town could publicly humiliate those who ran afoul of the law by tying them to a pillory in the main square and covering their faces in an iron mask of shame. Fanciful mask decorations indicated the crime: Chicken feathers meant promiscuity, horns indicated that a man's wife slept around (i.e., cuckold), and a snout suggested that the person had acted piggishly. A gossip might wear a mask with giant ears (heard everything), eyeglasses (saw everything), and a giant, wagging tongue (couldn't keep her mouth shut). The infamous "iron maiden" started out as more of a "shame barrel"; the internal spikes were added to play up popular lore when it went on display for 18th-century tourists. For more serious offenses, criminals were branded—so that even if they left town, they'd take that shame with them for the rest of their lives. When all else failed, those in charge could always turn to the executioner's sword.

To safely capture potential witches, lawmen used a device resembling a metal collar—with spikes pointing in—that was easy to get into but nearly impossible to get out of. A neck violin—like a portable version of a stock—kept the accused under control. (The double neck violin could be used to lock together a quarrelsome couple to force them to work things out.) The chastity belts were used to ensure a wife's loyalty (giving her traveling husband peace of mind) and/or to protect women from rape, then a commonplace crime.

The exit routes you through a courtyard garden to a **last building** with temporary exhibits and a café. If you must buy a *Schnee ball*, consider doing it here. A recent blind taste test among the town's tour guides deemed these the best. They're inexpensive; they come in regular, medium, and bite-sized; and you'll support the museum.

▲German Christmas Museum (Deutsches Weihnachtsmuseum)

This excellent museum, in a Disney-esque space upstairs in the giant Käthe Wohlfahrt Christmas Village shop, tells the history of Christmas decorations. There's a unique and thoughtfully described collection of tree stands, mini trees sent in boxes to WWI soldiers at the front, early Advent calendars, old-time Christmas cards, Christmas pyramids, and a look at the evolution of Father Christmas as well as tree decorations through the ages—including the Nazi era and when you were a kid. The museum is not just a ploy to get shoppers to spend more money but a serious collection managed by professional curator Felicitas Höptner.

Cost and Hours: €4 most of the year, €2.50 low-season rate available to my readers year-round with this book; daily 10:00-17:30, shorter and irregular hours Jan-March; Herrngasse 1, tel. 09861/409-365, www.christmasmuseum.com.

▲Tradesman's House
(Alt-Rothenburger Handwerkerhaus)
If all the higgledy-piggledy buildings make you curious about how people lived way back when, stop into this restored 700-year-old home to see the everyday life of a Rothenburger in the town's heyday. You'll crouch under low ceilings as you explore a house that doesn't seem to have a single right angle—kitchen (with soot-blackened ceilings); tight, shared bedrooms; and attic workshop. Ponder the rugged reality of medieval *Bürger* life. While the house itself is fascinating, information (in any language) is scarce; pick up the free, paltry English handout, or shell out some cash for a little more background.

Cost and Hours: €3, daily 11:00-17:00, closed Nov-Easter except in early Dec, two blocks east of Market Square, near Markus Tower at Alter Stadtgraben 26.

ALONG THE WALL
▲▲Walk the Wall
Just longer than a mile and a half around, providing great views and a good orientation, this walk can be done by those under six feet tall in less than an hour. The hike re-

quires no special sense of balance. Much of the walk is covered and is a great option in the rain. Photographers will stay very busy, especially before breakfast or at sunset, when the lighting is best and the crowds are gone. You can enter or exit the ramparts at nearly every tower.

While the ramparts circle the city, some stretches aren't walkable per se: Along much of the western side of town, you can't walk atop the wall, but you can walk right alongside it and peek over or through it for great views outward from street level. Refer to the

"Rothenburg" map at the start of this chapter to see which portions of the wall are walkable.

If you want to make a full town circuit, Spitaltor—at the south end of town, with the best fortifications—is a good starting place. From here it's a counterclockwise walk along the eastern and northern ramparts. After exiting at Klingentor you can still follow the wall for a bit, but you'll have to cut inland, away from the wall, when you hit the Rothenburg Museum and again near the Medieval Crime and Punishment Museum. At the Kohlturm tower, back at the southern end of town, you can climb the stairs and walk atop the remaining short stretch of wall to the Spitalhof quarter, where you'll need to exit again. Spitaltor, where you started, is just a *Schneeball*'s toss away.

The TI has installed a helpful series of English-language plaques at about 20 stops along the route. The names you see along the way belong to people who donated money to rebuild the wall after World War II, and those who've more recently donated €1,200 per meter for the maintenance of Rothenburg's heritage.

▲The Allergic-to-Tourists Wall and Moat Walk

For a quiet and scenic break from the tourist crowds and a chance to appreciate the marvelous fortifications of Rothenburg, consider this hike: From the Castle Garden, go right and walk outside the wall to the Klingentor. At the Klingentor, climb up to the ramparts and walk on the wall past the Galgentor to the Rödertor. Then descend, leave the old town, and hike through the park (once the moat) down to Spitaltor. Explore the fortifications here before hiking a block up Spitalgasse, turning left on Rossmühlgasse to pass the youth hostel, popping back outside the wall, and heading along the upper scenic reaches of the river valley and above the vineyards back to the Castle Garden. Note that on the west (cliff-top) side of town, some of the outside-the-wall sections are steeper and harder to hike than the wall-top walkway.

St. Wolfgang's Church

This fortified Gothic church (which feels like a pale imitation of St. Jakob's) is built into the medieval wall at the Klingentor. While it sounds intriguing—and looks striking from the outside—its dungeon-like passages and shepherd's-dance exhibit are pretty lame.

Cost and Hours: €2, July-Aug Wed-Mon 11:00-13:00 & 14:00-17:00, closed Tue; April-Oct Fri-Sat 9:30-17:00, Sun 9:30-13:00, closed Mon-Thu; closed Nov-March.

NEAR ROTHENBURG

▲A Walk in the Countryside

This pleasant stroll—easy and downhill at the start, with an uphill return at the end—takes you through the tranquil countryside below Rothenburg, including stops at a characteristic little "castle-ette," a *Biergarten*, and a historic church.

From the *Burggarten* (castle garden), head into the Tauber Valley. As you come through the Burgtor into the castle garden, veer left to find the path that leads out of the garden (via the archway below and to the left of the chapel). At the fork just beyond the arch, keep right and head down and around, keeping the castle garden on your right. A few minutes later, at the next big fork, continue downhill (the level path on the right leads around and back into the castle garden). From here the trail becomes quite steep, taking you down to the wooden covered bridge on the valley floor. Across the bridge, the road goes left to Toppler Castle (5 minutes away) and right (downstream, with a pleasant parallel footpath) to Detwang (20 minutes).

Tiny **Toppler Castle** (Topplerschlösschen) is cute, skinny, sky-blue, and 600 years old. It was the castle/summer home of the medieval Mayor Toppler. The tower's top looks like a house—a sort of tree fort for grownups. It's in a farmer's garden, and while generally closed to visitors these days, it's still worth a look from the outside (open to groups of at least 5 people—call ahead, €3 each, one mile from town center at Taubertalweg 100, tel. 09861/7358).

People say the mayor had this valley-floor escape built to get people to relax about leaving the fortified town...or to hide a mistress. After leaving the "castle," you can continue straight along the same road to reach the big bridge in the valley just below town; from here, various roads and paths lead steeply back up into town.

Or, to extend your stroll, walk back to the small footbridge and follow the river downstream (passing the recommended Unter den Linden beer garden) to the peaceful village of **Detwang.** One of the oldest villages in Franconia, Detwang dates from 968. Like Rothenburg, it has a Riemenschneider altarpiece in its **Church of Sts. Peter and Paul.** Founded more than a millennium ago, this church has a dimly lit Romanesque interior with some Gothic frills. Riemenschneider's *Altar of the Holy Cross* depicts the moment when Christ, up on the cross, takes his last breath. While the central figures carry the same level of detail and emotion as any of Riemenschneider's work, the side panels (praying in Gethsemane on the left, the Resurrection on the right) exhibit a bit less mastery than the altarpiece in St. Jakob's. Originally carved for a church in Rothenburg, the altar was later trimmed to fit this smaller space. Notice the soldier on the right looking at an angle into thin air.

Before being scooted in, his gaze fell on the dying Christ. Angels and other figures were cut out entirely.

From Detwang, it's a reasonably steep 15-minute hike back up into Rothenburg (arriving at the northern edge of town), or backtrack to the wooden footbridge—or all the way to Toppler Castle—and head up from there.

Franconian Bike Ride

To get a fun, breezy look at the countryside around Rothenburg, rent a bike (see "Helpful Hints," earlier). For a pleasant 10.5-mile, half-day pedal, do the first portion of the 60-mile "Delightful Tauber Valley" bike route. Escape the old town through the Rödertor, bike along Topplerweg to Spitaltor, and follow the curvy road down into the river valley. Turn right at the yellow *Leutzenbronn* sign to cross the double-arcaded bridge. From here a peaceful road follows the river downstream to Detwang, passing the cute Toppler Castle (described earlier). From Detwang, follow the main road to the old mill, and turn left to follow the *Liebliches Taubertal* bike path signs as far up the Tauber River (direction: Bettwar) as you like. About 5.2 miles from Rothenburg (and 2.5 miles after Detwang), you'll arrive in the sleepy farming town of Bettwar, where you can claim a spot among the chickens and the apple trees for a picnic or have a drink at one of the two restaurants in town. Ride back the way you came to return to Rothenburg.

Franconian Open-Air Museum (Fränkisches Freilandmuseum)

A 20-minute drive from Rothenburg—in the undiscovered "Rothenburgy" town of Bad Windsheim—is an open-air folk museum that, compared with others in Europe, is a bit humble. But it tries very hard and gives you a good look at traditional rural Franconia.

Cost and Hours: €7, Tue-Sun 9:00-18:00, shorter hours Nov-Feb, check website for schedule, last entry one hour before closing, tel. 09841/66800, www.freilandmuseum.de.

Shopping in Rothenburg

Take note...Rothenburg is one of Germany's best shopping towns. Do it here and be done with it. Lovely prints, carvings, wine glasses, Christmas-tree ornaments, and beer steins are popular. Rödergasse is the old town's everyday shopping street. There's also a modern shopping center across the street from the train station.

To find local artisans, pick up the *Handmade in Rothenburg* pamphlet at the TI or visit the group's website (www.rothenburg-handmade.com).

For an appealing string of family-run shops, follow my

"Schmiedgasse-Spitalgasse Shopping Stroll" (described earlier, under "Walks in Rothenburg"). Below are two shops not on that walk:

Käthe Wohlfahrt Christmas Headquarters

Rothenburg is the headquarters of the Käthe Wohlfahrt Christmas trinkets empire, which has spread across the half-timbered reaches of Europe. Rothenburg has six Wohlfahrts. Tourists flock to the two biggest, just below Market Square (Herrngasse 1 and 2). Start with the **Christmas Village** (Weihnachtsdorf) at Herrngasse 1. This Christmas wonderland is filled with enough twinkling lights (196,000—mostly LEDs) to require a special electrical hookup. You're greeted by instant Christmas mood music (best appreciated on a hot day in July) and tourists hungrily filling little woven shopping baskets with goodies to hang on their trees (items handmade in Germany are the most expensive). With this book, you'll get 10 percent off official wooden KW products (look for the *Käthes Original* tag; must show book to receive discount).

Let the spinning, flocked tree whisk you in, and pause at the wall of Steiff stuffed animals, jerking uncontrollably and mesmerizing little kids. Then head downstairs to find the vast and sprawling "made in Germany" section, surrounding a slowly spinning 15-foot tree decorated with a thousand glass balls. The fascinating **Christmas Museum** upstairs is described earlier, under "Sights in Rothenburg." The smaller shop (across the street at Herrngasse 2) specializes in finely crafted wooden ornaments. Käthe opened her first storefront here in Rothenburg in 1977. The company is now run by her son Harald, who lives in town (Christmas Village open Mon-Sat 9:00-18:00, Sun from 10:00 beginning in late April; shorter hours at other locations).

Friese Shop

Cuckoo with friendliness, trinkets, and reasonably priced souvenirs, the Friese shop has been open for more than 90 years—and they've been welcoming my readers for more than 30 of those years. They give shoppers with this book tremendous service: a 10 percent discount off all items and a free pictorial map. Run for many years by Anneliese Friese, it's now lovingly run by her son, Bernie, with help from his daughter Amber, nieces Dolores and Nicole, and their friend Elizabeth. They let tired travelers leave their bags in the back room for free (Mon-Sat 9:00-17:00, Sun from 10:00, 20 steps off Market Square at Grüner Markt 8—around the corner from TI and across from free public WC, tel. 09861/7166).

Sleeping in Rothenburg

Rothenburg is crowded with visitors, but most are day-trippers. Except for the rare Saturday night and during festivals (see page 358), finding a room is easy. Competition keeps quality high. If you want to splurge, you'll snare the best value by paying extra for the biggest and best rooms at the hotels I recommend. In the off-season (Nov and Jan-March), hoteliers may be willing to discount.

Train travelers save steps by staying in the Rödertor area (east end of town). Hotels and guesthouses will sometimes pick up tired heavy-packers at the station. If you're driving, call ahead to get directions and parking tips. Save some energy to climb the stairs: Only one of my recommended hotels has an elevator.

Keep your key when out late. As Rothenburg's hotels are small and mostly family-run, they often lock up early (at about 22:00) and take one day a week off, so you'll need to let yourself in at those times.

For locations, see the "Rothenburg" map at the beginning of this chapter.

IN THE OLD TOWN

$$$$ Hotel Herrnschlösschen prides itself on being the smallest (8 rooms) and most exclusive hotel in Rothenburg. If you're looking for a splurge, this is your best bet. This 1,000-year-old building has a beautiful Baroque garden and every amenity you'd ever want (including a sauna), but you'll pay for them (Herrngasse 20, tel. 09861/873-890, www.herrnschloesschen.de, info@herrnschloesschen.de).

$$$ Gasthof Goldener Greifen, once Mayor Toppler's home, is a big, traditional, 650-year-old place with 14 spacious rooms and all the comforts. It's run by a helpful family staff and creaks with rustic splendor (family rooms, free loaner bikes for guests, free and easy parking, half a block downhill from Market Square at Obere Schmiedgasse 5, tel. 09861/2281, www.gasthof-greifen-rothenburg.de, info@gasthof-greifen-rothenburg.de; Brigitte, daughter Ursula, and Klingler family). The family also runs a good restaurant, serving meals in the back garden or dining room.

$$$ Gästehaus am Klosterhof, offering four apartments with kitchenettes, provides splurge-worthy comfort. Three apartments are outfitted in contemporary German style and one in charming Bavarian decor. Breakfast at the Altfränkische Weinstube (listed later and run by the same people) is included for the three contemporary apartments but is extra for the Bavarian one (Klingengasse 8, tel. 15151/086-047, www.am-klosterhof.de, info@am-klosterhof.de).

$$ Hotel Kloster-Stüble, deep in the old town near the castle garden, is one of my classiest listings. Twenty-one rooms, plus two apartments, each with its own special touches, fill two medieval buildings connected by a modern atrium (family rooms, just off Herrngasse at Heringsbronnengasse 5, tel. 09861/938-890, www. klosterstueble.de, hotel@klosterstueble.de, energetic Erika).

$$ Hotel Spitzweg is a rustic-yet-elegant 1536 mansion (never bombed or burned) with 10 big rooms, new bathrooms, open beams, and endearing hand-painted antique furniture. It's run by gentle Herr Hocher, whom I suspect is the former Wizard of Oz—now retired and in a very good mood (apartment, inviting old-fashioned breakfast room, free but limited parking, Parade-isgasse 2, tel. 09861/94290, www.hotel-spitzweg.de, info@hotel-spitzweg.de).

$$ Hotel Gerberhaus mixes modern comforts into 20 bright and airy rooms—some with four-poster *Himmel* beds—that maintain a sense of half-timbered elegance. Enjoy the pleasant garden in back and the delightful breakfast buffet. It's just inside the town wall, a five-minute walk to the main square (family rooms, apartment, pay parking, pay laundry, Spitalgasse 25, tel. 09861/94900, www.gerberhaus.rothenburg.de, info@hotelgerberhaus.com, Inge).

$$ Hotel Altfränkische Weinstube am Klosterhof is *the* place for well-heeled bohemians. Mario and Hanne rent eight cozy rooms above their dark and evocative pub in a 650-year-old building. It's an upscale *Lord of the Rings* atmosphere, with modern plumbing, open-beam ceilings, and some canopied four-poster beds (off Klingengasse at Klosterhof 7, tel. 09861/6404, www. altfraenkische.de, altfraenkische-weinstube@web.de). Their pub is a candlelit classic—and a favorite with locals, serving hot food to Hobbits (see listing later, under "Eating in Rothenburg"). It also hosts the Wednesday evening English Conversation Club (see "Meet the Locals" on page 390).

$ Pension Elke, run by spry Erich Endress and his son Klaus, rents 12 comfy rooms above the family grocery store. Guests who jog are welcome to join Klaus on his half-hour run around the city every evening at 19:30 (RS%, cheaper rooms with shared bath, cash only; reception in grocery store until 19:00, otherwise go around back and ring bell at top of stairs; near Markus Tower at Rödergasse 6, tel. 09861/2331, www.pension-elke-rothenburg.de, info@pension-elke-rothenburg.de).

$ Gästehaus Raidel rents eight rooms in a 500-year-old house filled with beds and furniture all handmade by friendly, soft-spoken Norry Raidel. The ramshackle ambience makes me want to sing the *Addams Family* theme song, but the place has a rare, time-passed family charm. Norry, who plays in a Dixieland band, has invented a fascinating hybrid saxophone/trombone called the Norryphone...

and loves to jam (family rooms, cash only, pleasant terrace with small garden, Wenggasse 3, tel. 09861/3115, Norry asks you to use the reservations form at www.romanticroad.com/raidel).

$ Gasthof zum Breiterle offers 23 comfortable rooms with wooden accents above their spacious breakfast room near the Rödertor. Because the inn sits on a busy street, light sleepers may want to request a room not facing Wenggasse (apartment, reception in restaurant, pay parking, Rödergasse 30, tel. 09861/6730, www.breiterle.de, info@breiterle.de, Mike and Nicole).

$ Gästehaus Gerlinger, a fine value, has five comfortable rooms in a pretty 16th-century house with a small terrace for guests (family apartment, cash only, easy parking, Schlegeleinswcth 10, tel. 09861/87979, mobile 0171-690-0752, www.pension-gerlinger. de, info@pension-gerlinger.de, Hermann).

$ Kreuzerhof Hotel offers 11 decent rooms surrounding a courtyard on a quiet side street near the Rödertor (family rooms, pay parking in courtyard, Millergasse 2, tel. 09861/3424, www. kreuzerhof.eu, info@kreuzerhof.eu, Heike and Walter Maltz).

$ Gästehaus Liebler, run by Frau Liebler, rents two large, modern, ground-floor rooms with kitchenettes. They're great for those looking for real privacy close to the action. On the top floor is an attractive two-bedroom apartment (RS%, no breakfast but café nearby, cash only, behind Christmas shop at Pfäffleinsgässchen 10, tel. 09861/709-215, www.gaestehaus-liebler.de, info@gaestehaus-liebler.de). Frau Liebler has three more apartments a couple blocks away.

$ Pension Pöschel is simple, with six plain rooms in a concrete but pleasant building and an inviting garden out back. Five rooms have shared baths; one pricier room has a private shower and toilet (cash only, Wenggasse 22, tel. 09861/3430, mobile 0170-700-7041, www.pensionpoeschel.de, pension.poeschel@t-online. de, Bettina).

¢ Rossmühle Youth Hostel rents 182 beds in two institutional yet charming buildings. Reception is in the huge building with droopy dormer windows—formerly a horse-powered mill, it was used when the old town was under siege and the river-powered mill was inaccessible (private rooms available, all-you-can-eat dinner-€6.50, membership required, close to P-1 parking lot, entrance on Rossmühlgasse, tel. 09861/94160, www.rothenburg. jugendherberge.de, rothenburg@jugendherberge.de).

OUTSIDE THE WALL

$$ Wildbad provides a tranquil escape on the edge of the Tauber River. Built into the hillside and offering 58 stylish rooms, this historic building occupies the site of a former 10th-century spa. The owners promote mixing and mingling of guests (including pilgrims walking the Camino de Santiago)—TVs are found in common areas only. The vast park surrounding the hotel, replete with walking trails, offers free summer concerts and Sunday *Kaffee und Kuchen* on the terrace. There's even a covered *Kegeln* lane where you can rent 19th-century wooden pins and try your hand at ninepin bowling. An elevator covers the first seven floors, but you'll have to walk to the eighth, where there's a tiny chapel and library (family rooms, free parking, Taubertalweg 42, tel. 09861/9770, www.wildbad.de, info@wildbad.de). While it's walkable to town, those arriving by train can take a taxi for around €7.

$ Pension Fuchsmühle is charmingly located in a renovated old mill on the river below the castle end of Rothenburg, across from Toppler Castle. It feels rural but is a pleasant (though steep) 15-minute hike from Market Square or a €12 taxi ride from the train station. Alex and Heidi Molitor, a young couple with kids, offer eight bright, modern, light-wood rooms. The building's electric power comes from the millwheel by the entrance, with excess sold to the municipal grid (family rooms, healthy farm-fresh breakfast, free parking, Taubertalweg 101, tel. 09861/92633, www.fuchsmuehle.de, info@fuchsmuehle.de).

Eating in Rothenburg

My recommendations are all within a five-minute walk of Market Square. While all survive on tourism, many still feel like local hangouts. Your choices are typical German or ethnic. You'll see regional Franconian *(fränkische)* specialties advertised, such as the German ravioli called *Maultaschen* and Franconian bratwurst (similar to other brats, but a bit more coarsely ground, with less fat, and liberally seasoned with marjoram). Many restaurants take a midafternoon break and stop serving lunch at 14:00; dinner may end as early as 20:00.

For locations, see the "Rothenburg" map at the beginning of this chapter.

TRADITIONAL GERMAN RESTAURANTS

$$$ Reichsküchenmeister's interior is like any forgettable big-hotel restaurant's, but on a balmy evening, its pleasant tree-shaded terrace overlooking St. Jakob's Church and reliably good dishes are hard to beat, including the *Flammkuchen*—southern German flatbread (daily 11:30-22:30, reservations smart, Kirchplatz 8, tel. 09861/9700, www.hotel-reichskuechenmeister-rothenburg.de).

$$$ **Hotel Restaurant Kloster-Stüble,** on a small street off Herrngasse near the castle garden, is a classy place for delicious and beautifully presented traditional cuisine, including homemade *Maultaschen*. Chef Rudi cooks while head waitress Erika makes sure communication goes smoothly. Choose from their shaded terrace, sleek-and-stony modern dining room, or woody traditional dining room (daily 18:00-20:30, Sat-Sun also 12:00-14:30, Heringsbronnengasse 5, tel. 09861/938-890).

$$ **Gasthof Goldener Greifen,** in a historic building with a peaceful garden out back, is just off the main square. The Klingler family serves quality Franconian food at a good price...and with a smile. The wood is ancient and polished from generations of happy use, and the ambience is practical rather than posh (affordable kids' meals, Wed-Mon 11:30-21:00, closed Tue, Obere Schmiedgasse 5, tel. 09861/2281, Ursula).

$$ **Altfränkische Weinstube am Klosterhof** seems designed for gnomes to celebrate their anniversaries. At this very dark pub, classically candlelit in a 650-year-old building, Mario whips up gourmet pub grub (hot food served Wed-Mon 18:00-21:30, closed Tue, off Klingengasse at Klosterhof 7, tel. 09861/6404). If you'd like dinner company, drop by on Wednesday evening, when the English Conversation Club has a big table reserved from 18:30 on (see "Meet the Locals," page 390). You'll eat well and with new friends—both travelers and locals.

$$ **Zum Pulverer** ("The Powderer") is a very traditional *Weinstube* (wine bar) just inside the Burgtor gate that serves a menu of affordable and well-executed regional fare, some with modern flourishes. The interior is a cozy wood-hewn place that oozes history, with chairs carved in the shape of past senators of Rothenburg (daily 17:00-23:00 except Sat-Sun from 12:00, closed Tue, Herrengasse 31, tel. 09861/976-182).

$$ **Alter Keller** is a modest, tourist-friendly restaurant with an extremely characteristic interior and outdoor tables on a peaceful square just a couple blocks off Market Square. The menu has German classics at reasonable prices—*Spatzle*, schnitzel, and roasts—as well as steak (Wed-Sun 11:30-15:00 & 17:30-21:00, closed Mon-Tue, Alter Keller 8, tel. 09861/2268, Markus and Miriam).

A NON-FRANCONIAN SPLURGE

$$$$ **Hotel Restaurant Herrnschlösschen** is the local favorite for gourmet presentation and a departure from Franconian fare. They offer a small menu of international and seasonal dishes with a theme. There's always a serious vegetarian option and a €50 fixed-price meal with matching wine. It's perhaps the most elegant din-

ing in town, whether in the classy dining hall or in the shaded Baroque garden out back. Reservations are a must (Herrngasse 20, tel. 09861/873-890, Ulrika, www.hotel-rothenburg.de).

BREAKS FROM PORK AND POTATOES

$$ Pizzeria Roma is the locals' favorite for pizza and pastas, with good Italian wine. The Magrini family moved here from Tuscany in 1968 (many Italians immigrated to Germany in those years), and they've been cooking pasta for Rothenburg ever since (Thu-Tue 11:30-23:00, closed Wed and mid-Aug-mid-Sept, Galgengasse 19, tel. 09861/4540, Riccardo).

$ TobinGo, just off Market Square, serves cheap and tasty Turkish food to eat in or take away. Their *döner kebab* must be the best €4.20 hot meal in Rothenburg. For about €1 more, try a less-bready *dürüm döner*—same ingredients but in a warm tortilla (daily 10:00-22:00, Hafengasse 2).

SANDWICHES AND SNACKS

$ Brot & Zeit (a pun on *Brotzeit,* "bread time," the German term for snacking), conveniently located a block off Market Square, is like a German bakery dressed up as a Starbucks. In a bright, modern atmosphere just inside the super-picturesque Markus Tower gate, they sell takeaway coffee, sandwiches, and a few hot dishes, making it a good one-stop shop for grabbing a meal to go or to eat inside or outside at its few small tables (Mon-Sat 6:00-18:30, Sun 7:30-18:00, Hafengasse 24, tel. 09861/936-8701).

Bakery and Butcher Sandwiches: While any bakery in town can sell you a sandwich for a couple of euros, I like to pop into **$ Metzgerei Trumpp,** a high-quality butcher shop serving up cheap and tasty sausages on a bun with kraut to go (Mon-Fri 7:30-18:00, Sat until 16:00, usually closed Sun, a block off Market Square at Schmiedgasse 18).

Grocery Stores: A small grocery store is in the center of town at Rödergasse 6. Larger supermarkets are outside the wall: Exit the town through the Rödertor, turn left through the cobbled gate, and cross the parking lot to reach the **Edeka** supermarket; or head to the even bigger **Kaufland** across from the train station (grocery stores generally open Mon-Sat until 20:00, closed Sun).

BEER GARDENS

Rothenburg's beer gardens can be great fun, but they're open only when the weather is balmy. My first listing is just outside the gate; the second is a hike away in the valley.

$$ Gasthof Rödertor, just outside the wall through the Rödertor, runs a backyard *Biergarten* that's popular with locals. It's great for a rowdy crowd looking for pizza, classic beer garden fare, and good beer. Their passion is potatoes—the menu is dedicated to spud cuisine. Try a plate of *Schupfnudeln*—potato noodles with sauerkraut and bacon (May-Sept Tue-Sat 17:30-22:00, Sun until 21:00, closed Mon and in bad weather, table service only—no ordering at counter, Ansbacher Strasse 7, look for wooden gate, tel. 09861/2022). If the *Biergarten* is closed, their indoor restaurant, with a more extensive menu, is a good value (Tue-Sun 11:30-14:00 & 17:30-21:00, closed Mon).

$$ Unter den Linden is a family-friendly (with sandbox and swing), slightly bohemian *Biergarten* in the valley along the river. It's worth the 20-minute hike on a pleasant evening, or on Sunday morning for the breakfast buffet (in season with decent weather open Wed-Sun 10:00-22:00, Mon-Tue from 14:00, good food and good beer, order at the kiosk and they'll yell your name when it's ready, Kurze Steige 7, tel. 09861/5909). As it's in the valley on the river, it's cooler than Rothenburg; bring a sweater. Take a right outside the Burgtor, then a left on the footpath toward Detwang; it's at the bottom of the hill on the left.

DESSERT

Eis Café D'Isep, with a pleasant "Venetian minimalist" interior, has been making gelato in Rothenburg since 1960, using family recipes that span four generations. They proudly serve up cakes, drinks, fresh-fruit ice cream, and fancy sundaes. Their sidewalk tables are great for lazy people-watching (daily 10:00-22:00, closed early Oct-mid-Feb, one block off Market Square at Hafengasse 17, run by Paolo and Paola D'Isep and son Enrico).

The **Allegra Schokolade** chocolate shop is run by delightful Alex, a pastry chef-turned-chocolatier who trained in Switzerland. He makes artisan chocolates with local ingredients like mint, hazelnuts, and even beer, and can arrange group workshops for you to create your own chocolate Santa or animal (Tue-Sat 10:00-18:00, Sun from 11:00, closed Mon; workshops from €10, minimum 4 people, 1.5 hours, arrange in advance; Georgengasse 9, tel. 9861/688-0293, www.allegra-schokolade.de, info@allegra schokolade.de).

Pastries: Rothenburg's **bakeries** *(Bäckereien)* offer succulent pastries, pies, and cakes... but skip the bad-tasting *Rothenburger Schneeballen.* Unworthy of the heavy promotion they receive, *Schneeballen* are bland pie crusts crumpled into a ball and dusted with powdered sugar or frosted with sticky-sweet

glop. If the curiosity is too much to bear, avoid the slick places on the busier tourist avenues—instead, try a fresh *(frisch)*, handmade *(handgemacht)* one from a smaller bakery or a sweet mini-*Schnee* at the Medieval Crime and Punishment Museum's café. There's little reason to waste your appetite on a *Schneeball* when you can enjoy a curvy *Mandelhörnchen* (almond crescent cookie), a triangular *Nussecke* ("nut corner"), a round *Florentiner* cookie, a couple of fresh *Krapfen* (like jelly doughnuts), or a soft, warm German pretzel.

WINE-DRINKING IN THE OLD CENTER

$$$ Trinkstube zur Hölle ("Hell") is dark and foreboding, offering a thick wine-drinking atmosphere, pub food, and a few main courses. It's small and can get painfully touristy in summer (Mon-Sat 17:00-24:00, food until 22:00, closed Sun, a block past Medieval Crime and Punishment Museum on Burggasse, look for the devil hanging out front, tel. 09861/4229).

Altfränkische Weinstube am Klosterhof (listed earlier, under "Traditional German Restaurants") is the liveliest place and a clear favorite with locals for an atmospheric drink or late meal. When every other place is asleep, you're likely to find good food, drink, and energy here.

$$ Restaurant Glocke, a *Weinstube* (wine bar) with a full menu, is run by Rothenburg's oldest and only surviving winemakers, the Thürauf family. The very extensive wine list is in German only because the friendly staff wants to explain your options in person. Their special €5.60 flight lets you sample five Franconian white wines (Mon-Sat 11:00-21:00, Sun until 14:00, Plönlein 1, tel. 09861/958-990).

MEET THE LOCALS WEDNESDAY NIGHTS

For a rare chance to mix it up with locals who aren't selling anything, bring your favorite slang and tongue twisters to the **English Conversation Club** at Mario's Altfränkische Weinstube am Klosterhof (Wed 18:30-24:00, restaurant listed earlier). This group of intrepid linguists has met more than 1,000 times. Hermann the German and his sidekick Wolfgang are regulars. Consider arriving early for dinner, or after 21:00, when the beer  starts to sink in, the crowd grows, and everyone seems to speak that second language a bit more easily.

Rothenburg Connections

BY TRAIN

If you take the train to or from Rothenburg, you'll transfer at Steinach. A tiny branch train line shuttles back and forth hourly between Steinach and Rothenburg (15 minutes, generally departs Steinach at :35 and Rothenburg at :06). Train connections in Steinach are usually quick and efficient (trains to and from Rothenburg generally use track 5; use the conveyor belts to haul your bags smartly up and down the stairs).

Note that the last train from Steinach to Rothenburg departs at about 22:30. But all is not lost if you arrive in Steinach after the last train: A subsidized taxi service runs to Rothenburg (cheaper for the government than running an almost-empty train). To use this handy service, called AST *(Anrufsammeltaxi)*, make an appointment with a participating taxi service (call 09861/2000 or 09861/7227) at least an hour in advance (2 hours ahead is better), and they'll drive you from Steinach to Rothenburg for the cost of train fare (€4.70/person) rather than the regular €30 taxi fare.

The Rothenburg station has ticket machines for fare and schedule information and ticket sales. If you need extra help, visit the combined ticket office/travel agency in the station (€1-3 surcharge for most tickets, Mon-Fri 10:00-18:00, Sat 9:00-13:00, closed Sun, tel. 09861/7711). The station at Steinach is entirely unstaffed but has ticket machines. Train info: www.bahn.com.

From Rothenburg (via Steinach) by Train to: Würzburg (hourly, 70 minutes), **Cochem** (every 1-2 hours, 6 hours, 4 changes), **Nürnberg** (hourly, 1.5 hours, change in Ansbach), **Munich** (hourly, 3.5 hours, 2-3 changes), **Füssen** (hourly, 5 hours, often with changes in Treuchtlingen and Augsburg), **Frankfurt** (hourly, 3 hours, change in Würzburg), **Frankfurt Airport** (hourly, 3.5 hours, change in Würzburg), **Berlin** (hourly, 5.5 hours, 3 changes).

BY BUS

The **Romantic Road bus** stops in Rothenburg two to three times a week (April-Oct) on its way from Frankfurt to Munich (and vice versa). The bus stop is at Schrannenplatz, a short walk north of Market Square. See the description at the end of this chapter.

ROUTE TIPS FOR DRIVERS

The three-hour autobahn drive from **Frankfurt Airport** (and other points north) to Rothenburg is something even a jet-lagged zombie can handle. It's a 75-mile straight shot to Würzburg on the A-3 autobahn; just follow the blue autobahn signs toward *Würzburg*. Then turn south on A-7 and take the *Rothenburg o.d.T.* exit (#108).

For a back-roads alternative, consider driving along the Romantic Road—see "From Würzburg (or Frankfurt) to Rothenburg," later.

The Romantic Road

The countryside between Frankfurt and Munich is Germany's medieval heartland. Walls and towers ring half-timbered towns, and flowers spill over the windowsills of well-kept houses. Glockenspiels dance from town halls by day, while night watchmen still call the hours after dark. Many travelers bypass these small towns by fast train or autobahn. But consider an extra day or two to take in the slow pace of small-town German life. With a car, you can wander through quaint hills and rolling villages and stop wherever the cows look friendly or a town fountain beckons.

In the 1950s, towns in this region joined together to work out a scenic driving route for visitors that they called the Romantic Road (*Romantische Strasse*, www.romantischestrasse.de). Because local train service was poor, they also organized a bus along the route for tourists, from Würzburg in the north to Füssen in the south.

The Romantic Road is the oldest and most famous of Germany's two dozen signposted scenic routes. Others celebrate toys, porcelain, architecture (Swabian Baroque or brick Gothic), clocks, and baths—and there are even two separate *Spargelstrassen* (asparagus roads). The "Castle Road" that runs between Rothenburg and Mannheim sounds intriguing, but it's nowhere near as interesting.

Now that the A-7 autobahn parallels the old two-lane route, the Romantic Road itself has become less important, but its destinations are still worthwhile. For drivers, the Romantic Road is basically a set of scenic stepping stones to Rothenburg, which is the most exciting town along the way. You can make a day out of the drive between Würzburg (or Frankfurt) and Rothenburg, stopping in the small towns along the Tauber River valley. If linking Rothenburg and Munich, stop in Dinkelsbühl and/or Nördlingen. The drive from Rothenburg to Füssen on two-lane roads makes for a full day, but it's possible to squeeze in a quick visit to Dinkelsbühl, Nördlingen, the Wieskirche, or Landsberg am Lech, hop-

ping on the autobahn to speed up parts of the trip. If you're driving with limited time, just zero in on Rothenburg by autobahn.

A confusing web of roads crisscrosses the Romantic Road region, and drivers will find that the official, signposted route is rarely the fastest option. Using GPS or a mapping app to find your way is confusing, as you'll usually be routed to the nearest highway or autobahn. This is smart if your time is tight and you want to focus on a few carefully selected stopovers. But if your goal is to meander and explore, skip the GPS, get a good map, and follow the brown *Romantische Strasse* signs.

For those without a car, the tour bus that still runs along the Romantic Road route once a day during the summer is a way to connect Rothenburg with Frankfurt, Würzburg, and Munich, or to go between Munich and Füssen, while seeing more scenery than you'd get on the train.

Sights Along the Romantic Road

I've divided the Romantic Road into three sections. The stretch from Würzburg (or Frankfurt) to Rothenburg runs up the Tauber River valley, offering pleasant views. Rothenburg to Augsburg is fairly flat and dull. From Augsburg south to Füssen, the route follows the Lech River up to where the Alps begin, and the scenery gets more exciting at every turn. To help you find your way, I've included some driving directions. While you can reach some of these destinations by public transit, most aren't worth the hassle without a car (try the Romantic Road bus, though the schedule can be sparse—see end of chapter).

FROM WÜRZBURG (OR FRANKFURT) TO ROTHENBURG

To follow this scenic back-road approach from Frankfurt, take A-3, then turn south on A-81, get off at the Tauberbischofsheim exit, and track signs for *Bad Mergentheim*. Or stay on A-3 to the Heidingsfeld-Würzburg exit and follow *Stuttgart/Ulm/Road 19* signs south to Bad Mergentheim. From Würzburg, follow *Ulm/ Road 19* signs to Bad Mergentheim.

Bad Mergentheim

This town, one of the less romantic stops along this route, holds a unique footnote in Germanic history: In 1525, the Teutonic Knights (called the *Deutschorden*, or "German Order") lost their lands in East Prussia (today's Poland) and the Baltic states. The order's leadership retreated to their castle at Bad Mergentheim, which became their headquarters for the next three centuries.

Today the building houses the **German Order Museum**—practically a pilgrimage for German historians but underwhelming for casual visitors, who will find it dry and with limited English (www. deutschordensmuseum.de).

Leaving Bad Mergentheim, continue east. Turn into Weikersheim off the main road, following *Stadtmitte* and *Schloss* signs, then bear right to park in the large free lot. From there it's a couple minutes' walk to the town square.

▲Weikersheim

This picturesquely set town, nestled between hills, has a charming little main square offering easy access to a fine park and an impressive palace.

Weikersheim's **palace** (Schloss Weikersheim), across a moat-turned-park from the main square, was built in the late 16th century as the Renaissance country estate of a local count. With its bucolic location and glowing sandstone texture, it gives off a *Downton Abbey* vibe. The palace interior boasts an unusual triangular floor plan but is only viewable by a guided tour in German (tel. 07934/992-950, www.schloss-weikersheim.de).

I'd skip the tour and instead focus on exploring the palace's fine Baroque **gardens.** From the ticket office, cut through the courtyard and pop out at the finely manicured gardens, originally laid out in the early 18th century and populated by an army of whimsical stony statues (most of them mythological figures). Along the balustrade separating the palace from the gardens are the most photographed statues, the so-called "Dwarves' Gallery." At the far end of the complex is an orangery, offering fine views back over the gardens to the palace.

The **rose garden,** to the right as you face the palace, is free (but likely not at its best, as it's been recovering from an infestation). A gate off the rose garden leads to a spooky "alchemy garden" with plants used by medieval witches.

If you have time after your garden visit, Weikersheim's pleasant **town square** and cobbled old town are worth exploring. The **city park** (*Stadtpark,* enter off town square) is a fine picnic spot, and from it you can peer over the hedge into the palace gardens.

Creglingen

While Creglingen itself isn't worth much fuss (TI tel. 07933/631, www.creglingen.de), two quick and rewarding sights sit across the road from each other a mile south of town.

The 14th century **Herrgottskirche Church,** worth ▲, is graced with Tilman Riemenschneider's greatest carved altarpiece, completed sometime between 1505 and 1510. The church was built on the site where a local farmer found a seemingly miraculous communion host in a field. Centuries later, Riemenschneider graced the space with an impressive altar nearly 30 feet high—tall enough that its tip pokes up between the rafters. While Riemenschnei-

ROTHENBURG & THE ROMANTIC ROAD

der's altars in Rothenburg and Detwang (see pages 365, 367, and 380) are focused on Jesus, the star here is Mary, captured in the moment she ascends to heaven. Angels—with their angular wings jutting out in all directions—whisk Mary off into the sky as the 12 apostles watch in wonder. Just above Mary, appreciate the remarkably intricate tangle of vines. Higher up is the heavenly coronation of Mary, who is surrounded by God and Jesus (distinguished by the bushiness of their beards) and the Holy Spirit. The side panels show important scenes from Mary's life. The church's other, colorful (non-Riemenschneider) altars are also worth a peek (tel. 07933/338, www.herrgottskirche.de).

The **Fingerhut Museum,** showing off thimbles (literally, "finger hats"), is far more interesting than it sounds. You'll step from case to case to squint at the collection, which numbers about 4,000 (but still fits in a single room) and comes from all over the world; some pieces are centuries old. Owner Thorvald Greif got a head start from his father, who owned a thimble factory (tel. 07933/370, www.fingerhutmuseum.de).

FROM ROTHENBURG TO AUGSBURG

Dinkelsbühl and Nördlingen (via B-25) are the main attractions between Rothenburg and Augsburg. From Donauwörth, taking the B-2 highway (which parallels the Romantic Road here) can speed up your trip.

▲Dinkelsbühl

Rothenburg's little sister is cute enough to merit a short stop. A moat, towers, gates, and a beautifully preserved medieval wall all surround this town. Dinkelsbühl is pretty, and a bit less touristy than Rothenburg, but also less exciting. Still, it's a delight to simply stroll for an hour or two. Park at one of the free lots outside the town walls, which are well signed from the main road (parking inside the town is limited to one hour).

To orient yourself, head for the tower of **St. Georg's Cathedral,** at the center of town. This 15th-century church has a surprisingly light, airy interior and fine carved altarpieces. On good-weather summer weekends, you can climb to the top of the tower.

Back outside the church, follow the signs around the corner (first into Ledermarkt, then Altrathausplatz) to the **TI,** which offers a free "Tour of the Town" brochure (tel. 09851/902-440, www.dinkelsbuehl.de). In the TI, take a minute to watch the TV monitor showing the stork nest on top of the old Town Hall (also visible at www.storch24.de). Dinkelsbühl offers an evening Night Watchman Tour similar to Rothenburg's, but it's in German only (details at TI).

The TI doubles as the ticket office for the fine **City History Museum** (Haus der Geschichte) in the same building. This shiny, up-to-date museum fills three floors. Learn about Dinkelsbühl's location along important north-south travel routes in early times, its role in the Thirty Years' War, and how the tug-of-war between Catholics and Protestants ended in a power-sharing agreement and the loss of the town's medieval prosperity. The self-service movie theater shows short film clips about Dinkelsbühl. On the top floor is the large, recently restored town model (Stadtschaue) with only the walls and a few key buildings set up on a medieval street plan. There's also a kids' play area.

Sleeping in Dinkelsbühl: Dinkelsbühl has a good selection of hotels, many of them lining the main drag in front of the church (though more choices and lower prices are available in Rothenburg and Nördlingen). Options include: **$$$ Hezelhof Hotel** (modern rooms in an old shell at Segringer Strasse 7, tel. 09851/555-420, www.hezelhof.com), **$$$ Weisses Ross** ("White Horse," attached to a historic restaurant at Steingasse 12, tel. 09851/579-890, www.hotel-weisses-ross.de), and Dinkelsbühl's unique **¢ youth hostel** (in a medieval granary at Koppengasse 10—steps from the Schweinemarkt, where Romantic Road buses stop two to three times a week in each direction; tel. 09851/555-6417, www.dinkelsbuehl.jugendherberge.de).

▲Nördlingen

Though less cute than Dinkelsbühl, Nördlingen is a real workaday town that also has one of the best city walls in Germany, not to mention a surprising geological history. For centuries, Nördlingen's residents puzzled over the local terrain, a flattish plain called the Ries, which rises to a low circular ridge that surrounds the town in the distance. In the 1960s, geologists figured out that Nördlingen lies in the middle of an im-

pact crater blasted out 15 million years ago by a meteor, which hit earth with the force of 250,000 Hiroshima bombs.

Park in one of the big, free lots at the Delninger Tor and the Baldinger Tor, or in the free parking garage at the Berger Tor (parking inside the old town is time-limited).

After parking, head through one of the gates in the wall and into the center of town by zeroing in on the tower of **St. Georg's Church.** The inside is stripped-down austere—a far cry from the frilly Wieskirche two hours to the south. It's clear that Nördlingen and Wies straddle the Protestant-Catholic boundary.

Climb Nördlingen's **church tower** (which locals call "the Daniel") for sweeping views over the almost perfectly circular old town. The rickety 350-step climb up the tower rewards you with the very best view of the city walls and crater. You'll twist up a tight stone staircase, then tackle several flights of wooden ones—passing a giant wheel once used to winch materials up into the tower. Higher up is a modern winch used today. From the top, take a slow 360-degree spin; it's easy to visualize how the trees on the horizon sit on the rim of the meteorite crater.

The small square next to the church's main entrance is called Marktplatz, and just behind the step-gabled Rathaus (Town Hall) is the **TI** (tel. 09081/84116, www.noerdlingen.de).

Now walk out the bottom of Marktplatz and down Baldinger Strasse (past the Rathaus). At the traffic light, turn right and then left, past the skippable Stadtmuseum (town history, obscure local artists, and very little English), to the **Ries Crater Museum** (Rieskrater-Museum). Ask them to play the two 10-minute English films, which explain meteors. The exhibits are well presented but only described in German (tel. 09081/84710, www.noerdlingen.de).

With more time, walk all the way around on the top of the **town wall,** which is even better preserved than Rothenburg's or Dinkelsbühl's. Circle back to Baldinger Strasse and continue to the Baldinger Tor tower. This is one of five towers where you can climb the stairs to the walkway along the wall. From here, stroll atop the wall back to the lot where your car is parked. The city started building the wall in 1327 and financed it with a tax on wine and beer; it's more than a mile and a half long, has 16 towers and five gates, and offers great views of backyards and garden furniture. You could continue farther along the wall to the **City Wall Museum,** with a 108-step climb to the top—but the view from the church is better.

Sleeping in Nördlingen: Several small hotels surrounding St. Georg's Church offer mediocre but reasonably priced rooms. Try **$$ Hotel Altreuter** (over an inviting bakery/café at Marktplatz 11, tel. 09081/4319, www.hotel-altreuter.de).

Maypoles

Along the Romantic Road and throughout Bavaria, you'll see colorfully ornamented maypoles (*Maibaum*) decorating town squares. Many are painted in Bavaria's colors, white and blue. The decorations that line each side of the pole symbolize the craftspeople and businesses of that community (similar to the chamber of commerce billboards that greet visitors to small American towns today). Originally these allowed passing traders to quickly determine whether their services were needed in that town. The decorations are festively replaced each May Day (May 1). Traditionally, rival communities try to steal each other's maypole. Locals guard their new pole night and day as May Day approaches. Stolen poles are ransomed only with lots of beer for the clever thieves.

Harburg

You can't miss this town, thanks to the impressively intact, 900-year-old castle that looms high on a bluff over the river. Unusually well preserved from the Middle Ages (not a Romantic Age rebuild), it's still owned by the noble Wallerstein family. Locals enjoy repeating the story of how, years ago, Michael Jackson tried to buy this place—which he termed "the castle of my dreams."

Augsburg

Founded more than 2,000 years ago by Emperor Augustus, Augsburg enjoyed its heyday in the 15th and 16th centuries. Today, it's Bavaria's third-largest city (population 278,000). It lacks must-see sights, but the old town is pleasant, especially the small streets below the main square, where streams diverted from the River Lech run alongside pedestrians (www.augsburg.de).

FROM AUGSBURG TO FÜSSEN

From Augsburg, you can either continue south to Füssen on two-lane B-17, or you can hop on A-8, which brings you quickly into Munich (in about an hour).

Landsberg am Lech

Like many towns in this area, Landsberg (on the River Lech) has its roots in the salt trade. Every four years, the town hosts the Ruethenfest pageant, which brings Landsberg's medieval history to life. The town was shaped by the architect Dominikus Zimmermann (of Wieskirche fame). Adolf Hitler wrote *Mein Kampf* while serving his prison sentence here after the Beer Hall Putsch of 1923 (when Hitler and his followers unsuccessfully attempted to take over the government of Bavaria).

About 30 miles south of Landsberg, the nondescript village of **Rottenbuch,** near the Wieskirche, has an impressive church in a lovely setting.

▲▲Wieskirche

Germany's most glorious Baroque-Rococo church is beautifully restored and set in a sweet meadow. For details on the Wieskirche, including opening hours and a full description, see the Bavarian Alps chapter.

The Romantic Road Bus

From April through October, the Romantic Road Coach company runs tour buses that roughly follow the Romantic Road between Frankfurt and Munich. Buses run Wednesday and Sunday, with a third departure on Saturday from mid-May to early September. It's worthwhile mostly if you have no car but want to catch a fleeting glimpse of the towns along the Romantic Road, or if you're planning an overnight stay in a town that's poorly served by train (such as Dinkelsbühl). The bus also offers the convenience of a direct connection between towns where you'd have to transfer if traveling by train, such as between Rothenburg and the cities of Munich and Frankfurt.

Most riders take the bus in one direction, but you could also make day trips from either Frankfurt or Munich to Rothenburg and back. The Frankfurt-Rothenburg leg passes through the small towns in the Tauber River valley (Bad Mergentheim, Weikersheim, and Creglingen) but generally stops only to pick up and drop off passengers. You'll have a scheduled three-hour stop in Rothenburg, then transfer to another Romantic Road bus if continuing on to Munich (or take your same bus back to Frankfurt). The Rothenburg-Munich leg includes short stops to pick up or drop off passengers in towns such as Dinkelsbühl, Nördlingen, and Donauwörth. (Buses running from Munich to Rothenburg include a 45-minute stop in Harburg, allowing time to visit the town's 900-year-old castle.) Riders who wish to visit Augsburg and Füssen (instead of continuing to Munich) need to get off in Donauwörth and take the train.

Be aware that bus stops may not always be well signed, but their location in each town is listed in the bus brochure and on the website. Look for a small *Romantic Road* or *Romantische Strasse* sign.

Buses depart Frankfurt at 9:00 (from platforms A1-A3 outside the train station) and from Munich at 8:30 (from the tour-bus stop across the street from the train station's main entrance). If you want to stop (or be picked up) at one of the small towns along the route, you'll likely need to give the bus company at least 36 hours' notice (check their schedule).

Frankfurt to Rothenburg costs €45, and Munich to Rothenburg is also €45. The one-way ride (Frankfurt to Munich) costs €87. Students and seniors—without a rail pass—get a 10 percent discount. Rail-pass holders can get a 20 percent discount.

For tickets and information, go to www.romantischestrasse. de and choose "Bus & train," then "Romantic Road Bus"; or call 089/593-889 (Mon-Sat 9:00-13:00). You can also buy tickets at the Munich train station at the EurAide office located in the *Reisezentrum* (travel center), or on the bus in Frankfurt (if space is available; cash only).

WÜRZBURG

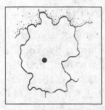

A historic midsized city, Würzburg (VE-WRTS-boorg) is worth a stop to see its stately prince-bishop's Residenz and the palace's sculpted gardens. Surrounded by vineyards and filled with atmospheric *Weinstuben* (wine bars), this tourist-friendly town is easy to navigate by foot or streetcar. Today, 25,000 of its 130,000 residents are students—making Würzburg feel young and very alive. It's also popular both with bike tourists (who enjoy the four-day pedal between Bamberg and here) and with river cruises.

While the town isn't all that charming (thanks to its unmistakable post WWII-rebuild vibe), its quiet and appealing old center is scenically surrounded by vineyard-laced hills, with a stout fortress looming overhead. At one end of town is Würzburg's palace, among the most enjoyable to tour in Germany. On the other end is its atmospheric old bridge, lined by stone statues that make it reminiscent of Prague's famous Charles Bridge.

PLANNING YOUR TIME

Würzburg has a few hours' worth of sightseeing. Begin by touring the Residenz (prince-bishop's palace), then take my self-guided walk through town to the Old Main Bridge. With more time, cross the bridge and hike up to the hilltop Marienberg Fortress. If you're overnighting here, be sure to stroll the bridge at sunset, when you can join the friendly local crowd that gathers there in good weather for a glass of wine and mellow mingling.

Würzburg's Beginnings

The city was born centuries before Christ at an easy-to-ford part of the Main River under an easy-to-defend hill. A Celtic fort stood where the fortress stands today. Later, three Irish missionary monks came here to Christianize the local barbarians. In AD 686 they were beheaded, and their relics put Würzburg on the pilgrimage map. About 500 years later, when the town was the seat of a bishop, Holy Roman Emperor Frederick Barbarossa came here to get the bishop's OK to divorce his wife. The bishop said "No problem," and the emperor thanked him by giving him secular rule of the entire region of Franconia. From then on, the bishop was also a prince, and the prince-bishop of Würzburg answered only to the Holy Roman Emperor.

Orientation to Würzburg

Würzburg's old town core huddles along the bank of the Main (pronounced "mine") River. The tourists' Würzburg is bookended by the opulent Residenz (at the east end of downtown) and the hill-capping Marienberg Fortress (at the west end, across the river). You can walk from the Residenz to the river (below the fortress) in about 15 minutes; the train station is a 15-minute walk to the north.

TOURIST INFORMATION

Würzburg's helpful TI is in the yellow Rococo-style Falken Haus on Market Square (Mon-Fri 10:00-18:00, Sat and Sun until 14:00; shorter hours and closed Sun off-season; Market Square, tel. 0931/372-398, www. wuerzburg.de). If you're continuing on the Romantic Road (see previous chapter), the TI has information on routes and accommodations along the *Romantische Strasse,* including a very helpful route plan. The TI also has tips about biking along the Main River.

Sightseeing Passes: The **Würzburg Welcome Card** offers minimal discounts on a few sights and restaurants—you'll have to visit at least four sights to make it pay off (€3, valid 3 days, sold at TI). Würzburg's Residenz and Marienberg Fortress are covered by Bavaria's 14-day *Mehrtagesticket* (sold at participating sights; details on page 141).

ARRIVAL IN WÜRZBURG

By Train: Würzburg's train station is user-friendly and filled with services, including pay lockers and a handy *Reisezentrum* office that sells tickets (long hours daily). Walk out of the train station to the small square in front. Between the tram tracks and the small building with shops (ahead and on the right) is a good city map showing the easiest walking route between the station and the Residenz (and to other sights in town). Farther right are pay WCs, the post office, and the Romantic Road bus stop (look for sign and schedule—usually platform 12).

From the tram cul-de-sac in front of the station, **tram** #1, #2, #3, or #5 will take you one stop to the Juliuspromenade stop, near most recommended hotels (easily walkable). Trams #1, #3, and #5 continue into town: The next stop (Dom) is close to Market Square, the TI, and the recommended Hotel zum Winzermännle. After that is the Rathaus stop, near the river and the recommended Hotel Alter Kranen.

To **walk** toward town (and some recommended hotels), cross over the busy Röntgenring and head up the shop-lined Kaiserstrasse. To reach the Residenz, it's simplest to walk (15 minutes), but you can get part of the way by taking tram #1, #3, or #5 to the Dom stop.

By Car: Drivers entering Würzburg can keep it simple by following signs to the *Residenz* and parking in the vast cobbled square that faces the palace. Cheaper parking is available in garages on the east bank of the river, just north of the old bridge.

HELPFUL HINTS

Festivals: Würzburg—always clever when it comes to trade—tightly schedules its biggest festivals in summer: Mozart (late May-June, with concerts in the Residenz, www.mozartfest-wuerzburg.de), wine (late May-early June, www.weindorf-wuerzburg.de), African music and dance (also late May-early June, www.africafestival.org), and the Kiliani Volksfest (first three weeks in July, www.wuerzburg.de/kiliani).

Supermarket: Kupsch, at Domstrasse 10, is just a few doors from City Hall (Mon-Sat 7:00-20:00, closed Sun). Another branch is on Kaiserstrasse, near the train station and recommended hotels.

Bike Rental: Ludwig Körner rents bikes right in the old town, a five-minute walk north of Market Square (€12/24 hours, Mon-Fri 9:00-18:00, Sat until 14:00, closed Sun, Bronnbachergasse 3, tel. 0931/52340).

Taxi: Call 0931/19410.

Local Guide: Julius Goldmann is a fine private guide in Würzburg (mobile 0175-873-2412, ju.goldmann@web.de). Rothen-

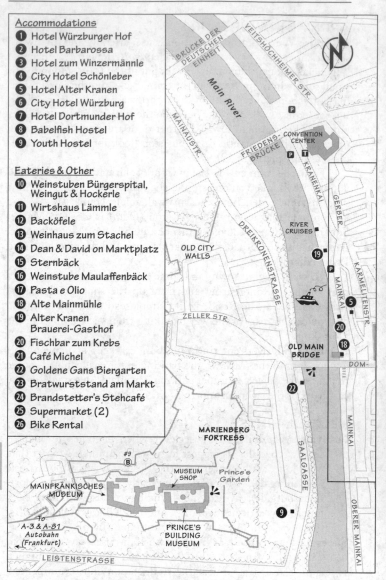

Accommodations

1. Hotel Würzburger Hof
2. Hotel Barbarossa
3. Hotel zum Winzermännle
4. City Hotel Schönleber
5. Hotel Alter Kranen
6. City Hotel Würzburg
7. Hotel Dortmunder Hof
8. Babelfish Hostel
9. Youth Hostel

Eateries & Other

10. Weinstuben Bürgerspital, Weingut & Hockerle
11. Wirtshaus Lämmle
12. Backöfele
13. Weinhaus zum Stachel
14. Dean & David on Marktplatz
15. Sternbäck
16. Weinstube Maulaffenbäck
17. Pasta e Olio
18. Alte Mainmühle
19. Alter Kranen Brauerei-Gasthof
20. Fischbar zum Krebs
21. Café Michel
22. Goldene Gans Biergarten
23. Bratwurststand am Markt
24. Brandstetter's Stehcafé
25. Supermarket (2)
26. Bike Rental

WÜRZBURG

burg guide **Martin Kamphans** also does tours in Würzburg (tel. 09861/7941, www.stadtfuehrungen-rothenburg.de, kamphans@posteo.de).

Tourist Train: While most of the city is easily walkable, the tourist train is worth considering for a quick 40-minute town loop (€9, buy tickets on board, English headphone commentary, departs at the top of the hour from in front of the Residenz, daily June-Sept 10:00-17:00, May and Oct until 16:00, fewer

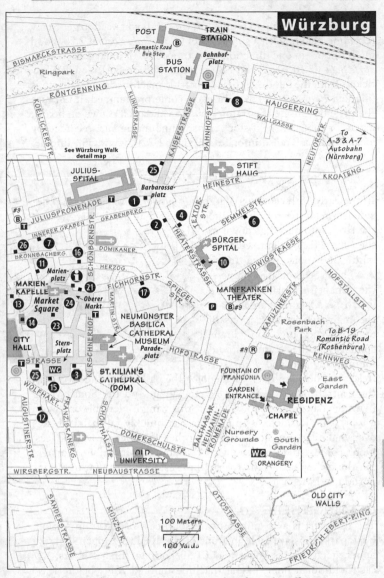

Würzburg

departures and sometimes weekends only off-season, www.
city-tour.info).

GETTING AROUND WÜRZBURG

You can easily walk to everything except the hilltop Marienberg
Fortress (doable, but a steep hike). For public transit, the same tickets work on all city bus and tram lines (including the bus up to the
fortress). Your options include a short-trip ticket (*Kurzstrecke Eins*

+4-€1.35, good for up to four stops; this is all you need to get to my recommended hotels), a single ticket (*Einzelfahrschein*-€2.70, good for 1.5 hours in one direction with transfers), or a day pass (*Tageskarte Solo*-€5.10, also valid Sun if purchased on Sat). You can buy tickets from the bus driver or at streetside machines near tram stops (marked *Fahrausweise*). Most tickets come prestamped; if not, use the little box inside the tram or bus to validate it. Once on board, listen for the cute "next stop" transit announcements, recorded by local children. Transit info: Tel. 0931/362-320, www.vvm-info.de.

Residenz Tour

In the early 18th century, Würzburg's powerful prince-bishop decided to relocate from his hilltop residence at Marienberg, across the river, into new digs down in the city. His opulent, custom-built, 360-room palace (rated ▲▲) and its associated sights—the chapel (Hofkirche; also worth ▲▲) and garden—are the main tourist attractions of today's Würzburg. This Franconian Versailles features grand rooms, 3-D art, and a massive

fresco by Giovanni Battista Tiepolo. The palace has three sections: the central main rooms, the North Wing, and the South Wing (with the dazzling Mirror Cabinet; this wing is viewable only with a tour). The Residenz is impressive, yet quickly taken in; it's less overwhelming to visit than many other European royal palaces. Don't confuse the Residenz with Würzburg's Marienberg Fortress (on the hilltop across the river). The Residenz is the far more important sight to visit.

GETTING THERE

The Residenz is a 15-minute walk southeast of the train station. Easy parking is available in front of the Residenz (open daily 24 hours, get ticket as you enter, €1.50/hour for first 2 hours, €1/ each additional hour, pay at machine marked *Kasse* before leaving). Enter the palace through the main door at the middle of the sprawling complex (directly behind the big fountain).

ORIENTATION TO THE RESIDENZ

Cost and Hours: Palace-€7.50, includes guided tour, daily April-
Oct 9:00-18:00, Nov-March 10:00-16:30; chapel-free, same
hours as palace; gardens-free, daily until dusk (20:00 at the

latest); tel. 0931/355-170 or 0931/355-1712, www.residenz-wuerzburg.de.

Sightseeing Strategies and Tours: A guided tour is included with your ticket and covers the main rooms (vestibule, Tiepolo fresco, White Hall, Imperial Hall), along with the otherwise inaccessible South Wing (tours last 45-60 minutes; English tours daily at 11:00 and 15:00, April-Oct also at 13:30 and 16:30; never full, just show up and wait in the vestibule—then be sure to request English; more tours in German: 2-3/hour). The English tour, while good, isn't worth planning your day around; you can see everything worthwhile in the Residenz on your own by following my self-guided tour (or consider the €5 English guidebook), and then, from the Imperial Hall, jump onto any German tour heading into the South Wing. You can do the history rooms behind the gift shop on your own.

Services: You'll find free WCs and self-service lockers (bags must be checked) on the right as you exit the ticket office. In the garden, WCs are to the right as you come in the main entrance, next to the orangery.

❯ SELF-GUIDED TOUR

This commentary gives you the basics to appreciate the palace (whether visiting on your own or with a tour), as well as an overview of the chapel and gardens.

Residenz Palace

• *Begin at the entrance.*

Vestibule and Garden Hall: This indoor area functioned as a grand circular driveway, exclusively for special occasions—just right for six-horse carriages to drop off their guests at the base of the stairs. This area is relatively dark and serves as a good springboard for the dazzling palace that awaits.

Before climbing the formal staircase, pop into the adjacent Garden Hall (if open). This lovely, airy space is where the garden and the palace meet. The ceiling was painted by Johann Zick in 1750. Notice how he portrays his subjects without Greek-style idealism; they're shown realistically and in high contrast—quite edgy for the time.

• *Now picture yourself dressed up in your fanciest imaginary finery...and ascend the stairs.*

Grand Staircase: The elegant stairway comes with low steps, enabling high-class ladies to glide up gracefully, heads tilted back to enjoy Europe's largest and grandest fresco opening up above them. Hold your lady's hand high and get into the ascending rhythm. Enjoy the climb.

• *As you reach the top of the stairs, look up at the...*

Tiepolo Fresco: In 1752, the Venetian master Giovanni Battista Tiepolo was instructed to make a grand fresco illustrating the greatness of Europe, Würzburg, and the prince-bishop. And he did—completing the world's largest fresco (more than 7,000 square feet) in only 13 months. (The prince-bishop was in a rush to finish furnishing his new home in time for a visit from Habsburg Empress Maria Theresa.) Tiepolo was a master of three-dimensional illusion—and here, he employs one of his favorite tricks, with actual 3-D feet and other features breaking the frame of his faux 3-D frescoes.

The ceiling celebrates the esteemed prince-bishop, who smirks in the medallion with a red, ermine-trimmed cape. This guy had a healthy ego. The ceiling features Apollo (in the sunburst) and a host of Greek gods, all paying homage to the P-B. Ringing the room are the four continents, each symbolized by a woman on an animal and pointing to the prince-bishop. Walk the perimeter of the room to study and enjoy the symbolism of each continent one by one:

America—desperately uncivilized—sits naked with feathers in her hair on an alligator among severed heads. (Notice the cannibal BBQ going on just to the right. Eeew.)  She's being served hot chocolate, a favorite import and nearly a drug for Europeans back then. The black cloud hovering ominously above her head symbolizes (with great subtlety) how unenlightened Europeans of the time considered this savage continent to be.

Africa sits on a camel in a land of trade (notice the blue vase, the ivory tusk, and the kneeling servant with wafting frankincense) and fantasy animals (based on secondhand reports, and therefore inaccurate—the ostrich has human-horse-like legs). Father Nile, with his blue cloak, represents the river by pouring water from a jug.

Asia rides her elephant (with the backward ear) in the birthplace of Christianity (notice the crosses on the hill) and the alphabet (carved into the block beneath the obelisk).

Europe, who rides a bull, is shown as the center of high culture. And here, Lady Culture points her brush not at Rome, but at

Würzburg. A few portraits are hiding out in this area. The big dog is sniffing the purple-clad architect of the Residenz building. And Tiepolo includes a self-portrait as well: Find the burgundy-clad fellow in the corner just to the left, between the heads of the two white statues.

White Hall: This hall—with four big paintings portraying various prince-bishops—is actually gray (to provide better contrast) and was kept plain to punctuate the colorful rooms on either side. Also completed at a breakneck pace to meet the Maria Theresa deadline, it's a Rococo-stucco fantasy. (The word "Rococo" comes from the Portuguese word for the frilly rocaille shell.) The stucco decorations (particularly in the corners) have an armor-and-weapons theme, as this marked the entrance to the prince-bishop's private apartments—which had to be carefully guarded. Even the cloth-like yellow decorations above those weapons, draped high in the corners, are made of painted stucco. As you observe the stucco, dripping with symbolism that celebrates the prince-bishop, notice how the Rococo style is free from the strict symmetry of the Baroque. Also notice the stove, which heated the room. There's one in each room, all stoked from service hallways behind. The four gold cupids symbolize the seasons.

• *Straight ahead is the palace gift shop, which leads to a few other interesting rooms. Instead, from the White Hall, continue to your left, following signs for* Rundgang/Circuit.

Imperial Hall: Enjoy the artistic ensemble of this fine room in its entirety and feel its liveliness. This glorious hall—which was smartly restored—is the ultimate example of Baroque: harmony, symmetry, illusion, and the bizarre; lots of light and mirrors facing windows; and all with a foundation of absolutism (absolute power vested in one ruler, inspired by Louis XIV). Take a moment to marvel at all the 3-D tricks in the ceiling. Here's another trick: As you enter the room, look left and check out the dog in the fresco (at the top of the pillar). When you get to the window, have another look...notice that he has gotten older and fatter while you were crossing the hall.

The room features three scenes: On the ceiling, find Father Main (the local river—I call him "Dirty Old Man River") amusing himself with a nymph, whose blue shroud breaks the frame as it flows and flutters down the wall (subtly shifting from 3-D illusion to three actual dimensions). The two walls recount more history. On one (to the right as you enter), the bishop presides over the marriage (in 1156, but with more modern dress) of a happy Barbarossa (whose bride was actually 12 years old, unlike the woman in the painting, who looks considerably older; for more on Barbarossa, see the "Würzburg's Beginnings" sidebar, earlier). The bishop's power is demonstrated through his oversized fingers (giving the benediction) and through the details of his miter (tall hat), which—unlike his face—is not shown in profile, to allow you to see his coat of arms. Opposite that (left wall as you enter) is the payoff: Barbarossa, now the Holy Roman Emperor, gives the bishop Franconia and the secular title of prince. Notice the bishop touching Barbarossa's scepter with two fingers, performing an oath of fealty. From this point onward, the prince-bishop rules. Also in the Imperial Hall, the balcony offers a great vantage point for surveying the Italian section of the garden.

• If you're not already on a guided tour, keep a lookout for any group headed from here into the South Wing—if you see one, join it. Otherwise, continue with me into the...

North Wing (Northern Imperial Apartments): This wing is a string of lavish rooms—evolving from fancy Baroque to fancier Rococo—used for the prince-bishop's VIP guests. It's a straight shot, with short descriptions in each room, to the **Green Lacquered Room** in the far corner. This room is named for its silver-leaf walls, painted green. The Escher-esque inlaid floor was painstakingly restored after WWII bombings. Have fun multiplying in the mirrors before leaving.

Keep going through a few more small rooms, which serve as a gallery for paintings, and then step out into the **hallway.** In this area, look for the little four-foot-tall doors that were used by tiny servants who kept the stoves burning, unseen from inside the walls. Also in the hallway are photos of the building's destruction in the 1945 firebombing of Würzburg, and its subsequent restoration. While about three-quarters of the Residenz was destroyed during World War II, the most precious parts—the first rooms on this tour, including the Tiepolo frescoes—were unscathed, partly because these important halls were located in a stout stone structure rather than a more fragile wooden one. A temporary roof saved the palace from total ruin, but it was not until the late 1970s that it was returned to more or less its original condition.

• If you haven't yet joined a tour but want to see the South Wing, find your way back to the Imperial Hall and wait until a group comes along. Then tag along for about 15 minutes as you stroll the...

South Wing (by Tour Only): The dark and woody South Wing feels more masculine than the North Wing. In this wing's string of rooms, you'll first come to the waiting room (antechamber), the audience chamber/throne room (with circa-1700 Belgian tapestries showing scenes from the life of Alexander the Great), and the Venetian Room (which was a bedroom; note the three tapestries, made around 1740 in Würzburg). The rooms become progressively more ornate until you reach the South Wing's climax: the Mirror Cabinet.

The 18th-century **Mirror Cabinet** was where the prince-bishop showed off his amazing wealth. It features six lavish pounds of gold leaf, lots of Asian influence, an allegory of one of the four continents in each corner, and painted figures on the reverse side of glass. Because it couldn't be removed, it was destroyed by WWII bombing raids in 1945. The doors in this room are original, but everything else was restored in the 1980s based on photos taken by the Nazis, who knew that regardless of how the war turned out, Germany would be rebuilding.

The **Art Gallery** room is next, with portraits of different prince-bishops who ruled until the early 1800s, when Napoleon said, "Enough of this nonsense" and secularized politics in places like Franconia.

You can leave the escorted tour at this point and explore the **history exhibit,** including Napoleonic-age furniture and a barbaric carousel where children competed to lop off papier-mâché heads and noses—illustrating child-oriented violent games long before videogames were known. This route eventually leads to the **gift shop.**

• *Finish your tour of the Residenz at the Court Chapel. To get there, head back down the stairs, past the ticket office and through the locker room. Follow signs to the southern wing of the big complex. An arch leads left into a courtyard, from which a humble door leads toward the ornate chapel. Follow signs to Court Chapel/Hofkirche.*

Court Chapel (Hofkirche)

This sumptuous chapel was for the exclusive use of the prince-bishop (private altar upstairs with direct entrance to his residence) and his court (ground floor). The decor and design are textbook Baroque. Architect Johann Balthasar Neumann was stuck with the existing walls. His challenge was to bring in light and create symmetry—essential to any Baroque work. He did it

with mirrors and hidden windows. All the gold is real—if paper-thin—gold leaf. The columns are "manufactured marble," which isn't marble at all but marbled plaster. This method was popular because it was uniform, and the color could be controlled. Pigment was mixed into plaster, which was then rolled onto the stone or timber core of the column. This half-inch veneer was then polished. You can tell if a "marble" column is real or fake by resting your hand on it. If it warms up, it's not marble.

The faded painting in the dome high above the altar shows

WÜRZBURG

three guys in gold robes losing their heads (for more on these martyred Irish monks, see the "Würzburg's Beginnings" sidebar, earlier). The two side paintings are by the great fresco artist Tiepolo.
Since the fresco plaster wouldn't dry in the winter, Tiepolo spent
his downtime painting with oil.
• *To reach the garden, enter through the gate at the right of the Residenz
building.*

Residenz Garden
One of Germany's finest Baroque gardens is a delightful park
cradling the palace. It has three sections: the East Garden, the

South Garden, and the nursery
grounds. The South Garden, just
inside the gate, features statues of
Greek gods (with lots of kidnap-
ping action); carefully trimmed,
remarkably conical, 18th-century
yew trees; and an orangery (at the
far back). The nursery grounds
(to the right) is like a rough park.
The East Garden, directly behind
the palace around to the left, is grand—à la Versailles—but uses
terraces to create the illusion of spaciousness (since it was originally
hemmed in by the town wall). Behind the orangery is the replanted
palace kitchen garden.

Würzburg Walk

This one-hour self-guided walk takes you from the Residenz
(which you may want to tour first) to the Old Main Bridge (Alte
Mainbrücke) via the key old-town sights. (If you're not touring the
Residenz before taking this walk, you can start at St. Kilian's Ca-
thedral.)
• *Begin at the fountain in front of the Residenz palace.*

Fountain of Franconia
In 1814, the prince-bishop got the boot, and the region of Fran-

conia was secularized and given
to the Bavarian Wittelsbach dynasty. Technically, Franconia is
a part of Bavaria, but calling a
Franconian a Bavarian is something like calling a Scot an Englishman. This statue—a gift from
the townspeople to their then-
new royal family—turns its back

Würzburg Walk

to the palace and faces the town. It celebrates the artistic and intellectual genius of Franconia with statues of three great hometown boys (a medieval bard, the woodcarver Tilman Riemenschneider, and the Renaissance painter Matthias Grünewald).

• *If Franconia hopped down and ran 300 yards ahead on Hofstrasse, she'd hit the twin-spired cathedral. Meet her there. As you walk, think about how the city was essentially destroyed in 1945 and later rebuilt. At the cathedral, circle around the right, and enter the church through its heavy bronze side door (before the underground passage and across from the modern cathedral museum).*

St. Kilian's Cathedral (Dom)

This building's core is Romanesque (1040-1188), with Gothic spires and Baroque additions to the transepts. It was built as a Catholic church and stayed that way after the Reformation.

Cost and Hours: Free, Mon-Sat generally 10:00-19:00, Sun 13:00-18:00, daily Easter-Oct closes midday for brief services, tel. 0931/3866-2900, www.dom-wuerzburg.de.

Visiting the Church: The cathedral was destroyed in World War II and rebuilt in the 1960s with a passion for mixing historic and modern styles. Before 1945, the entire church was slathered in Baroque stucco decor, as the apse is today. The nave has a cohesive design, progressing from the menorah (representing the Old Testament) in the back, past tombstones of centuries of prince-bishops and a crucified Jesus (above the high altar), to the apse, where a resurrected Christ, riding a golden disc, welcomes you into a hopeful future. The skulls of Würzburg's three favorite saints—those Irish monks martyred in the seventh century—lie in a box within the altar (see "Würzburg's Beginnings" sidebar, earlier).

Halfway along the nave (on the left side, as you face the altar) is a fine memorial to the 15th-century Prince-Bishop Rudolf von Scherenberg, whose name means "scissors mountain" (see his coat of arms). Scherenberg ruled until he was 94 years old. Carved by Tilman Riemenschneider, this tombstone is an example of late-Gothic realism. Back then, it was outrageous to portray an old bishop as...an old bishop (looking at the tombstone, you can tell he needs dentures). The next prince-bishop, whose tomb is to the right of Scherenberg's, saw how realistic his predecessor's was and insisted on having an idealized portrait (also by Riemenschneider) done to his satisfaction before he died. (He's looking implausibly dashing.)

• *Leave the church the way you entered. Outside, look up at the three martyrs (before they were beheaded), high on the building opposite. Walk a few steps downhill (to the left) and notice, embedded in the cathedral wall, the tomb of the great local artist Riemenschneider, placed here after the church's cemetery was moved. If you're interested in a fresh take on religious art, go into the modern Cathedral Museum across the way. Otherwise, skip ahead and continue downhill through the tunnel on your way to the basilica.*

Cathedral Museum (Museum am Dom)

This museum features a refreshing, poignant juxtaposition of old and new religious art, managing to be provocative in a constructive way. It pairs 11th- to 18th-century works with modern interpretations, sprinkles it all with a Christian theme, and wraps it in a shiny modern building. With an emphasis on more cutting-edge contemporary works, it does an impressive job of respecting "religious art" for both its artistic and spiritual qualities.

Cost and Hours: €4, €5 combo-ticket includes Cathedral

Treasury, Tue-Sun 10:00-17:00, closed Mon, tel. 0931/3866-5600, www.museum-am-dom.de.
• *Upon leaving the museum, hook right through a tunnel, which emerges on a delightful urban scene. Straight ahead, Domstrasse leads down to the spire of the City Hall and the Old Main Bridge (where this walk ends). But we're looping right. Go a block up Kürschnerhof, where a staircase leads into the...*

Neumünster Basilica

Like the cathedral, this church has a Romanesque body with a Baroque face. Climb the stairs to take a look inside, appreciating the church's rounded Romanesque nave decorated (like the outside) with bubbly Baroque stucco.

Return to Kürschnerhof and continue up the street, noticing the vineyards in the distance. Appreciate the relative quiet here in the heart of town. Locals wouldn't have it any other way—electric trolleys, bikes, and pedestrians in a thriving and car-free commercial zone.
• *Enter the square on the left with the lacy, two-tone church.*

Upper Market Square (Oberer Markt)

Imagine this square during the wine fest in June—with 75 vintners showing off their best wines—or during the Christmas market, when the square is full of quaint stalls selling holiday goodies. The fancy yellow-and-white, Rococo-designed Falken Haus (House of the Falcon) dates from 1751, when the landlady gave a wandering band of stucco artists a chance to show their stuff (inside are the TI and library).
• *Continue past the Falken Haus, passing the church on your right, into...*

Market Square (Marktplatz)

Würzburg's Marktplatz is a great scene. The obelisk at its center, built in 1805, has a relief showing romantic maidens selling fruits, a hare, and other wares. To this day, the square is host to a bustling produce and flower market four days a week. Under the covered walkway, find a fountain with the modern statue nicknamed "Market Barbara" *(Markt Barbel)*, which recalls a traditional merchant woman. From there, a line often leads to the **Bratwurststand am Markt** (under the yellow-and-white awning, near the covered walkway), where cheap sausage sandwiches are made and sold to eager locals. Watch the wiener-folding action through the side window, or grab a wurst yourself (let them know whether you want yours "*mit*"—with mustard—or "*ohne*"—without). Beyond that, anchored like a Hansel-and-Gretel barnacle to the foot of the church, is **Brandstetter's Stehcafé,** a venerable choice for a coffee-and-cake break while you stand and watch the crowds.

Marienkapelle

The two-tone late-Gothic church was the merchants' answer to the prince-bishop's cathedral. Since Rome didn't bankroll the place, it's ringed with "swallow shops" (like swallows' nests cuddled up against a house)—enabling the church to run little businesses. The sandstone statues (in the small alcoves partway up the columns; they're replicas of Riemenschneider originals) depict the 12 apostles and Jesus. The famous Adam and Eve statues (flanking the side entrance to the church) show off Riemenschneider's mastery of the human body. Continue around the church to the west portal, where the carved Last Judgment (above the main doors) shows kings, ladies, and bishops—some going to heaven, others making up the chain gang bound for hell, via the monster's mouth. (This was commissioned by those feisty town merchants tired of snooty bluebloods.) Continue around to the next entry (which faces a *Biergarten* under chestnut trees) to see the Annunciation, with a cute angel Gabriel telling Mary (the lilies symbolize her virginity) the good news. Notice how God whispers through a speaking tube as Baby Jesus slips down and into her ear.

• *Go back around to the market (Adam-and-Eve side) and leave—passing the obelisk—in the direction of the yellow building. Follow Schustergasse, a pedestrian lane lined with shops that leads back to Domstrasse (with tram tracks). The cathedral is on your left, while the City Hall and Old Main Bridge are to the right. Head right to the City Hall's tower.*

City Hall (Rathaus)

Würzburg's City Hall is relatively humble because of the power of the prince-bishop. As you face the building, go around the left side to find the *Gedenkraum 16 März 1945* memorial (free, always open). This commemorates the 20-minute Allied bombing raid on March 16, 1945, and the resulting firestorm that destroyed—and demoralized—Würzburg six weeks before the end of World War II. The damage was almost as bad as in Dresden: Nearly every downtown building was reduced to a shell, with roofs, floors, and windows gone. Most residents survived in bomb shelters, but 5,000 died—largely women and children. Check out the model of the devastated town, and read the interesting panels about the rise of Nazism and the brutality of war and the hope brought by a spirit of reconciliation.

• *As you leave City Hall, notice the horizontal lines cut into the archway on your right. These mark the floodwaters* (Hochstand des Maines) *of the years 1342, 1682, and 1784. Now, find the bridge.*

Old Main Bridge (Alte Mainbrücke)

This isn't the town's "main" (as in primary) bridge; rather, it spans the Main (pronounced "mine") River, which flows through Frankfurt and into the Rhine.

The bridge, from 1133, is the second-oldest in Germany. The 12 statues lining the bridge are Würzburg saints and prince-bishops. Walk to the St. Kilian statue (with the golden sword)—one of the three monks who are shown being beheaded in the Residenz Palace's chapel. Squint up at Kilian, still with his head on, pointing to God. This is a great spot to linger with the locals as

you drink in the view and perhaps a glass of the local wine.

Beyond Kilian you may see river cruise ships moored by the next bridge. The rising popularity of river cruising (from Amsterdam to Budapest) is bringing lots of crowds and business to towns like Würzburg.

High above the city, capping the hill beyond the bridge, is the Marienberg Fortress (described at the end of this walk). And downstream are three stacks marking a power plant. Between here and there find the old crane, built in 1770 to further the city's desirability as a river trading port. Along the embankment near the crane are a recommended beer garden (named for the crane) and a fish-and-chips boat—and lots of people picnicking (all described later, under "Eating in Würzburg").

The hillside (beyond the crane) is blanketed with grapevines destined to become the fine Stein Franconian wine. Goethe, the

great German author, ordered 900 liters of this vintage annually. A friend once asked Goethe what he thought were the three most important things in life. He said, "Wine, women, and song." The friend then asked, "If you had to give one up, which would it be?" Without hesitating, Goethe answered "Song." Then, when asked what he would choose if he had to give up a second item, Goethe paused and said, "It depends on the vintage."

• *Consider stopping here and having lunch at the recommended Alte Mainmühle restaurant, with a terrace overlooking the bridge (at the near end). On warm summer evenings, the restaurant sets up a little wine stand at the start of the bridge—worth returning to at sunset to buy a glass of wine to sip while you do laps around the bridge. Or you can continue on to the fortress on the hill above you.*

Marienberg Fortress (Festung Marienberg)

This 13th-century fortified retreat was the original residence of Würzburg's prince-bishops (before the opulent Residenz across the river was built). After being stormed by the Swedish army during the 17th-century Thirty Years' War, the fortress was expanded in Baroque style.

Cost and Hours: Grounds-free; Prince's Garden-free, daily 9:00-17:30 except Mon until 16:00, closed Nov-March; Prince's Building Museum-€4.50, €6.50 combo-ticket includes Mainfränkisches Museum, different €6 combo-ticket includes tour—described next, Tue-Sun 9:00-18:00, closed Mon and Nov-March, tel. 0931/355-1750, www.schloesser.bayern.de; Mainfränkisches Museum-€4, €6.50 combo-ticket includes Prince's Building Museum, Tue-Sun 10:00-17:00, Nov-March until 16:00, closed Mon year-round, tel. 0931/205-940, www.mainfraenkisches-museum.de.

Tours and Information: On weekends from April to October, a 45-minute English-language tour brings the fortress to life (€3.50 or €6 combo-ticket that includes Prince's Building Museum, Sat-Sun at 15:00, none off-season, buy tickets at museum shop in the inner courtyard). The inexpensive *Marienberg Castle* booklet, sold throughout the fortress, is well-written and has basic information on both museums.

Getting There: To walk there, cross the Old Main Bridge and follow small *Festung Marienberg* signs to the right uphill for a heart-thumping 20 minutes. Or take infrequent bus #9 (direction: Festung) from the middle of town—not the bridge—to the last stop (Schönborntor) and walk through the tunnel to enter the fortress (runs every 30 minutes daily 9:30-18:00, times listed at stops, departs from Residenzplatz and Juliuspromenade). Consider taking the bus up and walking down (follow *Fussweg zur Altstadt* signs). Taxis wait near the Old Main Bridge (€10 to fortress).

Visiting the Fortress: The **fortress grounds** provide fine city views and a good place for a picnic. You can wander freely through the fortress courtyards and peek into the bottom of the original keep (tower stronghold at the center of the complex) and the round church, where carved relief monuments to former bishops decorate the stone floor. For the best views of the town, go through the archway off the inner courtyard (next to church entrance) into the **Prince's Garden**—look for the *Fürstengarten* sign.

The fortress houses two museums: The **Mainfränkisches Museum,** which highlights the work of Tilman Riemenschneider, Germany's top woodcarver and onetime mayor of Würzburg, is in the red-and-white building at the back of the fortress, near the bus stop. Riemenschneider fans will also find his work throughout Würzburg's many churches (such as in the cathedral, described on page 415). A visitor's guide (in English) directs the way, but it provides little real information.

The **Prince's Building Museum** (Fürstenbaumuseum) is in the inner courtyard. The first floor shows off relics of the prince-bishops (some signs in English), and the second floor focuses on the history of Würzburg (German only). You'll wander through big, mostly empty rooms with a few sparse exhibits and Würzburg views through hazy windows.

Sleeping in Würzburg

Würzburg's hotels and hostels are a stress-free option for a first or last night when flying into or out of Frankfurt. Trains run at least hourly between Würzburg and Frankfurt's airport; the journey takes 1.5 hours. Hotels tend to discount the prices listed during slow months—November to April, and sometimes in August as well.

As Würzburg is a convention town, it has ample chain hotels that can be a great value in slow times—consider searching online for the dates you're in town. My listings are smaller places with more personality and rates that are less likely to fluctuate. In these hotels, quieter rooms are in back, front rooms have street noise, and all rooms are entertained by church bells.

Most of these listings are less than a 10-minute walk from the train station and perfectly situated for sightseeing. To reach nearly all of them, head up Kaiserstrasse from the station to Barbarossaplatz (with the circular awning) or take the tram one stop to Juliuspromenade. Hotel zum Winzermännle and Hotel Alter Kranen are closer to the river; consider riding a tram to the Dom or the Rathaus stops, respectively. If you're driving, you'll likely have to park in a garage near your hotel (about €8/day) as street parking is scarce.

$$$ Hotel Würzburger Hof has an elegant lobby and 34 large, Baroque rooms right at the Juliuspromenade tram stop. They have two types of rooms: smaller but perfectly fine "comfort" rooms and larger "superior" rooms (elevator, good windows that dampen street noise, Barbarossaplatz 2, tel. 0931/53814, www.hotel-wuerzburgerhof.de, info@hotel-wuerzburgerhof.de).

$$ Hotel Barbarossa, tucked away on top of a tall medical-office building above the busy Barbarossaplatz intersection, has a more modern, youthful sensibility than the others listed here and is a good value. Its 18 rooms combine sleek minimalism and a respect for traditional design (RS%, rooftop terrace, elevator, Theaterstrasse 2, fourth floor, tel. 0931/3291-9091, www.hotelbarbarossa-wuerzburg.de, info@hotelbarbarossa-wuerzburg.de, run by hard-working Christine).

$$ Hotel zum Winzermännle has 20 bright rooms along a busy pedestrian street in the city center, but its double-paned windows keep things quiet. The atmosphere is simple but tastefully done, in a hotel the Fick family has run for three generations (elevator, reception up one floor from street, Domstrasse 32, tel. 0931/54156, www.winzermaennle.de, info@winzermaennle.de, friendly Alexandra and her parents).

$$ City Hotel Schönleber has 33 simple, up-to-date rooms fronting a busy street—in open-window weather, it's worth requesting a room on the courtyard (cheaper rooms with shared bath, elevator, from Barbarossaplatz angle left down Theaterstrasse to #5, tel. 0931/304-8900, www.cityhotel-schoenleber.de, reservierung@cityhotel-schoenleber.de, Ulrich Kölbel).

$$ Hotel Alter Kranen has 16 standard rooms with a tidy, business-class vibe right along the river (but only three rooms have views—try requesting one when you reserve). This hotel is farther from the train station than the others listed here, but a bit handier to the Market Square/Old Main Bridge action (air-con in top-floor rooms only, elevator, Kärrnergasse 11, tel. 0931/35180, www.hotel-alter-kranen.de, mail@hotel-alter-kranen.de).

$$ City Hotel Würzburg has 33 comfortable rooms on a street with a pleasant neighborhood feel (no elevator, from Barbarossaplatz follow Theaterstrasse and take your first left onto Semmelstrasse, Semmelstrasse 28, tel. 0931/780-0990, www.cityhotel-wuerzburg.de, info@cityhotel-wuerzburg.de, Ulrich Kölbel).

$ Hotel Dortmunder Hof offers 13 simple, bright, slightly musty rooms on a quiet back street. Mellow jazz tunes sometimes play in the cozy restaurant and wine bar, where you'll check in and enjoy a warm welcome (wonderful breakfast, elevator, reception in wine bar to right of entrance; from train station, turn right onto Juliuspromenade, then jog left a block onto Innerer Graben, Innerer Graben 22, tel. 0931/56163, www.dortmunder-hof.de, info@dortmunder-hof.de, Hennig-Rink family).

¢ Babelfish Hostel, across the street from the station, welcomes travelers of all ages to its 18 colorful rooms. This laid-back place is eco-friendly, modern, and feels safe (private rooms available—some with kitchenettes, breakfast extra, roof deck, wheelchair-accessible, reception on second floor, Haugering 2, tel.

0931/304-0430, www.babelfish-hostel.de, info@babelfish-hostel. de).

¢ Würzburg's official **youth hostel** (*Jugendherberge*) is across the river in a former women's prison (private and family rooms; 20-minute walk from station: cross Old Main Bridge and turn left on Saalgasse to Fred-Joseph-Platz 2; or take tram #3 or #5 to Löwenbrücke stop, then follow *Jugendherberge* signs; tel.0931/4677-860, www.wuerzburg.jugendherberge.de, wuerzburg@jugendherberge. de).

Eating in Würzburg

IN THE CENTER

The **Bürgerspital** is a grand Baroque complex that once housed one of the city's medieval charity hospices. Back then, rich Würzburgers created charitable foundations to support the city's elderly and poor. They began making and selling wine to fund their charity work, and this tradition continues today. Still occupying grand Baroque complexes, the foundations have restaurants, wine shops, and extensive wine cellars. These are no longer basic soup kitchens but well-respected, quite elegant eateries that also happen to support a good cause. The Bürgerspital—the oldest and best-known of these foundations—now cares for about a hundred local seniors and also provides two eating options:

$$ Weinstuben Bürgerspital is a candlelit but informal restaurant that serves beautifully presented Franconian specialties. Depending on the weather, you can dine outside in a fine old courtyard or indoors in traditional or modern rooms (daily 10:00-24:00, enter at Theaterstrasse 19, tel. 0931/352-880).

$$ Weingut Bürgerspital, an unintimidating wine shop/ tasting room on a busy corner, serves up small dishes in a contemporary setting. The staff is happy to educate you on the basics of Franconian wine (flights available, Tue-Sat 9:00-24:00, Sun-Mon 11:00-18:00, Theaterstrasse 19, tel. 0931/350-3441).

The Bürgerspital's fun, drinks-only place, **Hockerle,** is described later, under "Places for a Memorable Snack or Drink."

Other Central Options

$$ Wirtshaus Lämmle is just right for a wine garden serving traditional Franconian dishes under chestnut trees with a view of the back side of the Marienkapelle (Mon-Sat 11:00-22:00, Sun until 16:00, Marienplatz 5, tel. 0931/54748).

$$$ Backöfele is a fun hole-in-the-wall (literally, though it's quite big once you enter). Named "The Oven" for its entryway, this place is a hit with Germans, offering a rustic menu full of traditional meat and fish dishes. You can sit inside or in the delightful, glassed-in, cobbled courtyard (daily 12:00-23:00, reservations smart; a couple of blocks beyond City Hall, Ursulinergasse 2; tel. 0931/59059, www.backoefele.de).

$$$ Weinhaus zum Stachel, Würzburg's oldest *Weinhaus,* originated as the town's tithe barn—where people deposited 10 percent of their produce as tax. In 1413, it began preparing that produce and selling wine. Today, its stone-and-ivy courtyard is one of the city's most elegant settings for enjoying fresh fish and gourmet Franconian meals. In bad weather, you'll eat in the woody medieval dining room, where the ceiling depicts a *Stachel* (mace) in deadly action (Tue-Sat 11:30-22:00, Sun until 16:00, closed Mon, reservations smart, Gressengasse 1, tel. 0931/52770, www. weinhaus-stachel.de).

$ Dean & David on Marktplatz, part of a national chain, is deservedly a favorite for a fast, inexpensive, and healthy meal with views of the market action. They have a pleasant modern interior and tables on the square (super-fresh salads, veggie dishes, curries, soups, wok plates, sandwiches, smoothies, Mon-Sat 10:00-21:00, Sun 11:00-19:00, look for modern building kitty-corner from church, Marktplatz 4, tel. 0931/4522-8303).

$$ Sternbäck is an inviting *Kneipe* (pub) with rickety tables spilling onto a busy square. This is where locals from all walks of life gather for a drink and cheap eats. The hip, friendly staff can recommend something that will satisfy you, including Franconian classics and curries (daily 9:00-late, breakfast served until 13:00, Sternplatz 4, tel. 0931/54056).

$ Weinstube Maulaffenbäck, hidden in an alley near Market Square with a few outdoor tables, is a characteristic place for cheap Franconian meals and good wine. In accordance with a unique Würzburger tradition, if you order wine at lunch between 10:00 and 12:00, you're welcome to bring your own cold cuts and bread (the butcher next door is open until 18:00)—they'll provide the plate and fork (Mon-Thu 10:00-22:00, Fri-Sat until 23:00, closed Sun in summer, otherwise 10:00-16:00, Maulhardgasse 9, tel. 0931/4677-8700).

Lunch: A couple of blocks east of Market Square, **$ Pasta e Olio** may look like an anonymous fast-food stand, but here the pasta is made fresh daily by the same family that's been running the place for three generations. The limited menu usually includes a pasta dish, lasagna, a vegetarian option, and mixed *antipasti*. Place your order cafeteria style, then eat standing at one of the tables (Mon-Fri 8:00-17:00, Sat until 16:00, closed Sun, no WC, Eich-hornstrasse 6, tel. 0931/16699). Lots of other cheap, fast, stand-up lunch places—serving various cuisines—are nearby, between here and Market Square.

ON THE RIVERFRONT

$$$ Alte Mainmühle, on the bridge in a converted mill, is a great place to end your walking tour or enjoy a sunset. On a warm day, nothing beats a cold beer on their deck, which over-looks the river and the for-tress—choose from their sunny top-floor terrace or the shade below. (They also run a wine stand on the Old Main Bridge on summer evenings.) If din-ing inside, I'd sit upstairs

rather than on the lower level. They have fresh fish specials and tra-ditional fare with a Franconian twist. Their homemade sourdough bread *(Natursauerteigbrot)* is a delicious nod to their milling history (daily 11:00-22:00, Mainkai 1, tel. 0931/16777).

$$ Alter Kranen Brauerei-Gasthof is a youthful eatery with a big beer hall interior and outdoor tables around the old crane overlooking the river (try the local brew—Würzburger Hofbräu, table service only, daily 11:00-24:00, a couple of blocks down from the Old Main Bridge at Kranenkai 1, tel. 0931/9913-1546). They kick off evenings with a popular happy hour (cheap beer and cock-tails, 17:00-19:00).

$ Fischbar zum Krebs, a fun-loving little fish-and-chips boat, is permanently tied up a bit downstream from the Old Main Bridge. With a commotion of funky tables and lots of riverside park benches nearby, it caters to a youthful crowd and is the cheapest meal on the water. They serve local fish—trout, pike-perch, and carp—with English-style malt vinegar and sea salt. Place your order at the counter onboard. You'll have to fetch your own beer, and if ordering beer or wine you have to stay on the boat (likely daily 14:00-23:00 in summer, closed in bad weather and Nov-April).

Riverfront Picnic: A parklike stretch of riverbank from the Old Main Bridge to the crane is made-to-order for picnicking. There are plenty of benches and a long, inviting concrete embank-ment to spread out your meal. It comes with beer-drinking stu-dents, the down-and-out collecting their bottles, and great views of the river, bridge, and castle.

PLACES FOR A MEMORABLE SNACK OR DRINK

$ Café Michel, right on Upper Market Square and next to the TI, is a family-oriented bakery and teahouse with quiet indoor seating and tables on the square. They offer soups, sandwiches, and an im-pressive selection of cakes and strudels (daily until 18:00, Markt-platz 11).

WÜRZBURG

$ Goldene Gans Biergarten is a sloppy riverside beer garden on the west side of the river, with wooden benches, shaded views of the Old Main Bridge, forgettable food, and good beer (daily 11:00-23:00—weather permitting, closed off-season; to the left about a block after you cross the Old Main Bridge).

Hockerle, a funky little time warp, is a pub tucked away right next to Weingut Bürgerspital (listed earlier). It serves wine on tap to locals and outgoing tourists who bring in their own food. The regulars start drinking early (no food, wines listed on blackboard, Mon-Fri 9:00-18:00, Sat until 15:00, closed Sun).

Würzburg Connections

From Würzburg by Train to: Rothenburg (hourly, 70 minutes, transfer in Steinach; 45 minutes to Steinach, then 15 minutes to Rothenburg; tiny Steinach-Rothenburg train leaves usually from track 5 shortly after the Würzburg train arrives), **Frankfurt Airport** (1-2/hour, 1.5 hours), **Frankfurt** (1-2/hour, 70 minutes, or 2 hours on cheaper RE trains), **Nürnberg** (2-3/hour, 1 hour), **Munich** (1-2/hour, 2 hours), **Cologne** (hourly, 2.5 hours by ICE; also 3/day by IC, 4 hours), **Leipzig** (hourly, 3 hours, some transfer in Fulda or Bamburg), **Berlin** (hourly, 4 hours, change points vary). Train info: www.bahn.com.

FRANKFURT

Frankfurt, while low on Old World charm, offers a good look at today's no-nonsense, modern Germany. There's so much more to this country than castles and old cobbled squares. Ever since the early Middle Ages, when—as the city's name hints—this was a good place to ford the river, people have gathered here to trade. Frankfurt is a pragmatic city, and its decisions are famously based on what's good for business. Destroyed in World War II? Make that an opportunity to rebuild for trade better than ever. And that's what they did.

With trade came people from around the world. Cosmopolitan Frankfurt—nicknamed "Bankfurt"—is a business hub of the united Europe and home to the European Central Bank. Especially in the area around the train station, you'll notice the fascinating multiethnic flavor of the city. A quarter of its 700,000 residents carry foreign passports, representing 200 different nationalities. Though Frankfurt is often avoided by tourists who consider it just a sterile business and transportation hub, the city's modern energy, fueled in part by the entrepreneurial spirit of its immigrant communities, makes it a unique and entertaining city. And if you visit on a Sunday, when Frankfurt takes the day off from its usual hustle and bustle, you'll find a city cloaked in a village-like charm.

PLANNING YOUR TIME

You might fly into or out of Frankfurt am Main, or at least pass through, as this glossy city links the best wine-and-castles stretch of the Rhine to the north with the fairy-tale Romantic Road to the south. Even two or three hours in Frankfurt leaves you with some powerful impressions: The city's main sights can be enjoyed in a half-day by using its train station (a 12-minute ride from the airport) as a springboard. At a minimum, ride up to the top of the Main Tower for commanding city views and wander through the pedestrian zone to the Old Town area (Römerberg). My self-guided walk provides a framework for your explorations. With more time or an overnight, Frankfurt has plenty of museums and other attractions to choose from.

Orientation to Frankfurt

Frankfurt, with its forest of skyscrapers perched on the banks of the Main (pronounced "mine") River, has been dubbed Germany's "Mainhattan." The city is Germany's trade and banking capital, leading the country in high-rises (mostly bank headquarters)...and yet, a third of Frankfurt is green space.

The convention center *(Messe)* and the red light district are near the train station. Just to the east is the skyscraper banking district and the shopping and pedestrian area around the distinctive Hauptwache building. Beyond that is what remains of Frankfurt's Old Town, around Römerberg, the city's central market square. A short walk across the river takes you to a different part of town: Frankfurt's top museums line the south bank of the Main, and nearby is Sachsenhausen, a charming residential neighborhood and schmaltzy restaurant zone.

TOURIST INFORMATION

Frankfurt has several TIs. The handiest is just inside the **train station**'s main entrance (Mon-Fri 8:00-21:00, Sat-Sun 9:00-18:00, tel. 069/212-38800, www.frankfurt-tourismus.de). Another TI is on **Römerberg square** (Mon-Fri 9:30-17:30, Sat-Sun 10:00-16:00); there's also one at the **airport.** At any TI, buy the city/subway map (the inexpensive basic version is fine). The TI also offers city bus tours and walking tours (see "Tours in Frankfurt," later).

Discount Deals: Two passes sold at TIs are good deals and worth considering if you'll be taking public transportation and visiting several sights. The **Museumsufer Ticket** covers 34 museums (€21, €32 family ticket; valid 2 consecutive days but can be used Sun and Tue since many are closed Mon). The **Frankfurt Card** gives you a transit pass (including connections to and from the airport), up to 50 percent off major museums, and 20 percent off the TI's walking tours, which virtually pays for the pass (€10.50/1 day,

€15.50/2 days; group rate for 2-5 people-€22/1 day, €32/2 days).
A third pass, the **RheinMainCard,** is worthwhile only for travelers with time and interest for farther-flung destinations (€26, €46 group rate for 2-5 people valid 2 days).

ARRIVAL IN FRANKFURT

By Train: Frankfurt's main train station (Hauptbahnhof) bustles with travelers. The TI is in the main hall just inside the front door on the left and lockers are along track 24. Pay WCs and showers are down the stairway by tracks 9 and 10. Inquire about train tickets in the *Reisezentrum,* off the main hall (long hours daily).

Getting out of the station can be a bit tricky. Use the underground passageway *(Bahnhofspassage)* and follow the signs, or better yet, exit straight out the main door located in the middle of the terminal to reach a crosswalk. The station is a 20-minute walk from the convention center *(Messe),* a three-minute subway ride or 20-minute walk from Römerberg, and a 12-minute train ride from the airport. A taxi stand is just outside the main entrance of the train station to your left.

By Car: Follow signs for *Frankfurt,* then *Messe,* and finally *Hauptbahnhof* (train station). The Hauptbahnhof garage (€35/day) is under the station, near most recommended hotels. For information on parking elsewhere in Frankfurt, visit www.parkhausfrankfurt. de.

By Plane: See "Frankfurt Connections," at the end of this chapter.

HELPFUL HINTS

Museum Hours: Most museums are closed Monday. Many stay open until 20:00 on Wednesday.

Festivals and Events: Frankfurt keeps a busy and fun-loving calendar of events. When you're here, be sure to check out what's happening.

Laundry: Located near the train station, **Miele Wash World** is small and often crowded, with loud music from the next-door kiosk likely at night (Moselstrasse 17, by the corner of Münchener Strasse, signs in English). In Sachsenhausen, by the recommended Fichtekränzi restaurant, is a **Wasch Treff** (Wallstrasse 8, instructions in German only). Both are open Monday-Saturday 6:00-23:00 (closed Sun).

Theater: The most active English-language theater on the Continent, **English Theatre Frankfurt** hosts companies from the UK and the US. The quality is good and the delightful theater is small, so it books up well in advance (Gallusanlage 7, closed July-Aug, tel. 069/242-31620, www.english-theatre.de).

Helpful Website: For highlights of the best Frankfurt events

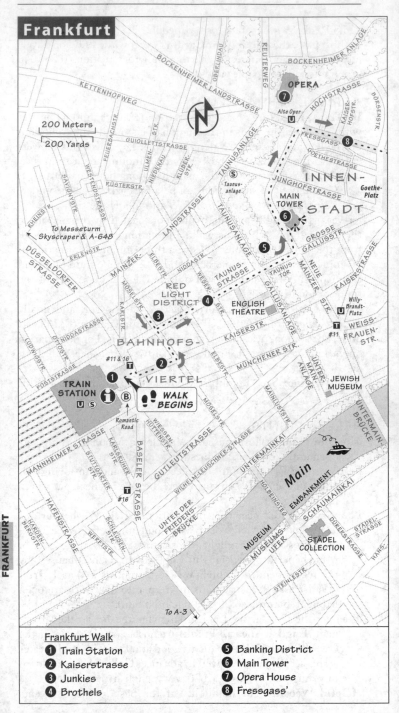

Frankfurt

200 Meters
200 Yards

To Messeturm
Skyscraper & A-648

OPERA

Alte Oper

INNEN-
STADT

Goethe-
Platz

MAIN
TOWER

RED
LIGHT
DISTRICT

ENGLISH
THEATRE

Willy-
Brandt-
Platz

WEISS-
FRAUEN-
STR.

BAHNHOFS-

VIERTEL

TRAIN
STATION

WALK
BEGINS

Romantic
Road

JEWISH
MUSEUM

Main

EMBANKMENT

MUSEUM

STÄDEL
COLLECTION

To A-3

Frankfurt Walk

1 Train Station
2 Kaiserstrasse
3 Junkies
4 Brothels

5 Banking District
6 Main Tower
7 Opera House
8 Fressgass'

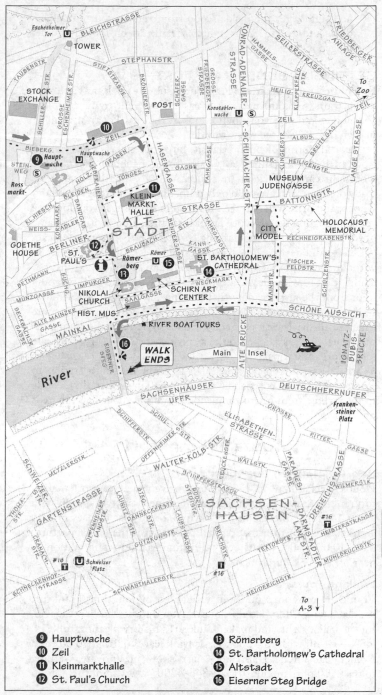

9 Hauptwache

10 Zeil

11 Kleinmarkthalle

12 St. Paul's Church

13 Römerberg

14 St. Bartholomew's Cathedral

15 Altstadt

16 Eiserner Steg Bridge

and sights, get the inside scoop from veteran tour guides Jo-dean and David Ator at http://frankfurt-on-foot-cityguide.blogspot.com.

GETTING AROUND FRANKFURT

By Public Transportation: Frankfurt's subway (U-Bahn) and sub-urban train (S-Bahn) network is easy to use, but trams are more convenient and give you a better look at the city. For transit information in English, see www.rmv.de.

For all forms of public transit, buy your tickets *(Fahrkarten)* from an RMV machine (carry cash, some machines don't accept US credit cards). Tickets are issued with a validating stamp already on them, and are valid only immediately after they're bought. Choose the British flag to see the menu in English. If you don't see your destination listed, type "Frankfurt" first, along with the name of your stop. Choose a regular single ticket (€2.75), short ride ticket (€1.85—valid destinations listed on machines), all-day pass (€5.35 without the airport, €9.55 with), or all-day group ticket (up to 5 adults, €11.30 without the airport, €16.80 with). If you'll be going to or from the airport, note that the one-day Frankfurt Card (described earlier, under "Tourist Information") costs just a bit more than the all-day transit pass and includes sightseeing discounts. An individual one-way ticket to the airport costs €4.90 (no group rate for airport-only trips).

By Taxi: A typical ride, such as from the train station to Römerberg square, costs about €7 (up to €10 in slow traffic). A ride to the airport from my recommended hotels is about €30. There is no Uber in Frankfurt.

Tours in Frankfurt

Hop-On, Hop-Off Bus Tours

Double-decker hop-on, hop-off buses give you an easy orientation to Frankfurt. Two bus companies offer one-hour tours, each with about 14 stops. There's also a "Skyline Tour" that focuses on city architecture. For information and tickets, visit the TI (departures daily 10:00-17:00, about every 30 minutes from train station or near St. Paul's Church).

Walking Tours

Frankfurt on Foot's 3.5-hour walks, led by longtime Frankfurt residents (and Ohio natives) Jodean Ator and her husband David, hit the major sights and make Frankfurt's history meaningful (€14, RS%—€1 off with this book, basic walk leaves daily at 10:30 from Römer/Paulskirche tram stop—just show up, private walking tours—€55/hour, mobile 01520-846-4200, www.frankfurtonfoot.

com, info@frankfurtonfoot.com). Their flexible **"Frankfurt Layover Tour"** is ideal for those with long Frankfurt Airport layovers and includes pickup and drop-off at the airport.

The **TI** offers one-hour walking tours of the historic center (€10.90, daily at 10:30 and sometimes at 14:30, less frequent off-season). They also give 1.5-hour tours of the reconstructed Dom-Römer Quarter at 14:30 (€12.90, daily June-Oct). Reserve ahead by phone, online, or via email (20 percent discount with Frankfurt Card, tours depart from the Römerberg TI; tel. 069/2123-8800, www.frankfurt-tourismus.de, info@infofrankfurt.de).

Local Guide

Elisabeth Lücke loves her city and shares it very well (€70/hour, cash only, reserve in advance, tel. 06196/45787, mobile 0173-913-3157, www.elisabeth-luecke.de, elisabeth.luecke@t-online.de). She enjoys tailoring tours (for example, to the IG Farben building, a.k.a. the "Pentagon of Europe") for military personnel once based around here.

River Boat Tours

These tours are relaxing but pretty boring (with no medieval castles in sight). You can go an hour in either direction or take a grand two-hour ride (departures from near the Eiserner Steg pedestrian bridge). You'll see the impressive skyline, but a river ride in the Romantic Rhine gorge is far more interesting.

Frankfurt Walk

This self-guided sightseeing walk, worth ▲▲, shows you the new Frankfurt and the old, as well as its hard edges and softer side. Starting at the main train station (Hauptbahnhof), it takes you past junkies and brothels, up the Main Tower, through the modern shopping and eating districts, and into the lively square at the center of the Old Town (where you could continue on to the Jewish Holocaust Memorial), before finishing on a bridge overlooking the city and its river. Allow three leisurely hours to complete the full walk. Ideally, do the walk in the morning when the streets are relatively quiet, and you'll finish near lots of great lunch options. To trace the route, see the "Frankfurt" map in this chapter.

Train Station

Frankfurt has Germany's busiest train station: 350,000 travelers make their way to 24 platforms to catch 1,800 trains every day. Hop a train and you can be in either Paris or Berlin in around four hours. While it was big news when it opened in the 1890s, it's a dead-end terminus station, which, with today's high-speed trains, makes it outdated. Complaining that it takes an extra 20 minutes to stop here, railway officials threatened to have the speedy ICE trains bypass Frankfurt altogether unless it dug a tunnel to allow for a faster pass-through stop. But this proved too expensive, and—while some trains stop only at the pass-through airport station—most fast trains begrudgingly serve downtown Frankfurt.

Leaving through the front door, walk directly away from the station to the traffic island facing the pedestrian Kaiserstrasse, and turn to look back at the building's Neo-Renaissance facade—a style popular with Industrial Revolution-era architects. This classic late-19th-century glass-and-iron construction survived World War II. High above, a statue of Atlas carries the world—but only with some heavy-duty help: Green copper figures representing steam power and electricity pitch in. The 1890s were a confident age, when people believed that technology would solve the world's problems.

• *With your back to the station, look down...*

Kaiserstrasse

This grand 19th-century boulevard features appropriately elegant facades that were designed to dress up the approach to what was a fine new station. Towering above and beyond the 100-year-old buildings are the skyscrapers of Frankfurt's banking district. Until a few years ago, the street was rife with local riffraff. But city officials have directed that crowd a couple of blocks to the left, and Kaiserstrasse is fast becoming a people-friendly eating zone.

Warning and Alternate Route: This walk now goes into a neighborhood of hard-drug users and sex workers. If you use common sense, it's not dangerous, but it can be unnerving and creepy at any time of day.

If you'd rather **go directly to the Banking District** and the Main Tower, simply walk straight down Kaiserstrasse four blocks to the park and skip ahead to the "Banking District" section, later in this walk.

• *Walk down Kaiserstrasse, one block away from the station. If you're*

*game, jog left on Moselstrasse and walk a block to the corner of Tau-
nusstrasse. This is where the city contains and controls its sex-and-drug
scene. To the right, Taunusstrasse is lined half with brothels and half
with bank towers. And across Taunusstrasse and farther down Moselstrasse is a heroin-maintenance clinic, known here as a "drug-consumption room."*

▲Junkies

A half-block down Moselstrasse, you'll probably see a gang congregating near one of several **"junkie cafés"** in Frankfurt (no photos allowed). In the 1980s Frankfurt was plagued by one of the
largest open drug markets in Europe. Its parks (and police) were
overwhelmed with needle addicts. Then Frankfurt decided to get
creative, take the crime out of the equation, and go for a pragmatic
harm-reduction approach.

In 1992, Frankfurt began offering "pump rooms" to its hard-
drug users. The idea: Provide a safe haven for addicts (mostly heroin, but also crack and methadone) to hygienically maintain their
habit. Heroin addicts still buy their stuff on the street, but inject
it here with clean needles, with medical help standing by, and a
place to stay if needed. It's strictly not for first-time users and no
dealing or sharing of drugs is allowed. These centers provide a safe
and caring place for addicts to go to maintain their habit and get
counseling and medical help.

These days, overdose deaths are down 75 percent in general,
and there's never been a death in a drug-consumption room. Locals consider the program a success and are accustomed to wasted
people congregating in neighborhoods like this one. While un-
sightly, the compassionate harm-reduction approach that much of
Europe uses to deal with this problem saves lives. Meanwhile, the
US continues to suffer about double the heroin-related deaths per
capita as Europe.

• *Now for the sex. Take a right on Taunusstrasse and walk to Elbestrasse.*

▲▲Brothels

From Taunusstrasse, look (or detour)
left down Elbestrasse, to see a row of
high-rise brothels, or **"eros towers."**
With all the businessmen coming into
town, Frankfurt found there was no effective way to outlaw prostitution. So
the city (like any German city over a
certain population threshold) decided
to funnel sex workers into what it calls
a "tolerance area."

FRANKFURT

About 20 five-story brothels fill original, late-19th-century apartment flats within a block of this spot. Legal since 2002, prostitution is big business here. The women, who are mostly from Eastern Europe, Latin America, and Thailand (only about 2 percent are from Germany), essentially run their own little businesses. They charge around €20 for services and rent their rooms for about €130 a day. It's said that they cover their rent by the end of the businessmen's lunch break (look at the bank towers nearby). German sex workers get health care just like any other workers and pay taxes (on €14 billion of declared income each year).

Crazy Sexy, at Elbestrasse 51, is the biggest of these brothels, with 180 rooms. The first three floors are for women. The fourth floor is for transsexuals. (I was told, "A sex change is expensive, and many workers are making money to pay for their operation.") While it's safe to discreetly climb through these towers, the experience isn't for everyone. And the aggressive women at the neighboring strip shows can be unsettling.

Ever since the Middle Ages, Frankfurt's prostitution industry has gone hand-in-hand with its trade fairs. Today, prostitution thrives with the *Messe* (convention center). Both hotels and sex workers double their prices during big trade fairs, and business varies with the theme of the trade show—the auto show is boom time and the butchers' convention is famously hungry, but Frankfurt's massive book fair is a bust.

To the right of Taunusstrasse, at Elbestrasse 31, is a strip joint called **Pik-Dame.** Old-timers are nostalgic about this lone remnant from "the good old days" in the years after World War II, when 30,000 US soldiers stationed in Frankfurt provided a stimulus for this neighborhood's economy. When the troops left, the Russian mob moved in, replacing any old-time gentility with a criminal and thuggish edge. (Note that there's another drug-consumption center across the street from Pik-Dame.)

Also across the street (at Elbestrasse 34), look for an inconspicuous, dark door, which leads to a cocktail bar, **The Kinly.** Like a Prohibition-era speakeasy, it has no signs, just a call button by the door. Press it, wait for the door to open, then descend the stairs into a cozy, softly lit salon right out of the 1920s (Mon-Sat 19:00-late, closed Sun).

• *Enough sex and drugs. Back on Taunusstrasse, continue out of the red light district and into the banking district. Look up and see why this city (on the Main River) is nicknamed "Mainhattan." Cross the street to the park.*

▲Banking District

Find the statue of the poet Schiller (a Romantic and friend of Goethe), on your left. This park is part of a greenbelt that encircles the old center and marks the site of Frankfurt's medieval moat and fortifications. These walls (along with many castles on the Rhine) were destroyed by the French in 1806. Napoleon had just beaten the Austrians and Russians at Austerlitz, and, since he had the upper hand, he figured it was wise to preemptively obliterate any German fortifications that might haunt him if the Germans turned against France in the future.

The park is the center of Frankfurt's banking district. The post-WWII Marshall Plan was administered from here—requiring fancy money-handling. And the mighty deutsche mark was born in a 1930s-era building facing the park (in the third building, a low Art Deco mansion, now a Deutsche Bundesbank headquarters, on the left of the square as you entered). After World War II, Germany's economy was in chaos. In 1948, the US gave it a complete currency transfer—like a blood transfusion—literally printing up the new deutsche marks and shipping them across the Atlantic to inject them from here directly into the German economy. As if catching water from a fountain, banks naturally grew up around this square.

But Frankfurt was "Bankfurt" long before World War II. This was the Rothschilds' hometown. Born in Frankfurt's Jewish ghetto in 1744, Mayer Rothschild went from being a pauper to the richest banker in the world. His five sons set up businesses in Rome, London, Paris, and Vienna, and in two generations the Rothschild banking dynasty was established. (Their former palace now houses Frankfurt's Jewish Museum, described later, under "Sights in Frankfurt"). Today, locals call Frankfurt's legion of bankers "penguins," as they all dress the same. Tour guides here talk of banks as part of the cultural soil (the way French Riviera guides talk of the big yachts).

Beyond the statue of Schiller stand the twin towers of the Deutsche Bank (not to be confused with the DB—Deutsche Bahn—tower to your left). This country's #1 bank, its assets are greater than the annual budget of the German government. If money makes the world go round, the decisions that spin Germany are made in Frankfurt.

Make a 360-degree spin and survey all the bank towers. Notice the striking architecture. By law, no German worker can be kept out of natural light for more than four hours, so work environments are filled with windows. And, as you can see, Germans like their skyscrapers with windows that open.

• *Find the skyscraper with the red-and-white candy cane on top. That's your destination—the Main Tower. To reach it, continue straight along Taunustor a block, then turn left on Neue Mainzer Strasse and look for the tower symbol on the doors on the right.*

▲▲Main Tower

Finished in 2000, this tower houses the Helaba Bank and offers the best (and only public) open-air viewpoint from the top of a Frankfurt skyscraper. A 55-second, ear-popping elevator ride to the 54th floor (watch the meter on the wall as you ascend) and then 50 stairs take you to the rooftop, 650 feet above the city.

Cost and Hours: €7.50, 20 percent discount with Frankfurt Card; Sun-Thu 10:00-21:00, Fri-Sat until 23:00; closes earlier off-season and during bad weather; enter at Neue Mainzer Strasse 52, between Taunustor and Junghofstrasse, tel. 069/3650-4878, www.maintower.de.

⊘ **Self-Guided Spin-Tour:** Here, from Frankfurt's ultimate viewpoint, survey the city by circling clockwise, starting with the biggest skyscraper (with the yellow emblem).

Designed by Norman Foster (of Berlin Reichstag and London City Hall fame), the **Commerzbank building** was finished in 1997. It's 985 feet high, with nine winter gardens spiraling up its core and windows that open. It's considered the first ecological skyscraper...radically "green" in its day. Just to the left is Römerberg—the Old Town center (the half-timbered houses huddled around the red-and-white church with a green spire; we'll visit there soon).

The **Museum Embankment** (see "Sights in Frankfurt," later) lines Schaumainkai on the far side of the Main River, just beyond the Taunus Tower.

The Rhine-Main **airport,** off in the distance (like a city in the forest), is the largest employment complex in Germany, with 70,000 workers. Frankfurt's massive train station dominates the foreground. From the station, the grand Kaiserstrasse cuts through the city to Römerberg.

The **Frankfurt fair** *(Messe),* marked by the brown skyscraper with the pointy top, is a huge convention center—the size of 40 soccer fields. It sprawls behind the skyscraper that looks like a classical column sporting a visor-like capital. (The protruding lip of the capital is heated so that icicles don't form, break off, and impale people on the street below.) Frankfurt's fair originated in 1240, when the emperor promised all participating merchants safe passage. The glassy black twin towers of the Deutsche Bank in the foreground (nicknamed "Debit and Credit") are typical of mid-1980s mirrored architecture.

The **West End,** with vast green spaces and the telecommunications tower, is Frankfurt's priciest residential quarter. The city's most enjoyable zone cuts from the West End to the right. Stretching from the classic-looking Opera House below are broad and people-filled boulevards made to order for eating and shopping. Find the "Beach Club" filling the rooftop of a parking garage with white tents, two pools, and colorful lounge chairs. This is a popular family zone by day and a chic club after dark.

From here, you can see how the city walls, demolished in 1806, left a string of green zones arcing out from the river. This defined the city limits in the 19th century.

Take a moment from this vantage point to trace the rest of this walk: from the Opera House, along the tree-lined eating and shopping boulevards to St. Paul's Church and Römerberg. After side-tripping from Römerberg out to the cathedral, we'll finish on Eiserner Steg, the iron pedestrian bridge over the Main River.

Now look east, farther out along the river, to the glistening twin towers (standing all alone). At 600 feet tall, these are the striking headquarters of the **European Central Bank.**

As you leave the Main Tower, step into the **Helaba Bank** lobby (next door over from base of elevator). A black-and-white mosaic filling the wall shows cultural superstars of 20th-century Frankfurt, from composer Paul Hindemith to industrialist and humanitarian Oskar Schindler to Anne Frank (see the key on the post nearby for a who's who).

• *Exit right from the Main Tower and continue walking along Neue Mainzer Strasse (crossing Junghofstrasse) for a couple of blocks, to where you see a large square open to your left. Across the square is the Opera House.*

Frankfurt's Good-Living People Zone

Opera House (Alte Oper): Finished in 1880, Frankfurt's opera house celebrated German high culture and the newly created nation. Mozart and Goethe flank the entrance, reminders that this is a house of both music and theater. On a hot day, people of all ages cool their heels in the refreshing fountain in the plaza out front. The original opera house was gutted in World War II. Over the objections of a mayor nicknamed "Dynamite Rudi," the city rebuilt it in the original style, and it opened in 1981. Underneath is a U-Bahn station (Alte Oper).

• *Facing the Opera, turn right down Frankfurt's famous...*

Fressgass': The official names for this pedestrian street are Grosse Bockenheimer Strasse and Kalbächer Gasse...but everyone in Frankfurt calls it the Fressgass', roughly "Feeding Street." Herds of bank employees come here on their lunch breaks to fill their bellies before returning for another few hours of cud-chewing at their computers. It's packed gable-to-gable with eateries and shoulder-to-shoulder with workers wolfing cheap sandwiches, plates of

Asian food, and more. It also offers great people-watching. Join in if you're hungry—or wait for more eating options in a couple of blocks.

• *Fressgass' leads to a square called Rathenauplatz, but it's known as Goethe Platz for its central statue. Cross the square and continue straight—the pedestrian street is now called Biebergasse—another block to the...*

Hauptwache: The small, red-and-white building—which has given its name to the square (and the subway station below it)—was built in 1730 to house the Frankfurt city militia. Now it's a café. The square, entirely closed to traffic, is one of the city's hubs.

• *To the right, at the south side of the square, is the Protestant Katharinenkirche, which was destroyed in the bombing raids of March 1944 and rebuilt after the war. Straight ahead of you is a boulevard called the...*

Zeil: This tree-lined pedestrian drag is Frankfurt's main shopping street. Crowds swirl through the Galeria Kaufhof department store, the Zeil Galerie, and the MyZeil shopping center (the one with the glassy hole in its wall) along the left side of the street. MyZeil has a huge glass atrium shaped like two massive funnels—and can be a mesmerizing sight on a rainy day. A really long escalator, claiming to be the longest in Germany (behind the much shorter twin set by the door) leads straight to the top-floor food court (with good, free WC). On your way, stop on the fourth floor and head toward the streetside windows to see a huge aerial photo of Frankfurt on the floor. This top-down view shows the surprising amount of green space there is in this city.

Lunch and Views at Department Stores: The Galeria Kaufhof has a recommended rooftop cafeteria, Leonhard's (good for lunch or just the views). There's a supermarket with a snack stand and seating in the basement of the MyZeil shopping center (Mon-Sat 7:00-24:00, closed Sun).

• *Continue down Zeil a block to the fountain at the next intersection. Turn right on Hasengasse. In the distance is the lacy red-brick spire of the cathedral. Halfway there, after about two blocks, find the low-key green entrance to Kleinmarkthalle on the right. Enter the market (pay WC downstairs at entry).*

Kleinmarkthalle: This delightful, old-school market was saved from developers by local outcry, and to this day it's a neighborhood favorite. Explore and sample your way through the ground floor. It's an adventure in fine eating (with a line of simple eateries upstairs, too; see "Eating in Frankfurt," later) and a delight for photographers. The far wall is filled with a fun piece of art offering a bird's-eye view of Frankfurt over a charming montage of the many ways locals love their hometown.

• *Exit the Kleinmarkthalle opposite where you entered. Angle right, and climb five steps into a square (Leibfrauenberg) with a red-brick fountain and the 14th-century Church of Our Lady (rebuilt after World War II). On the far side is Lebkuchen-Schmidt, a fun shop selling traditional gingerbread, a local favorite. Turn left and head downhill on Neue Kräme, then cross Berliner Strasse to Paulsplatz.*

▲St. Paul's Church (Paulskirche)

To your right, the former church dominating the square is known as the "cradle of German democracy." It was here, during the political upheaval of 1848, that the first freely elected National Assembly met and the first German Constitution was drafted, paving the way for a united Germany in 1871. Following its destruction by Allied bombs in 1944, the church became the first historic building in the city to be rebuilt. This was a symbolic statement from the German people that they wanted to be free (as they had demonstrated here in 1848), democratic...and no longer fascist. Around the outside of the building, you'll see reliefs honoring people who contributed to the German nation, including Theodor Heuss, the first president, and John F. Kennedy, who spoke here on June 25, 1963.

Step inside; the entrance is around to the left (free, daily 10:00-17:00). Displays described in English tell the story of 1848. Check out the circular mural from the 1980s. Called *The March of Members of Parliament*, it was controversial when unveiled. Commissioned to honor the political heroes of 1848, the portraits are cartoonish figures, with faces hinting of contemporary politicians. Political leaders seem to sneer at the working class, and two naked men who look like they're having sex represent the forces of democracy and monarchy fighting within Germany. Upstairs is a 900-seat assembly hall with no decor except the flags of the 16 states of the Federal Republic of Germany.

FRANKFURT

• *Walk across the square. If you need a break, a variety of eateries offer inviting seating that's perfect for some fun people-watching. Then, cross the next street and tram tracks and you'll enter what's left of Frankfurt's Old Town.*

▲Römerberg

Frankfurt's market square was the birthplace of the city. This is the site of the first trade fairs (12th century), bank (1405), and stock exchange (1585). Now, crowds of tourists convene here. Römerberg's central statue is the goddess of justice without her customary blindfold. She oversees the Town Hall, which itself oversees trade. The Town Hall *(Römer)* houses the *Kaisersaal,* or Imperial Hall, where Holy Roman Emperors celebrated  their coronations. Today, the *Römer* houses the city council and mayor's office. Marriages must be performed in a civil ceremony here to be legal, so you'll see lots of brides and grooms celebrating outside. The cute row of half-timbered homes (rebuilt in 1983) opposite the *Römer* is typical of Frankfurt's quaint old center before the square was completely destroyed in World War II.

The Gothic red-and-white Old Nikolai Church (Alte Nikolaikirche, with fine stained glass from the 1920s by a local artist) dates from the 13th century and was restored after the war. Behind it, closer to the river, is the new **Frankfurt Historical Museum** (€8, Tue-Fri 10:00-18:00, Wed until 21:00, Sat-Sun 11:00-19:00, closed Mon).

Hosting everything from Christmas markets to violent demonstrations, this square is the beating heart of Frankfurt. In its center, the metal plaque that looks like a large manhole cover reminds us that a Nazi book-burning took place in the square on May 10, 1933. Around the edge of the plaque is a quote from the German poet Heinrich Heine, who presciently pointed out that it's a short step from burning books to burning people.

• *Facing the Town Hall, the river and the bridge where this walk ends are just two blocks to the left. But first, we'll take a short detour. Turn left past the Old Nikolai Church and walk through the courtyard of the Schirn Art Center to the big red...*

St. Bartholomew's Cathedral (Kaiserdom)

Holy Roman Emperors were elected at this Catholic church starting in 1152 and crowned here between 1562 and 1792. The cathedral was gutted by fire in 1867 and had to be rebuilt. It was seriously damaged in World War II, but repaired and reopened in 1953. Though the cathedral is free, you must pay to access two sights within the church: a museum (not particularly interesting) and a 328-step tower climb with city views at the top.

Cost and Hours: Cathedral-free, Mon-Thu and Sat 9:00-20:00, Fri and Sun from 13:30, www.dom-frankfurt.de; museum-€4, Tue-Fri 10:00-17:00, Sat-Sun from 11:00, closed Mon, enter from church vestibule, www.dommuseum-frankfurt.de; tower-€5, daily 9:00-18:00, weather permitting, shorter hours Nov-March; tel. 069/7808-9255, www.domturm-frankfurt.de.

Visiting the Cathedral: Enter on the side opposite the river. Note the painted white lines that imitate mortar between stones.

This illusionist architecture was a popular technique for churches. Frescoes from the 15th century survive (flanking the high altar and ringing the choir). They show 27 scenes from the life of St. Bartholomew. The Electors Chapel (to the right of the altar) is where the electors convened to choose the Holy Roman Emperor in the Middle Ages. Everything of value that could be moved was taken out of the church before the WWII bombs came. The delightful sandstone Chapel of Sleeping Mary (to the left of the high altar), carved and painted in the 15th century, was too big to move—so it was fortified with sandbags. The altarpiece and stained glass next to it survived the bombing. As you wander, appreciate the colorful and extravagant tombstones embedded in the walls when the church's cemetery was emptied.

• *Exit the cathedral where you entered and turn left, passing the red-and-white half-timbered, gold-trimmed house that marks the start of the...*

Altstadt ("New Old Town")

This "new" development (officially called the DomRömer Quarter)—70 years in the making—is a reconstruction of the half-timbered Old Town destroyed during World War II. Following the war, some locals wanted to rebuild the original buildings, while others wanted to modernize. The compromise was an ugly concrete building in typical 1970s style that remained until 2010, when reconstruction of this more modern version of the Old Town began.

Pause at the fountain in the center of the main square (a former poultry market), featuring a statue of Friedrich Stoltze, a writer and poet who was born in the former Old Town. Notice the buildings' eclectic mix of colors and styles, some with slate roofs, others with red sandstone facades, and others with doors made from

300-year-old oak. This mix of new and old architecture is a microcosm of today's Frankfurt.

Before the war, this was a lively center of pubs, small businesses, and workshops. While today's Altstadt feels a bit saccharin, the city hopes this mix of reconstructed and new buildings will return the square to something close to its former character.

As you pass Stoltze, turn left to do a loop around the development, checking out the red sandstone columns at #9. Keep turning left until you're parallel with the Schirn Art Center. Look for an opening behind the last set of new buildings on the right: The Stadthaus am Markt is a public area and event space floating above the "Franconofurd"—Roman ruins that were revealed by the Old Town's destruction.

• *Returning to the cathedral, you can turn left on Weckmarkt and continue a couple of blocks to visit the Jewish Holocaust Memorial, and/or the Frankfurt City Model (both free and described later, under "Sights in Frankfurt"). Or head down to the river, turn right, and walk along the pleasant riverfront park to the next bridge. Head out to its center.*

Eiserner Steg Bridge

This iron bridge, the city's second oldest, dates to 1869. (The oldest is just upstream: the Alte Brücke, site of the first "Frank ford"—a fifth-century crossing.) From the middle of the bridge, survey the skyline and enjoy the lively scene along the riverbanks of Frankfurt. These grassy areas are some of the most pleasant parts of the city.

• *For a quick return to your starting point at the main train station (Hauptbahnhof), walk back to Römerberg and take the U-Bahn or board tram #11 or #12.*

Sights in Frankfurt

NEAR RÖMERBERG
▲Goethe House (Goethehaus)

Johann Wolfgang von Goethe (GUH-teh; 1749-1832), a scientist, minister, poet, lawyer, politician, and playwright, was a towering figure in the early Romantic Age; his two-part tragedy, *Faust,* is a masterpiece of world literature. His birthplace, now a fine museum, is furnished as it was in the mid-18th century, when the boy destined to become the "German Shakespeare" grew up here.

Borrow a laminated card at the bottom of the stairs for a refreshingly brief commentary on each of the 16 rooms. Since nothing's roped off and there are no posted signs, it's easy to picture real people living here. Goethe's father dedicated his life and wealth to cultural pursuits, and his mother told young Johann Wolfgang fairy tales every night, stopping just before the ending so that the boy could exercise his own creativity. Goethe's family gave him all the money he needed to travel and learn. His collection of 2,000 books was sold off in 1795. In recent decades, more than half of these have been located and repurchased by the museum (you'll see them in the library). This building honors the man who inspired the Goethe-Institut, which is dedicated to keeping the German language strong.

Cost and Hours: €7, Mon-Sat 10:00-18:00, Sun until 17:30, €3 high-tech but easy-to-use and informative audioguide, English booklet has same info as free laminated cards—worthwhile only as a souvenir; 15-minute walk from Hauptbahnhof up Kaiserstrasse, turn right on Am Salzhaus to Grosser Hirschgraben 23; tel. 069/138-800, www.goethehaus-frankfurt.de.

Schirn Art Center (Schirn Kunsthalle)

This facility is one of Europe's most respected homes of modern and contemporary art. Rotating exhibits pay homage to everything and everyone from Kandinsky and Kahlo to contemporary artists, movements, and topics.

Cost and Hours: €7-10 depending on exhibits, Tue-Sun 10:00-19:00, Wed-Thu until 22:00, closed Mon, Römerberg, tel. 069/299-882-112, www.schirn.de.

IN THE FORMER JEWISH GHETTO

During the early Middle Ages, the most important Jewish communities north of the Alps were along the Rhine, in towns like Cologne, Speyer, Worms, and Frankfurt. Even after the center of Jewish life moved east to Poland and Lithuania, Frankfurt had a large and prominent Jewish community, which included the Rothschilds (the famous banking family).

You can get a feel for Frankfurt's Jewish history with a visit to the Museum Judengasse and the nearby Jewish Holocaust Memorial (at the old Jewish cemetery, just down Battonnstrasse). These sights are a short walk (or one tram stop) east of Romerberg and St. Bartholomew's Cathedral.

▲Jewish Holocaust Memorial, Jewish Cemetery, and Museum Judengasse

This memorial to Frankfurt's Jewish community—devastated by the Holocaust—marks the site of the old Jewish ghetto and where the city's main Börneplatz Synagogue once stood. Commemorating 12,000 murdered Jews, it's a powerful and evocative collection of images.

Museum Judengasse's permanent exhibit focuses on Jewish life in Frankfurt, covering everything from work and school to the arts to relations between the community and Frankfurt's government. The exhibit is built around and within a section of excavated ruins of Europe's oldest Jewish ghetto, where 4,000 people once lived on a quarter-mile stretch of street. You'll see artifacts found in the ruins. Interactive exhibits let you listen to evocative music and Jewish hymns.

Back outside, around the old Jewish cemetery is the Wall of Names, with a tiny tombstone for each Frankfurt Jew deported and murdered by the Nazis (with location and date of death, if known). Pebbles atop each tomb represent Jewish prayers. The memorial gives each victim the dignity of a tombstone and of being named, while a databank inside the adjacent Museum Judengasse keeps their memory alive with a record of everything  known about each person. The markers are alphabetical by last name: Look for Anne Frank (Annelies Marie Frank) about halfway between the cemetery entrance and the end of the wall. The Frank family left Frankfurt for Amsterdam in 1933 and eventually went into hiding. Upon discovery by the Nazis, Anne and her sister were sent to Bergen-Belsen, where she died of typhus.

By peeking through the locked black-metal gate into the cemetery, you can see a few original tombstones that survived the Nazi rampage. In the tree-filled square is a stone tower, built with foundation stones from homes excavated from the Jewish ghetto. The gravel is designed to evoke train tracks and the deportation of so many people to concentration camps.

The paved section marks the footprint of the Börneplatz Synagogue, destroyed on November 9, 1938—a night traditionally known as Kristallnacht. (Because people's lives were also destroyed on that night along with lots of windows and glass, the preferred name is "Pogrom Night.") A plaque on the wall opposite recalls this terrible event. In the wake of World War II, American troops made Frankfurters memorialize each synagogue they destroyed with a plaque like this.

Cost and Hours: Wall of Names and cemetery-always free and viewable (key for cemetery available when museum is open); museum-€6, Tue 10:00-20:00, Wed-Sun until 18:00, closed Mon; Battonnstrasse 47, tel. 069/212-70790, www.museumjudengasse.de.

▲Frankfurt City Model

This ever-evolving model, unrelated to the Jewish story, is next to the Jewish Holocaust Memorial in the City Planning Office (Stadtplanungsamt), located in the same building as the Museum Judengasse. Enter through the frosted sliding doors and step left past the receptionist into an atrium to view a 30-by-20-foot layout on a 1:500 scale. Frankfurt's inner-city skyscrapers are marked *Planungsdezernat*. Since 1960 this model has helped planners envision and track the development of the city and its many massive building projects—even seeing where shadows of new buildings

will fall. Red buildings are those under construction (the city has plans for 20 more skyscrapers in the next decade).

Cost and Hours: Free, Mon-Fri 8:30-18:00, closed Sat-Sun, Kurt-Schumacher-Strasse 10.

NEAR THE RIVER, ON THE NORTH BANK
Jewish Museum (Jüdisches Museum)

This museum, which may be open after a lengthy renovation when you visit, is housed in the former Rothschild family palace, along the river between Römerberg and the train station (Untermainkai 14, tel. 069/2123-5000, www.juedischesmuseum.de).

Riverside Promenade

Just across the road from the Jewish Museum is a lovely riverside promenade—a perfect place to rest your feet and watch people and planes go by.

ACROSS THE RIVER, ON THE SOUTH BANK
▲Schaumainkai and Frankfurt's Museum Embankment (Museumsufer)

The Schaumainkai riverside promenade (across the river from Römerberg over the Eiserner Steg pedestrian bridge, and then to the right) is great for an evening stroll or people-watching on any sunny day. Keep your eyes peeled for nude sunbathers. Every other Saturday, the museum strip street is closed off for a sprawling flea market, and in late August a weekend cultural festival brings food, art, and music to "museum row."

Nine museums in striking buildings line the Main River along Schaumainkai. In the 1980s, Frankfurt decided that it wanted to buck its "Bankfurt" and "Krankfurt" (*krank* means "sick") image. It went on a culture kick and devoted 11 percent of the city budget to arts and culture. The result: Frankfurt has become a city of art. These nine museums (covering topics such as architecture, film, world cultures, and great European masters—the Städel Collection) and a dozen others are all well-described in the TI's *Museum-*

sufer brochure. Of these, a visit to the Städel (listed next) is most worthwhile.

Cost and Hours: All museums here are covered by the Museumsufer Ticket (for details see "Tourist Information," earlier in this chapter); most museums open Tue-Sun 10:00-17:00, Wed until 20:00, closed Mon; www.kultur-frankfurt.de.

Getting There: Take tram #15 or #16 to the Otto-Hahn-Platz stop; bus #46 to the Städel stop; or U-1, U-2, U-3, or U-8 to the Schweizer Platz stop. Or, walk: It's 15 minutes from the Hauptbahnhof via Holbeinsteg Bridge, or just a few minutes' walk over the Eiserner Steg pedestrian bridge from the center of Frankfurt.

▲Städel Museum

With an enormous yet approachable collection spanning Old Masters to modern day, this museum offers up a one-stop European art retrospective.

Cost and Hours: €14, open Tue-Sun 10:00-18:00, Thu-Fri until 21:00, closed Mon; audioguide-€4, on-site restaurant; Schaumainkai 63, tel. 069/605-098-0299, www.staedelmuseum.de.

Visiting the Museum: Begin with Old Masters on the top floor, where you'll find a huge Rembrandt canvas in Room 6— *The Blinding of Samson*—depicting Delilah gleefully making off with a handful of locks, scissors in hand, while one man handcuffs the now-powerless Samson and another gouges out one of his eyes.

The floor below has works by Renoir, Paul Klee, and Marc Chagall, as well as a female head sculpture by Picasso and his 1909 Cubist portrait of Fernande Olivier. Don't miss the canvases by Max Beckmann, who lived in Frankfurt for nearly 20 years before the Nazis banned his work, classifying his art as "degenerate." *Frankfurt Main Station*—looking not at all seedy—was done from memory while Beckmann lived in exile in Amsterdam. In Room 11, *Dog Lying in the Snow* by Franz Marc (who founded the Blue Rider group with Kandinsky—see page 88) is one of the museum's most popular paintings.

On the museum's lower level, you'll find contemporary work— including more by Picasso, a skinny Giacometti sculpture, and avant-garde installations.

Sleeping in Frankfurt

Sleeping in Frankfurt is a gamble: The city's numerous trade fairs *(Messe)* send hotel prices skyrocketing—a €70 double can suddenly shoot up to €300. For an exact schedule, visit www.messefrankfurt. com (scroll down to "Messe Frankfurt Calendar"). During trade fairs, it's best to skip Frankfurt altogether and stay in Würzburg, Bacharach, or St. Goar.

When trade fairs aren't in town, room prices in most Frankfurt hotels fluctuate €10-50 with the day of the week. If you'll be staying overnight in Frankfurt during a nonconvention summer weekend, you can land a great place relatively cheaply. Frankfurt hotels are business-oriented, so many are empty and desperate for guests from Friday night to Monday morning. Although the price categories listed are typical, varying demand may skew them higher or lower.

Keep overnights in Frankfurt to a minimum: Pleasant Rhine and Romantic Road towns are just a quick drive or train ride away, offering a mom-and-pop welcome that you won't find here in the big city.

NEAR THE TRAIN STATION

The following places are within a few blocks of the train station and its fast and handy train to the airport (to sleep even closer to the airport, see "Sleeping at or near Frankfurt Airport," later in this chapter). The Hamburger Hof, Bristol, and Topas hotels are on the north (and most sedate) side of the station. The Manhattan, Concorde, and EasyHotel are along the busy streets just to the northeast of the station. The Victoria, Holiday Inn Express, Ibis Styles, and Five Elements hostel are in the multiethnic neighborhood east of the station. The Ibis Hotel Frankfurt Centrum is south of the station, close to the Main River and within walking distance of the Museum Embankment (Museumsufer). For locations, see the "Frankfurt Hotels & Restaurants" map.

All these listings are well-run and feel safe and respectable. I like staying in this colorful and convenient neighborhood (which gets more gentrified every year). But the red light district is close by, with gritty clubs and hard-drug users. Don't wander into seedy-feeling streets, and use care and common sense after dark.

$$ Hotel Concorde, across the street from the station and then a few doors down Karlstrasse in a restored 1890s building, offers 45 air-conditioned rooms and four-star comfort and professionalism, all at a reasonable price (breakfast extra, elevator, Karlstrasse 9, tel. 069/242-4220, www.hotelconcorde.com, info@ hotelconcorde.de, Marc is manager). Exit the station by track 24, cross the street and head right, walking past the Manhattan Hotel and around the corner to the Concorde. A REWE supermarket is across the street.

$$ Hotel Hamburger Hof, right next to the train station but in a quiet and safe-feeling location, has a classy, shiny lobby and 62 modern rooms. The side facing the station is cheerfully sunny, while rooms on the other side are quieter (air-con, elevator, Poststrasse 10, tel. 069/2713-9690, www.hamburgerhof.com, info@hamburgerhof.com). Exit the station by track 24, cross the street, turn left, and walk to the end of the block.

$$ Bristol Hotel is a swanky 145-room place that serves up style and flair, from its nod to Pacific Rim architecture to its spacious breakfast room and relaxing patio bar. It's just two blocks from the station and enjoys quiet and respectable surroundings (air-con, elevator, huge breakfast buffet, Ludwigstrasse 15, tel. 069/242-390, www.bristol-hotel.de, info@bristol-hotel.de). Exit the station by track 24, cross the street, turn left, then right on Ottostrasse, then left on Niddastrasse to Ludwigstrasse.

$$ Victoria Hotel, two blocks from the station along the grand Kaiserstrasse, has 73 rooms and feels a world apart from the red light district a block away (air-con, elevator, Kaiserstrasse 59, entrance on Elbestrasse, tel. 069/273-060, www.victoriahotel.de, info@victoriahotel.de). From the station, go down the escalators to the underground passageway below the station and follow the *Kaiserstrasse* signs.

$$ Manhattan Hotel, with 55 rooms and an energetic vibe, is a few doors from the station on a busy street. Friendly manager Robert tries to greet all of his guests personally (RS%, air-con, elevator, Düsseldorfer Strasse 10, tel. 069/269-5970, www.manhattan-hotel.com, info@manhattan-hotel.com). Exit the station by track 24, cross the street, and go right until you see the hotel; to cross Düsseldorfer Strasse safely, walk up to the tram stop.

$$ Holiday Inn Express Hauptbahnhof has 116 fresh rooms two blocks from the station, in a quiet location just off Münchener Strasse in the Turkish district (air-con, elevator, Elbestrasse 7, tel. 069/8700-3883, www.fmhos.com, frankfurt@fmhos.com). From the front of the station, use the crosswalk by the tram stop and follow the tracks down Münchener Strasse two blocks to Elbestrasse and turn right.

$$ Ibis Styles Frankfurt City is a small step up from the Ibis Hotel (next listing) and is centrally located just a few blocks from the station. Its 96 funky, colorful rooms help you forget that this is a popular chain hotel (air-con, elevator, Moselstrasse 12, tel. 069/6925-6110, https://ibis.accorhotels.com, H7561@accor.com). From the front of the station, use the crosswalk by the tram stop and follow the tracks down Münchener Strasse one block to Moselstrasse and turn right.

$$ Ibis Hotel Frankfurt Centrum is a good value, with 233 rooms on a quiet riverside street away from the station (breakfast extra, elevator, pay parking, Speicherstrasse 4, tel. 069/273-030, https://ibis.accorhotels.com, h1445@accor.com). Exit the station by track 1 and follow busy Baseler Strasse three blocks, then turn right before the river; it's across the street from the green office tower and park.

$ Hotel Topas, a decent budget choice with 33 rooms, is a block north of the train station. Ask for one of the eight back-facing rooms, as they're quieter and cooler in summer (elevator, Niddastrasse 88, tel. 069/230-852, www.hoteltopas.de, hoteltopas@t-online.de). From the station, follow the same directions as for the Bristol Hotel (listed earlier), two doors away.

$ EasyHotel Frankfurt's tiny, no-frills rooms feel as if they were popped out of a plastic mold, right down to the ship's head-style "bathroom pod." Rates can be low if you book early, but are nonrefundable and you'll be charged for add-ons that are normally included at most other hotels (air-con, pay Wi-Fi, pay TV, elevator, pay parking, no breakfast but 20 percent discount at bakery next door, Düsseldorfer Strasse 19, www.easyhotel.com). Exit the station by track 24 and follow Düsseldorfer Strasse two blocks to the Platz der Republik tram stop, which is directly in front of the hotel.

Hostel: A block from the train station, **¢ Five Elements** is clean and modern and feels very safe inside. But because it's smack in the middle of the red light district, families might feel more comfortable elsewhere. Here, too, prices skyrocket during conventions (breakfast extra, private rooms available, elevator, Moselstrasse 40, tel. 069/2400-5885, www.5elementshostel.de, welcome@5elementshostel.de). From the station, exit the underground passage onto Taunusstrasse and go one block to the corner of Moselstrasse; the hostel is across the intersection to your left.

ELSEWHERE IN FRANKFURT

If you're in Frankfurt for one night, stay near the station—but if you're in town for a few days and want to feel like you belong, choose one of the following listings. Hotel Neue Kräme and Hotel Zentrum are near Römerberg, and the Maingau Hotel and the hostel are in the Sachsenhausen district, with lots of local shops and cafés (see "Eating in Frankfurt," later). For locations, see the "Frankfurt Hotels & Restaurants" map.

$$ Hotel Neue Kräme is a quiet little 21-room oasis tucked away above the center of Frankfurt's downtown action, just steps from Römerberg. Friendly staff welcome guests in this bright and cheerful place (two apartments with kitchen across street, elevator, Neue Kräme 23—look for blue-and-white *hotel* sign out

Frankfurt Hotels & Restaurants

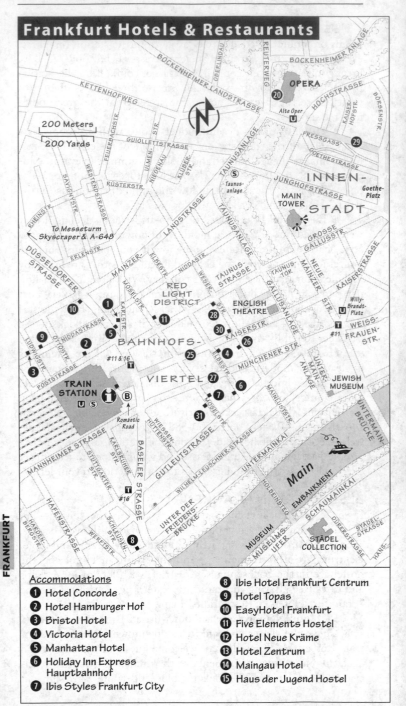

Accommodations

1 Hotel Concorde
2 Hotel Hamburger Hof
3 Bristol Hotel
4 Victoria Hotel
5 Manhattan Hotel
6 Holiday Inn Express Hauptbahnhof
7 Ibis Styles Frankfurt City
8 Ibis Hotel Frankfurt Centrum
9 Hotel Topas
10 EasyHotel Frankfurt
11 Five Elements Hostel
12 Hotel Neue Kräme
13 Hotel Zentrum
14 Maingau Hotel
15 Haus der Jugend Hostel

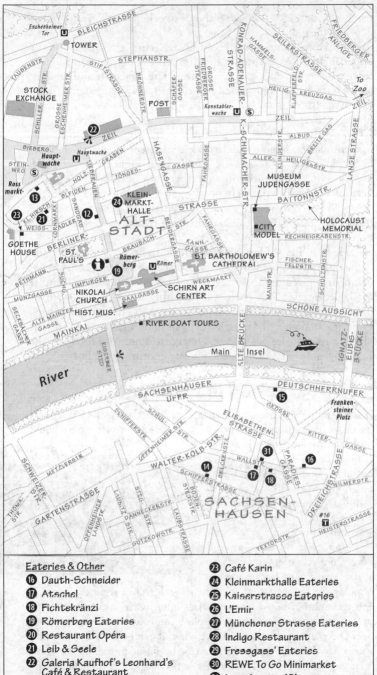

FRANKFURT

Eateries & Other

- ⑯ Dauth-Schneider
- ⑰ Atschel
- ⑱ Fichtekränzi
- ⑲ Römerberg Eateries
- ⑳ Restaurant Opéra
- ㉑ Leib & Seele
- ㉒ Galeria Kaufhof's Leonhard's Café & Restaurant
- ㉓ Café Karin
- ㉔ Kleinmarkthalle Eateries
- ㉕ Kaiserstrasse Eateries
- ㉖ L'Emir
- ㉗ Münchener Strasse Eateries
- ㉘ Indigo Restaurant
- ㉙ Fressgass' Eateries
- ㉚ REWE To Go Minimarket
- ㉛ Launderette (2)

front, tel. 069/284-046, www.hotel-neuekraeme.de, info@hotel-neuekraeme.de).

$$ Hotel Zentrum offers industrial-chic style hidden on the upper floors of a downtown building. With 29 colorful, modern rooms, it's in a great location near the Hauptwache (family rooms, elevator, free afternoon coffee and cake in lobby, Rossmarkt 7, tel. 069/5050-0190, www.hotel-zentrum.de, info@hotel-zentrum.de, manager Sascha).

$ Maingau Hotel, located across the river in the Sachsenhausen district, is on a quiet residential street facing a neighborhood park. The 78 rooms are simple and bright. If you're looking for a little tranquility in an authentic residential setting, stay here (elevator, pay parking in nearby garage, Schifferstrasse 38, tel. 069/609-140, www.maingau.de, info@maingau.de). From the station, take tram #16 to the Lokalbahnhof/Textorstrasse stop; the hotel is three blocks away.

Hostel: The ¢ **Haus der Jugend** is right along the river and is the only place I list where prices don't go up during conferences (membership required, private rooms available, lunch and dinner available, elevator, 2:00 curfew, Deutschherrnufer 12, tel. 069/610-0150, www.jugendherberge-frankfurt.de, info@hellofrankfurt.de). From the station, exit through the front door, turn right to the bus platforms, and take bus #46 (2/hour, direction: Mühlberg) to the Frankensteiner Platz stop, which is one door from the hostel.

Eating in Frankfurt

Instead of beer-garden ambience, Frankfurt entices visitors and locals to its Sachsenhausen district, across the river, where you'll find lots of characteristic apple-wine pubs (and plenty of other options). This cobbled and cozy neighborhood is the city's traditional eating-and-drinking zone—a great place to spend a warm summer evening.

Apfelwein, drunk around here since Charlemagne's time 1,200 years ago, became more popular in the 16th century, when local grapes were diseased. It enjoyed another boost two centuries later, when a climate change made grape-growing harder. Apple wine is about the strength of beer (5.5 percent alcohol), but like wine, it can be served spiced and warm in winter. This hard cider can be an acquired taste—good luck enjoying it. You'll see locals, who've spent a lifetime learning to like it, grasping their apple wine in *geripptes*—characteristic hatched glasses (which go back to its early days, when this tax-free drink was slurped by greasy-fingered sausage munchers on the streets).

Sachsenhausen is also a good place to sample local cuisine. The culinary pride of Frankfurt is *Grüne Sosse,* a green sauce made of sour cream blended with seven herbs (parsley, chives, watercress, sorrel, borage, chervil, and burnet); it's frequently served with beef, schnitzel, or halved hard-boiled eggs. Another widely available local specialty (for the adventurous) is *Handkäse mit Musik* ("hand cheese with music"—the "music" comes tomorrow), an aged, cylindrical ricotta-like cheese served with onions and vinegar. You can also satisfy your craving for *Leiterchen* here ("miniladders," or spare ribs—surprisingly meaty and salty).

APPLE-WINE PUBS IN SACHSENHAUSEN

The three apple-wine pubs I've listed below all have indoor and outdoor seating in a woodsy, rustic setting. Not just for tourists, these characteristic places are truly popular with Frankfurters, too. To reach them, take bus #46 from the train station (direction: Mühlberg) to Frankensteiner Platz. Or to walk from downtown (20 minutes), cross the river on the pedestrian-only Eiserner Steg bridge or Alte Brücke bridge. For locations, see the "Frankfurt Hotels & Restaurants" map.

$$ Dauth-Schneider has lots of tables outside on the shady, tree-covered square, a large indoor section, and a big and accessible menu. It's my first choice for eating outside on a balmy evening (daily 11:30-24:00, Neuer Wall 5, tel. 069/613-533). Families appreciate the big-city playground across the square from the outdoor tables.

$$ Atschel, across the street and a few doors down, is my Sachsenhausen choice for eating inside. They serve "Frankfurter Schnitzel" with green sauce and other local standards in a handsome dining room and cozy back garden (daily 12:00-24:00, kitchen closes at 22:30, cash only, Wallstrasse 7, tel. 069/619-201).

$$ Fichtekränzi, across the alley from Atschel, is open evenings only. It offers the typical specialties and some lighter fare, both in its cozy, bench-filled beer hall and outside under the trees. The atmosphere is young and relaxed—expect to share a table and make some new friends (Mon-Sat 17:00-23:00, Sun from 16:00, cash only, Wallstrasse 5, tel. 069/612-778).

Pub Crawl: Irish pubs and salsa bars clutter the pedestrian zone around Grosse Rittergasse and Frankensteiner Strasse; if you're looking for a place to do a pub crawl, this is it.

DINING DOWNTOWN
On or near Römerberg

Römerberg, Frankfurt's charming, traffic-free, and historic market square, is the focal point of any visit. As you can imagine, it's lined with the typical array of touristy and overpriced restaurants. Still, if you'd like to eat here (especially nice if eating outside), your best bets are listed below.

$$ Weinstube im Römer, in the bottom of the Town Hall, is a classic old place serving good schnitzel and the local Frankfurt white wine, a Riesling, still produced in vineyards owned by the city (Tue-Fri 16:00-23:00, Sat-Sun from 11:30, closed Mon, Römerberg 19, tel. 069/291-331).

$ Alten Limpurg, next to the Town Hall, is a very simple and basic option with the cheapest menu on the square and easy to spot: Look for the big sausages displayed out front. Choose from the comfy pub inside or order from the sausage window and enjoy sitting on the square (daily 9:00-24:00, Römerberg 17, tel. 069/9288-3130).

$$ Cafébar im Kunstverein, while a few steps off the square and without the memorable views, is a fine value and hosts more locals than tourists in a kind of retro elegance under medieval vaults. They serve organic meals, excellent salads, and homemade cakes (daily 10:00-19:00, Thu until 24:00, cash only, adjacent modern-art gallery at Markt 44, tel. 069/8477-0863).

In the Old Center near the Hauptwache

$$$$ Restaurant Opéra is a great place for a dressy splurge, with white tablecloths and formal service both inside, under gilded arches and circa-1900 decor, or out on a terrace over the opera's grand entry (daily 12:00-15:00 & 18:00-23:30, Opernplatz 1, tel. 069/134-0215). Enter through Café Rosso at street level, then take the elevator or stairs up to the third floor.

$$ Leib & Seele is a modern place a block toward the river from the Hauptwache. Its name means "body and soul," and this local favorite serves lots of hearty and creative salads, serious vegetarian plates, and traditional dishes in a modern pub interior with fine outside tables (daily 11:30-24:00, Kornmarkt 11, tel. 069/281-529).

$ Galeria Kaufhof's Leonhard's Café and Restaurant is a huge, sleek, modern cafeteria serving good buffet-style food (at restaurant prices), with nice city views from its top-floor perch. It's super-efficient, with lots of healthy options, air conditioning, and sofas on the rooftop terrace for those just having a drink (Mon-Sat 9:30-20:00 or 21:00, closed Sun).

$ Café Karin, a local institution, serves one of the best breakfasts in town until 18:00 (including the yummy, homemade Bircher Muesli). Located right next to Goethe House, it's also a convenient place for a coffee break (Mon-Fri 9:00-21:00, Sat until 19:00, Sun 10:00-19:00, cash only, Grosser Hirschgraben 28, tel. 069/295-217).

$ The **Kleinmarkthalle** is one of the most charming and inviting indoor market halls you'll find anywhere in Germany, and a great place for a simple lunch. Strolling its ground floor, you can graze through a world of free samples (call that the first course). Once you've made your selection (fish, Italian, oyster bar), find a place to sit down at the far end opposite the entrance, or go upstairs (Mon-Fri 8:00-18:00, Sat until 16:00, closed Sun). Or assemble a picnic to eat on the adjacent square, Liebfrauenberg, near the fountain.

$$ **Kleinmarkthalle Markt-Stubb** (breakfast and lunch only) is the only real restaurant in the market hall. It's upstairs at the east end and is a hit with local seniors for its traditional home cooking with fresh-from-market ingredients (Tue-Sat 9:00-16:00, closed Sun-Mon).

Kleinmarkthalle Weinterrasse is a lively wine garden upstairs at the market hall, serving every wine but apple to locals. It stays open for two hours after the market is closed (Mon-Fri 10:00-20:00, Sat until 18:00, closed Sun).

NEAR THE TRAIN STATION, ON AND NEAR KAISERSTRASSE

A grand boulevard connecting the train station with the old center, **Kaiserstrasse** is a venerable, linden-tree-lined, four-block stretch of once-dazzling buildings (circa 1880) that once saw some seedy times (but the sex and drugs have moved a block or two to the north). It's emerging as a fun eating-and-drinking zone—especially if you need a break from traditional German fare. The parallel **Münchener Strasse** is less upscale but up-and-coming, with some hip newer restaurants popular with locals (such as Maxie Eisen) and with a cheaper selection of ethnic eateries. And the train station itself is a veritable mall of shops and restaurants with long hours.

I recommend strolling around first to enjoy the scene and survey your options (as things are steadily evolving upward in quality). Here are a few places to consider (starting nearest the station).

$$ **Der Fette Bulle Hamburger Restaurant** (the "Fat Bull") is a trendy burger joint with a modern and fun interior and good seating on the street. If you're in the mood for a fancy burger, this is the place (daily 11:30-23:00, Kaiserstrasse 73, tel. 069/9075-7004).

$$ **Urban Kitchen** is chic and modern. It serves creative global food (everything from pizza to sushi) from a fun and healthy menu

FRANKFURT

to a cool crowd (daily 11:00-late, Kaiserstrasse 53, tel. 069/2710-7999).

$$$ BonaMente is the local choice for red meat, with a sleek and modern steakhouse ambience inside and good on-the-street tables. The portions are big, and so is the selection (daily 11:00-24:00, Kaiserstrasse 51, tel. 069/2562-7566).

$$$ L'Emir, just off Kaiserstrasse inside a cheap hotel on Weserstrasse, is a good Lebanese place. Choose from their endless appetizer options or try their popular lamb dishes (daily 12:00-24:00, Weserstrasse 17, tel. 069/2400-8686).

$ Der Thai is good, quick, and inexpensive. Dine inside the small, modern interior or eat your food streetside (Mon-Fri 11:00-23:00, Sat-Sun from 12:00, Kaiserstrasse 38, tel. 069/2695-7957).

$ Dean & David is a favorite for a fast, inexpensive, and healthy meal with views of the skyscrapers of "Bankfurt." It has a pleasant modern interior and streetside tables (Mon-Fri 10:00-20:30, Sat 12:00-18:00, closed Sun; Kaiserstrasse 31, tel. 069/8008-8363).

$$ Merkez Kebab Haus is the best place for Turkish food. With a wood-fired grill, it's a cut above the usual *Döner Kebab* shop, with an inviting ambience and good service at a great price (try the wonderful *sütlaç*—rice pudding, Mon-Sat 8:00-late, Sun from 10:00, Münchener Strasse 33, tel. 069/233-995).

$$ Maxie Eisen, named after a 1920s Chicago racketeer with German roots, is a deli/diner and bar located on the light-flooded corner of Münchener Strasse and Weserstrasse. If you're craving a pastrami or Reuben sandwich, you'll find it here, along with other Jewish dishes like matzo ball and kreplach soups, plus delicious seasoned fries (Mon-Sat 11:30-23:00, bar open later, closed Sun, Münchener Strasse 18, tel. 069/7675-8362).

$$ Indigo Restaurant, a block north of Kaiserstrasse at the corner of Weserstrasse and Taunusstrasse, is a bit closer to the red light district, but their Indian food is considered among the best in town. This is a good place for takeout (daily 12:00-14:30 & 17:30-23:30, Taunusstrasse 17, tel. 069/2648-8878).

SUPERMARKETS

A small but well-stocked **REWE** is near the station, across the street from the recommended Hotel Concorde (Mon-Sat 7:00-22:00, closed Sun, Karlstrasse 4, use Kaiserstrasse exit from underground passageway). For a quick snack, a **REWE To Go** minimarket offers a salad bar and sandwich counter (Mon-Fri 6:00-24:00, Sat-Sun 8:00-22:00, Kaiserstrasse 48). A larger **REWE** is in the basement of the MyZeil shopping center near the Hauptwache, in the center of town (Mon-Sat 7:00-24:00, closed Sun). On Sundays (when many stores are closed), you'll find a grocery store and pharmacy in the underground section of the train station (open until 20:00).

Frankfurt Connections

BY TRAIN

German Destinations: Rothenburg (hourly, 3 hours, transfer in Würzburg and Steinach; the tiny Steinach-Rothenburg train often leaves from track 5, shortly after the Würzburg train arrives), **Würzburg** (1-2/hour, 70 minutes, or 2 hours on cheaper RE trains), **Nürnberg** (1-2/hour, 2 hours), **Munich** (hourly, 3.5 hours), **Baden-Baden** (hourly, 1.5-2 hours, direct or transfer in Karlsruhe), **Bacharach** (hourly, 1.5-2 hours, transfer in Mainz or Bingen), **Freiburg** (hourly, 1.5-2 hours), **Cochem** (hourly, 2.5 hours, transfer in Koblenz), **Cologne** (direct ICE trains hourly, 1-1.5 hours; cheaper, less frequent IC trains take 2.5 hours and show you more of the Rhine), **Erfurt** (1-2/hour, 2.5 hours), **Leipzig** (hourly, 3 hours), **Berlin** (at least hourly, 4 hours), **Hamburg** (hourly, 4 hours). Train info: www.bahn.com.

International Destinations: Amsterdam (6/day direct, 4 hours; more with transfers, 5-7 hours), **Bern** (hourly, 4 hours, most with transfer in Basel), **Zürich** (hourly, 4.5 hours, most transfer in Basel), **Brussels** (6/day by direct ICE, 3 hours, reservation not required; more with transfers, 5 hours), **Copenhagen** (5/day, 9.5 hours, transfer in Hamburg, reservation required in summer), **Paris** (about hourly, 4-5 hours, many with 1 change, reservation required in France), **Vienna** (6/day direct, 6.5 hours), **Prague** (6/day, 6 hours, change to bus in Nürnberg).

BY ROMANTIC ROAD BUS

The bus departs at 9:00 (Wed and Sun late April-early Oct, also Sat mid-May-early Sept) from the Romantic Road Coach bus stop outside the Frankfurt train station. Exit the station through the main entrance and turn right; look for platforms A1-A3 with signs for *Romantic Road* or *Romantische Strasse*. If you haven't booked in advance, you can pay in cash on board if seats are available. For tickets and information, go to www.romantischestrasse.de (choose "Bus & train," then "Romantic Road Bus") or call 089/593-889 (Mon-Sat 9:00-13:00). Frankfurt to Rothenburg costs €45; from Frankfurt to Munich is €87 (20 percent discount available with rail pass). If you're heading to Füssen and the King's Castles instead of Munich, you'll have to transfer to a train in the town of Donauwörth (and you must notify the bus company 36 hours in advance so they'll stop). For more information, see page 400.

BY PLANE
Frankfurt Airport

Frankfurt's airport *(Flughafen),* just a few stops by S-Bahn from the city center, has its own long-distance train station, which makes it a snap to connect from a flight here to other German cities (airport code: FRA, tel. 01806-372-4636, www.frankfurt-airport.com).

There are two separate terminals (know your terminal—check your ticket or the airport website). **Terminal 1,** a multilevel maze of check-in counters and shops, is linked to the train station. **Terminal 2** is small and quiet, with few services. A SkyLine train connects the two terminals in less than five minutes. Pick up the free brochure *Airport Guide* for a map and detailed information (available at the airport and at most Frankfurt hotels).

The airport has three pay **baggage-storage** desks *(Gepäckaufbewahrung;* the branch in Terminal 1B, level 1 is open 24 hours). Among the other services are a **post office** (in Terminal 1B, level 1), a **pharmacy** (in Terminal 1B, level 2, and also in Terminal 2), a 24-hour **medical clinic** (on level 1 between terminals 1B and 1C), public **showers** (one in Terminal 2 and four in Terminal 1, €6, shampoo and towel included), and free **Wi-Fi.** A good-sized, fairly priced **Tegut supermarket** is handy for last-minute shopping (Terminal 1C, level 0; tricky to find: Go down the escalators from the underpass on level 1 between terminals 1B and 1C, or up the escalators from train platforms 1-3). There are **customs desks** in both terminals for VAT refunds (daily 7:00-21:00; after hours, ask the information desk to page a customs officer for you). There's even McBeer at four McDonald's, one of which is allegedly among Europe's largest. McWelcome to Germany.

Frankfurt Airport Train Station

The airport's train station has two parts, both reachable from Terminal 1. Regional S-Bahn trains to downtown Frankfurt and nearby towns and suburbs depart from platforms 1-3. Long-distance trains leave from the slightly more distant *Fernbahnhof,* platforms 4-7.

Getting to Downtown Frankfurt: The airport is a 12-minute train ride on the **S-Bahn** from Frankfurt's main train station, or Hauptbahnhof (4/hour, €4.80, ride included in €10.50 Frankfurt Card and €9.10 individual/€15.80 group version of all-day *Tageskarte Frankfurt* transit pass, but not in cheaper version of *Tageskarte Frankfurt*). Figure about €30 for a **taxi** from the airport to any of my recommended hotels.

Getting to Other Destinations by Train: Train travelers can validate rail passes or buy tickets at the *Reisezentrum* on the level above the long-distance train platforms. Handy ticket machines are easy to use and allow you to print a schedule even if you aren't buying a ticket—great for those traveling with a rail pass. Destinations include **Rothenburg** (hourly, 3.5 hours, change in Würzburg and Steinach), **Würzburg** (1-2/hour, 1.5 hours), **Nürnberg** (1-2/hour, 2.5 hours), **Munich** (1-2/hour, 3.5 hours), **Baden-Baden** (roughly hourly, 1.5 hours, change in Karlsruhe and/or Mannheim), **Cologne** (1-2/hour, 1 hour; trains along Rhine go less often and take 2.5 hours), **Bacharach** (hourly, 1 hour, change in Mainz or Bingen, some depart from regional platforms), **Berlin** (1-2/hour, 4.5-5 hours, most with 1 change). There are also many **international connections** from here (such as Paris, London, Brussels, Amsterdam, Zurich, Bern, and Prague).

Sleeping at or near Frankfurt Airport

Because train connections to Frankfurt Airport are so good, if your flight doesn't leave too early, you can sleep in another city and make it to the airport for your flight. If you wake up in Cologne, Baden-Baden, Würzburg, or Bacharach, you can catch a late-morning or midday flight; you can often make it from Nürnberg, Rothenburg, Freiburg, the Mosel, and even Munich for an early afternoon flight. Plan ahead and leave room for delays; don't take the last possible connection.

Thanks to these easy connections—and because downtown Frankfurt is just 12 minutes away by frequent train—it makes little sense for train travelers to sleep at the airport. Drivers who do want to stay near the airport the night before returning a rental car can stay in Kelsterbach, just across the expressway from the airport, at the **$ Ibis Frankfurt Airport Hotel** (breakfast extra, Langer Kornweg 9a, tel. 06107/9870, https://ibis.accorhotels.com/). If you're desperate, the **$$$ Sheraton Frankfurt** is conveniently connected to Terminal 1 (tel. 069/69770, www.sheraton.com/frankfurt, reservationsfrankfurt@sheraton.com).

"Frankfurt" Hahn Airport

This smaller airport, misleadingly classified as a "Frankfurt" airport for marketing purposes, is a nearly two-hour drive away in the Mosel region. Hahn Airport is popular with low-cost carriers (such as Ryanair). To avoid confusion, double-check the three-letter airport code on your ticket (FRA for Frankfurt Airport, HHN for Frankfurt Hahn). Regular buses connect Frankfurt Hahn Airport to Bullay (for trains to Cochem), Trier, Mainz, Cologne, and Frankfurt (more info at www.hahn-airport.de).

RHINE VALLEY

Best of the Rhine • Bacharach • Oberwesel • St. Goar • Koblenz

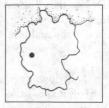

The Rhine Valley is storybook Germany, a fairy-tale world of legends and "robber-baron" castles. Cruise the most turret-studded stretch of the romantic Rhine as you listen for the song of the treacherous Loreley. For hands-on thrills, climb through the Rhineland's greatest castle, Rheinfels, above the town of St. Goar. Connoisseurs will also enjoy the fine interior of Marksburg Castle near Koblenz. Spend your nights in a castle-crowned village, either Bacharach or St. Goar.

PLANNING YOUR TIME

The Rhineland is magical, but doesn't take much time to see. Both Bacharach and St. Goar are an easy one-hour train ride or drive from Frankfurt Airport, and make a good first or last stop for travelers flying in or out.

The blitziest tour of the area is an hour looking at the castles from your train window—use the narration in this chapter to give it meaning. The nonstop express runs every hour, connecting Koblenz and Mainz in 50 scenic minutes. (Super-express ICE trains between Cologne and Frankfurt bypass the Rhine entirely.) For a better look, cruise in, tour a castle or two, sleep in a medieval town, and take the train out.

Ideally, if you have two nights to spend here, sleep in Bacharach, cruise the best hour of the river (from Bacharach to St. Goar), and tour Rheinfels Castle. If rushed, focus on Rheinfels Castle and cruise less. With more time, add a visit to Koblenz or Oberwesel, or ride the riverside bike path. With another day, mosey through the neighboring Mosel Valley or day-trip to Cologne (both covered in different chapters).

There are countless castles in this region, so you'll need to be selective in your castle-going. Aside from Rheinfels Castle, my favorites are Burg Eltz (see the next chapter; well preserved with medieval interior, set evocatively in a romantic forest the next valley over), Marksburg Castle (rebuilt medieval interior, with commanding Rhine perch), and Rheinstein Castle (a 19th-century duke's hunting palace overlooking the Rhine). Marksburg is the easiest to reach by train.

If possible, visit the Rhine between April and October. The low season (winter and spring) is lower here than in some other parts of Germany. Many hotels and restaurants close from November to February or March. Only one riverboat runs, sights close or have short hours, and neither Bacharach nor St. Goar have much in the way of Christmas markets.

CHOOSING A HOME BASE

Bacharach and St. Goar, the best towns for an overnight stop, are 10 miles apart, connected by milk-run trains, riverboats, and a riverside bike path. Bacharach is a much more interesting town, but St. Goar has the famous Rheinfels Castle. In general, the Rhine is an easy place for cheap sleeps. B&Bs and *Gasthäuser* with inexpensive beds abound (and normally discount their prices for longer stays). Rhine-area hostels offer cheap beds to travelers of any age. Finding a room should be easy in high season (except for Sept-Oct wine-fest weekends). Note: Rhine Valley towns often have guesthouses and hotels with similar names—when reserving, double-check that you're contacting the one in your planned destination.

Best of the Rhine

Ever since Roman times, when this was the empire's northern boundary, the Rhine has been one of the world's busiest shipping rivers. Although the name "Rhine" derives from a Celtic word for "raging," the river you see today has been tamed and put to work. You'll see a steady flow of barges with 1,000- to 2,000-ton loads. Cars, buses, and trains rush along highways and tracks lining both banks.

Many of the castles were "robber-baron" castles, put there by petty rulers (there were 300 independent little countries in medieval Germany, a region about the size of Montana) to levy tolls on passing river traffic. A robber baron would put his castle on, or even in, the river. Then, often with the help of chains and a tower on the opposite bank, he'd stop each ship and get his toll. There were 10 customs stops in the 60-mile stretch between Mainz and Koblenz alone (no wonder merchants were early proponents of the creation of larger nation-states).

Some castles were built to control and protect settlements, and others were the residences of kings. As times changed, so did the lifestyles of the rich and feudal. Many castles were abandoned for more comfortable mansions in the towns.

Most Rhine castles date from the 11th, 12th, and 13th centuries. When the pope successfully asserted his power over the German emperor in 1076, local princes ran wild over the rule of their emperor. The castles saw military action in the 1300s and 1400s, as emperors began reasserting their control over Germany's many silly kingdoms.

The castles were also involved in the Reformation wars, in which Europe's Catholic and Protestant dynasties fought it out using a fragmented Germany as their battleground. The Thirty Years' War (1618-1648) devastated Germany. The outcome: Each ruler got the freedom to decide if his people would be Catholic or Protestant, and one-third of Germans died. (Production of Gummi Bears ceased entirely.)

The French—who feared a strong Germany and felt the Rhine was the logical border between them and Germany—destroyed most of the castles as a preventive measure (Louis XIV in the 1680s, the Revolutionary army in the 1790s, and Napoleon in 1806). Many were rebuilt in the Neo-Gothic style in the Romantic Age—the late 1800s—and today are enjoyed as restaurants, hotels, hostels, and museums.

GETTING AROUND THE RHINE

The Rhine flows north from Switzerland to Holland, but the scenic stretch from Mainz to Koblenz hoards all the touristic charm. Studded with the crenellated cream of Germany's castles, it bustles with boats, trains, and highway traffic. Have fun exploring with a mix of big steamers, tiny ferries *(Fähre)*, trains, and bikes.

By Boat: While some travelers do the whole Mainz-Koblenz trip by boat (5.5 hours downstream, 8.5 hours up), I'd just focus on the most scenic hour—from Bacharach to St. Goar. Sit on the boat's top deck with your handy Rhine map-guide (or the kilometer-keyed tour in this chapter) and enjoy the parade of castles, towns, boats, and vineyards.

Two boat companies take travelers along this stretch of the Rhine. Boats run daily in both directions from early April through October, with only one boat running off-season.

Most travelers sail on the bigger, more expensive, and romantic **Köln-Düsseldorfer (K-D) Line** (recommended Bacharach-St. Goar trip: €15.40 one-way, €17.40 round-trip, bikes-€2.80/day; discounts: up to 30 percent if over 60, 20 percent with connecting

Rhine Overview

UNROMANTIC RHINE

BEST OF THE RHINE

See detail map

---

train ticket, 20 percent with rail passes and does not count as a flex
ipass day; tel. 06741/1634 in St. Goar, tel. 06743/1322 in Bacharach, www.k-d.com). I've included an abridged K-D cruise schedule in this chapter. Complete, up-to-date schedules are posted at
any Rhineland station, hotel, TI, and www.k-d.com. (Confirm
times at your hotel the night before.) Purchase tickets at the dock
up to five minutes before departure. The boat is never full. Romantics will enjoy the old-time paddle-wheeler *Goethe*, which sails each
direction once a day (noted on schedule, confirm time locally).

The smaller **Bingen-Rüdesheimer Line** is slightly cheaper
than the K-D, doesn't offer any rail pass deals, and makes three trips
in each direction daily from mid-March through October (Bacharach-St. Goar: €13.40 one-way, €15.40 round-trip, bikes-€2/day,
buy tickets at ticket booth or on boat, ticket booth opens just before
boat departs, 30 percent discount if over 60; departs Bacharach
at 10:10, 12:00, and 15:15; departs St. Goar at 11:00, 14:00, and
16:15; tel. 06721/308-0810, www.bingen-ruedesheimer.de).

By Car: Drivers have these options: 1) skip the boat; 2) take a
round-trip cruise from St. Goar or Bacharach; 3) draw pretzels and

let the loser drive, prepare the picnic, and meet the boat; 4) rent a bike, bring it on the boat, and bike back; or 5) take the boat one-way and return to your car by train. When exploring by car, don't hesitate to pop onto one of the many little ferries that shuttle across the bridgeless-around-here river.

By Ferry: As there are no bridges between Koblenz and Mainz, you'll see car-and-passenger ferries (usually family-run for generations) about every three miles. Bingen-Rüdesheim, Lorch-Niederheimbach, Engelsburg-Kaub, and St. Goar-St. Goarshausen are some of the most useful routes (times vary; St. Goar-St. Goarshausen ferry departs each side every 20 minutes daily until 22:30, less frequently Sun; one-way fares: adult-€1.80, car and driver-€4.50, pay on boat; www.faehre-loreley.de). For a fun little jaunt, take a quick round-trip with some time to explore the other side.

By Bike: Biking is a great way to explore the valley. You can bike either side of the Rhine, but for a designated bike path, stay on the west side, where a 35-mile path runs between Koblenz and Bingen. The eight-mile stretch between St. Goar and Bacharach is smooth and scenic, but mostly along the highway. The bit from Bacharach to Bingen hugs the riverside and is car-free. Some hotels have bikes for guests; Hotel an der Fähre in St. Goar also rents to the public (reserve in advance).

Consider biking one-way and taking the bike back on the riverboat, or designing a circular trip using the fun and frequent shuttle ferries. A good target is Kaub (where a tiny boat shuttles sightseers to the better-from-a-distance castle on the island) or Rheinstein Castle.

By Train: Hourly milk-run trains hit every town along the Rhine (Bacharach-St. Goar in both directions about :50 after the hour, 10 minutes; Mainz-Bacharach, 40 minutes; Mainz-Koblenz, 1 hour). Express trains speed past the small towns, taking only 50 minutes nonstop between Mainz and Koblenz. Tiny stations are unstaffed—buy tickets at machines. Though generally user-friendly, some ticket machines claim to only take exact change; others may not accept US credit cards. When buying a ticket, be sure to select "English" and follow the instructions carefully. The ticket machine may give you the choice of validating your ticket for that day or a day in the near future—but only for some destinations (if you're not given this option, your ticket will automatically be validated for the day of purchase).

The **Rheinland-Pfalz-Ticket** day pass covers travel on milk-run trains to anywhere in this chapter—plus the Mosel Valley and Trier chapters (and also Remagen, but not Frankfurt, Cologne, or Bonn). It can save heaps of money, particularly on longer day trips or for groups (1 person-€24, up to 4 additional people-€5/each, buy at station ticket machines—may need to select Rhineland-Palatinate, good after 9:00 Mon-Fri and all day Sat-Sun, valid on trains labeled *RB, RE,* and *MRB*). For a day trip between Bacharach and Burg Eltz (normally €35 round-trip), even one person saves with a Rheinland-Pfalz-Ticket, and a group of five adults saves €130—look for travel partners at breakfast.

Best of the Rhine Tour
by Train or Boat

One of Europe's great train thrills is zipping along the Rhine enjoying this self-guided blitz tour, worth ▲▲▲. Or, even better, do it while relaxing on the deck of a Rhine steamer, surrounded by the wonders of this romantic and historic gorge. This quick and easy tour (you can cut in anywhere) skips most of the syrupy myths filling normal Rhine guides. You can follow along on a train, boat, bike, or car. By train or boat, sit on the left (river) side going south from Koblenz. While nearly all the castles listed are viewed from this side, train travelers need to clear a path to the right window for the times I yell, "Cross over!"

You'll notice large black-and-white kilometer markers along the riverbank. I erected these years ago to make this tour easier to follow. They tell the distance from the Rhine Falls, where the Rhine leaves Switzerland and becomes navigable. (Today, river barge pilots also use these markers to navigate.) If you're doing the tour by train and are stuck on the wrong side, keep an eye out for green-and-white signs that also show these numbers.

We're tackling just 36 miles (58 km) of the 820-mile-long (1,320-km) Rhine. Your Best of the Rhine Tour starts at Koblenz and heads upstream to Bingen. If you're going the other direction, it still works. Just hold the book upside-down.

🎧 Download my free Best of the Rhine audio tour—it works in either direction.

KOBLENZ TO BINGEN

Of the major sights and towns mentioned here, Marksburg and Rheinstein castles and the Loreley Visitors Center are described in more detail under "Sights Along the Rhine" (see next section); the others—Koblenz, St. Goar (and Rheinfels Castle), Oberwesel, and Bacharach—are covered later in this chapter. For Burg Eltz, see the next chapter.

Km 590—Koblenz: This Rhine blitz starts with Romantic Rhine thrills, at Koblenz. Koblenz isn't terribly attractive (it was hit hard in World War II), but its place at the historic Deutsches Eck ("German Corner")—the tip of land where the Mosel River joins the Rhine—gives it a certain patriotic charm. A cable car

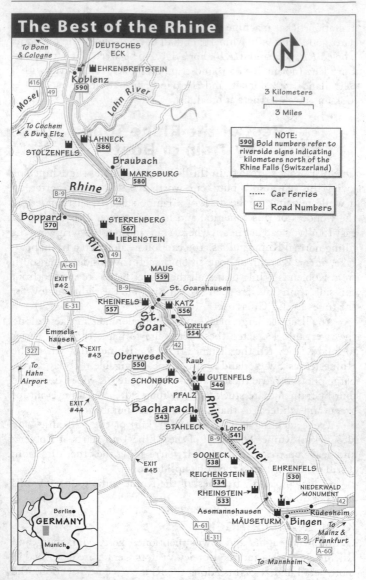

The Best of the Rhine

To Bonn & Cologne

DEUTSCHES ECK

EHRENBREITSTEIN

Koblenz
590

416
49

Mosel

Lahn River

To Cochem & Burg Eltz

LAHNECK
586

STOLZENFELS

Braubach

MARKSBURG
580

Rhine

B-9

42

Boppard
570

River

STERRENBERG
567

LIEBENSTEIN

A-61

EXIT #42

49

MAUS
559

E-31

B-9

St. Goarshausen

RHEINFELS
557

KATZ
556

St. Goar

LORELEY
554

Emmels-hausen

EXIT #43

42

327

Oberwesel
550

Kaub

To Hahn Airport

SCHÖNBURG

GUTENFELS
546

EXIT #44

PFALZ

Bacharach
543

STAHLECK

Rhine River

Lorch
541

B-9

EXIT #45

SOONECK
538

REICHENSTEIN
534

EHRENFELS
530

RHEINSTEIN
533

NIEDERWALD MONUMENT

42

Assmannshausen

Rüdesheim

MÄUSETURM

Bingen

To Mainz & Frankfurt

A-61

E-31

B-9

To Mannheim

A-60

3 Kilometers

3 Miles

NOTE:
590 Bold numbers refer to riverside signs indicating kilometers north of the Rhine Falls (Switzerland)

.... Car Ferries
42 Road Numbers

Berlin
GERMANY
Munich

links the Deutsches Eck with the yellow Ehrenbreitstein Fortress across the river.

Km 586—Lahneck Castle: Above the modern autobahn bridge over the Lahn River, this castle *(Burg)* was built in 1240 to defend local silver mines. The castle was ruined by the French in 1688 and rebuilt in the 1850s in Neo-Gothic style. Burg Lahneck faces another Romantic rebuild, the yellow Schloss Stolzen-

K-D Line Rhine Cruise Schedule

Boats run from early April through October (usually 5/day, but 3-4/day in early April and most of Oct). From November through March, one boat runs daily for groups, but individuals can tag along if they know you're coming—call the boat directly (tel. 0172/1360-335) or the main office in Cologne (tel. 0221/2088-318). The times listed below are based on the 2018 schedule. Check www.k-d.com for the latest.

Koblenz	Boppard	St. Goar	Bacharach
—	9:00	10.20	11:30
*9:00	*11:00	*12:20	*13:30
—	13:00	14:20	15:30
—	14:00	15:20	16:30
14:00	16:00	17:20	18:30
13:10	11.50	10:55	10:15
—	12:50	11:55	11:15
—	13:50	12:55	12:15
18:10	16:50	15:55	15:15
20:10	*18:50	*17:55	*17:15

These sailings are on the 1913 paddle-wheeler Goethe.

fels (€5, out of view above the train, Tue-Sun 10:00-18:00, closed Mon, Sat-Sun only and shorter hours off-season, closed Dec-Jan, a 10-minute climb from tiny parking lot, www.schloss-stolzenfels. de). Note that a *Burg* is a defensive fortress, while a *Schloss* is mainly a showy palace.

Km 580—Marksburg Castle: This castle stands bold and white—restored to look like most Rhine castles once did, with their slate stonework covered with stucco to look as if made from a richer stone. You'll spot Marksburg with the three modern smoke-stacks behind it (these vent Europe's biggest car-battery recycling plant just up the valley), just before the town of Spay. This is the best-looking of all the Rhine castles and the only surviving medieval castle on the Rhine. Because of its commanding position, it was never attacked in the Middle Ages (though it was captured by the US Army in March 1945). It's now a museum with a medieval interior second only to the Mosel Valley's Burg Eltz.

If you haven't read the sidebar on river traffic (later in this chapter), now's a good time.

Km 570—Boppard: Once a Roman town, Boppard has some impressive remains of fourth-century walls. Look for the Roman towers and the substantial chunk of Roman wall near the train station, just above the main square. You'll notice that a church is a big part of each townscape. Many small towns have two tow-ering churches. Four centuries ago, after enduring a horrific war, each prince or king decided which faith his subjects would follow (more often Protestant to the north and east, Catholic to the south and west). While church attendance in Germany is way down, the towns here, like Germany as a whole, are still divided between Catholic and Protestant.

If you visit Boppard, head to the fascinating Church of St. Severus below the main square. Find the carved Romanesque crazies at the doorway. Inside, to the right of the entrance, you'll see Christian symbols from Roman times. Also notice the painted arches and vaults (originally, most Romanesque churches were painted this way). Down by the river, look for the high-water *(Hochwasser)* marks on the arches from various flood years. You'll find these flood marks throughout the Rhine and Mosel valleys.

Km 567—Sterrenberg Castle and Liebenstein Castle: These neighboring castles, across from the town of Bad Salzig, are known as the "Hostile Brothers". Notice how they're isolated from each other by a low-slung wall. The wall was built to improve defenses from both castles, but this is the *romantic* Rhine so there has to be a legend: Take one wall between castles, add two greedy and jealous brothers and a fair maiden, and create your own legend. **$$$ Burg Liebenstein** is now a fun, friendly, and reasonably af-fordable family-run hotel (9 rooms, giant king-and-the-family room, easy parking, tel. 06773/251, www.castle-liebenstein.com, info@burg-liebenstein.de, Nickenig family).

Km 560: While you can see nothing from here, a 19th-cen-tury lead mine functioned on both sides of the river, with a shaft actually tunneling completely under the Rhine.

Km 559—Maus Castle: The Maus (mouse) got its name be-cause the next castle was owned by the Katzenelnbogen family. (*Katz* means "cat.") In the 1300s, it was considered a state-of-the-art fortification...until 1806, when Napoleon Bonaparte had it blown apart with then-state-of-the-art explosives. It was rebuilt true to its original plans in about 1900. Today, Burg Maus is open for concerts, weddings, and guided tours in German (20-minute walk up, weekends only, reservations required, tel. 06771/2303, www.burg-maus.de).

Km 557—St. Goar and Rheinfels Castle: Cross to the other side of the train. The pleasant town of St. Goar was named for a sixth-century hometown monk. It originated in Celtic times (i.e., really old) as a place where sailors would stop, catch their breath, send home a postcard, and give thanks after surviving the seduc-tive and treacherous Loreley crossing. St. Goar is worth a stop to explore its mighty Rheinfels Castle.

Km 556—Katz Castle: Burg Katz (Katzenelnbogen) faces St.

Goar from across the river. Together, Burg Katz (built in 1371) and Rheinfels Castle had a clear view up and down the river, effectively controlling traffic (there was absolutely no duty-free shopping on the medieval Rhine). Katz got Napoleoned in 1806 and rebuilt in about 1900.

In 1995, a wealthy and eccentric Japanese man bought it for about $4 million. His vision: to make the castle—so close to the Loreley that Japanese tourists are wild about—an exotic escape for his countrymen. But the town wouldn't allow his planned renovation of the historic (and therefore protected) building. Stymied, the frustrated investor abandoned his plans. Today, Burg Katz sits empty...the Japanese ghost castle.

Below the castle, notice the derelict grape terraces—worked since the eighth century, but abandoned in the last generation. Yet Rhine wine remains in demand. The local slate absorbs the heat of the sun and stays warm all night, resulting in sweeter grapes. Wine from the steep side of the Rhine gorge—where grapes are harder to grow and harvest—is tastier and more expensive.

About Km 555: A statue of the Loreley, the beautiful-but-deadly nymph, combs her hair at the end of a long spit—built to give barges protection from vicious ice floes that until recent years raged down the river in the winter. The actual Loreley, a landmark cliff, is just ahead.

Km 554—The Loreley: Steep a big slate rock in centuries of legend and it becomes a tourist attraction—the ultimate Rhinestone. The Loreley (name painted near shoreline), rising 450 feet over the narrowest and deepest point of the Rhine, has long been important. It was a holy site in pre-Roman days. The fine echoes here—thought to be ghostly voices—fertilized legend-tellers' imaginations.

Because of the reefs just upstream (at km 552), many ships never made it to St. Goar. Sailors (after days on the river) blamed their misfortune on a *wunderbare Fräulein*, whose long, blond hair almost covered her body. Heinrich Heine's *Song of Loreley* (the CliffsNotes version is on local postcards, and you'll hear it on K-D boats) tells the story of a count sending his men to kill or capture this siren after she distracted his horny son, who forgot to watch where he was sailing and drowned. When the soldiers cornered the nymph in her cave, she called her father (Father Rhine) for help. Huge waves, the likes of which you'll never see today, rose from the river and carried Loreley to safety. And she has never been seen since.

But alas, when the moon shines brightly and the tour buses are parked, a soft, playful Rhine whine can still be heard from the Loreley. As you pass, listen carefully ("Sailors...sailors...over my

Rhine River Trade and Barge-Watching

The Rhine is great for barge-watching. There's a constant parade of action, and each boat is different. Since ancient times, this has been a highway for trade. Today, Europe's biggest port (Rotterdam) waits at the mouth of the river.

Barge workers are almost a subculture. Many own their own ships. The captain lives in the stern, with his family. The family car is often parked on the stern. Workers live in the bow.

In the Rhine town of Kaub, there was once a boarding school for the children of the Rhine merchant marines—but today it's closed, since most captains are Dutch, Belgian, or Swiss. The flag of the boat's home country flies in the stern (Dutch—horizontal red, white, and blue; Belgian—vertical black, yellow, and red; Swiss—white cross on a red field; German—horizontal black, red, and yellow; French—vertical red, white, and blue). Logically, imports go upstream (Japanese cars, coal, and oil) and exports go downstream (German cars, chemicals, and pharmaceuticals). A clever captain manages to ship goods in each direction. Recently, giant Dutch container ships (which transport five times the cargo) have been driving many of the traditional barges out of business, presenting the German economy with another challenge.

Going downstream, tugs can push a floating train of up to five barges at once, but upstream, as the slope gets steeper (and the stream gradient gets higher), they can push only one at a time. Before modern shipping, horses dragged boats upstream (the faint remains of towpaths survive at points along the river). From 1873 to 1900, workers laid a chain from Bonn to Bingen, and boats with cogwheels and steam engines hoisted themselves upstream. Today, 265 million tons travel each year along the 530

bounding mane"). Today a visitors center keeps the story alive; if you visit you can hike to the top of the cliff.

Km 552—The Seven Maidens: Killer reefs, marked by red-and-green buoys, are called the "Seven Maidens." OK, one more goofy legend: The prince of Schönburg Castle (*über* Oberwesel—described next) had seven spoiled daughters who always dumped men because of their shortcomings. Fed up, he invited seven of his knights to the castle and demanded that his daughters each choose one to marry. But they complained that each man had too big a nose, was too fat, too stupid, and so on. The rude and teasing girls escaped into a riverboat. Just downstream, God turned them into the seven rocks that form this reef. While this story probably isn't entirely true, there was a lesson in it for medieval children: Don't be hard-hearted.

Km 550—Oberwesel: Cross to the other side of the train. The town of Oberwesel, topped by the commanding Schönburg Castle

miles from Basel on the German-Swiss border to the Dutch city of Rotterdam on the Atlantic.

Riverside navigational aids are of vital interest to captains who don't wish to meet the Loreley (see Km 554 on the "Best of the Rhine" tour). Boats pass on the right unless they clearly signal otherwise with a large blue sign. Since ships heading downstream can't stop or maneuver as freely, boats heading upstream are expected to do the tricky do-si-do work. Cameras monitor traffic all along and relay warnings of oncoming ships by posting large triangular signals before narrow and troublesome bends in the river. There may be two or three triangles per signpost, depending upon how many "sectors," or segments, of the river are covered. The lowest triangle indicates the nearest stretch of river. Each triangle tells whether there's a ship in that sector. When the bottom side of a triangle is lit, that sector is empty. When the left side is lit, an oncoming ship is in that sector.

The **Signal and River Pilots Museum** (Wahrschauer- und Lotsenmuseum), located at the signal triangles at the upstream edge of St. Goar, explains how barges are safer, cleaner, and more fuel-efficient than trains or trucks (free, May-Sept Wed and Sat 14:00-17:00, outdoor exhibits always open).

(now a hotel), boasts some of the best medieval wall and tower remains on the Rhine.

Notice how many of the train tunnels along here have entrances designed like medieval turrets—they were actually built in the Romantic 19th century. OK, back to the riverside.

Km 547—Gutenfels Castle and Pfalz Castle, the Classic Rhine View: Burg Gutenfels (now a privately owned hotel) and the shipshape Pfalz Castle (built in the river in the 1300s) worked very effectively to tax medieval river traffic. The town of Kaub grew rich as Pfalz raised its chains when boats came, and lowered them only when the merchants had paid their duty. Those who didn't pay spent time touring its prison, on a raft at the bottom of its well. In 1504, a pope called for the destruction of Pfalz, but the locals withstood a six-week siege, and the castle still stands. Notice the overhanging outhouse (tiny white room between two wooden ones). Pfalz (also known as Pfalzgrafenstein) is tourable but bare and dull (€2.50 ferry from Kaub, €3 entry, Tue-Sun 10:00-18:00, closed Mon; shorter hours in March; Nov and Jan-Feb Sat-Sun only, closed Dec; last entry one hour before closing, mobile 0172-262-2800, www.burg-pfalzgrafenstein.de).

In Kaub, on the riverfront directly below the castles, a green statue (near the waving flags) honors the German general Gebhard von Blücher. He was Napoleon's nemesis. In 1813, as Napoleon fought his way back to Paris after his disastrous Russian campaign, he stopped at Mainz—hoping to fend off the Germans and Russians pursuing him by controlling that strategic bridge. Blücher tricked Napoleon. By building the first major  pontoon bridge of its kind here at the Pfalz Castle, he crossed the Rhine and outflanked the French. Two years later, Blücher and Wellington teamed up to defeat Napoleon once and for all at Waterloo.

Immediately opposite Kaub (where the ferry lands, marked by blue roadside flags) is a gaping hole in the mountainside. This marks the last working slate mine on the Rhine.

Km 544—"The Raft Busters": Just before Bacharach, at the top of the island, buoys mark a gang of rocks notorious for busting up rafts. The Black Forest, upstream from here, was once poor, and wood was its best export. Black Foresters would ride log booms down the Rhine to the Ruhr (where their timber fortified coal-mine shafts) or to Holland (where logs were sold to shipbuilders). If they could navigate the sweeping bend just before Bacharach and then survive these "raft busters," they'd come home reckless and horny—the German folkloric equivalent of American cowboys after payday.

Km 543—Bacharach and Stahleck Castle: Cross to the other side of the train. The town of Bacharach is a great stop. Some of the Rhine's best wine is from this town, whose name likely derives from "altar to Bacchus" (the Roman god of wine). Local vintners brag that the medieval Pope Pius II ordered Bacharach wine by the cartload. Perched above the town, the 13th-century Burg Stahleck is now a hostel. Return to the riverside.

Km 541—Lorch: This pathetic stub of a castle is barely visible from the road. Check out the hillside vineyards. These vineyards once blanketed four times as much land as they do today, but modern economics have driven most of them out of business. The vineyards that do survive require government subsidies. Notice the small car ferry, one of several along the bridgeless stretch between Mainz and Koblenz.

Km 538—Sooneck Castle: Cross back to the other side of the train. Built in the 11th century, this castle was twice destroyed by people sick and tired of robber barons.

Km 534—Reichenstein Castle and **Km 533—Rheinstein Castle:** Stay on the other side of the train to see two of the first castles to be rebuilt in the Romantic era. Both are privately owned, tourable, and connected by a pleasant trail. Go back to the river side.

Km 530—Ehrenfels Castle: Opposite Bingerbrück and the Bingen station, you'll see the ghostly Ehrenfels Castle (clobbered by the Swedes in 1636 and by the French in 1689). Since it had no view of the river traffic to the north, the owner built the cute little *Mäuseturm* (mouse tower) on an island (the yellow tower you'll see near the train station today). Rebuilt in the 1800s in Neo-Gothic style, it's now used as a Rhine navigation signal station.

Km 528—Niederwald Monument: Across from the Bingen station on a hilltop is the 120-foot-high Niederwald monument, a memorial built with 32 tons of bronze in 1877 to commemorate "the re-establishment of the German Empire." A lift takes tourists to this statue from the famous and extremely touristy wine town of Rüdesheim.

From here, the Romantic Rhine becomes the industrial Rhine, and our tour is over.

Sights Along the Rhine

▲▲Marksburg Castle (Marksburg)

Medieval invaders decided to give Marksburg a miss thanks to its formidable defenses. This best-preserved castle on the Rhine can be toured only with a guide on a 50-minute tour. In summer, tours in English normally run daily at 13:00 and 16:00. Otherwise, you can join a German tour (3/hour in summer, hourly in winter) that's almost as good—there are no explanations  in English in the castle itself, but your ticket includes an English handout. It's an awesome castle, and between the handout and my commentary, you'll feel fully informed, so don't worry about being on time for the English tours.

Cost and Hours: €7, family card-€16, daily 10:00-18:00, Nov-mid-March 11:00-16:00, last tour departs one hour before closing, tel. 02627/206, www.marksburg.de.

Getting There: Marksburg caps a hill above the village of Braubach, on the east bank of the Rhine. By **train**, it's a 10-minute trip from Koblenz to Braubach (1-2/hour); from Bacharach or St. Goar, it can take up to two hours, depending on the length of the layover in Koblenz. The train is quicker than the **boat** (downstream from Bacharach to Braubach-2 hours, upstream return-3.5 hours; €30.40 one-way, €36.40 round-trip). Consider taking the downstream boat to Braubach, and the train back. If traveling with luggage, store it in the convenient lockers in the underground passage at the Koblenz train station (Braubach has no enclosed station—just platforms—and no lockers).

Once you reach Braubach, **walk** into the old town (follow *Altstadt* signs—coming out of tunnel from train platforms, it's to your right); then follow the *Zur Burg* signs to the path up to the castle. Allow 25 minutes for the climb up. Scarce **taxis** charge at least €10 from the train platforms to the castle. A green **tourist train** circles up to the castle, but there's no fixed schedule (Easter-mid-Oct Tue-Sun, no trains Mon or off-season, €3 one-way, €5 round-trip, leaves from Barbarastrasse, confirm departure times by calling 06773/587, www.ruckes-reisen.de). Even if you take the tourist train, you'll still have to climb the last five minutes up to the castle from its parking lot.

Visiting the Castle: Your guided tour starts inside the castle's first gate.

Inside the First Gate: While the dramatic castles lining the Rhine are generally Romantic rebuilds, Marksburg is the real McCoy—nearly all original construction. It's littered with bits of its medieval past, like the big stone ball that was swung on a rope to be used as a battering ram. Ahead, notice how the inner gate—originally tall enough for knights on horseback to gallop through—was made smaller to deter enemies on horseback. Climb the Knights' Stairway, carved out of slate, and pass under the murder hole—handy for pouring boiling pitch on invaders. (Germans still say someone with bad luck "has pitch on his head.")

Coats of Arms: Colorful coats of arms line the wall just inside the gate. These are from the noble families who have owned the castle since 1283. In that year, financial troubles drove the first family to sell to the powerful and wealthy Katzenelnbogen family (who made the castle into what you see today). When Napoleon took this region in 1803, an Austrian family who sided with the French got the keys. When Prussia took the region in 1866, control passed to a friend of the Prussians who had a passion for medieval things—typical of this Romantic period. Then it was sold to the German Castles Association in 1900. Its offices are in the main palace at the top of the stairs.

Romanesque Palace: White outlines mark where the larger

original windows were located, before they were replaced by easier-to-defend smaller ones. On the far right, a bit of the original plaster survives. Slate, which is vulnerable to the elements, needs to be covered—in this case, by plaster. Because this is a protected historic building, restorers can use only the traditional plaster methods... but no one knows how to make plaster that works as well as the 800-year-old surviving bits.

Cannons: The oldest cannon here—from 1500—was back-loaded. This was advantageous because many cartridges could be preloaded. But since the seal was leaky, it wasn't very powerful. The bigger, more modern cannons—from 1640—were one piece and therefore airtight, but had to be front-loaded. They could easily hit targets across the river from here. Stone balls were rough, so they let the explosive force leak out. The best cannonballs were stones covered in smooth lead—airtight and therefore more powerful and more accurate.

Gothic Garden: Walking along an outer wall, you'll see 160 plants from the Middle Ages—used for cooking, medicine, and witchcraft. *Schierling* (hemlock, in the first corner) is the same poison that killed Socrates.

Inland Rampart: This most vulnerable part of the castle had a triangular construction to better deflect attacks. Notice the factory in the valley. In the 14th century, this was a lead, copper, and silver mine. Today's factory—Europe's largest car-battery recycling plant—uses the old mine shafts as vents (see the three modern smokestacks).

Wine Cellar: Since Roman times, wine has been the traditional Rhineland drink. Because castle water was impure, wine—less alcoholic than today's beer—was the way knights got their fluids. The pitchers on the wall were their daily allotment. The bellows were part of the barrel's filtering system. Stairs lead to the...

Gothic Hall: This hall is set up as a kitchen, with an oven designed to roast an ox whole. The arms holding the pots have notches to control the heat. To this day, when Germans want someone to hurry up, they say, "give it one tooth more." Medieval windows were made of thin sheets of translucent alabaster or animal skins. A nearby wall is peeled away to show the wattle-and-daub construction (sticks, straw, clay, mud, then plaster) of a castle's inner walls. The iron plate to the left of the next door enabled servants to stoke the heater without being seen by the noble family.

Bedroom: This was the only heated room in the castle. The canopy kept in heat and kept out critters. In medieval times, it was impolite for a lady to argue with her lord in public. She would wait for him in bed to give him what Germans still call "a curtain lecture." The deep window seat caught maximum light for needlework

Rhein in Flammen

During the annual "Rhine in Flames" festival, spectacular displays of fireworks take place along the most scenic stretches of the Rhine, while beautifully illuminated ships ply the river, offering up-close views of the fireworks above. Held on five days between May and September, the festival rotates between several Rhine towns. Traditional wine festivals and other local celebrations are often timed to coincide with the Rhein in Flammen (in Bonn in May, Rüdesheim in July, Koblenz in August, and Oberwesel and St. Goar in September; confirm dates at www.rhein-in-flammen.com).

and reading. Women would sit here and chat (or "spin a yarn") while working the spinning wheel.

Hall of the Knights: This was the dining hall. The long table is an unattached plank. After each course, servants could replace it with another pre-set plank. Even today, when a meal is over and Germans are ready for the action to begin, they say, "Let's lift up the table." The action back then consisted of traveling minstrels who sang and told of news gleaned from their travels.

Notice the outhouse—made of wood—hanging over thin air. When not in use, its door was locked from the outside (the castle side) to prevent any invaders from entering this weak point in the castle's defenses.

Chapel: This chapel is still painted in Gothic style with the castle's namesake, St. Mark, and his lion. Even the chapel was designed with defense in mind. The small doorway kept out heavily armed attackers. The staircase spirals clockwise, favoring the sword-wielding defender (assuming he was right-handed).

Linen Room: About the year 1800, the castle—with diminished military value—housed disabled soldiers. They'd earn a little extra money working raw flax into linen.

Two Thousand Years of Armor: Follow the evolution of armor since Celtic times. Because helmets covered the entire head, soldiers identified themselves as friendly by tipping their visor up with their right hand. This evolved into the military salute that is still used around the world today. Armor and the close-range weapons along the back were made obsolete by the invention of the rifle. Armor was replaced with breastplates—pointed (like the castle itself) to deflect enemy fire. This design was used as late as the start of World War I. A medieval lady's armor hangs over the door. While popular fiction has men locking up their women before heading off to battle, chastity belts were actually used by women as protection against rape when traveling.

The Keep: This served as an observation tower, a dungeon (with a 22-square-foot cell in the bottom), and a place of last refuge. When all was nearly lost, the defenders would bundle into the keep and burn the wooden bridge, hoping to outwait their enemies.

Horse Stable: The stable shows off bits of medieval crime and punishment. Cheaters were attached to stones or pillories. Shame masks punished gossipmongers. A mask with a heavy ball had its victim crawling around with his nose in the mud. The handcuffs with a neck hole were for the transport of prisoners. The pictures on the wall show various medieval capital punishments. Many times the accused was simply taken into a torture dungeon to see all these tools, and, guilty or not, confessions spilled out of him. On that cheery note, your tour is over.

The Loreley Visitors Center (Besucherzentrum Loreley)

Easily reached from St. Goar, this lightweight exhibit reflects a little on Loreley, but focuses mainly on the landscape, culture, and people of the Rhine Valley. Though English explanations accompany most of the geological and cultural displays, the information about the famous mythical *Mädchen* is given in German only. The 3-D movie is essentially a tourist brochure for the region, with scenes of the grape harvest over Bacharach that are as beautiful as the sword-fighting is lame.

Far more exciting than the exhibit is the view from the cliffs themselves. A five-minute walk from the bus stop and visitors center takes you to the impressive viewpoint overlooking the Rhine Valley from atop the famous rock.

Cost and Hours: €2.50, daily April-Oct 10:00-17:00, closed Nov-March, café, tel. 06771/599-093, www.loreley-besucherzentrum.de.

Getting There: For a good hour's **hike,** catch the ferry from St. Goar across to the village of St. Goarshausen (€1.80 each way, every 20 minutes daily until 22:30, less frequent on Sun). Then follow green *Burg Katz* (Katz Castle) signs up Burgstrasse under the train tracks to find steps on the right *(Loreley über Burg Katz)* leading to Katz Castle (privately owned) and beyond. Traverse the hillside, always bearing right toward the river. You'll pass through a residential area, hike down a 50-yard path through trees, then cross a wheat field until you reach the Loreley Visitors Center and rock-capping viewpoint.

If you're not up for a hike, catch **bus #535** from just left of the St. Goarshausen ferry ramp (€2.90 each way, departs almost hourly, Easter-Oct Mon-Fri 8:45-18:45, Sat-Sun from 9:45).

To return to St. Goarshausen and the St. Goar ferry, you can take the bus (last departure 19:00), retrace your steps along the Burg Katz trail, or hike a steep 15 minutes directly down to the river, where the riverfront road takes you back to St. Goarshausen.

Loreley-Bob Luge Ride

Next to the Loreley Visitors Center is the Loreley-Bob, a summer luge course *(Sommerrodelbahn)*, with wheeled carts that seat one or two riders and whisk you down a stainless-steel track. It's a fun diversion, especially if you don't plan to visit the Tegelberg luge near Neuschwanstein or the scenic Biberwier luge in Austria. For hints on riding a luge, see the sidebar on page 204.

Cost and Hours: €3/ride, €13 shareable 6-ride card; daily 10:00-17:00, closed mid-Nov-mid-March, may close in bad weather—call ahead, no children under age 3, ages 3-8 may ride with an adult, tel. 06771/959-4833 or 06651/9800, www.loreleybob.de.

▲▲Rheinstein Castle (Schloss Burg Rheinstein)

This castle seems to rule its chunk of the Rhine from a commanding position. While its 13th-century exterior is medieval as can be, the interior is mostly a 19th-  century duke's hunting palace. Visitors wander freely (with an English flier) among trophies, armor, and Romantic Age decor.

Cost and Hours: €6; mid-March-Oct Mon 10:00-17:30, Tue-Sun 10:00-18:00; Nov-mid-March Sat-Sun only 12:00-16:00; tel. 06721/6348, www.burg-rheinstein.de.

Getting There: This castle (at km 533 marker, 2 km upstream from Trechtingshausen on the main B-9 highway) is easy by **car** (small, free parking lot on B-9, steep 5-minute hike from there), or **bike** (35 minutes upstream from Bacharach, stick to the great riverside path, after km 534 marker look for small *Burg Rheinstein* sign and Rösler-Linie dock). It's less convenient by **boat** (no K-D stop nearby) or **train** (nearest stop in Trechtingshausen, a 30-minute walk away).

Bacharach

Once prosperous from the wine and wood trade, charming Bacharach (BAHKH-ah-rahkh, with a guttural *kh* sound) is now just a pleasant half-timbered village of 2,000 people working hard to keep its tourists happy. Businesses that have been "in the family" for eons are dealing with succession challenges, as the allure of big-city jobs and a more cosmopolitan life lure away the town's younger generation. But Bacharach retains its time-capsule quaintness.

RHINE VALLEY

Orientation to Bacharach

Bacharach cuddles, long and narrow, along the Rhine. The village is easily strollable—you can walk from one end of town to the other along its main drag, Oberstrasse, in about 10 minutes. Bacharach widens at its stream, where more houses trickle up its small valley (along Blücherstrasse) away from the Rhine. The hillsides above town are occupied by vineyards, scant remains of the former town walls, and a castle-turned-hostel.

TOURIST INFORMATION

The bright and well-stocked TI, on the main street a block-and-a-half from the train station, will store bags and bikes for day-trippers (April-Oct Mon-Fri 9:00-17:00, Sat-Sun 10:00-15:00; Nov-March Mon-Fri 9:00-13:00, closed Sat-Sun; from the train station, exit right and walk down the main street with the castle high on your left—the TI will be on your right at Ober-

strasse 10; tel. 06743/919-303, www.bacharach.de or www.rhein-nahe-touristik.de, Herr Kuhn and his team).

HELPFUL HINTS

Carry Cash: Although more places are accepting credit cards, come prepared to pay cash for most things in the Rhine Valley.

Shopping: The **Jost** German gift store, across the main square from the church, carries most everything a souvenir shopper could want—from beer steins to cuckoo clocks—and can ship purchases to the US (RS% with €10 minimum purchase: 10 percent with cash, 5 percent with credit card; open daily 9:00-18:00, closed Nov-Feb; Blücherstrasse 4, tel. 06743/909-7214).

Laundry: The **Sonnenstrand campground** may let you use their facilities even if you're not staying there, but priority goes to those who are. Call ahead (tel. 06743/1752).

Picnics: You can pick up picnic supplies at **Tomi's,** a basic grocery store (Mon-Fri 8:00-12:30 & 14:00-18:00, Sat 8:00-12:30, closed Sun, Koblenzer Strasse 2). For a gourmet picnic, call the recommended **Rhein Hotel** to reserve a "picnic bag" complete with wine, cheese, small dishes, and a hiking map (€15/person, arrange a day in advance, tel. 06743/1243).

Bike Rental: Some hotels loan bikes to guests. For bike rental in town, head to **Rent-a-Bike Weber** (€10/day, Koblenzer

Strasse 35, tel. 06743-1898, mobile 0175-168073, heidi100450@aol.com).

Parking: It's simple to park along the highway next to the train tracks or, better, in the big public lot by the boat dock (€4 from 9:00 to 18:00, pay with coins at *Parkscheinautomat*, display ticket on dash, free overnight).

Local Guides: Thomas Gundlach happily gives 1.5-hour town walks to individuals or small groups for €35. History buffs will enjoy his "war tour," which focuses on the town's survival from 1864 through World War II. He also offers 4- to 10-hour hiking or biking tours for the more ambitious (mobile 0179-353-6004, thomas_gundlach@gmx.de). Also good is **Birgit Wessels** (€45/1.5-hour walk, tel. 06743/937-514, wessels.birgit@t-online.de). The **TI** offers 1.5-hour tours in English with various themes, including a night tour (prices vary, gather a group). Or take my self-guided town walk or walk the walls—both are described next.

Taxi: Call Dirk Büttner at 06743/1653.

Bacharach Town Walk

• *Start this self-guided walk at the Köln-Düsseldorfer ferry dock (next to a fine picnic park).*

Riverfront: View the town from the parking lot—a modern landfill. The Rhine used to lap against Bacharach's town wall, just over the present-day highway. Every few years the river floods, covering the highway with several feet of water. Flat land like this is rare in the Rhine Valley, where towns are often shaped like the letter "T," stretching thin along the riverfront and up a crease in the hills beyond.

Reefs farther upstream forced boats to unload upriver and re-load here. Consequently, in the Middle Ages, Bacharach was the biggest wine-trading town on the Rhine. A riverfront crane hoisted huge kegs of prestigious "Bacharach" wine (which, in practice, was from anywhere in the region). Today, the economy is based on tourism.

Look above town. The **castle** on the hill is now a hostel. Two of the town's original 16 towers are visible from here (up to five if you look really hard). The bluff on the right, with the yellow flag, is the **Heinrich Heine Viewpoint** (the end-point of a popular hike). Old-timers remember when, rather than the flag marking the town as a World Heritage site, a swastika sculpture 30 feet wide and tall stood there. Realizing that it could be an enticing target for Allied planes in the last months of World War II, locals tore it down even before Hitler fell.

Nearby, a stone column in the park describes the Bingen to Koblenz stretch of the Rhine gorge.

• *Before entering the town, walk upstream through the...*

Riverside Park: The park was originally laid out in 1910 in the English style: Notice how the trees were planted to frame fine town views, highlighting the most pic-
turesque bits of architecture. Erected in 2016, a Picasso-esque sculpture by Bacharach artist Liesel Metten—of three figures sharing a bottle of wine (a Riesling, perhaps?)—celebrates three men who brought fame to the area through poetry and prose: Victor Hugo, Clemens Brentano, and Heinrich Heine. Other new elements of the park are designed to bring people to the riverside and combat flooding.

The dark, sad-looking monu-
ment—its "eternal" flame long snuffed out—is a **war memorial.** The German psyche is permanently scarred by war memories. Today, many Germans would rather avoid monuments like this, which recall the dark periods be-
fore Germany became a nation of pacifists. The military Maltese cross—flanked by classic German helmets—has a W at its center, for Kaiser Wilhelm. On the opposite side, each panel honors sons of Bacharach who died for the Kaiser: in 1864 against Denmark, in 1866 against Austria, in 1870 against France, in 1914 during World War I. Review the family names below: You may later recognize them on today's restaurants and hotels.

• *Look upstream from here to see (in the distance) the...*

Trailer Park and Campground: In Germany, trailer vacation-
ers and campers are two distinct subcultures. Folks who travel in motorhomes, like many retirees in the US, are a nomadic bunch, cruising around the countryside and paying a few euros a night to park. Campers, on the other hand, tend to set up camp in one place—complete with comfortable lounge chairs and TVs—and stay put for weeks, even months. They often come back to the same spot year after year, treating it like their own private estate. These camping devotees have made a science out of relaxing. Tourists are welcome to pop in for a drink or meal at the campground café (see "Activities in Bacharach," later).

• *Continue to where the park meets the playground, and then cross the highway to the fortified riverside wall of the Catholic church, decorated with...*

High-Water Marks: These recall various floods. Before the

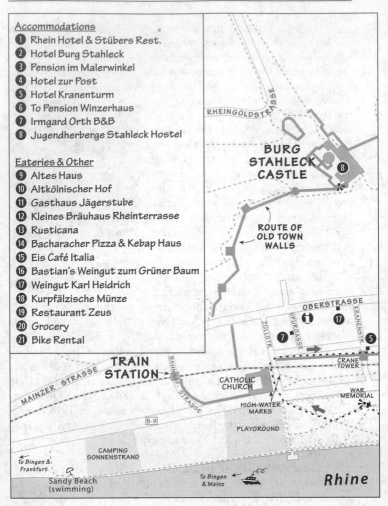

Accommodations
1 Rhein Hotel & Stübers Rest.
2 Hotel Burg Stahleck
3 Pension im Malerwinkel
4 Hotel zur Post
5 Hotel Kranenturm
6 To Pension Winzerhaus
7 Irmgard Orth B&B
8 Jugendherberge Stahleck Hostel

Eateries & Other
9 Altes Haus
10 Altkölnischer Hof
11 Gasthaus Jägerstube
12 Kleines Bräuhaus Rheinterrasse
13 Rusticana
14 Bacharacher Pizza & Kebap Haus
15 Eis Café Italia
16 Bastian's Weingut zum Grüner Baum
17 Weingut Karl Heidrich
18 Kurpfälzische Münze
19 Restaurant Zeus
20 Grocery
21 Bike Rental

RHEINGOLDSTRASSE

BURG STAHLECK CASTLE

ROUTE OF OLD TOWN WALLS

OBERSTRASSE

KRANENSTR.

ZOLLSTR.

SPURGASSE

BURGGASSE

CRANE TOWER

WAR MEMORIAL

TRAIN STATION

MAINZER STRASSE

BAHNHOF-STRASSE

CATHOLIC CHURCH

HIGH-WATER MARKS

PLAYGROUND

B-9

CAMPING SONNENSTRAND

To Bingen & Frankfurt

Sandy Beach (swimming)

To Bingen & Mainz

Rhine

1910 reclamation project, the river extended out to here, and boats would tie up at mooring rings that used to be in this wall.

• From the church, go under the 1858 train tracks (and past more high-water marks) and hook right up the stairs at the yellow floodwater yardstick to reach the town wall. Atop the wall, turn left and walk under the long arcade. After 30 yards, on your left, notice a...

Well: Rebuilt as it appeared in the 17th century, this is one of seven such wells that brought water to the townsfolk until 1900. Each neighborhood's well also provided a social gathering place and the communal laundry. Walk 50 yards past the well along the wall to an alcove in the medieval tower with a view of the war memorial in the park. You're under the crane tower (Kranenturm). After barrels of wine were moved overland from Bingen, avoiding

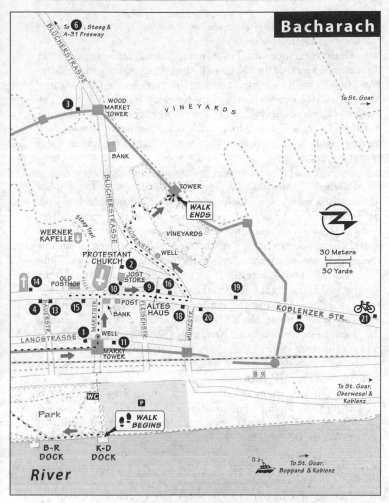

Bacharach

dangerous stretches of river, the precious cargo could be lowered by cranes from here into ships to continue more safely down the river. The Rhine has long been a major shipping route through Germany. In modern times, it's a bottleneck in Germany's train system. The train company gives hotels and residents along the tracks money for soundproof windows.

• *Continue walking along the town wall. Pass the recommended Rhein Hotel just before the...*

Markt Tower: This marks one of the town's 15 original 14th-century gates and is a reminder that in that century there was a big wine market here.

• *Descend the stairs closest to the Rhein Hotel, pass another well, and follow Marktstrasse away from the river toward the town center, the two-tone church, and the town's...*

Main Intersection: From here, Bacharach's main street (Oberstrasse) goes right to the half-timbered red-and-white Altes Haus (which we'll visit later) and left 400 yards to the train station. Spin around to enjoy the higgledy-piggledy building styles. The town has a case of the doldrums: The younger generation is moving to the big cities and many long-established family businesses have no one to take over for their aging owners. In the winter the town is particularly dead.

• *To the left (south) of the church, a golden horn hangs over the old...*

Posthof: Throughout Europe, the postal horn is the symbol of the postal service. In olden days, when the postman blew this, traffic stopped and the mail sped through. This post station dates from 1724, when stagecoaches ran from Cologne to Frankfurt and would change horses here, Pony Express-style. Notice the corner-stones at the Posthof entrance, protecting the venerable building from reckless carriage wheels. If it's open, inside the old oak doors (on the left) is the actual door to the post office that served Bacharach for 200 years. Find the mark on the wall labeled *Rheinhöhe 30/1-4/2 1850.* This recalls a historic flood caused by an ice jam at the Loreley just downstream. Notice also the fascist eagle in the al-cove on the right (from 1936; a swastika once filled its center). The courtyard was once a carriage house and inn that accommodated Bacharach's first VIP visitors.

Two hundred years ago, Bacharach's main drag was the only road along the Rhine. Napoleon widened it to fit his cannon wag-ons. The steps alongside the church lead to the ruins of the 15th-century Werner Chapel and the castle.

• *Return to the church, passing the recommended Italian ice-cream café* **(Eis Café Italia),** *where friendly Mimo serves his special invention: Riesling wine-flavored gelato.*

Protestant Church: Inside the church (daily 10:00-18:00, closed Nov-March, English info on a stand near door), you'll find grotesque capitals, brightly painted in medieval style, and a mix of round Romanesque and pointed Gothic arches. The church was fancier before the Reformation wars, when it (and the region) was Catholic. Bacharach lies on the religious border of Germany and, like the country as a whole, is split between Catholics and Prot-estants. To the left of the altar, some medieval (pre-Reformation) frescoes survive where an older Romanesque arch was cut by a pointed Gothic one.

If you're considering bombing the town, take note: A blue-and-white plaque just outside the church's door warns that, accord-ing to the Hague Convention, this historic building shouldn't be targeted in times of war.

• *Continue down Oberstrasse to the...*

Altes Haus: Dating from 1389, this is the oldest house in town. Notice the 14th-century building style—the first floor is made of stone, while upper floors are half-timbered (in the ornate style common in the Rhine Valley). Some of its windows still look medieval, with small, flattened circles as panes (small because that's all that the glass-blowing technology of the time would allow), pieced together with molten lead (like medieval stained glass in churches). Frau Weber welcomes visitors to enjoy the fascinating ground floor of the recommended Altes Haus restaurant, with its evocative old photos and etchings (consider eating here later).

• *Keep going down Oberstrasse to the...*

Old Mint (Münze): The old mint is marked by a crude coin in its sign. As a practicality, any great trading town needed coinage, and since 1356, Bacharach minted theirs here. Now, it's a restaurant and bar, **Kurpfälzische Münze,** with occasional live music. Across from the mint, the recommended **Bastian** family's wine garden is another lively place in the evening (see "Nightlife in Bacharach" and "Wine Tasting," later). Above you in the vineyards stands a lonely white-and-red tower—your final destination.

• *At the next street, look right and see the mint tower, painted in the medieval style, and then turn left. Wander 30 yards up Rosenstrasse to the **well**. Notice the sundial and the wall painting of 1632 Bacharach with its walls intact. Study the fine slate roof over the well: The town's roof tiles were quarried and split right here in the Rhineland. Continue another 30 yards up Rosenstrasse to find the tiny-stepped lane on the right leading up into the vineyard and to the...*

Tall Tower: The slate steps lead to a small path through the vineyard that deposits you at a viewpoint atop the stubby remains of the medieval wall and a tower. The town's towers jutted out from the wall and had only three sides, with the "open" side facing the town. Towers were covered with stucco to make them look more impressive, as if they were made of a finer white stone. If this tower's open, hike up to climb the stairs for the best view. (The top floor has been closed to give nesting falcons some privacy.)

Romantic Rhine View: Looking south, a grand medieval town spreads before you. For 300 years (1300-1600), Bacharach was big (population 4,000), rich, and politically powerful.

From this perch, you can see the ruins of a 15th-century chapel and six surviving **city towers.** Visually trace the wall to the Stahleck Castle. The castle was actually the capital of Germany for a couple of years in the 1200s. When Holy Roman Emperor Frederick Barbarossa went away to fight the Crusades, he left his brother (who lived here) in charge of his vast realm. Bacharach was home to one of the seven electors who voted for the Holy Roman Emperor in 1275. To protect their own power, these prince electors did their best to choose the weakest guy on the ballot. The elector from Bacharach helped select a two-bit prince named Rudolf von Habsburg (from a no-name castle in Switzerland). However, the underestimated Rudolf brutally silenced the robber barons along the Rhine and established the mightiest dynasty in European history. His family line, the Habsburgs, ruled much of Central and Eastern Europe from Vienna until 1918.

Plagues, fires, and the Thirty Years' War (1618-1648) finally did in Bacharach. The town has slumbered for several centuries. Today, the castle houses commoners—40,000 overnights annually by hostelers.

In the mid-19th century, painters such as J. M. W. Turner and writers such as Victor Hugo were charmed by the Rhineland's romantic mix of past glory, present poverty, and rich legend. They put this part of the Rhine on the old Grand Tour map as the "Romantic Rhine." Hugo pondered the chapel ruins that you see under the castle: In his 1842 travel book, *Excursions Along the Banks of the Rhine*, he wrote, "No doors, no roof or windows, a magnificent skeleton puts its silhouette against the sky. Above it, the ivy-covered castle ruins provide a fitting crown. This is Bacharach, land of fairy tales, covered with legends and sagas." If you're enjoying the Romantic Rhine, thank Victor Hugo and company.

• *Our walk is done. To get back into town, just retrace your steps. Or, to extend this walk, take the level path away from the river that leads along the once-mighty wall up the valley to the next tower, the...*

Wood Market Tower: Timber was gathered here in Bacharach and lashed together into vast log booms known as "Holland rafts" (as big as a soccer field) that were floated downstream. Two weeks later the lumber would reach Amsterdam, where it was in high demand as foundation posts for buildings and for the great Dutch shipbuilders. Notice the four stones above the arch on the uphill side of the tower—these guided the gate as it was hoisted up and down.

• *From here, cross the street and go downhill into the parking lot. Pass the recommended* **Pension im Malerwinkel** *on your right, being careful not to damage the old arch with your head. Follow the creek past a delightful little series of half-timbered homes and cheery gardens known as* "**Painters' Corner**" *(Malerwinkel). Resist looking into some weirdo's peep show (on the right) and continue downhill back to the village center.*

RHINE VALLEY

Activities in Bacharach

Walk Along the Old Town Walls

A steep and rocky but clearly marked walking path follows the remains of Bacharach's old town walls and makes for a good hour's workout. There are benches along the way where you can pause and take in views of the Rhine and Bacharach's slate roofs. The TI has maps that show the entire route. The path starts near the train station, climbs up to the hostel in what was Stahleck Castle (serves lunch from 12:00-13:30), descends into the side valley, and then continues up the other side to the tower in the vineyards before returning to town. To start the walk at the train station, find the house at Oberstrasse 2 and climb up the stairway to its left. Then follow the *Stadtmauer-Rundweg* signs. Good bilingual signposts tell the history of each of the towers along the wall—some are intact, one is a private residence, and others are now only stubs.

Swimming, Eating, and Drinking at Camping Sonnenstrand

This campground, a 10-minute walk upstream from Bacharach, has a sandy beach with water as still as a lake, and welcomes non-campers (especially if you buy a drink at their café). On hot summer days you can enjoy a dip in the Rhine at the beach at your own risk (free, no lifeguard—beware of strong current). This is a chance to see Euro-style camping, which comes with a sense of community. Campers are mostly Dutch, English, Belgian, and German, with lots of kids (and a playground). The **$ terrace café** overlooking the campsites and the river is the social center and works well for a drink or meal (inside or outside with river view, daily 17:00-21:00, closed Nov-March, tel. 06743/1752, www.camping-rhein.de).

Sleeping in Bacharach

The only listings with parking are Pension im Malerwinkel, Pension Winzerhaus, and the hostel. For the others, you can drive in to unload your bags and then park in the public lot (see "Helpful Hints," earlier). If you'll arrive after 20:00, let your hotel know in advance (many hotels with restaurants stay open late, but none have 24-hour reception desks).

$$ Rhein Hotel, overlooking the river with 14 spacious and comfortable rooms, is classy, well-run, and decorated with modern flair. This place has been in the Stüber family for six generations and is decorated with works of art by the current owner's siblings. The large family room downstairs is über stylish, while the quaint "hiker room" on the top floor features terrific views of both the town and river. You can sip local wines in the renovated room where owner Andreas was born (river- and train-side rooms come with quadruple-paned windows and air-con, in-room sauna, packages available including big three-course dinner, ask about "picnic bags" when you check in, free loaner bikes, directly inland from the K-D boat dock at Langstrasse 50, tel. 06743/1243, www.rhein-hotel-bacharach.de, info@rhein-hotel-bacharach.de). Their recommended Stübers Restaurant is considered the best in town.

$$ Hotel Burg Stahleck, above a cozy café in the town center, rents five big, bright rooms, more chic than shabby. Birgit treats guests to homemade cakes at breakfast (family rooms, view room, free parking, cheaper rooms in guesthouse around the corner, Blücherstrasse 6, tel. 06743/1388, www.urlaub-bacharach.de, info@urlaub-bacharach.de).

$ Pension im Malerwinkel sits like a grand gingerbread house that straddles the town wall in a quiet little neighborhood so charming it's called "Painters' Corner" *(Malerwinkel).* The Vollmer family's super-quiet 20-room place is a short stroll from the town center. Here guests can sit in a picturesque garden on a brook and enjoy views of the vineyards (cash only, family rooms, elevator, no train noise, bike rentals, easy parking; from

Oberstrasse, turn left at the church, walkers can follow the path to the left just before the town gate but drivers must pass through the gate to find the hotel parking lot, Blücherstrasse 41; tel. 06743/1239, www.im-malerwinkel.de, pension@im-malerwinkel.de, Armin and Daniela).

$ Hotel zur Post, refreshingly clean and quiet, is conveniently located right in the town center with no train noise. Its 12 rooms are a good value. Run by friendly and efficient Ute, the hotel offers more solid comfort than old-fashioned character, though the lovely wood-paneled breakfast room has a rustic feel (family room, Oberstrasse 38, tel. 06743/1277, www.hotel-zur-post-bacharach.de, h.zurpost@t-online.de).

$ Hotel Kranenturm, part of the medieval town wall, has 16 rooms with rustic castle ambience and *Privatzimmer* funkiness right downtown. The rooms in its former *Kranenturm* (crane tower) have the best views. While just 15 feet from the train tracks, a combination of medieval sturdiness and triple-paned windows makes the riverside rooms sleepable (RS%, family rooms, Rhine views come with train noise—earplugs on request, back rooms are quieter, closed Jan-Feb, Langstrasse 30, tel. 06743/1308, mobile 0176-8056-3863, www.kranenturm.com, hotel.kranenturm@gmail.com).

$ Pension Winzerhaus, a 10-room place run by friendly Sybille and Stefan, is just outside the town walls, directly under the vineyards. The rooms are simple, clean, and modern, and parking is a breeze (cash only, family room, laundry service, parking, nondrivers may be able to arrange a pickup at the train station—ask in advance, Blücherstrasse 60, tel. 06743/1294, www.pension-winzerhaus.de, winzerhaus@gmx.de).

¢ Irmgard Orth B&B rents three bright rooms, two of which share a small bathroom on the hall. Charming Irmgard speaks almost no English, but is exuberantly cheery and serves homemade honey with breakfast (cash only, Spurgasse 2, tel. 06743/1553—speak slowly; she prefers email: orth.irmgard@gmail.com).

¢ Jugendherberge Stahleck hostel is a 12th-century castle on the hilltop—350 steps above Bacharach—with a royal Rhine view. Open to travelers of any age, this gem has 36 rooms, eight with private showers and WCs. The hostel offers hearty all-you-can-eat buffet dinners (18:00-19:30 nightly); in summer, its bistro serves drinks and snacks until 22:00. If you arrive at the

train station with luggage, it's a minimum €10 taxi ride to the hostel—call 06743/1653 (pay Wi-Fi, reception open 7:00-20:00—call if arriving later, tel. 06743/1266, www.diejugendherbergen.de, bacharach@diejugendherbergen.de, Samuel). If driving, don't go in the driveway; park on the street and walk 200 yards.

Eating in Bacharach

RESTAURANTS

Bacharach has several reasonably priced, atmospheric restaurants offering fine indoor and outdoor dining. Most places don't take credit cards.

The recommended Rhein Hotel's **$$$ Stübers Restaurant** is Bacharach's best top-end choice. Andreas Stüber, his family's sixth-generation chef, creates regional plates prepared with a slow-food ethic. The menu changes with the season and is served at river- and track-side seating or indoors with a spacious wood-and-white-tablecloth elegance. Consider the William Turner pâté starter plate, named after the British painter who liked Bacharach. Book in advance for the special Tuesday slow-food menu (discount for hotel guests, always good vegetarian and vegan options, daily 17:00-21:30 plus Sun 11:30-14:15, closed mid-Dec-Feb, call or

RHINE VALLEY

email to reserve on weekends or for an outdoor table when balmy, family-friendly with a play area, Langstrasse 50, tel. 06743/1243, info@rhein-hotel-bacharach.de). Their Posten Riesling is well worth the splurge and pairs well with both the food and the atmosphere.

$$$ Altes Haus, the oldest building in town (see the "Bacharach Town Walk," earlier), serves classic German dishes within Bacharach's most romantic atmosphere. Find the cozy little dining room with photos of the opera singer who sang about Bacharach, adding to its fame (Thu-Tue 12:00-14:30 & 18:00-21:30, Mon dinner only, limited menu and closes at 18:00 on weekends, closed Wed and Dec-Easter, dead center by the Protestant church, tel. 06743/1209).

$$$ Altkölnischer Hof is a family-run place with outdoor seating right on the main square, serving Rhine specialties that burst with flavor. This restored 18th-century banquet hall feels formal and sophisticated inside, with high ceilings and oil paintings depicting the building's history. Reserve an outdoor table for a more relaxed meal, especially on weekends when locals pack the place (Tue-Sun 12:00-14:30 & 17:30-21:00, closed Mon and Nov-Easter, Blücherstrasse 2, tel. 06743/947-780, www.altkoelnischer-hof.de).

CASUAL OPTIONS

$$ Gasthaus Jägerstube is every local's nontouristy, good-value hangout. It's a no-frills place run by a former East German family determined to keep Bacharach's working class well-fed and watered. Next to the WC is a rare "party cash box." Regulars drop money into their personal slot throughout the year, Frau Tischmeier banks it, and by year's end...there's plenty in the little savings account for a community party (Wed-Mon March-Nov 11:00-22:00, food served until 21:30; Dec-Feb from 15:00, food served until 20:30; closed Tue year-round; Marktstrasse 3, tel. 06743/1492, Tischmeier family).

$$ Kleines Brauhaus Rheinterrasse is a funky microbrewery serving hearty meals, fresh-baked bread, and homemade beer under a 1958 circus carousel that overlooks the town and river. Sweet Annette cooks while Armin brews, and the kids run free in this family-friendly place. For a sweet finish, try the "beer-liquor," which tastes like Christmas. Don't leave without putting €0.20 in the merry-go-round-in-a-box in front of the Rhine Theater next door (Tue-Sun 13:00-22:00, closed Mon, at the downstream end of town, Koblenzer Strasse 14, tel. 06743/919-179). The little flea market in the attached shed seems to fit right in.

$$ Rusticana, draped in greenery, is an inviting place serving homestyle German food and apple strudel that even the locals swear by. Sit on the delightful patio or at cozy tables inside (daily 11:00-20:00, credit cards accepted, Oberstrasse 40, tel. 06743/1741).

$ Bacharacher Pizza and Kebap Haus, on the main drag, is the town favorite for *döner kebabs*, cheap pizzas, and salads. Imam charges the same to eat in or take out (daily 11:00-22:00, Oberstrasse 43, tel. 06743/3127).

Camping Sonnenstrand, a 10-minute walk from town, has a café (dinner only) with great river views inside and out (see "Activities in Bacharach," earlier).

Gelato: Right on the main street, **Eis Café Italia** is run by friendly Mimo Calabrese, who brought gelato to town in 1976. He's known for his refreshing, not-too-sweet Riesling-flavored gelato. He also makes one with rose petals from a nearby farm. Eat in or take it on your evening stroll (no tastes offered, homemade, Waldmeister flavor is made with forest herbs—top secret, daily 13:00-19:00, closed mid-Oct-March, Oberstrasse 48).

WINE TASTING

Bacharach is proud of its wine. Two places in town—Bastian's rowdy and rustic Grüner Baum, and the more sophisticated Weingut Karl Heidrich—offer visitors an inexpensive tasting memory. Each creates carousels of local wines that small groups of travelers (who don't mind sharing a glass) can sample and compare. Both places offer light plates of food if you'd like a rustic meal.

At **$$ Bastian's Weingut zum Grüner Baum,** pay €29.50 for a wine carousel of 12 glasses—nine different white wines, two reds, and one lonely rosé—and a basket of bread. Your mission: Meet up here after dinner with others who have this book. Spin the Lazy Susan, share a common cup, and discuss the taste. The Bastian family insists: "After each wine, you must talk to each other" (daily 12:00-22:00, Nov-Dec closed Mon-Wed, closed Jan-Feb, just past Altes Haus, tel. 06743/1208). To make a meal of a carousel, consider the *Käseschmaus* (seven different cheeses—including *Spundekäse*, the local soft cheese—with bread and butter). Along with their characteristic interior, they have three nice terraces (front for shade, back for sun, and a courtyard).

$$ Weingut Karl Heidrich is a fun family-run wine shop and *Stube* in the town center, where Markus and daughters Magdalena and Katharina proudly share their family's centuries-old wine tradition, explaining its fine points to travelers. They offer a variety of €14.50 carousels with six wines, English descriptions, and bread—ideal for the more sophisticated wine taster—plus light meals and a meat-and-cheese plate (Thu-Mon 12:00-22:00, kitchen closes at 21:00, closed Tue-Wed and Nov-mid-April, Oberstrasse 16, will ship to the US, tel. 06743/93060, info@weingut-karl-heidrich.

de). With advance notice, they'll host a wine tasting and hike for groups (€185/up to 15 people).

Nightlife in Bacharach

Bacharach goes to bed early, so your options are limited for a little after-dinner action. But a handful of local bars/restaurants and two wine places (listed in "Wine Tasting," above) are welcoming and can be fun in the late hours.

$$ Kurpfälzische Münze (Old Mint) has live music some nights, ranging from jazz and blues to rock to salsa, and pairs local wines with meat-and-cheese plates and other local specialties (daily 12:00-24:00, Nov-March from 18:00). **Gasthaus Jägerstube** (described earlier) is a good pick for those who want to mix with a small local crowd. **$$ Restaurant Zeus**'s delicious Greek fare, long hours, and outdoor seating add a spark to the city center after dark (daily 17:30-24:00, cash only, Koblenzer Strasse 11, tel. 06743/909-7171). For something a bit off the beaten path try **Jugendherberge Stahleck**—Bacharach's hostel—where the bistro serves munchies and drinks with priceless views until 22:00 in summer (listed earlier, under "Sleeping in Bacharach").

Bacharach Connections

BY TRAIN

Milk-run trains stop at Rhine towns each hour starting as early as 6:00, connecting at Mainz and Koblenz to trains farther afield. Trains between St. Goar and Bacharach depart at about :50 after the hour in each direction (buy tickets from the machine in the unstaffed stations, carry cash since some machines won't accept US credit cards).

The durations listed below are calculated from Bacharach; for St. Goar, the difference is only 10 minutes. From Bacharach (or St. Goar), to go anywhere distant, you'll need to change trains in Koblenz for points north, or in Mainz for points south. Milk-run connections to these towns depart hourly, at about :50 past the hour for northbound trains, and at about :05 past the hour for southbound trains (with a few more on the half hour). Train info: www.bahn.com.

From **Bacharach by Train to: St. Goar** (hourly, 10 minutes), **Moselkern** near Burg Eltz (hourly, 1.5 hours, change in Koblenz), **Cochem** (hourly, 2 hours, change in Koblenz), **Trier** (hourly, 3 hours, change in Koblenz), **Cologne** (hourly, 2 hours with change in Koblenz, 2.5 hours direct), **Frankfurt Airport** (hourly, 1 hour, change in Mainz or Bingen), **Frankfurt** (hourly, 1.5 hours, change in Mainz or Bingen), **Rothenburg ob der Tauber** (every 2 hours,

4.5 hours, 3-4 changes), **Munich** (hourly, 5 hours, 2 changes), **Berlin** (every 2 hours with a transfer in Frankfurt, 5.5 hours; more with 2-3 changes), **Amsterdam** (hourly, 5-7 hours, change in Cologne, sometimes 1-2 more changes).

ROUTE TIPS FOR DRIVERS

This area is a logical first (or last) stop in Germany. If you're using Frankfurt Airport, here are some tips.

Frankfurt Airport to the Rhine: Driving from Frankfurt to the Rhine or Mosel takes about an hour (follow blue autobahn signs from airport—major cities are signposted).

The Rhine to Frankfurt: From St. Goar or Bacharach, follow the river to Bingen, then autobahn signs to *Mainz*, then *Frankfurt*. From there, head for the airport *(Flughafen)* or downtown (signs to *Messe*, then *Hauptbahnhof*, to find the parking under Frankfurt's main train station—see "Arrival in Frankfurt—By Car" on page 429).

Oberwesel

Oberwesel (OH-behr-vay-zehl), with more commerce than St. Goar and Bacharach combined, is just four miles from Bacharach. Oberwesel was a Celtic town in 400 BC, then a Roman military station. It's worth a quick visit, with a charming main square, a fun-to-walk medieval wall, and the best collection of historic Rhine artifacts I've found within the Rhine Valley. From the river, you'll notice its ship's masts rising from terra firma—a memorial to the generations of riverboat captains and sailors for whom this town is famous. Like most towns on the Rhine, Oberwesel is capped by a castle (Schönburg, now a restaurant, hotel, and youth hostel with a small museum). The other town landmark is its 130-foot-tall crenellated Ochsenturm (Oxen Tower), standing high and solitary overlooking the river.

Oberwesel is an easy stop by boat, train, bike, or car from Bacharach. There's free parking by the river (as is often the case in small towns, you must display a plastic clock—see page 1017).

Exploring Oberwesel is a breeze when you follow my self-guided walk. Start out by picking up a map from the **TI** on the main square (closed Sun, 10-minute walk from the train station at Rathausstrasse 3—from the station turn right and follow Liebfrauenstrasse to Marktplatz, tel. 06744/710-624, www.oberwesel. de). Maps are also available at the Kulturhaus and Stadtmuseum Oberwesel, and posted around town—just snap a photo of one to use as a guide.

Oberwesel Walk

I've laced together Oberwesel's sights with this self-guided walk. Allow at least an hour without stops. Here's an overview: Starting at the Marktplatz, you'll visit the museum and hike the lower wall to the Ochsenturm at the far end of town, then climb to the top of the town and walk the upper wall, passing through the Stadtmauergarten and Klostergarten (former monastery) before returning to the Marktplatz, where you can get a bite to eat at one of several cafés.

• *Begin at the Marktplatz in front of the TI.*

Marktplatz: For centuries this has been Oberwesel's social and commercial center. That tradition continues today in the Mark-

tplatz's tourist-friendly cafés and wine bars. If you're here in the summer, you can't miss the oversized wine glass declaring that Oberwesel is a winegrowers' town. Around harvest time, the city hosts a huge wine festival and elects a "Wine Witch." Why? It's pure marketing. After World War II, the Rhine's wine producers were desperate to sell their wine, so they hosted big parties and elected a representative. All the other towns picked wine queens, but Oberwesel went with a witch instead.

• *Continue along the main drag, passing several cafés, until you see the entrance (marked* Eingang*) for the museum on the left.*

Kulturhaus and Stadtmuseum Oberwesel: This is the region's best museum on local history and traditions, with lots of artifacts and interesting exhibits. The ground floor retraces the history of Oberwesel, from the Romans to the 19th-century Romantics.

Upstairs you'll learn how salmon were once fished here, and timber traders lashed together huge rafts of wood and floated them to the Netherlands to sell. You'll see dramatic photos of the river when it was jammed with ice, and review wine witches from the past few decades (€3, Tue-Fri 10:00-17:00, Sat-Sun from 14:00, closed Mon; Nov-March Tue-Fri until 14:00, closed Sat-Mon; borrow the English descriptions, Rathausstrasse 23, tel. 06744/7147-26, www. kulturhaus-oberwesel.de).

• *Return to the Marktplatz, turn toward the river and walk to the...*

Town Wall: The walls in front of you are some of the best-preserved walls in the Middle Rhine Valley, thanks to the work of a group of local citizen volunteers.

• *Turn right on Rheinstrasse, climb the narrow steps on the left to the top of the wall, and start walking downstream (left), toward the leaning tower.*

Hospitalgassenturm (Hospital Tower) and Vineyards: This tower was initially constructed to rest on the wall. But it was too heavy. In an attempt to "fix it," they straightened out the top.

Notice the vineyards along the banks of the Rhine. They've been part of the landscape here for centuries. Recently, many vintners have been letting the vineyards go untended, as they are just too expensive to keep up. The hope is that a younger generation will bring new energy to the Rhineland's vineyards. But the future of these fabled vineyards remains uncertain.

• *Continue walking until you come to the...*

Werner-Kapelle (Hospital Chapel): This chapel was built into the wall in the 13th century and remains part of the hospital district to this day. The sick lay in bed here with their eyes on the cross, confident that a better life awaited them in heaven. Today this chapel serves the adjacent, more modern hospital (free, daily 9:00-17:00).

• *Continue walking along the wall to reach the next tower. Climb up if you'd like.*

Steingassenturm: This tower is named for the first paved road in town, just ahead. Inside the tower, notice the little holes about six feet up. This is where they placed the scaffolding during construction. If you climb to the top, consider how many Romantic painters and poets in centuries past enjoyed this same view.

As Victor Hugo wrote, "This is the warlike Oberwesel whose old walls are riddled with the havoc of shot and shells. Upon them you easily recognize the trace of the huge cannon balls of the bishops of Treves, the Biscayans of Louis XIV, and the revolutionary grape shot of France. At the present day Oberwesel resembles an old veteran soldier turned winemaker, and what excellent wine he produces."

RHINE VALLEY

• *Carry on toward the two towers in the distance. Just before the break in the wall, stop to take in the view.*

View of the Katzenturm (Cat Tower) and Ochsenturm (Oxen Tower): These were among the 16 towers that once protected Oberwesel. The farthest tower, Ochsenturm, was built in the 14th century as a lookout and signal tower, but its eight-sided design and crenellated top were also a status symbol for the archbishop, declaring his power to all who passed here along the Rhine. The tower still impresses passersby today.

Take a moment here, with all the ships and trains going by, to think about transportation on the Rhine across the centuries. The Rhine has been a major transportation route since Roman times, when the river marked the northern end of the empire. The Rhineland's many castles and fortifications, like the one above Oberwesel, testify to its strategic importance in the Middle Ages. The stretch from Koblenz to Bingen was home to no fewer than 16 greedy dukes and lords—robber barons running two-bit dukedoms, living in hilltop castles and collecting tolls from merchant vessels passing by in the river below.

Between you and the river are: a bike lane (once a towpath for mighty horses pulling boats upstream), a train line (one of the first in Germany), and the modern road (built in the 1950s). Until modern times there was just one small road through Oberwesel—the one you walked along to get to the center of town.

Have you heard the trains passing by? Increasing rail traffic has made nearly constant train noise quite an issue for Rhinelanders. It's estimated that, on average, a train barrels down each side of the Rhine every three minutes. That's 500 trains a day. Landowners complain that it's nearly impossible to sell a piece of property along this stretch due to the train noise.

• *A set of stairs takes you down to street level. Notice the white church on the hilltop to your left—that's where you're headed, to continue this walk with a visit to the upper town walls. To get there, walk straight ahead along Niederbachstrasse. Go under the arch and make an immediate left to walk through the Kölnischer Torturm (Cologne Gate Tower). Follow Kölnische Turmgasse two blocks to find a staircase to your right, leading up to the church. Ascend the stairs and stop at the top to enjoy the view.*

St. Martin's Church: Built in the 14th century, this is one of two major churches in town and is known to townspeople as the "white church." Although it looks like sandstone, it's actually made of more readily available slate. Notice the picturesque little church-caretaker's house to the left, then ascend the small set of stairs to the church.

• *Walk around the left side of the church and peek inside. Then continue around the back of the building through the gate to the gardens overlooking the Rhine.*

Gardens: The church garden to the right, with the green cross, was planted in the 17th century. The garden to the left is much more modern; step into it to enjoy this secret oasis. Before leaving the garden, turn around and notice the tower attached to the back of the church. Set on a hilltop, the tower was part of the town's defensive wall—built long before the church. Later, when it came time to build a church, the townsfolk incorporated the tower into the new structure.

• *Exiting the gardens, head through the gate across from the church entrance, cross the street, and merge onto the dirt path bordering the outside of the upper town wall. Follow the wall to the first of two towers.*

Michelfeldturm I and II: This stretch is the oldest part of the town wall. Of the 23 original towers, 16 remain today. If you're looking for a summer home along the Rhine, here's a real-estate tip. The city leases these towers for €1 for 100 years. The hitch? You have to agree to restore them. Notice the house set atop the first tower.

• *Continue walking until you come to the next tower.*

Kuhhirtenturm (Cowherder's Tower): This is now a private home with a fanciful drawbridge. If the bridge is down you'll know they're home. According to local folklore, a teenage son of the tower's owners once had a rowdy graduation party here. With all the noise, neighbors complained. But when the police came, they just hoisted up the drawbridge and partied on.

• *Enjoy the views along this last stretch of the wall. To the left you'll see the Rathaus (Town Hall), with the clock on top. That's where this walk ends. Pass the Pulverturm (Powder Tower) and start downhill, stopping just beyond the miniature house.*

View of Schönburg Castle: You can't help but take in the castle view from here. There's been a castle in Oberwesel since the 10th century. Destroyed by the French in 1689, it stood in ruins for 200 years before being rebuilt. Today it houses a hotel/restaurant, youth hostel, and small museum. While there's not much to see at the castle itself, the hike to reach it (along the Elfenley trail) is scenic.

RHINE VALLEY

• *Turning away from the castle, continue downhill and take the first set of stairs to your left, bordering a vineyard. At the bottom of the stairs follow the path past the beautiful backyard gardens. Continue down another small set of stairs, passing a well on your left, and then immediately ascend another set of stairs (along Rasselberg). When you reach the ivy-lined wall, enter the gardens to your left.*

Stadtmauergarten (Town Wall Gardens): These beautiful gardens were made possible by a local lad who left town to pursue his fortune but never forgot where he came from. Upon his retirement, he returned to Oberwesel to establish a private foundation and spent his last years back in his old childhood home...our next stop.

• *Exit the gardens, turn left, and walk downhill. At the dead-end, turn right and walk until you see the cross (on the left) at the next intersection. Take a left and walk to the entrance of the monastery.*

Klostergarten (Monastery Garden): For 600 years Franciscan monks lived, worked, and prayed here. During Napoleon's reign this monastery was vacated and later fell victim to fire. The poor took refuge in what was left and built their homes inside the former cloister, sacristy, and other remnants. At its peak, after World War II, about 70 people were living here. Only a dozen remain today in this very unique (and cramped) living space.

• *Feel free to enter and explore a bit, but be respectful and remember that this is a private residence. When you reach the information board (in English) beside the church entrance, you know you're done. Retrace your steps back to the entrance and walk downhill until you reach the Marktplatz.*

St. Goar

St. Goar (sahnkt gwahr) is a classic Rhine tourist town. Its hulk of a castle overlooks a half-timbered shopping street and leafy riverside park, busy with sightseeing ships and contented strollers. Rheinfels Castle, once the mightiest on the river, is the single best Rhineland ruin to explore. While the town of St. Goar itself is less interesting than Bacharach, be sure  to explore beyond the shops: Thoughtful little placards scattered around town explain factoids (in English) about each street, lane, and square. St. Goar also makes a good base for hiking or biking the region. A tiny car ferry will shuttle you back and forth across the busy Rhine from here. (If you run out of things to see, a great pastime in St. Goar is simply chatting with friendly Heike at the K-D boat kiosk.) For train connections, see "Bacharach Connections," earlier.

Orientation to St. Goar

St. Goar is dominated by its mighty castle, Rheinfels. The village—basically a wide spot in the road at the foot of Rheinfels' hill—isn't much more than a few hotels and restaurants. From the riverboat docks, the main drag—Heerstrasse, a dull pedestrian mall without history—cuts through town before ending at the road up to the castle.

TOURIST INFORMATION

The helpful St. Goar TI, which stores bags for free, is on the main pedestrian street (Mon-Fri 9:00-13:00 & 14:00-18:00, Sat-Sun 10:00-13:00; shorter hours and closed Sat-Sun off-season; from train station, go downhill around church and turn left after the recommended Hotel Am Markt, Heerstrasse 127; tel. 06741/383, www.st-goar.de).

HELPFUL HINTS

Picnics: St. Goar's waterfront park has benches perfect for a picnic. You can buy picnic fixings on the pedestrian street at the tiny **St. Goarer Stadtladen** grocery store (Tue-Fri 8:00-19:00, Sat until 16:00, closed Sun-Mon, Heerstrasse 106) or at the recommended **Café St. Goar.**

Shopping: The Montag family runs two shops (one specializes in steins and the other in cuckoo clocks), both at the base of the castle hill road. The stein shop under Hotel Montag has Rhine guides and fine steins. The other shop boasts "the largest free-hanging cuckoo clock in the world" (RS%—10 percent discount, €10 minimum purchase; both locations open daily 9:00-18:00, shorter hours Nov-April). They'll ship your souvenirs home—or give you a VAT form to claim your tax refund at the airport if you're carrying your items with you. A couple of other souvenir shops are across from the K-D boat dock.

Laundry: **Helmut Dubrulle** can pick up and drop off your laundry, or you can drop it off. There's no self-service (Mon-Fri 9:00-12:30, also Tue and Thu-Fri 14:00-17:00, closed Sat-Sun, one street above the main drag between the train station and TI, Herpellstrasse, tel. 06741-512).

Bike Rental: Call ahead to reserve a bike at **Hotel an der Fähre,**

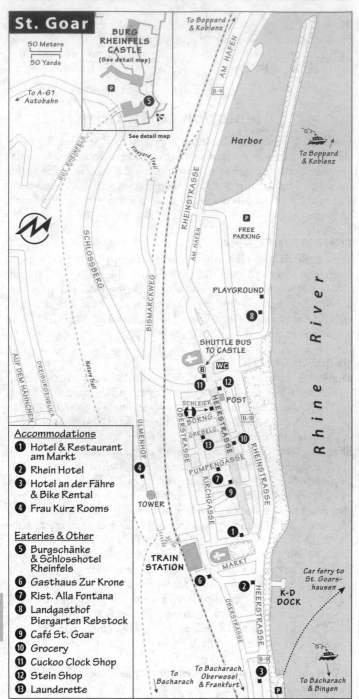

St. Goar

50 Meters
50 Yards

BURG RHEINFELS CASTLE
(See detail map)

To Boppard & Koblenz

To A-61 Autobahn

AM HAFEN

B-9

Harbor

To Boppard & Koblenz

GUT RHEINFELS

See detail map

Vineyard Trail

SCHLOSSBERG

BISMARCKWEG

RHEINSTRASSE

AM HAFEN

FREE PARKING

Rhine River

AUF DEM HÄHNCHEN

DREIBURGENBLICK

Nature Trail

PLAYGROUND

8

SHUTTLE BUS TO CASTLE

B   WC

11   12

SCHLEIER
OBERSTRASSE   BORNG.   HEERSTRASSE   POST   B-9

GREBELG.

13

10

ULMENHOF

PÜMPENGASSE

7

9

KIRCHGASSE

TOWER

1

Accommodations

1 Hotel & Restaurant am Markt

2 Rhein Hotel

3 Hotel an der Fähre & Bike Rental

4 Frau Kurz Rooms

Eateries & Other

5 Burgschänke & Schlosshotel Rheinfels

6 Gasthaus Zur Krone

7 Rist. Alla Fontana

8 Landgasthof Biergarten Rebstock

9 Café St. Goar

10 Grocery

11 Cuckoo Clock Shop

12 Stein Shop

13 Launderette

4

TRAIN STATION

MARKT

6

2

OBERSTRASSE

HEERSTRASSE

K-D DOCK

Car ferry to St. Goarshausen

To Bacharach

To Bacharach, Oberwesel & Frankfurt

B-9

3

To Bacharach

To Bacharach & Bingen

which rents wheels to the public (€10/day, pickup after 10:00, Heerstrasse 47, tel. 06741/980-577).

Parking: A free lot is at the downstream end of town, by the harbor. For on-street parking by the K-D boat dock and recommended hotels, get a ticket from the machine *(Parkscheinautomat)* and put it on the dashboard (€4/day, daily 9:00-18:00, coins only, free overnight). Make sure you press the button for a day ticket.

Sights in St. Goar

Rheinfels Castle is St. Goar's only real sight. For day trips from here, see "Sights Along the Rhine," earlier.

▲▲▲Rheinfels Castle (Burg Rheinfels)

Perched proudly atop the hill above St. Goar, the ruins of this once mightiest of Rhine River castles still exude a hint of menace. Built

in the 13th century, Rheinfels ruled the river for more than 500 years. The castle you see today, though impressive and an evocative sight to visit, is but a shadow of its former sprawling self. This hollow but interesting shell offers your single best hands-on ruined-castle experience on the river. The free castle map shows which areas are accessible without a guided tour, and my self-guided tour, next, covers most everything worth seeing.

Cost and Hours: €5, family card-€10, daily 9:00-18:00, Nov-mid-March possibly Sat-Sun only 11:00-17:00 (call ahead), last entry one hour before closing—weather permitting.

Information: Tel. 06741/7753, in winter 06741/383, www.st-goar.de.

Tours: Due to a multiyear restoration, parts of the castle grounds, including the tunnels, can only be seen with a guided tour. Tours are run in both German and English but determined on the day by who shows up; to arrange an English tour for a group, call 1-2 days in advance. If you plan to take a tour, you must bring a flashlight for the dark tunnels.

Services: A handy WC is immediately across from the ticket booth (men take note of the guillotine urinals—stand back when you pull to flush). There are also WCs in the hotel across from the entrance.

Getting to the Castle: A **taxi** up from town costs €5 (tel. 06741/7011). Or take the shuttle bus (€2 one-way, generally April-

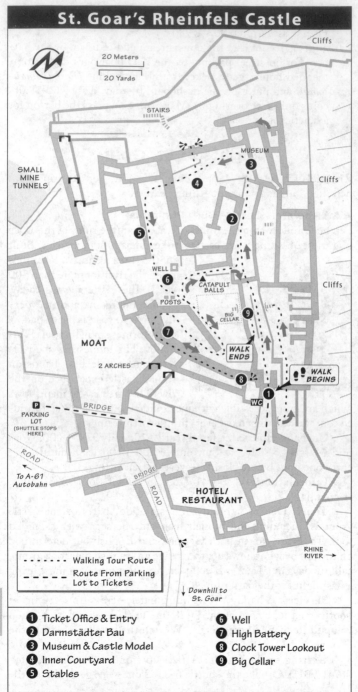

St. Goar's Rheinfels Castle

20 Meters
20 Yards

CLIFFS

STAIRS

MUSEUM

SMALL MINE TUNNELS

CLIFFS

3

4

2

5

CLIFFS

WELL

6

CATAPULT BALLS

POSTS

BIG CELLAR

9

MOAT

7

WALK ENDS

2 ARCHES →

8

WALK BEGINS

1

WC

BRIDGE

P
PARKING LOT
(SHUTTLE STOPS HERE)

ROAD

To A-61 Autobahn

BRIDGE

ROAD

HOTEL/ RESTAURANT

RHINE RIVER →

- - - - - Walking Tour Route

- - - Route From Parking Lot to Tickets

↓ Downhill to St. Goar

RHINE VALLEY

1 Ticket Office & Entry
2 Darmstädter Bau
3 Museum & Castle Model
4 Inner Courtyard
5 Stables

6 Well
7 High Battery
8 Clock Tower Lookout
9 Big Cellar

Oct daily 10:55-16:55, departs roughly every 30 minutes or when full). The shuttle departs from the Catholic church just past the top end of the pedestrian street. **Parking** at the castle costs €1/hour, cash only.

To **walk** up to the castle, simply follow the main road up through the railroad underpass at the top end of the pedestrian street (5 minutes). But it's more fun to **hike** the nature trail: Start at the St. Goar train station. Take the underpass under the tracks at the north end of the station, climb the steep stairs uphill, turn right (following *Burg Rheinfels* signs), and keep straight along the path just above the old city wall. Small red-and-white signs show the way, taking you to the castle in 15 minutes.

Background: Burg Rheinfels *was* huge—for five centuries, it was the biggest castle on the Rhine. Built in 1245 to guard a toll station, it soon earned the nickname "the unconquerable fortress." In the 1400s, the castle was thickened to withstand cannon fire. Rheinfels became a thriving cultural center and, in the 1520s, was visited by the artist Albrecht Dürer and the religious reformer Ulrich Zwingli. It saw lots of action in the Thirty Years' War (1618-1648), and later became the strongest and most modern fortress in the Holy Roman Empire. It withstood a siege of 28,000 French troops in 1692. But eventually the castle surrendered to the French without a fight, and in 1797, the French Revolutionary army destroyed it. For years, the ruined castle was used as a source of building stone, and today—while still mighty—it's only a small fraction of its original size.

● Self-Guided Tour: Rather than wander aimlessly, visit the castle by following this tour. We'll start at the museum, then circulate through the courtyards, up to the highest lookout point, finishing in a big cellar. To walk around the fortified ramparts, and to access the dark tunnels that require a flashlight, you'll need to book a tour (see earlier). If it's damp, be careful of slippery stones.

Pick up the free map and use its commentary to navigate from red signpost to red signpost through the castle. My self-guided tour route is similar to the one marked on the castle map. That map, the one in this book, and this tour all use the same numbering system. (You'll notice that I've skipped a couple stops—just walk on by signs for ❷ *Darmstadter Bau* and ❺ *Stables.*)

• *Buy your ticket and walk through the castle's clock tower, labeled* ❶ *Uhrturm. Continue straight, passing a couple points of interest (which we'll visit later), until you get to the* ❸ *museum.*

Museum and Castle Model: The pleasant museum is located in the only finished room of the castle. It features a sweeping history exhibit with good English descriptions and Romantic Age etchings that give a sense of the place as it was in the 19th century (daily 10:00-12:30 & 13:00-17:30, closed Nov-mid-March).

The seven-foot-tall carved stone immediately to the right inside the door (marked *Flammensäule*)—a tombstone from a nearby Celtic grave—is from 400 years before Christ. There were people here long before the Romans...and this castle.

The massive fortification was the only Rhineland castle to withstand Louis XIV's assault during the 17th century. At the far left end of the room is a model reconstruction of the castle, showing how much bigger it was before French Revolutionary troops destroyed it in the 18th century. Study this. Find where you are. (Hint: Look for the tall tower.) This was the living quarters of the original castle, which was only the smallest ring of buildings around the tiny central courtyard (13th century). The ramparts were added in the 14th century. By 1650, the fortress was largely complete. Since its destruction by the French in the late 18th century, it's had no military value. While no WWII bombs were wasted on this ruin, it served St. Goar as a stone quarry for generations. The basement of the museum shows the castle pharmacy and an exhibit of Rhine-region odds and ends, including tools, an 1830 loom, and photos of icebreaking on the Rhine. While once routine, icebreaking hasn't been necessary here since 1963.

• *Exit the museum and walk 20 yards directly out, slightly uphill and halfway into the castle courtyard. At the first opening on the right, step up for a peek out at the...*

Corner of Castle: Look right. That's the original castle tower. A three-story, half-timbered building originally rose beyond the tower's stone fortification. The two stone tongues near the top supported the toilet. (Insert your own joke here.) Lean and look left.

Thoop...You're Dead: Notice the smartly placed crossbow slits. While you're lying there, notice the stonework. The little round holes were for the scaffolds they used as they built up, which indicate that this stonework is original.

• *Pick yourself up and walk back into the inner courtyard,* (❹ Innenhof).

Medieval Castle Courtyard: Five hundred years ago, the entire castle encircled this courtyard. The place was self-sufficient and ready for a siege, with a bakery, pharmacy, herb garden, brewery, well (top of yard), and livestock. During peacetime, 300-600 people lived here; during a siege, there would be as many as 4,000. The walls were plastered and painted white. Bits of the original 13th-century plaster survive.

• *Continue through the courtyard under the Erste Schildmauer (first*

shield wall) sign, turn left, and walk straight toward the two old wooden upright posts. Find the pyramid of stone catapult balls on your left just before you reach the posts.

Castle Garden: Catapult balls like these were too expensive not to recycle—they'd be retrieved after any battle. Across from the balls is a well (**6** *Brunnen*)—essential for any castle during the age of sieges. Look in. Thirsty? The old posts are for the ceremonial baptizing of new members of the local trading league. While this guild goes back centuries, it's now a social club that fills this court with a huge wine party every year on the third weekend of September.

• *Climb uphill to the castle's highest point by walking along the cobbled path (look for the* To the Tower *sign) up past the high battery (**7** Hohe Batterie) to the castle's best viewpoint—up where the German flag waves (signed **8** Uhrturm).*

Highest Castle Tower Lookout: Enjoy a great view of the river, the castle, and the forest. Remember, the fortress once cov-

ered five times the land it does today. Notice how the other castles (across the river) don't poke above the top of the Rhine canyon. That would make them easy for invading armies to see.

From this perch, survey the Rhine Valley, cut out of slate over millions of years by the river. The slate absorbs the heat of the sun, making the grapes grown here well-suited for wine. Today the slate is mined to provide roofing. Imagine St. Goar himself settling here 1,500 years ago, establishing a place where sailors—thankful to have survived the treacherous Loreley—would stop and pray. Imagine the frozen river of years past, when the ice would break up and boats would huddle in man-made harbors like the one below for protection. Consider the history of trade on this busy river—from the days when castles levied tolls on ships, to the days when boats would be hauled upstream with the help of riverside towpaths, to the 21st century when 300 ships a day move their cargo past St. Goar. And imagine this castle before the French destroyed it...when it was the mightiest structure on the river, filled with people and inspiring awe among all who passed.

• *Return to the catapult balls, walk downhill and through the tunnel, and pause to look back up and see the original 13th-century core of the castle. Now go right toward the entrance, first veering down to see the...*

Big Cellar: This **9** *Grosser Keller* was a big pantry. When the castle was smaller, this was the original moat—you can see the

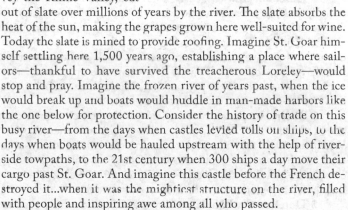

rough lower parts of the wall. The original floor was 13 feet deeper. The drawbridge rested upon the stone nubs on the left. When the castle expanded, the moat became this cellar. Halfway up the walls on the entrance side of the room, square holes mark spots where timbers made a storage loft, perhaps filled

with grain. In the back, an arch leads to the wine cellar (probably blocked off) where finer wine was kept. Part of a soldier's pay was wine...table wine. This wine was kept in a single 180,000-liter stone barrel (that's 47,550 gallons), which generally lasted about 18 months.

The count owned the surrounding farmland. Farmers got to keep 20 percent of their production. Later, in more liberal feudal times, the nobility let them keep 40 percent. Today, the German government leaves the workers with 60 percent...and provides a few more services.

• *You're free. Climb out, turn right, and leave. For coffee on a terrace with a great view, visit Schlosshotel Rheinfels, opposite the entrance.*

Sleeping in St. Goar

For parking advice, see "Helpful Hints," earlier.

$ Hotel am Markt, run by Herr and Frau Marx and their friendly staff, is a decent value with all the modern comforts. It features 15 rustic rooms in the main building (think antlers with a pastel flair), 10 classier rooms right next door, and a good restaurant. It's a stone's throw from the boat dock and train station (family rooms, some rooms with river view, two apartments also available, closed Nov-Feb, pay parking, Markt 1, tel. 06741/1689, http://hotel-sankt-goar.de, dashotel@t-online.de).

$ Rhein Hotel, on the other side of the church from Hotel am Markt and run with enthusiasm by young and energetic Gil Velich, has 10 bright and stylish rooms in a spacious building (some rooms with river view and balconies, family rooms, pay laundry, closed mid-Nov-March, Heerstrasse 71, tel. 06741/981-240, www.rheinhotel-st-goar.de, info@rheinhotel-st-goar.de).

$ Hotel an der Fähre is a simple place on the busy road at the end of town, immediately across from the ferry dock. It rents 12 cheap and colorful rooms (cash only, some view rooms, cheapest rooms with shared bath, street noise but double-glazed windows, parking, closed Nov-Feb, Heerstrasse 47, tel. 06741/980-577, www.

hotel-stgoar.de, info@hotel-stgoar.de, friendly Alessya). They also offer rental bikes by reservation (see "Helpful Hints," earlier).

$ Frau Kurz has been housing my readers since 1988. With the help of her daughter, Jeanette, she offers St. Goar's best B&B, renting three delightful rooms (sharing 2.5 bathrooms) with bathrobes, a breakfast terrace with castle views, a garden, and homemade marmalade (cash only, free and easy parking, ask about apartment with kitchen, Ulmenhof 11, tel. 06741/459,  www.gaestehaus-kurz.de, fewo-kurz@kabelmail.de). If you're not driving, it's a steep five-minute hike from the train station: Exit left from the station, take an immediate left under the tracks, and go partway up the zigzag stairs, turning right through an archway onto Ulmenhof; #11 is just past the tower.

Eating in St. Goar

$$ Hotel Restaurant am Markt serves tasty traditional meals with plenty of game and fish (specialties include marinated roast beef and homemade cheesecake) at fair prices with good atmosphere and service. Choose cozy indoor seating, or dine outside with a river and castle view (daily 9:00-21:00, closed Nov-Feb, Markt 1, tel. 06741/1689).

$$$ Burgschänke is easy to miss on the ground floor of Schlosshotel Rheinfels (the hotel across from the castle entrance—enter through the souvenir shop). It offers the only reasonably priced lunches up at Rheinfels Castle, is family-friendly, and has a Rhine view from its fabulous outdoor terrace (*Flammkuchen* and regional dishes, Sun-Thu 11:00-21:00, Fri-Sat until 21:30, tel. 06741/802-806).

The **$$$$ Schlosshotel Rheinfels** dining room is your Rhine splurge, with an incredible indoor view terrace in an elegant, dressy setting. Call to reserve for weekends or if you want a window table (daily 7:00-11:00, 12:00-14:00 & 18:00-21:00, tel. 06741/8020, www.schloss-rheinfels.de).

$$ Gasthaus Zur Krone is the local choice for traditional German food in a restaurant off the main drag. There's no river view, but it's cozy and offers some outdoor seating on weekends (Thu-Tue 11:00-14:30 & 18:00-21:00, closed Wed, cash only, next to the train station and church at Oberstrasse 38, tel. 06741/1515).

$$ Ristorante Alla Fontana, tucked away on a back lane and busy with locals, serves the best Italian food in town at great prices in a lovely dining room or on a leafy patio (Tue-Sun 11:30-14:00 & 17:30-21:30, closed Mon, cash only, dinner reservations smart, Pumpengasse 5, 06741/96117).

$$ Landgasthof Biergarten Rebstock is hidden on the far end of town on the banks of the Rhine. They serve schnitzel and plenty of beer and wine. A nice playground and minigolf course on either side keeps the kids busy (April-Oct long hours daily— weather permitting, Am Hafen 1, tel. 06741/980-0337).

$ Café St. Goar is the perfect spot for a quick lunch or *Kaffee und Kuchen*. They sell open-face sandwiches, strudel, tiny cookies, and a variety of cakes to satisfy any appetite. Grab something for a picnic or enjoy seating on the pedestrian-only street out front (Mon-Sat 9:00-18:00, Sun from 10:00, Heerstrasse 95, tel. 06741/1635).

Koblenz

The main town on this stretch of the Romantic Rhine is Koblenz— situated where the Mosel River flows into the Rhine. The word "Koblenz" comes from the Roman word for confluence—a reminder that 2,000 years ago, this was the northern border of the Roman Empire. The city has long been a strategic base. A transportation hub with a key bridge and a mighty fortress, it was heavily bombed in World War II. The city feels rebuilt today and has little of the charm that most are looking for when they visit the Rhineland. All I would do here is check out the modern center (Zentralplatz, with its Forum Confluentes and Rhineland museum), trek out to the Deutsches Eck ("German Corner") for a little Deutschland patriotism, ride the cable car over the Rhine (from the Deutsches Eck to the castle), and tour the Ehrenbreitstein Fortress, if only for the views.

The **TI** is inside the Forum Confluentes cultural center on Zentralplatz (daily 10:00-18:00, tel. 0261/19433, www.koblenz-touristik.de).

Arrival in Koblenz: If you're driving a **car,** go directly to the Deutsches Eck and park. If arriving by **train,** walk (or catch bus #1) from the station through the town center to the Deutsches Eck, with a stop at Zentralplatz on the way. K-D Rhine sightseeing **boats** stop right at the Deutsches Eck (2-3/day, 3.5 hours upstream to St. Goar, 2.5 hours downstream from St. Goar, www.k-d.com).

Sights in Koblenz

Zentralplatz and Forum Confluentes

The city's once bombed-out center now sparkles with sleek modern architecture. On the main square, Zentralplatz, you'll find the striking Forum Confluentes. This bright, modern cultural center houses the TI; the Romanticum, an interactive museum with fun Romantic-era portrayals of Rhine towns and exhibits on the Rhineland culture; and the Mittelrhein Museum, with art from medieval to modern. You can also catch an elevator ride to the roof terrace for sweeping city views. (Romanticum-€6, daily 10:00-18:00, tel. 0261/19433; Mittelrhein-€6, Tue-Sun 10:00-18:00, closed Mon; elevator-€1, daily 9:00-20:00; Zentralplatz 1, tel. 0261/129-2520, www.forum-confluentes.de). It's a short walk from here to the Deutsches Eck.

Deutsches Eck

The actual tip of land where the two rivers meet is the legendary "Deutsches Eck"—the "German Corner." For many Germans, this spot stirs their nationalis-tic spirit. While *"Deutschland über alles"* ("Germany above all"—a line from the German national anthem) is often associated with Hitler and German expansionism in the 20th century, the phrase actually refers to the fragmentation of German-speaking states before unity in 1871. The *Song of Germany* celebrated the notion of the little German states uniting in one German nation.

When Germany finally was united, it was the Johnny-come-lately of European superpowers and scrambled to establish its legitimacy. The allure of this strategic spot made it a natural staging ground to symbolize unity. Notice how the flags of the many German states all converge on the flag of a united Germany at the tip of the peninsula. While, historically, there was a lack of clarity about the French/German border (and under Napoleon, it was actually right here), today the "German Corner" is seen not as a border but as the heart of a great nation. Beyond the flag-lined plaza is a reconstructed memorial to Kaiser Wilhelm. Germans come here to feel good about their country while enjoying the organ grinders and buskers playing accordions in this park-like atmosphere.

Seilbahn Cable Car

Koblenz's cable car runs above the Rhine River, stretching a half-mile from the Deutsches Eck to the Ehrenbreitstein Fortress high above. As you glide over the river you'll get fine views of the point where the Rhine and the Mosel rivers converge. This is the only convenient way to get from the city to the fortress.

Cost and Hours: €7.20 one-way, €9.90 round-trip, €13.80 round-trip combo-ticket with fortress entry; daily 9:30-19:00, Nov-March Sat-Sun only 9:30-17:30; tel. 0261/2016-5850, www.seilbahn-koblenz.de.

Ehrenbreitstein Fortress

While a castle has stood on this strategic point much longer, what you see today is not your classic Rhine castle standing tall, but a squat and sprawling, bombshell-hardened 19th-century fortress. The exhibit is poorly signposted, with little English describing a vast space that is not very inviting. As you enter you'll get a map with 20 points of (little) interest. But the views are grand and it's a chance to roam free in a castle.

Cost and Hours: €7, €13.80 combo-ticket with round-trip cable-car ride, daily 10:00-18:00, Nov-March until 17:00, tel. 0261/6675-4000, www.diefestungehrenbreitstein.de.

MOSEL VALLEY

Cochem • Burg Eltz • Beilstein

The misty Mosel is what some visitors hope the Rhine will be— peaceful, sleepy, romantic villages slipped between impossibly steep vineyards and the river; fine wine; a sprinkling of castles (Burg Eltz is tops); and lots of friendly small pensions. Boat, train, and car traffic here is a trickle compared with the roaring Rhine. While the swan-speckled Mosel (MOH-zehl in German; Moselle/moh-ZEHL in French) moseys 300 miles from France's Vosges mountain range to Koblenz (where it dumps into the Rhine), the most scenic piece of the valley lies between the towns of Bernkastel-Kues and Cochem. I'd savor only this section. Cochem and Trier (see next chapter) are easy day trips from each other (an hour by train, 60 miles by car). Cochem is the handiest home base, unless you have a car and want the peace of Beilstein.

GETTING AROUND THE MOSEL VALLEY

By Train and Bus: Fast trains zip you between Koblenz, Cochem, Bullay, and Trier in a snap. Other destinations require changing to a slow train or bus. Beilstein is a 20-minute ride on bus #716 from Cochem (see "Getting to Beilstein," later). Burg Eltz is a scenic 1.5-hour hike or €28 taxi ride from the tiny Moselkern train station (or about a €55 taxi ride from Cochem). For bus times, pick up printed schedules at train stations and TIs, or check the regional transit website (www.vrminfo.de) or Germany's train timetable (www.bahn.com).

By Boat: Thanks to its many locks, Mosel cruises feel more like canal-boat rides than the cruises on the mighty Rhine. The Kolb Line has the most frequent departures, and cruises the most scenic stretch of the Mosel (tel. 02673/1515, www.moselrundfahrten.de).

A simple and fun outing is the one-hour cruise between **Cochem** and **Beilstein**, passing through the Fankel lock (4-5/day in each direction May-Oct, weekends only in April, no boats off-season, first departure from Cochem at about 10:30, last departure from Beilstein at about 17:30, €12 one-way, €16 round-trip). Another option is the boat in the other direction (downstream) from **Cochem** to **Treis-Karden** (3/day, runs mid-July-Aug daily; May-mid-July and Sept-Oct Wed and Sat-Sun only; no boats off-season; 40 minutes, €11 one-way, €14 round-trip). From Karden, you can get to Burg Eltz via

a long hike (2 hours, steep in places), train-and-hike combination, weekend bus (May-Oct only, 4/day, www.burg-eltz.de), or taxi ride—though it's generally easier to reach Burg Eltz from the Moselkern train station. Kolb also runs one-hour **sightseeing cruises** and two-hour "Tanz Party" **dancing cruises** from Cochem (€11 sightseeing cruises 5/day Easter-Oct; €18 dancing cruises with live music at 20:15, May-Oct Sat only, Aug-Sept also Tue).

The K-D (Köln-Düsseldorfer) line sails the lower Mosel, between **Cochem** and **Koblenz**—but only Friday to Sunday, and only once a day in each direction (€38.20 one-way, May-Sept only, none off-season, Koblenz to Cochem 9:45-15:00, Cochem to Koblenz 15:40-20:00; 20 percent discount with a German rail pass and does not count as the use of a flexipass day, possible discounts with Eurail pass—ask; tel. in Cochem 02671/980-023, www.k-d.com).

Each year in May or June, the Mosel locks close for a week or more of maintenance, and none of the boats listed here run. In 2020, this is scheduled to happen May 12-19.

By Car: Two-lane roads run along both riverbanks. While these riverside roads are a delight, the river valley is very windy. Overland shortcuts can "cut the corners" and save you serious time—especially between Burg Eltz and Beilstein (see page 529) and if you're driving between the Mosel and the Rhine (note the Brodenbach-Boppard shortcut). Both Koblenz and Trier have car-rental agencies. A new mile-long, 500-foot-high, €456 million expressway bridge (called Hochmoselbrücke) has been built near the town of Ürzig, just southwest/upstream of Cochem and Beilstein. It should be open by the time you visit.

By Bike: Biking along the Mosel is all the rage among Dutch and German tourists. You can rent bikes in most Mosel towns (I've listed options in both Cochem and Beilstein). A fine bike path follows the river from Koblenz to Zell (some bits share the road with

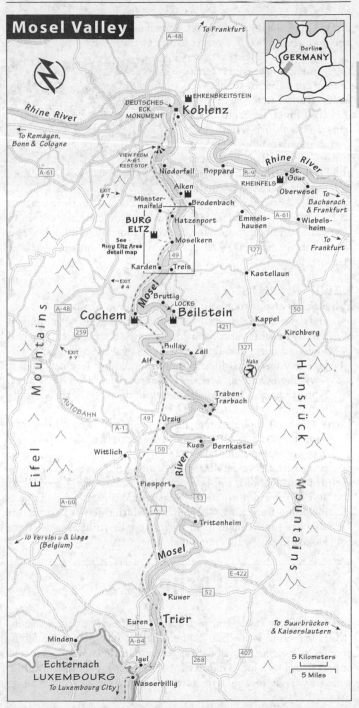

Mosel Valley

To Frankfurt

A-48

Berlin
GERMANY

Rhine River

To Remagen,
Bonn & Cologne

DEUTSCHES
ECK
MONUMENT

EHRENBREITSTEIN

Koblenz

A-61

VIEW FROM
A-61
REST STOP

EXIT
7

Niederfell

Boppard

Alken

Münster-
maifeld

Brodenbach

Rhine River

R-9

St.
Goar

RHEINFELS

Oberwesel

To
Bacharach
& Frankfurt

A-61

Wiebels-
heim

**BURG
ELTZ**

See
Burg Eltz Area
detail map

Hatzenport

Moselkern

Emmels-
hausen

327

To
Frankfurt

49

Karden

Treis

Kastellaun

EXIT
4

Mosel

Bruttig

LOCKS

Cochem

Beilstein

A-48

259

421

Kappel

50

Kirchberg

EXIT
?

Bullay

Zell

327

Hahn

Alf

Hunsrück

AUTOBAHN

Traben-
Trarbach

49

Ürzig

A-1

50

Kues

Bernkastel

Wittlich

River

Piesport

53

A-60

A-1

Trittenheim

To Verviers & Liège
(Belgium)

Mosel

E-422

Mountains

52

Ruwer

Eifel

Mountains

To Saarbrücken
& Kaiserslautern

Euren

Trier

Minden

A-64

Igel

268

407

5 Kilometers

Echternach
LUXEMBOURG

Wasserbillig

To Luxembourg City

5 Miles

cars). Allow one hour between Cochem and Beilstein. Many pedal one-way, then relax on a return cruise or train ride.

By Ferry: About a dozen small car-and-passenger ferries *(Fähre)* cross the Mosel between Koblenz and Trier.

By Plane: The confusingly named Frankfurt Hahn Airport, a popular hub for low-fare airlines such as Ryanair, is actually located near the Mosel (airport code: HHN, www.hahn-airport.de). You can ride bus #750 from the airport to Bullay (about €8, runs every 2 hours, 50 minutes) where you can take a train to Cochem (10 minutes). Groups of five or more should book ahead for this bus (tel. 0800-724-1370, www.airportshuttle-mosel.de/AirportHahn).

HELPFUL HINTS

Wine Festivals: Throughout the Mosel region on summer weekends and during the fall harvest, wine festivals with oompah bands, dancing, and colorful costumes are powered by good food and wine. You'll find a wine festival in some nearby village any weekend, June through September (see calendar at www.mosellandtouristik.de). The tourist season lasts from April through October. Things close down tight through the winter.

Carry Cash: Although more places are accepting credit cards, come prepared to pay cash for many services in the Mosel Valley—including food, hotels, and transportation—especially at Burg Eltz and in smaller villages along the river,

Helpful Guidebook: The booklet *The Castles of the Moselle* (sold at TIs) offers information on castles from Koblenz to Trier—including Burg Eltz, Cochem, and Metternich in Beilstein. It also has some drawings of what the now-ruined castles once looked like.

Cochem

With a majestic castle and picturesque medieval streets, Cochem (KOHKH-ehm) is the hub of the middle Mosel. Home to 5,000 people, it's a larger, more bustling town than Beilstein, Bacharach, or St. Goar. Duck into a damp wine cellar to sample the local white wine (*Weinprobe* means "wine tasting"). Stroll pleasant paths along the idyllic riverbank, hike through vineyards for a panoramic view, or just grab a bench and watch Germany at play. River-cruise passengers clog the old town during the day, but evenings are peaceful.

Orientation to Cochem

Long and skinny Cochem stretches along both banks of the Mosel. The main part of town, on the west bank, sits below vineyards and the town's showpiece castle. From the river, the town bunny-hops up various small valleys.

TOURIST INFORMATION

The information-packed TI is by the bridge at the main bus stop on Endertplatz. Find out about special events, wine tastings, public transportation to Burg Eltz, and area hikes. Consider the six-foot-long *Mosellauf* poster/ brochure (Mon-Sat 9:00-17:00, Sun 10:00-15:00; Sat until 15:00 and closed Sun May-mid-July; off-season shorter hours and closed Sat-Sun; Endertplatz 1, tel. 02671/60040, www.ferienland-cochem.de).

ARRIVAL IN COCHEM

By Train: Cochem's train station is often unstaffed and has no lockers, but you can pay to leave your bags at the Gleis 9 café off the station hall (Mon-Fri 7:30-19:00, Sat-Sun from 10:00).

To reach town, make a hard right out of the station and walk about 10 minutes along cobbled Ravenéstrasse, keeping to the right at the busy intersection past the supermarket. You'll soon see a safe crosswalk; take it to find the TI and bus station (both on your left, before the bridge). To continue to the main square (Markt) and colorful medieval town center, continue under the bridge (with pay WC on your left), then stay straight to follow Bernstrasse.

By Car: Drivers can park in a lot behind the train station (€5/ day, reach it by circling around on Ravenéstrasse and Pinnerstrasse). There's also a multistory garage just up Endertstrasse from the bridge (€8/day).

HELPFUL HINTS

Festival: Cochem's biggest wine festival is held the last weekend in August. High season for wine aficionados lasts from August through October.

Laundry: Frau Huntscha at **Wäscherei Huntscha** will wash, dry, and fold your clothes, and the location is handy, but she speaks no English (Mon-Tue and Thu-Fri 9:00-14:30, Sat from 10:00, closed Wed and Sun, entrance just down the alley around Ravenéstrasse 31 opposite the supermarket, tel. 02671/3493).

Bike Rental: Consider taking a bike on the boat or train and pedaling back. **Radverleih Schaltwerk,** between the station and TI, offers helmets with rentals (€10/day, €20/day for electric bikes; Mon-Fri 9:00-13:00 & 14:00-18:00, Sat 9:00-13:00, Sun 10:00-12:30—except closed Sun Nov-March; drop-off after 18:00 possible, Ravenéstrasse 18, tel. 02671/603-500). The ticket office at the **K-D boat dock** also rents bikes (€9/day, €18/day for electric bikes, daily May-Sept 9:00-18:00, tel. 02671/980-023).

Tours: To explore Cochem town, consider one of the **TI**'s tour offerings: one-hour walking tours run twice a week at 11:00 (€3.50, Mon and Sat March-Dec, Sept-Oct also Wed); night watchman tours run on Saturdays (€5, at 20:30; tel. 02671/60040, www.ferienland-cochem.de).

Taxi: Taxis usually wait at the taxi stand in front of the church on Moselpromenade; if not, call 02671/8080.

Sights in Cochem

Cochem Castle (Reichsburg Cochem)

This pretty, pointy castle on a hill above town is the work of overly imaginative 19th-century restorers. Like many castles along the Rhine and Mosel, Cochem's— dating from the year 1000—was blown up by French troops in 1689. For almost two hundred years it stood in ruins (much like Beilstein's) until it caught the attention of Louis Ravené, a rich Berliner who'd made a fortune in the steel industry. He bought the castle dirt-cheap in 1868 and  spared no expense in turning it into a luxurious private residence furnished with tasteful antiques. Today, the castle can only be visited on a 40-minute tour (these run more frequently in German, but guides pass out a helpful English info sheet that makes the visit worthwhile). You'll see seven beautiful rooms, complete with antlers on the wall and hidden doors leading to secret passages. The other 43 rooms are empty, as Ravené's descendants took most of their stuff with them in 1942 when they were forced to sell the castle to the Nazi government (which then used it as a training

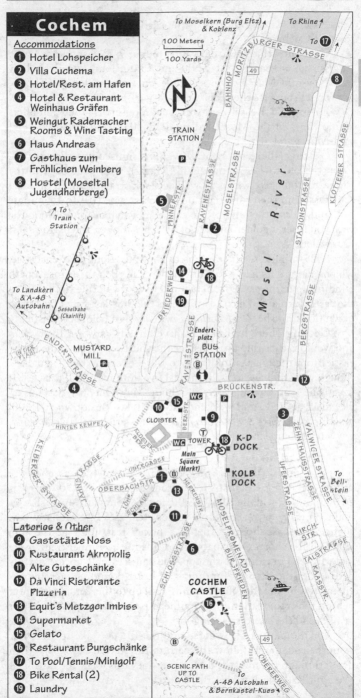

Cochem

Accommodations
1 Hotel Lohspeicher
2 Villa Cuchema
3 Hotel/Rest. am Hafen
4 Hotel & Restaurant Weinhaus Gräfen
5 Weingut Rademacher Rooms & Wine Tasting
6 Haus Andreas
7 Gasthaus zum Fröhlichen Weinberg
8 Hostel (Moseltal Jugendherberge)

Eateries & Other
9 Gaststätte Noss
10 Restaurant Akropolis
11 Alte Gutsschänke
12 Da Vinci Ristorante Pizzeria
13 Equit's Metzger Imbiss
14 Supermarket
15 Gelato
16 Restaurant Burgschänke
17 To Pool/Tennis/Minigolf
18 Bike Rental (2)
19 Laundry

center for lawyers). Since 1978 the castle has been owned by the town of Cochem.

Cost and Hours: €6, daily, first tour at 9:00, last tour at 17:00, English tours generally at 12:00 and 15:00, tours run irregularly mid-Nov–mid-March—see schedule on website, tel. 02671/255, www.reichsburg-cochem.de.

Eating: $$ Restaurant Burgschänke serves lunch and offers scenic views of the Mosel Valley (daily 10:00-18:00, closed Nov–mid-March, tel. 02671/255).

Getting There on Foot: *Zur Burg* signs point the way up. From the old town's main square (Markt), with your back to the tower, the quickest way is to walk a block straight ahead on Herrenstrasse and then turn right up Schlossstrasse (10- to 15-minute huff and puff with views of the castle above vineyards). Along the way, you'll see a golden mosaic of St. Christopher, the patron saint of travelers.

A 25-minute scenic route is to continue along Herrenstrasse, which changes its name to Burgfrieden and then turns into a path winding up to the castle from behind. Even if you ride the bus up to the castle (explained next), this trail is the prettiest way to get back down (look for the *Zur Mosel und zur City* sign below the castle).

Getting There by Bus: If you've already *probed* a little *Wein* and would rather ride up, consider the shuttle bus that runs to the castle from the bus station (next to the TI) or the main square—though you still have to walk the last five minutes uphill (bus #781, €2.50 one-way, €4 round-trip, 1-3/hour, May-Oct only, first bus up weekdays at 10:30 and weekends at 10:10, last bus down at 18:00, look for *Reichsburg Shuttle-Bus* sign at bus station, tel. 02671/7647, www.reichsburg-cochem.de).

Chairlift and Hikes

For great views, ride the *Sesselbahn* (chairlift), which ascends the hill on the opposite side of town from the castle (€4.90 one-way, €6.90 round-trip, daily 10:00-18:00, longer hours July-Aug, shorter hours on rainy days, closed off-season, tel. 02671/989-065, www.cochemer-sesselbahn.de). There's a pricey restaurant at the top, along with a short, rocky path that leads to the Pinnerkreuz overlook. Instead of riding to the top, you can scramble up the narrow path under the lift for 20 minutes of heart-pounding, aerobic excitement. Or take the long, winding trail up to the same point from behind the train station (find trailhead past Weingut Rademacher just beyond the station parking lot).

For the best of all worlds, ride the lift up, take in the view from the restaurant, follow the path to the station *(Bahnhof),* then down through the forest and then the vineyards to a wine tasting at Weingut Rademacher (described next).

Wine Tasting

At **Weingut Rademacher,** near the train station, you can taste four local wines for €6 (usually open April-Oct Mon-Sat 10:00-18:30, closed Sun, different hours during festivals, call ahead to confirm, open by arrangement Nov-March, Pinnerstrasse 10, tel. 02671/4164, www.weingut-rademacher.de; they also rent rooms—see "Sleeping in Cochem," later). Other wine cellars in town also offer tastings.

If you have a car, consider going upriver to the town of **Zell,** famous for its Schwarze Katze ("Black Cat") wine. That's where English-speaking Peter Weis runs **F. J. Weis** winery and gives a clever, entertaining tour of his 60,000-bottle-per-year wine cellar (€18, includes tasting, book ahead by phone, April-mid-Nov daily 10:00-18:00, open by arrangement mid-Nov-March, tel. 06542/41398, mobile 0172-780-7153, www.weingut-weis.de). You'll find his *Weinkeller* south of Zell, 200 yards past the bridge toward Bernkastel (on the riverside at Notenau 30). Peter also rents two luxurious **$$** apartments with kitchen facilities (breakfast extra).

Mustard Mill (Historische Senfmühle)

Just down the road from the chairlift, you can see one of the oldest mills (c. 1810) of its kind still operating in Europe. Run by Wolfgang Steffens and his helpful staff, they use only natural spices and follow centuries-old recipes to produce some of Germany's best mustard. You may also want to try their homemade spirits or, for a unique treat, look for the Roter-Weinbergs-Pfirsich Likör—a local cordial made from the small, tart "red peaches" that are unique to the Mosel Valley.

Cost and Hours: Free mustard tasting of 8-10 varieties plus jams and chutney, 30-minute guided tours in German only-€2.50, daily 10:00-18:00, Enderstrasse 18, tel. 02671/607665, www.senfmuehle.net.

Swimming, Tennis, and Golf

Cochem's leisure center (Freizeitzentrum) offers an array of family-friendly activities: an indoor wave pool, an outdoor pool, a sauna, tennis courts, and minigolf (30 minutes on foot from the center of town, or take bus #702 from outside the TI, 9/day Mon-Fri).

Cost and Hours: Indoor pool-€7/3 hours, generally Tue-Sun 10:00-19:00, closed Mon; hours and prices vary for other activities; 10 minutes beyond youth hostel at Moritzburger Strasse 1, tel. 02671/97990, www.moselbad.de.

Cruise

The Kolb Line offers one-hour sightseeing cruises and schmaltzy two-hour dancing cruises with live music (see "Getting Around the Mosel Valley—By Boat," earlier in this chapter).

Sightseeing Train

A little green-and-yellow tourist train leaves from under the bridge at the TI and does a 20-minute sightseeing loop through town with commentary in German and English. Since Cochem is such a pedestrian-friendly town, this is worth it only on a rainy day, or if you're bored and lazy.

Cost and Hours: €6, includes a coupon for a souvenir glass of wine in the train company's nearby wine shop, 1-2/hour, daily 10:00-17:00, Nov-March weekends only.

Sleeping in Cochem

Cochem is a good base for train travelers. Most of my recommendations are within a 10- to 15-minute walk or a €6 taxi ride from the station. August is very tight on rooms, with various festivals and generally inflated prices.

$$ Hotel Lohspeicher, an upscale-rustic hotel just off the main square on a street with tiny steps, is for those willing to pay a bit extra for quality lodgings in the thick of things. Its nine high-ceilinged rooms have modern comforts, and the owner is a gourmet chef who offers cooking classes as well as hiking and biking excursions—book in advance (includes classy breakfast in a fine stone-and-timber room, elevator, pay parking, Obergasse 1, tel. 02671/3976, www.lohspeicher.de, service@lohspeicher.de, Ingo and Anna Beth).

$$ Villa Cuchema's 12 fresh and beautifully decorated rooms fill a handsome 1904 row house two convenient blocks from the station, along the street leading into town. Guests enjoy a pleasant roof terrace overlooking the river (laundry, local wines/beers available, free parking—entrance on Moselstrasse, Ravenéstrasse 34, tel. 02671/910-224, www.villa-cuchema.de, info@villa-cuchema.de; energetic Peter and Ann-Kathrin).

$$ Hotel am Hafen, across the bridge from the TI, offers a mellow atmosphere with views over the river to Cochem. Some of the 18 rooms have balconies (restaurant/terrace with seafood specialties, limited free parking, pay parking garage, closed Dec-Jan, Uferstrasse 3, tel. 02671/97720, www.hotelamhafen.de, info@hotelamhafen.com).

$ Hotel & Restaurant Weinhaus Gräfen, run by the friendly and helpful Vatlav family, has a mix of 14 comfortable rooms, a nicely decorated terrace, and a recommended restaurant downstairs (family rooms, elevator, discounted parking at nearby public garage; near chairlift at Endertstrasse 27, tel. 02671/4453, www.weinhaus-graefen.de, info@weinhaus-graefen.de).

$ Weingut Rademacher rents six simple ground-floor rooms that share a lounge with a fridge and a microwave. It's wedged between vineyards and train tracks, with a pleasant garden (free parking—exit station at rear and walk diagonally across the municipal parking lot to Pinnerstrasse 10; tel. 02671/4164, www.weingut-rademacher.de, info@weingut-rademacher.de). Their wine tastings—free for guests—are open to the public (described earlier, under "Sights in Cochem").

$ Haus Andreas has 10 clean rooms at fair prices in the old town (cash only, pay Wi-Fi, pay parking but free lot nearby, Schlossstrasse 9, reception is often across the street in shop at #16, tel. 02671/1370 or 02671/5155, www.hausandreas.de, info@hausandreas.de, kind Frau Pellny speaks a little English). From the main square, take Herrenstrasse, after a block, angle right up the steep hill on Schlossstrasse.

¢ Gasthaus zum Fröhlichen Weinberg, near a quiet, colorful courtyard just above the main square, is a relaxed jumble of nine clean, inexpensive rooms, some with low ceilings and tiny bathrooms and most with sunny balconies. Topped by a fun roof garden with a view over town, it's run by friendly Jutta and her mother, who makes jam from vineyard peaches fresh from the garden (cash only, fan available, family rooms, lots of stairs, pay parking, Schlaufstrasse 11, tel. 02671/4193, www.zum-froehlichen-weinberg.de, weinberg-cochem@t-online.de). From the main square, go up Oberbachstrasse (in the far-right corner if coming from the station) and then left up tiny Schlaufstrasse.

Cochem's **¢ hostel (Moseltal Jugendherberge)** is a huge, family-friendly complex just across the river from the train station, with picnic tables, a grill pit, a playground, and a sundeck over the Mosel (private rooms available, box lunches available, game room, bar, restaurant, fills up—reserve in advance, Klottener Strasse 9, tel. 02671/8633, www.diejugendherbergen.de/cochem, cochem@diejugendherbergen.de). To reach it from the train station, take an immediate left up the hill and walk parallel to the train tracks until you reach the "new bridge" on your right; the hostel is to the right immediately after the bridge.

Eating in Cochem

In addition to the following listings, cafés at both the castle and the chairlift serve lunch (see "Sights in Cochem," earlier) and there are plentiful pizza, Turkish, and Asian options in the old town.

$$$ Gaststätte Noss is one of several restaurants along the riverside promenade. It's open later than most—and supplies meat from its own butcher shop. Don't confuse it with the hotel of the same name; look for the awning draped in vines, which cover the sign (Fri-Wed 10:00-20:00, open later Fri-Sun, closed Thu, Mosel-promenade 4, tel. 02671/7067).

$$$ Hotel am Hafen's restaurant is a comfortable, well-respected riverfront eatery that specializes in seafood. From their terrace you can enjoy gorgeous views of the river and castle (indoor and outdoor seating, daily 12:00-21:00, Uferstrasse 3, tel. 02671/97720).

$$$ Restaurant Akropolis sits hidden away upstairs in a cozy room with a modern take on an old Greek cave house. Their extensive menu ranges from simple gyros and souvlaki to pricier steak, lamb, and seafood dishes. Try to score a seat under the twinkling ceiling that imitates the night sky (daily 11:30-14:30 & 17:00-22:00, reservations smart, Liniustrasse 7, tel. 02671 9153780, www.akropolis-cochem.de).

$$ Alte Gutsschänke, better known as "Arthur's place," is where locals go for a glass of wine in a cozy cellar. Seating is at long, wooden, get-to-know-your-neighbor tables (extensive wine list and very basic pub food, Easter-Oct Tue-Fri from 18:00, Sat-Sun from 14:00, closed Mon and in winter, just uphill from the old town's Markt square at Schlossstrasse 6, tel. 02671/8950).

$$ Hotel & Restaurant Weinhaus Gräfen is where you can meet the locals while enjoying freshly prepared traditional food (Fri-Wed 10:00-22:00, closed Thu and last 2 weeks of Nov and Feb, below recommended hotel at Endertstrasse 27, tel. 02671/4453).

$$ Da Vinci Ristorante Pizzeria serves good, reasonably priced Italian fare at its hard-to-miss location just across the bridge from the TI. Grab a seat on the covered terrace for city, river, and castle views while rubbing elbows with locals and fellow travelers (Tue-Sun 17:30-22:00, Fri and Sun also 12:00-14:00, closed Mon except mid-July-Aug, Bergstrasse 1, tel. 02671/916-195).

$ Equit's Metzger Imbiss is a great and inexpensive alternative for lunch or an early dinner. Local butcher Thomas Equit offers tasty sausages, schnitzel, and other regional dishes—as well as burgers—for a reasonable price. The interior is modern, clean, and very inviting. In summer, the big front windows are opened up, and you'll feel like you're sitting right on the main square (daily 10:00-18:00, cash only, Markt 10, tel. 02671/910-710).

Picnics: The **Diewald supermarket** stocks everything you need for a fabulous picnic (Mon-Fri 7:30-20:00, Sat 8:00-18:00, closed Sun). Located between the train station and TI, it's just off Ravenéstrasse, up a little side street at #33, behind a clothing store.

Gelato: For good quality, inexpensive scoops, **Gelateria**

Fratelli Bortolot brings a taste of Italy to the Rhine. They run a sprawling café on the corner facing the Brückenstrasse bridge, but stick to their smaller shop closer to the main square just inside the old town (daily 11:00-late, Bernstrasse 25).

Cochem Connections

From Cochem by Train to: Moselkern (for hike to Burg Eltz; hourly, 16 minutes), **Trier** (2/hour, 1 hour), **Frankfurt Airport** (hourly, 2.5 hours, change in Koblenz and sometimes Mainz), **Cologne** (hourly, 2.5 hours, most change in Koblenz), **Bacharach** (hourly, 2 hours, change in Koblenz), **Rothenburg** (every 1-2 hours, 6 hours, 4 changes), **Berlin** (roughly hourly, 7 hours, 1-2 changes), **Paris** (roughly every 2 hours, 4-5 hours, transfer in Saarbrücken or in Trier and Luxembourg). Train info: www.bahn.com. Bus info: Tel. 02671/8976, www.vrminfo.de.

Burg Eltz

My favorite castle in all of Europe—worth ▲▲▲—lurks in a mysterious forest. It's been left intact for 700 years and is decorated and furnished throughout much as it was 500 years ago. Thanks to smart diplomacy, clever marriages, and lots of luck, Burg Eltz (pronounced "boorg elts") was never destroyed (it survived one five-year siege). It's been in the Eltz family for 850 years. The scenic 1.5-hour walk up the Elz Valley to the castle makes a great half-day outing if you're staying anywhere along the Mosel—and a worthwhile day trip if you're staying on the Rhine.

GETTING THERE

The castle is a pleasant 1.5-hour **walk** from the nearest train station, in the little village of Moselkern—the walk is not only easy, it's the most fun and scenic way to visit the castle.

Alternatively, if the weather is bad, or you prefer not to walk, you can take a **taxi** (or, on summer weekends only, the **bus**) to the castle from the village of Karden (see "By Bus from the Treis-Karden Station," later).

Cars (and taxis) park in a lot near, but not quite at, Burg Eltz.

MOSEL VALLEY

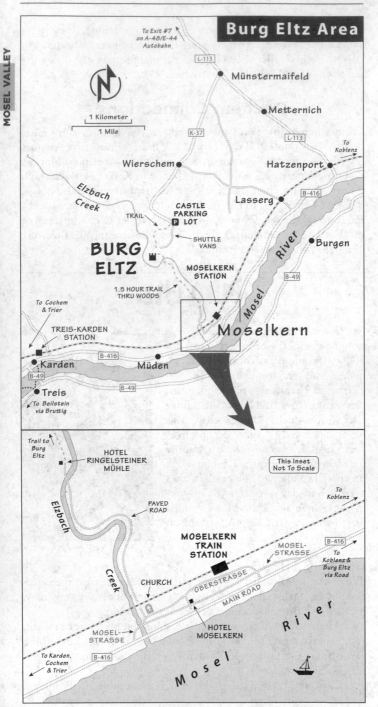

To Exit #7
on A-48/E-44
Autobahn

L-113

Burg Eltz Area

Münstermaifeld

N

1 Kilometer

1 Mile

Metternich

K-37

L-113

To
Koblenz

Wierschem

Hatzenport

Elzbach
Creek

Lasserg

B-416

TRAIL

CASTLE
PARKING
LOT

P

Mosel River

Burgen

SHUTTLE
VANS

B-49

**BURG
ELTZ**

MOSELKERN
STATION

1.5 HOUR TRAIL
THRU WOODS

To Cochem
& Trier

Moselkern

TREIS-KARDEN
STATION

B-416

Karden

Müden

B-49

B-49

Treis

To Beilstein
via Bruttig

Trail to
Burg
Eltz

HOTEL
RINGELSTEINER
MÜHLE

This Inset
Not To Scale

To
Koblenz

Elzbach

PAVED
ROAD

**MOSELKERN
TRAIN
STATION**

MOSEL-
STRASSE

B-416

To
Koblenz &
Burg Eltz
via Road

Creek

OBERSTRASSE

CHURCH

MAIN ROAD

MOSEL-
STRASSE

HOTEL
MOSELKERN

Mosel River

To Karden,
Cochem
& Trier

B-416

Mosel

From the lot, hike 15 minutes downhill to the castle or wait (10 minutes at most) for the red castle shuttle bus (€2 each way).

Each of your options is explained next.

Hiking from Moselkern

The hike between the Moselkern train station and Burg Eltz runs through a magical pine forest, where sparrows carry crossbows, and maidens, disguised as falling leaves, whisper "watch out." You can do the hike in 75 minutes at a steady clip, but allow an extra 20 minutes or so to enjoy the scenery. The trail is mostly gentle, except for a few uneven parts that are slippery when wet and the steep flight of stairs leading up to the castle at the end. The overall elevation gain from the river to the castle is less than 400 feet.

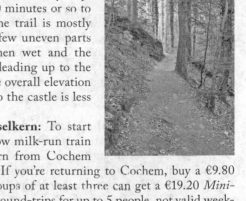

Getting to Moselkern: To start the hike, take the slow milk-run train (hourly) to Moselkern from Cochem (16 minutes, €4.90). If you're returning to Cochem, buy a €9.80 round-trip ticket; groups of at least three can get a €19.20 *Mini-gruppenkarte* (covers round-trips for up to 5 people, not valid weekdays before 9:00). You can reach Moselkern by train from towns on the Rhine (including Cologne and Bacharach) with a change at Koblenz.

Storing Luggage: The Moselkern train station is unstaffed and has no lockers, phones, or taxis. You can store luggage at Hotel Moselkern, on the river a five minute walk from the station (see "Sleeping near Burg Eltz," later); call the hotel in advance to make arrangements (tel. 02672/1303). There's no charge for storage, but consider thanking them by eating at their restaurant (food served 12:00-21:00, reasonable prices) or buying a drink at the hotel bar.

The Hike: The path up to the castle begins at the other end of Moselkern village from the station. Turn right from the station along Oberstrasse, cross the intersection with Weinbergsstrasse, and continue straight along narrow Oberstrasse. In about five minutes, you'll pass the village church. Keep going straight a few houses past the church; then, as the street ends, turn right through the underpass. On your left is the Elzbach stream that you'll follow all the way up to the castle. Follow the road straight along the stream through a mostly residential neighborhood. Just before the road crosses the stream on a stone bridge, take either the footpath (stay right) or the bridge—they join up again later.

About 30 minutes into your walk, the road ends at the parking lot of the Hotel Ringelsteiner Mühle. Stay to the right of the hotel and continue upstream along the easy-to-follow trail, which starts out paved but soon changes to dirt. From here, it's another 45 minutes through the forest to the castle.

Hiking from Karden (with Optional Boat Trip)

If you don't mind a longer hike, consider a boat ride to the village of Karden, then walk to Burg Eltz from there. (Karden is also on the train line between Cochem and Moselkern.) This two-hour hike is steep in places, and harder to follow and less shady than the hike from Moselkern.

Getting to Karden: Kolb Line riverboat cruises run between Cochem and Karden three times a day in July-Aug and less frequently in spring and fall (see "Getting Around the Mosel Valley" near the beginning of this chapter). Make sure to get off the boat in Karden (not in Treis, across the river). If you come by train, get off at the Treis-Karden stop, which is in Karden but serves both villages.

Storing Luggage: The elegant Schloss-Hotel Petry, across from the Treis-Karden station, is happy to guard your bags if you eat at their **$$$** restaurant (lunch daily 12:00-14:00, St. Castorstrasse 80, tel. 02672/9340, www.schloss-hotel-petry.de).

The Hike: The path from Karden to Burg Eltz starts at the far end of Karden village, beyond the white-towered St. Castor's church (follow *Burg Eltz* signs). Get a trail map (available locally), and be prepared for full sun when the hike travels through open fields.

Shortcuts: To ride the boat but avoid the lengthy hike to Burg Eltz, you can either hop the hourly train from Treis-Karden to Moselkern and take the shorter 1.5-hour hike from there (described earlier); take the bus from the Treis-Karden station straight up to Burg Eltz on weekends (May-Oct only, described next); or take a taxi from Karden to the castle (see later).

By Bus from the Treis-Karden Station

From May through October on Saturdays and Sundays only, bus #330 runs to Burg Eltz from the Treis-Karden railway station (4/day, 40 minutes; leaves Treis-Karden station at 9:10, 11:15, 15:10, and 17:15; leaves Burg Eltz at 10:30, 12:30, 16:30, and 18:30; confirm times at Cochem TI, with bus operator at tel. 02671/8976, or at www.burg-eltz.de). To make the best use of your time, take the 9:10 or 15:10 bus from Treis-Karden to Burg Eltz, and return to Treis-Karden on either the 12:30 or 18:30 bus. This allows you about 2.5 hours to explore the castle.

By Taxi

You can taxi to the castle from **Cochem** (30 minutes, about €55 one-way for up to 4 people, Cochem taxi tel. 02671/8080), **Moselkern** (€28 one-way, taxi tel. 02672/1407), or **Karden** (€30 one-way, taxi tel. 02672/1407). Remember: Even with a taxi, you'll still have a 15-minute walk from the parking lot to the castle. If you're planning to taxi from Moselkern, call ahead and ask the taxi to meet your train at Moselkern station. Consider taxiing up to Burg Eltz and then enjoying the hike downhill back to the train station in Moselkern.

By Car

Be Careful: Signs direct drivers to two different "Burg Eltz" parking lots—some deceptively take drivers far from the castle, while

others get you right there. From Koblenz, leave the river at Hatzenport, following the white *Burg Eltz* signs through the towns of Münstermaifeld and Wierschem. From Cochem, follow the *Münstermaifeld* signs from Moselkern. The castle parking lot (€2/ day, daily 9:00-18:30) is just over a mile past Wierschem. (Note that the *Eltz* signs at Moselkern lead to Hotel Ringelsteiner Mühle and the trailhead for the hike to the castle—see next. To drive directly to the castle, ignore the *Eltz* signs until you reach Münstermaifeld.)

Drive/Hike Combo: If you're driving but would enjoy walking part of the path from Moselkern up to the castle, drive to Moselkern, follow the *Burg Eltz* signs up the Elz Valley, park at the Hotel Ringelsteiner Mühle (buy ticket from machine), and hike about 45 minutes up the trail to the castle (full hike described earlier).

Shortcut to Beilstein: If driving from Burg Eltz to Beilstein, you'll save 30 minutes with this shortcut: Cross the river at Treis-Karden, go through town, and bear right at the swimming pool (direction: Bruttig-Fankel). This overland route deposits you in Bruttig, a scenic three-mile riverside drive from Beilstein.

ORIENTATION TO BURG ELTZ

Cost and Hours: €10 castle entry (includes guided tour and treasury), April-Oct daily from 9:30, last tour departs at 17:30, closed Nov-March. Pick up the free English descriptions at entry. Tel. 02672/950-500, www.burg-eltz.de.

Tours: The only way to see the castle is with a 40-minute tour (included with admission). Guides speak English and thoughtfully collect English speakers into tour groups—well worth waiting for (usually a 30-minute wait at most; visit treasury in the meantime).

Bring Cash: The castle (including the parking lot and café) doesn't accept credit cards—only cash. There's no ATM, so make sure you bring enough. (There's one exception: If you spend at least €30 at the ticket desk they will accept Visa and MasterCard.)

Eating: The $ castle café downstairs serves lunch, with soups and bratwurst-and-fries cuisine (April-Oct daily 9:30-16:30; snacks available upstairs until 18:00, cash only).

VISITING THE CASTLE

Elz is the name of a stream that runs past the castle through a deep valley before emptying into the Mosel. The first record of a *Burg* (castle) on the Elz is from 1157. By about 1490, the castle looked like it does today, with the homes of three big landlord families gathered around a tiny courtyard within one formidable fortification. Today, the excellent tour winds you through two of those homes, while the third is still the residence of the castellan (the man who maintains the castle).

This is where members of the **Eltz family** stay when they're not at one of their other feudal holdings. The elderly countess of Eltz—whose husband's family goes back 33 generations here (you'll see a photo of their family)—enjoys flowers. Each week for 40 years, she made the grand arrangements that adorned the public castle rooms. Nowadays a local florist continues the tradition.

It was a comfortable castle for its day: 80 rooms made cozy by 40 fireplaces and wall-hanging tapestries. Many of its 20 toilets were automatically flushed by a rain drain. The delightful **chapel** is on a lower floor. Even though "no one should live above God," this chapel's placement was acceptable because it filled a bay window, which flooded the delicate Gothic space with light. The three families met—working out common problems  as if sharing a condo complex—in the large "conference room." A carved jester and a rose look down on the big table, reminding those who gathered that they were free to discuss anything ("fool's freedom"—jesters could say anything to the king), but nothing discussed could leave the room (the "rose of silence"). In the **bedroom,** have fun with the suggestive decor: the jousting relief carved into the canopy, and the fertile and phallic figures hiding in the lusty green wall paintings.

Near the exit, the **treasury** fills the four higgledy-piggledy floors of a cellar with the precious, eccentric, and historic mementos of this family that once helped elect the Holy Roman Emperor and, later, owned a sizable chunk of Croatia (Habsburg favors). The silver and gold work—some of Germany's best—is worth a close look with the help of an English flier.

SLEEPING NEAR BURG ELTZ

Although I prefer the bustle of Cochem or the charm of Beilstein, staying in tiny, sleepy Moselkern is a workable option. You can set off to Burg Eltz right after breakfast to beat the heat on a warm day. **$ Hotel Moselkern,** set alongside the river a five-minute walk from the train station, has 25 comfortable rooms in a solid, 1970s-era building. All rooms have balconies, most of them overlooking the river (cash only, elevator, restaurant with outdoor seating, free parking, bowling alley in basement, tel. 02672/1303, www.hotel-moselkern.de, hotel-moselkern@t-online.de, Wanda Ketsila).

Beilstein

Just upstream from Cochem is the quaintest of all Mosel towns. Cozy Beilstein (BILE-shtine) is Cinderella-land touristy but tranquil, except for its territorial swans. Beilstein has no food shops, ATMs (bring cash), or public restrooms (you'll have to use a café's or restaurant's). It does have one bus stop, one  mailbox, and 180 residents who run about 30 guesthouses and eateries. It's nicknamed the "Sleeping Beauty of the Mosel" because until about 1900, it was inaccessible except by boat. Beilstein also has no TI, but there is an information board by the bus stop, and cafés and guesthouses can give you town info.

PLANNING YOUR TIME

Car travelers use Beilstein as a base, day-tripping from here to Cochem, Trier, Burg Eltz, and the Rhine. Overnighting in Beilstein without a car is doable, as long as you check the bus and boat schedules in advance and plan carefully. If you're staying in Cochem and using public transportation, you can day-trip to Beilstein: Take the bus to Beilstein, follow my self-guided walk up to the castle, have lunch, and then return by boat. While the town is peaceful and a delight in the evening, midday crowds in peak season can trample all its charm and turn it into a human traffic jam. In the winter (mid-Nov until Easter), Beilstein is dead as a doornail.

GETTING TO BEILSTEIN

Beilstein has no train station, but it's easy to reach from Cochem—either on **bus #716** (May-Oct hourly Mon-Fri, 8-10/day Sat, less frequent Sun and Nov-April, 20 minutes; last bus departs between 21:00-22:00 except Sun 18:00-19:00, €3.80, www.vrminfo.de), by **taxi** (about €20), or by one-hour **river cruise** (4-5/day in each direction May-Oct, weekends-only in April, no boats off-season, first departure from Cochem at about 10:30, last departure from Beilstein at about 17:30, €12 one-way, €16 round-trip). If **driving**, there's a free lot along the river just upstream from town, under the castle hill. Parking spaces closer-in cost €1/hour during the day (4-hour maximum, use coins to buy ticket from *Parkscheinautomat* machine by town info board).

Two helpful tips: When looking up schedules on www.bahn.com (the Deutsche Bahn website), Beilstein's bus stop appears as "Moselstrasse (Beilstein)." On weekends when bus #716 runs infrequently and the Ellenz Fähre ferry is running (see "Beilstein's Riverfront," later), you can reach Beilstein from Cochem via bus #711 along the other side of the river. (This alternative is slightly more expensive, and the ferry's irregular hours and early closing time complicate it, so I prefer taking the direct #716 bus.) If you go this way, take bus #711 to the Ellenz Fähre stop, then ride the ferry across the river to Beilstein.

Beilstein Walk

Explore the narrow lanes, ancient wine cellar, resident swans, and ruined castle by following this short self-guided walk.

• *Stand along the riverfront, by the town info board.*

Beilstein's Riverfront

In 1963, the big road and the Mosel locks were built, making the river peaceful today. Before then, access to Beilstein was limited to a tiny one-way lane and the small ferry. Originally, the ferry was motorless and the cables that tethered it allowed the craft to cross the river powered only by the current and an angled rudder. However, since the river was tamed by locks, the current is so weak that the ferry needs its motor. Today, the funky little **Ellenz Fähre** ferry shuttles people, bikes, and cars constantly (€1.50, Easter-Oct daily 9:00-18:00, no ferries off-season, wave to summon ferry if captain has paused on opposite bank).

The campground across the river is typical of German campgrounds—nearly all of its residents set up their trailers and tents at Easter and use them as summer homes until October, when the regular floods chase them away for the winter. If you stood where you are now through the winter, you'd have cold water up to your crotch five times.

Look inland. The town was given market rights in 1310 and was essentially an independent city-state for centuries (back when

there were 300 such petty kingdoms and dukedoms in what we now call "Germany"). The Earl of Beilstein ruled from his castle above town. He built the Altes Zollhaus in 1634 to levy tolls from river traffic. Today, the castle is a ruin, the last monk at the once-mighty monastery (see the big church high on the left) retired in 2009, and the town's economy is based only on wine and tourists.

Beilstein is so well preserved because it was essentially inaccessible by road until about 1900. And its tranquility is a result of Germany's WWI loss, which cost the country the regions of Alsace and Lorraine

(now part of France, these provinces have flip-flopped between the two nations since the Thirty Years' War). Before World War I, the Koblenz-Trier train line—which connects Lorraine to Germany—was the busiest in the country, tunneling through the grape-laden hill across the river in what was the longest train tunnel in Germany. The construction of a supplemental line designed to follow the riverbank (like the lines that crank up the volume on the Rhine) was stopped in 1914. After Alsace and Lorraine went to France in 1918, the new line no longer made any sense, and the plans were scuttled.

• *Follow the main "street" up into town. You'll notice blue plaques on the left marking the high-water (Hochwasser) points of historic floods. At the first corner, after the Wirtshaus Alte Stadtmauer, go left and find house #13 in the corner.*

Former Synagogue

In the 1300s, several Jewish families were invited to Beilstein after being persecuted and expelled from towns on the Rhine. By 1840, a quarter of the town's 300 inhabitants were Jewish. The synagogue (which dates from

1310) and the adjacent rabbi's home were at #13. The medallion above the door shows the Star of David embedded in the double-headed eagle of the Holy Roman Emperor, indicating that the Jews would be protected by the emperor. This was perhaps of some comfort, but not reliable. Of the town's many Jews, most moved away (to larger German towns or abroad) in the 1800s and early 1900s. Others assimilated, marrying Gentiles and raising their children as Christians (among these was the Lipmann family, whose descendants run the riverfront hotels). By 1933, only one Jewish family was left in Beilstein to deal with the Nazis. There are no practicing Jews in town today. The cemetery above the castle is another interesting Jewish sight (see "Beilstein's Castle," later).

• *Continue right (uphill) from the synagogue, and then with the church high above, go right again. You'll reach a long flight of stairs (marked Klostertreppe) that leads to the monastery. Look up (it's only worth actually going up the stairs if you like good views, Baroque churches...or you're a hungry masochist).*

Although the last Carmelite monk retired several years ago, Rome maintains a handsome but oversized-for-this-little-town **Catholic church** that runs a restaurant with a great view. It's a screwy situation that seems to make locals uncomfortable when you ask them about it.

• *Continue back to the main street, called...*

Bachstrasse ("Creek Street")

The town's main drag runs straight inland through Beilstein, passing through the tunnel you see to the left. It covers up the brook that once flowed through town and used to provide a handy 24/7 disposal service. Today, Bachstrasse is lined with wine cellars. The only way for a small local vintner to make any decent money these days is to sell his wine directly to customers in inviting little places like these.

• *Cross Bachstrasse and walk a few steps ahead to the...*

Market Square (Marktplatz)

For centuries, neighboring farmers sold their goods on Marktplatz. The *Zehnthaus* (tithe house) was the village IRS, where locals would pay one-tenth *(Zehnte)* of their produce to their landlord (either the Church or the earl). Pop into the **Zehnthauskeller.** Stuffed with peasants' offerings 400 years ago, it's now packed with vaulted medieval ambience. It's fun at night for candlelit wine-tasting, soup and cold cuts, and schmaltzy music (often live Fri and Sat). The adjacent **Bürgerhaus** (above the fountain) had nothing to do with medieval fast food. First the village church, then the residence of the *Bürger* (like a mayor), and later the communal oven and the village grade school, today it's where locals hold a big party or wedding (upstairs) and a venue for local craftspeople to show their goodies (below). **Haus Lipmann** (on the riverside, now a recommended hotel and restaurant) dates from 1727. It was built by the earl's family as a residence after the French destroyed his castle. Haus Lipmann's main dining hall was once the knights' hall.

• *Leave the square going uphill and follow the main street through the tunnel and up to the top end of town. Then bear right up the stairs (follow signs for* Burgruine Metternich*) to...*

Beilstein's Castle

Beilstein once rivaled Cochem as the most powerful town on this part of the Mosel. Like so much around here, it was destroyed by the French in 1689. Its cas-  tle (officially named Burg Metternich) is a sorry ruin today, but those who make the steep 10-minute climb are rewarded with a postcard Mosel view and a chance to hike even higher to the top of its lone sur-viving tower for a 360-de-gree view (€2.50, daily 9:00-18:00, closed Nov-Easter, view café/ restaurant, tel. 02673/93639, www.burgmetternich.de).

For more exercise and an even better **viewpoint,** exit through the turnstile at the rear of the castle. Take the uphill (left-hand)  road, and after 100 yards, fork right. Here you'll find the ulti-mate "castle/river bend/carpets of vineyards" photo op. The derelict vineyard in front of you is a sign of recent times—the younger generation is abandon-ing the family plots, opting out of all that hard winemaking work.

From this viewpoint, continue another 100 yards farther up the road to the small but poignant **Jewish cemetery** (*Jüdische Fried-hof*).

To reach the viewpoint and the cemetery without going through the castle, continue up the road past the castle entrance, then follow the signs for *Jüdische Friedhof*.

• *From here, you can return to the castle gate, ring the bell (Klingeln), and show your ticket to get back in and retrace your steps; or continue on the road, which curves and leads downhill (a gravel path at the next bend on the left leads back into town).*

Activities in Beilstein

Biking and Boating

Boats come and go several times a day for extremely relaxing river trips (for details, see "Getting Around the Mosel Valley" at the beginning of this chapter). While scenic, these rides can take longer than you'd like because of the locks. I prefer a riverside bike ride (perhaps combined with a boat trip). Biking is very popular along the Mosel, and roads are accompanied by smooth and perfectly flat bike lanes. The lanes are separate from the car traffic, letting you really relax as you pedal through gorgeous riverside scenery. To rent a quality bike in Beilstein, visit Herr Nahlen (€9/day, daily 9:00-12:00, return bikes between 16:00 and 19:00, no rentals Nov-March, reservations smart for groups, Bachstrasse 47, tel. 02673/1840, www.fahrradverleih-in-beilstein.de).

Five-Hour Trip to Zell and Back: You could rent a bike in Beilstein, catch the 9:20 boat to Zell (2.5-hour ride), enjoy that pretty town, and cycle 15 miles back to Beilstein along the sleepy and windy riverside bike path.

Hour-and-a-Half Loop: For a shorter bike trip, ride the little ferry across the river from Beilstein, explore the campground, continue left past Poltersdorf, cycle under vineyards to Senhals, cross the bridge to Senheim, and return to Beilstein on the other side of the river. At the edge of Mesenich, leave the road and take the peaceful bike lane along the river, explore another campground, and head for Beilstein, with its castle in the distance encouraging you home.

Sleeping in Beilstein

Beilstein's hotels shut down from at least December through mid-March. All the listings here are just steps from the bus stop and boat dock, except for Hotel Lipmann am Klosterberg. All accept credit cards except Gasthaus Winzerschenke an der Klostertreppe.

$$$ Hotel Lipmann Altes Zollhaus is run by one of three Lipmann sisters carrying on an eight-generation-long tradition in town. The nine bright rooms right on the riverfront feel fresh and cheery (closed mid-Nov-Easter, tel. 02673/1850, www.hotel-lipmann.de, lipmann@t-online.de, family rooms, free parking at Hotel Lipmann Am Klosterberg, also has a restaurant—see "Eating in Beilstein," later).

$$ Hotel Lipmann Am Klosterberg, run by Joachim Lipmann and his wife Marlene, is a big, modern place with 16 comfortable rooms at the extremely quiet top of town (elevator, easy free parking, Auf dem Teich 8, up the main street 200 yards then a sharp left before the stairs to the castle, same contact info as Altes Zollhaus).

$$ Hotel Haus Lipmann is your chance to live in a medieval mansion with hot showers and TVs. A prizewinner for atmosphere, it's been in the Lipmann family since 1795. The creaky wooden staircase and the elegant dining hall, with long wooden tables surrounded by antlers, chandeliers, and feudal weapons, will get you in the mood for your castle sightseeing, but the riverside terrace may mace your momentum. There are six guest rooms in the main building, six larger rooms in an equally old building next door, and, across the square, four **$$$$** spacious, sleek studios with luxe bathrooms and an elevator. David and his wife Anja work hard for their guests (some rooms with Mosel views, family rooms, closed Nov-Easter, Marktplatz 3, tel. 02673/1573, www.hotel-haus-lipmann.com, hotel.haus.lipmann@t-online.de).

$ Gasthaus Winzerschenke an der Klostertreppe is welcoming and a great value, with four sharp rooms right at the bottom of the stairs to the church cloister (cash only, family rooms, closed Nov-Easter, take a few steps up the main street and take second left—after the second building—onto Fürst-Metternich-Strasse, reception in restaurant, tel. 02673/1354, www.winzerschenke-beilstein.de, winzerschenke-beilstein@t-online.de, young and eager Stefanie and Christian Sausen).

$ Hotel Gute Quelle, straddling the main street and the square, offers half-timbers, a good restaurant, and 13 inviting rooms up a narrow stairway, plus seven more in an annex across the street (free Gäste-Ticket for guests —good for buses and trains between Koblenz and Traben-Trarbach, closed Nov-mid-March, Marktplatz 34, tel. 02673/1437, www.hotel-gute-quelle.de, info@hotel-gute-quelle.de, helpful Susan speaks Irish). The hotel also has five bigger, very quiet family rooms and an apartment that sleeps up to four in an adjacent building.

Eating in Beilstein

You'll have no problem finding a characteristic dining room or a relaxing riverview terrace in Beilstein.

$$ Restaurant Haus Lipmann serves good, fresh food with daily specials on a glorious, leafy riverside terrace. For a wonderful trip memory, enjoy a slow meal here while watching the lazy riverside action and the changing light on the distant vineyards (daily 10:00-21:30, last meal order at 20:00, closed Nov-Easter).

The daughters Lippman run two **$$$** restaurants and a **$$** wine bar all within steps of each other. **Hotel Lipmann Altes Zollhaus,** run by Julia, serves specialties cooked on a lava-stone grill (Thu-Tue 11:00-22:00, closed Wed). You could toss a dinner roll across to **Alte Stadtmauer,** run by Kristina, with a relaxed terrace overlooking the river (Wed-Mon 11:00-22:00, closed Tue and mid-Nov-Easter). And **Zehnthauskeller** on the Marktplatz is *the* place for wine tasting, a light meal, and lively *Schlager* music (kitschy German folk-pop). Hang with old locals on holiday, sitting under a dark medieval vault or out in the Marktplatz (try the *Flammkuchen*—German version of white pizza, Tue-Sun 11:00-22:00, closed Mon and Nov-Easter, run by Joachim Lipmann's other daughter Sabine).

The recommended **$$ Hotel Gute Quelle** runs a popular restaurant with classic, well-presented German dishes (daily 11:00-21:00, closed Nov-mid-March, Marktplatz 34).

TRIER

Germany's oldest city lies at the head of the scenic Mosel Valley, near the border with Luxembourg. An ancient Roman capital, Trier brags that it was inhabited by Celts for 1,300 years before Rome even existed. Today, Trier (rhymes with clear) is thriving and feels very young. A short stop here offers you a look at Germany's oldest Christian church, one of its most enjoyable market squares, and its best Roman ruins.

Founded by Augustus in 16 BC, Trier was a Roman town called Augusta Treverorum for 400 years. When Emperor Diocletian (who ruled AD 285-305) divided his overextended Roman Empire into four sectors, he made Trier the capital of the west: roughly modern-day Germany, France, Spain, and England. For most of the fourth century, this city of 80,000—with a four-mile wall, four great gates, and 47 round towers—was a favored residence of Roman emperors. Emperor Constantine lived here, spending lavishly on urban projects. As a military town in a god-forsaken corner of the empire, Trier received lots of perks from Rome to make it livable for those assigned here. But when the last emperor checked out in AD 395, the money dried up, and that was the end of Trier's ancient glory days. In the late 400s, when Rome fell to the barbarians, so did Trier.

Roman Trier was much bigger than medieval Trier. The pedestrian center of town—containing nearly all of your sightseeing and browsing—is defined by the medieval wall (which encloses only half the area the Roman wall did). Trier's Roman sights include the huge city gate (Porta Nigra), basilica, baths, and amphitheater.

Trier's main draw is the chance to experience Germany's Roman and early Christian history, which deserve at least a full day to appreciate. Poly-sci junkies should try to visit Karl Marx's House. If you're more interested in wine tasting and scenery, stay elsewhere on the Mosel River (see previous chapter).

Orientation to Trier

The mid-size city of Trier, with more than 100,000 people, has a broad, rectangular footprint hemmed in by the Mosel River and gentle hills. Many visitors never even see the river, and stick to the city's central core: From the landmark Porta Nigra, the main drag (Simeonstrasse) runs south to the Market Square (Hauptmarkt) and beyond. Most sights—including the cathedral and its museum, the Basilica/Imperial Throne Room, and the Archaeological Museum—are within a five-minute walk of this artery. The train station is about a 10-minute walk east of the Porta Nigra.

TOURIST INFORMATION

Trier's cramped and busy TI is just through the Porta Nigra. The TI sells a useful little city guide called *Trier: History and Monuments* (€4). Also consider the booklet *Trier in One Day* (€3), which has little information on sights but a great map and suggested walking routes (Roman, medieval, Jewish, rainy day). The TI also offers tours—see "Tours in Trier," later (Mon-Sat 9:00-18:00, Sun 10:00-17:00, shorter hours off-season, tel. 651/978-080, www.trier-info.de).

ARRIVAL IN TRIER

By Train: The *Reisezentrum* at the train station can answer your train-schedule questions and book tickets (long hours daily). The station also has lockers, a pay WC (coins only), and bike rental (see "Helpful Hints," below). To reach the town center from the train station, walk 10 boring minutes and four blocks up Theodor-Heuss-Allee to the big black Roman gate (Porta Nigra), and turn left under the gate to find the TI. From here, the main pedestrian mall (Simeonstrasse) leads right to the sights: Market Square and the cathedral (a five-minute walk), and the basilica (five more minutes).

By Car: Drivers get off the A-602 at Trier Verteilerkreis and follow signs to *Zentrum*. Parking is near the Porta Nigra and TI.

HELPFUL HINTS

Sightseeing Passes: The Antique Card, available at the TI and participating sights, can save you a few euros. The €12 version covers the Archaeological Museum and any two of Trier's four paid Roman sights (Porta Nigra, Imperial Baths, Viehmarkt Baths Museum, and amphitheater); for €18 you get all four Roman sights. The Trier Card, which includes free use of city buses and sightseeing discounts, is not worth it if you're staying in the center of this small, walkable town.

Laundry: A well-maintained self-service launderette is just beyond Karl Marx's House (daily 8:00-22:00, last load at 20:30, instructions in English, Brückenstrasse 19).

Bike Rental: A local citizens' group called **Bürgerservice** rents bikes for reasonable daily rates. Find them at the train station, just off track 11 (€12/up to 24 hours, spiffy 27-gear bikes-€14, show ID and leave €30 as deposit; daily 9:00-18:00, shorter hours and closed Sun in off-season; tel. 0651/148-856, www.bues-trier.de).

Tours in Trier

Walking Tours

The TI offers an €8, informative 75-minute walking tour in English daily at 13:00 (May-Oct, may also be offered Nov-April—ask) and can put you in touch with local guides who do private tours (€100/2 hours, tel. 0651/978-080).

Hop-On, Hop-Off Bus Tour

The hop-on, hop-off City Sightseeing bus leaves Porta Nigra every 30 minutes. The route has seven stops—including the amphitheater, Basilica/Imperial Throne Room, and Karl Marx's House—and takes you as far as Petrisberg, a recreational area with great views over the city and the Mosel Valley. Tickets are valid for 24 hours; buy them onboard, at any stop, or at the TI (€13, April-Oct daily 2/hour 10:00-17:00, recorded commentary in 8 languages, Luxembourg tel. 352-3565-75888, www.city-sightseeing.com).

Tourist Train

I'd skip the expensive, hokey red-and-yellow tourist train, which does a pointless 35-minute loop of Trier's major old-town sights (€9, recorded narration in English, departs from TI, www.roemer-express.de).

Sights in Trier

I've laced together the historic city's top sights on this fascinating self-guided walk, offering a taste of Trier old, new, and in-between.

▲Porta Nigra

Roman Trier was built as a capital. Its architecture mirrored the grandeur of the empire. Of the four-mile town wall's four huge

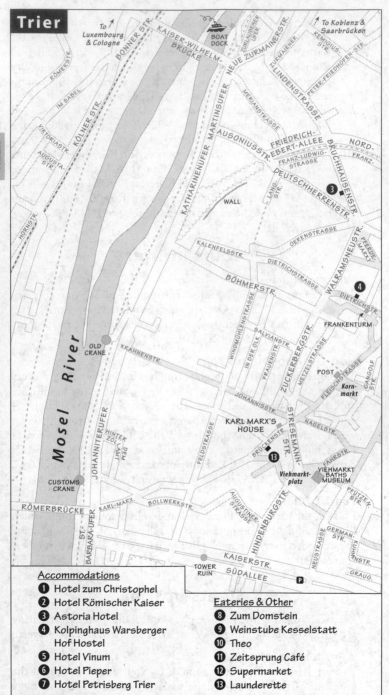

Trier

TRIER

To Luxembourg & Cologne

BOAT DOCK

To Koblenz & Saarbrücken

RÖMERSTR.

IM SABEL

VIKTORIASTR.

AUGUSTA-STR.

KÖLNER STR.

BONNER STR.

KAISER-WILHELM-BRÜCKE

HORNSTR.

NEUE ZURMAINERSTR.

ZURLAUBENER UFER

ZURMAINER.

LINDENSTRASSE

REMIGIUS-STR.

PETER-FRIEDHOFEN-STR.

MERIANSTRASSE

FRIEDRICH-EBERT-ALLEE

NORD-FRANZ.

BRUCHHAUSENSTR.

FRANZ-LUDWIG-STRASSE

3

DEUTSCHHERRENSTR.

KATHARINENUFER

MARTINSUFER

AUSONIUSSTR.

LANG-STR.

WALL

OBERENSTRASSE

WALRAMSNEUSTR.

PFERDE-MARKT

KALENFELSSTR.

DIETRICHSTRASSE

BÖHMERSTR.

4

DIETRICHSTR.

FRANKENTURM

WINDMÜHLENSTRASSE

IN DER OLK

SALVIANSTR.

FRAUENSTR.

ZUCKERBERGSTR.

METZELSTRASSE

FLEISCHSTRASSE

POST

GANGOLF-STR.

Kornmarkt

OLD CRANE

KRAHNENSTR.

JOHANNISSTR.

JOHANNITERUFER

HINTER DEM ZOLLAMT

FELDSTRASSE

KARL MARX'S HOUSE

BRÜCKENSTR.

STRESEMANN-STR.

NAGELSTR.

13

FAHRSTR.

Viehmarkt-platz

VIEHMARKT BATHS MUSEUM

PÜTZEN-STR.

CUSTOMS CRANE

RÖMERBRÜCKE

ST.-BARBARA-UFER

KARL-MARX-UFER

BOLLWERKSTR.

AUGUSTINER-STRASSE

HINDENBURGSTR.

GERMAN-STR.

NEUSTRASSE

KUNNSTR.

GRAUG.

Mosel River

TOWER RUIN

KAISERSTR.

SÜDALLEE

P

Accommodations

1 Hotel zum Christophel

2 Hotel Römischer Kaiser

3 Astoria Hotel

4 Kolpinghaus Warsberger Hof Hostel

5 Hotel Vinum

6 Hotel Pieper

7 Hotel Petrisberg Trier

Eateries & Other

8 Zum Domstein

9 Weinstube Kesselstatt

10 Theo

11 Zeitsprung Café

12 Supermarket

13 Launderette

TRIER

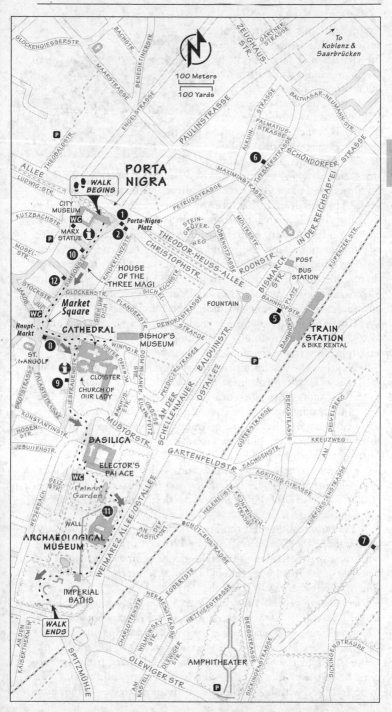

Sights in Trier map. Features labeled include:

To Koblenz & Saarbrücken

PORTA NIGRA

WALK BEGINS

100 Meters
100 Yards

CITY MUSEUM
WC
MARX STATUE
1 Porta-Nigra-Platz
2
10
12
HOUSE OF THE THREE MAGI
6

Market Square
WC
Haupt-Markt
CATHEDRAL
BISHOP'S MUSEUM
FOUNTAIN
5
8
ST. GANGOLF
9
CLOISTER
CHURCH OF OUR LADY

POST
BUS STATION

TRAIN STATION
& BIKE RENTAL

BASILICA
ELECTOR'S PALACE
WC
Palace Garden
11

ARCHAEOLOGICAL MUSEUM
WALL

7

IMPERIAL BATHS
WALK ENDS

AMPHITHEATER

gates, only this northern gate survives. This is the most impressive Roman fortification in Germany, and it was built without mortar—only iron pegs hold the sandstone blocks together. While the other three gates were destroyed by medieval metal and stone scavengers, this "black gate" (originally lighter sand-

stone, but darkened by time) survived because it became a church. St. Simeon—a pious Greek recluse—lived inside the gate for seven years. After his death in 1035, the St. Simeon monastery was established, and the Roman gate was made into a two-story church—lay church on the bottom, monastery church on top. The 12th-century Romanesque apse—the round part at the east end—survives. You can climb around inside the gate, but there's little to see other than a fine town view. Enter through the adjacent City Museum (described below). As you go in, look for pictures of how the gate looked during various eras, including its church phase.

Cost and Hours: €4; daily 9:00-18:00, March and Oct until 17:00, Nov-Feb until 16:00; videoguide-€2 but free download to smartphone, www.trier-info.de.

Nearby: The remaining arcaded courtyard and buildings of the monastery of St. Simeon, next to the Porta Nigra, are now home to the TI and a **City Museum** (Stadtmuseum Simeonstift). The museum's mildly interesting collection seems to be largely made up of anything old that turned up in townspeople's basements. The third level, however, holds a fascinating model—painstakingly constructed over 19 years—of Trier as it looked in 1800. Families will appreciate the entertaining audioguide designed especially for children—there's one for adults, too (€5.50, includes audioguide, Tue-Sun 10:00-17:00, closed Mon; tel. 0651/718-1459, www.museum-trier.de).

The busy road beyond the Porta Nigra follows what was a dry moat outside the Roman wall. In the 19th century, Trier's wealthy built their mansions along this belle époque promenade. Today, it's a people's park lined with fine old buildings, interrupted by newer construction where WWII bombs hit.

• *Trier's main pedestrian drag, which leads from the gate into the town center, is named for St. Simeon. As you walk to Market Square, you'll follow the main north-south axis of the grid-planned Roman town.*

Before heading toward the square, look left to the small pink house (at #8, by the bus stop) where Karl Marx lived from age one until he left for college at 17—nearly his entire childhood. (Not to be confused with his birthplace on Brückenstrasse—a museum for Marx enthusiasts, described later.) Next, detour (or just look) right immediately after the TI to see a large and highly controversial statue of Marx gifted to Trier by China and erected in 2018 to commemorate Marx's 200th birthday (an event that drew local protests).

• *Continue down Simeonstrasse. On your left, at #19, is the...*

House of the Three Magi (Dreikönigenhaus)

Now home to a coffee shop and café, this colorful Venetian-style building was constructed in the 13th century as a keep. Before the age of safe banking, rich men hoarded their gold and silver inside their homes...and everyone knew it. Understandably paranoid, they needed fortified houses like this one. Look for the floating door a story above the present-day entrance. A wooden staircase to this door—once the only way in or out—could be pulled up when necessary.

• *Continue down the pedestrian street. As you walk, ignore street-level storefronts—instead, look up to appreciate the variety and richness of the town's architecture. Eventually you'll reach the...*

▲▲Market Square (Hauptmarkt)

Trier's Hauptmarkt is a people-filled swirl of fruit stands, flowers, painted facades, and fountains (plus stairs down to a handy public

WC). This is one of Germany's most in-love-with-life market squares.

For an orientation to the sights, go to the square's centerpiece, a market cross, and stand on the side of the cross closest to the big gray-stone **cathedral** a block away. This cathedral (which we'll visit in a bit) was the seat of the archbishop. In medieval times, the cathedral was its own walled city, and the archbishop of Trier was one of the seven German electors who chose the Holy Roman Emperor. This gave the archbishop tremendous political, as well as spiritual, power.

The pink-and-white building (now an H&M store) on the corner of the lane leading to the cathedral was a **palace** for the archbishop. Notice the seal above the door: a crown flanked by a crosier (representing the bishop's ecclesiastical power) and a sword (demonstrating his political might). This did not sit well with the townspeople of Trier. The square you're standing in was the symbolic battlefield of a centuries-long conflict between Trier's citizens and its archbishop.

The stone market **cross** (a replica of the AD 958 original, now in the City Museum) was the archbishop's way of bragging about the trading rights granted to him by King Otto the Great. This was a slap in the face to Trier's townspeople. They'd wanted Trier to be designated a "free imperial city," with full trading rights and beholden only to the Holy Roman Emperor, not a local prince or archbishop.

Look across the square. Facing the cathedral is the 15th-century **Town Hall** (Steipe). The people of Trier wanted a Town Hall, but the archbishop wouldn't allow it—so they built this "assembly hall" instead, with a knight on each second-story corner. The knight on the left, facing Market Square, has his mask up, watching over his people. The other knight, facing the cathedral and the archbishop, has his mask down and his hand on his sword, ready for battle.

Just below the knights are four brightly painted 16th-century statues of Christian figures nestled between the arches (right to left): St. Paul, with his sword, was the patron saint of Trier's university in the 15th century. St. Peter, with his bushy beard and key, is the patron saint of Trier. St. Helena, Emperor Constantine's mom and a devout Christian, lived in Trier and brought many super relics here from the Holy Land, giving the town lasting importance. And St. James, with his staff and scallop shell, is the patron saint of pilgrims—a reminder that Trier was the staging point for northern European pilgrims heading south on the spiritual trek to Santiago de Compostela (in northwest Spain).

Elsewhere on the square are more indications of tension between the archbishop and the townsfolk. Look to the left, at the tall white steeple with yellow trim. This is the Gothic tower of the **Church of St. Gangolf,** the medieval townspeople's church and fire-watchman's post. (From medieval times until the present day, a bell has rung nightly at 22:00, reminding drunks to go home. When the automatic bell-ringer broke a few years back, concerned locals flooded the mayor with calls.) In 1507, Trier's mayor built this new Gothic tower to make the people's church higher than the cathedral. A Bible verse in Latin adorns the top in gold letters: "Stay awake and pray." In retaliation, the archbishop raised one tower of his cathedral (all he could afford). He topped it with a threatening message of his own, continuing the Town Hall's verse: "For you never know the hour when the Lord will come."

Look farther to the left, to the Renaissance **St. Peter's Fountain** (1595). This fountain symbolizes thoughtful city government, with allegorical statues of justice (sword and scale), fortitude (broken column), temperance (wine and water), and prudence (a snake and, formerly, a mirror—but since the mirror was stolen long ago, she's now empty-handed). The ladies represent idealized cardinal virtues—but notice the rude monkeys hiding on the column behind them, showing the naughty way things are really done. The recommended **Zum Domstein** restaurant is next to the fountain.

The rest of the square is a textbook of architectural styles. Look for the Art Deco hotel that now houses a McDonald's (forced to keep its presence low-key). The half-timbered houses at the north end of the square (toward the Porta Nigra) mark Trier's 14th-century Jewish ghetto. Judengasse ("Jews' Alley") led under these facades into a gated ghetto where 60 families earned enough from moneylending to buy protection from the archbishop. But the protection only went so far—in 1418, Trier's Jews were expelled. (They tried to collect interest owed them by the prince, but rather than pay up, he sent them packing.) The buildings lining Judengasse today, while quaint, date only from the 18th century.

• *From the square, head down Sternstrasse to the...*

▲▲Cathedral (Dom)

This is the oldest Christian church in Germany. After Emperor Constantine legalized Christianity in the Roman Empire in AD 312, his mother, Helena (now a saint), allowed part of her palace in Trier to be used as the first church on this spot. In AD 326, to celebrate the 20th anniversary of his reign, Constantine began the construction of two great churches: St. Peter's in Rome and this huge cathedral in Trier—also called St. Peter's.

Cost and Hours: Cathedral-free, daily 6:30-18:00, Nov-March until 17:30. Treasury-€1.50, Mon-Sat 10:00-17:00, Sun from 12:30, shorter hours off-season.

Information: The Dom Information Office (on the square facing the church) runs a gift shop, has a pay WC, and provides services for Santiago de Compostela-bound pilgrims (Mon-Sat 9:30-17:00, Sun 12:00-16:00; shorter hours and closed Sun in off-season; tel. 0651/979-0790, www.dominformation.de).

Visiting the Cathedral: Begin your visit in the cathedral's large front courtyard. As you face the cathedral, look in the corner behind you and to your left (in front of the pink palace); you'll see a large patch of light-colored bricks in an L shape in the ground. The original Roman cathedral was more than four times its present size; these light-colored bricks mark one corner of this massive "double cathedral." (The opposite corner was at the back of the smaller Church of Our Lady, waaay across the courtyard.) The plaque by the corner shows the floor plan of the original Roman cathedral (from AD 380).

The cathedral's mighty **facade** is 12th-century Romanesque. To the right is the more delicate 13th-century Gothic facade of the Church of Our Lady, which we'll visit later.

As you walk toward the cathedral entrance, you'll pass an evocative bit of Roman scrap stone (just outside the door on the left). This was part of a 60-ton ancient granite column quarried near Frankfurt—one of four columns used in the fourth-century Roman church.

Enter the cathedral (English info brochure in racks on right). The many **altars** lining the nave are dedicated not to saints, but to bishops. These ornate funeral altars were a fashionable way for the powerful archbishop-electors to memorialize themselves. Even the elaborate black-and-white altar at the back of the church (above where you entered) is not a religious shrine, but a memorial for a single rich archbishop. (His black 1354 tomb dominates the center of that chapel.)

The "pilgrim's walk" (the stairway to the right of the altar) leads to the chapel at the far east end of the church that holds the cathedral's most important relic: the supposed **Holy Robe of Christ,** thought to have been found by St. Helena on a pilgrimage to Jerusalem (rarely on view, but you can see its reliquary; look for photos of the robe itself as you approach, after the first flight of stairs).

Midway along the "pilgrim's walk," you'll find the entrance to the **treasury** (Schatzkammer), displaying huge bishops' rings, medieval Bibles, St. Andrew's sandal (in a box topped with a golden foot), and a holy nail supposedly from the Crucifixion. At the base of the steps below the treasury, pause and look back up at the statues of St. Helena and Emperor Constantine.

Back down the stairs, the door on your immediate left marked *Kreuzgang* leads to the peaceful 12th-century Domkreuzgang **cloister** between the Dom and the Church of Our Lady.

When you're ready to leave the cathedral, head back toward the main door, where you'll see two controversially modern (1972) paintings at the back of the church, representing the Alpha (Paradise/Creation, to the left) and the Omega (the Last Judgment, to the right). The archbishop pushed this artwork through, arguing that a living church needs contemporary art, and overriding objections from the congregation's conservative old guard.

Once outside the cathedral, go left to find the entrance to the adjoining **Church of Our Lady** (Liebfrauenkirche), which dates from 1235 and claims to be the oldest Gothic church in Germany. This church was built when Gothic was in vogue, so French architects were brought in—and paid with money borrowed from the bishop of Cologne when funds ran dry. Pop in to see the interior, filled with colorful, modern stained glass.

Exit the Church of Our Lady and go right, passing the cathedral entrance, and then turn down the first street on your right (Windstrasse). As you walk with the cathedral on your right, you'll be able to see the different **eras of its construction.** The big red cube that makes up the back half of the present-day cathedral is all that remains of the enormous, original fourth-century Roman construction (at one time twice as tall as what you see here). Arched bricks in the facade show the original position of Roman windows and doors. Around this Roman nucleus, chunks were grafted on over a millennium and a half of architectural styles: the front half of the cathedral facing the big courtyard, added in the 11th century; the choir on the back, from the 12th century; and the transept and round Baroque shrine on the far back, from the 18th century.

If you look at the original Roman construction squarely, you'll see that it's not perfectly vertical. Locks were built along the Mosel River in the 1960s, depleting groundwater—which was the only thing preserving the church's original wooden foundation. When dry, the foundation disintegrated, and the walls began to settle. Architects competed to find a way to prevent the cathedral from collapsing. The winning solution: a huge steel bracket above the main nave, holding the walls up with cables.

• *Just past the cathedral on Windstrasse (to the left) is the...*

▲Bishop's Museum (Museum am Dom)

This museum focuses on the history of the cathedral. Its highlight is the pieced-together remains of exquisite ceiling frescoes from St. Helena's palace. The vivid reds, greens, and blues of the restored works depict frolicking cupids, bejeweled women, and a philosopher clutching his scroll. The 15 panels are displayed in such a way that you feel mysteriously transported back to when they were made, in AD 320. The frescoes were discovered in 50,000 pieces while cleaning up from WWII bombs. Incredibly, with the help of computers (and using patterns from the wattle-and-daub work on the back sides of the pieces), the jigsaw puzzle was put back together. There are no English descriptions, but you can—and should—borrow the book in English that explains the frescoes and their restoration (or you can buy a copy). Elsewhere in this small, modern museum, you'll see an interesting model of the original Roman church, stone capitals, gold chalices, vestments, and icons.

Cost and Hours: €3.50; Tue-Sat 9:00-17:00, Sun from 13:00, closed Mon; audioguide-€1, Bischof-Stein-Platz 1, tel. 0651/710-5255, www.bistum-trier.de/museum.

• *Return to the front of the cathedral and head two blocks south (passing the Church of Our Lady, under an arch capped by a Crucifixion scene—*

indicating that you're leaving the archbishop's walled ecclesiastical city).
Bear left on An der Meerkatz, to the 200-foot-by-100-foot...

▲▲Basilica/Imperial Throne Room (Konstantin Basilika)

This building is the largest intact Roman structure outside Rome. It's best known as a basilica, but it actually started out as a throne room. The last emperor moved out in AD 395, and petty kings set up camp in the building throughout the Middle Ages. By the 12th century, the archbishops had taken it over, using the nave as a courtyard and converting the apse into a five-story palace. The building became a Lutheran church in 1856, and it remains the leading Protestant church in Trier. It was badly damaged by WWII bombs, (as illustrated by photographs at the cashier's desk), and later restored.

Cost and Hours: Free; Mon-Sat 10:00-18:00, Sun from 13:00; Nov-March Tue-Sat 10:00-12:00 & 14:00-16:00, Sun 13:00-15:00, closed Mon; €4 *Basilica of Trier* booklet brings the near-empty shell to life; tel. 0651/9949-1200, www.evangelisch-trier.de.

Visiting the Basilica: Standing inside the vast structure, you see the genius of Roman engineering. Notice the 65-foot-wide round arch over the apse. The small rectangular holes between the windows were chimneys, which vented the hot air that circulated below the floor, heating the place. It's a huge expanse to span without columns. Each of the squares in the ceiling above you measures 10 feet by 10 feet—as big as your hotel room. While today's roof cheats, using concrete girders, the Roman original was all wood, relying on triangular trusses above the flat ceiling. Today's windows match the Roman originals—small frosted panes held in place by a wooden frame. The place is enormous—so big that the Porta Nigra could fit comfortably inside.

Picture this throne room in ancient times, decorated with golden mosaics, rich marble, colorful stucco, and busts of Constantine and his family filling the seven niches. The emperor sat in majesty under a canopy on his altar-like throne. The windows in the apse around him were smaller than the ones along the side walls, making his throne seem even bigger.

When you turn around, face the wall where you entered and check out the huge new organ with 6,006 pipes. It's located in the same spot as the basilica's original organ, which was destroyed in World War II. Building the new €3.4 million organ was the final step in the decades-long reconstruction of the basilica, finished in 2014. (See website for listings of organ recitals.)

Nearby: A pink Rococo wing, the Elector's Palace, was added to the basilica in the 18th century to house the archbishop-elector; today, it holds local government offices (closed to the public).

• *The Rococo wing faces a fragrant, picnic-rific garden. Beyond the garden are three more sights: the Archaeological Museum (with a handy lunch spot, the recommended Zeitsprung Café), the remains of a Roman bath, and a 16,000-seat Roman amphitheater. Cut across the garden, heading toward Weimarer Allee (the main street in the distance), and veer right to pass through the medieval city wall to the entrance of the...*

TRIER

▲▲Archaeological Museum (Rheinisches Landesmuseum)

Trier's top museum has arguably the best collection of Roman art in Germany. The museum tells the town's story from prehistoric times to today. The best pieces are all from the Roman period, including funeral art, mosaics, coins, and a fine model of Roman Trier.

Cost and Hours: €8, Tue-Sun 10:00-17:00, closed Mon, tel. 0651/97740, www.landesmuseum-trier.de. Get a map as you enter and a free English audioguide.

Visiting the Museum: *Rundgang* signs guide you through the museum's 19 exhibition rooms in a logical order. I'll focus just on the museum's most important collections. Brief English overviews are posted in each room.

Start by walking down the round staircase to the basement level. Head through three rooms of displays on prehistoric Trier, then back up and through two rooms on the Romanization of the area's Celtic population.

Find the rich collection of **funerary art** (in Room 6, a big room at the back of the courtyard). Originally these were all painted in vibrant colors. For pagan Roman big shots, the closest thing to eternal life was to be remembered after they died. Consequently, those who could afford it erected big memorials to their own lives and accomplishments along the road leading into Trier. When Roman Trier went Christian in AD 320, these pagan ideals were no longer respected. The memorials were scavenged for their stones, which were then used as a foundation for a nearby fortress and forgotten. In 1890, a resident of the modern village sitting on the ruins of that Roman fortress dug up one of these stones, the museum paid a handsome price for it, and everyone in the village went wild digging up old Roman stones to cash in.

Browse around, finding glimpses of everyday Roman life: the tax collector at work, the boys with their Latin teacher, a woman visiting a beauty salon, and a ship laden with barrels of Mosel wine. Behind the wine ship, a wall painting shows how the mausoleum-lined road into Roman Trier might have looked. Archaeologists have learned a lot about life in this corner of the Roman Empire by studying these artifacts.

Another highlight are the **Roman mosaics** (in Room 8, just beyond the wine ship). On the right wall is a mosaic of four horses surrounding the superstar charioteer Polydus, discovered intact at the Imperial Baths. Mosaic floors were the *Sports Illustrated* covers of the Roman world.

Leave the room on your left, cross the next two rooms, and find the stairs on the far right. Room 11 displays a **map** showing Trier's position in the Roman Empire. You can see how Gaul (Gallia, roughly modern France) was divided into three parts, with Trier (Treveri) in the northern ("Belgian") section. Roads led from Trier south toward Rome via modern-day Lyon (Lugdunum) and Marseille (Massilia).

Upstairs, in Room 12, don't miss the huge **model** of Roman Trier—a thriving city of 80,000. Notice the grid street plan, and pick out the sights you're visiting today: Porta Nigra, the cathedral, basilica, baths, and amphitheater.

Back down a flight, in the small, darkened Room 13, is an exhibit of **coins** through the centuries of Roman rule. In 1993, some Trier construction workers dug up a bag holding 2,600 golden Roman coins; the coins are in the central display case. Experts used the emperor's face on each coin to date the finds. Look closely and you can follow the steady progression of emperors and their coins from Nero (AD 54) to Septimius Severus (AD 211). It's impressive that over 150 years of coinage were in circulation when this bag was lost.

Finally, Rooms 15-16 show how medieval Trier was built on the ruins of the Roman town. A model (in Room 15) lets you see how the Porta Nigra looked as a church.

• *Exit the Archaeological Museum, walk right (paralleling the main Weimarer Allee through the trees), then follow the* Tourist Route *signs through the archway in the wall to the modern, red-brick entry arcade of the...*

Imperial Baths (Kaiserthermen)

Built by Constantine, these were destined to be the biggest of Trier's three Roman baths and the most intricate baths of the Roman world. Trier's cold northern climate, the size of the complex, and the enormity of Constantine's ego meant that these Imperial Baths required a two-story subterranean complex of pipes, furnaces, and slave galleys to keep the water at a perfect 47 degrees Celsius (120 degrees Fahrenheit). But the grandiose vision was never finished. When Constantine left Trier in AD 316, the huge and already costly project was scuttled. Later the site was used as a military

barracks. The giant court-yard—originally for exer-cising and lounging—be-came a parade ground for the Praetorian Guard.

Stepping into the un-finished building section, you can imagine the in-tended pools (cold, tepid, and hot) and the heated floor. Thirty years of construction left nearly a mile of underground tunnels and foundation work, which are fun to explore. Imagine the engineering, slave labor, and wood that would have been neces-sary to make all this work, if it had ever been completed. A literal river of water was planned to flow into the baths via an aqueduct. And the surrounding land would ultimately have been deforested as it supplied enough wood to keep the ovens going to heat the water.

Cost and Hours: €4; daily 9:00-18:00, March and Oct until 17:00, Nov-Feb until 16:00; videoguide-€2, good €2.50 English booklet, tel. 0651/436-2550, www.trier-info.de.

• *To finish your tour of Trier's Roman sights, hike from the baths about 10 minutes farther to the amphitheater. Or you can skip it (just look at amphitheater photos in shop postcard racks), head back to Market Square, and enjoy the town.*

To reach the amphitheater, backtrack through the arch in the wall, follow the signs through the pedestrian underpass, then follow Her-messtrasse as it curves up the hill, and turn left on Olewiger Strasse.

Amphitheater

Roman Trier's amphitheater, built around AD 200, seated at least 16,000. The city was largely inhabited by Celts who learned Latin and wanted to adopt the Roman lifestyle. And any self-respecting Roman town needed an amphitheater. While Trier's amphitheater had some gore, it didn't usually feature Roman degenerates egging on gladiators—it was more often used for less bloody spectacles, assemblies, and religious festivals.

Cost and Hours: €4; daily 9:00-18:00, March and Oct until 17:00, Nov-Feb until 16:00; tel. 0651/73010, www.trier-info.de. It's OK to picnic discreetly in the amphitheater grounds (free WC inside entrance).

Visiting the Amphitheater: You'll enter where grand proces-sions did. Pick up the free map when you buy your ticket, and go left up the stairs to a handy illustrated diagram of ancient Trier that helps put the amphitheater into context with the city. After enjoying this high vantage point, continue along the left side of

TRIER

the amphitheater for 20 yards, then turn left on the downhill path. Enter the amphitheater through one of its grand entries (called *vomitoria*, these were named for the way crowds could spew out quickly after events). Then descend a staircase in the center of the amphitheater into the cellar, where gear for the spectacles was kept (it's below the water table, so it's always wet). After Rome fell, the amphitheater was used as a refuge from barbarian attacks, a quarry, and a vineyard.

SIGHTS NEAR VIEHMARKTPLATZ
▲Karl Marx's House

Communists can lick their wounds at Karl Marx's birthplace, an 18th-century house with three floors of exhibits spanning the influential economist/philosopher's life and the impact his ideas still have today. The museum was completely overhauled to celebrate Marx's 200th birthday in 2018, and is now a vibrant and thoughtful exploration of Marx and his historical legacy.

Cost and Hours: €4, includes audioguide and brochure, daily 10:00-18:00, from Market Square follow signs for 10 minutes to Brückenstrasse 10, tel. 0651/970-680, www.fes.de/Karl-Marx-Haus.

Visiting the Museum: You'll see a mix of historical artifacts, colorful illustrations, contemporary art, and interactive displays, with good English explanations. Start with the video just past the ticket office, which traces the building's history as it changed hands from Marx's family to the Social Democratic Party (SPD) to the Nazi party and back to the SPD, eventually becoming a museum.

The museum details Marx's life chronologically, but focuses largely on the lingering effects of his ideas long after his death, from revolutions against communism to skepticism of capitalism, demonstrating how societies around the world have interpreted his beliefs differently to fit their own agenda. On the third floor, a color-coded world map shows the range of socialist and communist governments in the 1980s and the "spheres of influence" attributed to Marxist beliefs.

The house spans two sections divided by a courtyard. Inside

the courtyard you'll find a large Marx head sculpted by his grandson. Also explore the garden in back, with some interesting Marx-related art.

Viehmarkt Baths Museum

A beautiful modern glass building covers the ruins of a Roman bath, mixed with stone monastery foundations and medieval waste-wells. It's certainly historic, but almost meaningless unless you have a good guide and a freakish interest in Roman stones. You can see nearly everything without paying just by looking in from the entry and through the many windows. The best thing about going here is walking down Fahrstrasse to the museum—a block away, you'll pass a cool fountain showing Trier craftsmen at work.

Cost and Hours: €4, Tue-Sun 9:00-17:00, closed Mon, Viehmarktplatz, tel. 0651/994-1057, www.trier-info.de.

Sleeping in Trier

NEAR THE PORTA NIGRA

$$ Hotel zum Christophel, with a kind owner, offers top comfort in 11 mostly large and classy rooms next to the Porta Nigra. Billing itself as a "coffee hotel," they're serious about their beans and invite you to hang out in their attached café. It's an easy roll from the train station with your luggage (breakfast extra, elevator, pay parking, Simeonstrasse 1, tel. 0651/979-4200, www.mondos-kaffeehotel.de, info@mondos-kaffeehotel.de).

$$ Hotel Römischer Kaiser, next door, is also nice, but a lesser value—charging more for a polished lobby and 43 comparable rooms (breakfast extra, family rooms, elevator, free parking, Am Porta-Nigra-Platz 6, tel. 0651/977-0100, www.friedrich-hotels.de, rezeption@friedrich-hotels.de).

$ Astoria Hotel, two blocks west of Porta Nigra, is a 15-room family-run place in a quiet area just beyond the tourist crowds. Rooms are colorfully decorated, and a rose-filled terrace beckons outside the light and cheery breakfast room (no elevator, pay parking, Bruchhausenstrasse 4, tel. 0651/978-350, www.astoria-hotel.de, info@astoria-hotel.de). American-born Paula and her husband Sudhir like to offer guests a choice of welcome drinks on arrival.

NEAR MARKET SQUARE

¢-$ Kolpinghaus Warsberger Hof, run by a Catholic foundation and its friendly staff, is a clean, simple hostel and budget hotel two blocks from Market Square. It has 168 beds and private rooms. This is your best value for cheap sleeps in town (breakfast extra, bike rental, showers down the hall, no elevator, laundry service, limited courtyard pay parking—reserve ahead, Dietrichstrasse 42, tel. 0651/975-250, www.kolpinghaus-warsberger-hof.de, info@ kolpinghaus-warsberger-hof.de).

NEAR THE TRAIN STATION

$$ **Hotel Vinum,** with 31 rooms directly across from the train station, is owned and run by the Lutheran Church and has a wine theme (all guests get a small free bottle). It's conveniently located if you're not bothered by the square's train-station ambience (family rooms, elevator, pay parking, Bahnhofsplatz 7, tel. 0651/994-740, www.hotelvinum.de, info@hotelvinum.de).

$$ **Hotel Pieper,** a good value, is run by the friendly Becker family. They rent 20 comfortable rooms, some with air-conditioning (buffet breakfast, no elevator, free parking; 8-minute walk from station, 2 blocks off main drag at Thebäerstrasse 39; tel. 0651/23008, www.hotel-pieper.com, info@hotel-pieper-trier. de). From the station, follow Theodor-Heuss-Allee (toward Porta Nigra) to the second big intersection, angle right onto Göbenstrasse, and continue as the road curves and becomes Thebäerstrasse.

OUTSIDE THE CENTER

$$ **Hotel Petrisberg Trier,** up a steep road behind the amphitheater, is charming, reasonably priced, and ideal if you have a car. It's on a hillside overlooking the city, exuding old-school elegance without being stuffy. The Pantenburg family takes great care to spoil all their guests: Helpful Helmut and brother Wolfgang preside, whipping up tasty egg breakfasts, and niece Christina—the 1999 Trier Wine Queen—sometimes works reception. A pleasant footpath brings you downhill to the cathedral in 20 minutes (35 rooms, elevator, free parking, Sickingenstrasse 11, tel. 0651/4640, www.hotel-petrisberg.de, info@hotel-petrisberg.de).

Eating in Trier

$$ **Zum Domstein,** right on Market Square, serves standard German fare at decent prices and also has a special, pricier menu of dishes based on ancient Roman recipes. The Roman menu was inspired during renovations, when the owner discovered a Roman column in her cellar. (In Trier, you can't put a rec room in your basement without tripping over Roman ruins.) The finished cellar dining room incorporates the column, plus a mini museum of Roman crockery (Roman dishes usually served in cellar 18:00-21:00, open daily 8:30-24:00, last orders at 21:30, Am Hauptmarkt 5, tel. 0651/74490).

$$ **Weinstube Kesselstatt,** a wine tavern in the historic Palais Kesselstatt, features a pleasant garden and friendly staff. For 25 years, Dieter Hilgers has been offering up a variety of regional and

seasonal dishes and local wines (order at the counter, daily 10:00-24:00, located just across from the Church of Our Lady at Liebfrauenstrasse 10, tel. 0651/41178).

At **$$ Theo,** right at Porta Nigra, locals and tourists enjoy popular local dishes and daily specials. The outdoor patio, with a huge sunshade sail, has a pleasant view overlooking the square (daily 11:00-22:00, Simeonstrasse 59, tel. 0651/44888).

$ Zeitsprung Café, run by enthusiastic and friendly Anja, is at the rear of the Archaeological Museum building and is very popular with locals. The place offers good-value lunches and salads in a pretty setting overlooking the Elector's Palace and fountain (Tue-Sun 9:00-18:00, closed Mon, outdoor seating available, Weimarer Allee 1, tel. 0651/994-5820).

Picnics: One of several supermarkets in the center is in the basement of the **Karstadt** department store on Simeonstrasse (Mon-Sat 9:30-20:00, closed Sun).

Trier Connections

From Trier by Train to: Cochem (2/hour, 1 hour), **Cologne** (at least hourly, 3 hours, some change in Koblenz), **St. Goar/Bacharach** (hourly, 3 hours, change in Koblenz), **Frankfurt Airport** (hourly, 3 hours, change in Koblenz and sometimes Mainz), **Paris** (hourly, 3.5 hours, best with change in Saarbrücken or Luxembourg, reservation required for France section). Train info: www. bahn.com.

COLOGNE & THE UNROMANTIC RHINE

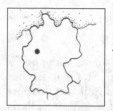

Romance isn't everything. Cologne (Köln—pronounced "kurln"—in German) is an urban Jacuzzi that keeps the Rhine churning. It's home to Germany's greatest Gothic cathedral, one of the country's best collections of Roman artifacts, a world-class art museum, and a healthy dose of German urban playfulness.

Peaceful Bonn, which offers good people-watching and fun pedestrian streets, used to be the capital of West Germany. The small town of Remagen had a bridge that helped defeat Hitler in World War II, and unassuming Aachen, near the Belgian border, was once the capital of Europe.

Cologne

Germany's fourth-largest city, Cologne has a compact, lively center. The Rhine was the northern boundary of the Roman Empire, and, 1,700 years ago, Constantine—the first Christian emperor—made what was then called "Colonia" the seat of a bishopric. (Five hundred years later, under Charlemagne, Cologne became the seat of an archbishopric.) With 40,000 people within its walls, Cologne was the largest German city and an important

cultural and religious center throughout the Middle Ages. Today, the city is most famous for its toilet water: Eau de Cologne was first made here by an Italian chemist in 1709.

During World War II, bombs destroyed 95 percent of Cologne—driving its population from 800,000 down to an estimated 30,000 at its lowest ebb. But with the end of the war, the city immediately began putting itself back together (the population rebounded to about 400,000 by Christmas 1945). Today, it's a bustling commercial and cultural center that still respects its rich past.

PLANNING YOUR TIME

Cologne makes an ideal on-the-way stop; it's a major rail junction, and its top sights are clustered near the train station. With a couple of hours, you can toss your bag in a locker, take my self-guided town walk, zip through the cathedral, and make it back to the station for your train. If you're planning that short of a stop, make sure you'll be here when the whole church is open (in between its services—see the sight listing for times). More time (or an overnight) allows you to delve into a few of the city's fine museums and take in an old-time beer pub.

Orientation to Cologne

Cologne's core was bombed out, then rebuilt in mostly modern style with a sprinkling of quaint. The city has two areas that matter to visitors: One is the section right around the train station and cathedral. Here you'll find most sights and most of my recommended hotels, plus the TI and plenty of eateries and services. Hohe Strasse, Cologne's pedestrian shopping street, begins near the cathedral. The other area—called the "old town"—is between the river and the Alter Markt, a few blocks to the south. After the war, this section was rebuilt in the old style, and today pubs and music clubs pack the restored buildings.

TOURIST INFORMATION

Cologne's energetic TI is opposite the cathedral entrance (Mon-Sat 9:00-20:00, Sun 10:00-17:00, Kardinal-Höffner-Platz 1, tel 0221/346-430, www.koelntourismus.de). For information on Cologne's museums, visit www.museenkoeln.de.

City Bus Tours: The TI sells tickets and is the departure point for city bus tours offered by two competing companies (1.5-hour tour-€15; hop-on, hop-off tour-€18; departures at least hourly in summer, most have recorded commentary in both German and English, but Kölner CityTour has live guides every 2 hours—see www.cityfahrten.de).

ARRIVAL IN COLOGNE

Cologne couldn't be easier to visit—its three important sights cluster within two blocks of the TI and train station. This super pedestrian zone is a constant carnival of people.

By Train: Cologne's busy train station has everything you need: drugstore, bookstore, food court, juice bar, grocery store, pricey 24-hour "McClean" pay WC with showers, travel center (*Reisezentrum,* long hours daily), and high-tech lockers (next to *Reisezentrum;* insert coins or bills and wait for door to open; your luggage—up to four pieces—is transferred to storage via an underground conveyor belt and retrieved when you reinsert your ticket). Exiting the front of the station (the end near track 1), you'll find yourself smack-dab in the shadow of the cathedral. Up the steps and to the right is the cathedral's main entrance (TI across street).

By Car: Drivers should follow signs to *Zentrum,* then continue to the huge Parkhaus am Dom garage under the cathedral (€2.40/hour, €24/day). The lot outside the garage has a cheaper day rate (€4/hour, €15/day). There's also the Parkhaus am Heumarkt, centrally located at the south end of the old town area (€2.50/hour, €20/day).

By Boat: If you're arriving on a K-D Line boat, exit the boat to the right, then walk along the waterside park until just before the train bridge, when the cathedral comes into view on the left.

HELPFUL HINTS

Closed Day: Note that most museums are closed on Monday (though the cathedral remains open). The cathedral is off-limits to sightseers during services.

Sightseeing Cards: The **MuseumsCard** is valid for two consecutive days (or a Sun and Tue, as museums close Mon). It covers all local public transit on the first day and includes the Roman-Germanic Museum, Museum Ludwig, and Wallraf-Richartz Museum, plus several lesser museums (but not the cathedral sights). If you're visiting all three museums, this card will save you money (€18/person, €30 family pass includes 2 adults and 2 kids up to age 18, sold at participating museums, www.museenkoeln.de). Skip the **KölnCard;** its small discounts aren't worth it.

Festivals: Though **Carnival** is celebrated all over Germany, Cologne's celebration is famously exuberant. Join the locals as they dress up, feast, and exchange *Bützje*—innocent pursed-lip kisses. Festivities start on the Thursday before Ash Wednesday and culminate with a huge parade on the following Monday ("Rose Monday," or *Rosenmontag*). The parade draws musicians from all over Germany, and families line the parade route to grab pieces of candy tossed off the floats (www.

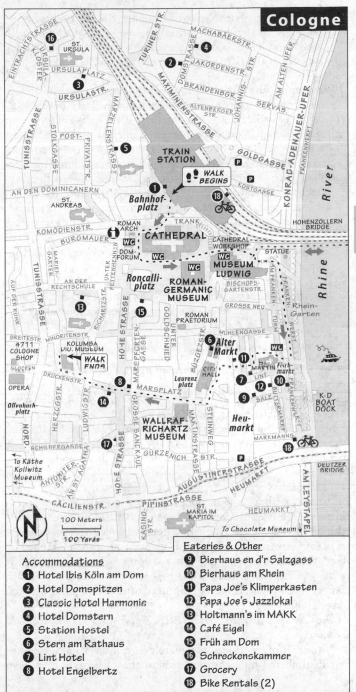

Cologne

Map labels:

EINTRACHTSTRASSE · URSULA KLOSTER · ST. URSULA · URSULAPLATZ · URSULASTR. · TURINER STR. · MACHABAERSTR. · DOMSTRASSE · JAKORDENSTR. · BRANDENBGR. STR. · AM ALTEN UFER · KONRAD-ADENAUER-UFER · JOHANNIS · SERVAS · TUNISSTRASSE · STOLKGASSE · POST · PRIVAT-R. · MAXIMINENSTRASSE · MARZELLENSTRASSE · ALTENBERGER STR. · TRAIN STATION · GOLDGASSE · FRANKENWERFT · River · WALK BEGINS · AN DEN DOMINICANERN · ST. ANDREAS · Bahnhof-platz · KOSTGASSE · Rhine · HOHENZOLLERN BRIDGE · KOMÖDIENSTR. · BURGMAUER · ROMAN ARCH · TRANKG. · CATHEDRAL · DOM-FORUM · CATHEDRAL WORKSHOP · STATUE · MARIEN-GARTEN · WC · WC · WC · MUSEUM LUDWIG · Roncalli-platz · ROMAN-GERMANIC MUSEUM · BISCHOFS-GARTENSTR. · Rhein-Garten · AUF DER RUHR · AN DER RECHTSSCHULE · RICHARTZSTR. · UNTER FETTENHENNEN · GOLDSCHMIED · ROMAN PRAETORIUM · GROSSE NEU. · FRANKEN TURM · FRANKEN WERFT · BREITESTR. · MINORITENSTR. · KOLUMBA DIÖ. MUSEUM · HOHE STRASSE · MARSPFORTEN-GASSE · BÜRGERSTR. · MÜHLENGASSE · WL · 4711 COLOGNE SHOP · WALK ENDS · Alter Markt · Fischmarkt · GLOCKEN · DRUCKSTR. · HERZOGSTR. · Laurenz-platz · CITY HALL · MARTIN LINT. · BUTTERMARKT · SALZG. · K-D BOAT DOCK · OPERA · MARSPLATZ · GROSSE SANK KAUL · Heu-markt · Offenbach-platz · LUDWIGSTR. · WALLRAF-RICHARTZ MUSEUM · MARTINSTRASSE · STEINWEG · MARKMANNS · DEUTZER BRIDGE · SCHILDERGASSE · GÜRZENICH · STR. · To Käthe Kollwitz Museum · NORD · ANTONITER-STR. · ST. AGATHA · HOHE STRASSE · AUGUSTINERSTRASSE · HEUMARKT · AM LEYSTAPEL · CÄCILIENSTR. · PIPINSTRASSE · KASINO STR. · ST. MARIA IM KAPITOL · HEUMARKT · To Chocolate Museum · 100 Meters · 100 Yards

Accommodations

1. Hotel Ibis Köln am Dom
2. Hotel Domspitzen
3. Classic Hotel Harmonie
4. Hotel Domstern
5. Station Hostel
6. Stern am Rathaus
7. Lint Hotel
8. Hotel Engelbertz

Eateries & Other

9. Bierhaus en d'r Salzgass
10. Bierhaus am Rhein
11. Papa Joe's Klimperkasten
12. Papa Joe's Jazzlokal
13. Holtmann's im MAKK
14. Café Eigel
15. Früh am Dom
16. Schreckenskammer
17. Grocery
18. Bike Rentals (2)

koelnerkarneval.de). Cologne's annual **Kölner Lichter** festival lights up the sky on a mid-July weekend, with fireworks, music, and lots of boats on the river (www.koelner-lichter.de). It's part of the Rhein in Flammen regional festival (see page 478).

Bike Rentals and Tours: Convenient bike rental is available at two branches of the friendly **Radstation** (€6/3 hours, €12/day; tel. 0221/139-7190, mobile 0171-629-8796, www.radstationkoeln.de). One branch is tucked under the train-track arcade (long hours daily, ID and €50 deposit required; from the station, exit out the back by track 11 to Breslauer Platz, turn right, cross the street, and look toward the train tracks). The other is along the river a 10-minute walk from the station, on Markmannsgasse (daily April-Oct 10:00-18:00, leave photo ID as security deposit, 100 yards upstream from the K-D Line dock). Consider biking the path along the Rhine River up past the convention center *(Messe)* to the Rheinpark for a picnic.

Radstation also offers German/English guided city tours by bike (€22.50, 3 hours, April-Oct daily at 13:30, includes bike rental, about 10 people per guide, reservations smart).

Cologne Walk

Cologne lends itself to a fine orientation walk, worth ▲▲. The old town, towering cathedral, and most of the sights cluster near the train station. Starting at the train station, this self-guided walk takes less than an hour and provides a good introduction. The main sights on this walk—the cathedral, Roman-Germanic Museum, Museum Ludwig, Wallraf-Richartz Museum, and Kolumba Diocesan Museum—are described in more detail later, under "Sights in Cologne."

Bahnhofsvorplatz: Stepping out of the train station, you're confronted with a modern hodgepodge of post-WWII architecture and the towering icon of Cologne, its cathedral. The city feels rebuilt—because it was. The Allies bombed Cologne hard in retaliation for Germany's bombing of London. Your gaze is grabbed by the cathedral. While it was built according to the original 13th-century plans, and the left (east) part was completed in the 13th century, the right half wasn't built until after German unification, in the 1880s.

• *Climb the steps and circle right, to the people-filled square facing the cathedral.*

Roncalliplatz (Roncalli Square): In centuries past, a clutter of half-timbered huts crowded around the cathedral. They were cleared out in the late 1800s so the great building would have a suitable approach; in the late 1960s the plaza was pedestrianized.

This has been a busy commercial zone since ancient times. The Roman arch was discovered nearby and set up here as a reminder of the town's Roman roots. This north gate of the Roman city, from AD 50, marks the start of Cologne's nearly 2,000-year-old main shopping street, Hohe Strasse.

Look for the life-size replica tip of a spire. The real thing is 515 feet above you. The cathedral facade, while finished in the 1880s, is exactly what was envisioned by the original church planners in 1280.

• *Continue around the right side of the church, passing modern buildings and public spaces. Step up to the window of the* **Roman-Germanic Museum** *to see a...*

Roman Mosaic: Through the Roman-Germanic Museum's generous window, you can get a free look at the museum's prize piece—a fine mosaic floor. Once the dining-room floor of a rich Roman merchant, this is actually in its original position (the museum was built around it). It shows scenes from the life of Dionysus...wine, women, and song, Roman-style. The mosaic is quite sexy, with several scenes showing a satyr seducing and ultimately disrobing a half-goddess, half-human maenad. First he offers her grapes, then he turns on the music. After further wining and dining—all with an agenda—the horny satyr finally scores. The cupid on a lion's back symbolizes the triumph of physical love.

The mosaic is at the original Roman street level. The tall monument above and left of the mosaic is the mausoleum of a first-century Roman army officer. Directly across from you (at eye level, beyond the mosaic) are beautifully carved stone reliefs—an indication of what a fine city Roman Cologne must have been.

• *Walk 20 steps beyond the mosaic farther along the cathedral and look down to see the...*

Cathedral Workshop: Any church of this size is a work in progress, requiring constant renovation, repair, and care. Sandstone blocks are stacked and waiting to be shaped and plugged in wherever needed. The buttresses above are the church's showiest, because they face the bishop's palace, city center, and original entrance (south transept). For 500 years, the church was left unfinished, simply capped off midway. You're facing the functional part of the church, where services were held from the 1300s until the late 1800s.

• *From the cathedral, walk past the* **Museum Ludwig** *and continue left onto the...*

Hohenzollern Bridge (Hohenzollernbrücke): This is the busiest railway bridge in the world (30 trains an hour all day long). A classic Industrial Age design from around 1900, the bridge was destroyed in World War II and later rebuilt in its original style. These days, the bridge is a landmark for its "love locks"—couples come here, mark a little padlock with their names and the date, chain it to the bridge railing, and throw away the key as proof of their everlasting love.

• *Walk back in the direction of Museum Ludwig, then head down the stairs toward the river.*

Riverfront: The statue (to your left) honors Kaiser Wilhelm II, who paid for the Hohenzollernbrücke (named after his family). Stairs lead down to a people-friendly riverside park. This is urban planning from the 1970s: Real and forward-looking. The riverside, once a noisy highway, is now a peaceful park. All that traffic still courses through the city, but flows unnoticed below you in a tunnel. A bike-and-pedestrian path follows the riverside in each direction, and families let their children frolic in the fountain.

Turn right, and walk away from the bridge for a few blocks along the Frankenwerft, Cologne's riverside restaurant district, until you are even with the tower of the Romanesque church. (Cologne's famous chocolate museum is a five-minute walk farther downstream.)

Notice a strip of sockets for a metal flood wall (on the inland side of the grassy stretch; an eight-foot-high structure can be erected here when needed). Locals see a definite climate change: They say that "floods of the century" now happen every decade, thunderstorms are 10 times more prevalent, and for the first time, this part of Europe has witnessed small tornadoes.

• *At the foot of the church is the Fischmarkt, a tiny square.*

Fischmarkt and "Old Town": Right below Great St. Martin Church, this little square—once the fish market—faces the river. It's ringed by medieval-looking buildings from the 1930s. In the early 20th century, Cologne's entire old town was a scruffy, half-timbered slum where prostitutes and their clients mingled. To the disgusted Nazis, prostitutes were human dirt. Their vision for old towns all over Germany: Clear out the clutter,  boot the riffraff, and rebuild in the clean, tidy, stone-and-stucco style you see here. After World War II, Cologne decided to rebuild in a faux-medieval style to approximate what had once been. This square and the streets around the church are from that period.

• *Walk inland, circling around the right (downstream) side of the church. From the church's front door, a passageway leads away from the river directly to Alter Markt (Old Market Square).*

Alter Markt and City Hall: The ornate City Hall tower symbolized civic spirit standing strong against the power of the bishops in the 15th century. Circle around the tower to see the City Hall's fine Renaissance porch—the only historic facade left standing after the 1945 bombings. Its carvings stress civic independence. The busts of emperors bring to mind Cologne's strong Roman past; the lions symbolize the evil aspect of church authority. If it's viewable, look above the door to see the mayor killing the lion (thus establishing independence from church government for his city). This scene is flanked by biblical parallels: the angel saving Daniel from the lions (on right), and Samson fighting lions (on left).

In front of City Hall, an archaeological site has uncovered both Roman ruins and the remains of Cologne's old Jewish quarter.

• *Head back down the steps and turn right to walk around the modern side of the building, looking out for flying rice—the City Hall is often busy with civil wedding parties. Turn right again, passing the* **Wall-raf-Kollwitz Museum.** *Continue up Marsplatz until you reach Hohe Strasse.*

Shopping, Church Art, and Eau de Cologne: Look left and right to see the hustle and bustle of the town's main pedestrian shopping street. **Hohe Strasse** thrived during the Middle Ages, when Cologne was a major player in the heavyweight Hanseatic League of northern European merchant towns. The street was rebuilt after its complete destruction in World War II and was Germany's first pedestrian shopping mall. Today it's a rather soulless string of chain stores—most interesting for its seas of shoppers (the big MediaMarkt electronics store, Germany's version of Best Buy, is a couple of blocks down to the right).

Continue straight ahead on Brückenstrasse to the modern white building, set atop the ruins of a bombed-out Gothic church. This is the **Kolumba Diocesan Museum.** Inside, from the corner, you can grab a free peek at what was the church interior.

Across busy Tunisstrasse stands Cologne's circa-1960s **Opera House** (a big deal in Germany when built). And across the street from that, on the right, is a historic building at **Glockengasse 4.** When Cologne's houses were renumbered in a single series during the Napoleonic era in 1796, this building was given the number 4711—which the perfume-making firm based here later adopted as its trademark. A shop on the ground floor has Cologne water running in a fountain by the door—sample this year's new fragrances for free at the counter. A small, free exhibit is upstairs (Mon-Sat 9:30-18:00, closed Sun, tel. 0221/2709-9910, www.glockengasse. de).

Sights in Cologne

▲▲▲COLOGNE CATHEDRAL (DOM)

The Gothic *Dom*—Germany's most exciting church—looms immediately up from the train station in one of the country's starkest

juxtapositions of the modern and the medieval. The church is so big and so important that it has its own information office, the Domforum, in a separate building across the street (described later).

Cost and Hours: Free, Mon-Sat 9:30-11:30 & 12:30-16:30, Sun 12:30-16:30; closed to tourists during services (generally Mon-Sat at 6:30, 7:15, 8:00, 9:00, 12:00, and 18:30; Sun at 7:00, 8:00, 9:00, 10:00, 12:00, 17:00, and 19:00; confirm times at Domforum office or at www.koelner-dom.de).

Tours: The one-hour English-only tours are reliably excellent (€8, Mon-Sat at 10:30 and 14:30, Sun at 14:30, meet inside front door of *Dom*, tel. 0221/9258-4730). Your tour ticket also covers the 20-minute English video in the Domforum directly following the tour.

◉ **Self-Guided Tour:** If you don't take the guided tour, follow this seven-stop walk (note that stops 3-7 are closed off during confession Sat 14:00-18:00, and any time services are underway).

❶ **Cathedral Exterior:** The cathedral—the most ambitious Gothic building project north of France in the 13th century—was stalled in the Middle Ages and not finished until 1880. Even though most of it built in the 19th century, it's still technically a Gothic church (not "Neo-Gothic") because it was finished according to its original plans.

• *Step inside the church. Grab a pew in the center of the nave.*

❷ **Nave:** If you feel small, that's because you're supposed to. The 140-foot-tall ceiling reminds us of our place in the vast scheme of things. Lots of stained glass—enough to cover three football fields—fills the church with light, which represents God.

The church was begun in 1248. The choir—the lofty area from the center altar to the far end ahead of you—was inaugurated in 1322. Later, during the tumultuous wars of religious reformation, Catholic pilgrims

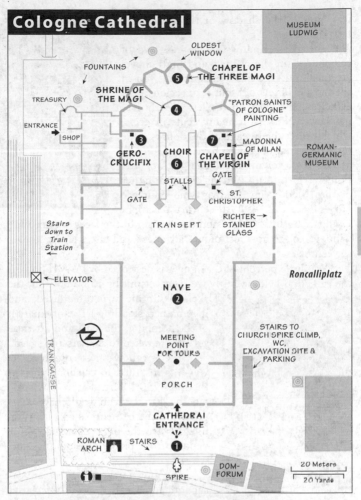

Cologne Cathedral

MUSEUM LUDWIG

OLDEST WINDOW

CHAPEL OF THE THREE MAGI

FOUNTAINS

5

SHRINE OF THE MAGI

TREASURY

4

"PATRON SAINTS OF COLOGNE" PAINTING

ENTRANCE

SHOP

3

7

MADONNA OF MILAN

GERO-CRUCIFIX

CHOIR

6

CHAPEL OF THE VIRGIN

ROMAN-GERMANIC MUSEUM

STALLS

GATE

GATE

ST. CHRISTOPHER

Stairs down to Train Station

TRANSEPT

RICHTER STAINED GLASS

ELEVATOR

Roncalliplatz

NAVE

2

TRANKGASSE

MEETING POINT FOR TOURS

STAIRS TO CHURCH SPIRE CLIMB, WC, EXCAVATION SITE & PARKING

PORCH

CATHEDRAL ENTRANCE

ROMAN ARCH

STAIRS

1

20 Meters

20 Yards

SPIRE

DOM-FORUM

COLOGNE & THE UNROMANTIC RHINE

stopped coming. This dried up funds, and eventually construction stopped. For 300 years, the finished end of the church was walled off and functioned as a church, while the unfinished nave (where you now sit) waited. For centuries, the symbol of Cologne's skyline was a huge crane that sat atop the unfinished west spire.

With the rise of German patriotism in the early 1800s, Cologne became a symbol of German unity. And the Prussians—the movers and shakers behind German unity—mistakenly considered Gothic (which actually originated in France) a German style. They paid for the speedy completion of this gloriously Gothic German church. With nearly 700 workers going at full speed, the church was finished in just 38 years (1842-1880). The great train station was built in the shadow of the cathedral's towering spire.

The glass windows at the east end of the church (in the chapels and high above) are medieval. The glass surrounding you in the nave is not as old, but it's precious nevertheless. The glass on the left is early Renaissance. Notice the many coats of arms, which depict the lineage of the donors. One of these windows would have cost as much as two large townhouses. The glass on the right—a gift from Ludwig I, grandfather of the "Mad" King Ludwig who built the fairy-tale castles—is 19th-century Bavarian. Compare both the colors and the realism of the faces between the windows to see how techniques advanced and tastes changed over the centuries.

While 95 percent of Cologne was destroyed by WWII bombs, the cathedral held up fairly well. (It was hit by 15 bombs, but the

skeletal Gothic structure flexed, and it remained standing.) In anticipation of the bombing, the glass and art treasures were taken to shelters and saved.

The "swallow's nest" organ above you was installed to celebrate the cathedral's 750th birthday in 1998. Attaching it to the wall would have compromised the cathedral's architectural integrity, so the organ is actually suspended from precarious-looking steel wires.

The guys in the red robes are cathedral cops, called *Schweizer* (after the Swiss guard at the Vatican); if a service is getting ready to start, they hustle tourists out (if you'd like, you can stay for the service if you're already inside).

• *Leave the nave to the left and step through the gate at the far end (beside the transept), into the oldest part of the church.*

As you enter, look down at the 19th-century **mosaic** *showing a saint holding the Carolingian Cathedral, which stood on this spot for several centuries before this one was built. Ahead of you on the left is the...*

❸ **Gero-Crucifix:** The Chapel of the Cross features the oldest surviving monumental crucifix north of the Alps. Carved in the 970s with a sensitivity 300 years ahead of its time, it shows Jesus not suffering and not triumphant—but with eyes closed...dead. He paid the price for our sins. It's quite a twofer: great art and powerful theology in one. The cathedral has three big pilgrim stops: this crucifix, the Shrine of the Magi, and the *Madonna of Milan*.

• *Continue to the front end of the church, stopping to look at the big golden reliquary in the glass case behind the high altar.*

❹ **Shrine of the Magi:** Relics were a big deal in the Middle Ages. Cologne's acquisition of the bones of the Three Kings in the 12th century put it on the pilgrimage map and brought in enough money to justify the construction of this magnificent place. By some stretch of medieval Christian logic, these relics also justified the secular power of the German king. This reliquary, made in about 1200 of gilded silver, jewels, and enamel, is the biggest and most splendid I've seen. On the long sides, Old Testament prophets line the bottom, and 12 New Testament apostles—with a wingless angel in the center—line the top. The front looks like three stacked coffins, showing scenes of Christ's flagellation, Crucifixion, and Resurrection.

Inside sit the bones of the Magi...three skulls with golden crowns. So what's the big deal about these three kings (of Christmas-carol fame)? They were the first to recognize Jesus as the Savior and the first to come as pilgrims to worship him—inspiring medieval pilgrims and countless pilgrims since. For a thousand years, a theme of this cathedral has been that life is a pilgrimage...a search for God.

• *Opposite the shrine, at the far-east end of the church, is the...*

❺ **Chapel of the Three Magi:** The center chapel, at the church's far end, is the oldest. It also features the church's oldest window (center, from 1265). The design is typical: a strip of Old Testament scenes on the left with a parallel strip of New Testament scenes on the right that matches theologically and visually (such as, on bottom panels: to the left, the birth of Eve; to the right, the birth of Mary with her mother Anne on the bed).

Later glass windows (which you saw lining the nave) were made from panes of clear glass that were painted and glazed. This medieval window, however, is actually colored glass, which is assembled like a mosaic. It was very expensive. The size was limited to what pilgrim donations could support. Notice the plain, budget design higher up.

• *Peek into the center zone between the high altar and the carved wooden central stalls. (You can't usually get inside, unless you take the tour.)*

❻ **Choir:** The choir is surrounded by 13th- and 14th-century art with carved oak stalls, frescoed walls, statues painted as they would have been, and original stained glass high above. Study the fanciful oak carvings. The woman cutting the man's hair is a Samson-and-Delilah warning to the sexist men of the early Church.

• *The nearby chapel holds one of the most precious paintings of the important Gothic School of Cologne.*

❼ **Chapel of the Virgin:** *The Patron Saints of Cologne* was painted around 1440, probably by Stefan Lochner. Notice the photographic realism and believable

depth. There are literally dozens of identifiable herbs in the grassy foreground. During the 19th century, the city fought to move the painting to a museum. The Church went to court to keep it. The judge ruled that it could stay in the cathedral—as long as a Mass was said before it every day. For more than a hundred years, that happened at 18:30. Now, 21st-century comfort has trumped 19th-century law: In winter, services take place in the warmer Sacrament Chapel instead. (If you like this painting, you'll enjoy the many other fine works from the School of Cologne at the Wallraf-Richartz Museum.)

Overlooking the same chapel (between the windows), the delicate *Madonna of Milan* sculpture (1290), associated with miracles, was a focus of pilgrims for centuries. Its colors, scepter, and crown were likely added during a restoration in 1900. The reclining medieval knight in the cage at the back of the chapel (just before the gate) is a wealthy but childless patron who donated his entire county to the cathedral.

Pass through the gate and look back above the tomb with the cage to find the statue of **St. Christopher** (with Jesus on his shoulder and the pilgrim's staff). He's facing the original south transept entry to the church. Since 1470, pilgrims and travelers have looked up at him and taken solace in the hope that their patron saint is looking out for them.

As you head for the exit, look into the transept on your left. The **stained-glass windows** above you are a random and abstract pattern of 80 colors, "sampled" from the church's more-historic windows. The local artist Gerhard Richter designed these windows to create a "harmony of colors" in 2007.

• *Go in peace.*

More Cathedral Sights
Church Spire Climb (Dom-Turm)
An exterior entry (to the right of the church as you face the west facade) takes you into a modern excavation site, where you can see an arch and the foundations from the cathedral's predecessor (free), and pay to climb the cathedral's dizzying south tower. For a workout of 509 steps, you can enjoy a fine city view. From the belfry (*Glockenstube;* only 400 steps up), you can see the *Dom*'s nine huge bells, including *Dicke Peter* (24-ton Fat Peter), claimed to be the largest free-swinging church bell in the world.

Cost and Hours: €4, €8 combo-ticket with treasury, daily 9:00-18:00, closes earlier off-season.

Treasury
The treasury sits outside the cathedral's left transept (when you exit through the front door, turn right and continue right around the building to the gold pillar marked *Schatzkammer*). The six dim, hushed rooms are housed in the cathedral's 13th-century stone cellar vaults. Spotlights shine on black cases filled with gilded chalices and crosses, medieval reliquaries (bits of chain, bone, cross, and cloth in gold-crusted glass capsules), and plenty of fancy bishop garb: intricately embroidered miters and vestments, rings with fat gemstones, and six-foot gold crosiers. Displays come with brief English descriptions; the little *Cologne Cathedral* book sold inside the adjacent cathedral shop *(Domladen)* provides extra information.

Cost and Hours: €6, €8 combo-ticket with spire climb, daily 10:00-18:00, tel. 0221/1794-0530.

Domforum
This helpful visitors center, across from the cathedral's entrance, is a good place to support the Vatican Bank (notice the Pax Bank ATM just outside), or to take a break from the crowds. The staff offers plenty of cathedral info, and the welcoming lounge has inexpensive coffee and juice. The English "multivision" video about the church starts slow but gets a little better.

Cost and Hours: Visitors center-free, Mon-Fri 9:30-18:00, Sat until 17:00, Sun 13:00-17:00, may close for special events, clean pay WC downstairs; video-€2, included with church tour, runs Mon-Sat at 11:30 and 15:30, Sun at 15:30 only, 20 minutes; tel. 0221/9258-4720, www.domforum.de.

Kolumba Diocesan Museum
This museum contains some of the cathedral's finest art. Built around the Madonna in the Ruins church, the museum is conceived as a place of reflection. There are no tours or information or noise. It's just you and the art in a modern building built upon the

rubble of war. The daring modernist rebuild is a statement: We lost the war. Just accept it.

Cost and Hours: €5, Wed-Mon 12:00-17:00, closed Tue; on Kolumbastrasse, which runs between Minoritenstrasse and Brückenstrasse, a few blocks southwest of the cathedral; tel. 0221/933-1930, www.kolumba.de.

NEAR THE CATHEDRAL
▲▲Roman-Germanic Museum
(Römisch-Germanisches Museum)

One of Germany's top Roman museums, with an elegant and fascinating display of Roman artifacts, may be closed for renovation during your visit--check their website for the latest. If open, the pieces on display are evidence of Cologne's status as an important site of civilization long before the cathedral was ever imagined. Temporary exhibits are usually on the ground floor. Upstairs is an original, reassembled arched gate to the Roman city with the Roman initials for the town, CCAA, still legible, and incredible glassware that Roman Cologne was famous for producing. The museum's main attraction, described in my self-guided walk, is the Roman-mosaic floor--which you can see from the street for free through the large window.

Cost and Hours: €6.50, €9 combo-ticket with Roman Praetorium; Tue-Sun 10:00-17:00, first Thu of month until 22:00, closed Mon; Roncalliplatz 4, tel. 0221/2212-4438, www.roemisch-germanisches-museum.de.

Nearby: The **Roman Praetorium** houses the ruins of the fourth- century palace of the Roman governor in Lower Germania (same hours as Roman-Germanic Museum, tiny entrance off Kleine Budengasse).

▲▲Museum Ludwig

Next door to the Roman-Germanic Museum and more enjoyable, this museum—in a slick and modern building—offers a stimulating trip through the art of the last century, including American Pop and post-WWII art. Head upstairs to find the Haubrich collection. Josef Haubrich managed to keep his impressive collection of German Expressionist art out of Nazi hands (they considered it "decadent art") and eventually gave it to the city. The collection includes works by the great German Expressionists Max Beckmann, Otto Dix, and Ernst Ludwig Kirchner. Their paintings capture the loss of idealism and innocence following World War I and helped take art into the no-holds-barred modern world. Also upstairs is a Picasso collection spanning the artist's entire career. The lower level is mostly contemporary and abstract paintings.

Cost and Hours: €12; Tue-Sun 10:00-18:00, first Thu of

month until 22:00, closed Mon; audioguide-€3, free WC in entry hall, pricey cafeteria, Heinrich-Böll-Platz, tel. 0221/2212-6165, www.museum-ludwig.de.

FARTHER FROM THE CATHEDRAL

These museums are several blocks south of the cathedral.

▲▲Wallraf-Richartz Museum

Housed in a cinderblock of a building near the City Hall, this minimalist museum—Cologne's oldest—features a world-class collection of old masters, from medieval to northern Baroque and Impressionist. You'll see the best collection anywhere of Gothic School of Cologne paintings (1300-1550), offering an intimate peek into those times. Also included are German, Dutch, Flemish, and French works by masters such as Albrecht Dürer, Peter Paul Rubens, Rembrandt, Frans Hals, Jan Steen, Vincent van Gogh, Pierre-Auguste Renoir, Claude Monet, Edvard Munch, and Paul Cézanne.

Cost and Hours: €8-13 depending on special exhibits; Tue-Sun 10:00-18:00, first and third Thu until 22:00, closed Mon; on Obenmarspforten, tel. 0221/2212-1119, www.wallraf.museum.

▲Imhoff Chocolate Museum (Schokoladenmuseum)

Chocoholics love this place, cleverly billed as the "MMMuseum." Three levels of displays follow the cocoa bean from its origin to the finished product. Local historians, noting the "dumbing-down" of this generation of tourists, complain that this museum gets more visitors than all of Cologne's other museums combined—in fact, it's the only sight in Cologne worth booking in advance. You'll see displays on the history, culture, and business of chocolate from the Aztecs onward, step into a hot and muggy greenhouse to watch the beans grow, and follow sweet little treats as they trundle down the conveyor belt in the functioning chocolate factory, the museum's highlight. The top-floor exhibit on chocolate advertising is fun. Some find that the museum takes chocolate too seriously, and wish the free samples weren't so meager—you'll have to do your indulging in the fragrant, choc-full gift shop.

Cost and Hours: €11.50; Mon-Fri 10:00-18:00, Sat-Sun 11:00-19:00, last entry one hour before closing; lines—though fast-moving—can be long in high-season, book online in advance; Am Schokoladenmuseum 1a, tel. 0221/931-8880, www.

schokoladenmuseum.de. It's a pleasant 15-minute walk south from the cathedral along the riverfront, between the Deutzer and Severins bridges.

Käthe Kollwitz Museum

This museum contains the largest collection of the artist's powerful Expressionist art, welling from her experiences living in Berlin during the tumultuous first half of the 20th century.

Cost and Hours: €5; Tue-Fri 10:00-18:00, Sat-Sun from 11:00, closed Mon; Neumarkt 18, tel. 0221/227-2899, www.kollwitz.de. From Hohe Strasse, walk west on Schildergasse for about 10 minutes to Neumarkt; go past the Neumarkt Gallerie shopping center to Neumarkt Passage, enter Neumarkt Passage, and walk to the glass-domed center courtyard, where you'll take the glass elevator to the fifth floor.

Sleeping in Cologne

Cologne is *the* convention town in Germany. Consequently, hotels are either jam-packed (rates double or even triple), or they're empty and hungry for guests. An updated list of convention dates is posted at www.koelnmesse.de (choose English, then "Trade fairs and events," then "Trade fairs in Cologne"). Unlisted smaller conventions can also lead to small price increases, and big conventions in nearby Düsseldorf can fill rooms and raise rates in Cologne. Outside of convention times, prices are soft, so ask the hotel for its best offer.

All the options listed here are an easy roll from the train station with your luggage.

NEAR THE STATION

$$$ Hotel Ibis Köln am Dom, a 71-room chain hotel, offers predictability and tidiness, and you can't beat the location—inside the station building—though it lacks personality (breakfast extra, air-con, elevator, Bahnhofsvorplatz, entry across from station's *Reisezentrum,* tel. 0221/912-8580, https://ibis.accorhotels.com, h0739@accor.com).

$$ Hotel Domspitzen is the 30-room sister hotel to the Domstern (listed later). Its convenient location, whimsical wallpapered rooms, and sun terrace with a peek-a-boo view of the cathedral make it a good value (elevator, pay parking; from the train station, take the Breslauer Platz exit by track 11 and walk a half-block up Domstrasse to #23; tel. 0221/998-930, www.hotel-domspitzen.de, info@hotel-domspitzen.de).

$ Classic Hotel Harmonie's 72 business-class rooms include some very small, nicely priced singles as well as luxurious "superior" rooms, which have hardwoods and swanky bathrooms with heated floors. It's plenty pricey during conventions, but becomes affordable on weekends and is a downright steal when business is slow (more expensive rooms have air-con, elevator, limited pay parking, Ursulaplatz 13, tel. 0221/16570, www.classic-hotel-harmonie.de, info@classic-hotel-harmonie.com). It's a five-minute walk northwest of the station: Exit by track 1 and walk straight to the roundabout, then go right on Marzellenstrasse and bear left on Ursulaplatz, toward the church.

$ Hotel Domstern is a 16-room boutique hotel with fresh, pleasant rooms above a colorful lobby with funky furniture, located in a fine townhouse just steps from the station (elevator, pay parking; from the train station, take the Breslauer Platz exit by track 11 and walk two blocks up Domstrasse to #26; tel. 0221/168-0080, www.hotel-domstern.de, info@hotel-domstern.de).

¢ Station Hostel is a five-minute walk from the train station and has a clean and welcoming vibe (private rooms available, breakfast extra, elevator, next-door restaurant, no curfew, tel. 0221/912-5301; exit station on cathedral side, walk along right side of the church one block, turn right on Marzellenstrasse to #44; www.hostel-cologne.de, station@hostel-cologne.de).

IN THE TOWN CENTER

$$ Stern am Rathaus has nine stylish rooms on three floors in a quiet location just around the corner from Alter Markt and the City Hall. The staff and breakfast room are equally cheery (family rooms, air-con, no elevator, pay parking; Bürgerstrasse 6, tel. 0221/2225-1750, www.stern-am-rathaus.com, hotelstern@mailbox.org).

$$ Lint Hotel, a small place with 18 modern rooms and hardwood floors, is comfortably located in a little alley between Fischmarkt and Alter Markt. It's expensive during conventions and in high season, but offers affordable deals at other times (includes breakfast with homemade Bircher Muesli, no elevator, pay parking, Lintgasse 7, tel. 0221/920-550, www.lint-hotel.de, contact@lint-hotel.de).

$ Hotel Engelbertz is a fine, family-run, 40-room enterprise. It's simple and feels dated, but it's clean and in a good location, at the end of the pedestrian mall (RS%, elevator, some rooms with street noise, public pay parking; just off Hohe Strasse at Obenmarspforten 1, coming from station turn left at Hohe Strasse 96; tel. 0221/257-8994, www.hotel-engelbertz.de, info@hotel-engelbertz.de).

Eating in Cologne

The city's distinct type of beer, called *Kölsch*, is pale, hoppy, and fermented in a way more typical of wheat-based beers, lending it a slight sweetness. Beer halls tend to have similar menus but distinguish themselves by which brand of beer they serve (usually Gaffel, Päffgen, Peters, or Früh). Beers come in delicate glasses (by Bavarian standards) and are shuttled around in small wreath-like trays *(Bierkränze)*. Cologne's waiters, called *Köbes*, have a reputation for grumpiness, and some beer halls have a sloppy, sticky-tabled feeling, but others have helpful and attentive service and attractive interiors. This is the place to satisfy your cravings for blood sausage *(Blutwurst)* and kidneys *(Nierchen)*...or, for something a little more mainstream, look for the tasty *Rheinischer Sauerbraten* with *Klössen* (dumplings) and applesauce. Pub after pub advertise yard-high beer glasses and yard-long bratwurst.

NEAR ALTER MARKT

The area around Alter Markt, a square a few blocks from the cathedral, is home to dozens of beer halls, most with both outdoor and indoor seating. Wander from Alter Markt through Heumarkt (an adjacent square) and down Salzgasse to Frankenwerft (along the river) to catch the flavor.

$$$ Bierhaus en d'r Salzgass, cozy and stylishly decorated, is where locals have been coming for beer since the 19th century. Today it belongs to Päffgen brewery and serves authentic German dishes (Mon-Thu 16:00-24:00, Fri from 12:00, Sun from 11:00, Salzgasse 5, tel. 0221/800-1900). Päffgen's nearby **$$$ Bierhaus am Rhein** has the same menu and offers views of the Rhine and park at Frankenwerft (Mon-Thu 15:00-24:00, Fri-Sun from 11:00, Frankenwerft 27, tel. 0221/800-1902).

If you're more interested in music and beer than in food, check out **$$ Papa Joe's Klimperkasten,** a dark pub packed with memorabilia and live jazz daily (Gaffel on tap, live piano jazz Sun-Thu from 20:00, Alter Markt 50, tel. 0221/258-2132). A couple of minutes' walk away is its rowdier sibling, **Papa Joe's Jazzlokal** (live bands Mon-Sat from 20:30, Sun from 19:30 except closed Sun June-Aug, Buttermarkt 37, tel. 0221/257-7931, www.papajoes.de for jazz schedule—American jazz and Dixieland have a big following in Germany). The pubs on the Frankenwerft, along the river across from the K-D boat dock, tend to be a bit more expensive.

ELSEWHERE IN COLOGNE

$$ Holtmann's im MAKK, a museum café with sophisticated locals enjoying light fare, is a good option for a non-*Brauhaus* lunch. If you eat here on a Sunday morning, be sure to sit outside and enjoy a free organ concert al fresco—the courtyard abuts a church (Tue-Sun 11:00-17:00, closed Mon, on other side of Hohe Strasse from the cathedral in Museum of Applied Arts—Museum für Angewandte Kunst—at An der Rechtschule 1, inside front door and down the stairs, no museum ticket needed, tel. 0221/2779-8860).

$ Café Eigel, just off Hohe Strasse near the recommended Hotel Engelbertz, is a good option for *Kaffee und Kuchen* (afternoon cake and coffee) or for a light lunch (including salads and omelets). In the same location for many years, it's been remodeled in a fresh, sleek, modern style. Enjoy delicious pastries in the airy atrium, and be sure to pick up some homemade chocolates. Order your *Kuchen* at the counter first, then find a table and a server will take the rest of your order (Mon-Fri 9:00-19:00, Sat until 18:00, Sun 14:00-18:00, Brückenstrasse 1, tel. 0221/257-5858).

$$ Früh am Dom, near the cathedral, is the closest beer hall to the train station. Popular with both locals and tourists, it offers three floors of traditional German drinking and dining options. In the adjoining delicatessen on the left, check out a painting of what the city looked like in 1531 (daily 8:00-24:00, Am Hof 12, tel. 0221/261-3211).

$$ Schreckenskammer is a down-home joint and might be the least touristy beer hall in central Cologne. It's located just behind the St. Ursula church, near the recommended Harmonie hotel. The sand on the floor, swept out and replaced each morning, buffs the hardwood and also keeps it clean. The *kammer* is small and cozy, so be prepared to share a table and make new friends over a *Kölsch* or two. Most meals (choose from the *Tageskarte*, or daily specials) start with a complimentary cup of *Brühe* (broth). Don't mistake this as an act of hospitality—it only serves to make you thirstier. This eatery is popular, so arrive early or make a reservation (Tue-Sat 11:00-13:45 & 16:30-22:30, closed Sun-Mon, Ursulagartenstrasse 11, tel. 0221/132-581, www.schreckenskammer.com).

Groceries: For a quick snack or picnic essentials, there's a **Rewe To Go** along the city's main drag (long hours daily, Hohe Strasse 63).

Cologne Connections

From Cologne by Train to: Bonn (5/hour, 30 minutes), **Remagen** (2-3/hour, 50 minutes), **Aachen** (2-3/hour, 1 hour), **Frankfurt** (direct ICE trains almost hourly, most leave from Cologne's Köln-Messe-Deutz station—a 2-minute trip across river by S-Bahn, 1.5 hours; slower, cheaper, less frequent IC trains along Rhine are better for enjoying scenery, 2.5 hours), **Frankfurt Airport** (1-2/hour, 1 hour; trains along Rhine go less often and take 2.5 hours), **Bacharach/St. Goar** (hourly; 2 hours with change in Koblenz,

2.5 hours direct), **Cochem** (hourly, 2.5 hours; most change in Koblenz), **Trier** (at least hourly, 3 hours, some change in Koblenz), **Würzburg** (hourly, 2.5 hours by ICE; also 3/day by IC, 4 hours), **Hamburg** (hourly direct, 4 hours), **Munich** (2/hour, 4.5 hours, some with 1 change), **Berlin** (hourly, 4.5 hours, night train possible), **Paris** (5/day direct, 3.5 hours, Thalys train—requires seat reservation), **Amsterdam** (every 2 hours direct, 3 hours). Night trains are possible to Berlin, Innsbruck, Munich, and Vienna. Train info: www.bahn.com.

The Unromantic Rhine

HIGHLIGHTS
▲Bonn

Bonn was chosen for its sleepy, cultured, and peaceful nature as a good place to plant West Germany's first post-Hitler government. Since the two Germanys became one again in 1989, Berlin has taken back its position as the capital.

Today, Bonn is sleek, modern, and, by big-city standards, remarkably pleasant and easygoing. The pedestrian-only old town stretching out from the station will make you wonder why the US can't trade in its malls for real, people-friendly cities. The market square and Münsterplatz—filled with street musicians—are a joy. People-watching doesn't get much better, though the actual sights are disappointing.

The **TI** is a five-minute walk from the station (Mon-Fri 10:00-18:00, Sat until 16:00, Sun until 14:00, go straight on Windeckstrasse, next to Karstadt department store, tel. 0228/775-000, www.bonn.de).

If you're a classical-music fan, you can stop by **Beethoven's Birthplace,** with its sparse exhibits (€6; daily 10:00-18:00, shorter hours Nov-March; free tours run Mon, Thu, and Sat at 14:30; Bonngasse 18, tel. 0228/981-7525, www.beethoven-haus-bonn.de).

▲Remagen

Midway between Koblenz and Cologne are the scant remains of the Bridge at Remagen, of WWII (and movie) fame. But the memorial and the bridge stubs are enough to stir the emotions of Americans who remember when, in 1945, it was the only bridge still standing on the Rhine, allowing the Allies to pour across the river and race toward Berlin. The bridge was built during World War I to help supply the German forces on the Western Front. (Ironically, one war later, General Eisenhower said the bridge was worth its weight in gold for its service *against* Germany.) An American unit captured the bridge on March 7, 1945, just after two failed attempts to demolish it (Hitler executed four generals for this failure). Ten days after US forces arrived, the bridge did collapse, killing 28 American soldiers. Today you can pay your respects here and visit the **Peace Museum**, which tells the bridge's fascinating story (€3.50, daily 10:00-18:00, off-season until 17:00, closed mid-Nov-early March; it's on the Rhine's west bank, south side of Remagen town, follow *Brücke von Remagen* signs; tel. 02642/20159, www.bruecke-remagen.de). Remagen **TI:** Tel. 02642/20187.

▲Aachen (Charlemagne's Capital)

This city was the capital of Europe in AD 800, when Charles the Great (Charlemagne) called it Aix-la-Chapelle. The remains of his rule include an impressive Byzantine- and Ravenna-inspired church, with his sarcophagus and throne. Enjoy the town's charming historic pedestrian center and festive Christmas market. See the headliner newspaper museum and great fountains, including a clever arrange-'em-yourself version.

LOWLIGHTS

Heidelberg

This famous old university town attracts hordes of Americans. Any surviving charm is stained almost beyond recognition by commercialism. It doesn't make it into Germany's top three weeks.

Mainz, Wiesbaden, and Rüdesheim

These towns are all too big or too famous. They're not worth your time. Mainz's Gutenberg Museum is also a disappointment.

NÜRNBERG

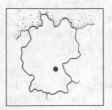

Nürnberg ("Nuremberg" in English), Bavaria's second city, is known for its glorious medieval architecture, important Germanic history museum, haunting Nazi past, famous Christmas market (Germany's biggest), and little bratwurst (Germany's tiniest and perhaps most beloved).

Nürnberg (NEWRN-behrg) was one of Europe's leading cities around 1500, and its large Imperial Castle marked it as a stronghold of the Holy Roman Empire. Today, though Nürnberg has a half-million residents, the charming Old Town—with its red-sandstone Gothic buildings—makes visitors feel like they are in a far smaller city. Thanks to an enlightened city-planning vision that rebuilt the town in a modern yet people-friendly style after the war, and policies that ensured that lots of residents chose to live in the center, Nürnberg's downtown is lively and inviting day and night.

PLANNING YOUR TIME

Nürnberg is an easy add-on to any itinerary that includes Munich, Würzburg, or Rothenburg (each about an hour away by frequent trains), and a handy stop on the way to Frankfurt, Berlin, or Dresden. Keep in mind that nearly all its museums (except those relating to World War II) are closed on Monday.

For the sightseer, Nürnberg is a city of the First Reich (Holy Roman Empire sites in the Old Town) and the Third Reich (Nazi-period sites outside the town center).

If you're staying just one night (or day-tripping), follow my self-guided walk from the train station through the Old Town up to the castle, then visit the farther-flung Nazi sites. If you have two days (most worthwhile if you have a serious interest in German history, especially the Nazi years), spend one day at the Nazi Documentation Center and the nearby Rally Grounds, and the other in the Old Town, with time for the outstanding Germanic National Museum.

Orientation to Nürnberg

Nürnberg's Old Town is surrounded by a three-mile-long wall and moat, with a ring road beyond that. At the southeast corner of the ring is the train station; across the street, just inside the ring, is the medieval Königstor gate. Sights cluster along Königstrasse downhill from the Königstor to the small Pegnitz River, then back uphill through the main market square (Hauptmarkt) to the Imperial Castle (Kaiserburg). The former Nazi Rally Grounds are southeast of the center (easily reached by tram or bus).

TOURIST INFORMATION

Nürnberg's handy and helpful TI is across the ring road from the station, in the modern building just opposite the Königstor gate (Mon-Sat 9:00-19:00, Sun 10:00-16:00, Königstrasse 93, tel. 0911/233-6132, www.tourismus.nuernberg.de). Pick up the free *See and Enjoy* city-guide booklet (with updated sights, hours, and prices) and get information about bus and walking tours. The TI also sells transit passes and the Nürnberg Card. A small branch TI is located at #18 on the Hauptmarkt (Mon-Sat 9:00-18:00, Sun 10:00-16:00, longer hours during the Christmas market) and at the airport (daily 6:00-23:00).

Sightseeing Passes: When you buy a ticket at any of Nürnberg's city-run museums—including the Nazi Documentation Center, Nurnberg Trials Courtroom, Albrecht Dürer House, Toy Museum, and the City Museum—you can pay an additional €3 for a **Discount Day Pass** that lets you visit all the others free of charge on the same day (www.museen.nuernberg.de).

If you're staying at least two days, the **Nürnberg Card** is a good value and gets you into a wider range of sights (€28/2 days, sold at TI and most hotels, covers local public transit and admission to the Germanic National Museum, Imperial Castle, Nürnberg Transport Museum, and the Historic Art Bunker tours, plus many others; www.tourismus.nuernberg.de).

ARRIVAL IN NÜRNBERG

By Train: Nürnberg's stately old Hauptbahnhof—with a contemporary interior—is conveniently located just outside the old city walls and ring road. The busy station has WCs, lockers, ATMs, and lots of shops. You can get train information and buy tickets at

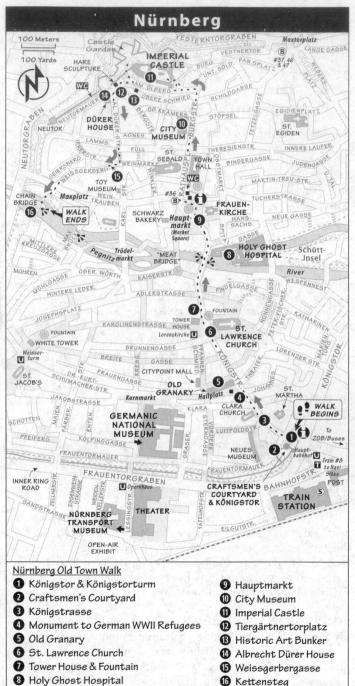

Nürnberg Old Town Walk

1. Königstor & Königstorturm
2. Craftsmen's Courtyard
3. Königstrasse
4. Monument to German WWII Refugees
5. Old Granary
6. St. Lawrence Church
7. Tower House & Fountain
8. Holy Ghost Hospital
9. Hauptmarkt
10. City Museum
11. Imperial Castle
12. Tiergärtnertorplatz
13. Historic Art Bunker
14. Albrecht Dürer House
15. Weissgerbergasse
16. Kettensteg

the travel desk *(Reisezentrum)* in the main hall (center of building, long hours daily) or at handy *Fahrkarten* machines throughout the station.

To reach the **Königstor** (the medieval city's southern gate)—near most recommended hotels and the starting point for exploring the Old Town—follow signs for *Ausgang/City* down the escalator, then signs to *Altstadt* in the underpass. When you emerge, the TI is on your right and the Königstor tower (Königstorturm) is on your left.

To go directly from the station by tram to the **Nazi Documentation Center** and the **former Nazi Rally Grounds,** follow pink *Tram* signs in the underpass and head up the escalators to the stop in front of the Postbank Center. Get your ticket from the red vending machine (marked *VAG Fahrausweise,* near the stairwell for the U-Bahn) and catch tram #8 (direction: Doku-Zentrum, every 10 minutes, 10-minute trip).

By Long-Distance Bus: Long distance buses arrive at the central bus terminal (ZOB) at Bahnhofstrasse 11, just east of the train station and a five-minute walk from the Königstor.

By Car: A handful of public garages are located within the city walls (most around €16/day and well-signed); cheaper on-street parking is available in the neighborhoods that lie a 5- to 10-minute walk from the city walls.

By Plane: Nürnberg's small airport is just 3 miles north of the city center (airport code: NUE, tel. 0911/937-00, www.airport-nuernberg.de). The U-Bahn subway line #2 makes the 13-minute trip to the central train station every 10 minutes (€3.10). A taxi between the airport and the center costs around €20.

GETTING AROUND NÜRNBERG

Most of Nürnberg's sights are in the strollable Old Town, but you'll need to use public transit to reach the Nazi Rally Grounds and the Nürnberg Trials Courtroom, which are far beyond walking distance. Nürnberg has the typical German lineup of trams, buses, U-Bahns (subways), and S-Bahns (faster suburban trains). All work on the same tickets, which you can buy at vending machines (marked *VAG Fahrausweise*) on the tram platform or before entering the U- or S-Bahns, or on board (buses only). Everything in this chapter is within Zone *(Preisstufe)* A.

A **single ticket** *(Einzelfahrkarte,* €3.20) is good for 1.5 hours of travel in one direction, including transfers. The **four-trip ticket** *(4er-Ticket;* €11) has the same restrictions and is shareable; stamp one strip per person per trip. The **short-stretch ticket** *(Kurzstreckefahrkarte,* €1.70) is a cheaper option for a trip no more than three stops away. The **day ticket** *(TagesTicket Solo,* €8.30) is good for one calendar day (or both Sat and Sun; €12.30 *TagesTicket Plus* covers

NÜRNBERG

two adults and up to four children; day tickets also sold at TI). Vending machines time-stamp single and day tickets, so you don't need to validate them separately. For more information, see www. vag.de.

HELPFUL HINTS

Festivals: Summer music festivals cater to different crowds in late July and early August: **Klassik Open Air** is a series of free classical concerts and fireworks at Luitpoldhain park, near the Nazi Documentation Center (www.klassikopenair.de), and **Bardentreffen Nürnberg** (also free) hosts all kinds of world-music acts right in the city center (www.bardentreffen. de). On the first Saturday in May, Nürnbergers stay out all night for **Die Blaue Nacht** ("The Blue Night"), which celebrates art and music with museum open houses, outdoor video projections, and much more (www.blauenacht.nuernberg.de). Two **city fairs** happen every spring and fall, also at Luitpoldhain park, with rides, traditional costumes, and the works (www.volksfest-nuernberg.de). The annual **Christmas market** *(Christkindlesmarkt),* with more than two million annual visitors, engulfs the Hauptmarkt (starts the Fri before the first Sun in Advent—November 27 in 2020, www.christkindlesmarkt. de).

Laundry: A **Schnell & Sauber** self-service launderette is at Allersberger Strasse 89 (daily 6:00-22:00, until 23:00 in summer, English instructions, near Schweiggerstrasse stop for tram #8, two stops from train station in same direction as Nazi Documentation Center; from tram stop, head 200 yards away from downtown along Allersberger Strasse to find launderette on left).

Tours in Nürnberg

Walking Tours

English-language tours of Nürnberg's Old Town leave daily at 11:00 in peak season from the branch TI at Hauptmarkt 18 (€10, mid-April-early Jan, kids under 14 free, 2 hours, buy ticket from TI, www.nuernberg-tours.de).

Historic Art Bunker and Beer Cellar Tours

The intriguing "Historic Art Bunker" tour takes you deep into the sandstone cellars under Castle Hill to learn how the city protected its art treasures (plus some plundered from elsewhere in Europe) from World War II's most devastating bomb attacks. The underground bunkers are largely empty now, except for photos posted at each stop of the tour. You'll get some background on the pieces that were kept here, and hear a lot about the air raids and the citywide rebuilding process that followed. While most live guides give the tour only in German, the good included audioguide is in English. Even with the audioguide, stick close to the live guide so they can lock the doors as the group exits (€8.80, daily at 14:30, Fri-Sat also at 17:30, 1.5 hours, buy tickets at the Brauereiladen brewery shop—under the *Nürnberger Altstadthof* sign—at Bergstrasse 19, tel. 0911/2360-2731, www.felsengaenge-nuernberg.de). Meet your guide and pick up your audioguide at the cellar entrance, near the Tiergärtnertorplatz at Obere Schmiedgasse 52.

If you're interested in just the cellars, consider the more frequent "Historic Rock-Cut Beer Cellars" tour, which takes you through more than a half-acre of passages burrowed right under the city streets (about a tenth of the city's vast network). Originally dug in the Middle Ages to store beer, these cellars sheltered people, not art, during the WWII air raids. The tour ends with a brief sales pitch (and a tasting) from the host brewery, but you can easily skip out once you're above ground (€8, includes tasting; daily on the hour from 11:00-17:00; all tours in German except additional English tour Sat-Sun at 11:15, English audioguide, 1.5 hours). Buy tickets at the Brauereiladen brewery shop (where art bunker tour tickets are sold).

Bus Tours

These tours, which include a 30-minute walk through the Old Town, leave daily at 10:00 from the Old Granary (Mauthalle) at Hallplatz, two blocks up from the Königstor TI (May-Oct and Dec, €17, buy ticket on bus or at TI, 2.5 hours, in German and English, tel. 0911/202-290, www.neukam.de).

Tourist Train

A goofy little tourist train makes the rounds in the Old Town (€9, 40 minutes, audio narration in English, schedule posted at the Beautiful Fountain; leaves from Hauptmarkt near the fountain April-Oct about hourly 10:30-17:15; Feb-March and Nov weekends only with shorter hours; also runs daily during the Christmas market from the Old Granary, no trips Jan; www.nuernberg-stadtrundfahrt.de).

Private Guides

For a good and charming local guide (who covers Nürnberg and Bamberg), call **Doris Ritter** (€150/2 hours, mobile 0176-2421-5863, www.nuernberg-city-tours.de, nuernberg-city-tours@gmx.de). The **Geschichte für Alle** ("History for All") association can set you up with a good private guide who is enthusiastic about the town's history (office open Mon-Fri 9:00-12:30, also Mon, Tue, and Thu afternoons, closed Sat-Sun; tel. 0911/307-360, www.geschichte-fuer-alle.de, info@geschichte-fuer-alle.de). Guides can

NÜRNBERG

also be booked through the TI (tel. 0911/233-6123, fuehrung@ctz-nuernberg.de).

Nürnberg Old Town Walk

Many of Nürnberg's top sights are conveniently clustered along a straight-line thoroughfare connecting the train station (Hauptbahnhof) with the main market square (Hauptmarkt) and the Imperial Castle (Kaiserburg). For a good orientation, take the following self-guided stroll, worth ▲▲. Plan on an hour, not including stops. Use the "Nürnberg" map to trace this route.

• *Begin at the Königstor (where you emerge from the Hauptbahnhof underpass).*

❶ Königstor and the Königstorturm

This tower *(turm)* guards one of the four main medieval entrances (*tor* means door, gate, or portal) to Nürnberg's Old Town. Of the three miles of wall that once surrounded the city, 90 percent survives. The sandstone was quarried locally, and you can still see the little dimples made by the construction tongs as they hoisted the stones into place. Many Central European cities tore down their walls to make way for expansion in the 1800s, and Nürnberg nearly did the same. Now the city is glad it didn't: It's better for tourism.

• *Between the walls just next to the gate, you'll see the entrance to the...*

❷ Craftsmen's Courtyard (Handwerkerhof)

This hokey collection of half-timbered houses was built in 1971 to celebrate craftsmanship and to honor the 500th birthday of Nürnberg's favorite son, Albrecht Dürer. Nürnberg didn't have abundant natural resources or a navigable waterway, so its citizens made their living through trade and crafts (such as making scientific instruments, weapons, and armor). Dürer, arguably Germany's best painter, was considered the ultimate craftsman.

While a bit kitschy, this courtyard—originally a holding zone for carriages waiting to enter the "free imperial city"—is good for picking up a medieval vibe as you enter the Old Town. It's packed with replicas of medieval shops, where artisans actually make—and, of course, sell—leather, pottery, and brass goods. In the Middle Ages, this area between the walls was not a medieval mall but a *Passkontrolle*—a customs and security checkpoint zone where all visitors had to register before they could enter the town.

At the back of the courtyard, step through the old gate and out onto a bridge over what was once the moat. This was one of four major entries into the medieval town. Admire the double eagle over the entry—a reminder to all who approached that this was a free city under the direct control of the Habsburgs, who were the Holy Roman Emperors. Look over at the mighty, round Königstorturm (King's Gate Tower). It was originally square, but as better cannons were developed, the tower was given a round casing (so cannon balls would glance off). Imagine cannons lined up under the eaves of the tower, set to defend the city.

• *When you're finished poking around the courtyard, head into town (with the train station at your back) along...*

❸ Königstrasse

Though it had always been one of the four primary entrances to Nürnberg, this street became the city's main drag only after the train station was built in the early 20th century. It's lined with key sights, several recommended hotels and restaurants, and some wonderful Gothic and Neo-Gothic architecture.

Nürnberg hit its peak in the 14th century. In 1356 Emperor Charles IV issued a decree from Nürnberg called the Golden Bull, which regularized many aspects of imperial government. From then on, throughout the Middle Ages, German emperors were elected in Frankfurt, crowned in Aachen, and were supposed to hold their first Imperial Diet (a gathering of German nobles and VIPs) right here in Nürnberg, though not all bothered to follow through on such democratic and inclusive notions.

Nürnberg's low point came during World War II. By the end of the war, 90 percent of the Old Town was destroyed. Damaged buildings were repaired in the original Gothic style, but some structures were beyond repair. Instead of replicating these exactly as they had been, or re-placing them with modern-style buildings, postwar Nürnberg architects compromised. Look 50 yards down the street to #71. This is a good example of the city's "traditional modern" ethic of rebuilding in a modern style while preserving the medieval city's footprint and using traditional building materials (such as native sandstone). The blemishes on the older sandstone buildings all around are patched bullet scars from 1945.

Ahead, on the left, is the small **Clara Church** (Klarakirche). Step inside—first into a candlelit spiritual decompression chamber, and then into the modern and peaceful nave. The rear door leads to the old cloister area—a tranquil oasis and another good example of how the city retooled with respect for its history as it rebuilt. In the Middle Ages, Nürnberg had nine monasteries like this one. When the Reformation hit, Nürnberg turned Lutheran, and most of its monasteries were converted into practical municipal buildings such as hospitals and homes for the poor. As the monasteries fell, so did Nürnberg's importance: The city was now Lutheran, but the emperors were still Catholic. They moved the increasingly frequent Imperial Diet meetings—once Nürnberg's claim to fame—to more Catholic-friendly Regensburg. (Today, this church is an "ecumenical free church"—meaning it's neither Lutheran nor Catholic and welcomes worshippers of all stripes.)

Just after the church, above the recommended Istanbul Restaurant, look for Mary on the second-story corner. Statues like this grace houses all over Nürnberg.

• Continue down Königstrasse to Hallplatz, where the pedestrian stretch begins, and stop at the modern metal arch on the left. This is the...

❹ Monument to German WWII Refugees

This minimalist metal doorway, erected in 1999, remembers the German refugees of World War II and the hospitality of the Bavarians who took them in. Walk through the doorway and find a metal plaque in the pavement 30 steps beyond. It lists regions to the east once populated by Germans. In the years after the war, nearly a third of Bavaria's population was made up of German citizens who had fled west—or who'd been expelled from lands lost in the east. As a new generation of Germans comes into its own, memorials like this reflect a delicate challenge: to remember those who suffered in the war without forgetting that Germany was the aggressor.

• To visit the excellent Germanic National Museum now (see "More Sights in Nürnberg," later), detour left at Hall-platz (with the monument to your back) and walk 200 yards. Otherwise, continue down the main drag and look left to check out the...

❺ Old Granary (Mauthalle)

Medieval Nürnberg had 11 of these huge granaries to ensure that residents would have enough food in case of famine or siege. The grain was stored up above in the attic (behind all those little dormer windows, which provided ventilation). Imagine the wealth and resources this imperial town must have had to erect such a massive structure. Today, the cellar is home to a lively beer hall, Barfüsser. There are better places to eat in town, but pop in for a look or a drink.

Continue down pedestrian-only Königstrasse. Check out the Brezen Kolb stand, which sells pretzels local-style: as sandwiches with butter and cold cuts—never with mustard.

Look ahead to the street just beyond and across from the big church, notice another fine example of "traditional modern" architecture, and feel the energy of this healthy urban center. This drag used to have more cars and trams than any other street in town. But when the U-Bahn came in the 1970s, this part of the street became traffic-free.

• *After another two blocks, you'll see...*

❻ St. Lawrence Church (Lorenzkirche)

This once-Catholic, now-Protestant church is a massive house of worship, worth ▲▲. It was never a cathedral because Nürn-

berg never had a bishop (a fact locals were very proud of—a bishop would have threatened their prized independence). The name Königstrasse ("King Street")—where you've been walking—is a misnomer. When royals processed into town, they actually preferred to come through the west gate, so they could approach this church's magnificent Gothic facade head-on.

Cost and Hours: €2 donation requested, Mon-Sat 9:00-17:30, Sun 10:00-15:30, www.lorenzkirche.de.

❍ **Self-Guided Tour:** Stand in front of St. Lawrence's west portal, its **main door.** Flip around and imagine the Holy Roman Emperor parading—right past Starbucks—toward this tremendous Oz-like church.

Study the 260-foot-tall **facade** (completed c. 1360). Adam and Eve flank the doors (looking for a sweater). In the first row above the left door are two scenes: an intimate take on Jesus' birth on top, and the visit from the Magi on the bottom (with the Star of Bethlehem shining from above). Over the right door are the slaughter of the innocents (with a baby skewered by a Roman sword—classic medieval subtlety), and below that the presentation of Jesus in the temple and the flight to Egypt. Above those scenes is the Passion story (from left to right: trial, scourging, carrying the cross, Crucifixion, deposition, entombment, Resurrection, and, above that row, people rising from their graves). In the next row up, the saved (Peter—with his huge key—and company) stand on the left, while the sorry chain gang of the damned (including some kings and bishops) is shuttled off literally into the jaws of hell on the right. Above it all stands the triumphant resurrected Christ, with the sun and moon at his feet, flanked by angels tooting horns to announce Judgment Day.

• *Step inside (enter around right side).*

The **interior** wasn't completely furnished until more than a century after the church was built—just in time for the Reformation (so the Catholic decor adorned a now-Lutheran church). Most of the decorations inside were donated by wealthy Nürnbergers trying to cut down on their time in purgatory. Through the centuries, this art survived three separate threats: the iconoclasm of the Reformation, the whitewashing of the Baroque age, and the bombing of World War II. While Nürnberg was the first "free imperial city" to break with the Catholic Church and become Lutheran, locals didn't go wild (like Swiss Protestants did) in tearing down the rich, Mary-oriented decor of their fine churches. Luther (who, despite some flaws, was still very cool for his time) told the iconoclasts, "Tear the idols out of your heart, and you'll understand that these statues are only pieces of wood."

Suspended over the altar, the sculptural *Annunciation* is by a Nürnberg citizen and one of Central Europe's best woodcarvers, Veit Stoss. Carved in 1517, the 360-degree piece shows the angel Gabriel telling Mary that she'll be giving birth to the Messiah. Startled, she drops her prayer book. This is quite Catholic (notice the rosary frame with beads, and a circle of roses—one for each Hail Mary, and with a medallion depicting the "Joys of Mary"). A dove sits on Mary's head, and God the Father—looking as powerful as a Holy Roman Emperor—looks down. The figures are carved from the wood of linden trees. The piece survived the Reformation covered in a sack, revealed only on special occasions. Around back, enjoy more details—Mary's cascading hair and the sun and the moon. Nearby, the painting at the very front of the church (behind the altar) shows Mary and baby Jesus sitting with the city of Nürnberg in 1483 in the background (before the city's square towers were made round).

To the left of the altar, the frilly **tabernacle** tower is the "house of sacraments" that stored the consecrated Communion wafer. After the Mass, leftovers needed a worthy—even heavenly—home, and this was it. The cupboard behind the gold grate was the appropriate receptacle for what Catholics considered literally "the body of Christ." The theme of the carving is the Passion. The scenes ascend in chronological order: Last Supper, Judas' kiss, arrest, Crucifixion, and so on. Everything is carved of stone except for the risen Christ (way up high). He was living, and so was this—it's made of wood. The man holding the tabernacle on his shoulders is the artist who created it, Adam Kraft (with his curly black beard, chisel in hand). In the Middle Ages, artists were faceless artisans, no more important than a blacksmith or a stonemason. But in the 1490s, when this was made, the Renaissance was in the air, and artists like Kraft began putting themselves into their works. Kraft's contemporary, the painter Albrecht Dürer, actually signed his works—an incredible act in Germany at that time (for more on Dürer, see the "Albrecht Dürer House," later on this walk). In anticipation of the Allied bombs of World War II, this precious work was encased in protective concrete, except for the top 22 feet—which was the only part destroyed when the church was hit.

Look slightly above and to the left of Kraft's likeness to find the church's namesake—St. Lawrence—cradling the grill on which he was barbequed alive (as punishment for distributing treasures to the poor instead of handing them over to a greedy Roman official). Legend says the martyr's last brave words to the Romans were, "I'm done on this side. Turn me over!"

Following Adam Kraft's gaze, turn around and look up to a **plaque** honoring American philanthropist brothers Samuel and Rush Kress, who donated nearly a million Deutschmarks in 1950 to help rebuild the church. The bottom half of the plaque is in English, but it's hard to read, as it's written in an old-style black-letter font. Though the church was devastated by WWII

bombs, everything movable had been hidden away in bunkers right here in Nürnberg (which we'll pass later), including the stained glass you see today.

• *Wander slowly to the rear of the church.*

As you walk, notice the many **side chapels**, each a private chapel for a leading Nürnberg family. Also note the dozen or so wooden boxes with finely carved symbols representing various trades and craft guilds. After Mass, these were manned by a leading master of that trade who shamed parishioners into donating to needy widows and others in his organization. In a society without government-organized welfare, this was a way to cope.

In the last chapel on your right, an **interactive screen** features a digital copy of an illuminated (illustrated) handwritten manuscript, the *Das Gänsebuch* (*The Geesebook*, 1510). Named for one of its satirically provocative drawings, the book chronicles the entire Mass liturgy. Take a few moments to browse the "pages" of the manuscript, looking at close-ups of the ornate, often quirky illuminations. Put on the headphones and play one of the *chorale*, then face the nave and imagine yourself as a faithful parishioner listening to your local church choir.

At the rear of the church are **photos** of WWII destruction and postwar reconstruction.

• *Head back outside.*

❼ Tower House and Fountain

As you exit the church, look for the castle-like building on the corner across from the church facade. This is the only remaining **tower house** in Nürnberg. When it was built, in 1200, there was no city wall, and locals had to defend their own homes. It's basically a one-family castle. The ornate church-like structure protruding halfway up the wall is a reminder that while rich families could afford their own chapel, not even the very wealthy could live above God. Their personal chapels had to be "outside" the house. The house also sports two sundials. While they only bother to show daylight hours, they still work (as long as you adjust for the fact that there was no Daylight Saving Time back then).

• *Walk downhill, toward the river.*

American moralists might shield their eyes from the kinky 16th-century **Fountain of the Seven Virtues** (Tugendbrunnen). Otherwise, play a game: Circle the sprightly fountain and try to identify the classic virtues by the symbolism: justice (on top), faith, love, hope (anchor), courage (lion), moderation, patience. Are any birds sipping? Notice that, aside from faith's cross, there's no religious symbolism here, as this fountain was made during the Renaissance, when artists celebrated humanism and secular values.

• *Continue down the street toward the river. Caution: On your left, you'll pass **Kaiserstrasse**—the most expensive shopping street in town (with a little shop filled with insanely expensive Steiff teddy bears). When you get to the bridge, look to the right to see the...*

❽ Holy Ghost Hospital (Heilig-Geist-Spital)

This river-spanning hospital was donated to Nürnberg in the 14th century by the city's richest resident, eager to do his part to help the poor—and hopefully skip purgatory altogether. (A modern statue of this donor hangs out on the second-story corner of the Spital Apotheke, the first building after the bridge.) He funded this very scenic hospital to care for ill, disabled, and elderly Nürnbergers. The wing over the river dates from the

16th century. The dove beneath the middle window under the turret represents the Holy Ghost, the hospital's namesake.

Cross to the other side of the bridge, and look at the next bridge over (the Fleischbrücke—**"Meat Bridge"**). This is the narrowest point of the river. When it was built in 1596, this was considered the most high-tech bridge in Central Europe, an engineering feat inspired by Venice's single-span Rialto Bridge (though with a much flatter profile to accommodate carriage traffic, which Venice, of course, didn't have). Flooding along the river was a big concern until a fix was constructed after World War II.

There are a few handy lunch spots in the arcade between the two bridges (see "Eating in Nürnberg," later). The arrival of a big Starbucks, just beyond the Meat Bridge, is credited with cleaning up what had been a dodgy part of the riverbank. (In this land of cake-and-coffee, the Dunkin' Donuts and Starbucks chains—wildly popular among younger Germans—are shaking up tradition.)

Continue across the bridge and study the monument depicting characters from a 15th-century satire called *The Ship of Fools (Das Narrenschiff)*. It's adapted to follies that plague modern society: violence, technology, and apathy. Hey, how about the quiet, people-friendly ambience created by making this big city traffic-free in the center? Do a slow 360-degree spin and imagine this back home.

• *Continue ahead another 50 yards and enter the...*

❾ Hauptmarkt (Main Market Square)

When Nürnberg began booming in the 13th century, it consisted of two distinct walled towns separated by the river. As the towns grew, they merged and the middle wall came down. This square, built by Holy Roman Emperor Charles IV and worth ▲▲, became the center of the newly united city. Though Charles is more often associated with Prague (he's the namesake for the Charles Bridge and Charles University), he also loved Nürnberg—and visited 60 times during his reign.

The Gothic-style **Frauenkirche** on the square is located on the site of a former synagogue. When Nürnberg's towns were separate, Jewish residents were required to live in this swampy area close to the river and outside the walls. When the towns merged and the land occupied by the Jewish quarter became valuable, Charles IV allowed his subjects to force out the Jews. In the process, 562 were killed—a somber reminder that anti-Semitism predated the Nazis. (Inside the church, there's a Star of David on the floor, behind the main altar. In the apse, below the medieval altar, is a tabernacle that's reminiscent of a Torah scroll.) Charles IV, the most powerful man in Europe in his time, oversees the square from a perch high on the church facade. He's waiting for noon, when the electors dance around him.

Year-round, the Hauptmarkt is lively every day but Sunday with fruit, flower, and souvenir stands. For a few weeks before Christmas, it hosts Germany's largest **Christmas market.**

Walk across the square to the pointy gold **Beautiful Fountain** (Schöner Brunnen). Medieval tanneries, slaughterhouses, and the hospital you just saw dumped their by-products into the river. So this fountain brought clean drinking water into the square. Of course, it's packed with allegorical meaning. Step up to the iron railing. The outermost figures ringing the bottom represent the earthly arts (such as philosophy, music, and astronomy). On the pillars sitting behind each of these characters are the four church fathers and the four evangelists, showing that religion is higher than the arts. On the column itself, the lowest figures are the seven electors of the Holy Roman Emperor and nine heroes: three Christian (including King Arthur and Charlemagne); three Jewish (such as King David); and three heathen (such as Julius Caesar). At the very top are eight prophets, hovering above—but granting legitimacy to—worldly power. On the side of the fountain facing the McDonald's, you'll probably see tourists fussing over a gold ring. If you believe in such silly tour-guide tales, spinning this ring three times brings good luck...OK, go ahead and spin it.

While there are plenty of grilled sausage vendors on the square during market times, connoisseurs will want to take a short side-trip from here: Head a block down Waaggasse (the street leading left, away from the Beautiful Fountain) and take a quick left on Winklerstrasse to find the recommended **Schwarz Bakery** one block down, at the corner of Winklerstrasse and Tuchgasse. This is paradise for lovers of sausage and dark bread (i.e., Nürnbergers). Step in and inhale. This old-school place, open since 1923 and still family-run, selects the best wursts and breads from producers in the surrounding countryside, and brings the bounty into the city. They can make the German sandwich of your dreams. When Franconians travel, what they miss most is their homeland's dark bread and variety of high-quality sausages.

• *Return to the fountain on the Hauptmarkt. (Note that bus #36, which goes directly to the Nazi Documentation Center, departs from a stop facing the recommended Sorat Hotel Saxx.) Now climb uphill, heading for the Imperial Castle. After a block, you'll pass the* **Bratwursthäusle** *(on the left), a recommended sausage restaurant. For another local taste treat—my favorite in town—step inside, pay €3 at the half-door, take your receipt to the beechwood grill, and trade it for three sausages in a bun.*

Hiking farther uphill, you'll pass **St. Sebald** *(Sebaldkirche), Nürnberg's second great Gothic church. The imposing Renaissance building on your right is Nürnberg's Town Hall* (Rathaus)*, which was partially designed and decorated by Albrecht Dürer. About 100 yards farther up the hill, on the left, you'll see the...*

❿ City Museum (Stadtmuseum Fembohaus)

This fine museum, packed with historic artifacts, fills a former Dutch silk merchant's house dating from the late Renaissance.

Cost and Hours: €6, includes essential (if long-winded) audioguide, Tue-Fri 10:00-17:00, Sat-Sun until 18:00, closed Mon, Burgstrasse 15, tel. 0911/231-2595, www.museen.nuernberg.de.

Visiting the Museum: Start on the top floor—where you'll get an overview of the town and its history via a 12-minute video and a massive model of Nürnberg, which took four master woodcarvers four years to create, finishing in 1939 (look for the synagogue, which was destroyed by the Nazis before the model was even completed). Working your way down, you'll see the surprisingly humble Holy Roman Emperor's throne (from 1520), other reminders of Nürnberg's privileged history as an imperial city and market town, and more town models.

At the far end of the second floor is a thought-provoking painting titled *The Peace Banquet of 1649*, which documents the pan-European negotiations that took place in Nürnberg the year after the Thirty Years' War finally ended. Find headsets on the bench and listen to an emotional nine-minute account of the peace conference—the fictional narrator is the man wearing a blue cape in the painting on the opposite wall. Many of the people of his era had only known hunger, sickness, misery, and war. This historic meeting of political and diplomatic minds in Nürnberg was a sign of hope.

On the first floor, check out the maps drawn here when cartographer Johann Baptist Homann turned this merchant home into a publishing house. His heirs continued the family business for 150 years, publishing more than 3 million maps. In the Music Room, take a moment to enjoy works by Johann Pachelbel and other Nürnberger composers from the 1500s through the 1700s. A

NÜRNBERG

neighboring room has photographs of pre- and postwar Nürnberg that are are worth a quick peek.

• *Now hike the rest of the way up to the Imperial Castle. The cobbled path forks at the castle's base. The right fork leads to the castle garden and youth hostel. The left fork leads to the courtyard (with its big, round tower) of the...*

⓫ Imperial Castle (Kaiserburg)

In the Middle Ages, Holy Roman Emperors stayed here when they were in town, and the imperial regalia, including the imperial cross, imperial sword, and crown, were stored here from 1424 until 1796. While this huge complex (worth ▲) has 45 buildings, only a few are open to the public. The part on the right, which housed the stables and stockpiles of grain, is now a youth hostel.

Cost and Hours: €5.50 for castle only, €3.50 for Deep Well and Sinwell Tower, €7 combo-ticket, €2 audioguide has more background than you likely want, daily 9:00-18:00, Oct-March 10:00-16:00, tel. 0911/244-6590, www.kaiserburg-nuernberg.de.

Visiting the Castle: Start in the ticket office, where you can enjoy a 16-minute virtual-reality tour of the castle through the centuries. Then continue across the courtyard to the museum entrance. For a no-way-to-get-lost, one-way route, just follow the *Rundgang* signs. If you don't see a sign, give the closest door a nudge; it'll likely lead you to the next room.

The **Lower Hall** is empty of furniture because, in the 12th century, the imperial court was mobile. Royal roadies would arrive and set things up before the emperor got there. If you happen to be in here at :20 or :40 past the hour, you can watch a cutesy toy parade of the emperor and his entourage complete with an elephant, several feet above eye level. Through the door at the end of the hall, find the **Romanesque church**—one of few buildings that wasn't destroyed during World War II. It has a triple-decker design: lower nobility on the lower floor, upper nobility above that, and the emperor worshipping from the topmost balcony.

The **Upper Hall** (also called the Imperial Hall) is most interesting, with interactive screens and artifacts that show what the heck the Holy Roman Empire actually was. Then comes a series of creaky-floored **former living quarters,** with painted ceilings (many dismantled and stored in bunkers during the war—they're that precious), and a copy of the imperial crown (the original is in Vienna). The final exhibit is on **old weapons.**

After leaving the main exhibit area you can visit a few more parts of the castle; the most interesting are the castle well and gardens (separate or combo-ticket required for Deep Well and Sinwell Tower).

The **Deep Well** is indeed deep—165 feet (that's more than half a football field). Visits are simple, fun, and only possible with a guide (10-minute English tours leave on the hour and half-hour). You'll see water poured way, waaay down—into an incredible hole dug in the 14th century. Then the guide lowers down small candles until they almost disappear into the water table. Video monitors track its progress. A climb up the **Sinwell Tower** offers only a higher city view and lots of exercise—113 steps.

When you're finished, walk out around the round tower to enjoy a commanding **city view** from the rampart just behind it. Then backtrack down the ramp and hang a sharp right down the stairs at the small Burgwächter restaurant. Find your way to the first lane (Am Ölberg). Follow it slightly uphill, then keep right at the fork, which leads to the fine **castle garden** *(Burggarten).* Wrapped around the back of the castle, the garden offers great views of the town's 16th-century fortifications and former moat.

• *Head back out the way you came. Take the stairs immediately to your right, just outside the garden, and follow the switchback downhill. On the right and directly below you, about a block away, is a lively cobbled square called...*

⑫ Tiergärtnertorplatz

Near the top of the square, inspect the giant rabbit. While it looks like roadkill with mice gnawing at it, it's actually a modern interpretation of *The Hare,* one of the best-known paintings by medieval Nürnberg artist Albrecht Dürer. (The original painting is in Vienna.) This square is Nürnberg's de facto living room throughout the day and kicks into high gear on good-weather evenings. When the nearby restaurant and café tables are full, people find plenty of space to sit and mingle on the ground. At the bottom of the square, **Der Senfladen** (The Mustard Store) sells really good mustard, which they'll happily slather onto one of their freshly grilled Nürnberger sausage sandwiches.

• *About 20 yards beyond the well on the square, at Obere Schmiedgasse 52, is the...*

⑬ Historic Art Bunker

Behind these doors, a series of cellars worth ▲▲ are buried deep inside the rock of Castle Hill. This is where precious artworks were carefully safeguarded from the WWII air raids that devastated the city. Unfortunately, the only way to visit the bunker is with a once-daily tour (see "Tours in Nürnberg," earlier).

Nürnberg was bombed relatively late in the war, which allowed its citizens time (and experience gained from already-bombed cities to the north) to prepare for the aerial attack they knew would be coming. While many other cities sent their most important works away from the urban centers (obvious targets), Nürnberg was able to safely shelter everything right here. The art wasn't just stashed in the bunker, but carefully battened up inside wooden crates and padded with sandbags, safeguarded in a climate-controlled environment behind layer upon layer of thick fireproof doors.

Rich in art, Nürnberg had long been known as the "treasure chest of the German Empire." The pieces stored here included regalia of the Holy Roman Empire and the city's own treasures, evacuated from nearby buildings (such as the tabernacle in St. Lawrence Church, as well as all of that church's stained glass). Other pieces had been plundered by the Nazis from conquered lands, such as the Veit Stoss Altar from Kraków, Poland (later recovered by the "Monuments Men," as described in Robert Edsel's 2009 book and the 2014 movie based on it).

• *Turning back to the rabbit statue on the square, notice that it faces a half-timbered building (at the square's bottom). That's the...*

⑭ Albrecht Dürer House

Nürnberg's most famous resident lived in this house, worth ▲, for the last 20 years of his life. Albrecht Dürer (1471-1528), a contemporary of Michelangelo, studied in Venice and brought the Renaissance to stodgy medieval Germany. He did things that were unthinkable to other northern European artists of his time—such as signing his works and painting things like rabbits simply for study (not on commission). As a painter of exquisite detail, Dürer's patrons included Emperors Maximilian I and Charles V as well as King Christian II of Denmark, but he gained his steady income and international fame from the "mass production" of his prints.

Nothing in the museum is original (except the house itself, which survived WWII bombs)—all the paintings are replicas; the only Dürer originals in Nürnberg are in the Germanic National Museum (described later). But the museum does a fine job of capturing the way Dürer actually lived, and it includes a replica of the workshop, with a working printing press, where he painted and printed his woodcuts and metal engravings. Another room is a gallery with copies of Dürer's most famous paintings and woodcuts.

Cost and Hours: €6 includes overly detailed audioguide; Mon-Wed and Fri 10:00-17:00, Thu until 20:00, Sat-Sun until 18:00, closed Mon Oct-June; "Agnes" (Mrs. Dürer) leads one-hour tours in English on Sat at 14:00 for €3; ask about daily art demonstrations, Albrecht-Dürer-Strasse 39, tel. 0911/231-2568, www.museums.nuremberg.de.

• *With Albrecht's Haus on your right, head down Albrecht-Dürer-Strasse. When the street bends to the left, continue straight down the stairs, cross the street at the recommended Sebald Bistro, and veer right onto cobblestoned...*

⑮ Weissgerbergasse

"Tanners' Lane" is lined with Nürnberg's finest collection of half-timbered houses to survive the war. Such well-crafted homes, sev-

eral stories tall and many with their own wells and gardens, attest to medieval Nürnberg's considerable prosperity. What's that dark-red color so common in the painted beams of houses like these? Ox blood, which helped prevent rot and termite damage. Stop at #35 and turn around for one of the city's best photo ops. On this end of the lane, note the many small bars that turn this quiet street into a busy nightlife zone after dark.

• *Cross the wider Am Hallentor and through the recommended Biergarten Kettensteg to its namesake, the...*

⑯ Kettensteg (Chain Bridge)

This iron footbridge—the oldest on the Continent—comes with a great river view. Notice the mix of medieval fortification and

Industrial Age brickwork around here. This wasn't always considered such a picturesque quarter—it was the industrialized, downstream end of town, where you'd find water-mills, stinky industries (like the tanneries we just passed on Weissgerber-

gasse), and graphite factories. (In Germany, Nürnberg is famous for its pencils.)

NÜRNBERG

• *Our tour is over. To return to the heart of town, continue across the bridge, then head left toward the green twin towers in the distance, which mark St. Lawrence Church. Once you hit Königstrasse, it's a short walk (left) to the Hauptmarkt, with its convenient bus #36 to the Nazi sites (stops around the corner from the Beautiful Fountain).*

Or, for more sightseeing in the city center, consider a visit to one or more of the museums listed in the next section.

More Sights in Nürnberg

IN AND NEAR THE OLD TOWN
▲▲▲Germanic National Museum (Germanisches Nationalmuseum)

This sprawling, sweeping museum is dedicated to the cultural history of the German-speaking world. It's gorgeously presented, nicely lit, and well-described by its audioguide. For German history buffs, this museum alone makes a visit to Nürnberg worthwhile. It occupies an interconnected maze of buildings, old and new, in the southern part of the Old Town, near the station and recommended hotels. Approaching the museum along Kartäusergasse, you'll walk along the "Way of Human Rights." Designed by an Israeli artist, its pillars trumpet the provisions of the United Nations' Universal Declaration of Human Rights, each in a different language.

Cost and Hours: €8, free Wed after 18:00; open Tue-Sun 10:00-18:00, Wed until 21:00, closed Mon; worthwhile audioguide-€2 (ID required), check website for occasional English tours, two blocks west of Königstrasse at Kartäusergasse 1, enter through the modern glass lobby in middle of street, tel. 0911/13310, www.gnm.de.

Eating: The lower-level cafeteria, while pricey, is top quality, with elegant and artfully presented dishes.

Visiting the Museum: To avoid feeling overwhelmed by this vast museum, pick up the English floor plan/brochure and use it to choose things you're particularly interested in. I'd go more or less chronologically, starting on the ground floor with the Holy Roman Empire and Middle Ages artifacts, then to the first floor's Renaissance/Baroque collection of German art and gadgets.

The **entry hall** is dominated by a wall displaying street signs from East Germany—complete with a little politically motivated spray paint—dating from the time when the Soviets had renamed the main drag in many towns *Strasse der Befreiung* ("Street of the Liberation" from the Nazis and capitalism).

Facing the signs wall, enter the museum wing to your left for a glimpse at some evocative medieval artifacts, including a gilded reliquary shrine and a series of well-preserved tapestries depicting courtly love.

As you turn to head up to the first floor, *Germania*—a 19th-century painting of the motherland incarnate—proudly greets you, as if she can't wait for you to see what's next. The museum's star attraction is its **German art collection** in the Renaissance/Baroque exhibit. Starting in Room 114, you'll find Albrecht Dürer's meticulously detailed paintings (the only originals in town) of Charlemagne, Emperor Sigismund, and Dürer's mother. Look for the delicate wooden *Nürnberg Madonna* (1515). This intimate, anonymous carving of the favorite hometown girl was the city's symbol during the 19th-century Romantic Age. Farther on, Lucas

Cranach the Younger's polyptych *Heart-Shaped Winged Altarpiece* (Room 110)—as well as his father's *Ill-Matched Pair* (Room 111)—are worth a gander. Works on display by woodcarver Tilman Riemenschneider hint at the skills he used to make masterpieces such as the *Altar of the Holy Blood* at Rothenburg's St. Jacob's Church.

Another highlight is the oldest surviving **globe** in the world, crafted by Nürnberg's own Martin Behaim (since it dates from 1492, the Americas are conspicuously missing; Room 103a). For those interested in the Reformation, there's a wonderful Martin Luther section (Room 117). One non-German painting of note is of—and by—the young Rembrandt. Only recently did experts determine that this is a true **self-portrait** by the Dutch artist and not a copy, as originally believed (Room 123).

Of Nürnberg's 200 churches, only one escaped the WWII bombs. Return downstairs to see the historic core of the museum building, an old monastery filled with original, surviving **statues** from the city's bombed-out churches and fountains. The rest of this huge museum covers a vast spectrum of German culture, from fine arts to prehistory to science to musical instruments, plus regular temporary exhibits.

▲▲Nürnberg Transport Museum

Just outside the city walls, within the mighty Nürnberg Transport Museum building, are the Deutsche Bahn's German Railway

(DB) Museum and the Communications Museum. As you'll end up weaving in and out of both museums—and your ticket includes both—think of them as one sight.

Cost and Hours: €6, €5 with any same-day transit ticket, free with valid rail pass; Tue-Fri 9:00-17:00, Sat-Sun 10:00-18:00, closed Mon; reasonably priced café, near the Germanic National Museum at Lessingstrasse 6; DB Museum tel. 0800-326-87386, www.dbmuseum.de.

Visiting the Museum: Pick up the free English booklet as you enter and ask about the model train demo (runs hourly). The €1 audioguide is essential for the ground floor, where no English descriptions are posted.

Start on the ground floor, where you'll discover the modest origins of Germany's now impressive rail system and learn about the railways' influence on German history. Skip the halls with the original trains until later (you'll pass them on your way out) and find the exhibit "Serving Dictatorship," which explains the role of the rail system during the Nazi regime.

After your ground floor visit, return your audioguide and head up one level for an exhibit on the evolution of rail travel and the massive and fascinating-to-watch model railway demonstration.

The top floor hosts the Kibala Kids' Railwayland, where young visitors can play dress-up, try out simulators, and ride a five-gauge minitrain. Another wing covers the story of human communication with lots of activities that are both kid- and adult-friendly: Write a letter with a quill, see the evolution of telephony, play postman with pneumatic tubes, and watch some German TV.

Back on the ground floor, check out the original trains you missed before, including "Mad" King Ludwig's crown-topped *Salonwagen*—practically a palace on wheels. Like his equally grandiose Neuschwanstein Castle, this train was barely used by Ludwig—who preferred to travel incognito.

At the far end of the hall, near the glass doors, admire the replica of the *Adler*—the first steam-powered locomotive in Germany (the original debuted in Nürnberg in 1835 and had a cruising speed of 35 kilometers per hour). It's displayed side-by-side with an Inter-City Express train (which tops out at 300 kilometers per hour). It's fun to ponder how far train technology has come in less than 200 years.

Pass through the glass doors, cross the street, go through a tunnel, and find a display hall just to your right, filled with handcarts and other railway contraptions. If you continue through the hall, you'll find an open-air exhibit with lots more trains.

Neues Museum

Nürnberg's "new museum" of contemporary art fills a striking glass building right by the town wall (near the train station), with two quiet, bright, and air-conditioned floors of sleek design pieces, installations that might make you go "Hmmm," and edgy Pop and abstract artworks.

Cost and Hours: €5, €1 on Sun, additional fees for special exhibits; open Tue-Sun 10:00-18:00, Thu until 20:00, closed Mon; behind recommended Hotel Victoria on Klarissenplatz, tel. 0911/240-2069, www.nmn.de.

Toy Museum (Spielzeugmuseum)

This museum's chronological/thematic display makes for a breezy and nostalgic history lesson, starting from the wooden toys on the ground floor that exemplify German woodworking traditions, and culminating with the corporate-branded toys three floors up (the top floor has a play zone). For many, the highlight is the miniature replica of the Omaha train station (third floor up), while others are fascinated, or perplexed, by the display of pro-Nazi toys.

Cost and Hours: €6, €1.50 for kids; Tue-Fri 10:00-17:00, Sat-Sun until 18:00, closed Mon; the €1 audioguide is worth it, Karlstrasse 13, near Albrecht Dürer House, tel. 0911/231-3164, www.museen.nuernberg.de.

NAZI SITES

Though Nürnberg tries to present itself as the "City of Human Rights," its reputation as Hitler's favorite place for a really big party is hard to shake. To understand the city's place in the Nazi era, visit Hitler's vast Nazi Party Rally Grounds (Reichsparteitagsgelände) and the excellent museum—the Nazi Documentation Center—set amid the mute remains of the Third Reich.

The courtroom where the Nürnberg Trials were held is across town from the Documentation Center and Rally Grounds and has much less to offer visitors.

Planning Your Time: With half a day, spend two hours in the museum, peek into the courtyard of the Congress Hall, and walk to Zeppelin Field and back. History buffs can easily spend an entire day here. The map in this book is enough to guide you around the site, but you can buy a more detailed map and guide from the museum counter. Also consider the small English-language book (€7). For lunch, skip the disappointing museum café and try the excellent Gutmann's beer garden at the lake (midway between the museum and Zeppelin Field).

If you opt to also visit the courtroom and its exhibit, allow another two hours, including travel time from the train station.

Getting to the Nazi Documentation Center and Rally

NÜRNBERG

Grounds: The sprawling complex is wrapped around a lake called Dutzendteich, southeast of the Old Town. Take tram #8, which leaves from the front of the Postbank Center next to the train station (Hauptbahnhof) every 10 minutes (direction: Doku-Zentrum, 10-minute trip). From the Hauptmarkt (around the corner from the fountain, on Waaggasse) or Rathaus (City Hall), you can hop on bus #36, which ends at the Doku-Zentrum stop. Both options go about every 10 minutes. For ticket options, see "Getting Around Nürnberg," earlier. Stepping off either the tram or bus, you'll see the Documentation Center.

▲▲▲Nazi Documentation Center (Dokumentationszentrum)

Visitors to Europe's Nazi and Holocaust sites inevitably ask the same question: How could this happen? This superb museum does its best to provide an answer. It  meticulously traces the evolution of the National Socialist movement, focusing on how it both energized and terrified the German people (the exhibit's title is "Fascination and Terror"). Special attention is paid to Nürnberg's role in the Nazi movement, including the construction and use of the Rally Grounds, where Hitler's largest demonstrations took place. This is not a WWII or Holocaust museum; those events are almost an afterthought. Instead, the center frankly analyzes the Nazi phenomenon to understand how it happened—and to prevent it from happening again.

Cost and Hours: €6, includes essential audioguide, Mon-Fri 9:00-18:00, Sat-Sun from 10:00, last entry at 17:00, Bayernstrasse 110, tel. 0911/231-7538, www.museen.nuernberg.de.

Services and Information: Use the lobby WC before or after your visit as there are none within the exhibit. Inside the museum, the exhibit is a one-way walk; allow at least two hours. WWII history buffs should plan on an extra hour for the various 10-minute videos that play continuously throughout the exhibit, offering excellent insights into the mass hypnosis of the German nation. Descriptions are in German only, so the English audioguide is a must (turns on automatically at video presentations; dial room numbers for overviews and specific numbers for details of displays—if rushed, listen to the overviews only).

Visiting the Documentation Center: The museum is housed in one small wing of Hitler's cavernous, unfinished Congress Hall—the largest surviving example of Nazi architecture. The

Nazi Documentation Center & Rally Grounds

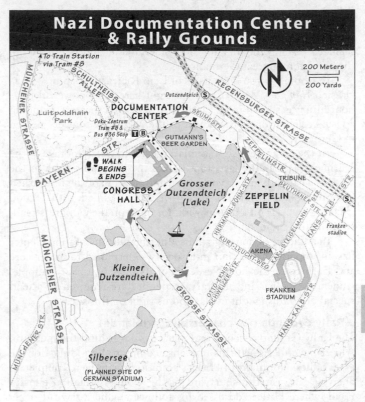

To Train Station via Tram #8 — SCHULTHEISS ALLEE — MÜNCHENER STRASSE — Luitpoldhain Park — DOCUMENTATION CENTER — Doku-Zentrum Tram #8 & Bus #36 Stop — BAYERN-STR. — WALK BEGINS & ENDS — CONGRESS HALL — Dutzendteich — REGENSBURGER STRASSE — SEUMESTR. — GUTMANN'S BEER GARDEN — ZEPPELINSTR. — Grosser Dutzendteich (Lake) — TRIBUNE — BEUTHENER-STR. — ZEPPELIN FIELD — HERMANN-PÖHLM.-STR. — KURT-LEUCHT-WEG — ARENA — Kleiner Dutzendteich — GROSSE STRASSE — OTTO-ERNST-SCHWEKER-STR. — KARL-STEIGELMANN-STR. — HANS-KALB-STR. — FRANKEN STADIUM — Franken-stadion — Silbersee — (PLANNED SITE OF GERMAN STADIUM) — MÜNCHENER STR.

200 Meters / 200 Yards

NÜRNBERG

building was planned to host the mammoth annual Nazi Party gatherings. Today, it has been symbolically cut open by its modern entryway—exposing the guts and brains of the Nazi movement.

The museum's purpose-built structure is sometimes called "a spear through Speer"—it's a jolt of glassy, modern construction that slices through the original Albert Speer-designed building. (Just as post-WWII doctors didn't want to take advantage of medical knowledge gained through Nazi torture, modern architects who designed the museum didn't want to utilize anything the Nazis had built.)

The somewhat dated introductory video has you following two skateboarding kids on a dreamy now-and-then tour of the entire complex. Once inside, you'll see copies of *Mein Kampf* (the sale of which was forbidden in Germany until 2015). Photos and video show Hitler-mania and how the cult of Hitler was created, which included placing the dictator alongside Goethe and Beethoven in the pantheon of great Germans.

In Room 14, you'll see parts of Leni Riefenstahl's propaganda classic *Triumph of the Will,* filmed right here. This powerful two-hour film was shown in all German schools and theaters, bringing a visual celebration of the power of the Nazi state to every person in Germany.

At the end, you'll sit in a small theater to watch footage of the Nürnberg Trials. The last stop (before the long ramp back to the start) is a catwalk giving you a look into the core of the unfinished Congress Hall (an artist's sketch of the hall filled with 50,000 cheering Nazis is on a nearby wall; for more on the Congress Hall, see its listing, below).

In addition to housing a museum, the Documentation Center has an important function in a society determined to underscore and learn from the horrible deeds of its dark past. For example, students at police and military academies are required to attend special programs taught in classrooms right on this site.

▲Rally Grounds (Reichsparteitagsgelände)

The Rally Grounds occupy four square miles behind the museum. Albert Speer designed this immense complex of buildings for the Nazi rallies. Not many of Hitler's ambitious plans were completed, but you can visit the courtyard of the Congress Hall, Zeppelin Field (where Hitler addressed his followers), and a few other remains. The easiest way to see them is to follow the circular route around the lake that's shown on the "Nazi Documentation Center & Rally Grounds" map and on the museum's free bilingual area plan *(Geländeplan).* The numbers on the plan correspond to the information pillars that you'll find on-site (this information also available at www.kubiss.de).

Figure a 1.5-hour round-trip from the Documentation Center for the full circuit. If you have less time, just look into the courtyard of the Congress Hall from the perch at the end of your museum visit and then walk the short way around the lake directly to Zeppelin Field and back. If you're really short on time, skip this walk, as you'll get the best sense of the Rally Grounds and how they were used simply from the videos and exhibits inside the Documentation Center.

❍ **Self-Guided Walk:** I've listed the main sites here in the order you reach them while circling the lake.

Congress Hall (Kongresshalle): This huge building—big enough for an audience of 50,000—was originally intended to be topped with a roof and skylight. The Nazi Documentation Center occupies part of the hall. To see the vast, Colosseum-like courtyard, turn right as you leave the Documentation Center, and walk along the side of the building. Dip through the archway into the courtyard to appreciate its dimensions. Notice the

stacked stones still awaiting further construction, untouched since the 1930s. Part of the hall is now used by the Nürnberg symphony orchestra.

• *Turn around and return to the lakeside path and continue walking with the Congress Hall on your right. Just after you round the first corner to the right, look across the lake. The lights you see in the distance hover above Franken Stadium (a 1928 soccer field before Hitler used it for Nazi rallies and, more recently, a venue of the 2006 World Cup).*

Continue past the end of the building, and then turn left (under the Kommen Sie gut nach Hause *sign) onto the...*

Great Road (Grosse Strasse): At 200 feet wide, the Great Road was big enough to be used as a runway by the Allies after the war. Now it's a parking lot for trucks serving the nearby conference center. The road points toward Nürnberg's Imperial Castle—Hitler's symbolic connection to the Holy Roman Empire (the First Reich).

Ahead and to the right was to be the site of the **German Stadium** (Deutsches Stadion)—the biggest in the world (with 400,000 seats). They got as far as digging a foundation before funding was redirected to the war effort. Today, the site is a park surrounding a lake, Silbersee—which filled the hole for the never-built stadium's foundation. Even farther ahead, where you can see the rooflines of a nearby suburb, the Nazis had a campground filled with 400 huge tents holding up to 100,000 rally participants. The campers bonded through a regimented communal experience that emphasized military discipline.

• *From here, you can detour across the road to an information sign about the stadium. Otherwise, follow the (main) Dutzendteich lakeshore to the left for about 15 minutes until you hit a parking lot. To your right is the huge...*

Zeppelin Field (Zeppelinwiese): This was the site of the Nazis' biggest rallies, including those (in)famously filmed by Leni Riefenstahl. You can climb up on the decaying grandstand and stand on the platform in front of the Zeppelin Tribune, where Hitler stood to survey the masses (up to 150,000 people at a time). The Tribune is based on the design of the ancient Greek Pergamon Altar

NÜRNBERG

Nazis in Nürnberg

It makes sense that Nürnberg appealed to Hitler. Nürnberg is centrally located in Germany, making it a handy meeting point for Nazi supporters. And, Hitler had a friend here, Julius Streicher (a.k.a. the "Franconian Führer"), who fanned the flames of Nazism and anti-Semitism with his inflammatory newspaper *Der Stürmer* (The Storm Trooper).

More importantly, Nürnberg was steeped in German history. Long before Nazism, the city—once home to Albrecht Dürer and the Holy Roman Emperor, and packed with buildings in the German Gothic style—was nicknamed the "most German of German cities." As one of the most important cities of medieval Europe, Nürnberg appealed to Hitler as a way to legitimize his Third Reich by invoking Germany's glorious past. Hitler loved the idea of staging rallies within sight of the Imperial Castle, a symbol of the "First Reich" (the Holy Roman Empire).

When Hitler took power in 1933, he made Nürnberg the site of his *Reichsparteitage*—**Nazi Party Rallies.** Increasingly elaborate celebrations of Nazi culture, ideology, and power took place here annually for the next six years. The chilling images from Leni Riefenstahl's documentary *Triumph of the Will* were filmed at the 1934 rallies and then shown in every theater and schoolroom in the country. At

the 1935 rallies, the Nazis devised the first laws—which came to be known as the **Nürnberg Laws**—that legally defined Jews as second-class citizens.

Hitler and his favorite architect, Albert Speer, designed massive buildings (such as a stadium seating 400,000 spectators) to host the proceedings. Only a few were completed before World War II broke out. Today, it's possible to walk around the still-unfinished remains of the megalomaniacal super-structures. The Rally Grounds were the ultimate example of Hitler's preferred architecture style: stark, huge, and Neoclassical. (Historians are hesitant to use the term "Nazi architecture," as much of it was stolen from other styles and simply enlarged. For example, Hitler adored the Roman Colosseum so he had his Congress Hall built at double the scale.)

Near war's end, the world puzzled over what to do with the Nazis who had overseen some of the most gruesome atrocities in the history of humankind. It was finally decided that they should be tried as war criminals by an international tribunal (spearheaded by the US and based on the Anglo-American code of law). These trials took place in the **Nürnberg Trials Courtroom.** The Nürnberg Trials—the first international war-crimes tribunal—brought about a new concept of international law, which continues today in The Hague, Netherlands.

(now in Berlin's Pergamon Museum); it was originally topped by a towering swastika (which was blown up by the Allies at the end of the war) and flanked on either side by massive colonnades. For night-time rallies Speer created a dramatic "Cathedral of

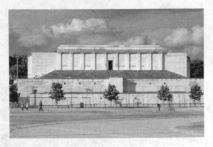

Light"—with 130 searchlights surrounding the field pointed skyward. *Warning:* Clowning around on the speaking platform with any Nazi gestures is illegal and taken seriously by the police.

• *From Zeppelin Field, continue the rest of the way around the lake, past Gutmann's beer garden (a good lunch option), and back to the Documentation Center (and the bus and tram stop).*

Nürnberg Trials Courtroom and Museum (Memorium Nürnberger Prozesse)

Across town from the Documentation Center and Rally Grounds is the courtroom where the Nürnberg Trials were held.

In 1945, in Room 600 of Nürnberg's Palace of Justice, 21 Nazi war criminals stood trial before an international tribunal of judges appointed by the four victorious countries. It was during these trials that the world learned of the full scale of the Holocaust and heard firsthand accounts from victims and perpetrators alike. The trials were also legally novel, setting a precedent for international law that has since been followed in a number of post-atrocity tribunals (think South Africa, Rwanda, Bosnia). Before the Nürnberg Trials, there was no such legal concept as a "crime against humanity."

After a year of trials and deliberations, 12 Nazis were sentenced to death by hanging, 3 were acquitted, and the rest were sent to prison. One of the death sentences was for Hitler's right-hand man, Hermann Göring. He asked to be shot by firing squad—a proper military execution—but his request was denied. Instead, two hours before his scheduled hanging, Göring committed suicide with poison he had smuggled into his cell, infuriating many who thought that this death was too easy for him.

Cost and Hours: €6, includes audioguide; Wed-Fri and Mon 9:00-18:00, Sat-Sun from 10:00, closed Tue, last entry one hour before closing; tel. 0911/3217-9372, www.memorium-nuremberg. de.

Getting There: The building is a five-stop subway ride from the Hauptbahnhof: Take the U-1 subway line (direction: Fürth Hardhöhe) to Bärenschanze, exit the station following signs for *Sielstrasse,* and continue 200 yards along the main street (Fürther

Strasse) to the huge court building, turning right at the corner with the tall signs showing the four national flags. It's at Bärenschanz-strasse 72.

Visiting the Courtroom and Museum: There are two parts to the experience here: the courtroom (upstairs from the entrance) and the museum (farther up on the top floor). You can usually enter the courtroom itself, but as it's still in occasional use, you could find it closed, especially if you come on a weekday. You're pretty much assured of getting to see the courtroom on a Saturday or Sunday. If it's important to you, call the museum (no more than a week in advance) to ask about the court schedule.

Unfortunately, the museum displays are almost all in German, and there's little here in the way of artifacts. The outrageously long-winded audioguide gives exact translations of the printed information.

Sleeping in Nürnberg

Prices spike during major conventions in the spring and fall, and in December—when the Christmas market brings visitors from around the world. Nürnberg gets a lot of business travelers, so some hotels drop their rates on weekends. July and August are generally low season and come with the lowest prices. See the "Central Nürnberg Hotels" map for locations.

NEAR THE KÖNIGSTOR, ON KÖNIGSTRASSE

These hotels, clustered along Königstrasse—just inside the Königstor and the city walls—are convenient to both the train station and city sightseeing. From the station, you can roll your luggage here in five minutes without a single stair.

$$$ Hotel Drei Raben is an artsy and fun splurge, with a stylish lobby, 22 comfortable rooms, a huge breakfast buffet (eggs and cappuccino by request), and lots of elegant and whimsical touches. Friendly Ralph and his staff offer free wine tastings and music nightly, and Matti happily shares info on his favorite local beers and hangouts. In this "theme hotel," you might get the Dürer room, the soccer room (equipped with a foosball table), the toys room, or even the graffiti room (family rooms, nearby apartment, air-con, elevator, pay valet parking, Königstrasse 63, tel. 0911/274-380, www.hoteldreiraben.de, info@hoteldreiraben.de).

$$ Hotel Victoria offers a friendly staff and 65 fresh, new-

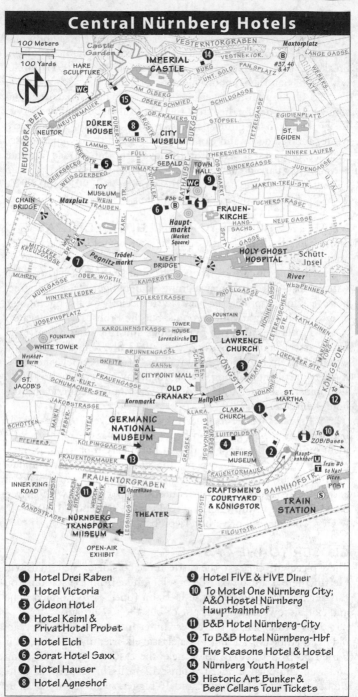

Central Nürnberg Hotels

100 Meters
100 Yards

Castle Garden
VESTERNTORGRABEN
Maxtorplatz
LANGE GASSE
HARE SCULPTURE
IMPERIAL CASTLE
VESTNEKTOR.
#37, 46 & 47
WEBERS PLATZ
BURG
UNT. SOLD. PAN. SPLATZ
AM OLBERG
WC
OBERE SCHMIED
SCHILDGASSE
AL. DÜRER-STR.
OB. KRAMERS.
BURGSTR.
STÖPSEL.
TETZELGASSE
EGIDIENPLATZ
DÜRER HOUSE
BERGSTR.
AGNES.
CITY MUSEUM
ST. EGIDEN
KREBS.
LÄMMS.
FÜLL
THERESIENSTR.
INNERE LAUFER
GEIERSBERG
WEISSGERBER
WEINMARKT
ST. SEBALD
OBSTMARKT
BINDERGASSE
JUDENGASSE
U. TAL
NEUTORGRABEN
NEUTOR
WINKLER.
RATHAUSPL.
TOWN HALL
MARTIN-TREU-STR.
TOY MUSEUM
WEIN.
WC
Maxplatz
KARL.
KRAUBEN.
#56
TUCHERSTRASSE
CHAIN BRIDGE
MITTLERE KREUZGASSE
MAX BRÜCKE
Pegnitz
Trödelmarkt
Haupt-markt (Market Square)
FRAUEN-KIRCHE
HANS-SACHS-
NEUE GASSE
HOLY GHOST HOSPITAL
Schütt-Insel
Hotel Hauser
OBER. WÖRTH.
"MEAT BRIDGE"
SEITAL G.
River
MÜHREN.
MÜHLGASSE
KAISERSTR.
WESPENNEST.
HINTERE LEDER.
ADLERSTRASSE
FINDELGASSE
JOSEPHSPLATZ
KAROLINENSTRASSE
TOWER HOUSE
FOUNTAIN
NONNENGASSE
KATHARINEN.
FOUNTAIN
WHITE TOWER
Weisser-turm
Lorenzkirche
ST. LAWRENCE CHURCH
PETER-VISCHER-STR.
MARIEN-TOR-G.
KÖNIGS-OR.
ST. JACOB'S
BREITE.
BRUNNENGASSE
FRAUENGASSE
DR. KURT-SCHUMACHER-STR.
KREBS.
GASSE
CITYPOINT MALL
FARHEN-SCHIED.
KÖNIGSTR.
LORENZER STR.
To
JAKOBSTR.
KORNMARKT
OLD GRANARY
Hallplatz
JOHANNE.
ST. MARTHA
SCHOTTEN
MAIEN.
FARBER.
ENTEN.
GERMANIC NATIONAL MUSEUM
GRASER.
KLARA.
STERNGASSE
CLARA CHURCH
To ZOB/Buses
&
PFEIFER.
KOLPINGGASSE
LUITPOLDSTR.
NEUES MUSEUM
Haupt-bahnhof
tram #8 to Nazi Sites
INNER RING ROAD
FRAUENTORMAUER
VORDERE
BAHNHOFSTR.
POST
EISENMANN-STRASSE
WEBER-KELLERSTR.
U
Opernhaus
FRAUENTORGRABEN
FRAUENTORMAUER
CRAFTSMEN'S COURTYARD & KÖNIGSTOR
TRAIN STATION
SANDSTRASSE
ZELTNERSTR.
LESSINGSTR.
TÄFEL.O.F.STR.
THEATER
FILGUTSTR.
NÜRNBERG TRANSPORT MUSEUM
OPEN-AIR EXHIBIT

NÜRNBERG

1 Hotel Drei Raben
2 Hotel Victoria
3 Gideon Hotel
4 Hotel Keiml & PrivatHotel Probst
5 Hotel Elch
6 Sorat Hotel Saxx
7 Hotel Hauser
8 Hotel Agneshof

9 Hotel FIVE & FIVE Diner
10 To Motel One Nürnberg City; A&O Hostel Nürnberg Hauptbahnhof
11 B&B Hotel Nürnberg-City
12 To B&B Hotel Nürnberg-Hbf
13 Five Reasons Hotel & Hostel
14 Nürnberg Youth Hostel
15 Historic Art Bunker & Beer Cellars Tour Tickets

feeling rooms behind its historic 1896 facade just inside the König-stor. The standard rooms are a better value than the slightly big-ger business rooms (rooms with air-con extra, elevator, indulgent breakfast, pay parking garage, Königstrasse 80, tel. 0911/24050, www.hotelvictoria.de, book@hotelvictoria.de).

$$ Gideon Hotel, overlooking the main pedestrian drag, has somewhat less personality than the Drei Raben but plenty of style. Its 27 rooms, many quite spacious, are decked out in a chic black, white, and red decor and can often be had at a good value. In nice weather, breakfast is served on the lovely rooftop terrace (air-con, elevator, pay parking at Parkhaus Katharinenhof, Grasersgasse 25 but enter around the corner on Theatergasse, tel. 0911/660-0970, www.gideonhotels.de, info@gideonhotels.de, friendly Nadine).

NEAR THE KÖNIGSTOR, ON LUITPOLDSTRASSE

These two affordable, family-run hotels are next door to each other, around the corner from the ones just described, set amidst a harm-less sprinkling of casinos, strip clubs, and sex shops. Either hotel will do just fine if you're watching your budget. To avoid street noise, ask for a room on the back side (especially for Fri-Sat nights). The Keiml has slightly nicer rooms, but the Probst has an elevator.

$ Hotel Keiml is run by gracious and tiny Frau Keiml, who has been welcoming guests here since 1975. She rents 22 bright and worn rooms up two long, smoky flights of stairs (no elevator) in a former apartment building (RS%, worth paying extra for breakfast, Luitpoldstrasse 7, tel. 0911/226-240, www.hotel-keiml.de, garni@hotel-keiml.de).

$ PrivatHotel Probst has been run for over 70 years by the hardworking Probst family on floors 2-4 of an 18th-century apart-ment building. They rent 29 decent but musty rooms, some more recently renovated than others. The family's been slowly updat-ing the space and now there's a modern breakfast room (breakfast extra, no air-con but fans on request, cheaper rooms with shared bath, elevator to third floor, Luitpoldstrasse 9, tel. 0911/203-433, www.probst.bayern, privathotel@probst.bayern).

CLOSER TO THE CASTLE

These places are closer to the castle at the far side of the Old Town. Getting here is a €10 taxi ride or a long hike from the station. You can get partway by taking the U-Bahn (line #1) to Lorenzkirche and exiting toward Kaiserstrasse or bus #36 to Rathaus.

$$$ Hotel Elch, the oldest hotel in town (with 500-year-old exposed beams adding to its classic elk-friendly woodiness), is buried deep in the Old Town near the castle. It rents charming and well-equipped modern rooms: 12 in its original 1342 half-timbered "History" building, and 16 bigger, swankier rooms in its

"Boutique" wing next door (pay parking, near St. Sebald Church at Irrerstrasse 9, tel. 0911/249-2980, www.hotel-elch.com, info@hotel-elch.com).

$$ Sorat Hotel Saxx, from its sleek lobby up to its 103 rooms, is professionally run. Most rooms aren't terribly big, but they're stylish, fresh, often reasonably priced, and in the middle of town, right on the Hauptmarkt (breakfast extra, family rooms, elevator, pay parking, at Hauptmarkt 17 but enter at Waaggasse 7, tel. 0911/242-700, www.sorat-hotels.com, saxx-nuernberg@sorat-hotels.com).

$$ Hotel Hauser offers 21 stylishly sleek yet comfortable rooms bedecked in green-and-purple velvet. Located on a charming square on the west side of town, it's a quiet oasis with boutique elegance at a good price (pay parking, Unschittplatz 7, tel. 0911/214-6690, www.hotel-hauser.com, info@hotel-hauser.com).

$$ Hotel Agneshof is tastefully casual with 74 no-frills, clean rooms. I'd spring for the slightly more expensive fourth-floor castle-view rooms. The spa and sauna are free for guests (family rooms, limited pay parking, Agnesgasse 10, tel. 0911/214-440, www.sorat-hotels.com, agneshof-nuernberg@sorathotels.com).

$ Hotel FIVE sports 16 rooms that match the natural wood-and-earth tones of the FIVE Diner, its trendy burger bar on the ground floor. Most rooms are fairly spacious, and some have balconies—all are a good value (Obstmarkt 5, tel. 0911/223-375, www.hotelfive.de, info@hotelfive.de).

JUST BEYOND THE CITY WALLS

$ Motel One Nürnberg City is part of a German chain offering cookie-cutter style and virtually no amenities. Despite its location with train tracks on one side and a busy street on the other, only a few travelers will need earplugs. It's low-cost modern, an easy walk to the city center, and generally less crowded on weekends (breakfast extra, no air-con, pay parking, Bahnhofstrasse 18, tel. 0911/274-3170, www.motel-one.com, nuernberg-city@motel-one.com).

$ B&B Hotel Nürnberg-City isn't a B&B by any stretch, but its 135 pleasant rooms are a solid value. Though it feels more like an IKEA catalogue than most hotels, its accommodations are a few steps above most hostels' private rooms (breakfast extra, air-con, elevator, family rooms, wheelchair-accessible room, limited pay parking, across from city walls at Frauentorgraben 37, from station take U-2 one stop to Opernhaus, tel. 0911/378-510, www.hotelbb.de, nuernberg-city@hotelbb.com). Their second location, **B&B Hotel Nürnberg-Hbf,** with the same rates, is about 500 yards from the station at Marienstrasse 10 (tel. 0911/367-760, nuernberg-hbf@hotelbb.com).

NÜRNBERG

HOSTELS

Budget travelers beyond traditional backpacker-age should consider private rooms offered by the Five Reasons Hostel, where those of any age will feel comfortable.

¢ **Five Reasons Hotel & Hostel** is the best kind of budget accommodation: clean, bright, centrally located, and run with care. None of the rooms here has its own bath, but the shared bathrooms are some of the swankiest hostel bathrooms I've seen (breakfast extra, private rooms available, family apartments, elevator, pleasant terrace, bike rentals, limited pay parking, facing the town walls around the corner from the Germanic National Museum at Frauentormauer 42, tel. 0911/9928-6625, www.five-reasons.de, booking@five-reasons.de).

¢ **Nürnberg Youth Hostel**—once the imperial stables and granary—is romantically situated at the top of the Old Town inside the castle complex (at the far right as you face it). It's scenic but expensive for a hostel, and can be crowded with school groups in the summer. For the best views, request an eighth- or ninth-floor tower room (private rooms available, family rooms, lunch/dinner available, elevator, Burg 2, tel. 0911/230-9360, www.nuernberg.jugendherberge.de, nuernberg@jugendherberge.de). To reach the hostel from the train station, take the U-3 subway three stops to Maxfeld, then walk (level, 12 minutes) or take the #37, #46, or #47 bus two stops back to Maxtor.

¢ **A&O Hostel Nürnberg Hauptbahnhof,** just outside the medieval city center on busy Bahnhofstrasse, is vast and institutional. The hostel caters to a wide range of travelers, from backpackers to families. To avoid street noise, ask for a room facing the courtyard (breakfast extra, private rooms available, fans for rent but no air-con, bar and lounge in lobby, some pay parking, Bahnhofstrasse 13, tel. 0911/309-168-4401, www.aohostels.com, booking@aohostels.com).

Eating in Nürnberg

SOUTH OF THE RIVER, NEAR THE STATION

Königstrasse, the main pedestrian boulevard leading from the train station into the old center, is lined with enticing places to eat. All along this street you'll find department stores, many with efficient cafeterias, popular restaurant chains, and memorable one-offs. The following places are my favorites on or just off Königstrasse, working from the station to the center.

$$$ Istanbul Restaurant, across from the recommended Hotel Drei Raben, is a local favorite for Turkish food, including *döner kebabs* and fresh *ayran* (yogurt drinks), with late-night hours, friendly service, and great outdoor seating for people-watching

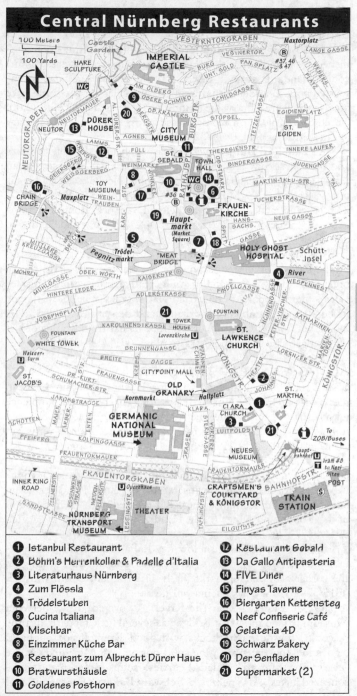

Central Nürnberg Restaurants

1. Istanbul Restaurant
2. Böhm's Herrenkeller & Padelle d'Italia
3. Literaturhaus Nürnberg
4. Zum Flössla
5. Trödelstuben
6. Cucina Italiana
7. Mischbar
8. Einzimmer Küche Bar
9. Restaurant zum Albrecht Dürer Haus
10. Bratwursthäusle
11. Goldenes Posthorn
12. Restaurant Sebald
13. Da Gallo Antipasteria
14. FIVE Diner
15. Finyas Taverne
16. Biergarten Kettensteg
17. Neef Confiserie Café
18. Gelateria 4D
19. Schwarz Bakery
20. Der Senfladen
21. Supermarket (2)

(daily 8:00-5:00 in the morning, air-con on upper floor, Königstrasse 60, tel. 0911/2124-8330).

$$$ Böhm's Herrenkeller is cozy, with a hunting-room ambience. It's proudly traditional but not kitschy, serving classic Franconian standards at good prices. Try the *Schweineschäufele* (oven-roasted pork shoulder with dumplings and salad) or the fixed-price meals, which are a fine value (Mon-Sat 11:30-14:30 & 17:30-22:00, closed Sun, a block off Königstrasse across from the Old Granary at Theatergasse 9, tel. 0911/224-465).

$$ Padelle d'Italia serves up reasonably priced and tasty pizza and pasta in a cozy and lively setting. Their sizable classic Italian dishes and daily seasonal specials are splittable, but seafood here is pricey. Reserve ahead for dinner (Mon-Sat 11:30-14:00 & 17:30-23:00 except open all day Fri-Sat, closed Sun, near Böhm's Herrenkeller at Theatergasse 17, tel. 0911/274-2130, www.padelleditalia.de).

$$ Literaturhaus Nürnberg is a casual Parisian-style café run by the local book club and popular for readings. It serves theme breakfasts (daily until 15:00) and creative international dishes. Locals like to order several varied plates, tapas-style, or just enjoy its bookish café ambience for drinks and desserts (Mon-Fri 7:00-24:00, Sat from 9:00, Sun 9:00-18:00, 2 blocks from Königstor just off Königstrasse at Luitpoldstrasse 6, tel. 0911/234-2658).

ALONG AND NEAR THE RIVER

$$$ Zum Flössla is packed with locals who like heavy German meals with an international flair. It's got a "been around" ambience with rustic, red-and-white-checked decor. With tables shoehorned into a tight space and elbow room at a premium, it can get warm (Tue-Sat 16:30-22:30, closed Sun-Mon, Unterer Bergauerplatz 12, tel. 0911/227-495).

$$ Trödelstuben is chock-full of kitschy and intriguing knick-knacks (*trödel* means "stuff" or "junk") and serves up basic, hearty Franconian dishes that go well with their selection of local beers and wines (daily 11:00-23:00, Trödelmarkt 30, tel. 0911/3677-2767).

$$ Cucina Italiana is a low-key Italian restaurant with splittable pizzas (plenty for two), fresh pastas, and sidewalk seating on the corner of the Haupmarkt (daily 11:30-23:00, Obstmarkt, tel. 0911/378-51956, www.cucina-online.de).

Quick Lunches near the River: A covered arcade between Museum Bridge and Meat Bridge has several little modern, healthy places in a row near a Starbucks, with good seating inside, out back, or overlooking the river. One solid option is **$ Mischbar,** where "everything's mixed" (salads, curries, soups, smoothies, fresh-squeezed juices). Also nearby, **$ Schwarz Bakery** serves traditional

The Nürnberger Bratwurst

Nürnberg is famous for its pinkie-sized bratwurst (called, like a city resident, a "Nürnberger"). Local butchers churn out 1.3 billion of the little buggers every year. Nürnbergers—the people—insist that size doesn't matter; they maintain that *in der Kürze liegt die Würze* ("in the shortness lies the tastiness"). All over town, signs read *3 im Weckle* (or *im Weggle*), meaning "three Nürnberger bratwurst in a blankie" (a good snack for about €3). Restaurant menus often offer them in 6-, 8-, or 10-weenie servings accompanied by *Beilagen* (side dishes, generally potato salad and/or kraut). Six Nürnberger with sauerkraut and bread will run you about €7. Old-timers go for mustard, while children like ketchup. (I'm a mustard guy.)

dark breads and sausages in a family-run setting (Mon-Fri 8:30-18:00, Sat until 16:00, closed Sun; Winklerstrasse 10, entrance on Tuchgasse, see description on page 594).

Picnicking in the Center: The **Aldi** supermarket on Königstrasse is a block from the TI and near recommended hotels (Mon-Sat 8:00-20:00, closed Sun). There's a more upscale supermarket in the subbasement of the **Karstadt** department store at the Lorenzkirche U-Bahn entrance (enter store at Karolinenstrasse 6 and take the escalators down two flights, Mon-Sat 9:30-23:00, closed Sun). The farmers market on the **Hauptmarkt** is another smart option (Mon-Sat 7:00-18:00, no market Sun).

NORTH OF THE RIVER, NEAR THE CASTLE

$$$ Einzimmer Küche Bar is my choice for a romantic splurge in a cozy interior where *House and Garden* meets *Architectural Digest*. Chef-owner Tim and sous chef Vadim make modern German dishes with locally sourced ingredients in a trendy open kitchen. Order à la carte or opt wisely for the four- or five-course fixed-price meal; there's also a smaller lunch *menu* (Tue-Sat 12:00-14:00 & 18:00-22:00, closed Sun-Mon, evening reservations required, Schustergasse 10, tel. 0911/6646-3875, www.einzimmerkuechebar.de).

At **$$ Restaurant zum Albrecht Dürer Haus,** you can dine with a view of half-timbered buildings and town-wall towers at a reasonable price. The dark-wood interior has three floors, and there are also outside tables. The menu is updated Franconian. Try the *Augustiner Bierschmankerl*—selections of traditional small plates served alongside beer (Tue-Sun 12:00-21:30, closed Mon, Obere Schmiedgasse 58, tel. 0911/2114-4940).

$ Bratwursthäusle is a high-energy, woody place with a leafy terrace (and enjoyable people-watching). Its cozy interior—small, crowded, and touristy—feels like a big farmhouse with tables gathered around an open grill. The menu is very limited, with little more than bratwurst, sides (pretzels, tasty potato salad, kraut), and some nasty pickled animal parts. Come here for the best bratwurst in town—all made in-house by the *Häusle*'s own butcher, cooked on a beechwood grill, and dished up with efficient service (Mon-Sat 11:00-22:00, closed Sun, midway between the Hauptmarkt and castle on the main drag, Rathausplatz 1, tel. 0911/227-695). For a bratwurst sandwich to go, head inside, pay €3 at the half-door on your right, take your receipt to the grill...and in seconds, you'll be on your way with Nürnberg's "Little Mac" (three *Nürnberger* in a fresh roll). Their nearby sister restaurant, **Goldenes Posthorn,** has the same to-go deal, a more varied sit-down menu, vegetarian options, and fewer tourists (daily 11:30-23:30, Glöckleinsgasse 2 at Sebalderplatz, tel. 0911/225-153).

$$$$ Restaurant Sebald is ideal for an elegant meal without sausage or dumplings. They serve excellent modern German dishes in a classy interior, with tables outside under the trees (Mon-Sat 11:00-23:00, Sun 12:00-22:00, a block west of St. Sebald Church at Weinmarkt 14, tel. 0911/381-303, www.restaurant-sebald.de).

$ Da Gallo Antipasteria is a treat for pasta lovers, who enjoy generous portions amid a welcoming atmosphere stoked by enthusiastic owner Giovanni (who serves everyone himself). Fun photos and a perpetual showing of classic Italian comedies make it feel like a tiny slice of Italy tucked between the river and Castle Hill (Mon-Sat 17:00-23:00, closed Sun, reservations smart for this small space, Radbrunnengasse 2, tel. 0911/238-8538, www.dagallo-antipasteria.de).

$ FIVE Diner, at the recommended FIVE Hotel, might be too trendy for its own good, but it's got a fun vibe and tasty eats. The menu includes gourmet burgers, veggie alternatives, and "bio"-friendly options. American-style breakfast is served until 15:00 (daily 8:00-23:00, Obstmarkt 5, tel. 0911/223-375).

Drinks and Pub Grub: Likely the town's most atmospheric drinking hole, **$ Finyas Taverne** has a medieval feel—from the animal-pelt seats to the music, food, drink (mead), even the wait-staff's attire—yet doesn't quite cross the kitsch line. The upstairs communal tables are popular nightly with tabletop board-game players and collectible card-traders (geeks of the world, unite!). You can eat a full meal here (build-your-own *Flammkuchen* and cheap stews), but I wouldn't (Tue-Sat 17:00-late, closed Sun-Mon, Weissgerbergasse 18, tel. 0911/2373-5122).

$$ Biergarten Kettensteg is a sloppy place with good drinks and simple traditional plates set like a riverside oasis under trees (daily 11:30-23:00, tel. 0911/2358-5808, just inside the town wall at the Kettensteg bridge, Maxplatz 35).

Sweets: The **Neef Confiserie Café** is *the* Nürnberger's go-to spot for an afternoon coffee-and-cake break. You can even get a marzipan version of the town's famous three-sausages-in-a-bun (Mon-Sat 8:30-18:00, closed Sun, Winklerstrasse 29, tel. 0911/225-0179).

Of the many *Eiscafés* in town, **Gelateria 4D** is the most likely to have locals lined up at the counter for a scoop (just off the Hauptmarkt on the corner of Königstrasse and Spitalgasse, long hours daily).

Nürnberg Connections

From Nürnberg by Train to: Rothenburg (hourly, 1.5 hours, transfer in Ansbach and Steinach), **Würzburg** (2-3/hour, 1 hour), **Munich** (2/hour, 1 hour on fast train), **Frankfurt** (1-2/hour, 2 hours), **Frankfurt Airport** (1-2/hour, 2.5 hours), **Dresden** (hourly, 3.5 hours hours, transfer points vary), **Erfurt** (hourly, 1.5 hours), **Leipzig** (hourly, 2 hours, half with transfer in Erfurt), **Berlin** (hourly, 3.5 hours), **Salzburg** (hourly with change in Munich, 3 hours), **Prague** (3 slow trains/day, 5 hours with connections; better to take express bus, nearly hourly, 4 hours, covered by rail passes, leaves from front door of train station). Train info: www.bahn.com.

LUTHERLAND

Erfurt • Wartburg Castle • Wittenberg

Martin Luther—pious monk, fiery orator, and religious whistle-blower—came from a humble, pastoral corner of Germany's heartland. In the charming university town of Erfurt, Luther was a student before casting his former life aside to become a monk. At Wartburg Castle, he hid out to translate the New Testament. And he eventually made his home in Wittenberg, where he worked as a university professor, nailed his 95 Theses to the church door, and enjoyed married life with Katharina von Bora.

Located in the present-day states of Saxony and Thuringia, this chapter's three destinations—Erfurt, Wartburg Castle, and Wittenberg—form the cradle of the Protestant Reformation. Luther's groundbreaking work here set into motion a chain of events that would split Western Christian faith, plunge Europe into a century of warfare, cause empires to rise and fall, and inspire new schools of art and thought.

OK, I'll admit it—I'm a Lutheran. So I have a special reason for enjoying this area. But anyone with an appreciation for history will likely be interested as well. Even without their Luther connections, Erfurt is pleasant for a stroll, and Wartburg is a fine castle. And anyone—including atheists—will appreciate Wittenberg's excellent Luther sights, demonstrating the dramatic impact this courageous monk had on European history—which went far beyond his original intent to reform the church—and the enduring example he set for those who dare to speak truth to power. (For more on Martin Luther's significance, read the background information about him starting on page 622; or watch my TV special *Rick Steves' Luther and the Reformation* at www.ricksteves.com/

luther. For more on the destinations, skip to the section on Erfurt, which starts on page 626).

If you're connecting the Luther towns, you'll almost certainly pass through the city of Leipzig, which also has a few Luther ties and is worth a visit in its own right (see next chapter).

Throughout the region that I call "Lutherland," keep an eye out for the Luther rose, a symbol of the man who became known as the Great Reformer: a black cross in a red heart (symbolizing the Crucifixion) inside a white rose (the peace and joy of faith), all within a golden ring that symbolizes the infinite nature of heaven.

PLANNING YOUR TIME

Lutherland is easy to visit on the way between the Frankfurt/Würzburg area to the west and the Berlin/Dresden area to the east. Luther pilgrims may want several days to linger at the historic sights. You can see Wittenberg on its own as a day trip from Berlin, or follow this two-day plan en route to Berlin:

Day 1: Ride the train to Eisenach, throw your bag in a locker, and visit Wartburg Castle. In the evening, continue by train 30-45 minutes to Erfurt, where you'll enjoy a charming evening and sleep.

Day 2: Spend the morning sightseeing in Erfurt; at midday, head to Wittenberg, see the sights there, and then take an evening train to Berlin. (If you'd also like to visit Leipzig, do it today and stay the night, then see Wittenberg on the morning of Day 3 on the way to Berlin.)

Background on Martin Luther

Luther lived a turbulent life. In early adulthood, the newly ordained Catholic priest suffered a crisis of faith before finally emerging as "born again." In 1517, he openly protested against Church corruption and was later excommunicated. Defying both the pope and the emperor, he was declared a heretic and hid out in a friendly prince's castle, watching as his ideas sparked peasant riots. In his castle refuge he translated the New Testament from Greek to German. He later composed hymns such as "A Mighty Fortress is Our God," sparred with fellow Reformers, and tried to harness and guide the religious, social, and political firestorm he helped ignite.

Early Life

Luther was born on November 10, 1483, in Eisleben, south of Berlin. His dad owned a copper smelter, affording Luther a middle-class upbringing—a rarity in the medieval hierarchy of nobles, clergy, and peasants.

Luther enrolled at the University of Erfurt in 1501. There he earned a liberal-arts degree, entered law school, and earned himself two nicknames—"the philosopher" for his wide-ranging mind, and "the king of hops" for his lifelong love affair with beer.

Then came July 2, 1505. While riding through the countryside, Luther was caught up in an intense thunderstorm, and a bolt of lightning knocked him to the ground. Luther cried out, "St. Anne, save me, and I will become a monk!" Surviving the storm, Luther was determined to make good on his promise. He returned to Erfurt, sold his possessions, and told his friends, "After this day,

you will see me no more." The next morning, he knocked on the door of Erfurt's Augustinian Monastery and dedicated his life to Christianity.

But Luther soon realized that pious monastic life did not suit his inquisitive nature. He returned to academia, was ordained a priest in 1507 in Erfurt's cathedral, and by 1508 was teaching theology part-time at the university in nearby Wittenberg.

In 1509, Luther set out for Rome on foot, a pilgrimage that would change him forever. Upon arriving in the Eternal City, he was dismayed to find rich, corrupt priests and bishops selling "indulgences," which supposedly guaranteed entry to heaven to those able to pay the price. This was the Rome of Pope Julius II, who was in the midst of an expensive, over-the-top remodel of Vatican City—and the lucrative sale of indulgences helped refill the papal treasury. At the time of Luther's visit, Michelangelo was lying aloft on his back in the Sistine Chapel, executing detailed frescoes on the ceiling, while Raphael was slathering nearby hallways with his own Renaissance masterpieces.

This traffic in indulgences and luxury clashed violently with Luther's deeply held belief that people's faith, not their pocketbook, would determine the final destination of their souls. Indulgences were an insult to his worldview—and, to Luther, a betrayal of the Christian faith.

Professor and Preacher

After returning to Germany in 1512, Luther received his doctorate and got a job teaching theology at the university in Wittenberg. The prince elector of Saxony, Frederick the Wise, had decided to make this backwater town his royal seat, so he invited the region's best and brightest to populate his dynamic new burg. Here, Luther mingled with other great thinkers (including fellow professor Philipp Melanchthon) and artists (most notably Lucas Cranach the Elder).

During these early years, Luther was consumed with the notion that he was a sinner. He devoured the Bible, looking for an answer and finding it in Paul's letter to the Romans. Luther concluded that God makes sinners righteous through their faith in Jesus Christ, not by earning it through good deeds. As this concept of "unearned grace" took hold, Luther said, "I felt myself to have been born again."

Energized, he began a series of Bible lectures at Wittenberg's Town Church of St. Mary. The pews were packed as Luther quoted passages directly from the Bible. Speaker and audience alike began to see discrepancies between what the Bible said and what the Church was doing. Coincidentally, a friar happened to arrive in Wittenberg around this time, selling letters of indulgence that promised "forgiveness for all thy sins, transgressions, and excesses, howsoever enormous they may be"...a bargain at twice the price.

Outraged at the idea that God's grace could be bought, Luther thought the subject should be debated openly. On October 31, 1517, he nailed his now-famous 95 Theses (topics for discussion) to the door of Wittenberg's Castle Church. The theses questioned indulgences and other Church practices and beliefs. Thesis #82 boldly asked: "If the pope redeems a number of souls for the sake of miserable money with which to buy a church, why doesn't he empty purgatory for the sake of holy love?" With the newfangled printing presses belonging to Lucas Cranach, Luther's propositions were turned into pamphlets that became the talk of Germany.

Excommunication

Luther didn't set out to start a new church; he wanted to reform the existing one. He preached throughout the region, spreading his provocative ideas and publicly debating his positions in such venues as Leipzig's town hall. In 1520, a furious Pope Leo X sent the rebellious monk a papal bull threatening excommunication. Luther burned the edict on the spot, and soon after, Leo X formally excommunicated him.

Luther was branded a heretic and ordered to Rome to face charges, but he refused to go. Finally, the most powerful man in Europe, Emperor Charles V, stepped in to arbitrate, calling an Imperial Diet (congress) at Worms in 1521. Luther made a triumphal entry into Worms, greeted by cheering crowds. The Diet convened, and Luther took his place in the center of the large hall, standing next to a stack of his writings. Inquisitors grilled him while the ultra-conservative Charles looked on. Luther refused to disavow his beliefs.

The infuriated emperor declared Luther an outlaw and a heretic. Being "outside the law" meant that he could be killed at will. After leaving Worms, Luther disappeared. He was kidnapped—by supporters—and given refuge in Frederick the Wise's Wartburg Castle. There Luther wore a beard to disguise himself as Junker Jörg ("Squire George"). He spent 10 months fighting depression and translating the Bible's New Testament from the original Greek into German. This "September Testament" was revolutionary, bringing the Bible to the masses and shaping the modern German language.

Meanwhile, Luther's ideas caught on back home in Wittenberg, where his followers had continued to pursue reform. By the time Luther returned to the city in 1522, popular uprisings led by more radically-minded reformers were undermining law and order.

Later Life

In 1525, Luther's friend and follower Thomas Müntzer used Luther's writings to justify an uprising known as the Peasants' Revolt. Poor farmers attacked their feudal masters with hoes and pitchforks, fighting for more food, political say-so, and respect. Thousands of peasants died, and Müntzer was executed. Luther decried the uprising, preaching that Church corruption did not justify outright societal rebellion. In fact, he supported the violent suppression of the Peasants' Revolt.

In 1525, the 41-year-old ex-priest married a 26-year-old ex-nun, Katharina von Bora, "to please my father and annoy the pope." (Their wedding set the precedent of allowing Protestant clergy to marry.) They moved into the former Wittenberg monastery where Luther had once lived (today's Luther House, the best museum anywhere on the Reformation and Luther), where they rented rooms to students. Luther turned his checkbook over to "my lord Katie," who ran the family farm and raised their six children and 11 adopted orphans.

Luther traveled, spreading the Protestant message. In 1529, at Marburg Castle (just north of Frankfurt), he attended a summit of leading Protestants to try and forge an alliance against Catholicism. They agreed on everything except a single theological point: whether Christ was present in the wine and bread of Communion in a physical sense (according to Luther) or symbolic sense (per the Swiss reformer Ulrich Zwingli). The disagreement doomed the Protestant movement to splinter into dozens of sects.

In 1534, Luther finished translating the Bible. Lucas Cranach illustrated it with woodcuts and published it on his printing presses. The Martin Luther Bible was to German-speaking Christians what the King James Bible would be to English-speaking Christians—essentially codifying an entire language. Luther also wrote a German Mass, catechisms, and several hymns, including the still-beloved "A Mighty Fortress is Our God."

In his fifties, Luther's health declined and he grew bitter, a fact made clear in such writings as "Against the Papacy at Rome Founded by the Devil" and "Of the Jews and Their Lies." A general tone of anti-Judaism pollutes his later work. Luther was less concerned with the ethnicity of Jews—as the Nazis later were—than he was by their refusal to accept Christianity. Luther's words were later invoked to justify anti-Semitic speech and actions during the early days of Nazism.

Martin Luther died on February 18, 1546, and was buried in Wittenberg. To read more about the Protestant Reformation, see the "Luther's Legacy" sidebar, later. And watch my one-hour public television special, *Rick Steves' Luther and the Reformation* (www. ricksteves.com/luther).

Erfurt

A half-timbered, many-steepled medieval townscape with a shallow river gurgling through its middle, Erfurt (AIR-foort) is an inviting destination. The capital of the Thuringia region, this is where Martin Luther spent his early years. While its Luther sights aren't as exciting as those at Wartburg Castle or Wittenberg, the town itself more than makes up for it. You can see the monastery where Luther became a monk and the cathedral where  he became a priest, stroll across an atmospheric medieval bridge lined with characteristic shops, ogle an unearthed treasure-trove in one of Europe's oldest surviving synagogues, hike up to the citadel for views over town, or just bask in Erfurt's quaintness.

Sitting on an important medieval trade route, Erfurt boomed in the Middle Ages thanks largely to its production of woad, a plant-based blue dye. In the 16th century, trade with India flooded the market with less expensive dyes made from true indigo, and Erfurt's fortunes tumbled, leaving it a well-preserved backwater for centuries. It enjoyed another boom after the creation of a united Germany in 1871. Unlike the nearby cities of Berlin, Dresden, and Leipzig, Erfurt emerged from World War II relatively unscathed. This imbues Erfurt with a delightful time-capsule quality—rare for an eastern German city of its size.

These days, Erfurt is very popular among German tourists and Martin Luther pilgrims, but largely undiscovered by American visitors (meaning English information can be hard to come by). Erfurt provides a handy launch pad for visiting Wartburg Castle, where Luther hid out while translating the New Testament (in Eisenach, 30-45 minutes west by train).

PLANNING YOUR TIME

Erfurt deserves a day's visit, and possibly an overnight. You can get the gist of the town in a few hours: Take my self-guided walking tour, then drop into your choice of other sights—the twin churches are enjoyable, the citadel offers great views over town, Luther fans appreciate the Augustinian Monastery, and the truly old Old Synagogue interests historians.

Orientation to Erfurt

Although it has about 200,000 people, Erfurt feels smaller—particularly its downtown core, where you'll spend most of your time. Erfurt's Old Town, huddled picturesquely at a bend in the Gera River, is loosely bound by a ring road. The train station sits just beyond the southeastern edge of the ring, and the cathedral and citadel perch at the western edge. The Old Town core is a short walk (or speedy tram ride) from the train station; once there, virtually all points of interest are within a 10-minute walk of each other.

TOURIST INFORMATION

Erfurt's TI is in the town center, between the Merchants' Bridge and Town Hall. They sell a self-guided tour booklet and rent an audioguide—see "Helpful Hints," later (Mon-Sat 10:00-18:00, Sun until 15:00; Benediktplatz 1, tel. 0361/66400, www.erfurt-tourismus.de). The TI's website helps put visitors in touch with residents renting private rooms.

ARRIVAL IN ERFURT

The Erfurt Hauptbahnhof (main train station) has a few shops and eateries, and luggage lockers (below track 2). There's no city TI at the station, but a regional (Thuringia) TI is directly across the square from the main door.

From the station, you can walk into the heart of town in about 10-15 minutes (a few minutes farther to Domplatz or the Augustinian Monastery), or you can hop a tram part of the way.

To **walk,** exit through the main door and bear left until you reach Bahnhofstrasse, with the tram tracks. Turn right and head five short blocks until you pop out at the shopping square called Anger (marked by a glassy modern building). This is the starting point for my self-guided walk; most of the hotels I list are within a 10-minute walk of Anger.

Or, to take a **tram,** exit out the side of the station, toward Ausgang Bahnhofstrasse; you'll run right into the tram stops. You can take trams #1, #3, or #5 to Anger, then to Domplatz; tram #1 goes first to Anger, then continues to the Augustinerkloster (Augustinian Monastery and recommended hotels). Tram #5 also goes to Augustinerkloster.

GETTING AROUND ERFURT

For most visitors, the only reason to use Erfurt's trams is to haul luggage to or from the station (particularly to lodgings near the Augustinian Monastery) or to reach the Egapark gardens. One ride is €2; a day pass is €5.30. There are coin-op ticket machines (in-

LUTHERLAND

Erfurt

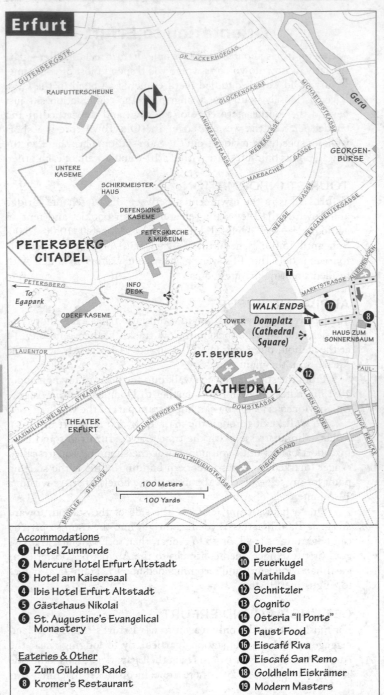

LUTHERLAND

GUTENBERGSTR.

GR. ACKERHOFGAS.

RAUFUTTERSCHEUNE

N

GLOCKENGASSE

MICHAELISSTRASSE

Gera

ANDREASSTRASSE

WEBERGASSE

MARBACHER GASSE

GEORGEN-
BURSE

UNTERE
KASEME

SCHIRRMEISTER-
HAUS

DEFENSIONS-
KASEME

WEISSE GASSE

PERGAMENTERGASSE

PETERSKIRCHE
& MUSEUM

PETERSBERG
CITADEL

← PETERSBERG

To
Egapark

INFO
DESK

OBERE KASEME

ALLERHEILIGEN

T

MARKTSTRASSE

WALK ENDS

17

8

TOWER

Domplatz
(Cathedral
Square)

T

HAUS ZUM
SONNERNBAUM

LAUENTOR

ST. SEVERUS

CATHEDRAL

12

PAUL-

MAXIMILIAN-WELSCH STRASSE

MAINZERHOFSTR.

AN DEN GRABEN

LANGE BRÜCKE

THEATER
ERFURT

DOMSTRASSE

HOLTZHEIENSTRASSE

FISCHERSAND

100 Meters

100 Yards

BRÜHLER STRASSE

Accommodations
1 Hotel Zumnorde
2 Mercure Hotel Erfurt Altstadt
3 Hotel am Kaisersaal
4 Ibis Hotel Erfurt Altstadt
5 Gästehaus Nikolai
6 St. Augustine's Evangelical
  Monastery

Eateries & Other
7 Zum Güldenen Rade
8 Kromer's Restaurant
9 Übersee
10 Feuerkugel
11 Mathilda
12 Schnitzler
13 Cognito
14 Osteria "Il Ponte"
15 Faust Food
16 Eiscafé Riva
17 Eiscafé San Remo
18 Goldhelm Eiskrämer
19 Modern Masters

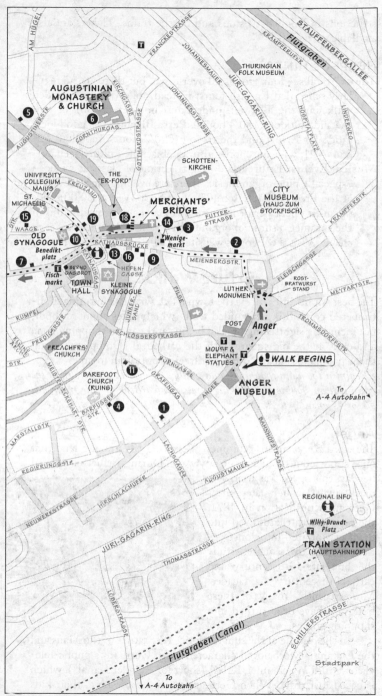

LUTHERLAND

Erfurt map labels:

STAUFFENBERGALLEE
Flutgraben
KRÄMPFERUFER
AM HÜGEL
FRANCKESTRASSE
"JOHANNESMAUER
JURI-GAGARIN-RING
THURINGIAN FOLK MUSEUM
HOSPITALPLATZ
LINDERWEG
KIRCHGASSE
AUGUSTINIAN MONASTERY & CHURCH
5
6
AUGUSTINERSTR.
CORNTHURGAS.
GOTTHARDSTRASSE
JOHANNESSTRASSE
SCHOTTEN-KIRCHE
KÄMPFERSTR.
UNIVERSITY COLLEGIUM MAIUS
THE "ER-FORD"
KREUZAND
CITY MUSEUM (HAUS ZUM STOCKFISCH)
ST. MICHAELIS
MERCHANTS' BRIDGE
FUTTER-STRASSE
STR.
15
WAAGE
19
18
14
3
2
OLD SYNAGOGUE
10
Wenige-markt
FLEISCHGASSE
ROST-BRATWURST STAND
MEYFARTSTR.
Benedikt-platz
RATHAUSBRÜCKE
MEIENBERGSTR.
7
13
16
9
Fisch-markt
BERND DAS BROT
HEFEN-GASSE
LUTHER MONUMENT
TROMMSDORFFSTR.
TOWN HALL
KLEINE SYNAGOGUE
JUNKER-SAND
PILSE
RUMPEL
PREDIGERSTR.
SCHLÖSSERSTRASSE
POST
Anger
KRÄME STR.
PREACHERS' CHURCH
MEISTERECKHART STR.
BURGGASSE
MOUSE & ELEPHANT STATUES
WALK BEGINS
To A-4 Autobahn
BARFÜSSER STR.
BAREFOOT CHURCH (RUIN)
11
GRAFENGAS
ANGER
ANGER MUSEUM
4
1
MARSTALLSTR.
REGIERUNGSSTR.
LACHSGASSE
BAHNHOFSTRASSE
AUGUSTMAUER
REGIONAL INFO
Willy-Brandt Platz
NEUWERKSTRASSE
HIRSCHLACHUFER
JURI-GAGARIN-RING
TRAIN STATION (HAUPTBAHNHOF)
THOMASSTRASSE
LÖBERSTRASSE
SCHILLERSTRASSE
Flutgraben (Canal)
Stadtpark
To A-4 Autobahn

structions in English) at stops and on the trams. Tickets are also available at the TI.

HELPFUL HINTS

Tours: You'll see tour groups all over town, but there are no regularly scheduled English tours; instead, follow my self-guided walk, buy the TI's self-guided tour booklet (€2.50), or rent the audioguide (€7.50/4 hours). **Petra Bischoff** is a good local guide for Erfurt and the region (€90/2 hours, mobile 0172-354-7021, www.bischoff-kultur.de, bischoff-kultur@web.de).

Musical Events: Erfurt has a long tradition of classical music—especially pipe-organ music. There are evening organ concerts at the Preachers' Church (€5, May-Sept Wed at 20:00), plus open-air opera performances on the steps of the cathedral in the summer, a summer organ festival, and a Bach festival each spring. Visit the TI or its website for a listing of musical events.

Erfurt Walk

The best "sight" in Erfurt is the town itself, with its charming, half-timbered core. This self-guided walk (which takes about an hour, not including sightseeing breaks) begins at the main shopping zone and ends at the big square with the cathedral (Domplatz); along the way, it passes nearly every sightseeing option in town.

• *Begin in the main shopping square, called Anger. To get here from the train station, follow my walking directions (earlier), or ride trams #1, #3, or #5 one stop to Anger.*

Anger

The word *Anger* means "commons," evoking the grazing land that once sprawled just outside the city walls. During Erfurt's medieval heyday, this space was used as a marketplace. Much later, after Germany's unification in 1871, the new wealth that flowed into town was poured into construction around this square. Study the fine late-19th-century and early-20th-century facades. More recently, many of these buildings have been turned into shopping spaces.

In the middle of the square, notice the statues of the Maus and the Elefant—two beloved characters from Germany's public-television children's channel, **KiKA** (short for "Kinder Kanal"), which is based in Erfurt. When German families come here, their kids can't wait to pose with figures like these—you'll see them scattered around town.

The palatial yellow building, across the tram tracks from the glassy, modern building, hosts the **Anger Museum** (described later, under "Sights

in Erfurt"). This building was restored to showcase the city's marginally interesting collections of paintings, applied arts, and medieval artifacts.

• *Facing the mouse and elephant, follow the tram tracks 100 yards to the right and look for a church with a statue in front, depicting...*

Martin Luther

Luther came to Erfurt in 1501 to enroll at the university. After graduating, the smart young student pursued a doctorate at the

prestigious law faculty, but after a close call with a lightning storm, Luther had a change of heart and became a monk at Erfurt's Augustinian Monastery for several years. This walk passes a few blocks from the monastery. The church in front of you is where Jo-

hann Sebastian Bach's parents were married in 1668.

• *To the right of the statue is a...*

Rostbratwurst Stand

Locals are extremely proud of what they stress is "originale" *Thüringer* bratwurst—a long, skinny, relatively low-fat pork sausage amply seasoned with pepper, marjoram, and other spices. When you buy one, grab a roll and hold it open, and they'll serve the wurst straight from the grill. While there's ketchup standing by, purists put only the locally made Born brand mustard *(Senf)* on their weenie.

• *As you munch, go around the left side of the church, then turn left up Meienbergstrasse, and walk for a couple of blocks—passing a line of ethnic eateries. (Erfurt's population seems have a huge appetite for cheap foreign food.) Soon you reach...*

LUTHERLAND

Wenigemarkt

This "Little Market Square" is one of Erfurt's most charming, encircled with al fresco cafés and watched over by the fortified tower of the Methodist church of St. Aegidius (which you can climb for a town view).

• *Head toward that church tower, and go through the large gateway in the green building just to its right. Jog left with the cobbled lane, and you'll pop out at...*

The "Er-Ford"

Notice the ramp that goes right down into the Gera River, out the other side, then continues through the far branch of the river. Like any German town with "-furt" in its name, Erfurt is named for a shallow point where ancient travelers could ford a river. (The "Er" part comes from an old German word for "dirty"—the water was muddied when people would cross.) In centuries past, this sleepy brook powered 50 water mills and therefore did much to power the economy of Erfurt.

Spanning the river on your left is the **Merchants' Bridge.** Notice that—unlike the famous shop-lined Ponte Vecchio in Florence—people actually make their homes along this bridge (see the flower boxes on the lived-in balconies). As in ages past, the residents live upstairs and run shops downstairs.

• *Climb the narrow staircase on your left to get onto the bridge.*

Merchants' Bridge (Krämerbrücke)

The bridge dates from 1325, but the shops that line it (*Krämer* means "shopkeeper") first sprouted around the late 15th and early 16th centuries, about Martin Luther's time. Today, the shops on the bridge are quaint, albeit a bit touristy, and a pleasure to browse. Window shop your way across the bridge.

Across from the steps, at #19, is a shop dealing in Thuringian specialties, including wine, mustard, cheese, and sausage. Across from that (on the right, marked by the golden helmet) is the **Goldhelm Schokolade shop,** selling chocolates and delicious ice cream (the chocolate flavor is tasty, but the caramel is *wunderbar*).

At #31 is the office of the foundation that cares for the bridge, with a tiny, free exhibit. You're welcome to pop in and climb downstairs and upstairs. An English flier describes their work (small donation requested, daily 10:00-18:00).

Near the end, at #2 on the right, don't miss the window marked **Theatrum Mundi.** This is the brilliant work of local puppetmaker Martin Gobsch—go in, say hi, and observe him at work. It's well worth popping in a €1 coin to see the evil queen open her green eyes and pull back her arm to reveal an intricately detailed, fully articulated rendering of the Snow White story—it plays for a few minutes, just long enough for you to take in all the delightful details. Happily, the prince takes Snow White away.

• *At the end of Merchants' Bridge, you emerge at...*

Benediktplatz

Originally Merchants' Bridge was guarded at either end by fortified churches; the one on this end—St. Benedict's—was torn down by Napoleonic troops, but its name survives. The TI is at the bottom of this square. At the end of the bridge, immediately on the right, is **Backstube,** a bakery proudly selling handmade breads in the traditional style (with a tasty selection of still-warm rolls and drinks).

• *Let's take a detour up...*

Michaelisstrasse

Historically the core of the university district, today this drag hosts some of the town's most popular restaurants and bars. After a block (at Waagegasse), go down the first lane on the left, then look left to find the entrance to the **Old Synagogue**—one of Europe's earliest surviving synagogues, displaying a rediscovered treasure in its cellar (see "Sights in Erfurt," later).

Back on Michaelisstrasse, continue left. At Zum Güldenen Krönbacken (#10), go through the fine arch. Walk 25 paces to a big aluminum planter filled with leafy **woad plants.** Growing to four feet, and with yellow flowers, woad (*Waid* in German) was converted into a highly valuable, brilliant blue dye, which buoyed Erfurt's economy in the Middle Ages. This courtyard is one place where the woad was processed and warehoused. After being mashed up, the plant was fermented with urine for two months. (How they worked out this procedure, I don't care to know.) The mixture was dried, then ground into a fine powder that was literally worth its weight in gold. Leading woad merchants were local tycoons.

Continuing up Michaelisstrasse, you'll come to an intersection shared by a church and an old pink building—both related to the **University of Erfurt.** Founded in 1379,  the university was the third in present-day Germany and counts Martin Luther and Johannes Gutenberg as alums. The pink building, called the Collegium Maius, was the town's first university building (though it's mostly a reconstruction—the original was one of Erfurt's few WWII casualties in the last months of the war). Medieval students had a rough life: They got up at 4:00 in the morning to attend Mass, ate two meals a day (breakfast at 10:00 and dinner at 16:00), and bathed once a month. On the upside, students were rationed one liter of beer per meal (it was purer than the water). Notice the modern stained-glass windows above the door depicting the four traditional areas of study: theology (cross and fish), law (weights), medicine (snake on staff), and philosophy (eye).

• *Head back to Benediktplatz and the TI, and turn right (in the direction you were originally going) toward...*

Fischmarkt

On the left just before you reach the square, in front of the Town Hall, look for another KiKA character—a morose, SpongeBob-looking slice of bread named **Bernd das**  **Brot.** In what surely ranks among the most dramatic art heists in European history, this statue was stolen in 2009 by squatters protesting an eviction notice. They even put a tongue-in-cheek ransom video on YouTube. Several days later, Bernd was discovered by kids in an abandoned building, and returned to his rightful home.

Just past Bernd, enter the **square** itself, dominated by the Town Hall building. The statue in the center of the square holds a flag and shield, both with the city symbol—a wheel in a shield. Erfurt, which was never a free city, spent much of its history as part of the Archbishop of Mainz's holdings, so this wheel is based on that city's symbol.

The stately **Town Hall,** built in 1880 in the Neo-Gothic style, welcomes visitors (free and open daily, WC inside). In the lobby, the fine staircase ahead of you leads up two stories to the festival hall. Along the stairs and in the hall are melodramatic 19th-century Romantic paintings of Wagnerian opera themes and city history (all thoughtfully described in English).

Back out on the square, survey the building **facades** and enjoy the variety of architectural styles taking you from the 13th to the 20th century. Notice in particular two fine Renaissance facades owned by affluent woad merchants hell-bent on showing off their wealth: Zum Breiten Herd (1584, celebrates the five senses: from left to right, look, listen, smell, taste, and touch), and the Red Oxen (#7, from 1562, with a round arch and "gossip stones" where women would sit flanking the doorway and gossip while keeping an eye on the city).

Finally, notice the modern addition to the Town Hall, built around 1930 in the bold and early-modern Bauhaus style. The German Bauhaus movement marked the beginning of functionalism—the "form follows function" aesthetic that became the norm for the last half of the 20th century. The statues here, which also date from the 1930s, show bad human characteristics (greed, narcissism, laziness, stupidity, and so on). The Nazi-era relief celebrates solid, traditional family roles.

· *Stand with the Town Hall at your back. Now follow the tram lines ahead and to your right up...*

Marktstrasse

At the tall white steeple (after passing Werner's Head Shop on your left—pop in if you need a gift for your mother), turn left and walk down the street to **Haus zum Sonneborn** (a big yellow house with brown timbers and trim). At this popular venue for weddings, notice the intertwined golden rings on the grate over the window to the right of the door, and to the left, the cage (whose symbolism is obvious).

· *From here, head right, down Mettengasse, imagining the old days when the higgledy-piggledy backsides of these half-timbered buildings were teeming with activity. Passing the biggest potted plant you'll ever see, you reach the...*

Domplatz (Cathedral Square)

This vast square, often full of market stalls, is dominated by twin churches: the **cathedral** (on the left) and **St. Severus** (right).

While Erfurt's history is tied to religion, the atheistic East German government successfully smothered the faith: These days, just 7 percent of Erfurters profess to be Catholic, 14 percent are Protestant, and the rest are unchurched. On the hill to the right, you can see the base of **Petersberg Citadel,** a gigantic fortress that's free to explore and offers sweeping views over Erfurt. (The churches and citadel are described later, under "Sights in Erfurt.")

The street leading away from Domplatz to the right, **Andreasstrasse,** was called "the longest street in Erfurt" during communist times. Just past the end of the square, on the left, the bright red-brick building behind the wall was a prison run by the Stasi, East Germany's secret police, reserved for those who were caught trying to escape to the West. Why was it the longest street? "It takes five minutes to go in, and five years to get out."

• *Our tour is finished. Visit the churches and citadel, then enjoy exploring the town. Or, if you're ready to head back to the train station, you can hop on a tram.*

Sights in Erfurt

MARTIN LUTHER SIGHTS
▲Augustinian Monastery and Church (Augustinerkloster und Augustinerkirche)

On July 17, 1505, a young student knocked on the door of this monastery and declared that he wished to become a monk. Martin Luther lived here for several years—even after becoming a priest and a part-time professor—until he settled in Wittenberg in 1512. Inside the still-active complex, you can see the church, a small museum of Luther artifacts, and the cell where Monk Martin lived. While the museum and cell are more accustomed to German-speaking groups, they welcome individuals, and their exhibits are explained in English.

Cost and Hours: Church-free, museum-€3.50, daily 9:00-18:00, Augustinerstrasse 10, tel. 0361/576-600.

Tours: €7.50, one-hour guided tours in German depart roughly at the top of the hour (Mon-Sat 9:30-16:00, Sun at 11:00,

14:00, and 15:00). Tours include the church, peaceful cloister, exhibition, and Luther's cell.

Getting There: The monastery is an easy 10-minute walk along Johannesstrasse from Anger square. To get there by tram from either the Hauptbahnhof or Anger, take the #1, #3, or #5 to the Augustinerkloster stop.

Visiting the Monastery: As the Augustinians were a "begging order," life here was just the basics: *"ora et labora"* (pray and work). That's why this monastery, while important, had no great spire and just a humble cloister. Entering through the door, you emerge into a tranquil, park-like **courtyard**. On the right, the modern building (housing offices and a conference center) marks the site of an earlier library, where 267 people suffocated while hiding in the cellar to escape WWII bombs. The new building is connected by an elevated walkway to the main part of the complex, with two major sights: the church and the Martin Luther museum and cell.

The **church,** dating from the late 13th century, is where Martin Luther worshipped as a monk. The stained-glass windows (c. 1330) include (in the lower left corner) a motif of lions (symbolizing Jesus) flanking a rose (Mary). This window, which monks used as a focal point for meditation, must have made a deep impression on Luther: He later adopted a similar rose icon for his personal coat of arms. In front of the main altar, the tomb of Johannes Zacharias, a prominent priest, was a place where monks (including Luther) would meditate overnight—lying on their backs, with their arms outstretched. The deeply introspective Luther struggled with all this piety, and eventually he returned to academic life.

Oddly enough, it was Zacharias who had the Czech reformer Jan Hus burned in 1415 for his proto-Reformation ideas. Just before his execution, Hus had defiantly cried, "You can burn me—I'm just a little goose—but in one century a white swan will come and defeat your thinking." A century later, Luther, meditating on that tomb, kindled the ideas of the Reformation. As a priest, Luther performed the Mass here and would sit on the bench under the arch on the right.

Today, this monastery and church form a center of ecumenism, and it was in that spirit that Pope Benedict XVI came here in 2011.

To see the **museum and cell,** go to the reception of the on-site hotel, buy a ticket, and pick up a map. You'll head through the cloister and upstairs to find exhibits about the history of the Bible and a working model of a

Catholic and Protestant Differences

The differences between Protestant and Catholic doctrines have split Christians for centuries, ever since the Luther-sparked "protest" against Catholic corruption and rigidity. Both faiths see Jesus Christ as the central figure in bringing salvation, but they take different approaches.

Protestants emphasize the direct relationship between the individual and God, established through Bible study and personal prayer. With this one-on-one connection at the core of their worship, church rituals and doctrines aren't all that essential, and Protestant clergy (who can marry) are lay people or pastors hired to facilitate worship.

To Catholics, church rituals and an ordained clergy are key conduits for creating and maintaining an individual's connection to God. Catholics receive forgiveness for their sins through the act of Confession, which must be conducted with a priest. Unlike Protestants, they venerate saints and the Virgin Mary, and consider official pronouncements by the pope to be the word of God. Catholic priests must be celibate, and the Church recognizes organizations of monks and nuns.

15th-century printing press. It was the combination of humanism, Gutenberg, and Luther that resulted in affordable Bibles in the vernacular rather than Latin. Another room dedicated to Martin Luther contains a few original artifacts, as well as replicas of his straw bed, gown, book, lute, and so on. The room is lined with small cells where monks would meditate. (The monks all slept together on the main floor.) The cell at the far corner (called the Lutherzelle) was Martin Luther's. Inside the cell is a writing table, similar to the one Luther used for carrying out the monastic task of copying Bibles.

The **cloister** is simple, in keeping with Augustinian values. In the adjoining chapter hall, monks would convene for meetings and to confess before each other.

Georgenburse

A couple of blocks away, just across the stream, is the dorm where Luther lived as a student. The renovated building is basically one big room with information about university life and the U. of E.'s most famous alum, Luther.

Cost and Hours: €3.50; Mon, Wed, and Fri 9:00-14:00; Tue and Thu 13:00-17:00; closed Sat-Sun; Augustinerstrasse 27, tel. 0361/576-6094, www.augustinerkloster.de.

▲Preachers' Church (Predigerkirche)

This church, founded by the Catholic Dominicans in the 14th century, whose mission was teaching and preaching, is now Erfurt's main Protestant church. Its architecture is stunning (it has undergone multiple rebuildings). Colorful keystones honor guilds that paid to build the original church in Gothic times (find symbols for the baker, hatter, goldsmiths, and *schneider*—that's a tailor...indicated by scissors). You'll see a rare surviving wall, which separated people from the clergy before the Reformation. The finely carved choir stalls date from 1320. And the windows behind the altar are an abstract kaleidoscope of colors—pieced together from the original medieval glass windows that were shattered in World War II. The church also has a glorious circa-1650 Baroque pipe organ that you can hear in action (see "Helpful Hints," earlier).

Cost and Hours: Free, Tue-Sat 11:00-16:00, Sun from 12:00, closed Mon and Nov-March, Predigerstrasse 4.

OTHER SIGHTS IN THE TOWN CENTER
▲Old Synagogue (Alte Synagogue)

One of the oldest surviving synagogues in Europe, the original identity of this building was forgotten for several centuries before

being rediscovered in the 1980s. Today it has been restored to highlight its medieval heyday, while preserving its other layers of history. The exhibit inside explains the history of the building, examines the relationship between Jews and Christians in medieval Erfurt, and shows off a cache of coins and jewelry that was discovered nearby.

Cost and Hours: €8, includes wordy audioguide, Tue-Sun 10:00-18:00, closed Mon, mandatory bag check, Waagegasse 8, tel. 0361/655-166, www.juedisches-leben.erfurt.de.

Background: With sections dating back to around 1100, this building was the religious center of Erfurt's bustling medieval Jewish community. Erfurt's Jews mixed freely with their Christian neighbors. In fact, the synagogue's location was one of the most desirable in town, situated near the main trading routes.

All of that changed during the Black Death pandemic of 1348-1349, which killed a third of Europe's population. In the hysteria that ensued, Jewish communities, including Erfurt's, were accused of spreading the disease and faced appalling persecution. Hundreds of Erfurt Jews died and the rest were expelled in a single horrible day of violence.

The Jews returned to Erfurt in the 1350s, but from that point on they were relegated to a ghetto. By about 1450 the Jews had again moved out of Erfurt. The abandoned synagogue building was taken over by the town and sold. Over the next several centuries,

LUTHERLAND

it was used first as a warehouse, then (in the late 19th century) as a restaurant, bowling alley, and dance hall. Finally, in 1988, historians realized that it had once been a synagogue, and it was restored.

Visiting the Synagogue: On the **ground floor,** models illustrate how the original synagogue building grew over time. The rail high on the wall once held lamps. The octagon in the center of the room marks the location of the bema, a raised platform for reading the Torah. A projection on the wall shows the niche where the Torah was kept.

Now go **upstairs.** Nothing here is original—it looks more like the colorfully decorated dance hall that was here from 1876 through the 1930s. The balcony ringing the room was the so-called dragon's watch, where mothers could keep an eye on their daughters dancing with would-be suitors. Imagine young Nazis waltzing here, oblivious to the fact that they were partying in a former synagogue. Among the replicas of parchment scrolls and important books is a copy of the biggest handwritten Hebrew Bible in the world (notice that the illustrations are made up of tiny Hebrew characters). The originals are in a Berlin museum.

Finally, head into the **cellar.** In 1998, a remarkable collection of gold, silver, and jewels—some 60 pounds—was discovered in the cellar of a nearby building. Called the "Erfurt Treasure," this almost certainly belonged to a wealthy local Jew who was killed in the 1349 pogrom. Display cases show off brooches, tableware, and golden decorations for a belt and other garments. The wheel-shaped necklace was used for perfume. (They've reformulated this original medieval perfume—you can ask to sniff it at the ticket desk upstairs.) The museum's prize piece is a finely detailed golden wedding ring from the early 14th century. Around the ring's central pillar is the hard-to-see inscription *mazel tov,* indicating that this belonged to a Jewish woman. Peer into the mirror beneath the ring to see the clasped hand that allows the ring to be adjusted.

Nearby are mannequins dressed as a Jewish bride and groom from that period—wearing rich materials and draped in gold. The stacks of coins come from all over Europe, especially from France. The chunks of silver, called ingots, are marked with the seal of an Erfurt goldsmith.

Anger Museum

This modern, well-presented museum, almost completely lacking in English information, displays paintings, applied arts, and artifacts from the Middle Ages. The ground-floor medieval collection includes wood-carved statues, altarpieces, and a huge collection of shields. The Heckelarium is a small room slathered with frescoes by painter Erich Heckel (1883-1970). Part of the early-1900s art movement called Die Brücke, Heckel strove to create a bridge between two emotional, artistic styles: dramatic Romanticism and edgy Expressionism. The first floor features the good applied arts collection (Kunsthandwerke, featuring historical room interiors with period furnishings, a treasury of precious items, and a collection of glass and porcelain) and a painting gallery (mostly Romantic canvases by largely unknown artists). Temporary exhibits fill the top floor.

Cost and Hours: €6, Tue-Sun 10:00-18:00, closed Mon, Anger 18, tel. 0361/655-1651, www.angermuseum.de.

DOMPLATZ AND NEARBY

Erfurt's grandest square is watched over by three giant structures: a pair of churches on the small hill called Domberg (the cathedral on the left, St. Severus on the right) and the Petersberg Citadel.

Climb up the 70 steps to enter the two churches, whose entrances face each other. Both churches are Catholic and Gothic, dating from the 14th century and later expanded after a fire in the 15th century.

▲▲Cathedral (Dom)

The seat of a bishopric founded in the eighth century by St. Boniface, Erfurt's cathedral is the church where Martin Luther was ordained a priest. It sticks out from the hill on a massive substructure to level out the foundation. Inside you'll find a gorgeously carved choir and a few interesting pieces of ecclesiastical art.

Cost and Hours: Free; Mon-Sat 9:30-18:00, Sun from 13:00; Nov-April daily until 17:00; Domstufen 1, tel. 0361/646-1265, www.dom-erfurt.de.

Visiting the Cathedral: Upon entering, turn left to reach the **choir,** with its intricately carved oak seats. Designs on the benches, built about 50 years after the Black Death, demonstrate that anti-Semitic feelings were still running high. To the left, near the entrance to the choir (about waist-high), find the carving depicting a duel between two knights—one on a horse, the other on a swine. The *Schweinereiter* (swine knight) caricature, wearing a Jewish helmet, was intended to both insult Jews (particularly because the Jewish faith considers pigs unclean) and to emphasize the triumph of Christianity over Judaism. Opposite, on the right, are a series of intimate and playful carved scenes from the world of winemaking. Look up to take

in the stained-glass windows (c. 1370-1410), depicting Old and New Testament stories, and missionaries in the region of Thuringia.

Directly across from the main entrance, find the remarkably old (c. 1160) bronze **candelabra** shaped like a man holding up a pair of candles, fighting off evil with light. Nearby, the light hanging from the ceiling was stolen from the Jewish synagogue during the 1349 pogrom. Behind the candelabra in a simple niche is another exquisite example of 12th-century art—Mary and Jesus on the throne of wisdom.

Filling the wall to the right, a giant **fresco** shows St. Christopher using Erfurt's namesake ford to walk Christ to safety (notice this cathedral's steeples over his shoulder). Pictorial depictions such as this helped make the saints' stories real to medieval congregations.

Below St. Christopher is a **tomb** relief panel showing the Duke of Gleichen flanked by two women. This gravestone gave

rise to a popular (but almost certainly fabricated) local tale: Supposedly "the only man allowed to have two wives," this influential knight went to the Holy Land to fight in the Crusades, was captured and enslaved, and was forced to toil in the garden of the sultan. He married the sultan's daughter in exchange for her help in escaping, then brought her back with him to Erfurt...where he introduced her to his first wife. (Awwk-waaard.) The new bride was accepted by the first one, the knight received special dispensation from the pope to be a bigamist, and the valley where the three of them lived in wedded bliss is still called Freudenthal ("Happy Valley").

Church of St. Severus (Severikirche)

This early Gothic "hall church" has five parallel naves (notice the two narrow ones flanking the main nave) and no perpendicular transept. To the left of the fine Baroque organ is a 14th-century sarcophagus containing the remains of the church's namesake. (Some of the relics of St. Severus, bishop of Ravenna, were brought to Erfurt in the ninth century.) On the sides of the tomb, see

the scenes of Severus' life (a poor craftsman being designated as the chosen one by a white dove over his head—representing the Holy Spirit—and then being "crowned" the bishop of Ravenna) and the Three Magi bringing gifts to the Baby Jesus.

Cost and Hours: Free, same hours as cathedral.

▲Petersberg Citadel (Zitadelle Petersberg)

This sprawling fortress complex, occupying the hill just above Domplatz, is an enjoyable place to go for a stroll and enjoy views over the rooftops of Erfurt (grounds are free and always open). Built from the 17th to the 19th century, this is one of the best-preserved citadels of its kind in Europe.

For a quick visit, walk up the ramp from Domplatz, pausing at the gatehouse, and continue up into the main courtyard of the castle complex. The glassy

building on your right is a visitors center with a helpful info desk, a view café, and panoramic terrace offering sweeping views over Domplatz and the rest of Erfurt. The visitors center hands out a helpful, free map and miniguide of the entire complex.

To visit the Military History Museum (a couple of rooms with mannequin soldiers and other displays, well-explained in English) and to tour the underground tunnels (in German only), you have to make a reservation (inquire at the TI, or tel. 0361/664-0120). Across the field from the center is a large church building with an exhibit of interesting "concrete art"—modern art with 3-D optical illusions (Tue-Sun 11:00-18:00, closed Mon).

ON OR NEAR THE RING ROAD
Thuringian Folk Museum
(Museum für Thüringer Volkskunde)

This former hospital contains folk artifacts and old photos illustrating "The Fascination of Everyday Life" in the region of Thuringia. You'll climb up rickety stairs to see representations of various walks of life, including church, school, bars, farming, shops, kitchen, and home life. The top floor features clothing and dress-up dolls from the 19th through the early 20th century. While charming, the museum has not a word of English.

Cost and Hours: €6, Tue-Sun 10:00-18:00, closed Mon, Juri-Gagarin-Ring 140A, tel. 0361/655-5607, www.volkskundemuseum-erfurt.de.

City Museum (Stadtmuseum)

Filling the historic Haus zum Stockfisch town house, this old-fashioned collection shows off items relating to the history of Erfurt and a small exhibit on Martin Luther. You'll also see a model of the town, dusty cases of artifacts, military uniforms, collections of guns and typewriters (both manufactured in Erfurt), and a film about the growth of Erfurt over time. Look for the wall of street signs from Erfurt's time as part of the former German Democratic Republic (communist East Germany). Under the communists, Erfurt's main drags were renamed Karl-Marx-Allee, Waffenbrüderschaft ("Brothers in Arms"—i.e., the Warsaw Pact), Völkerfreundschaft ("Peoples' Friendship"—a favorite buzzword of Stalin's), and October 7 Street (celebrating the date, in 1949, when the republic was officially formed). In a display case, you can compare banknotes from West Germany and East Germany.

Cost and Hours: €6, Tue-Sun 10:00-18:00, closed Mon, Johannesstrasse 169, tel. 0361/655-5650, www.stadtmuseum-erfurt.de.

ON THE OUTSKIRTS OF TOWN
Egapark

When the flowers are blooming (April through October), garden lovers travel from all over Germany to this sprawling green space at the western edge of town. You can stroll through various gardens (perennials, roses, dahlias, irises, sculptures, Japanese rock and water), visit the houses (for butterflies, tropical plants, and more), climb the observation tower, and tour the museum.

Cost and Hours: €8, €2 after 17:30, 20 percent discount with Deutsche Bahn train ticket, free Nov-mid-March; daily 9:00-18:00, shorter hours off-season; Gothaer Strasse 38, ride tram #2 from the train station, tel. 0361/564-3737, www.egapark-erfurt.de.

NEAR ERFURT

Two other interesting sights are close to Erfurt—the town of **Eisleben,** where Luther was born, and the **Peasants' War Panorama** (in Bad Frankenhausen), a monumental painting that depicts the final battle of the 1525 uprising. Both Eisleben and Bad Frankenhausen can be reached by public transportation, but these sights are most easily visited by those with cars. For driving directions, check with the TI in Erfurt.

Luther's Birth House in Eisleben

Luther pilgrims will enjoy a short stop in the town where he was born and died—Eisleben. Luther's father was a miner, and Eisleben is still in a mining district. A small and rough town of 25,000, it has a fine market square under a Gothic church with a Martin Luther statue marking the center. The house where Luther was born in 1483 burned down, and the "birth house" (a 1689 reconstruction) contains a good museum (they claim it's the oldest in Germany) with lots of artifacts.

Cost and Hours: €4, daily 10:00-18:00, Nov-March Tue-Sun 10:00-17:00, closed Mon, located next to the TI at Lutherstrasse 15, tel. 0347/560-2124.

Panorama Museum/Peasants' War Panorama (Bauernkriegspanorama)

Located in the town of Bad Frankenhausen, about 30 minutes north of Erfurt, this museum holds a massive, 400-foot-long painting in the round showing vividly (and with an old, East German communist slant) the bloody Peasants' War of 1525. It's housed in a 007-looking building at the top of the hill where 6,000 peasants, armed with shovels and axes, were slaughtered while battling the well-armed troops of the Holy Roman Emperor, marking the end of the Peasants' War.

Cost and Hours: €6, includes essential audioguide, Tue-Sun 10:00-18:00, Nov-March until 17:00, closed Mon year-round, good cafeteria, tel. 034/671-6190, www.panorama-museum.de.

Visiting the Museum: This monumental artwork (officially titled *Frühbürgerliche Revolution in Deutschland* a.k.a. *Early Bourgeois Revolution in Germany*) portrays more than just a horrible battle. It shows the bloody transition between the medieval and modern worlds. At the panorama's base, 20 great humanists—change agents from the end of the Middle Ages (Luther, Erasmus, other Protestant reformers, Copernicus, Dürer, and more)—gather around a well. Above them a colossal battle takes place under a rainbow, with the Emperor's troops on the left, and the doomed rabble on the right. Farther to the right is an elegant couple (with their backs to us), who dance before a gallows. The message: The elites continue to win.

LUTHERLAND

This painting was done in the 1980s, during the last years of Communist rule, by Werner Tübke. The government of East Germany wanted to celebrate the struggle of peasants 500 years ago as a reminder of the same struggle being valiantly fought by the modern working class.

Sleeping in Erfurt

Like many other former East-German cities, Erfurt is short on characteristic little family-run inns. The accommodations here are mostly sterile business-class hotels offering predictable comfort in the Old Town core. Note that Erfurt charges a 5 percent "cultural tax" on all overnight stays in town.

$$$ Hotel Zumnorde, buried in the Anger shopping district, has 54 spacious, somewhat overpriced rooms and ample public spaces, including a roof garden and wine bar (air-con in some rooms, family apartments, elevator, free sauna, pay parking, Anger 50 but enter on the side street at Weitergasse 26, tel. 0361/56800, www.hotel-zumnorde.de, info@hotel-zumnorde.de).

$$$ Mercure Hotel Erfurt Altstadt, part of the Europe-wide business-class chain, has 141 rooms on a nondescript street between the Anger shopping district and the main sightseeing zone (breakfast extra, elevator, pay parking, Meienbergstrasse 26, tel. 0361/59490, www.mercure.com, h5375@accor.com).

$$ Hotel am Kaisersaal offers 90 business-class rooms in an inviting, quiet location, just a few steps off the charming Wenigemarkt restaurant square (air-con in most rooms, elevator, pay parking, Futterstrasse 8, tel. 0361/658560, www.hotel-am-kaisersaal.de, info@hotel-am-kaisersaal.de).

$$ Ibis Hotel Erfurt Altstadt offers 105 centrally located rooms with cookie-cutter comfort. Considering the dearth of characteristic hotels in town, if you're going to sleep in an Ibis, it might as well be here (breakfast extra, air-con, elevator, pay garage parking, Barfüsserstrasse 9, tel. 0361/66410, https://ibis.accorhotels.com, h1648@accor.com).

$$ Gästehaus Nikolai, run by the Augustinian Monastery, has 17 old-fashioned rooms along the river, just up the street from the monastery (family room, limited free parking, Augustinerstrasse 30, tel. 0361/598-170, www.augustinerkloster.de, gaestehaus-nikolai@augustinerkloster.de). This place is far enough from the station that you might want to bring your luggage there by tram (three stops on the #1, #3, or #5 to Augustinerkloster).

$ St. Augustine's Evangelical Monastery, a conference center where Luther prayed, studied, and taught, is calm, peaceful, and feels very Lutheran. They rent simple, modern rooms—26 singles and 25 twin-bedded doubles—all with private bathrooms (Augustinerstrasse 10, tel. 0361/576-600, www.augustinerkloster.de, info@augustinerkloster.de).

Eating in Erfurt

A Thuringian staple is the distinctive potato dumpling called a *Kloss* (plural: *Klösse*). About the size of a tennis ball, these are soft and light, though generally drenched in gravy, and served with meat dishes and sometimes in soups. Many Erfurt menus include an array of dumpling dishes. Thuringians are also proud of their own special type of peppery sausage.

Most of Erfurt's restaurants are quite plain-Jane—don't expect culinary variety here. Since little distinguishes one place from the next, the stakes are low—just look for an ambience that appeals.

$$ Zum Güldenen Rade ("At the Golden Wheel") has an appealing beer garden out back—under trees and surrounded by half-timbers (with both table service and self-service sections). To eat cheaply, order self-serve grub at the counter—cheap beer, bratwurst, pork chops, potato salad. There's also indoor seating. Understandably touristy, it offers classic German and Thuringian cuisine, including a few vegetarian *Klösse* options (Mon-Sat 11:00-24:00, Sun until 22:00, Marktstrasse 50, tel. 0361/561-3506).

$$ Kromer's Restaurant serves "Thuringian slow food"—traditional dishes, great salads, and vegetarian meals with local ingredients in a classy and untouristy setting. They have a small courtyard, a charming dining room, and a romantic barrel-vaulted cellar (Tue-Sun 17:00-23:00, Sat-Sun also 11:30-14:30, closed Mon, near Preachers' Church at Kleine Arche 4, tel. 0361/6447-7211).

$$ Übersee ("Over the Water") is a lively restaurant and bar with tables on a terrace over the river, just upstream from the Merchants' Bridge. It has an eclectic international menu and seating that sprawls through two adjacent buildings—one new, one old—and out onto the best riverfront terraces in town (Mon-Sat 9:00 until late, Sun 10:30-14:00, Kürschnergasse 8, tel. 0361/644-7607).

$$ Feuerkugel serves up good, traditional Thuringian cooking, supposedly from the recipe book of "Oma Käthe" (Granny Katie). Its cozy, warm, woody interior is particularly inviting. For balmy evenings, they have a small terrace out back and pleasant tables on the cobbled lane in front (daily 11:00-24:00, Michaelisstrasse 3, tel. 0361/789-1256).

$$$ Mathilda has a country-chic interior and a dedication to simple, quality ingredients on its Mediterranean menu. Pick a pour from the top-notch wine list to pair with their handmade pasta or catch of the day (Mon-Thu 17:00-22:00, Fri-Sat from 11:00, closed Sun, reservations smart, Barfüsserstrasse 1, tel. 0361/216-9096, www.mathilda-restaurant.de).

$ Schnitzler, true to its name, serves schnitzel in many varieties—huge and splittable—along with other options. It's right on Domplatz, with a nondescript interior and fine outdoor tables looking toward the cathedral and St. Severus (daily 11:00-23:00, Domplatz 32, tel. 0361/644-7557).

$ Cognito offers a fresh, healthy, self-service alternative with plenty of vegetarian options right next to the Merchants' Bridge. This student-vibe place dishes up soups, curries, salads, and coffee drinks. Get it to go or enjoy the comfortable, hip lounge interior on two floors (daily 7:30-22:30, Hefengasse 1, tel. 0361/660-4666).

Wenigemarkt Eateries: The characteristic "little market square" is ringed with inviting cafés, bars, and restaurants. For a good Italian meal consider **$$ Osteria "Il Ponte,"** with fine seating inside and on the square (daily 10:00-24:00, Wenigemarkt 2, tel. 0361/5415-7426).

Fast Food: To grab a quick *Thüringer* bratwurst, stop by **$ Faust Food,** which grills up sausages and other meats at low prices (€3 or less). Pick a table inside or out. A hit with students, it's on a forgotten lane in the middle of town—so near all the tourists, yet so far away (Wed-Sat 11:00-23:00, Sun until 19:00, closed Mon-Tue, Waagegasse 1, tel. 0361/786-9969).

Ice Cream: Two popular places are **Eiscafé Riva** (on the east end of Rathaus Bridge) and **Eiscafé San Remo** (at Marktstrasse 21, a block off Domplatz). On the Merchant's Bridge, **Goldhelm Eiskrämer** serves inventive seasonal flavors such as port wine with chocolate or buttermilk passionfruit.

Late-Night Drinks: Modern Masters is the favorite in this student town for cocktails, with a sophisticated yet unsnooty atmosphere. Its historic interior is cool and inviting, and its outdoor tables are great for people-watching (no food—only drinks, Tue-Sat 18:00 until late, closed Sun-Mon, right at the start of Michaelisstrasse at #48, tel. 0361/550-7255).

Erfurt Connections

From Erfurt by Train to: Eisenach and **Wartburg Castle** (2/hour, 30 minutes on IC or ICE train, 45 minutes on regional train), **Leipzig** (hourly, 45 minutes on ICE train), **Wittenberg** (hourly, 1.5 hours), **Dresden** (hourly, 2 hours, some with transfer in Leipzig), **Berlin** (1-2/hour, 2 hours), **Hamburg** (hourly, 4 hours), **Frankfurt** (1-2/hour, 2.5 hours), **Würzburg** (2/hour, 2 hours, many with a transfer), **Nürnberg** (hourly, 1.5 hours), **Munich** (hourly, 2.5 hours). Train info: www.bahn.com.

Wartburg Castle

Just west of Erfurt is another important Martin Luther sight: Wartburg Castle (VART-boorg), perched over the town of Eisenach (EYE-zehn-nahkh). When Luther spoke out against Church corruption, he made enemies of the pope and emperor, and put his life in jeopardy. Luther was given refuge by a sympathetic prince in this easily defended castle, and—hidden away in a small room—he diligently translated the New Testament from original Greek sources. Although Luther's translation was not the first version of the Bible printed in German, it was the first translated from Greek rather than Latin (and therefore more accurate). It was so widely circulated that it helped shape the development of standard written German—making Wartburg, in a sense, the birthplace of the modern German language.

PLANNING YOUR TIME

Wartburg Castle works well either as a side-trip from Erfurt or on the way between Erfurt and points west (such as Frankfurt or Würzburg). You can try to time your visit around the castle's hour-long, once-daily English tour (at 13:30). But the tour isn't essential unless you're here to see the castle's few fine late-19th-century rooms. Otherwise, you can see the castle courtyard and little museum, including the room where Luther worked, at any time during open hours.

GETTING THERE

First head for the town of Eisenach, which is 30-45 minutes west of Erfurt on the main train line. (The Eisenach train station has large lockers in the main hall, with storage up to 72 hours.) From the station, you can take the bus, catch a taxi, or hike up to Wartburg.

Bus #10 (€1.70) runs from the parking lot across the street from the station up to Wartburg at the top of each hour (Easter-Oct only, daily 9:00-17:00, 20-minute trip). A taxi costs about €10. Drivers can park in the lot by the castle bus stop (€5). With any of these options, you'll still have a steep 15-minute climb up the stairs to Wartburg itself—or you can hop on the shuttle bus for €2.

It's at least a 45-minute walk from the train station to Wartburg, with an elevation gain of about 650 feet. Exiting the station, turn right and walk about 10 minutes into the Eisenach town center; then hike up into the hills (following signs for *Wartburg;* get detailed directions at TI).

Returning to Eisenach: Bus #10 departs Wartburg at :25 past each hour for the train station (Easter-Oct 9:25-17:25). Walking downhill to Eisenach is quick (30 minutes) and pleasant if you have strong knees. The broad dirt path starts at the bend in the road below the castle bus stop and takes you through the woods back into town: Follow signs for *Markt* to reach the main square, then wind your way through town to the station.

ORIENTATION TO WARTBURG CASTLE

Cost and Hours: Castle courtyard-free, museum-€6, grounds open daily April-Oct 8:30-20:00 (last museum entry at 17:30), Nov-March 9:00-17:00 (last entry at 15:30).

Information: Tel. 03691/2500, www.wartburg.de.

Tours: A one-hour English tour departs daily at 13:30, year-round. Tours in German run every 10-20 minutes (April-Oct 8:30-17:00, Nov-March 9:00-15:30). Tours are €10 and include museum admission and access to the 19th-century rooms. The castle offers a tiny-print English handout to English-speaking visitors on a German tour.

Eating: The café in the castle courtyard serves *Flammkuchen* (German flatbread) and cakes. Halfway up the stairs from the parking lot, the self-serve **$ Wartburg-Terrasse** has dumpling-based dishes. The wurst stands by the parking lot and bus stop close around 18:00.

OVERVIEW

Dramatically capping a forested ridgeline high above Eisenach, Wartburg Castle is famous among Luther lovers as a place that gave shelter and solace to the recently excommunicated young scholar who was determined to translate the New Testament into his own living language. Pilgrims come here to see the room where Martin Luther carried out that important work. But Luther aside, Wartburg is a fine fortress in its own right, with a few opulent rooms that were lavishly redecorated during a surge of German pride in the late 1880s. In the castle courtyard, you can climb the tower *(Südturm)* for €0.50 by inserting coins into the turnstile.

BACKGROUND

Wartburg has an impressive history. In 1130, the castle became the seat of Thuringia's landgraves (counts who ruled the region on behalf of the Holy Roman Empire). Most of the castle's days were peaceful (read: dull), but it was an important center of power—and notable as the site of a contest of minstrels in 1207, a story later famously dramatized by Richard Wagner in his opera *Tannhäuser.*

In May of 1521, Luther came to the castle, disguised as a bearded man named Junker Jörg (Squire George). He spent the next year secretly translating the New Testament from Greek into German. His short visit helped put Wartburg on the map.

In October of 1817, shortly after German-speaking armies helped defeat Napoleon, recently formed fraternal organizations from around the region came together at this castle to celebrate German unity. It was one of the first occasions when German speakers began to band together and forge a common pride. In fact, the flag of one of those fraternities (from Jena) was later adopted as the flag of a united Germany, which still flies all over the country.

VISITING THE CASTLE

In the **museum,** placards tell a bit of the story of the castle, and paintings show how it looked before reconstruction. You get the chance to peek into one small "royal bedroom" that shows the sumptuous 19th-century restoration work, and there's also a collection of historical cutlery. One room displays a few paintings of Luther and his family (mostly mass produced

ones from Lucas Cranach's workshop). Find the images of Luther's parents—note the family resemblance. Compare the portraits of Luther at various stages in his life—in the garb of an Augustinian monk, wearing the cap of a distinguished professor, in the bearded disguise of Junker Jörg—as well as the portraits of some of his notable contemporaries.

After the museum exhibit comes the highlight for Luther pilgrims: Walk along the gallery with low timber arches to find the humble **Luther Room** (Lutherstube). This was the site of one of the greatest intellectual revolutions in human history: For 10 months, Luther hunkered down at a desk here and used original Greek sources to translate the New Testament into everyday German. For centuries Christian worship had been passed through the obscure Latin-speaking filter of the Roman Catholic Church. Luther's widely distributed translation gave Germans, even peasants, direct access to the Word of God. Luther's work also helped to codify the evolving German language—setting the foundation for the tongue still being spoken by the people around you. The furnishings you see aren't original and were placed in the room long after Luther's time.

The guided **tour** (which ends in the museum) is the only way to visit 10 rooms in the part of the castle that was restored in the

19th century. Highlights include spectacular, glittering Neo-Byzantine mosaics from the early 1900s; the Elisabeth Gallery (decorated with beautiful frescoes about the life of St. Elisabeth); the Hall of Minstrels (with walls decorated with the text of a poem about Wartburg's famous contest of minstrels—this room was the setting for part of Wagner's *Tannhäuser*); and the vast Banquet Hall (decorated in an exuberant Historicist style rivaling the creations of "Mad" King Ludwig, who had a replica of this room created at his Neuschwanstein Castle).

TOWN OF EISENACH

Squatting in the valley below Wartburg, this town is worth a quick stroll for those with extra time. The TI is on the main square, called the Markt (Mon-Fri 9:00-17:00, Tue from 10:00, Markt 24, tel. 03691/79230, www.eisenach. info). A building where Martin Luther lived for three years while attending high school here has been turned into a museum (Lutherhaus), as has the house once thought to be the birthplace of Johann Sebastian Bach (Bachhaus).

Eisenach Connections: Trains run to **Erfurt** (2/hour, 30 minutes on IC or ICE, 45 minutes on regional train), **Leipzig** (hourly, 75 minutes on ICE, more with transfer in Erfurt), **Wittenberg** (8/day direct, 2 hours; more with transfer in Erfurt or Leipzig, 2.5 hours), **Berlin** (every 2 hours direct, 2.5 hours; more with transfer in Erfurt), **Frankfurt** (hourly, 2 hours), **Würzburg** (hourly, 1.5 hours, transfer in Fulda), and **Munich** (every 2 hours direct, 5.5 hours; more with change in Erfurt or Fulda, 4 hours). Train info: www.bahn.com.

Wittenberg

You need only look at its official name—Lutherstadt Wittenberg—to know this small city's claim to fame. The adopted hometown of Martin Luther, and the birthplace of his Protestant Reformation, little Wittenberg has a gigantic history that belies its straightforward townscape. With a pair of historic churches—the Town Church of St. Mary, where Luther preached, and the Church of All Saints (Castle Church), where he famously hammered his 95 Theses to the door—and an excellent museum about Luther's life (Luther House), Wittenberg can be a worthwhile stop even for those unfamiliar with the Great Reformer. And for Lutherans, it's a pilgrimage. The notable painter Lucas Cranach the Elder, a contemporary and friend of Luther who also lived and worked in Wittenberg, left behind a slew of masterful paintings and woodcuts, and you can see where he lived as well.

Centuries of Germans have celebrated Wittenberg for its ties to Luther. In 1983, which marked Martin Luther's 500th birthday, Wittenberg was part of communist East Germany, whose atheistic regime was tearing down proud old churches elsewhere. But ignoring the Luther anniversary would have made the East German government, already unpopular, seem woefully out of touch. (The government also sensed an opportunity to attract Luther tourists and much-needed hard Western currency.) So the communists swallowed hard and rehabilitated the memory of Luther, tidying up the sights devoted to him. This may be why Wittenberg emerged from communism in better shape than many other East German towns.

The city received another round of upgrades in 2017, when it celebrated the 500th anniversary of Luther's famous 95 Theses—it's newly spiffed up and sparkling. Most tourists here are Germans (and American Lutherans), and the town is also a stop for riverboat cruise groups heading from Hamburg to Dresden and Prague. And yet, Wittenberg isn't unpleasantly touristy. Its pedestrianized main street feels quiet—sometimes almost deserted—and its sights are satisfying and quickly seen. Wittenberg works perfectly as a side-trip from Berlin (offering a refreshing small-town break from the intense city), and also works well on the way between Berlin and Leipzig, Erfurt, or even Dresden (handy lockers at Wittenberg train station).

GETTING TO WITTENBERG

It's a speedy 40 minutes from Berlin on ICE trains, or 1.5 hours on cheaper regional (RE) trains. All trains depart from the Berlin Hauptbahnhof; some regional trains also stop at Potsdamer

Wittenberg in the Early 1500s

As you explore Wittenberg, mentally time-travel to the days of Luther—the first few decades of the 16th century. The Renaissance was percolating to the south in Italy (where Michelangelo and Raphael were hard at work redecorating the Vatican), and a spirit of new ideas was also beginning to take hold in Germany.

The influential prince elector Frederick III "the Wise" (1463-1525), who had inherited half of Saxony from his father, chose sleepy Wittenberg as his royal seat. He built a stout castle here in 1492 (not open to visitors, but viewable from the park just beyond the town gate), and began remaking this humble fishing village into a proper Renaissance town. (That explains Wittenberg's grid of streets, compared with the twisty medieval muddle of many other German towns.) Frederick the Wise hired Lucas Cranach the Elder to be his official court painter. Cranach—along with his wife, Barbara, and son Lucas Cranach the Younger—lived in a big mansion on Market Square (today a museum; his statue—pictured above—is in the courtyard). Frederick also founded a university here (in 1502) and stocked it with some of the brightest minds of his time, including the promising young theologian Martin Luther and the brilliant classical-languages specialist Philipp Melanchthon. Cranach, Luther, Melanchthon, and others were good friends who regularly socialized and swapped ideas.

Although he remained a devout Catholic until the end of his life, Frederick the Wise supported Luther and the reformers in their darkest hour, likely saving them from obscurity or worse. Wittenberg would not be famous if not for Luther—but, most likely, if not for Frederick the Wise, Luther would not be famous, either.

Platz. If you're a small group day-tripping from Berlin, and are willing to take the slower regional trains, you can save a bundle with the **Brandenburg-Berlin-Ticket** (not valid on ICE). Available through Deutsche Bahn, this covers unlimited regional train travel throughout the Brandenburg region during one day, for up to five people, all for €29.

PLANNING YOUR TIME

Wittenberg's sights can be seen in just a few hours. For an efficient visit, from the train station ride the public bus to Marktplatz, start at the TI and Castle Church, then work your way downhill through town—sightseeing and possibly having lunch as you go. From the last couple of sights—Luther House and Asisi's Wittenberg 360 Panorama—it's about a 15-minute, downhill walk back to the train station.

Orientation to Wittenberg

Literally "White Hill," Wittenberg (Germans say VIT-tehn-behrk, pop. 50,000) sits atop a gentle rise above the Elbe River. The tourists' Wittenberg is essentially a one-street town: Its main drag runs about three-quarters of a mile from the Luther House (where the street is called Collegienstrasse) to the Castle Church (where it's called Schlossstrasse). The rest of the Old Town consists only of a few side streets. The modern part of town sprawls mostly to the north and east.

Don't confuse Wittenberg with Wittenberge, a town north of Berlin. (The correct Wittenberg sometimes shows up as "Kleinwittenberg" on GPS maps or "Lutherstadt Wittenberg" on some websites.)

TOURIST INFORMATION

Wittenberg's TI is at the far end of town from the train station, across the street from Castle Church (daily 9:00-18:00; Nov-March daily 10:00-17:00, Schlossplatz 2, tel. 03491/498-610, www.lutherstadt-wittenberg.de). The TI rents a town audioguide (€7, 2 hours of commentary—must return before closing time), and there's a pay WC next door. A second, less comprehensive branch of the TI is at the northern edge of the Old Town, in the Stadthaus (shorter hours than main TI).

ARRIVAL IN WITTENBERG

Wittenberg's **main train station** (listed on schedules as Lutherstadt Wittenberg) is a dull 15-minute walk from the Luther House and a 25-minute walk from the

TI and Castle Church. (The smaller Lutherstadt Wittenberg Altstadt station, while closer to the Old Town, only serves trains on a small branch line.) The station building has handy lockers, a café, and a ticket office. Nearby

(on the other side of the big, white tent) are **bus** stops for the ride into town. Look for bus #300 (toward Coswig) or bus #301 (toward Straach); these leave from bus stop #1 (every 30 minutes, 10-min-

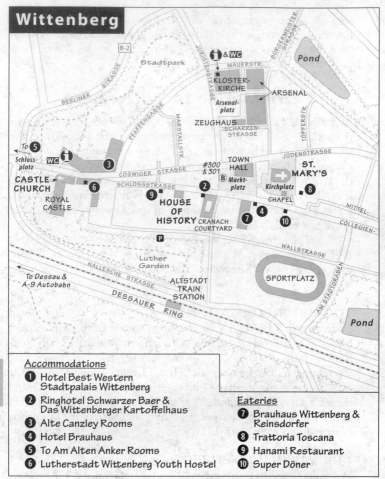

Accommodations
1. Hotel Best Western Stadtpalais Wittenberg
2. Ringhotel Schwarzer Baer & Das Wittenberger Kartoffelhaus
3. Alte Canzley Rooms
4. Hotel Brauhaus
5. To Am Alten Anker Rooms
6. Lutherstadt Wittenberg Youth Hostel

Eateries
7. Brauhaus Wittenberg & Reinsdorfer
8. Trattoria Toscana
9. Hanami Restaurant
10. Super Döner

ute ride, €1.30/ride, €2.50/day pass, buy tickets from driver). Stops aren't announced; you want the Marktplatz stop, right at the Old Town's main square (ask the driver to confirm). A **taxi** from the station to Schlossplatz (near the TI) should cost about €10 (if no taxis are waiting, call 03491/666-666). To **walk,** head left from the station, walk beneath the overpass, and look for signs directing you to the city center.

Drivers will find plenty of free on-street **parking** just outside the mostly pedestrianized town center.

HELPFUL HINTS

Festivals: Various festivals dot Wittenberg's calendar, including a three-day celebration of the wedding of Luther and Katharina (second weekend in June) and special events for **Reformation**

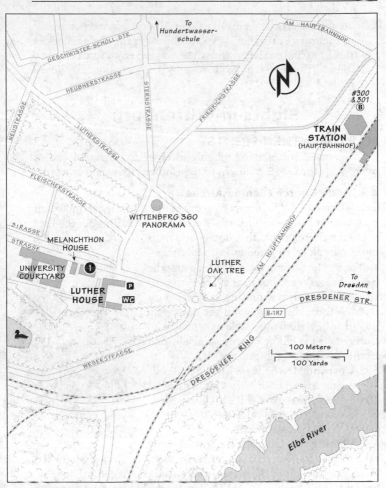

Day (Oct 31, when Luther nailed his 95 Theses to the church door).

Tours: Most walking-tour options (you'll likely see costumed Martin Luthers and Katharina von Boras leading groups through town) are in German only. For an English tour, hire your own local guide—gracious **Katja Köhler** does a great job telling Wittenberg's story (€80/2-hour tour, €130/4-hour tour, mobile 0177-688-8218, katjakochler@gmx.net).

English Worship Services: Local Lutherans offer English-language services in historic Wittenberg churches during the summer (April-Oct Wed-Fri at 16:00 in small Corpus Christi chapel next to Town Church of St. Mary; Sat at 17:00 in either Castle Church or Town Church of St. Mary; confirm times at www.wittenbergenglishministry.com).

Classical Concerts: It seems like there's always a concert on in one of the town's churches. If you're spending the night, check at the TI to find out when and where you can enjoy some classical music. (Luther—who said "to sing is to pray double"—loved music.)

Sights in Wittenberg

MARTIN LUTHER SIGHTS

I've organized these sights roughly in order from the TI end of town (with the Castle Church) to the Luther House end of town.

▲▲Castle Church (Schlosskirche)

This Church of All Saints was the site of one of the most important moments in European history: Martin Luther nailing his 95 Theses to the church door. That door—and most of the church as it existed in Luther's time—are long gone (destroyed in 1760, during the Seven Years' War). But in the late 19th century, as Germany was uniting as a nation for the first time, the church and the door were rebuilt in the Romantic style as a temple to Luther and his fellow reformers. You'll find Luther's humble tombstone inside.

Cost and Hours: Free; Mon-Sat 10:00-18:00, Sun from 11:30; Nov-March Tue-Sat 10:00-16:00, Sun from 11:30, closed Mon; Schlossplatz, tel. 03491/506-9160, www.schlosskirche-wittenberg.de.

Visiting the Church: Before entering, take a close look at that famous **side door** (in the middle of the church, to the left of the present-day entrance). According to most accounts, on October 31, 1517, a frustrated Martin Luther nailed a handwritten copy of 95 Theses—topics for discussion—to the wooden door that was here then. (What you see is a 19th-century bronze door engraved with the Latin theses.) The act wasn't quite as defiant as it sounds—the door served as a sort of community bulletin board. But the strong arguments Luther made about ending the practice of indulgences and other forms of Church corruption were revolutionary...as was his timing. Normally, Wittenbergers worshipped at the Town Church of St. Mary, but the day after Luther's act—All Saints' Day—was the one day each year that the Castle Church's interior was open to the public, who were invited to come inside, view Frederick the Wise's vast collection of relics, and purchase indulgences. Historians quibble over the exact day Luther made his theses public and whether he actually nailed them to the door, but there's no doubt that his work spurred a nascent sentiment of reform and cemented his role as that movement's leader.

Above the door is a glittering image of the crucified Christ flanked by Luther (on the left) and his fellow Reformer Philipp Melanchthon (on the right), with the skyline of Wittenberg behind them.

Go inside, walk down the **nave,** and look up. Notice the colorful coats of arms on the upper stained-glass windows, which represent German cities that became Protestant when they joined Luther's Reformation. The carved coats of arms on the railing honor larger principalities that also adopted Protestantism. The lower stained-glass windows, with images of Reformers, were grudgingly added for Luther's 500th birthday, in 1983, by the aggressively atheistic East German government...and it shows.

In the middle of the church, to the right (in front of the pulpit, with a raised plaque), you'll see the flower-bedecked **tomb of Martin Luther.** On the wall behind it is a replica of the large bronze tomb marker that originally covered Luther's remains. While this wasn't his home church (that would be the Town Church of St. Mary, just up the street and described later), this university church was traditionally where professors like Luther were entombed. On the left side of the nave is a similar raised plaque marking the grave of Luther's right-hand man and fellow professor, **Philipp Melanchthon.**

Proceed to the front of the church. In front of the high altar are large tomb markers for the **prince electors** who called Wittenberg home and provided safe harbor for Luther's provocative ideas. On the left is Frederick the Wise, and on his right is his younger brother, John the Steadfast. While Frederick remained devoutly Catholic throughout his life, his support for Luther, Melanchthon, and the early Protestant Reformers never wavered. Frederick's successor, John, converted to Protestantism and, in a fit of iconoclasm, destroyed his brother's impressive collection of relics.

Flanking these markers are larger plaques and statues (from the original church) that depict these important brothers.

▲Market Square (Marktplatz)

This wide square is much the same today as it was in Luther's time. An all-purpose space back then, it was used for everything from tournaments to executions. The square is dominated by the Renaissance-style **Town Hall** (Rathaus). Notice the seven small, filled-in doors at the right side of the building, which led to a shopping gallery back when the building's cellar hosted a little marketplace (today the Town Hall houses a 20th-century Christian art collection). In one corner of the square you'll find a metal model of Wittenberg's Old Town. In the middle of the square are 19th-century **statues** of Martin Luther (pictured here) and Philipp Melanchthon (pictured on next page).

The main street through town is lined by delightful gurgling **canals,** as in a few other German cities, like Freiburg and Augsburg. When Luther first moved to Wittenberg, he was disgusted by these, which carried drinking water (on the way into town) and smelly sewage (on the way out). Years later, they were covered over by the modern street. But recently they were opened up to the air to evoke the ambience of Luther's time.

Cranach Courtyard (Cranachhof)

Find the big beige Renaissance building at Schlossstrasse 1, in one corner of the square, with a pharmacy (the Lucas-Cranach-Apotheke) on the ground floor.

This building, circling a surprisingly large courtyard, was the residence of the artist Lucas Cranach the Elder. Enter the courtyard to see a statue of Cranach sketching at the far end.

As the official court painter for Frederick the Wise, Cranach was one of the most esteemed men in town, but he was also an entrepreneur who dabbled in endeavors like printing and running a pharmacy. Cranach and Luther were fast friends. The artist was the only painter who had permission to do portraits of Luther and his family (Cranach and his school produced and reproduced some 2,000 Luther portraits), and he was one of the first printers of Luther's writings. Cranach's house is also where Luther's future bride, Katharina von Bora, lived when she first came to Wittenberg (fresh out of the convent).

Philipp Melanchthon (1497-1560)

While everyone who comes to Wittenberg has heard of Martin Luther, many are surprised to find another important figure celebrated here with almost equal reverence: Philipp Melanchthon. The Garfunkel to Luther's Simon, Melanchthon was a brainy university professor who also played a critical role in the Protestant Reformation.

Born Philipp Schwartzerdt in southern Germany, he later changed his name to its Greek translation, Melanchthon ("black soil"). Although he was short, young, sickly, and notoriously unattractive, Melanchthon impressed everybody in Wittenberg with his keen intellect. In fact, when Melanchthon became disillusioned with Wittenberg and threatened to move away, Frederick the Wise persuaded him to stay by arranging a marriage for him (to the mayor's daughter, no less). While Luther was no intellectual slouch, Melanchthon was even more brilliant—he taught several topics (specializing in ancient languages, pedagogy, and theology) and encouraged women to pursue university study. Particularly gifted with languages, he provided Luther with invaluable assistance when translating the Bible into German from the original Greek and Hebrew texts.

For decades, this space sat in ruins (see the pre-1989 photo in the entry arch.) But it's been converted into a kind of cultural center, hosting artists' studios, a small bar, a gift shop, comfortable hotel rooms, and—at the far end of the courtyard—an old-fashioned print shop *(Druckerstube)*. Operated by a quirky printer who speaks some English and enjoys explaining the importance of Luther's statement, "This is a German nation—the people speak German," the shop uses traditional methods to create postcards and replicas of works by Luther and Cranach (closed Sun). There's a small Cranach museum a few doors away (at #4 on Market Square).

▲▲Town Church of St. Mary (Stadtkirche St. Marien)

Towering over a row of buildings at the end of Market Square, this is the oldest building in town and an impressively historic place to be surrounded by Luther lore.

Before stepping inside, notice that the tops of the twin towers don't quite match the rest of the building. Formerly pointy Gothic steeples, these were knocked down during a 1546 battle. They were

later rebuilt in the round Renaissance style you see today.

Cost and Hours: Free to enter, Mon-Sat 10:00-18:00, Sun from 11:30, Nov-Easter until 16:00, free organ concerts May-Oct Fri at 18:00, tel. 03491/62830, www.stadtkirchengemeinde-wittenberg.de.

Visiting the Church: The interior of the Town Church of St. Mary is striking for its pure, uncluttered feel. Once ornately painted and slathered with chapels, statues, and ornamentation, it was cleaned out when it became Lutheran. Sit in a pew and enjoy the Doublemint freshness of the space.

For most of his life, this was Luther's home church—where he was married, where his children were baptized, and where he preached over 2,000 times. This is where what many consider to be the first-ever Protestant service took place, on Christmas Day in 1521 (although Martin Luther wasn't in attendance—he was hiding out at Wartburg Castle). The readings were in German (not Latin), communion was taken by everyone (not just priests), and hymns were sung by the congregation—actually quite radical at the time.

At the front of the church, the **baptismal font** is where Luther's own children were baptized. Notice the tube extending from the basin directly down toward the ground. This allowed water, after having washed away sin, to be drained directly into what was a sandy floor, so it could be transmitted, unimpeded, to hell. Around the lower legs of the font, notice the many demons attempting to reach the baby being baptized up top—but their progress is blocked by the righteous saints.

The focal point of the church is the colorful, engaging, almost whimsical **altar painting** by Lucas Cranach the Elder, the Younger, and their school (completed in 1547, the year after Luther died). The gang's all here: All the big-name early Protestants and their buddies have showed up to reenact classic ecclesiastical scenes. In the spirit of the Reformation, these aren't saints or royals—they're just people.

The bottom panel shows Martin Luther preaching from a pulpit, one hand on the Bible and the other pointing to Christ, as he engages an enthralled group of worshippers. The fluttering loincloth of Jesus helps to convey the message from preacher to parishioner. But notice that, true to life, some of those people aren't paying attention—they're chatting and looking around. The woman watching Luther most intently is his wife, Katha-

rina. She's surrounded by their many children. Cranach (with the big white beard) is in the back.

The panel on the left shows Philipp Melanchthon (who was not a priest) baptizing a baby. The early reformers believed that lay people—not exclusively priests—could perform baptisms. In the foreground, the extravagantly dressed woman with her back to us is Cranach's wife, Barbara. Supposedly, she grew frustrated that her husband was always painting Luther, Katharina, and others, but never her. "Fine," he said. "I'll include you in the altarpiece."

On the right panel, Johannes Bugenhagen (among reformers, he ranks third after Luther and Melanchthon) is hearing confession from two very different people. Over the head of the obviously distraught and repentant man on the left, Bugenhagen holds the key of heaven—the sinner has done right by confessing and will reap eternal rewards. The man on the right, however, is trying to buy his way into heaven—but his hands are tied and the key of heaven is behind him, indicating he can't purchase paradise.

The central panel features the Last Supper, with the reformers standing in for the apostles. Notice the round table, which symbolizes how, in Protestantism, all are equal. People from all walks of life are actively engaging each other. It's easy to pick out Judas in the foreground (he wears yellow, as evildoers often do in Cranach paintings). On the opposite side of the table, Martin Luther (clad in black, wearing the bearded disguise of Junker Jörg) is being handed a chalice by Lucas Cranach the Younger. In contrast to Catholic worship at the time, Protestant services invited everybody to participate in communion.

Circle behind the painting and look at the lower panel, which appears as though it's been defaced by some no-good teenagers. It was...centuries ago. Around Luther's time, students of theology came here at the end of their studies and scratched their names or initials into the painting: on the left, in the river of knowledge, if they'd done well—or on the right, in hell, if they'd flunked. Looking carefully among the damned (higher up, on a skull), you can find the name "Johannes Luther"—Martin's son. (Thankfully, he had more success after he switched to law.)

The zone behind the altar has several interesting paintings. Most important is a painting labeled *Epitaph for Paul Eber and his Family* (better known as **The Vineyard of the Lord**), by Lucas Cranach the Younger. This work's propaganda-for-the-Reformation motives are obvious: On the right, the reformers tend to the garden of the Lord (that's Martin Luther raking and Philipp Melanchthon pulling water from the well—just as the reformers went back to the original source to translate their Bible). On the left, the pope and his cronies (in their excessively opulent robes) trash all their hard work. In the lower-

left corner, everyone lines up to receive their reward from Jesus. The pope (wearing yellow, again symbolizing evil) has already received his, but keeps his hand outstretched, expecting more than his share. In the lower right, the reformers (in their simple black robes) pray reverently.

As you head back up the nave to exit, look up: The grand **organ** dates from the communist period (1983), and booms out short organ concerts in summer. Luther's greatest musical hit, "A Mighty Fortress is Our God," was first sung here.

Exiting the way you came in, turn left and go to the back corner of the church. Look up at the bottom of the roofline to find the relief of a pig, called the **Judensau** ("Jewish sow"). This bit of medieval anti-Semitic propaganda was designed to intimidate Wittenberg's Jews, who lived in the area just behind the church. Look carefully at the pig, which is considered unclean in the Jewish faith: Jewish children are suckling from it, and

a rabbi seems to be peering inquisitively into its rear end. When restoring the church, church authorities asked the Jewish community in Berlin what they should do with this painful remnant of a less-enlightened time. Rather than cover it, they suggested leaving it here as a part of the town's heritage, and adding a modern monument: Look for the plaque in the cobbles directly below the pig, where four paving stones look as if they're being pried apart by something bubbling up from beneath. The message: You can't hide uncomfortable facts; they will find a way to see the light of day. The adjacent cedar tree was donated by students in Tel Aviv.

Behind you, go through the gap between the buildings near

the pig to see one of Wittenberg's 16th-century **fountains.** Part of Frederick the Wise's improvements, this network of fountains (with wooden pipes) still works—but nobody knows quite how.

▲▲Luther House (Lutherhaus)

Luther's former home has been converted into an excellent museum displaying original paintings, manuscripts, and other Luther-era items—including the

pulpit from which Luther preached, famous portraits of Luther and the other reformers by Lucas Cranach, and Luther's original New Testament and Bible translations into High German. Everything is fully described, and touch-screen stations provide more depth.

Cost and Hours: €8, €10 combo-ticket with Melanchthon House; daily 10:00-18:00; Nov-March Tue-Sun 10:00-17:00, closed Mon; Collegienstrasse 54, tel. 03491/420-3171, www. martinluther.de.

Visiting the House: From the street, step through the passage (at #59) into the inner courtyard to see the giant, turreted

building. Not really a "house," this was originally a monastery. Luther lived here first as a monk and again later, after he had married Katharina von Bora (the building was a wedding gift from a prince elector who took Luther under his wing). Katharina rented out rooms to students, and kept the family fed and watered by cultivating a garden, brewing beer, and even breeding cattle. In the middle of the courtyard is a **statue of Katharina.** Erected on her 500th birthday in 1999, the sculpture symbolizes her leaving her former life at a nunnery and beginning a new one with Martin Luther.

Head inside through the gateway on your right. From the ticket desk, go straight into the first room to see a simplified model of Wittenberg during Luther's time; paintings by Lucas Cranach (including a portrait of Frederick the Wise, the prince elector who supported Luther); and a woodcut print of a knights' tournament at Market Square.

The next room juxtaposes several **historic items.** Flanking the door are an indulgence chest and an original letter of indulgence *(Ablassurkunde),* from 1492. Those who bought indulgences would supposedly be rescued from their sins...while generating substantial income for the Catholic Church. Money raised was applied directly to an ambitious building project at the Vatican: On the right, see the engraving of St. Peter's Basilica, with its spectacular dome still under construction. Albrecht of Brandenburg (as the archbishop of Mainz, he was Luther's direct superior) and Pope Leo X (both pictured at right), stunningly influential and wealthy, were part of

a finely tuned business of selling forgiveness to mostly illiterate Christians frightened they'd spend eons in purgatory...or worse.

In contrast to the opulence in Roman Catholic churches, see Martin Luther's original lindenwood **pulpit** from the Town Church of St. Mary. Notice how relatively humble it is—imagine him climbing up to the top and bringing the Reformation message to a packed church. Nearby is the first printed version of Luther's troublemaking 95 Theses.

Continue into the **refectory,** where students would sit around a long table to dine. At the far end of this great hall is Cranach's wonderful painting *The Ten Commandments* (1516). This was originally designed for the Town Hall so that anybody could see it; and today, as then, it's handy for a review of Sunday school lessons. See if you can identify each of the 10 commandments being broken (and followed)—and note that the

same nobleman (in yellow and black) is responsible for half the sins. In each panel, an eerie-eyed demon prods the sinners.

In a side passage near the refectory, you can peruse a small but endearing exhibit with wood-carved figures acting out daily life in Luther's time.

Up on the **first floor** is a rare painting of a relatively young Martin Luther by Cranach (1520). In the little dimly lit alcove, find the Cranach-printed first edition (1522) of Luther's German translation of the New Testament, illustrated with Cranach woodcuts. Nearby is the "community chest," the first systematized charity for poor people—Protestants began steering donations to the needy rather than into Church coffers. (Compare this to the Church's indulgence chest we saw earlier.)

Pass through a lecture hall dominated by a fancy gilded lectern into the actual private **residence** of the Luther family (which still smells like the 16th century). Look for his-and-hers Cranach paintings of Martin and Katharina, three years after their wedding. Imagine the lifestyle of these newlyweds—he a former monk and priest, she a former nun. While the idealistic Luther took little or no payment for preaching and writing, and depended on the charity of wealthy local supporters, Katharina was a businesswoman who balanced the books and kept this huge household going. Look for the lockbox they used to protect their valuables. Katharina kept the key so Luther wouldn't give everything they owned to the poor.

The centerpiece is the **"Lutherstube"**—the room with benches, a stove, and the table where Luther engaged in spirited conversations with his colleagues. Notice the names scratched into the ceiling, left behind by visiting VIPs (on the door, protected by glass, is the John Hancock of Russian czars, Peter the Great). Luther's adjoining study contains a collection of his beer mugs (Luther loved his suds).

In the final room, see Luther's translation of the complete Bible from 1534, printed and illustrated by Cranach with 266 woodcuts, and a tiny hymnal from 1533. Luther, who believed that music should be an important part of worship, composed hymns that are still sung today.

An adjacent room features an old printing press and cases filled with booklets that Luther authored and Cranach illustrated. In this room you can find (on the wall) an etching of "the pope as Satan," a case full of anti-Jewish-themed books Luther wrote late in his life, and covers with more of Cranach's political cartoon etchings—designed so even the illiterate could get the gist of Luther's message. Perhaps the first PR genius to "go viral," Luther sold more than a quarter million books and was the best-selling German author of the 16th century.

Now climb the stairs to the **top floor,** which features a small treasury filled with 16th-century documents (including a small printed indulgence from 1515 with empty blanks for the purchaser to fill in, and a big indulgence from 1492 worth 100 fewer days in purgatory). This exhibit finishes with an intriguing exhibit of

Luther's Legacy

It'd be difficult to overstate the impact Luther and the Protestant Reformation he led had on European history.

Even during Luther's lifetime, the Reformation raged across northern Europe. In Holland, Protestant extremists marched into Catholic churches, lopped off the heads of holy statues, stripped gold-leaf angels from the walls, and shattered stained-glass windows in a fit of anti-Catholic iconoclasm.

Switzerland—with its deep roots in democracy and self-rule—was a haven for free thinkers, led by Ulrich Zwingli (1484-1531) and the exiled Frenchman John Calvin (1509-1564), who established a theocratic government and inspired French followers called Huguenots.

When England's charismatic King Henry VIII (r. 1509-1547) was excommunicated for divorcing Catherine of Aragon so he could marry Anne Boleyn, Henry "divorced" England from the Catholic Church, established the Church of England (or "Anglican Church") and "dissolved" (destroyed) England's many countryside abbeys.

The Vatican responded to these Protestant revolutions with the Counter-Reformation, which was an attempt to put the universal Catholic Church back together using a carrot-and-stick approach. On the one hand, the Church worked diligently to eliminate corruption from within, reach out to alienated members, do missionary work, and inspire the faithful with exalted Church art. This "Counter-Reformation" art, Baroque and bubbly, gave worshippers a glimpse of the heaven that awaited those who remained faithful. On the other hand, when need be, the Church resorted to propaganda, intimidation, and outright force—as doled out by the dreaded Inquisition.

The Reformation spawned a century of Catholic-versus-Protestant wars, with each side convinced that God favored them. When these wars finally ended, Western civilization realized what it should have known from the start: Catholics and Protestants would have to live together. The Peace of Westphalia (1648) decreed that the leader of each country would decide the religion of his nation. Ultimately this divided Europe in half: the generally Protestant north (Scandinavia, the Low Countries, northern Germany, and England), and the predominantly Catholic south (Spain, Portugal, Italy, and southern Germany).

It's clear that Luther's legacy lives on. If you are a Lutheran, Presbyterian, Methodist, Baptist, Episcopalian—or any one of a number of other Protestant faiths—you're the spiritual descendant of this German monk.

images showing how Luther has been represented in the centuries after his death. At the very end, check out Luther posters from Hitler's time and from communist days (including the 1982 East German illustration showing Luther conversing at a table with Che Guevara and other revolutionaries). The East German government decided that it was OK to tell Luther's story—as long as it was linked to the ideals of socialist revolution.

Luther Sights near Luther House

Several other Reformation sights cluster along Collegienstrasse, at the Luther House end of town:

Leaving the Luther House, turn right down Collegienstrasse with your back toward the town center (toward the ring road). At the big roundabout (see map), at the edge of the park on the left, is the famous **"Luther Oak" tree** marking the spot where Luther burned the papal bull that threatened him with excommunication.

About a block toward Market Square from the Luther House are two other buildings of interest to Lutherans. At #60 (with the rounded gables) is the **Melanchthon House** (Melanchthonhaus)—given to Philipp Melanchthon to persuade him to stay in Wittenberg when he threatened to move elsewhere, and now a museum about his life. Nothing survives from Melanchthon's household, but the museum tries hard to bring him to life, and everything is described in English (€5, €10 combo-ticket with Luther House; daily 10:00-18:00; Nov-March Tue-Sun until 17:00, closed Mon; tel. 03491/420-3171).

At #62a, duck through the doorway into the **university court-yard.** These are some of the original buildings where Luther, Melanchthon, and their colleagues worked. Wall plaques ringing the courtyard celebrate famous professors and alumni.

▲Wittenberg 360 Panorama: Luther 1517

Berlin artist Yadegar Asisi—who has created these immersive, 360-degree panorama paintings around eastern Germany—has arrived in Wittenberg. A giant bunker-like structure in a park near the Luther House is home to this nearly 12,000-square-foot work that wraps entirely around the viewer. Using a combination of photographed models and digitally reconstructed historic buildings, Asisi recreates a day in the life of the grubby, crowded, and colorful town on the cusp of the Reformation—standing right in front of the Castle Church. Light and sound effects highlight different parts of the giant illustration, inviting you to tune into various details (pick up the leaflet, which explains some of the tableaus you'll see). You can climb up the metal tower in the middle of the room for a higher vantage point. Panorama paintings like this one were all the rage in the 19th century, and Asisi does a good job of updat-ing the magic for the modern era. While certainly overpriced, this could be worth the splurge to round out your Luther experience.

Cost and Hours: €11, daily 9:00-18:00, Lutherstrasse 42, www.wittenberg360.de.

Luther Garden

This orchard of ecumenism, a short walk just south of Market Square, is a leafy statement that Christian communities—Protestant, Catholic, and Orthodox—can cooperate. Hundreds of trees from many Christian communities from all over the world have been planted, and each has a sister tree planted in its community of origin.

OTHER WITTENBERG SIGHTS

▲House of History (Haus der Geschichte)

Those intrigued by the communist chapter of Wittenberg's history will enjoy this museum's three floors of everyday items from East German times (1949-1989). For Cold War buffs, it's worth ▲▲.

The *Wende* (German reunification) in 1989 erased an entire culture, and in the space of a few years East German toys, food brands, cars, schoolbooks, and much more were replaced by Western ones—awakening nostalgia even in those who otherwise welcomed the end of communism. Over the past two decades, a dedicated staff has collected thousands of items that memorialize the world of their youth. The museum also includes a few rooms showing furnishings and fashions from the 1920s and 1930s. On the ground floor, you'll find a fully stocked communist-era grocery store, a cozy DDR pub, and an exhibit (German only) on the life of Soviet troops posted to East Germany. The museum is directed at nostalgic German visitors, but the €1 audioguide makes it more meaningful to outsiders.

Cost and Hours: €6, daily 10:00-18:00; Nov-Feb Tue-Sun until 17:00, closed Mon; Schlossstrasse 6, tel. 03491/409-004, www.pflug-ev.de.

Historical Town Information Center (Historisches Stadtinformation)

This slick new facility—in two buildings facing Arsenalplatz, a couple of blocks north of Marktplatz—illustrates the history of Wittenberg beyond the life of its most famous resident. The Zeughaus (former armory) displays a large model of Wittenberg in 1873, offering a good look at its earthen ramparts and moat. Across the square—displayed in the enclosed ruins of the Klosterkirche (former Franciscan monastery)—are exhibits on the Ascanian dukes of Saxony, who ruled this area before Luther. (This building adjoins the Stadthaus, with a branch TI, a concert hall, and a free WC.) While presented with modern flair, there's only so much to say—making this, mostly, a "so what?" experience.

Cost and Hours: €2; daily 9:00-18:00; Nov-March Tue-Sun 10:00-17:00, closed Mon; Zeughaus at Juristenstrasse 16a, Klosterkirche at Mauerstrasse 18.

Hundertwasserschule

This formerly drab communist-era public school, on the northeast outskirts of town, was redecorated in 1993 with wildly colorful and imaginative flair by Austrian architect Friedensreich Hundertwasser. Most intriguing to architecture buffs, it's a long 30-minute walk from the city center (interior closed to the public but exterior viewable anytime, officially called "Luther-Melanchthon-Gymnasium," Schillerstrasse 22a, www.hundertwasserschule.de).

Cruises and Biking the Elbe River Valley

While you can pay to take a brief cruise on the Elbe River, there's not much to see other than a panoramic view of town (details at TI). The Elbe Valley also attracts many bicycle tourists, following the bike path called the Elberadweg (cycling route info at www.elberadweg.de).

Sleeping in Wittenberg

Wittenberg has a wide range of charming hotels at fine prices. My listings (except Am Alten Anker) are right in the heart of the Old Town. Air-conditioning is rare.

$$$ Hotel Best Western Stadtpalais Wittenberg is a professional-feeling place with 78 rooms offering predictable business-class comfort right on the main drag, near the Luther House (some rooms have air-con, elevator, pay parking, Collegienstrasse 56, tel. 03491/4250, www.stadtpalais.bestwestern.de, info@stadtpalais.bestwestern.de).

$$ Ringhotel Schwarzer Baer ("Black Bear") has 32 modern, comfortable rooms—each a bit different, but all of them stylish—in a period building with hardwood floors right off Market Square (elevator, free parking, Schlossstrasse 2, tel. 03491/420-4344, http://schwarzer-baer-wittenberg.de, info@schwarzer-baer-wittenberg.de).

$$ Alte Canzley, right next to the TI and across from the Castle Church, has nine enormous, well-equipped (if somewhat dated) rooms above a restaurant in a historic building from 1391. You'll pay extra for a small kitchenette or a view of the Castle

Church (elevator, free parking, Schlossplatz 3, tel. 03491/429-110, www.alte-canzley.com, info@alte-canzley.de).

$$ Hotel Brauhaus, a lesser value, rents 34 straightforward rooms over a restaurant and antique shop fronting Market Square (lots of stairs with no elevator, free parking, Markt 7, tel. 03491/443-3130, www.brauhaus-wittenberg.de, info@brauhaus-wittenberg.de).

$ Am Alten Anker, above a restaurant in a drab area at the far end of town (about a 15-minute walk beyond the TI, or a 30-minute walk or quick taxi ride from the train station), has 20 basic but comfortable rooms at a reasonable price (Dessauer Strasse 286, tel. 03491/768-760, www.amaltenanker.de, info@amaltenanker.de).

¢ Lutherstadt Wittenberg Youth Hostel, an official HI hostel, has 160 beds in 3- to 6-bed dorms, each with its own bath. This modern hostel is perfectly located, filling a sleek building by the Castle Church (private rooms available, elevator, pay Wi-Fi, lots of school groups, doors close at 22:00, lunch or dinner available, tucked behind Castle Church at Schlossstrasse 14, tel. 03491/505-205, www.jugendherberge-wittenberg.de, wittenberg@jugendherberge.de).

Eating in Wittenberg

You'll find a fun variety of good, affordable restaurants within a couple blocks of Market Square.

$$ Brauhaus Wittenberg serves up traditional meals and great local beer in a fun-loving beer garden that feels closer to Bavaria than to Saxony. From Market Square, you'll enter the classic old courtyard filled with jovial tables; at the end, go inside to find comfortable seating on two levels, surrounding big copper vats where they brew their own "Wittenberger Original" pilsner. The menu includes big portions of tasty German standards (daily 11:00-22:30, Markt 6, tel. 03491/433-130).

$$ Das Wittenberger Kartoffelhaus serves up hearty, heavy skillets piled high with potatoes, potatoes, potatoes, prepared in fun and creative ways. The interior is cozy and brimming with kitschy decor, and the outdoor seating is on the relaxing pedestrian drag, just off Market Square (Schlossstrasse 2, daily 11:00-22:00, tel. 03491/411-200).

$$ Trattoria Toscana is a popular choice for Italian meals. Tucked in a "Little Italy" corner of town behind the Town Church of St. Mary, it has a fancy interior, romantic piazza seating, and down-to-earth prices (kid-friendly, daily 11:00-24:00, Mittelstrasse 1, tel. 03491/433-188).

$ Hanami, a family-run spot with a classy dining room, specializes in Vietnamese cooking and sushi. Like many Asian restaurants in eastern Germany, the Vietnam connection dates back to the communist days (cash only, usually daily 11:00-15:00 & 17:00-21:00, Schlossstrasse 8, tel. 03491/459-7068).

$ Reinsdorfer is good for a quick lunch on the go—there's a bakery on one side of the shop (sandwiches made to order) and a butcher's counter on the other (grilled sausages and prepared side dishes sold from the counter's back end, take out or eat at simple tables, Mon-Fri 8:00-18:00, Sat until 12:00, closed Sun, Markt 6).

$ Super Döner serves up super *döner kebabs* to go from a hardworking little hole-in-the-wall just off Market Square at Collegienstrasse 86 (Mon-Sat 10:30-19:00, closed Sun).

Wittenberg Connections

From Wittenberg by Train to: Berlin (hourly on ICE, 40 minutes; also every 2 hours on slower regional train, 1.5 hours), **Leipzig** (hourly, 30 minutes on ICE; also hourly on regional trains, 70 minutes), **Erfurt** (hourly, 1.5 hours), **Eisenach** and Wartburg Castle (8/day direct, 2 hours; more with transfer in Erfurt or Leipzig, 2.5 hours), **Dresden** (hourly, 2.5 hours, transfer in Leipzig), **Frankfurt** (6/day direct, 3.5 hours; more with 1 transfer, 4 hours), **Hamburg** (hourly, 2.5 hours, some with transfer in Berlin), **Nürnberg** (hourly, 3 hours, some with transfer in Erfurt), and **Munich** (hourly, 4 hours, half transfer at Erfurt). Train info: www.bahn.com.

LUTHERLAND

LEIPZIG

Music, education, and business are Leipzig's claims to fame. Johann Sebastian Bach spent his adult years at the St. Thomas Church here, and today the city is home to the Gewandhaus Orchestra and a famous boys' choir. Luminaries such as Goethe gave the city's university (established in the 1400s) a reputation as one of Germany's best. Before World War II, Leipzig was known for its textile, piano making, and printing industries—and after the war, for its entrepreneurial spirit.

Although the city is one of the most architecturally drab destinations in this book and attracts more business travelers than tourists, there's plenty to do in Leipzig (LYPE-tsikh). It's one of the best places to learn about the communist era in East Germany (known as the "DDR"—*Deutsche Demokratische Republik*): the excellent Stasi Museum documents the atrocities of the DDR's secret police, and the exhibits at the Contemporary History Forum juxtapose life in the East and West. Music lovers make a pilgrimage to Bach's tomb at the St. Thomas Church and the excellent Bach Museum across the street. Art lovers enjoy exploring the Museum of Fine Arts, beer lovers seek out the Bayerischer Bahnhof's unique Gose brew, history buffs trek to the Napoleonic battle site and monument at the edge of town, and those looking for hipster hangouts flock to the Karli district just south of downtown.

PLANNING YOUR TIME
Conveniently located between east (Berlin, Dresden) and west (Frankfurt, Nürnberg), Leipzig easily fills a day or more. But even a visit of just a few hours can be satisfying. If your train comes through Leipzig, throw your bag in a locker at the station and enjoy

a short tour. With limited time, focus on the city center—the best options are the Bach sights (St. Thomas Church and Bach Museum) and the Cold War sights (Augustusplatz, Stasi Museum, Contemporary History Forum, St. Nicholas Church). With more time, visit the City History Museum or worthwhile outlying sights: the lively Karli restaurant and nightlife zone and the Monument to the Battle of the Nations.

Orientation to Leipzig

The city's most important sights lie within or very near the ring road—called simply the Ring—which follows what once was the city wall. You can walk across this compact downtown core (known as Mitte—the "Middle") in about 15 minutes. At the center is Market Square (Markt); at the east end is the communist-style Augustusplatz, with the main university buildings and venues for the opera and orchestra. The gigantic main train station (Hauptbahnhof) rises at the northeastern edge of the Ring.

The central core has little cobbled charm—it's mostly shopping malls and massive old buildings. For more local color, head to the "Karli," a stretch of Karl-Liebknecht-Strasse that's a 20-minute walk or five-minute tram ride due south from downtown. Several other worthwhile attractions are a tram ride from downtown: the Monument to the Battle of the Nations, the Bayerischer Bahnhof brewpub, and the Spinnerei artists' complex.

TOURIST INFORMATION

Leipzig's TI, next to the Museum of Fine Arts, gives out self-guided walks and a map that shows gallery passages. You can also ask about local tours (Mon-Fri 9:30-18:00, Sat until 16:00, Sun until 15:00; Katharinenstrasse 8, tel. 0341/710-4260, www.leipzig.travel).

The skippable **Leipzig Card** covers local transit, entry to a few sights (including the City History Museum), and yields minor discounts at most others.

Tours: The TI's Leipzig Erleben service offers a 1.5-hour **guided walking tour** of the city (€9, April-Sept daily at 13:00 in German and English, departs from TI, smart to reserve ahead on weekends, tel. 0341/710-4280, www.leipzig-erleben.com). This same service can hook you up with a local guide, or specialty tours that focus on music, Jewish life, literature, or other topics.

Engaging **Gisa Schönfeld** is a good local guide (€80/2 hours, mobile 0176-210-67204, gisa.schoenfeld@gmail.com).

ARRIVAL IN LEIPZIG

By Train: One of Europe's biggest train stations, **Leipzig Hauptbahnhof** is breathtaking and a bit intimidating. As you arrive, count the six giant arches along the concourse at the end of the tracks. Under your feet are two stories of shops with hundreds of stores open until 22:00.

Two cavernous, mirror-image arrival halls (Westhalle and Osthalle) are linked by the *Reisezentrum* (ticket office) and Burger King. Both halls have lockers; a WC is opposite track 22. To exit the station, take any elevator or escalator down one floor, to the upper shopping level, and follow signs for *Tram* or *City*.

Out through the front door you'll find waiting taxis and the busy, multilane Ring. Cross the busy street to the Hauptbahnhof tram stop. From here, **trams** generally head north from the first set of platforms, and south—including to Augustusplatz and the Karli—from the second set.

You can also take the **S-Bahn** into town. The S-Bahn is one story lower than where you arrive. All lines run under the city center and conveniently connect the train station to Markt (Market Square), Wilhelm-Leuschner-Platz (central rail), Bayerischer Bahnhof station (with a recommended restaurant), and Völkerschlachtdenkmal (Monument of the Battle of the Nations).

To **walk** into the town center (about 15 minutes), cross the busy street (past the tram stop and public-transit kiosk), and keep going straight on Nikolaistrasse. After one block, turn right onto Brühl (you'll see a colorful mural honoring the 1989 Peaceful Revolution up ahead). Walking a block along Brühl, you can't miss the giant glass box holding the Museum of Fine Arts; the TI is on the museum's far side, and the main Market Square is two blocks beyond that.

By Bus: Long-distance buses come and go from the bus depot (ZOB) on the east side of the train station.

By Car: Parking is fairly easy in Leipzig, which has a number of garages (most €10/day) and affordable but limited on-street parking (€1.50 first hour, then €1/hour, cheaper outside Ring). For day-trippers, parking at the train station (Parking West or Ost) will run you €7 between 7:00 and 23:00.

GETTING AROUND LEIPZIG

Leipzig's tram system is easy to use and essential for all but the shortest visit. The S-Bahn system, while quicker and more frequent, is a bit more limited (useful stops include the train station, Market Square, and Völkerschlachtdenkmal, near the Monument of the Battle of the Nations). Each ride costs €2.60 (or €1.90 for a *Kurzstrecke*—"short stretch"—of four stops or less, including start point). A day ticket costs €7.40 and is good for 24 hours from initial validation. Tickets are available from machines at platforms and on most trams. You must stamp your ticket in the machines on board.

The main train station (Hauptbahnhof) is the tram network's main hub. A secondary hub is one stop south, at Augustusplatz (most trams connect these two central stops). Transit info: Tel. 0341/19449, www.lvb.de.

HELPFUL HINTS

Events: Market Square hosts a lively **farmers market** each Tuesday and Friday (9:00-17:00). Check the TI's website for other events: www.leipzig.travel.

Baggage Storage: The train station has lockers for rent.

Laundry: Tipptopp Schnellreinigung is an affordable coin launderette in the Karli district (daily 8:00-21:00, no English but staff can assist Mon-Fri 8:00-18:00, Karl-Liebknecht-Strasse 76, by the Karl-Liebknecht/Karl-Eisner-Strasse stop for trams #10 and #11, tel. 0341/252-2794).

Sights in Leipzig

WITHIN THE TOWN CENTER

These sights are in the heart of town (Mitte), within the Ring.

▲▲Old Town Hall (Altes Rathaus) and City History Museum (Stadtgeschichtliches Museum)

The Renaissance-style Old Town Hall, overlooking the bustling Market Square, houses the good City History Museum upstairs.

Although there are English descriptions throughout the museum, the audioguide is necessary for non-German speakers to fully appreciate the lower level.

Cost and Hours: €6, Tue-Sun 10:00-18:00, closed Mon, audioguide-€1, Markt 1, tel. 0341/965-1420, www.stadtgeschichtliches-museum-leipzig.de.

Visiting the Museum: You'll enter through a grand hall, lined with ornate benches and giant portraits of judges who presided here. The extremely detailed town model shows Leipzig in 1823.

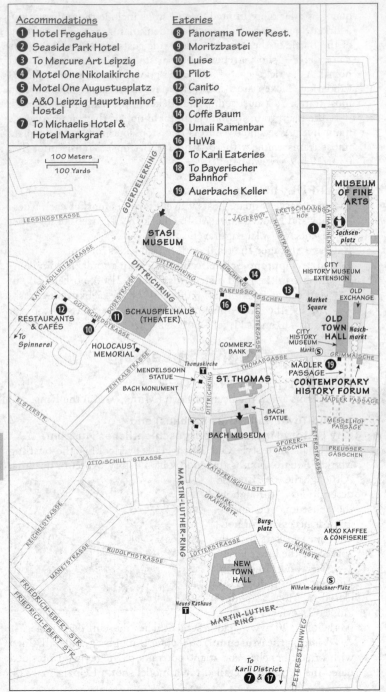

Accommodations
1 Hotel Fregehaus
2 Seaside Park Hotel
3 To Mercure Art Leipzig
4 Motel One Nikolaikirche
5 Motel One Augustusplatz
6 A&O Leipzig Hauptbahnhof Hostel
7 To Michaelis Hotel & Hotel Markgraf

Eateries
8 Panorama Tower Rest.
9 Moritzbastei
10 Luise
11 Pilot
12 Canito
13 Spizz
14 Coffe Baum
15 Umaii Ramenbar
16 HuWa
17 To Karli Eateries
18 To Bayerischer Bahnhof
19 Auerbachs Keller

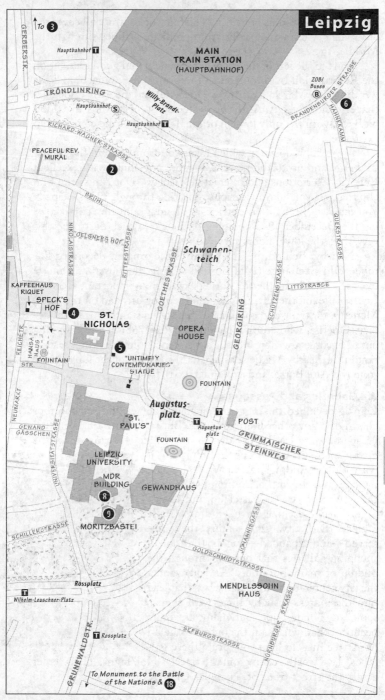

Smaller exhibit rooms branching off from the central hall cover the city's history chronologically, from prehistoric times through the Middle Ages.

Start to the left of the entry, where you'll find good sections on the Reformation (with portraits of reformers by Cranach, and the wedding ring Martin Luther gave his wife) and the early trade fairs that enriched the city. At the opposite end of this floor is an exhibit on Bach, with the only known original portrait of the composer in existence.

The exhibit upstairs, which takes you from 1815 in the Industrial Age and up to the present, is more engaging, with excellent English descriptions and interactive displays. Don't miss the film clip that lets you take a vicarious tram ride through 1930s Leipzig. You can also climb into the attic to see loud, grainy film clips showing the December 1943 bombing of the city, which destroyed this very attic (the lower floors survived).

Nearby: Behind the Town Hall is the ornately decorated Baroque **Old Exchange** (Alte Börse) building, now used as a meeting hall. Statues in the top corners symbolize important facets of Leipzig life: on the left, Apollo, representing art; and on the right, Mercury, for trade and commerce. The statue standing in front depicts Goethe, who studied law here (1765-1768) before dropping out to become a writer. Goethe set a scene from *Faust* in a restaurant in the nearby Mädler Passage (at the far end of the long square from the Alte Börse, and explained next).

▲▲Galleries and Passages

Leipzig once had the higgledy-piggledy cobbles-and-red-rooftops charm of many other German cities. But in the late 19th century, prosperous city leaders decided to modernize—tearing down the quaint medieval townscape and replacing it with bulky buildings. After WWII bomb damage and decades of communist neglect, the city center was a wasteland, but in just a generation, Leipzigers have dramatically remade their city. One feature they preserved—and expanded—was the tradition of shopping galleries that burrow through the middle of many buildings. As you wander the city center, don't miss doorways that lead into these areas (usually lined with shops); some are nondescript, but many are more beautiful than what's on the outside. The TI has a free map to help you locate these galleries. Two worth seeking out are Speck's Hof/Hansa Haus (enter across the street from St. Nicholas Church or from near the Old

Exchange behind the Old Town Hall) and Mädler Passage (enter roughly across the street from the Old Town Hall).

Just inside **Mädler Passage,** at the end nearest the Old Town Hall, statues (in front of the famous and touristy Auerbachs Keller restaurant) enact a scene from *Faust* that Goethe set here: The brilliant thinker Faust (wearing a scholar's gown and floppy hat) has made a deal with Mephistopheles (gesturing skyward) to experience as much as possible of the world—but if anything so impresses Faust that he refuses to move on, the devil gets his soul. Mephistopheles brings Faust to Auerbachs Keller to show him the simple pleasures of revelry with friends ("Before all else, I bring thee hither / Where boon companions meet together, / To let thee see how smooth life runs away. / Here, for the folk, each day's a holiday"). Across the passage are drunken students who have been bewitched by Mephistopheles.

Inside the **Speck's Hof/Hansa Haus** passage (the oldest passage in the city) is a cool "sound fountain"—a bronze bowl of water with brass handles, which, if rubbed just right with dampened hands, produce a loud ringing that reverberates as the water bubbles—give it a shot. Below, a sunken "art clock" sundial shows the time with a green laser projected onto the ground. The inscription around the basin has a line from a beloved children's book: "Just as you have eyes to see light with, and ears to hear to sounds with, so you have a heart to appreciate time."

Museum of Fine Arts (Museum der Bildenden Künste)

Located in a fancy glass house in the center of town, this museum displays Leipzig's eclectic collection of fine arts. Instead of being organized chronologically, items are displayed thematically—juxtaposed by some clever curator to create a "dialogue" between otherwise unrelated works. While this treatment thrills a certain breed of museumgoer, it's sometimes alienating to lowbrows (like me), and its split-level floor design can be confusing. There's also very little English (aside from a thick catalog), so the audioguide is essential.

Cost and Hours: €10, includes special exhibits, half-price one hour before closing, Tue and Thu-Sun 10:00-18:00, Wed 12:00-20:00, closed Mon, audioguide-€2, a short block north of Market Square at Katharinenstrasse 10, tel. 0341/216-990, www.mdbk.de.

Visiting the Museum: Within the vast, glassy building, the basement features temporary exhibits; the first floor displays excellent works by local sculptor Max Klinger, as well as other 20th-century and Leipzig art; the second floor has mostly Dutch and Flemish works from the 15th to 18th century; and the third floor shows predominantly Romanticism, 19th-century works, and contemporary pieces.

Leipzig History

Although it's the biggest city in Saxony, Leipzig has long been overshadowed by its glamour-girl sister, Dresden. While Dresden was the prettified capital of the rulers of Saxony, Leipzig was its down-and-dirty economic engine.

Leipzig first boomed in the 15th century. Its trade fairs attracted medieval vendors and businesspeople from throughout the region, and rich deposits of silver in the nearby Erzgebirge hills boosted the mining industry. While Dresden's glories were funded by princes who collected, then squandered, their subjects' wealth, Leipzig was imbued with a strong civic sensibility—its citizens took pride in voluntarily funding musicians and artists. Among the beneficiaries was an organist, choirmaster, and composer named Johann Sebastian Bach, who went largely unappreciated in his lifetime but whose works were later rediscovered and popularized by another Leipzig composer, Felix Mendelssohn.

Leipzig's university attracted great minds. Martin Luther came here to work with local printers and publishers to distribute his writings and to debate one of the Catholic Church's chief theologians (an event called the Leipzig Disputation) in what is today's New Town Hall. And Goethe, the "German Shakespeare"—who studied law at Leipzig U. before following his muse into literature—set a famous scene from his verse drama *Faust* at a cellar restaurant here. German Chancellor Angela Merkel is also a Leipzig U. alumna.

Leipzig's cityscape is a victim of its own success. In the late 19th century, the city boomed once again when it innovated the idea of a "sample fair." Instead of toting along their full inventory, vendors brought samples of their wares, allowing them to take orders and sell in much larger volumes. Never architecturally oriented, the newly flush people of Leipzig tore down most of their characteristic medieval Old Town. The city center—defined by a busy ring road that marks the former course of the city wall—features large, hulking buildings that are visually dull but shot through with fun-to-explore passages.

The museum's highlight is Leipzig artist **Max Klinger**'s (1857-1920) sculpture of Beethoven (1902, restored 2004). The marble and bronze piece—depicting the great composer pensively hunched over on a throne, nude, legs crossed, with Prometheus' eagle in clouds at his feet—took Klinger some 15 years to complete. Installed as the centerpiece of a 1902 Vienna Secession exhibit devoted to Beethoven, the sculpture was surrounded by Gustav Klimt's famous *Beethoven Frieze* (still displayed in Vienna). On the same floor, look for Expressionist works by another Leipzig artist, Max Beckmann, including *Portrait of a Carpet Dealer* (1946). The rest of the collection features minor works by major artists (such

After World War II, Leipzig became the second city, after East Berlin, of communist East Germany (DDR). The infamous Berlin Wall was built under DDR premier Walter Ulbricht, a Leipzig native. But the city's size and historical importance didn't protect it from communist neglect. Damaged by WWII bombs, postwar Leipzig fell into abhorrent disrepair. Making matters worse, an open-pit coal mine at the edge of town and belching Trabant cars covered everything in soot. People who lived here in the 1980s say they never wore white clothes outside, because they'd turn gray in minutes.

The people of Leipzig were also at the forefront of the so called "Peaceful Revolution" that toppled the communist regime. The famous scenes of Berliners joyfully partying atop the Wall were made possible by protests that first began in Leipzig in 1982 and eventually came to a head in the series of civil-disobedience actions that caught the regime completely off guard in 1989. Expecting an armed insurrection, DDR leaders were so flummoxed by the peaceful tone of the protests that they simply allowed them to continue. A month later, the Wall was history. (For more, see "The Peaceful Revolution" sidebar, later.)

As Germany moved toward reunification, DDR television broadcast a provocative documentary asking: Can ragtag Leipzig be salvaged? (Their conclusion: No.) But salvaged it was—and then some. Pictures from just 20 years ago show a different city. The area within the ring road has been rejuvenated with shiny new shopping malls and university buildings. In other zones—such as the colorful stretch south of downtown called the Karli—trendy young entrepreneurs have turned decrepit buildings into a world of funky, appealing bars and restaurants—earning the town its latest nickname "Hypzlg" and comparisons to hip Berlin. Leipzig may lack half-timbered and lederhosen charm, but its welcome urban contrast and fascinating history certainly live up to the hype.

as Frans Hals' *The Mulatto* and Rembrandt's *Head of an Old Man*) and some genuinely interesting pieces from lesser-known artists. For example, Paul de la Roche's evocative *Napoleon at Fontainebleau* shows the pudgy, diminutive Frenchman dejected after learning that he's lost Paris.

▲Augustusplatz

This somewhat dramatic square is home to Leipzig's university and its two most respected musical institutions. Renamed Karl-Marx-Platz during the DDR period, the square became a showcase for the communist aesthetic. In September of 1989, protesters against the communist regime gathered here—and were dispersed by the police. Today it's a busy people zone and a hub for trams around the city.

Stand between the fountain with the obelisk and the tram stops, and face the tallest skyscraper. This is the **MDR building** (named after the radio and TV station that's based here), which was erected in the 1970s as part of the university. Though it was designed to resemble an open book, locals affectionately refer to the skyscraper as *Weisheitszahn* (wisdom tooth). You can ride to the 29th floor and pay €3 at the turnstile to go out on the rooftop terrace for the best view in town (daily 9:00-22:30, Fri-Sat until 23:30, tel. 0341/710-0590, www.panorama-leipzig.de). Enjoy a similar view from the Panorama Tower restaurant on the same floor (affordable €10 three-course lunch served Mon-Fri 11:30-14:30). Hiding behind this building (not quite visible from here) is the **Moritzbastei.** This bastion is all that survives from Leipzig's former city wall,

which was torn down in the early 19th century to build the ring road. Today it hosts a happening student pub.

Stretching to the right is a complex of glassy buildings housing **Leipzig University**—the second oldest in present-day Germany. The pointed facade marks the new **University Church of St. Paul's**—a 2009 building replacing the 13-century church dynamited by the communists in 1968. The new church pays homage to the site's former purpose but is used for secular assemblies as well as religious services.

At either end of this square, two of Leipzig's main cultural institutions are housed in communist-era buildings. At the south end (to the left) is the **Gewandhaus,** home to the city's world-renowned orchestra. (If you step into the lobby, you'll see models

of the three different buildings that have housed the orchestra, including the original location in the clothmakers' guild hall—which is what *Gewandhaus* means.) At the north (right) end is the **Opera House.** Facing the Opera House, the tall building on the left with the two bell-ringers is Leipzig's earliest "skyscraper."

If you're intrigued by quirky public art, head a few steps up the pedestrianized shopping street, Grimmaische Strasse (to the left as you face the Opera House), and find the sculpture *Untimely Contemporaries* (a pun that works better in German), with insulting, exaggerated caricatures of hypocritical DDR figures. For example, the teacher (on the right) clutches a mallet

used to pound communist ideology into her students; the fourth guy over, with the oversized laurel wreath covering his eyes, is detonating St. Paul's Church.

COLD WAR SIGHTS

These attractions are scattered around the city center, but are all within about a 10-minute walk of each other.

▲St. Nicholas Church (Nikolaikirche)

Leipzig's oldest church (1165) played a pivotal role in recent German history. In the 1980s, prayer meetings held here every Monday gradually became a forum for those deeply dissatisfied with the

communist status quo. As anticommunist sentiment grew, the church became a major staging ground for the Peaceful Revolution that would ultimately topple the regime. During these protests, people would bravely go inside the church to meet—not knowing what would happen to them when they came back out.

The church sits in what was once a market square—appropriate, since its namesake, St. Nicholas, is the patron saint of traders. The ornate interior echoes the church's importance in recent history. In the 1780s, the church was redecorated in a very clean, bright Neoclassical style, with a pastel pink-and-green color scheme and fluted columns that sprout green fronds at the top. Above the door is the largest organ in Saxony, which booms out 45-minute concerts each Saturday at 17:00 (€2). Look for the free English flier that explains the church's role in the peace prayers and historic events of 1989 (see "The Peaceful Revolution" sidebar).

Outside and behind the church, find the single column with green leaves at the top. This column, mimicking the decoration in-

Leipzig, Coffee, and Classic Cafés

Over the centuries, coffee has played a vital role in Leipziger culture. In 1670, coffee beans made their debut at the Leipzig Trade Fair. As far back as 1695, coffeehouses have been an essential part of the Leipzig cityscape, and the people of Leipzig have long since been known as *Kaffeesachsen*—the coffee drinkers of Saxony. The city's movers and shakers often gathered in a *Kaffeehaus* to discuss literature, philosophy, politics, and art. To see Richard Wagner, Goethe, the painter Max Klinger, or the revolutionary Karl Liebknecht was commonplace. Coffee even stimulated the mind of Johann Sebastian Bach, who was so inspired that he wrote his "Coffee Cantata" about the energizing elixir. And in 1990, it was coffee that brought West German Chancellor Helmut Kohl and East German Prime Minister Lothar de Mazière together at Coffe Baum to discuss German reunification.

With all this history, visiting a coffeehouse in Leipzig is a delight. Formally known as **Zum Arabischen Coffe Baum** (the second oldest café in Europe after Paris's Le Procope), this café still serves coffee and cakes as it has since the early 1700s, and also houses a free museum dedicated to all things coffee (café open daily 11:00-24:00, museum open until 19:00, just off Market Square at Kleine Fleischergasse 4). Two other classic cafés with old-timey interiors are **Kaffeehaus Riquet** (decorated with elephants, daily 9:00-19:00, Schuhmachergässchen 1) and **Arko** at Petersstrasse 43 (part of a chain now occupying the elegant former home of Kaffee Richter, Mon-Fri 9:30-20:00, Sat 10:00-18:00, closed Sun).

Anywhere you go, you'll find many coffee styles, including Viennese, French, American, and Italian. Traditionally, Leipzigers prefer their coffee sweet and strong. A Catholic cardinal once said:

The coffee must be
As black as the devil
As hot as hell
As pure as an angel
As sweet as love

But Leipzigers have put up with weak or *Plempe* coffee over the years, especially when times were tough and coffee beans were hard to come by. To this day, there's even a special name—*Blümchenkaffee*—for coffee so light you can see the flower design at the bottom of the porcelain cup. And when Napoleon's troops came to town, they brought with them a coffee mixed heavily with malt or chicory. While the French called it *moka faut* (fake coffee), the people of Leipzig butchered the phrase and dubbed it *Muggefukk*.

side the church, is dedicated to the people of Leipzig and memorializes the anticommunist protests that began here.

Cost and Hours: Free, daily 10:00-18:00 (closes during Sunday services), Nikolaikirchhof 3, tel. 0341/124-5380, www.nikolaikirche.de.

▲Contemporary History Forum (Zeitgeschichtliches Forum)

Funded by the German government, this center examines life in a divided Germany (1945-1990), focusing mainly on the East but dipping into the West to provide contrast. The statue out front represents Germany's two 20th-century dictatorships: the flat-palmed *Sieg Heil!* Nazi salute and the proletariat's raised communist fist. The poor fellow—whose form resembles an abstracted swastika—has his head scrunched down, hoping to somehow get through it all.

Cost and Hours: Free, Tue-Fri 9:00-18:00, Sat-Sun 10:00-18:00, closed Mon, Grimmaische Strasse 6, tel. 0341/22200, www.hdg.de/leipzig.

Visiting the Museum: The exhibit is modern and well-presented, although there's little in English (translations sometimes available at the gift-shop counter where you enter—ask).

Ride the elevator (with patriotic DDR songs and voice clips piped in) up to the second floor, where the circular permanent exhibit spins off from a central timeline. Displays include photographs, propaganda posters, a mock-up of a DDR-era apartment, film footage of DDR authorities destroying churches and Soviet tanks putting down a 1953 protest at Berlin's Brandenburg Gate, a van used by the secret police to transport prisoners, an original "You are leaving the American sector" sign from an East/West border crossing, a simple airplane used to escape to the West, heads from several Stalin statues, protest signs from the fall of 1989, and the long table where the East German politburo met to hash out their plans for the country.

Temporary exhibits, which can give a stimulating peek at contemporary German life, fill the third floor.

▲▲Stasi Museum in the "Runde Ecke"

In the notorious so-called "Round Corner" building, the communist secret police (Stasi) detained and interrogated those suspected of being traitors to the state. That same building—once

The Peaceful Revolution

While the fall of the Berlin Wall got all the press, the end of communism in East Germany arguably began seven years earlier and a hundred miles to the south, in Leipzig.

In 1982, parishioners at Leipzig's St. Nicholas Church began gathering on Monday evenings to pray for peace and a better world. This continued until 1989, when a series of events sparked citizens to action. That spring, the Tiananmen Square protests in China inspired East Germans who felt similarly oppressed. And that summer, Hungary opened its border to the West, offering an enticing glimmer of hope to East Germans.

By September of 1989, the St. Nicholas prayer meetings started taking on an increasingly political bent, and more people joined, regardless of religious belief. DDR government officials watched with concern; after the October 2 gathering, they warned that deadly force would be authorized to stop any uprisings.

On October 7, Mikhail Gorbachev came to Berlin to celebrate the 40th anniversary of the founding of the DDR. He made a cryptic remark implying that the people of Eastern Europe had a right to bring about change. A huge demonstration ensued in Leipzig on October 9. An estimated 100,000 protesters carried banners bellowing *Wir sind das Volk!* ("We are the people!").

The Stasi (secret police) embedded undercover agents in the crowds to stoke the protesters to violence—but it didn't work. One official said, "We were ready for anything...except candles and prayer." With no excuse for clamping down on the demonstration, DDR officials for the first time allowed a major protest to continue—a turning point in the struggle to topple the Berlin Wall.

On October 16, an estimated 320,000 people participated in demonstrations. Two days later, DDR premier Erich Honecker and several other top officials resigned. The government was in disarray, and within two and a half weeks, people were dancing on top of the Berlin Wall.

While cameras were rolling in Berlin, the heroics in Leipzig were hardly documented. But today Leipzig remains fiercely proud of the crucial role it played in ousting the communists through nonviolent means. Around town, look for "89" plaques that explain sites relating to the Peaceful Revolution.

the Stasi headquarters—now houses a humble but worthwhile exhibit about the Stasi's activities. A citizens' committee created the museum in 1990—just months after their protests helped spark the fall of the Wall—as a temporary exhibit to document Stasi atrocities, with the goal of preventing such things from happening again. Decades later, the museum and its committee are still going strong. The museum is not fancy—basically one long hallway and a few rooms, with dusty hand-lettered exhibits—but it's a fascinating record of this dark chapter of German history. And it's chilling to see all of this while walking through the actual perpetrators' offices.

In the same building is the Stasi Records Agency—one of several satellite offices scattered throughout Germany that archive Stasi surveillance records (the central office is in Berlin). This is also worth a visit.

Cost and Hours: Museum-free, daily 10:00-18:00, €4 for the excellent and essential audioguide, Dittrichring 24, tel. 0341/961-2443, www.runde-ecke-leipzig.de; Records Agency-free, Mon-Fri 9:00-18:00, Sat-Sun from 10:00, http://bstu.de.

Background: Initially formed to investigate and prosecute Nazi crimes, the DDR government's Ministerium für Staatssicherheit (MfS, "Ministry for State Security")—nicknamed the "Stasi" (SHTAH-zee)—quickly became a means of suppressing dissent as civil liberties dwindled in communist Germany. The Stasi considered themselves "the sword and shield of the party."

Modeled after the Soviet Union's secret police, the Stasi recruited informants from every walk of life, often intimidating them into cooperating by threatening their jobs, their children's education, or worse. They eventually gathered an army of some 600,000 "unofficial employees" *(inoffizielle Mitarbeiter)*, nearly 200,000 of whom were still active when communism fell in 1989. At its peak, an estimated one in seven East Germans was cooperating with the Stasi. These "employees" were coerced into reporting on the activities of their coworkers, friends, neighbors, and even immediate family members.

Preoccupied with keeping track of "nonconformist" behavior, the Stasi collected whatever bits of evidence they could—including saliva, handwriting, odors, and voice recordings—and wound up with vast amounts of files.

What was the Stasi's goal? Quite simply, to be in control...

of everything. Sometimes they'd pursue criminal prosecution and imprisonment. The worst offenders might be deported. Most often, the Stasi simply harassed. They wanted suspects to *know* they were being watched—to destabilize and marginalize them. Often no formal accusation ever came of these investigations, but lives were ruined nonetheless.

Soon after the Wall fell, DDR authorities scrambled to destroy the illicit information their agents and informants had collected. But the new government mandated that these records be preserved as evidence of DDR crimes, and the documents are now managed by the Federal Commissioner for Stasi Records.

These days, German citizens can read the files once kept on them. It's a hard choice: Request their record—and likely find out that friends and loved ones had reported on them—or never know the truth. For a film that brilliantly captures the paranoid Stasi culture, see the 2006 Oscar winner *The Lives of Others*.

Visiting the Museum: As the museum exhibits are entirely in German, rent the audioguide before you start: Go partway down the hall and ask in the office on your left. Then return to the entrance to view the permanent exhibit.

The exhibit's title, "Power and Banality," invokes scholar Hannah Arendt's notion of the "banality of evil"—the idea that if horrific acts are systematized and repeated, they become routine and therefore more acceptable to the perpetrator. The first section of the exhibit documents the pivotal protest of October 9, 1989 (see "The Peaceful Revolution" sidebar, earlier), with shields and batons, and photos of the candles that stymied riot police who were expecting Molotov cocktails. It's an important reminder that the West can't take sole credit for the freedoms won that year—Leipzigers rightly take pride in what they helped accomplish as ordinary citizens, often at great risk to themselves.

Inside, **surveillance cameras** mounted overhead and a wall of monitors suggest just how closely the secret police observed the East German people. In the hallway, look for the copy of a 14-year-old student's essay questioning aspects of communist life, and its extensively documented consequences. It's chilling to see how this free-thinking assignment was on track to bar this schoolboy from university and ruin his life; fortunately, he wrote it in 1989, just before the Wall fell.

The **former offices** contain several items and tools used by the Stasi, such as a camera that could easily be concealed in a briefcase, microphones that could be hidden just about anywhere, disguises (including a fake beer belly with a hidden camera), and forged documents. One display case holds several jars with pale yellow cloths impregnated with "odor samples." Stasi agents would sit suspects on cloths to interrogate them, then save the sweat-drenched swatch for trained dogs to identify the scent. (For example, the dog would sniff an anti-DDR propaganda leaflet, then smell several odor samples and bark at the one that matched.) The police also used under-car mirrors to check for potential escapees at border

crossings. The **replica prison cell,** with original fixtures, illustrates what life was like in a detention center. All mail and packages coming into the country were searched for contraband—inspectors would steam them open, read them, then reseal them. Stasi mail inspectors stole millions in West German marks (sent to East German relatives) and confiscated piles of cassette tapes containing Western pop music—which officials then re-used to record interrogation sessions.

Stasi Records Agency: When you finish your audioguide tour, a visit to the Stasi Records Agency will fill in some gaps about what you just learned with thought-provoking exhibits described in English (inside the same building; door is across from the museum entrance). Let the bureaucrat behind the desk know that you're there "just to look." German citizens have a right to view their files, but not everyone chooses to learn the truth about family or friends who aided the Stasi. Visitors are welcome to explore the permanent and temporary exhibitions that shed light on the structure, tactics, and methods employed by the secret police.

Begin by following the displays in the stairwell. See how the Stasi targeted those on the fringe of society: skinheads, Goths, and heavy metalers. Each floor is dedicated to a different subgroup. Back downstairs, the second-floor exhibit explores the origin and ideology of the Stasi. The ground-floor rooms deal with the documentation process, "unofficial collaborators," and the logistics of secret surveillance.

Snooping on citizens was a huge industry. Eventually the Stasi outgrew this building. As you exit, walk to the right to see the Stasi headquarters expansion—a dreadfully ugly, gray and brown, prefabricated annex that's typical of the DDR.

BACH SIGHTS

These sights cluster along the west side of the Ring.

▲St. Thomas Church (Thomaskirche)

At this historic church, Martin Luther introduced Leipzig to Protestantism, and Johann Sebastian Bach conducted the boys' choir.

The most famous boys' choir in Germany—the Thomanerchor—still performs here.

Cost and Hours: Free, daily 9:00-18:00; pick up English flier about the church's history, artwork, organ, and choir for a small donation; Thomaskirchhof 18, tel. 0341/222-240, www.thomaskirche.org.

Concerts and Events: The St. Thomas boys' choir performs Fridays at 18:00 and Saturdays at 15:00, unless they are traveling (€3). The Bach Organ Festival is held here each summer (concerts Saturdays late June-early Aug).

Visiting the Church: Before entering the church, look (just outside the church door) for the **statue of Bach** standing in front of his favorite instrument, a pipe organ. Bach was the leader of the boys' choir here from 1723 until 1750. While here, Bach was remarkably prolific—for a time, he even composed a new cantata every week.

Examine the details of his portrait: He's holding a rolled-up sheet of music, which he used as a baton. Notice the button open on his vest—he could stick the "baton" into his shirt, if necessary, to free up his hands. His jacket pocket is turned out—Bach was famously always scrounging for more money to feed his huge family and the boys in the choir. His dedication to the arts led him to advocate tirelessly for the funding of local musicians.

Inside, the clean, white, stripped-down Neo-Gothic interior evokes the Protestant aesthetic of uncluttering the congregation's communion with God. On Pentecost in 1539, Martin Luther came here to perform Leipzig's first Protestant service. Look up at the 19th-century **stained-glass window** on the wall above the door through which you entered. In the panel to the left, Martin Luther is flanked by his supporter, prince-elector Frederick the Wise (on the left) and fellow reformer Philipp Melanchthon (on the right). Keeping them company in neighboring stained-glass windows (from left to right) are a WWI memorial, Sweden's King Gustavus Adolphus (champion of Protestantism during the Thirty Years' War), Johann Sebastian Bach, Felix Mendelssohn, and Kaiser Wilhelm I (Germany's first emperor when it unified).

The **main altar** actually comes from a different historic church,

St. Paul's on Augustusplatz, which was demolished by the communist regime in 1968 to make way for the expansion of university buildings (for the rebuilt version of that church, see the Augustusplatz listing, earlier).

In front of the altar is the **tomb of Bach**—or is it? Largely unappreciated in his own time and forgotten shortly after his death, Bach was buried in a humble graveyard. But after his music regained popularity in the 19th century, aficionados tracked down what they thought were his remains. Three cadavers that could have been Bach were compared to portraits of the composer to determine which one was most likely to be the real Johann Sebastian.

From the center of the church, facing the altar, look up and to the left (opposite the pulpit) to see the new **organ,** built in 2000 but designed to sound like a much older, Bach-era organ.

Sights near the Church

On the Ring side of the church (to the right as you leave, around the corner, and across the street), look for the **statue of Felix Mendelssohn** (1809-1847). Mendelssohn came to Leipzig at age 26 to conduct the Gewandhaus Orchestra, which he led to great success, putting Leipzig on the world musical map. Mendelssohn is remembered today primarily as a composer, but perhaps his greatest contribution was to popularize the works of Bach, which had become unfashionable after his death. If not for Mendelssohn, the name "Bach" would probably mean nothing to you today. Because he was Jewish, Mendelssohn's statue was torn down and used for scrap metal by the Nazis; this replica was erected here in 2008.

The busy ring road just beyond the Mendelssohn statue was the fortified city wall that once marked the end of town. When the wall was torn down in the 19th century, the west portal of St. Thomas Church suddenly stood in full view of the townsfolk, who were inspired to add the fancy Neo-Gothic facade you see today.

Turn around and go a bit farther along the park (with the Ring on your right) to find another, much older **monument to Bach.**

Johann Sebastian Bach (1685-1750)

Johann Sebastian Bach was a man of many musical trades—composer, musical director, organist, organ builder, and violinist. Born in 1685, he lived immersed in music from the very beginning. His  father was the director of the town musicians (because the family was so musically talented, people from Erfurt—where Bach senior was from—used the word *Bache* to describe any musician). After his parents' early deaths, Bach lived with his older brother, Johann Christoph, who helped him develop his musical skill.

In 1723, Bach was selected as the cantor of St. Thomas Church in Leipzig. He spent the last 27 years of his life in the city, working as the director of music for the city's four main churches and directing the St. Thomas boys' choir, the Thomanerchor. Responsible for providing Sunday music at the churches, in just five years Bach composed some 150 cantatas, two great Passions, and numerous other sacred pieces for his choir to perform.

In addition to shepherding the 50 boys in the choir, Bach, who married twice, had a number of his own children—seven with his first wife and another thirteen with the second. Of the twenty children, only nine survived into adulthood. And of those, six had musical careers of their own.

Mendelssohn was so dedicated to honoring the genius of the Baroque composer that he personally funded the construction of this monument. In the reliefs around the pillar, see Bach depicted as an organist, a good Christian, and a teacher (of the boys' choir).

Across the Ring from here, and a block up Gottschedstrasse (which is also lined with some great restaurants—see "Eating in Leipzig," later), you'll find an evocative **Holocaust memorial,** with 140 chairs on the site of the city's former main synagogue. The empty seats encourage people to "stand up" for what's right.

▲▲Bach Museum

Across the little square from St. Thomas is this small but very well-presented museum about Leipzig's favorite composer. Its good interactive exhibits are mostly displayed in 12 rooms on two manageable floors. With the help of the excellent, included audioguide, this museum is an absolute delight for music lovers.

Cost and Hours: €8, includes audioguide, Tue-Sun 10:00-18:00, closed Mon, Thomaskirchhof 15, tel. 0341/913-7207, www.bachmuseumleipzig.de.

While living in Leipzig, Bach began directing a group of university-student musicians who were more interested in convivial entertainment than somber church music. Their crowd-pleasing performances of his secular compositions drew attention to the composer's work, elevating his status in Leipzig.

Later in life, Bach became more withdrawn and reflective, composing complex, abstract Baroque pieces. He enjoyed entertaining guests with private concerts in his personal music room. But his eyesight began failing near the end of his life, and he died in 1750 after suffering a stroke. He was buried in an unmarked grave and soon forgotten.

In 1829, the musician and composer Felix Mendelssohn received from his grandmother a copy of Bach's manuscript for *St. Matthew Passion*. When Mendelssohn conducted and performed Bach's profoundly expressive music in Berlin, it was an instant hit. Mendelssohn's concert sparked a newfound appreciation for Bach's music that began in Germany, took over Europe, and soon spread around the world.

In the mid-1800s, several Bach fans and Leipzig scholars succeeded in rediscovering what they thought to be Bach's remains and moved them to Leipzig's Johanneskirche. After that church was destroyed by WWII bombs, the composer's remains were laid to rest, for a third time, at St. Thomas Church—where appreciative pilgrims and Bach admirers still bring flowers to honor the man whom *The New York Times* named "the most influential composer of all time."

Visiting the Museum: At the entry is a replica of a famous portrait-bust of the great composer. Inside and up the stairs, the family tree makes it clear that Bach came from a very musical family. In the organ room, touch the organ pipes to hear music, or settle in at a station to listen on headsets to one of Bach's many compositions. You'll see an actual organ console where Bach played his favorite instrument, an iron chest that came from his household, and original manuscripts. The orchestra exhibit explains Baroque music by letting you press buttons to isolate the different instruments and sounds. The Leipzig room shows sights in town associated with the composer—including a model of the residence (in the boarding school for his 50 choirboys) where he lived with his huge family. Film clips show the many cinematic depictions of Bach, and documentary footage from *Bach and Friends* includes American jazz musician Bobby McFerrin discussing the influence of Bach's improvisational style on his music.

Back on the ground floor, the Research Laboratory provides informative and interactive displays about the physical elements of

LEIPZIG

making music, as well as a listening station where you can "play" with Bach's scores. The highlight of the softly lit Treasury is the original manuscripts written by Bach. Because of their fragility, different documents are regularly rotated into and out of the display.

OUTSIDE THE RING
▲▲The Karli

Just south of the Ring, Karl-Liebknecht-Strasse—"Karli" for short—hosts a funky zone of boutiques, cafés, restaurants, and nightclubs (a.k.a. the Südmeile—"South Mile").

Renamed "Adolf-Hitler-Strasse" during the Führer's reign, today's Karli would make Hitler spin in his grave. Parts of the street

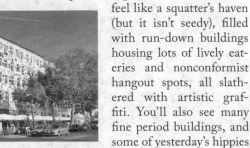

feel like a squatter's haven (but it isn't seedy), filled with run-down buildings housing lots of lively eateries and nonconformist hangout spots, all slathered with artistic graffiti. You'll also see many fine period buildings, and some of yesterday's hippies are now environmentally aware parents biking down the sidewalk with their children.

After the generally stern architecture of downtown Leipzig, a stroll here is good for the soul and flat-out fun. You can walk here from downtown (across the Ring, south of the New Town Hall), but it doesn't get interesting until the Hohe Strasse tram stop. The core of the zone is the four-block stretch between the Südplatz and Karl-Liebknecht-/Kurt-Eisner-Strasse stops. For more details, see the description under "Eating in Leipzig," later.

Getting There: Ride tram #10 (direction: Lössnig) or #11 (direction: Markkleeberg-Ost) about 5 minutes south from downtown (to the Hohe Strasse, Südplatz, or Karl-Liebknecht-/Kurt-Eisner-Strasse stops).

▲Monument of the Battle of the Nations (Völkerschlachtdenkmal)

This gigantic, heavy-handed monument—Europe's biggest—commemorates a pivotal battle in 1813 that involved forces from all over Europe. It was the first time Napoleon was decisively defeated in a major battle. While it's on the outskirts of town and a bit anticlimactic (it looks like a giant pedestal missing a statue on top), the monument is worth an ogle for its sheer size and chillingly patriotic design, especially if you're a history buff.

The year 2013 marked the 200th anniversary of the battle and the 100th anniversary of the monument. Today, nicknamed "Volki" by Leipzig's youth, the monument is most appreciated as a venue for concerts and outdoor events. Below the monument is the Forum 1813 museum.

Cost and Hours: €8 ticket covers both monument and museum, daily 10:00-18:00, Nov-March until 16:00; informative, if wordy, audioguide-€1; Strasse des 18 Oktober 100, tel. 0341/241-6870, www.voelkerschlachtdenkmal.eu.

Getting There: Ride tram #15 from the Hauptbahnhof or Augustusplatz (direction: Meusdorf) to the Völkerschlachtdenkmal stop, which is right next to the big park surrounding the monument. Or hop on S-Bahn lines S-1, S-2, or S-4 to Völkerschlachtdenkmal. "You can't miss it" is an understatement.

Background: In October 1813, the Battle of the Nations (*Völkerschlacht,* also called the Battle of Leipzig) pitted Napoleon's army against a united force of Prussian, Austrian, Russian, and Swedish fighters. With more than a half-million men involved and casualties approaching 100,000, it was the largest battle in European history until World War I. The Battle

of the Nations marked the turning point in the fight against Napoleon, who was routed and forced to retreat to France. It was the ultimate victory of predominantly German forces against French invaders.

A century later—during a surge of nationalism following the unification of the modern nation of Germany—Leipzig city leaders built this 300-foot-tall memorial on the site of the bloodiest warfare. Looming over a huge reflecting pool, the concrete monument has a granite facade and is decorated inside and out with gigantic, heroic (almost mythical) statues of faceless soldiers and other archetypes celebrating German might. Not surprisingly, it later became a favorite backdrop for Hitler's speeches. The Soviet puppet government of East Germany wasn't thrilled with its German nationalistic overtones, but decided to let it stand as a monument to German-Russian cooperation.

Visiting the Monument: A visit here has several parts: viewing the massive monument (ideally from the far end of the reflecting pool); entering the atmospheric crypt; riding the elevator up to the viewing platform; and visiting the Forum 1813 museum.

On the **exterior,** the Archangel Michael straddles the main door with the same tiresome message that accompanies most military monuments: "God with us." Circling the rounded top of the monument, a dozen stoic 40-foot-tall soldiers lean menacingly on their swords—which they will use, if necessary, to protect their nation.

Buy your ticket at the building to the left, then head through the main door and ride the elevator up to **floor 1.** A 13-minute video guides you through the history of the Battle of the Nations and its namesake monument, from Napoleonic entanglements in 1812 to the

restoration and reopening of the monument in 2013. From there, go to **floor 3.** Guards direct you to the exterior stairs leading to an upper gallery where four gigantic 30-foot-tall statues represent the virtues of the German people during wartime: bravery (flexing muscles), faith (an idealistic child), strength (a mother nursing two young children—more fodder for the battlefield), and sacrifice (holding out a piece of fruit). Rocketing up 225 feet from the crypt below is a dome decorated with hundreds of life-sized cavalry triumphantly returning from battle.

Head back down a level to the **crypt.** The atmospheric atrium is ringed by 16 soldiers with their heads respectfully bowed to honor the sacrifice of those lost in battle. From the crypt or atrium, continue up the elevator to the **viewing balcony** for a commanding open-air view. From there you can climb more steps to summit the monument and stand on the tip-top **platform,** enjoying more sweeping (if distant) views over Leipzig.

Back on the ground, the Forum 1813 **museum,** in the smaller building to the right of the monument, narrates the story of the battle with paintings, models, uniforms, weapons, lots of artifacts from 1813, and a large diorama (all in German, but explained by the English audioguide).

Spinnerei

Formerly Europe's largest cotton mill—in the 19th century, it was a self-contained community of both factories and homes—this industrial complex has transitioned from a 1990s squatter haven into a sprawling artistic venue with more than 10 galleries and dozens of artists' studios. Many showcase the "New Leipzig" art movement (contemporary eastern German art from after reunification). Gallery hoppers, or anyone interested in the gentrification of old industrial wastelands, may find this place (with the slogan "from cotton to culture") worth a visit. There are even four fun, industrial apartments for rent if you'd like to soak in the creative vibes overnight.

Cost and Hours: Most galleries are free to enter, generally Tue-Sat 11:00-18:00, closed Mon, email ahead to request a guided tour in English, Spinnereistrasse 7, tel. 0341/498-0222, mail@spinnerei.de, www.spinnerei.de, apartment information: www.meisterzimmer.de.

Getting There: It's about three miles southwest of the town center. From the Hauptbahnhof, take tram #14 or S-Bahn line S-1 to the Plagwitz stop. Cross under the tracks, and turn left at Spinnereistrasse. Spinnerei will be on your left.

Nightlife in Leipzig

Music lovers can look into performances at the **Opera House** or **Gewandhaus,** home of the city's orchestra (both on Augustusplatz). Nearby, the **Moritzbastei** is a popular-with-students place for cultural events (described later, under "Eating in Leipzig"; check events schedule at www.moritzbastei.de).

Leipzig's most happening nightlife zone is the **Karli,** loaded with trendy restaurants, cafés, and bars (see "Eating in Leipzig," later). A well-established venue here is **die naTo,** a cultural center presenting theater, film, poetry slams, and music as well as a bar with drinks and food (events nightly from 18:30, cover charge, Karl-Liebknecht-Strasse 48, tel. 0341/391-5539, www.nato-leipzig.de).

Sleeping in Leipzig

Thanks to the one-two punch of being both a convention town and a post-communist one, Leipzig is short on the characteristic, family-run little pensions I favor in other parts of Germany. With a few exceptions, I've listed functional, business-oriented hotels. Rates are typically higher on weeknights than weekends, and soft both in midsummer (July-Aug) and winter (Nov-March). Prices skyrocket during conventions and fairs—concentrated during the months of April-June and Sept-Oct (for a schedule, see www.leipziger-messe.com).

WITHIN OR NEAR THE RING

$$ Hotel Fregehaus is a real find. Just across from the TI, through a flowery courtyard, this historic merchant's house-turned-boutique hotel dresses its 17 rooms, two apartments, and one suite in an antique-chic-meets-low-key-mod look. The classy ambience and regional breakfast feel indulgent without having a high price tag (breakfast extra, elevator, Katharinenstrasse 11, tel. 0341/2639-3157, http://hotel-fregehaus.de, kontakt@hotel-fregehaus.de).

$$ Seaside Park Hotel has an anonymous, business-class vibe but an extremely convenient location (albeit nowhere near any seashore), just across the busy Ring from the train station and an easy walk to anywhere in the town center. With 288 rooms and a lot of marble, mirrors, and brass in the lobby, it feels elegant for the price. Note that many rooms come with open-plan bathrooms, with the shower or tub visible from the whole room (breakfast extra, air-con, elevator, pay parking, bistro, train-themed restaurant, Richard-Wagner-Strasse 7, tel. 0341/98520, www.parkhotelleipzig.de, info@parkhotelleipzig.de).

$ Mercure Art Leipzig, part of a stylish European chain, has 72 comfortable, minimalist rooms decorated with bright paintings of action heroes by a local artist. It's in a dull urban neighborhood one tram stop (or a 10-minute walk) north of the train station, but the prices are reasonable for what you get (breakfast extra, air-con, elevator, pay parking; from station ride tram #10, #11, or #16 one stop north to Wilhelm-Liebknecht-Platz, hotel is across street, on other side of triangular park; Eutritzscher Strasse 15, tel. 0341/303-840, www.mercure.de, h8847@accor.com).

$ Motel One Nikolaikirche, part of a German chain, is the most central hotel in Leipzig (facing St. Nicholas Church) and the best deal for well-located comfort. Its 194 rooms are cookie-cutter, modern, and sleek, and the staff is professional (breakfast extra, walkable from train station at Nikolaistrasse 23, tel. 0341/337-4370, www.motel-one.com, leipzig-nikolaikirche@motel-one.com). A second **Motel One,** located just off Augustusplatz, also has family rooms (Ritterstrasse 4, tel. 0341/252-7980, www.motel-one.com, leipzig-augustusplatz@motel-one.com).

¢ A&O Leipzig Hauptbahnhof Hostel fills the former post office with 163 rooms, ranging from dorms to private rooms. Vast and institutional, it caters to a wide range of travelers, from backpackers to families. Ask for a room away from the street (private rooms available, breakfast extra, elevator, bar and lounge in lobby, Brandenburger Strasse 2, tel. 0341/2507-94900, www.aohostels.com, booking@aohostels.com). From the train station, take the Wintergartenstrasse exit (by track 23); you'll see the hostel to the left, across the street from the bus parking lot.

KARLI DISTRICT

This area, along Karl-Liebknecht-Strasse, has Leipzig's best bar and nightclub scene, and some of its most appealing restaurants. Staying here puts you close enough to the sightseeing while helping you escape the relatively characterless downtown for a funkier, more colorful people zone. These listings are just off the main drag, so night noise is minimal, though you may hear rowdy people and rumbling trams in the distance—ask for a quieter back room. To get here from the train station (or Augustusplatz), ride south on tram #10 (direction: Lössnig) or #11 (direction: Markkleeberg-Ost).

$$ Michaelis Hotel is a class act, with 95 big rooms spread across two neighboring buildings, sophisticated decor, and good service. It's a particularly good value in July and August (apartments available, pay parking, tram stop: Hohe Strasse—then walk 100 yards ahead, turn left at intersection, and it's on the left, Paul-Gruner-Strasse 44, tel. 0341/26780, www.michaelis-leipzig.de, info@michaelis-leipzig.de).

$ Hotel Markgraf is simple but professionally run, offering 57 straightforward, sometimes musty rooms with sterile comfort at fair rates just a half block from the Südplatz tram stop—close but not *too* close to the Karli action (breakfast extra, elevator, free street parking in front of hotel, tram stop: Südplatz, Körnerstrasse 36, tel. 0341/303-030, www.markgraf-hotel-leipzig.com, hotel@markgraf-leipzig.de).

Eating in Leipzig

NEAR AUGUSTUSPLATZ AND THE UNIVERSITY

Getting "High" for Lunch: The towering MDR skyscraper (described on page 684), just off Augustusplatz, is capped with the elegant **$$$ Panorama Tower restaurant,** serving modern, international cuisine in a classy setting with a dramatic view. While dinner can be pricey, they serve a very affordable three-course "business lunch" for €11.50, and free rooftop access is included (available Mon-Fri 11:30-14:30; restaurant open Mon-Fri 9:00-21:00, Sat-Sun 10:00-20:00; take elevator to 29th floor, tel. 0341/710-0590, www.panorama-leipzig.de).

Student Grub: Behind the skyscraper, **$ Moritzbastei** is a maze of vaulted cellars that were once part of the city fortifications. After World War II, these passages were covered with dirt until a group of students—including, reportedly, Angela Merkel—organized to excavate them. Today the complex is filled mostly with students enjoying its indoor and outdoor seating, bars, basic bar food, sandwiches, design-your-own salads, weekday lunch specials, and live entertainment (daily until 24:00, closed Sat mornings and some Sun in summer, Universitätsstrasse 9, tel. 0341/702-590).

DOWNTOWN "RESTAURANT ROWS"

Two downtown streets to either side of the busy Dittrichring are lined with restaurants that cater to the lunch-break crowd and are also open for dinner. **Barfussgässchen** ("Barefoot Lane"), just inside the Ring, is closer to Market Square and has a higher concentration of bars and eateries. It's touristy, but even locals enjoy the drinks and people-watching here. I recommend walking another five minutes across the Ring and checking out **Gottschedstrasse**, which has somewhat better variety and value. Choose the cuisine and ambience you like best: Thai, tapas, Italian, Vietnamese, trendy lounge, and so on. Just about the only thing you won't find is a German beer hall.

Gottschedstrasse

$$ Luise, a big, lively, red-and-yellow bar with happening outdoor seating, serves international dishes, burgers, and big salads (daily 9:00-24:00, breakfast served until 15:00, at Gottschedstrasse and Bosestrasse at Bosestrasse 4, tel. 0341/961-1488).

$$ Pilot, attached to the Central Theater, is hip yet accessible, offering eclectic German and international food with seasonal ingredients in a relaxed setting accented by mismatched used furniture (daily 9:00-late, at intersection with Gottschedstrasse at Bosestrasse 1, tel. 0341/126-8117).

$$ Canito is a classy wine bar serving light *antipasti* meals, with live piano music, a wall of wines, and a Mediterranean deli case in back (Mon 12:00-15:00, Tue-Fri 12:00-24:00, Sat 15:00-24:00, closed Sun, Gottschedstrasse 13, tel. 0341/993-8011).

Barfussgässchen

$ Spizz is a jazz bar with an easy menu serving popular pasta and offering lots of outside seating on Market Square (daily 9:00-late, Markt 9).

$ Coffe Baum, which claims to be the oldest coffeehouse in Germany, is now a quality restaurant—and coffee museum—serving traditional Saxon and other German food as well as lots of coffees and cakes (daily 11:00-24:00, Fleischergasse 4; see the "Leipzig, Coffee, and Classic Cafés" sidebar, earlier).

$ Umaii Ramenbar serves big Asian noodle soups (Mon-Thu 11:30-10:30, Fri-Sat until 24:00, closed Sun; Klostergasse 7), and the **$ HuWa** is a mod pub offering breakfast until late, light meals, and drinks (daily 8:00-late, Barfussgässchen 15).

IN THE KARLI

Leipzig's avant-garde epicenter takes a bit more effort to reach but is still accessible. This several-block stretch of Karl-Liebknecht-Strasse is filled with artfully dilapidated, graffitoed buildings hosting eccentric and upscale boutiques, bars, restaurants, and venues for concerts and other creative happenings. You can walk here from downtown (across the Ring, south of the New Town Hall), but I'd hop on tram #10 (direction: Lössnig) or #11 (direction: Markkleeberg-Ost) at the train station or Augustusplatz, ride to the Karl-Liebknecht-/Kurt-Eisner-Strasse stop, and walk back until you find something you like.

Burgers are popular in the Karli, and there are plenty of vegetarian places too. Most eateries here are bars with decent food and indoor or outdoor seating. Here are some standout sit-down eateries notable for their funky vibe or fun cuisine.

$$ Pata Negra (#75) serves up tasty Spanish main dishes, but I'd go for a mix of tapas and call it dinner (choose between inside seating, cozy courtyard, or streetside tables, reservations smart, daily 17:00-late, tel. 0341/306-7103, www.patanegra.de).

$$ LuLu Lottenstein (#63) is your elegantly understated option in this part of town. Their focus is on regional specialties, with a menu that changes seasonally, in a comfy rustic-chic setting with a cozy fireplace (Mon-Fri 15:00-23:00, Sat 10:00-24:00, Sun 10:00-23:00, tel. 0341/308-2613).

$$ Maître (#62) is a brasserie serving a hodgepodge of German interpretations of French dishes including shareable salads, crêpes and galettes, quiche, and meat dishes. Locals enjoy their varied breakfast menu and pastry selection (Mon-Fri 8:00-24:00, Sat from 9:00, Sun 9:00-20:00, tel. 0341/3032-8924).

$$ L'Angolo d'Italia has solid Italian basics like pasta and pizza—as well as more creative and seasonal main courses with fish or meat—in a setting that aims for romance. Outside tables are less intimate and flanked by two busy streets (daily 11:30-14:30 & 17:30-23:00, Koschstrasse 1, tel. 0341/3068-6211).

$ Volkshaus (#30), a classic smoky pub with a beer garden out back, prides itself on its *Flammkuchen* (a kind of German pizza with white sauce) and offers standard international dishes like pastas and burgers (daily 9:30-late, tel. 0341/212-7222).

$ Gaststätte Kollektiv (#72) is an "Ostalgic" hoot with its classic—and filling—DDR dishes like *Omu* used to make. Try the "Strammer Max"—black bread with fried ham. Even if you dine on their terrace, be sure to take a time-travel stroll through each dining room filled with kitschy, authentic memorabilia and decor, including a cool model train set (daily 11:00-late, tel. 0341/306-7004).

$ Killiwilly Irish Pub (#44) slings beers and plates of typical pub grub, along with seasonal German classics and big salads, in a convivial locale (daily 10:00-late, tel. 0341/211-4322).

$ Casual or On-the-Go Options: These places are all open every day until at least 24:00. **Burgermeister der Grill** (Südplatz

1, at Südplatz tram stop), a trendy hamburger stand filling a circa-1900 public toilet kiosk, has a wide selection of made-to-order burgers with veggie options that go great with a side of sweet-potato fries or truffle-cheese fries. Be prepared to share a table. **El Amir** (#59) is the go-to *döner* joint with a chaotic menu of cheap, filling, and tasty dishes. Skip the salads and go for one of the *döner* or vegetarian specialties. **Olive Tree** (#38) is a slightly classier, if yuppier, venue with a simpler *döner* menu, splittable pizzas, and filling vegetarian options.

CHARACTERISTIC LEIPZIG BRAUHAUS

$$ Bayerischer Bahnhof is the city's main draw for beer pilgrims eager to sample the local brew, Gose (GOH-zeh). Originating in the town of Goslar, this ex-

tremely acidic-tasting light brew (to which coriander is added in the final stage) became a Leipzig favorite. But through the tumultuous 20th century, the recipe was all but lost, and Gose was forgotten. In the 1980s, a Berlin brewer dusted off the recipe and started making Gose once more. Its fizziness makes Gose especially refreshing on a hot day and also helps it mix well with various shots and flavors (you'll see a list on the menu; for example, the *Frauenfreundliche*—"women friendly"—has a shot of cherry syrup). Adding a shot isn't a bad idea, as first-timers sometimes find Gose sour and a bit salty.

True to its name, the restaurant is inside one wing of the old Bayerischer Bahnhof ("Bavarian train station," where trains from Bavaria first reached all the way north to Saxony). Built in 1842, this station has been renovated to become part of the city's S-Bahn system, allowing it to retain its title as the "world's oldest functioning train station." Besides beer, the restaurant also has a full menu of tasty beer-hall dishes. Choose between several brewpub seating sections—some with a view of the giant copper vats—or the delightful beer garden (daily 11:00-24:00, kitchen open until 23:00, Bayerischer Platz 1, take the S-Bahn from Hauptbahnhof or Market Square or ride tram #16 from Hauptbahnhof or Augustusplatz a few minutes to Bayerischer Platz, tel. 0341/124-5760).

Leipzig Connections

Leipzig is a major rail hub for eastern Germany; if you're traveling between towns in the western part of the country (Frankfurt, Würzburg, Nürnberg) and towns in the east (Berlin, Dresden), you'll likely pass through here. If traveling to the Luther towns or Dresden, you can save some money (but not time) with the Sachsen-Ticket, which is valid on slower RE trains.

From Leipzig by Train to: **Berlin** (hourly, 1.5 hours), **Dresden** (1-2/hour, 1.5 hours), **Erfurt** (hourly, 45 minutes on ICE), **Eisenach** and Wartburg Castle (hourly, 75 minutes on ICE, more with transfer in Erfurt), **Wittenberg** (hourly, 30 minutes on ICE; also hourly on regional trains, 70 minutes), **Frankfurt** (hourly, 3 hours), **Würzburg** (hourly, 3 hours, some transfer in Fulda or Bamberg), **Hamburg** (hourly, 3 hours, some transfer in Berlin), **Nürnberg** (hourly, 2 hours, half with transfer at Erfurt), **Munich** (8/day direct, 3 hours; more with transfer in Nürnberg, Erfurt, or Halle/Saale), **Prague** (every 2 hours, 4 hours with transfer in Dresden; 9:30 departure is a direct bus, 3 hours). Train info: www.bahn.com.

DRESDEN

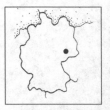

Dresden surprises visitors with fanciful Baroque architecture in a delightful-to-stroll cityscape, a dynamic history that mingles tragedy with inspiration, and some of the best museumgoing in Germany—rivaling the sights in Berlin and Munich (and that's saying something). Today's Dresden is an intriguing and fun city, filled with proud locals, cheery visitors, and students. Although it's crawling with German tourists, Dresden winds up on far fewer American itineraries than it deserves to. Don't make that mistake.

At the peak of its power in the 18th century, this capital of Saxony ruled most of present-day Poland and eastern Germany from the banks of the Elbe River. Dresden's answer to France's legendary King Louis XIV was Augustus the Strong. As both prince elector of Saxony and king of Poland, Augustus imported artists from all over Europe, peppering his city with fine Baroque buildings and filling his treasury with lavish jewels and artwork. Dresden's grand architecture and dedication to the arts earned it the nickname "Florence on the Elbe."

Outside Germany, Dresden is better known for its nearly complete destruction by Allied firebombing in World War II. In the postwar years under communist rule, Dresden patched up some of its damaged buildings, left many others in ruins, and replaced even more with modern, ugly sprawl. Later, after Germany was reunited, Dresden undertook a more systematic rebuilding, especially of the city's landmark structures, most notably the Royal Palace and the Frauenkirche.

The transformation over the last generation has been astonishing. Even so, Dresden still suffers somewhat from its wartime flattening. The historic core, while gorgeous, lacks personality—with plenty of hotels and touristy restaurants, but little real local life. The modern, rebuilt areas that fan out from the Old Town are tainted by a severe Soviet aesthetic.

However, the bombs missed most of the New Town, across the river. This well-worn area retains its prewar character and has emerged as the city's most engaging, lively neighborhood—especially the Outer New Town, north of Bautzner Strasse. Most tourists never cross the bridge away from the famous Old Town museums, but a visit to Dresden isn't complete without a wander through the New Town.

PLANNING YOUR TIME

Dresden merits spending at least one night (though two is better) and makes a good overnight stop between Nürnberg and Berlin. With one day, follow my self-guided walk, and visit your pick of museums. Reserve ahead to visit one of Dresden's top sights, the Historic Green Vault.

More time lets you dig even deeper into the city's fine museums, explore the thriving Outer New Town after-hours scene, or consider side trips to the "Blue Wonder" bridge or Saxon Switzerland National Park.

Orientation to Dresden

With a half-million residents, Dresden is big. The Old Town (Altstadt) hugs a curve on the Elbe River, so most of its sights are within easy strolling distance along the south bank of the river. South of the Old Town (a 5-minute tram ride or 20-minute walk away) is the main train station (Hauptbahnhof). North of the Old Town, across the river, you'll find the more residential New Town (Neustadt). While the New Town boasts no great sights, it's energetic, colorful, and fun to explore—especially after dark, when the funky, cutting-edge Outer New Town (Äussere Neustadt) sets the tempo for Dresden's nightlife scene.

TOURIST INFORMATION

Dresden has a good TI right in the heart of the Old Town (Mon-Fri 10:00-19:00, Sat until 18:00, Sun until 15:00; Neumarkt 2—enter under *Passage* sign across from door D of Frauenkirche, and go down escalators). A smaller TI kiosk is in the main train station (daily 9:00-21:00, under tracks 1-2). The TIs share a phone number and website (tel. 0351/501-501, www.dresden.de/tourismus). Both TIs hand out a good transit map, which includes an adequate street map, and the free *Theater Konzert Kunst* entertainment guide (in German only).

Discount Deals: Dresden offers a variety of combo-tickets that fully cover most of the city's top museums: at the Zwinger, in the Royal Palace, and the Albertinum (all operated by Staatliche Kunstsammlungen Dresden). None of these tickets includes the Historic Green Vault.

To cram a lot of sightseeing into one day, the €19 **Day Ticket** sold by the museums is an easy choice. For two days, skip the museums' own two-day Day Ticket (€27); instead, buy the cheaper €22 **Dresden Museums Card,** which covers the same museums and offers discounts on other attractions (sold only at TI; www.dresden.de/dresdencard).

ARRIVAL IN DRESDEN

Dresden has two major train stations: Dresden Hauptbahnhof and Dresden-Neustadt. Most trains stop at both stations (coming from Berlin, first at Neustadt, then at Hauptbahnhof). If you're visiting for the day, use the Hauptbahnhof for the easiest access to Dresden's sights. S-Bahn trains, as well as trams #3 and #11, connect the two stations (see "Getting Around Dresden," later).

By Train at the Hauptbahnhof: Dresden's main train station has a chic roof designed by Norman Foster (of Berlin's Reichstag Dome fame). In the bright, white arrivals hall, you'll find a *Reisezentrum* (travel desk). Under tracks 1-2 are pay WCs, lockers, and the TI.

To reach the beginning of my self-guided walk by **tram,** exit the station following *Ausgang 1* signs, cross the tram tracks, and take tram #11 to Postplatz in the Old Town (three stops) and walk ten minutes up Sophienstrasse to Theaterplatz. For those who'd rather **walk,** the 20-minute stroll to the Old Town gives you a look at communist-era architecture as you head down Prager Strasse (described under "More Sights in Dresden," later): From the station, exit toward *Ausgang 2/City/Prager Strasse,* and continue straight along Prager Strasse, then Seestrasse and Schlossstrasse until you emerge at the river.

To reach other points from the station by tram, note your line number and ask for help finding your platform. Lines #3, #8, #9 and #11 (linking to the New Town) depart from the Hauptbahnhof Nord tram stop: Exit the arrivals hall via *Ausgang 2,* cross the tram tracks, then angle right through the passage in the long, glassy building (look for *Hbf Nord* signs).

By Train at Neustadt: The Neustadt train station serves the New Town north of the river and is near some recommended hotels. It has lockers and WCs, and a *Reisezentrum.* To reach the Old Town from Neustadt Station, take tram #11 (direction: Zschertnitz) four stops to Postplatz.

By Plane: From Dresden's airport (airport code: DRS, tel.

351/881-3360, www.dresden-airport.de), S-Bahn line #2 runs to both train stations for the price of a regular public-transit ticket (€2.30, 2/hour, 20 minutes). A taxi between the airport and the center should cost around €20.

By Bus: Long-distance buses come and go from a cluster of stops just behind the Hauptbahnhof.

By Car: The city center has several well-marked parking garages with reasonable daytime rates (€10/day 8:00-20:00 on Mon-Sat, €3/day on Sun).

HELPFUL HINTS

Sightseeing Strategies: Note that many of Dresden's top museums are closed either Monday or Tuesday. Reserve ahead for the Historic Green Vault (closed Tue), where a limited number of people are admitted every half-hour. Otherwise, line up early to buy a same-day ticket (ticket office opens at 10:00; see listing later, under "Sights in Dresden"). Once you have your Historic Green Vault visit time, plan the rest of your day around it (it's conveniently located right in the center of the Old Town).

Entertainment, Organ Concerts, and Masses: The city has lots going on. Ask about events across the river at the big amphitheater (concerts, movies, sports broadcasts; almost nightly June-Aug). Both big churches—the Catholic Hofkirche and the Lutheran Frauenkirche—have a worship service or Mass with pipe-organ music every day (check schedule and buy tickets at TI and/or church); the Hofkirche also hosts free pipe-organ concerts (usually Wed and Sat evenings; check schedule at door).

Christmas Market: Dresden's huge "Striezelmarkt" **Christmas market** takes over Altmarkt square throughout Advent (www.dresden.de/striezelmarkt).

Laundry: These coin-operated launderettes are in the New Town (generally Mon-Sat 6:00-23:00, last load at 22:00, closed Sun): **Eco-Express Waschsalon** is just off Albertplatz (Königsbrücker Strasse 2) and **Waschmeister** is on the east end of the Outer New Town (Louisenstrasse 2)

Bike Rental: Roll on Dresden rents bikes and will gladly deliver and pick up bikes at your hotel for a small fee (€10/day; in summer Mon-Fri 9:00-14:00 & 17:00-19:00, Sat-Sun 9:00-13:00 & 18:00-19:00; returns available 24 hours; in New Town, near Albertplatz tram stop at Königsbrücker Strasse 4a, mobile 0152-2267-3460, www.rollondresden.de).

GETTING AROUND DRESDEN

As soon as you master the **trams,** you'll understand why so many Dresdeners never learn how to drive. Trams are cheap, easy, and go

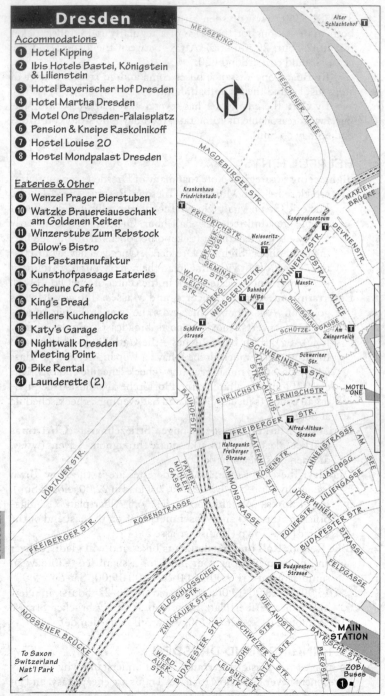

Dresden

Accommodations

1. Hotel Kipping
2. Ibis Hotels Bastei, Königstein & Lilienstein
3. Hotel Bayerischer Hof Dresden
4. Hotel Martha Dresden
5. Motel One Dresden-Palaisplatz
6. Pension & Kneipe Raskolnikoff
7. Hostel Louise 20
8. Hostel Mondpalast Dresden

Eateries & Other

9. Wenzel Prager Bierstuben
10. Watzke Brauereiausschank am Goldenen Reiter
11. Winzerstube Zum Rebstock
12. Bülow's Bistro
13. Die Pastamanufaktur
14. Kunsthofpassage Eateries
15. Scheune Café
16. King's Bread
17. Hellers Kuchenglocke
18. Katy's Garage
19. Nightwalk Dresden Meeting Point
20. Bike Rental
21. Launderette (2)

DRESDEN

To Saxon Switzerland Nat'l Park

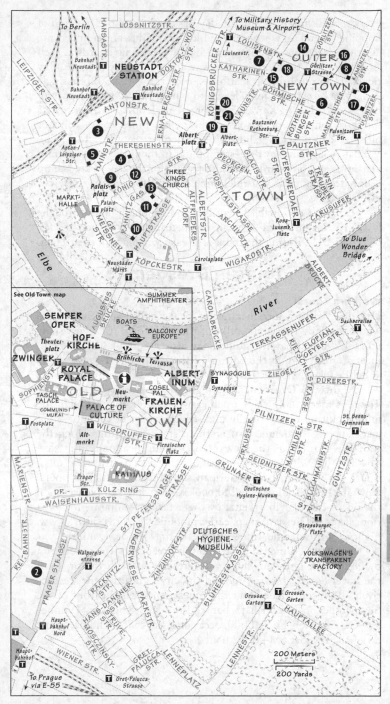

DRESDEN

every several minutes. Buy the day pass and enjoy the freedom of hopping on and off whenever you like. Tram lines and numbers are clearly marked on city maps, and handy electronic boards at each stop say which trams are on the way and when they'll arrive. Buy tickets from machines at platforms or on trams (€2.30 for a single *Einzelfahrkarte* ticket for rides up to 1 hour; €8.20 for a 4-pack of tickets, called a *4er-Karte;* €5.50 for a 4-pack of *Kurzstrecke* tickets for short journeys of 4 stops or fewer; machines accept coins or bills). A day ticket is valid for one calendar day (*Tageskarte,* €6). Validate your ticket by date-stamping it in the little boxes on train platforms and on board buses and trams (for the day ticket, stamp it only the first time you ride). For transit information, see www. vvo-online.de.

Taxis are reasonable, plentiful, and generally honest (roughly €8-10 ride in town—get an estimate before you hop in; tel. 0351/211-211). Riding the trams is so easy, you may not need a taxi.

Tours in Dresden

Walking Tours
Dresden Walks is a cooperative of local English-speaking guides who offer daily two-hour walks of the Old Town (€12, just show up at 12:00 and pay the guide, may also run at 14:30 June-Sept, meet at green sign at the bottom of the Brühlsche Terrasse stairs at Schlossplatz, mobile 0163-716-9886, www.dresdenwalks.com).

Nightwalk Dresden, a late-night tour of the city's Outer New Town, is much more than a pub crawl; it's a journey through the unique culture of a virtually undiscovered part of the city—that just happens to include two or three stops for drinks along the way. This tour brings the prewar (and prereunification) Outer New Town to life with fascinating details that you'd otherwise miss. Tours run in English and German simultaneously (€17, 3 hours, daily at 21:00—call or email to book a spot; starts in Neustadt on the north end of Albertplatz, by the artesian fountain—for location, see the "Dresden" map, earlier; mobile 0172/781-5007, www. nightwalk-dresden.de, info@nightwalk-dresden.de, Danilo).

The **Kurt Vonnegut Tour** and the **Street Art Tour,** both run by Nightwalk Dresden, show you Dresden through the prism of the novel *Slaughterhouse-Five* and the city's graffiti scene, respectively. Both tours meet near the equestrian statue in front of the Semperoper on Theaterplatz, but require advance booking (Vonnegut-€13.50, Mon-Fri at 11:00, occasional Sat tours, 2 hours; Street Art-€13, Tue-Sat at 14:00, 2 hours).

DRESDEN

Dresden at a Glance

▲▲Historic Green Vault Fairy-tale Baroque halls filled with sparkling gems and curiosities collected by the rulers of Saxony. **Hours:** Wed-Mon 10:00-18:00, closed Tue. See page 731.

▲▲New Green Vault More Saxon treasures, but displayed in sleek modern spaces. **Hours:** Wed-Mon 10:00-18:00, closed Tue. See page 732.

▲▲Old Masters Gallery Grand collection of paintings in the Zwinger Palace featuring top pieces from the most prominent late Gothic and Renaissance masters. **Hours:** Tue-Sun 10:00-18:00, closed Mon. See page 726.

▲▲Royal Armory Some of Europe's finest medieval armor, much of it posed as if in action, plus a historic coin collection. **Hours:** Wed-Mon 10:00-18:00, closed Tue. See page 734.

▲▲Albertinum Paintings and sculpture from the Romantic era through present day. **Hours:** Tue-Sun 10:00-18:00, closed Mon. See page 735.

▲▲Frauenkirche Landmark Baroque church whose exquisite restoration has come to symbolize Dresden's rebirth. **Hours:** Mon-Fri 10:00-12:00 & 13:00-18:00, Sat-Sun hours vary. See page 737.

▲▲Military History Museum Germany's largest museum, covering more than 800 years of Germanic war-making with a focus on understanding the costs of violence. **Hours:** Thu-Tue 10:00-18:00, Mon until 21:00, closed Wed. See page 742.

▲Mathematics-Physics Salon Fun collection of old-time scientific gadgets in the Zwinger Palace. **Hours:** Tue-Sun 10:00-18:00, closed Mon. See page 728.

▲Porcelain Collection World's largest array of decorative ceramics, with enough variety and sheer artistry to interest most. **Hours:** Tue-Sun 10:00-18:00, closed Mon. See page 728.

▲Turkish Chamber Augustus the Strong's impressive collection of Turkish swag, housed in the Royal Palace. **Hours:** Wed-Mon 10:00-18:00, closed Tue. See page 733.

▲Katholische Hofkirche Huge Catholic church at the foot of the Augustus Bridge, home to a stirring memorial to the 1945 firebombing. **Hours:** Mon-Fri 8:30-17:00, Sat 10:30-17:00, Sun 12:00-16:00. See page 739.

▲New Town and Outer New Town Stately, never-bombed neighborhood of restaurants and shops just across the river from the Old Town, with an edgy, proudly countercultural district stretching north from Albertplatz. See page 742.

Hop-On, Hop-Off Bus Tours

Red-and-white double-decker buses (labeled *Stadtrundfahrt*) connect nearly two dozen of the city's main sights (including the Blue Wonder bridge) in a 2-hour loop (€20, €2 more per extra day; in summer up to 4/hour, Nov-March 2/hour; tel. 0351/899-5650, www.stadtrundfahrt.com/dresden).

Local Guides

Liane Richter (€80/2-hour tour, lianerichter@gmx.net) and **Anke Winkler** (€90/2-hour tour, mobile 0151-1196-8770, info@dresden-citytour.de) are two good local guides who enjoy sharing the story of their hometown and region.

Old and New Dresden Walk

Dresden's major Old Town sights are conveniently clustered along a delightfully strollable promenade next to the Elbe River. From there, the city's oldest bridge leads into the energetic New Town. Lace these sights together by taking this self-guided walk, worth ▲▲▲. You'll get to know the four eras that have most shaped the city: Dresden's Golden Age in the mid-18th century under Augustus the Strong; the city's destruction by firebombs in World War II; the communist regime (1945-1989); and the current "reconstruction after reunification" era.

This walk takes about 1.5 hours, not counting museum stops. It passes by three major sights: the Zwinger, the Royal Palace and its Green Vault treasuries, and the Frauenkirche. These three and several other sights on this walk are described in more detail later, under "Sights in Dresden." If you visit the sights as you go, this walk will fill your day. Your stroll ends in the New Town, a great area for evening exploring or dining.

• *Begin at Theaterplatz (a 10-minute walk from the #11 tram stop on Postplatz).*

❶ Theaterplatz

In the middle of the square, face the equestrian statue of King John,

an intellectual mid-19th-century ruler who recognized and preserved Saxon culture—and paid for the opera house behind the statue. The Saxon State Opera House is nicknamed the **Semperoper** after its architect, Gottfried Semper (visits only with a 45-minute tour-€11, in English generally daily at 15:00, book

ahead, www.semperoper-erleben.de). Three opera houses have stood in this spot: The first was destroyed by a fire in 1869, the second by firebombs in 1945. The rebuilt Semperoper continues to be a world-class venue. Notice how the two greatest figures in German literary culture—Goethe and Schiller—flank the entry, welcoming all who enter to German high culture. Tickets for performances go on sale a year in advance and are hard to come by (tel. 0351/491-1705, www.semperoper.de, or drop by the box office in the Schinkelwache—described next).

As you face the Opera House, the big building to your left is the vast Zwinger complex (your next stop). The smaller Neoclassical building farther to your left is a former guardhouse called the **Schinkelwache.** If it looks out of place, that's because it was designed in a Prussian Classicist style by the architect Karl  Friedrich Schinkel, who was also responsible for some of Berlin's most impressive Neoclassical buildings. Today the Schinkelwache functions as a popular café and the opera's box office.

Behind you, across the square from the Opera House, are the Hofkirche (with its distinctive green-copper, onion-domed steeple) and the sprawling Royal Palace, both worth visiting and described later. All the buildings you see here—Dresden's Baroque treasures—are thorough reconstructions. The originals were destroyed in a single night by American and British bombs, with only walls and sometimes just foundations left standing (see "The Firebombing of Dresden" sidebar, later). Dresden has been rebuilding ever since.

A number of the Old Town's historical buildings, both original and rebuilt, are made from local sandstone—most of it looking really sooty. It's not from pollution or firebombing (as many visitors presume), but natural oxidation that turns the stone black in about 50 years. Many facades and statues, once restored, are now given a silicon treatment that lets the stone breathe but keeps it from going black.

• *Head to the gap between the Semperoper and the Zwinger. Standing in front of the recommended Alte Meister Café is a statue of Carl Maria von Weber, the composer whose Der Freischütz was the last opera performed in the Semperoper before its destruction in 1945—and the first opera performed when the building reopened in 1985.*

To the right of Weber, go up the stairs and hang a left up the path. Head past the adorable fountain at the top of the path to the balcony with a breathtaking view of the grand...

DRESDEN

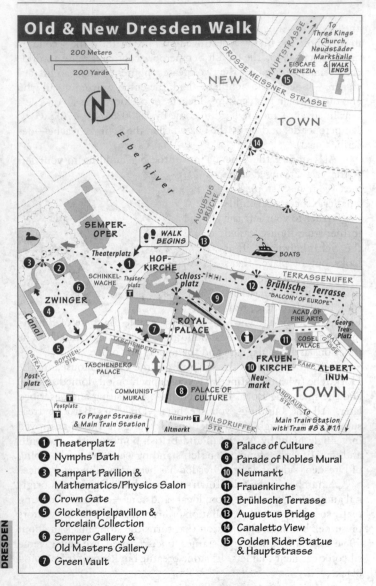

Old & New Dresden Walk

200 Meters
200 Yards

NEW TOWN

Elbe River

To Three Kings Church, Neustädter Markthalle
EISCAFÉ VENEZIA
WALK ENDS

15

14

SEMPER-OPER

WALK BEGINS

Theaterplatz
1
HOF-KIRCHE

SCHINKEL-WACHE
Theater-platz

3
2

ZWINGER
6
4

Canal

5

SOPHIEN STR.
OSTRA-ALLEE

TASCHENBERG-STR.

TASCHENBERG PALACE

Post-platz

Postplatz

To Prager Strasse & Main Train Station

AUGUSTUS BRÜCKE

13

BOATS

Schloss-platz

TERRASSENUFER

12 Brühlsche Terrasse
"BALCONY OF EUROPE"

9

ROYAL PALACE

7

ACAD. OF FINE ARTS

Georg-Treu-Platz

COSEL PALACE

SALZ-GASSE

11

10

FRAUEN-KIRCHE

Neu-markt

RAMP.

ALBERT-INUM

OLD TOWN

COMMUNIST MURAL

8 PALACE OF CULTURE

Altmarkt

WILSDRUFFER STR.

Altmarkt

LANDHAUS-STR.

To Main Train Station with Tram #8 & #11

1 Theaterplatz
2 Nymphs' Bath
3 Rampart Pavilion & Mathematics/Physics Salon
4 Crown Gate
5 Glockenspielpavillon & Porcelain Collection
6 Semper Gallery & Old Masters Gallery
7 Green Vault

8 Palace of Culture
9 Parade of Nobles Mural
10 Neumarkt
11 Frauenkirche
12 Brühlsche Terrasse
13 Augustus Bridge
14 Canaletto View
15 Golden Rider Statue & Hauptstrasse

DRESDEN

Zwinger

This Baroque masterpiece, once the pride and joy of the Wettin dynasty, is today filled with fine museums. The Wettins ruled Saxony for more than 800 years, right up until the end of the First World War (just like the Romanovs in Russia and the Habsburgs in Austria). Saxony wasn't ruled by a king, but by a prince elector—one of a handful of nobles who elected the Holy Roman Emperor.

The prince elector of Saxony was one of Germany's most power-ful people. In the 18th century, the larger-than-life Augustus the Strong—who was both prince elector of Saxony and king of Po-land—kicked off Saxony's Golden Age.

The word "Zwinger" refers to the no-man's-land moat between the outer and inner city walls. As the city expanded, the pavilions and galleries you see today were built. Although the Zwinger buildings might look like a palace to us commoners, no one ever lived here—it was solely for pleasurable pursuits. By Augustus' time, the Zwinger was a venue for Saxon court celebrations

(note how the decor—cherubs, wine grapes, comely maidens—is all about royal partying, rather than royal power). Imagine an over-the-top royal wedding in this setting. The courtyard served as a spot for open-air festivities, complete with gardens and orange trees in huge Chinese porcelain pots. Even today, the courtyard hosts the occasional gala or classical concert.

As you stand on the balcony, imagine yourself as one of Dres-den's 18th-century burghers, watching one of Augustus' wild par-ties in the courtyard below. If you visit the Old Masters Gallery (described later), you'll see the 1752 version of this balustrade view in Bernardo "Canaletto" Bellotto's *Zwinger Courtyard in Dresden.*
• *Cross the balcony to the left to enjoy a view of the enclosed Nymphs' Bath from above, then take the small stairs at the top down to its pool.*

❷ Nymphs' Bath

Here, at what is perhaps the city's favorite fountain, 18th-century aristocrats relaxed among cascading waterfalls and an open air grotto, ringed by sexy sandstone nymphs. It's textbook Baroque, with its pilasters and poolsides evoking falling water and an invis-ible wind machine conveniently blowing open the robes of eager-to-frolic maidens.
• *From the pool, cross through the glassy orangery (housing the Franzö-sische Pavillon, a branch of the Alte Meister Café) and all the way into the middle of the huge...*

Zwinger Courtyard

Stand in place here to survey the four wings, starting with the ❸ **Rampart Pavilion** (Wallpavillon)—the one you just came from, marked up top by Hercules hoisting the earth. The first wing of the complex to be built, it includes an orangery capped with a sun pavilion built for Augustus' fruit trees and parties. Hercules—the ultimate strongman (who happens to have Augustus' features)—is a fitting symbol for Augustus the Strong. The other side of this wing (on the left) houses the fun **Mathematics-Physics Salon.**

Turn farther to the left, facing the ❹ **Crown Gate** (Kronentor). The gate's golden crown is topped by four golden eagles supporting a smaller crown—symbolizing Polish royalty (since Augustus was also king of Poland).

Turn again to the left to see the ❺ **Glockenspielpavillon.** The glockenspiel near the top of the gate has 40 bells made of Meissen porcelain (bells chime every 15 minutes and play a sweet 3-minute melody at 10:15, 14:15, and 18:15, plus 20:15 in summer). If you're here when they play, listen to the delightful chimes of the porcelain—far sweeter than a typical metal bell. Tunes range from Vivaldi to Mozart and Weber. This wing of the Zwinger also houses Augustus the Strong's **Porcelain Collection.**

Turn once more to the left (with the Crown Gate behind you) to see the stern facade of the ❻ **Semper Gallery.** This Zwinger wing was added to the original courtyard 100 years later by Gottfried Semper (of Opera House fame). It houses Dresden's best painting collection, the **Old Masters Gallery.**

You are surrounded by three of Dresden's top museums. Anticipating WWII bombs, Dresdeners preserved their town's art treasures by storing them in underground mines and cellars in the countryside. This saved these great works from Allied bombs...but not from the Russians. Nearly all the city's artwork ended up in Moscow until after Stalin's death in 1953, when it was returned by the communist regime to win over their East German subjects. Today, Russians invade Dresden only as tourists.

• *Now's a good time to visit your choice of the Zwinger museums. When you're ready to move on, exit the courtyard through the Glockenspielpavillon.*

Halfway through the corridor, look for the engraved **timelines** telling the history of the Zwinger in German: to the right, its construction, and to the left, its destruction and reconstruction. It's got a Soviet spin: On February 13, 1945, "gangs" of Anglo-American bombers "obliterated" the city. On May 8, 1945, the Soviet army "liberated" Dresden from "fascist tyranny," and from 1945 to 1964, the Zwinger was rebuilt with the "power of the workers and peasants."

• *As you exit the corridor, cross the street and the tram tracks and turn*

Augustus the Strong (1670-1733)

Friedrich Augustus I of the Wettin family exemplified royal excess, and made Dresden one of Europe's most important cities of culture. Legends paint Augustus as a macho, womanizing, powerful, ambitious, properly Baroque man—a real Saxon superstar. A hundred years after his death, historians dubbed Augustus "the Strong." Today, tour guides love to impart silly legends about Augustus, who supposedly fathered 365 children and could break a horseshoe in half with his bare hands.

As prince elector of Saxony, Augustus wheeled and dealed—and pragmatically converted from his Saxon Protestantism to a more Polish-friendly Catholicism—to become King Augustus II of Poland. (You'll notice the city center features both the fancy Protestant Frauenkirche and the huge, prominent Catholic Hofkirche, as Augustus was finessing it both ways to be acceptable to both realms.) Like most Wettins, Augustus the Strong was unlucky at war, but a clever diplomat and a lover of the arts.

The Polish people blame Augustus and his successors—who were far more concerned with wealth and opulence than with sensible governance—for Poland's precipitous decline after its own medieval Golden Age. According to Poles, the Saxon kings did nothing but "eat, drink, and loosen their belts" (it rhymes in Polish).

Whether you consider them the heroes of history, or the villains, Augustus and the rest of the Wettins—and the nobles who paid them taxes—are to thank for Dresden's rich architectural and artistic heritage.

DRESDEN

*left, then curve right, walking down the street called Taschenberg, with the yellow Taschenberg Palace on your right. Built for Augustus' mistress, it eventually housed the crown prince. This building was ruined until 1990, but today it's a five-star hotel. The yellow-windowed sky bridge ahead connects the Taschenberg with the prince electors' **Royal Palace**. The gate on your left is one of several entrances to the palace, with its ❶ **Green Vault** treasuries and other sights.*

Continue along Taschenberg and under the sky bridge. Ahead of you and to the right, the blocky modern building is the...

❽ Palace of Culture (Kulturpalast)

Built by the communist government in 1969, today this hall is used for concerts. The building's exterior mural depicts communist themes: workers, strong women, well-cared-for elders, teachers and students, and—of course—the red star and the seal of the former East Germany. Check out the bronze doors on the street side that give a Marxist interpretation of the history of Dresden. Little of this propagandist art, which once inundated the lives of locals, survives in post-communist Germany (what does survive, like this, is protected). The refurbished concert hall inside is home to the Dresden Philharmonic.

• *Now turn left (leaving the Palace of Culture behind you). Walk along Schlossstrasse, with the Royal Palace on your left (noticing the postwar construction on your right, a mix of new and old). After passing through a tunnel with (likely Russian) musicians taking advantage of the fine acoustics, you emerge onto* **Palace Square.** *Ahead and to the left is the* **Katholische Hofkirche** *and another elevated passage, designed to allow royalty to go to church without the hassle of dealing with the public. (For a description of the interior, see "Sights in Dresden," later.)*

Now turn around and face the gate you just came through. You're looking at the palace complex entry, with the **Watchman's Tower** *above on the right. To the left, next to one of the palace's entrances, walk toward the long, yellow mural called the...*

❾ Parade of Nobles (Fürstenzug)

This mural is painted on 24,000 tiles of Meissen porcelain. Longer than a football field, it illustrates seven centuries of Saxon royalty.

It was built to commemorate Saxon history and heritage after Saxony became a part of Germany in 1871.

The very last figure in the procession (the first one you see, coming from this direction) is the artist himself, Wilhelm Walther. In front of him are commoners (miners, farmers, carpenters, teachers, students, artists), and then the royals, with 35 names and dates marking more than 700 years of Wettin rule. Walk the length of the mural to appreciate the detail. The artist carefully studied armor and clothing through the ages, accurately tracing the evolution of weaponry and fashions for seven centuries.

Before you get too far along, stop at 1694. That's Augustus the Strong (August II), the most important of the Saxon kings. His horse stomps on the rose (symbol of Martin Luther, the Protestant movement, and the Lutheran church today) to gain the Polish crown. The first Saxon royal, still farther along, is Konrad der Grosse ("the Great"). And waaay up at the very front of the parade, an announcer with a band and 12th-century cheerleaders excitedly herald the arrival of this wondrous procession. The porcelain tiles are originals (from 1907)—they survived the Dresden bombing. They were fired three times at 2,400 degrees Fahrenheit when created...and then fired again during the 1945 firestorm, at only 1,800 degrees.

• *When you're finished looking at the mural, dogleg right and walk into the big square, where a statue of Martin Luther stands tall.*

❿ Neumarkt

This "New Market Square" was once a central square ringed by the homes of rich merchants. After many years of construction,

it is once again alive with people and cafés, and even a few frilly facades that help you picture what the square looked like in its heyday. The statue of Martin Luther shows him holding not just any Bible, but the Word of God in German, which he personally translated from Hebrew and ancient Greek so that regular people could wrestle with it directly (this is, in a sense, what the Protestant Reformation was all about). When translating, Luther used colloquial, everyday German, forming the basis for what's now considered "High German." So besides being the Great Reformer, Luther is considered the father of the modern German language. (For more on Luther—who came from this part of Germany and spent most of his life in nearby Erfurt and Wittenberg—see the Lutherland chapter.) Toppled in 1945, Luther was cleaned up and is now back on his feet again.

• *The big church looming over the square is the...*

⓫ Frauenkirche (Church of Our Lady)

This church is the symbol and soul of the city. When completed in 1743, this was Germany's tallest Protestant church (310 feet high). Its unique central-stone-cupola design gave it the nickname "the stone bell." While it's a great church, this building garners the world's attention primarily because of

its tragic history and phoenix-like resurrection: On the night of February 13, 1945, the firebombs came. When the smoke cleared the next morning, the Frauenkirche was smoldering but still standing. It burned for two days before finally collapsing. After the war, the Frauenkirche was left a pile of rubble and turned into a peace monument. Only after reunification was the decision made to rebuild it completely. It reopened to the public in 2005.

Circle around the left side of the church to find a big hunk of the bombed **rubble** (near door E, river side of church). Notice the small metal relief of the dome that shows where this piece came from.

• *With your back to the rebuilt church, head right to find the nearby dome nicknamed "the lemon juicer." This caps the exhibition hall of the **Academy of Fine Arts**. Walk past that and hook left into the small, grassy Georg-Treu-Platz, which is surrounded by imposing architecture. The grand Neo-Renaissance building to the right is the **Albertinum**. Long the home of the Saxon armory, it was rebuilt in the 1880s in Neo-Renaissance style. Today it's an art gallery with the city's best collection of 19th- and 20th-century art.*

Walk through the square and climb the ramparts, now a park. Head through the park toward the banister for an Elbe River view. Each summer, the city sets up a popular amphitheater on the bank directly across the Elbe (offering nearly nightly events—such as concerts and movies). Now continue along the walkway back towards the tower of the Katholische Hofkirche and the Royal Palace to stroll the length of the...

⑫ Brühlsche Terrasse

This delightful promenade overlooking the river was once a defensive rampart—look along the side of the terrace facing the Elbe River to see openings for cannons. Later, it was given as a reward to a Saxon minister named Brühl, who had distinguished himself as a tax collector, raising revenue for Frederick Augustus II's state treasury. In the early 1800s, it was turned into a public park, with a leafy canopy of linden trees, and was given the nickname "The Balcony of Europe."

Look out over the Elbe River. Dresden claims to have the world's largest and oldest fleet of historic paddleboat steamers: nine riverboats from the 19th century. The hills in the distance (to the left) are home to vineyards, producing some of Germany's northernmost wine. Because only a small amount of land is suitable for

The Firebombing of Dresden

On the night of February 13, 1945, during the final months of World War II, American and British bomber crews firebombed Dresden to near-ruin. More than 3,500 tons of explosives decimated the city over three waves of attacks. Hot hurricane-force wind tunnels tore through the streets.

With few air-raid shelters in the city, civilians had little place to take cover: More than 25,000 people were killed in just one night, and 75 percent of the historical center was destroyed. American Kurt Vonnegut, who was a POW in Dresden during the firebombing, later memorialized the event in his novel *Slaughterhouse-Five*.

The ruthlessness of the civilian firebombing made it one of the war's most controversial attacks.

Why Dresden was targeted is debated. The city had no obvious strategic military importance. The Allies claimed the bombing was an effort to disrupt Nazi communication and to facilitate a Soviet invasion. More likely, the bombing was an act of vengeance and an attempt to demoralize the German population.

As you walk through Dresden, look for circa-1946 photos showing the devastation. An inscription on Altmarkt square calls Dresden "a place of remembrance" and asks passersby to recall that "thousands of victims' bodies were burnt here" in the raids. It concludes: "Thus the horrors of war, unleashed by Germany upon the whole world, came back to be visited upon our city."

Reconstruction under the communists was lackluster. But after the Berlin Wall fell and Germany was reunited, new funding became available for Dresden to restore its historic center. The city rebuilt the Royal Palace and Frauenkirche. Bombed-out blocks and derelict parking lots became huge department stores and apartment complexes with deep underground garages. The transition into a thriving cultural center is well underway, but the city remains a poignant reminder of the destruction caused by war.

DRESDEN

grape growing, the area's respected, expensive wine (mostly white) is consumed almost entirely by locals.

• *At the far end of the terrace, stop at the grove of linden trees with a fountain at the center, and look out at the...*

⑱ Augustus Bridge

The Augustusbrücke has connected Dresden's old and new towns since 1319, when it was the first stone bridge over the river. During

massive floods in August 2002, the water reached nearly to the top of the arches. Under the arches, you can see the distinct edge of the discoloration showing the high-water mark.

At the far end of the Augustus Bridge is a golden equestrian statue, a symbol of Dresden. It's Augustus the Strong, nicknamed the **"Golden Rider"** (Goldene Reiter). Beyond that is the spire of the Three Kings Church.

• *We're back near where we started, which makes this a good stopping point if you want to end this walk here. But for a balanced Dresden visit, you need to cross the river. Don't worry about having to walk all the way back; we'll wrap up at a tram stop from where you can effortlessly whisk back to the Old Town or the main train station.*

To continue, walk across the bridge (on its right side), enjoying the Elbe scene. Before leaving the bridge, stop at the last pedestrian turnout.

⓮ Canaletto View

Enjoy the grand city view from the bridge: the glass "lemon juicer" dome of the Academy of Fine Arts, capped by a trumpeting gold angel, and the other venerable facades, domes, and spires of regal Dresden. This is known as the "Canaletto view" for the Italian painter (Bernardo Bellotto, nephew of the Venetian master) who spent 12 years here immortalizing city vistas while on the Wettin payroll as a court painter; you can see his canvases

at the Old Masters Gallery. The broad riverbank below, called the Elbe Meadow, provides flood protection.

Downstream (far right), the interesting mosque-shaped building in the distance is called Yenidze. Originally a tobacco factory designed to advertise Turkish cigarettes, today it's an office building with restaurants.

• *At the end of the bridge, cross the street toward the stone building with five arched windows, then cross Grosse Meissner Strasse and head toward the golden statue.*

⓯ The Golden Rider and Hauptstrasse

Since its construction in 1736, the gleaming statue of Augustus the Strong—the Golden Rider—has faced east, toward Augustus' kingdom of Poland and trade routes to Warsaw and Kiev.

The broad, inviting, and tree-lined Hauptstrasse stretches from here into the New Town (Neustadt). On the left is Watzke, a popular (and recommended) peoples' brewery/restaurant. On the right is Eiscafé Venezia, an ice-cream parlor since 1979 and a reminder of the communist heritage here. A monument in the wall (just past the ice-cream palace) marks the 30th anniversary of the creation of the communist "German Democratic Republic" (or DDR) in 1949. On that important anniversary, in 1979, Hauptstrasse was opened as a showpiece of DDR urban design—a landscaped utopian workers' district with the best shops, affordable apartments, and delicious ice cream—everything a communist worker could want.

Stroll down Hauptstrasse a few blocks (past more recommended restaurants) until you see the towering Three Kings Church (Dreikönigskirche) on the left. Immediately across Hauptstrasse from the church stands the Neustädter Markthalle. This busy neighborhood market, a 19th-century iron-and-steel structure, is filled with fun shops selling local handicrafts and pleasant eateries (Mon-Sat 8:00-20:00, closed Sun).

While three-quarters of Dresden's Old Town was decimated by Allied firebombs, much of the New Town survived. Some of Dresden's 18th-century apartment buildings still stand, such as those facing the charming square that lies under the church's tower, a few steps down An der Dreikönigskirche from where you're standing (several recommended restaurants face this square).

This walk ends where Hauptstrasse ends: at the grand Albertplatz (flanked by twin Art Nouveau fountains).

• *Just beyond Albertplatz lies the Outer New Town, a bohemian district of swap shops, pubs, cafés, and galleries (described under "Nightlife in Dresden," later).*

From Albertplatz you can stop for a meal or hop on a handy tram (for a quick return to the Frauenkirche or main train station, take tram #3 or #7; tram #8 goes near the Albertinum and Frauenkirche before also heading to the main station; tram #11 stops at the Neustadt train station, then the Zwinger on its way to the main station).

Sights in Dresden

MUSEUMS IN THE OLD TOWN

Dresden's three most established museums are in the center of the Old Town: the Zwinger, the Royal Palace, and the Albertinum. For ticket options, see "Discount Deals" on page 708. For ticketing at the Historic Green Vault, see its listing under the Royal Palace.

Zwinger Museums

Three museums are located off the Zwinger courtyard: the Old Masters Gallery (with the stern facade), Mathematics-Physics Salon (under Hercules holding the earth), and Porcelain Collection (under the clock). All exhibits are well described in English, but their audioguides will enrich your visit. At each museum you'll need to show your ticket and check large bags.

Cost: €12 combo-ticket covers all three museums; €6 to visit either the Mathematics-Physics Salon or the Porcelain Collection; Old Masters Gallery requires the €12 combo-ticket (whether you visit the others or not).

Hours: Tue-Sun 10:00-18:00, closed Mon.

Information: Tel. 0351/4914-2000, www.skd.museum.

▲▲Old Masters Gallery (Gemäldegalerie Alte Meister)

Dresden's best collection of paintings, housed in the Zwinger's Semper Gallery, features works by Raphael, Titian, Rembrandt, Rubens, Vermeer, and more. It feels particu-

larly enjoyable for its "quality, not quantity" approach to showing off great art. Old-timers remember the Old Masters Gallery as the first big public building reopened after the war, in 1956.

Visiting the Museum: As you enter, pick up a map from the ticket desk (in the basement) to help you navigate, and get the excellent €3 audioguide. Then head up into the collection. Note that the building is undergoing an extensive years-long renovation project; while most of the major works mentioned here should be on display, they may move around.

From the ticket desk (level -1), you'll climb up to level 0, with art from the 15th and 16th centuries. Augustus the Strong and his son, Augustus III, supported much of the purchasing of the art for this collection. Their agents traveled across Europe to add to their holdings, but they also systematically included German works of the **late Gothic** and **early Renaissance** periods. In this section, look for lesser-known works by big Italian names, from Botticelli to Mantegna to Correggio, as well as German painters including Albrecht Dürer—and especially several works by Lucas Cranach the Elder. Hiding just above the staircase are Cranach's matching *Adam* and *Eve* portraits (from 1531).

Pass several more large Cranach works on the way upstairs. Floor 1 features the collection's highlights, from the 16th through 18th century. Most of the top names fill the three big rooms in

the middle of the wing. Among these is the museum's prized piece: Augustus charged his agents with finding a good painting by the Renaissance genius **Raphael,** and they succeeded. The masterful *Sistine Madonna* features the Madonna and Child, two early Christian martyrs (Saints Sixtus and Barbara), and wispy (and creepy) angel faces in the clouds. Mary is in motion, offering the Savior to a needy world. Note Mary's pensive gaze—this Madonna was originally part of a larger altarpiece, and her eyes were once
directed at a painting of the Crucifixion. These days, the gaze of most visitors is directed at the pair of whimsical angels in the foreground—which Raphael added after the painting was completed, just to fill the empty space. These lovable tykes—of T-shirt and poster fame—are bored...just hanging out, oblivious to the exciting arrival of the Messiah just behind them. They connect the heavenly world of the painting with you and me.

In another big hall, enter the Baroque world of **Peter Paul Rubens**—everything is richly textured, vividly colored, and lushly emotional. Belgian Baroque works are also on display, as well as the work of Venetian master **Giorgione,** who died in 1510 while in the middle of painting his sumptuous *Sleeping Venus* (Titian stepped in to finish it). Giorgione's idealized Venus sleeps soundly, at peace with plush nature.

In the third of the big halls, the star is a locally beloved artist named **Bernardo Bellotto.** His paintings of mid-18th-century Dresden offer a great study of the city, showing the Hofkirche (still under construction) and the newly completed Frauenkirche. Compare them with how the city appears today—it's especially amazing how familiar it looks when you consider how heavily the city was bombed. Bellotto sometimes goes by the nickname "Canaletto," which is confusing but understandable: His uncle and teacher was Antonio Canal (a.k.a. the more famous Canaletto), who painted similar landscapes of Venice.

More fine works are in the smaller rooms that line the corridor. Here the mood shifts with the humbler, quieter art of the Dutch Masters, including **Rembrandt.** Included in the fine collection of his works is a jaunty self-portrait—with wife Saskia on his lap and a glass of ale held aloft. Nearby are fine works by **Anthony van Dyck,** Rubens' talented apprentice who brought a focus and refinement to his master's sloppy brushstrokes.

Finally, head upstairs to level 2 and more works from the

DRESDEN

17th and 18th centuries. You'll see some Venice landscapes by the "real" Canaletto; small-scale Northern European works; gauzy aristocratic portraits; and Johann Alexander Thiele's two *Caroussel Comique* paintings depicting fanciful celebrations in the Zwinger. But the real highlight on this level—rivaling the *Sistine Madonna* in the collection—is **Johannes Vermeer**'s pristine and rare *Girl Reading a Letter at an Open Window* (it may be undergoing restoration when you visit). This pensive scene, executed with Vermeer's characteristic touch, is a fine way to wrap up this museum.

▲Mathematics-Physics Salon (Mathematisch-Physikalischer Salon)

This fun collection (at the end of the courtyard with the Hercules-topped pavilion; ascend the staircase in the left corner) features scientific gadgets from the 16th to 19th century, including measuring, timekeeping, and surveying instruments, as well as globes and telescopes—all displayed like dazzling works of art. Anyone with even a modest scientific bent will find something of interest. An audioguide app is available to download using the museum's free Wi-Fi.

Visiting the Museum: As you enter, most of the exhibits are in long halls to the left (measurement) and right (timekeeping). Start in the left hall, with its collection of automatons, including an elaborate music box and a mechanical bear who plays the drums—pretty exciting stuff in 1625 (a video shows the wind-up action). This wing also has compasses, rulers, protractors, primitive encoding devices, scales, an astrolabe, and Augustus the Strong's elaborate astronomical clock.

In the right hall—amidst a wide variety of clocks—look for the mechanical adding machine devised by French mathematician Blaise Pascal, which could do sums like a modern calculator back in 1650. A clever touch-screen replica lets you try it out and shows how the machine "carried the tens." The side room *(Neuer Saal)* has a large collection of old globes.

The small upper floor, reached only by the glass elevator in the atrium, displays "Instruments of the Enlightenment": telescopes (the salon was originally part of the Saxon state observatory); an early 18th-century vacuum pump; and "burning mirrors" that were valued for their ability to focus the sun's rays and, like a magnifying glass, create high-temperature light beams for use in scientific experiments. (I imagine a few 18th-century bugs were burnt along the way.)

▲Porcelain Collection (Porzellansammlung)

Every self-respecting European king had a porcelain works, and the Wettins had the most famous one, at Meissen (a charming town 10 miles north of here on the Elbe River). They inspired other

Saxony's White Gold

In the early 18th century, porcelain was considered "white gold"—an incredibly valuable and difficult-to-produce material. Only the Chinese had perfected the secret of its manufacture—which they jealously guarded. To acquire his initial collection, Augustus the Strong famously traded 600 soldiers (and their horses) for 151 Chinese vases belonging to Friedrich Wilhelm I of Prussia. Hungry for more, Augustus commissioned an alchemist named Johann Friedrich Böttger to solve the mystery of making the finicky stuff. Böttger was reluctant—he'd already failed at creating actual gold—but Augustus persuaded him by locking him up until he complied. Eventually Böttger came up with a recipe for "true" porcelain, and the Saxon prince electors became pioneers in European porcelain production.

royal courts to get into the art form. They also collected porcelain from around the world—from France to Japan and China.

Augustus the Strong was obsessed with the stuff...he liked to say he had "porcelain sickness" (for more on his porcelain fixation, see "Saxony's White Gold" sidebar). Here you can enjoy some of his symptoms, under chandeliers in elegant galleries flooded with natural light from the huge windows over the Zwinger courtyard. Today it's the largest specialist ceramics collection in the world.

Visiting the Museum: The royal porcelain collection fills the end of the Zwinger marked by the clock tower. Before entering, look closely at the clock with 40 white porcelain bells, which ring out classical music several times a day. Just above the clock is Augustus' coat of arms, with the two crossed swords in the center that eventually became the famous trademark (one of the world's oldest) of the royal Meissen porcelain factory. The collection is in two wings (some to the left, but with the lion's share to the right). Upstairs, behind the clock, is a pricey café with fine courtyard view tables.

Peruse the long halls of vases, tracing porcelain's development through the outstanding collection of locally produced Meissen wares. A special attraction is the hall of white Meissen porcelain animals: life-size (or near-life-size) peacocks, eagles, emoting lions, monkeys, rhinos, and lapdogs.

Royal Palace (Residenzschloss)

This palace, the residence of the Saxon prince electors and kings, was one of the finest Renaissance buildings in Germany before its destruction in World War II. It's currently being rebuilt in a years-long project, with galleries opening to the public as they are

DRESDEN

completed. The palace is highlighted by the Saxon treasuries: the Historic Green Vault (Augustus' goodies displayed in reconstructed Baroque halls) and the New Green Vault (more royal treasures in contemporary display cases). Other attractions include the Royal Armory, showing off sumptuous armor for horse and rider, and the Turkish Chamber, one of the oldest collections of Ottoman art outside Turkey.

Cost: All sights in the palace—except the Historic Green Vault—are covered by a €12 ticket (or the €19 combo-ticket for all state museums—a better value).

The Historic Green Vault requires a separate ticket, with two choices: the €12 standard, timed-entry ticket (€2 surcharge to book in advance), or the €20 VIP-Ticket (which lets you skip the line anytime).

Hours: The entire complex is open Wed-Mon 10:00-18:00, closed Tue.

Information: Tel. 0351/4914-2000, www.skd.museum.

Historic Green Vault Reservations: To protect these priceless items, the number of visitors each day is carefully controlled. If you must get in at a certain time, or if you'll be here at a busy period (weekend, holiday, or any time in December), book your ticket in advance. You'll be given a 15-minute entry window (strictly enforced; once inside, you can stay as long as you like). Book online (www.skd.museum) or reserve by email (besucherservice@skd.museum), then print out your ticket—an electronic version won't work.

If you haven't booked ahead, your chances of getting a same-day slot are usually good, especially if you show up in the morning (90 tickets are available every half-hour). The number of spots still available *(Karten)* and for what entry times *(Einlasszeit)* are indicated on screens over each ticket desk.

Tours: The sights are all well explained by good, included **audio-guides**—one covering the Historic Green Vault, and a different one for the rest of the complex. Be sure to ask for these (leave ID in exchange). Also pick up a palace map to navigate the sprawling complex. **Guided tours** in English run only once a week (€18.50, includes entrance fees, Sat at 14:00); book ahead online.

Orientation: The palace complex has three entrances, each leading to a glass-domed inner courtyard, where you'll find the ticket windows and restrooms. Inside, the ground floor is home to the Baroque halls of the Historic Green Vault (where bag check is required); the first floor up has the New Green Vault, and the next floor up houses the Giant's Hall, with the bulk of the Royal Armory, and the Turkish Chamber.

▲▲Historic Green Vault (Historisches Grünes Gewölbe)

This famed, glittering Baroque treasury collection was begun by Augustus the Strong in the early 1700s. Over the years it evolved into the royal family's extravagant trove of ivory, silver, and gold knickknacks, displayed in rooms as opulent as the collection itself. Damaged in the firebombing, the Green Vault has been painstakingly restored—including re-engineering the mirrors using the original methods, with tin and mercury.

Visiting the Historic Green Vault: Your visit is designed to wow you in typically Baroque style—starting easy and crescendoing to a climax, taking a quick break, and finishing again with a second climax. Following the included audioguide, you'll spend about an hour progressing through the exhibition's rooms. Most of the treasures are not behind glass. Inside, it feels like an almost sacred space, with people speaking in no more than whispers.

Your audioguide also describes treasures in the **foyer** (where you pick up and drop off the audioguide). Don't miss the photos of the vault before the war and the small room in the corner with Reformation treasures, including Martin Luther's signet ring.

Before entering the vault, cross to the end of the foyer and duck into the octagonal room 1a. Here you'll glimpse finely detailed wood reliefs, including Peter Dell the Elder's 16th-century *Resurrection of Christ* (perhaps the first depiction of Jesus Christ Superstar).

The rest of your visit is a one-way route through the vault's lavish rooms.

The **Amber Cabinet** serves as a reminder of just how many different things you can do with fossilized tree sap (in a surprising range of colors), and the **Ivory Room** does the same for elephant tusks, with some strikingly delicate hand-carved sculptures. The **White Silver Room,** painted its original vermillion color, holds a goblet carved from a rhino horn. During the firebombing of Dresden, much of this room survived thanks to the iron grates encasing the windows. The **Silver-Gilt Room** displays tableware and gold-ruby glass.

The wide variety of items in the largest room—the aptly named **Hall of Precious Objects**—includes mother-of-pearl sculptures, ostrich-egg and conch-shell goblets, and old portraits of Saxon rulers.

The oak cupboards that line the **Coats-of-Arms Room** are emblazoned with copper-and-gold coats-of-arms boasting of the various territories in Augustus the Strong's domain.

The vault's highlight is the grandly decorated **Jewel Room**—

essentially, Saxony's crown jewels. The incredible pieces in here, collectively, are considered a *Gesamtkunstwerk*—an artwork whose perfection comes from the coordinated sum of its parts. The two statues titled *Moor with Emerald Tier*—a "Moor" clad in jewels and gold (and a Native American headdress)—were designed to carry a chunk of rock embedded with large gems. Nearby, an ornately decorated obelisk trumpets the greatness of Augustus the Strong.

The exhibit concludes in the relatively subdued **Room of Bronzes,** with its equestrian statue of Augustus the Strong (designed to compete with similar depictions of his rival, the French Sun King Louis XIV), as well as a statue of Apollo surrounded by six women. The last room is filled with Renaissance bronze statues, including Giambologna's *Mercury.*

• *The rest of the Royal Palace museums are upstairs. Before heading up, return downstairs to pick up the second essential and included audioguide.*

Directly upstairs from the Historic Green Vault, on level 1, is the...

▲▲New Green Vault (Neues Grünes Gewölbe)

If you consider only the objects on display—not the setting—this is even more impressive than the Historic Green Vault. The collection is arranged in a modern museum space, chronologically from the Renaissance to the 19th century, in nine rooms in a clockwise route.

Visiting the New Green Vault: In the **Hall of Works of Art** (the first room you enter), look for the gilded **rolling ball clock,** an engineering delight from about 1600. One rock crystal ball twists down and around 16 bends of the tower-like clock in precisely 60 seconds, while a second ball is raised inside the clock case. As this happens, the minute hand advances, and Saturn strikes a bell with his mighty hammer. Nearby, the **Drinking Vessel in the Shape of Daphne** has a magnificent coral crown. Farther into the room, an **ivory column** from 1589 (which looks like Berlin's TV Tower) is another elaborate clock: The golden Cupid on top points to the hour with a wand. It also incorporates a music box featuring a dining scene carved inside an ivory sphere, ship-in-a-bottle-style. In the **Micro-Cabinet** in the corner, a magnifying glass helps you marvel at an earring from 1589 featuring a cherry pit carved with 185 minuscule faces.

The precious centerpiece of the **Crystal Cabinet** is a serving bowl in the shape of a galley ship, with intricate scenes carved on the side—it's hard to imagine anyone filling it with gravy (and they probably never did; items like this were made just for showing off).

The **First Elector's Room** features Renaissance treasures, such as an ivory frigate with delicately carved, nearly transparent sails and golden rigging, all of it supported by a heroic Neptune, riding his sea horses.

Past the Second Elector's Room, the **Room of Royal Precious Objects** holds a collection of irregular pearls fashioned into amusing figures, such as a fat fiddler and an ice skater. The nobles of this era were fascinated with gems and precious stones, which they prized much more than the craftsmanship exhibited in the Renaissance items we saw earlier. To see more of the aristocracy's playful side, find the intricately inlaid 17th-century wooden chess board.

The **Dinglinger Hall** features the masterpieces of court jeweler Johann Melchior Dinglinger. His 145-piece golden coffee set is pure gold (circa 1700), iced with enamel to imitate porcelain and crusted with thousands of precious stones. At the other end of the room is his ornate, captivating ensemble from 1708 depicting the Grand Mogul Aurengzeb, who sits enthroned on his birthday awaiting his presents (including a white elephant). Like a royal dollhouse, the 132 figurines and 32 gift items—all of pure gold glazed with enamel—are movable for the king's pleasure.

The **Traveling Treasures Room** contains the custom leather cases the king used to pack his favorite playthings to Poland. A few rooms farther, in the **Watzdorf-Kabinett,** the Dresden Green diamond sparkles all on its own—one huge green stone decorated with more than 400 twinkling white diamonds.

• *The next three collections are upstairs, on floor 2. If you head up directly from the New Green Vault, you'll find them in this order.*

▲Turkish Chamber (Türkische Cammer)

From the 16th through 19th century—as Ottomans pecked away at the southeastern corner of Europe—Western European elites were crazy about all things Turkish, and Augustus the Strong was no exception. (Clearly people are fascinated by what they fear.) Augustus collected Ottoman art with a passion, even dressing up as a sultan in his own court. This exceptional (if  dimly lit) collection of Ottoman art started as war booty from the Habsburgs—given as thanks for Saxon support in holding off invasions—and then grew over several centuries through diplomatic gifts, trades, and shopping trips to Constantinople.

Among the armor, swords, guns, saddles, and tapestries, one highlight is a 60-foot-long, three-poled ornamented silk tent from the 17th century—the most complete three-masted Ottoman tent on display in Europe. In the adjoining room, look for the *Relief of Vienna 1683* painting, showing the epic battle when, for the first time, Ottoman forces were turned back from Christian lands— with the help of the Saxons, of course.

• *Continue directly into the Giant's Hall (Reisensaal), which holds the...*

▲▲Royal Armory (Rüstkammer)

Dazzling, original, centuries-old armor fills the biggest space in the palace—once the scene of medieval war games. Today, its exhibits recall those breathtaking pageants of the 16th century with jousting models (something rich boys did when there was no war to fight). This is the largest collection of armor by 16th-century Europe's leading designer, Anton Peffenhauser, and it's an unusual chance to see armor displayed in dynamic fighting stances (instead of stiffly standing). The parade armor of King Erick XIV of Sweden (on horseback, with red-and-yellow plume)—from 1565, slathered in Herculean symbolism and coordinated perfectly with his horse—is considered the "Sistine Madonna" of the collection. Stand before it and imagine this coming at you. The black, no-nonsense, Darth Vader suits at the end of the hall were actually used in the Thirty Years' War (around 1620). Near the back of the room, check out the wee training suits of armor for little electoral princes.

• *A doorway in the corner at the far end of the room leads to the...*

Coin Cabinet (Münzkabinett)

This beautifully presented collection of historical coins is one of the best and largest in Europe, smartly organized to tell the story of how money as we know it came to be. If you have any interest in seeing a huge collection of coins, this is the one to visit—but these rooms are easily skippable for all but the most numismatically inclined.

• *To reach the final Royal Palace sight, head back down to the ground level through another floor of armor and weaponry, and cut through the courtyard.*

Watchman's Tower (Hausmannsturm)

This palace tower (closed in winter) is completely rebuilt and feels entirely modern. You can see the refurbished medieval clock mechanism from behind, peruse an extensive series of dome-damage photos, and earn a good city view after a long climb. In bad weather, the view terrace is closed, and you'll peer through small windows—a big disappointment. If you'll be climbing the Frauen-kirche dome (which affords the best view in town), skip this.

▲▲Albertinum

This museum's excellent collections feature artwork from the Romantic period (late 18th and early 19th centuries) to the present. The included audioguide does a beautiful job of explaining the art. The museum's ticket desk is in the building's old courtyard, which has been roofed over into a cavernous, minimalist, white atrium.

Cost and Hours: €12, includes audioguide (ID required), Tue-Sun 10:00-18:00, closed Mon, tel. 0351/4914-2000, www.skd.museum.

Visiting the Museum: Entrances are on the Brühlsche Terrasse and on Georg-Treu-Platz. Most visitors come to see the New Masters Gallery on the museum's top floor (elevator and stairs are behind the ticket desk). Moving down from there, contemporary and turn-of-the-20th-century art is on the first floor, and sculpture on the ground floor.

New Masters Gallery (Galerie Neue Meister): On the top level (floor 2), take a counterclockwise walk around this chrono-logically organized col-lection, showcasing most-ly German (and some French) paintings from the Romantic era, 20th-century Modernism, and contemporary art.

In Caspar David Friedrich's 19th-century landscapes, notice that people are small and are overwhelmed by the background: German Romanticism is all about man's place as a small part of nature—not its dominating force. Friedrich's Norwegian counterpart and friend, Johan Christian Dahl—who moved to Dresden later in life—captures his adopted hometown in his lovely *View of Dresden at Full Moon*, which seems not so different from today's reconstructed city. (The buildings across the river aren't on fire; the glow is from the hearths inside these rooms.)

Take a breather with Ludwig Richter's bucolic scenes of the Italian countryside, then move into the top-notch Modernist wing, which proceeds with late-19th- and early-20th-century works by artists including Edgar Degas (*Little Dancer Aged Fourteen*—one of 29 bronzes cast from the wax original), Paul Gauguin (Polynesian women), Vincent van Gogh *(Still Life with Quinces)*, Max Liebermann (insightful portraits and landscapes), Oskar Kokoschka (vibrantly colored, almost garish portraits), Claude Monet, and

Edouard Manet. You'll also spot pieces by modern masters Pablo Picasso, Paul Klee, and Marc Chagall. Some of the lesser-known works are also worth a good look, such as Max Slevogt's evocative paintings of North Africa.

Give yourself a moment to really take in Otto Dix's haunting, frank images—particularly his stirring triptych *The War*, rooted in his firsthand experience fighting in the trenches of France and Flanders during World War I. This vision, modeled after a medieval altarpiece, has a circular composition that's kept moving by the grotesque pointing skeleton. In this fetid wasteland, corpses are decomposing, and helmets and gas masks make even the intact bodies seem inhuman. Dix painted this in the 1930s, when Adolf Hitler was building a case for war (ostensibly to reclaim territory Germany lost after World War I). The Führer didn't care for Dix's pacifist message, dismissing the artist from his teaching job at Dresden's art academy and adding Dix's works to his collection of "degenerate art."

The collection wraps up with a quick fast-forward through mid-century modernism and contemporary works. New media (sound and video) are also represented.

Mosaiksaal and Klingersaal: Head down the stairs, to floor 1, where the Mosaiksaal features sculpture from the Classicist era on up to Ernst Rietschel's mid-19th-century depictions of historically important Germans. Pop into the library-like room showcasing a vast collection of ancient pottery and sculpture, including several Egyptian sarcophagi.

The Klingersaal shows slinky fin-de-siècle paintings and sculptures. Look for Gustav Klimt's atmospheric *Buchenwald*, a tranquil beech forest that shimmers with color. Next to it, in Ferdinand Hodler's *Portrait of Madame de R.*, the subject regards us with a steely gaze; nearby, Oskar Zwintscher's *Lady with Cigarette* is equally unfazed by our presence.

Sculpture Collection (Skulpturensammlung): Gathered in one huge *Skulpturhalle* on the ground floor, this easy-on-the-eyes collection covers 5,000 years of Western sculpture, with a special focus on the last 200 years. There are several plaster casts by Auguste Rodin, including a *Thinker*. Towards the center, find local sculptor Helmut Heinze's Giacometti-esque bronze *Nude Boy Standing* (1976). At the contemporary end of the spectrum is Tony Cragg's *Ever After* (2010), a 10-foot-tall wooden sculpture that appears to be melting; look closely (particularly interesting seen from the bottom, up) to see profiles of human faces emerge on the left side.

CHURCHES IN THE OLD TOWN
▲▲Frauenkirche (Church of Our Lady)

When this landmark Lutheran church was first built in the 18th century, it was financed largely by local donations expressive of

Protestant pride. Destroyed by Allied firebombing in World War II, it sat in ruins for decades. Rebuilding of the church finally began in 1992, following carefully considered guidelines: Stay true to the original design; use as much original material as possible; avoid using any concrete or rebar; maximize modern technology; and make it a lively venue for 21st-century-style worship. The remnants of the destroyed church were fitted together like a giant jigsaw puzzle, with about a third of the darker original stones placed lovingly in their original spots. The reconstruction cost more than €100 million, 90 percent of which came from donors around the world

Cost and Hours: Free but donation requested, Mon-Fri 10:00-12:00 & 13:00-18:00, Sat-Sun hours vary depending on service and concerts, 45-minute audioguide-€2.50 (available inside and to the left); worship services followed by a free guided tour in German normally Mon-Sat at 12:00, Mon-Wed & Friday also at 18:00, enter through door D; tel. 0351/6560-6701, www. frauenkirche-dresden.de.

Climbing the Dome: Get a great view over the city by hiking to the top of the dome. After an elevator takes you half of the way,

you still have a long ramp to climb (€8—consider it a donation to the church, Mon-Sat 10:00-18:00, Sun from 12:30, Nov-Feb until 16:00 daily, enter through door G, follow signs to *Kuppelaufstieg*).

Film: A 25-minute movie (€3) called *Fascination Frauenkirche* tells the story of the church and its reconstruction. It plays in German at :15 after the hour (10:15-17:15); they'll play the English-language version after the German showing (only until 16:45) if you ask at least 10 minutes ahead at the audioguide desk.

Visiting the Church: The Frauenkirche is as worthwhile for its glorious **interior** as for its tragic, then uplifting, recent history. Stepping inside, you're struck by the shape—not so wide (150 feet) but very tall (inner dome 120 feet, under a 225-foot main dome). The color scheme is pastel, in an effort to underline the joy of faith and enhance the festive ambience of the services and ceremonies held here. The curves help create a feeling of community. The seven entrances are perfectly equal (as people are, in the eyes of God). When the congregation exits, the seven exits point to all quarters—a reminder to "go ye," the Great Commission to spread the Word everywhere. The glassed-in "box seats" are just that. Like the rich get their own sections in a stadium, generous patrons of the church got their own VIP worship areas.

The Baroque sandstone **altar** shows Jesus praying in the Garden of Gethsemane the night before his Crucifixion. Soldiers, led by Judas, are on their way, but Christ is firmly in the presence of God and his angels. Eighty percent of today's altar is from original material—in the form of 2,000 individual fragments that were salvaged and pieced back together by restorers. If this feels more ornate than your typical Lutheran church, it's because of the taste of the king—who had to be Catholic to rule Poland.

The **Cross of Nails** at the high altar is from Coventry, England—Dresden's sister city. Two fire-blackened nails found in the smoldering rubble of Coventry's bombed church are used as a symbol of peace and reconciliation. Coventry was flattened as thoroughly as Dresden (so thoroughly, it gave the giddy Luftwaffe a new word for "bomb to smithereens"—to "coventrate"). From the destroyed town of Coventry was born the Community of the Cross of Nails, a worldwide network promoting peace and reconciliation through international understanding.

Near the exit stands the church's **twisted old cross,** which fell 300 feet and burned in the rubble. Lost until restorers uncovered it from the pile of stones in 1993, it stands exactly on the place it was found, still relatively intact. A copy—a gift from the British people in 2000 on the 55th anniversary of the bombing—crowns the new church. It was crafted by an English coppersmith whose father had dropped bombs on the church on that fateful night. Visitors are invited to light a candle before this cross and enter a wish for peace in the guest book.

Before you leave the church, go downstairs to the **cellar,** which is a maze of rooms and exhibits. In a separate room (on the left as you climb into the crypt) is a modest exhibit about the history of the building. In the center is a modern-feeling, very stark chapel under vaulted ceilings. In each stairwell, plaques list the names of donors who helped resurrect this church from the rubble.

▲Katholische Hofkirche
(Catholic Church of the Royal Court)

Why does Dresden, a stronghold of local boy Martin Luther's Protestant Reformation, boast such a beautiful Catholic church? When Augustus the Strong died, his son wanted to continue as king of Poland, like his father. The pope would allow it only if Augustus Junior built a Catholic church in Dresden. Now, thanks to Junior's historical kissing-up, the mere 5 percent of locals who are Catholic get to enjoy this fine church.

Cost and Hours: Free, Mon-Fri 8:30-17:00, Sat 10:30-17:00, Sun 12:00-16:00, Mass daily at 18:00 and several times on Sun—check at church for complete schedule and for pipe organ concert times, enter through side door facing palace, tel. 0351/484-4712, www.kathedrale-dresden.de.

Visiting the Church: Inside the cathedral, on the right side of the main nave, is the fine Baroque **pulpit,** carved from linden

wood and hidden in the countryside during World War II. The church was designed with a grand ambulatory that kept ritual Roman Catholic processions within the church, to avoid provoking the Lutheran populace.

The glorious 3,000-pipe **organ** filling the back of the nave is played for the public for free on Wednesdays and Saturdays at 11:30 (and occasionally at other times as well, posted at door).

The **Benno Chapel** (on the right as you face the organ) recalls the only Saxon saint (that's his 11th-century bishop's hat on the altar). It's the only part of the church that still survives from the architect's original vision and the style of the day—helpful in imagining the intended, initial look of the entire place.

The **Memorial Chapel** (on the left as you face the organ) is dedicated to those who died in the WWII firebombing and to all victims of violence. Its evocative, abstract pietà altarpiece (reminiscent of Picasso's *Guernica*) was constructed in 1976 of white Meissen porcelain. Mary offers the faithful the crown of thorns made from Dresden's rubble, as if to remind us that Jesus—on her lap, head hanging lifeless on the left—died to save humankind. Jesus' open heart shows us his love, offers us atonement for our sins, and proves that reconciliation is more powerful than hatred. The sculpture sits on an altar with the dates *30-1-33* and *13-2-45*, marking the dark period between Hitler's rise to power and the night Dresden was destroyed. Another altar (freestanding, in front) shows multiple abstract, flaming heads. It seems to symbolize how Dresdeners suffered...in the presence of their suffering savior.

MORE SIGHTS IN DRESDEN
Prager Strasse
This street, connecting the main train station and the historic center, was in ruins until the 1960s, when communist planners redeveloped it as a pedestrian mall. The design is typical of Soviet bloc architecture—there are similar streets in Moscow—and it reflects communist ideals: Buildings are big, blocky, and functional, without extraneous ornamentation. As you stroll down Prager Strasse, imagine these buildings without much  color or advertising (which were unnecessary back in the no-choices days of communism). Today, the street is filled with corporate logos, shoppers with lots of choices, and a fun summertime food circus. The street has developed into exactly what the communists envisioned for it, but never quite achieved: a pedestrian-friendly shopping area, where people can stroll and relax, with residential and office space above. The huge department stores, like the vast Altmarkt-Galerie, charge the German norm, which means things here are expensive for locals, who still earn only about 80 percent of what Germans farther to the west make. However, the gender pay gap here is much smaller, thanks to a socialist past that had most women working outside the home far earlier than in the west.

German Hygiene Museum (Deutsches Hygiene-Museum)

This curious museum is devoted to the wonders of the human body (don't take the word "hygiene," its historical title, too literally). It brings a frank, Germanic approach to anatomy...warts and all. Visitors with strong stomachs get a kick out of this highly inter-

active museum, but those easily grossed out should stay away—or at least plan meal times accordingly. File this under "Europe's offbeat sights."

Cost and Hours: €9 includes audioguide, €14 family ticket, 16 and under free, Tue-Sun 10:00-18:00, closed Mon; Lingnerplatz 1, take tram #1, #2, or #4 to the Deutsches Hygiene-Museum stop or tram #10 or #13 to Grosser Garten, then walk five minutes; tel. 0351/484-6400, www.dhmd.de.

Visiting the Museum: The massive building was completed in 1930; a few years later, it briefly became a center for Nazi eugenics and "racial studies." The permanent exhibit on the upper floor is loaded with exhibits on various aspects of life, health, and death—from sexuality to cognition to eating and drinking. Watch for cutaway models of organs, faces showing skin ailments, a housefly magnified 500 times, little wooden anatomical figures with removable parts (complete with strategically placed fig leaves), X-ray machines from the 1930s, wax models of venereal diseases, and the "transparent woman" *(Gläserne Frau)*—a life-size plastic model with bones, veins, and interior organs visible. The museum offers sparse English explanations, but most exhibits speak (or shriek) for themselves. While this all sounds extremely graphic by American standards, the museum is designed for German families. Seeing local parents earnestly introducing their young kids to this stuff offers a chance to reflect on why we Americans are so squeamish about our own bodies.

Your ticket also gets you into good temporary exhibits on the main floor; and Dresden's **children's museum,** in the basement, which stays with the general theme by focusing on the five senses.

Volkswagen's Transparent Factory (Gläserne Manufaktur)

Two floors of this transparent building are open to visitors interested in the assembly of VW's new line of electric vehicles (especially the e-Golf). During weekday working hours, it's free to gaze at the slowly moving assembly line from the building's atrium, or you can pay to take a tour, which lets you see the process at close range, get

a first look at futuristic "concept
cars," and use touchscreens to
learn more.

Cost and Hours: Atrium-
free, Mon–Sat 9:00–19:00, Thu
until 21:00, Sun 10:00-18:00;
guided 75-minute tour–€7, English tours Mon-Fri at 10:00,
12:00 & 15:00; Sat at 12:00,
15:00 & 17:00; Sun at 12:00 &
15:00—but confirm hours and tour times before you go; expensive
onsite café, tel. 0351/420-4411, www.glaesernemanufaktur.de.

Getting There: Take tram #1, #2, or #4 (from the Old Town)
or tram #10 (from the Hauptbahnhof) to the Strassburger Platz
stop. Look for the plant on one corner of the intersection; enter off
Lennestrasse.

▲New Town (Neustadt) and Outer New Town (Äussere Neustadt)

A big sign across the river from the old center declares, "Dresden
continues here"—directed at tourists who visit the city without ever
crossing the river into the New Town and Outer New Town. Don't
be one of them: While there are no famous sights here, it's the only
part of Dresden that looks as it did before World War II. Today,
it's thriving with cafés, shops, clubs, and—most important—actual
Dresdeners. On a warm summer evening, experiencing the vibe
here is a must. A fine destination is the Kunsthofpassage, a lovely,
fun, inviting series of courtyards with shops and eateries. For more
on this neighborhood, see "Nightlife in Dresden," later.

▲▲Military History Museum (Militärhistorisches Museum der Bundeswehr)

This huge museum covers more than 800 years of German military
history and focuses on the causes and consequences of war and violence. At over 180,000 square feet, it's the largest museum in Germany. The museum is housed in Dresden's Neoclassical former arsenal building, forcefully severed by a Daniel Libeskind-designed
wedge of glass and steel (signaling the break from Germany's militaristic past and its hope for a transparent government and peaceful
future). For a complete visit, you could spend the better part of a
day; allow a couple of hours for a "quick" visit.

Cost and Hours: €5, includes audioguide; Thu-Tue 10:00-
18:00, Mon until 21:00, closed Wed; onsite café; take tram #7 or
#8 to Stauffenbergallee stop (beyond the New Town), then follow
the diagonal, tree-lined path through the park to Olbrichtplatz 2;
tel. 0351/823-2803, www.mhmbundeswehr.de.

Visiting the Museum: The museum is long on design, and

uses creative juxtapositions to get visitors thinking in critical ways about war. Rather than glorifying soldiers and their bravery, the museum dissects our ideas about war, asks where those ideas come from, encourages us to question them, and ultimately sends a pacifist message.

The exhibits demand a thorough visit, and the audioguide provides solid context and background for the well-organized displays. Most of the exhibits are loosely organized into two categories: a chronological look at Germany's military history since the Middle Ages; and themed exhibits that try to provoke deep thought about various aspects of war and peace.

Start by taking the elevator to the fourth floor, which has a distant **view** of Dresden's Old Town and two visually arresting, thought-provoking pieces commemorating similarly war-damaged cities.

Next, walk down the stairs to the third floor to the first of the **themed exhibits**—"War and Memory," which considers how people remember and commemorate war (whether to glorify it, or to push it into the background). The second floor has further themed exhibits on politics, music (Marlene Dietrich's military uniform for entertaining Allied troops), fashion, language (find out what "08/15" means to Germans—and why), and toys and games (see the East German and Soviet dolls who famously "got married" on an international space mission in 1978).

On the first floor are the topics of suffering and animals (with a menagerie of taxidermied beasts who have been recruited into military service since Hannibal crossed the Alps on his elephants). The ground floor looks at technology (including a test tube of Pervitin, the meth-like performance-enhancing drug dispensed by the Nazi military) and the "Protection and Destruction" exhibit—a sobering reminder that the stated aims of military intervention are often sidetracked. You'll also see the first German submarine (the people-powered *Brandtaucher*, from 1850), a Nazi-era V-2 rocket (the first capable of entering space), and the Russian Soyuz manned space capsule that carried the first German into space (Sigmund Jähn).

But wait—there's more. If you prefer a more linear approach, you can follow extensive **chronological exhibits** telling the story of German military activity from 1300 to 1914 (ground floor, skippable for most visitors), from 1914 to 1945 (first floor up), and after 1945, including the founding of the Bundeswehr (German armed forces, also on the first floor). With tons of uniforms, portraits, vintage weapons, tanks, and much more, it's a lot to get through. Plus there's an outdoor collection of **military vehicles,** with even more filling the adjacent buildings.

DAY TRIPS NEAR DRESDEN

The sights listed in this chapter can keep you busy for (at least) two full days. With more time, consider getting out of the city. For more details on either of these trips, ask the TI.

One popular excursion is to ride a bike downriver to the **Blue Wonder bridge** (a.k.a. Loschwitzbrücke)—a classic old Indus-

trial Age bridge, untouched by WWII bombs, with a beloved local *biergarten* (Schiller Garten, unfiltered *Zwickel* beer, self-service buffet and full-service restaurant, www.schillergarten. de). The 3.5-mile path gives you a great slice-of-life glimpse of Germans at play as you hug the riverbank. The bridge is also connected to the Old Town by steam-powered paddleboats and by tram #12 (Schillerplatz stop).

For a longer excursion that really gets you out into nature, ride a train into **Saxon Switzerland National Park** (Sächsische

Schweiz Nationalpark). Twenty miles southeast of Dresden, the Elbe River cuts a scenic swath through beech forests and steep cliffs. Take S-Bahn line 1 to the Kurort Rathen stop (runs at least hourly, 35 minutes), where you'll walk downhill through the town, hop on a ferry for the two-minute crossing over the Elbe, and hike 30 minutes up-hill to the Bastei Bridge and stunning views of gray sandstone sentries rising several hundred feet above forest ridges. (This sandstone was used to build Dresden's finest buildings, as well as Berlin's famous Brandenburg Gate.) Higher up are the scant remains of the 13th-century Felsenburg Neurathen fort, and a hotel with a panoramic restaurant. Another lunch option is the **$$ Sonniges Eck Restaurant** (at the far end of town from the ferry dock, near the base of the trail up to the bridge).

Nightlife in Dresden

OUTER NEW TOWN (ÄUSSERE NEUSTADT)

To really connect with Dresden, you need to go to the Outer New Town—a popular neighborhood for young people and progressive families, reminiscent of Berlin's Prenzlauer Berg in its pre-yuppie days. This is a fun place to eat dinner, then join the action, which picks up after 22:00. Eateries range from the merely creative to the truly unconventional. You'll find lots of cheap international food, mini beer gardens (but not your grandfather's oompah bands), and young adults hanging out on the curb, nursing beer bottles. The neighborhood generally feels more exuberant than rough.

One of the best ways to experience this scene—and to learn a bit more about the neighborhood's history—is to take the Night-walk Dresden Tour (listed under "Tours in Dresden," earlier). I've sketched out a few highlights below for those who'd rather explore on their own.

Getting There: From the Old Town, take tram #7 or #8 to Louisenstrasse. Night trams bring you back to the center even in the wee hours.

Background: This area was built, with elegant facades, in the 19th century to accommodate workers of the Industrial Age. Despite the devastation wrought upon the area south of the river, this neighborhood wasn't bombed in World War II—but during communist times it became so dilapidated that officials made plans to just tear it all down. Today locals recall a time when no one ventured out on balconies fearing they'd fall off. A popular slogan for people disillusioned with the DDR was, "We create ruins without any weapons."

After the end of the DDR in 1989, the area sprouted the first entrepreneurial cafés and bistros. Now it's a bohemian-chic mix of cheap apartments, galleries, cafés, bars, and swap shops, filled with a clientele that's young, hip, pierced, and tattooed. While gentrification is kicking in, you'll find no chain stores, brick-and-mortar banks (only ATMs), or corporate-run businesses. Everything is independently run.

Visiting the Outer New Town: Get to the epicenter—at the corner of Görlitzer Strasse and Louisenstrasse—and enjoy wandering. If you arrive a little before nightfall, begin at the Kunsthofpassage while you still have light for photos. Then explore the nearby streets to feel the real vibe of Dresden's alternative neighborhood. Here are a few places and bars worth checking out.

The **Kunsthofpassage** is a series of five fanciful, imaginatively decorated courtyards surrounded by boutiques, eateries, a craft-beer pub, and art galleries (see "Eating in Dresden" for my recommendations). This is a delightful fantasy world, tucked improbably between lively urban streets (enter at Görlitzer Strasse 21, 23, or 25, or at Alaunstrasse 70; www.kunsthof-dresden.de). The Elements Courtyard (enter at Görlitzer Strasse 25) features artwork representing earth, wind, fire, and water. On one wall the downspouts have been reworked into a fountain made of musical-instrument shapes (water). The opposite wall sports large golden

DRESDEN

aluminum shavings, designed to reflect the ambient light (fire). The Animals Courtyard (enter at Görlitzer Strasse 21) feels whimsical, with its Noah's ark-like balconies, monkeys swinging from the windows, and gentle giraffe stretching its neck to join the fun. Nearby, look for a sculpture titled *Mensch und Artensterben* (Man and Species Extinction). Animal silhouettes are integrated into the shape of a human body, a reminder that all creatures must coexist. At night, shine your smartphone light onto the sculpture to make the silhouettes dance on the wall.

Another major nightlife zone here is along Alaunstrasse, specifically near the **$$ Scheune Café**—a longstanding restaurant, beer garden, and cultural center filling a big orange building, with food trucks on the plaza out front. They also host live performances (open long hours daily, Alaunstrasse 36, tel. 0351/802-6619, www. scheunecafe.de). Next door, on the corner of Alaunstrasse and Louisenstrasse, **Katy's Garage** really was once a garage ("Katy" wasn't a woman but a Land Rover), and is now a funky *Biergarten* speckled with eclectic art (long hours daily, Alaunstrasse 48, tel. 0351/656-7701).

A half-block off Lutherplatz at Böhmische Strasse 34, **$$ Kneipe Raskolnikoff,** in the same building as the recommended Pension Raskolnikoff, is a charming, just-the-right-kind-of-funky pub/bistro serving a small menu of Russian specialties... and lots of drinks (Mon-Sat 11:00-24:00, Sun from 9:00, tel. 0351/804-5706).

Sleeping in Dresden

Hotels in Dresden tend to be big chains (particularly near the Old Town). Characteristic, family-run places are rare. Peak season for hotels is May, June, September, and October. Prices soften at midsummer and drop in winter. Rates shoot up in December when the Christmas market (Striezelmarkt) is on.

IN AND NEAR THE OLD TOWN

$$$ Heinrich Schütz Residenz enjoys a prime location on the Neumarkt square facing the Frauenkirche. They rent 16 well-equipped apartments—each with a kitchen and separate bedroom—that feel luxurious but are reasonably priced (elevator, no parking, Frauenstrasse 14, tel. 0351/263-5960, www.heinrich-schuetz-residenz.de, info @ heinrich-schuetz-residenz.de).

$$$ Star Inn fills a stately old building on the Altmarkt (a short walk from the Old Town) with 123 modern rooms featuring American-style comforts (breakfast extra, air-con, elevator, bike rental, pay parking nearby, Altmarkt 4, tel. 0351/307-110, www. starinnhotels.com, dresden.altmarkt@starinnhotels.com).

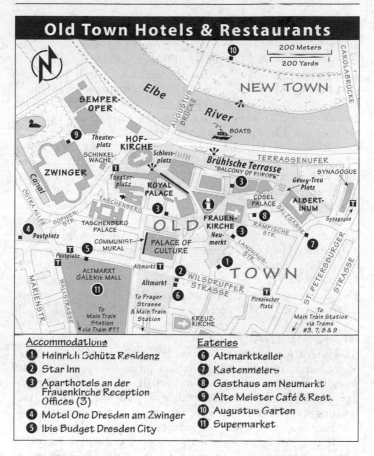

Old Town Hotels & Restaurants

Accommodations

1. Heinrich Schütz Residenz
2. Star Inn
3. Aparthotels an der Frauenkirche Reception Offices (3)
4. Motel One Dresden am Zwinger
5. Ibis Budget Dresden City

Eateries

6. Altmarktkeller
7. Kastenmelers
8. Gasthaus am Neumarkt
9. Alte Meister Café & Rest.
10. Augustus Garten
11. Supermarket

$$ **Aparthotels an der Frauenkirche** rents 108 units in five restored houses (many with views) in the heart of the Old Town. Designed for longer stays but also welcoming one- or two-nighters, these comfortable, if somewhat dated, apartments (from studios to 3-room apartments) come with kitchens and lots of amenities. Two buildings ("Neumarkt" and "Altes Dresden") overlook the pleasant Neumarkt square in front of the Frauenkirche, another is on the touristy Münzgasse restaurant street, a fourth is on Schössergasse, and the fifth is on less-interesting Altmarkt square (breakfast extra at nearby café, elevator in all buildings, pay parking at nearby garage, reception for Neumarkt and Altmarkt units is in gift shop at Neumarkt 7, reception for Münzgasse apartments is at Münzgasse 10, reception for Schössergasse at Schössergasse 16/Sporergasse 7; for locations see map; tel. 0351/438-1111, www.aparthotels-frauenkirche.de, info@aparthotels-frauenkirche.de).

$ Motel One Dresden am Zwinger looms over a corner of Postplatz, within cherub-fountain-spitting distance of the Zwinger. Some of its 288 aqua-and-brown, posh-feeling but small rooms peek right into the palace's courtyard. Outside you'll find mini fountains, swing-chairs, and the hotel's motto—emblazoned across its roofline: "A life without joy is like a long trip without an inn" (breakfast extra, air-con, elevator, pay parking; Postplatz 5—from left side of main station hop tram #11 to Postplatz, direction: Bühlau; for a slightly longer walk take tram #3, #7, #8, or #9 to Kaditz Riegelplatz; see "Old Town Hotels & Restaurants" map, earlier, for location; tel. 0351/438-380, www.motel-one.com, dresden-am-zwinger@motel-one.com).

$ Ibis Budget Dresden City, with 203 small, simple rooms, is conveniently situated right by the Postplatz tram stop, steps from the major sights. The oddly designed, hospital-like rooms provide only minimal bathroom privacy (breakfast extra, air-con, elevator, pay parking, rental bikes, Wilsdruffer Strasse 25—hop tram #3, #7, #8, #9, or #11 from main station—see tram details for Motel One, earlier; see map on previous page, tel. 0351/8339-3820, www.ibisbudget.com, h7514@accor.com).

NEAR THE TRAIN STATION

$$ Hotel Kipping, with 20 dated but quiet and tidy rooms 100 yards behind the Hauptbahnhof, is professionally run by the friendly and proper Kipping brothers, Rainer and Peter, whose grandfather owned the building during World War II. The original building was one of very few in this area to survive the 1945 fire-bombing—in fact, people took shelter here during the attack (elevator, free parking, air-con in most rooms; exit station following signs for *Bayerische Strasse* near track 1, it's at Winckelmannstrasse 6, from here trams #3, #8, and #11 whisk you to the Old Town; tel. 0351/478-500, www.hotel-kipping.de, reception@hotel-kipping.de). Their restaurant serves good dinners (closed Sun). For location, see the "Dresden" map, earlier.

$$ Hotels Bastei, Königstein, and **Lilienstein** are cookie-cutter members of the Ibis chain, goose-stepping single-file up Prager Strasse (listed in order from the station to the center). Each place is practically identical, and all together they have 918 rooms. Nobody will pretend they have charm, but they're fairly priced and handy to the Hauptbahnhof (a longish walk from the Old Town; see the "Dresden" map, earlier). They're historic, too—a chance to experience communist designers' revolutionary, if warped, vision of urban life (breakfast extra, elevator, air-con, rental bikes, pay public parking, reservations for all: tel. 0351/4856; individual receptions: tel. 0351/4856-5445, tel. 0351/4856-6445, and tel. 0351/4856-7445, respectively; www.ibis-dresden.de, reservierung@ibis-dresden.de).

IN THE NEW TOWN

These hotels are in the tidy residential neighborhood between the Neustadt train station and the Augustus Bridge (figure a 15-minute walk or quick tram ride to the historical center). For locations, see the "Dresden" map, earlier.

$$$ Hotel Bayerischer Hof Dresden, 100 yards toward the river from the Neustadt train station, offers 56 spacious rooms with antique decor. While a bit old-fashioned, its inviting public spaces and quaint courtyard fill a grand old building on a busy street—be sure to ask for a room facing the courtyard (elevator, free parking, family apartments, Antonstrasse 33, yellow building to the right and across from station, tel. 0351/829-370, www.bayerischer-hof-dresden.de, info@bayerischer-hof-dresden.de).

$$ Hotel Martha Dresden is well-run and a better value than the Bayerischer Hof. Its 50 neatly maintained rooms are in a quiet location a five-minute walk from Neustadt train station. The two old buildings that make up the hotel have been smartly renovated and connected in back with a glassed-in winter garden and a pleasant outdoor breakfast terrace (some cheaper rooms with shared bath, family apartments, elevator, pay parking; Nieritzstrasse 11; tel. 0351/81760, www.hotel-martha-dresden.de, rezeption@hotel-martha-dresden.de).

$ Motel One Dresden-Palaisplatz stands on a busy but convenient street a short walk from the prettiest part of the New Town and right on a tram line to the Old Town. This hotel's 228 rooms share the same stylish design sense as its sister hotel on Postplatz (breakfast extra, pay parking; Palaisplatz 1—a 6-minute level walk from Neustadt station, or ride tram #9 in direction: Leutewitz or tram #11 in direction: Zschertnitz one stop to Anton-/Leipziger Strasse; tel. 0351/655-7380, www.motel-one.com, dresden-palaisplatz@motel-one.com)

BUDGET BEDS IN THE OUTER NEW TOWN

$ Pension Raskolnikoff is your chance to sleep in relative comfort amid the Neustadt alternative scene. Eight basic rooms—all different and creatively designed—are on the top floors and in the back building of this café and art-gallery complex on a quiet side street. Originally slated for demolition at the end of the DDR years, the building was taken over by an artists' cooperative, two of whose members are the current owners (lots of stairs, no breakfast on weekdays but bakery around corner and good breakfast served a few doors down at Lloyd's; take tram #11 from Hauptbahnhof Nord or #11 or #6 from Neustadt Station to Bautzner/Rothenburger Strasse, then walk one block up Rothenburger Strasse and turn right to reach Böhmische Strasse 34; tel. 0351/804-5706, www. raskolnikoff.de, pension@raskolnikoff.de).

¢ **Hostel Louise 20** is in the middle of the Outer New Town action. Though located in this wild-and-edgy nightlife district, it feels safe, solid, clean, and comfy. The bright, IKEA-furnished rooms, guest kitchen, cozy common room, friendly staff, and 78 cheap beds make it a good budget choice, even for those older than the backpacker crowd (private rooms available, restaurant below, in courtyard at Louisenstrasse 20, tel. 0351/889-4894, www. louise20.de, info@louise20.de).

¢ **Hostel Mondpalast Dresden** is young and laid-back, above a trendy bar in a historic building (it's the city's oldest hostel) in the heart of the Outer New Town. Its super-groovy vibe—each room is named for a constellation—is good for backpackers with little money and an appetite for late-night fun (private rooms available, communal kitchen, rental bikes, near Kamenzer Strasse at Louisenstrasse 77, take tram #11 from Hauptbahnhof or Neustadt Station to Pulsnitzer Strasse stop, tel. 0351/563-4050, www. mondpalast.de, info@mondpalast.de).

Eating in Dresden

Dresden's Old Town restaurants tend to be nice but touristy, and quite expensive. For cheaper prices and authentic local character, leave the famous center, cross the river, and wander through the New Town.

Many Dresden restaurants serve a Russian-style soup called *Soljanka,* which usually includes finely chopped meat and pickled vegetables in a light tomato-based broth. A special local dessert sold all over town is *Dresdner Eierschecke,* an eggy cheesecake with vanilla pudding, raisins, and almond shavings.

IN THE OLD TOWN

For locations, see the "Old Town Hotels & Restaurants" map, earlier.

$$ Altmarktkeller (a.k.a. Sächsisch-Böhmisches Bierhaus), a few blocks from the river on Altmarkt square, is a festive beer cellar that serves nicely presented Saxon and Bohemian food (from separate menus) and has good Czech beer on tap. The lively crowd, cheesy brass-band music (most Sat nights, except in June-July), and jolly murals add to the fun. While the on-square seating is fine, most choose the vast-but-stout air-conditioned cellar. The giant mural inside the entryway portrays the friendship between Dresden and Prague, proclaiming that "the sunshine of life is drinking and being merry" (daily 12:00-22:00, Altmarkt 4, to the right of McDonald's, tel. 0351/481-8130).

$$$$ Kastenmeiers is a good bet if you're loaded, fond of fish, and want an elegant, near-Michelin-star dining experience in the old town center. Under stony modern vaults, diners surrounded by modern artwork feel a romantic vibe. The striking white-on-white courtyard is livelier (Mon-Sat 16:00-23:00, closed Sun; reservations smart, Tzschirnerplatz 3, tel. 0351/4848-4801, www.kastenmeiers.de).

$$ Gasthaus am Neumarkt, a sleepy and inviting little place with an almost tearoom ambience one floor above street level (but with a few outdoor tables), serves hearty Saxon cuisine with a passion for local wine (always fish, meat, and vegetarian; daily 12:00-21:00, stays open later Sat-Sun; be sure to go upstairs, just off Neumarkt at An der Frauenkirche 13, enter on Salzgasse, tel. 0351/3236-7210).

$$$ Alte Meister Café and Restaurant, with delightful garden seating, is pricey but convenient for your Zwinger sightseeing—it's built right into the wall of the royal courtyard (daily 11:00-24:00, facing the Opera at Theaterplatz 1, tel. 0351/481-0426). They also have a small, cozy winter-garden branch facing the Zwinger's main courtyard.

Groceries: A REWE supermarket is in the bottom level of the Altmarkt-Galerie shopping center. Enter the mall off Altmarkt, take the escalator down, and head left to the end of the corridor (Mon-Sat 9:00-21:00, closed Sun).

IN THE NEW TOWN

Venture to these eateries—across the Augustus Bridge from the Old Town—for lower prices and a more local scene. Unless otherwise noted, for locations see the "Dresden" map, earlier.

$$ Augustus Garten is a lazy, crude-yet-inviting beer garden open only in good weather with super-cheap self-service food (pork knuckle, wurst, kraut, cheap beer, and lots of mustard). You'll eat among big bellies—and few tourists— with a good view back over the river to the Old Town (daily 11:00-23:00, Fri-Sat until 24:00, closed in bad weather, tel. 0351/404-5531). For location, see the "Old Town Hotels & Restaurants" map, earlier.

$$ Wenzel Prager Bierstuben serves country Bohemian cuisine in a woodsy bar that spills out into an airy, glassed-in gallery—made doubly big by its vast mirror. Stepping inside, you'll be immediately won over by the interior. There's also peaceful streetside seating. The menu is fun and Bohemian, with two Czech Staropramen beers on tap (daily 11:30-22:00, stays open later Fri-Sat, Königstrasse 1, tel. 0351/804-2010).

$$ Watzke Brauereiausschank am Goldenen Reiter, just

DRESDEN

over the Augustus Bridge and facing the Golden Rider statue, is run by a local brewery, with seating that spills out into the square. A hit with Dresdeners (and a world away from the touristy kitsch of the Old Town), it serves German and Saxon beer-hall fare, including pork knuckle *(Haxe),* lots of kraut, and its own unfiltered beer (daily 11:00-24:00, Hauptstrasse 1, tel. 0351/810-6820).

$$ Winzerstube Zum Rebstock is a cozy and popular pub serving Saxon cuisine with seasonal specials in a small romantic interior or in a leafy and quiet "Baroque garden" courtyard (daily 11:30-23:30, enter through passageway at Hauptstrasse 17, tel. 0351/563-3544).

Near the Three Kings Church (Dreikönigskirche): At the top of Hauptstrasse, in an 18th-century zone that survived World War II intact, several good eateries cluster around the towering spire of the Three Kings Church (Dreikönigskirche). **$$$$ Bülow's Bistro,** in the fancy Hotel Bülow Palais, shares the same kitchen as the Michelin star-quality Carousel Restaurant. With just 14 tables off the hotel lobby, it offers elegantly presented seasonal, international dishes and one of the nicest dining experiences in town—reservations are smart; it's also a swell place for coffee and homemade cakes (daily 11:00-23:00, Königstrasse 14, tel. 0351/800-3140, www.buelow-palais.com). **$ Die Pastamanufaktur,** a fun and romantic little place for pasta lovers, has a minimalist interior and nice seating out back with its own little fountain (daily 10:00-21:30, Karl-Liebknecht-Strasse 56, tel. 0351/323-7797).

OUTER NEW TOWN

The trendy Outer New Town is thriving with creative and youthful places to eat and drink. While I enjoy exploring this ever-changing scene at night (see "Nightlife in Dresden,") these recommended eateries are fun options any time of day.

In the Kunsthofpassage

In this exuberantly decorated courtyard (enter at Görlitzer Strasse 21, 23, or 25, or at Alaunstrasse 70), you'll find a handful of eateries, including these options.

$$ Lila Sosse serves *junge deutsche Küche* ("young German cooking") at rustic wooden tables in a mellow setting. Most of their dishes—a trendy, updated take on German classics—are served in mason jars (Mon-Fri 16:00-23:00, Sat-Sun 12:00-23:00, in the "Courtyard of Legendary Creatures"—*Fabelwesen*—closest to entrance at Alaunstrasse 70, tel. 0351/803-6723).

$ Teestube im Feng Shui-Haus is a teahouse and quirky shop with courtyard seating, serving simple but filling pastas, sandwiches, soups and salads, plus homemade desserts. Their *Sächsische Eierschecke*—a custardy Saxon cake—is popular with locals (Mon-Fri

11:00-19:00, Sat 10:00-18:00; Sun 13:00-18:00 in spring, in the Animals Courtyard, tel. 0351/810-5498).

$ Tiki Eis & Cocktail Bar serves snacks, but most people pop in for the authentic seasonal gelato (in both standard and eclectic flavors) and their shakes (made with or without alcohol; Mon-Thu 9:00-20:00, Fri-Sat until late, Sun 10:00-20:00, street-front access at 21 Görlitzer Strasse).

On Louisenstrasse

These choices are just a few of many scattered along, or near, Louisenstrasse, which is the busy thoroughfare of the Outer New Town.

$$ Scheune Café, near the intersection with Alaunstrasse, is a large space serving an eclectic menu of vegetarian dishes—German, Indian, and Italian—and a beer garden (long hours daily, Alaunstrasse 36–40, tel. 0351/802-6619).

$ King's Bread is a casual, slow-food spot serving made-to-order beef, salmon, vegan burgers, and more. Run by German chef Stefan Flüge, the focus is on natural and high-quality ingredients and inventive combinations (Sun-Thu 11:00-22:00, Fri-Sat until late, Louisenstrasse 58).

$ Hellers Kuchenglocke is a classy gathering space on the pleasant square called Martin-Luther-Platz. They serve teas, fresh-baked pastries, salads, *Flammkuchen,* and sandwiches on rustic bread. It's popular with the new-mom crowd during the week (Tue-Sun 8:00-19:00, closed Mon, Pulsnitzer Strasse 1, tel. 0341/8996-2500).

Dresden Connections

From Dresden by Train to: Leipzig (1-2/hour, 1.5 hours), **Berlin** (direct every 2 hours, 2 hours; more with transfer in Leipzig, 3 hours), **Erfurt** (hourly, 2 hours; some with transfer in Leipzig), **Wittenberg** (hourly, 2.5 hours, transfer in Leipzig), **Hamburg** (5/day direct, 4.5 hours; otherwise hourly with transfer, 5 hours), **Frankfurt** (hourly, 4.5 hours, half with change in Leipzig), **Nürnberg** (hourly, 3.5 hours, transfers vary), **Munich** (every 2 hours, 5 hours, change in Leipzig), **Prague** (every 2 hours, 2.5 hours), **Vienna** (6/day 7.5 hours with change in Prague; or catch night train in Prague), **Budapest** (4/day, 9 hours, 1 direct and 3 via Prague; or catch night train in Prague). Train info: www.bahn.com.

BERLIN

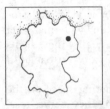

Berlin is a city of leafy boulevards, grand Neoclassical buildings, world-class art, glitzy shopping arcades, and funky graffitied neighborhoods with gourmet street food. It's big and bombastic—the showcase city of kings and kaisers, of the Führer and 21st-century commerce.

Of course, Berlin is still largely defined by its WWII years, and the Cold War. The East-West division was set in stone in 1961, when the East German government surrounded West Berlin with the Berlin Wall. Since the fall of the Wall in 1989, Berlin has been a constant construction zone. Standing on ripped-up streets and under a canopy of cranes, visitors have witnessed the city's reunification and rebirth. Today Berlin is a world capital once again—the nuclear fuel rod of a great nation.

In the city's top-notch museums, you can walk through an enormous Babylonian gate amid rough-and-tumble ancient statuary, fondle a chunk of the concrete-and-rebar Berlin Wall, and peruse canvases by Dürer and Rembrandt. A series of thought-provoking memorials confront Germany's difficult past. And some of the best history exhibits anywhere—covering everything from Prussian princes to Nazi atrocities to life under communism—have a knack for turning even those who claim to hate history into armchair experts.

Beyond its tangible sights and its enthralling history, Berlin is simply a pleasurable place to hang out. A recent mayor called it "poor but sexy"—a slogan that became a hit on local T-shirts. Berlin is captivating, lively, fun-loving—and easy on the budget. Go for a pedal in a park, or a lazy cruise on the delightful Spree River. Step across what was the Berlin Wall and through the iconic Bran-

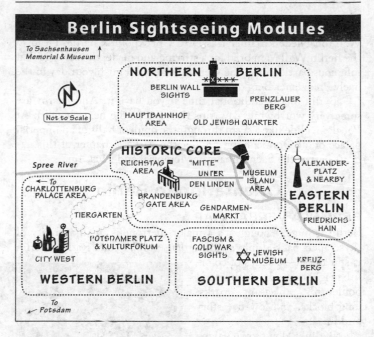

Berlin Sightseeing Modules

NORTHERN BERLIN
BERLIN WALL SIGHTS
PRENZLAUER BERG
HAUPTBAHNHOF AREA
OLD JEWISH QUARTER

To Sachsenhausen Memorial & Museum

Not to Scale

Spree River

HISTORIC CORE
REICHSTAG AREA
"MITTE"
UNTER DEN LINDEN
MUSEUM ISLAND AREA
BRANDENBURG GATE AREA
GENDARMEN-MARKT

To CHARLOTTENBURG PALACE AREA

TIERGARTEN

EASTERN BERLIN
ALEXANDER-PLATZ & NEARBY
FRIEDRICHS-HAIN

POTSDAMER PLATZ & KULTURFORUM

CITY WEST

WESTERN BERLIN

FASCISM & COLD WAR SIGHTS
JEWISH MUSEUM
KREUZ-BERG

SOUTHERN BERLIN

To Potsdam

denburg Gate. Nurse a stein of brew in a rollicking beer hall, slurp a bowl of ramen at a foodie hotspot, or dive into a cheap *Currywurst*. Ponder present-day "street art" (a.k.a. graffiti) on your way to see the famous bust of Nefertiti or a serene Vermeer. Grab a drink from a sidewalk vendor, find a bench along the river, watch the sun set over a skyline of domes and cranes...and simply bask in Berlin.

PLANNING YOUR TIME

On all but the shortest trips through Germany, I'd give Berlin three nights and at least two full days, and spend them this way:

Day 1: Begin your day getting oriented to this huge city. For a quick and relaxing once-over-lightly tour, jump on one of the many hop-on, hop-off buses that make two-hour narrated orientation loops through the city. Use the bus to get off and on at places of interest (such as Potsdamer Platz). Then walk from the Reichstag (reservations and passport required to climb its dome), under the Brandenburg Gate, and down Unter den Linden following my "Berlin City Walk." Tour the German History Museum, and cap your sightseeing day by catching a one-hour boat tour (or pedaling a rented bike) along the parklike banks of the Spree River.

Day 2: Spend your morning touring the great museums on Museum Island (note that the Pergamon Museum's famous altar is out of view until about 2025). Dedicate your afternoon to sights of the Third Reich and Cold War: After lunch, hike to the To-

BERLIN

pography of Terror exhibit and along the surviving stretch of the Wall (on Niederkirchnerstrasse) to Checkpoint Charlie. Head to the Berlin Wall Memorial for a stirring and in-depth survey of that infamous barrier, or to the Gemäldegalerie. Finish your day in the lively Prenzlauer Berg district.

Berlin merits additional time if you have it. And nearby are some very worthwhile day trips (covered in the next chapter): At Potsdam, glide like a swan through the opulent halls of an imperial palace or, at Oranienburg, ponder the darkest chapter of this nation's past at the Sachsenhausen Memorial and Museum.

Orientation to Berlin

BERLIN: A VERBAL MAP

Berlin is huge. Though it's a major metropolis, it's not a city of skyscrapers packed into a single, dense urban core. Rather, Berlin is spread out—a series of colorful neighborhoods, with broad boulevards, pleasant parks, long blocks, and low five-story buildings.

Berlin's "downtown" alone stretches five miles, following the west-to-east flow of the Spree River. In the center sits the vast park called Tiergarten.
Most tourist sights lie east of the park, in the historic core known locally as "Mitte." To make sprawling Berlin easier to digest, this chapter's coverage is organized by compass direction, radiating out from the center. (This organization has nothing to do with the old, Cold War-era "East Berlin" and "West Berlin" designations; in fact, virtually everything mentioned here other than "Western Berlin" was in the former East.)

Historic Core: Berlin's 1.5-mile sightseeing axis runs west-to-east along **Unter den Linden** boulevard, with a mix of 19th-century Neoclassical grandeur and 21st-century glitz. At the western edge, you'll find the **Reichstag** (Germany's domed parliament), the historic **Brandenburg Gate,** and a scattering of poignant memorials. Unter den Linden passes the grand squares called Gendarmenmarkt and Bebelplatz before it terminates at **Museum Island**—the birthplace of Berlin and today home to a cluster of the city's top museums: the ancient wonders of the Pergamon and Neues museums, and German paintings in the Old National Gallery.

Besides art, within this core are Berlin's towering Cathedral, the German History and DDR museums, and the re-creation of Berlin's former royal palace.

Northern Berlin: The trendy **old Jewish quarter,** near the Hackescher Markt transit hub, is a short walk north of Unter den Linden; here you'll find eateries, shopping, and Jewish history. Farther out is the even hipper **Prenzlauer Berg** residential area, with recommended hotels, restaurants, and shopping. Also in this zone are the **Berlin Wall Memorial**—the best place in town to learn more about the Wall—and the **Hauptbahnhof** (main train station).

Southern Berlin: South of Unter den Linden, **fascism and Cold War sights** dominate, anchored by Checkpoint Charlie (the former Wall border crossing) and the Topography of Terror (documenting Nazi atrocities). Further south and east is the diverse and fun-to-explore **Kreuzberg** neighborhood, with a flourishing Turkish community and the Jewish Museum Berlin.

Eastern Berlin: East of Museum Island, Unter den Linden changes its name to Karl-Liebknecht-Strasse and leads to **Alexanderplatz**—formerly the hub of communist East Berlin, still marinated in brutal architecture, and marked by its impossible-to-miss TV Tower. Farther east sits the gentrifying **Friedrichshain** neighborhood, with the East Side Gallery (a graffiti-slathered stretch of surviving Berlin Wall).

Western Berlin: Just west of the Brandenburg Gate is the entrance to Berlin's huge central park, **Tiergarten.** South of the gate, **Potsdamer Platz** is home to Berlin's 21st-century glitz, with skyscrapers and shopping plazas. Down the street, the **Kulturforum** is a cluster of museums, including the impressive Gemäldegalerie (starring Rembrandt, Dürer, and more).

West of the park is **City West**—the former heart of communist-era West Berlin, lined up along the boulevard named Kurfürstendamm ("Ku'damm" for short). This modern area feels like a classy suburb, with a few sights (Kaiser Wilhelm Memorial Church, Berlin Zoological Garden) and several recommended hotels. Finally, to the north of Ku'damm is the mediocre **Charlottenburg Palace,** with good 20th-century art museums nearby.

TOURIST INFORMATION

Berlin's TIs are for profit agencies that are only marginally helpful (tel. 030/250-025, www.visitberlin.de). You'll find them at the **Hauptbahnhof** (daily 8:00-21:00, by main entrance on Europaplatz) and in City West at **Europa Center** (Mon-Sat 10:00-20:00, closed Sun, hidden inside the shopping mall ground floor at Tauentzienstrasse 9). You'll also find "info box" kiosks at the **Brandenburg Gate** (daily 9:30-19:00, Nov-March until 18:00), at Alexanderplatz in the **Park Inn lobby** (Mon-Sat 7:00-21:00; Sun 8:00-18:00), and at **Tegel Airport's main hall** (daily 7:00-22:00). A separately run TI—focusing on Prenzlauer Berg, and generally

The History of Berlin

Berlin was a humble, marshy burg until prince electors from the Hohenzollern dynasty made it their capital in the mid-15th century. Gradually their territory spread and strengthened, becoming the powerful Kingdom of Prussia in 1701. As the leading city of Prussia, Berlin dominated the northern Germanic world—both militarily and culturally—long before there was a united "Germany."

Thanks largely to Frederick the Great (1712-1786), the enlightened despot who was both a ruthless military tactician and a cultured lover of the arts, Prussia was well-positioned to lead the German unification movement in the 19th century. And when Germany became a unified modern nation in 1871, Berlin was its natural capital. The city boomed with Germany's industrialization, quadrupling its population over the next 40 years. After Germany's humiliating defeat in World War I, Berlin thrived as an anything-goes cultural capital of the Roaring Twenties. During World War II, the city was Hitler's headquarters—and the place where the Führer drew his final breath.

When the Soviet Army reached Berlin in 1945, the protracted fighting left the city in ruins. Berlin was divided by the victorious Allied powers—the American, British, and French sectors became West Berlin, and the Soviet sector, East Berlin. The city became the main battlefield of the nascent Cold War. In 1948, the Soviets tried to starve the 2.2 million residents of the western half in an almost medieval-style siege, which was broken by the Allies' Berlin Airlift. Later, with the overnight construction of the Berlin Wall in 1961, an Iron (or, at least, concrete) Curtain completely encircled West Berlin—cutting Berlin in half. While East Berliners lived through difficult times, West Berlin became a magnet for artists, punks, squatters, and free spirits.

Finally, on November 9, 1989, the Wall came down. After wild celebrations, Berlin faced a fitful transition to reunification. Two cities—and countries—became one at a staggering pace. Some "Ossies" (impolite slang for Easterners) missed their security. Some "Wessies" missed military deferrals, subsidized rent, and tax breaks for living in an isolated city surrounded by the communist world.

Today, going on 30 years later, the old East-West divisions are a distant memory. Berlin's local government has been eager to charge forward, with little nostalgia for the past. Big corporations and the national government have moved in, and the dreary swath of land that was the Wall has been transformed. Berlin is a new city—ready to welcome visitors.

BERLIN

more useful—is at the **Kulturbrauerei** (daily 11:00-19:00, ask for the free *Pankow Entdecken* booklet, with lots of local insights). See the color maps at the back of this book for most locations.

Skip the TI's €1 map, and instead browse the walking tour company brochures—many include nearly-as-good maps for free. Most hotels provide free city maps. If interested in cultural happenings, pick up a copy of the current month's *Exberliner* (in English, €4, free at some hotels, www.exberliner.co).

ARRIVAL IN BERLIN

For a detailed rundown of the city's train stations and airports, see the "Berlin Connections" section at the end of this chapter.

HELPFUL HINTS

Closures: Many museums are closed on Monday, including the Berlin Wall Memorial Visitors Center and Documentation Center, Old National Gallery, Bode Museum, Altes Museum, Gemäldegalerie, Palace of Tears, Museum of Decorative Arts, and Charlottenburg Palace. The Deutsche Kinemathek Film and TV Museum is closed on Tuesdays. Many museums stay open late on Thursdays.

Sightseeing Strategies: Visiting the Reichstag dome is free, but you must make a reservation in advance (and bring your passport). It's also smart to book in advance for the Pergamon, Neues, and DDR museums.

The €29 **Museum Pass Berlin** is best for serious museum-goers—it covers nearly all the city sights for three consecutive days (including everything covered by the one-day Museum Island Pass; see details at www.visitberlin.de). It gets you into more than 30 museums, including the national museums and most of the recommended biggies. Covered sights include the five Museum Island museums (Old National Gallery, Neues, Altes, Bode, and Pergamon), German History Museum, and the Gemäldegalerie (and other Kulturforum museums). Buy it at any participating museum or a TI. The pass generally lets you skip the line and go directly into the museum—except at the Pergamon and Neues, where you should prebook a time slot on their websites.

The €18 **Museum Island Pass** (not sold at TIs; see www.smb.museum) covers all sights on Museum Island and is a fine value if you're touring at least two of the collections (though for just €11 more, the three-day Museum Pass Berlin described above gives you triple the days and many more entries). This pass also does not let you skip the line at the Pergamon and Neues—book a time slot in advance.

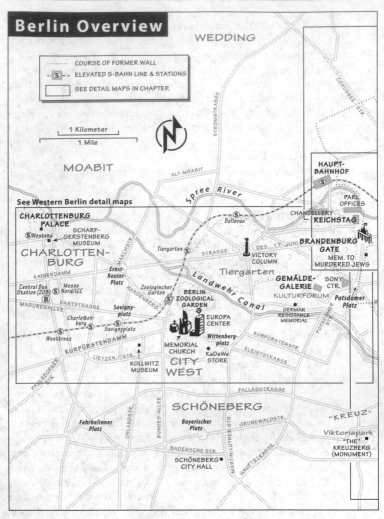

Berlin Overview

WEDDING

.... COURSE OF FORMER WALL

-⑤- ELEVATED S-BAHN LINE & STATIONS

☐ SEE DETAIL MAPS IN CHAPTER

1 Kilometer

1 Mile

MOABIT

ALT-MOABIT

Spree River

See Western Berlin detail maps

CHARLOTTENBURG PALACE

⑤ Westend

SCHARF-GERSTENBERG MUSEUM

CHARLOTTEN-BURG

KAISERDAMM

Ernst-Reuter-Platz

Central Bus Station (ZOB) ⑬ Messe Nord/ICC

MASURENALLEE

KANTSTRASSE

Savigny-platz

Charlotten-burg ⑤

⑤ Savignyplatz

Westkreuz ⑤

KURFÜRSTENDAMM

PAHLSBORNER STR.

LIETZEN. STR.

Bellevue ⑤

Tiergarten ⑤

STRASSE

Zoologischer Garten ⑤

BERLIN ZOOLOGICAL GARDEN

EUROPA CENTER

MEMORIAL CHURCH

Wittenberg-platz

KaDeWe STORE

KLEISTSTRASSE

CITY WEST

KOLLWITZ MUSEUM

PALLASSTRASSE

SCHÖNEBERG

Fehrbelliner Platz

UHLANDSTR.

BUNDES-ALLEE

Bayerischer Platz

BADENSCHE STR.

SCHÖNEBERG CITY HALL

MARTIN-LUTHER-STR.

GRUNEWALDSTR.

HAUPTSTRASSE

CHANCELLERY

HAUPT-BAHNHOF ⑤

PARL. OFFICES

REICHSTAG

BRANDENBURG GATE

MEM. TO MURDERED JEWS

GEMÄLDE-GALERIE

KULTURFORUM

SONY CTR.

Potsdamer Platz

GERMAN RESISTANCE MEMORIAL

KURFÜRSTENSTR.

"KREUZ-

Viktoriapark

"THE KREUZBERG (MONUMENT)

DES 17 JUNI

VICTORY COLUMN

Tiergarten

Landwehr Canal

STROMSTRASSE

CHAUSSEE-STR.

MARCHSTR.

HARDENBERG

Festivals: Berlin hosts a near-constant string of events; see the appendix for key dates.

Cold War Terminology: What Americans called "East Germany" was technically the German Democratic Republic—the Deutsche Demokratische Republik, or DDR. You'll still see those initials around what was once East Germany. The name for what was "West Germany"—the Federal Republic of Germany (Bundesrepublik Deutschland, or BRD)—is now the name shared by all of Germany. Former East or West? Here's a tip: The former communist sector has more tram tracks in the pavement.

Laundry: You'll find several self-service launderettes near my rec-

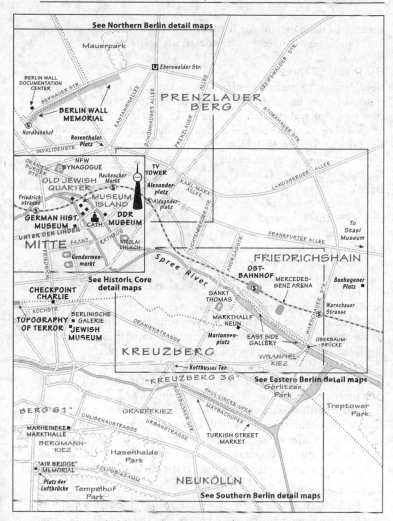

See Northern Berlin detail maps

ommended hotels (generally daily 6:00-22:00). In Prenzlauer Berg, try **Eco-Express Waschsalon** (Danziger Strasse 7) or **Schnell & Sauber Waschcenter** (Oderberger Strasse 1); for locations see the map on page 850. In the old Jewish quarter, there are two launderettes around the corner from Rosenthaler Platz: **Waschsalon 115** (Wi-Fi, Torstrasse 115) and **Eco-Express Waschsalon** (Torstrasse 109); for locations see the map on page 854.

GETTING AROUND BERLIN

Berlin's sights spread far and wide. Right from the start, commit yourself to the city's fine public-transit system. This vast city is

BERLIN

committed to bikes, and you'll notice smart and efficient bike lanes. This can be very dangerous for pedestrians, so be alert.

By Public Transit

Berlin's transit system uses the same ticket for its many modes of transportation: buses, trams *(Strassenbahn)*, and trains. There are two types of trains: The U-Bahn—like a subway, making lots of short hops around town—is run by the local transit authority (BVG); the S-Bahn, a light rail that goes faster and stops only at major stations, is operated by German Railways (Deutsche Bahn).

For all types of transit, there are three lettered zones: A, B, and C. Most of your sightseeing will be in zones A and B (the city proper); you may enter zone C if you're going to Potsdam, Sachsenhausen, Schönefeld airport, or other outlying areas.

Sections of the U-Bahn or S-Bahn sometimes close temporarily for repairs, with a bus route replacing the train *(Ersatzverkehr,* or "replacement transportation"; *zwischen* means "between").

Within Berlin, Eurail passes are good on connections from the train station when you arrive and to the station when you depart on counted rail pass days (both S-Bahn and U-Bahn).

Information: Timetables, prices, and trip planning are available on two helpful websites: BVG (www.bvg.de) or VBB (www.vbb.de). Both offer handy, free apps with on-the-go trip routing for U-Bahn, S-Bahn, tram, and bus connections. For an overview of the transit system, see the color map at the back of this book.

Ticket Options

The €2.80 **basic single** ticket *(Einzelfahrschein)* covers two hours of travel in one direction. It's easy to make this ticket stretch to cover several rides...as long as they're in the same direction.

The €1.70 **short-ride** ticket *(Kurzstrecke Fahrschein)* covers a single ride of up to six bus/tram stops or three subway stations (one transfer allowed on subway). You can save on short-ride tickets by buying them in groups of four (€5.60).

The €9 **four-trip** ticket *(4-Fahrten-Karte)* is the same as four basic single tickets at a small discount.

The **day pass** *(Tageskarte)* is good until 3:00 the morning after you buy it (€7 for zones AB, €7.70 for zones ABC). For longer stays, consider a seven-day pass *(Sieben-Tage-Karte;* €30 for zones AB, €37.50 for zones ABC), or the WelcomeCard (described next).

The *Kleingruppenkarte* lets groups of up to five travel all day (€19.90 for zones AB, €20.80 for zones ABC).

If you've already bought a ticket for zones A and B, and later decide to go to zone C (such as to Potsdam), you can buy an **"extension ticket"** *(Anschlussfahrschein)* for €1.60, which covers two hours of travel in that zone.

If you plan to cover a lot of ground using public transportation during a two- or three-day visit, the **WelcomeCard** is usually the best deal (available at TIs—including both airport locations—and U-Bahn/S-Bahn ticket machines; www.visitberlin.de/welcomecard). It covers all public transportation and gives up to 50 percent discounts off lots of minor and a few major museums, sightseeing tours (including 25 percent off the recommended Original Berlin Walks and Insider Tour), and music and theater events. The Berlin-only card covers transit zones AB (€20/48 hours, €29/72 hours).

Buying Tickets

You can buy U-Bahn/S-Bahn tickets from machines at stations (coins and bills accepted). Tickets are also sold at BVG pavilions at train stations and at the TI, from machines onboard trams (coins only), and on buses from drivers, who give change.

To use a ticket machine, start by pressing the British flag icon for English instructions. Next, select the zone (AB, ABC, or "short trip journey" for a zoneless short-ride ticket) and the type of ticket you want (single, day, or four-trip; for seven-day tickets, select the "other tickets" option), then pay. Most travelers want the AB ticket —either single or all-day ticket. Note that "adult" *(Erwachsener)* means anyone 14 or older.

Boarding Transit

As you board the bus or tram or enter the subway, validate your ticket in a clock machine (or risk a €60 fine; with a pass, stamp it only the first time you ride). Tickets are checked periodically, often by plainclothes inspectors. You may be asked to show your ticket when boarding the bus. Note that not all tram stops (marked by a sign with a green *H* in a gold circle) have designated platforms on raised sidewalks, and not all trams pull right up to the curb. When the tram arrives, be ready to step into the road to hop aboard.

Useful Transit Lines

Learning a few key transit lines will help shrink this vast city.

U-Bahn: Line **U2** cuts diagonally across the city from Prenzlauer Berg (hotels) to Potsdamer Platz, stopping near Checkpoint Charlie at Stadtmitte. Other handy U-Bahn lines include **U6** (runs north-south through downtown, offering a quick connection to Kreuzberg) and **U1** (cuts east-west through southern Berlin, connecting City West, Kreuzberg, and Friedrichshain). Line **U5** (likely open in 2020) will connect the Hauptbahnhof, Reichstag, and strategic stops along the city's main sightseeing spine: Brandenburger Tor, Unter den Linden (near Bebelplatz), Museum Island, Rotes Rathaus (City Hall, near the Nikolai Quarter), and Alexanderplatz.

S-Bahn: Several S-Bahn lines flow like a high-speed river through the heart of Berlin. Lines **S3, S5, S7,** and **S9** zip quickly east-west between key stops: Savignyplatz (hotels in western Berlin), Zoologischer Garten—also known as "Zoo Station" (zoo, City West, Ku'damm), Hauptbahnhof, Friedrichstrasse (near the heart of Unter den Linden), Hackescher Markt (Museum Island, old Jewish quarter, connection to Prenzlauer Berg), and Alexanderplatz (east end of the historic core).

Lines **S1** and **S2** travel north-south between Nordbahnhof (Berlin Wall Memorial), Friedrichstrasse, Brandenburger Tor, and Potsdamer Platz (Kulturforum).

Trams: Trams connect several of my recommended neighborhoods in East Berlin. **#M1** is helpful for getting to and around Prenzlauer Berg—connecting the Hackescher Markt S-Bahn station with key stops along the main drag Kastanienallee; **#12** overlaps with the middle part of #M1; and **#M10** is handy for connecting Cold War sights—it starts at the Hauptbahnhof, goes to Nordbahnhof (Berlin Wall Memorial), connects stops along the Berlin Wall Memorial (Mauerpark, Alexanderplatz, and Frankfurter Tor), and finishes at Warschauer Strasse (for the East Side Gallery).

Buses: Handy bus **#100, #200,** and **#TXL** travel east-west along Unter den Linden between the Reichstag/Brandenburg area on one end and Alexanderplatz on the other. There are stops every few blocks, with buses every 10 minutes or so.

By Taxi and Uber

Cabs are easy to flag down, and taxi stands are common. A typical ride within town costs around €10, and a crosstown trip (for example, Savignyplatz to Alexanderplatz) will run about €20.

Tariff 1 is for a *Kurzstrecke* ticket (short-stretch ride). This ticket can save you several euros for any ride of less than two kilometers (about a mile). To get this rate, you must flag down the cab on the street—not at a taxi stand—and ask for the *Kurzstrecke* rate as soon as you hop in. Confidently say *"Kurzstrecke, bitte"* (KOORTS-shtreh-keh, BIT-teh); your driver will grumble and flip the meter to a fixed €5 rate (for a ride that would otherwise cost €8). If your ride exceeds two kilometers, the meter kicks on and the regular rate takes over.

All other rides are tariff 2 (€3.90 drop plus €2/km for the first seven kilometers, then €1.50/km after that). If possible, use cash: Credit card payment comes with a surcharge. If a taxi looks empty but doesn't stop, it's likely on its way to a pick-up requested through one of many ride-sharing apps.

While Germans have better local ride apps, Uber works in Berlin like it does in the US (but rates are tied to taxi fares so you don't really save any money).

Private Car and Driver: Michael Rogowski is a private chauffeur with a very comfortable eight-seat minivan. He speaks decent English, knows Berlin and environs well, has a knack for finding parking for spontaneous sightseeing, and is a delight to be with (€50/hour, cheaper for longer gigs, m-rogowski@t-online.de).

By Bike

Flat Berlin is a very bike-friendly city, but be careful—motorists don't brake for bicyclists (and bicyclists don't brake for pedestrians). Fortunately, many roads and sidewalks have special red-painted bike lanes. Don't ride on the regular sidewalk—it's *verboten* (though locals do it all the time).

Fat Tire Bikes rents good bikes at the base of the TV Tower near Alexanderplatz (€14/day, cheaper for 2 or more days, trekking bikes available, free luggage storage, daily 9:30-20:00, shorter hours off-season, tel. 030/2404-7991, www.berlinbikerental.com; for location, see the map on page 864).

Take a Bike—near the Friedrichstrasse S-Bahn station—is owned by a knowledgeable Dutch-German with a huge inventory (3-gear bikes: €8/4 hours, €12.50/day, €19/2 days, slightly cheaper for longer rentals, more for better bikes, includes helmets, daily 9:30-19:00, Nov-March closed Tue-Thu, Neustädtische Kirchstrasse 8—see the map on page 864, tel. 030/2065-4730, www.takeabike.de). To find it, leave the S-Bahn station via the Friedrichstrasse exit, turn right, go through a triangle-shaped square, and hang a left on Neustädtische Kirchstrasse.

Bike Rental Berlin is a good option in Prenzlauer Berg (€10/day, helmets-€1, kids' bikes and child seats available, daily 10:00-18:00, often closed off-season—call ahead, Kastanienallee 55—see the map on page 850, tel. 030/7153-3020, http://bike-rental-berlin.de).

Simple **Rent a Bike** stands outside Berlin shops, restaurants, and hotels charge €12/day (no maps, no helmets); I prefer the full-service rental shops listed above.

Tours in Berlin

BY BUS

Berlin lends itself to a bus-tour orientation (worth ▲▲). Several companies offer essentially the same routine: a circuit of the city with unlimited, all-day hop-on, hop-off privileges for around €25 (two days for a few euros more, check for WelcomeCard discounts). Buses make about a dozen stops at the city's major tourist spots (Potsdamer Platz, Museum Island, Brandenburg Gate, Kaiser Wilhelm Memorial Church, and so on). For specifics, look for brochures in your hotel lobby or at the TI, or check the websites for the dominant outfits: **CitySightseeing Berlin,** a.k.a. Berlin City Tour, runs red buses and yellow-and-green buses (www.berlin-city-tour.de). **City Circle Sightseeing,** a.k.a. BEX, runs yellow-and-black buses marked with a "Grayline" logo (www.berlinerstadtrundfahrten.de).

Buses come with cursory narration in English and German by a live, sometimes tired guide, or a dry recorded commentary. Try to catch a bus with a live guide (buses generally run daily 10:00-18:00, 4/hour, last departure from all stops around 16:00, 2-hour loop; Nov-March 2/hour, last departure around 15:00). Due to heavy traffic, pick-up times are unreliable; you may find yourself waiting on the curb for a good part of your day.

BY BOAT
▲▲ Spree River Cruises

Several boat companies offer €15 trips up and down the river. In one relaxing hour, you'll listen to an excellent English audioguide, see lots of wonderful new government-commissioned architecture, and enjoy the lively park action fronting the river. Boats leave from docks clustered near the bridge behind the Berlin Cathedral (just off Unter den Linden, near the DDR Museum). For better views, go for a two-story boat with open-deck seating. While you have many interchangeable options, I enjoyed the Historical Sightseeing Cruise from **Stern und Kreisschiffahrt** (departures on the half-hour, mid-March-Nov daily 10:30-17:30, leaves from Nikolaiviertel Dock—cross bridge from Berlin Cathedral  toward Alexanderplatz and look right; RS%—show this book for free English audioguide, otherwise €2; tel. 030/536-3600, www.sternundkreis.de).

ON FOOT

Berlin's fascinating and complex history can be challenging to appreciate on your own, but a good Berlin tour guide and walking tour makes the city's dynamic story come to life (and can be worth ▲▲▲).

Unlike many European countries, Germany has no regulations controlling who can give city tours. As a result, guide quality is hit-or-miss, ranging from brilliant history buffs who've lived in Berlin for years, to new arrivals who've memorized a script. To improve your odds of landing a great guide, try one of my recommendations.

Most outfits offer walks that are variations on the same themes: general **introductory** walk, **Third Reich** walk (Hitler and Nazi sites), and day trips to **Potsdam** and the **Sachsenhausen Memorial and Museum.** Most tours cost about €12-15 and last 3-4 hours (longer for side trips to Potsdam and Sachsenhausen); public-transit tickets and entrances to sights are extra. For more details—including prices, schedules, and other themes—see each company's website or pick up brochures at TIs, hotel reception desks, cafés, and shops.

Original Berlin Walks

With a strong commitment to quality guiding, Original Berlin's "Discover Berlin" walk offers a solid overview with a smart itinerary in four hours (€14, RS%—€2 less with this book, daily at 10:30 and 14:00, May-Sept also daily at 9:00). Tours depart from opposite the Hackescher Markt S-Bahn station, outside the recommended Weihenstephaner restaurant (tel. 030/301-9194, www.berlinwalks.de).

Insider Tour

This well-regarded company runs the full gamut of itineraries, as well as a day trip to Dresden. Their tours have two meeting points: in Western Berlin, in front of the McDonald's outside the Zoologischer Garten station; and in the old Jewish quarter, outside the AM to PM Bar at the Hackescher Markt S-Bahn station (tel. 030/692-3149, www.insidertour.com).

Food Tours

Many companies offer food tours—a typical offering might start at Hackesche Höfe at 12:00, last 3.5 hours, cost €30, and make five stops (sampling German ravioli, *Currywurst,* Turkish treats, baked goodies, and some schnapps). Your guide will stoke your appetite with history, jokes, and cultural insights as you walk between stops. A good start is to check Original Berlin Walks' and Insider Tour's websites for the latest offerings.

BERLIN

Berlin at a Glance

▲▲▲**Reichstag** Germany's historic parliament building, topped with a striking modern dome you can climb (reservations required). **Hours:** Daily 8:00-24:00. See page 789.

▲▲▲**Brandenburg Gate** One of Berlin's most famous landmarks, a massive columned gateway, at the former border of East and West. See page 793.

▲▲▲**German History Museum** The ultimate swing through Germany's tumultuous story. **Hours:** Daily 10:00-18:00. See page 803.

▲▲▲**Berlin Wall Memorial** Museums with videos and displays, several outdoor exhibits, and lone surviving stretch of an intact Wall section. **Hours:** Museums open Tue-Sun 10:00-18:00, closed Mon; outdoor areas accessible daily 24 hours. See page 810.

▲▲**Memorial to the Murdered Jews of Europe** Holocaust memorial with almost 3,000 symbolic pillars, plus an exhibition about Hitler's Jewish victims. **Hours:** Memorial always open; information center Tue-Sun 10:00-20:00, Oct-March until 19:00, closed Mon year-round. See page 794.

▲▲**Unter den Linden** Leafy boulevard in the heart of former East Berlin, lined with some of the city's top sights. See page 794.

▲▲**Memorials near the Reichstag** Tributes to Nazi victims, including Jews, Roma, homosexuals, opposing politicians, and people with disabilities. See page 791.

▲▲**Pergamon Museum** World-class museum of classical antiquities on Museum Island (Pergamon Altar closed through 2025). **Hours:** Daily 10:00-18:00, Thu until 20:00. See page 796.

▲▲**Neues Museum** Egyptian antiquities collection and proud

"Free" Tours

You'll see ads for "free" introductory tours all over town. Popular with students (who've yet to learn you get what you pay for), it's a business model that has spread across Europe: English-speaking students (often Aussies and Americans) deliver a memorized script before a huge crowd lured in by the promise of a free tour. The catch: Guides expect to be "tipped in paper" (€5/person minimum is encouraged).

home of the exquisite 3,000-year-old bust of Queen Nefertiti. **Hours:** Daily 10:00-18:00, Thu until 20:00. See page 799.

▲▲**Old National Gallery** German paintings, mostly from the Romantic Age. **Hours:** Tue-Sun 10:00-18:00, Thu until 20:00, closed Mon. See page 800.

▲▲**DDR Museum** Quirky collection of communist-era artifacts. **Hours:** Daily 10:00-20:00, Sat until 22:00. See page 806.

▲▲**Courtyards** (Höfe) Interconnected courtyards with shops, eateries, and museums, best explored in the old Jewish quarter. See page 807.

▲▲**Prenzlauer Berg** Lively, colorful neighborhood with hip cafés, restaurants, boutiques, and street life. See page 809.

▲▲**Topography of Terror** Chilling exhibit documenting the Nazi perpetrators, built on the site of the former Gestapo/SS headquarters. **Hours:** Daily 10:00-20:00. See page 818.

▲▲**Kreuzberg** Eclectic, trendy neighborhood with diverse roots, popular eateries, and the Turkish street market. See page 821.

▲▲**Gemäldegalerie** Germany's top collection of 13th- through 18th-century European paintings, featuring Holbein, Dürer, Cranach, Van der Weyden, Rubens, Hals, Rembrandt, Vermeer, Raphael, and more. **Hours:** Tue-Fri 10:00-18:00, Thu until 20:00, Sat-Sun 11:00-18:00, closed Mon. See page 827.

▲**Museum of the Wall at Checkpoint Charlie** Stories of brave Cold War escapes, near the site of the famous former East-West border checkpoint; the surrounding street scene is almost as interesting. **Hours:** Daily 9:00-22:00. See page 817.

Local Guides

Berlin guides are generally independent contractors who work with tour companies (such as those listed here) but can also be hired privately. Most licensed local guides charge €65/hour or €200-300/day (confirm when booking). Guides can get booked up—especially in summer—so reserve ahead.

Most of these guides belong to a federation called Bündnis Berliner Stadtführer, which is a great source for connecting with even more guides (www.guides-berlin.org).

BERLIN

I've personally worked with and can strongly recommend each of the following guides:

Archaeologist **Nick Jackson** (mobile 0171-537-8768, www.jacksonsberlintours.com, info@jacksonsberlintours.com);

Lee Evans (makes 20th-century Germany a thriller, mobile 0176-6335-5565, lee.evans@berlin.de);

Torben Brown (a walking Berlin encyclopedia, mobile 0176-5004-2572, www.berlinperspectives.com, torben@berlinperspectives.com);

Holger Zimmer (a cultural connoisseur and public radio journalist, mobile 0163-345-4427, explore@berlin.de);

Carlos Meissner (a historian with a professorial earnestness, mobile 0175-266-0575, www.berlinperspectives.com, carlos@berlinperspectives.com);

Maisie Hitchcock (a young British international, mobile 01763-847-2717, maisiehitchcock@hotmail.com);

Caroline Marburger (a sharp historian who has lived and studied abroad, mobile 0176-7677-9920, www.berlinlocals.com, caroline@berlinlocals.com);

Bernhard Schlegelmilch (the only guide listed here who grew up behind the Wall, mobile 0176-6422-9119, info@steubentoursberlin.com);

Haşim Anik (who grew up with his Turkish family in Kreuzberg and specializes in that neighborhood, mobile 0163-916-2148, hasimanik@hotmail.com).

Be aware that several of these guides (Torben, Holger, Carlos, Maisie, and Caroline) lead Rick Steves Europe bus tours around Germany, Austria, and Switzerland, and are often out of town.

ON WHEELS

Fat Tire Bike Tours offers guided bike tours from April through October (around €28, 4-6 hours, 6-10 miles, check schedules at www.fattiretours.com/berlin). Topics include a City Tour, Berlin Wall Tour, Third Reich, evening food tour (€49), Modern Berlin Tour (countercultural, creative aspects of contemporary Berlin), an all-day Potsdam Gardens and Palaces Tour, and private tours for families and small groups. Meet at the TV Tower at Alexanderplatz (reservations smart, tel. 030/2404-7991).

Berlin on Bike offers a 3.5-hour introductory tour daily at 11:00. They also offer several themed tours, including Alternative Berlin, Street Art Berlin, and Nightseeing (most €24, 8-12 miles, private tours available, all tours leave from the Kultur-brauerei brewery in Prenzlauer Berg, tel. 030/4373-9999, https://berlinonbike.de).

Berlin City Walk

Trace Germany's turbulent 20th-century history on this two-mile self-guided walk, worth ▲▲▲. We'll start in front of the Reichstag, pass through the Brandenburg Gate, walk down Unter den Linden, and finish on Alexanderplatz, near the TV Tower. You'll want to visit some major sights along the route later or by taking a break from the walk. Follow the route on the "Berlin City Walk" map.

Length of This Tour: If you have just one day in Berlin, or want a good orientation to the city, simply follow this walk (allow 2-3 hours at a brisk pace, not counting museum visits). By the end, you'll have seen the core of Berlin and its most important sights.

If you have more time and want to use this walk as a spine for your sightseeing, entering sights and museums as you go, consider doing Part 1 and Part 2 on different days.

Part 1 goes from the Reichstag and takes you partway down Unter den Linden, with stops at the Brandenburg Gate, Memorial to the Murdered Jews of Europe, and Friedrichstrasse, the glitzy shopping street.

Part 2 continues down Unter den Linden, from Bebelplatz to Alexanderplatz, visiting Museum Island and the Spree River, the Berlin Cathedral, and the iconic TV Tower.

Tours: ∩ Download my free Berlin City Walk audio tour.

PART 1: THE REICHSTAG TO UNTER DEN LINDEN

• *Start in Platz der Republik and take in your surroundings. Dominating this park is a giant domed building.*

❶ Reichstag

The Reichstag is the heart of Germany's government. It's where the Bundestag—the lower house of parliament—meets to govern the nation (similar to the US House of Representatives).

When the building was inaugurated in 1895, Germany was still a kingdom. Back then, the real center of power was a mile east of here, at the royal palace. But after the emperor was deposed in World War I, the German Republic was proclaimed. Meanwhile, the storm of National Socialism was growing—the Nazis. Soon the Reichstag had dozens of duly elected National Socialists, and Adolf Hitler seized power. In 1933, the Reichstag building nearly burned down. Many believe that Hitler planned

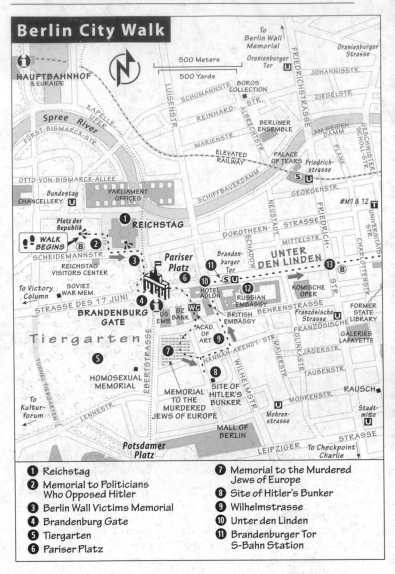

Berlin City Walk

1. Reichstag
2. Memorial to Politicians Who Opposed Hitler
3. Berlin Wall Victims Memorial
4. Brandenburg Gate
5. Tiergarten
6. Pariser Platz
7. Memorial to the Murdered Jews of Europe
8. Site of Hitler's Bunker
9. Wilhelmstrasse
10. Unter den Linden
11. Brandenburger Tor S-Bahn Station

the fire as an excuse to frame the communists and grab power for himself.

With Hitler as Führer and real democracy a thing of the past, the Reichstag was hardly used. But it remained a powerful symbol and was a prime target for Allied bombers during World War II. As the war wound down and Soviet troops advanced on the city, it was here at the Reichstag that 1,500 German troops made their last stand.

BERLIN

⑫ Russian Embassy

⑬ Intersection of Unter den Linden & Friedrichstrasse

⑭ Bebelplatz

⑮ Neue Wache

⑯ Museum Island

⑰ Spree River

⑱ Marx & Engels Statues

⑲ Karl-Liebknecht-Strasse & Plattenbau

⑳ Martin Luther Statue & Marien Church

㉑ TV Tower

㉒ Alexanderplatz

After the war, Berlin was divided and the Berlin Wall ran right behind the Reichstag. The building fell into disuse, and the West German capital was moved from Berlin to the remote city of Bonn.

After the Berlin Wall fell, the Reichstag again became the focus of the new nation. It was renovated by British architect Norman Foster, who added the glass dome. In 1999, the new Reichstag reopened, and the parliament reconvened. To many Germans, the proud resurrection of their Reichstag symbolizes the end of a terrible chapter in their country's history.

Look now at the Reichstag's modern **dome.** The cupola rises 155 feet above the ground. Inside the dome, a cone of 360 mirrors reflects natural light into the legislative chamber below, and an opening at the top allows air to circulate. Lit from inside after dark, it gives Berlin a memorable nightlight. If you make a reservation to visit the interior, you can climb the spiral ramp all the way to the top of the dome for a grand city view (for details on visiting, see the Reichstag listing under "Sights in Berlin," later).

Facing the Reichstag, do a 360-degree spin to find some other big landmarks. To the left of the Reichstag, at the Bundestag U-Bahn stop, the long, partly transparent building houses parliamentary offices. Beyond that, in the distance, is the tower of the huge main train station, the Hauptbahnhof (marked *DB* for Deutsche Bahn, the German rail company). Farther left is the mammoth, white, concrete-and-glass Chancellery (nicknamed "the Washing Machine"). This is the office of Germany's most powerful person, the chancellor. To remind the chancellor who he or she works for, Germany's Reichstag (housing the parliament) is about six feet taller than the Chancellery.

• *Approach the Reichstag, turn right, walk nearly to the street, and find a small memorial next to the shipping-container-like entrance buildings. It's a row of slate stones sticking out of the ground—it looks like a bike rack. This is the...*

❷ Memorial to Politicians Who Opposed Hitler

These 96 slabs honor the 96 Reichstag members who spoke out against Adolf Hitler and the rising tide of fascism. When Hitler became chancellor, these critics were persecuted and murdered. On each slab, you'll see a name and political party—most are KPD (Communists) and SPD (Social Democrats)—and the date and location of death (*KZ* denotes those who died in concentration camps).

• *Walk east, along the right side of the Reichstag, on busy Scheidemannstrasse, toward the rear of the building. When you reach the inter-*

section at the back of the Reichstag, turn right and cross the street. Once across, on the corner you'll see a humble row of white crosses that predate the fall of the wall.

❸ Berlin Wall Victims Memorial

The Berlin Wall once stood right here, running north-south down what is now busy Ebertstrasse, dividing the city in two. This side (near the crosses) was democratic West Berlin. On the other side was the Soviet-controlled East. The row of white crosses commemorates a few of the many brave East Berliners who died trying to cross the Wall to freedom. (For more, see the sidebar.)

Read some of the crosses. The last person killed was 20-year-old Chris Gueffroy. He died nine months before the Wall fell, shot through the heart just a few steps away from here.

Several other memorials dedicated to groups targeted by the Nazis (from Sinti/Roma to homosexuals) are in the vicinity. For details and where to find them, see page 791.

• *Continue south down Ebertstrasse toward the Brandenburg Gate, tracing the former course of the Berlin Wall. A thin strip of memorial bricks embedded in the street pavement indicates where it once stood. Ebertstrasse spills into a busy intersection dominated by the imposing Brandenburg Gate. To take in this scene, cross the Berlin Wall bricks to the piazza in front of the...*

❹ Brandenburg Gate

This massive classical-looking monument is the grandest—and last survivor—of the 14 original gates in Berlin's old city wall. (This one led to the neighboring city of Brandenburg.) The majestic four-horse chariot on top is driven by the Goddess of Peace.

When Napoleon conquered Prussia in 1806, he took this statue to the Louvre in Paris. Then, after the Prussians defeated Napoleon, they got it back (in 1813)...and the Goddess of Peace was renamed the "Goddess of Victory."

The gate straddles the major east-west axis of the city. The western segment—behind you—stretches four miles, running through Tiergarten Park to the Olympic Stadium. To the east—on the other side of the gate—the street is called Unter den Linden. That's where we're headed. In the distance (if you jockey for position), you can see the red-and-white spire of the TV Tower that marks the end of Berlin's main axis.

The Berlin Wall: The Basics

West Berlin was a 185-square-mile island of capitalism surrounded by East Germany. Between the establishment of the DDR (East Germany) in 1949 and construction of the Berlin Wall in 1961, an estimated three million East Germans emigrated (fled) to freedom. To stanch their population loss, the DDR erected the 96-mile-long "Anti-Fascist Protective Rampart" almost overnight, beginning on August 13, 1961.

The Berlin Wall (*Berliner Mauer*) was actually two walls. The outer was a 12-foot-high concrete barrier topped with barbed wire and a rounded, pipe-like surface to discourage grappling hooks. The inner wall was lower-profile. Sandwiched between was a no-man's-land ("death strip") between 30 and 160 feet wide.

There were eight points where you could legally cross between West and East Berlin, the most famous of which were Checkpoint Charlie and the Friedrichstrasse train station, with its so-called "Palace of Tears". In general, Westerners could temporarily enter the East, but not vice-versa.

Even after the Wall went up, people continued to try to escape. During the Wall's 28 years, there were about 5,000 documented successful escapes—and 565 of those were East German guards. An estimated 136 people were killed at the Wall while trying to escape. Meanwhile, living in West Berlin—surrounded by concrete, barbed wire, and enemy soldiers armed to the teeth—was no picnic.

The Berlin Wall came to symbolize the larger Cold War between East and West. President John F. Kennedy gave a speech of solidarity in West Berlin, declaring, *"Ich bin ein Berliner"*—I am a Berliner. A generation later, President Ronald Reagan stood in front of the Brandenburg Gate and demanded of his Soviet counterpart, "Mr. Gorbachev, tear down this wall."

Finally, one November night in 1989, the Berlin Wall came down, as suddenly as it went up.

Historically, the Brandenburg Gate was just another of this city's many stately Prussian landmarks. But in our lifetime, it became *the* symbol of Berlin—of its Cold War division and its reunification. That's because, from 1961 to 1989, the gate was stranded in the no-man's land between East and West. For an entire generation, scores of German families were divided—some on this side of the Wall, some on the other. This landmark stood tantalizingly close to both East and West...but was off-limits to all.

By the 1980s, it was becoming clear that the once-mighty Soviet empire was slowly crumbling from within. Finally, on November 9, 1989, the world rejoiced at the sight of happy Berliners standing atop the Wall. They chipped away at it with hammers, passed beers to their long-lost cousins on the other side, and adorned the Brandenburg Gate with flowers like a parade float. Six weeks later, on December 22, West German Chancellor Helmut Kohl led a triumphant procession through the Brandenburg Gate to shake hands with his (soon-to-be-defunct) East German counterpart—the literal opening of a big gateway that marked the symbolic closing of a heinous era.

• *Turn 180 degrees and take in the vast, green expanse of the park called...*

❺ Tiergarten

Look down the long boulevard (Strasse des 17. Juni) that bisects the 500-acre park called Tiergarten ("Animal Garden"). The boulevard's name comes from the 17th of June, 1953, when brave East Germans rose up against their communist leaders. The rebellion was crushed, and East Berliners had to wait another 36 years for the freedom to walk through the Brandenburg Gate. In the distance is the 220-foot **Victory Column,** topped with a golden statue that commemorates the three big military victories that established Prussia as a world power in the late 1800s—over France, Denmark, and Austria—and kicked off Berlin's golden age. (For more on Tiergarten and the Victory Column, see page 824.)

• *Walk through the Brandenburg Gate, entering what for years was forbidden territory. Just past the gate, there's a small TI on the right, and on the left is the Room of Silence, dedicated to meditation. As you cross through this historic but long forbidden gate, you enter a grand square known as...*

❻ Pariser Platz

Pariser Platz marks the start of Unter den Linden, the broad boulevard that stretches before you. "Parisian Square" was so named after the Prussians defeated France and Napoleon in 1813. The square was once filled with important government buildings, but all were bombed to smithereens in World War II. For decades, it was an unrecognizable, deserted no man's-land, cut off from both East and West by the Wall. But now it's rebuilt, and the banks and hotels that were here before the bombing have reclaimed their original places, with a few modern additions. And the winners of World War II—the US, France, Great Britain, and Russia—continue to enjoy this prime real estate: Their embassies are all on or near this square.

The **US Embassy** (on the right as you come through the gate) reopened here in its original location on July 4, 2008. To the left of the US Embassy is the **DZ Bank Building**, built as a conference center in 2001 by Canadian-American architect Frank Gehry (its low-profile exterior was designed so as not to draw attention away from the Brandenburg Gate). To get your fix of wild and colorful Gehry, step into the building's lobby. The undulating interior is like a big, slithery fish.

Two doors past the bank is the ritzy **Hotel Adlon.** Over the years, this place has hosted celebrities and VIPs from Charlie Chaplin to Albert Einstein. And yes, this was where pop star Michael Jackson shocked millions by dangling his infant son over the railing (from the second balcony up).

• *The most direct route to our next stop is by passing through the **Academy of Arts** (Akademie der Künst) building—it's between Hotel Adlon and the DZ Bank, at Pariser Platz 4. (If the Academy of Arts is closed, loop to the left, circling around the Hotel Adlon to Behrenstrasse.)*

Enter the glassy Academy of Arts (WC in basement) and head toward the back. Just past the ground-floor café (an oasis of calm) is the former office of Albert Speer, Hitler's chosen architect. Continue on, passing Speer's favorite statue, Prometheus (from around 1900). This is the kind of art that turned on Hitler: a strong, soldierly, vital man, defending the homeland.

As you exit out the back of the building, veer right on Behrenstrasse and cross the street. You'll wind up at our next stop, a sprawling field of stubby concrete pillars.

❼ Memorial to the Murdered Jews of Europe

This memorial consists of 2,711 coffin-shaped pillars covering an entire city block. More than 160,000 Jewish people lived in Berlin when Hitler took power. Tens of thousands fled, and many more were arrested, sent to nearby Sachsenhausen concentration camp and eventually murdered. The memorial remembers them and the other six million Jews who were killed by the Nazis during World War II. Completed in 2005 by the Jewish-American architect Peter Eisenman, this was the first formal, German-government-sponsored Holocaust memorial. Using the word "murdered" in the title was intentional, and a big deal. Germany, as a nation, was admitting to a crime.

Inside the **information center** (in the far-left corner), exhibits trace the rise of Nazism and tell the victims' stories (for details on visiting the information center, see page 794).

• *At the far-left corner, a little beyond the information center, you eventually emerge on the street corner. Our next stop is about a block farther. Carefully jaywalk across Hannah-Arendt-Strasse and continue straight (south) down Gertrud-Kolmar-Strasse. On the left side of the street, you'll reach a rough parking lot. At the far end of the lot is an information plaque labeled* Führerbunker. *This marks the...*

❽ Site of Hitler's Bunker

You're standing atop the buried remains of the *Führerbunker*. In early 1945, as Allied armies advanced on Berlin and Nazi Germany lay in ruins, Hitler and his staff retreated to this bunker complex behind the former Reich Chancellery. He stayed here for two months.

It was here, on April 30, 1945—as the Soviet army tightened its noose on the Nazi capital—that Hitler and Eva Braun, his wife of less than 48 hours, committed suicide. A week later, the war in Europe was over. The in-

formation board here explains the rest of the story. Though the site of Hitler's bunker is part of history, there really isn't much to see here. And that's on purpose. No one wants to turn Hitler's final stronghold into a tourist attraction.

• *Backtrack up Gertrud-Kolmar-Strasse, and turn right on Hannah-Arendt-Strasse. Take your first left (at the traffic light) on...*

❾ Wilhelmstrasse

This street was the traditional center of the German power, beginning back when Germany first became a nation in the 19th century. It was lined with stately palaces housing foreign embassies and government offices. This was the home of the Reich Chancellery, where the nation's chief executive presided. When the Nazis took control, this street was where Hitler waved to his adoring fans, and where Joseph Goebbels had his Ministry of Propaganda.

During World War II, Wilhelmstrasse was the nerve center of the German war command. From here, Hitler directed the war and ordered the Blitz (the air raids that destroyed much of London). As the war turned to the Allies' side, Wilhelmstrasse and the neighborhood around it were heavily bombed. Most of the stately palaces were destroyed, and virtually nothing historic survives today.

• *The pedestrianized part of the street is home to the **British Embassy**. The fun purple color of its wall represents the colors of the Union Jack mixed together. Wilhelmstrasse spills out onto Berlin's main artery, the tree-lined Unter den Linden, next to the Hotel Adlon.*

⑩ Unter den Linden

This boulevard, worth ▲▲, is the heart of imperial Germany. During Berlin's Golden Age in the late 1800s, this was one of Europe's grand boulevards—the Champs-Elysées of Berlin, a city of nearly two million people. It was lined with linden trees, so as you promenaded down, you'd be walking *"unter den Linden."* The street got its start in the 15th century as a way to connect the royal palace (a half-mile down the road, at the end of this walk) with the king's hunting grounds (today's big Tiergarten Park, out past the Brandenburg Gate). Over the centuries, aristocrats moved into this area so their palaces could be close to their king's.

Many of the grandest landmarks we'll pass along here are thanks to Frederick the Great, who ruled from 1740 to 1786, and put his kingdom (Prussia) and his capital (Berlin) on the map. We'll also see a few signs of modern times; after World War II, this part of Berlin fell under Soviet influence, and Unter den Linden was the main street of communist East Berlin.

• *Turn your attention to the subway stop in front of the Hotel Adlon (labeled Brandenburger Tor). We'll enter the station and reemerge a block or so farther down the boulevard.*

⑪ Brandenburger Tor S-Bahn Station

For a time-travel experience back to DDR days, head down the stairs into this station (no ticket necessary). Keep to the right as you descend (toward the S-Bahn, not the U-Bahn) to the subway tracks. As you walk along the platform about 200 yards, survey the historic black-and-white photos on the walls and feel the 1950s vibe of the station.

For decades, the Brandenburger Tor S-Bahn station was un-used—one of Berlin's "ghost stations." While you're down under, notice how mid-20th-century the station still looks. There's the original 1930s green tilework on the walls, and harsh fluo-rescent lighting. Some old signs (on the central ki-osks) still have *Unter den Linden* (the original name of this stop) written in old

Gothic lettering. During the Cold War, the zigzag line dividing East and West Berlin meant that some existing train lines crossed the border underground. To make a little hard Western cash, the East German government allowed a few trains to cut under East Berlin on their way between Western destinations. The only catch: No one could get on or off while the train was in East Berlin. For 28 years, stations like this were unused, as Western trains slowly passed through, and passengers saw only East German guards... and lots of cobwebs. Then, in 1989, within days of the fall of the Wall, these stations were reopened.

• *At the far end of the platform, ascend the escalator, bear right, and head up the stairs to exit. You'll emerge on the right side of Unter den Linden. Belly up to the bars and look in at the...*

⑫ Russian Embassy

Built from the ashes of World War II, this imposing building—it's Europe's largest embassy—made it clear to East Berliners who was now in charge: the Soviet Union. It was the first big postwar building project in East Berlin, built in the powerful, simplified Neoclassical style that Stalin liked. Standing here, imagine Unter den Linden as a depressing Cold War-era cul-de-sac, dead-ending at the walled-off Brandenburg Gate. After the fall of the Soviet Union in 1991, this building became the Russian Embassy, flying the white, blue, and red flag. Find the hammer-and-sickle motif decorating the window frames—a reminder of the days when Russia was part of the USSR.

• *Keep walking down the boulevard for two blocks. You'll pass blocks of dull banks, tacky trinket shops, and a few high-end boutiques, eventu-ally reaching cultural buildings—the university, the opera, and so on. That's intentional: The Prussian kings wanted to have culture closer to their palace. Pause when you reach the intersection with...*

⓭ Friedrichstrasse

You're standing at perhaps the most central crossroads in Berlin—named for, you guessed it, Frederick the Great. Before World War II, Friedrichstrasse was the heart of cultural Berlin. In the Roaring Twenties, it was home to anything-goes nightlife and cabarets where entertainers like Marlene Dietrich, Bertolt Brecht, and Josephine Baker performed. And since the fall of the Wall, it's become home to supersized department stores and big-time hotels.

Consider popping into the grand **Galeries Lafayette** department store (two blocks down to your right). Inside, you can ogle a huge glass-domed atrium—a miniature version of the Reichstag cupola. There's a WC and a handy designer food court in the basement—which you can see below the cupola viewpoint. (Note: If you were to continue down Friedrichstrasse from here, you'd wind up at **Checkpoint Charlie** in about 10 minutes.)

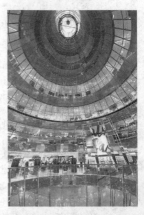

• *We've reached the end of Part 1 of this walk. This is a good place to take a break, if you'd like, and tackle Part 2 another time. But if you're up for ambling on, head down Unter den Linden a few more blocks, past the large equestrian statue of Frederick the Great, who ruled as king of Prussia in the mid-1700s. He turned his capital, Berlin, into a world-class city. Frederick is pointing east, toward the epicenter of Prussian imperial power, where his royal palace once stood. We're now entering the stretch of Unter den Linden that best represents Frederick's legacy.*

Turn right into Bebelplatz.

PART 2: BEBELPLATZ TO ALEXANDERPLATZ

• *Head to the center of the square, and find the square of glass window set into the pavement. We'll begin with some history and a spin tour, then consider the memorial below our feet.*

⓮ Bebelplatz: Square of the Books

Frederick the Great built this square to show off Prussian ideals: education, the arts, improvement of the individual, and a tolerance for different groups—provided they were committed to the betterment of society. This square was the cultural center of Frederick's capital. In many ways, it still is. Spin counterclockwise to take in the cultural sights, some of which date back to Frederick's time.

Start by looking across Unter den Linden. That's **Humboldt University,** one of Europe's greatest. Continue panning left. Fronting Bebelplatz is the **former state library**—which was funded by Frederick the Great. After the library was damaged in World War II, communist authorities decided to rebuild it in the original style...but only because Lenin studied here during much of his exile from Russia. The square's far end is marked by one of Berlin's swankiest lodgings—**Hotel de Rome,** housed in a historic bank building. Their trendy rooftop bar is a treat in good weather.

Next, the green-domed structure is **St. Hedwig's Church** (nicknamed the "Upside-Down Teacup"). It stands as a symbol of Frederick the Great's reli-

gious and cultural tolerance. The pragmatic king wanted to encourage the integration of Catholic Silesians into Protestant Prussia.

Up next is the **Berlin State Opera** *(Staatsoper)*—originally established in Frederick the Great's time. Frederick believed that the arts were essential to having a well-rounded populace. He moved the opera house from inside the castle to this showcase square.

Look down through the glass window in the pavement at what appears to be a room of empty bookshelves. This **book-burning memorial** commemorates a notorious event that took place here during the Nazi years. It was on this square in 1933 that staff and students from the university built a bonfire. Into the flames they threw 20,000 newly forbidden books—books authored by the likes of Einstein, Hemingway, Freud, and T. S. Eliot. Overseeing it all was the Nazi propaganda minister, Joseph Goebbels. Hitler purposely chose this square—built by Frederick the Great to embody culture and enlightenment—to symbolically demonstrate that the era of tolerance and openness was over.

• *Leave Bebelplatz toward Unter den Linden, cross to the university side, and continue heading east down Unter den Linden. You'll pass in front of Humboldt University's main gate. Immediately in front of the gate, embedded in the cobbles, notice the row of square, bronze plaques—each one bearing the name of a university student who was executed by the Nazis. You'll see similar* Stolpersteine *("stumbling stones") all over Berlin. Just beyond the university on the left, head for a building that looks like a Greek temple set in a small park filled with chestnut trees.*

⓯ Neue Wache

The "New Guardhouse" was built in 1816 as just that—a fancy barracks for the bodyguards assigned to the Hohenzollern palace just ahead (it's the Neoclassical building across the street, with four tall columns marking the doorway). Over the years, the Neue Wache has been transformed into a memorial for fallen warriors. Check out the pediment over the doorway: The goddess of Victory stands in the center amid the chaos of war, as soldiers fall.

The Neue Wache represents the strong, united, rising Prussian state Frederick created. It was just one of the grand new buildings built to line this stretch of Unter den Linden. The style was Neoclassical—structures that looked like Greek temples, with columns and triangular pediments.

Step inside. In 1993, the austere interior was fitted with the statue we see today—a replica of *Mother with Her Dead Son*, by Käthe Kollwitz, a Berlin artist who lived through both world wars. It marks the tombs of Germany's unknown soldier and an unknown concentration camp victim. The inscription reads, "To the victims of war and tyranny." (It's complicated to honor your war dead when you started and lost a great  war...or two. But you can honor the victims of your tyrant—both foreign and domestic.) The memorial, open to the sky, incorporates the elements—sunshine, rain, snow—falling on this modern-day pietà.

• *Continue down Unter den Linden, passing by the pink yet formidable Zeughaus (early 1700s), the oldest building on the boulevard. Built in the Baroque style as the royal arsenal, it later became a military museum, and today houses the excellent* **German History Museum** *(see page 803). When you reach the bridge, cross the Spree and step onto Museum Island.*

⓰ Museum Island and Former City Palace

This island, sitting in the middle of the Spree River, is Berlin's historic birthplace. Take in the scene: the lazy river, the statues along the bridge, and the impressive buildings all around you.

Berlin was born on this marshy island around the year 1200. As the city grew, this island remained the site of the ruler's castle and residence—from Brandenburg dukes and Hohenzollern prince-electors, to the kings of Prussia and the kaisers of the German Empire. At its peak under Prussian rulers (1701-1918), it was a splendid and sprawling Baroque palace called the Stadtschloss, topped at one end with a dome (as you see on the right side of Unter den Linden). It was considered the most important secular Baroque building north of the Alps.

After World War I, the last Prussian ruler was deposed, and the palace was gutted in a 1945 air raid in the last days of World War II. In 1950, the East Germans erected in its place the Palace of the Republic—a massive, blocky parliament building. In the early 21st century, that communist building was demolished, and for years this entire city block was a vacant lot—just a big grassy park.

Now, at great expense, Germany has rebuilt a palace on the site, creating the **Humboldt Forum,** a huge public space for business, a museum of art and artifacts from diverse cultures, and a place of higher education. The open "piazza" courtyard inside helps give it a community feel. This "palace for all" (which may be open by 2020) complements the cultural offerings on Museum Island, rounding out what this central place brings to Berlin.

The main facade fits beautifully with the Neoclassical architecture along Unter den Linden. The side facing the Spree River, however—in a nod to those feeling a little "Ost-algia"—has the stern functionalism of the Palace of the Republic from DDR days. On the back side, a round turret even harkens back to the original medieval fortress.

• *Now, turn your attention to the left side of Unter den Linden. There's a spacious garden, bordered on two sides by impressive buildings.*

Museum Island Sights

For 300 years, the **Lustgarten** has flip-flopped between being a military parade ground and a people-friendly park, depending on the political tenor of the time. In the Nazi era, Hitler enjoyed giving speeches here—from the top of the museum steps overlooking this square. At the far end of the Lustgarten is a cache of grandiose museum buildings that represent the can-do German spirit of the 1800s, when city leaders envisioned the island as an oasis of culture and learning. Today, these impressive buildings host five grand museums. The **Altes Museum** houses classical antiquities. Just beyond are the **Neues Museum** (Egyptian, prehistoric, and classical antiquities), the **Pergamon Museum** (classical antiquities), the **Old National Gallery** (German Romantic painting), and the **Bode Museum** (Byzantine art and mosaics).

Dominating the island is the towering, green-domed **Berlin Cathedral** (Berliner Dom). This is only a century old, built during the reign of Kaiser Wilhelm II—that jingoistic emperor in the spiked helmet who led Europe into World War I. The Wilhelmian style is over the top: a garish mix of Neoclassical, Neo-Baroque, and Neo-Renaissance, with rippling stucco and gold-tiled mosaics.

The church is at its most impressive from the outside. To see the extravagant interior and climb the dome (270 steps, sweeping views), you can pay the pricey admission (for details on visiting, see page 802).

• *Continue down Unter den Linden past the cathedral, and pause on the bridge over the Spree. Look left, past the cathedral.*

BERLIN

⓱ Spree River

The Spree River is people-friendly and welcoming. A parklike promenade leads all the way from here to the Hauptbahnhof.

Along it, you'll find impromptu "beachside" beer gardens with imported sand, BBQs in pocket parks, and lots of locals walking their dogs, taking a lazy bike ride, or jogging. Spree River boat tours depart from near here (for details, see page 766).

• *From here you could return to Museum Island to see the sights there or backtrack to the German History Museum. But we'll continue toward the TV Tower and Alexanderplatz (where this walk ends). Cross the bridge and find the* **statues of Marx and Engels,** *at the river-end of the big park. Note that as the boulevard crosses the river, Unter den Linden becomes Karl-Liebknecht-Strasse.*

⓲ Statues of Karl Marx and Friedrich Engels

These statues of the founders of Communism mark the Marx-Engels-Forum, a park dedicated in 1986 by the East German govern-

ment. During the heady days before the Berlin Wall and the Iron Curtain fell, a half-million Berliners gathered here to call for freedom and an end to the economic and social experiment preached by these two philosophers.

Marx and Engels were economists who studied at Berlin's Humboldt University in the early 1800s. They co-authored the landmark *Communist Manifesto* (1948), which ends with the famous line, "Workers of the world, unite!" Preoccupied with the "class struggle" through history—between the haves (bourgeoisie) and the have-nots (proletariat)—Marx and Engels believed that everyday working people should take control of the means of production. Over the next decades, Marx and Engel's ideas proved enormously influential. They caught on with a Russian named Vladimir Lenin. In 1917, Lenin led the Bolshevik Revolution that toppled the Russian czar and established the communist Soviet Union (USSR). Three decades later, Lenin's successor Josef Stalin sent the Red Army into Germany to defeat Hitler and the Nazis. After the war, the USSR occupied the eastern half of Germany and established a communist state: the DDR.

• *From here, with your back to the river, angle through the park veering left, in the direction of the TV Tower. As you emerge from the park and hit Spandauer Strasse, look right to see the red-brick* **city hall,** *where Berlin's mayor has an office. It was built after the revolutions of 1848 and was arguably the first democratic building in the city. Later it became the city hall of communist East Berlin—giving its nickname, "Rotes Rathaus" (Red City Hall), a dual meaning. At the intersection, a cute DDR-era* Ampelmännchen *("little traffic-light man") street light will tell you to stop or walk.*

Cross Spandauer Strasse. To your left is...

⑲ Karl-Liebknecht-Strasse and *Plattenbau*

This street is named for a founder of Germany's communist party: Karl Liebknecht, a martyr to the Marxist cause, and reminder of the communist regime. As you continue walking toward the TV Tower, notice the uniformity of the high-rise concrete buildings lining the boulevard to your left. These are *Plattenbau* ("panel buildings"). While the DDR government maintained a few token historic landmarks (like the Rotes Rathaus), their real architectural forte was prefabricated, high-capacity, low-aesthetics housing.

While the buildings' exteriors and public spaces are frightfully gloomy, residents prided themselves on creating cozy and welcoming little nests inside. Being invited to dinner at one of these apartments in DDR times showed you the stark contrast between cold, paranoid public life and colorful, gregarious private life. In their own homes, people could pursue hobbies and spend time with family.

• *Head for the old church up on the right.*

⑳ Martin Luther Statue and Marien Church

Approaching the church, you see a bold statue of **Martin Luther.** Marien Church, like the rest of Europe, was Roman Catholic until about 500 years ago when this solitary German monk rocked European history by kicking off the Protestant Reformation.

The **Marien Church,** with its prominent steeple, dates from 1270. Just inside the church, an artist's rendering helps you follow the interesting but very faded old "Dance of Death" mural that wraps around the narthex (dating from about 1470, the generation before Luther). The church's whitewashed interior is austere, with heavy oak pews. While originally Roman Catholic (like all churches in Europe before the Reformation), Marien Church has been Lutheran for about 500 years. In true Protestant style, the interior is dominated by the pulpit (for Protestants, it's all about the word of God) and the pipe organ (Luther said, "When you sing, you pray double").

• *Across the street and a half-block down is another Berlin memorial that's worth a detour—the* **Women's Protest Memorial***. It commemorates a courageous—and unusually successful—protest by the Gentile wives of Jewish men who were arrested by the Nazis. Remarkably, these brave women actually won the freedom of their husbands.*

Otherwise, gaze up at the 1,200-foot-tall...

㉑ TV Tower (Fernsehturm)

The communist regime is long gone, but it left this enduring legacy. The TV Tower—built in 1969 to celebrate the 20th anniversary of communist East Germany—was meant to show the power of the atheistic state at a time when DDR leaders were removing crosses from the country's church domes and spires. But when the sun hit the tower, the reflected light created a huge, bright cross on the mirrored ball. Cynics called it "The Pope's Revenge." East Berliners joked that if the TV tower fell over, they'd have an elevator to freedom in the West. (For a steep price you can ride to the top for a grand view.)

• *Return to the church side of the boulevard and continue walking east down Karl-Liebknecht-Strasse, passing the TV Tower on your right. You'll cross under a railway overpass, then walk alongside a mall called Galeria Kaufhof. Just past the mall, turn right onto a broad pedestrian street. It leads through a low tunnel and into a big square, surrounded by modern buildings. The blue U-Bahn station signs announce you've arrived at...*

㉒ Alexanderplatz

Alexanderplatz was built in 1805, during the Prussian Golden Age. Because this was a gateway for trade to Eastern Europe, it was named for a Russian czar, Alexander. In the Industrial Age, it became a transportation hub. In the roaring 1920s, it was a center of cabaret nightlife to rival Friedrichstrasse. And under the DDR, it was transformed into a commercial center. This was the pride and joy of East Berlin shoppers.

And then, on November 4, 1989, more than a half-million East Berliners gathered on Alexanderplatz to demand their freedom. Protesters chanted, *"Wir wollen raus!* We want out!" The winds of change were in the air; a week later, the Berlin Wall was history.

Today's square is a mix of old and new. Stand just beyond the first U-Bahn station entrance for the best view. Take a 360-degree, clockwise spin-tour—starting with Galeria Kaufhof, to the right of the TV Tower. In communist times, the Kaufhof department store was the ultimate shopping mecca...which wasn't saying much. In front is an abstract-sculpture fountain ringed with a colorful base that attracts sitters. Next, the tall, glassy skyscraper is a DDR-era hotel, now called the Park Inn. Primark, next door, is a major European discount clothing chain. If you see lots of young shoppers here, it's because of Primark.

Continuing clockwise past the Saturn electronics store and the colorful Kandinsky-esque Alexa building, notice the once-futuristic **World Time Clock,** a nostalgic favorite installed in 1969 that remains a popular meeting point.

• *We've seen Berlin go from a royal empire to a fascist state, from a country divided by communism to a center of democracy and capitalism, all in the space of one walk. From here, you can hike back a bit to catch the Spree riverboat tour, visit Museum Island or the German History Museum, venture into the colorful Prenzlauer Berg neighborhood, or extend your foray into eastern Berlin by way of Karl-Marx-Allee. These options are covered in detail in the next section.*

Alexanderplatz is a convenient transportation hub to the rest of Berlin. Or you can take bus #100 or #200 back along Karl-Liebknecht-Strasse and on to Unter den Linden.

Sights in Central Berlin (The Historic Core)

Much of Berlin's sightseeing is concentrated in this central strip, stretching over a mile-long corridor from the Tiergarten Park to Museum Island.

REICHSTAG AND BRANDENBURG GATE AREA
This area is covered in more detail in my "Berlin City Walk" (earlier; also available as a free 🎧 audio tour).

▲▲▲Reichstag
Germany's historic parliament building—completed in 1894, burned in 1933, sad and lonely in a no-man's-land throughout the Cold War, and finally rebuilt and topped with a glittering glass cupola in 1999—is a symbol of a proudly reunited nation. Visit here to

spiral up the remarkable dome and gaze across Berlin's rooftops, and to watch today's parliament in action. Because of security concerns, you'll need a reservation and your passport to enter.

Cost and Hours: Free, reservations required—see below, daily 8:00-24:00, last entry at 22:00, metal detectors, no big luggage allowed, Platz der Republik 1; S- or U-Bahn: Friedrichstrasse, Brandenburger Tor, or Bundestag.

Information: Tel. 030/2273-2152, www.bundestag.de.

Advance Tickets: You must make a free reservation. It's easy to do online, but book early—spots often book up several days in advance. Go to www.bundestag.de, and from the "Visit the Bundestag" menu, select "Online registration." You have two choices: "Visit to the dome" includes a good audioguide and is plenty for most; the 90-minute guided tour provides more in-depth information. After choosing your preferred date and time, you'll be sent an email link to a website where you'll enter details for each person in your party. A final email will contain your reservation (with a letter you must print out or download to your mobile device).

Without a Reservation: Tickets may be available even when online sales are "sold out"—inquire at the tiny visitors center on the Tiergarten side of Scheidemannstrasse, across from Platz der Republik (daily 8:00-20:00, until 18:00 Nov-March; bookings from 3 hours to 2 days in advance, go early to avoid lines). When booking, the whole party must be present and passports are required.

Another option is to have lunch or dinner at the pricey rooftop restaurant, **$$$$ Käfer Dachgarten** (daily 9:00-16:30 & 18:30-24:00, last access at 22:00, reserve well in advance at tel. 030/2262-9933 or www.feinkost-kaefer.de/berlin).

Getting In: Report 15 minutes before your appointed time to the temporary-looking entrance facility in front of the Reichstag, and be ready to show your passport and confirmation letter. After passing through a security check, you'll wait with other visitors for a guard to take you to the Reichstag entrance.

Visiting the Reichstag: The open, airy **lobby** towers 100 feet high, with 65-foot-tall colors of the German flag. See-through glass doors show the central legislative chamber. The message: There will be no secrets in this government. Look inside. Spreading his wings behind the podium is a stylized German eagle, the *Bundestagsadler* (affectionately nicknamed the "Fat Hen"), representing the Bundestag (each branch of government has its own symbolic eagle). Notice the doors marked *Ja* (Yes), *Nein* (No), and *Enthalten* (Abstain)...an homage to the Bundestag's traditional "sheep jump" way of counting votes by exiting the chamber through the corresponding door. (For critical votes, however, they vote with electronic cards.)

Germany's Bundestag (comparable to the US House of Representatives) meets here. Its 631 members are elected to four-year terms. They in turn elect the chancellor. Unlike America's two-party system, Germany has a handful of significant parties, so they must form coalitions to govern effectively. Bundestag members have offices in the building to the left of the Reichstag.

Ride the elevator to the base of the **glass dome** (where you'll pick up the *Berlin Panorama* flier and your audioguide). The dome is 80 feet high, 130 feet across, and weighs a quarter of a million pounds. It uses about 33,000 square feet of glass, or nearly enough to cover a football field.

Study the photos and read the circle of captions (around the base of the central funnel) telling the Reichstag story. Then study the surrounding architecture: a broken collage of new on old, torn between antiquity and modernity, like Germany's history. Notice the dome's giant and unobtrusive sunscreen that moves as necessary with the sun. Peer down through the

skylight to look over the shoulders of the elected representatives at work. For Germans, the best view from here is down—keeping a close eye on their government.

Walking up the **ramp,** you'll spiral past 360-degree views of the city, including the Tiergarten, the "green lungs of Berlin"; the Teufelsberg ("Devil's Hill"; famous during the Cold War as a powerful ear of the West—notice the telecommunications tower on top); Potsdamer Platz, the Brandenburg Gate; Frank Gehry's fishlike roof of the DZ Bank building; the Memorial to the Murdered Jews of Europe; the former East Berlin, with a forest of 300-foot-tall skyscrapers in the works; Berlin's huge main train station; and the blocky, postmodern Chancellery, the federal government's headquarters (the audioguide explains what you're seeing as you walk).

▲▲Memorials near the Reichstag

The area immediately surrounding the Reichstag is rich with memorials. Within a few steps, you'll find monuments to politicians

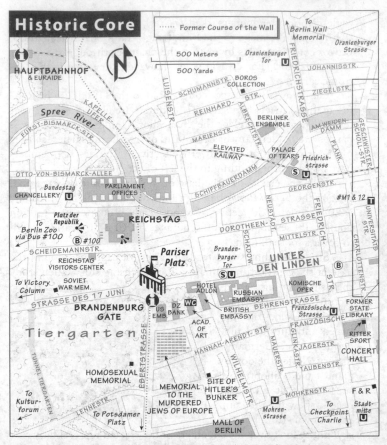

Historic Core

...... Former Course of the Wall

500 Meters
500 Yards

To Berlin Wall Memorial
Oranienburger Strasse
Oranienburger Tor
JOHANNISSTR.
FRIEDRICHSTRASSE
ZIEGELSTR.
GESCHWISTER-SCHOLL-STR.

HAUPTBAHNHOF & EURAIDE
LUISENSTR.
SCHUMANNSTR.
BOROS COLLECTION
REINHARD-STR.
ALBRECHTSTR.
BERLINER ENSEMBLE
AM-WEIDENDAMM
PLANCK

Spree River
KAPELLE-UFER
FÜRST-BISMARCK-STR.
MARIENSTR.
ELEVATED RAILWAY
PALACE OF TEARS
Friedrichstrasse
SCHIFFBAUERDAMM
NEUSTADT-STRASSE
GEORGENSTR.
#M1 & 12

OTTO-VON-BISMARCK-ALLEE
Bundestag
CHANCELLERY
PARLIAMENT OFFICES
DOROTHEEN-
MITTELSTR.
FRIEDRICH-STR.
UNIVERSITÄTS-STR.

Platz der Republik
To Berlin Zoo via Bus #100
SCHEIDEMANNSTR.
REICHSTAG VISITORS CENTER
(B) #100
REICHSTAG
Pariser Platz
Brandenburger Tor
SCHADOW
UNTER DEN LINDEN
CHARLOTTENSTR.

To Victory Column
SOVIET WAR MEM.
STRASSE DES 17 JUNI
BRANDENBURG GATE
HOTEL ADLON
US. EMB.
DZ BANK
WC
RUSSIAN EMBASSY
BRITISH EMBASSY
BEHRENSTRASSE
KOMISCHE OPER
Französische Strasse
FORMER STATE LIBRARY

Tiergarten
TUNNEL TIERGARTEN
ACAD. OF ART
HANNAH-ARENDT-STR.
MAUERSTR.
GLINKASTR.
FRANZÖSISCHE
JÄGERSTR.
RITTER SPORT
CONCERT HALL

To Kulturforum
HOMOSEXUAL MEMORIAL
LENNÉSTR.
EBERTSTRASSE
MEMORIAL TO THE MURDERED JEWS OF EUROPE
SITE OF HITLER'S BUNKER
WILHELMSTR.
TAUBENSTR.
MOHRENSTR.
Mohrenstrasse
To Checkpoint Charlie
Stadtmitte
F & R

To Potsdamer Platz
MALL OF BERLIN

who opposed Hitler and victims of the Berlin Wall (both described earlier, on the "Berlin City Walk").

In the park just behind the Berlin Wall Victims Memorial is the **Monument to the Murdered Sinti and Roma of Europe,** an opaque glass wall, with a timeline in English and German, commemorating the roughly 500,000 Holocaust victims who identified as "Sinti" and "Roma" (the main tribes and politically correct terms for the group often called "Gypsies"); these groups lost the same percentage of their population as the Jews.

Also in the park (in the opposite direction, toward the Victory Column) is the **Soviet War Memorial.** It honors the Soviet army soldiers who died in the bitter battle for Berlin, which brought World War II to a decisive conclusion.

Across the street from the Memorial to the Murdered Jews of Europe (described earlier, on the "Berlin City Walk"), tucked into a corner of the park, is the **Memorial to the Homosexuals Persecuted Under the National Socialist Regime.** Access it from

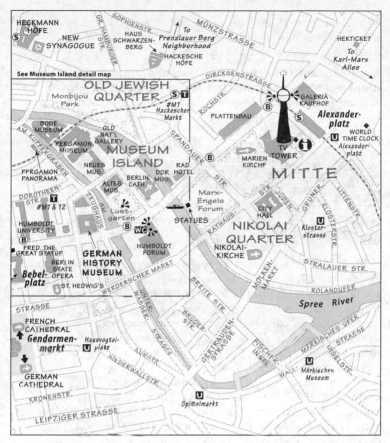

the Jewish memorial's southwest corner, across Ebertstrasse from Hannah-Arendt-Strasse. Through a small window, you can watch a film loop of same-sex couples kissing—a reminder that life and love are precious.

And finally, quite a bit farther south (in front of the philharmonic, facing the Tiergarten), is the **Memorial to the Victims of Nazi "Euthanasia."** Hitler sought to rid German society of people with physical and mental disabilities. Over time, the Nazis "euthanized" 300,000 German citizens.

▲▲▲Brandenburg Gate

The icon of Berlin, this majestic gateway has seen more than its share of history. Armies from Napoleon to Hitler have marched under its gilded statues, and for more than 25 years, it sat forlorn in the Berlin Wall's death strip. Today it's a symbol of Berlin's rejuvenated capital.

Just inside (east of) the Brandenburg gate is the tidy "Parisian

BERLIN

Square"—Pariser Platz. This prime real estate is ringed by governmental buildings, banks, historic plush hotels, the Academy of Arts, and the heavily fortified US Embassy.

▲▲Memorial to the Murdered Jews of Europe (Denkmal für die Ermordeten Juden Europas)

This labyrinth of 2,711 irregularly shaped pillars memorializes the

six million Jewish people who were executed by the Nazis. Loaded with symbolism, it's designed to encourage a pensive moment in the heart of a big city. Inside the **information center** (far-left corner), exhibits trace the rise of Nazism and how it led to World War II. Six portraits, representing the six million Jewish victims, put a human face on the numbers, as do diaries, letters, and final farewells penned by Holocaust victims. You'll learn about 15 Jewish families from very different backgrounds, who all met the same fate. A continually running soundtrack recites victims' names. To read them all aloud would take more than six and a half years.

Cost and Hours: Memorial—free and always open; information center—free, open Tue-Sun 10:00-20:00, Oct-March until 19:00, closed Mon year-round, last entry 45 minutes before closing, security screening at entry, audioguide-€3; S-Bahn: Brandenburger Tor or Potsdamer Platz, tel. 030/2639-4336, www.stiftung-denkmal.de.

UNTER DEN LINDEN
▲▲Strolling Unter den Linden

Berlin's main boulevard—"Under the Linden Trees"—has been the city's artery since the 15th century. Today, it's a well-tended place to stroll. This main drag and its sights are covered in my "Berlin City Walk" earlier (and also available as a free 🎧 audio tour).

Gendarmenmarkt

Berlin's finest square sits two blocks south of Unter den Linden (and one block south of Bebelplatz). The square, like its name ("Square of the Gens d'Armes," Frederick the Great's French guard), is a hybrid of Prussia and France. The square is bookended by two matching churches: the German Cathedral (with a free exhibit on the German parliamentary system) and the French Cathedral (dedicated to the French Huguenots who found refuge in Prussia). Gendarmenmarkt's centerpiece is the Concert Hall (Konzerthaus), commissioned by Frederick the Great and built by his favorite architect, Karl Friedrich Schinkel. In summer, Gendarmenmarkt hosts outdoor cafés, *Biergartens,* and occasional outdoor concerts.

MUSEUM ISLAND AREA

Filling a spit of land in the middle of the Spree River, Museum Island has perhaps Berlin's highest concentration of serious sightseeing. The island's centerpiece is the grassy square called Lustgarten, ringed by five museums and the hulking Berlin Cathedral.

This neighborhood is covered in more detail in my free ∩ Berlin City Walk audio tour. For cruises on the Spree River from near Museum Island, see "Tours in Berlin," earlier.

Museum Island (Museumsinsel)

Five of Berlin's top museums—featuring art and artifacts from around the world—are just a few steps apart on Museum Island.

Cost and Hours: Each museum has a separate admission (€10-19, includes audioguide). If you're visiting at least two museums here, get the €18 Museum Island Pass (which covers all 5; also consider the €29 Museum Pass Berlin—see page 759). The museums are open 10:00-18:00 (Thu until 20:00). The Pergamon and Neues museums are open daily; the Old National Gallery, Bode Museum, and Altes Museum are open Tue-Sun, closed Mon.

Information: Tel. 030/266-424-242, www.smb.museum.

Advance Tickets Recommended: To skip ticket-buying lines, purchase a timed ticket for the Pergamon or Neues Museum in advance at the museum website. If you have a Museum Island Pass or Museum Pass Berlin, you can book a free timed-entry reservation. The always-busy Pergamon is most crowded in the morning, on weekends, and when it rains; Thursday evenings are the least crowded.

Getting There: The island is a 10-minute walk from the Hackescher Markt or Friedrichstrasse S-Bahn stations. Trams #M1 and #12 connect to Prenzlauer Berg. Buses #100 and #200 run along Unter den Linden, stopping near the museums at the Lustgarten stop.

Expect Construction: A new visitors center (the James-Simon-Galerie) will connect the complex with tunnels, possibly by 2024.

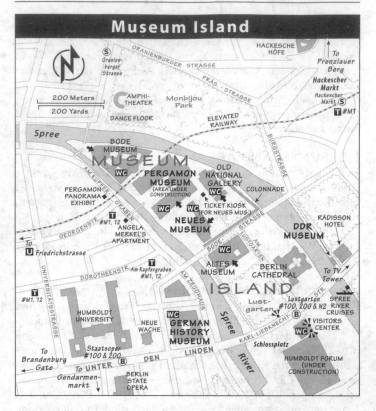

Museum Island

▲▲Pergamon Museum (Pergamonmuseum)

This world-class museum contains Berlin's Collection of Classical Antiquities (Antikensammlung)—in other words, full-sized build-ings from the most illustrious civilizations of the ancient world. Its namesake and high-light—the gigantic Pergamon Altar—is under renovation and off-limits to visitors until 2025 (a nearby pavilion hosts an exhibit about the altar—see the end of this listing). In the meantime, there's still plenty to see: the massive Babylonian

Processional Way and Ishtar Gate (slathered with glazed blue tiles, from the sixth century BC); artifacts from the Assyrians (7th-10th century BC); the full-sized market gate from the ancient Roman settlement of Miletus (first century BC); and, upstairs, an extensive collection of treasures from the Islamic world.

Visiting the Museum: The superb audioguide (included) helps broaden your experience. From the entry hall, head up to floor 1 and all the way back to 575 BC and Mesopotamia.

Processional Way and Ishtar Gate: The ruler Nebuchadnezzar II made sure that all who approached his city got a grand first impression. His massive blue Ishtar Gate stands 46 feet tall and 100 feet wide (counting its jutting facets). This was the grandest of Babylon's gates, one of eight in the 11-mile wall that encompassed this city of 200,000. In its day, the Ishtar Gate was famous—one of the original Seven Wonders of the World. All the pieces in this hall—the Ishtar Gate, Processional Way, and Throne Room panels—are made of decorative brick, glazed and fired in the ancient Egyptian faience technique. Decorations like the lions, which project outward from the surface, were carved or molded before the painted glaze went on. The colors—yellow, green, and blue (from rare lapis lazuli)—come from natural pigments, ground to a powder and mixed with melted silica (quartz). The chemicals bonded in the kiln fires, creating a sheen that's luminous, shiny, and even weather-resistant.

The museum's Babylonian treasures are meticulous reconstructions. After a Berlin archaeologist discovered the ruins in modern-day Iraq in 1900, the Prussian government financed their excavation. What was recovered was little more than piles of shattered shards of brick. It's since been augmented with modern tilework and pieced together like a 2,500-year-old Babylonian jigsaw puzzle. (You might peek into Room 6—if it's open—to see a model of Babylon.)

Assyrian Artifacts: The rooms at the opposite end of the Processional Way are filled with artifacts from the Babylonians' northern cousins, the Assyrians. Look for the Esarhaddon Stele, a ceremonial column marking the passing of the baton between the two great Mesopotamian powers, and the 10-foot-tall statue of the weather god Hadad. Browse through these rooms to get a sense of Assyrian grandeur, then return to the Ishtar Gate.

Market Gate of Miletus: You've flashed forward 700 years to ancient Miletus—the wealthy, cosmopolitan, Roman-ruled, and Greek-speaking city on the southwest coast of Asia Minor (modern Turkey). Dominating this room is the huge Market Gate of Miletus. This served as the entrance to the town's agora, or marketplace. Traders from across the Mediterranean and Middle East passed through the three arched doorways into a football-field-sized courtyard surrounded by arcades, where business was conducted.

Miletus was destroyed by an earthquake centuries ago. Around 1900, German archaeologists unearthed the rubble, and the gate was painstakingly reconstructed here in Berlin. This room also displays an exquisite mosaic floor of colored stone and glass

Pergamon Museum Tour

BABYLON
1. Processional Way
2. Ishtar Gate
3. Throne Room Facade (2)
4. Model of Babylon

ASSYRIA
5. Esarhaddon Stele

6. Statue of Hadad
7. More Assyrian Artifacts

ROME
8. Market Gate of Miletus
9. Model of Miletus
10. Orpheus Mosaic
11. Various Roman Artifacts

from the dining room of a Roman villa in Miletus, c. AD 200, and features the mythical Greek musician Orpheus.

The Rest of the Museum: To complete your tour of civilizations, on floor 1 you can see artifacts from several royal palaces of the Assyrian kings. Then find the stairs in front of the Ishtar Gate and head up to **floor 2,** which is dedicated to the **Museum of Islamic Art.** It demonstrates how—after Rome fell and Europe was mired in medievalism—the Islamic world carried the torch of civilization. The impressive Aleppo Room is illustrated with motifs from Christian, Arabic, Persian, and Jewish traditions.

What About the Pergamon Altar? The museum's name-

sake and most famous piece— the Pergamon Altar—is being stored out of view while the hall that houses it is slowly modernized. The altar likely won't be back until around 2025. (The "altar" is actually a temple, a masterpiece of Hellenistic art from the second century BC.) During the restoration, a special exhibit called *Pergamonmuseum—Das Panorama* is in a pavilion on Am Kupfergraben (directly across from Museum Island). The

BERLIN

main attraction here is a huge, wraparound panorama painting of the city of Pergamon in AD 129 by Berlin artist Yadegar Asisi. Some of the original sculpture from the altar, the largest piece of the altar frieze, and digital 3D models help visitors fill in the details (€19 combo-ticket with Pergamon Museum, €6 with Museum Island Pass or Museum Pass Berlin, open same hours as the museum).

▲▲Neues (New) Museum

This beautiful museum, featuring objects from the prehistoric (i.e., pre-Pergamon) world, contains three collections. Most visitors focus on the Egyptian Collection, with the stunning bust of Queen Nefertiti. But it's also worth a walk through the Museum of Prehistory and Early History and the Collection of Classical Antiquities (artifacts from ancient Troy). Everything is well-described in English (fine audioguide included with admission; for more on the museum, see www.neues-museum.de).

Visiting the Museum: The Neues Museum ticket desk is across the courtyard from the entrance. Ticket in hand, enter and pick up the floor plan. The main reason to visit is to enjoy one of the great thrills in art appreciation—gazing into the still young and beautiful face of Queen Nefertiti. If you're in a pinch for time, make a beeline to her (floor 2, far corner of Egyptian Collection in Room 210).

To tour the whole collection, start at the top (floor 3), the **prehistory section.** The entire floor is filled with Stone Age, Ice Age, and Bronze Age items. You'll see early human remains, tools, spearheads, and pottery.

The most interesting item on this floor (in corner of Room 305)—the tall, conehead-like **Golden Hat,** made of paper thin gold leaf—was likely worn by the priest of a sun cult popular among the Celtic people of central Europe around 1,000 BC. Admire the incredible workmanship of these prehistoric people. The hat, 30 inches tall, was hammered from a pound of gold into a single sheet of gold leaf less than a millimeter thick.

On floor 2, in a room all her own (Room 210), is the 3,000-year-old bust of **Queen Nefertiti,** wife of Akhenaton—the most famous piece of Egyptian art in Europe. Nefertiti has all the right beauty marks: long slender neck, perfect lips, almond eyes, symmetrical eyebrows, pronounced cheekbones, and a perfect spray-on tan. And yet, despite her seemingly perfect beauty,

Nefertiti has a touch of humanity. Notice the fine wrinkles around the eyes—these only enhance her beauty. She has a slight Mona Lisa smile, pursed at the corners.

The bust never left its studio, but served as a master model for all other portraits of the queen. (That's probably why the artist didn't bother putting the quartz inlay in the left eye.) Stare at her long enough, and you may get the sensation that she's winking at you.

Downstairs on level 1, make your way to Rooms 103-104. Text panels help explain the craze for antiquities that brought us the Neues Museum. Much of it can be traced to the man featured in these rooms: **Heinrich Schliemann** (1822-1890). Having read Homer's accounts of the Trojan War, Schliemann set out on a quest to find the long-lost ruins of the city of Troy. He (probably) found the capital of the Trojans (in Turkey), as well as the capital of the Greeks (Mycenae, in the Greek Peloponnese). Displays tell the fascinating story of how Schliemann smuggled the treasures out in fruit baskets, then their long journey until they were donated to the German government.

▲▲Old National Gallery (Alte Nationalgalerie)

Of Berlin's many top-notch art collections, this is the best for *German* art—mostly paintings from the 19th century, the era in which "German culture" first came to mean something. For a concise visit, focus on the Romantic German paintings (top floor), where Caspar David Friedrich's hauntingly beautiful canvases offer an insightful glimpse into German  landscapes...and the German psyche. With more time, peruse the French and German Impressionists and German Realists on the first and second floors.

Visiting the Museum: Start on the third floor and work your way down.

Casa Bartholdy Murals (Room 3.02): These frescoes tell the biblical story of Joseph. They were done by idealistic artists of the artistic brotherhood called the Nazarenes. It was the early 1800s, and the German people were searching for their unique national identity. In art, the Nazarenes were seeking a purer form of expression that was uniquely German. This almost religious fervor would inspire the next generation of German artists—the Romantics.

Karl Friedrich Schinkel (Room 3.05): Schinkel is best known as the Neoclassical architect who remade Berlin in the 1820s. But as a painter, Gothic cathedrals and castles dominate his scenes. Foliage grows over the buildings, and animals wander through. Nature rules. Where puny humans do appear, they are dwarfed by the landscape and buildings. Scenes are lit by a dramatic, eerie light, as though the world is charged from within by the power of God. Welcome to Romanticism.

Caspar David Friedrich (Room 3.06): The greatest German artist of the Romantic era was Caspar David Friedrich (1774-1840). A quick glance around this room gives you a sense of Friedrich's subjects: craggy mountains, twisted trees, ominous clouds, burning sunsets, and lone figures in the gloom. Rather than painting placid, pretty scenes as other landscape artists might, Friedrich celebrated Nature's awesome power. The few people he painted are tiny and solitary, standing with their backs to us. As they ponder the vastness of their surroundings, we're invited to see the world through their eyes, and to contemplate humankind's minuscule place in the grand scheme of things.

Biedermeier Style (Rooms 3.08-3.13): These rooms feature paintings in the so-called Biedermeier style (c. 1815-1848), the conservative flip side to Romanticism's individualism, turbulence, and political radicalism. Biedermeier landscapes are pretty, not dramatic. The style is soft-focus, hypersensitive, super-sweet, and sentimental. The poor are happy, the middle class are happy, and the world they inhabit is perfectly lit.

French Impressionists (Room 2.03): This one big room is lined with minor works by big-name French artists. Unlike the carefully composed, turbulent, and highly symbolic paintings of the German Romantics, these scenes appear like simple unposed "snapshots" of everyday life. Pan the room to see Renoir's pink-cheeked girls, Degas' working girls, Cézanne's fruit bowls, and Gauguin's Tahitian girls.

Rest of the Museum: In Room 2.14 are two well-known **portraits by Franz von Lenbach** of world-changing Germans: Otto von Bismarck (Germany's first prime minister) and the composer Richard Wagner.

Bode Museum

This fine building—at the northern tip of the island—contains a hodgepodge of collections: Byzantine art, historic coins, ecclesiastical art, sculptures, and medals commemorating the fall of the Berlin Wall and German

reunification. While this museum may be dull for casual sightseers, avid museumgoers find plenty to excite here—including the stunning Ravenna Mosaic, transplanted here from the Byzantine world of sixth-century Italy. For a free, quick look at its lavish interior, climb the grand staircase under a sweeping dome to the charming café on the first floor.

Altes (Old) Museum
Of the five Museum Island collections, this is the least exciting—unless you're an enthusiast of obscure Etruscan, Roman, and Greek art and artifacts.

Berlin Cathedral (Berliner Dom)
This bulky stone structure, with its rusted-copper dome, looms over Museum Island like the home church of a Prussian kaiser...because it was. It's a textbook example of Kaiser Wilhelm II's bigger-is-better aesthetic. While pricey to enter, the lavish interior has some fine details. The great reformers (Luther, Calvin, and company) stand around the brilliant dome  like stern saints guarding their theology. King Frederick I rests in an ornate tomb. Those who climb the 270 steps of the dome are rewarded with pleasant, breezy views of the city. The crypt downstairs is not worth your time.

Cost and Hours: €7 includes dome gallery access, not covered by Museum Island Pass, Mon-Sat 9:00-20:00, Sun from 12:00, daily until 19:00 Oct-March, closes around 17:30 on concert days, last entry one hour before closing, audioguide-€4, tel. 030/2026-9136, www.berliner-dom.de.

Humboldt Forum (Former Berlin Palace)
Communists replaced the Prussian palace on this site with a giant "brutalist" conference center. Now, that DDR-era building has been replaced with a cultural complex with a main facade that looks just like it did in the time of Frederick the Great. The new cultural center, called the Humboldt Forum, will be a huge public palace for business, culture, and higher education. By 2020, the forum should be open for business, including concerts under its dome (www.humboldtforum.com).

Near Museum Island
The German History Museum is on Unter den Linden, immediately west of Museum Island; and the DDR Museum is (fittingly)

just east of Museum Island, on the riverbank facing the back of the Berlin Cathedral. The Nikolai Quarter is a five-minute walk to the south, down the river (facing Museum Island).

▲▲▲German History Museum (Deutsches Historisches Museum)

This impressive museum offers the best look at German history under one roof, anywhere. The permanent collection packs 9,000 artifacts into two huge rectangular floors of the old arsenal building. You'll stroll through insightfully described historical objects, paintings, photographs, and models—all intermingled with multimedia stations. The 20th-century section—on the ground floor—is far better than any of the many price-gouging historical Nazi or Cold War "museums" all over town. A thoughtful visit here provides valuable context for your explorations of Berlin (and Germany).

Cost and Hours: €8, covered by Museum Pass Berlin, daily 10:00-18:00, worthwhile €3 audioguide, Unter den Linden 2.

Information: Tel. 030/2030-4751, www. dhm.de.

Getting There: It's immediately west of Museum Island (just across the river) at Unter den Linden 2. Buses #100, #200, and #TXL stop right in front (Staatsoper stop). By tram, the Am Kupfergraben stop (for trams #M1 and #12) is a block behind the museum. The nearest S-Bahn stops are Friedrichstrasse and Hackescher Markt, each about a 10-minute walk away.

Visiting the Museum: As you tour the collection, stay on track by locating the museum's historic chapters (pillars along the way marked with a date span) then browse the exhibits nearby. At the top of the stairs, consider taking 30 minutes for the dry but informative video on German history (with English subtitles).

First Floor (500-1918): This floor weaves its way through the centuries, with exhibits on early cultures, the Middle Ages, the Reformation, the Thirty Years' War, and the German Empire. Along the way you may see a medieval Saxon manuscript; a famous portrait along the right wall (by Albrecht Dürer) of Charlemagne, who was crowned "Holy Roman Emperor" in the year 800, uniting much of Europe into a Kingdom of the Franks—and marking the conversion of the Germans to Christianity; a portrait of Charles V, the most powerful Holy Roman Emperor, who ruled much of Europe during the Renaissance and Age of Discovery; and a copy of the 1492 globe Columbus used to plot his voyage (round and pretty accurate, except there's no America yet).

Several rooms are dedicated to the German monk Martin Luther, who in the 16th century shocked Europe with new and radical ideas, sparking the Protestant Reformation. You'll find a number of Luther artifacts, including the Edict of Worms (next to the portrait of Charles V), where Charles V condemned the Protestant heretic, and a Bible translated by Luther into everyday German. Luther's Bible helped to establish the "modern" German language spoken today (for more on Luther, see the Lutherland chapter).

Frederick the Great made Prussia (an area of northern Germany) a European power and Berlin a cultural capital. He brought the Age of Enlightenment to Germany. Science flourished (see scientific instruments) as did music (see early keyboards and a picture of the Mozart family). In the 1800s, Prussia took over Germany's destiny when Wilhelm I and his shrewd  prime minister, Otto von Bismarck (see their busts), used political wheeling-and-dealing and outright force to try to forge Germany's principalities and dukedoms together. In 1871, the German people united, and they waved an eagle flag (on display) of a new nation: Germany.

The handsome young ruler, Wilhelm II, reigned over a period of unprecedented wealth and prosperity. Germany was an industrial powerhouse, acquiring rich colonies in Africa and expanding its military might. Find the *Kaiser Panorama* display, with old photos of turn-of-the-century Berlin in its glory.

Ground Floor (20th Century): World War I pit Germany against France, England, and others. Photos show the grim reality of a war fought from defensive trenches, while posters (and a poignant woodcut by Berlin artist Käthe Kollwitz) capture the bitter and cynical mood that descended over Germany. By war's end, Germany had lost 1.7 million men, and 4 million came home wounded.

Europe's victors dealt harshly with Germany, sowing enormous resentment. In 1933, the Nazis took control of Germany under Adolf Hitler. Their propaganda convinced the German people that they were strong and good, but had been betrayed by a rigged system. To shore up support, Hitler appealed to Germans' sense of national and ethnic pride. He preached about the *Volksgemeinschaft*—a "people's community" of purely Germanic, Aryan ideals. Find the large, wall-sized church tapestry of cutesy German-style houses and common people marching in lock-(goose) step with Nazi-uniformed troops.

Hitler made plans to turn Berlin into "Welthaupstadt Germania," the "world capital" of his far-reaching Third Reich. The centerpiece would be the impossibly huge domed Volkshalle—950 feet high and able to accommodate 180,000 people. It would squat over the Spree River, just north of the Reichstag, as the anchor of a grandiose north-south axis called the Avenue of Splendors.

At the start of World War II, Germany's Blitzkrieg ("Lightning War") demolished its enemies. But then came several devastating, watershed battles, such as Stalingrad. A small theater shows the propaganda newsreels both sides produced and consumed each week, twisting understanding of what was actually happening.

Exhibits document the atrocities at Hitler's concentration camps, including registration photos of prisoners and a model of a crematorium at Auschwitz (in Nazi-occupied Poland) designed to exterminate Jews. By the end of the war, more than 60 million were dead, including 6 million Jews and 6 million non-Jewish Germans. Even before the last shots were fired in the war against Japan, Allied leaders had already met at the Potsdam Conference to divvy up a defeated Germany. Berlin and Germany were divided between the Soviet-leaning East and the US-leaning West. Right then, World War II became a protracted Cold War.

A border post marks the "inner German border" between West and East. Exhibits juxtapose slices of life in the two Germanys. The West's economy recovered (see the smart VW bug), while the East's languished (the clunky DDR-era Trabant cars known as Trabi). By the 1980s, the Soviet empire was cracking, and the German people longed to reunite. In 1989, the Berlin Wall—the most iconic symbol of division and oppression— began crumbling. You'll see videos of the celebrations, preserved sections of the wall, and clips of US president Ronald Reagan demanding they "tear down this wall."

Rest of the Museum: For architecture buffs, the big attraction is the modern annex behind the history museum, designed by American architect I. M. Pei, who is famous for his glass pyramid at Paris' Louvre. (To get there from the old building, cross through the courtyard, admiring the Pei glass canopy overhead.) This annex complements the museum with temporary, often-fascinating exhibits. A striking glassed-in spiral staircase unites four floors with surprising views and lots of light.

▲▲DDR Museum

While overpriced, crammed with school groups, and frustrating to local historians, the DDR Museum has a knack for helping out-

siders (rather than "Ost-algic" Germans) understand life in communist East Germany (the *Deutsche Demokratische Republik,* or DDR). The museum is well-stocked with kitschy everyday items from the DDR period, plus photos, video clips, and concise English explanations.

Cost and Hours: €9.80, buy online; daily 10:00-20:00, Sat until 22:00; just across the Spree from Museum Island at Karl-Liebknecht-Strasse 1, tel. 030/847-123-731, www.ddr-museum.de.

Advance Tickets Recommended: While you can get tickets at the museum, it's smart to purchase them online in advance to avoid waiting in a long line at the entrance.

Visiting the Museum: Inside, you can crawl through a Trabant car (known as a "Trabi"; take it for a virtual test drive) and pick up some DDR-era black humor ("East Germany had 39 newspapers, four radio stations, two TV channels...and one opinion"). You'll learn how many East Germans—with limited opportunities to travel abroad—vacationed on Hungary's Lake Balaton or on the Baltic Coast, where nudism was all the rage (as a very revealing display explains). Lounge in DDR cinema chairs as you view a subtitled propaganda film or clips from beloved-in-the-East TV shows, including the popular kids' show *Sandmännchen*—"Little

Sandman." The highlight is a tourable reconstructed communist-era home, where you can open drawers and cupboards to find both information panels and the trappings of a typical DDR home. You can even climb into a rickety old "elevator" and get jostled around.

Nikolai Quarter (Nikolaiviertel)

The Nikolai Quarter marks the original medieval settlement of Cölln, which would eventually become Berlin. Huddled around the twin spires of the Nikolaikirche, the area was destroyed during the war, then rebuilt for Berlin's 750th birthday in 1987. It has a cute and cobbled old-town feel...Middle Ages meets Socialist Realism. Today most of the buildings are occupied by touristy shops and restaurants. Perhaps the best reason to come here is to visit its old-fashioned beer hall—the recommended Brauhaus Georgbräu, with seating along the river.

Sights in Northern Berlin

OLD JEWISH QUARTER

Immediately northeast of the Spree River is the old Jewish quarter which, in addition to being packed with intriguing shops and fun eateries, is one of the most important areas for Berlin's historic Jewish community—offering insights into a culture that thrived here until the 1940s.

▲▲Courtyards *(Höfe)*

The old Jewish quarter is a particularly handy place to explore Berlin's unique *Höfe*—interconnected courtyards that burrow through city blocks, today often filled with trendy shops and eateries. Two starkly different examples are nearly next door, and just steps from the Hackescher Markt transit hub: the upscale, *Jugendstil* Hackesche Höfe (Rosenthaler Strasse 40), with eye-pleasing architectural flourishes and upscale shops; and the funky Haus Schwarzenberg (Rosenthaler Strasse 39), with a museum honoring Otto Weidt—a Berliner who defied the Nazis and saved many lives by employing blind and deaf Jews in his workshop.

New Synagogue (Neue Synagogue)

Marked by its beautiful golden dome, this large, mid-19th-century synagogue is now a museum memorializing the Berlin Jewish community that was decimated by the Nazis. Berlin was long the center of German Jewry and this small but moving exhibit (with good English descriptions) tells the story of this community through the centuries. You'll enter through a low-profile door in the modern building to the right of the synagogue facade and go through very tight security. A cutaway model shows the entire synagogue. This model, and the view across the vacant lot out back to the iron columns marking where the apse stood, helps you envision this space that once housed 3,200 worshippers. The upper floor personalizes

BERLIN

Northern Berlin

········ COURSE OF FORMER WALL

1/2 Kilometer
1/2 Mile

the Nazi terror with individual stories. Skip the climb to the dome; it's unimpressive from the inside and has ho-hum views.

Cost and Hours: €7; Sun-Fri 10:00-18:00, closed Sat; audioguide-€3, Oranienburger Strasse 28, S-Bahn: Oranienburger Strasse, tel. 030/8802-8300, www.centrumjudaicum.de.

The Kennedys Museum

This crisp collection (in a former Jewish girls' school building) recalls John F. Kennedy's 1963 Germany trip with photos and video clips, as well as a photographic shrine to the Kennedy clan in America. Among the interesting mementos are old campaign buttons and posters, and JFK's notes with the phonetic pronunciation "Ish bin ein Bearleener." The highlight: a newsreel of Kennedy's historic speech plays continuously, as does his 1960 presidential debate with Nixon.

Cost and Hours: €5, Tue-Fri 10:00-18:00, Sat-Sun from 11:00, closed Mon, tel. 030/2065-3570, www.thekennedys.de.

Getting There: Look for a huge red-brick building with red-and-white-striped doors (Auguststrasse 13, on the opposite end of the block from the New Synagogue, museum is on the second floor). For a shortcut from the synagogue, cut through the Heckmann Höfe courtyard (at Oranienburger Strasse 32) and turn right on Auguststrasse.

▲Palace of Tears (Tränenpalast) at Friedrichstrasse Station

Just south of the old Jewish quarter (cross the river on Friedrichstrasse at Weidendammer Brücke and bear right) stands this impactful Cold War site. The Friedrichstrasse train station—situated within East Berlin, but accessible by train from West Berlin—was one of the few places where Westerners were allowed to cross into the East. And when crossing back into the free world, this was where they'd take leave of their East German loved ones. The scene of so many sad farewells, it earned the nickname "Tränenpalast" (palace of tears). The 1962 building—an unassuming, boxy, bureaucratic structure that was once attached by a corridor to the station—has now been converted into a museum about everyday life in a divided Germany, with a fascinating peek into the paranoid border-control world of the DDR.

Cost and Hours: Free, includes excellent audioguide, Tue-Fri 9:00-19:00, Sat-Sun 10:00-18:00, closed Mon, on the river side of the Friedrichstrasse station—look for the building with large glass windows and blue trim, Reichstagufer 17, tel. 030/4677-7790, www.hdg.de/traenenpalast.

PRENZLAUER BERG AND NEARBY

The thriving Prenzlauer Berg district, worth ▲▲, offers an ideal opportunity to see a corner of today's "real Berlin," just beyond the core tourist zone but still easily accessible. Prenzlauer Berg (PRENTS-low-er behrk) was largely untouched by WWII bombs, fell into disrepair during DDR days, and has since been completely rejuvenated. Prenzlauer Berg is also a great place to sleep, eat, shop, and enjoy nightlife.

Kulturbrauerei

Prenzlauer Berg was once a wooded hill with dozens of breweries—including this one, the Schultheiss-Brauerei. By the 1920s, this was one of the largest breweries in the world. World War II put an end to that, as Nazis confiscated the brewery, turned it into a factory for the Wehrmacht (armed forces), and, in the closing days of war, barricaded themselves within the brewery grounds. Today the entire site has been renovated to maintain its historic buildings and to provide a venue for the cultural transformation of Prenzlauer Berg.

The "Culture Brewery" is a brewery-turned-cultural center that fills an evocative old industrial space with a handful of interesting shops, breezy restaurants, a movie theater, grocery store, and TI, plus a Sunday food market (12:00-18:00), winter Christmas market, and other outdoor events (Schönhauser Allee 36, tel. 030/4435-2170, www.kulturbrauerei.de). Of most interest is the museum described next.

▲Everyday Life in the DDR (Alltag in der DDR)

This museum, tucked in a passage at the northern end of the Kulturbrauerei, recounts the reality of communist East Germany. The thoughtful, well-curated collection—organized by theme—displays original artifacts, videos, photos, art, and mock storefronts that rise above the kitsch factor to give a real sense of the disparity between the socialist ideal and the grinding reality. It's designed not for casual tourists, but for aging Germans eager to teach their kids and grandkids about how they once lived. (The DDR Museum near Museum Island—described earlier—is less substantial, but also more tourist-friendly and therefore more crowded.) Although tricky to appreciate, this museum is free and well worth a visit, particularly if you're well-versed in DDR history.

Cost and Hours: Free, Tue-Sun 10:00-18:00, Thu until 20:00, closed Mon; enter at Knaackstrasse 97, tel. 030/4677 7790, www. hdg.de.

▲▲▲Berlin Wall Memorial (Gedenkstätte Berliner Mauer)

This is Berlin's most substantial and educational sight relating to its gone-but-not-forgotten Wall. As you visit the park, you'll learn about how the Wall went up, the brutal methods used to keep Easterners in, and the stories of brave people who risked everything to be free.

Exhibits line up along several blocks of Bernauer Strasse, stretching more than a mile northeast from the Nordbahnhof S-Bahn station (one of the DDR's "ghost stations") to Schwedter Strasse and the Mauerpark. For a targeted visit, focus on the engaging sights clustered near the Nordbahnhof: two museums (the Visitors Center and the Documentation Center)—with films, photos, and harrowing personal stories; various open-  air exhibits and memorials; original Wall fragments; and observation tower views into the only preserved, complete stretch of the Wall system (with a Cold War-era "death strip").

Cost and Hours: Free; outdoor areas accessible daily 24

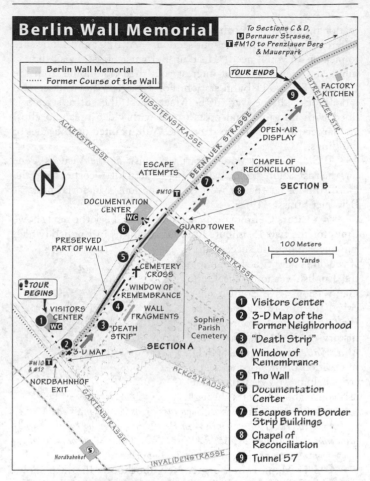

Berlin Wall Memorial

To Sections C & D,
Ⓤ Bernauer Strasse,
Ⓣ #M10 to Prenzlauer Berg
& Mauerpark

- Berlin Wall Memorial
- ...... Former Course of the Wall

TOUR ENDS

FACTORY KITCHEN

STRELITZER STR.

HUSSITENSTRASSE

ACKERSTRASSE

BERNAUER STRASSE

OPEN-AIR DISPLAY

ESCAPE ATTEMPTS

CHAPEL OF RECONCILIATION

⑦

SECTION B

⑧

#M10 Ⓣ

DOCUMENTATION CENTER

WC

⑥

GUARD TOWER

ACKERSTRASSE

100 Meters

100 Yards

PRESERVED PART OF WALL

⑤

CEMETERY CROSS

WINDOW OF REMEMBRANCE

TOUR BEGINS

VISITORS CENTER

WC

①

④

WALL FRAGMENTS

Sophien Parish Cemetery

SECTION A

③

"DEATH STRIP"

3-D MAP

#M10 & #12 Ⓣ

BERGSTRASSE

NORDBAHNHOF EXIT

GARTENSTRASSE

Nordbahnhof Ⓢ

INVALIDENSTRASSE

❶ Visitors Center
❷ 3-D Map of the Former Neighborhood
❸ "Death Strip"
❹ Window of Remembrance
❺ The Wall
❻ Documentation Center
❼ Escapes from Border Strip Buildings
❽ Chapel of Reconciliation
❾ Tunnel 57

hours; museums (Visitors Center and Documentation Center) both open Tue-Sun 10:00-18:00, closed Mon, memorial chapel closes at 17:00; on Bernauer Strasse at #119 (Visitors Center) and #111 (Documentation Center).

Information: Tel. 030/4679-86666, www.berliner-mauer-gedenkstaette.de.

When to Go: The outdoor part of this tour can be done in the evening, but it would be a shame to miss the two indoor exhibits, which close at 18:00.

Getting There: Take the S-Bahn (line S1, S2, or S25) to Nordbahnhof. Exit by following signs for *Bernauer Strasse*—you'll pop out at the memorial. You can also get there on tram #12 or #M10 (from near Prenzlauer Berg hotels).

Overview: Begin at the Nordbahnhof and pick up an infor-

BERLIN

mational pamphlet from the Visitors Center (note that there are different brochures for the four sections—A, B, C, and D; be sure to pick up all you'll need). Head up Bernauer Strasse, visit the exhibits and memorials that interest you, then ride home from the Bernauer Strasse U-Bahn station. For a longer visit, walk several more blocks all the way to the Mauerpark. The entire stretch is lined with informational posts (some with video or audio clips) and larger-than-life images from the Wall, painted on the sides of buildings.

● **Self-Guided Walk:** Start your visit at the Visitors Center, the rust-colored, blocky building located kitty-corner from the Nordbahnhof (at the far west end of the long Memorial park, at Bernauer Strasse 119).

❶ **Visitors Center** (Bezucherzentrum): Check the next showtimes for the two 15-minute introductory films in English (which run once an hour in succession). If you don't have time to wait for the English versions, the German versions have English subtitles. The film titled *The Berlin Wall* covers the four-decade history of the Wall. The other film, *Walled In!*, features a 3-D re-creation of the former death strip, helping you visualize what it is you're about to walk through.

• *Exit the Visitors Center, cross Bernauer Strasse, and enter the Memorial park. You're leaving former West Berlin and entering the no-man's-land that stood between East and West Berlin. Once in the park, find the rusty rectangular monument with a 3-D map.*

❷ **3-D Map of the Former Neighborhood:** The map shows what this neighborhood looked like back in the Wall's heyday. The shiny metal dot on the left marks where you're standing. Fifty years ago, you'd be right at the division between East and West Berlin—specifically, in the narrow strip between two sets of walls. One of those walls is still standing—there it is, stretching along Bernauer Strasse. As you gaze down the long park, West Berlin would be to your left (on the north side of Bernauer Strasse), and East Berlin to your right.

Now find the Nordbahnhof, both on the map and in real life—the entrance is across the street on your left. While the Wall stood, the Nordbahnhof station straddled both East and West—one of the "ghost stations" of Cold War Berlin (inside the station, photos compare 1989 with 2009).

• *Stroll along the path through this first section of the park ("Section*

A"). Along the way are small sights, remembrances, and exhibits. As you stroll, you're walking through the...

❸ **"Death Strip"** (Section A): Today's grassy park, with a pleasant path through it, was once the notorious "death strip" *(Todesstreifen)*. If someone was trying to escape from the East, they'd have to scale one wall (a smaller one, to your right), cross this narrow strip of land, and climb the main Wall (to your left, along Bernauer Strasse). The death strip was an obstacle course

of barbed wire, tire-spike strips to stop cars, and other diabolical devices. It was continually patrolled by East German soldiers leading German shepherds. Armed guards looked down from watchtowers, with orders to shoot to kill.

• *About midway through this section of the park, find the freestanding rusted-iron wall filled with photos.*

❹ **Window of Remembrance:** Find **Otfried Reck,** just 17 years old (eighth from the left, top row). On November 27, 1962, he and a friend pried open a ventilation shaft at the boarded-up Nordbahnhof, and descended to the tracks, where they hoped to flag down a passing westbound train. The police discovered them, and Reck was shot in the back. There's a memorial to him now directly across from the Visitors Center. **Ernst Mundt** (just left of Otfried) died directly behind you, at the cemetery wall. On September 4, 1962, he climbed the death strip's inner wall and ran across the top, headed in the direction of the Nordbahnhof and freedom. He was shot in the head, and his hat (the one in the picture) flew off. He died, age 40.

Continue walking through Section A. You're now walking along the original, preserved asphalt patrol path.

• *Now, walk across the grass and find a place to get a good close-up look at*

❺ **The Wall:** The Wall here is typical of the whole system: about 12 feet tall, made of concrete and rebar, and capped by a rounded pipe that made it tough for escapees to get a grip. The top would have been further outfitted with coils of barbed wire. This was part of a 96-mile-long Wall that encircled West Berlin, making it an island of democracy in communist East Germany. The West Berlin side of the Wall was typically covered with colorful graffiti by free-spirited West Berliners. A few bits of graffiti remain here.

• *Now, exit the park through the hole in the Wall, turn right along Ber-*

BERLIN

nauer Strasse, and make your way a short distance to the crosswalk.
Across Bernauer Strasse is a modern gray building with a view terrace,
located at #119 (labeled Gedenkstätte Berliner Mauer*). This is the...*

❻ **Documentation Center** (Dokumentationszentrum Berliner Mauer): This excellent museum is geared to a new generation of Berliners who can hardly imagine their hometown split so brutally in two. The two floors of exhibits have photos and displays to explain the logistics of the city's division and its effects. Listen to the riveting personal accounts of escapees—and of the border guards armed with machine guns and tasked with stopping them.

On the second floor, at the back of the room, be sure to watch the poignant seven-minute film, *Peaceful Revolution*. The video highlights the power of the people and traces the events that led to the Wall's collapse. From this floor, stairs lead to the rooftop **Tower** *(Turm)* where you're rewarded with a view. You can look across Bernauer Strasse and down at Berlin's last preserved stretch of the death strip with an original guard tower. More than 100 sentry towers like this one kept a close eye on the Wall. In the far distance, the communist-built TV Tower overlooks the scene.

• *Exit and continue on. Cross Bernauer Strasse (where it intersects with Ackerstrasse) and enter the next section of the Memorial park.*

❼ **Escapes from Border Strip Buildings** (Section B): Ahead, you'll see a group of information panels. The panels tell the story of what happened here: On August 13, 1961, the East German government officially closed the border. People began fleeing to the parts of Berlin controlled by other European powers—like the French, who held the neighborhood on the north side of Bernauer Strasse.

Over the next few weeks and months, bit by bit, the border hardened. Ackerstrasse was closed to traffic as East German soldiers laid down rows of barbed wire. People were suddenly separated from their West Berlin neighbors just across the street. During this brief window of time (summer of '61 to early '62), there were many escape attempts, and the residents of West Berlin did all they could to help.

• *Keep going up the path through Section B, to the round building up ahead.*

❽ **Chapel of Reconciliation** (Kapelle der Versöhnung): This modern chapel stands on the site of the old Church of Reconciliation. Built in 1894, the old Gothic-style church served the neighborhood parish. When the Wall went up, the church found itself stranded in the death strip. Border guards used the steeple as a watchtower. The church became famous in the West as a symbol of how the godless commies had driven out religion and turned a once-great culture into a bleak wasteland. The church itself was finally blown up by the East Germans in 1985.

After the Wall came down, this chapel was built to remember the troubled past and to try to heal the memory. Inside the church, the carved wooden altarpiece was saved from the original structure. The chapel hosts daily prayer services for the victims of the Wall.

• *Continue past the chapel into the second portion of Section B.*

Tunnels and More: Walk uphill then bear left to a large open-air display under a canopy (amid the ruins of a destroyed Bernauer Strasse home). Photos, info boards, and press-the-button audio clips explain what it was like to live here, so close to the front line of the Cold War. Head back up to the main path, turn left, and continue. You'll pass two parallel rows of metal slabs, labeled *Flucht-tunnel 1964*. This marks the route of the most famous tunnel of all: ❾ **Tunnel 57** (named after the 57 people who escaped through it). Its location is marked by rows of metal plates embedded in the ground.

• *The main part of our walk is done. From here you have several choices: To experience more of the Memorial, you could continue through more open-air exhibits. **Section C** focuses on the building of the Wall. **Section D**—nearly as long as the first three sections combined—covers everyday life in the shadow of the Berlin Wall.*

If you're ready to leave, the Bernauer Strasse U-Bahn station is just a block farther up Bernauer Strasse. Or you can backtrack to the Nordbahnhof. And tram #M10 follows Bernauer Strasse all the way to Eberswalder Strasse, in the heart of Prenzlauer Berg.

Sights in Southern Berlin

The following sights are listed roughly north to south (as you'd reach them from Unter den Linden)

FASCISM AND COLD WAR SITES NEAR CHECKPOINT CHARLIE

A variety of fascinating sites relating to Germany's tumultuous 20th century cluster south of Unter den Linden.

▲Checkpoint Charlie

Famous as the place where many visiting Westerners crossed into East Berlin during the Cold War, the original Checkpoint Charlie is long gone. But today a reconstructed guard station—with big

BERLIN

Southern Berlin

posters of American and Soviet guards, and a chilling "You are leaving the American sector" sign—attracts curious tourists for a photo op. Nothing here is original (except for the nearby museum—described next—and the whole area feels like a Cold War theme park, with kitschy communist-themed attractions, Trabi rides, hucksters, buskers, and sleazy vendors who charge through the nose for a DDR stamp in your passport. The

replica checkpoint is free to view and always open (but you'll pay to take photos with the "guards").

Background: For nearly three decades (1961-1989), this was a border crossing between East and West Berlin. It became known worldwide and stood as a symbol of the Cold War itself. The name "Charlie" came about because it was the third checkpoint in a series. Checkpoint A (Alpha) was at the East-West German border, a hundred miles west of here. Checkpoint B (Bravo) was where people left East Germany and entered the Allied sector of Berlin. This was Checkpoint C (Charlie). Its roots lie in the days immediately after World War II, when this intersection was the border between the US-occupied neighborhood and the Soviet zone. In 1952, the Soviets officially closed the border between East and West Germany with a fence, blocking East Germans from leaving.

But West Berlin was still open until the Wall went up here in 1961. Afterwards, this spot on Friedrichstrasse was one of the few places where people could legally pass between East and West—provided they had the proper documents, of course. That generally meant foreigners and officials from the Allies—not East Germans.

The East Germans fortified their side of the checkpoint heavily. There was the Wall, a watchtower, concrete barriers to prevent cars from speeding through, barbed-wire fences, and even a garage where vehicles could be checked for smuggled goods or people. (None of these structures stand today.)

On the US side, there was...Checkpoint Charlie. This was a humble shack for the document-checking GIs. It sat on a traffic island in the middle of Friedrichstrasse, fortified with a few piles of sandbags. While the actual checkpoint has long since been dismantled, you can see a **mock-up,** with a guard station, sandbags, and a US flag. Larger-than-life posters show an American soldier facing east and a young Soviet soldier facing west—look at these portraits and consider the decades of armed standoffs here.

▲Museum of the Wall at Checkpoint Charlie (Mauermuseum Haus am Checkpoint Charlie)

This ragtag but riveting celebration of the many ways desperate East Germans managed to slip through the Wall to freedom has stood here since 1963...

taunting DDR authorities. Today East Germany and its Wall are long gone, but the museum is still going strong. Some of the displays have yellowed, the place is cramped and confusing, and the ticket price is way too high, but the museum retains a special sense of history. Visiting here, you'll learn about the creation of the Wall and the many escape attempts (including several of the actual items used by clever escapees). If you're pressed for time, visit after dinner, when most other museums are closed. Compared to the soberly academic official Berlin Wall Memorial near the Nordbahnhof, this museum has more personality, buoyed by a still-defiant spirit.

Cost and Hours: €14.50, daily 9:00-22:00, last entry one hour before closing, audioguide-€5, U6 to Kochstrasse or U2 to Stadtmitte, Friedrichstrasse 43, tel. 030/253-7250, www.mauermuseum.de.

▲▲Topography of Terror (Topographie des Terrors)

A rare undeveloped patch of land in central Berlin, right next to a surviving stretch of Wall, was once the nerve center for the Gestapo and the SS—the most despicable elements of the Nazi government. Today this site hosts a modern documentation center, along with an outdoor exhibit in the Gestapo headquarters' excavated foundations. While there isn't much in the way of original artifacts, the exhibit does a good job of telling this

powerful story, in the place where it happened. The information is a bit dense, but WWII historians (even armchair ones) find it fascinating.

Cost and Hours: Free, includes audioguide, daily 10:00-20:00, outdoor exhibit closes at dusk, Niederkirchnerstrasse 8, U-Bahn: Potsdamer Platz or Kochstrasse, S-Bahn: Anhalter Bahnhof or Potsdamer Platz.

Information: Tel. 030/254-5090, www.topographie.de.

Visiting the Museum: Start in the lobby and study a **model** of the neighborhood showing the home of the German government at the outbreak of World War II. (We're standing at #20.) Back in the 1930s and '40s, this was just one of many governmental office buildings along Wilhelmstrasse. Seeing this sprawling bureaucratic quarter gives you a sense of how much mundane paperwork was involved in administering Hitler's reign of terror in an efficient, rational way. In the small theater nearby, the six-minute film provides context for the exhibit (and can be shown in English upon request).

The **ground floor** houses the permanent collection. Stepping in, you begin a chronological journey (with a timeline of events, old photographs, documents, and newspaper clippings) through the evolution of Nazism, the reign of terror, the start of World War II, and the Holocaust. Following the numbers, you'll trace: 1) the rise of Nazism and consolidation of power; 2) the institutionalization of terror; 3) the use of concentration camps and racism; 4) the spreading of Nazism with World War II; and 5) the end of the war and postwar life.

The displays illustrate how Hitler, Himmler, and their team expertly manipulated the German people to build a broadly supported "dictatorship of consent." You'll learn about the web of intersecting organizations whose duties were run from here. And you'll learn about the Gestapo and SS *(Schutzstaffel)*, and their brutal methods—including their chillingly systematic implementation of the Holocaust.

Some images here are indelible. Gleeful SS soldiers, stationed at Auschwitz, yuk it up on a retreat in the countryside (as their helpless prisoners were being gassed and burned a few miles away). A German woman, head shaved, is publicly humiliated for fraternizing with a Polish prisoner. On a street corner, jeering SS troops cut off the beard of an elderly Jewish man. A Roma woman's eye color is carefully analyzed by a doctor performing "racial evaluation." Graphic images show executions—by hanging, firing squad, and so on.

The exhibits end with the conclusion of the war in 1945. A photo shows this former building in ruins. The finale is a wall of colored cards used in collecting data for the postwar trials of the people who worked here. While the Nazi leadership was captured and prosecuted at the Nürnberg trials, the majority of midlevel bureaucrats who routinely facilitated genocide with the flick of a pen... were never brought to justice.

With more time, use the audioguide and posted signs to explore the grounds surrounding the blocky building. Around the corner (to the right facing the museum entrance) are the scant remains of the **House Prison** outlined in cement. The building was equipped with dungeons, where the Gestapo detained and tortured prisoners. The general public knew what went on here, and its very existence sent a message.

Nearby: Immediately next door is an unusually long surviving stretch of the Berlin Wall. A block beyond that is the looming, very fascist-style Former Air Ministry—built by Hitler to house his Luftwaffe (Nazi air force), later the DDR's "Hall of Ministries," today the German Finance Ministry, still adorned with cheery 1950s communist propaganda. A short walk away is a surviving DDR watchtower.

MUSEUMS SOUTH OF UNTER DEN LINDEN
▲Jewish Museum Berlin (Jüdisches Museum Berlin)

Combining a remarkable building with a thoughtful permanent exhibit, this is the most educational Jewish-themed sight in Berlin. The exhibit is undergoing a renovation that will likely last through April 2020. During this time, the top and middle floors of the museum will be closed. In the meantime, the building itself is still worth a look—it's packed with symbolism— and the memorials are still open during renovation.

Designed by American architect Daniel Libeskind (the master planner for the redeveloped World Trade Center in New York), the zinc-walled building has a zigzag shape pierced by voids symbolic of the irreplaceable cultural loss caused by the Holocaust. Enter the 18th-century Baroque building next door, then go through an underground tunnel to reach three memorial spaces. Follow the **Axis of Exile**—lined with the names of cities where the Jewish diaspora settled—to a disorienting slanted garden with 49 pillars. Next, the **Axis of Holocaust**—lined with names of concentration camps and artifacts from Jews imprisoned and murdered by the Nazis—leads to an eerily empty tower shut off from the outside world. Finally, the **Axis of Continuity** takes you to stairs and the main exhibit (if open). A detour partway up the long stairway leads (through temporary exhibits) to the Memory Void, a compelling space of "fallen leaves":

heavy metal faces that you walk on, making inhuman noises with each step.

Cost and Hours: €8, ask for discount if also going to Berlinische Galerie, daily 10:00-20:00, closed on Jewish holidays; tight security includes bag check and metal detectors; tel. 030/2599-3300, www.jmberlin.de.

Getting There: It's in a nondescript residential neighborhood (halfway between Checkpoint Charlie and the happening Kreuzberg scene). Take the U1/U6 to Hallesches Tor, find the exit marked *Jüdisches Museum*, exit straight ahead, then turn right onto Franz-Klühs-Strasse at the first corner. The museum is a five-minute walk ahead on your left, at Lindenstrasse 9.

Eating: The museum's **$$** restaurant offers good Jewish-style meals, albeit not kosher.

▲Berlinische Galerie

This gorgeous, well-presented museum (with an oversized word-search puzzle out front) showcases modern and contemporary art

created in this eclectic city. The main draw is the permanent exhibit upstairs, offering an intriguing, chronological, and easily digestible look at art generated in Berlin from 1880 to 1980. The collection begins with Conservative (i.e., realistic) art, then gives way to the shimmering Berlin Secession (starting in 1892), and evolves from there. You'll meet Margarette Kubicka (1891-1984), with her colorful, curvy, Cubist-inspired style; and Klimt-like, avant-garde Expressionism, including works by Otto

Dix (the biggest name here). You'll get a lesson in the Weimar-era "New Objectivity" (where artists focused on everyday scenes, intentionally objectifying their subjects in response to the abstraction trend). And you'll see how historical events shaped the art: works created under the Nazis (capturing confusion and alienation); scenes of postwar destruction; Cold War-era abstraction; and perspectives on the Wall from West Berlin artists.

Cost and Hours: €8, ask for discount if also visiting the Jewish Museum, Wed-Mon 10:00-18:00, closed Tue, Alte Jakobstrasse 124, tel. 030/7890-2600, www.berlinischegalerie.de.

KREUZBERG

Visitors who find downtown Berlin too tame head to Prenzlauer Berg, and those who find Prenzlauer Berg too tame fall in love with Kreuzberg (worth ▲▲). This huge, sprawling neighborhood (pop. 150,000) sits just south of central Berlin. For a representative look at this multicultural neighborhood, ride the U-Bahn (U1, U3, or U8) to **Kottbusser Tor**—the intersection at the heart of Kreuzberg—and explore. To the north is down-to-earth **Oranienstrasse,** lined with hole-in-the-wall shops and cheap eateries. Or wander south, crossing the Landwehr Canal to the increasingly trendy **Graefekiez** neighborhood. And if it's Tuesday or Friday, don't miss the vivid **Turkish Market,** with bustling street stalls that enliven the Maybachufer embankment near Kottbusser Brücke. All of these are within about a 10-minute walk of Kottbusser Tor. For recommended restaurants in this foodie-heaven neighborhood, see page 872.

Sights in Eastern Berlin

The first few sights listed here—Karl-Liebknecht-Strasse, Alexanderplatz, and the TV Tower— are also covered earlier, in my "Berlin City Walk" (available as a free 🎧 audio tour). To delve further into eastern Berlin, consider a walk along Karl-Marx-Allee, which stretches east from Alexanderplatz, or visit the neighborhood of Friedrichshain (just east of the historic core area). This quickly transforming neighborhood is where you'll find the East Side Gallery and Stasi Museum.

Karl-Liebknecht-Strasse

This wide boulevard—connecting Alexanderplatz to Museum Island, and named for an early German communist pioneer—is lined with DDR-era landmarks, including the TV Tower, Marien Church (historic church kept open—barely—during communism), Rotes Rathaus ("Red City Hall" of former East Berlin), and the

Marx-Engels-Forum, a park with statues of communism founders Karl Marx and Friedrich Engels, who studied in Berlin.

▲Alexanderplatz

Marking the eastern end of the Unter den Linden/Karl-Liebknecht-Strasse thoroughfare, this kitschy-futuristic space was the main square of DDR-era East Berlin. Named (fittingly) for a Russian czar, under communist rule the square was turned into a model of Soviet aesthetics—with stern, blocky facades; a showpiece department store; a transit hub for trams and trains; and a trippy "World Time Clock." Nearby is the start of the severely socialist-style Karl-Marx-Allee; originally named Stalinallee, it would have been more at home in Moscow than in Berlin.

TV Tower (Fernsehturm)

One of Berlin's landmarks, this 1,200-foot-tall massive spike is topped by a giant glittering disco ball. You'll see it from just about anywhere in the city, and riding the elevator to the observation deck comes with sweeping (but almost too-high) views. The tower also has a TI, and various walking and bike tours leave from here (€15.50, daily 9:00-24:00, Nov-Feb from 10:00, Panoramastrasse 1A, www.tv-turm.de).

Karl-Marx-Allee

This socialist-style boulevard was built after the original buildings here were leveled by the Red Army in 1945. As an expression of their adoration to the "great Socialist Father" (Stalin), the DDR government decided to rebuild the street better than ever (the USSR provided generous subsidies). They named it Stalinallee and lined it with apartment blocks ("workers' palaces") designed in the bold "Stalin Gothic" style so common in Moscow in the 1950s. The grand, showy boulevard was built in just four years and startled the West, as it gave them a peek at the potential future of Euro-Communism. Now renamed after Karl Marx, the street and its restored buildings provide a vivid look at architecture from Berlin's communist days.

The boulevard runs from Alexanderplatz to Frankfurter Tor. To see it, you can taxi or ride the U-Bahn to Alexanderplatz and hike east for a mile. Or, for a shorter walk, ride the U-Bahn to Weberwiese and walk to Frankfurter Tor (away from TV tower, along the right side). Strolling the boulevard, look for information posts along the way, and notice the Social Realism reliefs on the buildings and the lampposts, which incorporate the wings of a phoenix (rising from the ashes) in their design. From Frankfurter Tor you can ride the tram (#M10, direction: Warschauer Strasse) conveniently to the East Side Gallery, described next.

▲East Side Gallery

The biggest remaining stretch of the Wall is now the "world's longest outdoor art gallery." This segment of the Wall makes a memorable walk for those interested in street art and/or Berlin Wall history. The gallery stretches for nearly a mile and is covered with murals painted by artists from around the world. The murals (classified as protected monuments) got a facelift in 2009, when the city invited the original artists back to re-create their work for the 20th anniversary of the fall of the Wall. For the history of the East Side Gallery, see www.eastsidegallery-berlin.de.

From the Oberbaum Bridge, head along the most interesting stretch of the East Side Gallery. Just walking a hundred yards gives you the essence of the gallery and the tourist scene that enlivens it. Walk along as far as you'd like and return, or trek the  entire length, nearly a mile, to the Ostbahnhof S-Bahn station.

▲Stasi Museum

This extensive, thoughtfully presented exhibit tells the story of how the communist-era Ministry for State Security (a.k.a. Stasi)—headquartered in these very buildings—infiltrated all aspects of East German life. While the museum is quite dry and out of the way, it's the best place in Berlin to learn about the Stasi. Exhibits fill three floors of the building where Stasi Minister Erich Mielke had his office. Everything is described in English, with lots of reading and some interesting artifacts. At the entrance, check out the sprawling model of this neighborhood. The Stasi operation filled entire city blocks—essentially creating a city-within-the-city (54 acres, 50 buildings, 7,000 employees) for the sole purpose of surveilling its citizens. On official maps of East Berlin, this area showed up as blank space. For more on the Stasi, see the "Background" section on page 689.

Cost and Hours: €6, Mon-Fri 10:00-18:00, Sat-Sun from 11:00, tel. 030/553-6854, www.stasimuseum.de.

Getting There: It's a long haul from the center, at Ruschestrasse 103. Take the U5 to Magdalenenstrasse and exit toward *Ruschestrasse*. Up on the street, make a U-turn to the right up Ruschestrasse and look for the yellow sign—the museum is tucked far back in a courtyard.

Sights in Western Berlin

TIERGARTEN PARK

Berlin's "Central Park" stretches two miles from the Reichstag and Brandenburg Gate to Berlin Zoological Garden. This vast, 500-acre park, once a royal hunting ground, is now packed with cycling paths, joggers, and—on hot days—nude sunbathers.

The Tiergarten's centerpiece—faintly visible in the distance from the Brandenburg Gate—is the striking **Victory Column,** built to commemorate the Prussian defeat of Denmark in 1864... then reinterpreted after the defeat of France in 1870. The pointy-helmeted Germans rubbed it in, decorating the tower with French cannons and paying for it all with francs received as war reparations. The three lower rings commemorate Otto von Bismarck's victories (Germany's first chancellor). I imagine the statues of German military greats—which lurk among the trees nearby—goose-stepping around the floodlit angel at night.

Climbing the Victory Column's 270 steps earns you a breathtaking Berlin-wide view and a close-up of the gilded bronze statue of the

BERLIN

goddess Victoria (€3, daily 9:30-18:30, Sat-Sun until 19:00, Nov-March 10:00-17:00, closes for rain, no elevator). You might recognize Victoria from Wim Wenders' 1987 art-house classic film *Wings of Desire*, or the *Stay (Faraway, So Close!)* video he directed for the rock band U2.

SOUTH OF TIERGARTEN PARK

This area, a 15-minute walk from the Brandenburg Gate, is divided into the skyscraper zone of Potsdamer Platz and the arts-and-culture complex called the Kulturforum. For history buffs, the German Resistance Museum and the Silent Heroes Memorial sit just beyond the Kulturforum.

Potsdamer Platz Area

This immense, 150-acre square is home to sleek skyscrapers, shopping malls, a transportation hub, several major corporate headquarters, upscale restaurants, and a few museums.

▲Potsdamer Platz

The architectural face of Potsdamer Platz has changed drasti-

cally over time: Berlin's busiest intersection before World War II, it was bombed flat and remained a devastated wasteland until the 1990s, then quickly sprouted a forest of glassy skyscrapers, as if to trumpet the victory of capitalism. Visiting today, you'll see a skyscraper panorama, a replica of Europe's first traffic light, a boldly modern train station, a few chunks of the Berlin Wall, and the Sony Center shopping/entertainment complex. A good place to view it all is from the intersection of Potsdamer Strasse and Ebertstrasse. (From the S-Bahn or U-Bahn, exit following *Leipziger Platz* signs.) The next two sights are also nearby. A quick look at Potsdamer Platz also works well in conjunction with the nearby Kulturforum.

▲Deutsche Kinemathek Film and TV Museum

This exhibit is the most interesting place to visit within the Sony Center. Many early pioneers in filmmaking were German (including Fritz Lang, F. W. Murnau, Ernst Lubitsch, and the Austrian-born Billy Wilder)—and many became influential in Hollywood—making this a fun visit for cinephiles from anywhere. Your admission ticket gets you into several floors of exhibits made meaningful by the essential English audioguide. In the film section (floors 2 and 3), you'll walk back in time to the German film industry's beginnings, with an emphasis on the Weimar Republic period in the 1920s, when Berlin rivaled Hollywood; study the Nazi use of film as propaganda; and learn about today's influential German filmmakers. The TV section (floors 3 and 4) tells the story of *das Idioten Box* from its infancy (when it was primarily used as a Nazi propaganda tool) to today.

Cost and Hours: €8, free Thu 16:00-20:00; open Wed-Mon 10:00-18:00, Thu until 20:00, closed Tue; audioguide-€2, Potsdamer Strasse 2, tel. 030/300-9030, www.deutsche-kinemathek.de.

Nearby: The Kino Arsenal theater downstairs shows offbeat art-house films in their original language.

Panoramapunkt

Across Potsdamer Strasse from the Deutsche Kinemathek museum, you can ride what's billed as the "fastest elevator in Europe" to skyscraping rooftop views. You'll travel at nearly 30 feet per second to the top of the 300-foot-tall Kollhoff Tower in the Potsdamer Platz 1 building. Its sheltered-but-open-air view deck provides a fun survey of Berlin's changing skyline.

Cost and Hours: €7.50, €11.50 VIP ticket lets you skip the line, cash only, daily 10:00-20:00, until 18:00 in winter, in red-brick building at Potsdamer Platz 1, tel. 030/2593-7080, www.panoramapunkt.de.

Kulturforum

Berlin's *other* ensemble of museums (after Museum Island) fills a purpose-built facility just beyond Potsdamer Platz. Here you'll find a variety of impressive museums and other cultural institutions, including exquisite European Masters at the Gemäldegalerie, musical instruments, and decorative arts. Its New National Gallery (which houses modern art) is closed for renovation.

Combo-Tickets: All Kulturforum sights are covered by a €12 combo-ticket (can cost more if a special exhibit is on, www.kulturforum-berlin.de). They're also covered by the Museum Pass Berlin.

Getting There: Ride the S-Bahn or U-Bahn to Potsdamer Platz, then walk along Potsdamer Platz.

Getting Oriented: Locate the Kulturforum's various buildings by first finding the green steeple of the St. Matthäus Church. Just to the left and beyond the church is the glass-walled New National Gallery. To the right of the church is the low lying, sprawling Gemäldegalerie—this area's highlight. Farther right is the cubical Museum of Decorative Arts. Then comes the golden, angular Philharmonic concert hall and behind it, the Musical Instruments Museum (not really visible).

▲▲Gemäldegalerie

This "Painting Gallery" is one of Germany's top collections of great works by European masters. The Gemäldegalerie shows off fine works from the 13th through 18th century. While there's no one famous piece of art, you'll get an enticing taste of just about all the big names. In the North Wing are painters from Germany (Albrecht Dürer, Hans Holbein, Lucas Cranach), the Low Countries (Jan van Eyck, Pieter Brueghel, Peter Paul Rubens, Anthony van Dyck, Frans Hals, Johannes Vermeer), Britain (Thomas Gainsborough), France (Antoine Watteau), and an impressive hall of Rembrandts. The South Wing is the terrain of Italian greats, including Giotto, Botticelli, Titian, Raphael, and Caravaggio.

Cost and Hours: €14, includes audioguide; Tue-Fri 10:00-18:00, Thu until 20:00, Sat-Sun 11:00-18:00, closed Mon; clever little loaner stools, great salad bar in cafeteria upstairs, Matthäikirchplatz 4.

Information: Tel. 030/266-424-242, www.smb.museum.

Visiting the Museum: When you buy your ticket, pick up the current museum map for help locating specific paintings (artwork locations may change from descriptions below). Northern Art is on one side (where we'll begin) and Italian art is on the other (where we'll end). Note that inner rooms have Roman numerals (I, II, III), while adjacent outer rooms use Arabic numerals (1, 2, 3). We'll work counterclockwise (and roughly chronologically) through the collection.

Hans Holbein the Younger, 1497-1543 (Room 1): Holbein's portrait *Merchant Georg Gisze* (*Der Kaufmann Georg Gisze*, 1532) depicts a wealthy 34-year-old German businessman. His black beret and immaculate clothes mark him as a successful dealer in cloth. Around him are the tools of his trade—logbooks, business letters with wax seals, signet rings, scales, and coins. Typical of detail-rich Northern European art, the canvas is bursting with highly symbolic tidbits. The clock (on the table, inside the small gold canister) reminds the viewer that time passes and worldly success fades. The unbalanced scales suggest that wealth is fleeting. Those negative symbols are counterbalanced by the carnations and herbs in the vase, representing Gisze's upcoming marriage.

Albrecht Dürer, 1471-1528 (Room 2): In 1494, the young Dürer traveled from Germany to Italy, where he soaked up the technique and spirit of the burgeoning Renaissance movement. In his portrait *Hieronymus Holzschuher* (1526), Dürer captured the personality of a white-bearded friend from Nürnberg, right down to the sly twinkle in his sidelong glance. Dürer does not gloss over the 57-year-old's unflattering features like the wrinkles or receding hairline (with the clever comb-over).

Lucas Cranach the Elder, 1472-1553 (Room III): Cranach's *Fountain of Youth* (*Der Jungbrunnen,* 1546) depicts the perennial human pursuit of eternal youth. Ladies flock to bathe in the swimming pool of youth. They arrive (on the left) as old women—by wagon, on horseback, carried by men, even in a wheelbarrow. They strip and enter with sagging breasts, frolic awhile in the pool, rinse and repeat, then emerge (on the right) young again. Newly nubile, the women go into a tent to dress up, snog with noblemen in the bushes (right foreground), dance merrily beneath the trees, and dine grandly beneath a landscape of mountains and towers.

Rogier van der Weyden, 1400-1464 (Room IV): Dutch painters were early adopters of oil paint, and Van der Weyden was a virtuoso of the new medium. In *Portrait of a Young Woman* (*Bildnis einer jungen Frau,* 1440-1445), the subject wears a typical winged bonnet, addressing the viewer directly with her fetching blue eyes. In the same room is a remarkable, rare trio of three-panel altarpieces by Van der Weyden showing the life of the Virgin Mary, the life of John the Baptist, and the story of the Nativity. Savor the fine details in each panel.

Peter Paul Rubens, 1577-1640 (Room VIII): We've fast-forwarded a hundred years, and it's apparent how much the Protestant Reformation changed the tenor of Northern European art. Rubens' paintings represent the Catholic response, the Counter-Reformation. You'll see huge, brightly-colored canvases of Mary, alongside angels, bishops, and venerated saints (like the arrow-pierced martyr, St. Sebastian). This exuberant Baroque style trumpeted the greatness of the Catholic Church.

You'll also catch glimpses of Rubens' second wife, Helene Fourment, in mythological scenes such as *Andromeda* (1638). Helene, the amply-figured nymph with a sweetly smiling face, came to define the phrase "Ruben-esque."

Frans Hals, c. 1582-1666 (Room 13): Hals' *Portrait of Catharina Hooft with Her Nurse* (*Bildnis der Catharina Hooft mit ihrer Amme,* 1619-1620) presents a startlingly self-possessed baby (the newest member of a wealthy merchant family), dressed in the lacy, jeweled finery of a queen and clutching a golden rattle. At the other end of the social spectrum is Hals' *Malle Babbe* (1633-1635). The subject, a notorious barfly nicknamed "Crazy" Babbe, was well known in Hals' hometown. Hals captures her in a snapshot from the local pub, hefting her pewter beer stein and turning to laugh at a joke. The messy brushstrokes that define her collar and cap are as wild and lively as her over-the-top personality.

Rembrandt van Rijn, 1606-1669 (Room X): The ultimate Dutch master, Rembrandt was propelled to fame in his lifetime by his powers of perception and invention. Browse Room X and the adjoining galleries to get a taste of the range of Rembrandt's work. There are storytelling scenes, taut with pulse-racing emotion (*The Rape of Persephone,* 1631, Room 16). There are Bible scenes (*Samson and Delilah,* 1628-1629, Room 16; *Samson Threatens His Father-in-Law,* 1635, Room X).

And there are expressive portraits. In Room X, a *Self-Portrait* (1634) shows Rembrandt wearing a beret. The 28-year-old genius was already famous. He soon married the beautiful Saskia (*Portrait of Saskia,* 1643, Room 16), and seemed to have it all. But then Saskia died, Rembrandt declared bankruptcy, and his painting style went out of fashion...all of which contributed to his brooding, dark canvases.

Johannes Vermeer, 1632-1675 (Room 18): Vermeer was a master at conveying a complicated story through a deceptively simple scene with a few significant details. *Young Woman with a Pearl Necklace* (1664) is classic Vermeer. He lets us glimpse an intimate, unguarded moment in the life of an everyday woman. She wears a beautiful yellow coat with an ermine fur lining, ribbons in her hair, and pearl earrings. Vermeer tells us a bit about the woman with objects on the table: her comb, make-up brush, and water bowl.

Caravaggio, 1573–1610 (Room XIV): In the year 1600, living in Rome, Caravaggio burst onto the scene with a new and shocking art style. Even religious and allegorical subjects got his uncompromising, gritty, ultrarealistic treatment. In Caravaggio's *Amor Vincit Omnia* (1601-1602), "Love Conquers All." Cupid stands victorious over all the vain accomplishments of ambitious men: Military triumphs (symbolized by the fallen armor), Art (the discarded musical instruments), Literature (paper and pen), Science (a globe), Grand Architecture (compass and square), and Power (the crown). Cupid—a young, naked boy—mocks those grown-up ambitions. He laughs derisively and splays his genitals over the fallen symbols.

Now turn your attention to a painting in Room XIV by a different artist—**Giovanni Baglione**'s *Sacred and Profane Love* (1602-1603). Baglione was hired by a conservative cardinal to paint a moralizing response to Caravaggio. Here, the main figure is a more upright incarnation of love—Sacred Love—embodied by a radiant angel. He corners his rascally counterpart, the cowering and "Profane" little Cupid (lower right).

▲Musical Instruments Museum (Musikinstrumenten Museum)

Music lovers appreciate this beautifully displayed collection of 600 different items, going back to the 1500s. The included audioguide brings the collection to life and lets you actually hear a few of the instruments in action (€6, Tue-Fri 9:00-17:00, Thu until 20:00, Sat-Sun 10:00-17:00, closed Mon; Tiergartenstrasse 1—easy-to-miss entrance is down Ben-Gurion-Strasse, facing the back of the Sony Center; www.sim.spk-berlin.de).

Nearby: Berlin's yellow **Philharmonic Concert Hall** sits just beyond the Musical Instruments Museum (ticket office open Mon-Fri 15:00-18:00, Sat-Sun 11:00-14:00 except closed July-Aug, tel. 030/2548-8999, www.berliner-philharmoniker.de).

▲Museum of Decorative Arts (Kunstgewerbemuseum)
Berlin's answer to London's Victoria and Albert Museum shows off a thousand years of applied arts—from shimmering reliquaries (the Guelph Treasure) and delicate porcelain to Art Deco and *Jugendstil* furnishings, and much more. The highlights are the Dome Reliquary (an elaborately decorated, church-shaped container for saints' bones) and an appealing collection of women's fashions over the centuries (€8, Tue-Fri 10:00-18:00, Sat-Sun from 11:00, closed Mon; Matthäikirchplatz 5, www.smb.museum).

CITY WEST

The area now called City West has seen a lot of history. When Berlin's zoo was built here in the 1840s, this area was farm fields. It developed at a fast clip, and by the advent of the Cold War, Kurfürstendamm boulevard (nicknamed "Ku'damm") was West Berlin's main drag. The West German government poured funds into building Europa Center—glittering skyscrapers to house the headquarters of international businesses, a bold outpost of capitalism. The Schöneberg City Hall became the seat of West Berlin government, and the site of JFK's famous visit. But with the fall of the Wall, West Berlin became passé, and investors focused on developing previously inaccessible swaths of the East.

The following sights are in the heart of the former "West Berlin" (clustering near Kurfürstendamm boulevard). To get here, ride the S-Bahn to Zoologischer Garten. (For locations, see the "Western Berlin" map).

▲Kurfürstendamm
Nicknamed "Ku'damm," this boulevard starts at Kaiser Wilhelm Memorial Church and does a commercial cancan for two miles. In the 1850s, when Berlin became a wealthy and important capital, her "new rich" chose Kurfürstendamm as their street. In the 1870s, Bismarck made it Berlin's Champs-Elysées. In the 1920s, it was a stylish and fashionable drag of cafés and boutiques. During the Third Reich it was home to an international community of diplomats and journalists, and throughout the Cold War, economic subsidies from the West ensured that capitalism thrived here. Today, Berlin's focus has shifted east and Ku'damm feels more "international-touristy" than "authentic Berlin"—with a Hard Rock Café and a Käthe Wohlfahrt Christmas ornament superstore. But it remains a fine place to enjoy elegant shops (around Fasanenstrasse), department stores, and people-watching.

▲Kaiser Wilhelm Memorial Church (Gedächtniskirche)
This church was originally dedicated to the first emperor of Germany, Wilhelm I. Reliefs and mosaics show great events in the life of Germany's favorite kaiser, from his coronation in 1871 to

his death in 1888. The church is actually an ensemble of buildings: a new church, the matching bell tower, a meeting hall, and the ruins of the old church, with its Memorial Hall. The bombed-out ruins of the old church were left standing as a memorial to Berlin's destruction in World War II, with a new church constructed next door.

Cost and Hours: Church-free, daily 9:00-19:00—or until 18:00 if there's a concert; Memorial Hall-free, Mon-Fri 10:00-18:00, Sat until 20:00, Sun 12:00-17:30. Located on Breitscheidplatz, U2/U9 and S-Bahn: Zoologischer Garten or U1/U9: Kurfürstendamm, www.gedaechtniskirche-berlin.de.

Visiting the Church: Start your visit by picking up the English flier for information on both churches. Bullet holes dot the exterior of the **ruined church.** After the war, some Berliners wanted to tear down the ruins, but instead the ruins were kept as a Memorial Hall. Inside, under a Neo-Romanesque mosaic ceiling, you'll find a small photo exhibit and before-and-after models of the church.

To replace the ruined church, the authorities held a competition to design a contemporary annex. The winning entry—the short, **modern church** (1961) across from the Memorial Hall—offers a meditative world of 11,000 little blue windows. The blue glass was given to the church by the French as a reconciliation gift. As you enter, turn immediately right to find a simple charcoal sketch of the Virgin Mary wrapped in a shawl. During the Battle of Stalingrad, German combat surgeon Kurt Reuber rendered the Virgin on the back of a stolen Soviet map to comfort the men in his care. Though Reuber died in captivity, his sketch was flown out of Stalingrad on the last medical evacuation flight, and postwar Germany embraced it as a symbol of the wish for peace. Copies of the drawing, now known as the *Stalingrad Madonna,* hang in the Berlin Cathedral, in St. Michael's Cathedral in Coventry, England, and in the Kozan Cathedral in Russia's Volgograd (formerly Stalingrad) as a sign of reconciliation among nations.

Outside, a **golden crack** in the sidewalk stretches from the church toward Budapester Strasse, commemorating the December 2016 Christmas Market terrorist attack that took the lives of 12 people here. Look for the names of the victims on the steps.

Nearby: The lively square between the churches and the Europa Center attracts street musicians and performers—especially in the summer. Berliners call the funky fountain the "Wet Meatball." Overlooking the scene is the newly renovated Bikini Berlin shopping mall, with a mix of local and international shops, pop-up stores, and an upstairs terrace peering down into the zoo.

▲Käthe Kollwitz Museum

This local artist (1867-1945), who experienced much of Berlin's stormiest century, conveyed powerful, deeply felt emotions about motherhood, war, and suffering through the stark faces of her art. This small yet fine collection consists of three floors of charcoal drawings and woodcuts, dotted with a handful of sculptures. The museum may have moved by the time you visit; check the website before you go.

Cost and Hours: €7, daily 11:00-18:00, a block off Ku'damm at Fasanenstrasse 24, U-Bahn: Uhlandstrasse, tel. 030/882-5210, www.kaethe-kollwitz.de.

Visiting the Museum: Floor 1 focuses on the relatively happy first half of her life, when she drew from interactions with the poor to create some of her most moving works. You'll see how Kollwitz gained confidence and found her artistic voice in her depictions of the Peasants' Revolt (1520s) and the Weavers' Revolt (1844). **Floor 2** continues the story, with the turning point in her life: 1914, when Kollwitz's first-born son died in battle on Flanders Fields. You'll see her transition to a woodcut technique. Posters from this era show her social conscience—shaming Germans into helping feed their starving compatriots. Her self-portraits from the 1930s are imbued with a world-weariness that will only intensify with the death of her grandson, fighting in Russia, in World War II. (These losses inspired Kollwitz to create her most famous work, the powerful pietà inside Germany's war memorial at the Neue Wache—described on page 783.) Kollwitz's sculptures are spread across floors 1 and 2. While best known during her lifetime for her prints, Kollwitz favored sculpting. But lack of access to materials meant that she produced relatively few works.

Berlin Zoological Garden (Zoologischer Garten) and Aquarium

More than 1,500 kinds of animals call Berlin's famous zoo home... or so the zookeepers like to think. The zoo and the world-class adjacent aquarium draw gaggles of school kids and their frazzled chaperones. For a free look into the monkey enclosure, head inside the nearby Bikini Berlin shopping center, where the ground-floor windows offer an eye-level glimpse at the playful primates (or for a delightful bird's-eye view, head to the mall's rooftop terrace).

Cost and Hours: Zoo and aquarium €15.50 each, €21 for both, kids half-price, daily 9:00-18:30, until 16:30 in winter, aquarium closes at 18:00 year-round; feeding times—*Fütterungszeiten*—posted just inside entrance and listed on the zoo map (best feeding show is the sea lions—generally at 15:15); enter zoo near Europa

BERLIN

Center in front of Hotel Palace or opposite Zoologischer Garten station on Hardenbergplatz, Budapester Strasse 34, tel. 030/254-010, www.zoo-berlin.de, www.aquarium-berlin.de.

Kaufhaus des Westens (KaDeWe)

The "Department Store of the West" has been a Berlin tradition for more than a century. With a staff of 2,100 to help you sort through its vast selection of 450,000 items, KaDeWe claims to be the biggest department store on the Continent. You can get everything from a haircut (third floor) to souvenirs (fourth floor). The cash-only theater and concert box office on the sixth floor charges an 18 percent booking fee, but they know all your options. The sixth floor is a world of gourmet taste treats. The biggest selection of deli and exotic food in Germany offers plenty of classy opportunities to sit down and eat. Ride the glass elevator to the seventh floor's glass-domed Winter Garden, a self-service cafeteria—fun but pricey.

Hours: Generally Mon-Sat 10:00-20:00, closed Sun, S-Bahn: Zoologischer Garten or U-Bahn: Wittenbergplatz, tel. 030/21210, www.kadewe.de.

Nearby: The **Wittenbergplatz** U-Bahn station (in front of KaDeWe) is a unique opportunity to see an old-time station. The first subway station in Berlin (1902), its interior still has classic advertisements decorating its venerable walls. On the KaDeWe side of the station, a sign lists sites of Nazi concentration camps—one of many examples of present-day Germans ensuring that the crimes of their ancestors are never forgotten.

The Wittenbergplatz station also marks the boundary of the adjacent **Schöneberg** district, immediately southeast of the Ku'damm corridor. Here, you'll find the Schöneberg City Hall, which became the de facto seat of the West Berlin city government. It was on the city hall's front steps, on June 26, 1963, that John F. Kennedy stood in solidarity with the people of West Berlin: *"Ich bin ein Berliner."*

CHARLOTTENBURG PALACE AREA

Halfway to the airport, tucked in an upscale residential neighborhood at the northwestern edge of the city, sits Charlottenburg Palace—once a suburban residence of Prussian royalty (including Frederick the Great). While there are far better palaces in Germany—including just out of town in Potsdam (see the next chapter)—Charlottenburg offers an easy and accessible look at a royal interior. For art lovers, this area is even more appealing for its cluster of three museums just across the street from the palace, which combine to present a remarkable array of early-20th-century art: Surrealism (Scharf-Gerstenberg Collection); Picasso, Matisse, and

Klee (Museum Berggruen); and furniture and decorative arts in the *Jugendstil* and Art Deco styles (Bröhan Museum).

Getting There: Ride U7 to Richard-Wagner Platz or U2 to Sophie-Charlotte Platz and walk 10 minutes up the tree-lined boulevard Schlossstrasse (from either stop, follow signs to *Schloss*), or—much faster—catch bus #M45 (direction: Spandau) direct from Zoologischer Garten or bus #109 from along Ku'damm (direction: Flughafen Tegel). You can also take the S-Bahn to Westend, then ride bus #M45 (or walk 10 minutes). From any bus, you want the Schloss Charlottenburg stop.

Eating: For lunch on Luisenplatz just east of the palace, try the traditional German grub at Brauhaus Lemke brewpub or sample Russian specialties at Samowar (both open daily).

▲Charlottenburg Palace (Schloss Charlottenburg)

Charlottenburg Palace is the largest former residence of the royal Hohenzollern family in Berlin, and contains the biggest collection of 17th-century French fresco painting outside France. If you've seen the great palaces of Europe, this Baroque palace comes in at about number 10. I'd rate it behind Potsdam, too. The palace has several parts: The central "Old Palace" (Altes Schloss) is a mostly reconstructed look at Frederick's wife, Sophie Charlotte, that falls a bit flat on historic interest; the New Wing (Neue Flügel), with background on Frederick the Great, is the better palace experience. You'll also find a variety of other royal pavilions and sprawling gardens.

Cost and Hours: New Wing-€10, Old Palace-€10, prices include audioguides, smaller buildings-€4 each, combo-ticket for everything-€17; all buildings open Tue-Sun 10:00-17:30, Nov-March until 16:30, closed Mon year-round; tel. 0331/969-4200, www.spsg.de.

Visiting the Palace: The **New Wing** (Neue Flügel, a.k.a. the Knobelsdorff Wing) features Rococo royal apartments and fine

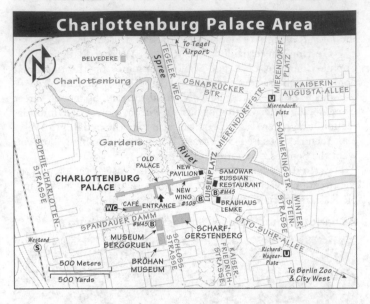

Charlottenburg Palace Area

paintings. First you'll head upstairs and walk through the sumptuous, gold-crusted State Rooms of Frederick the Great. The highlight is the 105-foot-long Golden Gallery, a real-life Cinderella ballroom with rich green walls, faux marble, gold flourishes, and glittering chandeliers. You'll also see Frederick's apartments (the concert chamber where he played the flute, and his study and bedroom). Retracing your steps, you'll enter the cozy Winter Rooms, dating from after Frederick's time. Rooms of royal portraits lead to the old wing, with more apartments and collections of silver, porcelain, and crown treasure. Back downstairs is a painting gallery, with two highlights: In the antechamber, look for the painting of a huge parade in front of Unter den Linden's Neue Wache. Then, at the end of this wing, don't miss the famous *Napoleon Crossing the Alps*—one of five originals of this scene done by Jacques-Louis David.

The **Altes Schloss** showcases Sophie Charlotte's state apartments—her portrait adorns most of the rooms and is the main theme of the audioguide—plus a lavish palace chapel that defied strict Protestant starkness in favor of Baroque supremacy befitting the Prussian Empire (an enormous royal crown sits opposite the altar, watching over the congregation). The highlight is its Porcelain Cabinet with over 2,700 pieces set against mirrored shelves reflecting natural light and a crazy melding of trompe l'oeil painting and 3-D stucco work.

Out back are sprawling **gardens** that are fun and free to wander in good weather, with a few skippable royal pavilions. The one that may be worth considering—past the end of the New Wing—is the **New Pavilion,** offering a concise and accessible look at the two big names of German Romanticism: the paintings of Caspar David Friedrich and Karl Friedrich Schinkel.

▲Scharf-Gerstenberg Collection

This pleasant museum houses more than 250 works of Surrealist and pre-Surrealist art, with works by big names including Joan Miró, Salvador Dalí, Paul Klee, Jean Dubuffet, and Francisco de Goya, juxtaposed with lesser-known German artists, such as Otto Dix, Max Ernst, and George Grosz. The *Surreal Worlds* exhibit shows just how freaky the world looks to artists—a jumbled existence of subjects and emotions. The collection is thoughtfully organized by theme, as if these great artists are in conversation. Note that these are "deep cuts" rather than "greatest hits," making this worth ▲▲ for someone with an affinity for this art, but not worth the trip for those with a casual interest.

Cost and Hours: €10 combo-ticket includes audioguide and Museum Berggruen, Tue-Fri 10:00-18:00, Sat-Sun from 11:00, closed Mon, Schlossstrasse 70, tel. 030/266-424-242, www.smb. museum.

▲Museum Berggruen

This tidy museum—with lesser-known works by some big-name modern artists (especially Picasso)—is a welcome surprise. The first floor features some of his earlier works: Blue Period, newspaper collages, and early Cubism (including a study for the seminal *Les Demoiselles d'Avignon*). The second (top) floor shows off how the prolific artist dabbled in virtually every medium: ceramic, mixed media, doodles, pencil sketches, and, of course, painting. The ground floor has a fine rotating collection intermixed with more Picasso sculptures. In the annex are notable works by Henri Matisse, Paul Cézanne, and a huge collection of pieces by Paul Klee. Everything is thoughtfully described in English.

Cost and Hours: €10 combo-ticket includes audioguide and Scharf-Gerstenberg Collection, Tue-Fri 10:00-18:00, Sat Sun from 11:00, closed Mon, Schlossstrasse 1, tel. 030/266-424-242, www.smb.museum.

▲Bröhan Museum

This beautifully understated museum displays decorative arts from the early 20th century on three floors (permanent exhibits on ground floor, temporary exhibits upstairs). This collection makes you wish you were furnishing a Berlin apartment in the year 1900. Wander through a dozen Jugendstil and Art Deco living rooms, a curvy and eye-pleasing organic world of lamps, glass, silver, and posters. English descriptions are posted in some rooms, and the included audioguide does a fair job describing temporary exhibits, featuring various subjects associated with the design history of the Art Deco and Art Nouveau movements.

Cost and Hours: €8, Tue-Sun 10:00-18:00, closed Mon, Schlossstrasse 1A, tel. 030/3269-0600, www.broehan-museum.de.

Entertainment in Berlin

Berlin has three opera companies, multiple symphonies and chamber orchestras, and organ concerts in churches nearly every day of the week. But you'll also find wild dance clubs, hipster ballrooms, dilapidated techno beach bars, and smoky jazz cellars.

Entertainment Info: The TI can provide basic information about what's on; for classical music, look for the free, monthly *Concerti* magazine. For good live music listings, see www.askhelmut. com or shell out a few euros for a Berlin magazine (sold at kiosks): *Zitty* (www.zitty.de) and *Tip* (www.tip-berlin.de) are the top guides to alternative culture (mostly in German); *Exberliner Magazine* is colorfully written in English (www.exberliner.com). Also pick up the free *030* schedule in bars and clubs (www.berlin030.de).

Half-Price Tickets: Berlin's ticket clearinghouse, **Hekticket,** offers advance tickets to concerts, cabaret, theater, etc. And every day after 14:00, they sell deeply discounted last-minute tickets (up to half off, ticket prices usually €10-40). You can either call or go online (tel. 030/230-9930, www.hekticket.de, pay by credit card), or visit one of their locations (cash only) to see what's on the push list for that evening. Booths are near Alexanderplatz (Mon-Fri 10:30-19:00, closed Sat-Sun, Alexanderstrasse 1 across from Hotel Park Inn) and in City West (Mon-Sat 12:00-20:00, Sun 14:00-18:00, across from Zoologischer Garten train station at Hardenbergstrasse 29).

Smoking: Berlin bars that don't sell food may allow smoking (unlike in much of Europe).

Late-Hours Sightseeing: Berlin's museums typically close at 18:00, but many stay open later at least one day a week. Three of the biggies are open late every day: the Reichstag (until midnight, last entry at 22:00), the Museum of the Wall at Checkpoint Charlie (until 22:00), and the Topography of Terror (until 20:00). All the Museum Island museums are open until 20:00 on Thursdays. Outdoor monuments such as the Berlin Wall Memorial and the Memorial to the Murdered Jews of Europe are accessible, safe, and well lit late into the night, though their visitor centers close earlier.

Classical Music
Berlin Philharmonic
Housed in a striking modern building at the Kulturforum cultural complex, the Berlin Philharmonic is among the world's top ten orchestras. Inexpensive and legitimate tickets are often sold on the street an hour before performances. You can also buy tickets at the box office, by phone, or online (ticket office open Mon-Fri 15:00-18:00, Sat-Sun 11:00-14:00 except closed

July-Aug, tel. 030/2548-8999, July-Aug until 16:00, www.berliner-philharmoniker.de). The philharmonic also presents a popular series of free lunch concerts (most Tue at 13:00 except in July-Aug, tickets handed out in person the same day—try to arrive by 12:00).

Other Classical Music Venues
In the historic core, these include the gorgeous, Schinkel-designed **Konzerthaus Berlin** on Gendarmenmarkt (home of the Konzerthausorchester symphony orchestra, popular 45-minute "espresso concert" series Wed at 14:00, tel. 030/203-092-101, www.konzerthaus.de) and the cutting-edge, Frank Gehry-designed **Pierre Boulez Saal** (theater-in-the-round chamber music, not far from Bebelplatz at Französische Strasse 33D, tel. 030/4799-7411, www.boulezsaal.de). To enjoy an affordable (sometimes free) recital by talented students, consider the **Hochschule für Musik Hanns Eisler,** with two venues in the historical center (facing Gendarmenmarkt at Charlottenstrasse 55, and on Museum Island at Schlossplatz 7, tel. 030/203-092-101, www.hfm-berlin.de).

Opera
The most historic opera venue is the stately **Staatsoper,** on Bebelplatz overlooking Unter den Linden (box office located at Unter den Linden 7, tel. 030/2035-4555, www.staatsoper-berlin.de). Quite different is Berlin's famous **Komische Oper,** with a long tradition for avant-garde, adventurous performances (near Unter den Linden and Friedrichstrasse at Behrenstrasse 55, tel. 030/4799-7400, www.komische-oper-berlin.de). The modern **Deutsche Oper** building (in Charlottenburg, near City West) houses both its own opera company and the Berlin State Ballet (Bismarckstrasse 35, U2: Deutsche Oper, tel. 030/3438-4343, www.deutscheoperberlin.de).

BERLIN

Concerts in Churches

Several Berlin churches and other venues offer frequent daytime and early-evening concerts. Even "free" concerts request a donation.

Marien Church: Along Karl-Liebknecht-Strasse near the TV Tower, free organ concerts twice weekly (Thu and Fri at 13:30, www.marienkirche-berlin.de), as well as a variety of other concerts.

Nikolaikirche: In the Nikolai Quarter, 30-minute organ concerts on Fridays at 17:00 (€4, www.en.stadtmuseum.de/nikolaikirche).

French Cathedral: On Gendarmenmarkt, 30-minute organ concerts on Tuesdays at 15:00 (€3, www.franzoesische-friedrichstadtkirche.de), plus a variety of other organ and choral worship services.

St. Hedwig's Catholic Cathedral: On Bebelplatz, free 30-minute organ concerts on Wednesdays at 15:00 (www.hedwigs-kathedrale.de).

Berlin Cathedral: On Museum Island, evening weekend concerts ranging from organ to choral (tickets at door—prices vary, starts between 18:00 and 20:00, www.berlinerdom.de).

Kaiser Wilhelm Memorial Church: In City West, quality concerts (some free, sporadic schedule, often choral, www.gedaechtniskirche-berlin.de).

Clärchens Ballhaus: Not a church but the old Jewish quarter's beloved classic ballroom, concerts most Sunday evenings in its twinkling upstairs Mirror Room, the Spiegelsaal (€12, often piano or small ensembles, usually begins at 19:00 or 19:30, www.sonntagskonzerte.de).

Modern Music and Theater
Jazz

Berlin has a lively jazz scene (for schedules, see www.jazzclubsinberlin.com). The following are close to my recommended accommodations; each has live music nightly from 21:00 (doors open at 20:00).

In City West (near Savignyplatz), consider **A Trane Jazz Club** (great stage and intimate seating, €10-25 cover depending on act, Bleibtreustrasse 1—see map on page 858, tel. 030/313-2550, www.a-trane.de).

Near the TV Tower, **B-Flat Acoustic Music and Jazz Club** has live shows and jam sessions (from free to €15, in Alexanderplatz at Dircksenstrasse 40—see map on page 864, tel. 030/283-3123, www.b-flat-berlin.de).

Kunstfabrik Schlot, northwest of the old Jewish quarter, is another respected venue (from free to €15, tucked in a cellar, in a courtyard at Invalidenstrasse 117, see map on page 854, U6:

BERLIN

Naturkundemuseum, tel. 030/448-2160, www.kunstfabrik-schlot. de).

Theater and Variety Shows

Since the cabaret days, Berlin has had a flair for the dramatic. Most of these offerings are in German only. For the big spectacles, the language matters less.

Bar Jeder Vernunft, in City West, offers modern-day cabaret a short walk from my recommended Savignyplatz hotels (€25-30, performances generally Mon-Sat at 20:00, Sun at 19:00, seating can be cramped, south of Ku'damm at Schaperstrasse 24—see map on page 858, U3 or U9: Spichernstrasse, tel. 030/883-1582, www. bar-jeder-vernunft.de).

Berliner Ensemble—a venerable company made famous under the direction of Bertolt Brecht—stages a dozen or so different productions each month ranging from classic to contemporary. The performances are housed in the majestic Theater am Schiffbauerdamm, across from the Friedrichstrasse Bahnhof, just off the river (€12-50, performances generally daily at 19:30 or

20:00, box office open Mon-Sat 10:00-18:30, Bertolt-Brecht-Platz 1, tel. 030/2840-8155, www.berliner-ensemble.de).

The **Friedrichstadtpalast** just north of Unter den Linden stages glitzy spectacles (Friedrichstrasse 107, www.palast.berlin). Nearby, a bit closer to Unter den Linden, the historic **Admiralspalast Theater** features lower-key concerts, plays, and musicals (including the Distel Cabaret Theater company—an East Berlin cabaret troupe, Friedrichstrasse 101, www.mehr.de/en/venues/admiralspalast-berlin).

Other venues to consider: **Theater RambaZamba,** in Prenzlauer Berg's Kulturbrauerei, highlights performers who are disabled and creatively transforms those "disabilities" into assets (www.theater-rambazamba.org). **Chamäleon,** inside Hackesche Höfe, channels the creative spirit of 1920s Berlin and bills itself as a contemporary circus, mixing acrobatics, theater, music, and dance (www.chamaeleonberlin.com). **Kookaburra,** between my old Jewish quarter and Prenzlauer Berg hotels, is a comedy club that regularly presents acts in English (usually Tue at 20:00, Schönhauser Allee 184, www.comedyclub.de). And the **Berliner Festspiele** often hosts Off Broadway-type fringe theater (www. berlinerfestspiele.de).

Live Music
Berlin has a staggering array of smaller music venues. Here's a sampling: **Frannz Club,** in Prenzlauer Berg's Kulturbrauerei, was a DDR-era hotspot; today it attracts talented rock and alternative bands (www.frannz.com). **Bassy Club,** near Senefelder Platz in Prenzlauer Berg, is a surreal cowboy-themed club boasting "wild music before 1969" (www.bassyclub.com). **Aufsturz,** the recommended pub in the old Jewish quarter, hosts jazz and other music (www.aufsturz.de). And **SO36,** on Oranienstrasse in Kreuzberg, is Berlin's most venerable punk venue (www.so36.de).

Big concerts are often held at **Olympic Stadium, Mercedes-Benz Arena** in Friedrichshain, the **Spandau Citadel,** and the outdoor **Waldbühne** ("Forest Stage").

Nightlife
Al Fresco Summer Fun
Great places to **stroll** while people-watching Berliners include the Spree riverbank (especially around Monbijoupark and Museum Island); Prenzlauer Berg's Kastanienallee, Oderberger Strasse, and Helmholtzplatz; and Kreuzberg's Paul-Lincke-Ufer, a leafy embankment on the Landwehr Canal with upscale homes and a lively *boules* court. The old Jewish quarter's Oranienburger Strasse (near the New Synagogue) and City  West's Europa Center/Kurfürstendamm boulevard are packed, but are more tourist-oriented.

To nurse a drink, stop by a ***Biergarten.*** Big, beloved, and lively choices include Prater Biergarten, in Prenzlauer Berg; Schleusenkrug in City West, tucked back in the park near the Zoologischer Garten train station; and Golgatha Gaststätten in Kreuzberg's Viktoriapark.

You can also start or end your evenings on a **rooftop bar.** Favorites include the posh **Hotel de Rome** (overlooking Gendarmenmarkt); **25hours Hotel's Monkey Bar** (with views into the zoo residents' enclosure); and **Hugos Restaurant** (inside the Intercontinental on the edge of Tiergarten).

An even more summery variation is Berlin's emerging **beach bar** scene—where people grab a drink along the riverfront and watch the excursion boats go by. The classic spot is the **Strandbar Mitte** in Monbijoupark, with a breezy and scenic setting overlooking the Bode Museum on Museum Island.

Dancing

The old ballroom **Clärchens Ballhaus** has been a Berlin institution since 1913. Every night from 21:00 on the DJ cranks it up and people dance like no one's watching. The music changes every day—swing, waltz, tango, or cha-cha. There's live music on Friday and Saturday (from 23:00, €5 cover, Auguststrasse 24—see map on page 854, S-Bahn: Oranienburger Strasse, tel. 030/282-9295, www.ballhaus.de). If you enjoy the *Ballhaus* scene, consider the campy (and less venerable) **Ballhaus Berlin,** just west of Prenzlau-er Berg (Chausseestrasse 102, U6: Naturkunde-museum, www.ballhaus-berlin.de).

Berlin boasts the largest **tango** scene outside Buenos Aires (well described at www.tangoberlin.de). In summer, it's easy to get a taste of tango on any balmy night in the riverside **Monbijoupark,** between Museum Island and Hackescher Markt.

Shopping in Berlin

Shops all over town stock the typical array of souvenirs (T-shirts, posters, bottle openers, etc.) emblazoned with icons of Berlin: Brandenburg Gate, TV Tower, Berlin Wall, bears (the namesake and official mascot of "Bear-lin"), and so on.

One big draw is **communist kitsch.** Gift shops at museums (such as the DDR Museum or the Museum of the Wall at Checkpoint Charlie) sell a variety of "East Berlin" paraphernalia: circa-1968 city maps that mysteriously leave out West Berlin, postcards and posters of DDR propaganda or famous Wall escapes, miniature Trabis, old DDR military armbands and medals, and defunct communist currency. For authentic communist artifacts, head to the flea market by the Ostbahnhof (Sun mornings, described later).

Maybe *the* top communist-kitsch souvenir is something—anything—with the image of the *Ampelmännchen* (traffic-light man), the DDR-era crossing-guard symbol that's become Berlin's unofficial mascot. The best selection is at the local chain of Ampelmann shops, with locations all over the city. The flagship store—with a hunk of Berlin Wall autographed by David Hasselhoff (no joke)—is along Unter den Linden at #35 (at the corner with Friedrichstrasse).

One communist-era souvenir to avoid is an **"authentic" chunk of the Berlin Wall**—enough of which have been sold since 1989 to encircle all of Germany. Don't trust any vendor who swears they chipped it off the Wall themselves. (And, because the few remaining stretches of Wall are now protected monuments, it's bad form to chisel off your own souvenir.)

Berlin's true forte is **design.** In this city of stylish young urbanites, the streets are lined with hipster gift shops that sell ironic T-shirts, clever kitchen or desk gadgets, snarky books and postcards, and so on.

Flea Markets and Farmers Markets

In such an outdoorsy city, some of the most enjoyable "shopping" experiences aren't in shopping malls or hole-in-the-wall boutiques, but at sprawling outdoor markets.

Flea Markets (Flohmarkt)

Virtually every Berlin neighborhood hosts a regular flea market.

Prenzlauer Berg: The Sunday rummage market in the **Mauerpark** isn't just about buying and selling—it's an excuse for a big, weekly, community-wide party. If it's nice out, people come here simply to chill, drink, barbecue, and socialize. You'll find lots of inventive snack stalls and, in the afternoon, karaoke in the park's amphitheater (Sun 10:00-18:00, U2: Eberswalder Strasse, www. flohmarktimmauerpark.de). On Sundays there's also a lively "junk market" *(Trödelmarkt)* several blocks south on **Arkonaplatz** (10:00-16:00, U8: Bernauer Strasse or a 10-minute walk from Mauerpark).

Old Jewish Quarter: Just across the Spree from Monbijoupark, the riverbank facing the **Bode Museum** hosts a weekend antique-and-book market (Sat-Sun 11:00-17:00, tram #M1 or #M12 to Am Kupfergraben or a 10-minute walk from Hackescher Markt or Friedrichstrasse S-Bahn stations, www.antik-buchmarkt.de). Nearby, **Hackescher Markt** hosts a twice-weekly market with an odd variety of produce, clothes, trinkets, jewelry, hats, and food stalls; while smaller, more touristy, and less funky than the best Berlin markets, it's conveniently located (Thu 9:00-18:00, Sat from 10:00).

Kreuzberg: Along the south bank of Landwehr Canal, the twice-weekly **Turkish street market** is a very local place to shop for everything from clothes and fabrics to basic housewares to produce and meat. The clientele is a mix of Turkish and Middle Eastern immigrants, Kreuzberg punks, and a smattering of tourists. I'd come here more for the

people-watching than for souvenirs (Tue and Fri 11:00-18:30, U8: Schönleinstrasse).

Friedrichshain: The swiftly gentrifying square **Boxhagener Platz** (affectionately called "Boxi" by locals) hosts a lively flea market on Sundays (10:00-18:00, U5: Samariterstrasse or major U- and S-Bahn hub Warschauer Strasse; also a Sat farmers market). On Sunday mornings, the **Antikmarkt Ostbahnhof** (9:00-17:00, on the north side of the Ostbahnhof S-Bahn station) is the place to pick through the Cold War knickknacks that keep turning up in the basements of former East Berliners.

Near Tiergarten Park: One of Berlin's largest flea markets is right next to the Tiergarten park on **Strasse des 17 Juni,** with great antiques, more than 200 stalls, collector-savvy merchants, and fun German fast-food stands (Sat-Sun 10:00-17:00, S-Bahn: Tiergarten, www.berlinertroedelmarkt.com).

Food and Farmers Markets

The city's best food market is Kreuzberg's **Markthalle Neun,** with a variety of vendors and even more activity during the thrice-weekly farmers market and on "Street Food Thursdays." Another local favorite is on **Boxhagener Platz** in Friedrichshain (farmers market Sat 9:00-15:30, see also Sunday flea market). Prenzlauer Berg also has options: **Kollwitzplatz** (Thu 12:00-19:00 and Sat 9:00-16:00) and in the courtyard of the **Kulturbrauerei** (Sun 12:00-18:00).

Browsing Areas
Prenzlauer Berg

My favorite hotel and dining neighborhood is also an enjoyable place to window-shop. It's a delight to simply wander colorful Kastanienallee between Eberswalder Strasse (with a U-Bahn station) and Weinbergspark.

The **Kulturbrauerei** brewery-turned-cultural center (described on page 809) has a smattering of little shops, including Green Living (with environmentally friendly housewares and home decor). The Kollwitzkiez (a few blocks east) is mostly residential, but you'll also find some pleasant shops here. For locally produced goods, stop by **Brandenburgerie,** with a variety of mostly edible products (meat, cheese, chocolate, juices, schnapps) made in the Brandenburg region that surrounds Berlin (closed Sun-Mon, Sredzkistrasse 36).

Rosenthaler Strasse

The otherwise nondescript street that connects the Hackescher Markt and Rosenthaler Platz areas (along the handy tram #M1 route) attracts those interested in Berlin's fashion and design scene. Most shops along here are **pop-up** spaces, giving you a glimpse at what local designers are up to right now. A couple of permanent fixtures are worth checking out: **Kauf Dich Glücklich,** a ramshackle Berlin café famous for its waffles (see page 868), but which has since moved into fashion (at #17, www.kaufdichgluecklich-shop.de); and **Schee,** with appealing handmade items, including prints and textiles (at #15, www.schee.net).

Hackesche Höfe

This delightfully restored old series of eight interlocking shopping courtyards sits in the heart of the old Jewish quarter. While not cheap, it's a convenient and tempting place to window-shop for everything from locally made porcelain to artisanal local foods to fashion (shops typically open Mon-Sat from 10:00 or 11:00 until 19:00, closed Sun, Rosenthaler Strasse 40, www. hackesche-hoefe.com).

Chocolate Shops on Gendarmenmarkt

The delightful square called Gendarmenmarkt—a short detour south of Unter den Linden—has two very different chocolate shops that are fun to browse: one bourgeois, and the other proletarian. For locations, see the "Historic Core Hotels & Restaurants" map.

Rausch claims to be Europe's biggest chocolate store. After 150 years of chocolatemaking, this family-owned business proudly displays its sweet delights—250 different kinds—on a 55-foot-long buffet. Truffles are sold for about €1 each and picked at your direction by white-gloved maidens (it's fun to compose the fancy little eight-piece box of your dreams). Upstairs is an elegant café with fine views (Mon-Sat 10:00-20:00, Sun from 11:00, corner of Mohrenstrasse at Charlottenstrasse 60—look for green awnings directly behind German Cathedral, tel. 030/757-882-440).

If you're a choco-populist, head to the opposite end of Gendarmenmarkt, near the French Cathedral, for the Volkswagen of candy. **Rittersport Bunte Schokowelt** is home to the flagship store of Rittersport, the famous chocolate company—*"quadratisch, praktisch, gut"* ("square, practical, good"). This is basically Germany's answer to the M&M's store (daily 10:00-19:00, Französische Strasse 24, tel. 030/200-950-810).

Big, Glitzy Department Stores

Central Berlin: Unter den Linden is lined with some high-end shops, but for a wider selection, head a few blocks south. The French department store **Galeries Lafayette** has a large outpost here with several floors of high-end goods under a glass dome (top-quality basement food court; Mon-Sat 10:00-20:00, closed Sun, Französische Strasse 23).

Several blocks west is the massive, recently opened, state-of-the-art **Mall of Berlin,** with 270 shops surrounding a cavernous glass-covered passageway (Mon-Sat 10:00-21:00, closed Sun, Vossstrasse 35, www.mallofberlin.de). Nearby, **Potsdamer Platz** and **Sony Center** have additional shops.

City West: Several swanky shops line **Kurfürstendamm,** the area's main boulevard. The trendy **Bikini Berlin** shopping center faces the Europa Center on one side and the Berlin Zoo on the other. This "concept mall" has a mix of international chains, artisan boutiques, temporary art exhibits, food stalls, a small Edeka supermarket, and "pop-up boxes" highlighting Berlin

vendors (plus a free glimpse of the zoo's monkeys; Mon-Sat 10:00-20:00, closed Sun, Budapester Strasse 38, www.bikiniberlin.de).

City West's most venerable shopping is a couple blocks east (near the Wittenbergplatz U-Bahn), at **KaDeWe**—one of Europe's fanciest department stores, in business since 1907 and a worthwhile sight in itself (for more, see page 834).

Sleeping in Berlin

Choosing the right neighborhood in Berlin is as important as choosing the right hotel. I've focused my recommendations in safe, colorful areas convenient to sightseeing. In northern Berlin, Prenzlauer Berg— my favorite area to sleep—offers a local neighborhood vibe, easy transit connections, and an excellent selection of eateries; the old Jewish quarter, also with good restaurants, is closer to the sights but more impersonal than Prenzlauer Berg. Farther out, City West—the heart of the former West Berlin—is an upscale, residential neighborhood. For some travelers, short-term, Airbnb-type rentals can be a good alternative to hotels; search for places in my recommended hotel neighborhoods.

A few notes about hotels in Berlin:

- Berlin charges a daily tourist tax (5 percent of the room rate). This may be included in the room price or may appear as an extra charge on your bill.
- Most hotels offer an optional **breakfast** buffet for about €15-20 per person, though it's often not included in their quoted rates (you can choose whether to add breakfast when book-

ing). Light eaters and budget travelers can opt out of the hotel breakfast and get coffee and a pastry at a neighborhood café for less.

- **Air-conditioning** is relatively rare (I've noted hotels that have it in all rooms). If it's important to you, ask about it when you book.
- Many hotels offer **bike rentals** to guests (usually €10-12/day).

I rank accommodations from **$** budget to **$$$$** splurge. To get the best deal, contact family-run hotels directly by phone or email. When you go direct, the owner may be able to offer you a discount (and avoids paying a big commission to a booking website). Book your accommodations well in advance if you'll be traveling during peak season or if your trip coincides with a major holiday or festival (see the appendix). Rooms can be in especially short supply when big trade shows are in town (including Green Week in mid-January and the ITB travel show in mid-March).

For information on hotel rates and deals, making reservations, finding a short-term rental, and more, see the "Sleeping" section in the Practicalities chapter.

PRENZLAUER BERG

My favorite Berlin neighborhood to call home, Prenzlauer Berg offers easy transit connections to sightseeing; diverse eateries, coffeehouses, and nightspots; and a welcoming personality. A onetime hipster mecca, this area is now gentrified and more sedate—yet it still retains a bit of its alternative edge (think of all that graffiti as just some people's way of saying they care).

Most of my recommended hotels are between Kastanienallee and Prenzlauer Allee. The area's transit hub is the Eberswalder Strasse U-Bahn station (U2 line). Trams also serve this neighborhood: The #M1 and #12 run up and down Kastanienallee, connecting to the Rosenthaler Platz U-Bahn (#M1 continues all the way to the Hackescher Markt S-Bahn station), while the #M10 heads west from Eberswalder Strasse along Bernauer Strasse to the Berlin Wall Memorial and eventually to the Hauptbahnhof.

$$$ Hotel Jurine (zhoo-REEN—the family name) is a pleasant and well-run 53-room business-style hotel on a peaceful street. Its good-value rooms are priced at the low end of this range. If you want calm atmosphere in a comfortable and quality building, with more German guests than tourists, your own peaceful back garden, and a very friendly staff, this is my choice (mention Rick Steves when you book for a free upgraded room, breakfast extra, elevator, pay parking—reserve ahead, Schwedter Strasse 15, 5-minute walk to #M1: Zionskirchplatz or U2: Senefelderplatz, tel. 030/443-2990, www.hotel-jurine.de, mail@hotel-jurine.de).

$$$ Hotel Oderberger has 70 modern rooms filling part of a Neo-Renaissance bathhouse complex (originally opened in 1902, renovated and reopened in 2016). From the reception, you can peek into the elegant old swimming pool area. It's a fine choice, with its understated elegance, historic aura, and good location, tucked away on a quiet side street near the most happening stretch of Kastanienallee (elevator, guest discount for swimming pool, Oderberger Strasse 57, tel. 030/780-089-760, www.hotel-oderberger.de, info@hotel-oderberger.berlin).

$$$ Linnen rents five rooms above a cozy and characteristic café, along a busy street between the Eberswalder Strasse U-Bahn station and Mauerpark. Linnen stays true to its motto, "more home, less hotel"—the vibe is casual, and the spacious, stylishly decorated rooms feel homey. This place pleases well-heeled hipsters (breakfast extra at downstairs café, Eberswalder Strasse 35, tel. 030/4737-2440, www.linnenberlin.com, booking@linnenberlin.com).

$$ Myer's Hotel rents 50 comfortable rooms decorated with lots of bold colors and gold accents. Located on a tranquil, tree-lined street, and overlooking a sleepy courtyard, Myer's is closer to charming Kollwitzplatz than to the Kastanienallee action. Staying at this peaceful hub, you'll find it hard to believe you're in the heart of a capital city. The gorgeous public spaces, including an art filled patio and garden, host frequent cultural events (air-con, elevator, sauna, Metzer Strasse 26—midway between U2: Senefelderplatz and #M2 tram; Prenzlauer Allee/Metzer Strasse, #M2 goes to/from Alexanderplatz, tel. 030/440-140, www.myershotel.de, info@myershotel.de).

$$ Hotel Kastanienhof feels less urban-classy and more like a traditional small-town German hotel. It's wonderfully located on the Kastanienallee #M1 tram line, with easy access to the Prenzlauer Berg bustle (but since trams run all night, ask for a room in the back). Its 44 rooms come with helpful service (breakfast extra, deluxe top-floor rooms offer air con and/or balcony, elevator, wheelchair-accessible room, pay parking, 20 yards from #M1: Zionskirchplatz at Kastanienallee 65, tel. 030/443-050, www.kastanienhof.berlin, info@kastanienhof.berlin). The hotel's recommended Ausspanne restaurant serves excellent German dishes with a modern twist.

¢ Hostels: A convenient branch of the hostel/budget hotel **Meininger** is at Senefelderplatz; for details, see page 861. **East-Seven Hostel** rents 100 of the best cheap beds in Prenzlauer Berg. Modern and conscientiously run, it offers all the hostel services plus an inviting lounge, guest kitchen, backyard terrace, and bike rental. Children are welcome. Easygoing people of any age are comfortable here (private rooms available, no curfew, 100 yards from U2: Senefelderplatz at Schwedter Strasse 7, tel. 030/9362-2240, www.eastseven.de, info@eastseven.de).

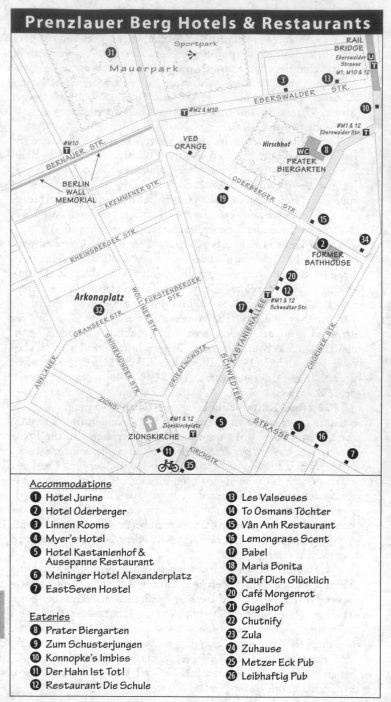

Prenzlauer Berg Hotels & Restaurants

Accommodations
1. Hotel Jurine
2. Hotel Oderberger
3. Linnen Rooms
4. Myer's Hotel
5. Hotel Kastanienhof & Ausspanne Restaurant
6. Meininger Hotel Alexanderplatz
7. EastSeven Hostel

Eateries
8. Prater Biergarten
9. Zum Schusterjungen
10. Konnopke's Imbiss
11. Der Hahn Ist Tot!
12. Restaurant Die Schule
13. Les Valseuses
14. To Osmans Töchter
15. Vân Anh Restaurant
16. Lemongrass Scent
17. Babel
18. Maria Bonita
19. Kauf Dich Glücklich
20. Café Morgenrot
21. Gugelhof
22. Chutnify
23. Zula
24. Zuhause
25. Metzer Eck Pub
26. Leibhaftig Pub

BERLIN

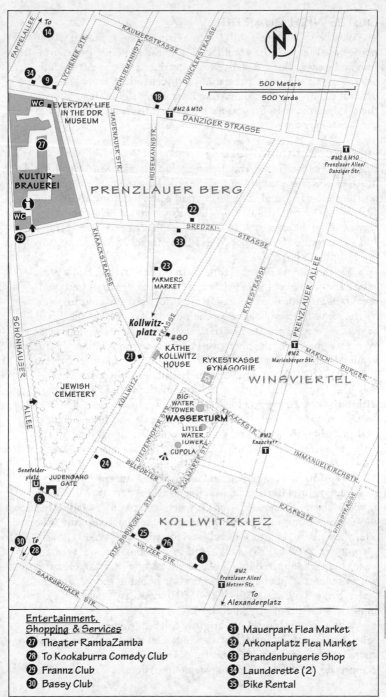

Entertainment, Shopping & Services

27 Theater RambaZamba
28 To Kookaburra Comedy Club
29 Frannz Club
30 Bassy Club

31 Mauerpark Flea Market
32 Arkonaplatz Flea Market
33 Brandenburgerie Shop
34 Launderette (2)
35 Bike Rental

OLD JEWISH QUARTER

The old Jewish quarter, south of Prenzlauer Berg, makes for a fine home base thanks to its good location (close to public transportation and easy walking distance to the center) and traveler-friendly offerings, including cozy restaurants, independent shops, the delightful Monbijoupark, and a few interesting sights. It's closer to the historic core than Prenzlauer Berg but feels less residential, and the hotels here are bigger and less personable.

Near Rosenthaler Platz

Rosenthaler Platz is halfway between Hackescher Markt and the heart of the Prenzlauer Berg scene (on Kastanienallee). Though bustling and congested, it makes a good base for getting around the city thanks to its U-Bahn stop (U8: Rosenthaler Platz) and tram service (#M1 heads north to Kastanienallee/Eberswalder Strasse and south to the Hackescher Markt S-Bahn hub; #M8 connects to the Hauptbahnhof).

$$ The Circus Hotel is fun, entirely comfortable, and a great value. The achingly hip lobby has a café serving delicious (optional) breakfasts, and the 60 rooms are straightforward and colorful. Run by the same folks who manage the popular Circus Hostel (listed below), it's service oriented, with a very "green" attitude and special events for guests. As the hotel overlooks a busy intersection, ask for a quieter back room (breakfast extra, elevator, Rosenthaler Strasse 1, tel. 030/2000-3939, www.circus-berlin.de, info@circus-berlin.de). The Circus also offers spacious, modern **$$$ apartments** within the hotel and two blocks away at Choriner Strasse 84.

$$ Amano Hotel, while big (163 rooms) and impersonal, is well-priced for what you get: chic contemporary design and all the little amenities you don't need but appreciate nonetheless (breakfast extra, air-con, elevator, pay parking, Auguststrasse 43, tel. 030/809-4150, www.amanogroup.de, amano@amanogroup.de).

$ EasyHotel Berlin Hackescher Markt is part of an unapologetically cheap, Europe-wide chain where you pay for exactly what you use—nothing more, nothing less. You're charged a low base rate, then pay à la carte for each service you add (Wi-Fi, housekeeping, etc.). The 125 orange-and-gray rooms are very small, basic, and feel popped out of a plastic mold (no breakfast, elevator, call to request a quieter back room after booking online, Rosenthaler Strasse 69, tel. 030/4000-6550, www.easyhotel-berlin.de, enquiries@berlinhm.easyhotel.com).

¢ The Circus Hostel is a brightly colored, well-run place with 250 beds, plenty of social networking, and a trendy lounge and microbrewery. It has typical hostel dorms as well as some hotel-like private rooms; for a few big steps up in comfort, consider the

Circus Hotel, listed earlier (no curfew, elevator, Weinbergsweg 1A, tel. 030/2000-3939, www.circus-berlin.de, info@circus-berlin.de).

By Hackescher Markt

Lively Hackescher Markt, just north of the river, is brimming with people, eateries, and on some days, an open-air market. It's also home to an S-Bahn station and is connected to Prenzlauer Berg by tram #M1.

Of the following listings, the first two (Adina and Hotel Alexander Plaza) are in a characterless glass-and-concrete zone just south of Hackescher Markt. The others face each other across the tracks of a tram depot (ask for a quieter room). These hotels are all bigger than they are charming.

$$$ Adina Apartment Hotel Berlin Hackescher Markt has 134 studio and one-bedroom apartments with kitchenettes, though breakfast is available for an extra fee (air-con, elevator, pay parking, An der Spandauer Brücke 11, tel. 030/209-6980, www.adinahotels.com, berlinhm@adina.cu).

$$$ Hotel Alexander Plaza offers 94 brightly appointed, business-style rooms (breakfast extra, elevator, pay parking, Rosenstrasse 1, tel. 030/240-010, www.hotel-alexander-plaza.de, frontoffice@hotel-alexander-plaza.de).

$$$ Monbijou Hotel's 101 rooms are small, but they make up for it with pleasing public spaces, a postcard-worthy rooftop terrace (with views of the cathedral and TV Tower), and a flair for design—from reclaimed wood and antique furnishings to plenty of natural light (breakfast extra, family rooms, air-con, elevator, pay parking, Monbijouplatz 1, tel. 030/6162-0300, www.monbijouhotel.com, info@monbijouhotel.com).

$$ Hotel Hackescher Markt, with 32 rooms, offers an inviting lounge and modern decor without being predictable or pretentious (breakfast extra, family rooms, elevator, Grosse Präsidentenstrasse 8, tel. 030/280 030, www.hotel-hackescher-markt.com, reservierung@hotel-hackescher-markt.com).

$$ Hotel Zoe by Amano, with 88 rooms and a pleasant rooftop bar, is a trendy and slightly more upscale branch of the Amano Hotel listed earlier (breakfast extra, air-con, elevator, Grosse Präsidentenstrasse 6, tel. 030/2130-0150, www.amanogroup.de, zoe@amanogroup.de).

On or near Auguststrasse

These good-value hotels are on or close to fun, art gallery-lined Auguststrasse, in an area that feels more characteristic than my other listings in the old Jewish quarter. They're located between the Oranienburger Strasse S-Bahn (S1/S2) and Oranienburger Tor U-Bahn (U6), and tram #M1 is nearby.

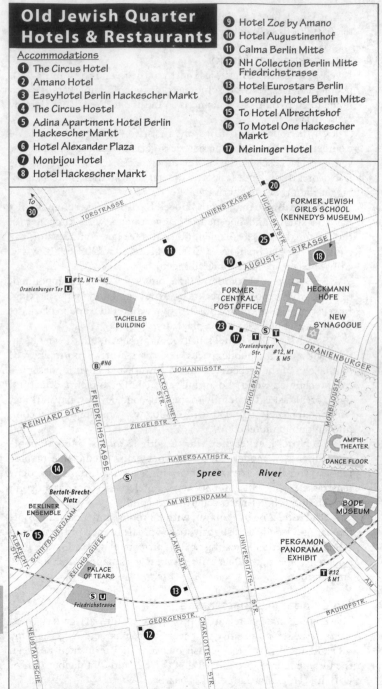

Old Jewish Quarter Hotels & Restaurants

Accommodations

1 The Circus Hotel
2 Amano Hotel
3 EasyHotel Berlin Hackescher Markt
4 The Circus Hostel
5 Adina Apartment Hotel Berlin Hackescher Markt
6 Hotel Alexander Plaza
7 Monbijou Hotel
8 Hotel Hackescher Markt
9 Hotel Zoe by Amano
10 Hotel Augustinenhof
11 Calma Berlin Mitte
12 NH Collection Berlin Mitte Friedrichstrasse
13 Hotel Eurostars Berlin
14 Leonardo Hotel Berlin Mitte
15 To Hotel Albrechtshof
16 To Motel One Hackescher Markt
17 Meininger Hotel

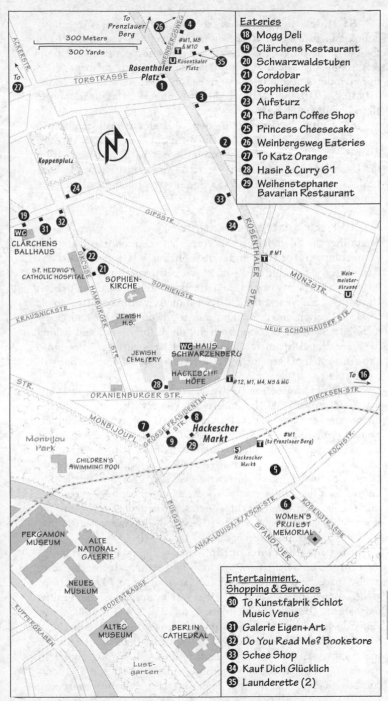

Eateries

- ⑱ Mogg Deli
- ⑲ Clärchens Restaurant
- ⑳ Schwarzwaldstuben
- ㉑ Cordobar
- ㉒ Sophieneck
- ㉓ Aufsturz
- ㉔ The Barn Coffee Shop
- ㉕ Princess Cheesecake
- ㉖ Weinbergsweg Eateries
- ㉗ To Katz Orange
- ㉘ Hasir & Curry 61
- ㉙ Weihenstephaner Bavarian Restaurant

Entertainment, Shopping & Services

- ㉚ To Kunstfabrik Schlot Music Venue
- ㉛ Galerie Eigen+Art
- ㉜ Do You Read Me? Bookstore
- ㉝ Schee Shop
- ㉞ Kauf Dich Glücklich
- ㉟ Launderette (2)

BERLIN

$$ Hotel Augustinenhof has 66 spacious rooms, nice woody floors, and firm beds. Rooms in front overlook the courtyard of the old Imperial Post Office (and its ongoing construction project), rooms in back are a bit quieter, and some rooms have older, thin windows (breakfast extra, elevator, Auguststrasse 82, tel. 030/3088-6710, www.hotel-augustinenhof.de, augustinenhof@albrechtshof-hotels.de).

$$ Calma Berlin Mitte, part of a small local chain, is a good budget bet. Its 46 straightforward but comfortable, modern rooms are tucked away on a tranquil courtyard, just steps from the lively Oranienburger Strasse scene (breakfast extra, elevator, Linienstrasse 139, tel. 030/9153-9333, www.lindemannhotels.de, calma@lindemannhotels.de).

Near Friedrichstrasse Station

Straddling the Spree River, this area—between the transit stations Oranienburger Tor (U6) and Friedrichstrasse (U6 and several S-Bahn lines)—feels big and sterile, with little personality. But hotels here have plenty of beds and are easy walking distance to both Unter den Linden and the old Jewish quarter. The first two hotels (NH Collection and Eurostars) are south of the river and closer to Friedrichstrasse Station; both are plush, high-end, and belong to international Spanish chains. The last two listings (Leonardo and Albrechtshof) are north of the river and a bit simpler, but still comfortable.

$$$ NH Collection Berlin Mitte Friedrichstrasse feels upscale and professional. Its 268 rooms come with sleek hardwood floors, high ceilings, and red accents (breakfast extra, air-con, elevator, gym, sauna, Friedrichstrasse 96, tel. 030/206-2660, www.nh-collection.com, nhcollectionberlinfriedrich@nh-hotels.com).

$$$ Hotel Eurostars Berlin is a classy hotel with 221 spacious, rich wood rooms towering over the everyday hustle and bustle. As it faces train tracks, ask for a quieter room—several face into the lobby atrium (breakfast extra, air-con, elevator, gym, spa, Friedrichstrasse 99, tel. 030/7017-36284, www.eurostarsberlin.com, info@eurostarsberlin.com).

$$ Leonardo Hotel Berlin Mitte occupies a modern building set back on a little park overlooking the river. It features retro public spaces and a mazelike floor plan leading to 309 tight, tidy, stylish rooms (breakfast extra, air-con, elevator, gym, spa, limited pay parking, Bertolt-Brecht-Platz 4, tel. 030/374-405-000, www.leonardo-hotels.com, info.berlinmitte@leonardo-hotels.com).

$$ Hotel Albrechtshof is a bit scruffier than its sister hotel, the Augustinenhof (described earlier), but still a good choice. It has the most personality of the hotels in this area. The 98 rooms come with a similar design, friendly staff, peaceful courtyard, and weekly chapel services. Martin Luther King Jr. once stayed here and attended one (breakfast extra, elevator, Albrechtstrasse 8, tel. 030/308-860, www.hotel-albrechtshof.de, albrechtshof@albrechtshof-hotel.de).

CITY WEST

City West—the heart of the former West Berlin—is a pleasant, upscale, low-impact residential neighborhood. While most travelers prefer to sleep closer to the center, City West can be an ideal home base if you don't mind a longer commute to sightseeing. The area retains an artsy aura, going back to the cabaret days of the 1920s, when it was the center of Berlin's gay scene. Today, City West feels sedate and posh (if quite touristy along Ku'damm). Travelers sleeping in City West have several transit options: Bus #100 is slow but scenic, while the S-Bahn zips much faster from Savignyplatz or Zoologischer Garten to the center.

Near Europa Center

$$$$ 25hours Hotel Bikini Berlin is your trendy hotel option overlooking Europa Center in the busiest and buzziest part of City West. Filling a high rise adjacent to the Berlin Zoo and the Bikini Berlin shopping mall, it has 149 plywood-and-concrete rooms and public spaces with an industrial-zoo ambience. This is where trendsetters sleep in City West (breakfast extra, air-con, elevator, Budapester Strasse 40, tel. 030/120-2210, www.25hours-hotels.com, bikini@25hours-hotels.com).

Around Savignyplatz

These listings huddle around the delightful, tree-lined Savignyplatz, which has a neighborhood charm and an abundance of simple, small, friendly, good-value places to sleep and eat. The first two hotels, located between Savignyplatz and Ku'damm, are close to the Uhlandstrasse U-Bahn station (U1). For the others, ride the S-Bahn directly to Savignyplatz—or get off at Zoologischer Garten (with more connections) and walk about 10 minutes.

$$ Hecker's Hotel is an excellent value, with 69 big, fresh, well-maintained rooms and all the Euro comforts. Herr Kiesel's "superior" rooms have air-conditioning and more-modern furnishings—and cost a bit more—than his "comfort" rooms (a few rooms with kitchenettes, free breakfast for Rick Steves readers, elevator, pay parking, Grolmanstrasse 35, tel. 030/88900, www.heckers-hotel.de, info@heckers-hotel.de).

$$ Hommage à Magritte is a spiffy, tidy B&B in a classic old apartment building on a quiet street. Its 17 rooms come with an artistic touch, inspired by its namesake, the Belgian Surrealist painter

City West Hotels & Restaurants

Accommodations
1 25hours Hotel Bikini Berlin
2 Hecker's Hotel
3 Hommage à Magritte B&B
4 Hotel-Pension Funk
5 Hotel Augusta
6 Pension Peters
7 Motel One Ku'damm

Eateries & Nightlife
8 Restaurant Marjellchen
9 Dicke Wirtin
10 Café im Literaturhaus
11 Heno Heno
12 Diener Tattersall
13 To Weyers
14 Bleibtreustrasse Eateries
15 Curry 36
16 Schleusenkrug Beer Garden
17 KaDeWe Winter Garden Buffet
18 A Trane Jazz Club
19 Bar Jeder Vernunft

BERLIN

René Magritte (Grolmanstrasse 32, tel. 030/8956-7087, www.hommage-a-magritte.com, info@hommage-a-magritte.com).

$$ Hotel-Pension Funk, the former home of a 1920s silent-movie star, is a delightfully quirky, only-in-Berlin time warp. Kind manager Herr Michael Pfundt and his right-hand man, Ding, offer 15 elegant old rooms with rich Art Nouveau furnishings and hardly any modern trappings. Most guests adore it; some are put off by its old-fashioned feel. Figure out which you'll be before you book (cheaper rooms with shared bath, cash preferred, no TVs, a long block south of Ku'damm at Fasanenstrasse 69, tel. 030/882-7193, www.hotel-pensionfunk.de, berlin@hotel-pensionfunk.de).

$$ Hotel Augusta, run by mother-and-daughter team Julia and Danuta—and their friendly staff—fills an early-20th-century building with 45 smartly decorated rooms, most with hints of the building's Jugendstil origins. Superior rooms come with coffee makers and air-con, while others have balconies overlooking Ku'damm

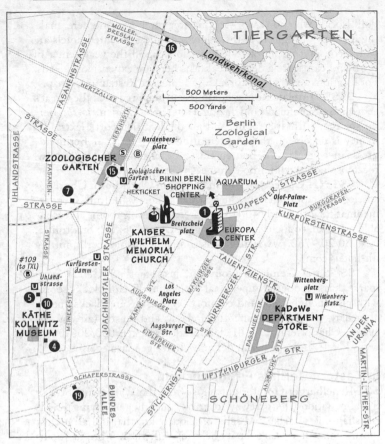

(breakfast extra, elevator, Fasanenstrasse 22, tel. 030/883-5028, www.hotel-augusta.de, info@hotel-augusta.de).

$ Pension Peters, run by a German-Swedish couple, is sunny and central, with a cheery breakfast room and super-friendly staff who go out of their way to help guests. With sleek Scandinavian decor and 33 rooms, it's a good choice. Some ground-floor rooms facing the back courtyard are a bit dark—and cheaper. If street noise bothers you, request a quiet room. Annika and Christoph (with help from his sister, Daisy, as well as Uwe and others) have been welcoming my readers for decades (breakfast extra, RS%, family rooms, 10 yards off Savignyplatz at Kantstrasse 146, tel. 030/312-2278, www.pension-peters-berlin.de, info@pension-peters-berlin.de).

OTHER SLEEPING OPTIONS
Business Hotels in the Historic Core
Berlin's historic core is handy to sightseeing, but—frankly—pretty

dull. Locals who don't work in this area rarely venture here, making it sleepy at night. But these large, business-oriented hotels are worth considering if you're looking to sleep in the very center of town and can score a deal. Breakfasts here are expensive add-ons. For locations see the "Historic Core Hotels & Restaurants" map.

$$$$ Hotel de Rome, holding court on Frederick the Great's showpiece Bebelplatz and facing Unter den Linden, is *the* Berlin splurge, with 108 rooms and all the luxurious little extras. If money is no object, this is a tempting choice for your Berlin address (air-con, elevator, Behrenstrasse 37, tel. 030/460-6090, www.roccofortehotels.com, info.derome@roccofortehotels.com).

$$$ NH Collection Berlin Mitte am Checkpoint Charlie is an elegant chain hotel on a busy street a short walk from Gendarmenmarkt, with nearly 400 fresh, interchangeable rooms at reasonable rates (air-con, elevator, Leipziger Strasse 106, U2: Stadtmitte, tel. 030/203-760, www.nh-hotels.com, nhcollectionberlinmitte@nh-hotels.com).

$$ Hotel Gendarm Nouveau, just steps off Gendarmenmarkt, has a modern, impersonal lobby and 47 Goldilocks rooms with just enough color and comfort. While the area lacks energy after dark, it's lively at lunchtime, classy, and central (air-con, elevator, Charlottenstrasse 61, U2: Stadtmitte, tel. 030/206-0660, www.hotel-gendarm-berlin.de, info@hotel-gendarm-berlin.de).

In Eastern Berlin's Friedrichshain

$$ Michelberger Hotel, right across from the Warschauer Strasse S-Bahn station (the gateway to gritty, quickly gentrifying Friedrichshain), is so artsy and self-consciously hip that it'd all be just too much...if it weren't for its helpful staff. Its 133 bright rooms are reasonably priced, and its common spaces—a bar/lounge and a breezy all-organic courtyard restaurant—are welcoming (breakfast extra, family rooms, elevator; from atop Warschauer Strasse S-Bahn station, turn left to cross the bridge—it's across from the U-Bahn station and #M10 tram stop at Warschauer Strasse 39; tel. 030/2977-8590, www.michelbergerhotel.com, reservations@michelbergerhotel.com).

Good-Value Chain Hotels

$ Motel One has multiple locations across Berlin; all have the same aqua-and-brown decor and posh-feeling but small rooms. The four most convenient locations are between Hackescher Markt and Alexanderplatz (Dircksenstrasse 36—see the "Old Jewish Quarter Hotels & Restaurants" map, tel. 030/2005-4080, berlin-hackeschermarkt@motel-one.com); near the Zoologischer Garten station (Kantstrasse 10—see the "City West Hotels & Restaurants" map, tel. 030/3151-7360, berlin-kudamm@motel-one.com);

just behind the Hauptbahnhof (Invalidenstrasse 54, tel. 030/3641-0050, berlin-hauptbahnhof@motel-one.com); and a few blocks east of Gendarmenmarkt (Leipziger Strasse 50, U2: Spittelmarkt, tel. 030/2014-3630, berlin-spittelmarkt@motel-one.com). For the last two locations, see the "Historic Core Hotels & Restaurants" map.

Meininger is a Europe-wide budget-hotel chain with several locations in Berlin. With both ¢ cheap dorm beds and $$ comfortable, hotelesque private rooms, Meininger is basic but lively, modern, and generally a solid budget option, even for nonhostelers. They have three well-located branches: in Prenzlauer Berg ("Alexanderplatz" branch, actually at Schönhauser Allee 19 on Senefelderplatz—see the "Prenzlauer Berg Hotels & Restaurants" map); in the old Jewish quarter (Mitte "Humboldthaus" branch, next to the recommended Aufsturz pub at Oranienburger Strasse 67—see the "Old Jewish Quarter Hotels & Restaurants" map); and near the Hauptbahnhof at Ella-Trebe-Strasse 9—see the "Historic Core Hotels & Restaurants" map (all locations have elevator and 24-hour reception, pay parking at some, tel. 030/666-36100, www.meininger-hostels.com, welcome@meininger-hostels.com).

Eating in Berlin

Berlin hosts a world of ever-changing restaurants. While the city abounds with traditional German eateries, Berliners consider this cuisine old-school; when they eat out, they're usually not looking for traditional local fare. Nouveau German is California cuisine with scant memories of wurst, kraut, and pumpernickel.

Berlin is also a place to venture beyond German cuisine. As one of Europe's primary melting pots, you'll find sushi, Turkish, Italian, Peruvian, Cuban, Thai, Georgian, Indian, Argentinian, and lots of Vietnamese—usually done quite well. In recent years, Michelin-star restaurants and fancy steak houses have attracted attention from celebrities and travelers who appreciate finer dining. The result: From simple to sophisticated, Berlin's cuisine scene has something for every taste bud—and budget.

EATING TIPS

I rank restaurants from $ budget to $$$$ splurge. For general advice on eating in Germany, including details on dining and tipping in restaurants, where to find budget meals, and descriptions of popular German dishes and beverages, see the "Eating" section in the Practicalities chapter.

Choosing Restaurants: Berlin has far more quality restaurants than could fit in any guidebook—and the scene changes so fast, anything in print is already dated. It's hard to go wrong by

BERLIN

just browsing a neighborhood until you find something that strikes your fancy.

Berlin Specialties: Don't be too determined to eat "Berlin-style." The city is best known for its street food—*Currywurst* and kebabs (see the "Berliner Street Food" sidebar).

But if you do eat German food in Berlin, popular dishes include *Buletten* and *Königsberger Klopse* (both meatball dishes), plus other meaty plates, such as *Schnitzel Holstein* (veal cutlet with egg), *Eisbein* (boiled ham hock), *Leber Berliner Art* (veal liver), *Kassler* (or *Kasseler;* smoked pork), and *Mett* (or *Hackepeter;* minced pork). Also popular are *Aal grün* (boiled eel), *Rollmops* (pickled herring), and *Senfeier* (hard-boiled eggs with potatoes). As for sweets, *Berliner Pfannkuchen* is the local jelly doughnut, and *Berliner Luft* is a popular dessert. These dishes are described in more detail in the Practicalities chapter (under "Traditional German Fare," starting on page 986).

HISTORIC CORE

While this government/commercial area is hardly a hotspot for eateries, I've listed a few places handy for your sightseeing, all a short walk from Unter den Linden.

On and near Museum Island

The Altes, Neues, and Bode museums all have simple cafés. My favorite Berlin museum restaurant is in the neighboring German History Museum. And the streets around Hackescher Markt, a 10-minute walk away in the old Jewish quarter, hold plenty of options (see that neighborhood description, later in this chapter).

$$ Deponie No. 3 is a rustic if touristy Berlin *Kneipe* (pub). Garden seating in the back is nice but comes with the noise of the S-Bahn passing directly above. The bar interior is a cozy and woody with several inviting spaces. They serve basic salads, traditional Berlin dishes, and hearty daily specials (daily 10:00-24:00, S-Bahn arch #187 at Georgenstrasse 5, tel. 030/2016-5740).

Near the TV Tower: $$ Brauhaus Lemke is a big, lively beer hall (modern but still in its 1970s DDR shell) that makes its own brews and offers a menu of Berliner specialties and Bavarian dishes. They have decent salads and serve a six-beer sampler board. You can venture upstairs any time to see the actual brewery (daily 12:00-24:00, across from the TV Tower and tucked a bit back from the street at Karl-Liebknecht-Strasse 13, tel. 030/3087-8989).

Nikolai Quarter: A short walk from Museum Island and Karl-Liebknecht-Strasse, Berlin's rebuilt "old town" (the Nikolai Quarter) feels pretty soulless by day but is a popular restaurant zone at night. **$$ Brauhaus Georgbräu,** a thriving beer hall teeming with German tourists, serves homemade suds on a picturesque courtyard overlooking the Spree River. Eat in the lively and woody but mod-feeling, hops-infused interior, or outdoors with fun riverside seating. It's a good place to try *Eisbein* (boiled ham hock) with sauerkraut and mashed peas with bacon, a typical Berlin dish. Their statue of St. George once stood in the courtyard of Berlin's old castle—until the Nazis deemed it not "German" enough (daily 12:00-24:00, 2 blocks south of Berlin Cathedral and across the river at Spreeufer 4, tel. 030/242-4244).

Near Gendarmenmarkt

South of Unter den Linden, Gendarmenmarkt, with its twin churches, is a delightful place for an al fresco meal. Here you'll find business-lunch-type places that offer midday specials, though they're pricey at night. For more options, browse the eateries along Charlottenstrasse.

$$$$ Lutter & Wegner Restaurant is a Berlin institution respected for its Austrian cuisine (*Schnitzel* and *Sauerbraten*). Popular with businesspeople, it's dressy, with fun sidewalk seating or a dark and elegant interior. Weekday €9 lunch specials are an affordable way to sample their cooking (daily 12:00-24:00, Charlottenstrasse 56, tel. 030/202-9515, www.l-w-berlin.de). Another location is inside the Sony Center.

$ Dom Curry, behind the German Cathedral, is a *Currywurst* stand that works for a quick bite out on the square (daily 12:00-20:00).

$$ Galeries Lafayette Food Circus is a French festival of fun eateries surrounding the glass atrium in the basement of the landmark department store—ideal for a quality lunch. You'll find sandwiches, savory crêpes, quiches, sushi bar, oyster bar, *les macarons,* and so on. Eat in or take advantage of their handy to-go items (Mon-Sat 10:00-20:00, closed Sun, Friedrichstrasse 76, U6: Französische Strasse, tel. 030/209-480).

PRENZLAUER BERG

Prenzlauer Berg is bursting with excellent restaurants, serving up every cuisine imaginable. Even if you're not staying in this area, it's worth venturing here for dinner. Before choosing a restaurant, I'd spend at least a half-hour strolling and browsing through this bohemian wonderland of creative eateries. Or consider one of my recommendations (for locations, see the "Prenzlauer Berg Hotels & Restaurants" map).

The epicenter of this neighborhood is Kastanienallee (between the Eberswalder Strasse U-Bahn station and Zionskirche), and surrounding streets. It's a youthful and trendy place to eat and drink. I've organized my recommendations in four categories: Ger-

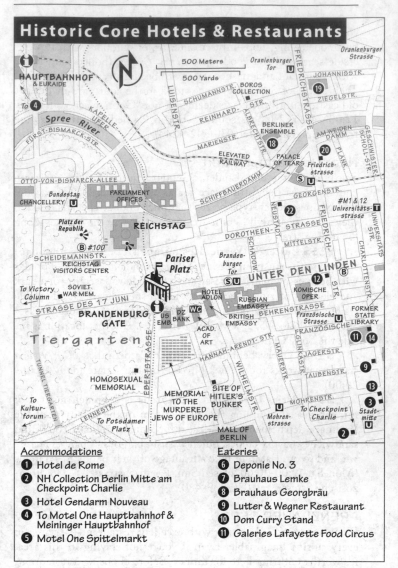

Historic Core Hotels & Restaurants

500 Meters
500 Yards

Accommodations

1 Hotel de Rome
2 NH Collection Berlin Mitte am Checkpoint Charlie
3 Hotel Gendarm Nouveau
4 To Motel One Hauptbahnhof & Meininger Hauptbahnhof
5 Motel One Spittelmarkt

Eateries

6 Deponie No. 3
7 Brauhaus Lemke
8 Brauhaus Georgbräu
9 Lutter & Wegner Restaurant
10 Dom Curry Stand
11 Galeries Lafayette Food Circus

man cuisine, international options, places for a drink or snack, and options in the gentrified Kollwitzkiez area, near a pleasant park.

German Food

$ **Prater Biergarten** has been in business since 1837—back when Prenzlauer Berg was a forested hill—and is Berlin's oldest beer garden. It's a classic *Gemütlichkeit* (cozy and convivial) scene—mellow, shaded, and super-cheap—with a family-friendly outdoor area, including a playground (no table service, order food at one counter,

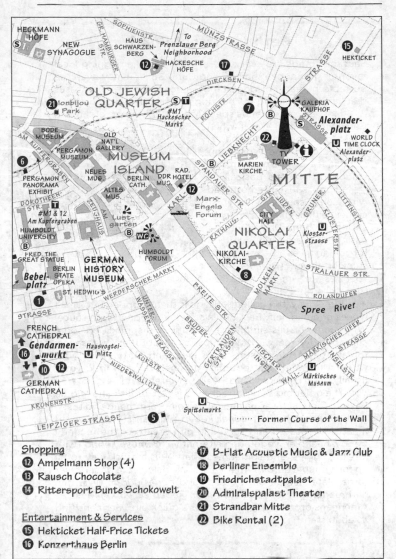

beer at the other). They serve just basic pub grub, but the price is right and there's a wide range of beers. Prater's rustic indoor restaurant (more expensive, with table service) serves well-executed German classics with proper veal schnitzel and good salads. Both sections proudly pour Prater's own microbrew (restaurant open Mon-Sat 18:00-24:00, Sun from 12:00; beer garden open daily in good weather 12:00-24:00, closed in winter; Kastanienallee 7, tel. 030/448-5688).

$$ **Zum Schusterjungen** ("The Cobbler's Apprentice") is a

Berliner Street Food

Sausage stands are everywhere—including the reigning local favorites, Konnopke's Imbiss and Curry 36. You may even see portable human hot-dog stands—cooks in clever harnesses that let them grill and sell hot dogs from under an umbrella.

Most sausage stands specialize in **Currywurst,** created in Berlin after World War II, when a fast-food cook got her hands on some curry and Worcestershire sauce from British troops stationed here. It's basically a grilled pork sausage smothered with curry sauce. *Currywurst* comes either *mit Darm* (with casing) or *ohne Darm* (without casing). If the casing is left on to grill, it gives the sausage a smokier flavor. (*Berliner Art*— "Berlin-style"—means that the sausage is boiled *ohne Darm,* then grilled.)

Either way, the grilled sausage is then chopped into small pieces or cut in half (East Berlin style) and topped with sauce. While some places simply use ketchup and sprinkle on some curry powder, real *Currywurst* joints use a proper *Currysauce:* tomato paste, Worcestershire sauce, and curry. With your wurst comes either a toothpick or small wooden fork; you'll usually get a plate of fries as well, but rarely a roll.

The other big Berlin street food is fast Turkish and Middle Eastern food. Schwarma and falafel joints are cheap and tasty. And the kebab—either **döner kebab** (Turkish-style skewered meat slow-roasted and served in pita bread) or the recently trendy, healthier, vegetarian alternative, **Gemüse kebab** (with lots of veggies, and sometimes falafel)—is a quick way to fill up for a couple euros. Other variations include the *döner teller* (on a plate instead of in bread) and *döner dürüm* (in a thin flatbread wrap, also called *dürüm kebab* or *yufka*). Just as Americans drop by a taco truck for a quick bite, Germans find a kebab stand.

classic, old-school, German-with-attitude eatery that retains its circa-1986 DDR decor. Famous for its filling meals (including various types of schnitzel and Berlin specialties such as pork knuckle), it's a no-frills place with quality ingredients and a strong local following. It serves the needs of those Berliners lamenting the disappearance of solid, traditional German cooking amid the flood of ethnic eateries (small 40-seat dining hall plus outdoor tables, daily 12:00-24:00, corner of Lychener Strasse and Danziger Strasse 9, tel. 030/442-7654).

$ Konnopke's Imbiss, a super-cheap German-style sausage

stand with a small section of covered picnic tables underneath the ever-rumbling U2 train tracks, has been a Berlin institution since 1930. It was family-owned even during DDR times. Loyal Berliners say Konnopke's cooks up some of the city's best  *Currywurst;* they also serve a wide variety of other wurst specialties (Tue-Sat 10:00-20:00, Sun 12:00-18:00, closed Mon; Schönhauser Allee 44A—underneath elevated train tracks where Kastanienallee dead-ends, tel. 030/442-7765). If you'd rather have very cheap, finger-licking-good, halal fried chicken, head across the street and join all the kids at Risa's.

$$$ Ausspanne looks like a traditional, uninspired hotel restaurant. But the small, always fresh menu boldly elevates German classics with surprising flourishes—such as a puff of habanero foam with duck breast and red cabbage. It offers an interesting and reasonably priced take on modern German cooking (daily 17:00-22:00, in recommended Hotel Kastanienhof at Kastanienallee 65, tel. 030/4430-5199)

$$$ Der Hahn Ist Tot! ("The Rooster Is Dead!") has whimsical style and cozy outdoor tables facing the Zionskirche, on a pleasant Prenzlauer Berg square. They serve only four-course, €24 dinners. The small menu is a thoughtful combination of rustic German and French dishes (always a fish, meat, and vegetarian option), and prices are decent. It's as tiny as it is popular—book ahead (Tue-Sun 18:30-23:00, closed Mon, Zionskirchstrasse 40, tel. 030/6570-6756, www.der-hahn-ist-tot.de).

$$$ Restaurant Die Schule is a dressy, spacious, modern eatery where you can sample €3 tapas-style plates of old-fashioned German food. They have several varieties of *Flammkuchen* (German pizza—a flatbread dish from the French borderlands) and seasonal main dishes. The vibe is sober and nondescript inside and out (daily 11:00-22:00, Kastanienallee 82, tel. 030/780-089-550).

International Eateries

$$$ Les Valseuses is a hole-in-the-wall French bistro with an open kitchen. Everything is simple and unpretentious, from the subway tile-clad exterior to the cozy, stripped-down interior, to the short menu (fish, meat or vegetarian). Reserve ahead (daily 18:30-23:00, Eberswalder Strasse 28, tel. 030/7552-2032, www.lesvalseuses.de).

$$$ Osmans Töchter ("Ottoman Daughters"), run by sisters from Istanbul, is a fun mash-up of industrial-mod interior and modern Turkish cuisine. Although the service can be a bit full of itself, this popular restaurant is the most appealing place in Prenzlauer Berg to sample well-executed Turkish dishes. Reservations are smart (daily 17:30-24:00, Pappelallee 15, tel. 030/3266-3388, www.osmanstoechter.de).

$$ Vân Anh Restaurant serves finer Vietnamese dishes than you might expect. Harried waiters barely take time to talk, but the creative menu—with dishes from stir fries to salads and steaks—makes ordering fun. It has a successful and youthful energy with stripped-down woody decor. You can enjoy the Oderberger Strasse and Kastanienallee action from sidewalk tables wrapping around a central corner of Prenzlauer Berg, or join the high-energy yet mellow tighter seating inside (daily 12:00-23:00, cash only, Oderberger Strasse 7, tel. 030/4171-7294).

$ Lemongrass Scent is a hardworking little spot on a quiet street serving fresh and tasty Asian dishes for a great price. It's fast, friendly, and has a comfy interior and tables with benches on the street (daily 12:00-23:00, Schwedter Strasse 12, tel. 030/4057-6985).

$$ Babel is a Lebanese restaurant popular with locals for its generous portions of shawarma, falafel, and kafta served at flower-bedecked sidewalk tables. Their mix-and-match lunch plates and two-person platters are an especially good value (daily 11:00-24:00, Kastanienallee 33, tel. 030/4403-1318).

$ Maria Bonita is an American-run Mexican bistro on a busy street offering some of the most authentic tacos in Berlin (daily 12:00-23:00, equidistant from Kollwitzplatz and Eberswalder Strasse U-Bahn stations at Danziger Strasse 33, tel. 030/2025-5338).

Browsing Kastanienallee: For other ethnic options, simply wander down Kastanienallee from the Eberswalder Strasse trestle. In just a few blocks, you'll see Italian, Vietnamese, falafel, *Gemüse kebab*, along with burgers, funky cafés, colorful *Kneipen*, and much more.

Waffles or a Hippy Bar in the Center of Prenzlauer Berg

The following places are good for lingering over a drink and/or snack, ideally at an outdoor table where you can soak up the essence of Prenzlauer Berg.

Kauf Dich Glücklich makes a great capper to a Prenzlauer Berg dinner. It serves an enticing array of sweet Belgian waffles and homemade ice cream in an inviting candy-sprinkled, bohemian lounge and a garden-like front terrace on a great street (or get your dessert to go, daily 10:00-23:00, Oderberger Strasse 44, tel. 030/4862-3292).

Café Morgenrot ("Red Dawn") is actually a bar. This Prenzlauer Berg classic, a holdover from the neighborhood's squatter days, brings together the community—gay, straight, local, foreign—and is still run by an artists' collective (Tue-Sun 11:00-24:00, closed Mon, vegan options, Kastanienallee 85, tel. 030/4431-7844).

Kollwitzkiez Area

This small neighborhood, a few blocks east of Kastanienallee, is Prenzlauer Berg's gentrified heart—quieter and more residential. Hip parents bring their hip kids to the hip leafy playground park at its center, Kollwitzplatz. The first listing (Gugelhof) is a pricier sit-down option right on the park; the others allow you to enjoy great food and this area on the cheap. Some of these (and many others in the neighborhood) offer takeaway; grab something to go, and find a bench on this prime square.

$$$$ Gugelhof is famous for its Alsatian German cuisine— French quality with German proportions. It has a kids' menu, a selection of *Flammkuchen* (Alsatian pizzas), fun fixed-price meals, and professional service. A smart local clientele fills its minimalist yet classy interior; in good weather, outdoor seating sprawls along its sidewalk (Mon-Fri 17:00-23:00, Sat-Sun from 10:00, reservations smart, where Knaackstrasse meets Kollwitzplatz, tel. 030/442-9229, www.gugelhof.de).

$ Chutnify offers a modern take on Indian street food. You can get a *dosa* (southern India's version of a burrito, with various fillings), a *thali* (mixed platter), or a curry, either to eat in the cozy interior or dine with the neighborhood street-side (daily 12:00-23:00, Sredzkistrasse 43, tel. 030/4401-0795).

$ Zula is handy for cheap hummus wraps to enjoy at an outside table on one of Prenzlauer Berg's finest streets, or take to Kollwitzplatz, just down the way (daily 11:00-23:00, Husemannstrasse 10, tel. 030/4171-5100).

$$ Zuhause specializes in picnic-perfect deli-style dishes. Choose from a fresh selection of salads, veggie dishes, or traditional Berlin comfort food—*Sauerbrauten*, *Buletten*, and *goulash*. Save room for a meal-capping slice of *kuchen* (Mon-Fri 11:00-21:00, Sat from 12:00, closed Sun, Kollwitzstrasse 26, tel. 030/6431-2315).

Pubs near Senefelderplatz: Two options—a few blocks south of Kollwitzplatz, handy to the Senefelderplatz U-Bahn—are good choices for beer with grub. **$ Metzer Eck** is a time-warp *Kneipe* with cozy charm and a family tradition dating to 1913. It serves cheap, basic, old-fashioned Berlin grub with five beers on tap (Mon-Fri 16:00-24:00, Sat from 18:00, closed Sun, Metzer Strasse 33, on the corner with Strassburger Strasse, tel. 030/442-7656). **$$ Leibhaftig** is the modern yin to Metzer's yang, serving their own brews and Bavarian tapas—small plates of nouveau German

Food Tours

Most Berlin culinary tours either focus on traditional German fare or the trendier foodie scene, some do a combination of both, and virtually all include a *Currywurst*. Some well-established tour operators—including **Original Berlin Walks** and **Fat Tire Bike Tours**—have added food and craft beer tours to their lineup (see "Tours in Berlin," earlier in this chapter). Meanwhile, an array of specialty companies focus on doing only food tours. As this is a quickly evolving scene, it's difficult to recommend a specific company. But for starters, consider the following: **Fork and Walk Tours** (higher-end, combines sightseeing with food stops, www.forkandwalktoursberlin.com), **Bite Berlin** (a smaller operation with thoughtful tours, www.biteberlin.com), and **The German Food Tour** (brief and affordable, www.thegermanfoodtour.de). Check their websites (and online reviews) to find a tour that suits your interests and travel philosophy.

cuisine, with plenty of vegetarian options (Mon-Sat 18:00-24:00, closed Sun, Metzer Strasse 30, tel. 030/5481-5039).

OLD JEWISH QUARTER

Of Berlin's trendy dining zones, this is the closest to the main sightseeing core. Most of these places are a reasonable walk from Unter den Linden and within 10 minutes of the Hackescher Markt S-Bahn station. For locations, see the "Old Jewish Quarter Hotels & Restaurants" map.

On and near Auguststrasse

The best place to find good eateries in the old Jewish quarter is along or near Auguststrasse, Berlin's "art gallery row" (close to the New Synagogue). Though the Hackescher Markt places are easier to reach, Auguststrasse has attracted a fun cross-section of creative chefs and is worth the short detour.

The nearby and much bigger Oranienburger Strasse is jammed with dime-a-dozen Indian, Cuban, and Singapore-themed restaurants serving tropical cocktails. While this street is trendy, the places I recommend here are more interesting and more respected by locals.

$$ Mogg Deli is a foodie favorite, serving a short but thoughtful menu of soups, salads, and sandwiches. While dishing up international cuisine, it's inspired by a New York deli. They're known for their home-cured pastrami, especially their monster, designed-to-be-shared Reuben (Mon-Sat 11:00-22:00, Sun until 20:00; inside the huge red-brick former Jewish girls school at Auguststrasse 11, tel. 030/330-060-770).

$$ Clärchens Restaurant fills the courtyard in front of Clärchens Ballhaus (a classic old Berlin ballroom) with twinkle

lights, ramshackle furniture, and a bohemian-chic atmosphere—especially nice on a balmy evening. They serve German and Italian dishes, including brats, pizza, and homemade cakes. You can also eat in the dance hall or in a garden out back. After

21:00, the DJ cranks up the music in the ground floor dance hall, creating a fun, high-energy yet neighborly scene (daily 12:00-22:00, Auguststrasse 24, tel. 030/282-9295).

$$$ Schwarzwaldstuben is a Black Forest-themed pub—which explains the antlers, cuckoo clocks, and painting of a thick forest on the wall. It's friendly, with good service, food, and prices. The staff chooses the music (often rock or jazz), and the ambience is warm and welcoming. If they're full, you can eat at the long bar (daily 12:00-23:00, Tucholskystrasse 48, tel. 030/2809-8084).

$$$ Cordobar is a cozy wine bar with a clean, trendy vibe and an appealing range of both German and international wines by the glass, paired with upscale small plates. Come here not for a filling meal, but to enjoy a posh local scene and try some interesting wines. It's popular, so reserve ahead (Tue-Sat 19:00-24:00, closed Sun-Mon, Grosse Hamburger Strasse 32, tel. 030/2758-1215).

$$ Sophieneck upholds its *Kneipe* roots as the neighborhood's ersatz living room, serving hearty Berliner specialties like *Buletten* and *Eisbein* on a breezy corner to a happy mix of locals and tourists (daily 12:00-22:30, Grosse Hamburger Strasse 37, tel. 030/283-4065).

$$ Aufsturz is a lively pub that's more for serious drinkers than serious eaters. It has a huge selection of beer and whisky and dishes up traditional Berliner pub grub to a young crowd (daily 12:00-24:00, Oranienburger Strasse 67, tel. 030/2804-7407).

Coffee: At **The Barn,** curt baristas serve up some of Berlin's best gourmet coffee with an extra shot of pretense. Hipster coffee snobs will be satisfied (Mon-Fri 8:00-18:00, Sat-Sun from 10:00, Auguststrasse 58).

Dessert: For your afternoon *Kaffee und Kuchen*, stop at **Princess Cheesecake,** beloved by locals and selling several varieties of cheesecake (daily 10:00-20:00, Tucholskystrasse 37, tel. 030/2809-2760).

Rosenthaler Platz Area

This busy neighborhood thrives with millennials and the youth hostel crowd and has some enticing options. It's roughly between the old Jewish quarter and Prenzlauer Berg, near the U8: Rosenthaler Platz station, and on the tram #M1 line that runs between Kastanienallee and the Hackescher Markt S-Bahn station.

Eclectic Eats on Weinbergsweg: Don't miss the first block of Weinbergsweg, the narrower, tram track-lined lane that heads north to Prenzlauer Berg. In just one block, you'll find cafés, bakeries, superfoods and organic juice, *Gemüse kebab, döner kebab,* an Italian deli, Mexican street food, Russian, Korean barbecue, a French bistro, Chinese dumplings, and gelato.

$$$$ Katz Orange is a mecca for foodies, and feels regal from the moment you enter its intimate courtyard. It's surprisingly affordable and delightfully cozy-chic. The menu is small and sharp, known for its "candy on the bone" slow-cooked meat, and changes with the season (daily 18:00-23:00, reservations recommended, Bergstrasse 22, tel. 030/9832-08430, www.katzorange.com).

Hackescher Markt Area

$$$ Hasir is a popular, upscale, somewhat stuffy opportunity to splurge on Turkish and Anatolian specialties amid candles and hardwood floors. While a bit past its prime and with hit-or-miss service, Hasir remains respected, and enjoys a handy location (large and splittable portions, daily 16:00-24:00, a block from the Hackescher Markt S-Bahn station at Oranienburger Strasse 4, tel. 030/2804-1616).

$$ Weihenstephaner Bavarian Restaurant serves traditional Bavarian food in an air-conditioned traditional-yet-sleek interior, down in an atmospheric cellar, on an inner courtyard, or on a busy people-watching terrace facing the delightful Hackescher Markt square; and, of course, it has excellent beer. If you want to eat right on Hackescher Markt, this is your best bet (daily 11:00-24:00, Neue Promenade 5 at Hackescher Markt, tel. 030/8471-0760).

$ Curry 61 serves up, for many, the best *Currywurst* in Berlin; vegetarians and vegans appreciate good options too. Eat in or grab a €5 meal to eat on a bench at the fine Monbijoupark across the street (daily, long hours, Oranienburger Strasse 6).

KREUZBERG

To dig into Berlin's up-and-coming food scene, head to Kreuzberg. This southern Berlin neighborhood—historically known for its large immigrant community and counterculture squatters—has taken off as *the* place for upwardly mobile young Berliners to eat out. As this is a very trendy destination, it's smart to reserve ahead

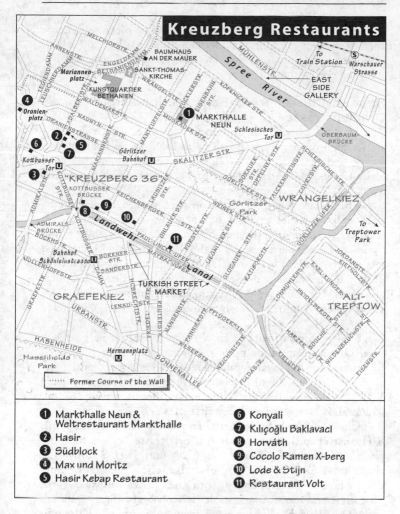

Kreuzberg Restaurants

1. Markthalle Neun & Weltrestaurant Markthalle
2. Hasir
3. Südblock
4. Max und Moritz
5. Hasir Kebap Restaurant
6. Konyali
7. Kılıçoğlu Baklavacı
8. Horváth
9. Cocolo Ramen X-berg
10. Lode & Stijn
11. Restaurant Volt

at most of my listings—especially on weekends—or avoid prime meal times. For locations, see the "Kreuzberg Restaurants" map.

Markthalle Neun

Kreuzberg's best foodie destination is this refurbished 19th-century market hall, filled with local producers and fun food stalls. You'll find gourmet butchers, wine shops, tapas, Berlin meatballs (Buletten), tofu sandwiches, fair trade spices, Turkish dishes, and a supermarket. It's most worthwhile on "Street Food Thursdays," when extra eateries open from 17:00 to 22:00 (most vendors open Mon-Sat 10:00-18:00, closed Sun, Eisenbahnstrasse 42, U1: Görlitzer Bahnhof, www.markthalleneun.de). Attached to the market is **$$$$ Weltrestaurant Markthalle,** with classic *Kneipe* decor and big portions of traditional German dishes (daily 12:00-24:00, Pücklerstrasse 34). Note: The Görlitzer Bahnhof area can feel seedy, especially at night.

Near Kottbusser Tor U-Bahn Station and Oranienstrasse

$$$ Hasir is a big, clean, and unstressful place tourists appreciate for high-quality Turkish cuisine at high prices. It's well-run, dressy, and spacious, with great energy and a big open kitchen (daily 12:00-24:00, Adalbertstrasse 10 at corner of Oranienstrasse, tel. 030/6165-9222, http://hasir.de).

$ Südblock, Kreuzberg's take on a beer garden, brings together all walks of local life: Turk, Berliner, gay, straight, and tourist. It's a convivial vibe, best when balmy, with shared tables filling a corner plaza under trees and umbrellas or inside with cramped seating under disco balls (the DJ turns up the music nightly at 21:00). The menu includes German standards, stuffed baked potatoes, Tex-Mex, *Flammkuchen*, vegan, and lots of booze (daily from 11:00, where Admiralstrasse hits Kottbusser Tor, tel. 030/6094-1853).

$$ Max und Moritz is an old-time *Wirtshaus* half a block from Oranienplatz. They pride themselves on doing traditional Berlin food the right way—with equal amounts respect for the origins, and disregard for anyone who might not like it that way (daily 17:00-23:00, cash only, reservations smart, Oranienstrasse 162, tel. 030/6951-5911, www.maxundmoritzberlin.de).

Cheap Turkish-Style Eats: Two doors down from Hasir, **$ Hasir Kebap Restaurant,** at Adalbertstrasse 12, is a bit more casual and has more kebab options (daily until late). **$ Konyali,** a cheap kebab joint just off Kottbusser Tor, offers the closest thing to an Istanbul vibe and crowd, with great prices and solid Turkish cuisine and fun seating outside (Reichenberger Strasse 10, tel. 030/6900-4567). For dessert, head down to the friendly **Kılıçoğlu Baklavacı** bakery for enticing honey-soaked sweets sold by weight (daily until late, Adalbertstrasse 9).

High-End Foodie Splurges on and near Paul-Lincke-Ufer

The Paul-Lincke-Ufer strip along the north bank of the Landwehr Canal (across from the Turkish market) is home to several top-tier Berlin eateries (U8: Schönleinstrasse). I've listed these in the order you reach them, heading east from Kottbusser Brücke.

$$$$ Horváth, a Michelin-star restaurant, serves elevated Austrian/international-fusion fare (Wed-Sun 18:30-22:00, closed Mon-Tue, #44a, tel. 030/6128-9992, www.restaurant-horvath.de).

$$ Cocolo Ramen X-berg, a wildly popular outpost of a high-end Japanese restaurant, dishes up slurpy noodle bowls (Mon-Sat 12:00-24:00, closed Sun, #39, tel. 030/9833-9073, www.kuchi.de).

$$$$ Lode & Stijn features the eclectic high-end cooking (without pretense) of two talented Dutch-transplant chefs (Tue-Sat 18:00-22:00, closed Sun-Mon, Lausitzer Strasse 25, tel. 030/6521-4507, www.lode-stijn.de)

$$$ Restaurant Volt serves upscale international dishes in a former power station (Tue-Sat 18:00-24:00, closed Sun-Mon, #21, tel. 030/338-402-320, www.restaurant-volt.de).

CITY WEST

I've listed these eateries primarily for travelers sleeping here. (In other words, they are not worth traveling across Berlin to enjoy.) For locations, see the "City West Hotels & Restaurants" map.

Near Savignyplatz

Many good restaurants are on or within 100 yards of Savignyplatz, near my recommended hotels. Savignyplatz is lined with attractive, relaxed, mostly Mediterranean-style places. Take a walk and survey the places I list here; continue your stroll along Bleibtreustrasse to discover many trendier, creative little eateries.

$$$ Restaurant Marjellchen is a trip to East Prussia, with big portions of hearty, delicious German/Polish cuisine. Dine in cozily cluttered elegance in one of two six table rooms. While it doesn't have to be expensive, plan to go the whole nine yards here, as this can be a great experience, with caring service. The menu is inviting, and the place family-run—all the recipes were brought to Berlin by the owner's East Prussian mother after World War II. Reservations are smart (daily 17:00-22:30, Mommsenstrasse 9, tel. 030/883-2676, www.marjellchen-berlin.de).

$$ Dicke Wirtin ("Fat Landlady") has a traditional old-Berlin *Kneipe* atmosphere, seven good beers on tap (including Andechs from Bavaria), and solid home cooking at reasonable prices—such as their famously cheap *Gulaschsuppe*. Their interior is fun and pubby, with soccer on the TV; their streetside tables are also inviting. Pickled eggs are on the bar—ask about how these can help you avoid a hangover (daily 11:00-23:00, dinner served from 18:00, just off Savignyplatz at Carmerstrasse 9, tel. 030/312-4952).

$$$$ Café im Literaturhaus sits above a rare-books shop on a delightfully tranquil garden courtyard, facing the Käthe Kollwitz Museum. It has the ambience of an Old World villa, with classy gold Art Deco accents—perfect for their evening poetry and other literary readings. While the full menu is quite pricey, you can enjoy the place far more affordably with a sandwich or coffee and cake (daily 9:00-24:00, reservations smart, Fasanenstrasse 23, tel. 030/882-5414).

$ Heno is a very popular Japanese hole-in-the-wall, serving a variety of rice bowls, noodle dishes, and soups (but no sushi) in a long, sleek, minimalist space (Mon-Sat 12:00-22:00, closed Sun, Wielandstrasse 37, tel. 030/6630-7370).

$ Diener Tattersall is a neighborhood favorite *Kneipe* with a complicated history. The building started as a horse riding school, later became a casino, and was eventually bought by the German heavyweight champion Franz Diener, who attracted an eclectic clientele of boxers and artists to his *Kneipe*. Today it's known for the affordable menu, specializing in homemade liver sausage (daily from 18:00, Grolmanstrasse 47, tel. 030/881-5329).

$$ Weyers offers modern German cuisine in a simple, elegant setting, with dining tables spilling out into the idyllic neighborhood park in the summer (daily 8:00-24:00, Pariser Strasse 16—facing Ludwigkirchplatz at intersection with Pfalzburger Strasse, tel. 030/881-9378).

On Bleibtreustrasse: On the stretch just south of the Savignyplatz S-Bahn tracks, Bleibtreustrasse is lined with an eclectic array of dining options—wander and take your pick: **$$ Zillemarkt,** an old-time beer hall with nice atmosphere and uninspired service (#48A); **$ Ali Baba,** with pizzas and outdoor seating (#45); **$ Repke Spätzlerei** (*Flamkuchen, Spätzle,* and buttery dumplings, #46); and **Nibs Cacao** (churros and chocolate, also at #46).

Near Zoologischer Garten Station

In addition to a beer garden and department-store cafeteria, there's plenty of fast food near the Zoologischer Garten station and on Ku'damm.

$ Curry 36—the locally beloved *Currywurst* vendor from Kreuzberg—has a handy outpost just outside of the station.

$$ Schleusenkrug beer garden is hidden in the park overlooking a canal between the Zoologischer Garten and Tiergarten stations. Choose from an ever-changing self-service menu of huge salads, pasta, and some German dishes (daily 11:00-24:00, food served 11:30-21:30, shorter hours and more basic menu off-season, cash only; from Zoologischer Garten station it's a 5-minute walk following the path into the park  between the zoo and train tracks; tel. 030/313-9909).

KaDeWe: The top floor of this famous department store holds the **$$ Winter Garden Buffet** cafeteria, while its sixth-floor deli/ food department is a picnicker's nirvana. Its arterials are clogged with more than 1,000 kinds of sausage and 1,500 types of cheese (Mon-Sat 10:00-20:00, closed Sun, U1/U2/U3: Wittenbergplatz, tel. 030/2121-2623).

Berlin Connections

BY PLANE

Berlin's airport situation is in flux. The completion of Willy Brandt Airport has been delayed for years; in the meantime, two older airports—Tegel and Schönefeld—do their best to handle Berlin's heavy air traffic. When heading to the airport, be very clear on which one you're flying from.

In addition to being well-served by Lufthansa and other big, traditional airlines, Berlin is also a destination for many budget airlines. These include **EasyJet** (www.easyjet.com), **Eurowings** (www.eurowings.com), **Condor** (with several long-haul routes, www.condor.com), **WizzAir** (with a handful of direct flights to southeastern Europe, www.wizzair.com), **TUIfly** (www.tuifly. com), and **Ryanair** (www.ryanair.com). For more on cheap flights, see the "Transportation" section in the Practicalities chapter.

Willy Brandt Berlin-Brandenburg International Airport

This state-of-the-art airport (airport code: BER), 11 miles south of central Berlin, has been under construction since 2006. Overdue and over budget, the airport may go into service in late 2020. When it finally does open, the airport should be connected to the city center by fast and frequent Airport Express trains. The airport station (Flughafen Berlin Brandenburg Bahnhof) sits directly under the terminal. A train (direction: Dessau or Nauen) will likely run to Alexanderplatz (for Prenzlauer Berg and old Jewish quarter hotels, 25 minutes), then continue to Zoologischer Garten (for City West hotels, 40 minutes). Additional trains will connect the airport to the main train station, via Potsdamer Platz (30 minutes).

Tegel Airport

Tegel (airport code: TXL), just four miles northwest of the center, serves as Berlin's "main airport" until Willy Brandt finally opens. Smaller and older than you'd expect for the airport of a huge city, it's limping along as well as it can. The easiest way to get downtown is by bus (follow the little bus icons to exit D).

To reach my **Prenzlauer Berg** or **old Jewish quarter** hotels, hop on bus #TXL, which stops at the Hauptbahnhof, then heads south down Friedrichstrasse before turning east on Unter den Linden, which it follows all the way to Alexanderplatz. Hop off just before Alexanderplatz—at the Spandauer Strasse/Marienkirche stop—then catch tram #M4 or #M6 to Hackescher Markt (you can also walk about 5 minutes north up Spandauer Strasse to Hackescher Markt). This is close to most old Jewish quarter hotels, and an easy ride on tram #M1 to most Prenzlauer Berg hotels.

To reach **City West** hotels, take bus #X9 directly to Zoologischer Garten (a.k.a. Zoo Station), or slower bus #109 by way of Ku'damm to Zoologischer Garten.

Any bus is covered by an AB zone transit ticket (€2.80 single ticket, buy from machine, validate before boarding). A taxi from Tegel Airport costs about €30 to Alexanderplatz or €20 to City West.

Schönefeld Airport

Most flights from the east and many discount airlines arrive at Schönefeld (airport code: SXF), 11 miles south of downtown and next to the under-construction Willy Brandt Airport. From the arrivals hall, it's a three-minute walk to the train station, where you can catch a regional express train or S-Bahn into the city. The S9 line is especially handy for Prenzlauer Berg and old Jewish quarter hotels: From the Schönhauser Allee stop, tram #M1 runs south along Kastanienallee, then all the way to Hackescher Markt. You can also take Airport Express RE and RB trains directly to Ostbahnhof, Alexanderplatz, Friedrichstrasse (near some old Jewish quarter hotels), Hauptbahnhof, and Zoologischer Garten (handy for City West hotels; train runs 2/hour, direction: Nauen or Dessau). Either train is covered by an ABC transit ticket (€3.40, buy at machine and validate before boarding). A taxi to the city center costs about €45.

BY TRAIN

Virtually all long-distance trains pass through the **Berlin Hauptbahnhof** ("Berlin Hbf" on schedules)—a massive, state-of-the-art temple of railroad travel in the heart of the city. This mostly underground train station is where the national train system meets Berlin's S-Bahn—unique for the way its major lines come in at right angles. Note that many arriving trains (especially regional ones) stop at multiple Berlin stations, one of which  may be more convenient to your hotel than the Hauptbahnhof. Before you arrive, figure out which station is best for you.

Orientation: The gigantic station has five floors, but its open layout makes it easy to navigate...once you understand the signage. The main floor, at street level, is labeled "EG" (for *Erdgeschoss*), or level 0. Below that are UG1 (level -1) and UG2 (level -2), while above it are OG1 (level +1) and OG2 (level +2). Tracks 1-8 are on UG2, while tracks 11-16 and the S-Bahn are on OG2. Shops and services are on the three middle levels. Enter and exit the station on level EG: The Washingtonplatz entrance faces south (toward the Reichstag and downtown, with a taxi stand). The north entrance is marked *Europaplatz*.

Services: On the main floor (EG), you'll find the **TI** (just inside the north/Europaplatz entrance) and the **"Rail & Fresh WC"** facility (public pay toilets, near the food court, follow gold signs). Up one level (OG1) are a 24-hour **pharmacy** and **lockers** (directly under track 14 on the east side). **Car rental** offices are down one level (UG1), near platforms 7-8.

Train Information and Tickets: The Deutsche Bahn *Reisezentrum* information center is up one level (OG1), between tracks 12 and 13 (on the west side; open long hours daily).

EurAide is an English-speaking information desk with answers to your questions about train travel around Europe. It's located at counter 12 inside the *Reisezentrum* on the first upper level (OG1). It's American-run, so communication is simple. This is an especially good place to make fast-train and *couchette* reservations (generally open Mon-Fri 11:10-18:50, until 20:00 May-Aug, check website for specific hours, closed Jan-Feb and Sat-Sun year-round; www.euraide.com).

Shopping: The Hauptbahnhof is home to 80 shops with long hours—some locals call the station a "shopping mall with trains" (many stores open Sun). The REWE City supermarket (UG1, follow signs for tracks 1-2) is handy for assembling a picnic for your train ride.

Getting into Town: Taxis and buses wait outside the station on the Washingtonplatz side, but the S-Bahn is probably your best bet for connecting to most hotels. It's simple: S-Bahn trains are on tracks 15 and 16 at the top of the station (level OG2). Trains on track 15 go east, stopping at Friedrichstrasse, Hackescher Markt, Alexanderplatz, and Ostbahnhof; trains on track 16 go west, toward Zoologischer Garten and Savignyplatz (best for City West hotels). Your train ticket to Berlin covers any connecting S-Bahn ride (but for the U-Bahn, trams, or buses, you'll need an additional ticket).

To reach most hotels in northern Berlin's **Prenzlauer Berg** neighborhood, it's fastest to take any train on track 15 two stops to Hackescher Markt. Once there, follow signs to *Hackescher Markt* down the stairs, then exit to Spandauer Strasse and cross the tracks to the tram stop. Here you'll catch tram #M1 north (direction: Schillerstrasse), which trundles north through Rosenthaler Platz and up Kastanienallee to Eberswalder Strasse. (For Rosenthaler Platz hotels, it's even more direct to hop on tram #M8, which leaves from in front of the Hauptbahnhof's Europaplatz entrance.)

For **old Jewish quarter** hotels, you'll also take the S-Bahn from track 15. Some of these hotels are closer to the Friedrichstrasse station (first stop), while others are closer to Hackescher Markt (second stop).

To reach **City West** hotels, catch any train on track 16 to Savignyplatz, where you're within a five-minute walk of most recommended hotels.

Bus #TXL to **Tegel Airport** leaves from in front of the Europaplatz exit.

The Berlin Hauptbahnhof is not well-connected to the city's **U-Bahn** (subway) system—yet. The station's sole U-Bahn line—U55—goes only two stops, to the Brandenburger Tor station, and doesn't really connect to the rest of the system. It's part of the extension of the U5 line beneath Unter den Linden to Alexanderplatz, which is scheduled to be finished in 2020.

From Berlin by Train to: Potsdam (2/hour, 30 minutes on RE1 train; or take S-Bahn from other points in Berlin, S7 direct, S1 with a change at Wannsee, 6/hour, 30-50 minutes—see next chapter), **Oranienburg** and Sachsenhausen Memorial and Museum (hourly, 25 minutes on the RE5; or take the S1 line from Friedrichstrasse or other stops in town, 2/hour, 50 minutes), **Wittenberg** (a.k.a. *Lutherstadt Wittenberg*, hourly on ICE, 40 minutes; also every 2 hours on slower regional train, 1.5 hours), **Dresden** (direct every 2 hours, 2 hours; more with a transfer in Leipzig, 3 hours), **Leipzig** (hourly, 1.5 hours), **Erfurt** (1-2/hour, 2 hours), **Eisenach** and Wartburg Castle (every 2 hours direct, 2.5 hours; more with transfer in Erfurt), **Hamburg** (1-2/hour, 2 hours), **Frankfurt** (at least hourly, 4 hours), **Bacharach** (every 2 hours with transfer in Frankfurt, 5.5 hours; more with 2-3 changes), **Würzburg** (hourly, 4 hours, transfer points vary), **Rothenburg** (hourly, 5.5 hours, 3 changes), **Nürnberg** (hourly, 3.5 hours), **Munich** (hourly, 4-5 hours), **Cologne** (hourly, 4.5 hours, night train possible), **Amsterdam** (every 2 hours direct, 6.5 hours; more with change in Hannover; wise to reserve in advance), **Brussels** (8/day, 7 hours with transfer, some require reservations), **Budapest** (1/day direct, more with transfer in Prague, 11 hours, via Czech Republic and Slovakia; if your rail pass doesn't cover these countries, consider a longer route via Nürnberg), **Copenhagen** (2/day, 8 hours, reservation required in summer, change in Hamburg; 1 direct bus 4/week at 11:30, daily in summer, accepts rail pass), **London** (4-6/day, 10 hours, 2 changes, reservations required), **Paris** (9/day, 8 hours with

1 transfer, reservations required in France), **Zürich** (hourly, 8-9 hours, transfer in Hannover or Basel; 1 direct 12-hour night train), **Prague** (6/day direct, 4 hours, wise to reserve in advance), **Warsaw** (4-6/day, 6.5 hours, reservations required), **Kraków** (transfer in Warsaw, 9 hours; 1 bus/day direct, accepts rail pass, 8 hours), **Vienna** (7/day, 8 hours via Nürnberg or 9 hours via Prague; others with 2 changes; trains with a change in Nürnberg or Munich avoid Czech Republic—useful if it's not covered by your rail pass).

Night trains run from Berlin to Cologne, Basel, and Zürich. A *Liegeplatz*, a.k.a. *couchette* berth (€15-36), is a great deal; inquire at EurAide at the Hauptbahnhof for details. Beds generally cost the same whether you have a first- or second-class ticket or rail pass. Trains are often full, so reserve your *couchette* a few days in advance from any travel agency or major train station in Europe.

BY BUS

The city's bus station, **ZOB** (Zentraler Omnibusbahnhof), is west of Zoologischer Garten (Berlin Zoo), in Charlottenburg (Masurenallee 4, U2: Kaiserdamm or S41/S42: Messe Nord, www.zob.berlin). **FlixBus, MeinFern,** and **Eurolines** all operate from here to locations around Germany and Europe.

BY CRUISE SHIP AT
THE PORT OF WARNEMÜNDE

Many cruise lines advertise a stop in "Berlin," but ships actually put in at the Baltic seaside town of Warnemünde—a whopping 150 miles north of downtown Berlin. By train, by tour bus, or by Porsche on the autobahn, plan on at least six hours of travel time round-trip between Warnemünde and Berlin. The easiest option is to book a package excursion from your cruise line. You can also book a tour with a local Berlin-based operator such as Original Berlin Walks; see contact information on page 767. Otherwise, several train connections run each day from Warnemünde's train station to Berlin (roughly every 2 hours, 3 hours, transfer in Rostock).

For more details on visiting Berlin while on a cruise, pick up the *Rick Steves Scandinavian & Northern European Cruise Ports* guidebook.

NEAR BERLIN

Potsdam • Sachsenhausen Memorial and Museum

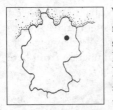

While you could spend days in Berlin and not run out of things to do, a few worthwhile side-trips are within an hour of downtown. Frederick the Great's opulent playground at Potsdam is a hit for its mix of Prussian history and ornate palaces surrounded by pretty parks; the town also has a fun-to-explore center and some interesting Cold War sights. On the opposite side of Berlin—and the sightseeing spectrum—the Sachsenhausen Memorial and Museum commemorates the tens of thousands of prisoners who died at this concentration camp during the Holocaust.

Other Berlin day-trip possibilities are covered elsewhere in this book: Wittenberg, with excellent Martin Luther-related sights (45 minutes by train), is covered in the Lutherland chapter. Dresden and Leipzig also work as day trips from Berlin; each has a separate chapter.

Potsdam

Squeezed between the Wannsee and a lush park strewn with the escapist whimsies of Frederick the Great, the once-important, now-sleepy town of Potsdam has long been Berlin's holiday retreat. Potsdam's palaces are your best opportunity to get a taste of Prussia's Hohenzollern royalty.

Beyond these royal retreats, Potsdam is simply enjoyable—a swanky bedroom community, where, thanks to its aristocratic heritage, everything seems bigger and better than it needs to be. Cold War buffs might focus on Cecilienhof (site of the famous post-

To Rostock & Warnemünde

SACHSENHAUSEN MEMORIAL & MUSEUM

Near Berlin

Oranienburg • Bus #804 & #821 or Walk

Note:
Map shows main rail lines.
Oranienburg/Sachsenhausen and
Potsdam can also be reached from
Berlin via S-Bahn (S1 & S7) line.

— City Limits
····· Former Course of the Wall

To Szczecin (Poland)

5 Kilometers
5 Miles

TEGEL AIRPORT

Tegelersee
Bus #X9 & #109

Bus #TXL

To Hamburg

SPANDAU

FRENZLAUER BERG

HAUPTBAHNHOF

CITY WEST

ZOOLOGISCHER GARTEN

OST-BAHNHOF

Berlin Center

Spree R.

To Warsaw (Poland)

KREUZBERG

Muggelsee

Peacock Island

Wannsee

Grünewald

NEW PALACE

CECILIENHOF

WANNSEE (STN.)

SANSSOUCI PALACE

To Frankfurt

Potsdam

Bus #695 or Walk or bike

Templinersee

To Wittenberg, Erfurt, Leipzig, Dresden & Nürnberg

WILLY BRANDT AIRPORT (UNDER CONSTRUCTION)

SCHÖNEFELD AIRPORT

WWII Potsdam Conference) and nearby KGB Prison Memorial. And anyone can enjoy Potsdam's well-manicured town center as a kind of sightseeing eye-candy. Don't come here just for the palaces—come here to escape the bustle of Berlin, and to spend a sunny day exploring a stately burg and its picnic-friendly park.

GETTING TO POTSDAM

Potsdam is 15 miles southwest of Berlin, easy to reach by train. You have two train options for zipping from the city to Potsdam's Hauptbahnhof, both covered by a Berlin transit day pass (€7.70, with zones ABC; if you have a pass for just zones AB, buy a €1.60 *Anschlussfahrausweis*—extension ticket—to get here, valid 2 hours).

Regional Express/RE1 trains go direct to Potsdam and depart twice hourly from three different Berlin stations: Zoologischer Garten (20 minutes to Potsdam), Hauptbahnhof (30 minutes), and Friedrichstrasse (35 minutes; any train to Brandenburg or Magdeburg stops in Potsdam). Note: Some RE1 trains continue past the Potsdam Hauptbahnhof to a stop called Park Sanssouci, which is closer to the New Palace.

The S-Bahn is slightly slower (30-50 minutes depending on starting point), but more frequent (6/hour) and handier from some areas of Berlin. The S7 line goes directly to Potsdam from downtown Berlin. Another option is to ride the S1 to the end of the line at Wannsee, cross the platform, and ride the S7 train three more stops to Potsdam.

Avid cyclists can rent a bike in Berlin, take it on the train (€1.90 extra), and combine a visit to Potsdam with an enjoyable ride along skinny lakes and through green parklands back into the city.

PLANNING YOUR TIME

There are three dimensions to a visit to Potsdam: the garrison town itself (centered near the main train station); Sanssouci Park with its many palaces and imperial delights; and a handful of Cold War sights a mile north of town. To see it all is a very long day with long walks, lots of biking, or plenty of bus rides.

Potsdam's main draw is its vast park dotted with frilly palaces. The two main palaces are the New Palace (no lines, smart to buy a combo-ticket with a Sanssouci timed-entry here) and the more famous and popular Sanssouci (long lines, required timed entry). Each comes with an audioguide and takes about an hour to tour. The two palaces are connected by the park—it's a pleasant 30-minute walk or a 10-minute bus ride between them.

While Sanssouci is an exquisite little palace with eight unforgettably lavish rooms, the New Palace is much bigger, more historic, and its state rooms are pleasantly plush. If one palace is plenty, you could happily tour the interior of the New Palace and enjoy the views and gardens around Sanssouci without bothering to go into the other palace. Keep in mind that Sanssouci is closed on Monday and the New Palace is closed on Tuesday.

Orientation to Potsdam

Potsdam (pop. 170,000) borders Berlin, on the lake called Wannsee. (During the Cold War, Potsdam was barely in East Germany, just outside West Berlin—the Wall ran right along the lakeshore.) Sights cluster in three areas, each a long walk or a short bus ride apart: the city center, just across the bridge from the train station; Sanssouci Park, a vast royal park at the western edge of town, peppered with grand Hohenzollern palaces; and, to the north, the park called  Neuer Garten, where Cecilienhof Palace looks out over Wannsee and a former KGB prison lurks nearby.

TOURIST INFORMATION

Potsdam has three handy TIs: inside Potsdam's **main train station** (near track 7, Mon-Sat 9:30-18:30, Sun until 15:00, tel. 0331/2755-8899, www.potsdamtourismus.de); on the old main square, **Alter Markt,** across the bridge from the station (Mon-Sat 9:30-19:00, Sun 10:00-16:00, Humboldtstrasse 1); and at **Luisenplatz,** on the eastern end of Sanssouci Park (Mon-Sat 9:30-18:00, Sun 10:00-16:00). While you're there, buy the TI's map of Potsdam—it's worth the minor fee.

ARRIVAL IN POTSDAM

Main Station (Potsdam Hauptbahnhof): This station has ample shops and services including a large Kaufland grocery store for picnic supplies (Mon-Sat 6:00-22:00, closed Sun). On arrival, to take the **bus or tram** to the palaces, head out the exit past track 4, labeled *Friedrich-Engels-Strasse;* here you'll find the tram stops, then the bus stops.

To **walk** into town—or rent a **bike**—use the opposite door, past track 7, labeled *Babelsberger Strasse.* Exiting, turn left to find the bike-rental office. To walk, keep going, turn right at the traffic light, cross a bridge and head for Alter Markt (with the huge dome).

Sanssouci Park Station: From this smaller station, simply walk straight out (or hop a local bus) and head up the boulevard called Am Neuen Palais, with the big park on your right. In about 10 minutes, you'll reach the New Palace.

GETTING AROUND POTSDAM

By Bike: Flat Potsdam is ideal by bike, and from the station it's a pleasant and well-signed 20-minute ride to Sanssouci Palace. There's one caveat: With-in Sanssouci Park you're restricted to a bike path between the palaces; you can't even walk with a bike anywhere else in the park. At the main train station, **Radstation/Pedales** rents bikes and provides a map showing recommended

routes (Mon-Fri 7:00-19:00, Sat-Sun 9:30-18:00, out the Babels-berg Strasse exit and on the left, tel. 0331/7480-057).

By Bus or Tram: Potsdam's public transit efficiently connects most points of interest. Potsdam is covered by a Berlin ticket with zones ABC, but not by one with just zones AB. You can either buy *Anschlussfahrausweis*/extension tickets (€1.60, valid 2 hours), or individual tickets covering Potsdam transit: €2.10/ride, €4.20 all day (buy tickets from machine on board). These are the buses you're most likely to take and the lane from which they depart at the main train station:

Bus **#695**—most handy for tourists—goes through the town center to Sanssouci Palace and then to the New Palace (3/hour, from lane 4).

Bus **#X15,** runs only on summer weekends, makes a beeline to Sanssouci Palace (3/hour, from lane 4).

Buses **#606** and **#605** go directly to the New Palace (3/hour, lane 4).

Bus **#603** runs on summer weekends from the main train station up to Cecilienhof Palace, then loops back down past the KGB Prison Memorial (Persiusstrasse stop) before returning to the station (3/hour, lane 6). If you visit during the week or off-season, catch bus #603 at Platz der Einheit, a 15-minute walk past the Alter Markt (reachable by multiple bus or tram lines from the station).

Tram **#91** is good for a scenic walk through the terraced palace gardens: Get off at Luisenplatz, then walk 20 minutes through the park, which lets you enjoy a classic view of Sanssouci Palace (3/hour from lane 1, direction: Bahnhof Pirscheide).

By Foot: It's a long (but scenic) 45-minute walk from the station to Sanssouci Palace (get a map at the TI). Tram #91, described above, shaves off the least interesting part of this hike.

By Taxi or Uber: A taxi can help link up otherwise difficult-to-connect sights (for example, €15 between the New Palace and Cecilienhof—avoiding a time-consuming bus connection).

Tours in Potsdam

Local Tours

Various bus tours (including hop-on, hop-off options) conveniently connect this town's spread-out sights. Most start at the main train station. Pick up brochures at the TI or check their website (www.potsdamtourismus.de).

Tours from Berlin

Original Berlin Walks and Insider Tour offer inexpensive all-day tours from Berlin to Potsdam. They rely on public transit, focus on the park and the palace exteriors, and don't actually go inside the palaces as a group (€17, admissions and public transportation not included; for contact info see "Tours in Berlin" in the previous chapter).

Sights in Potsdam

Potsdam's sights cluster in three areas: the city center; Sanssouci Park; and the Cold War sights near Neuer Garten.

POTSDAM'S TOWN CENTER

The easy-to-stroll town center has pedestrianized shopping streets lined with boutiques and eateries. For a small town, this was once a cosmopolitan place: Frederick the Great imported some very talented people.

▲Alter Markt

Potsdam's "Old Market Square" is marked by the massive dome of the Nikolaikirche—visible from all over town. This square, always pleasant, has been further rejuvenated by the opening of the Museum Barberini. It's worth a quick stroll through here to ogle the striking Hohenzollern architecture.

Stand in the middle of the square, facing the giant church. The obelisk dates from 1753 and is decorated with medallions celebrating Prussian kings. Remember, Potsdam was essentially a garrison town for the Hohenzollern dynasty. Do a clockwise spin-tour starting at the church to get oriented.

The **Nikolaikirche**, designed by architect Karl Friedrich Schinkel, is an icon of Potsdam. Step inside to see its austere, very Protestant, Neoclassical interior—a well-ordered world of perfectly formed domes and Corinthian columns. The flier explains how this was built following Schinkel's plans in 1850, destroyed in 1945, and rebuilt in 1981 (€2 donation, daily 10:00-21:00).

To the right sits the **Altes Rathaus** (Old Town Hall), with its frilly cupola topped by a "Goldfinger" Atlas supporting the world.

Next is the **Potsdam Museum** (rated ▲▲). This surprisingly interesting museum fills two floors with lots of well-described artifacts that give context to the town, its palaces, and its history. It shows life as a Hohenzollern, and everyday life under the dynasty. It also covers the tragic drama of Potsdam's bombing in 1945, postwar reconstruction, the Soviet era, and the spy-exchange drama on Glienicke Bridge (€5, Tue-Fri 10:00-17:00, Sat-Sun until 16:00, closed Mon, audioguide-€2, tel. 0331/289-6868, www.potsdam-museum.de).

The **Museum Barberini,** a state-of-the-art museum filling a beautifully restored old building, shows off temporary exhibits of world-class artists to the delight of Berlin art snobs. Check what's on (€14, Wed-Mon 10:00-19:00, closed Tue, audioguide-€2, www.museum-barberini.com).

Humboldtstrasse, further to the right, leads to the TI (and is the quickest route to the train station).

Next is the stately, salmon-colored **Stadtschloss** (Brandenburg State Capitol). Germany is made up of 16 states *(Länder)*. The city of Berlin is itself a state. And you're standing just outside the "state" of Berlin in the state of Brandenburg. Potsdam is the capital of Brandenburg, the *Land* that completely surrounds Berlin. Step inside the sterile courtyard, rebuilt after 1945, to see Brandenburg's state capitol and three flags: the EU, Germany, and Brandenburg.

Finally, spinning back toward the church, you see a construction site (or new building) where an ugly, concrete, functionalist building from the DDR once stood. It's now being replaced by a modern building designed to fit the historic tone of the city center. Bit by bit, the ugly communist-era architecture is being replaced.

Other Town Center Sights

Potsdam seems to have a museum for every interest, including a good film museum and a museum of Prussian history (both near Breite Strasse). I'd skip Potsdam's much promoted Wannsee boat rides, which are pretty dull.

FREDERICK THE GREAT'S PALACES AT SANSSOUCI PARK

The dynamic Frederick the Great put Prussia on the map in the 18th century with his merciless military prowess. Yet he also had tender affection for the finer things in life: art, architecture, gardens, literature, and other distinguished pursuits. During his reign,

Frederick built an impressive ensemble of palaces and other grand buildings around Sanssouci Park, with the two top palaces located at either end. Frederick's small, super-Rococo Sanssouci Palace is dazzling, and his massive New Palace was built to wow guests and disprove rumors that Prussia was running out of money after the costly Seven Years' War.

Getting Between the Palaces: It's about a 30-minute walk between Sanssouci and the New Palace, and about 10 minutes by bike. Otherwise hop on bus #695, which takes you between the palaces in either direction (€1.50 *Kurzstrecke* ticket). If you do walk, you'll find the park wilder, more forested, and less carefully manicured than those in other big-league European palace complexes (such as Versailles or Vienna's Schönbrunn). The park's €2 suggested donation gets you a helpful map.

Combo-Ticket: A €19 combo-ticket covers nearly all the royal buildings in the park. It's worthwhile only if you're visiting both Sanssouci and the New Palace (for most visitors, those two are more than enough). The combo-ticket is sold online and at the ticket offices at Sanssouci Palace and the New Palace and comes with an entry time for Sanssouci Palace.

Audio Tours: All tickets include an audioguide.

Information: Tel. 0331/969-4200, www.spsg.de.

▲▲Sanssouci Palace

Sans souci means "without a care," and this was the carefree summer home of Frederick the Great (built 1745-1747). Of all the palatial buildings scattered around Potsdam, this was his actual residence. While the palace is small and the audioguide does little to capture

the personality of its former resident, the palace is
worth seeing for its opu-
lence.

Cost and Hours:
€12, covered by combo-
ticket, Tue-Sun 10:00-
17:30, Nov-March until
16:30, closed Mon year-
round.

Crowd-Beating Tips: If you arrive right at 10:00, you can generally go right in. Arrive later and you'll be given an entry time a couple hours later in the day. If you buy a combo-ticket (described earlier), you'll also book a timed entry for Sanssouci. You can do this online in advance or the same day. A good plan is to go first to the New Palace, buy the combo-ticket with an entry time for Sanssouci later that day, tour the New Palace, and explore the garden until your Sanssouci appointment. If you need to kill time, the palace kitchen and the nearby windmill are both interesting.

Visiting the Palace: This cute little palace was where Frederick the Great spent his summers. You'll stroll through the classic Rococo interior, where golden grapevines climb the walls and frame the windows. First explore the Royal Apartments, containing one of Frederick's three libraries (he found it easier to buy extra copies of books rather than move them around), the "study bedroom" where he lived and worked, and the chair where he died. The domed, central Marble Hall resembles the Pantheon in Rome (on a smaller scale), with an oblong oculus, inlaid marble floors, and Corinthian columns made of Carrara marble.

Finally, you'll visit the guest rooms, most of which empty straight out onto the delightful terrace. Each room is decorated differently: Chinese, Italian, and so on; the niche at the back was for a bed. The happiest is the yellow Voltaire Room, where realistic animals and flowers dangle from the walls and ceiling. As you exit

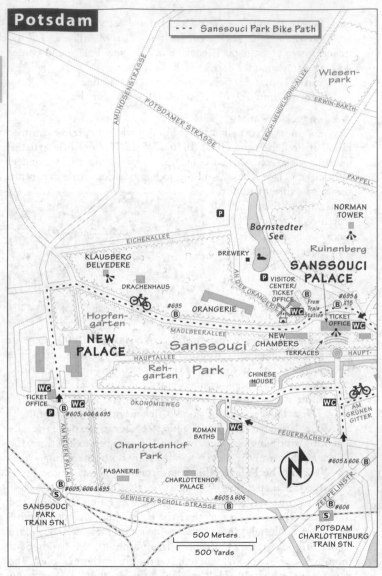

Potsdam

- - - Sanssouci Park Bike Path

(through the servants' quarters), keep an eye out for the giant portrait of Frederick by Andy Warhol.

Nearby: The **palace kitchen** (Schlossküche) gives a peek at a well-preserved and fully-equipped mid-19th-century royal kitchen. Hike down the tight spiral staircase to the wine cellar, with an exhibit about the grapes that were grown on the terraced vineyards out front (€4, covered by combo-ticket, Tue-Sun 10:00-17:30, closed Mon and Nov-March). The **historic windmill** was

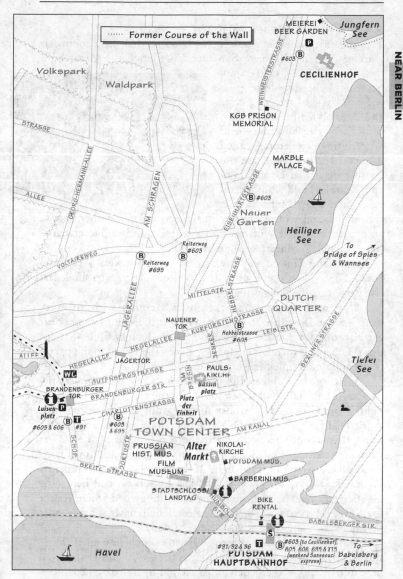

busy from 1787 on grinding grain for the royals. Today it's filled with a very vertical six floor exhibit (in German only). When the wind turns the sails, you can see the miller at work and feel the entire mill tremble (€4, covered by combo-ticket, daily 10:00-18:00, shorter hours off-season).

▲▲New Palace (Neues Palais)

This gigantic showpiece palace (with more than 200 rooms) is grander than the intimate Sanssouci. Frederick the Great built the New Palace (1763-1769), but he rarely stayed here—it was mostly used to host guests and dazzle visiting dignitaries. But other Prussian kings—and later German emperors—called it home. The highlights are the lavishly decorated Grotto Hall and Marble Hall, and several other fine apartments, each a

stunning example of the exuberant Rococo style. Together, they're an artistic ensemble with the same theme. And unlike at Sanssouci, there's no concern about a long line.

Cost and Hours: €8, covered by combo-ticket, Wed-Mon 10:00-17:30, Nov-March until 16:30, closed Tue year-round, last entry one hour before closing.

Getting In: Buy your ticket (which comes with an entry time—generally within 10 or 20 minutes) at the visitors center near the bus stop. I'd skip the eight-minute introductory film—but not the WC here, as there's none in the palace. Then head to the palace at the appointed time to pick up your audioguide.

Visiting the Palace: The audioguide takes you through the palace's ornate halls and state rooms. On the main floor, the highlight is the Grotto Hall, whose marble walls are encrusted with a quarter of a million seashells, semiprecious stones, and fossils. From there, continue on through the eight suites of the Lower Princes' Apartments, which accommodated guests and royal family members. In the 19th and early 20th century, German emperors Frederick III and Wilhelm II (the last kaiser) resided here. The Gentlemen's Bedchamber holds the red-canopy bed where Kaiser Frederick III died in 1888. The Ladies' Bedchamber is a reminder that noblemen and their wives slept separately.

Upstairs, the Upper Princes' Quarters include a small blue-tiled bathroom that was installed for Kaiser Wilhelm II (he lived here until 1918), and a bedchamber shared by a married couple—my, how times have changed. You'll also find Wilhelm's bedroom, as well as a small painting gallery with portraits of Frederick the Great and Russia's Catherine the Great (who was born a German princess). The grand finale is the sumptuous, 52-foot-high Marble Hall, with its dramatic ceiling painting and floors inlaid with Silesian marble. Through the windows, enjoy views of the gardens.

Other Palaces

The two main palaces (Sanssouci and the New Palace) are just the beginning. Sprawling Sanssouci Park contains a variety of other palaces and royal build-ings, many of which you can enter: the sprawling Italian-style **Orangery;** the **New Chambers** (a royal guesthouse); the **Chinese Tea House;** and other viewpoints, such as the **Klausberg Belvedere** and the **Norman Tower.**

Each has its own entry fee (€2-6; all but the Belvedere covered by the €19 combo-ticket). Some are open weekends and/or April-October only (get details at Potsdam TI, palace ticket office, or www.spsg.de).

COLD WAR SIGHTS

At the north end of town, another (much more modest) park, called Neuer Garten, is delightfully set on the idyllic Wannsee. This is where you'll find several stirring sights for those interested in Cold War history, and a fine lakeside brewery.

Getting There: While getting to these sights by public transit is possible, you'll do better with a bike or taxi. The Neuer Garten area is connected to the center by bus #603 (see "Getting Around Potsdam," earlier). Tram #93 takes you from the main train station to the Bridge of Spies. It's about a 20-minute walk between the Neuer Garten sights and the bridge.

▲Cecilienhof

This early-20th-century villa was the site of the historic Potsdam Conference for two weeks in the summer of 1945. For Cold War buffs, it's worth ▲▲. Touring the rooms with an audioguide, you'll hear how, during those meetings, Harry Truman, Winston Churchill, and Joseph Stalin negotiated how best to punish Germany for dragging Europe through another devastating war. It was here that the postwar map of Europe was officially drawn, setting the stage for a protracted Cold War that would drag on for more than four decades. There's no wait, and a stop here pairs well with a drink or meal at the fine Meierei brewery and a visit to the KGB Prison Memorial—each less than a 10-minute walk away.

Cost and Hours: €8, includes audioguide, Tue-Sun 10:00-17:30, Nov-March until 16:30, closed Mon year-round, tel. 0331/969-4200, www.spsg.de. Note: A separate ticket is required to visit the upper floor state rooms (hourly German-language tour).

Visiting the Palace: This Tudor-style villa—designed to appear smaller and more modest than it actually is—was built in 1912 to house Crown Prince Wilhelm and his wife Cecilie, who would have ruled Germany, had Kaiser Wilhelm II not lost World War I. It's certainly less striking than Potsdam's other palaces. The draw here is the 1945 history. You'll tour the palace using an excellent 45-minute audioguide, which does a marvelous job of re-animating history. You'll hear all about those tense days in July 1945, including sound bites from meeting participants. You'll see the private offices of Stalin,  Churchill, and Truman, as well as the grand meeting hall with the round table where they faced off to negotiate. It's both chilling and fitting to think that, just 20 years later, the Berlin Wall would run through the park right in front of the palace—cutting off idyllic views of the Wannsee. This was also where Truman told Stalin about the atomic bomb and issued the "Potsdam Declaration"—demanding that Japan unconditionally surrender to end the war once and for all. Japan refused—and the US dropped atomic bombs on Hiroshima and Nagasaki.

Eating: The **$ Meierei Biergarten,** named for a 19th-century creamery, now functions as a brewery. Delightfully set on the lake under an evocative industrial age chimney, it has two zones: a cheery, self-service beer garden (basic beerhall food and drink, open only in summer and good weather) and a more serious, pricier restaurant (with seating under vaults where cows were once milked and outside overlooking the lake). It's a short, thought-provoking walk from Cecilienhof as you pass through what was once the death strip of the Berlin Wall (Tue-Sun 12:00-22:00, closed Mon, a 10-minute stroll north of Cecilienhof—follow *Meierei* signs to Im Neuen Garten 10, tel. 0331/704-3211).

▲KGB Prison Memorial at Leistikowstrasse (Gedenkstätte Leistikowstrasse Potsdam)

Standing in stark contrast to all of Potsdam's pretty palaces and Hohenzollern bombast, this crumbling concrete prison has been turned into a memorial and documentation center to the Cold War victims of USSR "counterintelligence."

Cost and Hours: Free, Tue-Sun 14:00-18:00, Nov-March 13:00-17:00, closed Mon year-round, Leistikowstrasse 1, tel. 0331/201-1540, www.gedenkstaette-leistikowstrasse.de.

Visiting the Memorial: On the nondescript Leistikowstrasse, a few steps from the lakeside park, the KGB established a base in August 1945 (mere days after the Potsdam Conference), which remained active until the fall of the USSR in 1991. The centerpiece of their "secret city" was this transit prison in which enemies of the Soviet regime were held and punished in horrible conditions before entering the USSR "justice" system—to be tried, executed, or shipped off to notorious gulag labor camps. While most prisoners were Russian citizens, until 1955 the prison also held Germans who were essentially kidnapped by the USSR in retribution for their wartime activities.

From the blocky modern reception building at the corner, you'll enter the complex. In the yard find a model illustrating how

this was just the inner core of a walled secret city which (until 1991) was technically Soviet territory run by the KGB. Then head inside the prison, where the hallways and cells are an eerie world of peeling paint, faded linoleum, and rusted hinges. The two floors host a well-presented exhibit explaining the history of the building (which was a vicarage before being seized by the Soviets) and profiling several individuals who were held here.

Bridge of Spies

During the Cold War, the Havel River became the border between the US and Soviet sectors. Because this was a handy place to swap prisoners and spies, the Glienicke Bridge became known as the "Bridge of Spies." The bridge had long been part of a key transportation route between the royal residence in Potsdam and Berlin. A fine brick-and-wood bridge was built here in 1834, then replaced with a modern iron one in 1904. After serious bomb damage, it was rebuilt in 1949. After construction of the Berlin Wall in 1961, the bridge was closed to the public, and guarded as a border crossing.

Spies and dissidents—most famously Gary Powers (who piloted the U-2 spy plane shot down over the USSR in 1960) and Soviet activist Natan Sharansky—were traded on this bridge. The 1962 exchange of KGB agent Rudolf Abel for Powers inspired the Steven Spielberg film *Bridge of Spies*, starring Tom Hanks (2015). The Villa Schöningen at the west end of the bridge has an exhibit covering the historic border crossing (€5, Thu-Sun 12:00-18:00, closed Mon-Wed, Berliner Strasse 86, tel. 0331/200-1739, www. villa-schoeningen.org).

Sachsenhausen Memorial & Museum

About 20 miles north of downtown Berlin, the small town of Oranienburg was the site of one of the most notorious Nazi con-centration camps. Sachsen-hausen's proximity to the capital gave it special status as the place to train camp guards and test new procedures. It was also the site of the Third Reich's massive counterfeit-ing operation to destabilize Great Britain by flooding the monetary system with forged pound notes. Today the Sachsenhausen Memorial and Museum *(Gedenkstätte und Museum Sachsenhausen),* worth ▲▲, honors the camp's victims and survivors, and teaches visitors about the atroc-ities that took place here.

GETTING TO SACHSENHAUSEN

Take a train to the town of Oranienburg (20-50 minutes, covered by zone ABC ticket; if you have a pass for just zones AB, buy a €1.60 *Anschlussfahrausweis* extension ticket to get here—valid for 2 hours; from there, it's a quick trip by bus or taxi to the camp, or a 20-minute walk). The whole journey takes just over an hour each way.

From Berlin Hauptbahnhof, the **Regional Express/RE5** train speeds to Oranienburg (hourly, 25 minutes). Or you can take the S-Bahn (S1) line from various stops in downtown Berlin, in-cluding Potsdamer Platz, Brandenburger Tor, Friedrichstrasse, and Oranienburger Strasse (2/hour, 50 minutes).

At Oranienburg, the **bus** to the memorial departs from lane 4, right in front of the train station (on weekdays, hourly bus #804 is timed to meet most regional trains; on weekends it runs only every 2 hours, and doesn't sync with S-Bahn arrivals; direction: Malz; bus #821 also possible, runs 5/day, no buses Sat-Sun, di-rection: Tiergarten; €1.70, covered by Berlin transit day pass for zones ABC or *Anschlussfahrausweis,* get off at Gedenkstätte stop). You can also take a **taxi** (€8, ask for the *Gedenkstätte*—geh-DENK-shteh-teh).

To **walk** 20 minutes to the memorial, turn right from the train station and head up Stralsunder Strasse for about two blocks. Turn

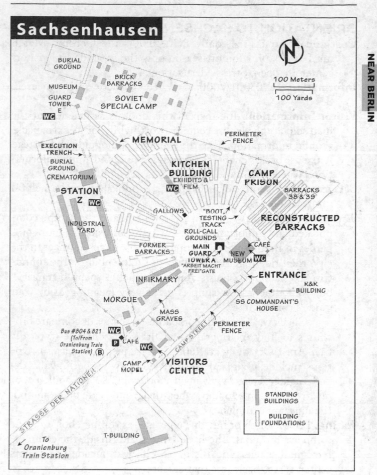

right under the railroad trestle onto Bernauer Strasse, following signs for *Gedenkstätte Sachsenhausen*. At the traffic light, turn left onto André Pican Strasse, which becomes Strasse der Einheit. After two blocks, turn right on Strasse der Nationen, which leads right to the camp.

PLANNING YOUR TIME

Make your pilgrimage to Sachsenhausen any day in summer. The museums are closed on Monday from mid-October to mid-March (the grounds are open daily year-round). You'll need at least three hours to appreciate the many worthwhile exhibits here. Factoring in transit time, give yourself at least five hours round-trip from central Berlin.

ORIENTATION TO SACHSENHAUSEN

Cost and Hours: Free, daily 8:30-18:00, mid-Oct-mid-March until 16:30, on Mon off-season only the grounds and visitors center are open, Strasse der Nationen 22.

Information: Tel. 03301/2000, www.gedenkstaette-sachsenhausen. de.

Visitor Information: The map in this book is sufficient, but the map sold at the visitors center is worthwhile for its extra background information. Skip the overlong audioguide and instead make use of this chapter's self-guided tour and ample information posted within the camp.

Services: The visitors center has WCs, a bookshop, and a helpful information desk.

Tours from Berlin: A tour helps you understand the camp's complicated and important story. Virtually all walking-tour companies in Berlin offer side-trips to Sachsenhausen (meet in the city, then ride together by train to Oranienburg). The round-trip takes about six hours, much of which is spent in transit— but your time at the camp is made very meaningful by your guide's commentary.

Check walking-tour companies' websites or compare brochures to find an itinerary that fits your schedule (typically €17, April-Oct daily at 10:00, less frequent off-season). Options include **Original Berlin Walks** (www.berlinwalks.de) and **Insider Tour** (www.insidertour.com). Don't book a tour on an off-season Monday, when the grounds are open, but not the museum exhibits.

Eating: Pack a lunch or buy one en route, as dining choices at the camp are minimal. The little "Info Café" inside the camp offers small snacks, and Bistro To Go, just outside the visitors center, serves basic fare (wurst, soup).

BACKGROUND

Completed in July 1936, Sachsenhausen was the first concentration camp built under SS chief Heinrich Himmler. The triangle-shaped grounds, contained by three walls, enabled observation of the entire camp from a single point, the main guard tower. The design was intended to be a model for other camps, but it had a critical flaw that prevented its widespread adoption: It was very difficult to expand without interfering with sight lines.

Sachsenhausen was not, strictly speaking, a "death camp" for mass murder (like Auschwitz); it was a labor camp, intended to wring hard work out of the prisoners. Many toiled in a brickworks, producing materials to be used in architect Albert Speer's grandiose plans for erecting new buildings all over Berlin.

Between 1936 and 1945, about 200,000 prisoners did time at

Sachsenhausen; about 50,000 died here, while numerous others were transported elsewhere to be killed (in 1942, many of Sachsenhausen's Jews were taken to Auschwitz). Though it was designed to hold 10,000 prisoners, by the end of its functional life the camp had up to 38,000 people. In the spring of 1945, knowing that the Red Army was approaching, guards took 35,000 able-bodied prisoners on a death march, leading them into the forest for seven days and nights with no rations. Rather than "wasting" bullets to kill them, SS troops hoped that the prisoners would expire from exhaustion. On the eighth day, after 6,000 had died, the guards abandoned the group in the wilderness. When Soviet troops liberated Sachsenhausen on April 22, 1945, they discovered an additional 3,000 prisoners who had been too weak to walk and were left there to die (all but 300 survived).

Just three months after the war, Sachsenhausen was converted into Soviet Special Camp No. 7 for the USSR's own prisoners. It was a notorious "silent camp," where prisoners would disappear—allowed no contact with the outside world and their imprisonment officially unacknowledged. The prisoners were Nazis as well as anti-Stalin Russians. By the time the camp closed in 1950, 12,000 more people had died here.

In 1961, Sachsenhausen became the first former concentration camp to be turned into a memorial. The East German government created the memorial mostly for propaganda purposes, to deflect attention from the controversial construction of the Berlin Wall and to exalt the USSR as the valiant antifascist liberators of the camp and all of Germany.

Since the end of the DDR, Sachsenhausen has been redeveloped into a true memorial, with updated museum exhibits and an emphasis on preservation—documenting and sharing the story of what happened here. While difficult to take in, as with all concentration camp memorials, the intention of Sachsenhausen is to share its story and lessons—and prevent this type of brutality from ever happening again.

❂ SELF-GUIDED TOUR

The camp's various exhibits are scattered throughout the grounds in various buildings, and offer more information than you probably have time to absorb. This outline covers the key parts of your visit.

Entrance

In the courtyard next to the visitors center, a **model** of the camp illustrates its unique triangular layout. Guards stationed in tower A (at the main gate) could see everything going on inside those three walls. Along the left (west) side of the triangle is the crematorium, called Station Z. Outside the main triangle are the workshops, factories, and extra barracks that were added when the camp ran out of room.

Walk up the dusty lane called Camp Street. On the right is the SS officers' R&R building, nicknamed the **"Green Monster,"** where prisoners dressed in nice clothes were forced to wait on their keepers. Officials mostly chose Jehovah's Witnesses for this duty, because they had a strong pacifist code and could be trusted not to attempt to harm their captors.

A left turn through the fence takes you into the courtyard in front of **guard tower A.** The clock on the tower is frozen at

11:07—the exact time that the Red Army liberated the camp. The building on the right—the **New Museum**—has an interesting DDR-era stained-glass window inside, as well as thoughtful temporary exhibits and a small café.

Go through the gate cruelly marked *Arbeit Macht Frei*— "Work will set you free."

Main Grounds

Entering the triangular field, you can see that almost none of the original buildings still stand. Following the war, locals salvaged the barracks here for much-needed building materials. Tracing the perimeter, notice the electric fence and barbed wire. A few feet in front of the wall is a gravel track called the **neutral zone**—any prisoner setting foot here would be shot. This became a common way for prisoners to attempt suicide. Guards quickly caught on:

If they sensed a suicide attempt, they'd shoot to maim instead of kill. It was typical upside-down Nazi logic: Those who wanted to live would die, and those who wanted to die would live.

Every morning, after a 4:15 wake-up call, prisoners would scramble to eat, bathe, and dress in time to assemble in the **roll-call grounds** in front of the guard tower by 5:00. Dressed in their thin, striped pajama-like uniforms and wooden clogs, prisoners would line up while guards, in long coats and accompanied by angry dogs, barked orders and accounted for each person, including those who had died in the barracks overnight. It could take hours, in any weather. A single misbehaving prisoner would bring about punishment for all others. One day, after a prisoner escaped, SS officer Rudolf Höss (who later went on to run Auschwitz-Birkenau) forced the entire population of the camp to stand here for 15 hours in a foot of snow and subzero temperatures. A thousand people died.

To the far right from the entrance, the wooden **barracks** (with good museum displays)  are reconstructed from original timbers. Barrack 38 focuses on the Jewish experience at Sachsenhausen, as well as the general mistreatment of German Jews under the Nazis (including anti-Semitic propaganda). Barrack 39 explains everyday life, with stories following 20 individual internees. You'll see how prisoners lived: long rows of bunks, benches for taking paltry meals, latrines crammed wall-to-wall with toilets, and communal fountains for washing. Inmates would jockey for access to these facilities. The strongest, meanest, most aggressive prisoners—often here because they had been convicted of a violent crime—would be named *Kapo*, the head of the barrack (to discourage camaraderie, the worst prisoners, rather than the best, were "promoted"). Like at many other camps, the camp leaders at Sachsenhausen ran a system of organized rape, whereby they brought in inmates from the women's-only Ravensbrück concentration camp and forced them to "reward good prisoners" at Sachsenhausen.

Next to the barracks is the **camp prison,** where political prisoners or out-of-line inmates were sent. It was run not by the SS, but by the Gestapo (secret police), who would torture captives to extract information. Other prisoners didn't know exactly what went on here, but they could hear screams from inside and knew it was no place they wanted to be. This was also where the Nazis held special hostages, including three Allied airmen who had participated in a bold escape from a Nazi prisoner-of-war camp (the basis for *The Great Escape;* they later managed to escape from Sachsenhausen as well, before being recaptured) and Joseph Stalin's son, Yakov Dzhugashvili, who had been captured during the fighting at Stalingrad. (The Nazis offered to exchange the young man for five German officers. Stalin refused, and soon after, Yakov died here under mysterious circumstances.) The cells contain exhibits about the prisoners and the methods used by their captors.

Just outside the back of the building stand three **posts** (out of an original 15) with iron pegs near the top. Guards cruelly executed people by tying their hands behind their backs, then hanging them on these pegs by their wrists until they died—a medieval method called *strappado*.

Walk around the inner semicircle toward the buildings in the middle of the camp. On this **"boot-testing track,"** prisoners were forced to put on boots two sizes too small and walk in a circle on uneven ground all day, supposedly to "test" the shoes for fighting at Stalingrad.

The rectangles of stones show where each of the original barrack buildings once stood. At the center, a marker represents the

location of the gallows, where prisoners would be publicly executed as a deterrent to others.

In the middle of the triangle, on the right, is the kitchen building, with exhibits that trace the chronological history of the camp. You'll learn how Sachsenhausen was built by prisoners and see original artifacts, including the gallows, a bunk from the barracks, uniforms, and so on. There are also photos, quotes, and a 22-minute film.

Memorial and Crematorium

Head back to the far end of the camp, which is dominated by the towering, 130-foot-tall, 1961 communist **DDR memorial** to the victims of Sachsenhausen. The 18 triangles at the top are red, the color designated for political prisoners (to the communists, they were more worthy of honor than the other victims who died here). At the base of the monument, two prisoners are being liberated by a noble

Soviet soldier. The prisoners are unrealistically robust, healthy, and optimistic (they will survive and become part of the proud Soviet proletariat!). The **podium** in front was used by the East German army for speeches and rallies—exploiting Sachsenhausen as a backdrop for their propaganda.

From here, head left and go through the gap in the fence to

find the execution trench, used for mass shootings. When this system proved too inefficient, the Nazis built "Station Z," the nearby **crematorium,** where they could execute and dispose of prisoners more systematically. Its ruins are inside the white building (prior to the camp's liberation by Soviet troops,

Nazi guards destroyed the crematorium to remove evidence of their crimes).

The crematorium's ramp took prisoners down into the "infirmary," while the three steps led up to the dressing room. This is where, on five occasions, the Nazis tested Zyklon-B (the chemical later responsible for killing hundreds of thousands at Auschwitz).

Most of the building's victims died in the room with the double row of bricks (for soundproofing; the Nazis also blasted classical music to mask noise). Victims would report here for a "dental check," to find out if they had gold or silver teeth that could be taken. They would then stand against the wall to have their height measured—and a guard would shoot them through a small hole in the wall with a single bullet to the back of the skull. (The Nazis found it was easier for guards to carry out their duties if they didn't have to see their victims face-to-face.)

Bodies were taken to be incinerated in the ovens (which still stand). Notice the statue of the emaciated prisoner—a much more accurate depiction than the one at the DDR monument. Outside, a burial ground is filled with ashes from the crematorium.

The Rest of the Camp

Back inside the main part of the camp you can head left, up to the tip of the triangle (behind the big monument) to find a museum about the postwar era, when Sachsenhausen served as a **Soviet**

Special Camp. Nearby is a burial ground for victims of that camp. At this corner of the triangle, the gate in the fence—called **tower E**—holds a small exhibit about the relationship between the camp and the town of Oranienburg.

Heading back toward the main guard tower, along the wall toward the front corner, are the long, green barracks of the **infirmary,** used for medical experiments on inmates (as explained by the exhibits inside). This was also where Soviet soldiers found the 3,000 remaining survivors when they liberated the camp. The small building in back was the morgue—Nazis used the long ramp to bring in the day's bodies via wheelbarrows. Behind that is a field with six stones, each marking 50 bodies for the 300 prisoners who died after the camp was freed.

HAMBURG

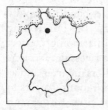

Hamburg is Germany's second-largest city, the richest judged by per-capita income, and its most important port—even though it is about 60 miles from the North Sea. Like other "second cities"—such as Chicago, Marseille, Glasgow, Antwerp, and St. Petersburg—Hamburg has a special pride. It's popular with German tourists, who come here to eat fish, watch soccer games, marvel at its mighty port, and experience the fabled nightlife of the Reeperbahn, the German answer to "Sin City" (and famous for launching the Beatles' career). On weekends year-round—and just about any time the weather is nice—the city comes alive. Foreign visitors are in the minority, and American tourists are rare. Like many port towns, Hamburg can have rough edges, but a short stay can be memorable.

Hamburg (HAHM-boork) lacks a quaint medieval center. Ye Olde Hamburg was flattened by a one-two punch that occurred over a 101-year span: First, a

devastating 1842 fire gutted the town center, and then an equally devastating firebombing by Allied forces in 1943 wiped out whole neighborhoods. Today the city center is a people-friendly collection of wide streets, outdoor cafés, office buildings, and shops—not unlike the downtown cores of many American cities. The most charming parts of Hamburg, however, are the neighborhoods outside the center, many of which show off Germany's economic prosperity in the 19th and 20th centuries.

The name "Hamburg" very loosely derives from "castle on wet ground"—and the city, with nearly 2,500 bridges, is built to accommodate a 13-foot tide. A century ago, Hamburg's seaport on the Elbe River was the third largest in the world. Today, the city's fishy maritime atmosphere—with a constant breeze and the evocative cries of seagulls—gives Hamburg an almost Scandinavian, Dutch, or English feel that's worlds away from the sun-drenched, Baroque joviality of Bavaria.

If you have German ancestors, there's a good chance they left for America from here: Between 1850 and 1930, more than five million Germans emigrated to the US from Hamburg's port. After the Iron Curtain cut off trade to the east, port traffic—and the city's influence—dwindled. But since reunification in 1990, Hamburg has been returning to its former status as one of the biggest trade centers in Central Europe, and the city is expanding rapidly as it focuses on redeveloping its old docklands. The burgeoning HafenCity district and its spectacular Elbphilharmonie concert hall are turning Hamburg back toward its Elbe riverside. No longer content to be famous merely for its lusty sailors' quarter and as the Beatles' springboard to stardom, the new Hamburg expects to be seen as a cultural capital rivaling other great cities throughout Europe.

PLANNING YOUR TIME

If you're passing through on your way between Germany and Denmark, Hamburg is certainly worth a quick stop. At the very least, toss your bag in a train-station locker and enjoy a 1.5-hour hop-on, hop-off bus tour and a harbor cruise before taking an evening train out.

But with its variety of attractions, Hamburg can easily fill a rewarding day (or more) of sightseeing. While you could see the sights in any order, consider this busy all-day plan using public transit (leave by 9:30 if you want to take the worthwhile noon harbor tour):

In the morning, visit the sights in the city center, starting at the City Hall (Rathaus). Have a look at the posh shops around Jungfernstieg and the Binnenalster lakefront. The St. Nikolai Memorial is a short walk in the opposite direction; from there make your way to the distinctive architecture of the Kontorhausviertel neighborhood. From the nearby Messberg U-Bahn stop, the U-3 line will take you to the Landungsbrücken stop, just above the waterfront where the harbor cruise starts.

After the cruise, decide how to spend your afternoon. To visit sights in the Speicherstadt warehouse district and go up to the Elbphilharmonie's Plaza viewing platform, take the #72 public ferry from the Landungsbrücken harborfront. Alternatively, you could walk from the harbor to the Hamburg History Museum, then return from the adjacent St. Pauli U-Bahn stop to the train station or your hotel via the U-3 line.

The U-3 will also take you to the Sternschanze stop, perfect for an evening stroll and dinner in the happening Schulterblatt neighborhood. Cap off your full day with the self-guided "Reeperbahn Walk" (see page 930) to see this nightlife area at full-tilt.

Orientation to Hamburg

Hamburg is big (1.8 million people, sprawling to 5 million in the surrounding metropolitan area). You can walk between some of its sights, but you'll need to use public transit to reach the top ones. The city center sits between the Elbe River to the south and a lake called the Binnenalster to the north, and is surrounded by a ring road that follows the route of the old city walls. Away from the City Hall and the pleasant pedestrian streets of Spitalerstrasse and Mönckebergstrasse, the center is fairly workaday. Most places of interest are just outside this downtown core: The train station and the St. Georg neighborhood (with good hotels and restaurants) are east of the center; the harbor, old Speicherstadt warehouse district, and the new HafenCity zone are to the south along the Elbe; the St. Pauli waterfront district and the red light/entertainment zone along the Reeperbahn lie to the west; and to the northwest is the lively Sternschanze quarter and Schulterblatt ("shoulderblade") neighborhood.

TOURIST INFORMATION

Hamburg's main TI—in the train station, above the north end of tracks 3-4—is a good place to buy a Hamburg Card (Mon-Sat 9:00-19:00, Sun 10:00-18:00, tel. 040/3005-1701—not answered Sun, www.hamburg-travel.com). There are also TIs at the St. Pauli Landungsbrücken harborfront (Sun-Wed 9:00-18:00, Thu-Sat until 19:00) and the airport (daily 6:00-23:00). Visit the TI website to download a free Hamburg tourism app with tips and an offline map.

Hamburg Card: If you plan to see at least two or three museums, especially with a travel partner (or two), this card is a sound investment. Sold at TIs and public-transit ticket machines, it covers a full day of public transit plus reduced-priced entry to many sights. While the discounts are modest (10-33 percent), the card costs only a little more than a transit pass (€10.50/day, €18.50/day for groups of up to 5; 2- and 3-day cards available).

ARRIVAL IN HAMBURG

By Train: Hamburg's main train station has a handsome interior with a classic steel-arch design. The station is within walking distance of Hamburg's City Hall and recommended hotels in the St. Georg neighborhood. For other destinations, use the subway and buses.

From the platforms, escalators lead up to bridges that span the tracks at the north and south ends of the building; at each end of each bridge is an exit (four exits in all). The northern bridge—look for the giant *Wandelhalle* sign in the middle—has most services, including ticket counters in the *Reisezentrum* (long hours daily). You'll also find the TI (above tracks 3-4), WCs, a left-luggage desk (next to the *Reisezentrum,* daily 8:00-20:00),

and several banks of lockers (one is above tracks 5-6). Exit from here to reach my recommended St. Georg neighborhood hotels.

By Bus: Long-distance buses come and go from the large covered bus terminal *(ZOB)* located just around the corner from the southern end of the main train station (across from the Arts and Crafts Museum).

By Plane: Hamburg's airport (code: HAM, tel. 040/50750, www.hamburg-airport.de) is a simple ride from the train station on the S-1 subway line. The journey takes only 30 minutes (6/hour, runs 4:30-24:00). A Hamburg *Grossbereich* ticket (€3.30) will cover your journey, but consider getting a transit day pass or a Hamburg Card if you'll be doing more travel that day. Note that if you're traveling *to* the airport, S-1 trains from the city divide at Ohlsdorf, one stop before the airport. Generally, the first three cars go to the airport—but pay attention to the signs and ask fellow passengers to be sure.

HELPFUL HINTS

Fischmarkt: If you're here on a Sunday, it's worth getting out of bed for this venerable market (about 5:00-9:30, though the action usually lingers at least an hour later). It's a rich sensory experience: Smell the fresh flowers (and even fresher fish), wander among colorful baskets of produce, hear the stall-keepers shout

out closing-time deals, enjoy the fun music-festival vibe, and marvel at the Germans drinking beer this early in the morning (many are wrapping up a night out in St. Pauli).

To reach the market from the St. Georg neighborhood, catch bus #112 and ride it to the Hafentreppe stop (leaves from other side of train station, across the street from the end of Spitalerstrasse; 2-3/hour on Sunday mornings, 15 minutes). Otherwise, take the S-1 or S-3 to the Reeperbahn stop, or the U-3 to Landungsbrücken, and walk a few blocks to the market.

Laundry: Near the train station and convenient to St. Georg hotels, **Express Wasch-Center** offers both self-service and full service (Mon-Fri 8:00-19:00, Sat until 18:00, closed Sun, facing Hansaplatz at Zimmerpforte 6—from Lange Reihe, walk down Baumeisterstrasse until you reach Hansaplatz, then continue left along the north side of the square to the next street, tel. 040/280-4655).

Bike Lanes and Pedestrians: The city is a delight to explore on two wheels. But be alert: Red-brick pavement on the sidewalk means it's a bike lane. Pedestrians should stay on the gray part of the sidewalk. Bicyclists show little patience for tourists who stray onto the brick.

Bike Rental: StadtRAD stocks distinctive red bikes at more than 100 automated rental stations. The first half-hour is free, but you must pay a €5 registration fee that gives you about an hour of additional credit (tel. 040/822-188-100, www. stadtradhamburg.de).

Taxi: Try **Hansa-Taxi** (tel. 040/211-211).

GETTING AROUND HAMBURG

Public transport makes sightseeing efficient in this spread-out city. Hamburg's subway system includes both the U-Bahn (with four lines, U-1 to U-4) and S-Bahn (commuter rail lines). Buses and public ferries, which are both covered by the various transit passes, round out the system.

The Hamburg transport association—known as HVV—has an information office next to the TI in the train station (long hours daily, tel. 040/19449, www.hvv.de). Buy tickets from machines marked *HVV* at any U-Bahn or S-Bahn stop (use coins and small bills). Buy bus tickets from the driver (will make change). Tickets bought from machines or drivers are already validated; you don't need to stamp them again.

Single ticket prices vary with ride length; the shortest trips cost €1.60, longer trips cost €2.20, and the longest trips (within the *Grossbereich*—greater city limits, including the airport) cost €3.30.

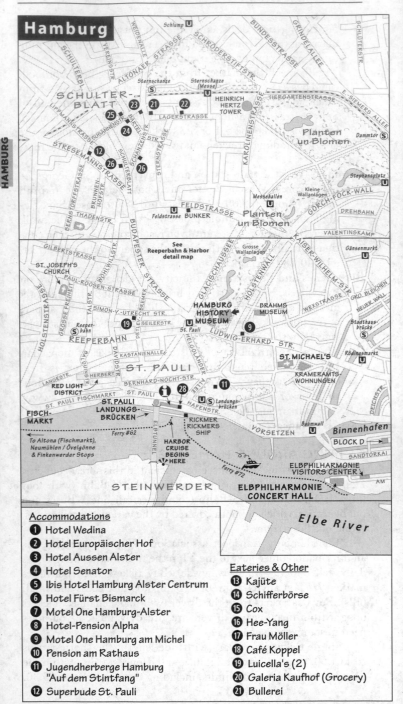

Hamburg

Accommodations
1. Hotel Wedina
2. Hotel Europäischer Hof
3. Hotel Aussen Alster
4. Hotel Senator
5. Ibis Hotel Hamburg Alster Centrum
6. Hotel Fürst Bismarck
7. Motel One Hamburg-Alster
8. Hotel-Pension Alpha
9. Motel One Hamburg am Michel
10. Pension am Rathaus
11. Jugendherberge Hamburg "Auf dem Stintfang"
12. Superbude St. Pauli

Eateries & Other
13. Kajüte
14. Schifferbörse
15. Cox
16. Hee-Yang
17. Frau Möller
18. Café Koppel
19. Luicella's (2)
20. Galeria Kaufhof (Grocery)
21. Bullerei

HAMBURG

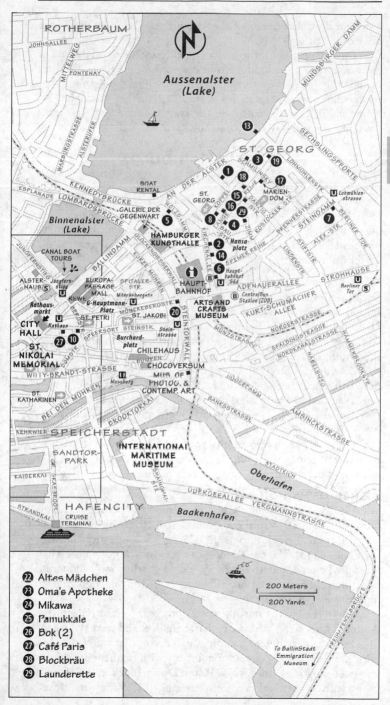

Key your destination into a ticket machine, and it will tell you the price of the ticket.

Day passes pay for themselves quickly and give you the run of the whole system, including ferry rides on the Elbe River. Options include the *9-Uhr-Tageskarte* day pass (€6.40) or the *9-Uhr-Gruppenkarte* for groups of up to five people (€12, neither valid Mon-Fri before 9:00). If you need to use the system before 9:00 on weekdays, buy the full-day pass (*Ganztageskarte*, €7.70).

Tours in Hamburg

Free Walking Tours

As in most big German cities, you'll find a variety of "free" walking tours (but guides hope for at least a €5/person tip). They all offer once-over-lightly walks through town with commentary that's more entertainment than history. Look for brochures or ask at the TI for information.

Do-It-Yourself Orientation Tour: U-3 Subway

For a brief orientation to the city, enjoy a short ride from the train station to the harborfront at Landungsbrücken. Starting at the Hauptbahnhof Süd U-Bahn stop, take the U-3 in the direction of Schlump/Barmbek. The first two stops are underground; then, at the Rödingsmarkt stop, you'll emerge onto elevated tracks that run past downtown office buildings (at this stop, look right to see the St. Michael's Church tower, and left to see the St. Nikolai Memorial tower). At the next stop, Baumwall, you can see Speicherstadt ("Warehouse City"), Hamburg's warehouse district, and the striking Elbphilharmonie concert hall. On the way to the next stop (Landungsbrücken), enjoy the view of the harbor, with its massive port and thriving riverfront. At Landungsbrücken you can detour to the harbor, return to the station, or continue to your destination.

▲▲Hop-On Hop-Off Bus Tours

With its most interesting sights scattered on the perimeter, Hamburg is well-suited to an above-ground orientation. Several companies run circular city bus tours (€17-19 for 1.5 hours, discount with Hamburg Card). The double-decker buses (which go topless when it's sunny) offer a smooth, high ride with a steady flow of sights and brief multilingual narration, allowing you barely enough time to identify what you're seeing.

The most logical starting points are at the train station (the double-decker buses park along Kirchenallee) and near the Landungsbrücken pier. Before boarding, make sure that you're on a bus with English commentary. One company with frequent departures and good English guides is **Die Roten Doppeldecker;** look for red buses with white *Stadtrundfahrt* lettering (€18.50 all-day ticket,

29 stops, departs every half-hour 9:30-17:00, less frequent Nov-March, tel. 040/792-8979, www.die-roten-doppeldecker.de). A €32.50 combo-ticket adds the recommended Rainer Abicht harbor boat tour; a different €32.50 combo-ticket adds the Maritime Circle hop-on, hop-off boat.

Boat Tours

To get out on the river, you can take a **tour** (runs in English once a day at noon), a **hop-on, hop-off boat** with English narration, or one of the less interesting (but cheaper and more frequent) public **ferries;** see page 924 for more details. Within the city center, **canal boats** leisurely circle the Binnenalster lake, with a few routes also swinging through the Speicherstadt/HafenCity development (described on page 926).

Local Guide

Consider Hamburg native **Tomas Kaiser** (€140/2 hours, €240/half-day, rates are suggestions and he's often flexible, mobile 0170-232-7749, tomas_kaiser@web.de). The professionals in the **Hamburg guide association** can cover everything from Hamburg highlights and historical sights to urban districts and boat trips. The association's website has a list of guides and their contact info; **Birgit Scheffner** is one of the most experienced (around €135/2 hours, www.hamburger-gaestefuehrer.de, info@hamburger-gaestefuehrer.de).

Sights in Hamburg

IN THE CITY CENTER
City Hall (Rathaus)

Hamburg's impressive City Hall, a mix of Historicist styles (from

1897), was designed to showcase the wealth and grandeur of turn-of-the-20th-century imperial Germany. While the building is called a "City Hall," Hamburg actually forms its own *Land* (state) within the Federal Republic of Germany, and the

council that meets in the City Hall chambers is more like a state legislature.

Cost and Hours: Free to enter entrance hall and inner courtyard, daily 10:00-18:00; daily €5 English-language tours run every 2 hours 11:15-15:15, plus Sat at 16:15 (45 minutes, canceled for special events, more frequent German-language tours); on Rathaus-markt, tel. 040/428-312-064, www.hamburg.de/rathausfuehrung.

Getting There: The City Hall has its own stop on the U-3 subway line (Rathaus); it's also very near the Jungfernstieg stop on the U-1, U-2, and U-4 lines. Enter under the archway into the lobby, where you'll find a desk with free info sheets and tour tickets.

Hamburg's Lakes

Hamburg's delightful lakes started as one big lake that formed when townsfolk built a mill that dammed the Alster River. During the Thirty Years' War, the city fortified itself behind a defensive wall that split the millpond in two.

To reach the first of these lakes from the square in front of City Hall, simply walk to the adjacent canal and turn right. From anywhere else in the city, ride the S-Bahn or U-Bahn to the Jung-fernstieg stop.

Binnenalster: The smaller and (as its name suggests) inner of the two lakes, the Binnenalster lies a long block from the plaza in front of City Hall. For a good look, head to the little viewpoint at the south corner of the lake (near the canal boat dock). Look left along the waterside **Jungfernstieg,** the city's most elegant prome-nade and home to its top-of-the-line shops, including a huge Apple Store (at #12) and the flagship showroom of Nivea (established in Hamburg in 1911, at #51). Along the shore to the right, you can see the headquarters of Hamburg's most important shipping com-pany, Hapag-Lloyd. This area gives you a good look at how the city rebuilt after a fire in the mid-19th century, when it turned its back on the Elbe to face this lake. For a better view, have lunch at the fourth-floor **$$** self-service restaurant inside the **Alsterhaus** department store (at #16) or visit the **Thalia** bookstore (inside the huge Europa Passage shopping mall).

Red-and-white Alsterschippern **canal boats** leave from the dock on Jungfernstieg for sleepy one-hour tours around the lakes (€16, every 30 minutes 10:00-18:00, less frequent Oct-March, guided commentary only in German, tel. 040/357-4240, www.alstertouristik.de). A two-hour version adds a trip through the Speicherstadt and HafenCity urban-renewal zone (€21, 3/day, 1/day off-season).

Aussenalster: The "outer Alster" is the bigger, more park-like and residential of Hamburg's lakes. In the past, when private gardens tumbled down from mansions lining the lake, much of the Aussenalster was off-limits to regular citizens. But a 1953 law guaranteed public lake access for everyone, and walking and biking paths now trace its nearly five-mile-long shore, providing Ham-burg—one of Germany's greenest cities—with sprawling parkland. On a nice day, the lake is jam-packed with sailboats. With extra

Hamburg at a Glance

▲▲▲**Harbor and Port Guided Boat Tour** Excellent chance to marvel at the city's mighty container port and burgeoning HafenCity. **Hours:** English tour daily at noon April-Oct. See page 923.

▲▲**Hop-On, Hop-Off Bus Tour** Convenient way to see the city's main sights. **Hours:** Departs every 30 minutes 9:30-17:00, less frequently Nov-March. See page 912.

▲▲**St. Nikolai Memorial** Bombed-out church memorializing the destruction of World War II, with excellent museum and view tower. **Hours:** Ruins always viewable; museum and tower open daily 10:00-18:00, Oct-April until 17:00. See page 916.

▲▲**Hamburg History Museum** Sprawling exhibit of the city's history since its founding in AD 800. **Hours:** Mon and Wed-Fri 10:00-17:00, Sat-Sun until 18:00, closed Tue. See page 921.

▲▲**St. Pauli Landungsbrücken Harborfront** Atmospheric people zone with boardwalk ambience, ferry docks, and views of the port. See page 922.

▲▲**HafenCity and Speicherstadt** Major urban development featuring striking Elbphilharmonie concert hall and historic, repurposed warehouses. **Hours:** Elbphilharmonie Plaza level open daily 9:00-24:00. See page 926.

▲▲**International Maritime Museum** Huge former warehouse filled with exhibits on nautical history, both military and civilian. **Hours:** Daily 10:00-18:00. See page 929.

▲▲**Reeperbahn Walk** A stroll through Hamburg's famous Red Light District, sizzling with nightclubs and street life. **Hours:** Best at night. See page 930.

▲**Hamburger Kunsthalle** Expansive art gallery with works by Old, New, and Modern Masters. **Hours:** Tue-Sun 10:00-18:00, Thu until 21:00, closed Mon. See page 918.

▲**Arts and Crafts Museum** Three floors filled with decorative arts. **Hours:** Tue-Sun 10:00-18:00, Thu until 21:00, closed Mon. See page 919.

▲**Miniatur Wunderland** Tiny world with German families thrilling to model trains. **Hours:** Daily at least 9:30-18:00. See page 928.

▲**BallinStadt Emigration Museum** Germany's version of Ellis Island, housing history exhibits. **Hours:** Daily 10:00-18:00, Nov-March until 16:30. See page 935.

time, you could take a bike ride (see "Helpful Hints," earlier) or rent a rowboat or sailboat at the small marina. Tiny arms of the lake stretch scenically into fancy residential neighborhoods at the north end.

▲▲St. Nikolai Memorial (Mahnmal St. Nikolai)

Before the mid-20th century, downtown Hamburg's skyline had five main churches, each with a bold tower. Today there are still five towers...but only four churches. The missing church is St. Nikolai. It was designed in the Neo-Gothic style by British architect George Gilbert Scott, and for a brief time after its completion in 1874, it was the world's tallest church (at 483 feet; its spire is still the fifth tallest in the world). The church was destroyed by the Operation Gomorrah firebombing in 1943. Its tower (open to visitors) and a few charred walls have been left as a ruin to commemorate those lost, and museum exhibits in the church cellar detail Hamburg's wartime destruction. As with similarly ruined churches in Berlin and Coventry (England), a stroll here, between the half-destroyed walls of a once-stunning church, is an evocative reminder of the horrors of war.

Cost and Hours: Ruins-free to explore and always viewable; tower and museum-€5, daily 10:00-18:00, Oct-April until 17:00; Willy-Brandt-Strasse 60, tel. 040/371125, www.mahnmal-st-nikolai.de. It's a five-minute walk from the Rödingsmarkt U-Bahn station—just follow busy Willy-Brandt-Strasse toward the tower—or a 10-minute walk from the Speicherstadt district or City Hall.

Visiting the Memorial: The **footprint** of the church has a few information posts as well as some modern memorials. Where the original altar once stood is now a simple concrete altar; behind it is a 1972 mosaic *(Ecce Homo)* based on a drawing by German Expressionist artist Oskar Kokoschka, showing Jesus on the cross being offered a vinegar-soaked sponge. To the right of the fresco, notice the **sculpture** *(Ordeal)* honoring people who died in the Nazi-era concentration camp Sandbostel, west of Hamburg. The bricks at the sculpture's base came from the camp barracks, and the plaque with the words of the theologian Dietrich Bonhoeffer are an important reminder for troubled political times: "No man in the whole world  can change the truth. One can only look for the truth, find it and serve it." The tower's 51-bell **carillon,** funded with local donations in 1993, plays music daily at 9:00, 12:00, 15:00, and 18:00. A live carillonneur plays 30-minute concerts every Thursday at noon.

HAMBURG

Operation Gomorrah: The Firebombing of Hamburg

With its port, munitions factories, and transportation links, Hamburg was a prime target for Allied bombers during World War II. After studying what the Luftwaffe did to Coventry in 1940, the British decided to use the same techniques against Hamburg on July 27, 1943. They hit targets first with explosive bombs to open roofs, break water mains, and tear up streets (making it hard for firefighters to respond), then followed up with incendiary bombs. Designed to destroy a city known for its licentious ways, the attack was given the codename Operation Gomorrah.

It had been a hot, dry summer, and when 700 RAF bombers concentrated their attack on a relatively small area, the result was an exceptionally intense firestorm. A tornado of flames raged at up to 150 miles per hour, reaching temperatures of 1500°F. Many inhabitants were baked to death huddling inside their air-raid shelters. Some who went outside were sucked off their feet, disappearing up into the superheated vortex. Roads and sidewalks caught on fire—the shoes of those who tried to run across the roadways became mired in boiling asphalt.

In three hours, the inferno killed an estimated 35,000 people, left hundreds of thousands homeless, and reduced eight square miles of Hamburg to rubble and ashes. At the end of the eight-day bombing campaign, which included US raids, about one million survivors had fled the city and over 40,000 were dead. The firebombing of Dresden two years later is better known, but far more people died in Hamburg. And while the earlier Nazi bombings of London, Rotterdam, and Coventry were deadly, some historians say the firebombing of Hamburg was World War II's first widespread destruction of a major city.

The **tower** still stands tall above the shell of the former church, and you can ride a speedy elevator 250 feet up to its observation platform. This vantage point provides a good visual orientation to Hamburg, with views of City Hall and lakes in one direction and the Speicherstadt warehouse district in the other (supplemented by a half-dozen informational panels).

The underground **museum** is modest yet effective, depicting the life, death, and resurrection of the church. Photos show the church's interior in all its pre-WWII glory alongside bits salvaged after the bombing (including some original stained-glass windows). Start in the hallway with a timeline of the church's history. In the first room, follow the counterclockwise display through a detailed retelling of the devastating firestorm. Then, in the second room, finish with a thoughtful examination of how the city came to grips with its aftermath—logistically, culturally, and morally. Consider that Hamburg's senior citizens experienced the firebombing firsthand—and yet the museum does not paint the Allied forces as bad guys, and reminds visitors that Hitler had done much the same to other cities (see the photos of a destroyed Warsaw) long before the destruction was visited upon German soil. One display invites visitors to imagine the fear and guilt experienced by the British bombers (many of whom were unaware they'd be attacking a civilian center).

▲Hamburger Kunsthalle (Hamburg Art Gallery)

Though not as renowned as art museums in Berlin or Munich, this sprawling and high-quality collection is worthwhile, especially for its many excellent paintings by German artists. The museum spreads over several buildings just north of the train station, showcasing Old Masters, New Masters, 19th-century artists, and Modern Masters.

Cost and Hours: €14, includes special exhibits; Tue-Sun 10:00-18:00, Thu until 21:00, closed Mon; audioguide-€3-4, café, Glockengiesserwall, tel. 040/428-131-200, www.hamburger-kunsthalle.de.

Visiting the Museum: In the spacious, light-filled foyer, notice the terrazzo floor from 1869, which had been hidden for many decades under linoleum. The core of the collection is displayed in the Lichtwark Gallery building, where visitors will find fine examples by 20th-century German Expressionists (Max Beckmann, Ernst Ludwig Kirchner) and 19th-century Romantics (Caspar David Friedrich, Philipp Otto Runge). Come appreciate one of the towering masterpieces of German painting, Friedrich's *Wanderer above the Sea of Fog,* dating from 1818. The Galerie der Gegenwart (Gallery of the Present) is the contemporary art annex, featuring German heavyweights like Gerhard Richter. The museum also presents excellent special exhibits, which can be reason enough to visit.

▲**Arts and Crafts Museum**
(Museum für Kunst und Gewerbe)

South of the train station, this museum has three floors of decorative and applied arts. The focus is on historical European items (ground floor), with more than 30,000 objects from the Middle Ages and on. The upper floors feature items from other periods and places, including Asian and Islamic pieces. Taken together, the sculptures, ceramics, textiles, furniture, jewelry, and musical instruments displayed here are a tangible timeline of human creativity and inventiveness. The temporary exhibits are often excellent.

Cost and Hours: €12, €8 on Thu after 17:00; open Tue-Sun 10:00-18:00, Thu until 21:00, closed Mon; café, Steintorplatz, tel. 040/428-134-880, www.mkg-hamburg.de.

Deichtorhallen (Museum of Photography and Contemporary Art)

Farther south from the Arts and Crafts Museum, at the end of Hamburg's *Kunstmeile* ("art mile"), you'll find one of the largest centers in Europe for contemporary art. Art fans will enjoy the often high-profile, changing exhibits, but the exhibition space itself is worth a look. Originally built around 1914 as market halls, the soaring steel-and-glass structure is a rare surviving example of industrial architecture transitioning between 19th-century Art Nouveau and 20th-century styles. Just across from the museum are the offices of Germany's leading newsmagazine *(Der Spiegel),* testifying to Hamburg's status as a media capital.

Cost and Hours: €15, Tue-Sun 11:00-18:00, closed Mon; café, Deichtorstrasse 1, tel. 040/321-030, www.deichtorhallen.de.

Kontorhausviertel Neighborhood and Chilehaus

The German name for this small neighborhood (which translates roughly as "office building quarter") undersells its architectural importance. The area is made up of unique buildings constructed in the "Brick Expressionist" school, mostly between 1920-30. The finest example is the **Chilehaus,** an immense flatiron-style building (north of Willy Brandt Strasse across the street from the Messberg U-Bahn station). Designed by Henry Sloman in 1922-1924, it's shaped like a ship, down to the railing-lined balconies on the upper floors that resemble decks, and comes to a razor-sharp point at the corner. The facade is especially impressive when it's illuminated at night. At the nearby Sprinkenhof building, study the exterior decoration all done in brick, including dozens of individual images of ships, castles, hands, and wheels. While there's no museum here, you can poke around the buildings' courtyards (with unpretentious cafés and shops that seem oblivious to the area's significance) and step into the entrance lobbies, still decorated with the Art Deco-style directories of the original tenants.

Chocoversum Chocolate Museum

This delightfully decadent chocolate universe is the sweet to Hamburg's salty. Most people find the museum's free shop—itself a tempting tribute to cocoa—enough of a treat. The museum is an expensive interactive experience: A mandatory 1.5-hour guided tour wraps history, tasting, and creation into one. You'll leave with your own handmade chocolate bar.

Cost and Hours: Shop free and open daily 10:00-18:00; €15 tours run every 30 minutes in German (ask for English handout), English tours usually offered several times a day—check website for times; Messberg 1—enter on Pumpen street, across from Chilehaus; tel. 040/4191-2300, www.chocoversum.de.

BETWEEN DOWNTOWN AND THE REEPERBAHN
St. Michael's Church

While unexceptional by European standards, Hamburg's most famous church, known simply as *"der Michel,"* is worth a look if you have time. The interior is bright and wide; the decoration, unusually ornate for a Protestant church, recalls its Baroque origins (it opened in 1768). A total rebuild after a 1906 fire—started by workers repairing the roof—lent the church a little of the flavor of an early-20th-century movie palace. The church has fine acoustics (a special channel brings the organ's sound through a latticed grate in the ceiling) and hosts many concerts. You can ascend its 350-foot-high, lantern-shaped tower (452 steps, or 52 steps plus an elevator) to see the clock and bell mechanics. While the views are fine, they're not spectacular—revealing how dull and modern Hamburg's urban core is.

Cost and Hours: Free but €2 requested donation, tower-€5, skippable crypt-€4, combo-ticket-€7; daily 9:00-19:30, Nov-April 10:00-17:30, closed to visitors during services; Englische Planke 1, tel. 040/376-780, www.st-michaelis.de. Several U- and S-Bahn stops are about a 10-minute walk away, including Baumwall, Rödingsmarkt, and Stadthausbrücke.

Nearby: At Krayenkamp 10, about 50 yards behind the church, duck through the archway for a glimpse of the **Krameramtsstuben**—a few half-timbered buildings along a narrow lane that form a rare surviving bit of the 17th-century city. Though today lined with kitschy souvenir shops, these were originally houses built for widows of Hamburg's guild members.

▲▲Hamburg History Museum (Museum für Hamburgische Geschichte)

Like the history of the city it covers, this museum is long, complex, and multilayered. Filling a giant old building with a stag-

gering variety of artifacts and historical re-creations, the modern, thoughtful exhibits work together to illuminate the full story of Hamburg (with an emphasis on its status as one of the world's biggest shipping ports). You'll learn about the city's industrial growth, devastating 1842 fire, WWII firebombing, development of its excellent infrastructure, and environmental conditions of the Elbe River. A highlight is the preserved bridge of an old steamship showing what life was like for the officers on board. Multiple large models of the city at various points in its history help you track how the place changed over time.

The core of the exhibit is on the first floor; the ground floor has exhibits on the 20th century and a delightful *Jugendstil* (Art Nouveau) café with seating in the glassed-in courtyard; and the top floor has large exhibits on Hamburg's Jewish community and beautifully re-created Baroque-era rooms. As the museum is close to the St. Pauli U-Bahn stop, it's easy to combine with a visit to the Reeperbahn (described later) for a day of contrasts.

Cost and Hours: €9.50, includes audioguide; Mon and Wed-Fri 10:00-17:00, Sat-Sun until 18:00, closed Tue; Holstenwall 24, tel. 040/428-132-100, www.hamburgmuseum.de.

Nearby: The museum sits within the inviting park around the Grosse Wallanlagen rampart in the Planten un Blomen gardens (described next), which curls around the route of the former moat, through the heart of town to the Binnenalster and Aussenalster lakes. For a nice approach to the museum from the St. Pauli U-Bahn stop, cut through the park and around the back of the museum (see orientation maps at park entrance).

Planten un Blomen

The wide strip of parkland called Planten un Blomen ("plants and flowers") stretches all the way from the harbor to the Binnenalster lake on the site of Hamburg's old city wall. Of the park's varied

sections, the most worthwhile is the northern stretch, near the Stephansplatz U-Bahn and Dammtor S-Bahn stops. It's an oasis of calm ponds, playful fountains, happy bunny rabbits, and colorful gardens (including a rose garden and a Japanese garden). Dotted with cafés, it's an ideal place to stroll with an ice-cream cone after a day of sightseeing—or sit back in an Adirondack chair under the shadow of the ray-gun TV tower.

Cost and Hours: Free; daily 7:00-20:00, later in summer, best before dark; S-11, S-21, or S-31 to Dammtor or U-1 to Stephansplatz; www.plantenunblomen.hamburg.de.

Brahms Museum

Although the composer was born in this part of Hamburg, Johannes Brahms' actual boyhood home is long gone. This museum has a modest collection that would interest only Brahms devotees (€5, Tue-Sun 10:00-17:00, closed Mon, about a block from Hamburg Museum at Peterstrasse 39, tel. 040/4191-3086, www.brahms-hamburg.de).

ST. PAULI LANDUNGSBRÜCKEN HARBORFRONT

Once Hamburg's passenger ship terminal, this half-mile-long floating dock, which parallels the waterfront, is now a thriving, touristy, borderline-tacky wharf that locals call "the Balcony of Hamburg." A visit is worth ▲▲. From here you can inhale the inviting aroma of herring and French fries while surveying the harbor and the city's vast port.

From the Landungsbrücken S- and U-Bahn stop (or from Davidstrasse, if you're walking down from the Reeperbahn), head toward the water. As you walk down, you'll be assailed by employees of the many tour-boat companies, each pitching their trips—ignore them (most are German language-only excursions). You'll see the venerable light-brown stone former terminal building (now filled with shops, a busy TI, and a Hard Rock Café), with its appropriately grandiose tower meant to evoke the ancient lighthouse in Alexandria, Egypt.

From the landing you can catch a public ferry, hop a guided boat tour, walk a short way to hike under the river, or tour a historic ship. Consider a lunch break at the harbor's own brewery, the recommended Blockbräu.

Cruising the Harbor

Facing the water behind the terminal building, nine numbered docks— a.k.a. the Landungsbrücken ("landing bridges")—stretch along the harbor. The numbers get larger from left to right—bridge 1 (with the *SS Rickmer Rickmers* museum ship and ferry #72) is to the far left; the Landungsbrücken S- and U-Bahn pedestrian overpass and ferry #62 are at bridge 3; and the terminal building and Rainer Abicht cruises are at bridges 1 and 4. Notice how this area, like the rest of Hamburg's waterfront, is designed to accommodate the Elbe's 13-foot tides.

On sunny days and most weekends the harbor swells with tourists eager to get on the water. Public ferries are crowded, and riders scrum at the gangway to fight their way onboard. If you're short on time or patience, consider taking one of the tour boats (listed below) instead.

▲▲▲Harbor and Port Guided Boat Tour

Of the hundred or so big-boat harbor tours that go daily here, only a few come with English narration. The best is **Rainer Abicht,** whose excellent tour (once a day in English) gives you a view from the water of all the construction in Hamburg. The industrial port is a major focus of the trip, and getting up close to all those massive container ships, cranes, and dry and wet docks is breathtaking.

The live commentary is fascinating and entertaining. You can order a drink to sip as you take it all in from the deck (bring a sandwich for a discreet picnic).

Cost and Hours: One-hour harbor tour–€20 (€32.50 combo-ticket with Roten Doppeldecker bus tour), English tour runs April-Oct daily at 12:00, few or no English tours off-season, tel. 040/317-8220, www.abicht.de. Their waterside ticket windows are by bridge 1 at the promenade and by bridge 4 (look for the blue-and-white boats).

Hop-On, Hop-Off Boat Trip

Maritime Circle Line operates a 1.5-hour journey with English narration three times a day covering the basic harbor highlights. The only real benefit of choosing this over a harbor tour is the freedom to disembark at any of its stops, including the BallinStadt Emigration Museum.

Cost and Hours: €16 (€30 combo-ticket with Roten Doppeldecker bus tour, discounts with Hamburg Card), April-Oct daily at 11:00, 13:00, and 15:00, some off-season tours with fewer stops, tel. 040/2849-3963, www.maritime-circle-line.de. Ticket windows and departure point are at bridge 10.

▲Harbor Tour by Public Ferry

Hamburg's ferries, which take the same tickets and passes as the S-Bahn and U-Bahn, give you a fine look at the harbor and a lot of the port action, but won't actu-

ally take you into the industrial port area—for that, you'll need to take one of the privately operated tour boats listed earlier. There's no point in riding this ferry if you're already taking a privately operated tour. Take ferry line #62 (3-4/hour 7:00-21:00, 2/hour 21:00-23:00), and use your transit-system day pass (ticket machines on the docks and on board) or Hamburg Card. The ride described below takes about one hour. Only bigger ferries have WCs and snack booths—but bringing a picnic on board is fully OK.

→ **Self-Guided Tour:** From the Landungsbrücken terminal building, go to bridge 3 and find the signs for ferry line #62 to Finkenwerder. With stops, it's a 28-minute trip downstream and another 28 minutes back—if you like, you can stay on the same ferry, but boats leave often enough for easy hopping on and off.

Riding toward Finkenwerder, the first stop is **Fischmarkt,** which hosts a popular market (produce, fish, flea market) that's only open on Sunday morning (see page 908).

The second stop is **Dockland,** also the name of the enormous office building designed to look like a gigantic yacht. Its "stern" is a series of climbable terraces that lead to a viewpoint rooftop.

Soon after Dockland, watch on the right for the *Schlepper* **(tugboat) station,** with a row of tugs lined up and ready to go. Because Hamburg sits about 60 miles inland from the sea, arriving ships have to traverse a long stretch of river—and at the regulated low speeds, very large ships can't gain enough momentum to steer, forcing them to rely on this fleet of plucky tugboats. Behind them, notice the red line on the quay. This was the high-water mark of the 1962 flood, which killed more than 300 people and destroyed about 6,000 buildings within the city.

As you pull into **Neumühlen,** the third stop, consider that you're cruising right over the eight lanes of autobahn traffic that speed through a tunnel (built in 1975). You could break your journey here, below hillside villas in the posh neighborhood of **Övelgönne.** You can see the modest "museum harbor" (Museumshafen) of retired boats bobbing near the ferry dock, eat lunch at one of the two reasonably priced cafés nearby (Elbterrassen and Museumshafen Café), or enjoy Hamburg's beach (a short walk downstream, visible from the ferry pier). Bus #112, which terminates at the Neumühlen pier, runs every 15 minutes and is an alternative way to get from Övelgönne back to St. Pauli and the train station (it also gives you a look at the suburb of Altona). Or, ride the boat all the way to Finkenwerder, then turn around to sail back to Landungsbrücken.

The **Finkenwerder** stop, where the ferry turns around, is on an island that's home to Airbus' test runway (closed to the public), which was used to develop the superjumbo A380.

Quickie Option: For a shorter ferry ride, try this: At Landungsbrücken, go to bridge 1 and catch line #72 toward the city center to HafenCity and the Elbphilharmonie concert hall (7-minute trip, 2-3/hour, Mon-Fri 9:00-21:30, Sat-Sun until 20:00).

Other Landungsbrücken Sights
St. Pauli Elbtunnel

Continental Europe's oldest underwater tunnel, built in 1911, is marked by a green-domed entry hall designed to resemble the Pantheon in Rome (just past the Hard Rock Café at the right end of the terminal building, close to bridge 6). To take a memorable look at some century-old technology, walk down the stairs or ride an elevator—ogling the big wooden industrial elevators that cars use (free entrance). At the bottom, look down the full quarter-mile length of the tunnel and wonder how it can safely lie just 40 feet under the surface of the Elbe (meaning big ships cannot go upstream past here). Inside, it's 15 feet high—just high enough for a coachman to hold his horse whip upright. For a little exercise, and a great view of Hamburg from across the river, walk or bike through the tunnel to the other side. Once across, ride the elevator or huff up the stairs to the surface. As you exit, turn right and head toward the back of the building and the water to find a terrace with a great panoramic view of Hamburg and a helpful orientation board that identifies the major landmarks.

SS *Rickmer Rickmers*

Sailboat enthusiasts will enjoy this three-masted, steel-hulled ship (moored near bridge 1). Built in Bremerhaven in 1896, it's been restored—largely by volunteers—and is now open to the public. You can explore the ship's four decks, including the crew quarters, engine room, and a handful of exhibits.

Cost and Hours: €5, daily 10:00-18:00, tel. 040/319-5959, www.rickmer-rickmers.de.

Nearby: In front of the ship is a café that's a little quieter than the others along the Landungsbrücken—it's a pleasant place to eat lunch while watching the ferries come and go.

HAMBURG

HAFENCITY AND SPEICHERSTADT

Together, the neighboring port districts of HafenCity and Speicherstadt are worth ▲▲. A century ago, Hamburg's port was the world's third largest, and in Europe it's still second only to Rotterdam's. The port was built right up next to the city center, as the small city-state of Hamburg couldn't defend a remote harbor. But with the advent of huge modern container ships, most marine business shifted to a larger and more modern port  nearby (you'll see these big container ships docking under the huge cranes after their North Sea voyage). All this prime real estate, just a half-mile from City Hall, suddenly became available and is now being redeveloped.

Getting to HafenCity and Speicherstadt: For an atmospheric approach, go to the Landungsbrücken S- and U-Bahn stop and take public ferry #72 one stop upstream (see page 922). You'll disembark by HafenCity's landmark Elbphilharmonie concert hall.

You can also take the U-3 subway line to Baumwall, walk across either of the Niederbaumbrücke bridges, and turn left onto Kehrwieder street and into the Speicherstadt district. After strolling between the canal (on your left) and a row of warehouses (on your right) for about five minutes, look for Block D (described later).

HafenCity

HafenCity is Europe's biggest urban development project (and, they claim, the biggest ongoing project in the world for the next 20 years). When it's done, downtown Hamburg will be 40 percent bigger, and the city will again face the Elbe River. Planners hope that 45,000 people will eventually work here and 12,000 will call it home. The area feels like a city in itself, with a maritime touch, interesting modern architecture, and a mix of business, culture, and leisure. On weekends locals flock here to take a stroll, bask in the sun, and enjoy a break from the city.

▲▲Elbphilharmonie Concert Hall

The centerpiece of the HafenCity development (and a building that promises to become a symbol of modern Germany) is the jaw-dropping Elbphilharmonie—a combination concert hall, hotel, and apartment complex, all contained in a towering and wildly beautiful piece of architecture. Though it was staggeringly behind schedule and over budget (costing €865 million instead of €77 million), it's nevertheless a source of pride and excitement

among Hamburg's citizens. Its daring design and huge size fit in well with the massive scale of the port around it—and when approached by water, it calls to mind the looming prows of the steamer ships that first put Hamburg on the world map.

For visitors, the heart of the complex is the Plaza level, which connects the renovated old harbor warehouse below with the modern glass tower above. From the main entrance of the 360-foot-tall, 360-foot-long structure, visitors ride a 270-foot-long escalator (dubbed the "Tube"). At the top you'll enjoy a spectacular view down the Elbe toward the harbor and docks. A second, shorter escalator takes you to the Plaza level, where you'll find an outdoor promenade that wraps around the entire level (plus a café and souvenir shop).

Cost and Hours: The Plaza level is open daily 9:00-24:00 to anyone with a Plaza ticket. Tickets are free for same-day visits but subject to availability (get tickets from machines in the entrance foyer, open daily 11:00-20:00). To guarantee you'll get in, buy timed-entry tickets a day or more in advance (€2, buy online or at the ground-floor ticket office, tel. 040/3576-6660, www.elbphilharmonie.de). Anyone with a concert ticket can enter the Plaza for no additional charge up to two hours before the event. It's at Platz der Deutschen Einheit 1.

Concerts: Tickets for events and concerts at the Elbphilharmonie can be booked by telephone, online, or by email (ticket tel. 040/3576-6666, www.elbphilharmonie.de, tickets@elbphilharmonie.de), or in person at the visitors center described earlier.

Guided Tours: Hour-long guided tours of the complex run in English daily, taking visitors through the old Kaispeicher warehouse, the Plaza, the foyer areas, and the Grand Hall. Tickets are released roughly 12 weeks out and can be purchased online or in person at the ground-floor ticket office (€15, schedule varies with performances, no tours during month-long break in July/Aug, www.elbphilharmonie.de/tours).

Speicherstadt and Block D

This "Warehouse City," between HafenCity and the city center, is a huge stand of red-brick riverside warehouses, and more interesting than the glitzy new buildings near the Elbphilharmonie for fans of historic architecture. It was originally built over a 40-year span, starting in the 1880s. Half of it, however, was destroyed in World War II. The area was rebuilt and officially remained part of Hamburg's port zone until 2003.

But after container terminals sprung up across the river, it no longer made sense to store goods here. Rather than tear down the warehouses, the city preserved them as part of the urban landscape, with a few museums and theme-park-like attractions catering mostly to German visitors. The redevelopment is still a work in progress, and the new buildings are not yet fully occupied, but the project is a great source of pride and interest among locals and German tourists (it's the best-known waterfront revival effort in this mostly landlocked country).

Wander around. Make sure to cross one of the side bridges to experience the length of the loading canals and to imagine this industrial area when it was full of barges and dockworkers. On the Pickhuben Bridge, at the corner of Pickhuben and Kannengiesserort, a plaque shows photographs of the warehouses after the WWII bombing. Each of the older Speicherstadt warehouses is labeled with a letter—such as Block D, home to the sights listed next.

▲Miniatur Wunderland

The most fun sight within the big Block D complex—and worth its high entry fee—Miniatur Wunderland claims to have the world's largest model railway, covering over 16,000 square feet with more than 9.5 miles of track. Marvel at the tiny airport (with model planes taking off), and watch  night fall every 15 minutes. Visit the Alps, Scandinavia, Italy, and the US in miniature (the latter complete with a shootout and Area 51). Little bits come to life with a press of a green-lit button—bungee jumpers leap, the drive-in plays a movie, and tiny Bavarians hoist teeny beer mugs to their mini mouths. Hamburg's harbor is lovingly rendered—including the building you're standing in—with a model of the Elbphilharmonie that lets you peek inside.

Cost and Hours: €15, daily 9:30-18:00, longer hours in peak season, Kehrwieder 4, Block D, tel. 040/300-6800, www. miniatur-wunderland.com.

Crowd-Beating Tips: The model railway is wildly popular, so it's a good idea to reserve online or via phone at least a couple of days in advance (no extra charge). If you haven't reserved, expect as much as a two-hour wait to get in. Check their website for estimated wait times and recommended arrival times for the day you want to visit. It's most crowded from midmorning through early afternoon, and swamped on school holidays.

Eating: Next door to the Miniatur Wunderland in Block D is the Speicherstadt Kafeerösterei, a convenient café and coffee roastery. It serves sandwiches, cakes, and desserts, and sells coffee by the bag and other small gifts (daily 10:00-19:00, tel. 040/3751-8683). You'll enter the café through a flood gate—which can be closed in high water. (Tidal bores are a real danger along the Elbe, so all new building in Hamburg is well above water level.) As you leave the café, look straight ahead across the canal into the city center to see a single short row of surviving half-timbered warehouses that still stand along Deichstrasse...and mentally expand this stretch across the harbor area to imagine the industrious, salty charm of 17th-century Hamburg.

▲▲International Maritime Museum (Internationales Maritimes Museum)

This state-of-the-art exhibit fills nine floors of a towering brick ex-warehouse with thousands of maritime artifacts—while reminding visitors that "the sail came before the wheel" and "rowing came before the saddle." Despite its name, its perspective is more German than international, but that's part of what makes it interesting (and nearly everything is well-described in English).

Ride the lift to the ninth "deck" (floor) to start with the world's biggest collection of miniature ship models, and then work your way down—each floor has a different military or civilian maritime theme: paintings and ship models; deep-sea research; the history of merchant shipping and cruise ships; exploration, colonization, and warfare (with good exhibits on the naval warfare of World Wars I and II); uniforms, medals, and insignias from around the world; the history of shipbuilding; global seafaring history; and navigation. Between the first and second decks is an enormous model of the RMS *Queen Mary 2* (which often sails from just a few blocks away)...made entirely of Legos.

Cost and Hours: €13, daily 10:00-18:00, audioguide-€3.50, Koreastrasse 1, Kaispeicher B, tel. 040/3009-2300, www.imm-hamburg.de.

REEPERBAHN NEIGHBORHOOD

Take New Orleans' Bourbon Street, Las Vegas' Strip, and Amsterdam's Red Light District, mix them up in a cocktail shaker, and you've got a tall glass of Reeperbahn ("roper's path"—pronounced

HAMBURG

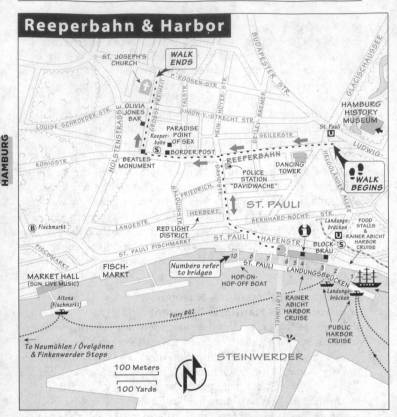

RAY-pehr-bahn). It's named after the legions of rope makers who once labored here to supply Hamburg's shipping industry. Now it's Germany's most famous nightlife district, home to some of Hamburg's musical theaters and a thriving prostitution scene.

Many tourists are understandably put off by the area's sleaziness—but consider that by concentrating all of it here, the Reeperbahn makes the rest of the city that much classier. The Reeperbahn may be less of a big deal in the age of online porn and internet-based prostitution, but the street remains a huge destination for Germans. Don't fear the Reeper...it's a fascinating look at a facet of German society.

▲▲Reeperbahn Walk

You can do the 30-minute walk described here at any time of day, but you'll find it much livelier after dark—the later the better. The area is generally safe (as long as you don't go looking for trouble), with a prominently located police station in the middle of the Reeperbahn.

⊙ Self-Guided Walk: Start at the St. Pauli U-Bahn station

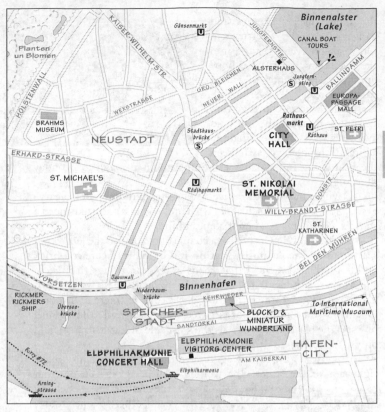

HAMBURG

(after hours, the stop announcement on the loudspeaker says, *"Nächste halt: St. Pauli...viel Spass!"*—Have fun!). Exit the platform following signs to *Reeperbahn.*

St. Pauli U-Bahn Station to Davidstrasse: Towering above the U-Bahn station is a landmark skyscraper nicknamed **"The Dancing Tower"** for the way one half of it leans romantically into the other.

Cross the street, keeping the Dancing Tower on your left, and begin walking down the busy Reeperbahn. Most of neighborhood action is along this main drag, a broad avenue with heavy car traffic that runs between the St. Pauli U-Bahn stop and the Reeperbahn S-Bahn stop. The east end of the avenue, which you'll see first, is fairly tame—it's gentrifying quickly, with high-rise buildings, chain hotels, and classier coffee shops, restaurants, and clubs going up—along with real-estate prices (this is some of the most expensive land in town). The west end (which you'll reach later) is more run-down.

As you stroll down the street, you'll see nightclubs, casinos, restaurants, fast-food joints, glitzy brothels, erotic theaters, and sex shops displaying toys and gadgets for every persuasion. On weekend evenings, and into the wee hours, this place is hopping with thousands of young partiers from all over north Germany, who've converged on Hamburg to dance the weekend away. Dance clubs coordinate in a kind of throbbing relay to keep

the beat going from Friday evening straight through to Monday morning.

Daylight makes the area feel seedy—the buildings look bleary-eyed, and the sidewalks, littered with broken glass and puke, need a shower. Nighttime is when it comes to life.

Red Light District: After a couple of blocks, on the left, you'll see the most famous **police station** in Germany: a cute red-brick building ("Davidwache") that keeps an eye on things (it's where the Reeperbahn meets the street called Davidstrasse, to the left, and Hein-Hoyer-Strasse, to the right). Turn left here and follow Davidstrasse a couple of blocks. Streetwalkers are only allowed in a few specific places here (such as the west side of Davidstrasse), and only after 20:00.

If you're a guy, expect aggressive flirtation after dark on the right side of the street. The women may be down-and-out, but

they're clever at helping each other; if one figures out your language, she'll whisper it to the next prostitute so she'll know how to engage you. If you walk on the left side of the street, you won't be hassled at all.

Except for the street-walkers and a few brothels nearby, Hamburg's Red Light District is limited to **Herbertstrasse,** one small lane set apart by two Nazi-era metal barriers (two blocks up Davidstrasse, on the right). The fascist ideal was a Germany with no prostitution, but the Third Reich pragmatically allowed it in Hamburg to accommodate the sailors who'd come ashore here after many lonely weeks at sea. The rest of society, however, was meant to be oblivious to the city's sex trade, so up went the barricades. Any man who wants to can scoot around them and stroll down the street, which is lined with glass-doored cabins where women try to entice prospective customers. Women, however, are by custom not allowed on Herbertstrasse (except the ones working here, of course), but I've seen female tourists walk around the barriers to gaze at the scene. Don't take photos here. The prostitutes are self-employed and run their businesses without pimps. Compared to the prostitutes on the streets and in the brothels, these are pricier and considered top-end.

From here you're a short walk to the St. Pauli Landungsbrücken harborfront (described on page 922); to visit it now, follow Davidstrasse—and the sound of seagulls—downhill as it curves and empties onto St. Pauli Hafenstrasse (landing you just across from the green-domed St. Pauli Elbtunnel entrance).

To finish this walk, return up Davidstrasse to the Reeperbahn, cross the boulevard, and turn left. A couple of blocks along, the brothel called **Paradise Point of Sex** is free to enter, open 24 hours—and staffed with security guards. In front you'll see an old, tall, iron lamppost in the sidewalk that looks like it might be a portal to another dimension; it marks the historic border between Denmark and Germany (the long entry corridor leading to the brothel actually traces the old border). Go a few more paces to the next corner, with the round vinyl record-shaped pattern in the pavement and the cheap tin statues of a certain four English rock-n-rollers. This cross street is...

Grosse Freiheit: The street's name means "Great Freedom"—a reference not to sexual liberation, but the religious and economic freedom of this formerly Danish border zone. For most of the 17th, 18th, and 19th centuries, Denmark was particularly powerful, with borders that extended farther south than they do today (and much, much farther north). What's now the Altona district (the area just west of the Reeperbahn S-Bahn stop) was, until 1864, the Danish city of Altona. In its heyday, it was Denmark's second city, a leading port, the southern terminus of the Danish railway system, and a magnet for Germans seeking free trade (unconstrained by the regulations of guilds) and religious tolerance.

Today, Grosse Freiheit is lined with noisy dance clubs and table-dancing bars. A nearby **monument** memorializes the long-gone Star Club, where the Beatles played a number of gigs (in a courtyard 30 yards before the church—behind the bar at #35 that features famous German transvestite Olivia Jones—go down the brick passage, follow *Kiez Alm Hamburg* signs, and look left).

Walk down Grosse Freiheit toward a church buried in all this sex and booze. Hamburg was an officially Protestant city, and, as elsewhere in Germany, any Christian denominations other than the locally established one were strongly discouraged. Danes, though also mostly Protestant, had a more tolerant attitude, and the street of "Great Freedom" was home to **St. Joseph's Church,** the first Catholic church built in northern Europe after the Reformation (in 1660). A fire destroyed that structure in 1713, so the current

HAMBURG

Das Beatlemania

For music lovers, the Reeperbahn's greatest significance is the role it played as the launching pad for the Beatles, who were unknowns when they arrived in Hamburg from Liverpool to play a season's worth of gigs in 1960. The group consisted of John, Paul, and George, plus drummer Pete Best (later replaced by Ringo Starr) and bassist Stuart Sutcliffe (who gave up music for art school in 1961, and died shortly thereafter).

Unpolished amateurs when they arrived, the band members became tight, hard-driving musicians by playing to a tough crowd night after night—they played 98 days straight at one point. While they were here, Ringo joined the band, and Sutcliffe's German girlfriend gave them their signature haircuts. By the time they left Hamburg for good in 1962, the Beatles had released several hit singles, had made their first TV appearance back in England, and were just months away from international stardom.

Baroque church dates from 1723. Hamburg's Catholics could sneak over the border to worship here at Grosse Freiheit 41.

The Reeperbahn S-Bahn and St. Pauli U-Bahn stops are nearby, and it's a quick and easy €12 taxi ride back to your hotel any time of day or night. You're also a short walk north to the youthful Schulterblatt ("Shoulderblade") area (described next).

NORTH OF THE REEPERBAHN
Schulterblatt ("Shoulderblade") Neighborhood

For a colorful slice of today's Hamburg and a breath of cultural fresh air (especially after walking the Reeperbahn), walk or ride the U- or S-Bahn to Sternschanze and explore a gentrifying but still funky neighborhood with so many cafés it's nicknamed "Latte Macchiato Boulevard." The broader area is known as the Schanzenviertel (for its main drag); the liveliest subsection is at the triangle formed by Susannenstrasse, Schulterblatt, and Schanzenstrasse. This trendy little area has piles of character, unique boutiques, and great places for a meal (for suggestions, see "Eating in Hamburg," later).

Join the cool young things for a leisurely, people-watching stroll; you'll find the streets filled with fun eateries and a clientele of hipsters and media/software/publicity-types. At the center of the neighborhood, roughly at the intersection of Schulterblatt and

Susannenstrasse, sits Rote Flora, a combination squatter hangout/ arts venue/progressive political center. Despite the red (Rote) in its name, the building's exterior is a changing kaleidoscope of graffiti and street art. Behind Rote Flora is an edgy-yet-charming park with a WWII-era bunker-turned-climbing wall also covered with street art. Look for the archway at Schulterblatt 58, where you'll see the sign *Pianoforte Fabrik*. Pop in for a look at the atmospheric courtyards of several well-preserved buildings from Hamburg's industrial past (including, as the name suggests, a piano factory).

On the southeastern edge of the Schanzenviertel, right next to the Feldstrasse U-Bahn stop, you'll see a monstrosity of gray concrete. This is one of the largest surviving urban bunkers of the Nazi era, and one of the very few you can freely enter. It was built in 1942 by forced laborers, and was designed to resist Allied air raids, with a roof that's over 15 feet thick. While not a tourist sight per se—the building now houses a large music store, a smattering of offices, and a nightclub—it's a rare chance for WWII buffs to peek inside this kind of relic.

OUTSIDE THE CITY CENTER
▲BallinStadt Emigration Museum

This engaging museum, a German counterpart to Ellis Island, tells the story of emigration to America through Hamburg from the mid-19th century up through World War II. Especially after 1890, many emigrants from the Austro-Hungarian and Russian empires—today's Eastern Europe—went first to Hamburg, by train or even on foot, before boarding a ship to cross

the ocean. The museum has less in the way of actual artifacts and more in the way of big, colorful re-creations of living conditions and interactive exhibits. It offers a dynamic and kid-friendly look at a powerful topic, and can be a moving experience for travelers with emigrant roots.

The museum complex is named after Albert Ballin, who was director of the Hamburg-America Line at the time the former emigration halls were built. Considered the father of the modern cruise industry, Ballin started his career working in his family's small emigration agency. He committed suicide in November 1918, worried (rightly, as it turned out) that his company's ships would be confiscated as reparations after World War I.

Cost and Hours: €13, daily 10:00-18:00, Nov-March until

HAMBURG

16:30, last entry one hour before closing, tel. 040/3197-9160; www. ballinstadt.de.

Getting There: BallinStadt is right by the Veddel S-Bahn station, two stops from the train station on the S-3 or S-31 (direction: Neugraben, Stade, Buxtehude, or Harburg Rathaus; about a 7-minute ride). From the S-Bahn platforms, follow the BallinStadt signs for about 200 yards across the parking lot and street to the museum. You can also get here on the Maritime Circle Line hop-on, hop-off boat (see page 913).

Visiting the Museum: The museum occupies three restored dormitory buildings that opened in 1901 to house and quarantine sick emigrants until they were healthy enough to ship out. Buy your ticket in Haus 1, "Port of Dreams," where you'll find the personal history of Albert Ballin on display (there may also be special exhibits).

The core of the museum is in Haus 2, "World in Transit." Creative themed exhibits give a look at the origins of the five million German emigrants who passed through here, the reasons they chose to leave (from poverty to pogroms), their experiences on the transatlantic ships, their arrival in New York City, and their challenges forging a new life in the new land. Haus 3, "Biographies," showcases the stories, fates, and personal memories of BallinStadt emigrants. The visit ends with a room where you can search genealogy databases (basically just Ancestry.com).

Eating: The museum's reasonably priced restaurant, in Haus 3, is a good place to try *Labskaus*, a Hamburg specialty similar to corned beef hash; see the "Eating in Hamburg" section, later.

Day Trips from Hamburg

Visitors disappointed by Hamburg's lack of a cute medieval old town could consider an outing to **Lübeck,** almost on the Baltic, 45 minutes northeast of Hamburg by train; or **Lüneburg,** a small university town that got rich off local salt mines, 30 minutes to the south. Both have classic, well-preserved old centers with typical North German/Hanseatic brick architecture.

Sleeping in Hamburg

Hamburg has plenty of reasonably priced places to stay and only a few of the special events that send prices skyrocketing in Frankfurt or Cologne. As the city is a popular musical theater destination, Friday and Saturday nights can be more expensive. Staying somewhere with good public transit links is helpful in this well-connected city. If you'll have a car in Hamburg, ask about parking rates and availability when reserving your room—many hotels in the city have dedicated garages. For hotel locations, see the map on page 910.

NEAR THE TRAIN STATION, IN ST. GEORG

The St. Georg neighborhood is a convenient place to sleep, thanks to its comfortable midrange hotels, proximity to the train station and walking paths around the Aussenalster, good restaurants, and lively street life. Some neighborhoods around European train stations are seedy at best; somehow St. Georg defies the stereotype. Its main thoroughfare, Lange Reihe, is busy with inviting eateries, cafés, and shops (reach it via the station's north exit by track 3 onto Kirchenallee). As you walk off Lange Reihe toward the water (the Aussenalster), the buildings become more and more elegant, with an upper-class, diamonds-and-poodles feel. Just a few streets in the other direction is Steindamm, St. Georg's other major avenue (reached from the station's south exit); it's a raucous immigrant boulevard that feels like Queens compared with Lange Reihe's Manhattan.

$$$$ Hotel Wedina—hip, full of character, and design-conscious—has 54 rooms in four renovated townhouses in a people-friendly neighborhood that's a 10-minute walk from the station. Each building has a different theme (such as literature, architecture, or Nordic style). Three of the buildings are connected; the fourth, with reception, breakfast room, and a tranquil garden oasis in back, is across the street (family rooms with kitchen, breakfast extra, lots of stairs, bike rental, pay parking; Gurlittstrasse 23, tel. 040/280-8900, www.hotelwedina.de, info@hotelwedina.de). From the station, walk up Lange Reihe, then go left on Gurlittstrasse. Or catch bus #6 (stop is across the street from the station, just right of Hotel Fürst Bismarck, direction: U Borgweg, leaves every 5-10 minutes) and hop off at the first stop (Gurlittstrasse). From the top of Gurlittstrasse, the hotel is just down the street on the right.

$$$$ Hotel Europäischer Hof is a business-class place with 275 rooms, a sixth-floor wellness center (complete with a 500-foot waterslide), and a striking resemblance to a casino. Choose between standard, standard-plus, or comfort room categories (includes 3-day transit ticket, elevator; Kirchenallee 45, tel. 040/248-248, www.europaeischer-hof.de, info@europaeischer-hof.de).

$$$ Hotel Aussen Alster, in a handsome lakeside townhouse, has 27 pleasant, straightforward rooms over a sometimes-smoky lobby. The hotel has loaner bikes for guests, as well as a sailboat that you can take out on the Aussenalster, just a block away (reserve ahead). The garden in back is a fine place to relax (elevator, pay parking, Schmilinskystrasse 11, tel. 040/284-078-570, www.aussenalsterhotel.de, info@aussen-alster.de). It's a 10-minute walk from the station up Lange Reihe, then left on Schmilinskystrasse. Or you can hop bus #6 from the station (see previous listing), and get off at the second stop (AK St. Georg), then backtrack a half-block to Schmilinskystrasse and turn right.

$$$ Hotel Senator, on Lange Reihe just down from the station, is a dated but quiet oasis with pastoral decor in each of its 56 airy rooms. Rooms on the fourth and fifth floors come with air-conditioning and a higher price; these "wellness rooms" also have waterbeds (the first I've seen in Europe) and some have balconies—though the views aren't worth the extra money (elevator, Lange Reihe 18, tel. 040/241-930, www.hotel-senator-hamburg.de, info@hotel-senator-hamburg.de).

$$$ Ibis Hotel Hamburg Alster Centrum has 165 reliable rooms right by the station. Ask for a front-side, street-facing room—they're quieter than those in back overlooking the tracks (breakfast extra, air-con, elevator, bike rental, pay parking; Holzdamm 4, tel. 040/248-290, www.accorhotels.com, h1395@accor.com). Exit the station at the north end of track 3 to Kirchenallee, then turn left and walk five minutes onto Holzdamm.

$$ Hotel Fürst Bismarck is old-fashioned and Old World, with regally carpeted halls and a marble lobby. Its 102 bright, contemporary rooms reflect the friendly staff's care and attention. You'll find yourself searching for Prince Bismarck himself checking in, as he once did 150 years ago (breakfast extra, includes 3-day transit ticket, elevator, Kirchenallee 49, tel. 040/790-251-640, www.fuerstbismarck.de, hotel@fuerstbismarck.de).

$ Motel One Hamburg-Alster, a monstrous, 460-room, inexpensive hotel with cookie-cutter but surprisingly stylish rooms and a friendly staff, is a good-value option especially if cozier places are booked (breakfast extra, air-con, elevator, guest iPad at front desk, pay parking; Steindamm 102, tel. 040/4192-4970, www.motel-one.com, hamburg-alster@motel-one.com). The hotel is right at the Lohmühlenstrasse U-Bahn stop (one stop from the station) or a 10-minute walk down a slightly seedy patch of Steindamm.

$ Hotel-Pension Alpha, a decent budget choice, has 21 rooms almost in sight of the station. The rooms are basic but more than adequate, and everything is well-kept by kindly Georg (breakfast extra, Koppel 4, tel. 040/245-365, www.alphahotel.biz, info@alphahotel.biz). From the station, exit by track 3 north onto Kirchenallee and look for the red-brick church (St. Georg); the hotel is across the street on the right side of the church. Confirm your arrival time in advance (if Georg won't be there, he'll give you a code for the door).

ELSEWHERE IN HAMBURG

These budget options are easy to reach from the train station by U-Bahn.

Near the Hamburg Museum: Part of the stylish and affordable chain, **$$ Motel One Hamburg am Michel** is located on a busy street but right next to the Grosse Wallanlagen area within Planten un Blomen gardens, steps from the Hamburg Museum, St. Pauli, and St. Michael's Church (breakfast extra, air-con, elevator, guest iPad at front desk, limited pay parking; Ludwig-Erhard-Strasse 26, tel. 040/3571-8900, www.motel-one.com, hamburg-am-michel@motel-one.com).

Near City Hall: True to its name, **$ Pension am Rathaus** is a long block from City Hall, in an appealing downtown neighborhood. The 15 rooms are simple and bright, and many share bathrooms (family room available, no breakfast, no elevator, reception open 9:00-15:00 & 16:00-19:00, Rathausstrasse 14, U-Bahn: Rathaus, tel. 040/337-489, www.pension-am-rathaus.de, info@pension-am-hamburg.de).

Near the Landungsbrücken: Located atop a hill right behind the Landungsbrücken S- and U-Bahn station, the **¢ Jugendherberge Hamburg "Auf dem Stintfang"** hostel has a super location and commanding view of the Elbe. It's big, bright, modern, and well-run. Choose from bunks in a dorm room or a private room with bath—but note that all the doubles are bunk beds (lunch and dinner available, elevator, Alfred-Wegener-Weg 5, tel. 040/570-1590, www.hamburg-stintfang.jugendherberge.de, stintfang@jugendherberge.de). From the train station, take the S-1 or S-3 three stops to Landungsbrücken, then follow the signs up the steep stairway, or—if you have wheeled luggage—take the long way, circling around back.

In the Schulterblatt Neighborhood: Though it has a hostel vibe, **$ Superbude St. Pauli** is really more of a funky budget hotel, and a good choice for this hip part of town. Its 99 rooms all have bathrooms and minimalist but creative decorative touches; ask for a room facing the courtyard to avoid street noise (breakfast extra, Juliusstrasse 1, U-Bahn: Sternschanze, tel. 040/807-915-820, www.superbude.de, stpauli@superbude.de).

Eating in Hamburg

Hamburg's food traditions have much in common with Scandinavia's. Fish is a fixture on local menus, even if little of it is actually caught in the nearby North Sea. Herring is common in sandwiches, as a main dish, and at breakfast (often rolled up with pickled vegetables inside and secured with a toothpick, called *Rollmops*). *Labskaus*, a traditional northern German dish, is not unlike corned beef hash; it's typically served with pickles, red beets, a fried egg, and sometimes a herring filet. For eatery locations, see the map on page 910.

After Dinner: To walk off your dinner, stroll the Reeperbahn area after dark, following my self-guided walk of that neighborhood (see page 930). Home to Hamburg's Red Light District, this is one of Germany's liveliest and most famous nightlife scenes.

NEAR THE TRAIN STATION, IN ST. GEORG

The main street through the St. Georg area, Lange Reihe, is lined with a great variety of shops and eateries. Dine here if you're sleeping at one of the nearby recommended hotels. Otherwise head to the Schulterblatt ("Shoulderblade") neighborhood for a better scene.

$$$$ Kajüte sits on pontoons on the Aussenalster (opposite Hotel Bellevue) and is good if you're willing to pay a little more for atmosphere. It has both indoor and outdoor seating. Come in the evening to watch sailboats and the setting sun across the water (daily 11:00-23:00, reservations smart, An der Alster 10a, tel. 040/243-037, www.kajuete.de).

$$$ Schifferbörse is right across the street from the train station. It's touristy and the service is surly, but it cooks up solid northern German food at fair prices. You'll eat in a fun dining room elaborately decked out like a Cubist take on a ship's galley (daily 11:30-23:00, Kirchenallee 46 between Bremer Reihe and Ellmenreichstrasse, tel. 040/245-240).

$$$ Cox is a well-regarded bistro with an understated classiness. Its menu leans toward culinary fusion, with influences from South Asia, North Africa, and the Mediterranean. Prices are quite reasonable for the quality (Mon-Fri 12:00-14:30 & 18:30-23:00, Sat-Sun 18:30-23:00, Lange Reihe 68, tel. 040/249-422).

$$ Hee-Yang, at the train-station end of Lange Reihe, is one of the many Asian restaurants in the neighborhood, and appeals to locals with sushi and Thai dishes (daily 11:30-24:00, Lange Reihe 15, tel. 040/2805-6227).

$ Frau Möller is a popular neighborhood hangout—a rollicking bar serving up very affordable, hearty Alsatian and Hamburger classics (sandwiches, huge salads, and daily specials that usually include one or two local specialties). The interior can be jammed and the service overwhelmed; try for one of the sidewalk tables, ideal for taking your time while people-watching (daily 11:30-late, Lange Reihe 96, tel. 040/2532-8817).

$ Café Koppel, a bright, inexpensive vegetarian café, occupies an art center just off Lange Reihe: through an archway and across a courtyard. Choose between two indoor floors or quiet garden seating; there are a couple of main courses available every day, as well as soups and big salads (daily 10:00-23:00, summer garden until 19:00, Lange Reihe 75, tel. 040/249-235).

Dessert: $ Luicella's is a step above other local ice cream joints, with their own homemade flavors produced with milk from local dairies (daily 11:00-20:00, Lange Reihe 113; another branch is a block off the Reeperbahn at Detlev Bremer Strasse 46, daily 12:00-20:00).

Supermarkets: The **Galeria Kaufhof** department store, by the train station, has a supermarket at basement level (Mon-Sat 10:00-20:00, closed Sun; exit the south bridge of the train station by track 14 toward Mönckebergstrasse and look for the entrance to your left). **REWE,** inside the Europa Passage shopping mall, has a good selection of prepared foods at affordable prices (Mon-Thu 7:00-22:00, Fri-Sat until 23:00, closed Sun). The **Edeka** supermarket inside the train station, on the upper level of the north bridge over the tracks, is smaller and more expensive (daily 7:00-23:00).

SCHULTERBLATT ("SHOULDERBLADE") NEIGHBORHOOD

Fun restaurants with good people-watching fill the streets just south and west of the Sternschanze U-Bahn stop. There's a world of options here: German, Asian, Turkish/Middle Eastern, Italian, Greek, French, Spanish, and more. Many places serve tapas or pizza and have generous outdoor seating. The highest concentration of good eateries is in the cross section between Schulterblatt, Schanzenstrasse, and Susannenstrasse. I'd just wander and browse. But if you're having a hard time deciding, here are some suggestions.

$$$$ Bullerei, right next to the Sternschanze U-Bahn stop, is the most serious restaurant in this neighborhood. The brainchild of German celebrity chef Tim Mälzer, it fills a gorgeously restored red-brick meatpacking hall with a vast, vibrant dining room and a cozy bistro—both stylish and dressy. There's also outdoor seating on a tree-lined brick patio. Their **bistro** is a bit more casual and less pricey. On the menu: meat, of course. Reservations are smart (bistro daily 11:00-23:00, restaurant daily 18:00-22:00, Lagerstrasse 34b, tel. 040/3344-2110, www.bullerei.com).

$$$ Altes Mädchen, just around the corner from Bullerei in a repurposed brick warehouse, serves up a short-but-refined menu alongside seemingly unlimited varieties of craft beer, much of it brewed right here at the Ratsherrn microbrewery (€6.40 sampler available). Dishes are made with locally sourced ingredients, and the bread's baked fresh in their wood oven. The expansive, retro-rustic **interior** houses a fireplace and lots of bare wood; the less-expensive **self-service tables outside** buzz on pleasant evenings (daily 12:00-24:00, Lagerstrasse 28, tel. 040/800-077-750).

$$ Oma's Apotheke is a cozy café-bar-restaurant. The decor is vintage, the mood is relaxed, and it's a good place to connect with locals. Their tasty, mostly German food comes in huge portions for a small price (weekday lunch specials, daily 9:00-24:00, Schanzenstrasse 87, tel. 040/43-6620).

$$ Mikawa sushi bar, a peaceful oasis in a happening neighborhood, offers a wide variety of nigiri, sushi, and bento boxes (daily 12:30-22:00, Susannenstrasse 15, tel. 040/430-0220).

$$ Pamukkale serves big portions of fresh, tasty, authentic Turkish food. It's a good choice for satisfying your craving for *döner kebab* or *pide* (Turkish pizza). If you're in a hurry, order from the takeaway counter—otherwise enjoy the cozy atmosphere and attentive service inside or out (long hours daily, Susannenstrasse 34, tel. 040/430-2411).

$$ Bok serves up well-executed Japanese, Thai, and Korean cuisine in an airy, modern space (daily 12:00-23:30, locations at Schulterblatt 3 and Schanzenstrasse 36, tel. 040/4319-0070).

ELSEWHERE

In the Center: A block from the City Hall, **$$$ Café Paris** boasts a gorgeous, white-tile Art Nouveau interior that's worth a look even if you're not eating here—though the *très français* menu has good options for breakfast, lunch, or dinner (daily 9:30-23:30, Rathausstrasse 4, tel. 040/3252-7777).

On the Harbor: $$ Blockbräu, a huge, modern beer hall, features local cuisine and its own beer in the Landungsbrücken terminal building. It has a thousand seats, including a great rooftop terrace with harbor views (daily 11:00-24:00, Landungsbrücken 3, tel. 040/4440-5000).

Lining the harborfront is a long row of equally marginal fast-food booths, selling big glasses of beer, paper cones of french fries, gut-bomb *Currywurst*, and more—to go, to stand up, or to sit down.

Hamburg Connections

From Hamburg by Train to: Berlin (1-2/hour, 2 hours), **Dresden** (5/day direct, 4.5 hours, otherwise hourly with transfer, 5.5 hours), **Erfurt** (hourly, 4 hours), **Leipzig** (hourly, 3 hours, some transfer in Berlin), **Cologne** (hourly direct, 4 hours), **Frankfurt** (hourly, 4 hours), **Munich** (hourly direct, 6.5 hours), **Copenhagen** (direct trains almost every 2 hours, 5 hours, requires reservation in summer), **Amsterdam** (every 2 hours, 5.5 hours, 1 change). Train info: www.bahn.com.

GERMANY: PAST & PRESENT

A united Germany has only existed since 1871, but the cultural heritage of the German-speaking people stretches back 2,000 years.

ROMANS (AD 1-500)

German history begins in AD 9, when Roman troops were ambushed and driven back by the German chief Arminius. For the next 250 years, the Rhine and Danube rivers marked the border between civilized Roman Europe (to the southwest) and "barbarian" German lands (to the northeast). While the rest of Western Europe's future would be Roman, Christian, and Latin, most of Germany followed a separate, pagan path.

In AD 476, Rome fell to the Germanic chief Theodoric the Great (a.k.a. Dietrich of Bern). After that, Germanic Franks con-

trolled northern Europe, ruling a mixed population of Romanized Christians and tree-worshipping pagans. Rome's imprint on Germany remains in place names like Cologne ("Colonia" was an important Roman city) and great monuments like Trier's Porta Nigra.

CHARLEMAGNE AND THE FRANKS (AD 500-1000)

For Christmas in AD 800, the pope gave Charlemagne the title of Holy Roman Emperor. Charlemagne, the king of the Franks, was the first of many German kings to be called *Kaiser* ("emperor," from "Caesar") over the next thousand years. Allied with the pope, Charlemagne ruled an empire that included Germany, Austria,

France, the Low Countries, and northern Italy.

Charlemagne (Karl der Grosse, or Charles the Great, r. 768-814) stood a head taller than his subjects, and his foot became a standard unit of measurement. The stuff of legend, Charlemagne had five wives and four concubines, producing descendants with names like Charles the Bald, Louis the Pious, and Henry the Quarrelsome. His eldest son, Pippin the Hunchback, led a failed coup against Charlemagne and was exiled to a monastery. When Charlemagne died of pneumonia (814), he lacked a clear heir. His united empire was divided into (what would become) Germany, France, and the lands in between (Treaty of Verdun, 843). As this treaty was signed not in Latin, but in the local languages, many mark 843 as the year Europe was born.

THE HOLY ROMAN EMPIRE (1000-1500)

Chaotic medieval Germany (about the size of Montana) was made up of more than 300 small, quarreling dukedoms ruled by the Holy Roman Emperor. The title was pretty bogus, implying that the German king ruled the same huge European empire as the ancient Romans. In fact, he was "Holy" because he was blessed by the pope, "Roman" to recall ancient grandeur, and the figurehead "Emperor" of what was an empire in name only.

Holy Roman Emperors had less hands-on power than other kings around Europe. Because of the custom of electing emperors by nobles and archbishops, rather than by bestowing the title through inheritance, they couldn't pass the crown from father to son. In addition, there were no empire-wide taxes and no national capital. This system gave nobles great power: Peasants had to huddle close to their local noble's castle for protection from attack by the noble next door.

When Emperor Henry IV (r. 1056-1106) tried to assert his power by appointing bishops, he was slapped down by the nobles, and forced to repent to the pope by standing barefoot in the alpine snow for three days at Canossa (in northern Italy, 1077). Ever since, the phrase "going to Canossa" has meant "to humble oneself."

Emperor Frederick I Barbarossa (1152-1190), blue-eyed and red-bearded (hence *barba rossa*), gained an international reputation as a valiant knight, gentleman, bon vivant, and lover of poetry and women. Still, his great victories were away in Italy and Asia (on the Third Crusade, where he drowned in a river), while back home nobles wielded the real power.

This was the era of Germany's troubadours *(Meistersinger),* who traveled from castle to castle singing love songs *(Minnesang)* and telling the epic tales of chivalrous knights (Tristan and Isolde, Parsifal, and the Nibelungen) that would later inspire German nationalism and Wagnerian operas.

While France, England, and Spain were centralizing power around a single ruling family to create nation-states, Germany lagged behind as a decentralized, backward, feudal battleground. It would remain so until the 19th century (and neighboring European powers preferred it that way).

MEDIEVAL GROWTH

Nevertheless, Germany was strategically located at the center of Europe, and trading towns prospered. Berlin was born when in-

habitants of the region of Brandenburg settled on a marshy island in the Spree River. Several northern towns (especially Hamburg and Lübeck) banded together into the Hanseatic League, promoting open trade around the Baltic Sea. To curry favor at election time, emperors granted powers and privileges to certain towns, which were designated "free imperial cities." Some towns, such as Cologne, Mainz, Dresden, and Trier, held higher status than many nobles, as hosts of one of the seven "electors" of the emperor. To this day, every German town keeps careful track of whether it was "free" during the Middle Ages—or answered to a duke, king, archbishop, or elector in another place.

Textiles, mining, and the colonization of lands to the east made German states relatively wealthy and enabled the growth of a thriving middle class. In towns, middle-class folks (burghers), not aristocrats, began running things. In about 1450, Johann Gutenberg of Mainz figured out how to use moveable type for printing, an innovation that would allow the export of a new commodity: ideas. Around this time, Berlin came under the rule of the powerful Hohenzollern family, who began a palace complex on what is now that city's "Museum Island." The Hohenzollern's influence soon spread throughout northern Germany (Prussia).

RELIGIOUS STRUGGLES AND THE THIRTY YEARS' WAR (1500-1700)

Martin Luther—German monk, fiery orator, and religious whistle-blower—sparked a century of European wars by speaking out against the Catholic Church. Luther's protests ("Protestantism")

GERMAN HISTORY

1000 Years · Each dashed line = 500 years · Each dashed line =100 years · Each dashed

1000 | 0 | 500 | 1000 | 1100 | 1200 | 1300 | 1400 | 1500 | 1600

Jesus

CELTS
ROMAN
Constantine
Julius Caesar
FRANKS
ROMANS COLONIZE, BUILD BATHS, PLANT VINES

Charlemagne
TREATY OF VERDUN
HENRY IV IN CANOSSA

Barbarossa

BLACK DEATH

HRE ruled by Habsburgs from 1438 until it ends in 1806

HOLY ROMAN EMPIRE

Luther

DIET OF WORMS
LUTHER'S 95 THESES
GUTENBERG BIBLE
PEASANTS REVOLT
COUNCIL OF TRENT

30 YEARS WAR

RELIGIOUS
PEACE OF AUGSBURG

HISTORY

SACK OF ROME
BARBARIANS
Attila
←To Neanderthal Era

CRUSADES

DUCHY ESTABLISHED

WITTELSBACH DYNASTY BEGINS

BAVARIA UNITED

BEER PURITY LAW

BAVARIA

Nefertiti (Berlin)
EGYPT
GREECE
Pergamon Altar (Berlin)

MUNICH FOUNDED
BERLIN FOUNDED

OTHER EMPIRES & EVENTS

HOHENZOLLERN RULE BEGINS
PRINCIPALITY

UNIFIED

BRANDENBURG-

HABSBURG
Max. I Charles V

HANSEATIC LEAGUE

CELTIC
Cologne Founded
ROMAN
Porta Nigra
Trier Basilica

Palatine Chapel Aachen

DARK

ROMANESQUE

Freiburg Cathedral

GOTHIC

Cologne Cathedral

Altdorfer
Grünewald
Riemenschneider

Holy Blood Altar Rothenburg

RENAISSANCE

Dürer
Cranach
Holbein

St. Michael's Munich

ARTS & ARCHITECTURE

Wartburg

CASTLES

Marksburg   Rheinfels

MANY CASTLES BUILT ALONG RHINE & MOSEL

Burg Eltz finished

1000 | 0 | 500 | 1000 | 1100 | 1200 | 1300 | 1400 | 1500 | 1600

German History & Art Timeline

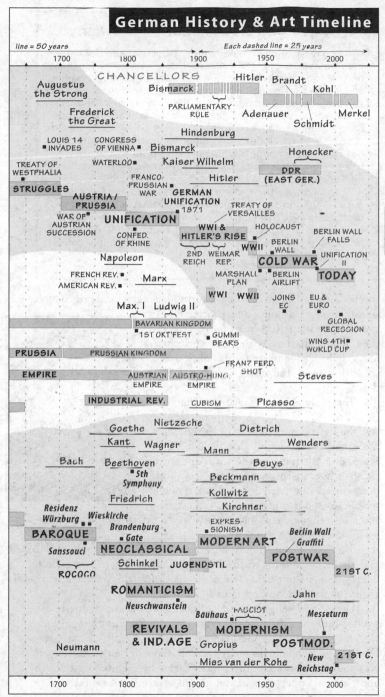

line = 50 years   Each dashed line = 25 years

1700   1800   1900   1950   2000

CHANCELLORS

Augustus the Strong

Bismarck   Hitler   Brandt   Kohl

PARLIAMENTARY RULE   Adenauer   Schmidt   Merkel

Frederick the Great

Hindenburg

LOUIS 14 INVADES   CONGRESS OF VIENNA   Bismarck

Honecker

TREATY OF WESTPHALIA   WATERLOO   Kaiser Wilhelm

DDR (EAST GER.)

STRUGGLES   FRANCO-PRUSSIAN WAR   Hitler

AUSTRIA/ PRUSSIA   GERMAN UNIFICATION 1871

TREATY OF VERSAILLES

WAR OF AUSTRIAN SUCCESSION   UNIFICATION   WWI & HITLER'S RISE   HOLOCAUST   BERLIN WALL FALLS

CONFED. OF RHINE   WWII   BERLIN WALL

Napoleon   2ND REICH   WEIMAR REP.   COLD WAR   UNIFICATION II

FRENCH REV.   MARSHALL PLAN   BERLIN AIRLIFT   TODAY

AMERICAN REV.   Marx   WWI   WWII   JOINS EC   EU & EURO

Max. I   Ludwig II   GLOBAL RECESSION

BAVARIAN KINGDOM   1ST OKT'FEST   GUMMI BEARS   WINS 4TH WORLD CUP

PRUSSIA   PRUSSIAN KINGDOM

FRANZ FERD. SHOT

EMPIRE   AUSTRIAN EMPIRE   AUSTRO-HUNG. EMPIRE   Steves

INDUSTRIAL REV.   CUBISM   Picasso

Goethe   Nietzsche   Dietrich

Kant   Wagner   Wenders

Mann

Bach   Beethoven   Beuys

5th Symphony   Beckmann

Friedrich   Kollwitz

Kirchner

Residenz Würzburg   Wieskirche   EXPRES- SIONISM

Brandenburg Gate   Berlin Wall Graffiti

BAROQUE   MODERN ART

Sanssouci   NEOCLASSICAL   POSTWAR

Schinkel   JUGENDSTIL

ROCOCO   21ST C.

ROMANTICISM   Jahn

Neuschwanstein   Bauhaus   FASCIST   Messeturm

REVIVALS & IND. AGE   MODERNISM

Neumann   Gropius   POSTMOD.   21ST C.

Mies van der Rohe   New Reichstag

1700   1800   1900   1950   2000

GERMAN HISTORY

Why We Call Deutschland "Germany"

Our English name "Germany" comes from the Latin *Germania,* the Roman name for the lands north of the Alps where "barbarian" tribes lived. The French and Spanish call it *Allemagne* and *Alemania,* respectively, after the Alemanni tribe. Italians call the country *Germania,* but in Italy the German language is known as *tedesco.* The Slavic peoples of Eastern Europe have a perhaps simpler approach, calling Germany *Německo* (Czech), *Niemcy* (Polish), and other variations of a word that basically means "people who can't speak right." The Hungarians borrowed this word from the Slavs and call anything German *német.*

To Germans, their country is *Deutschland,* their language is *Deutsch,* and they themselves are *Deutsche.* A few hundred years ago, this word was spelled *Teutsch* (later, the "t" changed to a "d"). The English word Teutonic, the Italian *tedesco,* and the Scandinavian *tysk* all come from this earlier form. *Alles klar?*

threw Germany into a century of turmoil, as each local prince took sides between Catholics and Protestants. In the 1525 Peasant Revolt, peasants attacked their feudal masters with hoes and pitchforks, fighting for more food, political say-so, and respect. The revolt was brutally put down.

The Holy Roman Emperor, Charles V (r. 1519-1556), sided with the pope. Charles was the most powerful man in Europe, having inherited an empire that included Germany and Austria, plus the Low Countries, much of Italy, Spain, and Spain's New World possessions. But many local German nobles took the opportunity to go Protestant—some for religious reasons, but also as an excuse to seize Church assets and powers.

The 1555 Peace of Augsburg allowed each local noble to decide the religion of his realm. In general, the northern and eastern lands became Protestant, while the south (today's Bavaria, along with Austria) and west remained Catholic.

Unresolved religious and political differences eventually expanded into the Thirty Years' War (1618-1648). This Europe-wide war, fought mainly on German soil, involved Denmark, Sweden, France, and Bohemia (in today's Czech Republic), among others. It was one of history's bloodiest wars, fueled by religious extremism and political opportunism, and fought by armies of brutal merce-

Germany Almanac

Official Name: Bundesrepublik Deutschland

Locals Call It: Deutschland

Size: 138,000 square miles (about half the size of Texas); population is 82 million people (almost three times the population of Texas)

Geography: The terrain gradually rises—from flat land in the north to the rugged Alps in the south, culminating in the 9,700-foot Zugspitze mountain. The climate is temperate.

Latitude and Longitude: 51°N and 9°E (similar latitude to Alberta, Canada)

Major Cities: Berlin (the capital, 3.5 million people), Hamburg (1.8 million), Munich (1.5 million)

Economy: The Gross Domestic Product is $4.1 trillion, Europe's largest; the GDP per capita is approximately $50,200. Germany's strength is in technology and manufacturing, producing steel, cars, chemicals, pharmaceuticals, consumer electronics, and more. Germany also has around 1,300 breweries (Bavaria boasts about half of them), but much of the production is consumed domestically. Germany trades almost equally with a half-dozen neighboring countries and the United States.

Government: Germany's chancellor, similar to a prime minister, is not elected by the people but is the head of the lead party in parliament. The less-powerful president is elected by parliament. The legislative branch includes the Bundestag (currently 630 seats, elected by both direct and proportional representation) and Bundesrat (69 votes by officials of Germany's 16 states).

Flag: Three horizontal bands of (from top to bottom) black, red, and gold

The Average Deutscher: The average German is 46 years old, has 1.4 kids, will live to be 80, is of Teutonic extraction (about 90 percent), lives in a household with two other people, watches 3.75 hours of TV a day, and drinks 27 gallons of beer a year.

naries who worked on commission and were paid in loot and pillage.

By the war's end (Treaty of Westphalia, 1648), a third of all Germans had died, France was the rising European power, and the Holy Roman Empire was a medieval mess of scattered feudal states. In 1689, France's Louis XIV swept down the Rhine, gutting and leveling its once-great castles, and Germany ceased to be a major player in European politics until the modern era.

(For an entertaining one-hour education on Luther, the Reformation, and the wars of religion, see my public-television special

GERMAN HISTORY

produced in 2017 to celebrate the 500th anniversary of the Reformation. You can stream it on YouTube or at www.ricksteves.com.)

AUSTRIA AND PRUSSIA (1700s)

The German-speaking lands now consisted of three "Germanys": Austria in the south, Prussia in the north, and the rest in between.

Prussia—originally a largely Slavic region colonized by celibate ex-Crusaders called Teutonic Knights—was forged into a unified state by two strong kings. Frederick I (the "King Sergeant," r. 1701-1713) built a modern state around a highly disciplined army, a centralized government (with Berlin as its capital), and national pride.

His grandson, Frederick II "The Great" (r. 1740-1786), added French culture and worldliness, preparing militaristic Prussia to enter the world stage. A well-read, flute-playing lover of the arts and liberal ideals, Frederick also ruled with an iron fist—the very model of the "enlightened despot." Meanwhile, Austria thrived under the laid-back rule of the Habsburg family. The Habsburgs gained power in Europe by marrying into it. They acquired the Netherlands, Spain, and Bohemia that way (a strategy that didn't work so well for Marie-Antoinette, who wed the doomed king of France).

In the 1700s, the Germanic lands became a cultural powerhouse, producing musicians (Bach, Haydn, Mozart, Beethoven), writers (Goethe, Schiller), and thinkers (Kant, Leibniz). Sophisticated Berlin became the epicenter of Prussian culture. But politically, fragmented Germany was no match for the modern powers.

After the French Revolution (1789), Napoleon swept through Germany with his armies, deposing feudal lords, emancipating Jews, confiscating church lands, and forcing the Holy Roman Emperor to hand over his crown (1806). After a thousand years, the Holy Roman Empire was dead.

GERMAN UNIFICATION (1800s)

Napoleon's invasion helped unify the German-speaking peoples by rallying them against a common foreign enemy. After Napoleon's defeat, the Congress of Vienna (1815), presided over by the Austrian Prince Metternich, realigned Europe's borders. The idea of unifying the three Germanic nations—Prussia, Austria, and the German Confederation, a loose collection of small states in between—began to grow. By mid-century, most German-speaking people favored forming a modern nation-state; the only question

Germany in the Early 1800s

SWEDEN

DENMARK

Danzig

SCHLESWIG
HOLSTEIN →

HANOVER

NETH.

P R U S S I A

Berlin

RUSSIA

BELG.

SAXONY

HESSE

BADEN-
WÜRT.

BAVARIA

Prague

ALSACE
LORRAINE →

Munich

AUSTRIA-

• Vienna

FRANCE

SWITZ.

HUNGARY

ITALY

Venice

was whether the confederation would be under Prussian or Austrian dominance.

Economically, Germany was becoming increasingly efficient and modern, with a unified trade organization (1834), railroads (1835), mechanical-engineering prowess, and booming factories benefiting from a surplus of labor. Berlin was changing into a world-class city graced by Neoclassical buildings designed by architect Karl Friedrich Schinkel (including many of today's museums). By 1850, with its Unter den Linden boulevard and the Brandenburg Gate, Berlin rivaled Paris as Europe's most elegant promenade.

Energetic Prussia took the lead in unifying the country. Otto

von Bismarck (served 1862-1890), the strong minister of Prussia's weak king, used cunning politics to engineer a unified Germany under Prussian dominance. First, he started a war with Austria, ensuring that any united Germany would be under Prussian control. (Austria remains a separate coun-

GERMAN HISTORY

Church Architecture

History comes to life when you visit a centuries-old church. Even if you wouldn't know your apse from a hole in the ground, learning a few simple terms will enrich your experience. Note that not every church has every feature, and a "cathedral" isn't a type of church architecture, but rather a designation for a church that's a governing center for a local bishop.

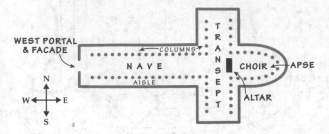

Aisles: The long, generally low-ceilinged arcades that flank the nave.

Altar: The raised area with a ceremonial table (often adorned with candles or a crucifix), where the priest prepares and serves the bread and wine for Communion.

Apse: The space beyond the altar, often bordered with small chapels.

Barrel Vault: A continuous round-arched ceiling that resembles an extended upside-down U.

Choir: A cozy area, often screened off, located within the church nave and near the high altar where services are sung in a more intimate setting.

Cloister: Covered hallways bordering a square or rectangular open-air courtyard, traditionally where monks and nuns got fresh air.

Facade: The front exterior surface of the church's main (west) entrance, viewable from outside and generally highly decorated.

Groin Vault: An arched ceiling formed where two equal barrel vaults meet at right angles. Less common usage: term for a medieval jock strap.

Narthex: The area (portico or foyer) between the main entry and the nave.

Nave: The long, central section of the church (running west to east, from the entrance to the altar) where the congregation sits or stands through the service.

Transept: In a traditional cross-shaped floor plan, the transept is one of the two parts forming the "arms" of the cross. The transepts run north-south, perpendicularly crossing the east-west nave.

West Portal: The main entry to the church (on the west end, opposite the main altar).

Typical Castle Architecture

Castles were fortified residences for medieval nobles. Castles come in all shapes and sizes, but knowing a few general terms will help you understand them.

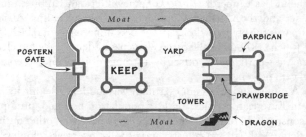

Barbican: A fortified gatehouse, sometimes a standalone building located outside the main walls.

Crenellation: A gap-toothed pattern of stones atop the parapet.

Drawbridge: A bridge that could be raised or lowered using counterweights or a chain-and-winch.

Great Hall: The largest room in the castle, serving as throne room, conference center, and dining hall.

Hoardings (or Gallery or Brattice): Wooden huts built onto the upper parts of the stone walls. They served as watch towers, living quarters, and fighting platforms.

Keep (or Donjon): A high, strong stone tower in the center of the complex; the lord's home and refuge of last resort.

Loopholes (or Embrasures): Narrow wall slits through which soldiers could shoot arrows.

Machicolation: A stone ledge jutting out from the wall, with holes through which soldiers could drop rocks or boiling water onto wall-scaling enemies below.

Moat: A ditch encircling the wall, sometimes filled with water.

Parapet: Outer railing of the wall walk.

Portcullis: An iron grille that could be lowered across the entrance.

Postern Gate: A small, unfortified side or rear entrance. In wartime, it became a "sally-port" used to launch surprise attacks, or as an escape route.

Towers: Square or round structures with crenellated tops or conical roofs serving as lookouts, chapels, living quarters, or the dungeon.

Turret: A small lookout tower rising from the top of the wall.

Wall Walk (or Allure): A pathway atop the wall where guards could patrol and where soldiers stood to fire at the enemy.

Yard (or Bailey): An open courtyard inside the castle walls.

try to this day.) Next, Bismarck provoked a war with France (the Franco-Prussian War, 1870-1871), which united Prussia and the German Confederation against their common enemy, France.

Fueled by hysterical patriotism, German armies swept through France and, in the Hall of Mirrors at Versailles, crowned Prussia's Wilhelm I as Emperor *(Kaiser)* of a new German Empire, uniting Prussia and the German Confederation (but excluding Austria). Berlin was the obvious choice as the new imperial capital. This Second Reich (1871-1918) featured elements of democracy (an elected *Reichstag*—parliament), offset by a strong military and an emperor with veto powers.

A united and resurgent Germany was suddenly flexing its muscles in European politics. Berlin's population boomed, prompting the construction of Prenzlauer Berg, Kreuzberg, and other outlying districts. With strong industry, war spoils, overseas colonies, and a large and disciplined military, Germany sought its rightful place at the global table.

Fueled by nationalistic fervor, patriotic *Volk* art flourished (Wagner's operas, Nietzsche's essays), reviving medieval German myths and Nordic gods. The rest of Europe saw Germany's rapid rise—and began arming themselves to the teeth. The old order was scrambled and peace was reliant upon a tenuous and confused web of bilateral treaties. In Berlin, the imposing Berlin Cathedral was built, announcing the über-nationalism of Kaiser Wilhelm II that would lead Europe into World War I.

WORLD WAR I AND HITLER'S RISE (1914-1939)

When Archduke Franz Ferdinand, the heir to the Austro-Hungarian Empire, was assassinated in 1914, all of Europe took sides as the political squabble quickly escalated into World War I. Germany and Austria-Hungary attacked British and French troops in France, but were stalled at the Battle of the Marne. Both sides dug defensive trenches, then settled in for four brutal years of bloodshed, boredom, mud, machine-gun fire, disease, and mustard gas.

More than four years later, at 11:00 in the morning of November 11, 1918, the fighting finally ceased. Germany surrendered, signing the Treaty of Versailles in the Hall of Mirrors at Versailles. The war cost the defeated German nation 1.7 million men, precious territory, military rights, reparations money, and national pride.

A new democratic government called the Weimar Republic (1919) dutifully abided by the Treaty of Versailles, and tried to maintain order among Germany's many divided political parties. But after the humiliating defeat, the country was in ruins, its economy a shambles, and the war's victors demanded heavy reparations. Berlin attracted the disillusioned as the center of decadent cabaret

Nazi Terminology

Many Nazi military terms are familiar to English speakers. "Nazi" is an abbreviation for *Nationalsozialismus* (National Socialism), Hitler's political party. Other terms you'll probably recognize are SS (short for *Schutzstaffel*, or "protective unit"), *Luftwaffe* (air force), and *Blitzkrieg* ("lightning war"). Nazis also devised the *Endlösung* ("final solution") for doing away with Jewish and other "undesirable" people, by interning and killing them in *Konzentrationslager* (KZ, concentration camps). The *Widerstand* (resistance) stood up against the Nazis. *Vergangenheitsbewaltigung* (coming to terms with the past) continues to be a major issue in Germany. Many concentration camps and other wartime symbols have been turned into *Gedenkstätte* (memorials). At a *Dokumentationzentrum* (documentation center), locals and visitors can learn about Nazi atrocities. The message of these sites is *Vergesst es nie*— "Never forget."

nightlife—especially near today's Ku'damm and along Friedrichstrasse. Elsewhere, communists rioted in the streets, fascists plotted coups, and inflation drove the price of a loaf of bread to a billion marks. War vets grumbled in their beer about how their leaders had sold them out. All Germans, regardless of their political affiliations, were fervently united in their apathy toward the new democracy. When the worldwide depression of 1929 hit Germany with brutal force, the nation was desperate for a strong leader with answers.

Adolf Hitler (1889-1945) was a disgruntled vet who had spent the post-World War I years homeless, wandering the streets of Vienna with sketchpad in hand, hoping to become an artist. In Munich, he joined other disaffected Germans to form the National Socialist German Workers' Party—the Nazis. In stirring speeches, Hitler promised to restore Germany to its rightful glory, blaming the country's current problems  on communists, foreigners, and Jews. After an unsuccessful coup attempt (the Beer Hall Putsch in Munich, 1923), Hitler was sent to jail, where he wrote an influential book of his political ideas, titled *Mein Kampf (My Struggle)*.

By 1930, the Nazis—now wearing power suits and working within the system—had become a formidable political party in Germany's democracy. They won 38 percent of the seats in the

Germany During World War II
(1939-1945)

1939: Soldiers singing *"Muss i denn, Muss i denn zum Städtele hinaus"* ("Must I, must I leave my city") march off to war. On September 1, Germany invades Poland to seize the free city of Danzig (Gdańsk), sparking World War II. Germany, Italy, and Japan (the Axis) would eventually square off against the Allies—which included Britain, France, the United States, and the USSR.

1940: The Nazi Blitzkrieg (lightning war) quickly sweeps through Denmark, Norway, the Low Countries, and France; later it also conquers Yugoslavia and Greece. With fellow fascists ruling Italy (Mussolini), Spain (Franco), and Portugal (Salazar), the Continent is now dominated by fascists, creating a "fortress Europe."

1941: Hitler invades his former ally, the USSR. Bombastic victory parades in Berlin celebrate the triumph of the Aryan race over the lesser peoples of the world.

1942: Allied bombs begin falling on German cities. That autumn and winter, German families receive death notices from the horrific Battle of Stalingrad. The German army suffers around 850,000 casualties (by comparison, the US had roughly 214,000 casualties for the entire Vietnam War). Back home, Nazi officials begin their plan for the "final solution to the Jewish problem"—systematic execution of Europe's Jews in specially built death camps.

1943: Germany fights a two-front war: against tenacious Soviets on the bitter Eastern Front, and against Brits and Yanks advancing north through Italy on the Western Front. Germany's industrial output tries desperately to keep up with that of the Allies.

Reichstag in 1932, and Hitler was appointed chancellor (1933). Two months later, the Reichstag building was mysteriously set on fire—an apparent act of terrorism with a September 11-sized impact—and a terrified Germany gave Chancellor Hitler sweeping powers to preserve national security.

Hitler wasted no time in using this Enabling Act to jail opponents, terrorize the citizenry, and organize every aspect of German life under the watchful eye of the Nazi Party. Plumbers' unions, choral societies, schoolteachers, church pastors, filmmakers, and artists all had to account to a Nazi Party official about how their work furthered the Third Reich.

For the next decade, an all-powerful Hitler revived Germany's economy, building the autobahns and rebuilding the military. Defying the Treaty of Versailles and world opinion, Hitler proceeded with his Four-Year Plan to re-arm Germany: He occupied the Saar region (1935) and the Rhineland (1936), annexed Austria and the Sudetenland (1938), and invaded Czechoslovakia (March 1939).

The average German suffers through shortages, rationing, and frequent trips to the bomb shelter.

1944: Hitler's no-surrender policy is increasingly unpopular, and

he narrowly survives an assassination attempt by members of his own military. After the Allies reach France on D-Day, Germany counterattacks with a last-gasp offensive (the Battle of the Bulge) that slows but doesn't stop the Allies.

1945: Soviet soldiers approach Berlin from the east, and Americans and Brits advance from the west. Adolf Hitler commits suicide, and families lock up their daughters to protect them from rapacious Soviet soldiers. When Germany finally surrenders on May 8, the country is in ruins, occupied by several foreign powers, divided into occupation zones, and viewed by the world as an immoral monster.

War's Aftermath: German citizens are faced with the scope of the mass killings and atrocities committed by their leaders and accomplices. Over 11 million people have been systemically murdered—6 million Jews, as well as people with disabilities, homosexuals, prisoners of war, political dissidents, and ethnic minorities.

The rest of Europe finally reached its appeasement limit—and World War II began—when Germany invaded Poland in September 1939 (see sidebar). When the war was over (1945), countless millions were dead and most German cities had been bombed beyond recognition. The Third Reich was over.

(For a one-hour program on this topic, see my public-television special, "The Story of Fascism in Europe," produced in 2018. You can stream it on YouTube and at www.ricksteves.com.)

TWO GERMANYS...AND REUNIFICATION (1945-2000)

After World War II, the Allies divided occupied Germany into two halves, split down the middle by an 855-mile border that Winston Churchill called an "Iron Curtain." By 1949, Germany was officially two separate countries. West Germany (the Federal Republic of Germany) was democratic and capitalist, allied with the powerful United States. East Germany (the German Democratic

GERMAN HISTORY

Postwar Berlin

Republic, or DDR) was a communist state under Soviet control. The former capital, Berlin, sitting in East German territory, was itself split into two parts, allowing a tiny pocket of Western life in the Soviet-controlled East. In 1961, the East German government erected a 12-foot-high concrete wall through the heart of Berlin—physically dividing the city in two, isolating West Berlin, and preventing East German citizens from fleeing to the West. Over the next decades, more than a

hundred East Germans would die or be arrested trying to cross that Wall. The Berlin Wall came to symbolize a divided Germany.

In West Germany, Chancellor Konrad Adenauer (who had suffered imprisonment under the Nazis) tried to restore Germany's good name, paying war reparations and joining international organizations of nations. Thanks to US aid from the Marshall Plan, West Germany was rebuilt, democracy was established, and its "economic miracle" quickly exceeded pre-WWII levels. Adenauer was eventually succeeded in 1969 by the US-friendly Willy Brandt.

Meanwhile, East Germany was a repressive communist state ruled with an iron fist by Walter Ulbricht (who had been exiled by the Nazis). In 1953, demonstrations and anti-government protests were brutally put down by Soviet—not German—troops. Erich Honecker (a kinder, gentler tyrant who had endured a decade of Nazi imprisonment) succeeded Ulbricht as ruler of the East in 1971.

Throughout the 1970s and 1980s, both the US and the Soviet Union used divided Germany as a military base. West Germans debated whether US missiles aimed at the Soviets should be placed in their country. Economically, West Germany just got stronger while East Germany stagnated.

As the Soviet Union collapsed, so did its client nation, East Germany. On November 9, 1989, East Germany unexpectedly opened the Berlin Wall. Astonished Germans from both sides climbed the Wall, hugged each other, shared bottles of beer, sang songs, and chiseled off souvenirs. At first, most Germans—West and East—simply looked forward to free travel and better relations between two distinct nations. But before the month was out, negotiations and elections to reunite the two Germanys had begun. October 3, 1990 was proclaimed German Unity Day, and Berlin reassumed its status as the German capital in 1991.

In the decade that followed, in reunified Berlin, Potsdamer Platz, formerly part of the Berlin Wall's "death strip," was redeveloped into a forest of skyscrapers. The glittering new dome atop the Reichstag—which had been damaged in World War II and sat unused for decades—formally opened, giving the German people a bird's-eye view of their government at work. Formerly dilapidated neighborhoods (first Prenzlauer Berg, then Kreuzberg, now Friedrichshain) rapidly gentrified, and the city erected several monuments to the victims of both the Nazis and the Cold War divide. Germany was ready to set its painful past behind.

GERMANY TODAY (2000-present)

Today Germany is a major economic and political force in Europe. It's a powerful member of the European Union—an organization whose original chief aim was to avoid future wars by embracing Germany in the economic web of Europe. Recently, however, Germany has outgrown its role as a mere member state to become, thanks to its economic might, the EU's de facto leader. (While many other European countries were hard hit by the economic  crisis of the last decade, Germany—with the largest economy in the EU—emerged relatively unscathed.)

German elections in 2005 resulted in no clear victory, and

both major parties formed a "Grand Coalition," sharing power equally under Germany's first female chancellor, Angela Merkel, who the media like to call "Mutti" (Mommy). While representing the center-right Christian Democratic Union, Merkel's cautious, centrist, pro-business policies earned her reelection in 2009, 2013, and 2017. Though she governs with coalition partners, she is considered one of the world's most powerful people. Returning for her fourth term in September 2017, Merkel became Europe's longest-serving elected female leader—breaking Margaret Thatcher's 11-year record.

Painfully aware of tensions that still linger even decades after World War II, many Germans have been reluctant to embrace their country's dominant role in Europe. But this hesitancy is slipping away. The 2006 World Cup is often cited as a turning point—not because Germany successfully hosted the huge event, but because that's when a new generation of Germans embraced their country's flag en masse. For the first time since World War II, Germans exhibited a national pride that they no longer feared would be confused with Nazi sentiment.

In 2014, the country's spirit got a huge boost when its soccer team won the World Cup, its first as a united nation. And while Chancellor Merkel's EU austerity measures are unpopular in many corners of Europe, her firm stance has been largely applauded by a German population that's increasingly comfortable calling the shots.

Merkel's popularity weakened somewhat in 2015 after she welcomed Syrian refugees fleeing that nation's civil war. About a million people were given asylum. Her decision was praised by some (she was named *Time* magazine's Person of the Year) but sparked a backlash among others, concerned about Germany's ability to absorb so many newcomers and the economic strain placed on the country's social services. Alternative for Germany (AfD), an anti-immigration right-wing party, gained momentum and became the third-largest party in Germany after the 2017 federal election.

Like the US and other European nations, Germany has been the target of isolated terrorist incidents. During New Year's Eve celebrations in 2015, an orchestrated series of sexual assaults and thefts rippled through German cities; many of the perpetrators were determined to have been North African migrants. And in 2016, a 24-year-old Tunisian man plowed a tractor-trailer into Berlin's Christmas market, killing 12. These events increased pressure on Germany's leaders to take a tougher stance on immigration, though the country's population remains generally welcoming.

The long-term viability of the EU is another challenge facing Germany. As the biggest and staunchest EU booster,

Germany must grapple with the implications of Brexit (Britain's decision to withdraw from the EU) and the rise of other European anti-EU movements.

For more on German history, consider *Europe 101: History and Art for the Traveler,* written by Rick Steves and Gene Openshaw (available at www.ricksteves.com). And for all the latest, travel to Germany, buy someone a beer, and ask, "So, what's going on here in Germany?"

PRACTICALITIES

This chapter covers the practical skills of European travel: how to get tourist information, pay for things, sightsee efficiently, find good-value accommodations, eat affordably but well, use technology wisely, and get between destinations smoothly. For more information on these topics, see www.ricksteves.com/travel-tips.

Tourist Information

Germany's national tourist office **in the US** is a wealth of information. Before your trip, scan their website (www.germany.travel) for maps and Rhine boat schedules, as well as information on festivals, castles, biking, and regions. Travel brochures can also be downloaded from their website.

In Germany, a good first stop is generally the tourist information office (abbreviated **TI** in this book). Throughout Germany, you'll find TIs are usually well-organized and have English-speaking staff. But be aware that TIs are in business to help you enjoy spending money in their town. A few TIs, notably in Berlin, have been privatized. This means they have become sales agents for big tours and hotels, and their "information" is unavoidably colored. Even so, I still make a point to swing by the local TI to confirm sightseeing plans, pick up a city map, and get information on public transit, walking tours, special events, and nightlife. An-

ticipating a harried front-line staffer, prepare a list of questions and a proposed plan to double-check.

Some TIs have information on the entire country or at least the region, so try to pick up maps and printed information for destinations you'll be visiting later in your trip.

Travel Tips

PRACTICALITIES

Emergency and Medical Help: For any emergency service—ambulance, police, or fire—call **112** from a mobile phone or landline. Operators, who in most countries speak English, will deal with your request or route you to the right emergency service. If you get sick, do as the Germans do and go to a pharmacist for advice. Or ask at your hotel for help—they'll know the nearest medical and emergency services. The US Embassy & Consulates website for Germany has a list of English-speaking doctors (tel. 030/83050, https://de.usembassy.gov, search for "Medical Assistance").

ETIAS Registration: Beginning in 2021, US and Canadian citizens will be required to register online with the European Travel Information and Authorization System (ETIAS) before entering certain European countries (quick and easy process, $8 fee, valid 3 years). A useful private website with more details is www.schengenvisainfo.com/etias/.

Theft or Loss: To replace a passport, you'll need to go in person to an embassy (see next). If your credit and debit cards disappear, cancel and replace them (see "Damage Control for Lost Cards," later). File a police report, either on the spot or within a day or two; you'll need it to submit an insurance claim for lost or stolen rail passes or travel gear, and it can help with replacing your passport or credit and debit cards. For more information, see www.ricksteves.com/help.

Embassies: US Embassy in Berlin—passport replacement by appointment only Wed-Thu, sign up online (Clayallee 170, tel. 030/83050, http://de.usembassy.gov). **Canadian Embassy** in Berlin—consular services open Mon-Fri 9:00-12:00, closed Sat-Sun (Leipziger Platz 17, tel. 030/2031-2470, www.germany.gc.ca).

Time Zones: Germany, like most of continental Europe, is generally six/nine hours ahead of the East/West Coasts of the US. The exceptions are the beginning and end of Daylight Saving Time: Europe "springs forward" the last Sunday in March (two weeks after most of North America) and "falls back" the last Sunday in October (one week before North America). For a handy time converter, use the world clock app on your mobile phone or download one (see www.timeanddate.com).

Business Hours: In Germany, most shops are open from about 9:00 until 18:00-20:00 on weekdays; smaller stores generally close earlier on Saturdays, and most stores are closed all day Sunday (shops and grocery stores in train stations often have longer hours). In small towns, shops may take a midafternoon break (roughly between 12:00 and 14:00 or 15:00). Banks are generally open Monday to Friday from 9:00 to 15:00 (or later, up to 19:00). Many museums and sights are closed on Monday. Catholic regions, including Bavaria, shut down during religious holidays (see the appendix).

Watt's Up? Europe's electrical system is 220 volts, instead of North America's 110 volts. Most newer electronics (such as laptops, battery chargers, and hair dryers) convert automatically, so you won't need a converter, but you will need an adapter plug with two round prongs, sold inexpensively at travel stores in the US. Avoid bringing older appliances that don't automatically convert voltage; instead, buy a cheap replacement in Europe.

Discounts: Discounts for sights are generally not listed in this book. However, seniors (age 60 and over), youths under 18, and students and teachers with proper identification cards (www.isic.org) can get discounts at many sights—always ask. Some discounts are available only to European citizens.

Online Translation Tips: Google's Chrome browser instantly translates websites; Translate.google.com is also handy. The Google Translate app converts spoken or typed English into most European languages (and vice versa) and can also translate text it "reads" with your phone's camera.

Money

Here's my basic strategy for using money in Europe:
- Upon arrival, head for a cash machine (ATM) at the airport and withdraw some local currency, using a debit card with low international transaction fees.
- Pay for most purchases with your choice of cash or a credit card. You'll save money by minimizing your credit and debit card exchange fees. The trend is for bigger expenses to be paid

---

> ## Exchange Rate
>
> **1 euro (€) = about $1.20**
>
> To convert prices in euros to dollars, add about 20 percent: €20 = about $24, €50 = about $60. (Check www.oanda.com for the latest exchange rates.) Just like the dollar, one euro (€) is broken down into 100 cents. Coins range from €0.01 to €2, and bills from €5 to €200 (bills over €50 are rarely used; €500 bills are being phased out).

by credit card, but cash is still the standby for small purchases and tips.
- Keep your cards and cash safe in a money belt.

PLASTIC VERSUS CASH

Although credit cards are widely accepted in Europe, cash is sometimes the only way to pay for cheap food, taxis, tips, and local guides. Some businesses (especially smaller ones, such as B&Bs and mom-and-pop cafés and shops) may charge you extra for using a credit card—or might not accept credit cards at all. Having cash on hand helps you out of a jam if your card randomly doesn't work.

I use my credit card to book and pay for hotel reservations, to buy advance tickets for events or sights, and to cover most other expenses. It can also be smart to use plastic near the end of your trip, to avoid another visit to the ATM. But keep in mind that some shops and restaurants in Germany accept only the local "EC" debit cards—not American credit cards. Larger hotels, restaurants, and shops that do take US cards more commonly accept Visa and MasterCard than American Express.

WHAT TO BRING

I pack the following and keep it all safe in my money belt.

Debit Card: Use this at ATMs to withdraw local cash.

Credit Card: Handy for bigger purchases (at hotels, shops, restaurants, travel agencies, car rental agencies, and so on), payment machines, and ordering online.

Backup Card: Some travelers carry a third card (debit or credit; ideally from a different bank), in case one gets lost, demagnetized, eaten by a temperamental machine, or simply doesn't work.

A Stash of Cash: I always carry $100-200 as a cash backup. A stash of cash comes in handy for emergencies, such as if your ATM card stops working.

What NOT to Bring: Resist the urge to buy euros before your trip or you'll pay the price in bad stateside exchange rates. Wait until you arrive to withdraw money. I've yet to see a European airport that didn't have plenty of ATMs.

BEFORE YOU GO

Use this pre-trip checklist.

Know your cards. Debit cards from any major US bank will work in any standard European bank's ATM (ideally, use a debit card with a Visa or MasterCard logo). As for credit cards, Visa and MasterCard are universal, American Express is less common, and Discover is unknown in Europe.

Know your PIN. Make sure you know the numeric, four-digit PIN for all of your cards, both debit and credit. Request it if you don't have one and allow time to receive the information by mail.

All credit and debit cards now have chips that authenticate and secure transactions. Europeans insert their chip cards into the payment machine slot, then enter a PIN. American cards should work in most transactions without a PIN—but may not work at self-service machines at train stations, toll booths, gas pumps, or parking lots. I've been inconvenienced a few times by self-service payment machines in Europe that wouldn't accept my card, but it's never caused me serious trouble.

Report your travel dates. Let your bank know that you'll be using your debit and credit cards in Europe, and when and where you're headed.

Adjust your ATM withdrawal limit. Find out how much you can take out daily and ask for a higher daily withdrawal limit if you want to get more cash at once. Note that European ATMs will withdraw funds only from checking accounts; you're unlikely to have access to your savings account.

Ask about fees. For any purchase or withdrawal made with a card, you may be charged a currency conversion fee (1-3 percent) and/or a Visa or MasterCard international transaction fee (1 percent). If you're getting a bad deal, consider getting a new debit or credit card. Reputable no-fee cards include those from Capital One, as well as Charles Schwab debit cards. Most credit unions and some airline loyalty cards have low-to-no international transaction fees.

IN EUROPE
Using Cash Machines

European cash machines have English-language instructions and work just like they do at home—except they spit out local currency instead of dollars, calculated at the day's standard bank-to-bank rate.

In most places, ATMs are easy to locate—in Germany ask for a *Geldautomat*. When possible, withdraw cash from a bank-run ATM located just outside that bank. Ideally use it during the bank's opening hours so if your card is munched by the machine, you can go inside for help.

If your debit card doesn't work, try a lower amount—your request may have exceeded your withdrawal limit or the ATM's limit. If you still have a problem, try a different ATM or come back later—your bank's network may be temporarily down.

Avoid "independent" ATMs, such as Travelex, Euronet, Moneybox, Cardpoint, and Cashzone. These have high fees, can be less secure than a bank ATM, and may try to trick users with "dynamic currency conversion" (see below).

Exchanging Cash

Avoid exchanging money in Europe; it's a big rip-off. In a pinch you can always find exchange desks at major train stations or airports—convenient but with crummy rates. Anything over 5 percent for a transaction is piracy. Banks generally do not exchange money unless you have an account with them.

Using Credit Cards

US cards no longer require a signature for verification, but don't be surprised if a European card reader generates a receipt for you to sign. Some card readers will accept your card as is; others may prompt you to enter your PIN (so it's important to know the code for each of your cards). If a cashier is present, you should have no problems. At self-service payment machines (transit-ticket kiosks, parking, etc.), results are mixed, as US cards may not work in unattended transactions. If your card won't work, look for a cashier who can process your card manually—or pay in cash.

Drivers Beware: Be aware of potential problems using a US credit card to fill up at an unattended gas station, enter a parking garage, or exit a toll road. Carry cash and be prepared to move on to the next gas station if necessary. When approaching a toll plaza, use the "cash" lane.

Dynamic Currency Conversion

If merchants offer to convert your purchase price into dollars (called dynamic currency conversion, or DCC), refuse this "service." You'll pay extra for the expensive convenience of seeing your charge in dollars. If an ATM offers to "lock in" or "guarantee" your conversion rate, choose "proceed without conversion." Other prompts might state, "You can be charged in dollars: Press YES for dollars, NO for euros." Always choose the local currency.

Security Tips

Pickpockets target tourists. Keep your cash, credit cards, and passport secure in your money belt, and carry only a day's spending money in your front pocket or wallet.

Before inserting your card into an ATM, inspect the front. If

PRACTICALITIES

anything looks crooked, loose, or damaged, it could be a sign of a card-skimming device. When entering your PIN, carefully block other people's view of the keypad.

Don't use a debit card for purchases. Because a debit card pulls funds directly from your bank account, potential charges incurred by a thief will stay on your account while the fraudulent use is investigated by your bank.

To access your accounts online while traveling, be sure to use a secure connection (see the "Tips on Internet Security" sidebar, later).

Damage Control for Lost Cards

If you lose your credit or debit card, report the loss immediately to the respective global customer-assistance centers. Call these 24-hour US numbers collect: Visa (tel. 303/967-1096), MasterCard (tel. 636/722-7111), and American Express (tel. 336/393-1111). In Germany, to make a collect call to the US, dial 0-800-225-5288. Press zero or stay on the line for an English-speaking operator. European toll-free numbers can be found at the websites for Visa and MasterCard.

You'll need to provide the primary cardholder's identification-verification details (such as birth date, mother's maiden name, or Social Security number). You can generally receive a temporary card within two or three business days in Europe (see www.ricksteves.com/help for more).

If you report your loss within two days, you typically won't be responsible for unauthorized transactions on your account, although many banks charge a liability fee of $50.

TIPPING

Tipping in Germany isn't as automatic and generous as it is in the US. However, tips are appreciated and expected. As in the US, the proper amount depends on your resources, tipping philosophy, and the circumstances, but some general guidelines apply.

Restaurants: You don't need to tip if you order your food at a counter. At German restaurants that have a wait staff, it's common to tip by rounding up (about 10 percent) after a good meal. For details on tipping in restaurants, see page 985.

Taxis: For a typical ride, round up your fare a bit (for instance, if your fare is €4.70, pay €5). If the cabbie hauls your bags and zips you to the airport to help you catch your flight, you might want to toss in a little more. But if you feel like you're being driven in circles or otherwise ripped off, skip the tip.

Services: In general, if someone in the service industry does a super job for you, a small tip of a euro or two is appropriate. If you're not sure whether (or how much) to tip, ask a local for advice.

GETTING A VAT REFUND

Wrapped into the purchase price of your German souvenirs is a value-added tax (VAT) of 19 percent. You're entitled to get most of that tax back if you purchase more than €25 (about $30) worth of goods at a store that participates in the VAT-refund scheme. Typically, you must ring up the minimum at a single retailer—you can't add up your purchases from various shops to reach the required amount. (If the store ships the goods to your US home, VAT is not assessed on your purchase.)

Getting your refund is usually straightforward...and worthwhile if you spend a significant amount on souvenirs.

Get the paperwork. Have the merchant completely fill out the necessary refund document, called a "Tax-Free Shopping Check." You'll have to present your passport. Get the paperwork done before you leave the store to ensure you'll have everything you need (including your original sales receipt).

Get your stamp at the border or airport. Process your VAT document at your last stop in the European Union (such as at the airport) with the customs agent who deals with VAT refunds. Arrive an additional hour before you need to check in to allow time to find the customs office —and wait. Some customs desks are positioned before airport security; confirm the location before going through security.

It's best to keep your purchases in your carry-on. If they're not allowed as carry-on (such as knives), pack them in your checked bags and alert the check-in agent. You'll be sent (with your tagged bag) to a customs desk outside security; someone will examine your bag, stamp your paperwork, and put your bag on the belt. You're not supposed to use your purchased goods before you leave. If you show up at customs wearing your new lederhosen, officials might look the other way—or deny you a refund.

Collect your refund. You can claim your VAT refund from refund companies, such as Global Blue or Planet, with offices at major airports, ports, or border crossings (either before or after security, probably strategically located near a duty-free shop). These services (which extract a 4 percent fee) can refund your money in cash immediately or credit your card (within two billing cycles). Otherwise, you'll need to mail the stamped refund documents to the address given by the shop where you made your purchase.

CUSTOMS FOR AMERICAN SHOPPERS

You can take home $800 worth of items per person duty-free, once every 31 days. Many processed and packaged foods are allowed, including vacuum-packed cheeses, dried herbs, jams, baked goods, candy, chocolate, oil, vinegar, mustard, and honey. Fresh fruits and vegetables and most meats are not allowed, with exceptions for some canned items. As for alcohol, you can bring in one liter duty-free (it can be packed securely in your checked luggage, along with any other liquid-containing items).

To bring alcohol (or liquid-packed foods) in your carry-on bag on your flight home, buy it at a duty-free shop at the airport. You'll increase your odds of getting it onto a connecting flight if it's packaged in a "STEB"—a secure, tamper-evident bag. But stay away from liquids in opaque, ceramic, or metallic containers, which usually cannot be successfully screened (STEB or no STEB).

For details on allowable goods, customs rules, and duty rates, visit http://help.cbp.gov.

Sightseeing

Sightseeing can be hard work. Use these tips to make your visits to Germany's finest sights meaningful, fun, efficient, and painless.

MAPS AND NAVIGATION TOOLS

A good map is essential for efficient navigation while sightseeing. The maps in this book are concise and simple, designed to help you locate recommended destinations, sights, and local TIs, where you can pick up more in-depth maps.

You can also use a mapping app on your mobile device. Be aware that pulling up maps or turn-by-turn walking directions on the fly requires an internet connection: To use this feature, it's smart to get an international data plan. With Google Maps or City Maps 2Go, it's possible to download a map while online, then go offline and navigate without incurring data-roaming charges, though you can't search for an address or get real-time walking directions. A handful of other apps—including Apple Maps, Off-Maps, and Navfree—also allow you to use maps offline.

PLAN AHEAD

Set up an itinerary that allows you to fit in all your must-see sights. For a one-stop look at opening hours, see the "At a Glance" sidebars for major cities (Munich, Salzburg, Dresden, Berlin, and Hamburg). Most sights keep stable hours, but you can easily confirm the latest by checking with the TI or visiting museum websites.

Don't put off visiting a must-see sight—you never know when a place will close unexpectedly for a holiday, strike, or restoration. Given how precious your vacation time is, I recommend getting reservations for any must-see sight that offers them (see page 25). Many museums are closed or have reduced hours at least a few days a year, especially on holidays such as Christmas, New Year's, and Labor Day (May 1). A list of holidays is in the appendix; check online for possible museum closures during your trip. In summer, some sights may stay open late; in the off-season, hours may be shorter.

Going at the right time helps avoid crowds. This book offers tips on the best times to see specific sights. Try visiting popular sights very early or very late. Evening visits (when possible) are usually peaceful, with fewer crowds.

If you plan to hire a local guide, reserve ahead by email. Popular guides can get booked up.

Study up. To get the most out of the self-guided tours and sight descriptions in this book, read them before you visit.

AT SIGHTS

Here's what you can typically expect:

Entering: Be warned that you may not be allowed to enter if you arrive less than 30-60 minutes before closing time. And guards start ushering people out well before the actual closing time, so don't save the best for last.

Many sights have a security check. Allow extra time for these lines. Most museums in Germany require you to check any bag bigger than a purse, and sometimes even purses. Museum lockers are free, but be prepared to pay a €1-2 deposit.

Photography: If the museum's photo policy isn't clearly posted, ask a guard. Generally, taking photos without a flash or tripod is allowed. Some sights ban selfie sticks; others ban photos altogether.

Temporary Exhibits: Museums may show special exhibits in addition to their permanent collection. Some exhibits are included in the entry price, while others come at an extra cost (which you may have to pay even if you don't want to see the exhibit).

Expect Changes: Artwork can be on tour, on loan, out sick, or shifted at the whim of the curator. Pick up a floor plan as you enter, and ask museum staff if you can't find a particular item.

Audioguides and Apps: Many sights rent audioguides, which generally offer useful recorded descriptions in English (about €2-5; often included with admission). Most of Berlin's top museums are run by the government, and include excellent audioguides with admission (you'll need to leave an ID as a deposit). Many audioguides have a standard output jack, so if you bring along your earbuds, you can often enjoy better sound. To save money, bring a Y-jack and share one audioguide with your travel partner.

PRACTICALITIES

Museums and sights often offer free apps that you can download to your mobile device (check their websites). And, I've produced free, downloadable audio tours for my Salzburg Town Walk, Berlin City Walk, Best of the Rhine Tour, Rothenburg Town Walk, and Munich City Walk; look for the ∩ in this book. For more on my audio tours, see page 26.

Services: Important sights usually have a reasonably priced on-site café or cafeteria (handy places to rejuvenate during a long visit). In Berlin, state-run museums offer free loaner stools, inviting you to camp out and really ponder your favorite work of art. The WCs at sights are free and generally clean.

Before Leaving: At the gift shop, scan the postcard rack or thumb through a guidebook to be sure that you haven't overlooked something that you'd like to see. Every sight or museum offers more than what is covered in this book. Use the information in this book as an introduction—not the final word.

Sleeping

Good-value accommodations in Germany are generally easy to find, comfortable, and include a hearty breakfast (typically an all-you-can-eat buffet). Choose from hotels; smaller, cheaper hotels and bed-and-breakfasts (called *Gasthof, Gasthaus,* or *Pension*); rooms in private homes (advertised with a *Zimmer Frei* sign); self-catering apartments rented by the week *(Ferienwohnung);* and hostels *(Jugendherberge).*

Extensive and opinionated listings of good-value rooms are a major feature of this book's Sleeping sections. Rather than list accommodations scattered throughout a town, I choose hotels in my favorite neighborhoods that are convenient to your sightseeing.

My recommendations run the gamut, from dorm beds to fancy rooms with all the comforts. I like places that are clean, central, relatively quiet at night, reasonably priced, friendly, small enough to have a hands-on owner or manager, and run with a respect for German traditions. I'm more impressed by a handy location and fun-loving philosophy than flat-screen TVs and a fancy gym. Most of my recommendations fall short of perfection. But if I can find a place with most of these features, it's a keeper.

Book your accommodations as soon as your itinerary is set, especially if you want to stay at one of my top listings or if you'll be traveling during busy times, such as Easter weekend, the first weekend and Ascension weekend in May, or Germany Unity Day on October 3. See the appendix for a list of major holidays and festivals in Germany.

Some people make reservations as they travel, calling ahead a few days to a week before their arrival. It's best to call hotels at

---

Sleep Code

Hotels in this book are categorized according to the average price of a standard double room with breakfast in high season.

$$$$	**Splurge:** Most rooms over €170
$$$	**Pricier:** €130-170
$$	**Moderate:** €90-130
$	**Budget:** €50-90
¢	**Backpacker:** Under €50
RS%	**Rick Steves discount**

Unless otherwise noted, credit cards are accepted, hotel staff speak basic English, and free Wi-Fi is available Comparison shop by checking prices at several hotels (on each hotel's own website, on a booking site, or by email). For the best deal, *book directly with the hotel*. Ask for a discount if paying in cash; if the listing includes **RS%**, request a Rick Steves discount.

---

about 9:00 or 10:00, when the receptionist knows which rooms will be available. Some apps—such as HotelTonight—specialize in last-minute rooms, often at business-class hotels in big cities. If you encounter a language barrier, ask the fluent receptionist at your current hotel to call for you.

RATES AND DEALS

I've categorized my recommended accommodations based on price, indicated with a dollar-sign rating (see sidebar). The price ranges suggest an estimated cost for a one-night stay in a standard double room with a private toilet and shower in high season, include breakfast, and assume you're booking directly with the hotel (not through a booking site, which extracts a commission). Room prices can fluctuate significantly with demand and amenities (size, views, room class, and so on), but these relative price categories remain constant.

Rates depend on the season and the day of the week, but peak times vary from one town to the next. Low season in Rothenburg is January-March, in Füssen it's October-May, and in Nürnberg it's July and August. While weekends are cheaper in Frankfurt and Nürnberg, weekdays are cheaper in Trier, Dresden, and Füssen. Munich hotels generally keep the same prices all week.

Room rates are especially volatile at larger hotels that use "dynamic pricing" to set rates. Prices can skyrocket during festivals and conventions, while business hotels can have deep discounts on weekends when demand plummets. Of the many hotels I recommend, it's difficult to say which will be the best value on a given day—until you do your homework.

Booking Direct: Once your dates are set, compare prices at

Using Online Services to Your Advantage

From booking services to user reviews, online businesses are playing a greater role in travelers' planning than ever before. Take advantage of their pluses—and be wise to their downsides.

Booking Sites

Hotel booking websites, including Priceline's Booking.com and Expedia's Hotels.com, offer one-stop shopping for hotels. While convenient for travelers, they present a real problem for small, independent, family-run hotels. Without a presence on these sites, these hotels become almost invisible. But to be listed, a hotel must pay a sizeable commission...and promise that its own website won't undercut the price on the booking-service site.

Here's the work-around: Use the big sites to research what's out there, then book directly with the hotel by email or phone, in which case hotel owners are free to give you whatever price they like. Ask for a room without the commission mark-up (or ask for a free breakfast if not included, or a free upgrade). If you do book online, be sure to use the hotel's website. The price will likely be the same as via a booking site, but your money goes to the hotel, not agency commissions.

As a savvy consumer, remember: When you book with an online booking service, you're adding a middleman who takes roughly 20 percent. To support small, family-run hotels whose world is more difficult than ever, book direct.

Short-Term Rental Sites

Rental juggernaut Airbnb (along with other short-term rental sites) allows travelers to rent rooms and apartments directly from locals, often providing more value than a cookie-cutter hotel. Airbnb fans appreciate feeling part of a real neighborhood and getting into a daily routine as "temporary Europeans." Depending on the host, Airbnb can provide an opportunity to get to know a local person, while keeping the money spent on

PRACTICALITIES

several hotels. You can do this by checking Hotels.com, Booking.com, and hotel websites. To get the best deal, contact family-run hotels directly by phone or email. When you go direct, the owner avoids the commission paid to booking sites, thereby leaving enough wiggle room to offer you a discount, a nicer room, or a free breakfast (if it's not already included). If you prefer to book online or are considering a hotel chain, it's to your advantage to use the hotel's website.

Getting a Discount: Some hotels extend a discount to those who pay cash or stay longer than three nights. And some accommodations offer a special discount for Rick Steves readers, indicated in this guidebook by the abbreviation **"RS%."** Discounts your accommodations in the community.

Critics view Airbnb as a threat to "traditional Europe," saying it creates unfair, unqualified competition for established guest-house owners. In some places, the lucrative Airbnb market has forced traditional guesthouses out of business and is driving property values out of range for locals. Some cities have cracked down, requiring owners to occupy rental properties part of the year (and staging disruptive "inspections" that inconvenience guests).

As a lover of Europe, I share the worry of those who see residents nudged aside by tourists. But as an advocate for travelers, I appreciate the value and cultural intimacy Airbnb provides.

User Reviews

User-generated review sites and apps such as Yelp and TripAdvisor can give you a consensus of opinions about everything from hotels and restaurants to sights and nightlife. If you scan reviews of a restaurant or hotel and see several complaints about noise or a rotten location, you've gained insight that can help in your decision-making.

But as a guidebook writer, my sense is that there is a big difference between the uncurated information on a review site and the vetted listings in a guidebook. A user-generated review is based on the limited experience of one person, who stayed at just one hotel in a given city and ate at a few restaurants there. A guidebook is the work of a trained researcher who forms a well-developed basis for comparison by visiting many restaurants and hotels year after year.

Both types of information have their place, and in many ways, they're complementary. If something is well reviewed in a guidebook and it also gets good online reviews, it's likely a winner.

PRACTICALITIES

vary: Ask for details when you reserve. Generally, to qualify for this discount, you must book direct (not through a booking site), mention this book when you reserve, show this book upon arrival, and sometimes pay cash or stay a certain number of nights. In some cases, you may need to enter a discount code (which I've provided in the listing) in the booking form on the hotel's website. Rick Steves discounts apply to readers with either print or digital books. Understandably, discounts do not apply to promotional rates.

Some cities require hoteliers to charge a daily tourist tax (about €1-5/person per night; in Berlin, it's 5 percent of the room rate). This may be included in the room price or may appear as an extra charge on your bill. In resort towns such as Baden-Baden and

Staufen, visitors pay a small spa tax (per person and per night) that's added to their bill.

Most hostels and some hotels and B&Bs offer half-board *(Halbpension)*, which means that dinner is included in the room price. This is often a good deal and gets you a hassle-free, value-priced three-course meal, but limits your choices. Many hotels (including the Ibis chain) give you the option of skipping breakfast and paying less. Although German hotel breakfasts are usually excellent, you can buy breakfast items easily and cheaply at a bakery or supermarket—the savings add up, especially for families.

TYPES OF ACCOMMODATIONS
Hotels

While I favor smaller, family-run hotels, occasionally a chain hotel can be a good value; the Europe-wide Ibis/Mercure chain has many options (www.accorhotels.com). I'm also impressed with the home-grown, Hamburg-based German chain called Motel One, which specializes in affordable style and has branches in Berlin, Munich, Nürnberg, Hamburg, Frankfurt, Cologne, Leipzig, Dresden, and other cities (www.motel-one.com). Because hotel chains tend to have multiple branches scattered across a city, be sure you're booking the location you want.

Because the train system in Germany is convenient and popular, both locals and foreigners have discovered that staying near the station saves hauling luggage. The concept of the train-station hotel, which went out of favor during the 20th century, is making a big comeback in Germany. Munich, Füssen, Baden-Baden, Frankfurt, Würzburg, Cologne, Nürnberg, Leipzig, and Dresden are among the destinations in this book that have good-value lodgings within steps of the train station.

In this book, the price for a double room in a hotel ranges from €50 (very simple, toilet and shower down the hall) to €400-plus (maximum plumbing and the works). In small towns, such as Bacharach or Rothenburg, you can find a good double with a private bath for under €80; in more expensive cities like Munich or Baden-Baden, you'll usually pay €100 or more. Breakfast is generally included in the quoted rate (except in Berlin), but you can usually add or remove a breakfast option when booking (sometimes continental, but often buffet; see "Eating," later in this chapter).

Some hotels can add an extra bed (for a small charge) to turn a double into a triple; some offer larger rooms for four or more people

(I call these "family rooms" in the listings). If there's space for an extra cot, they'll cram it in for you. In general, a triple room is cheaper than the cost of a double and a single. Three or four people can economize by requesting one big room.

Arrival and Check-In: Hotels and B&Bs are sometimes located on the higher floors of a multipurpose building with a secured door. In that case, look for your hotel's name on the buttons by the main entrance. When you ring the bell, you'll be buzzed in.

Hotel elevators are becoming more common, though some older buildings still lack them. When you're inside an elevator, press "E" to descend to the "ground floor" *(Erdgeschoss)*. You may have to climb a flight of stairs to reach the elevator (if so, you can ask the front desk for help carrying your bags up). Elevators are typically very small—pack light, or you may need to send your bags up without you.

The EU requires that hotels collect your name, nationality, and ID number. When you check in, the receptionist will normally ask for your passport and may keep it for anywhere from a couple of minutes to a couple of hours. (If you're not comfortable leaving your passport at the desk for a long time, ask when you can pick it up.)

If you're arriving in the morning, your room probably won't be ready. Check your bag safely at the hotel and dive right into sightseeing.

In Your Room: Most hotel rooms have a TV, telephone, and free Wi-Fi (although in old buildings with thick walls, the Wi-Fi signal might be available only in the lobby). Simpler places rarely have a room phone.

In Germany, beds usually come with a top sheet and blankets or a comforter. A double bed comes with two comforters—rather than one bigger one. It also frequently has two separate mattresses and sometimes two separate (but adjacent) frames—even if the bed is intended for couples. (A "real" double bed with a single mattress is called a *Französisches Bett*—a French bed.) Rooms with truly separate twin beds are less common in German hotels. When Americans request separate beds, German hotels sometimes give them normal doubles with complete sincerity—reasoning that the mattresses, though adjacent, are separate. More pillows and blankets are usually in the closet or available on request. Towels and linens aren't always replaced every day. Hang your towel up to dry.

Air-conditioning is rarely needed, and rare at smaller hotels. If you're here during a heat spell, ask to borrow a fan. Learn how the windows work: You'll often find the windows tipped open from the top to air out the room, with the window handle pointing up. To close the window, push it in and rotate the handle so it points down. The third handle position is horizontal, which lets you swing the entire window open.

Making Hotel Reservations

Reserve your rooms as soon as you've pinned down your travel dates. For busy national holidays, it's wise to reserve far in advance (see the appendix).

Requesting a Reservation: For family-run hotels, it's generally cheaper to book your room directly via email or a phone call. For business-class hotels, or if you'd rather book online, reserve directly through the hotel's official website (not a booking website). For complicated requests, send an email. Almost all of my recommended hotels take reservations in English.

Here's what the hotelier wants to know:

- Type(s) of rooms you want and size of your party
- Number of nights you'll stay
- Your arrival and departure dates, written European-style as day/month/year (18/06/20 or 18 June 2020);
- Special requests (en suite bathroom, cheapest room, twin beds vs. double bed, quiet room)
- Applicable discounts (such as a Rick Steves reader discount, cash discount, or promotional rate)

Confirming a Reservation: Most places will request a credit-card number to hold your room. If you're using an online reservation form, look for the *https* or a lock icon at the top of your browser. If you book directly, you can email, call, or fax this information.

Canceling a Reservation: If you must cancel, it's courteous—and smart—to do so with as much notice as possible, especially for smaller family-run places. Cancellation policies can be strict;

Most hotels have gone completely nonsmoking. Some hotels have nonsmoking rooms or floors—let them know your preference when you book.

Checking Out: While it's customary to pay for your room upon departure, it can be a good idea to settle your bill the day before, when you're not in a hurry and while the manager's in. That way you'll have time to discuss and address any points of contention.

Hotelier Help: Hoteliers can be a good source of advice. Most know their city well, and can assist you with everything from public transit and airport connections to finding a good restaurant, the nearest launderette, or a late-night pharmacy.

Hotel Hassles: Even at the best places, mechanical breakdowns occur: Sinks leak, hot water turns cold, toilets may gurgle or smell, the Wi-Fi goes out, or the air-conditioning dies when you need it most. Report your concerns clearly and calmly at the front desk.

If you find that night noise is a problem (if, for instance, your

From:	rick@ricksteves.com
Sent:	Today
To:	info@hotelcentral.com
Subject:	Reservation request for 19-22 July

Dear Hotel Central,

I would like to stay at your hotel. Please let me know if you have a room available and the price for:
- 2 people
- Double bed and en suite bathroom in a quiet room
- Arriving 19 July, departing 22 July (3 nights)

Thank you!
Rick Steves

read the fine print before you book. Many discount deals require prepayment, with no cancellation refunds.

Reconfirming a Reservation: Always call or email to reconfirm your room reservation a few days in advance. For B&Bs or very small hotels, I call again on my day of arrival to tell my host what time to expect me (especially important if arriving late—after 17:00).

Phoning: For tips on calling hotels overseas, see the "How to Dial" sidebar, later.

room is over a nightclub), ask for a quieter room in the back or on an upper floor. To guard against theft in your room, keep valuables out of sight. Some rooms come with a safe, and other hotels have safes at the front desk. I've never bothered using one and in a lifetime of travel, I've never had anything stolen from my room.

For more complicated problems, don't expect instant results. Above all, keep a positive attitude. Remember, you're on vacation. If your hotel is a disappointment, spend more time out enjoying the place you came to see.

Guesthouses

Guesthouses—the German equivalent to B&Bs—are small, warm, family-run accommodations. Known as *Pensionen, Gasthäuser,* or *Gasthöfe* in German, they are very common in areas popular with travelers (such as Germany's Rhine, Romantic Road region, and southern Bavaria, and Austria's Tirol and Salzburg). Compared to hotels, guesthouses give you double the cultural intimacy for half the price. While you may lose some of the conveniences of a hotel—such as in-room phones, frequent bed-sheet changes, and the ease of paying with a credit card—I happily make the trade-off for the lower rates and personal touches. If you have a reasonable but limited budget, skip hotels and look for smaller, family-run places.

Guesthouses range in size, with anywhere from 3 to 10 rooms (sometimes more), and many serve up a hearty breakfast. The smallest establishments are private homes with rooms *(Zimmer)* rented out to travelers for as little as €20 per person. In general, you can expect rooms in guesthouses to be clean, comfortable, and simple, though usually homey. Germans, especially in the south, are enthusiastic builders who like showing off their carpentry and decorating skills.

Rooms can run the gamut. Some are suite-like, with multiple rooms, separate entrances, and private baths. Others are spare bedrooms in family homes, with no in-room plumbing (but you have access to the bathroom and shower in the home).

Germans depend heavily on expensive imported fuel and are very aware of their energy use. You'll endear yourself to your hosts if you turn off lights when you leave and avoid excessively long showers.

Finding and booking a guesthouse is no different than reserving a hotel. Even most smaller places are listed on hotel-booking websites—but a direct booking is especially appreciated at mom-and-pop places, and will likely net you a better price. Private rooms are also available through Airbnb-type services (described next). If you haven't booked ahead, look for signs that say *Zimmer frei* (green), which means rooms are available; *Zimmer belegt* (orange) means no vacancy. TIs often have a list of guesthouses; use their list to book rooms yourself to avoid having the TI take a cut from you and your host.

Short-Term Rentals

A short-term rental—whether an apartment, house, or room in a local's home—is an increasingly popular alternative, especially if you plan to settle in one location for several nights. For stays longer than a few days, you can usually find a rental that's comparable to—and cheaper than—a hotel room with similar amenities. Plus, you'll get a behind-the-scenes peek into how locals live.

Many places require a minimum stay and have strict cancellation policies. And you're generally on your own: There's no hotel reception desk, breakfast, or daily cleaning service.

Finding Accommodations: Aggregator websites such as Airbnb, FlipKey, Booking.com, and the HomeAway family of sites (HomeAway, VRBO, and VacationRentals) let you browse properties and correspond directly with European property owners or managers. If you prefer to work from a curated list of accommodations, consider using a rental agency such as InterhomeUSA.com or RentaVilla.com. Agency-represented apartments typically cost more, but this method often offers more help and safeguards than booking direct.

Before you commit, be clear on the location. I like to virtually "explore" the neighborhood using the Street View feature on Google Maps. Also consider the proximity to public transportation and how well-connected the property is with the rest of the city. Ask about amenities (elevator, laundry, Wi-Fi, parking, etc.). Reviews from previous guests can help identify trouble spots.

Think about the kind of experience you want: Just a key and an affordable bed...or a chance to get to know a local? There are typically two kinds of hosts: those who want minimal interaction with their guests, and hosts who are friendly and may want to interact with you. Read the promotional text and online reviews to help shape your decision.

Confirming and Paying: Many places require you to pay the entire balance before your trip. It's easiest and safest to pay through the site where you found the listing. Be wary of owners who want to take your transaction offline to avoid fees; this gives you no recourse if things go awry. Never agree to wire money (a key indicator of a fraudulent transaction).

Apartments or Houses: If you're staying somewhere for four or more nights, it's worth considering an apartment or rental house (shorter stays aren't worth the hassle of arranging key pickup, buying groceries, etc.). Apartment or house rentals can be especially cost-effective for groups and families. European apartments, like hotel rooms, tend to be small by US standards. But they often come with laundry machines and small, equipped kitchens, making it easier and cheaper to dine in.

In rural areas, you can find reasonably priced vacation rentals *(Ferienwohnungen)*, ideal for families and small groups who want to explore a region. This kind of arrangement is very popular with German vacationers. You usually get a suite of two or three rooms with a kitchen. Owners discourage short stays and usually require a minimum rental period (3-5 days), and sometimes a deposit.

Rooms in Private Homes: Renting a room in someone's home is a good option for those traveling alone, as you're more likely to find true single rooms—with just one single bed, and a price to match. These can range from air-mattress-in-living-room basic to plush-B&B-suite posh. Some places allow you to book for a single night; if staying for several nights, you can buy groceries just as you would in a rental house. While you can't expect your host to also be your tour guide—or even to provide you with much info—

some may be interested in getting to know the travelers who come through their home.

Other Options: Swapping homes with a local works for people with an appealing place to offer (don't assume where you live is not interesting to Europeans). A good place to start is HomeExchange. To sleep for free, Couchsurfing.com is a vagabond's alternative to Airbnb. It lists millions of outgoing members, who host fellow "surfers" in their homes.

Hostels

A hostel *(Jugendherberge)* provides cheap beds where you sleep alongside strangers for about €25 per night. Travelers of any age are welcome if they don't mind dorm-style accommodations and meeting other travelers. Most hostels offer kitchen facilities, guest computers, Wi-Fi, and a self-service laundry. Hostels almost always provide bedding, but the towel's up to you (though you can usually rent one for a small fee). Family and private rooms are often available.

Independent hostels tend to be easygoing, colorful, and informal (no membership required; www.hostelworld.com). You may pay slightly less by booking directly with the hostel. **Official hostels** are part of Hostelling International (HI) and share an online booking site (www.hihostels.com). HI hostels typically require that you be a member or pay a bit more per night.

Eating

Germanic cuisine is heavy, hearty, and—by European standards—inexpensive. Each region has its specialties, which are often good values. Order house specials whenever possible. Though it's tasty, German food can get monotonous unless you look beyond the schnitzel and wurst. Fortunately, German chefs—especially in big cities—are increasingly adopting international influences, picking up previously unknown spices and ingredients to jazz up "Modern German" cuisine. Be adventurous.

For listings in this guidebook, I look for restaurants that are convenient to your hotel and sightseeing. When restaurant hunting, choose a spot filled with locals, not the place with the big neon signs boasting, "We Speak English and Accept Credit Cards." Venturing even a block or two off the main drag leads to higher-quality food for a better price.

RESTAURANT PRICING

I've categorized my recommended eateries based on the average price of a typical main course, indicated with a dollar-sign rating (see sidebar). Obviously, expensive specialties, fine wine, appetizers, and dessert can significantly increase your final bill.

The categories also indicate the personality of a place:

Budget eateries include street food, takeaway, order-at-the-counter shops, basic cafeterias, and bakeries selling sandwiches.

Moderate eateries are nice (but not fancy) sit-down restaurants, ideal for a straightforward, fill-the-tank meal. Most of my listings fall in this category—great for a good taste of local cuisine.

Pricier eateries are a notch up, with more attention paid to the setting, presentation, and (often inventive) cuisine. **Splurge** eateries are dress-up-for-a-special-occasion-swanky—typically with an elegant setting, polished service, intricate cuisine, and an expansive (and expensive) wine list.

BREAKFAST

Most German hotels and pensions include breakfast in the room price and pride themselves on laying out an attractive buffet spread. (However, in Berlin, hotels generally offer breakfast for an extra fee—it's usually not included in the base room price.) Even if you're not a big breakfast eater, take advantage of the buffet to fortify yourself for a day of sight-seeing.

Expect sliced bread, rolls, pastries, cereal, yogurt (both plain and with fruit), eggs, cold cuts, cheese, and fruit. You'll always find coffee, tea, and some sort of *Saft* (juice). Along with orange, apple, and grapefruit, multivitamin juice is popular. This sweet, smooth blend of various fruits is less acidic than a citrus juice. A bottle of mineral water is standing by to mix with any juice to turn it into a *Schorle* (spritzer).

For breakfast, most Germans prefer a sandwich with cold cuts and/or a bowl of *Müsli* (an oat cereal like granola, but less sweet), sometimes mixed with corn flakes. Instead of pouring milk over cereal, most Germans begin with a dollop of yogurt (or *Quark*—sweet curds that resemble yogurt), then sprinkle the cereal on top. If it's not sweet enough, drizzle on some *Honig* (honey). *Bircher Müsli* is a healthy mix of oats, nuts, yogurt, and fruit. To make a German-style sandwich for breakfast, layer *Aufschnitt* (cold cuts), *Schinken* (ham), *Streichwurst* (meat spread, most often *Leberwurst*—liver spread), and *Käse* (cheese) on a slice of bread or a roll.

If a buffet has eggs, they're most likely soft-boiled *(weichgekochte Eier)*. To eat it as the Germans do, set the egg in its stand,

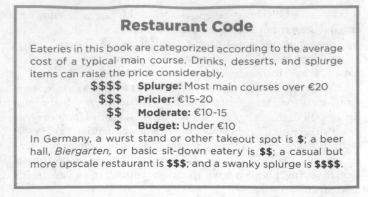

Restaurant Code

Eateries in this book are categorized according to the average cost of a typical main course. Drinks, desserts, and splurge items can raise the price considerably.

$$$$	**Splurge:** Most main courses over €20
$$$	**Pricier:** €15-20
$$	**Moderate:** €10-15
$	**Budget:** Under €10

In Germany, a wurst stand or other takeout spot is **$**; a beer hall, *Biergarten,* or basic sit-down eatery is **$$**; a casual but more upscale restaurant is **$$$**; and a swanky splurge is **$$$$**.

gently crack the shell around its perimeter and remove the top half, salt it, and eat it as if from a tiny bowl. Hard-boiled eggs *(hart-gekochte Eier)* are often served with rémoulade (similar to tartar sauce). Occasionally a buffet will have *Rühreier* (scrambled eggs) or *Spiegeleier* (fried eggs—literally "mirror eggs"—typically sunny-side up).

In some hotels, a small garbage can is set on the table for you to dispose of trash as you eat.

LUNCH AND DINNER

Traditional restaurants go by many names. For basic, stick-to-the-ribs meals—and plenty of beer—look for a beer hall *(Brauhaus)* or beer garden *(Biergarten). Gasthaus, Gasthof, Gaststätte,* and *Gasts-tube* all loosely describe an informal, inn-type eatery. A *Kneipe* is a bar, and a *Keller* (or *Ratskeller*) is a restaurant or tavern located in a cellar. A *Weinstube* serves wine and usually traditional food as well.

Germans are health-conscious and quite passionate about choosing organic *(Bio)* products: *Bio* fruits and vegetables, and even *Bio* bread, ice cream, and schnitzel. You'll often see footnotes on restaurant menus marking which dishes have artificial ingredients. However, despite Germans' healthy ways, many starchy, high-fat, high-calorie traditional foods remain staples of the national diet. (For a rundown of common German foods, see "Traditional German Fare," later.)

Most eateries have menus tacked onto their front doors, with an English menu inside. If you see a *Stammtisch* sign hanging over a table at a restaurant or pub, it means that it's reserved for regulars—don't sit here unless invited. Once you're seated, take your time—only a rude waiter will rush you. Good service is relaxed (slow to an American).

To wish others "Happy eating!" offer a cheery *"Guten Appetit!"* When you want the bill, say, *"Die Rechnung, bitte"* (dee REHKH-noong, BIT-teh).

Tipping: You only need to tip at restaurants that have table service. If you order your food at a counter, don't tip. At restaurants with wait staff, it's common to tip after a good meal by rounding up (roughly 10 percent). Rather than leaving coins behind on the table (considered slightly rude), Germans usually pay directly: When the server comes by with the bill, simply hand over paper money, stating the total you'd like to pay. For example, if paying for a €10 meal with a €20 bill, while handing your money to the server, say "Eleven, please" (or *"Elf, bitte"* if you've got your German numbers down). The server will keep a €1 tip and give you €9 in change.

Budget Tips

It's easy to eat a meal for €10 or less here. At lunchtime, locals grab a sandwich (around €2.50) and perhaps a pastry (€1-2) from one of the ubiquitous bakeries, which often have tables to sit at (but not table service). If there aren't any sandwiches on display at the bakery counter, ask to have one made for you.

Department-store cafeterias (usually on the top floor with a view) are common and handy, and they bridge the language barrier by letting you see your options. A *Schnellimbiss*—or simply *Imbiss*—is a small fast-food takeaway stand where you can get a bratwurst or other grilled sausage (usually less than €2, including a roll); for a rundown of common sausages, see the "Best of the Wurst," later.

All schnitzeled out? Ethnic restaurants provide a welcome break from Germanic fare. Italian, Turkish, and Asian food are generally a good value. A freshly baked pizza, a Turkish sandwich, or a rice or noodle dish will cost you €4-7, and can be packed up to enjoy on a park bench or in your room.

Stands and shops selling Turkish-style *döner kebab*—gyro-like, pita-wrapped rotisserie meat—are common (€4 at any time of day). Turkish cafés abound, selling not only the basic *döner kebab*, but also several variations, plus falafel (chickpea croquettes), "Turkish pizzas," and much more.

Some restaurants offer inexpensive €7-10 weekday hot-lunch specials that aren't listed on the regular menu (look for the *Tageskarte* or *Tagesangebot*, or just ask—sometimes available at dinner, too). For smaller portions, order from the *kleine Hunger* (small hunger) section of the menu. Simple dishes of wurst with sauerkraut and bread tend to run €6-8.

PRACTICALITIES

TRADITIONAL GERMAN FARE

Here are some typical dishes you'll see at German eateries.

Specialties

Traditional German dishes tend to be meat-heavy. The classic dish is sausage—hundreds of varieties of bratwurst, *Weisswurst,* and other types of wurst are served with sauerkraut as an excuse for a vegetable (for a list of common types of wurst, see the "Best of the Wurst" section, later).

Many traditional eateries serve some kind of meat on the bone, such as pork knuckle (called *Schweinshaxe* or *Eisbein* on menus) or shoulder, which has been boiled or roasted until tender. It goes down well with a big mug of beer. The fish and venison here are also good.

Another ubiquitous meat dish is schnitzel (a meat cutlet that's been pounded flat, breaded, and fried). Though traditionally made with veal, pork schnitzel is cheaper and more common.

You'll often see stuck on the beginning and end of menu items a form of the word *Braten* (which can mean "roasted" or "grilled" or "fried")—as in *Bratkartoffeln* (roasted potatoes), *Schweinebraten* (roasted pork), or *Bratwurst* (grilled sausage).

Here are a few other specialties—both regional and nationwide—to look for:

Aal Grün: Boiled eel served with *Spreewaldsauce* (parsley, dill, and cream sauce).

Dampfnudeln: Steamed bread roll with various toppings (also available sweet).

Eisbein (or **Hachse, Haxe, Schweinshaxe**): Boiled ham hock.

Flammkuchen (or **Dünnele**): German version of white pizza, on a thin, yeastless dough; the classic version is topped with bacon and onions.

Frikadellen (also called **Klopse;** in Berlin, **Buletten;** and in Bavaria, **Fleischpfanzerl**): Giant pan-fried meatball, sometimes flattened like a hamburger.

Geschnetzeltes: Strips of veal or chicken braised in a rich sauce and served with noodles.

Kassler (or **Kasseler**): Salted, slightly smoked pork.

Kohlrouladen: Cabbage rolls stuffed with minced meat.

Königsberger Klopse (or **Sossklopse**): Meatball with capers and potatoes in a white sauce (a staple of eastern Germany).

Kümmelbraten: Crispy roast pork with caraway.

Labskaus: Mushy mix of salted meat, potatoes, often beets, and sometimes herring, onions, and sour cream.

Leber Berliner Art: Pan-fried veal liver served with sautéed apple rings and onions.

Maultaschen ("mouth pockets"): Ravioli with various fillings, such as veal, cheese, and spinach.

Mett (or ***Hackepeter***): Raw, minced pork spread onto a roll.

Ratsherrentopf: Stew of roasted meat with potatoes.

Rollmops: Pickled herring fillets wrapped around a filling of pickled cucumber or onion. A popular hangover cure.

Rostbrätel: Marinated and grilled pork neck.

Rouladen (or ***Rinderrouladen***): Strip of beef rolled up with bacon, onion, and pickles, then braised.

Sauerbraten: "Sour"-marinated and roasted cut of beef (sometimes pork), typically served with red cabbage and potato dumplings.

Saure Zipfel: Bratwurst cooked in vinegar and onions.

Schäufele: Oven-roasted pork shoulder with gravy.

Schlachtplatte (or ***Schlachtschüssel***): "Butcher's plate"—usually blood sausage, *Leberwurst,* and other meat over hot sauerkraut.

Schnitzel Holstein: Schnitzel topped with a fried egg, capers, and anchovies.

Schweinebraten (or ***Schweinsbraten***): Roasted pork with gravy.

Senfeier: Hard-boiled eggs in mustard sauce served with potatoes (classic eastern German dish).

Spargel: Big, white or green asparagus in season in May and June.

Speckpfannkuchen: Large, savory crêpe with bacon.

Stolle (or ***Butterbrot***): Simple open-faced sandwich with butter and one topping.

Stolzer Heinrich: Grilled sausage in beer sauce (Berlin).

Best of the Wurst

Sausage (wurst) is a fast, tasty staple of the Germanic diet. Most restaurants offer it (often as the cheapest thing on the menu), but it's more commonly eaten at takeout fast-food stands (called *Würstchenbude* in Germany or *Würstelstand* in Austria). Options go far beyond the hometown hot dog. Most are pork-based. Generally, the darker the weenie, the spicier it is.

Sausages can be boiled or grilled. The generic term *Bratwurst* (or *Rostbratwurst*) simply means "grilled sausage." *Brühwurst* means boiled. *Kochwurst* describes sausage made of precooked ingredients, then lightly steamed. While some types of wurst can be found all over, others are unique to a particular area (as noted here).

When surveying your options at a sidewalk sausage stand or butcher *(Metzgerei),* these terms may help:

PRACTICALITIES

Blutwurst (or *Blunzen*): Made from congealed blood. Variations include *Schwarzwurst, Rotwurst,* and *Beutelwurst.*

Bockwurst: Thick pork-and-veal sausage with a mild, grassy flavor and a toothsome, smoky casing.

Bosna: Spicy sausage with onions and sometimes curry (Austrian).

Cervelat: Smoky, mild, chewy sausage that's butterflied at each end before grilling (mostly Swiss).

Currywurst: Grilled pork sausage (usually *Bockwurst*), often chopped into small pieces, with ketchup/curry sauce, served *mit* or *ohne Darm* (with or without skin; with skin tastes smokier).

Frankfurter: A skinny, pink, boiled sausage—the ancestor of our hot dog (also called *Wienerwurst, Wienerwürstchen,* or simply *Wiener*).

Jagdwurst: Baloney-like "hunter's sausage"—smoked pork with garlic and mustard.

Käsekrainer: Boiled, with melted cheese inside (Austrian).

Knackwurst (or *Knockwurst*): Short, stubby, garlicky, beef or pork sausage with a casing that "cracks" *(knackt)* when you bite into it.

Krakauer: Type of Polish sausage *(kiełbasa).*

Landjäger: Skinny, spicy, air-dried (almost withered and sometimes flattened, not round) salami. *Ahle Wurst* is similar.

Leberkäse: Finely ground corned beef, pork, bacon, and onions that's baked as a loaf (like a bologna sausage). *Leberkäsesemmel* is a pâté sandwich.

Leberwurst: Usually made from pig or calf livers and customarily served as a spread on open-face sandwiches, often with mustard or pickled cucumber.

Mettwurst: Made of minced pork that's cured and smoked.

Milzwurst: Made of pig spleen *(Milzstückchen).*

Nürnberger: Short and spicy grilled pork sausage from Nürnberg (also available throughout Bavaria), usually eaten three or six (or more) at a time, often lined up in a bun *(Drei im Weggla* means "three in bun").

Saumagen: "Sow's stomach" stuffed with meat, vegetables, and spices.

Teewurst: Air-dried, often smoked pork sausage similar to prosciutto, traditionally spread on bread and eaten at teatime (hence the name). It can also be grilled.

Thüringer: Long, skinny, peppery, and wedged into a much shorter roll. *Thüringer Rotwurst* is a blood-sausage variation.

Weisswurst: Boiled white sausage (peel off the casing before you eat it), served with sweet mustard and a pretzel (traditionally from Munich but served at any Bavarian-themed restaurant).

If it's *frisch* (fresh), you're supposed to "eat it before the noon bell tolls."

Zwiebelmettwurst: Spicy, soft sausage made with raw pork and onions; usually spread on bread, it comes *fein* (smooth) or *grob* (chunky).

Accompaniments: Sauces and sides include *Senf* (mustard; ask for *süss*—sweet; or *scharf*—spicy), ketchup, curry-ketchup, or *Currysauce* (a tasty curry-infused ketchup), *Kraut* (sauerkraut), and sometimes horseradish (called *Meerrettich* in the north, *Kren* in the south and Austria). *Grüne Sosse,* a green sauce made of sour cream blended with herbs, is a Frankfurt specialty.

At sausage stands, wurst usually comes with a roll (*Semmel*—not your typical hot-dog bun). The sausage might be inside the roll, or it may come on a plate with the roll to the side. You might be given the choice of a slice of bread *(Brot),* a pretzel *(Brezel),* or in restaurants, potato salad.

Starches

Besides bread *(Brot)* and potatoes (*Kartoffeln;* boiled, fried, or grilled), other typical starches include:

Kartoffelsalat: Potato salad.

Knödel: Large dumplings, usually made from potatoes but also from wheat, sourdough, semolina, or even liver; baseball-size dumplings are called *Klöss.*

Schupfnudeln: Stubby, diamond-shaped potato noodles.

Spätzle: Little noodles made from egg dough scraped through a wide-holed sieve; often served with melted cheese and fried onions as a standalone meal *(Käsespätzle).*

Salads

Germans make excellent salads, and most menus feature big, varied, dinner-size salad plates. Besides *grüner Salat* (mostly lettuce), you'll likely come across these options:

Bauernsalat: Greek salad, sometimes with sausage.

Bohnensalat: Bean salad.

Fleischsalat: Chopped cold cuts mixed with pickles and mayonnaise.

Gemischter Salat (or ***Bunter Salat***): A mixed salad of lettuce, fresh and (often) pickled veggies, and a tasty dressing.

Gurkensalat: Cucumber salad—usually just cukes in vinegar.

Nudelsalat: Pasta salad.

Ochsenmaulsalat: "Ox mouth salad" with vinegar, onion, and herbs.

Oliviersalat: Russian-style salad—potatoes, eggs, vegetables, and mayonnaise.

Wurstsalat: Chopped sausage in onion and vinegar.

Snacks

Pretzels *(Brezeln)*, either plain or buttered, make for an inexpensive snack. The brown crust comes from dunking them in water boiled with baking soda or lye.

Brotzeit ("bread time") is the all-purpose word for a light between-meals snack that's served cold. *Brotzeit* involves cold cuts, cheeses, breads, and other cold snacks, such as salads and some sausages. Other snack items include:

Kartoffelkäse: "Potato cheese" spread made of mashed potatoes, onion, and sour cream (but no cheese).

Krautsalat: "Coleslaw," basically cold sauerkraut.

Matjesfilet: Raw herring in yogurt.

Obatzda: Pungent Bavarian cheese spread with paprika and onions.

Schmalzbrot: Bread smeared with lard.

Schnittlauchbrot: Bread with cream cheese and diced chives.

Streichwurst: Meat spread; the most popular is *Leberwurst,* made from liver.

Sweets

Make sure to visit a bakery *(Bäckerei)* or pastry shop *(Konditorei)* to browse the selection of fresh pastries *(Feingebäck)* and cakes *(Kuchen)*. Pastries can include the familiar *Apfelstrudel* and croissant (sometimes called *Gipfel,* "peak"). Pastries often have a filling; these can include jam *(Marmelade* or *Konfitüre)*, apple *(Apfel)*, cherry *(Kirsche)*, raisins *(Rosinen)*, nut *(Nuss)*, almond *(Mandel)*, poppy seeds *(Mohn)*, or the sweet cheese curds called *Quark.* Don't mistake *Mohn* for cinnamon, which resembles *Mohn* but is far less common in German desserts. Here are some other sweets you might see:

Amerikaner: A flat, round doughnut with a thick layer of glaze frosting on top.

Berliner: A jelly-filled doughnut (also called *Krapfen* in Bavaria, or *Berliner Pfannkuchen* in Berlin).

Berliner Luft: An airy dessert made of cream, eggs, and gelatin, and served with raspberry sauce.

Rohrnudel: Roll-like sweet dumpling with raisins.

Schnecken: "Snail"-shaped pastry roll with raisins and nuts.

Gummi Bears from the German candy company Haribo are everywhere and taste better here close to the source. Ice-cream stores, often run by Italian immigrants, abound. While you can

PRACTICALITIES

always get a cone to go (ask for *eine Kugel,* a scoop—literally "ball"), many Germans sit down to enjoy their ice cream, ordering fancy sundaes in big glass bowls.

BEVERAGES
Water, Juice, and Soft Drinks

At restaurants, waiters aren't exactly eager to bring you *Leitungs-wasser* (tap water), preferring that you buy *Mineralwasser* (*mit/ohne Gas*—with/without carbonation). Half-liter mineral-water bottles are available everywhere for about €1. (I refill my water bottle with tap water.)

Popular soft drinks include *Apfelschorle* (half apple juice, half sparkling water) and *Spezi* (cola and orange soda). Menus list drink sizes by the tenth of a liter, or deciliter (dl): 0.2 liters is a small glass, and 0.4 or 0.5 is a larger one. Buy juice at a grocery store in cheap liter boxes, then drink some and store the extra in your water bottle.

At stores, most bottled water and soft drinks require a deposit (*Pfand;* usually €0.15 or €0.25—listed in small print on the shelf's price label), which is refunded if you return the bottle for recycling. You can generally return bottles to any supermarket, provided the bottle is a type they sell. Some supermarkets have vending machine-like bottle-return stations (marked *Leergutrück-gabe* or *Leergutannahme*) that issue a coupon after you insert your bottles (redeem when you pay for your groceries). If you don't want to bother getting your deposit back but do care about recycling, set the bottle on top of or right next to any trash can, whether on the street or in your hotel room. Chances are someone will collect it for the extra cash.

Beer

The average German drinks 40 gallons of beer a year and has a tremendous variety to choose from. *Flaschenbier* is bottled, and *vom Fass* is on tap. A typical bottle size is 33 centiliters (cl; about 12 ounces), and beer from the tap comes in 30 cl or 50 cl pours (10 or 17 ounces). When ordering beer in Bavaria, the standard order is *eine Mass* (a whole liter, or about a quart); for something smaller, ask for *eine Halbe* (a half-liter, not always available). For tips on visiting a *Biergarten,* see page 7.

Broadly speaking, most German beers fall into four main categories:

Helles Bier: Closest to American-style beer, this is the generic name for pale lager. Light-colored (but not "lite" as in low-calorie), a *helles Bier* is similar to a *Pilsner,* but with more malt. *Helles Bier* is usually served either in a straight glass (*Stange,*

PRACTICALITIES

meaning "rod," which its shape resembles) or a mug. Unfiltered lager (like cask ale) is *Kellerbier* or *Zwickelbier.*

Dunkles Bier: This is a general term for dark beer. Munich-style *dunkles* is sweet and malty, while farther north it's drier and hoppier. Variations include *Schwarzbier* (a "black" lager with a chocolaty flavor), *Rauchbier* (with a "smoky" flavor, from Bamberg), and *Weihnachsbier* (or *Festbier*—a seasonal Christmas beer). *Dunkles Bier,* like *helles Bier,* is typically served in a straight glass or mug.

Weissbier or **Weizenbier:** "White" or "wheat" beer (better known in North America as Hefeweizen) is a yeasty, highly caloric beer. It is poured slowly to build a frothy head in a tall, rounded-top glass and served with a lemon wedge. Unfiltered *Weissbier,* especially common in the south, is cloudy (and usually called *Hefeweizen*). *Kristallweizen* is a clear, filtered, yeast-free wheat beer. *Roggenbier* is darker colored and made with rye.

Pilsner (a.k.a. **Pilsener** or simply **Pils**): This is a barley-based, bottom-fermented, flavorful, hoppy, light-colored beer. Particularly common in the north, a *Pilsner* is usually served in a tall, slender, tapered, and sometimes stemmed glass. If it takes a while for the beer to arrive, it's because they're waiting for the head to die down.

Regional Specialties and Variations: *Kölsch* is Cologne's mild brew, served in trays of small, straight glasses. *Berliner Weisse* is a fizzy, slightly sour brew, often sweetened with a shot of syrup. The same approach helps sweeten *Leipziger Gose,* a very sour wheat beer. And Bavaria (Munich especially) has a wide array of special beers. Most famous are *Bockbier,* a high-alcohol, high-calorie, hoppy, bittersweet amber traditionally consumed during Lent (when monks were fasting and needed liquid nourishment); and *Märzenbier,* a light, malty, and highly alcoholic lager brewed in March *(März)* to be ready for Oktoberfest.

Other Beer Drinks: *Radler* (literally "bicyclist"—designed to be refreshing and not too intoxicating for a biker on a hot day) is half lager and half lemon soda. Wheat beer and lemon soda is *Russ* (or *Russ'n*). Cola-beer mixes are also common: *Diesel* (a.k.a. *Schmutziges* or *Krefelder*) is cola and lager, and *Colaweizen* is cola and wheat beer.

Nährbier ("Near Beer") is just that—low-alcohol lager. The closest thing to our "lite" beer is *leichtes Bier*—a low-calorie, low-alcohol wheat beer.

Nonalcoholic Beer: While virtually all nonalcoholic brews in the US are watery, bitter lagers, Germany produces some excellent alcohol-free white/wheat beers *(Weisses),* which have a somewhat sweeter flavor—very smooth drinking on a hot day. Teetotalers, or anyone who wants a refreshing beer at lunch without being tipsy all afternoon, can look for *"ohne Alkohol"* or *"alkoholfrei."* There's also the drink called *Malztrunk* (or *Malzbier*)—the sweet, malted beverage (resembling dark beer) that children quaff before they start drinking the real thing.

Wine

Though famous for its beer, Germany also has excellent wine. The best-known white wines are from the Rhine and Mosel, and there are some good reds (usually from the south), including *Dornfelder* (velvety, often oaky, sometimes sweet) and *Spätburgunder* (or *Blauburgunder;* German for "pinot noir").

Wein is commonly sold by the deciliter, with prices listed per 1 dl (sometimes written as 0.1 L on menus; 1 dl is about 3.5 ounces). You can order by the glass simply by asking for *ein Glas,* or to clarify that you don't want much, *eine Dezi* (one deciliter). For a mini-pitcher of wine, ask for *ein Viertel* (quarter-liter, about two glasses' worth). For a half-liter pitcher (about four glasses), request *ein Halber.* For white wine, ask for *Weisswein;* red wine is *Rotwein.* Order your wine *lieblich* (sweet), *halbtrocken* (medium), or *trocken* (dry).

Here are some of the white wines you may see:

Eiswein: Ultra-sweet dessert white made from frozen shriveled grapes.

Gewürztraminer: Aromatic, intense, and "spicy."

Grauburgunder: German for "pinot gris"—a soft, full-bodied white.

Liebfraumilch: Semisweet "beloved maiden's milk" blending Riesling with Silvaner and Müller-Thurgau.

Müller-Thurgau: Light and flowery, best when young, smooth, and semisweet.

Riesling: Fruity, fragrant, elegant.

Silvaner (or **Grüner Silvaner**): Acidic, fruity white from Franconia, comes in jug-shaped bottle.

Weinschorle: A spritzer of white wine pepped up with a little sparkling water.

Many hotels serve the inexpensive *Sekt,* or German champagne, at breakfast. Also keep an eye out for *Apfelwein* ("apple wine"—hard cider, especially popular in Frankfurt). In winter, *Gluhwein* (hot mulled wine) is popular.

Staying Connected

One of the most common questions I hear from travelers is, "How can I stay connected in Europe?" The short answer is: more easily and cheaply than you might think.

The simplest solution is to bring your own device—mobile phone, tablet, or laptop—and use it just as you would at home (fol-

Hurdling the Language Barrier

German—like English, Dutch, Swedish, and Norwegian—is a Germanic language, making it easier on most American ears than Romance languages (such as Italian and French). These tips will help you pronounce German words: The letter *w* is always pronounced as "v" (e.g., the word for "wonderful" is *wunderbar*, pronounced VOON-der-bar). The vowel combinations *ie* and *ei* are pronounced like the name  of the second letter—so *ie* sounds like a long *e* (as in *hier* and *Bier*, the German words for "here" and "beer"), while *ei* sounds like a long *i* (as in *nein* and *Stein*, the German words for "no" and "stone"). The vowel combination *au* is pronounced "ow" (as in *Frau*). The vowel combinations *eu* and *äu* are pronounced "oy" (as in *neu*, *Deutsch*, and *Bräu*, the words for "new," "German," and "brew"). To pronounce *ö* and *ü*, purse your lips when you say the vowel; the other vowel with an umlaut, *ä*, is pronounced the same as *e* in "men." (In written German, these can be depicted as the vowel followed by an *e—oe*, *ue*, and *ae*, respectively.) The letter Eszett (ß) represents *ss*. Written German capitalizes all nouns.

Though most young or well-educated Germans—especially those in the tourist trade and in big cities—speak at least some English, you'll get more smiles if you learn and use German pleasantries. Study the German survival phrases in the appendix. Give it your best shot. The locals will appreciate your efforts.

For more tips on hurdling the language barrier, consider the *Rick Steves German Phrase Book* (available at www.ricksteves.com).

lowing the tips below, such as getting an international plan or connecting to free Wi-Fi whenever possible). Another option is to buy a European SIM card for your US mobile phone. Or you can use European landlines and computers to connect. Each of these options is described below, and more details are at www.ricksteves.com/phoning. For a very practical one-hour talk covering tech issues for travelers, see www.ricksteves.com/mobile-travel-skills.

USING A MOBILE PHONE IN EUROPE

Here are some budget tips and options.

Sign up for an international plan. To stay connected at a lower cost, sign up for an international service plan through your carrier. Most providers offer a simple bundle that includes calling, messaging, and data. Your normal plan may already include international coverage (T-Mobile's does).

Before your trip, call your provider or check online to confirm that your phone will work in Europe, and research your provider's international rates. Activate the plan a day or two before you leave, then remember to cancel it when your trip's over.

Use free Wi-Fi whenever possible. Unless you have an unlimited-data plan, you're best off saving most online tasks for Wi-Fi. You can access the Internet, send texts, and even make voice calls over Wi-Fi.

Most accommodations in Europe offer free Wi-Fi, but some—especially expensive hotels—charge a fee. Many cafés (including Starbucks and McDonald's) have free hotspots for customers; look for signs offering it and ask for the Wi-Fi password when you buy something. You'll also often find Wi-Fi at TIs, city squares, major museums, public-transit hubs, airports, and aboard trains and buses.

Minimize the use of your cellular network. Even with an international data plan, wait until you're on Wi-Fi to Skype, download apps, stream videos, or do other megabyte-greedy tasks. Using a navigation app such as Google Maps over a cellular network can take lots of data, so do this sparingly or use it offline.

Limit automatic updates. By default, your device constantly checks for a data connection and updates apps. It's smart to disable these features so your apps will only update when you're on Wi-Fi. Also change your device's email settings from "auto-retrieve" to "manual" (or from "push" to "fetch").

When you need to get online but can't find Wi-Fi, simply turn on your cellular network just long enough for the task at hand. When you're done, avoid further charges by manually turning off data roaming or cellular data (either works) in your device's Settings menu. Another way to make sure you're not accidentally using data roaming is to put your device in "airplane" mode (which also disables phone calls and texts), and then turn your Wi-Fi back on as needed.

Use Wi-Fi calling and messaging apps. Skype, WhatsApp, FaceTime, and Google Hangouts are great for making free or low-cost calls or sending texts over Wi-Fi. With an app installed on your phone, tablet, or laptop, you can log on to a Wi-Fi network and contact friends or family members who use the same service. If you buy credit in advance, with some of these services you can call or send a text anywhere for just pennies per minute.

Some apps, such as Apple's iMessage, will use the cellular network if Wi-Fi isn't available: To avoid this possibility, turn off the "Send as SMS" feature.

How to Dial

International Calls

Whether phoning from a US landline or mobile phone, or from a number in another European country, here's how to make an international call. I've used one of my recommended Berlin hotels as an example (tel. 030/780-089-760).

Initial Zero: Drop the initial zero from international phone numbers—except when calling Italy.

Mobile Tip: If using a mobile phone, the "+" sign can replace the international access code (for a "+" sign, press and hold "0").

US/Canada to Europe

Dial 011 (US/Canada international access code), country code (49 for Germany), and phone number.

▸ To call the Berlin hotel from home, dial 011-49-30/780-089-760.

Country to Country Within Europe

Dial 00 (Europe international access code), country code, and phone number.

▸ To call the Berlin hotel from Spain, dial 00-49-30/780-089-760.

Europe to the US/Canada

Dial 00, country code (1 for US/Canada), and phone number.

▸ To call from Europe to my office in Edmonds, Washington, dial 00-1-425-771-8303.

Domestic Calls

To call within Germany (from one German landline or mobile phone to another), simply dial the phone number, including the initial 0 if there is one.

▸ To call the Berlin hotel from Munich dial 030/780-089-760.

More Dialing Tips

German Phone Numbers: Local phone numbers in Germany can vary in length (4-8 digits), as can area codes (3-5 digits). I keep it simple by always dialing the full number. Mobile phone numbers start with 015, 016, or 017, and cost more to

USING A EUROPEAN SIM CARD

With a European SIM card, you get a European mobile number and access to cheaper rates than you'll get through your US carrier. This option works best for those who want to make a lot of local calls, need a local phone number, or want faster connection speeds than their US carrier provides. It's simple: You buy a SIM card in Europe to replace the SIM card in your "unlocked" US phone or tablet (check with your carrier about unlocking it) or buy a basic cell phone in Europe.

call than landlines. Area codes are listed in this book, or you can get them from directory assistance (tel. 11833).

Toll and Toll-Free Calls: Some numbers, typically those that start with 018 (including some train and airline information numbers), are premium toll calls and cost more than a regular landline call. The per-minute charge should be listed in small print next to the phone number. International rates apply to US toll-free numbers dialed from Germany—they're not free.

More Phoning Help: See www.howtocallabroad.com.

European Country Codes		Ireland & N. Ireland	353 / 44
Austria	43	Italy	39
Belgium	32	Latvia	371
Bosnia-Herzegovina	387	Montenegro	382
Croatia	385	Morocco	212
Czech Republic	420	Netherlands	31
Denmark	45	Norway	47
Estonia	372	Poland	48
Finland	358	Portugal	351
France	33	Russia	7
Germany	49	Slovakia	421
Gibraltar	350	Slovenia	386
Great Britain	44	Spain	34
Greece	30	Sweden	46
Hungary	36	Switzerland	41
Iceland	354	Turkey	90

SIM cards are sold at department-store electronics counters, some newsstands, and vending machines. If you need help setting it up, buy one at a mobile-phone shop (you may need to show your passport). Costing about $5-10, SIM cards usually include prepaid calling credit, with no contract and no commitment. Expect to pay $20-40 more for a SIM card with a gigabyte of data.

There are no roaming charges for EU citizens using a domestic SIM card in other EU countries. Theoretically, providers don't have to offer Americans this "roam-like-at-home" pricing, but most do.

Tips on Internet Security

Make sure that your device is running the latest versions of its operating system, security software, and apps. Next, ensure that your device and key programs (like email) are password- or passcode-protected. On the road, use only secure, password-protected Wi-Fi hotspots. Ask the hotel or café staff for the specific name of their Wi-Fi network, and make sure you log on to that exact one.

If you must access your financial info online, use a banking app rather than accessing your account via a browser. A cellular connection is more secure than Wi-Fi. Avoid logging onto personal finance sites on a public computer.

Never share your credit-card number (or any other sensitive information) online unless you know that the site is secure. A secure site displays a little padlock icon, and the URL begins with *https* (instead of the usual *http*).

To be sure, buy your SIM card at a mobile-phone shop and ask if non-EU citizens also have roam-like-at-home pricing.

When you run out of credit, you can top your SIM card up at newsstands, tobacco shops, mobile-phone stores, or many other businesses (look for your SIM card's logo in the window), or possibly online.

WITHOUT A MOBILE PHONE

It's possible to travel in Europe without a mobile device. You can make calls from your hotel and check email or browse websites using public computers.

Most **hotels** charge a fee for placing calls—ask for rates before you dial. You can use a prepaid international phone card (usually available at newsstands, tobacco shops, and train stations) to call out from your hotel. Dial the toll-free access number, enter the card's PIN code, then dial the number. Even small hotels in Germany tend to have a direct-dial system, so callers can reach you without going through reception. Ask the staff for your room's specific telephone number.

You'll only see **public pay phones** in a few post offices and train stations. Most don't take coins but instead require insertable phone cards, which you can buy at a newsstand, convenience store, or post office. Except for emergencies, they're not worth the hassle.

Some hotels have **public computers** in their lobbies for guests to use; otherwise you may find them at public libraries (ask your hotelier or the TI for the nearest location). On a European keyboard, use the "Alt Gr" key to the right of the space bar to insert the extra symbol that appears on some keys. If you can't locate a special character (such as @), simply copy and paste it from a web page.

MAIL

You can mail one package per day to yourself worth up to $200 duty-free from Europe to the US (mark it "personal purchases"). If you're sending a gift to someone, mark it "unsolicited gift." For details, visit www.cbp.gov, select "Travel," and search for "Know Before You Go."

Get stamps at the neighborhood post office, or ask your hotel's front desk if they sell them. Some minimarts and card shops sell stamps as well. Avoid standing in line at the post office by using the handy yellow stamp *(Briefmarke)* machines found just outside the building. Warning: These machines give change only in stamps, not in coins.

The German postal service works fine, but for quick transatlantic delivery (in either direction), consider services such as DHL (www.dhl.com).

Transportation

Figuring out how to get around in Europe is one of your biggest trip decisions. **Cars** work well for two or more traveling together (especially families with small kids), those packing heavy, and those delving into the countryside. **Trains** and **buses** are best for solo travelers, blitz tourists, city-to-city travelers and those who want to leave the driving to others. Smart travelers can use short hop **flights** within Europe to creatively connect the dots on their itineraries. Just be aware of the potential downside of each option: A car is an expensive headache in any major city; with trains and buses you're at the mercy of a timetable; and flying entails a trek to and from a usually distant airport.

If your itinerary mixes cities and countryside, my advice is to connect cities by train (or bus) and to explore rural areas by rental car. Arrange to pick up your car in the last big city you'll visit, then use it to lace together small towns and explore the countryside. For more detailed information on transportation throughout Europe, see www.ricksteves.com/transportation.

I've included a sample itinerary for drivers (with tips and tweaks for those using public transportation) to help you explore Germany smoothly; you'll find it on page 20.

TRAINS

German trains—most operated by the Deutsche Bahn (DB), Germany's national railway—are speedy, comfortable, and nonsmoking. They cover cities and small towns well, but a few out-of-the-way places (such as Bavaria's Wieskirche) are only reachable by bus. Though German trains are fairly punctual, very tight connections can be a gamble. Once the obvious choice for long-distance travel

PRACTICALITIES

German Public Transportation

50 Kilometers
50 Miles

North Sea

Westerland • Tønder
• Tinglev • To Copenhagen

Niebüll • Flensburg

Husum • Schleswig
Heide • Rendsburg • Kiel
Neumünster

Cuxhaven
Norden • Wilhelmshaven
Emden • Bremerhaven
Groningen • Leer • Oldenburg • Bremen • Hamburg

Den Helder

NETHERLANDS
Lüneburg
Uelzen

Haarlem • Amsterdam • Schiphol
The Hague • Hengelo • Bad Bentheim • Celle • Wolfsburg
Rotterdam • Utrecht • Rheine • Osnabrück • Hannover
Arnhem • Emmerich • Münster • Braunschweig

Antwerp • Brussels
To Brussels • Maastricht • Duisburg • Essen • Dortmund • GERMA
Namur • Liege • Venlo • Mönchengladbach • Hagen • Göttingen
Aachen • Cologne • Wuppertal • Düsseldorf
Bonn • Siegen • Kassel
Siegburg

BELGIUM • Koblenz • Marburg • Bebra
Moselkern • (BURG ELTZ) • St. • Giessen • Eisenach
LUX. • Cochem • Hahn • Goar • Fulda • Meiningen
Luxembourg • Beilstein • Mainz • Frankfurt
Trier • Bacharach • Worms • Darmstadt • Würzburg
Metz • Mannheim • Heidelberg
To Paris • Forbach • Saarbrücken • Steinach • Nürnberg
Nancy • Rothenburg • ob der Tauber • Ansbach
Baden-Baden • Crailsheim • Dinkels-
Oos • Karlsruhe • Ellwangen • bühl
Strasbourg • Kehl • Baden- • Nördlingen • Treuchtlingen
Baden • Ingolstadt
FRANCE • Offenburg • Stuttgart
Colmar • Triberg • Ulm • Dachau
Titisee • Augsburg • Munich
Bad • Freiburg • Singen • Buchloe
Mulhouse • Kroz • Staufen • Fried. • Kempten • Ober-
Belfort • Konstanz • Lindau • ammergau
Basel • Bregenz • Murn.
SWITZERLAND • Zürich • Feldkirch • Reutte • Füssen
To • Bern • To • Luzern • To • LIECH. • Garmisch • Mitt.
Lausanne • Interlaken • Lugano • Innsbruck • To Italy

within Germany, trains now face competition from buses offering ultra-low fares (described later).

If you have a rail pass, you can hop on any train without much forethought (though for a small fee, you can reserve a seat on a fast train). Without a rail pass, you can save a lot of money by understanding the difference between fast trains and cheaper "regional" trains.

Types of Trains

Germany's three levels of trains differ in price, speed, and comfort. **ICE** trains (white with red trim and streamlined noses) are the fastest, zipping from city to city in air-conditioned comfort, and costing proportionately more. Midlevel **IC** and **EC** trains are also white with red trim, but look older than the ICEs. **Regional trains** (mostly red and labeled RB, RE, IRE, or S on schedules) are slowest but cost much less. Milk-run S and RB trains stop at every station.

If you have a rail pass, take the fastest train available; rail-pass holders don't pay a supplement for the fast ICE trains. If you're buying point-to-point tickets, taking a slower train can save a lot of money. You also save with day-pass deals valid only on slower trains.

Schedules

Schedules change by season, weekday, and weekend. Verify train times listed in this book at www.bahn.com. This website also includes public transport in cities (buses, trams, and subways). The handy DB Navigator app is also a useful tool for schedules.

At staffed train stations, attendants will print out a step-by-step itinerary for you, free of charge. You can also produce an itinerary yourself by using the trackside machines marked *Fahrkarten* (usually silver, red, and blue). The touch-screen display gives you an English option; choose "Timetable Information," indicate your point of departure and destination, and then hit "Print" for a personalized schedule, including transfers and track numbers.

If you're changing trains en route and have a tight connection, note the numbers of the platforms (*Bahnsteig* or *Gleis*) where you will arrive and depart (listed on itineraries). This will save you precious time hunting for your connecting train.

To reach Germany's train information number from anywhere

in the country, dial toll tel. 0180-699-6633 and ask for an English speaker.

Rail Passes

The single-country German Rail Pass can be a great value, often saving money while allowing you to hop on trains at your convenience (since most daytime routes in Germany, including fast ICE trains, do not require seat reservations). Rail passes are an even better deal if you're under 28 (you qualify for a youth pass) or traveling with a companion (you save with the "twin" rate). For only shorter hops, a rail pass probably isn't worth it, especially if you get discounts on point-to-point tickets and day passes (explained later).

If you're traveling beyond Germany (and beyond the international bus and train coverage of the German Rail Pass), consider the Eurail Global Pass, covering most of Europe. If you buy separate passes for neighboring countries, note that you'll use a travel day on each when crossing the border.

When choosing how many travel days you need for your rail pass, it can be worthwhile to buy an extra day (about $15-20 per person) even to cover short trips on regional trains--for instance, from Würzburg to Rothenburg--simply for the convenience of not having to buy tickets. Your rail pass covers certain extras, including travel on city S-Bahn systems (except in Berlin, where it's only good on S-Bahn lines between major train stations), German buses marked "Deutsche Bahn" or "DB" (run by the train company), and international express buses operated by Deutsche Bahn (covered by either a German Rail Pass or a pass for both countries of travel). Rail passes also get you a 20 percent discount on K-D Line boats on the Rhine and Mosel Rivers and the Romantic Road bus. Flexipass holders should note that fully covered ("free") trips start the use of a travel day, while discounted trips do not.

Because Salzburg, Austria is so close to the German border, traveling to or from the city on the main line from Munich counts as traveling within Germany, as far as your rail pass is concerned (Salzburg is the official border station on that line).

For more detailed advice on figuring out the smartest rail-pass options for your train trip, visit www.ricksteves.com/rail.

Point-to-Point Tickets

Ticket fares are shown in the "Rail Passes and Train Travel in Germany" sidebar, and for some journeys, at www.bahn.com and via the DB Navigator app (though not for most trains outside of Germany). Deutsche Bahn can charge a wide variety of fares for the same journey, depending on the time of day, how far ahead you

PRACTICALITIES

Rail Pass or Point-to-Point Tickets?

Will you be better off buying a rail pass or point-to-point tickets? It pays to know your options and choose what's best for your itinerary.

Rail Passes

A German Rail Pass lets you travel by train in Germany for three to fifteen days (consecutively or not) within a one-month period. Discounted "Twin" rates are offered for two people traveling together. Germany is also covered (along with most of Europe) by the classic Eurail Global Pass.

Discounted rates are offered for youths (ages 12-27). Up to two kids (ages 4-11) can travel free with each adult-rate pass (including the German Twin pass, but not with Eurail senior rates for ages 60 and up). All passes offer a choice of first or second class for all ages.

While most rail passes are best purchased outside Europe (through travel agents or Rick Steves' Europe), the German Rail Pass is also sold at main train stations and airports in Germany. For more on rail passes, including current prices, visit RickSteves.com/rail.

Point-to-Point Tickets

If you're taking just a couple of train rides, buying individual point-to-point tickets may save you money over a pass. Use this map to add up approximate pay-as-you-go fares for your itinerary, and compare that to the price of a rail pass. Keep in mind that significant discounts on point-to-point tickets may be available with advance purchase.

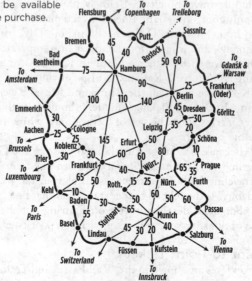

Map shows approximate costs, in US dollars, for one-way, second-class tickets on faster trains.

purchase the ticket, and other considerations. Know your options to get the best deal.

Kids: Kids ages 6-14 travel free with a parent or grandparent, but the ticket needs to list the number of children (unless purchased from a regional-train ticket machine). Kids under age 6 don't need tickets.

First Class vs. Second Class: First-class tickets usually cost 50 percent more than second-class tickets. While first-class cars are a bit more spacious and quieter than second class, the main advantage of a first-class ticket is the lower chance that the cars will fill up. Riding in second class gets you there at the same time, and with the same scenery. As second-class seating is still comfortable and quiet, most of my readers find the extra cost of first class isn't worth it. Germans tell me they never ride in first class unless someone else is paying for it.

Full-Fare Tickets *(Normalpreis):* The most you'll ever have to pay for a journey is the unrestricted *Normalpreis.* This full-fare ticket allows you to easily change your plans and switch to an earlier or later train, without paying a penalty. (If you buy a *Normalpreis* ticket for a slower train, though, you can't use it on a fast one without paying extra.)

Discount Fares *(Sparpreis):* If you reserve a ticket on a fast train at least a day in advance and are comfortable committing to specific departure times, you can usually save 25-75 percent over the *Normalpreis.* These tickets are more restrictive; you must take the train listed on the ticket (or pay a €19 fee to cancel at least one day ahead. Discounted fares go on sale nine months in advance and remain available until one day before departure, though the cheap seats often sell out earlier.

Savings on Slow Trains: You can always save money on point-to-point tickets if you're willing to skip Germany's high-speed trains (IC, EC, and ICE) and limit yourself to regional trains (most commonly labeled RB, RE, IRE, or S, but also a range of region-specific names). For example, Freiburg to Baden-Baden might cost €30 by ICE, €25 by EC, and €20 by RE train. To limit your search to these slower, cheaper trains, select "only local transport" on the Deutsche Bahn website or at ticket machines.

Day Passes

You may save even more with three types of extremely popular day passes valid only on slow trains: the various Länder-Tickets, the Schönes-Wochenende-Ticket, and the Quer-durchs-Land-Ticket. They are most cost-effective for groups of two to five people, but single travelers can benefit from them, too.

With a **Länder-Ticket,** up to five people traveling together get unlimited travel in second class on regional trains for one day at a very cheap price (generally €23-25 for the first person plus €4-6 for each additional person). There are a few restrictions: A Länder-Ticket only covers travel within a certain *Land* (Germany's version of a US state, such as Bavaria, Baden-Württemberg, Saxony, or Rheinland-Pfalz), doesn't work for the fastest classes of trains (ICE, IC, EC), and doesn't cover travel on weekdays before 9:00. Still, Länder-Tickets offer big savings, don't require advance purchase, and are also valid on local transit. For example, a Bayern-Ticket (the Bavarian version of a Länder-Ticket) not only gets you from Munich to Füssen, but also covers the bus from Füssen to Neuschwanstein and back.

Some scenarios: From Munich to Nürnberg, ICE express trains take one hour and 10 minutes and cost €56 at full fare; RE regional trains take at least 35 minutes longer and cost €38. However, a Bayern-Ticket lets one person ride the RE trains in Bavaria for only €25 (plus €6 for each additional person), provided you leave after 9:00. Plus, if you return that same day, there's no additional cost. The Baden-Ticket offers similar deals on the run from Freiburg to Baden-Baden, and the Rhineland-Pfalz-Ticket makes sense for longer day trips around the Rhine and the Mosel (for example, from Bacharach or Trier to Burg Eltz). Sometimes several smaller *Länder* are covered by a single ticket. For example, the Sachsen-Ticket covers trips in Saxony (including Dresden and Leipzig) as well as the neighboring *Länder* of Sachsen-Anhalt (Wittenberg) and Thuringia (Erfurt and Eisenach).

The **Quer-durchs-Land-Ticket** works like a Länder-Ticket, but gives you the run of the whole country. It's valid on any regional train anywhere in Germany, but doesn't include city transit (first person-€44, each additional passenger-€8, maximum of 5 travelers, only valid weekdays after 9:00).

The **Schönes-Wochenende-Ticket** is a cheaper weekend version of the Quer-durchs-Land Ticket, with looser conditions: It's valid on all regional trains on a Saturday or Sunday (starting at midnight, not 9:00), it does cover local transit in some areas (buses, trams, subways—check specifics when you buy), and additional travelers pay only €4 extra (first person-€40, maximum 5 travelers). Two people could make the four-hour trip from Frankfurt to Trier on regional trains for €52 with a Quer-durchs-Land ticket and for €44 with a Schönes-Wochenende-Ticket. This trip would otherwise cost €85 for two people. For even larger groups, these tickets save serious money.

Buying Tickets

Online: You can buy German train tickets online and print them out, or have them sent to your phone as an eticket; visit www.bahn.com and create a login and password. If you print out your ticket, the conductor may also ask to see your passport. You can also book seat reservations (optional) with a rail pass for trips within Germany—start to buy a regular ticket, then check the box for "reservation only." Another option is to use the DB Navigator app, which lets you buy tickets with your credit card—even for the same day of travel.

At the Station: Major German stations have a handy *Reisezentrum* (travel center) where you can ask questions and buy tickets (with a €2 markup for the personal service). You can also buy tickets from machines, which come in three types.

The silver, red, and blue touch-screen machines (marked with the Deutsche Bahn logo and *Fahrkarten*, which means "tickets") are user-friendly. They sell both short- and long-distance train tickets, and print schedules for free. Touch the flag to switch to English (some rare screens are German-only). You can pay with bills, coins, or credit cards—but US credit cards may not work.

There's one exception: Any trip that is entirely within the bounds of a regional transport network (i.e., Frankfurt-Bacharach or Nürnberg-Rothenburg) is considered local: Tickets can only be bought on the day of travel, and you must pay cash.

Each German city and region also has its own machines that sell only same-day tickets to nearby destinations (usually including Länder-Ticket day passes). In cities, these machines also sell local public transit tickets. At some smaller, unstaffed stations, these machines are the only ticket-buying option. You'll see the logo of the city or regional transport network on the machine. Increasingly, these machines are multilingual, with touch screens, and some even take American cards with a PIN (though others take only cash and German cards).

Some cities and regions still have older, silver ticket machines with smaller screens and plenty of buttons. To buy a train ticket from these machines, press the flag button until it gives you a screen in English. Then look for your destination on the long list of towns on the left side. If your destination isn't on the list (because it's too far away), you can buy the ticket on board (let the conductor know where you boarded so you won't have to pay the small markup for buying a ticket on the train). If your destination *is* on the list, note its four-digit code and enter it on the number pad. The machine defaults to a one-way *(Einfache)* second-class ticket, but you can alter that with the buttons below the keypad (press *Hin- und Rückfahrt* for a round-trip ticket, and *1./2. Klasse* for first class; also note the buttons for Länder-Ticket day passes and children's tickets). Feed the machine cash (small bills are OK, but it won't take credit cards), then collect your ticket and change. *Gut gemacht!* (Well done!)

On the Train: If you have enough cash, you can buy a ticket on board from the conductor for a long-distance journey by paying a small markup (US credit cards won't work unless they have a chip). But if you're riding a local (short distance) train, you're expected to board with a valid ticket...or you can get fined. Note that ticket checkers on local trains aren't necessarily in uniform.

Getting a Seat

As you board or exit a train, you'll usually have to push a button or flip a lever to open the door. Watch locals and imitate.

On the faster ICE, IC, and EC trains, it costs €4.50 extra per person to reserve a seat, which you can do at a station ticket desk, a touch-screen machine, or online (especially useful with a rail pass or a second-class ticket). If buying a first-class ticket on these trains, you can add a seat assignment for free at the time of purchase. German trains generally offer ample seating, but popular routes do fill up, especially on holiday weekends. If your itinerary is set, and you don't mind the small fee, seat reservations can be worth it for the peace of mind. They're especially smart for small groups and families (€9 reservation cap for families).

On ICE trains, families with small children can book special compartments called *Kleinkindabteil*, which have extra room for strollers and diaper changing, for the regular seat-reservation price.

With rare exceptions, there's no need to go through a US agent to make a seat reservation in advance of your trip; just do it online or at a German station. Reservations may be required on international trains and buses (specified in schedule). Slower regional trains don't even accept them.

If you have a seat reservation, while waiting for your train to arrive, note the departure time and *Wagen* (car) number and look along the train platform for the diagram *(Wagenstandanzeiger)* showing what sector of the platform the car will arrive at (usually A through F). Stand in that sector to avoid a last-minute dash to the right car or a long walk through the train to your seat. This is especially important for ICE trains, which are often divided into two unconnected parts.

If you're traveling without a reservation and are looking for an open seat, check the displays (or, in older trains, the slips of paper) that mark reserved seats. If you have a hard time finding an unreserved seat, take a closer look at the reservations—if you find a seat that's reserved for a leg of the journey that doesn't overlap with yours, you're free to take the seat. For example, if you're traveling from Frankfurt to Würzburg on a Munich-bound train, and you find a seat reserved only from Würzburg to Munich, it's all yours—you'll be getting off the train as the reservation holder boards in Würzburg.

In stations without elevators, you can take advantage of the luggage belts along the stairs to each platform. They start automatically when you put your bag on the bottom or top of the belt.

Bikes on Board

Your bike can travel with you for €5 per day on regional trains or €9 per trip on fast trains. Deutsche Bahn's helpful website even has a list of bike-rental shops that are in or near train stations. Rentals usually run about €10-15 a day, and some rental outfits offer easy "pick up here and drop off there" plans.

LONG-DISTANCE BUSES

While most American travelers still find the train to be the better option (mainly because rail passes make German train travel affordable and no-hassle), ultra-low-fare long-distance buses are worth considering. For example, a full-fare (second-class) train ticket from Munich to Nürnberg costs about €56, while a bus ticket for this route can cost €20 or less (as low as €6 if you're willing to buy a few days ahead and aren't picky about departure times).

While buses don't offer as extensive a network as trains, they do cover the most popular cities for travelers, often with a direct connection. The primary disadvantage to buses is a lack of travel flexibility: Buses are far less likely than trains to have a seat available for those who show up sans ticket (especially on either end of a weekend). And compared to trains, buses also offer fewer departures per day, though your options probably aren't too shabby on major routes served by multiple operators. Trains also beat buses in travel time and convenience, although often not by much. For the Munich-Nürnberg trip, bus travelers will spend about an hour longer en route than they would on the train (more if stuck in traffic—though train delays can happen, too).

Bus tickets are sold on the spot (on board and/or at kiosks at some bus terminals), but because the cheapest fares often sell out, it's best to book online as soon as you're sure of your plans (at a minimum, book a few days ahead to nab the best prices). The main bus operator is Flix-Bus (www.flixbus.de). Though not as comfortable as trains, their brightly colored buses are surprisingly well-outfitted and

PRACTICALITIES

make for a more pleasant ride than your average Greyhound trip. Most offer free Wi-Fi and on-board snack bars and WCs.

Bus terminals vary; you may find a true depot with ticket kiosks and overhead shelter, or just a stretch of street with a cluster of bus stops. Serious bus stations are labeled across Germany as "ZOB" (for *Zentraler Omnibusbahnhof*—central bus station). While most cities' bus terminals are usually a block or two from the train station, in some bigger cities (such as Munich and Berlin), bus travelers have to go a little farther afield to catch their ride.

TAXIS AND RIDE-BOOKING SERVICES

Most European taxis are reliable and cheap. In many cities, two people can travel short distances by cab for little more than the cost of bus or subway tickets. If you like ride-booking services such as Uber, their apps usually work in Europe just like they do in the US: Request a car on your mobile phone (connected to Wi-Fi or data), and the fare is automatically charged to your credit card.

RENTING A CAR

It's cheaper to arrange most car rentals from the US, so research and compare rates before you go. Most of the major US rental agencies (including Avis, Budget, Enterprise, Hertz, and Thrifty) have offices throughout Europe. Also consider the two major Europe-based agencies, Europcar and Sixt. Consolidators such as Auto Europe/Kemwel (www.autoeurope.com—or the sometimes cheaper www.autoeurope.eu) compare rates at several companies to get you the best deal.

Wherever you book, always read the fine print. Ask about add-on charges—such as one-way drop-off fees, airport surcharges, or mandatory insurance policies—that aren't included in the "total price."

Rental Costs and Considerations

Figure on paying roughly $250 for a one-week rental for a basic compact car. Allow extra for supplemental insurance, fuel, tolls, and parking.

Manual vs. Automatic: Almost all rental cars in Europe are manual by default—and cars with a stick shift are generally cheaper. If you need an automatic, request one in advance. When selecting a car, don't be tempted by a larger model, as it won't be as maneuverable on narrow, winding roads or when squeezing into tight parking lots.

Age Restrictions: Some rental companies impose minimum and maximum age limits. Young drivers (25 and under) and seniors (69 and up) should check the rental policies and rules section of car rental websites. If you're considered too young or too old, look into leasing (covered later), which has less stringent age restrictions.

Choosing Pick-up/Drop-off Locations: Always check the hours of the location you choose: Many rental offices close from midday Saturday until Monday morning and, in smaller towns, at lunchtime.

When selecting an office, plug the address into a mapping website to confirm the location. A downtown site is generally cheaper—and might seem more convenient than the airport. But pedestrianized and one-way streets can make navigation tricky when returning a car at a big-city office or urban train station. Wherever you select, get precise details on the location and allow ample time to find it.

Crossing Borders in a Rental Car: Be aware that international trips—say, picking up in Berlin and dropping off in Prague—can be expensive if the rental company assesses a drop-off fee for crossing a border.

Always tell your car-rental company exactly which countries you'll be entering. Some companies levy extra insurance fees for trips taken in certain countries with certain cars (such as BMWs, Mercedes, and convertibles). Double-check with your rental agent that you have all the documentation you need before you drive off (especially if you're crossing borders into non-Schengen countries, such as Croatia, where you might need to present proof of insurance).

Picking Up Your Car: Before driving off in your rental car, check it thoroughly and make sure any damage is noted on your rental agreement. Rental agencies in Europe tend to charge for even minor damage, so be sure to mark everything. Find out how your car's gearshift, lights, turn signals, wipers, radio, and fuel cap function, and know what kind of fuel the car takes (diesel vs. unleaded). When you return the car, make sure the agent verifies its condition with you. Some drivers take pictures of the returned vehicle as proof of its condition.

Car Insurance Options

When you rent a car in Europe, the price typically includes liability insurance, which covers harm to other cars or motorists—but not the rental car itself. To limit your financial risk in case of damage to the rental, choose one of these options: Buy a Collision Damage Waiver (CDW) with a low or zero deductible from the car-rental company (roughly 30-40 percent extra), get coverage through your credit card (free, but more complicated), or get collision insurance as part of a larger travel-insurance policy.

Basic **CDW** costs $15–30 a day and typically comes with a $1,000-2,000 deductible, reducing but not eliminating your financial responsibility. When you reserve or pick up the car, you'll be offered the chance to "buy down" the deductible to zero (for an additional $10–30/day; this is sometimes called "super CDW" or "zero-deductible coverage").

If you opt for **credit-card coverage,** you must decline all coverage offered by the car-rental company—which means they can place a hold on your card for up to the full value of the car. In case of damage, it can be time-consuming to resolve the charges. Before relying on this option, quiz your card company about how it works.

If you're already purchasing a **travel-insurance policy** for your trip, adding collision coverage can be an economical option. For example, Travel Guard (www.travelguard.com) sells affordable renter's collision insurance as an add-on to its other policies; it's valid everywhere in Europe except the Republic of Ireland, and some Italian car-rental companies refuse to honor it, as it doesn't cover you in case of theft.

For more on car-rental insurance, see www.ricksteves.com/cdw.

Leasing

For trips of three weeks or more, consider leasing (which automatically includes zero-deductible collision and theft insurance). By technically buying and then selling back the car, you save money on taxes and insurance. Leasing provides you a new car with unlimited mileage and a 24-hour emergency assistance program. You can lease for as little as 21 days to as long as five and a half months. Car leases must be arranged from the US. Two of several companies offering affordable lease packages are Renault Eurodrive and Auto Europe.

Navigation Options

If you'll be navigating using your phone or a GPS unit from home, remember to bring a car charger and device mount.

Your Mobile Phone: The mapping app on your phone works fine for navigation in Europe, but for real-time turn-by-turn directions and traffic updates, you'll need mobile data access. And driving all day can burn through a lot of very expensive data. The economical workaround is to use map apps that work offline. By downloading in advance from Google Maps, Apple Maps, Here WeGo, or Navmii, you can still have turn-by-turn voice directions and maps that recalibrate even though they're offline.

You must download your maps before you go offline—and it's smart to select large regions. Then turn off your data connection so you're not charged for roaming. Call up the map, enter your destination, and you're on your way. Even if you don't have to pay extra for data roaming, this option is great for navigating in areas with poor connectivity.

GPS Devices: If you want the convenience of a dedicated GPS unit, consider renting one with your car ($10-30/day). These units offer real-time turn-by-turn directions and traffic without the data requirements of an app. The unit may come loaded only with maps for its home country; if you need additional maps, ask. Also make sure your device's language is set to English before you drive off.

A less expensive option is to bring a GPS device from home. Be sure to buy and install the European maps you'll need before your trip.

Maps and Atlases: Even when navigating primarily with a mobile app or GPS, I always make it a point to have a paper map. It's invaluable for getting the big picture, understanding alternate routes, and filling in when my phone runs out of juice. The free maps you get from your car rental company usually don't have enough detail. It's smart to buy a better map before you go, or pick one up at European gas stations, bookshops, newsstands, and tourist shops.

Driving

Road Rules: Be aware of typical European road rules; for example, many countries require headlights to be turned on at all times, and nearly all forbid handheld mobile-phone use. In Germany, kids under age 12 (or less than about 5 feet tall) must ride in an appropriate child-safety seat. Seat belts are mandatory for all, and two beers under those belts are enough to land you in jail. You're required to use low-beam headlights if it's overcast, raining, or snowing. In Europe, you're not allowed to turn right on a red light, unless a sign or signal specifically authorizes it, and on expressways it's illegal to pass drivers on the right. Ask your car-rental company about these rules, or check the "International Travel" section of the US State Department website (www.travel.state.gov, search for your country in the "Country Information" box, then click on "Travel & Transportation").

Fuel: Unleaded gasoline comes in "Super" (95 octane) and "Super Plus" (98 octane). Pumps marked "E10" or "Super E10" mean the gas contains 10 percent ethanol—make sure your rental can run on this mix. You don't have to worry about learning the German word for diesel (it's *Diesel*). Your US credit and debit cards may not work at self-service gas pumps. Pay the attendant or carry enough euros.

Navigation: Use good local maps and study them before each drive. Learn which exits you need to look out for, which major cities you'll travel toward, where the ruined castles lurk, and so on.

Note: Your times may vary based on traffic, construction, and road conditions.

m = miles
h = hours
...... = ferry

North Sea

To Copenhagen 200m 4h

Flensburg

95m • 1.25h

Hamburg

NETHERLANDS

Amsterdam

165m • 2.5h

265m • 4.25h

310m • 4.5h

GER

360m • 5.5h

Brussels

Cologne

40m • .75h

90m • 1.5h

Aachen

230m • 3.5h

Erfurt

55m • .75h

BELGIUM

Koblenz

25m • .5h

140m • 2.25h

LUX.

Cochem

30m .5h

Bacharach

60m • 1h

Frankfurt

60m • 1h

125m • 2h

200m • 3.25h

55m 1h

Trier

70m • 1h

Würzburg

70m • 1.5h

175m • 2.5h

135m • 2.5h

40m .5h

Rothenburg

70m 1.25h

100m • 1.5h

Nürnberg

135m • 2h

Strasbourg

Baden-Baden

150m • 2h

100m • 1.75h

FRANCE

40m 1h

200m • 3.25h

Colmar

260m • 4h

35m 1h

Freiburg

175m • 3.75h

Munich

60m • 1.25h

Füssen

70m • 1.5h

95m • 1.75h

Zürich

55m • 1h

95m • 2.25h

70m 1.75h (via Reutte)

100m 1.5h

Appenzell

70m • 1.25h

Bern

SWITZERLAND

LIECH.

Innsbruck

20m 1.25h

To Brenner Pass

PRACTICALITIES

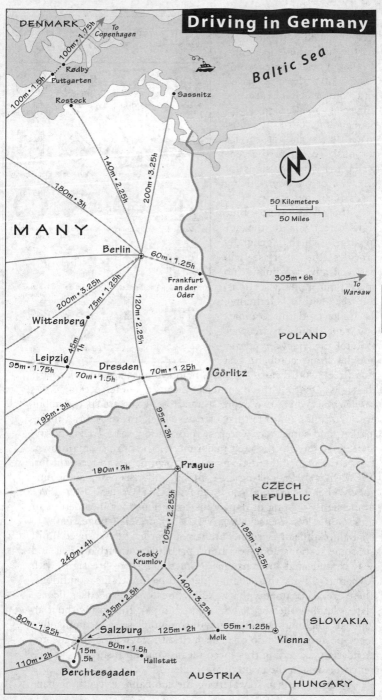

Every long drive between my recommended destinations is via the autobahn (super-freeway), and nearly every scenic backcountry drive is paved and comfortable. Learn the universal road signs (explained in charts in most road atlases and at service stations). To get to the center of a city, follow signs for *Zentrum* or *Stadtmitte*. Ring roads go around a city.

The Autobahn: Blue signs direct you to the autobahn, which generally provides the shortest trip between any two points (no speed limit in many sections, toll-free within Germany). To understand this complex but super-efficient freeway, look for the *Autobahn Service* booklet at any autobahn rest

STOP AND LEARN THESE ROAD SIGNS

Speed Limit (km/hr)	Yield	No Passing	End of No Passing Zone
One Way	Intersection	Main Road	Expressway
Danger	No Entry	Cars Prohibited	All Vehicles Prohibited
No Through Road	Restrictions No Longer Apply	Yield to Oncoming Traffic	No Stopping
Parking	No Parking	Customs or Toll Road	Peace

stop (free, lists all stops, services, road symbols, and more). Learn the signs: *Dreieck* ("three corners") means a Y-intersection; *Autobahnkreuz* is where two expressways cross. Exits are spaced about every 20 miles and often have a gas station, a restaurant, a minimarket, and sometimes a tourist information desk. Exits and intersections refer to the next major city or the nearest small town. Peruse the map and anticipate which town names to look out for. Know what you're looking for—miss it, and you're long autobahngone. When navigating, you'll see *Nord, Süd, Ost,* and *West*. Electronic signs warning of dangerous conditions may include one of these words: *Unfall* (accident), *Nebel* (fog), or *Stau* (congestion).

Autobahns in Germany are famous for having no speed limit, but some sections do have a limit, particularly in urban areas and near complicated interchanges. Sometimes there are signs with "dynamic" limits that change depending on traffic conditions. There are also cameras that take pictures of the speeder's license plate—so obey the law or be prepared to pay. In areas without an "official" maximum speed, you will commonly see a recommended speed posted. While no one gets a ticket for ignoring this recommendation, exceeding this speed means your car insurance no longer covers you in the event of an accident.

It's important to stay alert on the autobahn: Everything hap-

Key Phrases for Drivers

English	German
Exit	*Ausfahrt*
Gas station	*Tankstelle*
Traffic jam (ahead)	*Stau*
Detour	*Umleitung*
Toll	*Gebühr*
City center	*Zentrum/Stadtmitte*
Slow down	*Langsam*
Yield	*Vorfahrt beachten*
One-way street	*Einbahnstrasse*
No entry	*kein Einfahrt*
Pedestrian-only zone	*Füssgängerzone*
No parking	*Parken verboten*
(You're headed) out of town	*alle Richtungen*

pens much more quickly, and the speed differential between lanes can be dangerous for unaccustomed drivers. Watch for potential lane changers, whether from your right or from behind—a roaring Mercedes can appear out of thin air in your rearview mirror.

Even if you're obeying posted limits, don't cruise in the passing lane; stay right. Since it's illegal to pass on the right on the autobahn, drivers will angrily flash their lights, and possibly tailgate, if you drive in a passing lane. Obstructing traffic on the autobahn is against the law—so running out of fuel, or even cruising in the far-left lane—is not only dangerous, it can earn you a big ticket. In fast-driving Germany, the backed-up line caused by an insensitive slow driver is called an *Autoschlange*, or "car snake." What's the difference between a car snake and a real snake? According to locals, "On a real snake, the ass is in the back."

***Umweltplakette* for Driving in German Cities:** To drive into specially designated "environmental zones" *(Umweltzone)* in the centers of many German cities—including Munich, Freiburg, Frankfurt, Cologne, Dresden, Leipzig, and Berlin—you are required to display an *Umweltplakette* sticker. Literally "environmental sticker," these come standard with most German rental cars (ask when you pick up your car). If you're renting a car outside of Germany and plan to enter one of these cities, be sure you have one (sold cheap—around €10 at the border and at gas stations; you'll need the registration and legal paperwork that came with your rental; see www.umwelt-plakette.de).

Parking: To park on the street, pick up a plastic clock *(Parkscheibe,* available free at gas stations, police stations, and *Tabak* shops). Display your arrival time on the clock and put it on the dashboard, so parking attendants can see you've been there less than the posted maximum stay. Your US credit and debit cards may not work at automated parking garages—bring cash.

Theft: Thieves easily recognize rental cars and assume they are filled with a tourist's gear. Be sure all your valuables are out of sight and locked in the trunk, or even better, with you or in your room.

Driving in Austria: If you side-trip by car into Austria, bring your US driver's license and get an International Driving Permit (for details, go to www.ricksteves.com and search for "IDP"). Austria charges drivers who use their expressways. You'll need to have a *Vignette* sticker stuck to the inside of your rental car's windshield (€9 for 10 days, buy at border crossing, big gas stations near borders, or a rental-car agency). Place it on your windshield exactly as shown on the back of the sticker, and keep the lower tear-off portion—it's your receipt. Dipping into the country on regular roads—such as around Reutte in Tirol, or the less-direct route between the German border and Salzburg—requires no special payment. In Austria, green signs direct you to the autobahn, and autobahn speed limits are enforced.

FLIGHTS

To compare flight costs and times, begin with a travel search engine: Kayak.com is the top site for flights to and within Europe, easy-to-use Google Flights has price alerts, and Skyscanner.com includes many inexpensive flights within Europe.

Flights to Europe: Start looking for international flights about four to six months before your trip, especially for peak-season travel. Depending on your itinerary, it can be efficient and no more expensive to fly into one city and out of another. If your flight requires a connection in Europe, see my hints on navigating Europe's top hub airports at www.ricksteves.com/hub-airports.

Flights within Europe: Flying between European cities has become surprisingly affordable. Before buying a long-distance train or bus ticket, first check the cost of a flight on one of Europe's airlines, whether a major carrier or a no-frills outfit like EasyJet and Ryanair. Others with strong presence in Germany are Eurowings, Condor, WizzAir, and TUIfly. Be aware of the potential drawbacks of flying with a discount airline: nonrefundable and non-changeable tickets, minimal customer service, time-consuming treks to secondary airports, and stingy baggage allowances. To avoid unpleasant surprises, read the small print about the costs for "extras" such as reserving a seat, checking a bag, or checking in and printing a boarding pass.

Flying to the US and Canada: Because security is extra tight for flights to the US, be sure to give yourself plenty of time at the airport. It's also important to charge your electronic devices before you board because security checks may require you to turn them on (see www.tsa.gov for the latest rules).

Resources from Rick Steves

Begin Your Trip at RickSteves.com

My mobile-friendly **website** is *the* place to explore Europe in preparation for your trip. You'll find thousands of fun articles, videos, and radio interviews; a wealth of money-saving tips for planning your dream trip; travel news dispatches; a video library of my travel talks; my travel blog; my latest guidebook updates (www.ricksteves.com/update); and my free Rick Steves Audio Europe app. You can also follow me on Facebook, Instagram, and Twitter.

Our **Travel Forum** is a well-groomed collection of message boards where our travel-savvy community answers questions and shares their personal travel experiences—and our well-traveled staff chimes in when they can be helpful (www.ricksteves.com/forums).

Our **online Travel Store** offers bags and accessories that I've designed to help you travel smarter and lighter. These include my popular carry-on bags (which I live out of four months a year), money belts, totes, toiletries kits, adapters, guidebooks, and planning maps (www.ricksteves.com/shop).

Our website can also help you find the perfect **rail pass** for your itinerary and your budget, with easy, one-stop shopping for rail passes, seat reservations, and point-to-point tickets (www.ricksteves.com/rail).

Rick Steves' Tours, Guidebooks, TV Shows, and More

Small Group Tours: Want to travel with greater efficiency and less stress? We offer more than 40 itineraries reaching the best destinations in this book... and beyond. Each year over 30,000 travelers join us on about 1,000 Rick Steves bus tours. You'll enjoy great guides and a fun bunch of travel partners (with small groups of 24 to 28 travelers). You'll find European adventures to fit every vacation length. For all the details, and to get our tour catalog, visit www.ricksteves.com/tours or call us at 425/608-4217.

Books: *Rick Steves Germany 2020* is just one of many books in my series on European travel, which includes country and city guidebooks, Snapshots (excerpted chapters from bigger guides),

Pocket guides (full-color little books on big cities), "Best Of" guidebooks (condensed, full-color country guides), and my budget-travel skills handbook, *Rick Steves Europe Through the Back Door*. A more complete list of my titles—including phrase books, cruising guides, and more—appears near the end of this book.

TV Shows and Travel Talks: My public television series, *Rick Steves' Europe*, covers Europe from top to bottom with over 100 half-hour episodes—and we're working on new shows every year (watch full episodes at my website for free). Two *Rick Steves' Europe* TV shows worth viewing in particular are my *Berlin* episode and my one-hour special on *The Story of Fascism in Europe*. Or, try my free online video library, Rick Steves Classroom Europe, with a searchable database of short video clips on European history, culture, and geography (https://classroom.ricksteves.com). To raise your travel I.Q., check out the video versions of our popular classes (covering most European countries as well as travel skills, packing smart, cruising, tech for travelers, European art, and travel as a political act—www.ricksteves.com/travel-talks).

Radio: My weekly public radio show, *Travel with Rick Steves*, features interviews with travel experts from around the world. It airs on 400 public radio stations across the US, or you can hear it as a podcast. A complete archive of programs is available at www.ricksteves.com/radio.

Audio Tours on My Free App: I've produced dozens of free, self-guided audio tours of the top sights in Europe. For those tours and other audio content, get my free **Rick Steves Audio Europe app,** an extensive online library organized by destination. For more on my app, see page 26.

APPENDIX

Holidays and Festivals

This list includes selected festivals in major cities, plus national holidays observed throughout Germany. Many sights and banks close on national holidays—keep this in mind when planning your itinerary. Before planning a trip around a festival, verify the dates with the festival website, the Germany tourist office (www. germany.travel), or my "Upcoming Holidays and Festivals in Germany" web page (www.ricksteves.com/europe/germany/festivals). Austria's Salzburg has music festivals nearly every month (see the Salzburg chapter for more details).

Jan 1	New Year's Day
Jan 6	Epiphany (Heilige Drei Könige)
Early Jan	Perchtenlaufen (winter festival, parades), Tirol, Austria
Feb 20-26	Fasching (carnival season—parties, parades leading up to Ash Wednesday)
Spring	Thuringian Bach Weeks, Erfurt (3 weeks)
April 10-13	Easter weekend (Good Friday-Easter Monday)
Mid-April-early May	Spring Festival, Munich (Frühlingsfest, the "little sister of Oktoberfest") and Nürnberg

May 1	May Day with maypole dances, throughout Austria and Germany
Mid-May	International Dixieland Festival (www.dixielandfestival-dresden.com), Dresden
May 21	Ascension
Late May-early June	Weindorf wine festival and Mozartfest, Würzburg
Late May-early June	Fressgass' Fest, Frankfurt
May 29-June 1 (Pentecost weekend)	Carnival of Cultures (www.karneval-berlin.de), Berlin; Meistertrunk Show (play and market, medieval costumes, Biergarten parties, www.meistertrunk.de), Rothenburg
Mid-June	Luther's Wedding festival, Wittenberg
Mid-June	Stadtteilfest Bunte Republik Neustadt, Dresden (counterculture block party, www.brn-dresden.de)
June 11	Corpus Christi (Fronleichnam), southern and western Germany
Mid-June-mid-July	Tollwood, Munich (art, concerts, street theater, www.tollwood.de)
Late June	City Festival (www.elbhangfest.de), Dresden; Oberlindenhock (street food, beer and wine, live music), Freiburg; Midsummer Eve Celebrations, Austria
July	Kiliani Volksfest, Würzburg (county fair-type folk festival)
Early July	Open Air Festival, Berlin (music on Gendarmenmarkt, www.classicopenair.de)
Mid-July	Kinderzeche Festival (www.kinderzeche.de), Dinkelsbühl
Mid-July	Lichter Festival (fireworks and music, www.koelner-lichter.de), Cologne
Late July-early Aug	Schlossbergfest, Freiburg (music festival on Schlossberg mountain)
Late July-early Aug	Klassik Open Air (fireworks and classical music, www.klassikopenair.de), Nürnberg; Bardentreffen Nürnberg (world music, www.bardentreffen.de)
Early Aug	International Beer Festival, Berlin (www.bierfestival-berlin.de)
Aug 15	Assumption (Mariä Himmelfahrt)
Mid-Aug	Weindorf wine festival, Rothenburg

Late Aug	Museum Riverbank Festival, Frankfurt; wine festival, Cochem
Late Aug-early Sept	Rheingau Wine Festival, Frankfurt
Sept	International Literature Festival (www.literaturfestival.com), Berlin
Early Sept	Reichsstadt Festival (fireworks), Rothenburg
Sept 19-Oct 4	Oktoberfest (www.oktoberfest.de), Munich
Oct 3	German Unity Day (Tag der Deutschen Einheit), throughout Germany; party along Unter den Linden in Berlin
Mid-Oct	Festival of Lights, Berlin (landmark buildings artistically lit, www.festival-of-lights.de)
Oct 31	Reformation Day celebration, Wittenberg
Nov	Jazzfest Berlin (www.berlinerfestspiele.de)
Nov 1	All Saints' Day (Allerheiligen), southern and western Germany
Nov 11	St. Martin's Day (Martinstag, feasts)
Dec	Christmas markets throughout Germany, good ones in Nürnberg, Munich, Rothenburg, and Freiburg
Dec 6	St. Nikolaus Day (parades), throughout Germany
Dec 24	Christmas Eve (Heiliger Abend), when Germans celebrate Christmas
Dec 25	Christmas
Dec 31	New Year's Eve ("Silvester"), especially lively in Berlin

Books and Films

To learn more about Germany past and present, check out a few of these books and films.

NONFICTION

A Woman in Berlin: Eight Weeks in the Conquered City (Anonymous, 2006). This translated diary of a young German woman is a frank recounting of the post-surrender occupation of Berlin by Russian forces.

Berlin Diary: The Journal of a Foreign Correspondent (William Shirer, 1941). Stationed in Berlin from 1934 until 1940, CBS radio broadcaster Shirer delivers a vivid and harrowing day-by-day account of the rise of Nazi Germany.

Berlin Now—The City After the Wall (Peter Schneider, 2014). A long-time resident and journalist explores aspects of Berlin since 1989, including the Stasi legacy, the debate about how to preserve sections of the Wall, the city's frenetic club scene, thorny urban planning issues, and the ongoing BER airport debacle.

Berlin—Portrait of a City Through the Centuries (Rory MacLean, 2014). MacLean's colorful look at this pivotal and resilient city focuses on the people (from Frederick the Great to JFK to David Bowie) who were instrumental to its narrative—and its unique soul.

Boys in the Boat (Daniel James Brown, 2013). The true story of the University of Washington men's rowing team that defied the odds to win gold at Hitler's 1936 Berlin Olympics.

Culture Shock! Germany (Richard Lord, 2008). Lord provides cultural insights on German customs and etiquette.

Here I Stand: A Life of Martin Luther (Roland Bainton, 1950). Bainton delivers an authoritative biography of the man who initiated the Reformation.

In the Garden of Beasts (Erik Larson, 2011). Larson captures Berlin during the rise of the Nazis, as seen through the eyes of a reserved US ambassador to Germany and his socialite daughter.

Inside the Third Reich (Albert Speer, 1970). Based on 1,200 manuscript pages, this authoritative account of the years 1933-1945 was written by Hitler's chief architect and eventual armaments minister.

Martin Luther: A Life (Martin E. Marty, 2004). Marty offers a short, vivid biography of the irascible German reformer who transformed Western Christianity.

Night (Elie Wiesel, 1960). The Holocaust survivor and Nobel Peace Prize winner gives a candid and horrific account of existence in a Nazi concentration camp.

Peeling the Onion (Günter Grass, 2007). The Nobel Prize-winning author's memoir recounts his childhood in Danzig and his experiences as a soldier in the Nazi Waffen SS.

Stasiland: Stories from Behind the Berlin Wall (Anna Funder, 2002). Funder delivers a powerful account about the secrets of the Stasi, and how it affected the citizens of East Germany.

The Spy Who Came in From the Cold (John LeCarre, 1963). This spy novel about a British intelligence operation in Cold War East Germany was later made into a movie.

When in Germany, Do as the Germans Do (Hyde Flippo, 2002). Want to fit in? This lighthearted and helpful guide details the dos and don'ts of being German.

APPENDIX

FICTION

1632 (Eric Flint, 2000). This sci-fi/time travel series sends West Virginians back to 17th-century Germany.

Address Unknown (Kathrine Kressmann Taylor, 1939). Published before World War II and banished in Nazi Germany, this book warns of the terrors yet to come via a series of letters between a Jewish art dealer living in San Francisco and his former business partner.

All Quiet on the Western Front (Erich Maria Remarque, 1929). Young German classmates enlist in the German Army of World War I, only to find that war is not about glory and pride.

Berlin Noir (Philip Kerr, 1993). An ex-policeman turned detective struggles with secrets and crime in 1930s and '40s Berlin.

The Berlin Stories: The Last of Mr. Norris and Goodbye to Berlin (Christopher Isherwood, 1945). Composed of two novellas published in the 1930s, these stories capture the freewheeling early '30s Berlin and inspired the Broadway musical/motion picture *Cabaret*.

The Book Thief (Markus Zusak, 2007). This award-winning novel about a German girl who learns to read and then steals books the Nazis want to destroy is also a 2013 motion picture.

Floating in My Mother's Palm (Ursula Hegi, 1990). This best-selling novel follows the life of a young girl growing up in 1950s Burgdorf, a small German town on the Rhine. Hegi also wrote *Stones from the River*, based in the same small town.

The Magic Mountain (Thomas Mann, 1924). One of Germany's most influential and celebrated works of the 20th century takes place in a sanatorium in the Swiss Alps before and during World War I.

Marrying Mozart (Stephanie Cowell, 2008). Cowell's novel reveals a more intimate side of the famous composer.

Narcissus and Goldmund (Hermann Hesse, 1930). Hesse tells the story about two medieval men, one choosing life in a monastery and the other traveling the world. Also by the German-born Hesse is the popular *Siddhartha*, about a young man leaving his family.

The Reader (Bernhard Schlink, 1995). Told by a sympathetic narrator, this book challenges readers to ponder, "What if my loved ones had been Nazis?"

Saints and Villains (Denise Giardina, 1999). The author draws on the writings of Dietrich Bonhoeffer in this fictionalized account of the Protestant theologian who protested Hitler's rise.

The Silent Angel (Heinrich Böll, 1994). Soldier Hans Schnitzler returns from World War II unknowingly secreting a will that will change his life. Also by Böll: *Group Portrait with Lady*, about a war widow's attempt to save her Cologne apartment building from demolition.

The Tin Drum (Günter Grass, 1959). Grass' acclaimed novel tells the tale of a young boy who stands defiant against the Nazis, armed with only a drum and a piercing scream.

Winter (Len Deighton, 1987). Deighton's engrossing historical novel traces the lives of a German family from 1899 to 1945. The book also serves as a prequel to Deighton's masterful nine-part Cold War spy series, which kicks off with *Berlin Game* (1983).

FILM AND TV

The Baader Meinhof Complex (2008). Lightly fictionalized account of terrorism committed by radicalized Germans in 1967, rocking the still-fragile German democracy.

Backbeat (1994). This German/UK production chronicles the Beatles' time playing at dives in Hamburg, just before they hit it big.

Cabaret (1972). The multiple-Oscar-winning classic musical about 1930s Berlin, when Hitler and anti-Semitism was on the rise, and the only refuge was the cabaret.

The Counterfeiters (2007). This Oscar-winning film tells the story of Sachsenhausen Concentration Camp inmates forced to run a counterfeiting ring to undermine the British pound.

Das Boot (1981). Wolfgang Peterson's gritty film sinks any notion that war is glorious as it sails with the crew of a U-boat hunting Allied shipping during World War II.

Downfall (2004). Bruno Ganz delivers a frightening performance as Hitler in this story of Der Führer's final days in his Berlin bunker.

Good Bye, Lenin! (2003). In this funny, poignant film, a son struggles to re-create a pre-unification Berlin for his ailing communist mother.

Hannah Arendt (2012). This biographical drama examines the life of the German-Jewish philosopher who reported on Adolf Eichmann's 1961 Nazi war crimes trial for the *New Yorker*.

Head On (2004). Two mismatched Turkish-German lovers struggle with their heritage and personal issues in this culture-clash drama.

The Lives of Others (2006). In this gripping, Oscar-winning drama, a member of East Germany's secret police becomes too close to those whose lives he surveils.

Lore (2012). As the Allies swarm Germany at the end of World War II, a girl must lead her siblings to safety following their parents' disappearance.

The Marriage of Maria Braun (1979). Rainer Fassbinder's gritty meditation on post-WWII Germany is seen through the romantic woes of a young woman.

Mephisto (1981). This Oscar winner tells the tale of an actor who abandons his conscience and embraces the Nazis in order to further his career and standing. Bad move.

Metropolis (1927). Fritz Lang's landmark sci-fi epic (and silent film) is set in a futuristic city where the wealthy rule from high-rises while the underclass lives and toils underground.

The Miracle of Bern (2008). This popular film sets a moving father-son story against the backdrop of the West German soccer team's unexpected win in the 1954 World Cup in Bern, Switzerland.

North Face (2008). Gripping and grim, this historical drama set in 1936 centers on a pair of German mountain climbers attempting to be the first to conquer the deadly north face of the Eiger in the Swiss Alps.

Nowhere in Africa (2001). In this Academy Award winner, a Jewish family flees Germany in the 1930s and settles in Kenya.

Schindler's List (1993). Steven Spielberg's unflinching, Oscar-winning drama recounts a Nazi factory owner's inspirational efforts to save his Jewish employees from deportation to concentration camps.

Shoah (1985). This 9.5-hour Holocaust documentary includes no wartime footage, only interviews with those who lived through it.

Sophie Scholl: The Final Days (2005). This drama delivers a beautiful, devastating account of a German student who defied Hitler and paid with her life.

The Tin Drum (1979). This Academy Award-winning film is based on Günter Grass' seminal novel (see under "Fiction," earlier).

Triumph of the Will (1935). Leni Riefenstahl's infamous Nazi propaganda film shot during the 1934 Nazi Party rally in Nürnberg is notable for its groundbreaking cinematography.

Two Lives (2012). Bouncing between Norway and Germany, this film explores the struggle of children fathered by German soldiers in Norway during the Occupation.

Valkyrie (2008). This historical thriller chronicling the July 20, 1944 attempt to assassinate Hitler includes scenes shot on location in Berlin's Bendlerblock, the nerve center of the failed coup and now a memorial to the resistance effort.

The Wave (2008). Students at a high school quickly learn how easy it is to give in to the same social forces that enabled Nazi Germany (based on a real-life classroom experiment from 1967).

The White Ribbon (2009). A remote village in early-20th-century Germany, plagued by disturbing events, becomes a study in the roots of evil.

The White Rose (1982). This historical drama follows a group of Munich university students who form a resistance cell in defiance of the Nazis in 1942.

Wings of Desire (1987). Set in the former West Berlin, Wim Wenders' romantic fantasy tells the story of an angel who falls in love with a human. The story concludes in Wenders' 1993 sequel, *Faraway, So Close.*

Conversions and Climate

NUMBERS AND STUMBLERS

- Europeans write a few of their numbers differently than we do. 1 = 1, 4 = 4, 7 = 7.
- In Europe, dates appear as day/month/year, so Christmas 2021 is 25/12/21.
- Commas are decimal points and decimals are commas. A dollar and a half is 1,50, one thousand is 1.000, and there are 5.280 feet in a mile.
- When counting with fingers, start with your thumb. If you hold up your first finger to request one item, you'll probably get two.
- What Americans call the second floor of a building is the first floor in Europe.
- On escalators and moving sidewalks, Europeans keep the left "lane" open for passing. Keep to the right.

METRIC CONVERSIONS

A **kilogram** equals 1,000 grams (about 2.2 pounds). One hundred **grams** (a common unit at markets) is about a quarter-pound. One **liter** is about a quart, or almost four to a gallon.

A **kilometer** is six-tenths of a mile. To convert kilometers to miles, cut the kilometers in half and add back 10 percent of the original (120 km: 60 + 12 = 72 miles). One **meter** is 39 inches—just over a yard.

1 foot = 0.3 meter	1 square yard = 0.8 square meter
1 yard = 0.9 meter	1 square mile = 2.6 square kilometers
1 mile = 1.6 kilometers	1 ounce = 28 grams
1 centimeter = 0.4 inch	1 quart = 0.95 liter
1 meter = 39.4 inches	1 kilogram = 2.2 pounds
1 kilometer = 0.62 mile	32°F = 0°C

CLOTHING SIZES

When shopping for clothing, use these US-to-European comparisons as general guidelines (but note that no conversion is perfect).

Women: For pants and dresses, add 30 in Germany (US 10 = German 40). For blouses and sweaters, add 8 for most of Europe

(US 32 = European 40). For shoes, add 30-31 (US 7 = European 37/38).

Men: For shirts, multiply by 2 and add about 8 (US 15 = European 38). For jackets and suits, add 10. For shoes, add 32-34.

Children: Clothing is sized by height—in centimeters (2.5 cm = 1 inch), so a US size 8 roughly equates to 132-140. For shoes up to size 13, add 16-18, and for sizes 1 and up, add 30-32.

GERMANY'S CLIMATE

J	F	M	A	M	J	J	A	S	O	N	D
Berlin											
35°	37°	46°	56°	66°	72°	75°	74°	68°	56°	45°	38°
26°	26°	31°	39°	47°	53°	57°	56°	50°	42°	36°	29°
14	13	19	17	19	17	17	17	18	17	14	16
Munich											
35°	38°	48°	56°	64°	70°	74°	73°	67°	56°	44°	36°
23°	23°	30°	38°	45°	51°	55°	54°	48°	40°	33°	26°
15	12	18	15	16	13	15	15	17	18	15	16

First line, average daily high; second line, average daily low; third line, average days without rain. For more detailed weather statistics for destinations in this book (as well as the rest of the world), check www.wunderground.com.

APPENDIX

Fahrenheit and Celsius Conversion

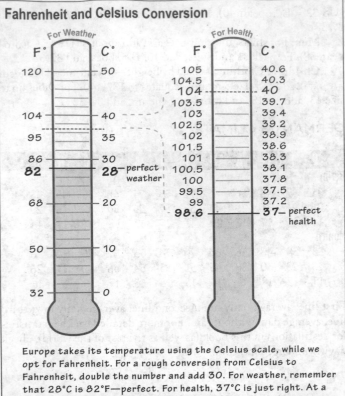

Europe takes its temperature using the Celsius scale, while we opt for Fahrenheit. For a rough conversion from Celsius to Fahrenheit, double the number and add 30. For weather, remember that 28°C is 82°F—perfect. For health, 37°C is just right. At a launderette, 30°C is cold, 40°C is warm (usually the default setting), 60°C is hot, and 95°C is boiling. Your air-conditioner should be set at about 20°C.

Packing Checklist

Whether you're traveling for five days or five weeks, you won't need more than this. Pack light to enjoy the sweet freedom of true mobility.

Clothing

- ☐ 5 shirts: long- & short-sleeve
- ☐ 2 pairs pants (or skirts/capris)
- ☐ 1 pair shorts
- ☐ 5 pairs underwear & socks
- ☐ 1 pair walking shoes
- ☐ Sweater or warm layer
- ☐ Rainproof jacket with hood
- ☐ Tie, scarf, belt, and/or hat
- ☐ Swimsuit
- ☐ Sleepwear/loungewear

Money

- ☐ Debit card(s)
- ☐ Credit card(s)
- ☐ Hard cash (US $100-200)
- ☐ Money belt

Documents

- ☐ Passport
- ☐ Tickets & confirmations: flights, hotels, trains, rail pass, car rental, sight entries
- ☐ Driver's license
- ☐ Student ID, hostel card, etc.
- ☐ Photocopies of important documents
- ☐ Insurance details
- ☐ Guidebooks & maps

Toiletries Kit

- ☐ Basics: soap, shampoo, toothbrush, toothpaste, floss, deodorant, sunscreen, brush/comb, etc.
- ☐ Medicines & vitamins
- ☐ First-aid kit
- ☐ Glasses/contacts/sunglasses
- ☐ Sewing kit
- ☐ Packet of tissues (for WC)
- ☐ Earplugs

Electronics

- ☐ Mobile phone
- ☐ Camera & related gear
- ☐ Tablet/ebook reader/laptop
- ☐ Headphones/earbuds
- ☐ Chargers & batteries
- ☐ Phone car charger & mount (or GPS device)
- ☐ Plug adapters

Miscellaneous

- ☐ Daypack
- ☐ Sealable plastic baggies
- ☐ Laundry supplies: soap, laundry bag, clothesline, spot remover
- ☐ Small umbrella
- ☐ Travel alarm/watch
- ☐ Notepad & pen
- ☐ Journal

Optional Extras

- ☐ Second pair of shoes (flip-flops, sandals, tennis shoes, boots)
- ☐ Travel hairdryer
- ☐ Picnic supplies
- ☐ Water bottle
- ☐ Fold-up tote bag
- ☐ Small flashlight
- ☐ Mini binoculars
- ☐ Small towel or washcloth
- ☐ Inflatable pillow/neck rest
- ☐ Tiny lock
- ☐ Address list (to mail postcards)
- ☐ Extra passport photos

German Survival Phrases

In the phonetics, ī sounds like the long i in "light," and bolded syllables are stressed.

English	German	Pronunciation
Good day.	Guten Tag.	**goo**-tehn tahg
Do you speak English?	Sprechen Sie Englisch?	**shprehkh**-ehn zee **ehgn**-lish
Yes. / No.	Ja. / Nein.	yah / nīn
I (don't) understand.	Ich verstehe (nicht).	ikh fehr-**shtay**-heh (nikht)
Please.	Bitte.	**bit**-teh
Thank you.	Danke.	**dahng**-keh
I'm sorry.	Es tut mir leid.	ehs toot meer līt
Excuse me.	Entschuldigung.	ehnt-**shool**-dig-oong
(No) problem.	(Kein) Problem.	(kīn) proh-**blaym**
(Very) good.	(Sehr) gut.	(zehr) goot
Goodbye.	Auf Wiedersehen.	owf **vee**-der-zayn
one / two	eins / zwei	īns / tsvī
three / four	drei / vier	drī / feer
five / six	fünf / sechs	fewnf / zehkhs
seven / eight	sieben / acht	**zee**-behn / ahkht
nine / ten	neun / zehn	noyn / tsayn
How much is it?	Wieviel kostet das?	**vee**-feel **kohs**-teht dahs
Write it?	Schreiben?	**shrī**-behn
Is it free?	Ist es umsonst?	ist ehs oom-**zohnst**
Included?	Inklusive?	in-kloo-**zee**-veh
Where can I buy / find ___?	Wo kann ich kaufen / finden...?	voh kahn ikh **kow**-fehn / **fin**-dehn
I'd like / We'd like...	Ich hätte gern / Wir hätten gern...	ikh **heh**-teh gehrn / veer **heh**-tehn gehrn
...a room.	...ein Zimmer.	īn **tsim**-mer
...a ticket to ___.	...eine Fahrkarte nach ___.	**ī**-neh **far**-kar-teh nahkh
Is it possible?	Ist es möglich?	ist ehs **mur**-glikh
Where is...?	Wo ist...?	voh ist
...the train station	...der Bahnhof	dehr **bahn**-hohf
...the bus station	...der Busbahnhof	dehr **boos**-bahn-hohf
...the tourist information office	...das Touristen-informations-büro	dahs too-**ris**-tehn-in-for-maht-see-**ohns**-**bew**-roh
...the toilet	...die Toilette	dee toh-**leh**-teh
men	Herren	**hehr**-rehn
women	Damen	**dah**-mehn
left / right	links / rechts	links / rehkhts
straight	geradeaus	geh-**rah**-deh-**ows**
What time does this open / close?	Um wieviel Uhr wird hier geöffnet / geschlossen?	oom **vee**-feel oor veerd heer göh **urf** neht / geh-**shloh**-sehn
At what time?	Um wieviel Uhr?	oom **vee**-feel oor
Just a moment.	Moment.	moh-**mehnt**
now / soon / later	jetzt / bald / später	yehtst / bahld / **shpay**-ter
today / tomorrow	heute / morgen	**hoy**-teh / **mor**-gehn

In a German Restaurant

English	German	Pronunciation
I'd like / We'd like...	Ich hätte gern / Wir hätten gern...	ikh **heh**-teh gehrn / veer **heh**-tehn gehrn
...a reservation for...	...eine Reservierung für...	ī-neh reh-zer-**feer**-oong fewr
...a table for one / two.	...einen Tisch für eine Person / zwei Personen.	ī-nehn tish fewr ī-neh pehr-zohn / tsvī pehr-**zoh**-nehn
Non-smoking.	Nichtraucher.	**nikht**-rowkh-er
Is this seat free?	Ist hier frei?	ist heer frī
Menu (in English), please.	Speisekarte (auf Englisch), bitte.	**shpī**-zeh-kar-teh (owf **ehng**-lish) **bit**-teh
service (not) included	Trinkgeld (nicht) inklusive	**trink**-gehlt (nikht) in-kloo-**zee**-veh
cover charge	Eintritt	**īn**-trit
to go	zum Mitnehmen	tsoom **mit**-nay-mehn
with / without	mit / ohne	mit / **oh**-neh
and / or	und / oder	oont / **oh**-der
menu (of the day)	(Tages-) Karte	(**tah**-gehs-) **kar**-teh
set meal for tourists	Touristenmenü	too-**ris**-tehn-meh-**new**
specialty of the house	Spezialität des Hauses	shpayt-see-ah-lee-**tayt** dehs **how**-zehs
appetizers	Vorspeise	**for**-shpī-zeh
bread / cheese	Brot / Käse	broht / **kay**-zeh
sandwich	Sandwich	**zahnd**-vich
soup	Suppe	**zup**-peh
salad	Salat	zah-**laht**
meat	Fleisch	flīsh
poultry	Geflügel	geh-**flew**-gehl
fish	Fisch	fish
seafood	Meeresfrüchte	**meh**-rehs-**frewkh**-teh
fruit	Obst	ohpst
vegetables	Gemüse	geh-**mew**-zeh
dessert	Nachspeise	**nahkh**-shpī-zeh
mineral water	Mineralwasser	min-eh-**rahl**-vah-ser
tap water	Leitungswasser	**lī**-toongs-vah-ser
milk	Milch	milkh
(orange) juice	(Orangen-) Saft	(oh-**rahn**-zhehn-) zahft
coffee / tea	Kaffee / Tee	kah-**fay** / tay
wine	Wein	vīn
red / white	rot / weiß	roht / vīs
glass / bottle	Glas / Flasche	glahs / **flah**-sheh
beer	Bier	beer
Cheers!	Prost!	prohst
More. / Another.	Mehr. / Noch eins.	mehr / nohkh īns
The same.	Das gleiche.	dahs **glīkh**-eh
Bill, please.	Rechnung, bitte.	**rehkh**-noong **bit**-teh
tip	Trinkgeld	**trink**-gehlt
Delicious!	Lecker!	**lehk**-er

For more user-friendly German phrases, check out *Rick Steves' German Phrase Book and Dictionary* or *Rick Steves' French, Italian & German Phrase Book.*

INDEX

MAP INDEX

Our website enhances this book and turns

Explore Europe

At ricksteves.com you can browse through thousands of articles, videos, photos and radio interviews, plus find a wealth of money-saving travel tips for planning your dream trip. And with our mobile-friendly website, you can easily access all this great travel information anywhere you go.

TV Shows

Preview the places you'll visit by watching entire half-hour episodes of Rick Steves' Europe (choose from all 100 shows) on-demand, for free.

your travel dreams into affordable reality

Radio Interviews

Enjoy ready access to Rick's vast library of radio interviews covering travel tips and cultural insights that relate specifically to your Europe travel plans.

Travel Forums

Learn, ask, share! Our online community of savvy travelers is a great resource for first-time travelers to Europe, as well as seasoned pros.

Travel News

Subscribe to our free Travel News e-newsletter, and get monthly updates from Rick on what's happening in Europe.

Classroom Europe

Check out our free resource for educators with 300+ short video clips from the Rick Steves' Europe TV show.

Audio Europe™

Rick's Free Travel App

Get your FREE **Rick Steves Audio Europe**™ app to enjoy…

- Dozens of self-guided tours of Europe's top museums, sights and historic walks
- Hundreds of tracks filled with cultural insights and sightseeing tips from Rick's radio interviews
- All organized into handy geographic playlists
- For Apple and Android

With Rick whispering in your ear, Europe gets even better.

Find out more at ricksteves.com

Pack Light and Right

Gear up for your next adventure at ricksteves.com

Light Luggage

Pack light and right with Rick Steves' affordable, custom-designed rolling carry-on bags, backpacks, day packs and shoulder bags.

Accessories

From packing cubes to moneybelts and beyond, Rick has personally selected the travel goodies that will help your trip go smoother.

Experience maximum Europe

Save time and energy

This guidebook is your independent-travel toolkit. But for all it delivers, it's still up to you to devote the time and energy it takes to manage the preparation and logistics that are essential for a happy trip. If that's a hassle, there's a solution.

Rick Steves Tours

A Rick Steves tour takes you to Europe's most interesting places with great

great tours, too!

with minimum stress

guides and small groups of 28 or less. We follow Rick's favorite itineraries, ride in comfy buses, stay in family-run hotels, and bring you intimately close to the Europe you've traveled so far to see. Most importantly, we take away the logistical headaches so you can focus on the fun.

travelers—nearly half of them repeat customers—along with us on four dozen different itineraries, from Ireland to Italy to Athens. Is a Rick Steves tour the right fit for your travel dreams? Find out at ricksteves.com, where you can also request Rick's latest tour catalog. Europe is best

Join the fun

This year we'll take thousands of free-spirited

experienced with happy travel partners. We hope you can join us.

See our itineraries at ricksteves.com

A Guide for Every Trip

BEST OF GUIDES

Full-color guides in an easy-to-scan format. Focused on top sights and experiences in the most popular European destinations

Best of England
Best of Europe
Best of France
Best of Germany
Best of Ireland
Best of Italy
Best of Scotland
Best of Spain

COMPREHENSIVE GUIDES

City, country, and regional guides printed on Bible-thin paper. Packed with detailed coverage for a multi-week trip exploring iconic sights and venturing off the beaten path

Amsterdam & the Netherlands
Barcelona
Belgium: Bruges, Brussels,
   Antwerp & Ghent
Berlin
Budapest
Croatia & Slovenia
Eastern Europe
England
Florence & Tuscany
France
Germany
Great Britain
Greece: Athens & the Peloponnese
Iceland
Ireland
Istanbul
Italy
London
Paris
Portugal
Prague & the Czech Republic
Provence & the French Riviera
Rome
Scandinavia
Scotland
Sicily
Spain
Switzerland
Venice
Vienna, Salzburg & Tirol

POCKET GUIDES
Compact color guides for shorter trips

Amsterdam
Athens
Barcelona
Florence
Italy's Cinque Terre
London
Munich & Salzburg

Paris
Prague
Rome
Venice
Vienna

SNAPSHOT GUIDES
Focused single-destination coverage

Basque Country: Spain & France
Copenhagen & the Best of Denmark
Dublin
Dubrovnik
Edinburgh
Hill Towns of Central Italy
Krakow, Warsaw & Gdansk
Lisbon
Loire Valley
Madrid & Toledo
Milan & the Italian Lakes District
Naples & the Amalfi Coast
Nice & the French Riviera
Normandy
Northern Ireland
Norway
Reykjavík
Rothenburg & the Rhine
Sevilla, Granada & Southern Spain
St. Petersburg, Helsinki & Tallinn
Stockholm

CRUISE PORTS GUIDES
Reference for cruise ports of call

Mediterranean Cruise Ports
Scandinavian & Northern European
 Cruise Ports

Complete your library with...

TRAVEL SKILLS & CULTURE
*Study up on travel skills and gain
insight on history and culture*

Europe 101
Europe Through the Back Door
European Christmas
European Easter
European Festivals
Postcards from Europe
Travel as a Political Act

PHRASE BOOKS & DICTIONARIES

French
French, Italian & German
German
Italian
Portuguese
Spanish

PLANNING MAPS

Britain, Ireland & London
Europe
France & Paris
Germany, Austria & Switzerland
Iceland
Ireland
Italy
Spain & Portugal

Credits

RESEARCHERS
For help with this edition, Rick relied on...

Ben Curtis

Ben is a native of the Pacific Northwest, but he's lived in the UK, Germany, Spain, Norway, Hungary, and a few other countries besides. He's worked as a professor of history and politics, a tour guide, and an advisor to the British government. These days, home is wherever he can go for a hike, listen to some Beethoven, and write.

Rosie Leutzinger

Rosie's love of travel was ingrained at an early age, thanks to family vacations to visit her British mother's family. Opportunities to play softball for Great Britain's national team, and professionally in Austria and Japan, turned that love of travel into an obsession. An editor at Rick Steves' Europe, she spends her time in Seattle trying all the hikes and baked goods time and appetite will allow.

Carrie Shepherd

After a childhood spent traipsing around New England, Carrie's college semester in London spurred her to explore and travel as much as her budget and employers allow. She's spent her career writing and editing arts and entertainment content, and now works as a guidebook editor and researcher for Rick Steves' Europe.

Robyn Stencil

Robyn's devotion to Germany began at a soccer camp watching the 1990 World Cup. Even after decades of forming deep connections to its language, land, and *Leute,* her heart still skips a beat whenever she sets foot in Deutschland. When not researching, trapezing, or running marathons, Robyn calls Everett, Washington home, and works as a tour product manager for Rick Steves' Europe.

Amanda Zurita

Amanda Zurita caught the travel bug early—she's been flying since before she could walk. For the last seven years she's worked in Europe as a researcher and tour guide for Rick Steves' Europe, exploring the rest of the world in the off-season. When she's not castle hopping on the Rhine, walking the walls in Rothenburg, or eating *Grüne Sosse* in Frankfurt, she lives in Seattle with her beloved Labrador, Hadrian.

CONTRIBUTORS
Cameron Hewitt

Born in Denver and raised in central Ohio, Cameron settled in Seattle in 2000. Ever since, he has spent three months each year in Europe, contributing to guidebooks, tours, radio and television shows, and other media for Rick Steves' Europe, where he serves as content manager. Cameron married his high school sweetheart (and favorite travel partner), Shawna, and enjoys taking pictures, trying new restaurants, and planning his next trip.

Gene Openshaw

Gene has co-authored a dozen *Rick Steves* books, specializing in writing walks and tours of Europe's cities, museums, and cultural sights. He also contributes to Rick's public television series, produces tours for Rick Steves Audio Europe, and is a regular guest on Rick's public radio show. Outside of the travel world, Gene has co-authored *The Seattle Joke Book*. As a composer, Gene has written a full-length opera called *Matter,* a violin sonata, and dozens of songs. He lives near Seattle with his daughter, enjoys giving presentations on art and history, and roots for the Mariners in good times and bad.

ACKNOWLEDGMENTS

Thanks to Ian Watson for writing the original version of the Hamburg chapter.

PHOTO CREDITS

914.304   Steves

Avalon Travel
Hachette Book Group
1700 Fourth Street
Berkeley, CA 94710

Printed in Canada by Friesens.
First printing September 2019

ISBN 978-1-64171-149-4

For the latest on Rick's talks, guidebooks, tours, public television series, and public radio show, contact Rick Steves' Europe, 130 Fourth Avenue North, Edmonds, WA 98020, 425/771-8303, www.ricksteves.com, rick@ricksteves.com.

Rick Steves' Europe
Managing Editor: Jennifer Madison Davis
Assistant Managing Editor: Cathy Lu
Special Publications Manager: Risa Laib
Editors: Glenn Eriksen, Julie Fanselow, Tom Griffin, Suzanne Kotz, Rosie Leutzinger, Teresa Nemeth, Jessica Shaw, Carrie Shepherd
Editorial & Production Assistant: Megan Simms
Editorial Interns: Maddy Smith, Maxwell Eberle
Researchers: Ben Curtis, Rosie Leutzinger, Carrie Shepherd, Robyn Stencil, Amanda Zurita
Contributors: Cameron Hewitt, Gene Openshaw
Graphic Content Director: Sandra Hundacker
Maps & Graphics: David C. Hoerlein, Lauren Mills, Mary Rostad
Digital Asset Coordinator: Orin Dubrow

Avalon Travel
Senior Editor and Series Manager: Madhu Prasher
Editors: Jamie Andrade, Sierra Machado
Copy Editor: Maggie Ryan
Proofreader: Denise Silva
Indexer: Stephen Callahan
Production & Typesetting: Lisi Baldwin, Jane Musser
Cover Design: Kimberly Glyder Design
Maps & Graphics: Kat Bennett, Mike Morgenfeld

Although every effort was made to ensure that the information was correct at the time of going to press, the author and publisher do not assume and hereby disclaim any liability to any party for any loss or damage caused by errors, omissions, lederhosen chafing, or any potential travel disruption due to labor or financial difficulty, whether such errors or omissions result from negligence, accident, or any other cause.

COLOR MAPS

Germany • Munich • Berlin • Bavarian Alps
• Berlin Public Transportation

Hamburg

BERLIN ⊛

POLAND

GERMANY

Wittenberg •

Leipzig •

NETH.

Cologne

Erfurt •

Dresden •

BELGIUM

Bacharach

LUX.

Beilstein

• Trier

Frankfurt

Nürnberg •

Würzburg

CZECH REPUBLIC

• Rothenburg

Baden-Baden

200 Kilometers

• Freiburg

Dachau •

MUNICH

300 Miles

• Staufen

FÜSSEN

• SALZBURG

FRANCE

Reutte

AUSTRIA

SWITZ.

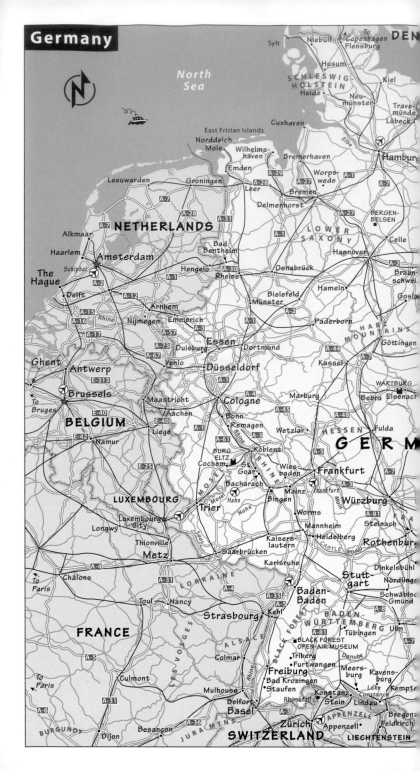

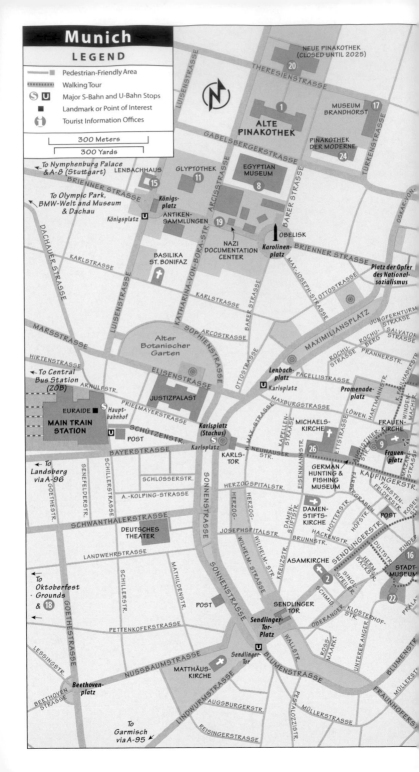

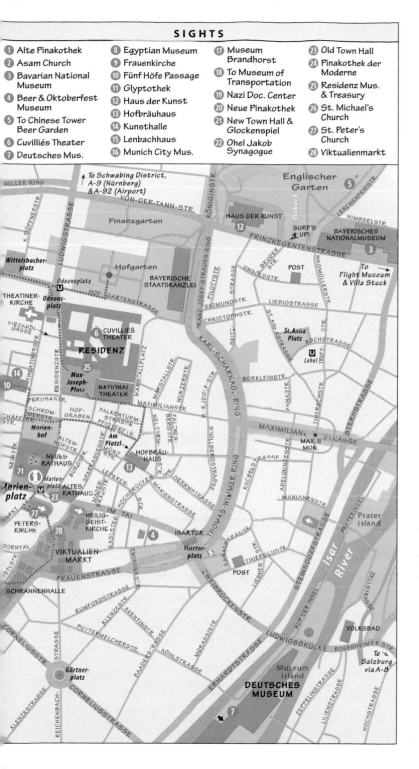

SIGHTS

1. Alte Pinakothek
2. Asam Church
3. Bavarian National Museum
4. Beer & Oktoberfest Museum
5. To Chinese Tower Beer Garden
6. Cuvilliés Theater
7. Deutsches Mus.
8. Egyptian Museum
9. Frauenkirche
10. Fünf Höfe Passage
11. Glyptothek
12. Haus der Kunst
13. Hofbräuhaus
14. Kunsthalle
15. Lenbachhaus
16. Munich City Mus.
17. Museum Brandhorst
18. To Museum of Transportation
19. Nazi Doc. Center
20. Neue Pinakothek
21. New Town Hall & Glockenspiel
22. Ohel Jakob Synagogue
23. Old Town Hall
24. Pinakothek der Moderne
25. Residenz Mus. & Treasury
26. St. Michael's Church
27. St. Peter's Church
28. Viktualienmarkt

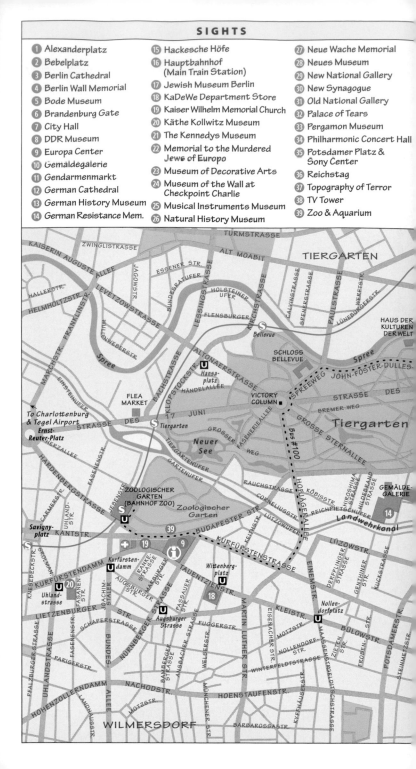

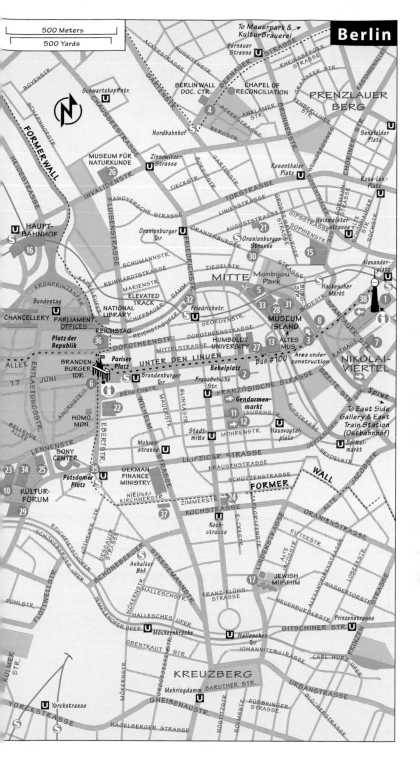

Berlin Public Transportation

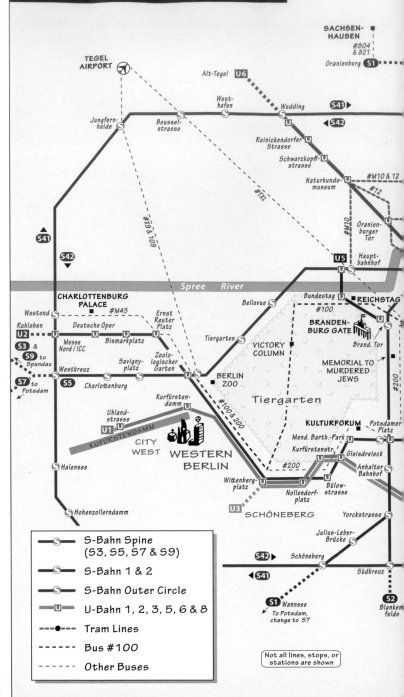

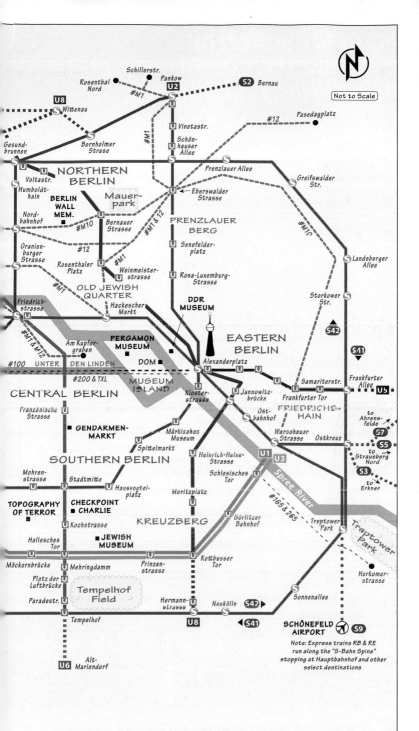

More for your trip!
Maximize the experience with Rick Steves as your guide

Guidebooks
Make side trips smooth and affordable with Rick's Vienna and Switzerland guides

Phrase Books
Rely on Rick's German Phrase Book & Dictionary

Rick's TV Shows
Preview your destinations with a wide variety of shows covering Germany

Rick's Audio Europe™ App
Get free self-guided audio tours for Germany's top sights

Small Group Tours
Take a lively, low-stress Rick Steves tour through Germany

For all the details, visit ricksteves.com